The Columbia Guide to the Literatures of Eastern Europe Since 1945

The Columbia Guides to Literature Since 1945

The Columbia Guide to the Literatures of Eastern Europe Since 1945

Harold B. Segel

Albania (and Kosovo), Bosnia-Herzegovina, Bulgaria, Croatia,
Czech Republic, German Democratic Republic, Hungary, Macedonia,
Poland, Romania, Serbia (and Montenegro), Slovakia, Slovenia

Columbia University Press
New York

Columbia University Press

Publishers Since 1893

New York   Chichester, West Sussex

Library of Congress Cataloging-in-Publication Data

Segel, Harold B., 1930–

  The Columbia guide to the literatures of Eastern Europe since 1945 / Harold B. Segel.

    p. cm. — (The Columbia guides to literature since 1945)

  Includes bibliographical references and index.

  ISBN 0-231-11404-4 (cloth : alk. paper)

  1. East European literature—20th century—Bio-bibliography. 2. German literature—Germany (East)—Bio-bibliography. 3. German literature—20th century—Bio-bibliography. 4. Authors, East European—20th century—Biography—Dictionaries. 5. Authors, German—Germany (East)—Biography—Dictionaries. 6. Authors, German—20th century—Biography—Dictionaries. I. Title

  Z2483 .S444 2002

  [PN849.E9]

  809′.8947—dc21   2002025661

∞

Printed in the United States of America

c 10 9 8 7 6 5 4 3 2 1

Contents

Preface

The purpose of this book is to equip the reader with a substantial reference work to the literatures of Eastern Europe, including the former East Germany, in the second half of the twentieth century, or, more specifically, from the end of World War II in 1945 to the beginning of a new century. No such reference work, embracing all the countries of the region including the German Democratic Republic for the duration of its existence, is currently available. Since the breakup of the Soviet Union, the reunification of East Germany and West Germany, the dissolution of Yugoslavia, and the division of Czechoslovakia into two separate states, Eastern Europe presents a more complex picture of peoples and cultures than ever before. By means of both its primary focus on the second half of the twentieth century—which brought a new world order to Eastern Europe and then witnessed its collapse—and its breadth of coverage, this book seeks to reduce such complexity to manageable proportions.

When the sole authorship of this book was proposed to me by then Assistant Director for Reference Publishing at Columbia University Press, James Raimes, it seemed a daunting task. How effectively, in fact, could one individual, even if appropriately equipped linguistically, deal with the variety of literatures involved? But the challenge, even with the risks it carried, was too enticing to turn aside without making at least a fair try. Further refining of language skills, extensive travel throughout the region, and far wider reading in the field than ever before rewarded this East Europeanist with a sense of gratification at coming to grips at last with the entirety of the area of his professional interest within the time frame of the book. In finally seeing this project through to its conclusion, I hope that notwithstanding the many obstacles and pitfalls, I have acquitted myself in a fair and balanced way. Although it may be restating the obvious to those who know me and my work, I have no ethnic, cultural, or professional biases that would in any way have impinged on the evenhandedness of this project. Having said this, I should make clear that this evenhandedness was defined by me as trying where possible and without any undue imbalance to give a little more weight to those literatures that are still not particularly well known within the Eastern European context. As the sole author of this book, I also bear the heavy weight of sole responsibility for any of its shortcomings—be they linguistic, interpretive, or factual—as well as for less than felicitous compromises inevitable in a text of this nature.

I was flattered that James Raimes originally invited me to undertake this project, and I enjoyed our working relationship for the time that he was at Columbia University Press. Further cooperation with his successor, James Warren, and especially my principal editor, Irene Pavitt, kept the project on an even keel; their support and encouragement have meant a great deal to me. I received much assistance from libraries, booksellers, and academics throughout Eastern Europe and offer a collective acknowledgment of gratitude to them.

The Organization of the Book

The principal parts of this book present a reasonably broad but concise overview of literary developments in Eastern Europe from 1945 to the present and almost 700 author entries, arranged in strict alphabetical order, that represent the various national literatures. The narrative overview is topical rather than chronological. The rationale for this is essentially practical. It obviously would have been impossible to do justice to the different literatures—thirteen since the fragmentation of Yugoslavia in the early 1990s and the official separation of the Czechs and Slovaks in 1993—in the format of the conventional literary history, in which authors are treated in chronological order and/or by literary genre. Moreover, this book is not intended to be a compilation of national literary histories in miniature. The topical division chosen as the ordering principle for the opening survey seeks primarily to relate literary developments to the defining moments in the post–World War II history of the Eastern European peoples.

The author entries are intended to provide the most salient information about the writers and their works. Although the effort was made to be as inclusive as possible, in view of the intended Anglophone readership for the book preference was given initially to writers available in English translation. Fortunately, a very large number of works by Eastern European writers have been translated into English, clearly attesting to the broad interest in the region both during and following the collapse of communism. The criterion of available English translations was soon discarded, however, and no writer judged worthy of being included in the book was excluded simply because his or her works have not been translated into English.

In considering authors for possible inclusion, I also established other criteria. Older writers whose careers developed primarily in the interwar period or largely in emigration, such as the Croatian Miroslav Krleža and the Pole Witold Gombrowicz, were omitted in order to better accommodate those authors who made their literary debuts only after World War II and, especially, younger writers who began coming to prominence in the last three decades of the twentieth century. The criterion for the older author was his or her literary activity after 1945. Needless to say, I would have liked to include an even larger number of authors than the nearly 700 now present. But choice had to be based on the individual writer's relative importance and the need to keep a fair and impartial balance in the representation of the national literatures covered by this book. This is especially important in the case of the former Yugoslavia, for which entries for Bosnian, Croatian, Macedonian, Serbian, and Slovenian writers would have been subentries under the single rubric of "Yugoslavia" before that country's breakup. Compromises also were inevitable in order to keep the book to a reasonable size. As it is, a larger volume evolved than had originally been planned.

Apart from basic biographical and literary historical information, the author entries include some descriptive and critical material, although for obvious reasons of space this had to be kept within strict limits. The more important the writer and the text, the more expansive the entry. The entries are not intended to be uniform throughout in either the scope of coverage or the order in which data are presented. Each entry also contains information about the secondary literature on the author, with preference, where possible, given to works in English. This material is grouped under the heading "Literature." The information on translations, grouped under the heading "Translations" at the end of each entry, is very comprehensive, since it was felt that such material would constitute an important resource of the book. The translations are listed in alphabetical order, beginning with books and followed by such individual works as poems, stories, and plays. For works that have not been translated into English, available French, German, Italian, and Russian translations are mentioned in light of the widespread knowledge of these languages, especially in the academic community.

Several sections of a practical nature follow the preface: a brief chronology of important political events, organized by country; a guide to the English translations of titles of Eastern European newspapers and periodicals in order to avoid duplication throughout the author entries; and a note on orthography, transliteration, and titles. A list of the authors included in the book, arranged by country, appears as the index.

A general bibliography appears at the end of the book. It lists references to books and articles only in English and is itself divided into two major parts. The first contains works of a general nature on Eastern Europe, primarily but not exclusively after 1945. The second cites works, listed by country, that fall into four categories: histories, literary histories, anthologies, and monographs on genres and movements. All information regarding translations and individual writers appears in the author entries.

Chronology of Major Political Events, 1944–2002

Albania

1944   May. The National Liberation Movement transforms itself into the National Liberation Front and deposes King Zog.

Autumn. The Germans withdraw from Albania, which is taken over by the communists under Enver Hoxha (1908–1985). Hoxha founded the Albanian Communist Party on 8 November 1921 and was Albania's most powerful figure in the twentieth century.

October. A congress at Berat establishes a provisional government, nine of whose eleven members are communists.

1946   November. The First Congress of the Communist Party is held. Mehmet Shehu (1913–1981) is dismissed from power. Shehu was commander of the First Partisan Brigade during World War II and chief of the general staff of the Albanian army. After the Tito–Cominform break in 1948, Shehu will regain power and become prime minister, retaining this position until his death in mysterious circumstances on 18 December 1981.

29 November. A constituent assembly forms a new government and chooses Hoxha as chairman of the Council of Ministers.

1948   1 July. Albania denounces all agreements with Yugoslavia in the wake of the Tito–Cominform split.

1961   Late December. Albania breaks off relations with the USSR and expels the Soviet navy from its bases on the Adriatic.

1967   All religions are officially banned by decree of Hoxha.

1982   Ramiz Alia (b. 1925), who will succeed Hoxha after his death, is elected chairman of the presidium of the People's Assembly, a position he holds until 1991.

1985   Hoxha dies and is replaced by Alia as the leading figure in the Communist Party and the government.

13 April. Alia is named first secretary of the Party.

30 April. Alia becomes president of Albania.

1990   Student demonstrations and related violence lead to the formation of the opposition Democratic Party, whose leader is Sali Berisha (b. 1944), a noted cardiologist and professor at Tirana University.

1991   The independent newspaper *Koha Jonë* is founded.

February. The first national congress of the Democratic Party is held.

1992   A series of economic reform measures is approved, transferring more state enterprises into the private sector. By 1995 at least 65 percent of such enterprises will have been privatized.

22 March. The Democratic Party defeats the Socialist Party (former communists) in national elections. Alia resigns the presidency and is replaced by Berisha.

12 September. Alia is placed under house arrest on charges of corruption.

1993   Berisha leads a campaign against communists and other parties loyal to Hoxha and Alia.

April. Albania recognizes the Former Yugoslav Republic of Macedonia (FYROM) as an independent state.

1994   April. Alia remains under house arrest.

6 November. A referendum on a proposed new constitution, which would have granted more power to Berisha, is defeated.

1995   September. Genocide and verification laws are passed, excluding from public life anyone who held office under the communists.

1996   5 March. Berisha is reelected president.

1997   The collapse of pyramid investment schemes results in the loss of savings of more than half the Albanian population, leading to economic and political instability. The country is racked by violence.

29 June. The Socialists win a majority in national elections.

23 July. Berisha resigns the presidency in order to lead the opposition in the parliament. Rexhep Mejdani (b. 1944), a physics lecturer at Tirana University, becomes president.

1998   18 September. A large but peaceful rally is led by Berisha against the government of Prime Minister Fatos Nano (b. 1952), the Socialist leader.

November. Nano resigns as prime minister and is replaced by Pandeli Majko (b. 1967).

1999   October. Majko resigns as prime minister to make way for a new coalition government led by fellow Socialist Ilir Meta (b. 1969).

2001   Meta is reelected prime minister.

Bulgaria

1944   8–9 September. A partisan brigade takes command of Sofia during the night. Colonel Kimon Georgiev (1882–1969), the founder of the Fatherland Front, comes to power and forms a government that includes communists.

1946	8 September. After a plebiscite, a republic is declared and the eleven-year-old King Simeon II and his family are sent into exile.
	The National Assembly passes the Agrarian Reform Law, by which large tracts of land are appropriated and included in the state land pool. Massive disruptions in the traditional patterns of agriculture and peasant life result.
1949–1953	The first Five-Year Plan is initiated.
1954	Todor Zhivkov (1911–1998) is appointed first secretary of the Bulgarian Communist Party.
1956	April. The "April line" rejecting the Stalinist "cult of personality" is instituted. Some political exiles are granted amnesty, and a number of victims of communist purges are rehabilitated. The "April line" remains in force until 1987, but its potential for liberalization is compromised by the fallout in Bulgaria from the Hungarian uprising of 1956.
1973	Zhivkov declares that henceforth Bulgaria and the Soviet Union will "act as a single body" and reiterates his suggestion of a decade earlier that Bulgaria be incorporated into the USSR.
1978	September. The dissident writer Georgi Markov (1929–1978) is murdered in London by a poisoned pellet fired from an umbrella.
1984	A wide-ranging and senseless anti-Turkish campaign is launched. The "regenerative process," as it is called, is aimed at the Bulgarization and Christianization of the large Turkish minority in the country (some 10 percent of the population as a whole), whom the communists declare to be Bulgarians who were forcibly converted to Islam during the long Ottoman Turkish occupation. All ethnic Turks are required to adopt Bulgarian names, and restrictions are passed against the public use of the Turkish language. Moreover, broadcasting, teaching, and publishing in Turkish are prohibited.
1989	May. Large-scale protests against the "regenerative process" are held. More than 300,000 ethnic Turks leave Bulgaria for Turkey.
	10 November. One day after the opening of the Berlin Wall, Zhivkov is deposed.
1990	Article 1 of the Bulgarian constitution, which assigned the Communist Party a leading role in the state and society, is abolished. The Union of Democratic Forces, led by Zheliu Zhelev (b. 1935), takes control of the country. Zhelev will serve as president of Bulgaria until 1996.
	3 April. The Bulgarian Communist Party changes its name to the Bulgarian Socialist Party.
	29 December. The "regenerative process" is rescinded, and full rights and equality under the law are restored to all Bulgarian Turks and Muslims.
1991	July. A new constitution is adopted.
	October. For the first time since 1944, a national election returns a government with no communist members.

2001	Former king Simeon II returns to Bulgaria to participate in national elections and is voted in as prime minister.

Czechoslovakia

1945	April. Edvard Beneš (1884–1948), leader of the government-in-exile, returns from London to a newly restored Czechoslovakia. A National Front government is formed, with Beneš as president and Klement Gottwald (1938–1953) of the Czechoslovak Communist Party, prime minister.
1946	May. The first postwar elections are held. The communists score impressive gains, winning 38 percent of the vote. They then agree to join a coalition government, which lasts for two years.
	May–summer 1947. Czechoslovakia enjoys a period of relative tranquillity.
1947	18 April. Monsignor Josef Tiso (1887–1947), the head of the wartime collaborationist Slovak state, is hanged.
	July–early January 1948. The popularity of the communists rapidly declines.
1948	25 February. The communists take over Czechoslovakia. Beneš accepts Gottwald's proposals for a new administration.
	Late February. Jan Masaryk (1886–1948), the son of Tomáš Garrigue Masaryk (1850–1937) and prime minister in the Beneš government, is found dead on the sidewalk underneath the window of his Prague office. All independent opposition to the communists now ceases.
	May. The communists succeed in fashioning an entirely dependent national assembly.
	6 June. Beneš resigns from office, paving the way for Gottwald to become president and Antonín Zápotocký (1884–1957), prime minister.
1948–1953	Czechoslovakia suffers under Stalinist rule.
1949–1954	Notorious purges are climaxed by the trial of Rudolf Slanský (1901–1952) and twelve other Party officials, the majority of them Jews.
1957–1968	Antonín Novotný (1904–1975) rules harshly as president, until he is replaced by the more liberal Ludvík Svoboda (1895–1979).
1963	May. Alexander Dubček (1912–1992) is named first secretary of the Slovak Communist Party .
1967	27–29 June. The historically important Czechoslovak Writers' Congress is held, during which the most powerful attacks on government cultural policies are delivered by Milan Kundera and Ludvík Vaculík.
1968	20–21 August. Czechoslovakia is invaded by Warsaw Pact armies under the leadership of the Soviet Union.
	28 August. Gustáv Husák (1913–1991) is named Slovak Party boss.
1969	17 April. Dubček is replaced as first secretary of the Communist Party by Husák.

1970s   Husák initiates a series of purges. Stagnation and regression of social life characterize the 1970s and early 1980s. Many thousands of Czechs and Slovaks flee the country.

1977   7 January. Charter 77, a declaration of human rights, is formulated, petitioning for greater democratization. The main author of the text is the writer Václav Havel, who will become president of Czechoslovakia and the Czech Republic. In a new government crackdown, signers of Charter 77 are allowed to leave Czechoslovakia between 1977 and 1987 or, in some cases, are summarily expelled from the country. Some 300 people leave, including such writers as the former communist Pavel Kohout and the noncommunist Jiří Gruša.

1989   December. The "Velvet Revolution," sparked by spreading student demonstrations, hastens the collapse of the communist government and initiates an irreversible move toward more rapid democratization.

1990   June. Vladímir Mečiar (b. 1942) becomes Slovak prime minister.

       29 December. Havel becomes president of Czechoslovakia.

1991   A screening resolution, barring former communists from holding important government positions, passes parliament.

       April. Mečiar is ousted as Slovak prime minister.

1992   June. Mečiar regains the prime ministership.

       25 November. Czechoslovakia is formally divided into two separate states, the Czech Republic and the Republic of Slovakia, effective 31 December.

1993   1 January. Slovakia becomes an independent republic after the peaceful dissolution of Czechoslovakia. Mečiar becomes de facto head of the government. The authoritarian and nationalistic Mečiar will dominate Slovak political life in the mid- and late 1990s, which witnesses a resurgence of interrelated nationalism, neofascism, and anti-Semitism.

1999   The election of the reform-minded Rudolf Schuster (b. 1934) as president of Slovakia and that of Mikuláš Dzurinda (b. 1955) as premier effectively ends Mečiar's grip on power.

       12 March. The Czech Republic becomes an official member of NATO.

German Democratic Republic

1945   July. The Soviet army establishes the Soviet Military Administration in those parts of Germany in its zone of occupation. The German Communist Party (KPD) is one of several antifascist parties permitted to operate.

1946   21–22 April. A KPD/ SPD (Social Democratic Party) congress establishes the Socialist Unity Party (SED) of Germany, which, for a time, includes representatives from western zones not within the zone of Soviet occupation.

1948   The SED is transformed into a Marxist-Leninist party with strong Soviet backing.

1949   October. The German Democratic Republic (GDR), with Wilhelm Pieck (1876–1960) as its first president and Otto Grotewohl (1894–1964) its first prime minister, is established.

1953   9 June. A 10 percent increase in work norms provokes large-scale destabilizing riots by workers and anticommunists.

17 June. The riots are suppressed by Soviet troops.

1961   The notorious Berlin Wall, which will separate the eastern and western parts of Berlin for almost thirty years, is built.

1971   May. Walter Ulbricht (1893–1973) is elected to the newly created chairmanship of the SED. His successor as head of the Party, Erich Honecker (1912–1994), who had supervised the building of the Berlin Wall, aggressively pursues a policy of *Abgrenzung*, the systematic isolation of the German Democratic Republic from western influences, especially those emanating from West Germany.

1976   The dissident poet Wolf Biermann is deprived of his East German citizenship while on a tour of West Germany, leading to widespread resentment and the emigration of a number of East German artists.

1989   9 November. The Berlin Wall falls.

Reunification of the two German states begins.

Hungary

1944   December. A provisional government with a Marxist-Leninist character is established in Debrecen.

1945   November. General elections are held, with the communists doing less well than expected. They begin laying the groundwork for the next elections.

1948   June. The Hungarian Workers' Party (communist) is formed from the old Hungarian Communist Party and the Social Democratic Party.

1949   General elections are held, with the communists completing their takeover of the government since no opposition candidates are fielded.

1949–1953   Hungary suffers under the Stalinist rule of Mátyás Rákosi (1892–1971), the Communist Party leader and head of the government.

1956   Summer. Rákosi is allowed to retain his position after a reprimand by the new Soviet leadership for his continued support of Stalinism after 1953. The less doctrinaire and more reform-minded Imre Nagy (1896–1958), however, is named prime minister.

18 July. Rákosi resigns.

24 October. The Hungarian uprising erupts.

4 November. Thousands of Soviet tanks roll into Hungary to crush the uprising, leading to intense street fighting.

7 November. János Kádár (1912–1989) arrives at Party headquarters to begin the political reconstruction of communist rule in Hungary.

1956–1968	Kádár institutes reforms.
1980s	Antigovernment demonstrations, largely protesting the state of the economy, increase across the country.
1985	May. A new electoral law allows independent candidates to oppose Party nominees in parliamentary elections.
1988	December–January 1989. A series of measures are enacted by the parliament allowing rights of association and assembly.
1989	February. A multiparty system is allowed, ending the hegemony of the Communist Party.
	16 June. The rehabilitated Nagy and several other victims of repression are removed from anonymous graves and reburied as national heroes.
	23 October. Communist rule virtually ends as a new open electoral system is instituted in which the president is to be elected by a direct vote, and the name of the state is changed to the Hungarian Republic, with the adjective "People's" dropped.
1990	March and April. General elections are held.
1999	12 March. Hungary becomes an official member of NATO.

Poland

1945	A government of national unity is established in Warsaw in the wake of the German defeat.
1948	The Polish United Workers' Party (communist) is formed.
1951	Władysław Gomułka (1905–1982) is arrested for "nationalist deviation."
1956	The Poznań riots, widely referred to as the "Polish October," erupt. Widespread workers' demands for economic reforms and the removal of Soviet troops from Poland result in Gomułka being returned to power.
1968	January. The National Theater production of the Romantic poet Adam Mickiewicz's play Forefathers' Eve (1833) triggers anti-Soviet outbursts. Subsequent student demonstrations are harshly suppressed.
	March. Government-sponsored anti-Semitic acts in the wake of the Six-Day War in the Middle East cause thousands of Jews to leave Poland voluntarily and involuntarily. The minister of foreign affairs, the highly respected Adam Rapacki (1909–1970), is deprived of his position.
1970	West Germany recognizes the Oder–Nysa line as the official border between Germany and Poland.
	Gomułka is brought down by workers' riots in Gdańsk and elsewhere. Edward Gierek (b. 1913) takes over the reigns of the Party and government.
1976	A new wave of workers' riots in the industrial cities of Radom and Ursus wins the support of intellectuals and leads to the establishment of the democratic-oriented Committee for the Defense of Workers (KOR).
1978	Karol Wojtyła (b. 1920), archbishop of Kraków, becomes Pope John Paul II.

| 1979 | John Paul II makes his first visit to Poland as pope. |

1980   New strikes, this time chiefly among workers at the Lenin Shipyards in Gdańsk, results in the formation of Solidarity, headed by the electrician Lech Wałęsa (b. 1943).

1981   13–14 December. Martial law is declared on orders of General Wojciech Jaruzelski (b. 1923), who justifies the action as the lesser of two evils, the greater being that of a Soviet invasion to suppress the movement for democratic reform spearheaded by Solidarity.

1982   January. The Polish Diet confirms the legality of martial law.

8 October. Solidarity is formally dissolved by the Diet.

1989   Solidarity is victorious. Jaruzelski is named president of Poland and Tadeusz Mazowiecki (b. 1927), the first noncommunist premier.

1990   Wałęsa is elected president.

The first free elections to the Diet are held.

1993   An election allows the coalition of the Democratic Left Alliance and the Polish Populist Party. Waldemar Pawlak (b. 1959) becomes premier.

1995   Aleksander Kwaśniewski (b. 1954) defeats Wałęsa for the presidency.

1997   Following a center-right electoral victory, Jerzy Buzek (b. 1940) becomes premier.

1999   Poland becomes an official member of NATO.

2000   Kwaśniewski is elected president for a second five-year term.

Romania

1944   23 August. The Romanian army turns against the Germans, hastening Romania's departure from the war.

1945   6 March. Petru Groza (1884–1958), leader of the procommunist Plowman's Front, becomes prime minister with Soviet approval and names communists to key cabinet posts.

1947   30 December. King Michael abdicates under pressure from Groza and Gheorghe Gheorghiu-Dej (1901–1965), secretary-general (1945–1954) and first secretary (1955–1965) of the Romanian Communist Party.

1948   21–23 February. The Romanian Workers' Party (communist) is formed, following the unification of the Communist Party and the Social Democratic Party. It has an avowedly Marxist-Leninist agenda.

13 April. A republican Soviet-style constitution is enacted.

Spring. The government bloc is enlarged to include other parties, among them the People's Democratic Front, which is dominated by communists.

1949   3–5 March. The Central Committee of the Workers' Party launches its program for the collectivization of agriculture, which would be completed only in the spring of 1962.

1955	14 May. Romania joins the Soviet-led Warsaw Pact military alliance.
	14 December. Romania becomes a member of the United Nations.
1956–1968	Romania rejects Soviet influences and pursues a policy of domestic Stalinism and Tito-style independence in foreign affairs.
1964	April. Romania begins to follow its own economic policy and greatly reduces its role in Comecom and the World Trade Organization.
1965	19 March. Gheorghiu-Dej dies and is succeeded by Nicolae Ceauşescu (1918–1989) as first secretary of the Workers' Party.
	19–24 July. At the Ninth Congress, the name of the Workers' Party is officially changed to the Romanian Communist Party, and Ceauşescu is elected secretary-general.
	21 August. A new constitution is adopted, and the name of the country officially becomes the Socialist Republic of Romania.
1968	21 August. Romania and Albania are the only Warsaw Pact members that refuse to take part in the Soviet-led intervention in Czechoslovakia. Ceauşescu condemns the invasion and demands that relations between states be governed by respect for national independence, sovereignty, and nonintervention in internal affairs.
1969	2–3 August. Richard Nixon (1913–1994) becomes the first American president to visit Romania.
1970	December. Nicolae and Elena Ceauşescu visit the United States, the first of three visits (the other two are in 1973 and 1978).
1971	14 November. Romania is admitted to General Agreement on Tariffs and Trade (GATT).
1972	9 December. Romania becomes the first Eastern European state admitted to the World Monetary Fund.
1974	28 March. Ceauşescu is elected the first president of Romania by the Grand National Assembly.
1975	2 April. Romania becomes the first communist country to receive most-favored-nation trade status by the United States.
1977	1–3 August. A large miners' strike becomes the first of a series of sporadic outbursts of worker unrest extending into the 1980s.
1980s	Romanians suffer under intensified police surveillance and ever-worsening privation.
1984	25 June. Ceauşescu launches the construction of the "House of the People" and the Boulevard of the Victory of Socialism, a gigantic project that necessitates the razing of an old central area of Bucharest and the destruction of churches and other historical buildings.
1987	15 November. Serious worker unrest at the Red Star tractor plant in the Transylvanian town of Braşov is suppressed by the army and Securitate (secret police).

1989 November. Ceauşescu is reelected secretary-general of the Communist Party at the Fourteenth Party Congress and refuses to accede to demands for a program of national reforms.

16 December. Demonstrations begin in Timişoara, sparked by the rumor that the Securitate intends to arrest a popular Hungarian preacher, Lászlo Tökés.

21 December. Ceauşescu is heckled during an address from the balcony of Commmunist Party headquarters in Bucharest.

22 December. Ceauşescu is again heckled in public, finally fleeing Party headquarters by helicopter. Open fighting breaks out in the streets of Bucharest and elsewhere in the country between diehard Ceauşescu loyalists in the Securitate and demonstrators and soldiers who join the protestors in increasing numbers.

25 December. Nicolae and Elena Ceauşescu are captured and shot.

After 28 December. The National Salvation Front is established under the leadership of former communist, now socialist, Ion Iliescu (b. 1930). A new government is formed with Petre Roman (b. 1946) as prime minister.

1990 12 January. The Communist Party is officially abolished.

20 May. In the first free elections after the 1989 revolution, the National Salvation Front wins two-thirds of the seats in both houses of parliament, and Iliescu is elected president.

1991 December. A new constitution is adopted by which Romania becomes a European-style parliamentary democracy.

1992 February. A shift to the Democratic Convention (CDR) results from the first multiparty elections on the local level.

27 September. A runoff general election keeps Iliescu in the presidency.

1993 28 September. Romania admitted as a member with full rights to the Council of Europe.

1995 18 January. Romania becomes an associate member of the European Union.

2000 December. Iliescu again is elected president of Romania.

Yugoslavia

1945–1953 Yugoslavia is ruled by the renowned wartime communist partisan leader Josip Broz Tito (1892–1980), who holds the positions of premier and minister of defense from 1945.

1948 28 June. The Yugoslav Communist Party is expelled from the Cominform over disagreements on economic policy with the Soviet Union. Yugoslavia will pursue a form of non-Soviet socialism and strict neutrality in foreign affairs.

1950 June. Workers' "self-management" is introduced with much fanfare. Although it appears to transfer significant power to workers in their factories and communities, the system is, if anything, pseudo-democratic and will collapse in the 1980s.

1953	Tito becomes president of Yugoslavia.
1953–1965	Yugoslavia enjoys a period of reform and major economic gains.
1964	A dissident Marxist group, affiliated with the journal *Praxis* and strongly committed to a policy of decentralization, emerges.
1971	Tito establishes a twenty-two-member collective presidency made up primarily of the presidents of the six constituent republics (Bosnia-Herzegovina, Croatia, Macedonia, Montenegro, Serbia, and Slovenia) to assume power after his death, thus settling the matter of succession.
1974	The constitution allows full cultural and limited political autonomy for Albanians in Kosovo, which is now recognized as an autonomous province of Yugoslavia.
1980	4 May. Tito dies.
1981	March. Anti-Yugoslav riots erupt among Albanian students at Priština University in Kosovo.
1985	December. Further protests by Albanians result in the deterioration of Albanian–Serb relations.
1987	Slobodan Milošević (b. 1941) becomes head of the Serbian Communist Party.
1988	November. Mass demonstrations by Albanians in Priština lead to a retaliatory march in Belgrade, involving an estimated 1 million participants, to protest discrimination against Serbs in Kosovo.
1989	Milošević becomes president of the Republic of Serbia. Kosovo de facto loses its autonomous status and is placed under direct Serbian military occupation.
1990	Summer. The Kosovo parliament is dissolved, and Albanian-language daily newspapers as well as Albanian radio and television broadcasting are banned.
1991	25 June. Assemblies in Croatia and Slovenia declare full national independence.
	Serbian military action against Slovenia ceases after a fruitless ten-day campaign.
	Summer. Bitter fighting next ensues as Serbian forces turn on Croatia, ostensibly to protect the Serbian minority of the country after their declaration of a separate Croatian Serbian political entity.
	Autumn. Teaching at Priština University is suspended, except for classes reserved for the small Serbian minority.
1992	March. A cease-fire is called to avert war between Croatia and Bosnia.
1993	Spring. The Vance–Owen plan, named for the American and British mediators Cyrus Vance and Lord David Owen, respectively, proposes to divide

Bosnia-Herzegovina into Muslim, Serb, Croat, and Muslim–Croat administrative areas, with Sarajevo having special status.

September. A Serbian plan for the partition of Bosnia-Herzegovina is mediated by Owen and Thorvald Stoltenberg, who has replaced Vance.

1995   November. The Dayton Agreement ends the Bosnian war by creating separate Muslim–Croat and Bosnian Serb republics.

1997   Milošević becomes president of a new Yugoslavia, composed of just Serbia and Montenegro.

1999   An "ethnic-cleansing" campaign follows the Serbian takeover of Kosovo.

24 March. NATO intervenes aggressively in the Kosovo situation, with heavy bombing strikes against Yugoslavia, mostly by American and British planes, lasting seventy-eight days.

10 June. Milošević agrees to NATO conditions to remove Serbian troops from Kosovo.

2000   Milošević is voted out of power, and a democratic government takes over under Vojislav Kostunica (b. 1944).

2001   10 March. Milošević is taken into custody by Serbian police and jailed, pending his indictment on charges of corruption and abuse of power. Kostunica continues to resist demands that Milošević be extradited to The Hague to stand trial for war crimes.

26 June. Milošević is finally extradited to The Hague and placed in detention.

2002   14 February. Milošević outlines his defense before the war crimes tribunal in The Hague.

Journals, Newspapers, and Other Periodical Literature

Albania

Bota e re	New World
Drita	The Light
Hosteni	The Prod
Jeta e re	New Life
Koha Jonë	Our Way
Kritika letrare	Literary Criticism
Nëntori	November
Rilindja	Renaissance
Shêjzat	The Pleiades
Ylli	The Star
Zëri i Popullit	The People's Voice

Bosnia

Izraz	The Word
Jugoslovenska pošta	Yugoslav Post
Jugoslovenski list	Yugoslav News
Život	Life

Bulgaria

Bulgarska misul	Bulgarian Thought
Bulgarski pisatel	Bulgarian Wrtiter
Bulgarski voin	Bulgarian Combatant
Demokratsiia	Democracy
Fokus	Focus
Frontovak	Frontline Fighter
Hudozhnik	Artist
Ikar	Icarus
Izkustvo	Art

Izkustvo i kritika	Art and Criticism
Kinoizkustvo	Film Art
Kooperativno selo	Village Cooperative
Kosmos	Cosmos
Literaturen front	Literary Front
Literaturen vestnik	Literary Herald
Literaturen zhivot	Literary Life
Literaturna misul	Literary Thought
Literaturni novini	Literary News
Lovets	The Hunter
Mladezhka iskra	Spark of Youth
Most	The Bridge
Narodna mladezh	The Nation's Youth
Nauka i tehnika	Science and Technology
Obzor	Review
Orbita	Orbit
Otechestven front	Fatherland Front
Otechestvo	Fatherland
Plamuche	Twinkle
Plamuk	Flame
Rabotnichesko delo	The Workers' Cause
Rodni krile	The Nation's Wings
Rodni prostori	National Expanses
Samokovska tribuna	The Samokov Tribune
Septemvri	September
Septemvriiche	Young Pioneer
Slaveiche	Little Nightingale
Slivensko delo	Sliven News
Studentska tribuna	Student Tribune
Sturshel	The Hornet
Suvremennik	The Contemporary
Trakiia	Thrace
Vecherni novini	Evening News
Vedrina	Bright Sky
Zlatorog	The Golden Horn

Croatia

Feral Tribune	Feral Tribune [The Beacon]
Hrvatski tjednik	Croatian Weekly
Izvor	The Source
Krugovi	Circles
Medjutim	On the Other Hand
Mogućnosti	Possibilities
Plima	Flux
Prosvjeta	Enlightenment
Razlog	Consideration
Savremenik	The Contemporary
Slobodna Dalmacija	Free Dalmatia
Studentski list	Student News
Tribuna	The Tribune
Vjesnik	The Courier
Zadarska revija	Zadar Review

Czech Republic

Československý rozhlas	Czechoslovak Broadcast
Dikobraz	The Porcupine
Domácí lekař	Home Doctor
Haló noviny	Hello News
Host do domu	Guest in the House
Kmen	The People
Kulturní tvorba	Cultural Creativity
Lídové noviny	The People's News
Listy	Folios
Literární listy	Literary Jottings
Literární noviny	Literary News
Mladý svět	Young World
Nová scéna	New Stage
Nové knihy	New Books
Občanské listy	Civic Sheets
Obrys/Kmen	Outline/The People
Orientace	Orientations
Práce	Labor

Rudé právo	Red Truth
Sedmička pionýrů	Seven Pioneers
Sešity	Notebooks
Stadion	Stadium
Světová literatura	World Literature
Trafika	Traffic
Tvář	Visage
Tvorba	Creativity
Vesmir	Universe
Vlasta	The Authority
Zítřek	Tomorrow

German Democratic Republic

Aktion	Action
Anschlag	Assault
Aufbau	Construction
Deutsches Volksecho	Echo of the German People
Freies Deutschland	Free Germany
Freiheit	Freedom
Junge Kunst	Young Art
Die Kunstblätter	Art Pages
Leipziger Volkszeitung	Leipzig People's News
Linkskurve	Left Turn
Literarische Welt	Literary World
Das Magazin	The Warehouse
Märkische Volkstimme	The People's Voice of the Mark (Brandenburg)
Mikado oder Der Kaiser ist nackt	Mikado or the Emperor Is Naked
Neue deutsche Literatur	New German Literature
Neue Deutschland	New Germany
Ost und West	East and West
Sinn und Form	Sense and Form
Sonntag	Sunday
Temperamente	Temperaments
tua res	your thing
Wochenpost	The Weekly Post

Zweite Person	Second Person

Hungary

Alföld	The Plain
Délmagyarország	Southern Hungary
Élet	Life
Élet és Irodalom	World and Literature
Életünk	Our Life
Előre	Forward
Igaz szó	The True Word
Jelenkor	Present Age
Kincskereső	Treasure Seeker
Kisdobos	Drummer Boy
Magyar Csillag	Hungarian Star
Magyar Hírlap	Hungarian Daily
Magyar Nemzet	Hungarian Nation
Mozgó Világ	Moving Earth
Négy Évszak	Four Seasons
Népszava	People's Choice
Pesti Napló	Pést Diary
Rádió	Radio
Sorsunk	Our Destiny
Szabad Szó	Free Word
Színház	Theater
Újhold	New Moon
Új Könyvék	New Books
Új Magyarország	New Hungary
Új Tükör	New Mirror
Válasz	The Answer
Valóság	Truth
Vigilia	Vigil

Macedonia

Flaka e vëllazërimit	The Flame of Brotherhood (in Albanian)
Makedonia denes	Macedonia Today
Makedonsko sonce	Macedonian Sun
Mlada literatura	Young Literature

Nova Makedonija	New Macedonia
Razgledi	Views
Sovremenost	Modernity
Stremež	Striving
Trudbenik	Worker
Večer	Evening
Večeren reporter	Evening Reporter

Poland

Arka	The Ark
Czas	Time
Dialog	Dialogue
Dziennik Polski	Polish Daily
Expres wieczorny	Evening Express
Głos Ludu	Voice of the People
Głos Wybrzeża	Voice of the Coast
Kurier Lwowski	Lwów Courier
Kurier Polski	Polish Courier
Kurier Poranny	Morning Courier
Kurier Poznański	Poznań Courier
Kuźnia Młodych	Forge of the Young
Kuźnica	The Forge
Literatura na Świecie	World Literature
Miesięcznik Literacki	Literary Monthly
Nasz Wyraz	Our Word
Nowa Kultura	New Culture
Nowa Sztuka	New Art
Nowe Widnokręgi	New Horizons
Nowiny Literackie	Literary News
Nowy Wyraz	New Expression
Nurt	The Current
Odra	The Oder
Odrodzenie	Rebirth
Pion	The Perpendicular
Pióro	The Pen
Pismo	Writing

Poezja	Poetry
Polityka	Politics
Po prostu	Straight from the Shoulder
Powściągliwość i Praca	Temperance and Hard Work
Prawda Wileńska	Wilno Truth
Przegląd Kulturalny	Cultural Review
Przekrój	The Cut
Puls	Pulse
Signały	Signals
Słowo Powszechne	The Universal Word
Świat	World
Sztandar Młodych	Standard of the Young
Trybuna Robotnicza	The Workers' Tribune
Trybunu Ludu	Tribune of the People
Twórczość	Creativity
Tygodnik Powszechny	Universal Weekly
Zapis	Notation
Żołnierz Polski	Polish Soldier
Życie Literackie	Literary Life
Życie Warszawy	Warsaw Life

Romania

Adevărul literar și artistic	The Literary and Artistic Truth
Albina	The Honeybee
Almanah literar	Literary Almanac
Amfiteatru	Amphitheater
Apostrof	Apostrophe
Azi	Today
Bilete de papagal	Notes from a Parrot
Caiete critice	Critical Notebooks
Contrapunct	Counterpoint
Convorbiri literare	Literary Conversations
Cotidianul	The Daily
Cuvântul	The Word
Dacia Literară	Literary Dacia
Dilema	Dilemma

Echinox	Equinox
Flacăra Roşie	The Red Flame
Gazeta literară	Literary Gazette
Gînderea	The Thought
Iaşul nou	The New Iaşi
Informaţia Bucureştului	Bucharest Informator
Liceu	Lyceum
Luceafărul	The Star
Lumea românească	Romanian World
Lumen	Lumen
Orizont	Horizon
Ramuri	Branches
Revista elevilor	The Students' Review
Revista Fundaţiilor Regale	Review of Royal Foundations
România liberă	Free Romania
România literară	Literary Romania
Săptămîna	The Week
Scînteia	The Spark
Scînteia tineretului	The Spark of Youth
Scrisul bănăţean	Writings of the Banat Region
Secolul 20	The 20th Century
Sportul	Sport
Steaua	The Star
Teatru	Theater
Tribuna	The Tribune
Vatra	The Hearth
Viaţa nouă	New Life
Viaţa românească	Romanian Life
Viaţa studenţească	Student Life

Serbia

Borba	Struggle
Delo	The Deed
Duga	The Rainbow
Književna reč	About Books
Književnost	Literature
Mladost	Youth

Narodna armija	The National Army
Narodna prosveta	National Enlightenment
Novi Albatros	New Albatross
Pionir	Pioneer
Politika	Politics
Savremenik	The Contemporary
Spomenica	Memorial
Srpski Književni Glasnik	Serbian Literary Herald
Znak	Sign

Slovakia

Borba	Struggle
Fragment K	Fragment K
Kamarát	Comrade
Kulturný Život	Cultural Life
Mladá tvorba	Young Creativity
Nové slovo	New Word
Nový rod	New Voice
Prameň	The Source
Slovenské pohl'ady	Slovak Views
Smena	Change
Smer	Direction

Slovenia

Beseda	Conversation
Dom in svet	Home and World
Križ	The Cross
Kurirček	The Little Courier
Literatura	Literature
Mladinska revija	Youth Review
Nova revija	The New Review
Osvobodilna fronta	Liberation Front
Perspektive	Perspectives
Problemi	Problems
Razgledi	Viewpoints
Revija 57	Review 57
Slovenec	The Slovenian

Note on Orthography, Transliteration, and Titles

With literatures in languages that employ the Latin alphabet, names and titles of works are given as they appear in the original; that is, all diacritics are faithfully preserved, with the exception of the Serbo-Croatian "đ," which I transliterate as "dj" (as in Djilas). Bulgarian, Macedonian, and Serbian are written in slightly different versions of the Cyrillic alphabet. Names and titles of works in Bulgarian and Serbian are transliterated according to widely used patterns of transliteration from Cyrillic. The exception is the distinctly Macedonian "ǵ" and "ḱ," which are found in a small number of words in the language. Although these letters represent the same phonemes as the Latinized Serbian and Croatian "đ" ("dj") and "ć," respectively, and are sometimes so transliterated, I thought it best to transliterate the first as "gj" and the second as "kj" at the beginning and in the middle of a word and as "ć" at the end of a word in order to avoid excessive distortion of Macedonian names. The surname of the Macedonian poet Katica Ḱulavkova, for example, is never rendered Ćulavkova, although this is how the name is pronounced. Hence I opted for the transliteration Kjulavkova, which, while not a perfect solution, seems better than simply Kulavkova. However, "ć" seemed preferable to "kj" at the end of the surname of the writer transliterated by me as Vlada Urošević. In the case of the Romanian vowel rendered variously as "â" or "î," the most practical approach seemed to be to follow the spelling of the given text rather than to make changes on the basis of the newer Romanian orthography.

Titles of works in the author entries appear first in their original form and then in English translation in parentheses. Italics are used only with works that have been published, whether the reference is to the original title or a translation. In order to avoid unnecessary duplication, titles of works mentioned in the Introduction appear only in translation.

The Columbia Guide to the Literatures of Eastern Europe Since 1945

Introduction:
The Literatures of Eastern Europe
from 1945 to the Present

If art thrives on adversity, as some argue—and there is ample evidence that it does—then it is certainly fair to say that the conditions of life in Eastern Europe from 1939 to 1945 and from 1945 to nearly the end of the twentieth century provided the inspiration for many literary works of considerable artistic achievement and enduring significance. With certain notable exceptions, and insofar as it may be possible to generalize about the matter, the achievements of Eastern European authors in the appreciably longer post–World War II period outweigh those of the interwar years, attested by the number of Nobel Prizes in Literature awarded to contemporary Eastern European writers. A reference work for Eastern European creative writing from 1945 to the fall of communism and the Balkan wars of the 1990s can no more ignore the political and ethnic context in which this literature developed than it can the artistic properties of texts if the genuine achievements of so many fine writers living and working in anything but optimal conditions are to be appreciated.

The Politics and the Peoples and Cultures of Eastern Europe

In order to resolve the sometimes thorny question of terminology as soon as possible, I want to make it clear from the outset that the term "Eastern Europe" as used in this book is geopolitical. That is why it appears in capitals as opposed to "eastern Europe," which would connote a primarily geographical entity. "Eastern Europe" hence refers to those countries that were absorbed into or became otherwise aligned with the Soviet orbit of power, the Soviet "bloc" as it has often been referred to, after 1945 and in direct consequence of the outcome of World War II, and were dominated by communist regimes until the late 1980s and early 1990s. Subsumed, then, under the rubric of "Eastern Europe" are such countries as Albania, Bulgaria, Czechoslovakia, Hungary, Poland, Romania, and the former Yugoslavia. As a state created wholly out of the political realities of the war, and to all intents and purposes a Soviet vassal state, East Germany, or, as it was formally known, the German Democratic Republic (GDR), is also included. Excluded from this book are the new states of Belarus (Belorussia), Estonia, Latvia, Lithuania, and Ukraine—former republics of the Soviet Union that achieved independence with the breakup of the USSR in 1991. Fully integrated into the political, economic, cultural, and social fabric of the Soviet system, these republics before independence lacked the patterns of resistance to Soviet rule common to the previously mentioned Eastern European states.

Virtually from the very beginning of imposed Soviet authority—indeed, even before the end of World War II, as in the case of Poland—this Sovietization met with serious opposition in Eastern Europe. So alien was the communist system perceived throughout the region after 1945 that it can be likened to a foreign body that an otherwise healthy organism tries to reject. From the workers' riots in East Germany in 1953 through the collapse of communism in 1989 to 1991, periodic spontaneous attempts to reform the system, achieve greater democratization, or overthrow the communist regimes entirely caused great unrest—and hardship—throughout Eastern Europe. Of greatest consequence were the Polish riots of 1956, the Hungarian uprising that same year, the events leading up to the "Prague Spring" of 1968, and the series of labor disturbances in Poland between 1970 and 1980 from which the Solidarity movement arose. In two countries, Hungary and Czechoslovakia, the challenge to Soviet authority was regarded as sufficiently menacing to warrant Soviet armed intervention. Had General Władysław Jaruzelski not imposed martial law in Poland in 1981, there is every reason to believe that the Soviets would have intervened militarily in that country as well. Indeed, troop and tank movements had already been initiated. In such countries as Albania and Yugoslavia, which had indigenous partisan movements during the war and were not liberated primarily by Soviet troops, autonomous forms of communist rule and resistance to Soviet dictates soon manifested themselves. In Albania, as well as Romania—which, of course, had been occupied by the Red Army as a state aligned with Germany in World War II—independence from Soviet authority went hand in hand with the development of the highly repressive communist regimes of, respectively, Enver Hoxha and Nicolae Ceaușescu. Yugoslavia, whose strong communist-dominated partisan movement acquitted itself well during the war, also avoided wholesale Soviet liberation and occupation, developed its own socialistic political-economic system, and stubbornly resisted integration into the Soviet model. The result was inevitable: ideological conflict with the Soviets and the now famous break between Yugoslavia and the USSR in 1948.

It is on the basis of this common history of the peoples of Eastern Europe between 1945 and the downfall of communism that a literary reference work of a synthetic nature—one, that is, that proposes to treat the region as a whole—can be rationalized. The thrust of this book is to show both the commonality of shared experiences and the diversity of literary response to those experiences. Eastern Europe has never been a monolith. Very different societies, with distinct cultures in the period from 1918 to 1939, found themselves uneasy bedfellows in essentially the same political camp after World War II. The imposition of a Soviet model throughout Eastern Europe after the war also imposed a temporary and, to a degree, inorganic complex of shared social and cultural experiences. Even World War II itself was not a uniform experience for the peoples of Eastern Europe. Some of the countries were occupied by German forces—the Czech lands, Poland, Yugoslavia absent Croatia—or by Italian as well as German forces, as was Albania. Others were allies of the Germans: Bulgaria, Hungary, Romania, the "independent" Slovak republic headed by a Nazi puppet, Monsignor Josef Tiso, and the similarly "independent" Croatian puppet state headed by Ante Pavelić. However much collaboration with the Germans during the war was in principle inexcusable, long-standing territorial ambitions and ethnic tensions within a given state go a long way toward explaining such collaboration. Hungarian claims against Romania concerning Transylvania, long a bone of contention between the two peoples; Bulgarian ambitions with respect to Macedonia and parts of neighboring Greece and Yugoslavia; Romanian grievances over Soviet control of Bessarabia; and ethnic tensions between Slovaks and Czechs, as well as among Croats, Serbs, and Bosnian Muslims, were for many sufficient motivation to throw their lots in with Hitler.

Although it may seem rudimentary in a book of this nature, it may be useful to review the ethnic and religious map of Eastern Europe. The vast majority of the peoples of Eastern Europe are Slavs: Bulgarians, Croats, Czechs, Macedonians, Poles, Serbs, Slovaks, and Slovenes. While not within the scope of this book, the Belarussians and Ukrainians, as well as the Russians, also belong to the immense Slavic family of nations. Three non-Slavic nations appear like islands in the Slavic sea: Albania, Hungary, and Romania. The languages and cultures of these three peoples are as different from one another as they are from those of the Slavs surrounding them. The Albanians speak an Indo-European language that is unlike any other in Europe; the Hungarians speak a non–Indo-European Ugric language, also unlike any other in Europe except, distantly, Finnish and Estonian; and the Romanians speak a Romance language that incorporates a number of Slavic, Greek, and Turkish words as well as structural features not found in other Romance languages. As for the Slavs themselves, despite the many similarities among their languages, and various attempts through the centuries to foster the ideal of Slavic unity, they are far from being a monolith.

The basic division of the Slavic world is geographical—east, west, and south—a division that applies as well to the Slavic family of languages. The Belarussians and Ukrainians, like the Russians, are East Slavs; the Czechs, Poles, and Slovaks are West Slavs; the Bulgarians, Croats, Macedonians, Serbs, and Slovenes are South Slavs. Religious differences, while similarly tripartite in nature, present a slightly more uneven picture. The Bulgarians, Macedonians, Russians, Serbs, and many Ukrainians belong to the Eastern Orthodox Church. A large number of Ukrainians also profess the Uniate faith, which combines elements of Eastern Orthodoxy and Roman Catholicism. The Croats, Czechs, Poles, and Slovaks are overwhelmingly Roman Catholic. Protestantism, however, has a long (and interesting) history among the Slavs of East Central Europe, as well as among the Hungarians, and Protestants of different denominations are still to be found in those countries. Two different alphabets are in use in the Slavic world, the Cyrillic and the Latin, their use determined by the prevailing religion. The Cyrillic alphabet is common to the Orthodox Slavs; the Latin alphabet is common to the Roman Catholic Slavs. Despite their historical and cultural differences, and some dialectal differentiation, the Croats and Serbs speak essentially the same language, commonly known as Serbo-Croatian. Since the breakup of Yugoslavia, however, it has become more politically correct to speak of separate Croatian and Serbian languages, and, to be sure, linguists primarily in Croatia have been working diligently to satisfy nationalistic aims by widening the gap between the two languages. Also adding to the separateness of Croatian and Serbian is the fact that the Croats use the Latin alphabet, and the Serbs, the Cyrillic.

The non-Slav peoples of Eastern Europe—the Albanians, Hungarians, and Romanians—are also distinguished along religious lines. The Albanians are overwhelmingly Muslim, although Albanian employs the Latin alphabet. Hungarians are Roman Catholics, and Romanians, Eastern Orthodox. And although Romanian now uses the Latin alphabet, it was written in Cyrillic until 1860 when Latin became the official Romanian alphabet (the Church, however, continued to use Cyrillic until 1890).

Ethnic minorities have long been part of the fabric of Eastern European societies. From the literary point of view, the most important are the Albanians and Bosnian Muslims in the former Yugoslavia, the Hungarians and Germans in Romania, the Jews throughout the entire region, and the Gypsies, like the Jews, throughout Eastern Europe as a whole. The Jewish communities of Eastern Europe collectively represented the largest Jewish population in the world outside the United States. Until World War II, the greatest number of them, some 3.5 million people, lived in Poland, making up 10 percent of the entire population of the country. The Bosnian Muslims, who became the focus of worldwide attention during the ethnic strife in the former Yugoslavia in the early 1990s, are not, as their name might suggest, a distinct Muslim people who have long inhabited the Bosnia-Herzegovina region of what was once Yugoslavia. The Bosnians are in fact South Slavs whose forebears, like the Bulgarian *pomaks,* converted to Islam in the days when virtually the entire South Slavic world had been conquered by the Turks and incorporated into the Ottoman Empire. Besides figuring prominently as literary subjects in the various Eastern European literatures, the German and Jewish ethnic minorities created their own literary cultures. Most Yiddish literature, for example, arose in Poland; the German community in Romania has its own literary tradition, which makes it possible to speak of a German-Romanian literature, just as a minority Hungarian literary culture has also long existed in Romania.

Despite the differences among them and their very different historical evolutions, the peoples of Eastern Europe shared a destiny in the second half of the twentieth century. The entire region was engulfed in World War II and experienced some of the bitterest fighting of the entire war. The mass destruction of the European Jewish community commonly referred to as the Holocaust took place in Eastern Europe, primarily in Poland, where the Nazis established their most extensive network of concentration camps and where random massacres of Jews by Poles were also perpetrated. But persecution and deportation to the death camps in Poland was also the common fate of most Jews in those states allied with the Germans during the war. Treatment of the Jews was the worst in Hungary, Romania, and the puppet states of Croatia and Slovakia. Croatia was dominated by the fascist Ustaša organization, which was led by Ante Pavelić and operated a notorious concentration camp of its own at Jasenovac. If generally less brutal toward Jews than Croatia, Hungary, and Romania, the Slovak republic, headed by the cleric Josef Tiso (who was hanged after the war), willingly carried out deportations of Jews ordered by the Germans. Bulgaria, alone of the Eastern European collaborationist states, managed to save the lives of virtually all its indigenous Jewish population—although this was not the fate of Jews in neighboring countries occupied by the Bulgarian army during the war—thanks especially to the intervention of the Bulgarian Orthodox Church. A somewhat similar claim has also been made by the Romanians with respect to the Jewish population of the historic Romanian lands. But the horrific slaughter of Jews in the areas of Bessarabia and Bukovina, and in the western Ukrainian region occupied by Romanian forces and known in Romanian as Transnistria, beggars description.

The defeat of Germany and the end of World War II in 1945 paved the way for the inclusion of Eastern Europe into the Soviet sphere of political control. Belarus and Ukraine, of course, had already been constituent republics of the Soviet Union, gaining independence only after the collapse of the Soviet Union in 1991. Neither country had ever been independent. By 1948, all of Eastern Europe was within the orbit of Soviet power. The one partial exception was Yugoslavia under the leadership of the former wartime communist guerrilla leader, Marshal Josip Broz Tito. As the dominant political element in the only state in Eastern Europe besides Albania that had not been overrun by the Red Army by the end of the war, the Yugoslav communists insisted on maintaining their independence from Moscow. This led in 1948 to a formal split with the Soviet-dominated Comintern (Communist International). Until the death of Marshal Tito and its eventual disintegration in the late 1980s and early 1990s, Yugoslavia had in some ways been the most liberal state in Eastern Europe and the most open to the West. For all its independence from Moscow, this was certainly not the case with Albania, which developed one of the most repressive and bizarrely austere political systems in the entire region.

Again with the exception of Yugoslavia, Eastern Europe was subject to intense Sovietization until the death of Joseph Stalin in 1953 and the Soviet Twentieth Party Congress of 1956. The period from the end of the war to the death of Stalin is generally regarded as the bleakest in the postwar history of the region. The economy of most of Eastern Europe was artificially, and inefficiently, molded to Soviet needs and policies, ties with the West were sharply curtailed, and social regimentation and cultural repression became facts of daily life.

Cracks in the façade of Eastern European communism began to appear even before the death of Stalin and Nikita Khrushchev's electrifying revelations in his now famous speech before the Twentieth Congress of the Communist Party of the Soviet Union in 1956. Seething resentment against Soviet domination, repressive domestic policies, and inefficient and corrupt economic practices led to the first serious challenge to communist authority in Eastern Europe in the widespread workers' strikes in East Germany in June 1953. The more threatening and by far the bloodiest manifestation of hostility to an indigenous communist regime—before the upheaval in Romania in 1989—was the Hungarian uprising of 1956, which was quelled only by the intervention of Soviet armed forces. The uprising began on 23 October 1956 and lasted until its suppression on 4 November. It resulted in the emigration of a large number of Hungarians, leading cultural figures among them, and stricter censorship and other repressive measures for several years. The Hungarian uprising virtually coincided with riots in Poznań, Poland, protesting the slow pace of de-Stalinization and the continued domination of the Polish military by the Soviets, and demanding the return to power of the ousted communist politician Władysław Gomułka. As the unrest in Poland widened into a protest against the pace of economic reforms, the very real danger of Soviet intervention existed. When the Soviets finally withdrew their opposition to Gomułka, threats of invasion were for the time muted and order gradually was restored.

The sterner measures to restore order in Hungary in the wake of the events of 1956 were paralleled by relative liberalization in Poland. This was most apparent in the cultural sphere, where censorship was eased and a new opening to the West became possible. The reactionary forces, which with the support of Soviet power successfully crushed the uprising in Hungary—although at great cost, primarily in terms of moral standing—and which were compelled to make concessions in Poland, reached their nadir in Romania, also in 1956, when the country fell into the hands of Nicolae Ceauşescu. Under Ceauşescu, and the Ceauşescu family, Romania entered one of its darkest periods in modern history, becoming a virtual police state dominated by an abysmally corrupt and exploitive communist regime. The Romanian nightmare ended in a popular uprising in 1989 that culminated in the summary execution of Ceauşescu and his wife. Less repressive, but still unpopular regimes similarly dominated Czechoslovakia and Bulgaria in the 1950s and 1960s. Todor Zhivkov, who ruled Bulgaria from 1954 to 1989, had the longest tenure of any political leader in Eastern Europe.

Censorship and other internal controls were gradually relaxed in Eastern Europe in the 1960s as the communists believed themselves firmly in control and well able to resist further challenges to their authority. However, they were rudely awakened by the events of the "Prague Spring" of 1968. Fearing the spread of what they regarded as the contagion of liberalization now emanating from Czechoslovakia, the Soviets abandoned hopes of resolving the matter to their satisfaction by applying pressure on the prime minister, Alexander Dubček, and invaded the country. As in Hungary, an indigenous and spontaneous reform movement was halted only by Soviet tanks.

The iron-fisted restoration of order Soviet-style was bound to encounter further challenges. The spirit of reform and democratization was like the genie let out of the bottle. Hardly had Czechoslovakia been brought to heel, when the first of a series of workers' strikes erupted in Poland on 14 December 1970 at the Lenin Shipyards in Gdańsk. These events were destined to lead to the formation of the Solidarity movement and bring the Gdańsk shipyards electrician Lech Wałęsa to prominence. Despite some concessions by the authorities, grievances continued to fester and surfaced again in June 1976 in the cities of Radom and Ursus. A new wave of strikes, now uniting workers and intellectuals, broke out in the summer of 1980 and resulted in the creation of the Solidarity union. The situation in Poland was in some respects beginning to resemble the mood in Czechoslovakia during the "Prague Spring" of 1968. The Soviets, convinced of the inability of the Poles to impose the appropriate restraints, threatened to invade the country and, in fact, undertook menacing military maneuvers. Rather than risk a full-fledged Soviet invasion and the bloody fighting that surely would have ensued with the entry of Soviet troops into the largest country in Eastern Europe, General Władysław Jaruzelski imposed a state of martial law on 13 December 1981. This was sufficient to appease the Soviets. Again, a stick-and-carrot approach restored a measure of calm, and Jaruzelski lifted martial law about a year later. Solidarity, of course, had been outlawed. When Mikhail Gorbachev took the reins of power in the Soviet Union in 1985, he initiated a series of limited economic reforms (perestroika) and greater openness in public life (glasnost), which eventually contributed to the breakup of the USSR. Gorbachev's reforms in the Soviet Union had the effect of encouraging the supporters of Solidarity in Poland. More strikes broke out in 1988, culminating in negotiations the following year between a revived Solidarity and the government, which paved the way for new elections and the end of communism in Poland. Also in 1989, Hungary's borders to the West were opened, and the Berlin Wall came down; in late 1990 the eminent playwright and political dissident Václav Havel was elected president of Czechoslovakia; and a new Bulgarian constitution took effect on 12 July 1991. The collapse of the Soviet Union came about in December 1991.

After the death in 1980 of Marshal Tito, who had the strength to hold the Yugoslav federation together, the largest and ethnically most complex South Slav state stumbled along an inexorable path to fragmentation. Slovenia and Croatia declared their independence of Yugoslavia in June 1991, followed by Macedonia in September 1991 and by the Croats and Muslims of Bosnia-Herzegovina in April 1992. Serbia lost no time in initiating war against them in an effort to maintain the integrity of the Yugoslav state (of course, under its domination) or at least to separate Serb-populated territories from the other republics—above all, Croatia and Bosnia-Herzegovina—and incorporate them into a greater Serbia. In a mercifully brief (ten-day) war, Slovenia succeeded in driving off the Serbs and preserving its territorial integrity. In bitter and protracted fighting, Croatia lost but later regained more than a third of its territory. Bosnia-Herzegovina, with its mix of Croatian, Serbian, and Muslim ethnic groups—and their conflicting political and territorial aims—fared the worst. The hapless land became the scene of the bloodiest fighting and the worst slaughter of the innocents in Europe since World War II. Only with the intervention of the United Nations and peace agreements among the warring parties signed in Dayton, Ohio, in 1995 that called for a remapping of Bosnia-Herzegovina along ethnic lines was the conflict brought to an uneasy halt. But that was still not the end of the Yugoslav tragedy. A relentless Serbian campaign of "ethnic cleansing" in the overwhelmingly Albanian Muslim province of Kosovo, undertaken in 1998, led to NATO intervention and seventy-eight days of American bombing of Serbia before the Serbian forces were driven back. Hundreds of thousands of Albanian refugees were able to return home from sanctuaries in Albania and Macedonia, and the road was paved for the eventual political demise of the nationalist Serbian leader, Slobodan Milošević, in democratic elections in November 2000. Following his arrest and imprisonment in March 2001, Milošević was extradited to The Hague on 28 June to stand trial for war crimes before an international tribunal.

In light of the history of Eastern Europe in the past sixty years, a question may now be raised: How should we view the development of imaginative literature in Eastern Europe and East Germany in the period 1945 to the fall of communism? Are these not literatures primarily of political interest, literatures that expose the nature of communism and offer glimpses into the daily life of people living under this system? The literatures of Eastern Europe from 1945 to the end of the 1990s—including the period of the Bosnian and Kosovo campaigns—are undeniably bound up with the political history of the region. In no small measure, they were shaped by and responded to the circumstances of the period. The time frame encompasses some of the most momentous events in Europe in the twentieth century. Interest in those events is neither negligible nor ephemeral and necessarily embraces cultural products. In assessing those products, the conditions of their genesis should not obscure the deep commitment of so many of the artists to the integrity and autonomy of their art despite the curtailments of freedom imposed on them.

World War II and the Holocaust

World War II, much of the action of which was waged on the territories of the Eastern European countries, resulted in the incorporation of the entire region into the Soviet orbit and the consequent imposition of a Soviet-style political and economic system. For nearly a half-century that system, despite several grave challenges to and modifications of it, remained in place and became responsible for a broad and in some instances wrenching transformation of the entire fabric of society. The impact of the war on Eastern Europe as a whole was enormous. Apart from the extensive loss of life and property, postwar Sovietization for a long time erected formidable barriers to the normal flow of East–West contacts, especially in the cultural and intellectual spheres. Sovietization also had a profound influence on patterns of social life in the countries of the region. Not only were the Eastern European states distanced from the West, but they were also distanced from the social, cultural, economic, and political structures that had existed within them during the interwar years. For nearly two decades after World War II, and in a few cases even longer, with hardly an exception the interwar period was dismissed as neo-feudal and dominated by right-wing regimes supported by conservative elements of society and the clergy. Even the early interwar avant-garde, despite the opposition to it by the same forces of conservatism derided by the communists in the postwar period, was made off-limits because of its enthusiasm for experimentation, its general disinterest in social issues, and its repudiation of representational art.

Because of its huge Jewish population, Eastern Europe also became the main killing fields for European Jewry. The Holocaust not only swept away the established Jewish communities of Eastern Europe that were steadily integrating into mainstream economic, cultural, and intellectual life, but also left a legacy of moral and philosophical questions with which the various Eastern European countries have had to deal since the end of the war. The most obvious of these questions addresses the degree of complicity in the Nazi campaign against the Jews on the part of those Eastern European states allied with Germany during the war: Bulgaria, Croatia, Hungary, Romania, and Slovakia. Although each of these countries was under the wartime leadership of right-wing or fascist regimes in alliance with Nazi Germany on ideological grounds or for opportunistic purposes of anticipated territorial expansion, there were differences among them in their treatment of the Jews. The subject of more than one book, Bulgaria's ability to spare its relatively small Jewish population the fate suffered by Jews elsewhere in Central and Eastern Europe has by now become fairly well known. Under the leadership of Admiral Miklós Horthy, Hungary managed to stave off the wholesale roundup of Jews intended for the gas chambers until 15 October 1944, when the extremist Arrow Cross Party of Ferenc Szálasi seized power and joined the Germans not only in a desperate three-month defense of Budapest against the approaching Red Army, but also in a frenzied extermination of the thousands of Jews who had survived previous roundups. From early in their unholy alliance with the Germans, the Nazi puppet states of Slovakia, under Monsignor Joseph Tiso, and Croatia, under the fascist and virulently anti-Serb and anti-Semitic Ustaša organization, enthusiastically collaborated in the German policy against the Jews. Romania, especially under the command of Marshal Ion Antonescu, pursued the paradoxical policy of trying to spare its indigenous Jewish population while sanctioning and participating in the slaughter of allegedly pro-Russian Jews in territories occupied by the Soviets or claimed by the Romanian state. The sensitivity in such countries as Croatia, Romania, and Slovakia to the subject of wartime collaboration with the Germans in the mass deportation and extermination of the Jews for a long time curtailed a frank literary engagement with the issue. Communist censorship also preferred to draw a veil over it both because it was embarrassing and because the communist regimes that came to power after 1945 had done so by virtue of the defeat of the wartime collaborationist states. Generally speaking, the literary response to the Holocaust was more forthcoming in those countries where there had been little or no collusion in the war against the Jews. These would include Bulgaria, the Czech lands, and Poland.

The mixed record of Hungary—the attempt on the part of the Horthy regime to spare the Jews as long as possible after the German invasion of 19 March 1944, including the officially tolerated efforts of the Swedish diplomat Raul Wallenberg to bring as many Jews as he could under the protection of neutral-country passes, followed by the frenzied bloodletting of Szálasi's Arrow Cross toughs—encouraged a somewhat more forthright literary representation of what befell the country's Jews before and after 15 October 1944. The Jewish writer Ernő Szép's memoir, *The Smell of Humans,* which was first published in 1945 and reprinted in 1984, is a chilling but emotionally restrained picture of conditions in Hungary under the Szálasi regime. Somewhat similar in nature, although with its focus on the concentration camp experiences of a young boy, is Imre Kertész's novel *Fateless* (1975), for which he was awarded the Nobel Prize in Literature for 2002. With the exception by and large of writers of Jewish background (in whole or in part), such as the Serbs Danilo Kiš and Aleksandar Tišma, and the Slovene Boris Pahor, Yugoslav literature from 1945 to 1990 tended to focus on the anti-German campaign of Marshal Josip Broz Tito's partisans and the simultaneous internecine struggle against Draža Mihailović's royalists. In this regard, a seriocomic war novel like the Montenegran Miodrag Bulatović's *Hero on a Donkey* (1965) or Milovan Djilas's compelling book of memoirs, *Wartime* (1977), might well have won a broader audience than, say, Kiš's *Psalm 44* (1962), Pahor's *Pilgrim Among the Shadows* (1967), or Tišma's *Book of Blam* (1972), *Use of Man* (1976), and *Kapo* (1987), with their focus on Jewish experience. Since the disintegration of Yugoslavia, the Balkan wars of the 1990s have created new national concerns capable, in literary terms, of pushing the events of the period 1940 to 1945 more into the background.

Although Antonescu remains a misunderstood national hero to a number of Romanians, and the expression of such sentiments became easier after the fall of the regime of Nicolae Ceaușescu in 1989, the firm grip in which Romanian literature was held captive in the Ceaușescu era severely limited the ability of writers to deal with the fate of the Romanian Jews during the war. By far the richest literary treatment of the plight of the Jews from 1939 to 1945 came in Czechoslovakia and, to a somewhat lesser extent, Poland. Among Slovak writers, both before and after the peaceful separation of Czechoslovakia into the Czech Republic and the Republic of Slovakia, the main focus in creative writing about World War II has been on the events surrounding the Slovak National Uprising of 1944 when, sensing the inevitability of German military collapse, the Slovaks sought to break free of German control. More than one Slovak writer—Ján Johanides, for example, in his novel *Elephants in Mauthausen* (1985) or Milo Urban in his book of memoirs, *Freedom Is No Joke* (1977)—has resisted the temptation to drape the uprising wholly in banners of national pride and has forthrightly confronted the less savory aspects of Slovak collaboration with the Germans during the war, especially regarding the treatment of the Slovak Jewish community. What the Slovaks did to the Jews "under German pressure," writes Urban in *Freedom Is No Joke,* "exceeded the limits of humanity." Among the Czechs, the most substantial body of writing about the Holocaust has come from writers of Jewish background—above all, Julius Fucík, Ladislav Fuks, Arnošt Lustig, and Jiří Weil—who had firsthand knowledge of the persecution of the Jews.

The case of the Poles is more complex. The Polish Jewish community, by far the largest in Europe, was mostly destroyed. Since it was liquidated on the territory of Poland, there has been an undeniable Polish sensitivity to the fate of the Polish Jewish community during the war and to the ability, and willingness, of many Poles to come to the aid of the Jews. This sensitivity has become all the more acute with revelations of apparently spontaneous massacres of Jews by Poles, as at Jedwabne in northeastern Poland in 1941. Although Polish heroism in fighting the Germans both in Poland and elsewhere in Europe has been the subject of much fiction, the Holocaust as such has generated few literary works. Of those dealing directly with the situation in the concentration camps, perhaps the most famous is the collection of stories by Tadeusz Borowski known in English as *This Way for the Gas, Ladies and Gentlemen* (1948). The poet Marian Piechal draws a chilling picture of Jewish humiliation and persecution at the hands of the Germans in his poem "Yankel's Last Concert" (1954). But the overriding issue for most Polish writers who have written about the war and the situation of the Jews in Poland at the time has been the nature of Polish attitudes toward the Jews and the nagging moral question as to whether indeed Poles could have done more to save Jewish lives. Jerzy Andrzejewski's novella *Holy Week* (1943) is set in the time of the Warsaw Ghetto Uprising and uses the event mainly to explore this issue. So, too, in a more expansive and complex way does Andrzej Szczypiorski's novel *The Beautiful Mrs. Seidenman* (1986). The ambivalence of some Poles toward the fate of the Jews, and the issue of Christian moral responsibility for what befell the Jews, are the subjects of the Nobel Prize winner Czesław Miłosz's wartime poems "Campo Fiore" and "A Poor Christian Looks at the Ghetto." This preoccupation with Polish moral responsibility, which is addressed as well in Jarosław Marek Rymkiewicz's *The Final Station: Umschlagplatz* (1988), is not difficult to understand in light of two incontrovertible facts: Poland became the principal locus of the Holocaust, and, unlike the situation among the Czechs, the overwhelming majority of Polish writers confronting the occupation and the plight of the Jews of Poland happen to have been Christian. Jewish losses in Poland during the war were of such magnitude that few Jews could be counted in the ranks of the immediate postwar literary community. Among the few was Adolf Rudnicki, whose huge *The Living Sea and the Dead Sea* (1952) stands as a monument to Jewish suffering in Poland under the Germans. Among non-Jewish writers, Urszula Kozioł's novel *Stations of Memory* (1965) is a poignant picture of life in a Polish village before, during, and after the war with haunting images of what the German occupation meant for the local Jews. With revelations surfacing about previously unimaginable local atrocities committed by Poles against Jews both during the war (the 1941 Jedwabne massacre) and in the aftermath of the war (the 1945 Kielce massacre), newer Polish literature faces yet graver challenges.

The literary response to the war itself, as distinguished from the Holocaust, replicates to a considerable degree the pattern of national response noted in the treatment of the Holocaust. Where active resistance to the German invaders was sustained over a period of time, as in the case of the Yugoslavs and, to a lesser extent, the Albanians, a body of fiction and other types of writing arose around the actual fighting. Novels and short stories by the Montenegran Miodrag Bulatović, the Serbs Branko Ćopić (*Breakthrough,* 1952) and Mihailo Lalić (*Reconnaissance Patrol,* 1948, and *The Wailing Mountain,* 1957), and the Croatian Vjekoslav Kaleb (*The Beauty of Dust,* 1954), as well as the memoirs of the Montenegran Milovan Djilas are wholly representative of this aspect. But the fighting in Yugoslavia was not confined to the campaign against the Germans. A parallel war, waged between Tito's partisans and the royalist *chetniks* under the leadership of Mihailović, also generated literary response, as in novels by Mihailo Lalić, where the emphasis is on the fratricidal fighting in his native Montenegro, and in the massive tetralogy *Turning Point* (1994–1998), by the Serbian writer Sava Janković. Since Tito and his partisans came out on top in this vicious domestic conflict, postwar Yugoslav writing about it had long been under a stern injunction against any favorable depiction of the *chetniks* or Mihailović (who was executed after the war). But it must be remembered that negative portrayals of the fascist Croatian state did not paint all Croatians with the same brush, for the Ustaša by no means commanded the loyalty of all Croatians. The ranks of Tito's partisans were multiethnic; that is, they included not only Serbs, but also Bosnians, Macedonians, Montenegrans, Slovenes, and Croatians. The Serb Oskar Davičo's lengthy novel, *The Poem* (1959), about the consequences of a young partisan's exaggerated moral standards, explores the extremes of which the partisan movement was capable.

The Albanian situation essentially resembled the Yugoslav in that Albania was invaded mainly by Italian forces and mounted a vigorous defense in the form of partisan warfare. Hence virtually all of Albanian postwar writing about World War II pivots on this resistance to the Italians and, later, Germans and on the impact of the Italian occupation on both the Albanians and the occupiers themselves. Two novels by the internationally acclaimed writer Ismail Kadare, *The General of the Dead Army* (1963) and *Chronicle in Stone* (1971), have World War II settings. For the latter, Kadare drew on his own memories of his native city of Gjirokastër under Italian occupation. Similarly, Petro Marko's *Ustica Night* (1989) is based on his wartime internment together with other Balkan prisoners on the island of Ustica in the Tyrrhenian Sea north of Sicily. Dritëro Agolli, a prominent poet, based two major novels on the partisan campaign, *Commissar Memo* (1970) and *The Man with a Cannon* (1975), as did Nasi Lera, in *The Blood of April* (1980). Of Fatos Arapi's novels about the war, *The Comrades* (1978) and *The Sea Between* (1986), the latter is particularly interesting in that it deals with the sufferings and tragic end of a group of Italian soldiers in the autumn of 1943. The ability of some Albanian writers to look at the war in terms also of its impact on the enemy had already been demonstrated by Kadare's *The General of the Dead Army*.

Although Polish resistance to the German invasion of September 1939 crumbled in a matter of weeks, that brief but ferocious struggle as well as underground action during the occupation and the service of thousands of Poles in Allied military units provided ample material for a rich Polish literature about the war. Among the most compelling are Leopold Buczkowski's *Black Torrent* (1954) and Tadeusz Konwicki's *A Dreambook for Our Time* (1963), both of which deal with the partisan campaign. Buczkowski's novel is notable as well for its treatment of the Jewish role in the resistance. The heroic but terribly costly Warsaw Uprising of 1944 created its own myths and came vividly to life in Miron Białoszewski's factual memoir, *A Memoir of the Warsaw Uprising* (1970), and the collection of poems under the title *Building the Barricade* (1974), by Anna Swir (real name Anna Świrszczyńska). Since the partisan fighting against the German occupiers in Poland was carried out both by units loyal to the London government-in-exile and by others of a pro-Soviet character, the rivalry and hostility between the two groups also operates as a subtheme in some of the Polish literature about the war.

Among the Eastern Europeans who fought with the Germans, there was understandable reluctance in a communist-dominated postwar period to confront the war except within the limits of anti-German resistance that developed in 1944 or 1945. The literary exploitation of such resistance was ideologically important in order to blunt the image of wartime collaboration and to extol communist opposition to fascism. From the standpoint of imaginative literature, arguably the most resonant of the national uprisings against the Germans was the Slovak insurrection in 1944, which, despite its weak organization and ultimate failure, grew even larger in the popular consciousness after the declaration of an independent Slovak republic in 1993. Beginning with Jozef Horák's novel *The Silence of Mountain Forests* (1947), the uprising has generated a large body of writing in which the event is seen from divergent points of view, ranging from the revisionist to the unabashedly mythopoeic. Among major texts inspired by the uprising are Jozef Ciger-Hronsky's *The World in the Peat-Bog* (1960), Ladislav Mňačko's *Death Is Called Engelchen* (1959), Ladislav Ťažký's *Herd of Ferocious Adams* (1965) and *I Buried Him Naked* (1970), Vladimír Mináč's *The Quick and the Dead* (1958), Dominik Tatarka's *The First and Second Blows* (1950), and Július Balco's *The Waxen-Yellow Apple* (1976), which carries the tendency toward sentimentalization of the role of hill-farmer partisans of a writer like Tatarka to near excess. Vincent Šikula's trilogy *The Master Carpenters* (1976–1979) is representative of the manner in which the Slovak wartime uprising has been transformed into the stuff of national mythology. The most open-minded Slovak writing about the role of the Slovaks during the war and the uprising has come in works of the 1980s and 1990s by such relatively younger writers as Ladislav Ballek, Ján Johanides, and Ivan Habaj (especially in his massive trilogy, *Colonists,* 1980, 1981, and 1986). As early as 1961, Rudolf Jašík, in *The Dead Do Not Sing,* painted a broad canvas of Slovakia during World War II, including the fate of Slovak troops on the eastern front.

The communist regime of Nicolae Ceaușescu would, one assumes, have encouraged positive writing about the late-in-the-war Romanian resistance to the Germans after the downfall of the government of Marshal Ion Antonescu. However, World War II has yielded a negligible Romanian literary harvest. The heavy weight of the past—the virulent and anti-Semitic nationalism of Corneliu Zelea Codreanu (1899–1938), founder of the Legion of the Archangel Michael, with its notorious Iron Guard military wing; the four-year reign (1940–1944) of the Hitler-loving Antonescu, who was hanged after the war; the horrendous massacres of Jews at the hands of the Romanians in Bessarabia, Bukovina, and Transnistria; and the disasters that befell the Romanian army in the campaign against the Soviets, including their participation in the battle of Stalingrad—proved so burdensome that literary engagement with the war years could only seem distasteful. Moreover, in the more repressive days of the Ceaușescu regime, writers had little choice but to advance the policies and goals of the government and to concentrate on the building of Romanian-style socialism, with its curious combination of nationalism and independence. And when one of the prime goals of the regime was attaining and retaining Most Favored Nation trading status in the U.S. Congress, Romania's distance from the Soviet Union during the Cold War and deflection of attention from Romanian fascism and anti-Semitism—the latter still a factor in the postwar period, as witness the meteoric political rise of Ceaușescu's "court poet," Corneliu Vadim Tudor, a presidential runoff candidate in the December 2000 elections—became paramount. Since the fall of the Ceaușescus, Romanian literary interest in World War II has taken a back seat to now possible revelations of the repression of artists and intellectuals under the communists.

The East German literary response to World War II is of particular interest in light of the official dissociation of the postwar German communist state from the Nazi past. During the darker days of the Cold War, moreover, East German propaganda was relentless in its portrayal of West Germany (Federal Republic of Germany) as a neo-Nazi state and the logical successor to Hitlerite Germany. For the East German authors who wished to write about the Nazi period and World War II, the path was relatively easy as long as certain proprieties were observed. As works by such well-known East German literary figures as Bruno Apitz, Franz Fühmann, Stephan Hermlin, and Arnold Zweig demonstrate, a favorite subject was the great battle of Stalingrad, which broke the back of the deep German advance into the USSR and was a devastating blow to the pride of the German military and Hitler's plans for the conquest of the Soviet Union. Notwithstanding its acknowledged literary merits, Fühmann's epiclike and autobiographical poem, *The Journey to Stalingrad* (1953), is ideologically typical in its praise of the heroic defenders of Stalingrad and postwar socialist construction. Apitz's greatest literary success was *Naked Among Wolves* (1957), which was not only the first East German novel about the wartime concentration camps, but the first GDR literary work to gain international recognition. Impressive in the realism of its depiction of conditions inside Buchenwald in March 1945, the novel was also politically correct at the time in its focus on the resistance to the German SS by a clandestine communist-led organization within the camp.

The battle of Stalingrad as a literary theme was exceptionally convenient for writers in that it afforded them the opportunity to paint in often very graphic terms the sheer horror and senselessness of the war while permitting description of the valor of the Russian soldier and the ultimate triumph of the Soviet forces over the German army. Perhaps more compelling for the foreign reader than the literature about the war itself was the writing about Germany in the 1930s after Hitler came to power: the rise of National Socialism and Hitlerite intolerance and what it meant, for example, to grow up German in the 1930s and be subjected to the relentless anti-Semitic propaganda of the Nazis. A classic story in this regard is Füh-mann's "The Jew Car," which is included in the collection *The Jew Car: Fourteen Days out of Two Seasons* (1968) and which ought to be a required text in studies of Nazi Germany and the Holocaust. So, too, should Hermlin's *Evening Light* (1983), a fine book of personal reminis-cences of the author's youth in Berlin in the 1930s, his entry into the Communist Party, the rise of National Socialism, and his participation in the struggle against fascism.

The Communist Takeover: The Individual versus the State in Postwar Society

Since the most momentous events of the twentieth century for the peoples of Eastern Eu-rope were World War II and the subsequent communist rule until the late 1980s and early 1990s, the literary preoccupation with those events and their ramifications is eminently un-derstandable. However, censorship, at its harshest in the first decade after the communist assumption of power, and cultural repression in general limited the freedom of writers to deal forthrightly with the political situation in the immediate aftermath of the war. In some instances, only writers who had become émigrés could write such works. The classical ex-ample of this is Czesław Miłosz's novel about the Soviet takeover of Poland, *The Seizure of Power* (1955), which he wrote and published when already a political defector in Paris. The war in Poland between the communists and their supporters and the anticommunist units of the Home Army, which remained loyal to the Polish government-in-exile in London, had begun in fact before the actual end of World War II. Long shrouded in official secrecy and a taboo subject for writers, this Polish "civil war" of 1945 to 1947 found literary expression in at least one famous Polish postwar text decades before the collapse of communism in Poland in 1989. The striking exception to the rule of silence was Jerzy Andrzejewski's novel, subsequently made into a well-known film, *Ashes and Diamonds* (1948). Were it not for Andrzejewski's portrait of a sympathetic local Communist Party official, the novel most surely would not have won the approval of censors for publication when it did. In one of her best prose texts, the novel *Dungeon* (1990), the Serbian writer Svetlana Velmar-Janković draws a vivid picture of the privations and repression attendant on the communist takeover of Yugoslavia after the victory of Tito's partisans. One of the strengths of the novel is the un-erring psychological accuracy in Velmar-Janković's portrayal of the impact of the changes on the outlook and behavior of various characters.

Once in power, the communists throughout Eastern Europe set about implementing their plans for the imposition of Soviet-model governments and economies. Besides ig-noring national cultural and institutional differences, they trampled on the rights of the individual citizen in the name of the collective and dealt harshly with attempts to assert the rights of the individual over those of the state. Before long, the anomalies and priva-tions of the great programs of communist postwar reconstruction, the severe dislocations brought on by mass agricultural collectivization, the offenses to human dignity and artis-tic creativity of social and cultural regimentation, the gross inequality in living standards between the newly privileged and the rest of society, and the paranoia underlying the walling off of East from West in both the figurative and the literal sense (as in the case of the Berlin Wall) gave rise to an extraordinary response in every genre of literature. Em-ploying whatever means at their disposal to circumvent a watchful and stern censorship, from Aesopian language to obscure poetic imagery to underground and foreign publica-tion, Eastern European writers throughout virtually the entire region put a human face on the implacable countenance of dogmatic communism. Sensitive to the absurd and grotesque aspects of everyday life under a communist regime, Czechoslovakia in its time being among the most repressive, Czech and Slovak writers such as Václav Havel, Bohumil Hrabal, Ivan Klíma, Milan Kundera, Ladislav Mňačko, and Josef Škvorecký were delighting—and in some instances terrifying—domestic as well as foreign readers with glimpses of the plight of the ordinary citizen up against the awesome machinery of the state. For Havel, Hrabal, Kundera, and Škvorecký, it was to the bizarre and Kafkaesque aspects of the everyday life and the robotlike nature of the communist bureaucracy to which their attention was drawn in such fine examples of Eastern European black humor as Havel's comedies *The Garden Party* (1963) and *The Memorandum* (1965); Hrabal's collection of short stories *The Death of Mr. Baltisberger* (1974); Kundera's short novel *The Joke* (1968) and story collection *Laughable Loves* (1968); and Škvorecký's novel *The End of the Nylon Age* (written 1950, first published 1967) and story collection *From the Life of High Society* (1965). In the land of Kafka, an understanding of the nightmarish aspects of totalitarianism came easy and was reflected in such Czech novels as Jiří Gruša's *The Questionnaire* (1974), Klíma's *An Hour of Silence* (1963), Zdena Salivarová's *Summer in Prague* (1973) and *Ashes, Ashes, All Fall Down* (1987), Škvorecký's *The Miracle Game* (1972), and Ludvík Vaculík's *Guinea Pigs* (1973), and in such Slovak novels as Mňačko's *The Taste of Power* (1967) and Martin M. Šimečka's *The Year of the Frog* (1993).

Absurdist and grotesque plays about the monstrously inefficient workings of the communist bureaucracy were hardly the province of the Czechs alone. Some of the most effective playwriting aimed at exposing the nature of power and the mechanisms of repression in a communist state were written as well by the Poles Sławomir Mrożek and Tadeusz Różewicz and by the Hungarian István Örkény, in whose *Stevie in the Bloodbath* (written 1969, premiere 1979) the experiences of the Hungarian and Eastern European Everyman, Stevie, and his three alter egos encapsulate the horrors of the twentieth century, with its wars, genocide, nuclear bomb, and massive social and political upheavals.

Some of the bleakest accounts of life under communism were written by the Hungarian author and sometime social worker György Konrád, whose novels *The Case Worker* (1969), *The City Builder* (1972), and *The Loser* (1980) dispel any romantic notions about the building of socialism under the leadership of the Communist Party. A confession of willing self-deception, such as the following by Konrád, could have been echoed many times over the length and breadth of Eastern Europe:

> But however much I would like to, I cannot fool myself; each station of my life was an error. I was forever up in arms, for something, against something, first as the officer of an occupying army, then as a party functionary of a satellite state. I helped establish an overcautious government that locked me up twice and is forced to keep on snooping and interfering—its obtuse subjects have yet to learn that it's good for them not to do what they would most like to do. I trained thousands of young people to become revolutionaries just like me; on some I did such a good job that they became my surliest interrogators at state security headquarters.

A deeper anguish attended the perception of betrayed idealism and exploitation, as conveyed so effectively in the Polish writer Kazimierz Brandys's novella *The Defense of the "Granada"* (1956), about a group of young theater people whose plans to stage an antibureaucracy satire by the early Soviet poet and playwright Vladimir Mayakovsky are thwarted by Machiavellian authorities.

Contrasting, either directly or indirectly, the high lifestyle of the communist privileged and the privations faced by the ordinary citizen also provided ample grist for the literary mills between 1945 and 1990, as exemplified by the Pole Leopold Tyrmand's *The Rosa Luxemburg Contraceptives Cooperative: A Primer on Communist Civilization* (1971) and the Romanian Petru Popescu's *Burial of the Vine* (1973).

Unmasking the Communist Party and the Mechanisms of Soviet Control

The widespread disillusionment in Eastern Europe with the postwar communist regimes gave rise to a large body of writing intended to reveal the true nature of communism while baring the mechanisms of Soviet control. Sometimes, this revelatory literature takes a historical perspective, as does the internationally renowned Serbian writer Danilo Kiš's *A Tomb for Boris Davidovich* (1976), in which patterns of Soviet cynicism, exploitation, and terror are traced to the immediate aftermath of the Bolshevik ascension to power in Russia in 1917. The revelations of a number of authors whose sights were trained on the period after World War II were made only from afar, from the safe havens attained through defection or emigration under political pressure. Perhaps the most famous, and one of the earliest, example of this is Czesław Miłosz's book of essays *The Captive Mind* (1951–1952). Written shortly after he had defected from Poland while serving as the cultural attaché of the Polish Embassy in Paris, *The Captive Mind* draws on Miłosz's own experiences as well as those of his contemporaries (who are easily identified, despite their fictionalized names) to depict the ways in which the communists sought to exploit the talents of artists and intellectuals for their own ends. In his memoir, *A World Apart* (1951), another distinguished Polish writer, Gustaw Herling-Grudziński, who chose to remain in the West after military service in World War II, describes his terrifying experiences in the Soviet concentration camp system (the gulag) from 1940 to 1942.

After Miłosz, the most notable Eastern European writer to share with readers his disillusionment in the postwar political and social order was a Yugoslav, Milovan Djilas. A former partisan intellectual and political figure, who was very close to Tito and knew the socialist system of Yugoslavia inside out, Djilas, a prolific writer, bared the nature of communist power and privilege in a series of incisive and extraordinarily revealing books such as *The New Class* (1957). They enjoyed almost immediate world fame and became required texts in colleges and universities. How close Djilas actually was to the seats of power in communist Yugoslavia is nowhere better exemplified than in his *Conversations with Stalin* (1962), a book of memoirs and an insider's account of what it was like to deal with the Soviet dictator at first hand. In 1969 Djilas followed up *The New Class* with *Unperfect Society: Beyond the New Class* and in 1977 published another book of memoirs, *Of Prisons and Ideas,* based in large measure on his own incarceration as a political prisoner. While neither a political figure nor a war veteran, as was Djilas, the Hungarian writer György Konrád, whose prose fiction has already been mentioned in another context, wrote some of the most cogent analyses of communist-era political culture. His essays have been collected in *The Intellectuals on the Road to Class Power* (1979) and *Antipolitics: An Essay* (1984).

Exposés of the reality of communist power in Eastern Europe often took the form of personal recollections and memoirs, as we have seen with Herling-Grudziński's *A World Apart,* a narrative of terror with few peers. Memoirs by émigrés and exiles such as Herling-

Grudziński and Miłosz as well as by writers who remained in Eastern Europe flourished especially from the late 1960s on. Typical examples of the genre are the Slovak Ladislav Mňačko's *Belated Reportages* (1968), the Czechs Jiří Mucha's *Living and Partly Living* (1968) and Pavel Kohout's *From the Diary of a Counterrevolutionary* (1969), the Bulgarian Georgi Markov's *The Truth that Killed* (1969), the Croatian Dubravka Ugrešić's *Fording the Stream of Consciousness* (1988), the Pole Kazimierz Brandys's *A Question of Reality* (1980), and the Serb Borislav Pekić's *The Years the Locusts Consumed: A Prison Memoir or Anthropopeia, 1948–1954* (1987), about his years in prison, and *Stripped of My Stripes: Daily Notes and Thoughts, 1954–1983* (1996), consisting of personal reflections from his postprison years.

Emigration and Exile

The ability of the creative artist—in this instance, the writer—to adapt to or accommodate the new postwar political realities varied, of course, with the individual. For most writers, the option of emigration did not exist even when the possibility itself existed. Nothing can be more traumatic for writers than separation from their own cultures, from the environments of their own languages. Faced with that prospect, Eastern European writers usually took the path of lesser resistance by avoiding direct confrontation with the communist literary authorities. Least resistance was the way of open collaboration with Party and state in the use of creative writing for ideological purposes, as was practiced by the otherwise talented Romanian poet Eugen Jebeleanu, who before the war had played a fairly prominent role in the Romanian literary avant-garde. Until the discrediting of Soviet-imported socialist realism, this often implied conformity to the goals and techniques of this peculiar fusion of realism and Soviet-style idealism. For writers lacking the stomach to turn themselves into producers of socialist realist potboilers, probing the outer limits of censorial tolerance was one way of trying to maintain artistic integrity. Compromises were usually inevitable, but for many they could be lived with for the sake of publication. Few, indeed, were the writers who managed to wholly avoid some accommodation with the officially mandated socialist realism of the late 1940s and 1950s, as the careers of such otherwise disparate writers as the fine Bulgarian poet Blaga Dimitrova and the Polish prose writer Kazimierz Brandys attest. The most offensive taboos, and the resultant consequences when they were breached, could be avoided by means of what has been referred to as "inner censorship"—a form of self-policing on the part of the writer before submitting the literary work to the censors.

Writers generally understood which subjects were taboo, such as the Communist Party's accession to power, its unquestioned authority, the legitimacy of the regime, and the primacy of socialism (to name only the more obvious), and which had to be dealt with in a circumspect manner, such as the role of communists during the war, collaboration with the Germans, the Soviet-imposed redrawing of national borders, the leadership role of the Soviet Union within the communist camp, and new socioeconomic realities like agricultural collectivization and the emphasis on heavy industry. Beyond the visible boundaries, writers felt free to explore uncharted territory and to hope for the best. Since experimentation with form and style was risky, especially in the days when a fairly rigid adherence to the tenets of socialist realism was demanded and expected, any literary work capable of being construed as abstract and nonrepresentational was deemed lacking in either social content or merit and was not tolerated. As can be imagined, this proved to be especially difficult and challenging for poets, for whom language and image are the principal tools of creativity.

The avant-garde art so well developed in interwar central and eastern Europe—particularly in Germany (until Hitler's rise to power), Hungary, Poland, and Romania—was also regarded with unconcealed suspicion because of its nonconformity and its defiance and rejection of political and cultural institutions. In periods of lesser cultural repression in the history of post–World War II Eastern Europe, the abject failure of the authorities to erect an insurmountable barrier between their own time and the interwar years of the avant-garde became painfully obvious. Formal experimentation involving everything from narrative structures to poetic language became widespread whenever domestic conditions provided some breathing space. Underlying much of this experimentation was the nurturing rediscovery of the interwar avant-garde as an antecedent tradition. In Romania, no such rediscovery was really necessary. An impressive and very cosmopolitan interwar surrealism was kept alive and cultivated even during the war years and afterward until, in 1947, the new regime felt itself sufficiently empowered to crack down on it. But one of its major representatives, the poet and prose writer Gellu Naum, returned to it with renewed vigor in the 1960s when literary repression eased. The impressive interwar Polish avant-garde, exemplified by such writers as Stanisław Ignacy Witkiewicz (Witkacy), who committed suicide in 1939 shortly after the German invasion, and Witold Gomborowicz, who was in South America when hostilities erupted and spent the war years in Argentina, was put under a strict ban by the communists until at least the early 1960s. As elsewhere in Eastern Europe, the works of the now repudiated and outlawed interwar avant-garde were no longer permitted to be reprinted or studied. When the situation changed in the 1960s, younger Polish writers who had grown up in ignorance of this legacy embraced it with the fervor of zealots.

The easing of prohibitions on the interwar avant-garde also occurred in the context of an easing of access to Western cultural products. Thus with such younger postwar Polish enthusiasts of the theater of the absurd as Sławomir Mrożek and Tadeusz Różewicz, the opportunity to familiarize themselves with the plays of Samuel Beckett, Eugène Ionesco, Harold Pinter, Max Frisch, and Bertolt Brecht (who despite his communist loyalties and resettlement in East Berlin was still long banned as a dramatist from many Eastern European stages) paralleled the discovery of their domestic predecessors. The now accessible Western tradition of the absurd in a sense validated the achievement of interwar Polish experimentalism, and both acted as a vigorous stimulant to a new postwar Polish dramatic art utterly incompatible with the by now largely discredited socialist realism.

Until the uprising of 1956 propelled thousands of Hungarians into emigration, arguably the most celebrated Eastern European political émigré was the Pole Czesław Miłosz, who has had a brilliant academic and literary career in the United States, capped by his winning the Nobel Prize in Literature in 1980. Other well-known Polish literary émigrés were Marek Hłasko, a rebellious young writer who could not be integrated into the system prevailing in Poland at the time, and Sławomir Mrożek, whose absurdist stories and plays take aim squarely at the gross inanities and inequities of the postwar communist police state. The prominent Romanian anthropologist and creative writer Mircea Eliade, who chose not to return home at the end of World War II from his diplomatic service in London and Lisbon, has had no less distinguished a career in the United States than Miłosz. Eliade was a long-time faculty member at the University of Chicago. As political émigrés, the Romanians Paul Goma and Norman Manea—the first in France, and the second in the United States—similarly became prominent members of the ever-growing Eastern European literary community in the West. They were followed by their fellow Romanians Gellu Naum, Petru

Popescu, Nina Cassian, Ion Caraion, and Herta Müller, the last a leading representative of the small German-language literary community in postwar Romania. The relatively more favorable political climate in Yugoslavia under Tito, in comparison with East Germany and the rest of Eastern Europe, was still no guarantee that conflicts with communist rule would not result in exile or voluntary emigration, as the careers of Danilo Kiš and Dubravka Ugrešić demonstrate. Among Bulgarians, the most notorious case of the dangers faced by a banished writer even in emigration is exemplified by Georgi Markov, who was murdered on Waterloo Bridge in London in 1978 by agents of the Bulgarian secret police using a poisoned projectile fired from a weapon disguised to look like an umbrella.

The stifling literary repression in communist Czechoslovakia created perhaps the largest community of émigré, exile, and underground writers. Before the legendary "Prague Spring" of 1968 was crushed by Soviet-led Warsaw Pact troops on the night of 20 August, the new prime minister, Alexander Dubček, the former Communist Party secretary of Slovakia, had set in motion a series of reforms embraced especially by younger members of the literary community, such as Pavel Kohout and Ladislav Mňačko, eager to test the limits of official tolerance. Even before the heady days of the "Prague Spring," the Fourth Congress of the Czechoslovak Union of Writers in June 1967, just after the Six-Day War in the Middle East, became a platform for the expression of outspoken views against continued state cultural repression, particularly on the part of writers opposed to the government's anti-Israel stance. In protest against this policy, Mňačko, for example, left Czechoslovakia and settled in Israel. In the ranks of the boldest speakers at the congress were communists and noncommunists alike, among them Kohout, Ludvík Vaculík, Jan Procházka, Ivan Klíma, Milan Kundera, and Václav Havel, who later became the first freely elected president of a post-communist Czechoslovakia. Kohout, Klima, Vaculík, Havel, and Jan Trefulka, representing the Circle of Independent Authors, soon became the core of the Charter 77 movement, which drew up a list of reforms to be submitted to the authorities. The failure to significantly alleviate the oppressive censorship under which Czech and Slovak literatures then labored resulted in the creation of an underground press the initiative for which came from the writer Ludvík Vaculík, who established Edice Petlice (Edition Padlock) in 1973. Two years later, Havel founded the similar Edice Expedice (Edition Expedition).

For writers who either were expelled from their countries as politically undesirable or were somehow able to emigrate, resuming a writing career in new and different cultural and linguistic circumstances was anything but easy. Some were never more than partially successful and drifted aimlessly. Others proved more resilient and better able to adapt to the uncertainties of emigration. Miłosz, a professor at the University of California in Berkeley since the early 1960s, returned to Poland even before the collapse of the communist regime and more times since, but has made the United States his permanent home. Like most other prominent Eastern European writers in emigration, Miłosz, although knowing English well and active in creating a readership for his own books in English translation, has pursued his literary career in a foreign land entirely in his native language. But the fame of his award-winning and widely translated *The Captive Mind* greatly eased his transition to life outside Poland and ensured a market for his writings during the so-called Cold War when works by Eastern European authors were much sought after for their presumed insights into communist society.

In 1975 the celebrated Czech writer Milan Kundera resettled in France, from where he brought out such works as *The Unbearable Lightness of Being* (1984), in which he explored the exquisite entanglements of eros while depicting the barbarism of the Soviet-led Warsaw

Pact invasion of Czechoslovakia in 1968. But when Czechoslovakia at last came out from under the communist yoke, Kundera, still nursing old resentments, showed no desire to return to his native land. He was criticized for this as well as for shifting from Czech subjects to wholly French settings and characters and for later writing in French, as in his recent novel *Ignorance* (2000), whose theme is emigration. The Czech writers Josef Škvorecký and his wife, Zdena Salivarová, immigrated to Canada in 1969. There he continued one of the most prolific literary careers of any contemporary Czech writer and became widely known in the English-speaking world. Once settled in Toronto, Škvorecký and Salivarová performed an immensely valuable service to Czechoslovak culture by establishing a modest émigré publishing house called Sixty-Eight Publishers, which became an outlet for émigré writers as well as for those banned from publishing in Czechoslovakia. With roots set deep in their adopted country, Škvorecký and Salivarová, like Kundera and Miłosz, if for different reasons, chose to remain there.

The distinguished Albanian writer Ismail Kadare presents an interesting case of an individual with close ties to the communist regime (and, indeed, favored by it) who at a certain point relatively late in his career chose to resettle in Paris as a form of protest against the oppressive conditions in which writers continued to live and work in his native Albania. But Kadare's literary reputation was already so firmly established outside Albania by the time he left for France that the transition for him was virtually seamless. Most of his major works published before and after his resettlement in Paris have been quickly published in French translation, thereby ensuring an international market for them, or they have appeared first in French before their subsequent publication either in Albania proper or by an Albanian émigré press. Kadare's reputation is indeed so formidable that no other contemporary Albanian writer even remotely approaches it.

Dissatisfied and unassimilable East German writers at odds with the regime for one reason or another were occasionally able to reestablish themselves in West Germany. But when the popular writer and singer Wolf Biermann was stripped of his GDR citizenship in 1976 while in Cologne, West Germany, for a concert, it was in a sense the straw that broke the camel's back. The insensitivity of the regime and the symbolism of the ban on Biermann's return to East Germany gave rise to widespread protest within the East German literary community and resulted in the immigration to West Germany of a number of East German writers. The freedom now to write candidly about conditions in the GDR prompted several of these authors to continue writing about the society and homeland they chose to leave. When this urgency played itself out, they undertook to write about their resettlement in West Germany, often venting frustration and discouragement over the conditions they found there, from crass materialism to open hostility to their fellow Germans from the East—a hostility that persists despite the enormous investment that the Federal Republic of Germany has made toward the still elusive goal of fully integrating the economies and societies of the two formerly autonomous German states.

As havens of free literary expression, the Slovene communities in Trieste, Italy, and especially in the Austrian province of Carinthia bore a certain superficial resemblance to West Germany or, perhaps better said, to West Berlin before reunification, and to the important Polish émigré literary communities in Paris and London. They have long been active centers of Slovenian-language writing and publishing and could thus be regarded as an alternative free Slovenian literary community to that within communist Slovenia in the time of the Titoist Yugoslav state. They thus represented a dimension of Slovenian literature while retaining the distinction of their separateness. To a certain extent, these Slovene communities just beyond the borders of Slovenia do constitute a diaspora and, indeed, served as places of refuge for those whose political views might have made problematic their continued residence in Slovenia under the communist regime. However, because they evolved just over the borders of Slovenia itself, they cannot be regarded as centers of exile comparable to those of Poles, Czechs, Romanians, or others in more distant lands. And because Slovenia had not been politically partitioned, as was Germany after World War II, the Slovenian communities in Austria and Italy were never viable candidates for incorporation into any Greater Slovenia.

Strategies of Refuge

In light of the harsh circumstances of the postwar era in Eastern Europe—the arduous task, after the horrendous destruction of the war, of rebuilding within the context of adjustment to the imposed orthodoxies and repression of communism across the broad spectrum of society—refuge held considerable appeal. It is thus easy to appreciate the temptation of the artist who ruled out emigration to flee the drabness and uncertainties of daily life under the communists into realms of recollection and imagination. In the aftermath of the costliest and most devastating war in human history, which Eastern European writers for long were unable to deal with in as wholly open a way as they might have liked, World War I proved in some instances an irresistible attraction. Its appeal lay primarily in the fact that the defeat of the Central Powers paved the way for the creation or reconstitution of such independent Eastern European states as Czechoslovakia, Poland, and Yugoslavia.

Recollections of World War I

It would seem entirely natural that the experience of World War II, which effectively wrote an end to interwar Eastern Europe, would eventually evoke recollections of that first "World War" of 1914 to 1918, out of which arose the new Eastern Europe of the 1920s and 1930s. The collapse of the Hapsburg, Wilhelmine, Romanov, and Ottoman dynasties drastically rewrote the map of Eastern Europe. Poland, which had lost its independence in the partitions of the late eighteenth century, rejoined the European family of nations as a sovereign state after World War I and in direct consequence of the war. The new country of Czechoslovakia, which would last until its peaceful division into the Czech Republic and the Republic of Slovakia in 1993, emerged from the ashes of the Austro-Hungarian (or Hapsburg) Empire. The new Kingdom of the Serbs, Croats, and Slovenes, later renamed Yugoslavia, also owed its existence to the disintegration of the Hapsburg Empire. Yugoslavia retained its integrity until the Balkan wars of the 1990s put an end to any dreams of a unified South Slavic state. The "Yugoslav idea" died in the horrors of "ethnic cleansing" (a term that arose in the context of the Balkan wars of the 1990s) and has been replaced by the separate entities of Bosnia-Herzegovina, Croatia, Macedonia, Slovenia, Yugoslavia (the combined state of Serbia and Montenegro), and a United Nations–controlled Kosovo, destined for either fragile independence or questionable partition between the overwhelming majority of Albanians and the few thousand Serbs who still live in the nominally Serbian province. Albania, long a province of the Ottoman Empire, achieved independence in 1912 during the Balkan wars of the early twentieth century.

Literary works with World War I settings appeared throughout Eastern Europe in the period 1945 to 2001. The important Romanian writer Zaharia Stancu set his novel *A Gamble with*

Death (1962) in the autumn of 1917 when a large part of Romania was under German and Austrian occupation. In his autobiographical novel, *The Issa Valley* (1987), Czesław Miłosz warmly evokes the daily routine of a boy on a provincial Polish estate when the distant drums of war can be heard (although not seen) in the background. But no Eastern European literature can boast of a literary monumentalization of World War I comparable to that of the Serbian. And this was to a great extent the creation of a single writer, Dobrica Ćosić, an ardent Serbian nationalist and later political figure whose four-volume epic, *A Time of Death*, written in the 1960s and 1970s and comprising *Into the Battle, A Time of Death, Reach to Eternity,* and *South to Destiny,* might well serve as required reading for anyone trying to understand Serbian political aspirations and the mentality of the Serbian leader Slobodan Milošević, who more than anyone else bears responsibility for the breakup of the Yugoslav state and the new Balkan wars of the 1990s, including the destruction of Kosovo.

The Remembrance of Things Past: National, Regional, and Family History

The solace of history, in the sense of buttressing a strong sense of national identity, has sown a rich literary harvest among the South Slavs apart from Dobrica Ćosić's monumental celebration of Serbian nationalism. Milovan Djilas made the sweep of Montenegran history the subject of his novel *Under the Colors* (1971), while the Nobel Prize winner Ivo Andrić wove a rich tapestry of Bosnian history in such novels from 1945 as *The Bridge on the Drina* and *The Days of the Consuls*. The Bosnian Turkish past also comes vividly to life in Meša Selimović's novel *Death and the Dervish* (1983). The Bulgarian Anton Donchev's major work of fiction, *Time of Parting* (1969), is a historical novel set in the seventeenth century in the period of Bulgarian–Turkish conflict. Rich in detail and exotic coloration, the novel also pleads the case for reconciliation and unity among all Bulgarians, be they Christian or Muslim. So, too, in a sense does the Bulgarian writer Nikolai Haitov's most famous collection of stories, *Wild Tales* (1969), which is set in his native Rhodope Mountains region and deals mostly with the life of the *pomaks* (descendants of Bulgarian converts to Islam). In 1974 it was voted the most popular work written by a living Bulgarian writer since the end of World War II. The outstanding Croatian writer Miroslav Krleža, most of whose career developed in the interwar years, similarly evoked a colorful panorama of Pannonia, Budapest, and Hungary in the early twentieth century in his huge novel *Banners* (1967). The Polish author Andrzej Kuśniewicz mined much the same trove for his more compact and effective novel, *The Kingdom of the Two Sicilies* (1978). The Slovak Peter Jaroš's most acclaimed work, the novel *The Millennial Bee* (1979), is an epic-style family chronicle spanning three generations and set in the second half of the nineteenth and the beginning of the twentieth centuries. In it, Slovak history is likened to a millennial beehive through love and work. Its sequel, *Deaf Ear, Deaf Eye* (1984), takes place after the establishment of the new Czechoslovak state in 1918. Departing from the idyllic and sentimental tradition of Romanian village literature, Zaharia Stancu aimed in his novel *Barefoot* (1948) for an unflinchingly realistic depiction of the struggle for survival of the poorest stratum of the peasantry in the first half of the twentieth century. Drawing on his own firsthand knowledge of peasant life, he wrote an entire series of novels along similar lines, including the five-volume *The Roots Are Bitter* (1958–1959), the previously mentioned World War I novel *A Gamble with Death* (1962), and the three-volume *The Wind and the Rain* (1969). Collectively, the series constitutes a sweeping lyrical epic panorama of Romanian peasant and small-town life from the early twentieth century until after World War II.

The enthusiasm for the national past so evident in works by South Slavic authors is rooted not just in a keen sense of national pride. There has also been a perceived need to reassert ethnic and regional uniqueness at a time in Titoist Yugoslavia when the emphasis was on the development of a supranational Yugoslav identity as the best means of holding together the federated Yugoslav state against the centrifugal pressures that lay not far beneath the surface and burst forth with a vengeance in the late 1980s and early 1990s.

Besides the rediscovery of an exotic and highly colorful past, as among the South Slavs who were long part of the Ottoman Empire, the dreariness and regimentation of much life under communism prompted an interest in the family past, invariably the youth of the writer, thus allowing an implied contrast between a different set of family and social values than those prevailing under the communists. In such patently autobiographical texts as Czesław Miłosz's *The Issa Valley* (1955), the Serbian writer Danilo Kiš's *Garden, Ashes* (1975), and the Polish author Tadeusz Konwicki's *A Hole in the Heavens* (1959), *The Anthropos-Spectre-Beast* (1969), *A Chronicle of Love Affairs* (1974), which was made into a film by the famous Polish director Andrzej Wajda, and *Bohin Manor* (1987), the lyricism, nostalgia, and warmth with which these pictures from the past are infused contrast vividly with the bleak images of communist reality depicted elsewhere in these writers' works.

The destruction in World War II of the once huge and distinct Jewish community of Poland has led, especially in recent years, to various evocations of the Jewish past by writers of Jewish and non-Jewish origin alike. This literary effort to reconstruct a vanished way of life began seriously after the war with the Polish Jewish writer Julian Stryjkowski's novel *The Inn* (1966), which recalls earlier Jewish life in provincial Poland. In more recent times, Piotr Szewc attracted no small attention in Poland with his novel *Annihilation* (1987), the goal of which is to capture the mood of a July day in 1934 in the Jewish district of the southeastern Polish town of Zamość. Although tiny in comparison with the Jewish community of pre–World War II Poland, the Sephardic Jewish enclave in Bosnia, centered primarily in Sarajevo, also found literary immortality in the stories of Isak Samokovlija, gathered in such collections as *Samuel, the Porter* (1946), *On Trial for Life* (1948), and *Solomon's Word* (1949).

Allegory: Historical and Contemporary

Of the various uses to which history could be put in Eastern European imaginative literature from 1945 to the collapse of communism, political allegory was both inevitable and certainly one of the most productive. Thus for his indictment of doctrinaire fanaticism in his novel *The Inquisitors* (1957), the Pole Jerzy Andrzejewski drew on Spain in the time of the Inquisition. In his best-known work, the novel *The Royal Hunt* (1973), a combination of allegory and parable set in a mythical Danubian county (likened to William Faulkner's Yoknapatawpha County), the Romanian Dumitru Radu Popescu clearly intended an indictment of the ruthless means employed by the new Romanian communist regime to achieve the collectivization of agriculture in the "dark days" of the 1950s. Although Marin Sorescu, another prominent contemporary Romanian writer, set his historical drama *The Third Stake* (1972)—which has been translated into English as *Vlad Dracula, the Impaler*—in mid-fifteenth-century Wallachia, the play has an obvious relevance to Romania in the Ceaușescu period. For his portrayal of the struggle of the Eastern European artist for freedom of expression in the face of relentless oppression and repression, the Hungarian dramatist György Spiró based his patently allegorical historical drama *The Impostor* (1982) on the career of Wojciech Bogusławski, the director of the Warsaw National Theater in the first half of the nineteenth century when Poland was partitioned and cultural repression was harshest under the Russians.

That allegory can function on a contemporary as well as a historical level is apparent from the books of reportage for which the Polish writer Ryszard Kapuściński has earned justifiable renown. A well-known journalist with a taste for the exotic and dangerous, Kapuściński has traveled the world in pursuit of upheaval, rebellion, and war. The book that first brought him international recognition, *The Emperor: Downfall of an Autocrat* (1978), is an intriguing, sometimes humorous glimpse of the inner workings of the court of the Ethiopian ruler, Haile Selassie, but has been read as well as an allegory of Poland under the communist leader Edward Gierek. In *The Official of the Palace of Dreams*, first published in Albania in 1981 and immediately banned, Ismail Kadare's subject is totalitarianism, but the setting is a fictional United Ottoman States where his protagonist, a bureaucratic functionary, works in a secret-police-like agency (the "Palace of Dreams") dedicated to stifling opposition to a totalitarian state by controlling people's dreams. A revised version of the novel appeared in 1996 under the abbreviated title *The Palace of Dreams*.

Flight from Reality

In both the historical and the contemporary context, a literature of the fantastic, occult, and supernatural is as well developed in Eastern Europe as elsewhere in the world. But the exceptional cultivation of this genre in the post–World War II period down to the collapse of communism must to a considerable degree be viewed as another way of exchanging the grimness of the everyday for the splendor of fantasy, of obliquely addressing issues of contemporary relevance, and of circumventing censorship. There is hardly an Eastern European literature that cannot boast of an outstanding writer or writers of a literature of the fantastic, occult, and supernatural. Some, obviously, are better known than others. This is especially true of the internationally acclaimed Polish writer Stanisław Lem, an acknowledged master of science fiction and the author of such widely translated novels as *Solaris* (1970), *The Futurological Congress* (1975), *Memoirs Found in a Bathtub* (1976), and *Mortal Engines* (1977). Certainly in the English-speaking world, the reputation of no Eastern European writer of such fiction can match that of Lem.

Although he is most highly regarded for his scholarly contributions to the study of myth, magic, and religion, virtually all of which are available in English, the Romanian Mircea Eliade was the author of two collections of stories of a fantastic and occult character, *Fantastic Tales* (1969) and *Two Tales of the Occult* (1970), which contain some of the best specimens of this type of literature. Regretfully poorly represented in English, Eliade's fellow Romanian Vasile Voiculescu similarly deserves recognition for his contributions to the world's treasure chest of a literature of the fantastic on the basis of two novels, long out of print, published jointly in 1966 under the title *Tales of Fantasy and Magic*. Among the Czechs, Josef Nesvadba continued the tradition of his great countryman Karel Čapek, the author of the world-famous *War of the Newts* (1921), with such works as *The Death of Tarzan* (1958) and *Einstein's Brain* (1960). In their anthology *Bulgarian Literature of the Fantastic* (1976), Stanka Pencheva, Liuben Dilov, and Ognian Saparev offer a number of rewarding examples of the genre as interpreted by, among others, such major writers as Iordan Radichkov and Pavel Vezhinov. Branimir Donat and Igor Zidić's *An Anthology of Croatian Fantasy in Prose and Painting* (1975), an abridgment of the prose part of which appeared in English in 1996 as *Croatian Tales of Fantasy*, does a similar service for Croatian literature, although one need not look much beyond Vesna Krmpotić's *Eyes of Eternity: A Spiritual Autobiography* (1979).

New Perspectives on East and West

The restricted access to Western culture during the more repressive periods of communist rule in Eastern Europe made the establishment of such contacts all the more urgent. This was especially true with respect to literary translations, the strictest ban being imposed on anything regarded as avant-garde. The Western theater of the absurd, for example, was kept as much at arm's length as the interwar domestic experimental and surrealistic art. When such prohibitions eased for the most part in the 1960s (only to reappear later), domestic experimentalism was embraced with as much fervor and sense of discovery as were Western cultural products. The Romanians Gherasim Luca, Gellu Naum, and Virgil Teodorescu—who had been among the leading representatives of prewar and immediate postwar Romanian surrealism—sought to revive the movement in the 1960s during a period of relative cultural thaw and thus create a bridge between writers of the postwar generation intent on preserving the freedom to experiment and the important prewar Romanian avant-garde of such figures as the writer known as Urmuz and the renowned sculptor Constantin Brancuși.

The stubborn insistence by Eastern European writers on their Europeanness, on the integral place of the national cultures within the Western tradition, and on the utter artificiality of the barriers separating them from the West are superbly exemplified by some of the prose writings of the courageously independent Polish poet Zbigniew Herbert. His two major collections of essays, *Barbarian in the Garden* (1985) and *Still Life with a Bridle* (1992), are wholly Western in content and orientation. In the first collection, the art and architecture of the West are freshly perceived through the eyes of an adoring Eastern European—the self-ironizing "barbarian in the garden"—whose rediscovery of a common patrimony acquires the sensuous intensity of lost love regained. The essays and "apocryphas" in *Still Life with a Bridle* to be sure demonstrate Herbert's breathtaking familiarity with seventeenth-century Dutch art, but more than that they validate the Polish traveler's sense that he has not strayed into an alien realm. As a teenager fighting the Germans as a member of the Polish underground, Herbert nourished the hope that with the conclusion of the war he would visit the Louvre in order to see the Mona Lisa—which to him was an image of Western civilization. In a similar spirit, another Polish poet, Adam Zagajewski, who lived as an émigré in Paris for several years, takes European culture as his native province in his book of reminiscences, *Another Beauty* (1998), and in his poems on such figures as Beethoven, Schopenhauer, and Schubert. Like Herbert, Zagajewski conveys the belief that the art and culture he celebrates may provide the spiritual strength to cope with the injustices of history.

Reflections on History, National and Otherwise

One way of coping with these injustices was to better understand them, which is what the Polish writer Tadeusz Konwicki attempts, for example, in his book *The Polish Complex* (1977) or in his very personal *Moonrise, Moonset* (1982), which could not be published in Poland. He speaks bluntly about the Poles' (and Russians') shortcomings as well as strengths and predicts the ultimate downfall of communism, which he describes in one place as "this terrible variation of totalitarianism." The temptation for Poles to indulge in such speculative ruminations on the twists and turns of the historical process has been difficult to resist in light of the collapse of a once great state that was made to endure dismemberment at the hands of its neighbors and nearly a century and a quarter of servitude. There was a time, long ago to be sure, when the balance of power between Poland and Russia was weighted on the side of the Poles. But then history misbehaved—the Poles were dealt cruel blows, and the balance of power shifted, never to be regained—and so after the horrors of World War II, Poland found itself once again a Russian vassal state.

The vicissitudes of Eastern European history are perhaps even more dramatically exemplified in the case of Yugoslavia. The disintegration of this once geopolitically important state a little more than a decade after the death of Marshal Tito in 1980 represents one of the saddest chapters in twentieth-century European history. Tito's unique ability to hold together the disparate elements out of which the immediate post–World War I Kingdom of the Serbs, Croats, and Slovenes and the post–World War II Federal Republic of Yugoslavia were created could not withstand his passing. While separatist tendencies among the larger ethnic communities of the country had long been apparent, they posed no real threat to the stability and continuity of Yugoslavia. That changed with the ascension to power of the Serbian leader Slobodan Milošević and his initiation of a campaign to dominate all of post-Titoist Yugoslavia by bringing the other republics in the federal state under Serbian domination. The clarity of the ambition of Milošević and other Serbian nationalists to finally realize the long-standing Serbian dream of a Greater Serbia was all the spark necessary to fan the flames of independence elsewhere in the country. Seeing the handwriting on the wall, Slovenia was the first to declare itself independent of Yugoslavia on 25 June 1991. Croatia unilaterally declared its own independence the very same day. Milošević's crude and hastily organized campaign to defeat Slovenia was short lived (hence referred to often as the "weekend war" or the "phony war"). Slovenia's access to neighboring Austria as a source of arms and the threat of possible European intervention intent on preventing a Serbian takeover of Yugoslavia's northernmost and most prosperous republic ended the Serbian threat, and Slovenia went the way of independence with a minimum of bloodshed. Croatia and Bosnia-Herzegovina were to be different. Larger in population and land than little Slovenia, with its population of somewhat over 2 million, Croatia had sizable pockets of Serbs living within its borders. To these Serbs, well aware of Croatian atrocities against the Serbs during World War II, an independent Croatia was anathema. When they moved to separate themselves from Croatia and appealed to Serbia for help, another, bloody phase of the Balkan wars of secession opened up. Serbian intervention widened the conflict and threatened to engulf all of Croatia. Even the pearl of the Adriatic, Dubrovnik, was not spared shelling and some damage to its splendidly preserved Renaissance old town. Before long, Serbs, Croats, and Muslims were all trying to carve out their own separate enclaves in a newly declared independent Bosnia-Herzegovina. Since the idea of living under a Muslim government in an independent Bosnia-Herzegovina was equally unacceptable to Serbs and Croats alike, it was inevitable that bitter fighting would ensue over territorial claims among all the involved parties: Serbs, Croats, and Muslims who represented the plurality population. The divisions, and weakness, within the emerging independent Bosnia-Herzegovina were too tempting for Serbia and Croatia not to try to exploit. Hence the outbreak of the Bosnian War and the bloodiest conflict Europe has known since World War II. The Dayton Peace Accords of 1995 finally put an end to the warring among Bosnia-Herzegovina's factions. But although these accords may have stopped the fighting as 1999 drew to a close and the world stood on the threshold of a new millennium, Bosnia-Herzegovina remained an ethnically divided country with no real functioning government. NATO troops were still enforcing the peace, as indeed they are in Yugoslavia's overwhelmingly Albanian province of Kosovo, where NATO's bombing of Serbia and threatened ground action finally put an end to the horrific campaign of ethnic cleansing.

Even as the Croatian president Franjo Tudjman lay close to death from stomach cancer in late November 1999 (he died on 10 December), there was little evidence of a relaxation of the strongly authoritarian government he had led since Croatia declared its independence from Yugoslavia in 1991. Apart from Bosnia-Herzegovina, Croatia bore most of the brunt of Serbian aggression in the wars of the Yugoslav secession of the early 1990s. The considerable hostility toward the Serbs extends as well to the matter of language. Referring to the essentially common language of the Serbs and Croats as "Serbo-Croatian" is no longer acceptable, and a concerted effort has been under way for several years to distance Croatian from Serbian as much as possible.

The Yugoslav wars of the 1990s have already given rise to a substantial literature. The most moving writing has come from Bosnian Muslims, who had firsthand experience of the siege of Sarajevo, writers such as Dževad Karahasan, the author of *Sarajevo: Portrait of an Inward City* (1993), and the impressive roster of writers included in the second volume of the unusual collection *Forgotten Country: War Prose in Bosnia-Herzegovina* (1992–1995), edited by Zlatko Topčić and published in Sarajevo in 1997 by the Association of Writers of Bosnia-Herzegovina. Some of the most thoughtful and sophisticated views of the Balkan conflicts are to be found in the widely translated Croatian writer Dubravka Ugrešić's *Have a Nice Day: From the Balkan War to the American Dream* (1994) and *Balkan Blues* (1994). The Macedonian playwright Goran Stefanovski's poignant *Sarajevo: Tales from a City,* a play written in English, was performed in London at the International Theatre Festival in 1993. Although Serbian writers have for obvious reasons been more conflicted in their approach to the Balkan wars, some insights into their outlook can be gauged from such texts as Slobodan Blagojević's *Here I Am!* (1993), in which he mocks both Serbian and Croatian nationalism. The reaction of the authorities was so hostile to the book that Blagojević left Serbia for Amsterdam, where, together with his fellow writers Hamdija Demirović and Predrag Dojčinović, he established Ex-Yu PEN to represent other Yugoslav writers in exile.

That demythification of nationalism and national pretensions has been a common response among opposition Serbian writers is evidenced also in the maverick Svetislav Basara's idiosyncratic (to put it mildly) *Looney Tunes: A Manic-Paranoiac History of Serbian Literature in the Period 1979–1990* (1997) and its sequel, *Holy Water: A Manic-Paranoiac History of Serbian Literature* (1998). Taking a Christian spiritual viewpoint, Dragan Jovanović Danilov's "novel-cenotaph" *Iconostasis at the End of the World* (1998) includes an epilogue in which he forecasts a time when the "Golden Cross of Christ" will shine, heralding an age of universal peace. While more distant from the conflict, the Hungarian writer Andor Szilágyi's novel *Shalim* (1997) offers an example of the kind of response possible from another quarter of Eastern Europe.

Publishing and Literature in Eastern Europe in the Postcommunist Period

Since the collapse of communism, radical changes have taken place in the literary culture of Eastern Europe as a whole. The difficult transition from a socialist to a free-market economic system has drastically altered the publication and marketing of literary products. Although the large state publishing houses have not entirely departed from the scene, they have been forced to become cost conscious, no longer enjoying the levels of state subsidies they did previously. To put the matter somewhat differently, they are far less willing now to carry authors whose works sell poorly or authors who were little more than ideologically correct literary hacks. The changing economic situation has also given rise to a large number of small independent publishing houses whose ephemerality in many cases rivals that of New York restaurants. While this has obviously opened up many new outlets for writers, it has stiffened competition among publishers and put greater pressure on writers to produce marketable, to say nothing of profitable, books.

The changes in the economics of book publishing and marketing in the new Eastern Europe have also been reflected in the cost of the literary product. No longer able to get by with the cheap paper and shoddy binding so common throughout Eastern Europe under the communists, publishers have had to upgrade their products and charge for them appropriately. In most instances, the spiraling cost of a book has outstripped wage increases, with the inevitable result that books in postcommunist Eastern Europe have become expensive and on average compare in price with their counterparts in such European countries as Germany and Austria. Although Eastern Europe previously had a very large reading public, in part because of the political situation (imaginative literature filling the void created by print journalism that was either devoid of substance or slanted) and in part because of state subsidies that made books relatively cheap, a decline in the book-buying public in the postcommunist period has undeniably occurred. Factor in the spread of computer literacy and ownership in the region, the enhanced role of revitalized mass media, and the large-scale influx of foreign literary works in translation, and the picture grows even darker.

The book market in Eastern Europe has also changed in a geopolitical sense. The cordial split of Czechoslovakia into the Czech Republic and the Republic of Slovakia and the calamitous disintegration of the former Federal Republic of Yugoslavia have altered the literary landscape, doubtless for all time. As the larger and better-known literary culture, Czech has had little to lose from the divorce of Czechs and Slovaks. The languages are close enough so that a popular Czech writer still has a chance of selling in Slovakia without the need for translation. But Slovakia has become a marginalized culture since the establishment of the Republic of Slovakia. Although traditionally burdened, if you will, by parochialism and regionalism, Slovak literature in the postcommunist era has been compelled to gauge the needs of a newly independent and small Slovak state with its own problems distinct from those of the Czech Republic. As a representative of a much less well known culture than his Czech counterpart, the Slovak writer today faces an uphill climb in attracting recognition beyond the borders of his own land. Of course it may be argued that this is a problem faced by the writer of any small country and that talent will eventually out. But the Slovaks have for so long lived in the shadow of the Czechs that the problem seems more acute in their case. This is all too evident in the extreme paucity of contemporary Slovak literary works in English. Indeed, at this writing not a single work by a major Slovak writer has become available in the world's most global language since Ladislav Mňačko's *Death Is Called Engelchen* (1961), *The Taste of Power* (1967), and *The Seventh Night* (1969) and Martin M. Šimečka's *The Year of the Frog* (1993).

In some respects, the situation in the Yugoslav successor states resembles that in the new Czech and Slovak republics; in other respects, it is quite different. When Yugoslavia was still a unified state and an important one geopolitically, the wartime mystique of Tito and the partisans, the break in 1948 with the Soviet Union, and Yugoslavia's relatively more open society when compared with the rest of Eastern Europe under the communists all generated considerable interest in Yugoslav culture. Writers such as Ivo Andrić, Milovan Djilas, Danilo Kiš, Vasko Popa, Miodrag Bulatović, Tomaž Šalamun, David Albahari, Milorad Pavić, and Dobrica Ćosić acquired international recognition and were widely translated. Andrić, in fact, was the winner of the Nobel Prize in Literature. And the prematurely deceased Kiš may well be the most respected of those writers who regarded themselves as Yugoslav before and immediately after the disintegration of the Federal Republic of Yugoslavia.

But the breakup of Yugoslavia has more than ever Balkanized the Balkans in terms of literary culture. With the days of the official promotion of a supranational Yugoslav identity now over, the foreign reader no longer faces the literature of a single, and important, country—notwithstanding its multicultural aspect—but the more bewildering literatures of five states. None of them commands the clout of the former Yugoslavia. In a few of these countries, notably Croatia, Macedonia, and Slovenia, the importance of translation has been recognized (as it has, for example, in Hungary), and a number of literary texts regarded as important are translated domestically into various languages, especially English, as a means of awakening foreign interest in the respective national culture and of enhancing national prestige. The success of such a program of indigenous, sometimes state-subsidized, translation depends on marketing skills. In most instances, the translations find their way into academic libraries, but rarely are picked up by major bookshop chains. Occasionally, a foreign-published translation comes to the attention of and is carried by small independent bookshops known for their broad range of interests. Without the promotional activity of a foreign scholar attracted to the particular culture or an indigenous translation program sponsored by the state or a major national publishing house, the post-Yugoslav Slovenian, Croatian, Serbian, Bosnian, or Macedonian writer would not have much of a chance in the international literary marketplace. One thing, however, has made a difference in attracting attention to the literatures of the Yugoslav successor states. Sad to say, the circumstances in which the former Yugoslavia disintegrated have generated extraordinary interest abroad, an interest that remains strong and has collaterally given greater visibility to literary and other cultural products to a large extent created and shaped by the events of 1991 to 1999. The situation in both Bosnia-Herzegovina and Kosovo is still far from settled, but the outpouring of articles, books, and translations of literary works dealing with these regions has been staggering. The understandable compulsion on the part of Croatian, Bosnian, and Serbian writers (more so than the Slovenes and Macedonians, who suffered the least in the upheaval) to give voice to their experiences has prepared a fertile field in the West for their works in translation. Even Albanian culture, by all means the most remote and least known of any in the Balkans, has received more attention than it would otherwise.

The Literary Scene from the End of Communism to the New Century

The remarkable breakdown of the communist order in Eastern Europe and in the Soviet Union, however inevitable, came earlier than almost anyone imagined possible. The dismantling of a largely discredited, feared, and loathed system came amid wrenching trauma. All the political and political-military upheavals of the 1950s, 1960s, 1970s, and 1980s were advance indications of a weak foundation, instability, and uncertainty. But the end, when it came, was still startling. The pictures flashed around the globe of the jubilant tearing down of the Berlin Wall seemed almost unbelievable, as did the scenes of bloody revolution in Romania in 1989 and the summary executions of the once seemingly omnipotent Ceauşescus.

The euphoria of the end of an order that had been imposed by force after World War II and kept in place by force, or the threat of force, was mitigated by the appalling disintegration of Yugoslavia in the 1990s, from which the dust still has not settled.

The sense of relief that accompanied the collapse of communism in Eastern Europe was soon overwhelmed by the sobering reality of necessary and very far-reaching change. Transforming the grossly inefficient centralized economies of Eastern Europe was a daunting challenge that, while met courageously by and large throughout the region, still has much to accomplish. In the conversion to a free-market economy, privatization led to the dismantling of wasteful anachronistic industrial plants, with an inevitable loss of jobs. Currencies had to be revalued in order to curb inflation, which in some countries began running rampant. The ending of the old system of state supports brought unavoidable hardships, and the attempt to establish democratic government proved anything but easy because of both the lack of experience and the surprising vitality and adaptability of former communists. The breakdown of civil order in Albania, in part caused by economic calamities, has created a situation resembling lawlessness and evokes memories of older patterns of clan rivalries. The incorporation of such countries as the Czech Republic, Hungary, and Poland into NATO, with the prospects of other Eastern European states eventually joining, was unthinkable only a few years ago. The social as well as the economic and political fallout of the vast changes overtaking Eastern Europe in the 1990s and the beginning of the new century has been considerable. Unemployment in some countries—for example, Albania, Romania, and the former East Germany—has been high and must still be dealt with. The collapse of the German Democratic Republic, the reunification of communist East Germany with the Federal Republic of Germany, and the establishment once again of a unified German state have created enormous problems for the Germans. However politically and emotionally desirable, the reunification of the two Germanys has been a logistical and economic nightmare. Euphoria over the reconstitution of Germany, with its national capital again in Berlin, for some time blinded Germans on both sides to the great difficulties and costs involved in the transformation. Absorbing the former East Germany into the West German economy has been more expensive than imagined. Unemployment in the cities and towns of what used to be the German Democratic Republic remains uncomfortably high and has given rise to an increase in the crime rate and expressions and acts of a neo-Nazi character. Xenophobia and crimes against immigrants as well as new manifestations of anti-Semitism have been a stain on the democratic balance sheet of the reunified Germany. But Germany is hardly alone in experiencing social unrest in the immediate postcommunist era. Crime has been on the rise throughout Eastern Europe as well as in the new states of the former Soviet Union. Without the apparatus of state police and the strict system of social controls of the communists, young people in particular have proved vulnerable to the negative influences of contemporary urban civilization. Drug use and venereal disease, including AIDS, have risen dramatically in the years since the collapse of communism. Minority problems, such as discriminatory practices against Gypsies in the Czech Republic and elsewhere, have attracted international attention. Ethnic tensions between the Slav and Albanian populations in tiny independent Macedonia were exacerbated by the fighting in Kosovo and erupted into open fighting in the winter and spring of 2001 over the issue of the Albanians' perceived second-class citizenship. Only European Union and NATO intervention halted a deadly worsening of the situation and cleared the way for a political solution acceptable to both sides. The toll of the conflicts in the former Yugoslavia has not yet been fully reckoned. If Slovenia is a success story, a much larger Croatia in the post-Tudjman era has yet to resolve grave economic problems. The overthrow of Slobodan Milošević in Serbia has brought an apparently democratic regime to power, but after intense NATO bombing during the Kosovo conflict the Serbian economy is in tatters and needs considerable outside assistance before even a semblance of health is restored. Moreover, the future of Kosovo is yet to be determined. A fragile peace holds in a devastated Bosnia-Herzegovina, and while life has slowly begun returning to normal and rebuilding has been undertaken, it is still too soon to predict the future of that badly torn multiethnic state.

It would be inconceivable to imagine that postcommunist writing in Eastern Europe would not reflect and in some ways be shaped by the extraordinary transformation that has taken place in the region with the collapse of the communist order and the turmoil in the former Yugoslavia. Perhaps the best way to get a sense of the literary climate in this the first decade after the fall of communism in Eastern Europe is by looking at a few texts by various writers who may be regarded as representative. These writers are usually described as "postmodern" or "post-postmodern." If the term "postmodern" has by now come close to wearing out its welcome in the critical idiom and in some instances has yielded to the still vaguer "post-postmodern," it may nonetheless be useful to consider those properties of these late communist or postcommunist literary texts that have encouraged critics and literary historians to situate them in the postmodernist landscape in the first place.

While exceptions, of course, may easily be found, this newer Eastern European literature is overwhelmingly urban as opposed to rural in its orientation, thereby eschewing an exceptionally important current, arguably the most important, in the pre– as well as post–World War II literary traditions of the predominantly agricultural Eastern European countries. For many writers in the communist period, the rural theme, so to speak, remained not only a major link with the prewar literary culture, but also a way of asserting and in a number of instances redefining traditional values brought under siege by the massive programs of agricultural collectivization introduced by the communists, often with severe repercussions. Even when supportive of the Party policy on collectivization, writers addressing the conflicts generated by its imposition on traditional village life invariably included powerful images of the tenacity of those values and the sense that rural life and the village were somehow bound up with a deep sense of nationhood. All too often in texts outwardly hewing to the official policy of the communists on the matter of collectivization, there is an undercurrent of regret, of a sense of loss, about the threatened extinction of rural culture.

To the younger Eastern European writers who began coming to prominence in the 1980s and 1990s, rural life matters little or has been irretrievably lost in terms of its traditions during the more than forty years of communist political, social, and economic transformation. For most of these writers, their hopes, aspirations, and important life experiences are bound up with the city. They are invariably chroniclers of city life. But if the city allures, it also repels. Absent the conformist pressures of communism, and its artificial and always suspect value system, the city in postcommunist Eastern European literature has become the locus of such perceived social maladies as rootlessness, the loss of illusions, and irreverence toward the traditional, as well as of such real dangers as crime (including murder and the extortions of a homegrown Mafia), xenophobia, considerable sexual license, substance abuse, and, in the new postcommunist economic reality, money-grubbing. The Czech writers Michal Ajvaz, Jáchym Topol, Michal Viewegh, and Martin Vopěnka are certainly among the best of this newer breed of Eastern European writers in this respect and, indeed, typify the newer literary urbanism.

Topol paints arguably the grimmest picture of postcommunist urban life of any of his contemporary fellow Czech writers. His first novel, the critically successful *Sister* (1994; translated as *City Sister Silver*), is a huge explosive work of the imagination, at times almost hallucinogenic, offering the best view yet of the amoral, hedonistic, hustling, and cynical postcommunist Czech youth. In his two novellas, both dating from 1995, *A Trip to the Train Station* and *Angel*, Topol is equally skillful at depicting the seamy underside of postcommunist Prague, with its foreign hustlers and its native criminal element. Viewegh's first novel, *Thoughts of Murder*, appeared in 1990. Narrated in the first person (as is almost all of Viewegh's fiction), the short work is about the mysterious death of a young schoolteacher. Typical of Viewegh's style is the feeling his works convey of contemporary Czech and, especially, Prague life. His leading characters are mostly young people and usually include offbeat individuals such as a few Vietnamese in *Thoughts of Murder* and a Mafia big shot in *Bringing Up Girls in Bohemia* (1994). Vopěnka's best-known work to date, the disturbing *Ballad of Descent* (1992), follows the mysterious Christmas Day journey of two young men from Prague who leave behind their own society of repressed individuality in order to reach "that other country," which is very near and is obviously intended to represent Romania. There they find far worse repression and the chaos of civil unrest. Ajvaz's first novel, *Another Place*, which appeared in 1993, spins a similarly intriguing yarn about an eerie realm just beyond the city in which the novel takes place. In both Vopěnka's and Ajvaz's novels, the city is the locus as well as the point of departure for journeys of Dantesque darkness.

Another characteristic feature of postcommunist Eastern European literature, already suggested by the novels of Vopěnka and Ajvaz, is the cultivation of the eerie, bizarre, grotesque, and magical. In "White Ants," the first story in Ajvaz's two-part *The Turquoise Eagle* (1997), he recounts the tale of a species of white ants that secrete a green fluid capable of curing sleeping sickness. When in danger, moreover, the entire colony merges and forms a living sculpture, usually a white tiger lying down with its jaws wide open. In the works of another Czech writer, Jiří Kratochvil, the bizarre and fantastic merge with the autobiographical in such novels as *Song in the Middle of the Night* (first published 1992) and *Avion* (1995). Kratochvil's prodigious appetite for the bizarre is amply demonstrated in his "carnival novel," *An Immortal Tale, or, The Life of Sonia Trocká-Sammlerová* (1997), and in the similarly unsettling *Nocturnal Tango, or, A Novel About a Single Year at the End of the Century* (1991). No less a postmodernist spellbinder is the Hungarian László Krasznahorkai, whose novel *The Melancholy of Resistance* (1989) exemplifies his fondness for conjuring surreal images of small-town Hungarian life as mired in drabness, stagnation, and decay. Scary and intriguing at the same time, the Polish writer Andrzej Zaniewski's well-known novel, *Rat* (1993)—which originally appeared in multiple translations—is an excruciatingly detailed account of the day-to-day struggle for survival of a rat during its life cycle. A deeply committed environmentalist, Zaniewski believes that rats are close to humans biologically and psychologically and can offer valuable lessons on the survival of the species. His grimly naturalistic novel is a compelling reading experience without overt preachment, and it anticipates his second novel, *The Civilization of Birds* (1996). Another younger Polish writer who came to prominence in the postcommunist period, Paweł Huelle, has attracted attention for his considerable imaginative power, on evidence especially in his first collection of stories, *Stories for a Walk* (1991; translated as *Moving House*). Huelle's domain is the unusual, mysterious, and puzzling, with overtones of the magical and supernatural. In the most intriguing of the stories, "Snails, Puddles, Rain," the narrator, as a boy, goes on expeditions with his unemployed father to catch snails for profit. They find their most abundant supply of snails in local cemeteries where the snails appear to stick out their horns ahead of them to catch the voices of the dead. In the story's eerie climax, father and son witness the spectacle of hundreds of snails marching up a hill at twilight in a vain ritualistic effort to scale the slippery sheer sides of a gigantic stone at the top. The Romanian writer Ştefan Agopian's short-story collections, *The Handbook of Happenings* (1984) and *Notes from Sodom: Portrait of the Artist Dying* (1993), brim with exotic and grotesque elements. The Pole Tomek Tryzna's first novel, *Miss Nobody* (1993), a sensual tale of lesbian love, features a fifteen-year-old Polish girl whose life gradually assumes a nightmarish aspect when her family moves to a new town. In her novel, *E. E.* (1995), which is set in Wrocław (formerly Breslau) in the first decade of the twentieth century, Olga Tokarczuk develops the intriguing character of another fifteen-year-old heroine who suddenly acquires parapsychological abilities.

Equally productive a facet of postcommunist literary culture in Eastern Europe is the postmodernist deconstruction especially of the novel form and widespread experimentation with various modes of narration. This was anticipated by, among others, the Serbian writer Milorad Pavić, whose postmodernist novels, *Dictionary of the Khazars* (1988), *Landscape Painted with Tea* (1990), and *The Inner Side of the Wind* (1991), assume the form of extravagant literary games and puzzles. The rise of contemporary feminism, the seriousness with which the gender issue is pursued now throughout society, and the birth in academia of gender studies have added another dimension to Pavić's deconstructive game playing. Besides its already formidable complexities, *Dictionary of the Khazars* was published in two editions—male and female—with a difference of only seventeen lines, since according to Pavić masculine and feminine stories cannot have the same ending. He followed nearly the same procedure in *The Inner Side of the Wind*, which is based on the classical legend of Hero and Leander, but this time more economically since the male and female versions of the story are accommodated within a single volume. Depending on which version he or she prefers to read first, the reader merely turns the book upside down to get the other version.

The Czech writer Daniela Hodrová, a highly intellectual writer who also happens to be a literary scholar, extends her professional interest in the literary process into her imaginative writing. In *Théta* (1992), arguably her best work of fiction to date, the narrator may or may not be the author but instead a fictionalized young woman writer trying to come to grips with the death of her father, a prominent actor. In rediscovering his identity, she also sets about recapturing her own past. The structure of the novel is complex, with situations and characters in constant flux and shifting or dissolving boundaries. Similar experimentation is characteristic as well of recent Polish fiction. In *Prawiek and Other Times* (1996) and *House of Day, House of Night* (1998), Tokarczuk, a writer of extraordinary inventiveness, uses the setting of small-town Polish life to defamiliarize conventional concepts of time and place and to probe the interconnection of dream and the everyday. Through a poetics of the fragmentary and digressive, she transforms the mundane into the mysterious and even mythical.

Dazzling postmodernist performances also have come from Romania during and after the Ceauşescu regime. Although unlikely ever to be translated because of its mammoth size, linguistic pyrotechnics, and Romanian referentiality, Mircea Horia Simionescu's tetralogy, *The Well-Tempered Innovator* (1969–1983), the first volume of which is subtitled *An Onomastic Dictionary*, aims at a subversion of socialism while dismantling traditional Romanian literary genres. It remains one of the tour de forces of post–World War II Romanian prose. In Mircea Cǎrtǎrescu's *The Dream* (1989; reprinted, 1993, as *Nostalgia*), which has been translated into several languages and earned its author a formidable reputation, a writer's dream to become Everything—a Creator who will in time replace the universe—is the novel's principal motivating force. Besides creative writing, Eastern European writers have contributed importantly to the postmodernist discourse through such formidable studies as the Slovene Aleš Debeljak's inquiry into modernity, postmodernity, and bourgeois society, *Postmoderna sfinga: Kontinuiteta modernosti in postmodernisti* (The Postmodern Sphinx: The Continuity of Modernism and the Postmodernists, 1989; translated, 1998, as *Reluctant Modernity: The Institution of Art and Its Historical Forms*), and Cǎrtǎrescu's exhaustive and thought-provoking *Romanian Postmodernism* (1999).

The great range of literary expression and experimentation so characteristic of the decade since the collapse of communism argues well for the present vitality of Eastern European literature. While critical of the past and the compromises imposed on creative artists by the political circumstances, there is scant evidence that younger writers are throwing out the baby with the bath water. Unlike in Russia, where revulsion toward three-quarters of a century of Soviet tyranny has led to a tendency to be overly dismissive of the past, the genuine and lasting achievements of their predecessors in the period 1945 to 1990 is acknowledged by the younger Eastern European writers of today. The dreary products of long discredited socialist realism are obviously rejected without a backward glance. But moral and ethical lapses, the compromises with repressive authoritarian regimes made by artists who tried to cope as best they could for the sake of careers, have been—and are being—reviewed critically in an effort to understand rather than to condemn out of hand. But the greatest respect and enthusiasm of the young is understandably reserved for those many poets, prose writers, and dramatists who through their art sought to expose totalitarianism for what it was; who used the power of their imagination and their pens to subvert and undermine it, above all by laying bare its contradictions, ironies, and absurdities; and who left a powerful legacy of courage and independence for future generations to build on. Despite censorship, oppression, privations, and, as in the Balkans in the 1990s, the horror of war and ethnic hatred all over again, it has been art and the independence of the spirit that have triumphed over the tyrannies that one by one have been driven from the stage of history.

The high hopes for the future raised in a ravaged Eastern Europe by the defeat of the Central Powers in World War I were ultimately dashed by the economic and political instability of the interwar years. And twenty years after the "war to end all wars" ended, a new war erupted, one far more devastating than any that preceded it. The joy of rebirth, of newly won independence, in Eastern Europe after World War I became an extraordinary stimulus to artistic creativity as the frenzied experimentation of the 1920s attests. Before long, however, dictatorship and conservatism imposed their restraints, and once again the stage was set for the contest of wills between the artist demanding the right to challenge tradition and convention and those institutions in society prepared to exact subservience at any cost. But the discomforts visited on the artist in Eastern Europe in the interwar period pale by comparison with the conditions of life during the years 1939 to 1945 and the dislocations and indignities of the postwar period until the collapse of communism. And yet, with everything that had to be endured from 1945 to 1990 and in some cases beyond, Eastern European writers created and continue to create an extraordinary body of writings in every form of literary expression. It is those achievements of the past half-century that this book seeks to preserve and, in some measure, honor.

Authors A–Z

A

Abdihoxha, Ali (b. 1923) Albanian novelist, short-story writer, and critic. A native of El-basan, where he received his early education, Abdihoxha took an active part in the Resis-tance movement in Albania during World War II, rising to the rank of battalion com-missar. In 1944 he joined the Albanian Com-munist Party, which had been founded in 1941. After the war, Abdihoxha worked as a journalist and for the Albanian Writers Asso-ciation and the Naim Frashëri publishing house. He subsequently held positions in the Ministry of Education and Culture. In 1957 he completed higher studies at the Gorky Insti-tute of World Literature in Moscow. A prolific and respected prose writer, Abdihoxha built his reputation primarily on a series of well-crafted works inspired by his wartime experiences and notable for the equation of patriotism and communism. His first novel, *Një vjeshtë me stuhi* (A Stormy Au-tumn, 1959), one of his very few texts to be translated into a foreign language, explores the moral and ideological crosscurrents within a group of young partisans who want to set up a clandestine press during the war. His next work was the four-part novel *Tri ngjyra të kohës* (Three Colors of Time), which was published between 1965 and 1972. It com-prises *Në prag të luftës* (On the Threshold of War, 1965); *Lufta* (The Battle, 1969); *Përsëri lufta* (The Struggle Renewed, 1969); and *Lufta vazhdon* (The War Continues, 1972) and fo-cuses, above all, on the impact of the war on the Albanian peasantry. Abdihoxha's subse-quent novels include *Dueli i madh* (The Great Duel, 1975), a contemporary social novel of particular interest for the centrality of a Jew-ish married couple (Agron and Meritë); *Vila në periferi* (Villa in the Suburbs, 1982), in-spired by the revolution of 1924, which ush-ered in the presidency of Ahmed Zogu (who reinvented himself on 1 September 1928 as Zog I, king of the Albanians); and *Kronika e një nate* (Chronicle of a Night, 1984), one of Abdihoxha's best novels, depicting both the last days of the war and the laying of the po-litical groundwork for Albania's entry into the communist camp in the postwar period. Apart from his novels, the most recent of which is *Sarajet* (Seraglios, 1997), Abdihoxha is the author of the short-story collections *Në malet tona* (In Our Mountains, 1952); *Ëndrra dhe dritë* (Dreams and Daylight, 1970); and *Tregime te zgjedhura* (Selected Stories, 1973) and of the novella *Mirazh* (Mirage, 1978). An eight-volume collected edition of Abdi-hoxha's works (*Vepra letrare*) was published in Tirana in 1983.

Translations: *Një vjeshtë me stuhi* is avail-able in French as *Automne d'orage* (Tirana: Naim Frashëri, 1968).

Adameşteanu, Gabriela (b. 1942) Romanian novelist and short-story writer. Adameş-teanu was born in Tîrgu Ocna and was educated through secondary school in Piteşti. From 1960 to 1965, she studied Romanian literature at Bucharest University, following which she held several editorial positions, including at the major book publisher Carta Românească (1983–1989). In 1990 she became editor in chief of the weekly magazine *22,* which was founded by former opponents of the regime of Nicolae Ceauşescu. Adameşteanu made her literary debut in 1971 with a fragment of her novel *Drumul egal al fiecărei zile* (Every Day an Equal Road), published in the review *Luceafărul.* The novel was published in book form in 1975. The same year, she won the Writers Union Prize for a literary debut. After Every Day an Equal Road, Adameşteanu published a volume of short stories, *Daruieşte-ţi o zi de vacanţă* (Give Yourself a Holiday, 1979), and her well-received second novel, *Dimineaţa pierdută* (A Wasted Morning, 1983). In 1989 she published a second volume of short stories under the title *Vară—primăvară* (Spring, Summer). Adameşteanu's strengths as a writer lie in her ability to draw psychologically convincing portraits against a broad social and political background, and in her narrative strategies. In Every Day an Equal Road, which is set in the 1960s, a grave injustice suffered by a professor who refuses to compromise his principles by arranging for an unearned college degree to be granted a member of the political establishment becomes a legacy to be grappled with by his niece, who is the novel's lead character. Constructed wholly out of the niece's memories, the novel encompasses the pre– and post–World War II years and deals realistically with both the fascist legionnaires of the 1930s and 1940s and the communists. Whereas memories shape the narrative structure of Every Day an Equal Road and also figure in the design of A Wasted Morn-ing, Adameşteanu experimented in her second novel primarily with multiple narrations through extensive use of inner monologues, diary entries, and long dialogues. The lead figure in the work is the liberal Professor Mironescu, whose recollections of the circumstances surrounding Romania's entry into World War I in 1916 under the government of Ion Brătianu (1864–1927) and growing doubts about his wife's fidelity form the context of a well-etched portrait of bourgeois society in a period encompassing pivotal moments in twentieth-century Romanian history.

Adameşteanu's most recent publication, a collection mostly of articles published in the newspaper *România liberă* and the journal *22* between 1992 and 2000 (most dating from 1999 and 2000) and dealing primarily with contemporary Romanian political issues, appeared in 2000 under the title *Cele două Românii: Articole şi fragmente memorialistice* (The Two Romanias: Articles and Fragments of Memoirs).

Translations: "A Common Path" (from *Vară—primăvară*), in *The Phantom Church and Other Stories from Romania,* ed. and trans. Georgiana Farnoaga and Sharon King (Pittsburgh: University of Pittsburgh Press, 1996), 148–52.

Adamović, Ratko (b. 1942) Serbian novelist and short-story writer. An intriguing and intellectually stimulating writer, Adamović seeks through his many fictional texts to point the way to an idealistic spiritual transcendence of human materialism. Religion, mythology, and mysticism intertwine in his writing, and his narrative style is a blend of the metaphoric and symbolic. A graduate in comparative literature from Belgrade University, Adamović made his literary debut in 1971 with the short-story collection *Žutna pomornica* (The Yellow Submarine), which won the Mladost Prize as the best first book of a Yugoslav prose writer. It was followed by the novel *Konopac* (The Rope) in 1977. In 1979 Adamović published a second short-story collection, *Svi umiru* (Everyone Dies), in which death links seven separate and distinct tales. *Gola garda* (The Naked Guard), a contemporary satirical novel with a science-fiction base, appeared in 1982. Adamović's next novel, *Pogon za ludilo* (The Workshop for Madness, 1986), is a first-person psycho-analytical narrative about the mad relationship between a father, a famous psychiatrist, and his son, who ends up committing suicide on his father's tomb. The novel *Sveti hrast* (The Sacred Oak), which appeared in 1990, handsomely exemplifies Adamović's attraction to myth and his ability to concretize it in a contemporary setting. *Karavan saraj* (Caravansary, 1993) brings together three novellas linked by the common story of a certain basilica.

Adamović's next three novels—*Paganski protokol* (The Pagan Protocol, 1995); *Besmrtni Kaleb* (The Immortal Kaleb, 1997); and *Kantarion* (1998)—represent the most expansive working out yet of his mystically philosophical views of humanity, death, and the afterlife. The best of the three, The Immortal Kaleb, won the Isidora Sekulić Award for 1997. In his latest novel, *Tumači gline* (Clay Readers, 2000), Adamović depicts a sterile futuristic society in which such alien concepts as "cigarette" and "pleasure" have to be searched on a computer for their meanings. Apart from his creative writing, Adamović has long been the editor and moderator of the "Francuska 7" readings at the Serbian Writers Union in which readings and discussions of Serbian and foreign literary works are held several times a week. "Francuska 7" was an important venue of dissident authors in the period of cultural repression in the former Yugoslavia. Adamović has lectured widely on Serbian literature, including in the United States and Canada.

Translations: "Souls of Stone," trans. Alice Copple-Tošić, in *The Prince of Fire: An Anthology of Contemporary Serbian Short Stories,* ed. Radmila J. Gorup and Nadežda Obradović (Pittsburgh: University of Pittsburgh Press, 1998), 202–13.

Agolli, Dritëro (b. 1931) Albanian poet, short-story writer, and novelist. A native of Menkulas, in the Devoll region of southeastern Albania, Agolli has been widely admired for both his poetry and his prose writing. After completing secondary school in Gjirokastër in 1952, he attended Leningrad University. When he returned to Albania, he settled on a career in journalism and began working for the daily newspaper *Zëri i Popullit.* He was president of the communist-controlled Albanian Union of Writers and Artists from 1973 until his retirement in 1992. A longtime member of the Central Committee of the Communist Party of Albania, Agolli succeeded to the presidency of the Union of Writers and Artists following the purge of a faction of liberals led by the dramatist Fadil Paçrami (b. 1922) and Todi Lubonja (b. 1923), the head of Albanian Radio and TV at the time and an early member of the Central Committee of the Party. With the fall of the Enver Hoxha dictatorship in 1990, Agolli joined the opposition Socialist Party.

Agolli's major verse collections include *Në rrugë dolla* (I Went Out on the Street, 1958); *Hapat e mija në asfalt* (My Steps on the Asphalt, 1961); *Devoll, Devoll* (1964); *Shtigje malesh dhe trotuare* (Mountain Paths and Sidewalks, 1965); *Çelësat e lumturise* (The Keys to Happiness, 1966); *Udhëtoj i menduar* (Pensive I Wander, 1985); *Pelegrini i vonuar* (The Belated Pilgrim, 1993), his first book following the collapse of communism in Albania; *Çudira dhe marrëzi: Fabula, epigrame* (Marvels and Madness: Fables and Epigrams, 1995); *Lypësi i kohës* (Begging for Time, 1995); *Vjen njeriu i çuditshëm* (An Unusual Man Is Coming, 1996); *Shpirti i gjyshërve: 101 këngë* (The Ancestral Spirit: 101

Songs, 1996); *Baladë për time atë dhe për vete* (Ballad for My Father and for Myself, 1997); *Shtigje dhe trotuare* (Paths and Sidewalks, 1998); *Fletorka e mesnatës* (Midnight Notes, 1998); *Kambana e largët* (The Distant Bell, 1998); *Këngët e buzëqeshjes* (Happy Songs, 1998); and *Gdhihet e ngryset* (It Dawns and It Grows Dark, 2000). At its best, Agolli's poetry is a refreshing union of bucolic themes reflective of his deep attachment to the soil, humor, and sophisticated, sometimes playful, metrics and imagery. If a single poem of the communist era can be taken as representative of Agolli's feelings toward the land and agricultural toil, it might well be "Work," in which he recalls the dirt on the hands and under the fingernails that his deceased father, a tiller of the soil his whole life, took to the grave with him:

My father's nails were blue with dirt
Even as he lay in his coffin.

The other side of Agolli, the communist-era "official" poet writing and promoting the Party's ideology, is much in evidence in such works as *Baballarët* (The Fathers, 1969) and *Nënë Shqipëri* (*Mother Albania*, 1974), a ten-chapter poem that extols the rugged beauty of his mountainous homeland while celebrating the achievements of the Communist Party:

. . . through pains and blood, under
    dense clouds over earth,
Thunderbolts foreboding, the working
    class gives birth
To her true genius,
To her great genius,
To her just genius,
The most wise and human, the
    Party. . . .

In The Belated Pilgrim, Agolli captures the sense of bewilderment, loss, and drift in Albania in the wake of the collapse of the most re-pressive and isolationist communist regime in post–World War II Europe. At the same time, he urges poets to look to the future while trying to make sense of the past and to help forge a new life as well as a new art.

Agolli's reputation as a prose writer rests mostly on novels and short stories with wartime settings. Although his collection of short stories *Zhurma e erërave të dikurshme* (The Noise of the Winds of the Past, 1964) was banned on grounds of Agolli's alleged "Soviet revisionism" of the time, he won literary acclaim for three novels published in the 1970s: *Komisari Memo* (Commissar Memo, 1970; translated as *The Bronze Bust*) and *Njeriu me top* (The Man with a Cannon, 1975; translated as *The Man with the Gun*), both of which deal with the partisan campaign during World War II, and Agolli's masterpiece, *Shkëlqimi dhe rënia e shokut Zylo* (The Splendor and Fall of Comrade Zilo, 1972). No prose work by Agolli has had the resonance of The Splendor and Fall of Comrade Zilo. The novel has not yet been translated into English; however, a French translation was published by Gallimard of Paris in 1990. At first glance, the novel would seem an unlikely work by a writer with Agolli's political credentials. It is an entertaining putdown of a bungling government official who heads a minor department of cultural affairs. Zilo's final undoing comes when he criticizes a play that is later praised by his superiors. On closer examination, the novel appears less a criticism of socialist realism or the communist system than an attempt—through the character of Zilo—to discredit a liberal journalist named Jusuf Alibali, who was a friend of Fadil Paçrami and General Mehmet Shehu (1913–1981). Alibali eventually went into exile. General Shehu ostensibly committed suicide, but was more likely the victim of foul play. Eleven volumes of Agolli's collected works (*Vepra letrare*) were published in Tirana from 1981 to 1987. His newest works of fiction are the novels *Trëndafilli në gotë* (The Rose in a Glass, 1980); *Dështaku* (The Aborted, 1991); *Njerëz të krisur: Tregime dhe novela* (Loony People: Stories and Novellas, 1995); *Kalorësi lakuriq: Roman* (The Naked Horseman: A Novel, 1996); *Arka e djallit: Roman* (The Devil's Trove: A Novel, 1997); and *Lutjet e kambanës* (Loud Prayers, 1998).

Translations: *The Bronze Bust* (Tirana: 8 Nëntori, 1975); *The Man with the Gun* (Tirana: 8 Nëntori, 1975); *Mother Albania: A Poem*, trans. Vasil Gjymshana (Tirana: 8 Nëntori, 1985); *Short Stories* (Tirana: 8 Nëntori, 1985); ten poems in *An Elusive Eagle Soars: Anthology of Modern Albanian Poetry*, ed. and trans. Robert Elsie (London: Forest, 1993), 44–56. *Shkëlqimi dhe rënia e shokut Zylo* is available in French as *Splendeur et décadence du camarade Zilo*, trans. Christian Gut (Paris: Gallimard, 1990).

Agopian, Ştefan (b. 1947) Romanian novelist and short-story writer. Agopian was born in Bucharest and studied chemistry at Bucharest University from 1965 to 1968. After leaving without earning a degree, he worked as a technician in Bucharest until devoting himself wholly to writing. He first appeared in print with a short story in *Luceafărul* in 1971. His first book was the novel *Ziua mîniei* (The Day of Anger, 1979), an intriguing reconstruction through fragments of a single day in the turbulent lives of two families in 1915. The Day of Anger set the pattern of Agopian's subsequent writing in its innovative approach to traditional Romanian epic narration. Through ambiguity, chronological distortions, fragmentariness, and irony, Agopian established himself as a writer respectful of but not subservient to the past. This is manifest in his subsequent novels, beginning with *Tache de catifea* (Velvet Tache, 1981). Set in the first half of the nineteenth century, the novel tells the story of Tache Vlădescu (nicknamed Velvet Tache), who together with friends sets out to join the uprising (against the Turks) of Tudor Vladimirescu, but tarries so much in inns along the way that he arrives after Vladimirescu has been slain. Agopian's next two novels, *Tobit* (1983) and *Sara* (1987), are closely related. *Tobit* is a work of high adventure set in the early eighteenth century and built around the adventures of its eponymous hero, a nobleman's son who is taken prisoner by the Austrians and tortured. The novel won the Bucharest Association of Writers award for prose. In *Sara*, a novel with comic and fantastic elements, the focus is on the love affair between Tobit and Sara, the adoptive daughter of the alchemist Israel Hübner from Sibiu, who brings her back to life after her death at the age of five. The novel was awarded the prize of the review *Amfiteatru* for the best literary work of the year. Agopian's short-story collections *Manualul întîmplărilor* (The Handbook of Happenings, 1984) and *Însemnări din Sodoma: Portret al artistul murind* (Notes from Sodom: Portrait of the Artist Dying, 1993), which brim with exotic and grotesque elements, follow along essentially the same chronological and aesthetic lines as his novels. The Handbook of Happenings won the Writers Union Prize for prose. Agopian has served as editor of the newspaper *Academia Caţavencu* in Bucharest and is a member of the Writers Union.

Translations: "The Art of War" (from *Manualul întîmplărilor*), trans. Florin Bican, in *Description of a Struggle: The Vintage Book of Contemporary Eastern European Writing*, ed. Michael March (New York: Vintage, 1994), 252–54.

Ahmeti, Mimoza (b. 1963) Albanian poet. A native of Krujë, north of Tirana, Ahmeti studied Albanian language and literature in the Albanian capital and was subsequently employed as a teacher of literature. Her first book of poetry, *Bëhu i bukur* (Become Beautiful), appeared in 1986, the year she graduated from Tirana University, and was favorably reviewed. In 1989 Ahmeti's second volume of verse, *Sidomos nesër* (Especially Tomorrow), containing fifty-nine poems, was published. Eschewing complex experimentation, Ahmeti writes in a mostly straightforward style distinguished by a firm grasp of poetic technique. Her subjects are at once highly personal and universal. Although not numerous, her short stories are well crafted and original. Ahmeti is also a well-known painter and graphic artist.

Translations: "The Secret of My Youth," trans. Robert Elsie, in *Description of a Struggle: The Vintage Book of Contemporary Eastern European Writing*, ed. Michael March (New York: Vintage, 1994), 262–66; six poems in *An Elusive Eagle Soars: Anthology of Modern Albanian Poetry*, ed. and trans. Robert Elsie (London: Forest, 1993), 201–7.

Ajvaz, Michal (b. 1949) Czech novelist, short-story writer, poet, and essayist. One of the most cerebral yet imaginative contemporary Czech writers, Ajvaz was born and educated in Prague. He graduated from Charles University in 1974 with a degree in Czech literature and aesthetics and in 1978 received his doctorate. He subsequently held a variety of odd jobs, including that of a pumper in the national waterworks (1986–1994), in connection with which he traveled throughout the Czech Republic measuring quantities of underground water. In 1994 Ajvaz became a full-time writer. He made his literary debut in 1989 with *Vražda v hotelu Intercontinental* (Murder in the Hotel Intercontinental), a small book of longish, colloquial poems on Prague themes (e.g., "Bufet U labužníka" ["Buffet at the Sign of the Epicure"]) or reflecting his strong interest in philosophy (e.g., "Teorie poznání" ["Theory of Knowledge"]). His next book was *Návrat starého varana* (Return of the Old Komodo Dragon, 1991), a collection of twenty-one short sto-

ries almost all narrated in the first person and characterized by the combination of high intellect and rich imagination (that inclines toward the strange) seen in all his writings. Ajvaz's first novel, *Druhé město* (The Other City), appeared in 1993 and spins an intriguing yarn about an eerie realm just beyond the city in which the novel takes place. It was followed by the novels *Tiché labyrinty* (Quiet Labyrinths, 1996) and *Tyrkysový orel* (The Turquoise Eagle, 1997). The latter is divided into two parts: "Bílí mravenci" ("White Ants") and "Zénónovy paradoxy" ("Zeno's Paradoxes"). "White Ants" is a story told by an ethnographer to an archaeologist about a species of white ants that secret a green fluid capable of curing sleeping sickness and have a remarkable way of defending themselves—when in danger, the entire colony merges and forms a living sculpture, usually a white tiger lying with its jaws wide open. In "Zeno's Paradoxes," Ajvaz (the narrator) recalls what happened to him on a snowy night on his way home from the Philosophical Faculty of Charles University when he dropped into a pub and overheard students discussing ancient philosophy. The most important of Ajvaz's writings in the areas of philosophy and aesthetics are *Tajemství knihy* (The Secret of the Book, 1997)—a collection of seventeen short, mostly philosophically oriented literary essays originally published between 1990 and 1997 on such writers as Jorge Luis Borges, Michel Foucault, Roger Gilbert-Lecomte, Witold Gombrowicz, Ernst Jünger, Petr Král, Gustav Meyrink, and Leo Perutz—and *Znak a bytí* (Sign and Existence), a short study of the French linguist Jacques Derrida's grammatology.

Translations: Excerpts from *Druhé město*, trans. Tatiana Firkušný and Veronique Firkušný-Callegari, in *Daylight in Nightclub Inferno: Czech Fiction from the Post-Kundera Generation*, selected by Elena Lappin

(North Haven, Conn.: Catbird, 1997), 87–97; "The Beetle," trans. Alexandra Büchler, in *This Side of Reality: Modern Czech Writing* (London: Serpent's Tail, 1996), 181–89.

Albahari, David (b. 1948) Serbian novelist, short-story writer, and translator. Born in Peć, Albahari's literary star rose in the 1970s when he came to be regarded as the most impressive of a group of young writers who followed the lead of Danilo Kiš in rejecting post–World War II Serbian nationalism. Instead of accepting the conventions of socialist realism, the postwar celebration of the heroism of Tito's partisans, and the historical struggle of the Serbs for national greatness, Albahari cultivated the unheroic, the unconventional, and the nature of literature and the creative process. Although he has published four novels, Albahari succeeds best as a writer of short pieces, which in itself is a rejection of monumentalism. Much of Albahari's inspiration derives from his recollections of family life, which he portrays in a series of vignettes—above all, in the collection *Opis smrti* (A Description of Death, 1982)—noteworthy for their emphasis on the odd and whimsical. Like Kiš, Albahari is of Jewish background and makes the now-extinct world of small-town Jewish life in the former Yugoslavia the subject of a number of his stories without ranging far beyond the ambiguous Jewishness of his own family. Albahari also shares Kiš's impulse to break out of the confines of traditional storytelling by experimenting with narrative composition. More particularly characteristic of Albahari is both his persistent questioning of the nature and limits of reality and his consideration of the place of language in the literary creative process and, by inference, in a totalitarian society. The strands of fantasy to be found in Albahari's works reflect his desire to move beyond the realistic and knowable. Many of his thoughts on language, and on the power of silence, appear in the context of

dialogues with his wife in which she assumes the role of a mocking, irreverent, and crabby doubting Thomas.

Widely traveled and a man of broad culture, Albahari frequently builds his stories around his experiences in such places as the United States, Israel, and Kenya, as well as his native Yugoslavia. Allusions to popular films (*The Man Who Shot Liberty Valance* and *Godzilla,* for example, in the story "The Movies") appear, as do references to such American writers Albahari has translated as the metafictionalists Robert Coover and Thomas Pynchon, by whom Albahari has obviously been influenced.

Besides the novels *Sudija Dimitrijević* (Judge Dimitrijević, 1978); *Cink* (Tsing, 1988); *Kratka knjiga* (Short Book, 1993); and *Snežni čovek* (Snow Man, 1995), Albahari has published several collections of shorter prose, among them *Porodično vreme* (Family Time, 1973); *Opis smrti*; *Fras u šupi* (Shock in a Shack, 1984); *Jednostavnost* (Simplicity, 1988); and *Pelerina* (The Cloak, 1993). His most recent work, and one of his best, the novel *Mamac* (The Bait, 1996), is set in western Canada and reflects Albahari's own resettlement in Canada in 1994 in the wake of the Yugoslav wars. It is patently autobiographical. A refugee in Canada for two years, the narrator has carried with him from Yugoslavia three cassette tapes of his mother recorded sixteen years earlier. As he replays the tapes, the narrator listens to his mother's voice recounting her life, the tragedy of which encapsulates that of Yugoslavia itself. Through discussions between the narrator and his friend Donald, a writer, which are interspersed throughout the novel, Albahari again manifests his interest in narrative structures by raising the question of the legitimacy of the taped memoirs as a novelistic form. At the same time, the discussions between the narrator and Donald add further substance to the historicity of the memoirs.

Literature: There is next to nothing on Albahari in English. "Words and Things: David Albahari's Prose in the Context of the Former Yugoslavia," the short afterword by Tomislav Longinović to the translation of Albahari's *Words Are Something Else,* is a useful introduction despite its brevity.

Translations: *Tsing,* trans. David Albahari (Evanston, Ill.: Northwestern University Press, 1997); *Words Are Something Else,* trans. Ellen Elias-Bursać (Evanston, Ill.: Northwestern University Press, 1996), a compilation drawn from Albahari's collections of short prose: *Porodično vreme, Opis smrti, Fras u šupi, Jednostavnost,* and *Pelerina. Mamac* is available in French as *L'Appât,* trans. Gojko Lukić and Gabriel Iaculli (Paris: Gallimard, 1999).

Albu, Florenṭa (1934–2000) Romanian poet. Born in the county of Ialomiṭa, Albu graduated in 1957 from the Faculty of Philology at Bucharest University, where she studied Romanian and French literatures. She worked briefly as a reporter for the daily *Scînteia tineretului* (1963–1964) and then became potery editor of the review *Viaṭa Românească.* Her first volume of poems, *Fără popas* (Without Rest), appeared in 1961. A prolific poet, Albu followed this volume with another twenty-two: *Cîmpia soarelui* (Plains of the Sun, 1962; 2nd ed. 1971); *Constanṭa* (Constancy, 1962); *Intrare în anotimp* (Entering the Season, 1964); *Fata Morgana* (1969); *Poeme* (Poems, 1969); *Măşti de priveghi* (Masks of a Death Vigil, 1968); *Himera nisipurilor* (Chimera of the Sands, 1969); *Austru* (Southwestern Wind, 1971); *Arborele vieṭii* (Trees of Life, 1971); *Petrecere cu iarbă* (Feast with Grass, 1973); *Elegii* (Elegies, 1973); *Ave, noiembrie* (Ave, November, 1975); *Întoarcere* (The Return, 1977); *Roata lumii* (The Wheel of Life, 1977); *65 de poeme* (65 Poems, 1978); *Umbră arsă* (Withered Shadow, 1980); *Epitaf* (Epitaph, 1981); *Poem în Utopia* (Poem on Utopia,

1983); *A fi—fire* (To Be—Nature, 1984); *Terase* (Terraces, 1985); *Efectul de seră* (The Greenhouse Effect, 1987); and *Kilometrul Unu* (Kilometer One, 1988). A poet with a wide range of interests from eros to war, Albu writes often of an intimacy with nature and a feeling of closeness to rural life. It is as if, in a number of her lyrics, the rhythms and traditions of village life reinforce the proximity of nature. Another of Albu's recurrent themes is old age, but there is no sense of dread; Albu is a poet of delicacy and tranquillity. And often images of old age are coupled with and modified by nostalgia for the bygone innocence of childhood. Albu is also the author of a book of travel impressions, *Banchet autumnal* (Autumnal Banquet, 1984).

Translations: Seven poems in *Silent Voices: An Anthology of Contemporary Romanian Women Poets,* trans. Andrea Deletant and Brenda Walker (London: Forest, 1986), 1–8.

Alexandru, Ioan (real name Ion Şandor; b. 1942) Romanian poet. Born in the village of Topa Mică near Cluj, in Transylvania, Alexandru graduated from high school in Cluj in 1962 and then entered Cluj University, where he studied for two years before continuing at Bucharest University from 1964 to 1968. He began teaching Romanian language and literature at Bucharest University in 1968 before receiving a scholarship to study in Germany from 1968 to 1972. During this period, he traveled throughout Western Europe as well as Greece and Israel. He received his doctorate in 1973. A scholar of classical and biblical literature, Alexandru has translated Pindar into Romanian as well as the Song of Songs from the Hebrew. Alexandru made his debut as a poet in 1964 with the publication of his book *Cum să vă spun* (How to Tell You). It was followed by such further volumes as *Viaṭa deocamdată* (Life for the Time Being, 1965); *Infernul dis-*

cutabil (Disputable Hell, 1967); *Vină* (Guilt, 1967); *Vămile pustiei* (The Toll-Gates of Wasteland, 1969); and *Poeme* (Poems, 1970) and by a series of hymns mostly to Romania and its various regions: *Imnele bucuriei* (Hymns of Joy, 1973); *Imnele Transilvaniei* (Hymns to Transylvania, 1976); *Imnele Moldovei* (Hymns to Moldavia, 1980); *Imnele Țării Românești* (Hymns to Wallachia, 1982); *Imnele iubirii* (Hymns of Love, 1983); *Imnele Putnei* (Hymns to Putnea, 1985); and *Imnele Maramureșului* (Hymns to Maramureș, 1988). A poet of vitalistic dynamism and philosophically close to the German Romantics and Martin Heidegger, whom he studied while in Germany, Alexandru also evinces an attraction for myth, which in some instances merges with a deep feeling for Romanian national history and tradition. In his later poetry, this "Romanianism" has also assumed a political character. Alexandru won the Writers Union Prize in 1965 and the Bucharest Writers Association Prize in 1981. After the Romanian revolution of December 1989, he became a senator representing the nationalist PNT Party.

Translations: Six poems in *An Anthology of Contemporary Romanian Poetry*, trans. Andrea Deletant and Brenda Walker (London: Forest, 1984), 1–7; eight poems in *46 Romanian Poets in English*, trans. and ed. Ștefan Avădanei and Don Eulert (Iași: Junimea, 1973), 296–302; four poems, trans. Andrei Bantaș and Dan Dușescu, in *Like Diamonds in Coal Asleep: Selections from Twentieth Century Romanian Poetry*, ed. Andrei Bantaș (Bucharest: Minerva, 1985), 347–51.

Anderson, Sascha (b. 1953) German poet, essayist, and popular-song writer. Anderson was born and educated in Weimar. After graduating from high school, he trained as a printer and typesetter, but soon switched his interest to film. In 1974 he went to work for the DEFA film studios and then spent the academic year 1978/1979 studying at the Film Institute in Potsdam Babelsberg. Anderson ran afoul of the authorities in the 1970s and on three separate occasions (1971, 1973, 1979) was imprisoned, presumably for political reasons. From 1981 on, he devoted himself entirely to his creative career and to publishing, in which he had taken a keen interest. He became closely identified with the art scene in East Berlin until his departure for West Berlin in 1986. In 1991, after he had been awarded a fellowship to the Villa Massimo in Rome, he was denounced as a Stasi informer by fellow East German writer Wolf Biermann—a charge that Anderson has denied, although few now dispute it—and was constrained to decline the award.

Anderson attracted much attention as a leading figure in the Prenzlauer Berg community of younger writers who sought refuge from the official literary culture in an alternative lifestyle, in political protest, and in personal relationships. They likened themselves (and have been likened) to the writers of the American Beat Generation. Besides the poems he wrote during this period, Anderson composed popular songs and sang with rock musical groups. Anderson was also active as a founder and publisher of independent avant-garde journals and publications, the best known of which was the series *Poe-Sie-All-Bum* (1978–1984). He also had a hand in the UND, USW, and Ariadnefabrik small-scale publishing organizations and was personally responsible for Edition S. A. (Sascha Anderson Editions), which put out twelve titles, including works by such writers as Elke Erb, Uwe Kolbe, Heiner Müller, and Bert Papenfuss-Gorek. Anderson's editions are of particular interest because of their graphics, and his enthusiasm for the visual arts shows up as well in some of his own volumes published both before and after he quit the GDR. Color, for example, assumes a symbolic meaning in *jeder satellit hat einen killer satelliten* (each satellite has a killer satellite, 1982), a collection of poems from the 1970s, some of which Anderson had recited publicly. The second edition of the little volume, published in 1997, comes with fourteen other poems from 1970 to 1980 and a CD with vocals by Anderson, Cornelia Schleime, and Michael Rom, with music by thirteen instrumentalists. The shape of the text in *totenreklame: eine reise* (death notice: a journey, 1983) was meant to convey the spiral movement of a 7,000-kilometer trip inside a small state surrounded by a wall. This was an obvious allusion to the GDR, the contradictions within which form the subject of the work as a whole.

Anderson's other books of poems include *Waldmaschine: Übung, vierhändig* (Wood Machine: Four-Handed Exercise, 1984), with the short-story writer Michael Wildenhain and the artists Ralf Kerbach and Cornelia Schleime; *Ich fühle mich in Grenzen wohle* (I'm Happy Inside Borders, 1985); *brunnen, randvoll* (Well, Brimming Over, 1988), with woodcuts by Ralf Kerbach; *jewish jetset* (1991; original title in English), with drawings by A. R. Penck; and *Rosa Indica vulgaris: Gedichte und ein Essay* (Rosa Indica vulgaris: A Poem and an Essay, 1994), with nine drawings by A. R. Penck. Of no small value for the study of the East German literature in the 1970s and 1980s is the anthology edited by Anderson and the poet Elke Erb and published in 1985 under the title *Berührung ist nur eine Randerscheinung: Neue Literatur aus der DDR* (Contact Is Only a Marginal Phenomenon: New Literature from the GDR). From 1990 to 1996, Anderson worked in the Galrev publishing company in Berlin as a publisher, an editor, and a reader. Here is a typical shorter Anderson poem, "eNDe VI" (eNd VI"), from each satellite has a killer satellite:

> comrade butzmann says yesterday
> evening we had with us
> the class enemy as guest.

Literature: "Sascha Anderson, I" and "Sascha Anderson, II," in *Literary Intellectuals and the Dissolution of the State: Professionalism and Conformity in the GDR*, ed. Robert von Hallberg, trans. Kenneth J. Northcott (Chicago: University of Chicago Press, 1996), 257–64, 295–303.

Andreev, Veselin (1918–1991) Bulgarian poet and essayist. A native of Pirdop, where he received his elementary education, Andreev completed secondary school in Sofia and studied law at Sofia University. He began publishing in journals in the 1930s and also worked as a newspaper editor. During World War II, he participated in the underground Bulgarian Resistance movement, becoming a partisan in 1943 and political commissar of a partisan brigade in 1944. After 9 September 1944, he served as editor in chief of the army newspaper *Narodna voiska* (1945–1949) and of *Literaturen front* (1949–1955). As a literary figure, Andreev is best known for his writings about the wartime partisans. They include, among others, his verse collection, *Partizanski pesni* (Guerrilla Songs, 1947), which has been reissued several times; *V Lopianskata gora* (In the Lopian Forest, 1947); *Partizanski dnevnik* (Partisan Diary, 1965); *Partizanski razkazi* (Guerrilla Stories, 1975); *Umirakha bezsmurtni* (They Died Immortal, 1973); and *V otriada, v brigadata: Iz partizanskiia epos "Umiraha bezsmurtni"* (In the Detachment, in the Brigade: From the Partisan Epic "They Died Immortal," 1981). Imbued with much the same spirit of wartime camaraderie and shared joys and sorrows are the literary miscellany Andreev collected and edited: *S kruvta si noshtite trevozhim* (I Fear the Nights with Their Blood, 1969), in honor of those Bulgarian writers "who fell in the struggle against fascism," and such collections of essays and reminiscences as *Razmisli* (Reflections, 1973); *Ne moga bez vas: Eseta i spomeni za nashi pisateli* (I Can't

Without You: Essays and Recollections About Our Writers, 1974); and *Nasame—s tebe: Razgovori* (Together with You: Conversations, 1979). Typical of the kind of sycophantic communist work that Andreev could turn out when needed is *Ima na sveta Moskva* (There Is Moscow in the World, 1951). In 1991 Andreev committed suicide, deeply pained by the revelations of what communism had wreaked on Bulgaria, especially in the time of Todor Zhivkov, whom he cursed in his suicide note.

Translations: *Guerrilla Stories and Poems by Vesselin Andreyev* [*sic*], trans. V. Izmirliev, ed. M. Pojarlieva (Sofia: Sofia Press, 1969).

Andreevski, Petre M. (b. 1934) Macedonian poet and short-story writer. Andreevski was born in Sloeštica, a village near Bitola, and went to school in both Bitola and Skopje. He worked for some time as a folk music editor for Skopje Radio and TV. Andreevski is most admired as a writer for his narrative poems based on Macedonian legends and myths and contained in such volumes as *Jazli* (Knots, 1960); *I na nebo i na zemja* (In Heaven and on Earth, 1962); *Denicija* (Denizia [a woman's name], 1968); *Dalni nakovalni* (Distant Anvils, 1971); *Pofalbi i poplaki* (Praises and Complaints, 1977); *Večna kukja: Tažalenki* (The Eternal Hearth: Mourners, 1987); *Ptica potajnica* (Bird of Mystery, 1980); *Poezija* (Poetry, 1984); and *Pesni* (1988). His well-known poem "Death of the Guiser" was honored at the Struga International Poetry Festival in 1971 as best poem of the year. Apart from his poetry, Andreevski has written a considerable amount of prose. His short stories are contained in the volumes *Sedmiot den* (On the Seventh Day, 1964); *Odbrani raskazi* (Collected Stories, 1970); and *Raskazi* (Stories, 1984). His well-received novel *Poslednite selani* (The Last Villagers, 1997) was inspired by the migrations of the last half-century that emptied the Macedonian villages, leav-

ing behind only old people in desolate circumstances. His other writings include *Neverni godini: Zapisi, iskazi i preraskazi* (Treacherous Years: Memoirs, Reports, Retellings, 1974), a book essentially of memoirs; *Volnato vreme* (The Time for Wool, 1982), a volume of literary criticism; and play texts and collections such as *Prolet za prikaz* (Spring for Performance, 1969), *Vreme za peenje: Piesa vo dva dela* (Time for Singing: A Play in Two Acts, 1975), *Skakulici* (Locusts, 1984), *Drami* (Plays, 1984), and *Neznaen strav* (Unknown Fear, 1988).

Translations: *Nikoja doba* (Skopje: Naša Kniga, 1988), a volume of Andreevski's poems that includes some translations into English, French, and Romanian; "The Vampire," in *The Big Horse and Other Stories of Modern Macedonia,* ed. Milne Holton (Columbia: University of Missouri Press, 1974), 113–19; three poems in *Contemporary Macedonian Poetry,* ed. and trans. Ewald Osers (London: Forest, 1991), 77–83; four poems, including excerpts from "Death of the Guiser," trans. by various hands, in *Reading the Ashes: An Anthology of the Poetry of Modern Macedonia,* ed. Milne Holton and Graham W. Reid (Pittsburgh: University of Pittsburgh Press, 1977), 85–90.

Andrić, Ivo (1892–1975) Bosnian Serb novelist, short-story writer, and essayist. The best-known Yugoslav writer to rise to prominence after World War II, Andrić achieved international celebrity when he was awarded the Nobel Prize in Literature in 1961. A native of Travnik, in Bosnia, he attended schools in Višegrad and Sarajevo. During World War I, Andrić was imprisoned for three years because of his involvement in the nationalistic, anti-Hapsburg Young Bosnia organization, which was implicated in the assassinations of Archduke Franz Ferdinand and his wife in Sarajevo in 1914. His complex emotions while in prison were recorded in a type of undated prison diary, which he composed between

1914 and 1918 and to which he gave the title *Ex ponto* (From the Bridge). When the first collected edition of Andrić's works was being prepared for publication in 1963, he staunchly refused permission for *Ex ponto* as well as his early collection of related prose poems, *Nemiri* (Disquiet), to be included and maintained this position until his death. Subsequent editions of Andrić's collected works do include them. After his release from prison, Andrić studied at the universities of Zagreb, Vienna, Kraków, and Graz (Austria). It was at Graz that he earned a doctorate in history in 1924 for his (later published) dissertation *Die Entwicklung des geistlichen Lebens in Bosnien unter der Einwirkung der türkischen Herrschaft* (*The Development of Spiritual Life in Bosnia Under the Influence of Turkish Rule*). Before receiving his doctorate, Andrić had begun a career in the Yugoslav diplomatic service beginning with his posting to Rome in 1920. Subsequent assignments took him to Bucharest, Trieste, Graz, Marseilles, Paris, Madrid, Geneva, and Berlin, where he was stationed at the time of the German invasion of Yugoslavia in 1941. By then, he held the rank of assistant to the Yugoslav minister of foreign affairs.

During the German occupation of Belgrade, Andrić lived in virtual isolation in his apartment, where he devoted himself to writing his "Bosnian trilogy": *Na Drini ćuprija* (*The Bridge on the Drina*); *Travnička hronika* (translated variously as *Bosnian Chronicle, Bosnian Story,* and *The Days of the Consuls*); and *Gospodjica* (translated as *The Woman from Sarajevo*). All three volumes of the trilogy were published in 1945, the year World War II ended. A superb storyteller, Andrić also wrote a large number of stories that were eventually gathered together and published as separate volumes in the various collected editions of his works under the titles *Prokleta avlija* (Devil's Yard; translated as *The Damned Yard*); *Nemirna godina* (Uneasy Year); *Žedj* (Thirst); *Jelena, žena koje nema* (Jelena, the Woman Who Was Not); *Znakovi* (Signs); *Deca* (Children); and *Mara milosnica i druge priče* (Mara the Concubine and Other Tales; translated as *The Pasha's Concubine and Other Tales*). *Prokleta avlija,* a novella, is one of Andrić's more compelling shorter works. Set in a prison courtyard (the "devil's yard") in Istanbul, the novella uses its principal characters (a priest, a Jew, and a Turk) as a means of exploring different narrative styles.

Andrić's abundant nonfiction prose oeuvre encompasses a series of mostly travel sketches incorporated into such collected editions of his works as *Staze, lica, predeli* (Paths, Faces, Landscapes, 1967); two collections of essays, one on the relevance of legend to history—*Istorija i legenda* (History and Legend, 1976)—and the other, *Umetnik i njegovo delo* (The Artist and His Work, 1976), a series of essays on Vuk Karadžić (1787–1864), the great reformer of the Serbian language, and the great Montenegrin poet Petar Njegoš (1813–1851); a collection of personal reflections titled *Znakovi pored puta* (Signs by the Roadside, 1976); and an essay on art in the form of an imaginary conversation with the Spanish painter Francisco Goya, published originally in 1935. All these collections of sketches and essays have been incorporated into the various editions of Andrić's collected works.

Much of Andrić's fiction revolves around his native region, Bosnia, and the towns of Travnik, Sarajevo, and Višegrad, a region that, until the disintegration of the former Yugoslavia in the conflicts of the 1990s, was a striking mosaic of different ethnicities, religions, and cultures. A student of history, Andrić drew inspiration for many of his works from the Bosnian past when Bosnia, as most of the South Slavic world, was part of the Ottoman Empire. The most renowned novel of the "Bosnian trilogy," *The Bridge on the Drina,* superbly exemplifies Andrić's love of the Bosnian past and his ability to re-create it with color and remarkable narrative skill.

The focus of the novel is the bridge over the Drina River in Travnik that was built in the sixteenth century on order of a Turkish grand vizier. Andrić follows the intertwining of destinies of the bridge and the people whose lives it touches from its initial construction to the merciless pounding it received in World War I. *The Days of the Consuls,* the second part of the "Bosnian trilogy," spans the seven-year period 1807 to 1814, when the Dalmatian litoral fell under French rule in the wake of Napoleon's conquests. The arrival in Travnik of a French consul was soon followed by the appearance of other consuls from such rival countries as Germany, Russia, and Austria. The interaction of the Europeans with one another, their relations individually and collectively with the Turkish viziers already in the town, and the reactions of the ethnically diverse townspeople to the foreign diplomats in their midst form the basis of the novel. In the third novel of the "Bosnian trilogy," *The Woman from Sarajavo,* history recedes in importance as Andrić shifts his attention now to the moral tale of a woman whose desire to live frugally after her father's financial decline and premature death turns into a pathological love of money that condemns her to a life of solitude and ultimately destroys her.

Literature: Celia Hawkesworth, *Ivo Andrić: Bridge Between East and West* (London: Athlone, 1984), the best critical study of Andrić in English to date; Želimir B. Juričić, *The Man and the Artist: Essays on Ivo Andrić* (Lanham, Md.: University Press of America, 1986); Vanita Singh Mikerji, *Ivo Andrić: A Critical Biography* (Jefferson, N.C.: McFarland, 1990); Wayne S. Vucinich, ed., *Ivo Andrić Revisited: The Bridge Still Stands* (Berkeley: University of California Press, 1995), a good collection of essays by scholars of South Slavic literatures originally presented at a conference at Stanford University on 22 November 1992, commemorating the centenary of Andrić's birth.

Translations: *Bosnian Chronicle,* trans. Joseph Hitrec (New York: Knopf, 1963); *Bosnian Story,* trans. Kenneth Johnstone (London: Lincolns-Prager, 1959, 1961); *The Bridge on the Drina,* trans. Lovett F. Edwards (London: Allen and Unwin, 1959, 1961); *Conversation with Goya: Bridges Signs,* trans. Celia Hawkesworth and Andrew Harvey (London: Menard, 1992); *The Damned Yard and Other Stories,* ed. Celia Hawkesworth (London: Forest, 1992); *The Days of the Consuls,* trans. Celia Hawkesworth, in collaboration with Bogdan Rakić (London: Forest, 1992); *The Development of Spiritual Life in Bosnia Under the Influence of Turkish Rule,* trans. and ed. Želimir B. Juričić and John F. Loud (Durham, N.C.: Duke University Press, 1990); *Letters,* trans. and ed. Želimir B. Juričić (Toronto: Serbian Heritage Academy, 1984), a small and not very interesting collection of Andrić's letters to various recipients from 1918 to 1973; *The Pasha's Concubine and Other Tales,* trans. Joseph Hitrec (New York: Knopf, 1968), which includes such well-known stories as "The Bridge on the Žepa," "The Journey of Ali Djerzelez," and "The Pasha's Concubine"; *The Woman from Sarajevo,* trans. Joseph Hitrec (New York: Knopf, 1965); *The Vizier's Elephant: Three Novellas,* trans. Drenka Willen (New York: Harcourt, Brace & World, 1962).

Andrzejewski, Jerzy (b. 1909) Polish novelist and short-story writer. Well represented in translation, Andrzejewski was born in Warsaw and studied Polish literature at Warsaw University. His first published literary effort was a collection of short stories titled *Drogi nieuniknione* (Unavoidable Roads), which appeared in 1936. In 1939 he was awarded the Young Authors Prize of the Polish Academy of Literature for his novel *Ład serca* (Mode of the Heart), which has been reprinted a number of times. During World War II, Andrzejewski worked as an underground cultural activist. After the war, he eventually settled in Kraków, where in 1951, he became editor in chief of the weekly *Tygodnik Powszechny*. From 1952 to 1957 he served as a delegate to parliament. Andrzejewski's first postwar publication, the short-story collection *Noc i inne opowiadania* (Night and Other Stories, 1945), won the City of Kraków Prize. His second novel, and by far his best-known, most popular, and most widely translated work, *Popiół i diament* (*Ashes and Diamonds*, 1948), was awarded the literary prize of the literary weekly *Odrodzenie*. The taut novel, set in 1945, reflects the political chaos in Poland in the immediate aftermath of the war, when the communists were not yet firmly in control and their authority was challenged by members of the Armia Krajowa (Home Army), operating on behalf of the Polish government-in-exile, based in London. The novel was made into a highly successful film by the renowned Polish director Andrzej Wajda. Andrzejewski's next novel was the political allegory *Ciemności kryją ziemię* (Darkness Covers the Earth, 1957; translated as *The Inquisitors*), which is set during the Spanish Inquisition but alludes to postwar Polish Stalinism. Next came *Bramy raju* (*The Gates of Paradise*, 1960), a stream-of-consciousness novel effectively evoking the atmosphere of the tragic Children's Crusade of 1212, and, after a long stay in Paris, *Idzie, skacząc po górach* (translated as *He Cometh Leaping upon the Mountains* and *A Sitter for a Satyr*), an entertaining, almost parodic work based on the life of Pablo Picasso and his putative relations with young girls. Andrzejewski also published another three collections of short stories—*Książka dla Marcina* (A Book for Martin, 1954), a book of reminiscences of Warsaw; *Niby gaj: Opowiadania, 1933–1958* (The Would-Be Grove: Stories, 1933–1958, 1959); and *Złoty lis* (The Golden Fox, 1955)—and several collections of speeches, articles, essays, and feuilletons generally supportive of the official ideology, among them *Aby pokój zwyciężył* (That

Peace May Triumph, 1950); *O człowieku radzieckim: Wrażenia z pobytu w ZSRR* (On Soviet Man: Impressions from a Trip to the USSR, 1951); *Partia i twórczość pisarza* (The Party and the Writer's Art, 1952); *Ludzie i zdarzenia 1951* (People and Happenings 1951, 1952); and *Ludzie i zdarzenia 1952* (People and Happenings 1952, 1953).

Literature: Wacław Sadkowski, *Jerzy Andrzejewski* (Warsaw: Agencja Autorska and Zjednoczenie Księgarska, 1973), a good introductory brochure dealing mostly with *Ashes and Diamonds*.

Translations: *The Appeal*, trans. Celina Wieniewska (Indianapolis: Bobbs-Merrill, 1971); *Ashes and Diamonds*, trans. D. F. Welsh (London: Weidenfeld and Nicolson, 1962; Evanston, Ill.: Northwestern University Press, 1991); *Ashes and Diamonds* [screenplay by Jerzy Andrzejewski and Andrzej Wajda], *Kanal* [screenplay by Jerzy Stefan Stawiński], *A Generation* [screenplay by Bohdan Czeszko]: *Three Films by Andrzej Wajda*, trans. Bolesław Sulik (London: Lorrimer, 1973); *The Gates of Paradise*, trans. James Kirkup (London: Weidenfeld and Nicolson, 1963); *He Cometh Leaping upon the Mountains*, trans. Celina Wieniewska (London: Panther, 1968); *The Inquisitors*, trans. Konrad Syrop (Westport, Conn.: Greenwood, 1976); *A Sitter for a Satyr*, trans. Celina Wieniewska (New York: Dutton, 1965).

Anóka, Eszter (1942–1994) Hungarian short-story writer, novelist, poet, and critic. Anóka, a native of Nagyhalász, graduated from Budapest University in 1975 with a degree in Hungarian and library science. She subsequently worked as a factory hand, an administrator, a librarian, and later a journalist specializing mostly in book reviews and criticism. Her first volume of stories, *Hála* (Gratitude), appeared in 1975. It was followed by another collection of stories, *Búcsú a nőktől* (Goodbye to Women, 1980); *Ostrom békében* (Assault in Peace, 1988), a novel;

Üzenet (Message, 1990), poetry; and *A mérték* (The Measure, 1990), a short novel. Anóka drew her material from contemporary Budapest big-city life, with a particular affinity for odd and unusual female characters.

Translations: "Illatos Street 5, Budapest: Childhood Memories of a Housing Estate," trans. Gillian Howarth, in *Present Continuous: Contemporary Hungarian Writing*, ed. István Bart (Budapest: Corvina, 1985), 215–32.

Apitz, Bruno (1900–1979) German novelist. A native of Leipzig, Apitz was born into a worker's family of twelve children. He had little formal schooling and began working at the age of fourteen. Soon thereafter, he became a member of the communist youth organization. In 1927 he joined the German Communist Party, and in 1930 entered the Union of Proletarian-Revolutionary Writers. When Hitler came to power in 1933, Apitz was confined to a concentration camp for three months. He was arrested again in 1934 for underground activity and incarcerated in Buchenwald from 1937 to 1945. After the war, Apitz worked mostly as an editor, a theater director in Leipzig, and a literary adviser to the DEFA film studios. From 1965 he devoted himself entirely to writing. His greatest literary success was the novel *Nackt unter Wölfen* (*Naked Among Wolves*, 1957). Not only was it the first novel about the wartime concentration camps to appear in the GDR, but it was the first GDR literary work to gain international recognition. Set in Buchenwald in March 1945, it deals with the resistance to the SS by a clandestine communist-led organization within the camp and its concealment of a Polish Jewish child. The shifting of the child from one hiding place to another also serves as a means by which Apitz familiarizes the reader with the landscape of the concentration camp along with its daily routine. *Naked Among the Wolves* was translated into over two dozen languages and in 1963 was made into a film by DEFA. Apitz's second novel, *Der Regenbogen* (The Rainbow, 1976), is a heavily autobiographical panorama of the world of the German working and lower middle classes from the end of the nineteenth century to the end of World War I. Apitz's novel *Der Schwelbrand* (Smouldering Fire), which was incomplete at his death, was edited for publication and appeared in 1984.

Literature: Renate Florstedt, ed., *Bruno Apitz, 1900–1979: Biographie, Texte, Bibliographie* (Leipzig: Die Bibliothek, 1990), a solid reference work.

Translations: *Naked Among Wolves*, trans. Edith Anderson (Berlin: Seven Seas, 1960).

Aralica, Ivan (b. 1930) Croatian novelist and short-story writer. One of the most prolific and respected writers of the post–World War II period, Aralica was born in Promina, Dalmatia. He was educated through high school in such nearby towns as Drniš and Knin, and in 1953 graduated from the Teachers Training College in Knin. At the age of twenty-six, he published his first story, "Smokva" ("The Fig"), in 1956 in the magazine *Prosvjeta* while he was a part-time student in South Slavic languages and literatures at Zadar University. He completed his studies in 1961 and then started teaching high school in Zadar. In 1964 he became director of the Zadar Teachers Training College. The following year, he became a member of the editorial board of the Zadar literary review *Zadarska revija* and president of the Zadar subcommitee of the Central Croatian Cultural and Publishing Society, Matica Hrvatska.

Throughout his immensely productive career, Aralica has drawn inspiration for a great many of his works from the people and history of his native Dalmatian region, beginning with his first major prose text, the World War II novel *Svemu ima vrijeme* (All in Good Time, 1967), and continuing through such subsequent works as the short novels *Nevjernik* (The Infidel) and *Oluje u tihom ozraču*

(Storms in the Stillness), both published in 1967; *A primer se zvao Laudina* (And the Example Was Named Laudina, 1969); *Filip* (Philip, 1970), for which he was awarded the Zadar Prize; and *Konjanik* (The Rider, 1971). It was in the late 1960s and early 1970s, when Aralica was already making a substantial name for himself as a writer, that he fell victim to Tito's crackdown of the "Croatian Spring," the term applied to the rapidly growing Croatian nationalism of the time. The aim of this nationalism was greater autonomy for Croatia, especially in the economic sphere, and greater decentralization. Aralica lost the position he had held since 1969 in the regional parliament of the Socialist Republic of Croatia and was prohibited from further political activity. His reaction to this banishment is reflected in his novel *Ima netko siv i zelen* (There Is Someone Gray and Raw, 1977) and in his story-story collection *Opsjene paklenih crteža* (Illusions of Hellish Sketches, 1977).

The appearance of Aralica's historical novel *Psi u trgovištu* (Dogs in the Market Town, 1979), which was honored with an INA Award, signaled the beginning of his return to a more visible role in public life as well as his growing interest in the genre of the historical novel. In *Psi u trgovištu* he drew on old chronicles of Franciscan friars and travelers' diaries to paint a vivid picture of Ottoman Turkish–Venetian conflict in the Dalmatian area. This focus on the Dalmatian past within the framework of the rivalry in the region between the Ottoman Empire and the Republic of Venice characterizes such subsequent and well-regarded novels as the historical trilogy *Put bez sna* (Dreamless Journey, 1982), which won the Šandor Gjalski Prize; *Duše robova* (The Souls of Slaves, 1984), for which Aralica received both the Goran Prize and the Award of the Miroslav Krlža Foundation in 1985; and *Graditelj svratišta* (The Inn-Builder, 1986). The trilogy is built around the fate of three generations of a Croatian family (Grabovac) from the seventeenth-century Ottoman–

Venetian conflicts through the early nineteenth century, when Dalmatia fell under Napoleon's control. Aralica took a temporary holiday from historical writing with his next novel, *Okvir za mržanju* (Framework for Hatred, 1987), which presents a grim picture of Yugoslav life in the first years after World War II. The main character of the novel, a scholar from the Teachers Training College in Knin, clearly embodies autobiographical elements. *Asmodeev šal* (The Scarf of Asmodeus), which followed *Okvir za mržanju* in 1988, marked a successful resumption of Aralica's historical writing. Beginning with the two-part *Tajna sarmatskog orla* (The Secret of the Sarmatian Eagle, 1989), Aralica's writing turned overtly political. *Tajna sarmatskog orla* is a curious analysis of the nature of Bolshevism, whereas in *Zadah ocvalog imperija* (The Stench of the Rotting Empire, 1991) and *Spletanije i raspletanje čvoroga* (The Tying and Untying of Knots, 1993), Aralica brought together political essays—occasioned by the collapse of communism in Yugoslavia and the outbreak of the Yugoslav wars of the early 1990s—previously published in the Zagreb daily *Vjesnik* and the Split newspaper *Sloboda Dalmacija* between December 1990 and April 1991 and from December 1992 to May 1993, respectively. By this time, Aralica had relocated from Zadar to Zagreb. In 1992/1993 he availed himself of the opportunity to visit the United States, Canada, and Australia when he accompanied the Croatian National Theater on tours largely of Croatian communities. His contact with Croatians away from their native land provided the inspiration for his novel *Majka Marija* (Mother Marija, 1991), about a rich Croatian émigré who returns to Croatia and tries to regain land given away by his aunt, known as Mother Marija. In this novel as well as in his short-story collection *Pir ivanjskih krijesnica* (The Wedding of the Midsummer Glowworms, 1992) and the novel *Sokak triju ruža* (The Street of Three Roses, 1992), Aralica brought more to the fore his concern about what he regarded as a growing indifference to matters of faith and tradition. His film script *Gospa* (Mother of God), which the director Jakov Sedlar brought to the screen in 1994, further convinced some critics of Aralica's deeper Catholic conservatism and traditionalism. Aralica's most recent works of prose fiction include *Knjiga gorkog projekora* (A Book of Bitter Reproach, 1994), a historical novel about Zadar under Venetian rule in the fourteenth century, and *Četverored* (By Rows of Four, 1997), a World War II novel dealing with the plight of Croatian Ustaša and other troops at Bleiburg, Austria, as they seek to flee the oncoming communist partisans. The novel was turned into a popular film directed by Jakov Sedlar. *Svetišni blud* (Debauchery at the Shrine), which appeared in 2000, is based on Aralica's story "Nevjernik" ("The Unbeliever," 1967). In 1986 Aralica was elected a member of the Yugoslav Academy of Science and Art.

Arapi, Fatos (b. 1930) Albanian poet. One of the most formidable contemporary Albanian literary figures, Arapi was born in Zvërmec, near the port of Vlorë on the Adriatic Sea. Growing up close to the sea, Arapi developed an affinity with it and draws on it—whether the Adriatic, the Ionian, or the Mediterranean—in a number of his poems. After a local secondary education, Arapi attended Sofia University in Bulgaria from 1949 to 1954, where he majored in economics. After settling in Tirana, he worked as a journalist and for a number of years also taught Albanian literature at Tirana University. With his first two collections of verse, *Shtigje poetike* (Poetic Paths, 1961) and *Poema dhe vjersha* (Poems and Verses, 1962), he signaled a clear desire to loosen the restraints of Stalinist socialist realism. This was made easier by Albania's break with the USSR in 1961 when a number of Albanian writers seized the moment to bid farewell to Soviet literary models. During the uncertain

period of Albania's close relations with communist China in the 1960s, Arapi continued writing poetry, publishing such volumes as *Ritme të hekurta: Vjersha dhe poema* (Iron Rhythms: Verse and Poems, 1968) and *Kaltërsira* (Blues, 1971), which his fellow poet Ali Podrimja published in Priština. However, he fared less well after the cultural purge initiated by Enver Hoxha in the early 1970s. His poetry collection *Më jepni një emër* (Give Me a Name, 1973), for example, was pulped after harsh criticism. Although he still turned out three more volumes of poetry—*Drejt qindra shekujsh shkojmë: Poema e vjersha* (We're Heading Toward Hundreds of Centuries: Poems and Verse, 1977); *Fatet* (The Fates, 1979); and *Poezi* (Poetry, 1983)—it was not until his symbolically titled collection, *Duke dalë prej ëndrrës: Poezi* (Emerging from a Dream: Poems, 1989), that Arapi returned to the path of sea-inspired luminosity. Since then, he has published six more volumes of verse in which he appears markedly more reflective and nostalgic. They include *Ku shkoni ju, statuja* (Where Are You Going, Statues, 1990); *Dafina nën shi* (Laurel in the Rain, 1991), an earlier version of the next volume, *Ne, pikëllimi i dritave* (We, the Grief of Lights, 1993), which Ali Podrimja published in Priština; *Unë vdiqa në brigjet ë Jonit* (I Died on the Shores of the Ionian, 1993); *Më vjen keq për Jagon: Poezi* (I Feel Sorry for Jag: Poems, 1994); and the two small volumes *In teneberis* (1996) and *Gloria victis: Poezi* (Gloria victis: Poems, 1997). Arapi has also published several volumes of prose, a collection of rather flat short stories under the title *Patat e egra* (Wild Geese, 1970), and two novels, both dealing with World War II in Albania: *Shokët* (The Comrades, 1978), about a villager who loses two sons in the Resistance, and *Deti në mes* (The Sea Between, 1986), about the fate of a unit of Italian soldiers in 1943 trying to return home after the Italian capitulation. As a literary critic and scholar, Arapi is the author of two studies of Albanian poetry, *Këngë të moçme shqiptare: Studime* (*Ancient Albanian Songs: Studies,* 1986) and *Fjalë për poezinë: Studime dhe artikuj* (Words on Poetry: Studies and Essays, 1987). A book by him on Albania and the Balkan crisis, *Çështja shqiptare dhe kriza balkanike* (The Albanian Question and the Balkan Crises), appeared in 1996.

Translations: *Ancient Albanian Songs: Studies,* trans. William Bland (Tirana: Encyclopedic Publishing House, 1996); seven poems in *An Elusive Eagle Soars: Anthology of Modern Albanian Poetry,* ed. and trans. Robert Elsie (London: Forest, 1993), 37–44.

Arsenijević, Vladimir (b. 1965) Serbian novelist. A native of Pula, in northern Croatia, Arsenijević was the youngest Serbian writer to win the prestigious NIN Prize in 1994 for his first novel, *U potpalublju* (In the Hold, 1994; translated as *Cloaca Maxima: In the Hold*), the first part of an intended tetralogy under the title *Cloaca Maxima.* Narrated in the first person by a young man whose wife is expecting the birth of their first child, the novel explores the psychological and emotional impact of the beginning Serb–Croat war of late 1991 on Belgrade youth for whom drug use, rock music, and sexual license underscore their alienation from the rest of society. As the novel draws to an end, the calling up of reservists, early casualties at the front, and deaths among those who chose to flee the country to escape the war become an inescapable reality to the young couple. The second part of *Cloaca Maxima, Andjela* (Angela), subtitled *Sapunska opera* (A Soap Opera), appeared in 1997. Against the events of 1992, including the siege of Sarajevo, the narrator tells the story of his life and the role played in it by a young woman named Andjela, with whom he flees Serbia to Greece at the end. Arsenijević's newest book, *Mexico: Ratni dnevnik* (Mexico: A Diary of the War, 2000), encompasses a diary of the period 26 March to 26 May 1999. The diary is framed by a prefatory narrative of his dialogue about the Balkan wars and the events in Kosovo with the Albanian writer Bashkim Shehu, whom Arsenijević met for the first time in 1998, and a much longer concluding discussion about the NATO bombing of Serbia during the Kosovo conflict between the author and Serbian and Albanian friends in Mexico City, where he arrived with a grant from the International Writers' Parliament.

Translations: *Cloaca Maxima: In the Hold,* trans. Celia Hawkesworth (London: Harvill, 1996; New York: Knopf, 1996).

Baczyński, Krzysztof Kamil (1921–1944) Polish poet. Baczyński was born in Warsaw into a literary family and studied Polish literature in the clandestine Warsaw University during World War II. In 1942 his first collection of poems, *Wiersze wybrane* (Selected Poems), for which he used the pseudonym Jan Bugaj, was distributed in mimeographed copies run off by the underground press. It was well received by critics at the time. Baczyński joined the Armia Krajowa (Home Army) in 1943 and took part in the Warsaw Uprising of 1944, during which he lost his life. His wife, Barbara, the subject of a number of his most sensitive lyrics, died a few weeks later of shrapnel wounds. Much of Baczyński's poetry deals understandably with the wartime occupation of Poland and the struggle against the Germans. It was patriotic, inspired in part by the messianic tradition of nineteenth-century Polish Romanticism, but also deeply pessimistic about the future and politically ambivalent. Almost all of Baczyński's poetry was published posthumously: *Śpiew z pożogi* (Song from the Conflagration, 1947); *Utwory zebrane* (Collected Works [in two volumes], 1961, 1970); *Utwory wybrane* (Selected Works, 1964); *Wybór poezji* (A Selection of Poems, 1966); and *Poezje wybrane* (Selected Poems, 1967). Baczyński was a fine, sensitive artist who could write about the spiritual dimension of romantic love as convincingly as he could of the duty of the soldier-poet. His early death cost Polish literature one of its most promising postwar poets.

Literature: Kazimierz Wyka, *Krzysztof Baczyński, 1921–1944* (Kraków: Wydawnictwo Literackie, 1961).

Băieşu, Ion (1933–1992) Romanian short-story writer and playwright. A leading humorist and satirist, Băieşu was born in the village of Aldeni, in the Buzău district. After attending local elementary schools in Aldeni and nearby Poponeţi, he studied at the commercial high school in Buzău from 1944 to 1951, and then pursued a literary interest at the Mihai Eminescu School of Literature. Băieşu subsequently studied philosophy and law at Bucharest University, from which he graduated in 1961. As early as 1952, Buzău held an editorial post at the journal *Albina* and between 1954 and 1968 was similarly affiliated with *Scînteia tineretului* and *Amfiteatru.* The appearance of his book of sketches, *Necazuri şi bucurii* (Sorrows and Joys), in 1956 immediately established his talent as a humorist. His reputation was enhanced by such subsequent books as *Cei din urmă* (The Last Trace, 1959); *Noaptea cu dragoste* (The Night of Love, 1962), in which he demonstrated a willingness to address contemporary social problems; *Oameni cu simţul humorului* (People with a Sense of Humor, 1964), one of his most popular collections of stories in which his humor takes a decidedly satirical turn; *Sufereau împreună* (They Suffered Together, 1965; 3rd ed. rev., 1971), in which occasionally absurdist humor and irony come together productively; *Pompierul şi opera* (The Fireman and the Opera, 1976); *Umorul la domiciliu* (Humor at Home, 1981); *Autorul e în sală* (The Author Is in the Auditorium) and *Întîmplări trăite de alţii* (Events Experienced by Others), both published in 1987; the novel *Balanţa* (The Scales, 1985); and his most recent collection of stories, *Acceleratorul* (The Accelerator, 1990).

Băieşu was a popular dramatist as well as prose writer. Social comedies, which afforded him the opportunity to demonstrate his considerable skill with colloquial speech, were his specialty. So considerable was his reputation as a humorist and satirist that he did not shrink from poking fun at various aspects of Romanian communism, including the stilted "officialese" of the time. Perhaps his single greatest succcess as a dramatic writer was the series of sketches he wrote for television and later published in book form in 1967 under the title *Iubirea e un lucru foarte mare* (Love Is a Really Big Thing). Also popular were his plays *Preşul* (The Door Mat, 1970); *Futbal—joc de bărbaţi* (Soccer, a Man's Game, 1971); *În cautarea sensului pierdut* (In Search of Lost Meaning, 1979); and *Autorul e în sală* (The Author Is in the Auditorium). In the development of his comic style, Băieşu freely mixed in elements of the absurd and fantastic and in some works showed an ability to tackle more profound problems of a moral and philosophical character.

Translations: "Death and the Major" (from *Sufeareau împreună*), in *The Phantom Church and Other Stories from Romania,* ed. and trans. Georgiana Farnoaga and Sharon King (Pittsburgh: University of Pittsburgh Press, 1996), 197–220.

Baka, István (1948–1995) Hungarian poet and short-story writer. A native of Szekszárd, in the Transdanubian region, Baka studied Russian language and literature at Szeged University. He served on the staff of the Szeged-based children's magazine, *Kincskereső,* from

1974 to 1993, when he became its deputy director. Baka published five volumes of poetry and a few longer stories in his lifetime. His first major collection of poems, *Tűzbe vetett evangélium* (The Gospel Cast into the Fire), appeared in 1981. It was followed by *Szekszárdi mise* (The Szekszárd Mass, 1984); *Égtájak célkeresztjén: Válogatott és új versek* (Points of the Compass in the Crosshairs: Selected and New Poems, 1990*); November angyalához* (To the Angel of November, 1995); and *Tájkép fohásszal: Versek, 1969–1995* (Landscape of Prayer: Poems, 1969–1995, 1996), a fine collection of arguably the best of his poetry. A poet of loneliness and anxiety, often gloomy and obsessed with images of death (see especially his 1990 cycle "Yorick monológjai" ["Yorick's Monologue"]), Baka often found inspiration in music (Liszt, Mahler, Rachmaninoff). He also felt affinities for twentieth-century Russian poets who were victimized by the Soviet regime—notably Nikolai Gumilëv, Sergei Esenin, and Marina Tsvetaeva—and composed poems about them. Baka's best prose work is the long story *A kisfiú és a vámpirok* (The Small Boy and the Vampires, 1979). He also wrote the introduction to the poets and poems included in the anthology *88 híres vers és értelmezése a világirodalomból* (88 Famous Poems from World Literature and Their Interpretations, 1994). In 1985 Baka won the Graves Prize; in 1987, the Radnóti Prize; in 1989, the Attila József Prize; in 1992, the Weöres Prize; and in 1993, the Tibor Déry Prize.

Translations: Eight poems in *The Colonnade of Teeth: Modern Hungarian Poetry,* ed. George Gömöri and George Szirtes (Newcastle upon Tyne: Bloodaxe, 1996), 223–26.

Balco, Július (b. 1948) Slovak novelist. Born in Cífera, Balco studied law at Comenius University in Bratislava but subsequently became the editor of the literary-cultural monthly *Romboid.* His first major piece of creative writing, and arguably his best work,

the short novel *Voskovožlté jablko* (The Wax-Yellow Apple), appeared in 1976. It is a simple and simply told tale about the intrusion of war into the otherwise tranquil traditional lives of Slovak mountain shepherds. It was followed in 1979 by *Husle s labutím krkom* (The Violin with a Swan's Neck). His story collection, *Ležoviská* (Places to Lie Down), containing seven stories, was published in 1986. The second longest story in the collection, "Cíganska poviedka" ("A Gypsy Tale"), is possibly the most intriguing. It recounts the hanging of a Gypsy by Hungarian gendarmes and the retribution taken years later against the officer in charge. The short novel *Cestujúci tam a spät* (Traveling There and Back) came in 1988. Balco is also the author of two popular children's books, *Strigôňove Vianoce* (The Yearling's Christmas) and *Strigôňove prázdniny* (The Yearling's Nameday, 1994).

Ballek, Ladislav (b. 1941) Slovak novelist and short-story writer. One of the most important Slovak novelists of the postwar era, Ballek grew up and was educated through high school in the southern town of Šahy, on the border with Hungary. From 1959 to 1963, he studied Slovak literature, history, and art education at the Teachers College in Banska Bystrica. In 1966 he became editor of Czechoslovak Radio in Banska Bystrica and in 1968 editor of the cultural section of the regional daily, *Smer.* He left this position in 1972 in order to join the Slovenský spisovatel' publishing house in Bratislava, which became his new home. In 1977 Ballek became head of the literary section of the Slovak Ministry of Culture. Recognized for his administrative as well as literary skills, in 1984 Ballek was appointed general secretary of the Slovak Writers Union, a post he held until the dissolution of the organization in 1989. After the collapse of communism in Czechoslovakia and then the division of the country into two separate states, Ballek served for two years (1992–1994) as a delegate to the Slovak National Council representing the Democratic Left Party. In 1998 he was an unsuccessful candidate for the presidency of the newly independent Republic of Slovakia, and recently has been considered for the post of Slovak ambassador to the Czech Republic.

After his first novel, *Útek na zelenú lúku* (Flight to a Green Meadow, 1967), and the novellas *Púť červená ako ľalia* (Journey Red as a Lily, 1969) and *Biely vrabec* (The White Sparrow, 1970), which deal mostly with the frustrations of the young, Ballek hit his stride as a writer with a series of novels set in his native southern Slovakia, an area largely ignored by Slovak writers. The first, and possibly best, of these, *Južna pošta* (Southern Mail, 1974), is a fictional autobiography that highlights the ethnic tensions between the Slovaks and the Hungarians. It was followed by *Pomocník: Kniha o Palánku* (The Assistant: A Book About Palánk, 1977) and *Agáty: Druhá kniha o Palánku* (Acacias: A Second Book About Palánk, 1981), in which the town of Palánk stands for Šahy. Although allusions to World War II, the Slovak National Uprising of 1944, and the growing political challenge of the communists are woven into the tapestry of these last two novels, Ballek's greater concern is with patterns of social behavior in southern Slovakia in the immediate postwar period, before the communist assumption of power in 1948. In *Pomocník: Kniha o Palánku*, for example, he explores these through the contrast between the novel's two principals— Štefan Riečan, a northern Slovak who comes to Palánk and prospers as a butcher, and Volent Lančarič, who becomes his assistant, his wife's lover, and eventually his daughter's husband and the father of his grandchildren. The temperamental differences between the two men are meant to point up the differences between the more stolid Slovak north and the more emotional Slovak south, where the spirit has been shaped by the multiculturalism of this border region and the greater harmony between its people and nature. Ballek's most significant subsequent work is the novel *Lesné divadlo* (The Playhouse of Trees, 1987), which forms a link with his preceding novels and deals in part with the uprising. Ballek's more recent books include *Čudný spač zo Slovenského raja* (The Strange Sleeper from the Slovak Paradise, 1990), a sociocritical analysis of the period of so-called normalization in Slovakia in terms of generational conflict; *Trinásty mesiac: Sen noci mesačných* (The Thirteenth Month: A Dream of Monthly Nights, 1995), which considers the impact of periods of upheaval on the human spirit; and *Letiace roky* (Years Fly By, 1998), on Slovak civilization.

Baltag, Cezar (b. 1939) Romanian poet and essayist. A native of Malineşti, in the Bukovina region, Baltag graduated from high school in Piteşti in 1955 and then studied philology at Bucharest University from 1955 to 1960. He subsequently became an editor at several prominent literary journals, among them *Gazeta literară* (until 1968), *Luceafărul* (1968–1974), and *Viaţa Românească*, of which he became editor in chief in 1990. He published his first book of poetry, *Comuna de aur* (The Golden Commune), in 1960. It was followed by *Vis planetar* (Planetary Dream, 1964); *Răsfrîngeri* (Reflections, 1966), for which he won the Writers Union Award in 1967; *Monada* (Monad, 1968); *Odihnă în ţipăt* (Rest amid Shrieks, 1969); *Şah orb* (Blind Shah, 1971); *Madona din dud* (The Madonna in the Mulberry Tree, 1973); *Unicorn în oglindă* (Unicorn in the Mirror, 1975); *Dialog la mal* (Dialogue by the Shore, 1985); *Euridice şi umbra* (Euridice and Shadow, 1988); and *Chemarea numelui* (The Calling of the Name, 1995). An intriguing, at times elusive poet, Baltag has covered a broad spectrum of poetic states in his writing. From earlier lyrics of a Romantic sentimental nature in which he euphorically contemplates the universe, he has progressed to greater abstraction, linguistic refinement, more ornamental metaphors, and a certain fondness for the imagery of mirrors. In *Madona din dud* he makes greater use of his interest in folk magic and children's games, whereas in his more recent collections of poems—*Dialog la mal, Euridice şi umbra,* and *Chemarea numelui*—his principal subject is the nature of poetry itself. Baltag's interest in mythology, religion, and popular beliefs is reflected in his complete translation (from English into Romanian) of Mircea Eliade's four-volume *A History of Religious Ideas* (1976–1983). Baltag's Romanian version of the work was published between 1981 and 1988.

Translations: Three poems in *46 Romanian Poets in English,* trans. and ed. Ştefan Avădanei and Don Eulert (Iaşi: Junimea, 1973), 264–66; two poems, trans. Dan Duţescu and Leon Leviţchi, in *Like Diamonds in Coal Asleep: Selections from Twentieth Century Romanian Poetry,* ed. Andrei Bantaş (Bucharest: Minerva, 1985), 337–39; nine poems, in versions by Derek Mahon, in *When the Tunnels Meet: Contemporary Romanian Poetry,* ed. John Farleigh (Newcastle upon Tyne: Bloodaxe, 1996), 17–24.

Bănulescu, Ştefan (1929–1998) Romanian short-story writer and novelist. Bănulescu was born in the Danubian village of Făcăieni. The village, his family, and his early years there later formed the subject of his memoiristic cycle, *Elegii la sfârşit de secol* (Elegies at the End of the Century, 1999). After completing secondary school in 1945, he studied law for the next three years at Bucharest University, ultimately receiving his doctorate from the university's Faculty of Philology in 1952. From 1949 to 1962, he was actively engaged as a journalist and critic, writing for such journals as *Viaţa Românească, Contemporanul, Gazeta literară, Tribuna,* and *Steaua.* One of his earliest critical pieces was devoted to the

Russian writer Nikolai Gogol, to whom Bănulescu was attracted because of his own predilection for the fantastic and grotesque. From 1954 to 1959, Bănulescu worked as an editor for *Gazeta literară,* which was then under the directorship of the writer Zaharia Stancu. Bănulescu's creative writing began with the publication of stories in the early 1960s in such journals as *Gazeta literară* and *Luceafărul.* His first major literary success was the collection of stories published in 1965 under the title *Iarna barbaţilor* (The Winter of the Men), for which he won the prize for prose of the Writers Union. The book has been translated into several languages, including French, German, Spanish, and Russian. In 1966 Bănulescu spent the academic year in Urbino, Italy, as a visiting scholar. The following year, the second volume of *Iarna barbaţilor* appeared. This was followed in 1968 by the publication of *Cântece de câmpie* (Songs of the Plains), a collection of poems that had appeared in journals between 1954 and 1964. From 1968 to 1971, Bănulescu served as editor in chief of the literary review *Luceafărul.* He left the position in 1972 when he spent a year as a guest of the University of Iowa's International Writing Program. After returning to Romania, he published a series of essays that appeared in book form in 1976 under the title *Scrisori Provinciale* (Provincial Writings). Bănulescu won his second prize from the Writers Union for the book.

In 1977 Bănulescu made his debut as a novelist with *Cartea de la metropolis* (The Book of the Metropolis), the first volume of a projected four-part cycle titled *Cartea milionarului* (The Millionaire's Book). The novel brought him yet another award from the Writers Union. In 1979 the fourth, definitive, edition of *Iarna barbaţilor* appeared with a foreword by the author and an addendum in the form of Songs of the Plains. After the publication of chapters from *Cartea de la metropolis* in the West German journal *Lite-*

ratur im technischen Zeitalter, in 1980, Bănulescu was invited in 1983 as a visiting scholar to the West Berlin Academy of Art. The following year, Literarisches Colloquium published a collection of his prose writings in German translation as *Verspätetes Echo* (Delayed Echo). In 1988 *Viaţa românească* began publication of fragments of the novel *Cartea Dicomesiei* (The Book of Dicomesia), which was intended to be the second volume of The Millionaire's Book cycle, but the book never appeared in its entirety, nor were additional volumes ever published. In 1994 Bănulescu came out with the volume *Scrisori din Provincia de Sud-Est* (Provincial Writings from the Southeast) and *O bătălie cu povestiri* (A Battle with Stories). The German publishing house Suhrkamp brought out a volume of Bănulescu's shorter fiction in 1995 under the title *Ein Schnmeesturm aus anderer Zeit* (A Snowstorm from Another Time). Bănulescu disappeared in mysterious circumstances in 1998. The year before his disappearance, he published the volume *Un regat imaginar* (An Imaginary Kingdom), for which he was awarded the National Prize for Literature. In 1999 his book of memoirs, Elegies at the End of the Century, appeared.

Translations: Bănulescu's works are unavailable in English, even though Romanian sources mention an English version of *Cartea de la metropolis*. Substantial excerpts from *Cartea de la metropolis* are available in German in *Literatur im technischen Zeitalter* (1980); a collection of his prose writings as *Verspätetes Echo,* trans. Oskar Pastior and Ernest Wichner (Berlin: Literarisches Colloquium, 1984); and some of his shorter fiction in *Ein Schneesturm aus anderer Zeit,* trans. Veronika Riedel (Frankfurt am Main: Suhrkamp, 1995).

Banuş, Maria (1914–1999) Romanian poet, playwright, and translator. A major figure in twentieth-century Romanian poetry, Banuş was born and educated in Bucharest. She graduated from Bucharest University in 1934 with a degree in philology and law. Banuş made her literary debut at the age of fourteen in 1928 when the prominent writer Tudor Arghezi (1880–1967) published her first poem in his satirical journal *Bilete de papagal.* Her first published collection of verse, *Ţara fetelor* (Girls' Land), came out in 1937. It constituted a remarkable literary debut, impressive especially for its sensuality and vitalistic femininity. After the war and the establishment of a communist government in Romania, Banuş embraced the new regime and the official literary creed of socialist realism. Her poetry of the late 1940s and 1950s—contained in such volumes as *Bucurie* (Joy, 1949); *Despre pămint* (Speaking of the Earth, 1954); *Ţie-ţi vorbesc, Americă* (I'm Speaking to You, America, 1955); and *Se arată lumea* (The World Surges, 1956)—conform to the Party ideology and address such common Cold War issues as the plight of the world poor and American imperialism. Smaller subsequent volumes such as *Torentul* (The Torrent, 1957); *La porţile raiului* (At the Gates of Heaven, 1957); *Poezii* (Poems, 1958); *Magnet* (Magnet, 1962); *Metamoforze* (Metamorphoses, 1963); and *Diamantul* (The Diamond, 1965), although retaining features of Banuş's previous socialist realism, suggest a gradual transition to a less politicized and more personal style of poetry. It was also in her socialist realist period that Banuş translated such left-wing poets as the Chilean Pablo Neruda, the Turk Nazim Hikmet, and the Bulgarian Nikola Vaptsarov. Long recognized as a talented translator from several languages, Banuş by no means devoted her energies to translating politically correct poets. She had translated Rimbaud and Rilke in the 1930s, and in the same period that she was translating Neruda and other "engaged" poets, she also turned her attention to Shakespeare, Goethe, Pushkin, and Robert Browning. She later published separate volumes of translations of German Romantic and modern poetry and Austrian modernism. In response to the relative cultural liberalization after 1965, Banuş's new writing demonstrated greater independence and variety and drew inspiration from her prewar lyricism and intimacy. Not unexpectedly, poems from the period 1949 to 1965 are not represented in her, arguably, most selective collection of poems, *Demon între paranteze* (*Demon in Brackets*, 1994). This is, in essence, a lyrical diary starting at the age of twenty and reminiscent of poems in *Ţara fetelor* and ending, with barely any transition, three decades later, with excerpts from such collections *as Tocmai ieşeam din arenă* (I Was Just Leaving the Arena, 1967); the highly regarded *Portretul din Fayum* (The Portrait of Fayum, 1970); *Oricine şi ceva* (Anyone and Something, 1972); *Orologiu cu figuri* (Clock with Figures, 1984); and *Carusel* (Carousel, 1989). Her 1974 anthology of world love poetry, *Din poezia de dragoste a lumii* (From the Love Poetry of the World), has gone through a number of editions. The lyrical-confessional dimension of much of Banuş's poetry also informs her book of essays and reminiscences, *Himera* (Chimera, 1980), her major prose contribution. Although the author of two plays, *Ziua cea mare* (The Great Day, 1951) and *Oaspeţi de la mansardă* (Guests of the Attic, 1978), Banuş never made much of an impression as a dramatist. Banuş has won several awards for her writing, among them the G. Coşbuc Prize of the Romanian Academy (1949); the State Prize (1949, 1951); the Special Prize of the Writers Union (1986); and the International Herder Prize (1989).

Translations: *Demon in Brackets,* trans. Dan Duţescu (London: Forest, 1994), a Romanian–English edition; six poems, trans. Kurt W. Treptow and Dan Duţescu, in *An Anthology of Romanian Women Poets,* ed. Adam J. Sorkin and Kurt W. Treptow (New York: East European Monographs, 1994), 51–59; two poems in *Anthology of Contemporary Romanian Poetry,* ed. and trans. Roy MacGregor-Hastie (London: Peter Owen, 1969), 112–15; ten poems in *Silent Voices: An Anthology of Contemporary Romanian Women Poets,* trans. Andrea Deletant and Brenda Walker (London: Forest, 1986), 9–19.

Barańczak, Stanisław (b. 1946) Polish poet, essayist, and literary scholar. A native of Poznań, Barańczak became recognized as a dissident poet during the Solidarity era and was a consistent opponent of the communist regime in Poland. He eventually succeeded in leaving Poland, where his position had become more precarious. He immigrated to the United States, where he accepted the Alfred Jurzykowski Professorship of Polish Language and Literature at Harvard University. Barańczak's poetic output is represented by such volumes of poetry as *Dziennik Poranny* (Morning News, 1972); *Ja wiem, że to niesłuszne: Wiersze z lat 1975–1976* (I Know It's Unfair: Poems from the Years 1975–1976, 1977); *Tryptyk z betonu, zmęczenia i śniegu* (A Triptych from Cement, Torment, and Snow, 1980); *Atlantyda i inne wiersze z lat 1981–1985* (Atlantis and Other Verses from 1981–1985, 1986); *Widokówka z tego świata i inne rymy z lat 1986–88* (A Little View from This World and Other Rhymes from the Years 1986–88, 1988); *Poezje wybrane* (Selected Poems, 1990); and *Podróż zimowa: Wiersze do muzyki Franza Schuberta* (Winter Journey: Verses to the Music of Franz Schubert, 1994). Barańczak's poetry is on the whole unpretentious, free of far-fetched imagery, conversational in tone, and deeply rooted in the political experiences and traumas of his generation in Poland. Although a talented poet, Barańczak enjoys an even more formidable literary reputation based on his literary essays, scholarly writings, and voluminous translations—above all, from American and English literatures. His books of literary sketches and essays—many of which date from the Solidarity period and were published illegally or by Polish émigré presses in London and Paris—include *Ironia i harmonia: Szkice o najnowszej literaturze polskiej* (Irony and Harmony: Sketches on the Newest Polish Literature, 1973); *Etyka i poetyka: Szkice, 1970–1978* (Ethics and Poetry: Sketches, 1970–1978, 1979); *Nie podlegać nicości i inne szkice* (Avoiding Oblivion and Other Sketches, 1980); *Książki najgorsze (1975–1980)* (The Worst Books [1975–1980], 1981); *Czytelnik ubezwłasnowolniony: Perswazja w masowej kulturze literackiej* (The Reader Deprived of Free Will: Persuasion in Mass Literary Culture, 1983); *Książki najgorsze i parę innych ekscesów krytycznoliterackich* (The Worst Books and a Few Other Literary Critical Excesses, 1990); *Poezja i duch uogólnienia: Wybór esejów, 1970–1995* (Poetry and the Spirit of Generalization: A Selection of Essays, 1970–1995, 1996); and *Geografioły: Z notatek globtrottera-domatora* (Geografixations: From the Notes of a Globetrotter-Stay at Home, 1998). Barańczak's essays are informed by a broad literary culture, a high sense of morality, and considerable wit. Among his more important literary-critical studies are *Język poeticki Mirona Białoszewskiego* (The Poetic Language of Miron Białoszewski, 1974); *Uciekinier z utopii* (A Fugitive from Utopia, 1984), on the poetry of the Polish poet Zbigniew Herbert; and *Pegaz zdębiał: Poezja nonsensu a życie codzienne. Wprowadzenie w prywatną teorię gatunków* (Pegasus Stopped in His Tracks: The Poetry of Nonsense and Daily Life. An Introduction to a Private Theory of Genres, 1995). Other volumes include *Nieufni i zadufani: Romantyzm i klasycyzm w młodej poezji lat sześćdziesiątych* (The Distrustful and the Conceited: Romanticism and Classicism in New Poetry of the 1960s, 1971); *Samobójstwo sandaueryzmu* (The Suicide of Sandauerism, 1984), a polemical reading of the Polish literary critic Artur Sandauer; *Przed i po: Szkice o poezji krajowej przełomu lat siedemdziesiątych i osiemdziesiątych* (Before and After: Sketches on Domestic Poetry of the Late 1970s and 1980s, 1988), a study of the impact of martial law on Polish

poetry); *Przywracanie porządku* (The Return of Order, 1983), on immediate post–martial law Poland; and *Pomyślane przepaście: Osiem intepretacji* (Imagined Abysses: Eight Interpretations, 1995).

Barańczak's prodigious efforts as a translator from English include almost all of Shakespeare's plays, a sizable body of seventeenth-century English metaphysical poetry, English and American love poetry, and such individual poets as Dylan Thomas, Emily Dickinson, e. e. cummings, and Charles Simic. He has also translated poems by the Russian poet Osip Mandelshtam and, into English, works by the Polish poets Tadeusz Borowski and Ryszard Krynicki. His book of essays on the art of translation, *Ocalone w tłumaczeniu: Szkice o warsztacie tłumacza poezji z dołączeniem małej antologii przekładów* (Rescued in Translation: Sketches on a Poetry Translator's Workshop Together with a Small Anthology of Translations), appeared in 1992. In 1995 Barańczak and the Irish poet Seamus Heaney, recipient of the Nobel Prize in Literature, published their new English version of the Polish Renaissance poet Jan Kochanowski's masterpiece, *Treny* (Laments). The volume appeared as a bilingual edition.

Literature: Dariusz Pawelec, *Czytając Barańczaka* (Katowice: Gnome, 1995).

Translations: POETRY: *Under My Own Roof: Verses for a New Apartment,* trans. Frank Kujawinski (Forest Grove, Ore.: Mr. Cogito, 1980); *The Weight of the Body: Selected Poems,* trans. Magnus J. Krynski, Richard Lourie, Robert A. Maguire, and Stanisław Barańczak (Evanston, Ill.: Triquarterly, 1989); *Where Did I Wake Up?,* trans. Frank Kujawinski (Forest Grove, Ore.: Mr. Cogito, 1978). LITERARY AND RELATED STUDIES: *Breathing Under Water and Other East European Essays* (Cambridge, Mass.: Harvard University Press, 1990); *A Fugitive from Utopia: The Poetry of Zbigniew Herbert* (Cambridge, Mass.: Harvard University

Press, 1987); seven poems in *Polish Poetry of the Last Two Decades of Communist Rule: Spoiling Cannibals' Fun,* ed. and trans. Stanisław Barańczak and Clare Cavanagh (Evanston, Ill.: Northwestern University Press, 1991), 161–66. SOUND RECORDING: A sound recording, dated 1982, of Barańczak's lecture on "poetry and tanks" is available at the Academy of American Poets, New York; a sound recording, dated 1983, of Barańczak reading his poetry is available at the Woodberry Poetry Room, Harvard University.

Barbu, Eugen (1924–1993) Romanian novelist, playwright, poet, journalist, and scriptwriter. Barbu was born in Bucharest, where he received his secondary-school education between 1933 and 1943. He then enrolled in cadet school, which he quit soon after in order to study law. In 1945 he gave up law and entered the Faculty of Literature and Philosophy of Bucharest University. After his graduation, he worked for several newspapers as a journalist while pursuing a sports career as a soccer player and coach. From 1962 to 1968, he was the editor in chief of the cultural weekly *Luceafărul.* In 1969 he became a member of the Central Committee of the Romanian Communist Party. In 1970 he assumed the position of editor in chief of the cultural and political weekly *Săptămîna* (Norman Manea refers to him as the "socialist boss" of *Săptămîna* in *On Clowns: The Dictator and the Artist*). Four years later, he was named a corresponding member of the Romanian Academy of Sciences.

Barbu's first major literary success, and the work still considered by many as his best, was *Groapa* (The Hollow, 1957), the novel on which he worked from 1945 to 1956 and which underwent many changes before its final version. Set in the slums of prewar Bucharest, it touched off heated debate among literary critics as much for its subject matter as for its innovations in style and structure. It is now regarded as Barbu's finest literary work. With its wartime theme, Barbu's next novel, *Șoseaua nordului* (The North Road, 1959), marked a return to more traditional writing. True to the tenets of socialist realism, Barbu highlighted the role of the proletariat in the struggle against fascism. *Facerea lumii* (The Making of the World), which appeared in 1964, is imbued with essentially the same spirit. It addresses the building of a new socialist society in the postwar period. But Barbu deviated from the socialist realist norm by emphasizing psychological considerations in human motivation. With his next novel, *Princepele* (The Prince, 1968), Barbu surpassed the success of *Groapă*. A splendidly written, evocative historical novel set in the time of the Phanariot rulers of Romania (1711–1821), the work is at the same time a parable on political power with contemporary relevance. In 1972 Barbu published a collection of source materials for *Princepele* under the title *Caietele Princepelui* (The Prince Notebooks). *Miresele* (The Bride and Groom), a collection of novellas related to *Princepele,* came out in 1975. Barbu's massive four-volume novel *Incognito: Cineroman* (Incognito: A Cinema Novel), a nationalistic overview of Romanian history between 1914 and 1944, also began appearing in 1976. The last volume was published in 1980. Apart from his novels and novellas, Barbu was the author of a collection of short stories with sports motifs published under the title *Balonul e rotund* (The Ball Is Round, 1956); a second collection of novellas, *Oaie și ai săi* (Oaie and His People, 1958); two interesting literary studies, *Măștile lui Goethe* (The Masks of Goethe, 1967) and *O istorie polemică și antologică a literaturii române de la începuturi pînă în prezent* (A Polemical History and Anthology of Romanian Literature from Its Origins to the Present, 1975); and several collections of articles and essays: *Cît în șapte zile* (In Just Seven Days, 1960); *Foamea de spațiu* (Hunger for Space, 1969); *Jurnal în China* (Journal About China, 1970); and *Cu o torța alergînd în fața nopții* (With a Torch Running Ahead of Night, 1973). Barbu has also published a volume of poems, *Osînda soarelui* (The Indictment of the Sun, 1968); two plays, *Să nuți faci prăvălie cu scară* (Don't Build Yourself a Shop with Stairs, 1959), a political work aimed at the support for the dictatorship of Ion Antonescu among the petite bourgeoisie and some elements of the working class, and *Sfîntul și labirintul* (The Saint and the Labyrinth, 1967); and some twenty film and television scenarios. Barbu was a recipient of the prestigious International Herder Prize.

Translations: "In the Rain," in *Introduction to Rumanian Literature,* ed. Jacob Steinberg (New York: Twayne, 1966), 314–31.

Bartušek, Antonín (1921–1974) Czech poet. One of the most respected poets of his generation, Bartušek was born in the western Moravian village of Želetava, near Třebíč. After graduating from high school in Třebíč in 1941, he left for Prague where he worked in a law office during the war. From 1945 to 1950, he studied comparative literature, history, and the plastic arts at Charles University. After receiving his doctorate in 1950, he went to work for the State Office of Historical Monuments. This proved to be no time-marking employment for Bartušek, as he became a serious student of Czech and Moravian historical properties and published extensively on the subject. Bartušek began writing poetry shortly after World War II. His first book of poems, *Fragmenty* (Fragments), appeared in 1945. His second book, *Sudba* (Destiny), came out in 1947 and, like his first, contained lyrics mostly of a spiritual and reflective nature. When during the dark days of Stalinism Bartušek was unable to publish poetry, he found a literary refuge in writings on Czech antiquities. In 1956, for example, he coauthored a multi-volume history of the town of Žd'ár on the Sázava River. The following year, he published a book on Czech historical monuments. In 1958 Bartušek was one of the contributors to a volume on Gothic mural painting in the Czech lands published by the Czechoslovak Academy of Sciences. When conditions improved for writers in the 1960s, Bartušek published his first volume of poetry in eighteen years. This was a collection of poems written between 1954 and 1964 and issued under the title *Oxymóron.* Bartušek continued his scholarly activity on Czech and Moravian antiquities even after he resumed publishing poetry. *Červené jahody* (Red Strawberries), his next volume of poems, came out in 1967, followed two years later by *Tanec ptáka Emu* (Dance of the Emu Bird) and *Antihvězda* (Antistar). That same year, 1969, Bartušek published a book on the historic monuments of Třebíč. Another volume of poetry, *Královská procházka* (A Royal Stroll), came out in 1970. Bartušek's last collections of poems, *Období mohyl* (The Season of Barrows) and *Změna krajiny* (Change of Scene), appeared posthumously in 1975 and 1977, respectively.

Much of Bartušek's poetry conveys a sense of compassion for humanity coupled with deep trepidation and detachment. A strongly suggestive poet with a fine sense of rhythm who is at his best in shorter verse forms, Bartušek is fond of contrasting the world of nature and that of man. Human society, cramped in drab cities, toward which the poet is clearly antipathetic, is viewed as a kind of bleak confinement compared with the beauty, freshness, and purity of nature. As he writes in one poem:

Streets amid streets
longing for white
snow, for the clean
obverse of mud.
Man waiting
for the quiet
melody lost under the grinding
wheels of the tram car.

Humans, to Bartušek, are exiles from paradise condemned to the banality and futility of everyday life. But the poetic art, he believes, has the power to lift them from the morass of their existence:

> Like silkworms
> we meet our poets
> for years cocooned
> in misfortune.
> For years shone the sun of darkness
> blood fell instead of rain,
> the mire of mud came
> up to our mouths.
> Then
> in the green mulberries of hope
> the quick eye could have discerned
> ever so slight a movement in the
>   branches.
> In the leafy mulberry groves
> in the cocoons of love
> they spun their words into silken
>   threads
> of silent speech.
> So we should not be naked
> when once more we emerge
> into the light
> of reality.

Translations: *The Aztec Calendar and Other Poems,* trans. Ewald Osers (London: Anvil, 1975); *Three Czech Poets: Vítězslav Nezval, Antonín Bartušek, Josef Hanzlík,* trans. Ewald Osers and George Theiner (Harmondsworth: Penguin, 1971), 67–116.

Basara, Svetislav (b. 1953) Serbian novelist, short-story writer, and playwright. Basara is one of the most imaginative and provocative of those Serbian writers who made their literary debuts in the early 1980s. He currently lives in Užice. After his first collection of short stories, *Priče u nestajanju* (Stories in the Making, 1982), he went on to publish such additional collections as *Peking by Night* (1985; original title in English);

Fenomi: Prepis spaljene knjige (Phenomena: A Copy of a Burned Book, 1989); and *Izabrane priče* (Selected Stories, 1994). The sardonic wit, flamboyant irreverence, iconoclastic humor, worldliness, and liberally displayed knowledge of American popular culture characteristic of the stories are also much in evidence in his novels. They include *Kinesko pismo* (The Chinese Letter, 1985); *Napuklo ogledalo* (The Cracked Mirror, 1986); *Fama o biciklistima* (A Tale About Cyclists, 1988) and its sequel, *Na Gralovom tragu* (In Quest of the Grail, 1990); *Mongolski bedeker* (Mongolian Guidebook, 1992); *Tamna strana meseca* (The Dark Side of the Moon, 1992); *De bello civili* (On the Civil War, 1995); *Ukleta zemlja* (The Cursed Land, 1996); and *Looney Tunes: Manično-paranoična istorija srpske književnosti u periodu 1979–1990 godine* (Looney Tunes: A Manic-Paranoic History of Serbian Literature in the Period 1979–1990, 1997) and its sequel, *Sveta mast: Manično-paranoična istorija srpske književnosti* (Holy Water: A Manic-Paranoic History of Serbian Literature, 1998).

Basara is at his liveliest when subverting Yugoslav and Serbian pseudo-mythologies, especially Serbian delusions of national grandeur. The contradictions and absurdities of communism Yugoslav-style, and what he refers to as the "Yugonostalgia" of the period after the breakup of Yugoslavia, are among his frequent targets—above all in his two-part Manic-Paranoic History of Serbian Literature. Anything but a literary history by any stretch of the imagination, and with the flimsiest of plots, Looney Tunes and Holy Water present Basara's takes on anything of interest to him, from Titoist Yugoslavia to political correctness in the terminology for homosexual men and women, to postmodernism. Declaring himself an "inveterate anticommunist," he mockingly wonders aloud how he might yet save communism and still be an anticommunist since there will be nothing after communism. Communism, he declares, is the last stage of decomposition of the "huge idiot succinctly called the nation," and its collapse will be followed only by absolute chaos. Mixing real and fictitious characters, Basara drags a host of post–World War II Yugoslav and Serbian literary and political figures into his work, among them Danilo Kiš (of whom he speaks reverently) and Miodrag Bulatović (who appears in some of the funniest sequences in the novel). At the end of Holy Water, by which time fighting has broken out in Kosovo, the American peacekeeper Richard Holbrook and the spokesman for the Kosovo Liberation Army, the "academic painter" Agim Kastrati, a recurrent figure in A Manic-Paranoic History of Serbian Literature, put in an appearance.

Virtualna kabala (Virtual Cabala), which immediately preceded Looney Tunes and Holy Water in 1996, is essentially a consideration of the collapse of Yugoslavia in somewhat less frivolous terms. With occasional allusions to Looney Tunes and other works by him, Basara tackles the subject of the negative impact of technology on the modern world and its responsibility for global feeble-mindedness (debilizacija) in Mašine iluzija (Machines of Illusions), the first of two books he published in 2000. Basara's fondness for the unconventional and idiosyncratic is much in evidence, with sections of the three-part work carrying such titles in English as "Setup Wizard" and "Art of Noise." Kratkodnevica (Winter Solstice), his second publication in 2000, is a sheer flight of Basaran fancy and a takeoff on the postmodern novel. It uses correspondence and other artifacts to reconstruct the life of his fictional central character, a young woman writer named Nana Lovejoy (her married name), who was born in Split, Croatia, in 1960 and died in Toronto in 1993. In her short life, she became such a celebrity in the United States under the name Belatrix that

the publisher Harcourt Brace offered her a contract to write a novel that never saw the light of day. As a dramatic writer, Basara is also the author of several black comedies in the vein of the absurd and fantastic. Dolce-Vita, Hamlet-Remake, Budibogsnama (God-Be-With-Us)—in which Samuel Beckett and Albert Einstein appear as characters—and Oximoron (Oxymoron) were published in a single collection in 1997 under the title Sabrane pozorišne drame (Collected Plays). Although clever and laugh-provoking, most of Basara's works, with the exception of his comedies, are so full of Yugoslav and Serbian topical allusions that they can best be appreciated only by a very knowledgeable reader.

Translations: "A Letter from Hell," trans. Ellen Elias-Bursać, in The Prince of Fire: An Anthology of Contemporary Serbian Short Stories, ed. Radmila J. Gorup and Nadežda Obradović (Pittsburgh: University of Pittsburgh Press, 1998), 326–31.

Baševski, Dimitar (b. 1943) Macedonian novelist and poet. A native of Giavato, near Bitola, Baševski graduated from the Faculty of Philosophy of Saints Cyril and Methodius University in Skopje. He has held the position of managing director and editor in chief of the Kultura publishing house in Skopje. As a writer, Baševski is known above all as a novelist who later in his career turned to poetry. His novels include the three very short texts (under 100 pages) Tudjinec (Stranger, 1969); Vrakjanje (Return, 1972); and Raska (1974) and the somewhat longer works Nema smrt dodeka dzvoni (There's No Death While the Bell Tolls, 1980); Edna godina od životot na Ivan Plevnes (A Year in the Life of Ivan Plevnes, 1985); Sarajanovskiot karanfil (The Sarajanovo Carnation, 1990); Dnevnikot na Anja (The Diary of Anja, 1994), a work for children; and Bunar (The Well, 2001). Written in a deceptively simple style, Baševski's prose fiction deals for the most part with the emotional and psychological trauma of the

Macedonian diaspora—that is, Macedonians, especially migrant workers, who left their homeland often for many years and eventually returned. Baševski's first book of poetry appeared in 1987, but has since been overshadowed by his much-acclaimed collection *Privremen prestoi* (*Temporal Stay*, 1995). The volume consists of thirty-eight fairly short, unpretentious, yet delicate poems of compassion for man's dreams and ambitions and gentle admonishment against aiming too high and wanting too much. He is clearly a poet of the modest and simple. Baševski's images from nature are often splendid miniatures. A few of his poems are inspired by ancient Greece; others are tinged with the fantasy of the fairy tale. Baševski was also the principal editor of a ten-part collection of Macedonian love lyrics, *Makedonska ljubovna lirika,* published in 1990.

Translations: *Temporal Stay,* trans. Brenda Walker (London: Forest, 1997).

Basha, Eqrem (b. 1948) Macedonian Albanian short-story writer and poet. Basha was born in Dibër, in western Macedonia, and studied Albanian and Romance languages and literatures at Priština University. In 1972 he began working as a journalist for the newspaper *Rilindja* and as editor of the cultural section of Priština TV until its closure by the Serbs in 1989. He currently holds the position of editor in chief of the Priština publishing house Dukagjini. A well-known poet and short-story writer, he has also translated extensively from twentieth-century French drama (Jean-Paul Sartre, Albert Camus, Eugène Ionesco). After his debut as a poet in 1971 with the volume *Opuset e maestros* (The Master's Works), Basha published several other collections of poetry. They include *Stacionet e fisnikëve* (Stations of the Nobles, 1972); *Polip-Ptikon* (1974); *Yjedet* (Starfish, 1977); *Atleti i ëndrrave të bardha* (The Athletes of White Dreams, 1982); *Udha qumështore* (The Milky

Way, 1986); *Brymë në zemër* (Frost in the Heart, 1989); *Poezi* (Poetry, 1990); and *Zogu i zi* (The Blackbird, 1995). Basha is a poet of light, colloquial verse who often writes of small, everyday things with a bent particularly toward the absurd and fantastic. But in his poems about the sufferings of the Kosovars in the 1990s and of the second-class citizenship of Albanians and their culture in Yugoslavia in general in the twentieth century, his writing often turns bitter and caustic. His first short-story collection, *Shëtitje nëpër mjegull* (A Walk in the Fog), appeared in 1971 and was followed by *Mëngjesi i një pasditeje* (The Morning of an Afternoon, 1978). Basha's fondness especially for the fantastic and surreal is reflected in a number of his stories, particularly in his newer collection *Marshi e kërmillit* (The Snail's March, 1994), in which the narrative technique intensifies the nightmarishness of the plight of the Kosovo Albanians in the 1990s.

Translations: Five poems in *An Elusive Eagle Soars: Anthology of Modern Albanian Poetry,* ed. and trans. Robert Elsie (London: Forest, 1993), 145–50. Stories, mostly from *Marshi e kërmillit,* are available in French as *Les Ombres de la nuit et autres récits du Kosovo,* trans. Christine Montécot and Alexandre Zotos (Paris: Fayard, 1999).

Bashev, Vladimir (1935–1967) Bulgarian poet. A native of Sofia, Bashev graduated from high school in 1953 and earned a degree in Bulgarian literature at Sofia University in 1958. From 1957 until the year of his death, he held editorial positions at such journals and periodicals as *Narodna mladezh* (1957–1958, 1963), *Puls* (1963), *Rabotnichesko delo* (1957–1963), and *Literaturen front* (1964–1967). He was also a member of the administrative council of the Bulgarian Writers Union and a member of the Central Committee of the Dimitrov Young Communist League. Bashev began his literary career as early as 1950 when his first poems appeared in the periodical

Samokovska tribuna. He thereafter became a regular contributor of poetry, translations, and literary and sociopolitical articles to leading journals and periodicals. His early poetry conformed to the tenets of socialist realism in the 1950s. It brimmed with youthful enthusiasm about the possibilities for people of his generation to improve their own country and, indeed, the world. Yet despite occasional rhetorical excesses, Bashev generally favored simple language and verse forms and conveyed a distinct sincerity in his poetry. In the 1960s, his range broadened and reflected both the experience of travel and a more mature intellectual grasp of the greater concerns of the age. He also demonstrated a new willingness to experiment with poetic language and form. Bashev's first published book of poetry was *Trevoshni anteni* (Anxious Antennae, 1957). It was followed by *Preodoliavane na gravitatsiiata* (Overcoming Gravitation, 1960); *Zheliazno vreme* (Iron Times, 1962); *Netselunati momicheta* (Unkissed Girls, 1963); *Magazin na chasovnitsi* (The Clock and Watch Shop, 1964); *Vuzrast* (Age, 1966); and *Atelie* (Studio, 1967). Several posthumous collections of his poetry have been published, among them *Izbrani stihotvoreniia* (Selected Poems, 1968); *Izbrani stihotvoreniia* (Selected Poems, 1974); *Stihotvoreniia za zhivite* (Poems for the Living, 1981); and *Otkrih zvezda: Izbrani stihotvoreniia* (I Discovered a Star: Selected Poems, 1986). A volume of Bashev's articles was also published posthumously under the title *Publitsistika* (Articles, 1972). Besides his poetry and journalistic essays, Bashev wrote several opera librettos and oratorios as well as the texts for popular songs. He had a good grasp of Russian and Modern Greek and translated extensively from both languages. A Bulgarian literary award for poetry was created in honor of Vladimir Bashev and bears his name.

Basheva, Miriana (b. 1947) Bulgarian poet. A native of Sofia, Basheva completed the English high school in that city in 1965 and earned a degree in English language and literature from Sofia University in 1972. She thereafter worked for a year with Bulgarian TV before becoming an editor at such journals as *Otechestvo,* the feature film studio Boiana, and the publishing house Fakel. Her first poems began appearing in the journal *Literaturen front* in 1975. She subsequently contributed to *Plamuk, Septemvri, Otechestvo, Studentska tribuna, Narodna kultura,* and *Narodna mladezh.* To date, Basheva has published four volumes of poetry: *Tezhuk harakter* (Bad Character, 1976); *Malka zimna muzika* (A Little Winter Music, 1979); *Sto godini sueta* (A Hundred Years of Vanity, 1992); and *Nie sme beznadezhden sluchai* (We're a Hopeless Case, 1998). A typical representative of younger Bulgarian poets who began publishing in the mid-1970s, Basheva strikes an antiauthoritarian pose without being overtly political and maintains an ironic distance from the banalities and falsehoods of the contemporary communist society. Disdainful toward what she regards as outmoded forms of poetic expression, she has also shown a willingness to experiment freely, especially in the area of language, borrowing heavily from the idiom of young people of her own generation. Her style is colloquial and with a devil-may-care street toughness. Several of her poems have been set to music by well-known performers and have become popular hits.

Translations: "Mondays," trans. John Balaban, in *Poets of Bulgaria,* ed. William Meredith (Greensboro, N.C.: Unicorn, 1986), 4; eight poems in *The Devil's Dozen: Thirteen Bulgarian Women Poets,* trans. Brenda Walker with Belin Tonchev, in collaboration with Svetoslav Piperov (London: Forest, 1990), 155–62.

Becher, Johannes Robert (1891–1958) German poet, novelist, essayist, and political figure. One of the most influential men of letters in the history of the German Democratic Republic, Becher was born in Munich and studied philosophy and medicine in Berlin. An early enthusiast of expressionism, he contributed to the expressionist journal *Aktion* and wrote two well-regarded volumes imbued with the expressionist ethos: *Der Ringende. Kleist-Hymne* (The Struggling. Kleist Hymns, 1911) and *Die Gnade des Frühlings* (The Grace of Spring, 1912). But as World War I and its immediate aftermath moved Becher closer to radical politics and revolution, he distanced himself from the expressionist movement. In 1918 he joined the radical communist organization Spartacus. In 1924 Becher was charged with treason on the strength of two of his publications: the volume of poetry *Der Leichnam auf dem Thron* (The Corpse on the Throne) and the novel *(CHC1 = CH)3 As (Levisite), oder, Der einzig gerechte Krieg* (Levisite or The Only Just War), about the use of poison gas in the war. But mass demonstrations of the political left and an amnesty by President Paul von Hindenburg reversed the sentence in 1925. Becher remained active in left-wing German politics and literature, publishing such activist works as *Am Grabe Lenins* (At Lenin's Grave, 1924) and *Der Bankier reitet über das Schlachtfeld* (The Banker Gallops over the Battlefield, 1926), and copublishing the journal *Linkskurve*.

When Hitler became chancellor in 1933, Becher immigrated to Prague and subsequently to Vienna and Paris. Following the revocation of his German citizenship in 1935, Becher resettled in the Soviet Union. His skills as a literary organizer stood him in good stead when he began publishing the German section ("Deutsche Blätter") of the Moscow-based international literary journal *Internationale Literatur*. While in the USSR, Becher also published such works as *Gewissheit des Siegs und Sicht auf grosse Tage: Gesammelte Sonnete, 1935–1938* (The Cer-

tainty of Victory and the Great Days Ahead: Collected Sonnets, 1935–1938, 1939) and the autobiographical novel *Der Abschied* (*The Departure*, 1940), in which reservations are insinuated concerning the radical politicization of literature Stalinist-style. Nevertheless, Becher still wrote such patently Stalinist literary works as *Der grosse Plan: Epos des sozialistischen Aufbaus* (The Great Plan: The Epoch of Socialist Construction, 1939). Becher returned to Germany in 1945, an event he made the subject of his verse collection *Heimkehr: Neue Gedichte* (Homecoming: New Poems, 1946). He settled in Berlin and almost immediately began assuming a commanding role in the organization of communist-oriented German literary culture. He was the cofounder and first president of the Kulturbund zur demokratischen Erneuerung Deutschlands (Cultural Federation for the Democratic Renewal of Germany). He also became president of the German Academy of Arts in Berlin and, in 1954, Minister of Culture of the GDR. The same year, Becher published *Poetische Konfession* (Poetic Confession). Further enhancing his authority in the cultural life of the GDR was his founding of the most respected literary journal in GDR history, *Sinn und Form*, as well as the journal *Sonntag*.

How far Becher had come in his efforts to find a compromise between the artistic and the political is evident his book *Verteidigung der Poesie* (In Defense of Poetry), where he expresses a preference for classical forms, and in a volume of collected poems from 1957. Because Becher himself had become keenly aware of contradictions and inadequacies in a dogmatic communist approach to literature, his prominent position in the GDR cultural establishment provided some breathing space for occasional literary breaches of orthodoxy.

Literature: For two respectable biographies of Becher, see Jens-Fietje Dwars, *Abgrund des Widerspruchs: Das Leben des*

Johannes R. Becher (Berlin: Aufbau, 1998), and Horst Haase, *Johannes R. Becher: Leben und Werk* (Berlin: Das europäische Buch, 1981); *Metamorphosen eines Dichters: Gedichte, Briefe, Dokumente, 1909–1945* (Berlin: Aufbau, 1992), an excellent sourcebook for Becher's pre–World War II career; *Der gespaltene Dichter: Johannes R. Becher. Gedichte, Briefe, Dokumente, 1945–1958* (Berlin: Aufbau, 1991), another sourcebook for Becher's activities in the first decade or so of the postwar period.

Translations: *The Departure*, trans. Joan Becker (Berlin: Seven Seas, 1970).

Bećković, Matija (b. 1939) Serbian poet, playwright, and essayist. Regarded as one of the best contemporary Serbian poets, Bećković was born in Senta, Vojvodina, of Montenegran parents, and studied Yugoslav literature at Belgrade University. He made his literary debut with *Vera Pavladoljska* (1962), a book of poems in the surrealist style dedicated to the woman who became his wife. This was followed a year later by a second collection of poems, *Metak lutalica* (The Wandering Bullet, 1963). Beginning with his third volume of poems, *Tako je govorio Matija: Pesme i poeme* (Thus Spake Matija: Longer and Shorter Poems, 1965), it became obvious that Bećković was destined to make his mark as a witty social and political satirist. It was also obvious that he was becoming increasingly more concentrated on his native Montenegro and its people as his principal source of inspiration. This is evident in such books of poetry as *Medja Vuka Manitoga* (The Border of Vuk Manitog, 1970); his highly regarded *Reče me jedan čoek* (A Fellow Told Me, 1970); *Lele i Kuku* (Lele and Kuku, 1978); and *Dva sveta* (Two Worlds, 1980), in which his poems are also written for the most part in Montenegran dialect. Arguably his most impressive poetic work (also written in dialect) is *Bogojavljenje* (*Epiphany*, 1985), a long poem commingling earthy humor and philosophical

musings about his fellow Montenegrans' search for God in the wake of the calamities of World War II. Although Bećković has written several plays, the only one that has achieved any real celebrity is *Če, tragedia koj traje* (*Che: A Permanent Tragedy*, 1970), with Dušan Radović, about the Argentinian-born Cuban revolutionary leader Che Guevara (1928–1967). Bećković 's other works include *Doktor Janez Paćuka o medjuvremenu* (Doctor Janez Paćuka on the Interim Period, 1969), a collection of witty satirical pieces about communist Yugoslavia in which Bećković speaks through the persona of a Dr. Janez Paćuka; *O medjuvremenu: Zapisi* (About the Interim Period: Notes, 1979; 2nd enl. ed., 1995) and *O medjuvremenu i još ponečemu* (About the Interim Period and Still to No Purpose, 1998), both of which follow up *Doktor Janez Paćuka o medjuvremenu*, but without the fictitious persona and are carried down to the collapse of the former Yugoslavia; *Kaža* (A Tale, 1988), an ambitious book of poems about a quack fortune-teller who spreads false happiness; and *Poslušanja* (Obediences, 2000), a collection of lectures and public addresses on Serbian literary and cultural topics delivered around the world.

Literature: *Ovako govori Matija* (Gornji Milanovac: Decje novine, 1990), a book of interviews with Bećković, conducted by Milos Jevtić, and a good source of information about him.

Translations: *Che: A Permanent Tragedy and Random Targets*, trans. Drenka Willen (New York: Harcourt Brace Jovanovich, 1970); *Epiphany*, trans. Sofija Škorić (Toronto: Serbian Literary Company, 1997), a Serbo-Croatian–English edition; three poems, trans. Bernard Johnson, in *New Writing in Yugoslavia*, ed. Bernard Johnson (Harmondsworth: Penguin, 1970), 136–38.

Beniuc, Mihai (1908–1988) Romanian poet, novelist, playwright, and essayist. Born in Sebiş, Transylvania, Beniuc studied psychology, philosophy, and sociology at Cluj University, graduating in 1931, and did postgraduate work in Berlin and Hamburg, Germany. A specialist in animal psychology, Beniuc is regarded as the first Romanian authority on both animal and comparative psychology and taught for a number of years at Cluj University. By and large a social poet, with a strong attachment to village life (he himself was of peasant background), Beniuc began his literary career not long before the outbreak of World War II with poems in the Romantic patriotic tradition then popular in Transylvania and of which a leading exponent was the poet Octavian Goga (1881–1938). Beniuc's first book of verse, *Cîntece de pierzanie* (Songs of Loss), appeared in 1938, followed two years later by the collection *Cîntece noui* (New Songs, 1940). During the war, Beniuc published an additional two books of poetry: *Oraşul pierdut* (The Lost City, 1943) and *Poezii* (Poems, 1943).

After the war, Beniuc threw his wholehearted support to the communist regime and its dogmatic espousal of socialist realism in literature. His loyalty was rewarded with several administrative posts, including a tour of diplomatic service as consul general to the Romanian Embassy in Moscow (1946–1948). He was also the secretary, first secretary, and president of the Romanian Writers Union (1949–1965); a delegate to the National Assembly; a professor of psychology in the Faculty of Philosophy of Bucharest University (1965–1974); and a member of the Romanian Academy (1955). His first volume of poetry to appear in the postwar period was *Un om aşteapta răsăritul* (A Man Waits for the Dawn, 1946). This was followed by *Versuri alese* (Selected Poems, 1949) and the sycophantic exercise *Cîntec pentru tovarăşul Gh. Gheorghiu-Dej* (Song for Comrade Gh. Gheorghiu-Dej, 1951). Gheorghe Gheorghiu-Dej was then head of the Romanian Communist Party. This set the tone for several other mil-

itant volumes, among them *Steaguri* (Banners, 1951); *O seamă de poeme* (A Handful of Poems, 1953); *Mărul de lîngă drum* (The Roadside Apple Tree, 1954); *Azimă* (Unleavened Bread, 1955); *Trăinicie* (Durable Goods, 1955); *Ură personală* (Personal Grudge, 1955); and *Partidul m-a-nvăţat* (The Party Trained Me, 1957). A two-volume collection of Beniuc's poems was published in 1955 as *Versuri alese* (Selected Poems). His literary activity continued undiminished until nearly the year of his death. Between 1957 and 1987, he published another three dozen volumes of poetry: *Călătorii prin constelaţii* (Travelers Through the Constellations, 1957); *Inimă bătrînului Vesuv* (The Heart of Ancient Vesuvius, 1957); *Cu un ceas mai de vreme* (An Hour Earlier, 1959); *Poezii* (Poems, 1960); *Cîntecele inimii* (Songs of My Heart, 1960), an anthology of his own work; *Materia şi visele* (Matter and Dreams, 1961); *Poezii* (Poems, 1962); *Culorile toamnei* (The Colors of Autumn, 1962); *Pe coardele timpului* (On the Ropes of Time, 1963); *Zi de zi* (Day by Day, 1965); *Alte drumuri* (Other Roads, 1967); *Lumini crepusculare* (Full Lights On, 1970); *Etape* (Stages, 1971); *Arderi* (Fires, 1972); *Turn de veghe* (Armed Vigil, 1972); *Pămînt! Pămînt . . .* (The Earth! The Earth . . . , 1973); *Focuri de toamnă* (Fires of Autumn, 1974); *Patrula de noapte* (Night Patrol, 1975); *Ţara amintirilor* (Land of Memories, 1976); *Aurul regelui Midas* (The Gold of King Midas, 1977); *Dialog* (Dialogue, 1977); *Glasul pietrelor* (The Voice of the Stones, 1978); *Vă las ca frunză* (I Leave You Like Leaves, 1978); *Luptă cu îngerul* (The Struggle with the Angel, 1980); *Apele se revarsă în mare* (The Waters Empty into the Sea, 1982); *Filon de aur* (Lode of Gold, 1984); *Iarna magnoliei* (The Winter of Magnolias, 1984); *Rugul poeziei* (The Pyre of Poetry, 1985), a collection of his poetry selected by him; *75 poeme* (75 Poems, 1985); *Vlasia mea* (My Vlasia, 1987); and *În voia vîntului* (At the Mercy of the Wind, 1987).

Not long after receiving a professorship at Bucharest University in 1965, Beniuc denounced his previous role as "the drummer of our times," with reference to his militant dogmatic poetry, and began finding other themes. This is especially apparent in such volumes as *Lumini crepusculare* and *Luptă cu îngerul*. Beniuc's first volume of prose fiction, *Ură personală* (Personal Grudge), a collection of stories, appeared in 1955. He then turned to novel writing, publishing his first work in this genre, the partly autobiographical *Pe muchie de cuțit* (On a Knife's Edge), in 1958. Two other similarly autobiographical novels followed, both set in the period of World War II: *Disparița unui om de rînd* (The Disappearance of an Ordinary Man, 1963) and *Explozie înăbușita* (Suffocating Explosion, 1971). As a dramatist, Beniuc wrote two plays, *În Valea Cucului* (In Cuckoo Valley, 1959) and *Întoacerea* (The Return, 1962), both of which deal with contemporary social issues, primarily the impact of communist policies on rural life.

Apart from his poetry and prose fiction, Beniuc wrote texts on the art and nature of poetry, among them *Despre poezie* (On Poetry, 1955) and *Poezia militantă* (Militant Poetry, 1972). In 1957 he published *Meșterul Manole* (Master Builder Manole), a book of literary essays. Beniuc's interest in Romanian minority questions is reflected in such books as *Frăția dintre poporul român și minoritățile naționale* (Brotherhood Between the Romanian People and the National Minorities, 1954) and *În frunte comuniștii* (Communists in the Lead, 1954). He was also the author of books on Romanian folklore and landscape: *Păcală slugă la primar* (Păcală in Grade School, 1955), Păcală being a jester figure in Romanian tales and legends; *Folclor din Transilvania* (Folklore in Transilvania, 1962), a two-volume work that Beniuc collected and edited; and a picture book on the Apuseni Mountains, *Munții Apusenii* (1966), for which Beniuc wrote the text and which was published in French translation (*Monts Apuseni*) the same year. Eight volumes of Beniuc's writings (*Scrieri*) were published between 1972 and 1979.

Translations: "Vîrnav's Floodland" (from *Ură personală*), in *Contemporary Rumanian Writers: Short Stories* (Bucharest: Foreign Languages Publishing House, 1956), 2:15–62; "The Emergent Nature of Poetry," trans. Anda Teodorescu and Andrei Bantaș, in *Romanian Essayists of Today* (Bucharest: Univers, 1979), 153–75; three poems in *Anthology of Contemporary Romanian Poetry*, ed. and trans. Roy MacGregor-Hastie (London: Peter Owen, 1969), 95–100; three poems in *46 Romanian Poets in English*, trans. and ed. Ștefan Avădanei and Don Eulert (Iași: Junimea, 1973), 110–12; seven poems, trans. Andrei Bantaș, Dan Duțescu, and Leon Levițchi, in *Like Diamonds in Coal Asleep: Selections from Twentieth Century Romanian Poetry*, ed. Andrei Bantaș (Bucharest: Minerva, 1985), 195–202. A collection of Beniuc's poetry is available in French as *Mihai Beniuc*, trans. Mihai Beniuc and (Eugene) Guillevic, ed. Alain Bosquet and Nicolae Tertulian (Paris: Seghers, 1966), and a collection in German as *Der Apfelbaum am Weg*, trans. Andreas Lillin, Alfred Margul-Sperber, and Georg Maurer (Berlin: Volk und Welt, 1957).

Benka, Urszula (b. 1955) Polish poet. Benka was born in Wrocław, where she studied psychology and Polish philology at Wrocław University. After making her debut as a poet in 1975 in the pages of the Wrocław cultural monthly, *Odra*, she published her first book of poems, *Chronomea*, in 1977. It won the Stanisław Grochowiak Prize for Poetry. Four volumes followed between 1978 and 1991: *Dziwna rozkosz* (Strange Ecstasy, 1978); *Nic* (Nothing, 1984); *Perwersyjne dziewczynki* (Perverse Little Girls, 1984); and *Ta mała tabu* (This Little Taboo, 1991), containing poems of a personal nature about love and parting written between 1985 and 1987 during her stay in Paris. The "Taboo" of the title is the name of Benka's pet cat. In general, Benka is a stylistically straightforward, highly personal poet of nocturnal moods much taken with close scrutiny of the emotions. Benka, who also writes essays and translates from French literature, left Poland for Paris in the early 1980s and subsequently immigrated to the United States. She lives in New York but still publishes in Poland.

Translations: Ten poems in *Young Poets of a New Poland: An Anthology*, trans. Donald Pirie (London: Forest, 1993), 90–104.

Beňo, Ján (b. 1933) Slovak novelist. Beňo was born in the village of Slatinka, where he completed his elementary schooling. He graduated from high school in Zvolena in 1952, studied Slovak and Russian at Bratislava University, and, after earning his degree, spent the next two years in the Teachers College in Banska Bystrica. In 1959 he became the editor of the newspaper *Smena* and in 1966 the editor of the journal *Romboid*. He was relieved of his duties in the late 1960s and granted a two-year creative writing stipend. In 1974 he joined the state publishing house Slovenský spisovateľ as an assistant editor in chief and two years later became deputy editor in chief. From 1993 to 1995, he worked in the Slovak Ministry of Culture as head of the literary section. Beňo made his literary debut in 1964 with *Každy deň narodeniny* (Every Day a Birthday), a book of unpretentious short stories about ordinary people in everyday situations. A similar collection, *Nad modrým svetom* (Above the Blue Earth), appeared in 1968. His next publication was the novella *Braček rozum, sestrička harmónia* (Brother Reason, Sister Harmony, 1971), a grotesque allegory about the Soviet-led invasion of Czechoslovakia in 1968. This was followed by two more collections of stories, *Alej lásky* (Avenue of Love, 1975) and *Život s tužbou* (Living with Desire, 1976), a gathering of sev-

enteen stories drawn from his first two books. *Druhý semester* (Second Semester, 1977), a psychological novel with an academic setting, appeared next, followed by *So synom* (With Son, 1978); *Predposledný odpočinok* (The Next to Last Repose, 1980), about the last months of World War II in Slovakia; and *Vyberanie hniezda* (Choosing a Nest, 1982), a volume of contemporary stories dealing with social and moral problems in urban and rural communities. The work of fiction for which Beňo may be best known is the bloated novel *Kým príde veľryba* (Waiting for the Whale, 1986), about the effects on a stable provincial community when homes are cleared to make way for a new hydroelectric plant. Arguably more interesting is his satirical novel, *Dobrodinec* (The Benefactor, 1988), which is set in the publishing milieu. *Vykrik* (The Shout), which appeared in 1990, recapitulates the unfulfilled ideals and tribulations of the generation that reached maturity in the late 1950s through the imaginary conversation of a son with his dead mother. In his next novella, *Žena v snehu* (The Woman in Snow, 1994), Beňo contrasts the destinies of two women of seemingly different backgrounds. *Na svoj narod nedám dopustiť* (You Can't Enter My Country), published in 1995, is a collection of aphorisms, feuilletons, and occasional pieces of a socially critical nature. *Maslo v hlave* (Butter in the Head), which appeared in 1997, brings together stories in which Beňo takes aim as contemporary social and moral decline. His most recently published book, *Prhľava pre speváčku* (A Nettle for a Singer, 2000), is a collection of thirty-three very short stories in which everyday events are often viewed through the prism of the absurd and grotesque. Beňo is also well known as a writer of children's literature with a keen interest in the fairy tale, as in his book *Starý husár a nočný čert* (The Old Hussar and the Night Devil, 1993), a literary reworking of oral tales passed on by the well-known folk storyteller Michal Pavlovič.

Beński, Stanisław (1922–1988) Polish short-story writer and novelist. Known, above all, for his later writings about Jewish survivors of the Holocaust in Poland, Beński, a Warsaw native, published his first volume of stories in 1965. These were in the then popular genre of World War II combat fiction and bore the title *Zwiadowcy* (Reconnaissance Scouts). The subject was one that Beński knew well. His father had been shot by the Germans in 1941; he lost his mother and brother during the Warsaw Ghetto Uprising of 1943, and he himself fought in the Polish army against the Germans and received a number of decorations. For the last twenty-five years of his life, Beński was the director of a nursing home, the State Social Welfare Home for the Aged, in Warsaw. His stories about the Jews who survived the Holocaust, many of them elderly people he encountered in nursing homes and similar institutions, are outwardly simple in form and style but moving. Dialogue is often their most prominent feature. Beński's first work in this vein was the story collection *Tyle ognia wokoło* (So Much Fire All Around, 1979). It was followed in 1980 by the two-part novella *Jeden dzień* (One Day); two more collections of stories, *Ta najważniejsza cząsteczka* (This Most Important Particle, 1982) and *Cesarski walc* (Imperial Waltz, 1985); the novel *Ocaleni* (The Saved, 1986); and a final volume of stories, *Strażnik świąt* (The Guardian of Holidays, 1987). Whereas most of Beński's Jewish stories have a Polish urban setting, a few are set in the United States or describe encounters between Jews who remained in Poland after World War II and American Jews, friends or relatives, who have come to visit them. *Ocaleni* is Beński's only work with a shtetl setting, a place that had become a ghost town because of the war.

Translations: *Missing Pieces,* trans. Walter Arndt (San Diego: Harcourt Brace Jovanovich, 1990).

Berceanu, Patrel (b. 1952) Romanian poet. After completing his obligatory military service, in 1980 Berceanu became a drama student in Bucharest. He currently holds the positions of literary secretary at the National Theater in Craiova and director of the Colibri Theater for young people in the same city. A poet of sensitive lyrics on the theme of disillusionment and resignation, Berceanu has published four collections of poems: *Sentimentul baricadei* (The Feeling of the Barricade, 1976); *Poeme în mărime naturală* (Life-Size Poems, 1983); *Întimplarea cea mare* (The Big Happening, 1984); and *Lacrimi civile* (Civilian Tears, 1991).

Translations: Five poems in *Young Poets of a New Romania: An Anthology,* trans. Brenda Walker with Michaela Celea-Leach, ed. Ion Stoica (London: Forest, 1991), 111–16.

Bereményi, Géza (b. 1946) Hungarian novelist, short-story writer, and playwright. Bereményi was born in Budapest and, as a child, was raised by his elderly maternal grandparents after the breakup of his parents' marriage. He later went to live with his mother and stepfather, a physician. These biographical facts illuminate his preoccupation with young boys who lose a sense of the past and whose alienation, as in his absurdist tragedy *Halmi* (1980), assumes a menacing aspect. After completing secondary school, Bereményi earned a degree in humanities at Eötvös Lóránd University and, although trained as a teacher, went to work in the book trade. He began writing at an early age and was published in various periodicals and anthologies. His first volume of short stories, *A svéd király* (The Swedish King), appeared in 1970 and demonstrated an interest in the lives of contemporary young people, a natural ability for dialogue, and, in some cases, a quirky, quasi-absurdist flair. *A svéd király* was followed in 1978 by the serialized novel *Legendárium* (Book of Legends), in which past and present history are brought together in such a way as to draw moral and political inferences. It has perhaps been Beremény's most popular work and has gone through several editions. Apart from his plays, which were published mainly in the volume *Trilógia* (Trilogy, 1982) and include *Légköbméter* (A Cubic Meter of Air, 1978) and *Halmi,* Beremény has written a few film scripts, among them *Romantika* (Romance, 1972) and *Megáll az idő* (Time Stands Still, 1982); a number of songs, some of which were heard in films by the prominent director Miklós Jancsó; and a musical under the title *Harmincéves vagyok* (I Am Thirty). Many of Beremény's songs satirize life in Hungary under the communists. His last published work is the parodic, ninety-nine-page *Kelet-nyugati pályaudvar: Három időjárásjelentés, ahogyan azt Cseh Tamás előadta az 1979, 1982, és 1992 években* (The East-West Railway Station: Three Weather Reports as Narrated by Tamás Cseh in the Years 1979, 1982, and 1992, 1993).

Translations: "Last Spin on the Water," trans. Georgia Lenart Greist, in *Ocean at the Window: Hungarian Prose and Poetry Since 1945,* ed. Albert Tezla (Minneapolis: University of Minnesota Press, 1980), 405–14; "The Turned-up Collar," trans. Eszter Molnár, in *Present Continuous: Contemporary Hungarian Writing,* ed. István Bart (Budapest: Corvina, 1985), 183–98; *Halmi,* trans. Georgia Greist, in *Three Contemporary Hungarian Plays,* ed. Albert Tezla (Budapest: Corvina, 1992; London: Forest, 1992), 57–141. VIDEO RECORDING: A videocassette of Péter Gothár (director) and Géza Beremény and Péter Gothár (screenwriters), *Megáll az idő* (Time Stands Still) (Budapest: Hungarofilm, 1982), is available in the Motion Picture/TV Reading Room, Library of Congress.

Bertha, Bulcsú (1935–1997) Hungarian journalist, novelist, and short-story writer. Bertha was born and grew up in the village of Nagykanizsa on Lake Balaton and was edu-cated through high school in the nearby towns of Balatonederics and Keszthely. His intimate knowledge of the large Lake Balaton area is reflected in several of his works—above all, a collection of literary reportage published in 1973 under the title *Balatoni évtizedek* (Decades on Balaton) and *A Teimel villa* (The Teimel Villa, 1976). After working for a few years as a printer, Bertha began his literary career as a journalist in the southern Hungarian city of Pécs in 1960; seven years later, he moved to Budapest. From 1971 to 1974, he served as the editor of the review *Új Írás,* and then the executive editor of *Élet és Irodalom.* Bertha's journalistic writings, which often deal with provocative social problems, were published in a separate volume in 1980 under the title *A fejedelem sírja felett* (Above the Prince's Grave). Consisting of a large number of small pieces, the book is divided into three sections: "Central European Personal Opinions," with texts dating back to 1968; "Living with History"; and "Writers, Books, States of Mind." Bertha's interest in writers and writing, manifest in the last section of *A fejedelem sírja felett,* extended throughout his career and motivated such publications as his two collections of literary portraits (*íróportrék*), *Meztelen a király* (The Naked King, 1972) and *Írók műhelyében* (Writers in the Workshop, 1973); a book of interviews, *Délutáni beszélgetések: Interjúk* (Afternoon Chat: Interviews, 1978); and the essay collections *Írók, színészek, börtönök* (Writers, Actors, Prisons, 1990) and *Egy író állatkertje* (One Writer's Zoo, 1992).

Bertha's first work of fiction was a volume of short stories, *Lányok napfényben* (Girls in Sunshine), which appeared in 1962. It demonstrates his concern with the problems of young people, a theme as well of his second collection of short stories, *Harlekin és szerelmese* (Harlequin and His Beloved, 1964). Bertha subsequently published another two volumes of short stories, *Fehér rozsda* (White Rust, 1982) and *Willendorfi*

Vénusz (The Venus of Willendorf, 1988), and a volume of selected stories titled *Különleges megbízatás* (Special Assignment, 1983). Bertha's first novel, *Tűzgömbök* (Fireballs, 1970), portrays the horrors of World War II through the eyes of a child. His second novel, *Kengurú* (Kangaroo, 1976), deals with the life of working-class youths. Bertha's subsequent novels include *A bajnok élete* (The Life of the Champion, 1969); *Át a Styx folyón* (Crossing the Styx, 1969); *Füstkutyák* (Smoke Dogs, 1965); *Ilyen az egész életed* (That's Your Whole Life, 1980); *Medvetáncoltatás* (Dancing with Bears, 1983); and *Árnyak és lovasok* (Ghosts and Horsemen, 1986). His last work, *Amerikai fiúk* (American Boys), was published posthumously in 2000. Bertha was a member of the Board of the Hungarian Writers Association and was a winner of the Attila József Prize.

Translations: "Babylonia," trans. Judit Házi, in *Present Continuous: Contemporary Hungarian Writing*, ed. István Bart (Budapest: Corvina, 1985), 289–308; "The Zither Player," trans. György Nagyajtay, in *Landmark: Hungarian Writers on Thirty Years of History*, ed. Miklós Szabolcsi (Budapest: Corvina, 1965), 327–29.

Białoszewski, Miron (1922–1983) Polish poet and playwright. Born in Warsaw, Białoszewski studied Polish literature informally and clandestinely during World War II and, later, journalism at Warsaw University. He worked as a correspondent from 1946 to 1972 and made his debut as a poet in 1947 in the literary press. Very much a literary and social nonconformist who seemed to be indifferent to the poverty in which he lived, Białoszewski was widely regarded as an eccentric. He scorned socialist realism, preferring instead to compose poems on a variety of everyday household objects (stoves, forks, teapots, keys), as in his first published volume of sixteen poems, *Obroty rzeczy* (*The Revolution of Things*, 1956). Along with an experimental

and playful approach to language and form, the world of things, to Białoszewski, became a means of preserving his artistic integrity in the face of Stalinist cultural policy that made art subservient to political needs. When *The Revolution of Things* appeared, it seemed symptomatic of the cultural revival that followed the death of Stalin in 1953 and the October disturbances beginning in Poznań in 1956. It was followed by three other volumes of poems: *Rachunek zachciankowy* (A Whimsical Account, 1959); *Mylne wzruszenia* (Erroneous Emotions, 1961); and *Było i było* (There Was and There Was, 1965), the worst received of any of his volumes.

When not writing poetry, Białoszewski, together with his friend Ludwik Hering, ran the small experimental Białoszewski Theater, for which better than half the plays staged were written by Białoszewski and Hering themselves. A collection of these play texts was published in 1971 under the title *Teatr osobny, 1955–1963* (A Separate Theater, 1955–1963). Although much maligned as a sort of literary freak, Białoszewski earned high praise (and a literary award) in 1970 for his idiosyncratic, if highly effective, account of the Warsaw Uprising of 1944, which he experienced at first hand: *Pamiętnik z Powstania Warszawskiego* (*A Memoir of the Warsaw Uprising*).

Literature: Stanisław Barańczak, *Język poetycki Mirona Białoszewskiego* (Wrocław: Zakład Narodowy im. Ossolińskich, 1974), a study of Białoszewski's poetic language.

Translations: *A Memoir of the Warsaw Uprising*, ed. and trans. Madeline Levine (Ann Arbor, Mich.: Ardis, 1977; Evanston, Ill.: Northwestern University Press, 1991); *The Revolution of Things: Poems by Miron Bialoszewski*, trans. Andrzej Busza and Bogdan Czaykowski (Washington, D.C.: Charioteer, 1974).

Biermann, Wolf (b. 1936) German balladeer, poet, playwright, and essayist. A Hamburg native, of working-class Jewish origin, Biermann lost his father, a dock worker and political activist, in Auschwitz in 1943. Both his parents were communists. In 1953 he settled in East Germany, where he began to study economics, but he soon left to work with the Berliner Ensemble of Bertolt Brecht. Eventually, he returned to academia from 1959 to 1963, studying mathematics and philosophy at Humboldt University. His first collection of poems, *Liebesgedichte* (Love Poems), appeared in 1962. Biermann had discovered his talent as a balladeer in the late 1950s, usually accompanying himself on the guitar. In 1961 he rekindled his interest in theater and founded the b. a. t. theater (Berliner Arbeiter- und Studententheater [Berlin Workers and Students Theater]), but it dissolved before its premiere.

The cynicism, antiauthoritarianism, antimilitarism, and bluntness of Biermann's songs soon earned him the disfavor of the authorities, beginning, above all, with his public poetry and song evening at the East German Academy of the Arts in December 1962. Although he was permitted to go on tour through West Germany in 1964 and to fulfill an engagement as a guest performer at the East Berlin cabaret Die Distel that same year, Biermann was soon prohibited from further public appearances in the German Democratic Republic, and from further trips out of the country. This was about the time of the publication of his first book of poetry in West Germany: *Die Drahtharfe* (*The Wire Harp*). At the Eleventh Plenum of the Central Committee of the SED (Socialist Unity Party), Biermann was held up as an example of a "dedicated opposition to true socialism," "sensuality," "pleasure seeking," and "anarchistic individualism." Undeterred as usual, Biermann continued publishing in West Germany. It was there that his next two volumes of ballads appeared: *Mit Marx- und Engelszungen* (From the Mouths of Marx and Engels, 1968) and *Für meine Genossen*

(For My Comrades, 1972). Despite opposition, he went ahead with the premiere of his musical fairy-tale play, *Der Dra Dra* (The Big Old Dragon) in Munich in 1971. The play provoked a considerable scandal less for its subject matter than for the intention of the director and performers to put out a theater program portraying local politicians as "dragons" responsible for the oppression of the people in East Germany. The fracas led to H. Kipphardt's loss of the artistic direction of the theater. Nevertheless, Biermann was allowed to perform before small audiences and eventually to travel again to West Germany. While in Cologne for a concert on 16 November 1976, he heard on the radio that he had been stripped of his citizenship in the GDR and barred from returning to the country. The "Biermann affair" triggered an unexpectedly huge response from his fellow artists in the GDR, many of whom resettled in West Germany. Biermann himself returned to his native Hamburg and took up residence there. By now something of an international celebrity, he was invited to perform in Paris, where he lived from 1981 to 1983. He visited the United States in 1983 on invitation from Ohio State University. Biermann was never far from controversy. During public appearances in Cologne on the occasion of his fiftieth birthday, he accused the East German writer Sascha Anderson of cooperating with the Stasi (GDR State Security police). A natural rebel and protester, he also made no special effort to ingratiate himself with the West German authorities, attacking the political establishment and its economic and social agenda with no more restraint than he had attacked the East German government. This is evident in two collections of poems published after his expulsion from the GDR: *Preussischer Ikarus* (The Prussian Icarus, 1978) and *Verdrehte Welt—das seh' ich gerne* (Crazy World—I'm Glad to See It, 1982). His more recent works include a volume of essays under the title *Der Sturz des*

Daedalus (The Fall of Daedalus, 1992) and a text on poetry, *Wie man Verse macht und Lieder: Eine Poetik in acht Gängen* (How to Write Poems and Songs: A Poetics in Eight Movements, 1997).

Literature: Dietmar Keller and Matthias Kirchner, eds., *Biermann und Kein Ende: Eine Dokumentation zur DDR-Kulturpolitik* (Berlin: Dietz, 1991), basically a documentation of Biermann's difficulties with the East German regime up to and including his loss of citizenship; Wolf Biermann, *Klartexte im Getümmel: 13 Jahre im Westen. Von der Ausbürgerung bis zur November-Revolution* (Cologne: Kiepenheuer & Witsch, 1991), a collection of Biermann's writings covering his thirteen-year "exile" in West Germany after he was stripped of his East German citizenship and forbidden to reenter the country; Oliver Schwarzkopf and Beate Rusch, eds., *Wolf Biermann: Ausgebürgert* (Berlin: Schwarzkopf & Schwarzkopf, 1996), a large-format photo album of Biermann by the photographer Roger Melis with running commentary by Biermann.

Translations: *Three Contemporary German Poets: Wolf Biermann, Sarah Kirsch, Reiner Kunze*, ed. Peter J. Graves (Leicester: Leicester University Press, 1985); *The Wire Harp*, trans. Eric Bentley (New York: Harcourt, Brace & World, 1968), which includes the music for several of Biermann's ballads; *Wolf Biermann: Poems and Ballads*, trans. Steve Gooch (London: Pluto, 1977), a German–English edition.

Bittel, Adriana (b. 1946) Romanian short-story writer and essayist. A generally well regarded prose writer known especially for her Chekhovian conciseness and fondness for cinematic collage techniques, Bittel is a graduate of the Faculty of Letters of Bucharest University. She broke into print as a poet in 1979 in the *Gazeta literară* review. Although she continued writing poetry as her career developed, she has made a name for herself primarily as a writer of urbane, cultivated prose focused mostly on women but without a feminist agenda as such and situated within a more cosmopolitan context. Her first book, *Lucruri întrun pod albastru* (Things in a Blue Attic), appeared in 1980. After a few years of publishing short stories and essays in leading literary and cultural reviews, above all *România literară*, Bittel turned out three volumes of short stories in a fairly short period of time: *Somnul după naştere* (Sleep After Birth, 1984); *Iulia in iulie* (Julia in July, 1986); and *Fototeca: Tema cu variaţiuni* (Phototeque: Variations on a Theme, 1989). Her latest volume of eleven stories, *Întîlnire la Paris* (Encounter in Paris), which includes mostly previously published texts such as "Visită în casa unui bărbat în absenţa soţiei sale" ("Visit in a Man's House in His Wife's Absence"), "'Chehov,' am cerut obosită" ("'Chekhov,' I'm Tired of Asking"), "Doctorul Blum" ("Dr. Blum"), and the title story, "Encounter in Paris," appeared in 2001. Bittel has held several editorial positions both at publishing houses and at literary reviews such as *România literară*. She is a member of the Romanian Writers Union and the Romanian PEN Club.

Blagojević, Slobodan (b. 1951) Bosnian Serb poet, short-story writer, playwright, essayist, and translator. Blagojević was born in Sarajevo but in 1986 moved to Belgrade, where he worked for several years as the editor of the literary journal *Delo*. His books of poetry include *Mene* (Of Me, 1976); *Slika bojnog saveznika* (Picture of a Fighting Ally, 1985); *Grči* (Cramps, 1995); and *Tri čiste obične pameti* (Three Pure and Ordinary Minds, 1996). He is also the author of the epistolary novel *Pisma prestoničkom listu* (Letters to the Metropolis, 1992), which he published under the pseudonym Aristid Teofanović. His book of literary essays, *Poezija, mistika, poviest* (Poetry, Mysticism, History), appeared in

1986. In 1993 Blagojević ran afoul of the authorities with a series of fragments grouped under the title *Here I Am!*, in which he pokes fun at Serbian and Croatian nationalism. He then moved to Amsterdam, where, together with his fellow writers Hamdija Demirović and Predrag Dojčinović, he established Ex-Yu PEN to represent other Yugoslav writers in exile. As a translator, Blagojević has published the collected works of Emily Dickinson and the Greek poet Konstantin Cavafy in Serbo-Croatian.

Translations: *Here I Am!*, trans. Hamdija Demirović, in *Storm Out of Yugoslavia*, ed. Joanna Labon (London: Carcanet, 1994), 191–209.

Blandiana, Ana (real name Otilia-Valeria Coman; b. 1942) Romanian poet, fiction writer, and essayist. One of the finest contemporary Romanian poets, Blandiana was born in Timişoara, Transylvania, and received her primary- and secondary-school education in Oradea. While still in her teens, in 1959, she published her first poems in the Cluj review *Tribuna*, but was thereafter forbidden to publish until 1963 as the result of her father having been declared "an enemy of the state." From 1963 to 1967, she studied Romance languages and literatures at the Babeş-Bolyai University in Cluj. Following her university education, she moved to Bucharest, where she worked for one year as editor of the journal *Viaţa studenţească* and, from 1968 to 1975, with the journal *Amfiteatru*. In 1968 she was invited to give a recital of her poetry during the regular season of the Theater of Nations in Paris. From December 1973 to May 1974, she and her husband, the writer Romulus Rusan, participated in the International Writing Program of the University of Iowa. Both writers then went on an extended bus tour of the United States. When in 1975 Blandiana was dismissed for two years from the staff of *Amf-*

iteatru for political reasons, she accepted the position of librarian at the Institute of Plastic Arts. Despite increasing pressure from the censors, from 1974 to 1988 she continued to write a weekly column under the pseudonym Atlas for the literary journal *România literară*.

Blandiana has published eleven collections of poetry, beginning with *Persoana întîia plural* (First-Person Plural) in 1964. Subsequent volumes include *Călcîiul vulnerabil* (The Vulnerable Heel, 1966); *A treia taină* (The Third Secret, 1969); and *Cincizeci de poeme* (Fifty Poems, 1970), a selection of previously published poems plus ten new ones. Blandiana won the Poetry Prize of the Writers Union that year. Other works include *Octombrie, noiembrie, decembrie* (October, November, December, 1972); *Poezii* (Poems, 1974), a collection of previously published poems with thirteen new pieces; *Somnul din somn* (The Sleep Within Sleep, 1977); a collection of verse (*Poeme*) in the series *Cele mai frumoase poezji* (The Choicest Poems, 1978); *Întîmplări din grădina mea* (Goings-on in My Garden, 1980); *Ochiul de greier* (The Cricket's Eye, 1981); *Ora de nisip* (The Hour of Sand, 1983), a selection of thirty-one previously unpublished poems as well as critical texts; *Stea de pradă* (Star of Prey, 1985); *Poezii* (Poems, 1989), which forms part of a new collection under the title *Arhitectura valurilor* (The Architecure of Waves, 1990); and *100 de poeme* (100 Poems, 1991). Blandiana has also written a number of essays collected in such volumes as *Calitatea de martor* (To Be a Witness, 1970; 2nd ed., 1971) and *Cea mai frumoasă dintre lumile posibile* (The Most Beautiful of All Possible Worlds, 1978). Three other volumes comprise prose pieces originally published in the journal *Contemporanul*: *Antijurnal* (Antijournal, 1975); *Eu scriu, tu scrii, el, ea scrie* (I Write, You Write, He, She Writes, 1976), a book of essays; and *Cele patru anotimpuri* (The Four Seasons, 1977). Her books of essays *Coridoare de oglinzi* (Hall of

Mirrors, 1984) and, especially, *Autoportret cu palimpsest* (Self-Portrait with Palimpsest, 1986) are at the same time a probe at an autobiography. *Oraşe de silabe* (Town Syllables, 1987), which appeared a year later, is an account of travel. As a writer of fiction, Blandiana has also cultivated the genre of fantasy so well represented in the Romanian literary tradition. Her tales in this vein appear in two volumes: *Cele patru anotimpuri* and *Proiecte de trecut* (Projects for the Past, 1982). Her novel along similar lines, *Sertarul cu aplauze* (The Applause Machine), appeared in 1992; the second edition came out in 1993.

Blandiana made her literary debut as a poet in the mid-1960s when Nicolae Ceauşescu's rise to power following the death of the communist premier Gheorghe Gheorghiu-Dej (19 March 1965) ushered in a brief period of relative cultural liberalism after the nightmare of Stalinization and collectivization from 1946 to 1959. Her poetry, which represents her major literary achievement, is largely apolitical. A delicate, vulnerable, and deeply personal writer, Blandiana in her poetry conveys the general impression of a profound desire to be free of the strife, deceptions, and "suspect sincerities" of the world. In straightforward, technically traditional forms, she expresses a yearning for purity—often conveyed by images of snow (a frequent image in Romanian poetry)—for stillness, where "not a footstep desecrates the light," for the refuge of dream, even for death. Not surprisingly, sleep and dream are among the most recurrent images in Blandiana's poetry. So, too, is the eye, which tends if anything to look away from the world, to see into the poet's dream world of animated plants and unpeopled landscapes.

The freshness of Blandiana's poetic vision won instant recognition and made her popular with critics and readers alike. In 1969 and 1970, she was twice awarded prizes for poetry by the Writers Union, and in 1970 by the Romanian Academy. Her work in prose

was honored in 1982 by the Prose Prize of the Association of Writers of Bucharest. The same year, in recognition of her international following, she was awarded the Herder Prize in Vienna. In 1988 at the Teatr Mic (Small Theater) in Bucharest, Irina Răchiţeanu-Şirianu performed a program of prose and verse pieces by Blandiana.

Despite the overwhelmingly apolitical character of Blandiana's writing, she did incur the enmity of the Ceauşescu regime with a few works in the 1980s in which she sought to comment on renewed cultural repression and the social hardships caused by the wretched state of the Romanian economy. Four poems in the journal *Amfiteatru* in December 1984 were suppressed, but circulated in samizdat ("the first Romanian samizdat") and were widely translated. The *Independent,* an English daily, devoted an entire page to it, in which each word of the poem "Totul" ("The Whole") was "decoded" in order to reveal the true picture of the Romanian dictatorship. In 1986 Blandiana was invited to give a recital at the Covent Garden Readings in London. But she was denied a visa, and her place on stage was taken by a tape recording of her and a letter of protest to the organizers. A book of poetry for children, *Întîmplări de pe strada mea* (Events on My Street), was withheld from publication until 1989 on suspicion of intended satire of the authorities. In November 1990, after the overthrow of the Ceauşescu regime, Blandiana was one of the founders and then president of the Alianţă Civica (Civic Alliance) in Sighet. Also in 1990 she became president of the newly reconstituted Romanian PEN. In 1994 she founded and became president of the Academia Civică Foundation. The following year, Blandiana came out with her most recent book of poetry, *Imitaţie de coşmar* (Imitations of Nightmare, 1995). The volume contains an excellent biobibliographical chronology, a collection of reviews of her works, and an afterword by the poet and critic Doina Uricariu, who also heads the publishing house Editura du Style, which published the collection.

Translations: *Ana Blandiana: Poeme/ Poems,* trans. Dan Duțescu (Bucharest: Eminescu, 1982), a Romanian–English edition; *Balanță cu un singur talger/Die Waage mit einer einzigen Schale/The Balance Scale with a Single Pan* (Bucharest: Style, 1997), a selection of poems in Romanian, German, and English; *Don't Be Afraid of Me* (*Nu-ți fie teamă de mine*) (Detroit: Spiritual Poetry Collection, 1985); *The Hour of Sand: Selected Poems, 1969–1989,* trans. Peter Jay and Anca Cristofovici (London: Anvil, 1990), a good selection of Blandiana's poetry accompanied by intelligent but brief commentary; twenty-two poems in *An Anthology of Contemporary Romanian Poetry,* trans. Andrea Deletant and Brenda Walker (London: Forest, 1984), 8–30; thirteen poems in *Silent Voices: An Anthology of Contemporary Romanian Women Poets,* trans. Andrea Deletant and Brenda Walker (London: Forest, 1986), 21–36; ten poems, in versions by Nobel laureat Seamus Heaney, in *When the Tunnels Meet: Contemporary Romanian Poetry,* ed. John Fairleigh (Newcastle upon Tyne: Bloodaxe, 1996), 25–32; "The Phantom Church" (from *Proiecte de trecut*), in *The Phantom Church and Other Stories from Romania,* ed. and trans. Georgiana Farnoaga and Sharon King (Pittsburgh: University of Pittsburgh Press, 1996), 91–111.

Blatnik, Andrej (b. 1963) Slovenian novelist, short-story writer, critic, essayist, and translator. One of the most impressive Slovenian writers to emerge in the 1980s, Blatnik was born and educated in Ljubljana. To date, he has published two novels, three collections of short stories, a number of radio plays, collections of essays and criticism, and translations from English. Blatnik made his debut as a writer of short stories with a tale

included in the anthology, *Mlada proza . . .* (Young Prose . . .), edited by Matjaž Potokar and published in 1983. This was followed the same year by *Šopki za Adama venijo* (Bouquets for Adam). His novel *Plamenice in solze* (Torches and Tears) appeared in 1987, and within the next few years Blatnik came out with two new collections of short stories, *Biografije brezimenih: Majhne zgodbe, 1982–1988* (Biographies of the Nameless: Short Stories, 1982–1988, 1989) and *Menjave kož* (*Skinswaps,* 1990); a novel, *Tao ljubezni* (Gentle Tao, 1996); and a book of essays, *Gledanje cez ramo: Komentarji kulturnih vsakdanjosti* (Looking over the Shoulder: Comments on Everyday Culture, 1996). *Zakon želje* (The Law of Desire), which appeared in 2000, is a collection of sixteen mostly first-person short narratives on the theme of love and desire based on his experiences in the United States. Blatnik's prose fiction for the most part revolves around personal relations, especially between men and women, in the here and now, neither as a reflection of the previous communist era— which no longer commands his interest— nor in terms of the developing postcommunist society. Although he brings a light touch and a sense of humor and irony to his writing, Blatnik's characters, who are usually young, move in a world seemingly bereft of ideals. People become emotionally drained in insensitive, callous, and sometimes even violent relationships. An able and versatile storyteller who likes experimenting with form and narrative techniques, Blatnik writes works with a distinct contemporary feel because of both their realism and his heavy use of colloquial dialogue. Notable also in his fiction are the reflections of his visit to Japan in 1987 on a Japanese government grant and his stay in the United States as the recipient of a Fulbright Fellowship in 1993. Blatnik writes of his participation in the International Writing Program of the University of Iowa in 1993 in his essay translated into English in 1995 under the title "The Future of Literature Can Be Discerned in the Last Sentence."

Translations: *Skinswaps,* trans. Tamara Soban (Evanston, Ill.: Northwestern University Press, 1998); "The Future of Literature Can Be Discerned in the Last Sentence," trans. Tamara Soban, in *The Slovenian Essay of the Nineties,* selected by Matevž Kos (Ljubljana: Slovene Writers Association, 2000), 81–92.

Bllaci, Jorgo (b. 1938) Albanian poet. Bllaci was born in Gjirokastër and was working as a teacher and translator when he was arrested and imprisoned in the early 1960s at the height of the campaign waged against intellectuals by the Albanian Communist Party. He was released from prison in 1967 but was unable to resume his literary career until 1990. In the interim, he was permitted to earn his living as a construction worker. Bllaci's first published book of verse, *Zërat e natës* (The Voices of the Night), appeared in 1993 and represents a collection of poems written between 1957 and 1990 that reflect the hardships he experienced. Well versed in and a translator of Russian verse (Pushkin, Aleksandr Blok, Sergei Esenin), Bllaci owes much to the formal influence of classical Russian poetry. Bllaci has also translated works from Chinese, Persian, Modern Greek, Polish, German, British (Burns, Keats, Byron), and American (Longfellow, Frost) literatures. A number of these translations appear as an appendix to *Zërat e natës.*

Bobrowski, Johannes (1917–1965) German poet, novelist, and short-story writer. Bobrowski, one of the most respected writers of the German Democratic Republic, was born in Tilsit, East Prussia, but resettled with his family in Königsberg in 1928. After graduating from secondary school in 1937, he began studying history in Berlin. He had to interrupt his studies for compulsory military ser-

vice and, after the outbreak of World War II, saw action on the eastern front. During the final months of the war, he was taken prisoner by the Soviets and spent four years working in a coal mine. When he returned home, he became an editor at a Berlin publishing house. In 1959 he joined the Christian publishing company Union-Verlag. Bobrowski began his literary career with several poems published in *Sinn und Form* in 1955. But serious critical and public recognition came only with the publication in 1961 in both Germanys of his collection of poems, *Sarmatische Zeit* (Sarmatian Time). "Sarmatian" here refers to the German-Slavic-Lithuanian border region between the lower bank of the Vistula River and the western border of Lithuania. Bobrowski was deeply interested in the history and culture of the different peoples of the area and made them the subject of a number of his poems, not only in Sarmatian Time but also in his major collection, *Schattenland Ströme* (1962; translated as *Shadow Lands*). Bobrowski's regionalism and fondness for local color stand out even more vividly in his novel *Levins Mühle* (*Levin's Mill,* 1964), by all means his most popular work of prose. Set in 1874, the novel tells the story of the mean-spirited and bigoted grandfather (Johann) of the novel's narrator who, feeling threatened by the mill that the Russian Jew Leo Levin buys in his village, schemes for the destruction of the mill and eventually drives Levin as well as a family of Gypsies from the village. Of particular interest in *Levin's Mill,* an inquiry of sorts into the nature of German xenophobia and prejudice, is the style of a narrator, who distances himself from the world emblematized by his grandfather by means of a sardonic wit, occasional moralizing, and commenting on his own narrative for the sake of the reader.

Besides his poems and novels, Bobrowski was a talented short-story writer, as evidenced by such collections as *Boehlendorff und andere* (Boehlendorff and Others) and *Maüsefest* (Mouse Party), both of which appeared in 1965. In order to gauge Bobrowski's total literary output, his posthumous publications have to be taken into account. They include two volumes of poetry, *Wetterzeichen* (Weathersigns, 1967) and *Im Windgesträuch* (Tumbleweed, 1970); a collection of satirical verses, *Literarisches Klima* (The Literary Climate, 1977); the novel *Litauische Claviere* (Lithuanian Clavichords, 1966); and a collection of short pieces published under the title *Der Mahner* (The Admonisher, 1968; new ed., 1981, under the title *Maüsefest/Der Mahner: Zweiundzwanzig Erzählungen* [Mouse Feast/The Admonisher: Twenty-two Stories]). Much appreciated for the lyricism of his poetry, his skill at plot construction and narration, and his sensitivity toward the plight of peoples long oppressed by the Germans, Bobrowski was the recipient of several prestigious literary awards: the (West German) Gruppe 47 Prize and the Austrian Alma Johanna Koenig Prize (1962); the Heinrich Mann Prize (1965); the Swiss Charles Veillon Prize (1965); and, posthumously, the F. C. Weiskopf Prize (1967).

Literature: Brian Keith-Smith, *Johannes Bobrowski* (London: Wolff, 1970), an introductory monograph that also contains twenty poems and seven prose pieces in translation; John P. Wieczorek, *Sarmatia and Socialism: The Life and Works of Johannes Bobrowski* (Amsterdam: Rodopi, 1999), the most solid study on Bobrowski in English.

Translations: *Boehlendorff: A Short Story and Seven Poems,* trans. Francis Golffing (Francestown, N.H.: Typographeum, 1989); *Darkness and a Little Light,* trans. Leila Vennewitz (New York: New Directions, 1994); *From the Rivers,* trans. Ruth Mead and Matthew Mead (London: Anvil, 1975); *I Taste Bitterness,* trans. Marc Linder (Berlin: Seven Seas, 1970); *Johannes Bobrowski. Horst Bienek: Selected Poems,* trans. Ruth Mead and Matthew Mead (Harmondsworth: Penguin, 1971); *Levin's Mill,* trans. Janet Cropper (London: Calder and Boyars, 1970); *Shadow Lands: Selected Poems,* trans. Ruth Mead and Matthew Mead (London: Anvil, 1984); *Yesterday I Was Leaving,* trans. Rich Ives (Seattle: Owl Creek Press, 1986); "Mouse Party," trans. Jan van Heurck, in *The New Sorrows of Young W. and Other Stories from the German Democratic Republic,* ed. Therese Hörnigk and Alexander Stephan (New York: Continuum, 1997), 225–27.

Bodor, Ádám (b. 1936) Transylvanian Hungarian novelist and short-story writer. A native of Cluj (Hungarian, Kolozsvár), Romania, Bodor served time in prison from 1952 to 1954. After his release, he earned his living for a while as a factory worker. He began publishing short stories in Hungary in 1965, but became a full-time writer in 1968. In 1984 he resettled permanently in Hungary. Bodor is credited with playing a major role in the revitalization of the literary life of the Transylvanian Hungarian community in the 1960s and 1970s. He has published several collections of short stories and novellas, among them *Megérkezés északra* (Arrival in the North, 1978); *Milyen is egy hágó?* (What Is a Mountain Pass Like Anyway?, 1980); *A Zengezur hegység* (Mount Zengezur, 1981); and *Az Eufratesz Babilonnál* (*The Euphrates at Babylon,* 1969). He is also the author of the novel *Sinistra körzet: Egy regény fejezetei* (The Sinistra District: A Novel in Chapters, 1992). Bodor is at his best in the short story and the short-short story (one to two pages). A master of the strange and bizarre, Bodor carries his often ordinary subjects to the brink of the absurd and fantastic. In one story, for example, a man arranges to get a false ear for a friend who was born without one from a well-off relative of the friend's in West Germany, and then discards the box containing the ear for fear that his "dealings" with the West Germans will bring him under suspicion. In another, a seemingly well regarded woman functionary is "promoted" by being sent off to an unbelievably primitive and remote station where her only real companions are weasels. In many instances, the political allusions are unmistakable. The secret police or their agents seem to be almost everywhere. The bizarre atmosphere of the typical Bodor tale mirrors the bizarre nature of state control and repression in the Romanian communist state, the more keenly felt by a member of the Hungarian minority.

Bodor's most important larger work of fiction is *Sinistra körzet: Egy regény fejezetei*, so subtitled to convey the relative autonomy of the novella-like chapters of the book. It takes place in a mysterious military zone known as "sector Sinistra," located in a high valley in the northern Carpathian Mountains, within the borders of Transylvania and Ukraine. It is a region peopled with exotic and even monstruous people where strange maladies and epidemics occur. Narrated by a character who is identified by the alias Andrei Bodor, *Sinistra körzet* has some superbly evoked landscapes and has been translated into a half-dozen languages (including French and German, but not English). However, it is less successful than Bodor's stories, since his taste for the bizarre is more effectively realized in the more concentrated form of the short story. Bodor's most recent publication is the short novel *Az érsek látogatása* (The Bishop Comes Calling, 1999).

Translations: *The Euphrates at Babylon*, trans. Richard Aczel (Edinburgh: Polygon, 1991); three sections of *Sinistra körzet: Egy regény fejezetei, Hungarian Quarterly* 39 (1998): 63–81; "Give or Take a Day," trans. Elizabeth Szász, in *Give or Take a Day: Contemporary Hungarian Short Stories,* ed. Lajos Szakolczay (Budapest: Corvina, 1997), 39–49; "The Outpost," trans. Judith Sollosy, in *The Kiss: Twentieth Century Hungarian Short Stories*, selected by István Bart (Budapest: Corvina, 1998), 311–30. *Az érsek látogatása* is

available in German as *Der Besuch des Erzbischofs,* trans. Hans Skirecki (Zurich: Ammann, 1999); *Sinistra körzet: Egy regény fejezetei* in French as *La Vallée de la Sinistra: Les chapitres d'un roman,* trans. Émilie Molnos Malaguti (Paris: Laffont, 1995), and in German as *Schutzgebiet Sinistra: Roman in Novellen,* trans. Hans Skirecki (Zurich: Ammann, 1994).

Bogza, Geo (b. 1908) Romanian poet and prose writer. A native of Ploieşti, Bogza completed secondary school there and then studied for a naval career in Galaţi and Constanţa (1921–1925). He lived in Buştenari in the Ploieşti region from 1926 to 1933. In 1928 he and other avant-garde intellectuals published the short-lived surrealist journal *Urmuz*, in which most of Bogza's early poetry first appeared. He also published in Tudor Arghezi's *Bilete de papagal* and for a while was associated with the circle of writers grouped around the avant-garde journal *Unu*. Between 1934 and 1939, he contributed to dozens of mostly left-wing journals. After World War II, Bogza received a number of awards and in 1955 became a member of the Romanian Academy of Science. Notwithstanding his avant-garde inclinations and his prewar surrealist poetry, Bogza eventually made his mark as a writer of literary reportage, of which he is Romania's acknowledged master in the twentieth century. Bogza's pre–World War II poetry includes the collections *Jurnal de sex* (Sex Diary, 1929); the patently antibourgeois *Poemul invectivă* (Offensive Poem, 1933); *Ioana Maria: 17 poeme* (Ioana Maria: 17 Poems, 1937); and *Cîntec de revoltă, dragoste şi moarte* (Song of Revolt, Love and Death, 1945).

Bogza's first book of reportage appeared in 1939 under the title *Ţări de piatră, de foc şi de pamînt* (Lands of Stone, Fire, and Clay; reprinted, 1946, as *Ţara de piatră* [*Land of Stone*]). It was followed by, among others, *Pe urmele războiului în Moldova* (On the Trail of the War in Moldavia, 1945); *Cartea Oltului* (The Book of the River Olt, 1945); *Oameni și cărbuni în Valea Jiului* (Men and Coal in the Jiu Valley, 1947); *Începtulul epopeii* (The Beginning of the Epic, 1950); *Porțile măreției* (The Gates of Glory, 1951); *Trei călătorii în inima țării* (Three Journeys into the Heart of the Land, 1951); *Anii împotrivirii* (Years of Resistance, 1953), a collection of reportage, pamphlets, and articles from 1934 to 1939; *Tablou geografic* (Geographical Survey, 1954); and *Pagini contemporane, 1944–1956* (Contemporary Pages, 1944–1956, 1957). Bogza's well-known novella, *Sfîrșitul lui Iacob Onisia* (The End of Jacob Onisia, 1949), describes the tragic circumstances surrounding the death of a mountain worker from Aninoasa and, like many of his works, is, in essence, a social protest. Although Bogza drew his subjects from the standard socialist realist repertoire, his style won him admirers for its highly intense, dramatic quality. Bogza also wrote the text accomanying an illustrated book on the Romanian sculptor Constantin Brancuși (1876–1957) published in 1965.

Literature: *Eu sunt ținta: Geo Bogza în dialog cu Diana Turconi* (Bucharest: Style, 1996), an excellent and revealing book on Bogza, with a number of photographs and illustrations, consisting in the main of conversations with the writer Diana Turconi between 18 July 1992 and 14 September 1993.

Translations: *Land of Stone: The Land of the Motzi* (Bucharest: Book, 1954); *Years of Darkness* (Bucharest: Book, 1955), a good collection of reportage, pamphlets, and articles written between 1934 and 1939, including pieces on the plight of the Basques during the Spanish Civil War; excerpt from *Sfîrșitul lui Iacob Onisia,* in *Introduction to Rumanian Literature,* ed. Jacob Steinberg (New York: Twayne, 1966), 281–98.

Boldizsár, Iván (1912–1988) Hungarian journalist, short-story writer, and diplomat. A native of Budapest, Boldizsár entered Bu-

dapest University in 1930 and began studying philosophy and medicine. From 1932 to the outbreak of World War II, he also held several newspaper editorial positions. He was taken prisoner during the war and after his release resumed his editorial career. In 1945/1946, he worked for *Szabad Szó* and from 1946 to 1948 for *Új Magyarország.* In 1947, while still practicing journalism, Boldizsár entered diplomatic service and became Hungarian undersecretary of state for foreign affairs and served as a member of the Hungarian delegation to the Paris peace negotiations. From 1951 to 1955, he held the position of editor of *Magyar Nemzet* and in 1960 became editor in chief of the English-language *New Hungarian Quarterly.* In 1968 he became editor in chief of the theater journal *Színház.* In 1979 Boldizsár became president of the Hungarian PEN Club; in 1972, vice president of the National Peace Council; and in 1984, head of the International PEN Club. His first published work and long considered his best was a collection of reportage based on a trip to Denmark: *A gazdag parasztok országa* (The Land of Rich Peasants, 1939). After World War II, he became a well-known writer based largely on his collections of political and sociographical essays, travel diaries (France, England, New York City), short stories, fairy tales, and novels. A volume of his selected short stories, *Örökké élni* (To Live Forever), was published in 1979. His memoirs about the period 1942 to 1947, also one of his better works, were published in 1982 under the title *Don—Budapest—Párizs* (The Don, Budapest, Paris).

Translations: "Meeting the General," trans. Kathleen Szasz, in *Present Continuous: Contemporary Hungarian Writing,* ed. István Bart (Budapest: Corvina, 1985), 32–43.

Borowski, Tadeusz (1922–1951) Polish poet and short-story writer. Widely known internationally on the basis of his graphic and unsentimental depictions of concentration camp life during World War II, Borowski was born in the city of Zhitomir, Ukraine. He began attending secondary school in Warsaw after his parents moved from the USSR, but because of the German invasion of Poland it was only in 1940 that he was able to complete his studies in the clandestine school system that operated in the occupied country. His first publication was an underground mimeographed volume of poetry titled *Gdzekolwiek Ziemia* (Wherever the Earth, 1942). From 1943 to 1945, Borowski was imprisoned, first in Auschwitz and then in Dachau. His experiences in the death camps shaped his subsequent literary career. After his liberation from Dachau by American troops, he lived for a while in nearby Munich, where he published a small volume of poems, *Imiona nurtu* (The Names of the Current), in 1945 and, the following year, a documentary account with Janusz Siedlecki and Krystyn Olszewski of their experiences in Auschwitz: *Byliśmy w Oświęcimiu* (We Were in Auschwitz). Back in Poland in 1946, Borowski became the editor of the monthly *Nurt.* In 1949 he spent a year in Berlin as an employee of the Polish Information Service, thereafter returning to Poland to join the staff of the periodical *Nowa Kultura* as editor of its journalism section. In 1950 he was awarded a State Prize, Third Class, for his story collection *Opowiadania z książek i gazet* (Stories from Books and Newspapers, 1949).

Borowski's literary fame rests principally on two collections of stories based on his experiences in Auschwitz: *Kamienny świat* (World of Stone, 1948) and *Pożegnanie z Marią* (Farewell to Mary, 1948). Despite their international fame as among the most compelling literary works dealing with the concentration camps and the Holocaust, *Pożegnanie z Marią* and *Kamienny świat* were roundly denounced by Marxist critics in Poland for their candid, unsentimental, and antiheroic depiction of everyday life in the camps. Borowski sought to appease his detractors by becoming an ardent champion of socialist realism, but when the contradictions in his life got the best of him he committed suicide in 1951. *Mała kronika wielkich spraw* (A Little Chronicle of Big Affairs), a collection of his feuilletons, was published in the year of his death, followed in 1952 by a posthumous anthology of his articles and reportage, *Na przedpolu* (On the Front Line). A collection of short stories, *Czerwony maj* (Red May), was also published posthumously in 1953, and a five-volume edition of his collected works (*Utwory zebrane*) appeared in 1959.

Translations: *Selected Poems,* trans. Tadeusz Pioro, with Larry Rafferty and Meryl Natchez (Walnut Creek, Calif.: Hit and Run Press, 1990); *This Way for the Gas, Ladies and Gentlemen and Other Stories,* ed. and trans. Barbara Vedder (New York: Viking, 1967; New York: Penguin, 1967, 1976).

Boruń, Katarzyna (b. 1956) Polish poet. A native Varsovian, Boruń studied at the Łódź Film School and in 1989 took part in the International Writing Program at the University of Iowa. She subsequently became an editor at the monthly *Powściągliwość i Praca.* Her first poems appeared in the journal *Nowy Wyraz* in 1974. *Wyciszenia* (Quietenings), her first published book of poetry, came out in 1977. It was followed by *Mały happening* (A Small Happening, 1979); *Życie codzienne w Państwie Środka* (Daily Life in the Middle Kingdom, 1985); and *Więcej—wiersze o zmroku* (More—Poems at Twilight, 1991). A poet in a very contemporary vein who writes with a real feeling for loneliness of the big city, Boruń rejects illusions and appeals for a poetry brought down from the ivory tower to confront everyday realities.

Translations: Seven poems in *Young Poets of a New Poland: An Anthology,* trans. Donald Pirie (London: Forest, 1993), 111–18.

Boškovski, Jovan (1920–1968) Macedonian short-story writer and novelist. Born in Skopje into a family of migrant workers, Boškovski was forced by the need to work to acquire most of his education in night schools after ending his formal education with elementary school. Although he discovered his talent for writing at an early age, his first work did not appear in print until 1944. His stories, often devoted to contemporary Macedonian history, were collected from various journals and newspapers and published in three collections: *Rastrel* (Gunfire, 1947); *Blokada* (Blockade, 1950); and *Ludje i ptici* (People and Birds, 1955). His one novel, *Salunskite atentatori* (Assassins of Salonika, 1961), is based on the well-known story of the Ilinden uprising of 1903 when the Macedonians revolted against the Turks and declared an independent republic, which lasted for only ten days. Boškovski was also active as an editor. In 1948 he brought out a collection of Macedonian epic songs under the title *Junak nad junaci: Epski narodni pesni za Marka Kraleta* (Hero of Heroes: National Epic Songs About King Marko) and in 1968 an anthology of Macedonian drama: *Makedonska drama.* Boškovski's interest in the drama was previously reflected in his book of reviews, *Oplemeneta igra: Teatarski razgledi* (The Tribalized Game: Theater Reviews, 1955). An edition of his collected works (*Izbrani dela*) was published in 1983.

Translations: "The Man on the Roof," in *The Big Horse and Other Stories of Modern Macedonia,* ed. Milne Holton (Columbia: University of Missouri Press, 1974), 107–12.

Boškovski, Jozo T. (b. 1933) Macedonian poet, short-story writer, essayist, and art critic. An idiosyncratic but well-known writer, Boškovski was born in the village of Ostrilitsi, near Kruševo. After his early schooling in his native village as well as in Kruševo, Boševski atttended the Brothers Miladinov Teachers College in Bitola, from which he graduated in 1954. He then worked for the next two years as a teacher of Macedonian language and music, first in Kruševo and then in the village of Obršani. After 1956 and until his early retirement for medical reasons, he worked as a journalist specializing in cultural and intellectual issues for Skopje Radio and TV and such newspapers and journals as *Večeren reporter, Trudbenik,* and *Večer.* When his health permitted him to pursue a university education, he studied the history of the literatures of the peoples of the former Yugoslavia as well as Macedonian language at Saints Cyril and Methodius University in Skopje. He graduated in 1969 and then went on to do further work in philosophy at the university.

Boškovski's first published book was the verse collection *Boj so Gadurija* (The Battle with Gadurija, 1963), which draws heavily on the Macedonian mythic and folkloric heritage. It was followed by *Aktiven poetgovornik* (The Activist Poet-Speaker, 1966); *Longing for the South: Contemporary Macedonian Poetry* (1981; original title in English), a two-volume anthology of translations of Macedonian poetry into English and of English poetry into Macedonian, undertaken with the Indian poet Sitakant Mahapatra and published in New Delhi; *Makedonska tragedija: Fantazmagorija* (The Macedonian Tragedy: Fantasmagoria, 1987), an augmented edition, two sections of which first appeared in *Boj so Gadurija,* came out in 1969; *Nov svet* (New World, 1990), a collection of essays; *Big Bang. Imperatorot na zloto: Poetska drama* (Big Bang. The Emperor of Gold: Poetic Drama, 1992); *Lek protiv smrtta* (Antidote for Death, 1994), a collection of poems, prose, mixed verse and prose, and a few short pieces by other writers about Boškovski and his work; and *Skopskata ovca* (The Macedonian Sheep, 1997), a collection of short stories.

Boškovski writes about Macedonia and its myths and traditions; the environment; the danger of nuclear catastrophe, as exemplified by the Chernobyl, Ukraine, incident; and, not the least, himself. Boškovski's style is that of a visionary—ecstatic, self-possessed, cosmic in scope. The typography of some of his poetry, as in the curious collection *Lek protiv smrtta,* recalls that of the early Soviet revolutionary poet Vladimir Mayakovsky, whose name Boškovski invokes on several occasions (and with whom he compares himself). Boškoski seems to emulate Mayakovsky's militant, exhortatory style, but outdoes the Russian poet in his use of words in capitals and multiple exclamation and question marks. In one poem Boškovski extols himself as the creator of new matter: POETRY.

Bošovski has been widely translated and has become well known through his own poetry readings. In 1986 he was awarded the gold medal of the Munich writers society, Littera, for his readings in that city through the years. He has also had appearances in Amsterdam and New York City (1987, 1990), including at the United Nations. Among distinctions claimed for Boškovski by bio-bibliographic accounts of him are an honorary doctorate of letters awarded in 1988 by a university in Benson, Arizona (where no such university exists), and his election in 1989 as a deputy to the World Parliament for Security and Peace.

Translations: Two poems, trans. Herbert Kuhner and Duško Tomovski, in *Reading the Ashes: An Anthology of the Poetry of Modern Macedonia,* ed. Milne Holton and Graham W. Reid (Pittsburgh: University of Pittsburgh Press, 1977), 83–84.

Bozhilov, Bozhidar (b. 1923) Bulgarian poet, novelist, playwright, essayist, and translator. Bozhilov, one of the most prolific of contemporary Bulgarian poets, was born in the Black Sea town of Varna. After completing his secondary schooling there, he studied medicine and law at Sofia University (1942–1946). The author of over thirty books of poetry, Bozhilov has also written novels, plays, and essays, and is well known for his translations from English. He has also served as director of the Narodna Kultura publishing house (1973–1980), editor in chief of *Puls* (1985) and *Fakel* (1985–1989), and secretary of the Bulgarian Writers Union (1966–1968). Bozhilov helped his career along with the political correctness demonstrated, for example, in his sycophantic *Chetiri sreshti s Lenin* (Four Meetings with Lenin: A Poem, 1971). Apart from such obvious ideological exercises, Bozhilov has written mainly about the great importance to him of poetry, love (the subject of several of his volumes), and the physical world around him. He is very much an urban poet. Known for a certain flamboyance and lust for life, he enjoys the reputation of a playboy poet, a reputation he has encouraged in life and in art. As he wrote in his collection, *Ars Poetica* (1973):

Not knowing
how to write poems,
I live them.

In 1979 Bozhilov published a lighthearted acount of his travels in the United States under the title *Putnitsite ot "Sivata Hrutka": Amerikanski skitsi* (Traveling with Greyhound: American Sketches, 1979). His translation of Shakespeare's *Richard II* appeared in 1974.

Translations: *American Pages,* trans. Cornelia Bozhilova (Athens: Ohio University Press, 1980); four poems, trans. Cornelia Bozhilova, in *Poets of Bulgaria,* ed. William Meredith (Greensboro, N.C.: Unicorn, 1985), 9–12; two poems, trans. Marvin Bell, in *Window on the Black Sea: Bulgarian Poetry in Translation,* ed. Richard Harteis, in collaboration with William Meredith (Pittsburgh: Carnegie Mellon University Press, 1992), 122–23.

Božič, Peter (b. 1932) Slovenian playwright and novelist. Božič was born in Bled, but completed his secondary-school education in Maribor before attending Ljubljana University. He made his literary debut with the novel *Izven* (Outdoors) in 1963. A second novel, *Na robu zemlje* (On the Edge of the Earth), followed in 1968. His subsequent works, all published in 1970, include *Kaznjenci* (Prisoners), a sixty-page novella; the one-act plays *Križišče* (Crossroads) and *Zasilni izhod* (Emergency Exit); and three full-length plays: *Človek v sipi* (Man in Sand), *Dva brata* (Two Brothers), and *Vojaka Jošta ni* (Soldier Jošta Is Missing). A contemporary murder mystery titled *Jaz sem ubil Anito* (I Killed Anita) appeared in 1972, followed in 1979 by the World War II novel *Očeta Vincenca smrt* (Father Vincent's Death). *Komisar Kris* (Commissar Chris, 1982), a tragedy, was Božič's last play for a while. In 1987 he published his highly popular *Chubby Was Here* (original title in English), subtitled *Notes from Memory* and dealing with the Ljubljana subculture of homeless youths, bohemians, and eccentrics in the 1960s and 1970s. His more recent novels, *Človek in senca* (Man and Shadow, 1990) and *Zdaj ko je nova oblast* (Now Who Is the New Authority, 1993), deal similarly with the dark undercurrent of contemporary urban life.

Brabcová, Zuzana (b. 1959) Czech novelist. One of the most promising writers of the 1980s, Brabcová was born in Prague, where she graduated from high school in 1978. Shortly thereafter, she began working as a librarian at Charles University, a position she held for no more than six months when her political noncomformity forced her into menial labor. She earned a living for a while as an assistant in a hospital, and from 1982 to 1988 was employed as a cleaning woman.

After marrying and bearing children, she devoted herself to her domestic routine and her writing. Her first novel, *Daleko od stromu* (Far from the Tree), was initially published in a samizdat edition in 1984 and in Prague only in 1991. Widely recognized as one of the most important texts to emerge from the generation that grew up in the repressive 1970s, the novel is a fragmentary, nonlinear first-person narrative by a young woman who is meant to typify the sense of despair and aimlessness of her generation. After attempting suicide, she is confined to an asylum where she retreats into her inner world and seeks solace in her memories and creative writing. The asylum also represents a refuge from the outside reality. Prague, where the novel is set, appears to be sinking in a deluge, a motif that crops up often in Czech prose of the 1970s and 1980s. Brabcová's second novel, *Zlodějina* (Thievery, 1996), is similarly constructed and comprises two stories that seem at first to have little in common, but ultimately merge. The first is about a man who is beaten by the police during demonstrations in Prague in November 1989; the second is about a store clerk who gets stuck in an elevator in a high-rise apartment house. The two seemingly disparate incidents assume a common hopeful conclusion at the end of the novel.

Translations: Excerpt from *Daleko od stromu,* trans. James Naughton, in *Allskin and Other Tales by Contemporary Czech Women,* ed. Alexandra Büchler (Seattle: Women in Translation, 1998), 15–28; "The Slaughtering" (from *Daleko od stromu*), trans. James Naughton, in *This Side of Reality: Modern Czech Writing,* ed. Alexandra Büchler (London: Serpent's Tail, 1996), 140–53.

Brandys, Kazimierz (1916–2000) Polish novelist and short-story writer. One of the best-known Polish writers of the postwar period, Brandys was born in Łódź. He completed his secondary-school education in Warsaw and then earned a master's degree in law at Warsaw University shortly before the outbreak of World War II. While at the university, he belonged to a student socialist organization and began publishing in the left-wing academic press. Although Jewish, he managed to live in Warsaw during the war without being forced into the ghetto and actually began his literary career under the German occupation. His first completed work was a novel titled *Urodziny* (The Birthday), written between 1940 and 1942, but never published in its entirety. Instead, his second novel, *Drewniany koń* (Hobby Horse), which was written between 1943 and 1945, became his first major publication when it appeared in 1946. It was followed that year by *Miasto niepokonane: Opowieść o Warszawie* (The Invincible City: A Tale of Warsaw), a fictionalized account of the Warsaw Uprising of 1944. Brandys's next project was a huge novel in four parts under the general title *Między wojnami* (Between the Wars) and comprising *Samson* (1948)—which was made into a film by Andrzej Wajda in 1961—*Antygona* (Antigone, 1948), *Troja miasto otwarte* (Troy, the Open City, 1949), and *Człowiek nie umiera* (Man Does Not Die, 1951). The tetralogy is, in essence, a communist-inspired putdown of the interwar intelligentsia for its delusions and indecisiveness. Even more fully in the mainstream of socialist realism was Brandys's novel *Obywatele* (Citizens, 1954), about high-school "vigilantes" ferreting out class enemies.

In the post-Stalinist era, Brandys switched gears and began writing about sincere, dedicated younger communists whose idealism is eventually destroyed by the cynicism and expedience of their Party superiors. Among his best works in this vein are the novella *Obrona "Granady"* (*The Defense of the "Granada,"* 1956) and the short novel *Matka Królów* (The Mother of the Króls, 1957; translated as *Sons and Comrades*),

which was also made into a film in 1987 by Jerzy Zaorski. *The Defense of the "Granada"* is about what happens when a group of young enthusiasts of revolutionary theater try to mount a production of Vladimir Mayakovsky's 1920s early Soviet antibureaucracy satirical comedy, *The Bathhouse*. In *Sons and Comrades*, a woman of proletarian origin loses all her sons either to the war against the fascists or as Party scapegoats when policies go wrong. Brandys's next major publication was the three-part *Listy do Pani Z.: Wspomnienia z teraźniejszości* (*Letters to Mrs. Z: Reminiscences of the Present*), which some critics have regarded as his best work. Drawing on the tradition of the epistolary novel, yet redefined innovatively, *Letters to Mrs. Z.* is a lively and intellectually stimulating parade of ideas about literary, social, political, and philosophical matters by a well-informed, thoughtful, and ironic man of letters with a good knowledge of East and West. The first volume covers the years 1959 and 1960 and was published in 1962; the second, the year 1961, was also published in 1962; and the third, the years 1957 to 1961, appeared in 1963. Brandys returned to the epistolatry tradition, this time in a more traditional way, in *Wariacje pocztowe* (Postal Variations, 1972). Covering a much longer time frame, the novel assumes the form of letters and one telegram dispatched over the years 1770 to 1970 from fathers to sons and vice versa in the (fictional) Zabierski family. A 1989 edition of the novel was augmented by the exchange of a letter on computer disk from Jacek Zabierski in Paris to his son Dawid in Warsaw and the son's reply in the form of a small letter. The additions were made by Jan Zieliński, a Warsaw philologist and literary critic who edited the volume, as a postscript to the new edition, with Brandys's permission.

Brandys's works from the late 1970s and the 1980s tend to be mostly autobiographical, such as *Nierzeczywistość* (Unreality,

1978; translated as *A Question of Reality*), in which he broaches, among other things, his own experience of anti-Semitism in Poland, or diary-like accounts of travels outside Poland (including the United States) after he had incurred the anger of the regime by his open support of Solidarity. The principal texts of this latter category are *Miesiące, 1978–1979* (Months, 1978–1979, 1981; translated as *A Warsaw Diary: 1978–1981*) and *Miesiące, 1982–1984* (Months, 1982–1984, 1984; translated as *Paris, New York: 1982–1984*). *Rondo,* set during World War II, appeared in 1982. Of Brandys's collections of short fiction, the best two are *Obrona "Grenady" i inne opowiadania* (The Defense of the "Granada" and Other Stories, 1966) and *Jak być kochana i inne opowiadania* (How to Be Loved and Other Stories, 1970). The title story of the second collection, "How to Be Loved," was very popular and was made into a film by the director Wojciech Has in 1963.

Translations: *Letters to Mrs. Z.,* trans. and ed. Morris Edelson (Highland Park, Ill.: December Press, 1987); *Paris, New York: 1982–1984,* trans. Babara Krzywicki-Herburt (New York: Random House, 1988); *A Question of Reality,* trans. Isabel Burzum (New York: Scribner, 1980); *Rondo,* trans. Jaroslaw Anders (New York: Farrar, Straus and Giroux, 1989); *Sons and Comrades,* trans. D. J. Welsh (New York: Grove, 1961); *A Warsaw Diary: 1978–1981,* trans. Richard Lourie (New York: Random House, 1983; New York: Vintage, 1985); *The Defense of the "Granada,"* trans. Jadwiga Zwolska, in *Contemporary Polish Short Stories,* selected by Andrzej Kijowski (Warsaw: Polonia, 1960), 68–127.

Bratić, Radoslav (b. 1948) Serbian novelist, short-story writer, and playwright. A native of Vidovdan, in Herzegovina, Bratić finished elementary school in Koritim and nearby Bileća, graduated from high school in Trebinja, and then studied Yugoslav and world literature at Belgrade University. Bratić started to write as a student and was one of the founders of the avant-garde literary journals *Znak* and *Književna reč.* He is currently on the editorial board of *Književnost.* His works include the short novel *Smrt spasitelja* (Death of the Savior, 1973), for which he won the prize awarded by the newspaper *Mladost*; the novel *Sumnja u biografiju* (Doubts About Biography, 1980), which was honored with the Isidora Sekulić Prize; the short-story collection *Slika bez oca* (A Picture Without Father, 1985), a "saga of Herzegovina" that conjures up Herzegovina as a mythic space and won the Ivo Andrić Prize; *Strah od zvona* (Fear of Bells, 1992), one of his best works, which won the Meša Selimović Prize and the Djamil Sijarić Prize; *Zima u Hercegovini* (Winter in Herzegovina, 1995); and *Ljubavnik Šeherezade* (Scheherezade's Lover, 1996). Bratić's works generally pivot on recollections of childhood and draw heavily on local legends and superstitions. Bratić has also edited works by Danilo Kiš as well as the correspondence and sermons of the Serbian patriarch Pavle, related to the Yugoslav wars of the 1990s: *Molitve i molbe: Besede, razgovori, propovedi, pisma i izjave* (Prayers and Supplications: Discussions, Conversations, Sermons, Correspondence, and Lectures, 1996). With Gabriel Arc, he edited anthologies of stories by American black writers, of writings by Lusatian Sorbs, of short Indian fables, and of Chinese literature in the past and present. He is also the author of the play *Rasturanje lika Grigorija Miketića* (The Dispersal of Grigori Miketić's Image), which was performed in 1973 by the Belgrade student experimental drama studio. In 1977 Radio Belgrade presented his play about Aleksi Šantić, and the same year Radio Sarajevo did a dramatic version of his novel *Sumnja u biografiju.*

Translations: "A Picture Without Father," trans. Christina Pribićević Zorić, in *The*

Prince of Fire: An Anthology of Contemporary Serbian Short Stories, ed. Radmila J. Gorup and Nadežda Obradović (Pittsburgh: University of Pittsburgh Press, 1998), 248–58.

Braun, Volker (b. 1939) German poet, novelist, essayist, and playwright. One of the most provocative and important East German writers, Braun was born in Dresden. Unable to enter a university after completing secondary school, he worked as a common laborer from 1958 to 1960. Finally, in 1960 he gained admission to Leipzig University, where he studied philosophy. After leaving university in 1964 and making an extensive trip to Siberia, he moved to Berlin, where he was the literary director of the Berliner Ensemble Theater for the 1965/1966 season. In 1972 he joined the Deutsches Theater. Braun's literary breakthrough came with the publication in 1965 of his book *Provokation für mich* (Provocation for Me), a volume of poems of a rebellious youth at odds with Marxist ideology. Adding to the sensational character of the volume was Braun's repudiation of traditional agitational rhetoric in favor of a style heavily indebted to the colloquial language and full of hyperbole and dramatic effects. His next books—*Das ungezwungene Leben Kasts: Drei Berichte* (The Uninhibited Life of Kast: Three Reports, 1972); *Hinze und Kunze* (Hinze and Kunze, 1973); and *Tinka* (1973)—were sharply critical of the bureaucratization in the German Democratic Republic and the concept of "socialist democracy." *Unvollendete Geschichte* (The Unfinished Story), a hugely popular work in both East and West Germany, was originally published by the journal *Sinn und Form* (after being rejected) in 1975. Its first official West German publication came in 1977, eight years before the work was allowed to be published in book form in the GDR. The novella tells the story of the troubled relationship between two young people: Karin, the daughter of a GDR state official, and Frank, the reformed delinquent son of a family of no apparent political interests. The political and police pressure on Karin to break with Frank and the resultant outcome sparked the great interest in the work.

Braun's essays, as in the volume *Es genügt nicht die einfache Wahrheit: Notate* (The Simple Truth Doesn't Suffice: Notes, 1976), follow the same pattern of his poems and novels. The same year, 1976, Braun traveled to Cuba and Peru. *Guevara oder der Sonnenstaat* (Guevara or The Sun State, 1975), the major literary product of the trip, is an analysis in dramatic form of the reasons for the revolutionary Che Guevara's failed campaign in Bolivia. Braun's other works include the plays *Grosser Frieden* (Big Peace, 1979), about a popular revolt in ancient China, and *Dmitri* (1983), and the poetry collections *Wir und nicht sie* (We and Not They, 1970); *Gegen die symmetrische Welt* (Against the Symmetrical World, 1974); *Training des aufrechten Gangs* (Training to Walk Straight, 1979); and *Der Wendehals* (The Renegade, 1995). In 1980, the year in which he was awarded the Heinrich Mann Prize, Braun gave readings in England. In 1983 he was named a member of the Academy of Arts of the GDR. He visited China in 1988 and the United States in 1990.

Literature: Andy Hollis, introduction to Volker Braun, *Unvollendete Geschichte,* ed. Andy Hollis (Manchester: Manchester University Press, 1988), is very informative, as is Rolf Jucker, ed., *Volker Braun,* Contemporary German Writers series (Cardiff: University of Wales Press, 1995), a collection of essays in English and German.

Translations: Nine poems, in German and English, trans. Gordon Brotherston, Gisela Brotherston, and Michael Hamburger, in *East German Poetry: An Anthology,* ed. Michael Hamburger (New York: Dutton, 1973), 188–207.

Breza, Tadeusz (1905–1970) Polish novelist. Breza was born in the village of Siekierzyńce in Volynia, then in eastern Poland. After completing his secondary-school education, he spent a year and a half in a Benedictine monastery in Belgium. After he returned to Poland, he earned a degree in philosophy at Warsaw University and then studied in London. Following his auspicious debut as a poet in 1925, he went into the Polish diplomatic service and served in London from 1929 to 1932. He published his first work of prose, the psychological novel *Adam Grywald,* in 1936. From 1932 to 1937, he headed the cultural section of the newspaper *Kurier Poranny.* During World War II, Breza was active in the cultural undergound in occupied Poland. From 1945 to 1946, he was literary director of the Teatr Stary in Kraków. In the next two years, he served as head of the theater section of the Warsaw weekly *Odrodzenie.* He subsequently returned to diplomatic service and from 1955 to 1959 held the position of cultural attaché of the Polish Embassy in Rome, and a similar position in the Polish Embassy in Paris from 1961 to 1965.

As a writer of fiction, Breza is known most for such works as *Mury Jerycha* (The Walls of Jericho, 1946) and its two-volume sequel, *Niebo i ziemia* (Sky and Earth, 1949), political novels aimed at the political right, which opposed the imposition of communism in Poland after the war; *Uczta Baltazara* (Balthazar's Feast, 1952), essentially an exercise in socialist realism; *Spiżowa brama: Notatnik rzymski* (The Bronze Gate: A Roman Notebook, 1960), a knowledgeable, even incisive and scrupulously objective, book about the inner workings of the Vatican that became a best-seller; and *Urząd* (The Office, 1960), a follow-up to *Spiżowa brama: Notatnik rzymski* that also deals with the Vatican, but in the form of a novel baring the workings of the Vatican bureaucracy. He was also the author of a book of Cuban reportage, *Listy hawańskie: Reportaże z Kuby* (Havana Letters: Reportage from Cuba, 1961), and a collection of reminiscences and essays published under the title *Nelly: O kolegach i o sobie* (Nelly: About My Colleagues and Myself, 1970).

Broda, Marzena (b. 1966) Polish poet. A native of Kraków, Broda began publishing in 1985 and was associated with the "Barbarian" poets, whose main outlet was the Kraków quarterly *bruLion.* Her first book of poetry, *Światło przestrzeni* (The Light of Space), appeared in 1990; it was awarded the Kazimiera Iłłakowiczówna Prize. Her next book, *Cudzoziemszczyzna* (Foreign Things, 1995), contains poems from 1989 to 1995 composed in such places as New York; New Jersey; Bar Harbor, Maine; and Sandy Hook, New Jersey. Broda is a poet of transcendant inclination willing to ask questions for which she knows no answers will be forthcoming and with a sensitive feeling for the world of nature. In her rhythmically prosaic poem "Dom Iguany" ("The Home of the Iguana"), she conveys a fascination with the Galápagos Islands, which have so far remained free of the spoiling effects of human habitation. Several of Broda's poems are addressed to other women writers, among them Marguerite Yourcenar (1903–1987) and the Russian Sofia Parnok (1885–1933). Broda also counts the Russian poet Marina Tsvetaeva as one of her mentors. The epigraph to *Cudzoziemszczyzna* is taken from the elegy to Tsvetaeva written by the German poet Rainer Maria Rilke. Moreover, Tsvetaeva dedicated her poetic cycle *Friend* to Sofia Parnok.

Bruyn, Günter de (b. 1926) German novelist, short-story writer, and essayist. A native of Berlin, de Bruyn became one of East Germany's most respected literary figures. He served in the army from 1943 to 1945, and suffered a serious head wound from which he eventually recovered. After release from a

POW camp, he worked as a farmhand in the Göttingen area. In 1946, in the Soviet zone of occupation, he completed a course for "new teachers" who would replace those dismissed for past Nazi Party affiliation. De Bruyn thereafter taught in a village school in Garlitz (Havelland), on the outskirts of Berlin. This lasted until 1949, when he left to study librarianship (which de Bruyn has referred to as his "true calling") until 1952. After a year as a librarian in East Berlin, he became a research assistant at the Central Institute of Library Science of the German Democratic Republic (Berlin). He held this position until 1961, when he gave it up to become a freelance writer.

De Bruyn's literary career began with the publication of a volume of short stories in 1960. Its success confirmed his decision to leave library work for a full-time literary career. His first, largely autobiographical, novel, *Der Hohlweg* (The Ravine, 1963), deals with the postwar fortunes of young men of his generation who grew up under Hitler, served in the army in World War II, and set out to create a true socialist utopia on the ruins of the defeated Nazi state. Although it was well written and well received, de Bruyn later disavowed the novel (in an essay published in 1974 under the title "Der Holzweg" ["The Wrong Path"]) because of its conformity to the precepts of a then obligatory Soviet-style socialist realism. "The Wrong Path" is included in the volume *Eröffnungen: Schriftsteller über ihr Erstlingswerk* (Openings: Writers on Their First Works, 1974), edited by Gerhard Schneider, and was reprinted in the collections *Frauendienst: Erzählungen und Aufsätze* (Serving Women: Tales and Essays, 1986) and *Lesefreuden: Über Bücher und Menschen* (The Joys of Reading: On Books and People, 1987).

The texts that established de Bruyn's formidable reputation were his subsequent novels, *Buridans Esel* (*Buridan's Ass*, 1968) and *Preisverleihung* (The Literary Award, 1972). Drawn from the life of the East German socialist intelligentsia, the novels are refreshingly free of ideology and concentrate on everyday human situations viewed with ironic detachment and a wry sense of humor. De Bruyn's only work to be translated into English, *Buridan's Ass* features a romantic triangle involving Berlin librarians in an obvious reflection of de Bruyn's own experiences. The focus of the work falls on the morally flawed senior librarian Karl Erp, whose affair with a fellow librarian causes the breakup of his marriage, until his tepid response to her transfer to another city ends that relationship and returns him to the family that now seems cooly indifferent to him. De Bruyn's irony, underscored by occasional discussion of the strategy of his novel with his readers, also addresses the breakdown of the former idealism of his own generation and the pursuit of petit-bourgeois comforts in the GDR's "little stabilization" of the 1960s. The underlying social concerns of *Buridan's Ass* are manifest as well in the strong female characters in the work—a reflection of de Bruyn's interest in the role of women in the new socialist society of the GDR—and in the moral and ethical compromises made for the sake of career by his central figure. *Buridan's Ass,* which attracted attention not least of all for the realism of its relatively rare (East Berlin) urban setting, was subsequently made into a stage play and a film under the title *Glück in Hinterhof* (Happiness in One's Own Backyard).

The social diagnosis of *Buridan's Ass* becomes even sharper in *Preisverleihung* and *Märkische Forschungen: Erzählung für Freunde der Literaturgeschichte* (Brandenburg Researches: A Story for Friends of Literary History, 1979), in which the focus is on the pampered and privileged academic and literary establishment of the GDR. The point of departure for *Märkische Forschungen,* the more compelling of the two works, was the lengthy study of the neglected early Romantic writer Jean Paul Friedrich Richter (1763–1825), by the prominent GDR scholar Wolfgang Harich. Published in 1974 to much critical acclaim, Harich's study, *Jean Pauls Revolutionsdichtung* (Jean Paul's Revolutionary Poetry), portrays Richter as an enthusiast of the French Revolution who seeks to inspire his fellow Germans to emulate the French. Harich must have been aware of de Bruyn's own interest in Richter but accords de Bruyn's research a single footnoted reference late in the book. De Bruyn's study, *Das Leben des Jean Paul Friedrich Richter,* was published in 1978 and takes a more qualified view of Richter's putative revolutionary ardor. Although *Märkische Forschungen* may first strike the reader as a a thinly disguised polemic with Harich, it is far more a probing analysis of the entire GDR cultural establishment.

De Bruyn has also published several collections of mostly literary essays: *Frauendienst: Erzählungen und Aufsätze,* a collection of short stories with the common theme of male–female relations, autobiographical pieces, and literary essays; *Lesefreuden: Über Bücher und Menschen* (The Pleasure of Reading: Collected Essays on Books and People, 1987), on a wide variety of topics from E. T. A. Hoffmann in Berlin to his own novels *Der Hohlweg* and *Märkische Forschungen*; and *Jubelschreie, Trauergesänge: Deutsche Befindlichkeiten* (Cries of Joy, Songs of Sorrow: German Conditions, 1991), a collection of literary essays and speeches published or delivered between 1986 and 1990.

Since the collapse of the GDR, de Bruyn has published several well-regarded works of an autobiographical nature, beginning with *Zwischenbilanz: Eine Jugend in Berlin* (Taking Stock: A Berlin Youth, 1992), which ends with the division of Germany in 1949. The sequel, describing de Bruyn's subsequent forty years in the GDR, appeared in 1996 under the title *Vierzig Jahre: Ein Lebensbericht* (Forty Years: A Report on One's Life). De Bruyn is also the author of a short book of a more theoretical nature on the art of biography, *Das erzählte Ich: Über Wahrheit und Dichtung in der Autobiographie* (As I Told It: On Truth and Poetry in Autobiography, 1995). Among the many honors that de Bruyn has received are the Heinrich Mann Prize (1964); the Lion Feuchtwanger Prize (1982); the Thomas Mann Prize (1989); the Heinrich Böll Prize (1990); and the Great Literary Prize of the Bavarian Academy of Fine Arts (1993). De Bruyn was also awarded an honorary doctorate from Freiburg University/Breisgau. In 1989 he rejected the National Prize of the GDR as a protest against the GDR's "rigidity, intolerance, and inability to engage in dialogue."

Literature: Günter de Bruyn, *Märkische Forschungen: Erzählung für Freunde der Literaturgeschichte,* ed. Dennis Tate (Manchester: Manchester University Press, 1990), which contains the original German text as well as extensive commentary and notes in English by the editor. In the absence of other works on de Bruyn in English, this must be regarded as most helpful on him in that language. Among German studies, the best are Uwe Wittstock, ed., *Günter de Bruyn: Materialen zu Leben und Werk* (Frankfurt am Main: Fischer, 1991), which contains essays by de Bruyn, interviews with him, and analyses by various critics; and Ingo Hermann, ed., *Günter de Bruyn: Was ich noch schreiben will* (Göttingen: Lamuv, 1995), an extended discussion between de Bruyn and Ingo Hermann covering the major facets of his life and career. Containing essays by de Bruyn, interviews with him, and critical analyses, this is the best general work in German on the writer.

Translations: *Buridan's Ass,* trans. John Paet (Berlin: Seven Seas, 1973).

Bryll, Ernest (b. 1935) Polish poet and play-wright. A native of Warsaw, Bryll received a degree in Polish literature from Warsaw University and pursued film studies at the State Institute of Art. He has served as a member of the editorial board of *Współczesność* (1959–1960), literary director of the film studios Kamera (since 1968) and Silesia (since 1978), literary director of the Teatr Polski in Warsaw (1971–1974), and director of the Polish Cultural Institute in London (1975–1978), and in 1991 was appointed Polish ambassador to Ireland. Bryll has been a highly prolific writer in several genres and has directed much of his energy to a deflation of the Polish Romantic-messianic tradition, with its exaggerated national ideals and lack of practical realism. Bryll began publishing poetry in 1952 but reached a broader audience with his first book of poems, *Wigilie wariata* (Christmas Eves of a Madman, 1958), for which he was awarded a prize at the Kraków Students Festival for the best literary debut of the year. He subsequently published such additional volumes of poems as *Autoportret z bykiem* (Self-Portrait with a Bull, 1960); *Twarz nie odsłonięta* (A Face Not Revealed, 1963); *Sztuka stosowana* (Applied Art, 1966); *Mazowsze* (Mazovia, 1967); *Muszla* (Conch, 1968); *Fraszka na dzień dobry* (A Joke for a Good Day, 1969); *Zapiski* (Notes, 1969); *Wybór wierszy* (Selected Poems, 1970); *Zwierzątko* (A Little Animal, 1975); and *Wiersze wybrane* (Selected Poems, 1978). *Adwent* (Advent), which was published in London in 1986, and the verse drama *Wieczernik* (The Cenacle), which was suppressed by the censors and published only in 1990, capture the moods of hope, frustration, and pessimism during the period of Solidarity and martial law in the 1980s. Both are notable for their religious elements. The renowned Polish film director Andrzej Wajda, a close friend of Bryll, wrote an afterword to *Adwent* and produced The Cenacle in several churches before its appearance in print in 1990.

Bryll has also published several volumes of prose, among them *Studium* (A Study, 1963); *Gorzko, gorzko* (Bitter, Bitter, 1965); *Ciotka* (Aunt, 1964); *Ojciec* (Father, 1964); *Rok polski* (The Polish Year, 1978); *Slowik* (Nightingale, 1978); *A kto się odda w radość* (But Who Can Be Happy?, 1980), *Czasem spotkam siebie: Lipiec 1974–czerwiec 1978* (I'll Meet Myself Sometime: July 1974–June 1978, 1981); and *Kropla w wodospadzie* (A Drop in the Waterfall, 1995). Bryll wrote the plays *Żołnierze* (Soldiers, 1968); *Rzecz listopadowa* (The November Affair, 1968); *Kurdesz* (Drinking Song, 1969); *Po górach, po chmurach* (Over Mountains, over Clouds, 1969); *Na szkle malowane* (Painted on Glass, 1970); *Kto ty jesteś—czyli małe oratorium na dzień dzisiejszy* (Who Are You, or a Small Oratorium for Today, 1971); and *Życie jawą* (Life in the Open, 1973). The most resonant of these has been *Rzecz listopadowa,* in which a perspective on post–World War II Poland is shaped by the evocation of the Polish November Uprising of 1830/1831, a failed Romantic revolution by young noble idealists. Although not a writer in the folk tradition as such, Bryll drew on this tradition in his biblical pastoral drama *Po górach, po chmurach* and in his folk-musical play about the legendary mountain brigand Janosik, *Na szkle malowane,* both of which imply a contrast between the earthy values of the folk and the emptiness of the dreams and illusions of the Romantics. A collection of Bryll's poetry and plays was published in 1973 under the title *Dramaty i wiersze* (Plays and Poems).

Bryll's literary awards include the Broniewski Poetry Prize (1964); the Fiction Prize, Second Class, of the Ministry of Culture and Art for his novels *Ciotka* and *Ojciec;* the Piętak Prize for his volume *Mazovia* (1968); and the Pietrzak Prize for his complete ouevre as a poet and playwright.

Translations: One poem, trans. Sylvester Domański, in *The New Polish Poetry: A*

Bilingual Collection, ed. Milne Holton and Paul Vangelisti (Pittsburgh: University of Pittsburgh Press, 1978), 68–69; three poems in *Polish Poetry of the Last Two Decades of Communist Rule: Spoiling Cannibals' Fun,* ed. and trans. Stanisław Barańczak and Clare Cavanagh (Evanston, Ill.: Northwestern University Press, 1991), 132–34. *Rzecz listopadowa* is available in French as *Le Remous de novembre,* trans. Suzanne Arlet (Paris: Arlet, 1975).

Buczkowski, Leopold (1905–1989) Polish novelist. Arguably the most memorable writer who dealt with the partisan fighting against the Germans in World War II, Buczkowski was born in the village of Nakwasza in Podole, in the eastern borderlands region of the interwar Polish republic. Much of his writing about the war and the role of Jews in it (both as victims and as partisan fighters) is set in his native Podole. After beginning a program of Polish studies at the Jagiellonian University in Kraków in 1931, Buczkowski moved to Poznań and began working as a journalist for the *Kurier Poznański.* However, he soon returned to Kraków and pursued a course of painting under the direction of the artist Julian Fałat. In 1932 he transferred to Warsaw, where he enrolled in the Academy of Fine Arts. In 1935 he returned to his native Podole, where, until the outbreak of war in 1939, he was actively involved in regional folklore and amateur theatricals.

Buczkowski's breakthrough in print came in the form of fragments of his novel *Wertepy* (Puppets), which appeared in the journal *Signały* in 1937. Set in Podole, the work is an extraordinarily graphic depiction of the culture and mores of the multiethnic (Ruthenians, Poles, Jews) region that historically served as a kind of buffer between the Russian and Hapsburg empires and was rife with political intrigue. Although he pursued a career in literature rather than in the vi-

sual arts, Buczkowski brought to his writing a great sense of the pictorial, which shows up handsomely in *Wertepy*. Its publication in book form was delayed by the war and by the reservations of doctrinaire communist critics in the immediate postwar period concerning its unorthodox narrative techniques. *Wertepy* finally appeared in 1947. New editions came out in 1957 and 1973.

A veteran of the campaign against the Germans in September 1939 and later of the partisan fighting in southeastern Poland as well as the Warsaw Uprising of 1944, Buczkowski knew war at first hand and drew on his experiences for most of his subsequent writing. His first postwar novel, *Czarny potok* (*Black Torrent*), first appeared in 1954 and has become his most famous. It is also his only work available in English. Depicting the partisan warfare against the Germans in Podole from June 1941 to 1943 in stark, unsentimental, and unheroic terms, and with particular attention to the Jewish aspect of the fighting, the novel is notable for the same fragmented and disharmonious narrative technique used by Buczkowski so effectively in *Wertepy*. There is also an important symbolic nexus in the work between the destruction of the communities ravaged by the Germans and the destruction by Buczkowski of traditional novelistic form.

Black Torrent was followed by a sequel, the novel *Dorycki krużganek* (The Doric Cloister, 1957), an outstanding piece of fiction in its own right; *Młody poeta w zamku* (The Young Poet in the Castle, 1959), a quasi-collection of stories anticipating Buczkowski's curious *Uroda na czasie* (Charm in Time, 1970), his sole postwar text unrelated to World War II and composed entirely of fragments of conversations that Polish scholars subsequently exposed as mostly authentic from both Polish and French nineteenth-century sources; *Pierwsza świetność* (First Splendor, 1966), which deals with the Bełżec concentration camp and is woven together almost entirely of monologues of the murderers and the victims; *Kąpiele w Lucca* (The Baths at Lucca, 1974), in which Buczkowski skillfully employs the technique of collage for the purpose of developing a synthetic view of European history and culture; and two "supplements" (so termed by Buczkowski) to *Kąpiele w Lucca: Oficer na nieszporach* (An Officer at Vespers, 1975) and *Kamień w pieluszkach* (A Stone in Diapers, 1978).

Translations: *Black Torrent*, trans. David Welsh (Cambridge, Mass.: MIT Press, 1969).

Bukovčan, Ivan (1921–1975) Slovak playwright. A mildly entertaining, "comfortable" dramatist who never challenged the political realities of his time and place, Bukovčan was a lawyer by training who also worked as an editor and a film director. As a creative writer, he is known mostly for the Slovak specificity of such plays as *Surovô drevo* (Raw Wood, 1954), which is notable for its use of songs and dances from the Slovak Tatra Mountain area; *Hl'adanie v oblakoch* (Searching in the Clouds, 1961), a psychological drama about small-town Slovak life on the eve of World War II; *Pštrosí večierok* (The Ostrich Party, 1967); and *Kým kohút nezaspieva* (Before the Cock Crows, 1969). In 1972 Bukovčan broke out of his own mold with *Prvý deň karnevalu* (The First Day of the Carnival), which took critics and theater-goers alike by surprise with its exotic Latin American anticapitalist revolutionary setting. The play was, in fact, inspired by Bukovčan's experiences in Cuba, where he lived for half a year in 1963 and which also served as the basis for his book of Cuban reportage, *Kuba bez brady* (Cuba Without a Beard, 1963). In such subsequent plays as *Slučka pre dvoch* (A Noose for Two, 1967); *Takmer božský omyl* (An Almost Divine Mistake, 1971); *Sneh nad limbou* (Snow on the Cedar Pines, 1974); and *Luigiho*

serdce (Luigi's Heart, 1974), ironically subtitled "An American Buffonade," Bukovčan widened his perspective yet again by addressing problems of more universal concern in the contemporary world. The grotesque *Luigiho serdce* is perhaps the most interesting and timely of this group in that it deals with rival claims for the use for a possible transplant of the heart of a gangster of Italian origin who is sentenced to die in the electric chair. Not long before his death in 1975 Bukovčan published the film script *Deň, ktorý neumrie* (The Day Which Will Not Die); his last play, *Mirage* (Fatamorgana), appeared posthumously in 1977.

Translations: *Before the Cock Crows* (Budapest: Centre Hongrois de l'I. I. T., 1977). VIDEO RECORDING: A videocassette of Ivan Bukovčan and Jiri Weiss (screenwriters), *Zabelec/The Coward* [from an original story by Bukovčan] (Chicago: Facets Video, 1966), is available.

Bulatović, Miodrag (b. 1930) Serbian novelist and short-story writer. A native of Montenegro, Bulatović had little formal education and is said not to have read his first full-length book until the age of sixteen. The impression made on him by this experience was such that he at once made up his mind to become a writer. His own first book, a collection of stories titled *Djavoli dolaze* (The Devils Are Coming, 1955), demonstrated a characteristic predilection for the offbeat, even bizarre, and a keen interest in marginal social types. *Djavoli dolaze* was followed by the "poeticized" novel *Vuk i zvono* (The Wolf and the Bell, 1958). Bulatović's fondness for the poetic and fantastic evident in this work is asserted even more strikingly in *Crveni petao leti prema nebu* (*The Red Cock Flies to Heaven*, 1959), a modern-day legend about a wretched Montenegran Muslim peasant named Muharem and the red cockerel that is eventually taken from him. Montenegro is also the setting of

Bulatović's best-known novel, *Heroj na magarcu* (*Hero on a Donkey*, 1965), but fantasy here gives way to the graphic realism of Montenegro under Italian occupation during World War II. Big, burly, and raunchy, *Hero on a Donkey* for some time seems a lighthearted treatment of a fairly benign Italian military presence in a Montenegran town. Interaction between the Italians and the Montenegran townspeople is casual, often amusing, and the Italians seem far more interested in sex than heroics. As in *The Red Cock Flies to Heaven*, Bulatović's protagonist is again a simple man—in this instance, a bar-cum-brothel-keeper named Malić—whom nobody takes seriously. But Malić metamorphoses into an ardent Marxist and a supporter of the partisans, who gradually close in on the Italians. In the aftermath of Malić's comico-serious transformation, the novel acquires a previously negligible nationalism as the Italians are finally brutally vanquished by the Yugoslav communist partisans.

Bulatović sought to repeat the success of *Hero on a Donkey* with a sequel, *Rat je bio bolji* (*The War Was Better*, 1968). But despite the reappearance of a now almost formulaic ribaldry, a frolicsome Italian military, and the new Marxist Malić, the sprawling almost phantasmagoric novel about the postwar communized Slavic "invasion" of Europe spearheaded by Malić is ultimately less successful than *Hero on a Donkey*—doomed, in a sense, by its own exhibitionism. Bulatović's less familiar literary works include the novels *Ljudi sa četiri prsta* (People with Four Fingers, 1975) and *Gullo Gullo* (1983); the short-story collection *Najveća tajna sveta: Izabrane pripovetka* (The Greatest Secret in the World: Collected Stories, 1971); two works of a romantic nature, *Jahač nad jahačima: Moje istrgnute ljubavne stranice* (Rider Above Riders: My Torn Out Pages of Love, 1983) and *Od ljubavi* (From Love, 1984); and *Godo je došao* (Godo Has Come, 1965), a takeoff on Beckett's *Waiting for Godot*. Bulatović eventually settled in Ljubljana, Slovenia.

Literature: Jevrem Brković, *Pjesnik s potjernice* (Zagreb: Aurora, 1997); Horst Bienek, *Borges, Bulatović, Canetti: Drei Gespräche* (Munich: Hauser, 1965), interviews (in German) with Bulatović and two famous writers.

Translations: *Hero on a Donkey*, trans. E. D. Goy (London: Secker & Warburg, 1966); *The Red Cock Flies to Heaven*, trans. E. D. Goy (New York: Geis, 1962); *The War Was Better*, trans. B. S. Brusar, adapted by Michael Wolfert (New York: McGraw-Hill, 1968).

Bulić, Vanja (b. 1947) Serbian journalist, television and film scriptwriter, and novelist. Bulić's journalistic writing has appeared mostly in the magazine *Duga*. His report of a ten-day siege during the Bosnian War, which grew into the novel *Tunel: Lepa sela lepo gore* (The Tunnel: Pretty Village, Pretty Flame, 1995), was first published there. The novel describes the Muslim siege of six Serbian soldiers trapped in a tunnel. Three of them escape. The focus is mostly on the Serb Milan and his prewar Muslim friend, Halil, from the same town, whom he now regards as a mortal enemy. Full of hatred for Muslims, Milan seeks to kill a wounded Muslim soldier in the same hospital where he has been taken but exhausts himself trying to reach him and bleeds to death. The novel, and even more graphically the highly successful 1996 film based on it directed by Srdjan Dragojević, spares none of the brutalities and atrocities committed by both sides as it targets the senselessness of the long-standing ethnic and religious hatreds from which the Bosnian conflict arose. In his newest work, *RS: Ratna sreća* (Remembrance of War, 2002), Bulić extends his deep interest in the Balkan wars of the 1990s into Serbia in the period after the Dayton Accords. His focus is on war profiteers in Belgrade and the new morality of exploitation and profit. The novel was published in the new series Dosije 011 (Dossier 011), which specializes in crime novels with contemporary Belgrade settings.

Bulka, Nonda (pseudonym Chri-Chri; 1906–1972) Albanian short-story writer. Bulka was born in the village of Leuse in the Përmet district. He studied in the French high school in Korçë and later in France. After his return from France, he taught Albanian and French language and literature in secondary schools, later becoming a professor of linguistics and literature at Tirana University. Although he continued writing up to the time of his death, Bulka's literary career developed mostly in the 1930s and 1940s, when his best work was written. Liberal and democratic in his outlook, Bulka ran afoul of the conservative regime of King Zog and in 1937 was interned for a while in a village deep in central Albania. A talented short-story and sketch writer, often inclined to satire, Bulka became well known for his lean, trenchant pieces illuminating the plight of the underprivileged in his country. A number of these were published in the volume *Kur qan e qesh bilbili* (When the Nightingale Cries and Laughs, 1934). His scorn was directed not only against the Zog regime, but against the conservative bourgeoisie whom he also held responsible for the status quo. Some of Bulka's indignation was reserved for those Albanian writers who seemed to be indifferent to the deteriorating social and economic conditions around them, tending instead to paint idealized pictures of the tribal and patriarchal way of life of the Albanian mountaineers. Bulka adopted as well an anticlerical stance in light of what he regarded as the reactionary policies of Albanian religious institutions at the time. Some of his pithiest sketches on the Muslim establishment in Albania are in the form of fables—a genre Bulka was

fond of—among them "Religious Mysticism" (1934).

A witness to the frantic efforts to forestall war in the 1930s and the Italian invasion of Albania on 7 April 1939, Bulka wrote about these events, as in the short-story collections *Skica dhe tregime* (Sketches and Short Stories, 1950) and *Në dritën e yllit* (In the Starlight, 1952) and in the volume of poems *Vargje satirike* (Satirical Verse, 1951), with irony and satire. After World War II and the communist rise to power in Albania, Bulka welcomed the new regime and sang the praises of its accomplishments in a number of pieces published in the periodical press, especially in the weekly *Hosteni*, of which he was one of the founders. In addition to his stories and sketches, published in such volumes as *Soditje* (Contemplation, 1957); *Maska të çjerra* (Torn Masks, 1966); and *Tregime të zgjedhura* (Selected Short Stories, 1972), Bulka wrote critical studies of Albanian and European writers, among them Naim Freshëri, Girolamo De Rada, Ando Zako Çajupi, Fan Noli, Migjeni (acronym of Millosh Gjergj Nikolla), Shakespeare, Cervantes, Diderot, Hugo, and Gorky. He also translated works by Balzac, Zola, Gorky, and Mark Twain. His collected works (*Vepra letrare*) appeared in a new edition in 1980.

Translations: *Sketches and Short Stories* (Tirana: 8 Nëntori, 1984).

Burmeister, Brigitte (b. 1940) German novelist, short-story writer, and literary scholar. Burmeister's first novel, *Anders oder Vom Aufenthalt in der Fremde* (Anders, or From a Stay Abroad), became a literary sensation in the German Democratic Republic after its publication in 1988. The novel takes its name from its narrator and principal character, David Anders (the name means "different" in German), a government employee who starts a new job in Berlin at the beginning of the year. The novel has fifty-three chapters, corresponding to the weeks of the year, and the first and last chapters are identical, as a new year begins. Anders appears to spend most of his spare time writing the text, which forms the novel, ostensibly "letters" to his family at home, but it is more reminiscent of a diary. He meets an author who encourages him, and at the end of the year he moves on to a new job. But such is the mystification of the text that nothing can be taken for granted, especially as concerns the role of the only real friends Anders seems to make in Berlin, a couple identified as "D" and his wife.

Essentially an experiment with the form and structure of the novel, and clearly aimed at GDR literary norms, *Anders oder Vom Aufenthalt in der Fremde* owes much to the French *nouveau roman* (Alain Robbe-Grillet, in particular). Burmeister brought to her novel a fine knowledge of the *nouveau roman*. From 1967 to 1983, she worked at the Central Institute for Literary History in Berlin, where she studied post– World War II French literature. Her academic research led, in fact, to a scholarly study of the *nouveau roman: Streit um den Nouveau Roman: Eine andere Literatur und ihre Leser* (Dispute over the *Nouveau Roman*: A Different Literature and Its Reader, 1983). Burmeister was also an authority on women's literature in France in the 1970s. In 1991, with Margarete Mitscherlich, she published *Wir haben ein Berührungstabu* (We Have a Taboo About Touching), which deals entirely with women's issues.

Burmeister returned to fiction in the mid-1990s. In 1994 she published a second novel, *Unter den Names Norma* (Under the Name Norma); in 1995, a collection of short stories, *Herbstfeste* (Autumn Festivals); and in 1999, another novel, *Pollok und die Attentäerin* (Pollok and the Lady Assassin).

Literature: "Brigitte Burmeister," in *Literary Intellectuals and the Dissolution of the State: Professionalism and Conformity in the GDR,* ed. Robert von Hallberg, trans. Kenneth J. Northcott (Chicago: University of Chicago Press, 1996), 125–33.

Buzea, Constanța (b. 1941) Romanian poet. A native of Bucharest, Buzea studied Romanian literature at Bucharest University from 1963 to 1969. After 1973 she worked as an editor for the journals *Amfiteatru* and *Viața studențească,* and in more recent times has held the post of editor for poetry and prose at *România literară.* Buzea made her literary debut in 1957 with several poems published in the collective work *Tînărul scriitor* (The Young Writer). Her first book of verse, *De pe pămînt* (From the Earth), was published in 1963. She has since published more than a dozen volumes, among them *La ritmul naturii* (Tuned to the Rhythm of Nature, 1966); *Norii* (The Clouds, 1968); *Agonice* (Agony, 1970); *Coline* (Hills, 1970); *Sala nervilor* (The Hall of Nerves, 1971); *Răsad de spini* (Thorny Seedlings, 1973); *Pasteluri* (Pastels, 1974); *Ape cu plute* (Rivers and Rafts, 1975); *Limanul orei* (Haven of the Hour, 1976); *Poeme* (Poems, 1977); *Ploi de piatră* (Rains of Stone, 1979); *Umbră pentru cer* (Shade for the Sky, 1981); *Cină bogată în viscol* (Supper Rich in Blizzard, 1983); *Planta memoria* (Plant Memory, 1985); *Cheia închisă* (The Locked Key, 1987); and *Pietre sălbatice* (Wild Stones, 1988). Buzea has also written books for children. A poet of exquisite delicacy and quiet modernity, Buzea often writes about human mortality, fear, loneliness, the bitterness in her soul, feelings of helplessness, the fragility and transitoriness of love, and the need for defenses against harsh reality. She finds such defenses in indifference, the complex allure of the word, and the sense that somehow even the bleakest moments harbor a remote hope of positive regeneration. Of particular note in her poetry are the often haunting images of nature that interwines and interacts with the destiny of man. As one Romanian critic put it, writing of Buzea's poetry, she has submitted herself to "imprisonment in gravity." In 1972 Buzea won the Writers Union Prize, and in 1974 the Mihai Eminescu Prize of the Romanian Academy.

Translations: *Tip of the Iceberg,* trans. Sergiu Celac (Bucharest: Eminescu, 1986), the best collection of Buzea's poetry in English; six poems in *An Anthology of Contemporary Romanian Poetry,* trans. Andrea Deletant and Brenda Walker (London: Forest, 1984), 31–36; ten poems in *Silent Voices: An Anthology of Contemporary Romanian Women Poets,* trans. Andrea Deletant and Brenda Walker (London: Forest, 1986), 37–47.

Buzura, Augustin (b. 1938) Romanian novelist. One of post–World War II Romania's most respected writers, Buzura was born in the village of Berinţa. He attended secondary school in Baia Mare, in northwestern Romania, subsequently earning a degree in medicine at Cluj University. He specialized in psychiatry. Buzura made his literary debut in 1963 with a volume of stories under the title *Capul Bunei Speranţe* (The Cape of Good Hope). It was followed in 1966 by another collection of stories, *De ce zboară vulturul?* (Why Does the Vulture Soar?). After these two volumes, Buzura devoted himself exclusively to the novel. In fairly rapid succession, he published the six novels that form the basis of his considerable reputation: *Absenţii* (The Absent, 1970); *Feţele tăcerii* (Faces of Silence, 1974); *Orgolii* (The Haughty, 1977); *Vocile nopţii* (Night Voices, 1980); *Refugii* (*Refuges,* 1984); and *Drumul cenuşii* (The Road of Ashes, 1988), the last two of which constitute his novelistic cycle: *Zidul morţii* (The Wall of Death). In 1981 Buzura published a volume of essays, *Bloc-Notes.* Confessional in nature, they attest to Buzura's inellectual nonconformity.

Beginning with *Absenţii,* Buzura's novels are characterized by his deep interest in psychology and a heavy use of first-person narrative and interior monologue, as the lead characters indulge in seemingly endless self-analysis. Typical among them are Mihai Bogdan, the doctor who stands at the center of *Absenţii,* and the woman in *Refugii* who is taken to a mental hospital after the breakup of her marriage and an automobile accident. The hospital in this case serves as the "refuge" in which the heroine, under the supervision of a sympathetic physician (a commonplace in Buzura's fiction), gradually overcomes partial amnesia and regains a sense of self-worth, enabling her to reenter society.

Translations: *Refuges,* trans. Ancuta Vultur and Fred Nadaban, rev. Andrei Bantaş (Bucharest: Editura Fundatiei Culturale Romane, 1993; Boulder, Colo.: East European Monographs, 1994). *Drumul cenuşii* is available in French as *Chemin des cendres,* trans. Jean-Louis Courriol (Montricher: Noir sur blanc, 1993).

C

Camaj, Martin (1925–1992) Albanian poet, novelist, and linguistic scholar. One of postwar Albania's most esteemed lyric poets, Camaj was born in Temali in the mountainous northern region of Albania known as Dukagjin, which provides the setting of a number of his many poems. He received a classical education at the Jesuit school of Shkodër (Xaverianum) and pursued university studies in Belgrade and Rome. While teaching Albanian in Italy, he earned a degree in linguistics at Rome University in 1960. Camaj lived abroad for most of his life, first in Italy and then in Munich, where he taught Albanian studies at Munich University from 1970 to 1990. In his Italian period, Camaj was active as editor of the Italo-Albanian journal *Shêjzat,* to which almost all the authors of the Albanian literary community in Italy contributed. *Shêjzat* was managed by Ernest Koliqi (1903–1975), an

Albanian writer of the older generation. Camaj's literary career had three major facets: lyric poetry, novels, and scholarly works on the Albanian language. His major collections of lyrics include *Një fyell ndër male* (A Flute in the Mountains, 1953), published in Priština, Kosovo; *Kënga e vërrinit* (Song of the Lowland Pastures, 1954), also published in Priština; *Legjenda* (Legend, 1964), published in Rome, and *Lirika mes dy moteve* (Lyrics Between Two Seasons, 1967), published in Munich, both containing revised versions of poems published previously in *Kënga e vërrinit*; *Njeriu me vete e me tjerë* (Man by Himself and with Others, 1978); *Dranja* (The Tortoise, 1981), a collection of prose poems published in Munich; and *Poezi, 1953–1967* (Poems, 1953–1967, 1981), a retrospective collection of poems published in Munich. Much of Camaj's early poetry is a kind of nostalgic evocation of the northern Albanian landscape and lore of his origins, from which he had long been separated by his exile. His later poetry, while still often drawing inspiration from his Albanian homeland, shows evidence of a broadening of horizons and a greater tendency toward obscurity. It also reveals the influence, in particular, of the Italian poet Giuseppe Ungaretti (1888–1970), whose classes at Rome University Camaj attended. Camaj wrote three novels: *Djella* (1959), published in Rome, a romantic tale in mixed prose and verse about a schoolteacher who falls in love with a village girl from the lowland country who eventually marries someone else; *Rrathë* (Rings, 1978), published in Munich, an interesting psychological novel about the impact of the Albanian mountain landscape and its mythology on a visiting writer and agronomist; and *Karpa* (1987), published in Munich, a parable of sorts set in Camaj's native Dukagjin region in the year 2338. Camaj's collection, *Shkundullima* (The Earthquake, 1981), contains five short stories and one play.

Apart from his lyric poetry and prose fiction, Camaj did extensive work on the Albanian language. Between 1966 and 1984, he published four studies in Germany: *Albanische Wortbildung: Die Bildungsweise der alteren Nomina* (Word Building in Albanian: The Structure of Older Nouns, 1966); *Lehrbuch der albanischen Sprache* (A Grammar of the Albanian Language, 1969); *Die albanische Mundart von Falconara Albanese in der Provinz Cosenza* (The Albanian Dialect of Falconara Albanese in the Cosenza Province, 1977); and, in English, *Albanian Grammar: With Exercises, Chrestomathy and Glossaries* (1984). The last work is a translation by Leonard Fox, the principal translator of Camaj's poetry into English, of an unpublished manuscript. Camaj's collected works (*Vepra letrare*) in five volumes were published in Tirana in 1997.

Literature: Koci Petriti, *Në poetiken e Martin Camajt: Studim* (Tirana: Dita, 1997).

Translations: *Palimpsest,* trans. Leonard Fox (New York: Camaj, 1991), a sixty-three-page collection of Camaj's poetry; *Selected Poetry,* trans. Leonard Fox (New York: New York University Press, 1990), an excellent Albanian–English edition of a good selection of Camaj's poetry.

Caraion, Ion (real name Stelian Diaconescu; 1923–1985) Romanian poet, essayist, and translator. Born into extreme poverty in the small village of Rușavăţ (Buzău district), whose contradictions he has alluded to in his writing, Caraion left it in order to pursue his education in Bucharest. He received his degree from the Faculty of Literature and Philosophy of Bucharest University in 1948. It was in the capital during World War II that he made his literary debut both as a poet and as a journalist. He was the author of sixteen volumes of verse, two of them for children, five volumes of essays, and several volumes of translations from twentieth-century American, Canadian, and French poetry. A greatly gifted poet with a fierce sense of independence and an utter contempt for totalitarianism in any form, Caraion paid heavily for his unwillingness to compromise his independence. His first volume, *Panopticum* (1943), was suppressed by the censors. Fearing arrest by the Gestapo for anti-German articles, he went into hiding for a while. In 1951, when Romania was already under communist control, he voluntarily surrendered the editorial position he held at *Scînteia tineretului,* the journal of the Communist Youth Union, because of his staunch refusal to renounce articles critical of the cultural policies of the new regime. He was arrested and sentenced to death; his wife, Valentina, who had been arrested with him, was given a five-year sentence because she had typed his poetry. Two years later, Caraion's sentence was commuted to eleven years of hard labor. He was freed in the political thaw of 1964. But his manuscripts were destroyed, he was kept under close surveillance, and it was extremely difficult for him to publish anything. Finally, in 1981, Caraion and his family went into voluntary exile, settling in Lausanne, Switzerland. He died four years later.

Caraion's several books of poetry published after *Panopticum* include *Omul profilat pe cer* (Man Outlined Against the Sky, 1945); *Cîntece negre* (Black Songs, 1946); *Eseu* (Essay, 1966); *Dimineața nimănui* (Nobody's Morning, 1967); *Neconoscutul ferestrelor* (The One Unknown to the Windows, 1969); *Cîrtiță și aproapele* (The Mole and His Kin, 1970); *Deasupra deasuprelor* (Above the Above, 1970); *Cimitirul din stele* (The Graveyard in the Stars, 1970); *Selene și Pan* (Selene and Pan, 1971); *Munții de os* (The Mountains of Bone, 1972); *Frunzele în Galaad* (The Leaves in Galahad, 1973); *Poeme* (Poems, 1974); *Lacrimi perpendiculare* (Perpendicular Tears, 1978); *Interogarea magilor* (The Interrogation of the Magi,

1978); *Cîntecul Singurei/Le Chant de l'Unique* (The Song of Solitude, 1979), a Romanian–French edition with a preface by the poet and critic Ov. S. Crohmălniceanu; *Dragostea e pseudonimul morții* (Love Is Death's Pseudonym, 1980); and *Apa de apoi* (The Water of Afterwards, 1991), published posthumously in an edition edited by Emil Manu. His best-known books of poetry for children, which provide glimpses into another side of Caraion's personality, are *Marta, fată cu povești în palme* (Marta, the Girl with Stories in Her Hands, 1974); *O ureche de dulceața și-o ureche de pelin* (Ear of Jam and Ear of Wormwood, 1976); and *Lucrurile de dimineața* (The Morning Things, 1978).

Caraion's voluminous prose writing was largely essayistic. It comprises such collections as *Duelul cu crinii* (Duel with Lilies, 1972); *Enigmatica noblețe* (The Enigmatic Nobility, 1974); *Pălărierul silabelor* (The Hatter of Syllables, 1976); and the posthumously published *Tristețe și cărți* (Sorrow and Books, 1995). Two of his collections of essays are devoted to other Romanian artists: *Masa tăcerii: Simposion de metafore la Brancuși* (The Table of Silence: A Symposium of Metaphors in the Work of Brancuși, 1970) deals with the celebrated Romanian sculptor Constantin Brancuși (1876–1957); *Bacovia: Sfîrșitul continuu* (Bacovia: The Continuous Ending, 1977) addresses the work of George Bacovia (1881–1957), one of the great Romanian poets of the twentieth century. Many of Caraion's most incisive thoughts on literature are to be found in his essay collection *Jurnal I: Literatură și contraliteratură* (Journal: Literature and Contra-Literature, 1980). *Insectele tovarășului Hitler* (Comrade Hitler's Insects, 1982) is a collection of sociopolitical pamphlets of a passionately antitotalitarian nature.

The surreal strangeness of much of Caraion's poetry is magnified by the circumstances in which it was written. Denied writing implements in prison, he could only compose poems in his own mind and then reconstruct and revise them years later, after he had been freed. Many of his poems are undated, and some were reprinted several times in different collections. Thus establishing an accurate chronology for Caraion's poetry is all but impossible, precluding any serious study of the evolution of his style and thought. However, the defiance and accusatory exuberance of his early poetry give way under the influence of his years of confinement to an understandable preoccupation with themes of isolation, desolation, solitude, and silence—as he writes, for example, in the poem "Vîntul şi zăpada" ("Wind and Snow"):

> Out of your mountains I made a
>   solitude
> thicker than freeze,
> thicker than solitude.

Caraion's indictment of his own time and place extends to the century as a whole, which he conveys through recurring images of death, putrefaction, and burial. The age is one hospitable only to lies and deceit, and the truth carries a terrible price.

An able translator of poetry and prose from French, Russian, and English, Caraion translated such English and American writers as Daniel Defoe, Mary Webb, Ezra Pound, Malcolm Lowry, and Edgar Lee Masters's *Spoon River Anthology*. He also published an anthology of contemporary Canadian poetry in 1978.

Translations: *The Error of Being: Poems*, trans. Marguerite Dorian and Elliott B. Urdang (London: Forest, 1994), a Romanian–English edition of *Greşeala de a fi* (*The Error of Being*); *Ion Caraion: Poems*, trans. Marguerite Dorian and Elliott B. Urdang (Athens: Ohio University Press, 1981).

Cârdu, Petru (b. 1952) Romanian poet and translator. Born in Vršac, Yugoslavia, of Romanian parents, Cârdu studied literature in Belgrade and history and theater in Bucharest. His first volume of poetry, *Menire în doi* (Double Meaning), appeared in 1970, followed by *Aducătorul ochiului* (The Bringer of the Eye) in 1974, *Pronume* (Book of the Year) in 1981, and *Capşuna in capcană* (*The Trapped Strawberry*) in 1988. In 1980 he was elected Young Poet of the Year at the Festival of Titograd. Cârdu also won a reputation for his translations of drama and prose as well as poetry. He has worked for Novi Sad (Yugoslavia) Radio as an interviewer and a critic and established the European Prize for Literature.

As a poet, Cârdu favors short forms, sometimes consisting of only a few lines, and a lexical and syntactic clarity that initially creates the impression of simplicity. But the simplicity is only outward and deceptive. An heir to the tenacious tradition of Romanian poetic surrealism, Cârdu conjures up tantalizingly provocative images drawn from classical antiquity to contemporary Serbian painting and covering a broad palette of European culture. Frequently compared with Rimbaud, Cârdu invokes the French poet in a few poems as well as writers as disparate as Isaac Babel, Jorge Luis Borges, Christine Ebner, and Yukio Mishima. However, his use of recognizable cultural and historical motifs is playful rather than overbearing, and where the personal voice of the poet makes an appearance the intrusion is usually accompanied by irony and humor. The provocativeness and elusiveness of Cârdu's style show up in a typical poem such as "Wind Speed," from *The Trapped Strawberry*:

> I seek an erotic asylum
> penetrating her through the attic
> in which a friend of mine
> exiled to sit among the walls of that
>   room
> is doing a tattoo of his poems

on his blushing penis.
radio reports
wind speed normal.

That Cârdu's irony and humor can extend even to contemporary politics is evident in another poem from *The Trapped Strawberry,* "The art of seizing windows":

New migrations begin
Jerusalem is moving to Constantinople
the NATO point of view has ideas to
    discourage
doubts
I'm smoking a peace pipe at an
    international
conference on the rose
this significant step aims at extending
the east–west dialogue
martial law in a glass of water
imposed in Greenwich at tea time in
    February . . .

Translations: *The Trapped Strawberry: Poems by Petru Cârdu,* trans. Brenda Walker and Dušica Marinkov, with an introduction by Daniel Weissbort (London: Forest, 1990), which includes translations from Cârdu's Serbo-Croatian as well as Romanian verse.

Cărtărescu, Mircea (b. 1956) Romanian poet and prose writer. The most prominent Romanian writer to emerge from the 1980s, and one often placed on the same level as the Serb Milorad Pavić and the Hungarian Péter Esterházy, Cărtărescu attended secondary school in his native Bucharest and in 1980 graduated from Bucharest University, where he had studied in the Faculty of Letters. In 1999 he received his doctorate with a thesis on Romanian postmodernism; an impressive, incisive study, it was published, also in 1999, as a nearly 600-page book under the title *Postmodernismul românesc.* From 1980 to 1989, he taught Romanian in a secondary school, subsequently joining the administra-

tion of the Writers Union and serving as editor of the review *Caiete critice.* He is now a lecturer in the Faculty of Letters of Bucharest University. Cărtărescu first appeared in print in 1978 with poetry published in the journal *România literară.* His first book, the poetry collection *Faruri, vitrine, fotografii* (Headlights, Shop Windows, Photos), appeared two years later. It was followed by six more poetry collections: *Aer cu diamante* (Air with Diamonds, 1982), an anthology of poetry together with the writers Traian T. Coșovei, Florian Iaru, and Ion Stratan; *Poeme de amor* (Love Poems, 1983); *Totul* (Everything, 1985); *Levantul* (The Levantine, 1990); *Dragostea* (Love, 1982); and *Dublu CD* (Double CD, 1998). *Visul* (The Dream), Cărtărescu's first major work of prose, appeared in 1989; it was reprinted in 1993 and in 1997 with a new title, *Nostalgia.* A dazzling postmodernist performance of extraordinary imagination and inventiveness, encompassing a writer's dream to become Everything, a Creator who will in time replace the universe, *Visul* has been translated into several languages and earned Cărtărescu a formidable reputation. It was followed by two novels, *Travesti* (In Disguise, 1994) and *Orbitor: Aripa stîngă* (Dazzling: The Left Wing, 1996), and an essay, *Visul chimeri: Subteranele poeziei eminesciene* (The Chimeric Dream: Subterranean Elements in the Poetry of Eminescu, 1992). The many prizes that Cătărescu has received include the Writers Union Prize for a first book of poetry (1980); the poetry award of the literary review *Flacăra* (1980); the Prize of the Romanian Academy for *Visul* (1989); the Writers Union Prize for Poetry (1990); the poetry award of the Romanian Academy for *Levantul* (1990); the prize of the Writers Union and that of the Association of Professional Writers in Romania (ASPRO) for *Travesti* (1994); and the Prize of the Writers Union of the Republic of Moldova (1994). In 1992 he was nominated for the Medicis Prize for the best foreign book published in France and, in 1993, for the award of the Latin Union.

Translations: Five poems in *Young Poets of a New Romania: An Anthology,* trans. Brenda Walker with Michaela Celea-Leach, ed. Ion Stoica (London: Forest, 1991), 27–32; excerpt from *Visul,* trans. Florin Bican, in *Description of a Struggle: The Vintage Book of Contemporary Eastern European Writing,* ed. Michael March (New York: Vintage, 1994), 235–41; "The Game" (from *Visul*), trans. Georgiana Farnoagă and Sharon King, in *Romanian Fiction of the '80s and '90s: A Concise Anthology,* ed. Calin Vlasie (Pitești: Mediana, 1999), 60–105.

Cassian, Nina (real name Renée Annie Ştefănescu; b. 1924) Romanian poet. One of Romania's most gifted, productive, and widely known contemporary poets, Cassian was born in the Danubian city of Galaţi. When she was eleven, her family moved to Bucharest where she attended secondary school, first at the fashionable Pompilian Institute and then at a high school for Jewish girls, to which she was forced to transfer by the right-wing Romanian authorities. It was while still a student that she became an ardent communist. One of her earliest poems was published in the Communist Party journal, *România liberă,* in 1945. She published her first book of poetry, *La scara 1/1* (On the Scale of 1:1), in 1948. The volume was inspired by her intense reading of such pre–World War II French and Romanian surrealists as Max Jacob, Guillaume Apollinaire, Ion Barbu, and Urmuz (Demetru Demetrescu-Buzău). But it was precisely Cassian's indebtedness to the different strands of surrealism in her first book that brought down the wrath of the communist authorities, who attacked her savagely and compelled her to seek out different means of expression. Her four books of poetry after *La scara 1/1*—*Sufletul nostru* (Our Soul, 1949); *An viu, nouă sute şi şaptesprezece* (Vital Year, 1917, 1949);

Horea nu mai este singur (Horea Not Alone Any More, 1952); and *Tinereţe* (Youth, 1953)—were clearly written to please the Party by showing conformity to the doctrine of socialist realism. After that—apart from children's books, which provided an outlet for her rich imagination—Cassian virtually stopped writing poetry. The volume *Versuri alese* (Selected Poems, 1955) is a collection of previously published verse, much of which Cassian has since rejected.

After Stalin's death and during the short-lived Romanian literary thaw of 1965 to 1970, Cassian had an extraordinary period of creativity, producing such collections as *Virstele anului* (The Measures of the Year, 1957); *Dialogul vîntului cu marea* (Dialogue of the Wind and the Sea, 1957); *Spectacol in aer liber—o monografie a dragostei* (Spectacle in the Open Air—A Monograph of Love, 1961); *Să ne facem daruri* (Let's Give Each Other Presents, 1963); *Disciplina harfei* (The Discipline of the Harp, 1964); *Singele* (The Blood, 1966); *Destinele paralele* (Parallel Destinies, 1967); *Ambitus* (Ambit, 1969); and *Cronofagie* (Time Devouring, 1969), a collection of poems written between 1944 and 1969. But even the return of more repressive conditions in Romania in the 1970s could no longer seriously diminish Cassian's poetic output. Between 1971 and 1983, she published another nine volumes of poetry: *Recviem* (Requiem, 1971); *Marea conjugare* (The Big Conjugation, 1971); *Loto-poeme* (Lotto Poems, 1972); *Suave* (Suave, 1974); *Spectacol in aer liber* (Spectacle in the Open Air: Selected Love Poems, 1974); *O sută de poeme* (One Hundred Poems, 1975); *Viraje* (Orbits, 1978); *De indurare* (For Mercy, 1981); and *Numărătoarea inversă* (Count Down, 1983), her last book of poetry to be published in Romania.

In 1985 Cassian received a Fulbright Fellowship to teach creative writing as a visiting professor at New York University for the academic year 1985/1986. While in the United

States, she learned of the arrest in Romania of her friend, the writer Gheorge Ursu, and that verses by her satirizing the regime of Nicolae Ceaușescu had been found among his papers. Ursu died of torture, and Cassian resolved to seek political asylum in the United States, which she received. As Cassian's poetry became better known in English, she was invited to give a number of readings. Apart from the two she gave at New York University in 1985 and 1986, she appeared with Czesław Miłosz in Berkeley, California, in 1986; again in New York City the same year at a PEN-sponsored public discussion with Stanley Kunitz; at the Cornelia Street Café in New York City in 1987; and at the University of Iowa and at Northern University in Cedar Falls, Iowa, in 1987. Cassian also held a Yaddo Fellowship in the summer of 1986, was a special guest at the 1986 PEN Congress, and participated in the International Writing Program at Iowa University in 1987. In her native Romania, she was awarded the State Prize in 1952, the Writers Union Prize in 1964 and 1983, and the Writers Association of Bucharest Prize in 1982.

Cassian's great appeal as a poet lies in her extraordinary range, her vivacity and sensuality, her wit, her fine sense of humor, and the appealing casualness of her style. An intensely personal poet, which she proclaims in a number of poems (for example, "Ars poetica—a polemic"), she also celebrates love, but has no illusions about its potential to cause pain and disappointment. Although most of her poems are small and simple in style, some of her longer poems—such as "Part of a Bird," "The First and Last Night of Love," "Postmeridian," and "Orbits"—are among her best. Cassian has also long been active as a translator, rendering into Romanian the works of such diverse writers as Paul Celan, Christian Morgenstern, Vladimir Mayakovsky, Max Jacob, Guillaume Apollinaire, Iannis Ritsos, and Shakespeare.

Translations: *Blue Apple,* trans. Eva Feiler, Cross-Cultural Review series (Merrick, N.Y.: Cross Cultural Communications, 1981); *Call Yourself Alive? The Love Poems of Nina Cassian,* trans. Andrea Deletant and Brenda Walker (London: Forest, 1988); *Cheerleader for a Funeral: Poems by Nina Cassian,* trans. Brenda Walker with Nina Cassian (London: Forest, 1992); *Lady of Miracles: Poems by Nina Cassian,* trans. Laura Schiff (Berkeley, Calif.: Cloud Marauder Press, 1982); *Life Sentence: Selected Poems,* ed. William Jay Smith (New York: Norton, 1990); *Take My Word for It: Poems* (New York: Norton, 1998), which includes primarily poems conceived in English, with the rest translated by Cassian; fifteen poems, including the long "Part of a Bird," in *Silent Voices: An Anthology of Contemporary Romanian Women Poets,* trans. Andrea Deletant and Brenda Walker (London: Forest, 1986), 49–66.

Čašule, Kole (b. 1921) Macedonian playwright, novelist, short-story writer, and essayist. A native of Prilep, Čašule trained to be a doctor in Belgrade, but his studies were interrupted by World War II. After the war, he combined a literary career with that of a diplomat, serving at various times as Macedonian consul in Canada and ambassador to Bolivia, Peru, and Brazil. His experiences in diplomatic service were recounted in *Proza: 1945–1967* (Prose: 1945–1967, 1968); *Kanadski fragmenti* (Canadian Fragments, 1985); *Konzulski pisma* (Consular Jottings, 1987); and *Novi zapisi* (New Notes, 1989). His first collection of short stories appeared in 1948 under the title *Prvite dni* (The First Days). A second collection, *Raskazi* (Stories), followed in 1953. Čašule, however, is known primarily as a playwright; he has also served as director of the Macedonian National Theater in Skopje. His plays include *Zadruga* (Village Commune, 1950); *Crnila* (*Darkness,* 1962); *Vejka na vetrot* (A Leaf on the Wind),

Gradskiot saat (The City Clock), and *Vitel* (Whirlpool), all published in 1967 in a single volume that also contains *Crnila; Igra ili Socialistička Eva* (The Game or Socialist Eve, 1969); *Partitura za eden Miron* (Partitura for a Certain Miron, 1970); *Sud* (Tribunal, 1980); and *Taka e (ako vi se čini): Antiparabola vo tri dejstvija so prolog i epilog* (So It Is [If You Think So]: An Antiparabola in Three Acts with a Prologue and an Epilogue, 1994).

Better at serious drama than comedy, Časule seems at his best as a playwright in *Vejka na vetrot* and *Darkness*. The first is a bleak work about the problems an immigrant Macedonian worker in the United States encounters when he imports a young bride from his homeland. In *Darkness*, a political play about the Macedonian independence struggle set in Sofia, Bulgaria, in 1921, Časule focuses on the treacherous rivalries among the Macedonians themselves as their major problem. Časule is also the author of the novels *Premreže* (Danger, 1977) and *Prostum* (Upright, 1970), perhaps his most popular work of prose fiction, which has been reprinted several times. Časule has also written several works of nonfiction dealing with Macedonian culture and politics, among them *Zapisi za naciata i literaturata* (Notes on the Nation and Literature, 1985); *Makedonski dilemi* (Macedonian Dilemmas, 1992); and *Rezime za mojata generacija* (A Résumé for My Generation, 1998).

Translations: *Darkness*, trans. Ilija Časule, in *Five Modern Yugoslav Plays*, ed. Branko Mikasinovich (New York: Cyrco, 1977), 268–322; excerpt from *Crnila; Igra ili Socialistička Eva*, trans. Dragan Milivojević, in *Introduction to Yugoslav Literature: An Anthology of Fiction and Poetry*, ed. Branko Mikasinovich, Dragan Milivojević, and Vasa D. Mihailovich (New York: Twayne, 1973), 634–42; "A Macedonian Girl," in *The Big Horse and Other Stories of Modern Macedonia*, ed. Milne Holton (Columbia: University of Missouri Press, 1974), 43–56.

Čejka, Jaroslav (b. 1943) Czech poet, novelist, and critic. Trained as a hydraulic engineeer, Čejka, a Prague native, was long interested in literature, a fact confirmed not only by his writing of poetry, but also by his assumption of the editorship of *Kmen*, the literary supplement of the weekly *Tvorba*, after its founding in 1982 and, in 1987, the chief editorship of *Tvorba* itself. Although he began writing and publishing poems as early as 1964, while employed in a waterworks before his university training as an engineer (1961–1967), his first volume of poetry, *Sentimentálni lásky* (Sentimental Loves), was published in 1979. His next volume, *Veřejné tajemství* (Public Secret, 1980), is also devoted to love, in much the same spirit and tone of unsentimentality as *Sentimentálni lásky*, but this time reflecting the personal experience of the termination of a love affair. With such subsequent books of poems as *Kniha přání a stižnosti* (Book of Requests and Complaints, 1981); *Kapesní sbírka zákonů, vět a definic: Básně z let 1979–1981* (Pocket Collection of Laws, Axioms, and Definitions: Poems from 1979–1981, 1983); *Milování se lví ozvěnou* (Loving with an Echo of Lions, 1985); *Čtení z ruky, aneb, chiromantické básně* (Palm Reading, or, Palmistry Poems, 1986); *Encyklopedické heslo: láska* (Encyclopedia Entry: Love, 1989); *Hotelové povídky* (Hotel Tales, 1989); and *Ryby táhnou proti proudu* (Fish Swim Against the Stream, 1992), Čejka abandoned the regular form and metrics (rhymed verse) of his earlier poetry in favor of free verse. Combining his training as a scientist with his verse writing, Čejka struck a responsive chord in readers by applying the language of physical and natural laws to human relationships in his newer poetry, an approach that, in its humor, some critics have traced to Miroslav Holub. In the cycle "Twelve Laws of the Heart," Čejka considers the laws of gravitation, probability, natural selection, action and reaction, inertia, mixture, conservation of energy, independent motion, and force, as well as Archimedes's principle, Pascal's law, and Ohm's law. Besides his poetry, Čejka has published a novel with a theatrical setting, *Kulisáci: Divadelní romans ukázkami* (Behind the Wings: A Theatrical Romance with Illustrations, 1985); a book of criticism, *Návod jak (ne) sbírat básně* (How [Not] to Compile Poems, 1988); and a memoir, *Aparát* (The Apparatus, 1991). In 1989 Čejka was named head of the cultural section of the Central Committee of the Czech Communist Party, but vacated the position after the November 1989 political changes.

Translations: Thirteen poems in *The New Czech Poetry: Jaroslav Čejka, Michal Černík, Karel Sýs*, trans. Ewald Osers (Newcastle upon Tyne: Bloodaxe, 1988), 13–35.

Černík, Michal (b. 1943) Czech poet. Černík was born in Čelákovice, where he graduated from high school in 1960. In 1964 he received his degree in Czech literature and history at the regional branch of Charles University in Brandýs nad Labem. He taught school for five years after leaving university and then became editor of the journal *Sedmička pionýrů* (1969–1980) and editor in chief of the children's literature division of the Panoráma publishing house (1981–1985). In 1987 he settled in Prague and soon held the position of secretary of the Czech Writers Union; in 1988/1989, he was chairman of the organization. In 1990, after the downfall of the communist regime in Czechoslovakia, he served as editor at the social-democratic publishing house L, then in 1992 at the journal *Vlasta*, and in 1992 and 1993 of the Saturday supplement of *Rudé právo*. In September 1993 he accepted the post of assistant editor in chief of *Vlasta*. Černík's first volume of poetry, *Náhradní krajina* (Spare Landscape), appeared in 1971. The central part of the collection consists of monologues, by inanimate objects or elements of nature, reflecting the poet's intimate relationship with na-

ture and, specifically, the North Bohemian Plain, with the legendary Říp Hill rising from it. A strong sense of family and personal and national identity across the generations runs through much of Černík's writing. Although his style tends toward the sparse, he has also composed several lengthy lyrical-epic cycles evoking the mystique of family and home, among them *Kdybychom nechodili po cestách* (If We Hadn't Walked the Roads, 1976); *Sklízeň srdce* (The Harvested Heart, 1974*); Milostná listování* (Love Letters, 1977); *Daleko stín, daleko sad* (Far Is the Shadow, Far Is the Garden, 1979), which reflects his relationship to his generation; *Mezivěk* (Mid-Century, 1981); *P. F.* (1984); and *Rozečtený život* (A Life Still Incomplete, 1987). Černík's other volumes of poetry include *Deset tisíc píšťal* (Ten Thousand Flutes, 1983); *Dluhy lásky: Výbor z milostných veršů* (Debts of Love: A Selection of Love Poems, 1984); *Řekni dům i otevři: Verse pro celou rodinou* (Say Home and Open: Poems for the Whole Family, 1987), a selection; *Kniha—dni* (Book, Days, 1987); *Nebudte smutni* (Don't Be Sad, 1989); and *Česká čítanka* (A Czech Reader, 1992). Besides his numerous books for children, Černík has translated Estonian and Lithuanian poetry for anthologies published in 1977 and 1982, as well as ancient Egyptian love lyrics based on scholarly translations (1982). He is also the author of *Tráva roste až k moři: Kniha českých reportaží* (Grass Grows Right Down to the Sea: A Book of Czech Reportage, 1979), a series of microessays on Prague and Czech themes; *Zrychlenýtep: Antologie mladé české poesie* (Accelerated Beat: An Anthology of Young Czech Poetry, 1980); and *33 životů* (33 Lives, 1994), a series of interviews with people from different walks of life, including artists and intellectuals.

Translations: Nine poems in *The New Czech Poetry: Jaroslav Čejka, Michal Černík, Karel Sýs*, trans. Ewald Osers (Newcastle upon Tyne: Bloodaxe, 1988), 39–50.

Chifu, Gabriel (b. 1954) Romanian poet and novelist. A native of the small Danubian town of Calafat, Chifu attended secondary school in Craiova and then went on to Craiova University, where he earned a degree in automation and computing in 1979. After working in his profession from 1979 to 1985 in Bucharest, Petroşani, and Craiova, Chifu became editor of the magazine *Ramuri*. He has also served as secretary of the Craiova branch of the Romanian Writers Union. Chifu's first book of poetry was published in 1976 under the title *Sălaş în inima* (Shelter in the Heart), and won the Writers Union Prize for a debut. Subsequent volumes of Chifu's poetry include *Realul eruptiv* (Eruptive Reality, 1979); *O interpretare a purgatoriului* (An Interpretation of Purgatory, 1982); *Lamură* (The Cream of the Crop, 1983), which won the Prize of the Central Committee of Communist Youth; and *Omul neţărmurit* (The Man Without Boundaries, 1987), which was awarded the Prize of the Craiova Writers Association. Apart from poetry lauded for its subtlety of expression, whether the subject is love, everyday life (which Chifu views from a certain ironic perspective), or the mystery of life, Chifu is also the author of two novels. The first, *Unde se odihnesc vulturii* (Where Vultures Rest, 1987), has been described as a Dostoevskian treatment of the Romanian provincial novel and features a young man whose life changes when he discovers during a vacation that he has cancer. The second, *Valul şi stînca* (The Wave and the Rock, 1989), is essentially an existential novel partly set in the nineteenth century and culminating in a suicide.

Translations: Four poems in *Young Poets of a New Romania: An Anthology*, trans. Brenda Walker with Michaela Celea-Leach, ed. Ion Stoica (London: Forest, 1991), 105–9.

Cibulka, Hanns (b. 1920) German poet. Born in Jägerndorf (Czech, Krnov), in the German-speaking northern border region of then Czechoslovakia, Cibulka studied in a business school as a young man and worked as a salesman until the outbreak of World War II. During the war, he was captured and imprisoned in Sicily. After his return to Germany in 1948, he studied librarianship in Berlin and Jena, and in 1952 became director of the Heinrich Heine City and District Library in Gotha. He began his literary career as a poet and has published seven volumes of poetry: *Märzlicht* (March Light, 1954); *Zwei Silben* (Two Syllables, 1959); *Arioso* (1962); *Windrose* (Compass Card, 1968); *Lichtschwalben* (Light Swallows, 1973); *Lebensbaum* (The Tree of Life, 1977); and *Rebstock* (The Vine, 1980). A retrospective collection of his poetry was published in 1986 under the title, *Losgesprochen: Gedichte aus drei Jahrzehnten* (Acquitted: Poems of Three Decades). Cibulka's classically inspired but unrhymed poetry often turns on the motif of a lost homeland and a nostalgia for his childhood in Czechoslovakia. A reverence for nature inclines him at times to a critical attitude toward contemporary civilization; in other poems, he confronts the problems involved in building a state on socialist principles. A number of Cibulka's poems have Czech and Slavic themes; others celebrate famous writers and musicians, among them Bach, Dvořák, Haydn, Mozart, and the Russian writer Osip Mandelshtam.

While respected as a poet, Cibulka became known, above all, for his autobiographical and memoiristic writing, most of which is in diary form. In some instances, the diary reads like fiction and is identified as "Tagebucherzählung" ("Diary Narrative"). In the first volume of his memoirs, *Sizilianisches Tagebuch* (Sicilian Diary, 1960), the Sicily of Cibulka's wartime internment takes on a highly poeticized and idealized character. Italy is also the setting of *Umbrische Tage* (Umbrian Days, 1963). Of two other books of diaries and travels also published in 1963, *Reisetagebuch* (Travel Book) and *Swantow:*

Die Aufzeichnungen des Andreas Flemming (Swantow: The Notes of Andreas Flemming), the latter is a fictional diary. *Eine Liebeserklärung in K.* (A Declaration of Love in K.), which Cibulka published in 1976, recalls travel to Poland and a tragic wartime love affair in a small town in eastern Poland. Cibulka's other books of memoirs include *Sanddornzeit: Tagebuchblätter von Hiddensee* (The Time of the Sea Buckthorn: Pages of a Diary from Lake Hidden, 1971); *Dornbürger Blätter* (Dornburg Pages, 1972); *Das Buch Ruth: Aus der Aufzeichnungen der Archäeologen Michael S.* (The Book of Ruth: From the Notes of the Archaeologist Michael S., 1978), in which the author presents himself as the editor of notes detailing a romance between the archaeologist Michael S., who eventually loses his life in an Israeli bombing raid on Damascus, and Ruth, a co-worker; *Seedorn: Tagebucherzählung* (Lake Buckthorn: A Diary Narrative, 1983); *Wegscheide: Tagebucherzählung* (Fork in the Road: A Diary Narrative, 1988); *Nachtwache: Tagebuch aus dem Kriege Sizilien* (Night Watch: A Sicilian War Diary, 1989); *Ostseetagebücher* (Baltic Diaries, 1991); *Am Brückenwehr: Zwischen Kindheit und Wende* (At the Dam Site: Between Childhood and the Turning Point, 1994); *Die Heimkehr des verratenen Sohne: Tagebucherzählung* (The Return of the Betrayed Son: A Diary Narrative, 1996); and *Tagebuch einer späten Liebe* (Diary of a Late Love, 1998), which in fact deals with the city of Erfurt. Cibulka's literary awards include the Louis Fürnberg Prize (1973); the Johannes R. Becher Prize (1978); the Francesco de Sanctis Prize (1978); and the Prize for Culture of the City of Gotha (1979).

Translations: *Not Marked on the Map*, trans. Ewald Osers (Portree, Scotland: Aquila, 1985), a small collection of Cibulka's poems.

Čingo, Živko (b. 1936) Macedonian short-story writer and novelist. Arguably the best-known Macedonian short-story writer, Čingo was born in Velgošti, a village uphill and inland from Lake Ohrid. A graduate of Skopje University, where he studied Yugoslav literature, Čingo published his first collection of short stories, *Paskvelia*, in 1962. Paskvelia is the name of a fictitious Macedonian village (somewhat akin to William Faulkner's Yoknapatawpha County), which serves as the setting for a number of Čingo's stories in which his emphasis is on a critical view of social relations in a representative Macedonian village in the first post–World War II years. Čingo is well known for his eye for the ironic and grotesque and for a style shaped in part by the oral tradition. A followup volume of stories, *Nova Paskvelia* (New Paskvelia), appeared in 1965. Čingo subsequently published an additional five volumes of stories: *Požar* (The Fire, 1970); *Kengurski skok* (Kangaroo Leap, 1979); *Prikazni od Paskvel* (Tales from Paskvelia, 1988); *Babagjan* (1989); and *Bunilo* (Delir-ium, 1989). He is also the author of three novels—*Golemata voda* (High Water, 1971), in which he takes a dim view of Stalinist-era methods of pedagogy and educational philosophy and for which he won the Racin Prize; *Srebrenite snegovi* (Silver Snows, 1984), a children's novel; and *Grob za dušata* (A Grave for the Soul, 1989)—and a book of literary criticism, *Obid za budenje* (Trying to Keep Awake, 1982). A two-volume edition of his selected works (*Odbrani dela*) was published in 1984.

Translations: "Argil's Decoration," in *The Big Horse and Other Stories of Modern Macedonia*, ed. Milne Holton (Columbia: University of Missouri Press, 1974), 71–78; "From's Daughter," trans. Michael Samilov, in *New Writing in Yugoslavia*, ed. Bernard Johnson (Harmondsworth: Penguin, 1970), 320–26; "Fromova Ćerka" and "The Medal," trans. Donald Davenport, in *Introduction to Yugoslav Literature: An Anthology of Fiction and Poetry,* ed. Branko Mikasinovitch, Dragan Milivojević, and Vasa D. Mihailovich (New York: Twayne, 1973), 627–33.

Claudius, Eduard (real name Eduard Schmidt, has also used the pseudonym Edy Brendt; 1911–1976) German novelist and short-story writer. Claudius was born into a worker's family in Buer bei Gelsenkirchen. He joined the Communist Party in 1932 and later fought with the International Brigades in the Spanish Civil War. During World War II, he was interned in Switzerland. He settled in Potsdam in 1947. Claudius made his debut as a prose writer in the German émigré periodical *Das Wort* in 1938. His strongly autobiographical novel *Grüne Oliven und nackte Bergen* (Green Olives and Naked Mountains), which deals with the Spanish Civil War (1936–1938) and, despite reservations about it in communist literary circles in the 1950s, is regarded as a forerunner of the socialist realist novel, appeared in Zurich in 1944. Although strikingly authentic in many places, the novel also tends toward the moralistic and the schematic. Claudius's second novel, *Menschen an unserer Seite* (People on Our Side, 1951), depicts the contradictions and tensions related to the "building of socialism" in the German Democratic Republic as seen from the perspective of a worker and could be published only after the intervention of high-placed authorities.

Apart from his novels, Claudius published several volumes of short stories, beginning with *Gewitter* (Thunderstorm) in 1948. This was followed by the collections *Früchte der harten Zeit* (Fruits of a Difficult Time, 1953); *Paradies ohne Seligkeit* (Paradise Without Blessedness, 1955); and *Saltz der Erde* (Salt of the Earth, 1969). An enthusiastic traveler, Claudius drew on his trips to the Far East and the Middle East for such collections of stories and travel books as *Aus den nahen und den fernen Städten* (From Cities Near and Far, 1964); *Hochzeit in den Alawitenbergen: Erzählungen aus Drei Jahrzehnten* (Wedding in the Alawite Mountains: Stories from Three Decades, 1964); *Mädchen "Sanfte Wolke": Erzählungen aus Dschungel und Wüste* (The Girl "Soft Cloud": Tales from Jungle and Desert, 1968); *Syrien: Reise in Sieben Vergangenheiten und eine Zukunft* (Syria: A Trip in Seven Pasts and One Future, 1975); and *Als die Fische die Sterne schluckten: Märchen und Legenden aus Vietnam, Laos und Kambodscha: An den Ufern des Roten Flusses und des Mekong* (When the Fish Swallowed the Stars: Fairy Tales and Legends from Vietnam and Cambodia: On the Banks of the Red River and the Mekong, 1976). When the Bitterfeld program, which sought to create a new relationship between artists and the working class, came into being, Claudius was one of the writers opposing it. In his autobiography, *Ruhelose Jahre: Erinnerungen* (Restless Years: Recollections, 1968), he came out squarely in opposition to some aspects of Stalinism. Claudius's collected works in separate editions were published between 1974 and 1986.

Comanescu, Denisa (b. 1954) Romanian poet. Born in Buzău, Comanescu studied Romanian and English language and literature at Bucharest University. After her graduation in 1977, she went to work for the Univers publishing house in Bucharest as editor of its English literature series. She made her debut in the review *România literară*. *Izgonirea din paradis* (Banishment from Paradise, 1979), her first volume of verse, won the debut prize of the Writers Union in 1979. She has since published three more volumes of poems: *Cuțitul de argint* (The Silver Knife, 1983); *Barca pe valuri* (The Boat on the Waves, 1987); and *Urmă focului* (Remains of the Fire, 1986). Comanescu has also translated from contemporary English and American poetry. In Comanescu's poetry, the misunderstandings and disappointments of everyday relationships, between family members and between lovers, and loneliness are addressed in a casual, colloquial style enlivened by unexpected, striking images.

Translations: Seven poems in *Silent Voices: An Anthology of Contemporary Romanian Women Poets,* trans. Andrea Deletant and Brenda Walker (London: Forest, 1986), 67–75; nine poems, in versions by Eiléan ní Chuilleanáin, in *When the Tunnels Meet,* ed. John Farleigh (Newcastle upon Tyne: Bloodaxe, 1996), 47–54; six poems in *Young Poets of a New Romania: An Anthology,* trans. Brenda Walker with Michaela Celea-Leach, ed. Ion Stoica (London: Forest, 1991), 33–39.

Ćopić, Branko (1914–1984) Bosnian Serb novelist, short-story writer, and poet. One of the most popular postwar Serbian writers, Ćopić was a native of the village of Hašani in western Bosnia. After elementary school in his native village, he attended secondary school in Bihać, Banja Kula, Sarajevo, and Karlovici. In 1940 he graduated from the Faculty of Philosophy of Belgrade University. After the German invasion of Yugoslavia, he was among the first to join Tito's partisans and eventually became a political commissar. In the early postwar period, he was the chief editor of the youth paper *Pionir* (1944–1949). Ćopić subsequently moved to Belgrade, where he spent the rest of his life as a professional writer.

Ćopić's literary career began in 1936 when the first short story signed with his own name, "Smrtno Soje Čubrilove" ("Burial Clothing of Soja Čubrilova"), appeared in the literary supplement of the newspaper *Politika.* Many of Ćopić's subsequent stories were published in the same paper. Ćopić's principal pre–World War II collections of stories included *Pod Grmečom* (At the Foot of Mount Grmeč, 1938); *Borci i bjegunci* (Fighters and Fugitives, 1939); and *Planinci* (Mountaineers, 1940). For the most part, the stories address the everyday life of poor rural folk in Ćopić's native Krajina region. Oppressed by monotony and loneliness, Ćopić's peasants yearn for another way of life, but are so mired in poverty and wretchedness that flight is impossible. Ćopić's wartime poetry, above all in the collection *Ognjeno rodjenje domovine* (Fiery Birth of the Homeland, 1944), combines elements of the old Serbian oral tradition and the militant exuberance of the Russian futurists. In his first collection published after the war, *Ratnikovo proljeće* (Springtime of War, 1947), Ćopić voices his optimism concerning Yugoslavia's postwar recovery. It was also in his early postwar period that Ćopić became an enthusiastic writer of poetry and prose for children, a genre to which he first contributed in 1939 with *U carstvu leptirova i medveda* (In the Kingdom of Butterflies and Bears). One of his best collections of verse for children was the volume *Ježeva kuća* (Porcupine's House, 1949). In his previous book of poems for children, *Armija odbrana tvoja* (The Army, Your Defense, 1947), Ćopić revealed a tendency at times toward ideological heavyhandedness.

The first of Ćopić's prose works for adults to gain recognition was the huge epic-style war novel *Prolom* (Breakthrough, 1952), dealing with the popular uprising in his native region against the invaders and their local collaborators. The well-known and popular story collection *Doživljaji Nikoletine Bursaća* (Adventures of Nikoletina Bursać) followed in 1956. The leading protagonist of the collection is the young peasant Nikoletina Bursać, a native of the Krajina, who joins the partisans, becomes a company commander, and reaches legendary fame for his exploits. The novel *Gluvi barut* (Deaf Gunpowder, 1957) appeared next as a sequel to *Prolom.* Of particular interest in the work is Ćopić's rejection of political extremism as he portrays ideological conflicts within the partisan movement. These incompatible views on the interrelationship between the liberation military struggle and the communist political revolution are embodied in Ćopić's main characters: Tigar, the commander of a partisan detachment and a dogmatic communist veteran of the Spanish Civil War; Vlado, the young student who serves as Tigar's political commissar; and Captain Radekić, Tigar's deputy commander, a peasant who became a prewar officer in the royalist army and espouses a flexibility and moderation Ćopić advances as the best way through the minefield of political extremes. In his next novel, *Ne tuguj, bronzana stražo* (Grieve Not, Bronze Sentry, 1958), Ćopić portrays the life of settlers from the Krajina who take over lands in the Banat region previously owned by ethnic Germans who were expelled as collaborators. Ćopić linked his new novel to his earlier stories about Nikoletina Bursać by having the peasants name their new village Bursaćevo, and by making the peasant characters Jovandeka Babić and Stanko Veselica of *Gluvi barut* the real "heroes" of *Ne tuguj, bronzana stražo*.

Osma ofansiva (The Eighth Offensive), a collection of short stories in which his wartime heroes are now functionaries of the new regime, appeared in 1964. The work, however, aroused considerable controversy because of its candid depiction of the drabness and squalor of postwar Yugoslav urban existence. His characters, all from the same Krajina village, find themselves unsuitable for bureaucratic life and cannot easily adjust to their new circumstances. One sketch, the satirical "Jeretička priča" ("Heretical Tale," 1950), about the estrangement of the new socialist state from the country's masses, became much the focus of the criticism leveled against Ćopić. He was expelled from the League of Communists, and by the mid-1970s the attacks on him and his vain

attempts to recover from his fall from grace took a heavy toll on his health. He suffered from depression and needed psychiatric treatment. His last two major works were *Bašta sljezove boje* (Garden of Mallow Color, 1970) and *Delije na Bihaću* (Heroes in the Assault on Bihać, 1975). The first consists of autobiographical tales of a largely lyrical and humorous character about his family and other people from his native region, covering the period from World War I to the end of the 1960s. The title of the collection derives from the flowering colors of the medicinal mallow plant and here assumes symbolic significance. *Delije na Bihaću*, in which Ćopić freely mixes historical and invented personages, recounts the successful partisan assault on Bihać during World War II, but the grim realities of wartime are decked out in the trappings of a modern fairy tale. After this book, Ćopić's mental health rapidly deteriorated, and he spent more time in psychiatric hospitals. In March 1984, he jumped to his death from the Sava River Bridge in Belgrade. A short autobiographical work, focused mainly on his childhood years, was published posthumously in 1994 under the title *12-XII-1939, uveče* (12-XII-1939, Evening).

Literature: Voja Marjanović, *Reč i misao Branka Ćopića: Ogledi i kritike* (Belgrade: Nova Knjiga, 1986), a good collection of articles that appeared in various journals in the 1970s and 1980s.

Translations: "An Awkward Companion" (from *Doživljaji Nikoletine Bursaća*), trans. Vida Janković, in *Death of a Simple Giant and Other Modern Yugoslav Strories*, ed. Branko Lenski (New York: Vanguard, 1965), 201–7; "Cruel Heart" (from *Doživljaji Nikoletine Bursaća*), trans. Branko Mikasinovich, in *Introduction to Yugoslav Literature: An Anthology of Fiction and Poetry*, ed. Branko Mikasinovich, Dragan Milivojević, and Vasa D. Mihailovich (New York: Twayne, 1973), 240–46.

Cosașu, Radu (real name Oscar Rohrlich, has also used the pseudonyms Radu Costin and Belphegor; b. 1930) Romanian journalist, essayist, short-story writer, poet, and playwright. Cosașu was born in Bacău. He attended a Bucharest secondary school from 1940 to 1948 and then spent the next year studying at the Faculty of Letters of Bucharest University. During this period, he worked as a reporter for the review *Revista elevilor,* the national school journal, where he made his literary debut in 1948. In 1949 he became editor of *Scînteia tineretului.* The next year, Cosașu worked as a milling-machine operator in a factory, after which he attended the Mihai Eminescu School of Literature in Bucharest from 1952 to 1953. From 1953 to 1956, he again served as editor of *Scînteia tineretului.* Throughout his career, Cosașu has collaborated with several prominent journals and reviews, among them *România literară, Tribuna,* and *Flacăra.* He also contributed to *Sportul* and *Informația Bucureștului,* and from 1968 to 1987 edited the film review *Cinema.* A number of his articles and reviews were published under the pen name Belphegor. Although he has also written poetry, prose fiction, and plays, Coșasu is undoubtedly best known for his collections of reportage, essays, and film reviews. They have been incorporated into such volumes as *Un august pe un bloc de gheața* (One August on a Block of Ice, 1971); *Viața în filmele de cinema* (Life in the Movies, 1972); *Alți doi ani pe un bloc de gheața* (Another Two Years on a Block of Ice, 1974); *Ocolul pămîntului în 100 de știri* (Around the World in 100 News Clips, 1974); *Cinci ani cu Belphegor* (Five Years with Belphegor, 1975); and *O viețuire cu Stan și Bran* (Living with Stan and Bran, 1981), about the film comedians Laurel and Hardy.

Although he subsequently developed a keen sense of the satiric and ironic, Cosașu began his career in the mainstream of so-cialist realism, as exemplified by such books as *Servim Republica Populară Română* (We Serve the Romanian People's Republic, 1952), published under the pseudonym Radu Costin; *Opiniile unui pămîntean* (Opinions of One Earthling, 1957); *Energii* (Energies, 1960); *Lumină!* (Light!, 1961); *Nopțile tovarașilor mei* (My Comrades' Nights, 1962); *A înțelege sau nu* (To Understand or Not, 1965); and *Omul după 33 de ani scapă* (The Man Rescued After 33 Years, 1966). By the late 1960s, beginning with his novel *Maimuțele personale* (Individual Monkeys, 1968), Cosașu had parted with socialist realism and was turning its dicta and methods into the stuff of ridicule.

Arguably, Cosașu's most significant literary achievement is the psychologically and sociologically engrossing multivolume autobiographical cycle *Supraviețuire I–VI* (Survivals I–VI), which he published between 1973 and 1989. Volumes I and II were titled simply *Supraviețuire,* whereas the subsequent volumes were given individual names: *Meseria de nuvelist* (The Handicrafts of a Novelist, 1980); *Ficționarii* (The Fictionalists, 1983); *Logica* (Logic, 1985); and *Cap limpede* (A Clear Head, 1989). In 1997 Cosașu published a seventh installment under the title *O supraviețuire cu Oscar* (Surviving with Oscar). Cosașu was also the author of two social comedies, *Mi se pare romantic* (It Seems Romantic to Me, 1961) and *Scurt program cu bossanove* (Short Program with Bossanovas, 1966), and one volume of poetry, *Povești pentru a-mi îmblînzi iubita* (Stories to Tame My Lover, 1978). In 1971 and again in 1981, Coșasu was awarded the Writers Union Prize, and in 1973 the Ion Creangă Prize of the Romanian Academy.

Translations: "Burials" (from *Ficționarii* [*Supraviețuire IV*]), in *The Phantom Church and Other Stories from Romania,* ed. and trans. Georgiana Farnoaga and Sharon King (Pittsburgh: University of Pittsburgh Press, 1996), 48–52.

Ćosić, Bora (b. 1932) Serbian novelist, short-story writer, essayist, translator, and screenwriter. Born in Zagreb, Ćosić moved with his family to Belgrade when he was five years old. Following his university education, he became affiliated with a number of journals, including the avant-garde review *Danas,* from 1961 to 1963. Although he published three novels between 1956 and 1959—*Kuća lopova* (House of Thieves, 1956); *Vsi smrtni* (All Are Mortal, 1958); and *Andjeo je došao po svoje* (The Angel Came for His Own, 1959)—it was with the humorous, somewhat absurdist, stories in his collection *Priča o zanatima* (Tale of the Trades, 1966) and, above all, the novella that grew out of it, *Uloga moje porodice u svetskoj revoluciji* (*My Family's Role in the World Revolution,* 1969), that Ćosić first attracted serious attention as a writer. Soon recognized as an original voice in Yugoslav literature, Ćosić also began to acquire an international reputation.

My Family's Role in the World Revolution, still Ćosić's best-known work, was originally published in 1969 at the author's expense. The large Belgrade publishing house Prosveta reissued it in 1970. A new edition, revised by the author and now regarded as definitive, was published in 1980. The novella is a young boy's comico-bizarre account of how his madcap family managed to survive the cataclysmic events in Central and Eastern European history from the late 1930s through the post–World War II period. Some critics have ascribed the device of the boy narrator-author to the German author Günter Grass's *The Tin Drum.* The freshness of Ćosić's method, compared with that of other Yugoslav writers who have also depicted the impact of the tragic events of the twentieth century (mostly on their own families), is that his focus is on a "small," insignificant family whose changing fortunes from the interwar Yugoslav monarchy through the German invasion and the communist postwar takeover reflect the great upheavals of the epoch. It is the uniqueness of his perspective, combined with his comic style and its bizarre elements, that creates so much of the appeal of Ćosić's work. Despite some official displeasure with the work and attempts to limit its dissemination, *My Family's Role in the World Revolution* was made into a film directed by Bato Čengić and was adapted for the stage and performed by the experimental Belgrade theater Atelje 212.

Ćosić's subsequent fiction has also sought to address the serious issues of his time in a deceptively playful manner. In such works as *Sadržaj* (Table of Contents, 1968); *Sodoma i Gomora* (Sodom and Gomorrah, 1968–1984); *Mixed Media* (1970; original title in English); *Tutori* (Guardians, 1978); *Bel tempo* (1982); *Intervju na Čiriskom jezeru* (An Interview on Lake Zurich, 1988); and *Musilov notates* (Musil's Notes, 1989), Ćosić mixes fact and fiction by introducing the writers Italo Svevo, James Joyce, and Robert Musil; the literary theorist György Lukács; and the surrealist Belgrade painter Marko Ristić. Strongly attracted to the figure of Miroslav Krleža, a distinguished man of letters and the most important Croatian intellectual of the twentieth century, Ćosić made him the subject of two books: *Poslovi, sumnje, snovi Miroslava Krleže* (The Works, Doubts, and Dreams of Miroslav Krleža, 1983), much of which deals with the fragmentary diary Krleža wrote during World War II; and *Doktor Krleža* (Doctor Krleža, 1988), a highly imaginative fictionalized biography of the writer. The "notes" in *Musilov notates* are similarly imaginary.

The Serb–Croat war of 1991/1992 was the inspiration for Ćosić's long essay "Dnevnik apatrida" ("Diary of a Stateless Person"), which was written in 1991, first serialized in the Belgrade newspaper *Borba* in 1992, and then published separately in 1993. It is built around parallels that Ćosić discovered between his own time and that of Marcel

Proust's novel *Le Temps retrouvé* (*Time Regained*). A shorter sequel, "Završni razgovor s gospodinom Verdurinom, rovinsjkim" ("Final Conversation with Mr. Verdurin, of Rovinj"), was published in the journal *Erasmus* in 1995. Similar parallels with another foreign literary work, Knut Hamsun's Norwegian novel *Hunger*, gave rise to the essay "Hamsunov Baedeker" ("Hamsun's Baedeker"). Directly related to the siege of Sarajevo during the Bosnian War in 1993/1994, the essay was also published in *Erasmus* in 1994. It was in 1992, during the Serb–Croat war, that Ćosić—refusing to align himself with either the Croats or the Serbs—left Belgrade for Rovinj, on the Istrian Peninsula, which previously had been his summer residence.

In his most recent published work, *Dobra vladavina* (The Art of Good Government, 1995), a collection of some forty short stories, Ćosić addresses the issue raised by him and, indeed, other Serbian writers (Dževad Karahasan, for example, in *Sarajevo: Exodus of a City*) of the complicity of intellectuals and of literature in an energized Serb nationalism ultimately responsible for the atrocities of the Balkan wars of the 1990s.

Translations: *My Family's Role in the World Revolution and Other Prose*, trans. Ann Clymer Bigelow (Evanston, Ill.: Northwestern University Press, 1997).

Ćosić, Dobrica (b. 1921) Serbian novelist. A native of Velika Drenova, near Kruševac, Ćosić fought with Tito's partisans during World War II and after the war became a member of the Central Committee of the Serbian Communist Party. He also served in the Yugoslav National Assembly. Although his first novel, *Daleko je sunce* (*Far Away Is the Sun*, 1951), is regarded as a classic text about the German occupation of Yugoslavia and the resistance movement during World War II, Ćosić's major literary achievement

remains a four-volume novel of epic proportions based on Serbia's trials in World War I. A vast panorama of people and places, *Vreme smrti* (*A Time of Death*) was originally published between 1972 and 1979 to wide acclaim. Overflowing with Serbian national pride, the novel deals harshly, however, with the cynicism and callous indifference to human suffering of high-placed political and military figures on both sides of the conflict and the shortsighted willingness of the Western allies (England, France, and Italy) to abandon the Balkans. Only Russia, the longtime Slav ally of Serbia, is shown in a favorable light. The tetralogy ends with the defeat of the ill-equipped Serbian army and the grim retreat of its survivors through a perilous Albania. Ćosić wrote two other novels along similar lines, *Koreni* (Roots, 1954) and *Deobe* (Divisions, 1961). He was also the author of two books on political subjects, both published in 1992: *Promene* (Changes), a collection of essays in which Ćosić is, as always, an apologist for Serbian political aspirations, Communist Party politics, and the emergence of Serbian nationalism in the wake of Tito's death, which led to the subsequent division of the country; and *Srpsko pitanje—demokratsko pitanje* (The Serbian Question—A Democratic Question), in large part a collection of correspondence addressing similar issues.

Literature: Miodrag Petrović, *Srbija u Vremenu smrti* (Niš: Prosveta, 1992), a study of Serbia in *A Time of Death;* Milan Nikolić, ed., *Šta je stvarno rekao Dobrica Ćosić* (Belgrade: Draganić, 1995), a book of wide-ranging interviews with Ćosić.

Translations: *Far Away Is the Sun,* trans. Muriel Heppell and Milica Mihajlović (Belgrade: Jugoslavia, 1963); *Into the Battle,* trans. Muriel Heppell (San Diego: Harcourt Brace Jovanovich, 1983); *Reach to Eternity,* trans. Muriel Heppell (San Diego: Harcourt Brace Jovanovich, 1980); *South to Destiny,* trans. Muriel Heppell (San Diego: Harcourt

Brace Jovanovich, 1981); *A Time of Death,* trans. Muriel Heppell (San Diego: Harcourt Brace Jovanovich, 1978).

Coşovei, Traian T. (b. 1954) Romanian poet and literary critic. The son of the poet Traian Coşovei (1921–1993), Coşovei was born in Bucharest and graduated from Bucharest University in 1978 with a degree in Romanian language and literature. While at the university, he was a member of Nicolae Manolescu's Cenaclul de Luni (Monday Literary Circle). His first published volume of poetry, *Ninsoarea electrica* (Electric Snowfall), won the debut prize of the Writers Union in 1979, the year of its publication. His next volume of poetry was *1, 2, 3 sau* (1, 2, 3 Or; 1980). It was followed by *Cruciada intreruptă* (Interrupted Crusade, 1982); *Poemele siameze* (Siamese Poems, 1983); *In aşteptarea cometei* (Waiting for the Comet, 1986); *Rondul de noapte* (The Late Night Round, 1987); *Bătrâneţile unui băiat cuminte* (The Old Age of a Good Boy, 1994), which won the Bucharest Writers Association Prize; *Mickey Mouse e mort* (Mickey Mouse Is Dead, 1994); *Ioana care rupe poeme* (Joana, the Ravisher of Poems, 1996), which won the Romanian Academy Prize and the Ion Vinea Prize; *Patineaza sau crapă* (Skate or Die, 1997); *Percheziţionarea îngerilor* (Bodily Search of the Angels, 1998); and *Lumină de la frigider* (Light from the Refrigerator, 1998). Coşovei also contributed to the anthology *Aer cu diamante* (Air with Diamonds, 1982), and in 1990 published a book of literary criticism, *Pornînd de la un vers* (Starting from a Verse). He has also worked as editor of the magazine *Contemporanul.* Coşovei is very much a contemporary poet attuned to the sounds and rhythms of his age, including American pop music. His haunts are those of the big city with its commercial and technical innovations, from which he oftens draws his imagery. He is most at home in longer, more discursive poems written in prosaic style and conveying a certain ironic and noncoformist attitude toward the life around him.

Translations: Five poems in *Young Poets of a New Romania: An Anthology,* trans. Brenda Walker with Michaela Celea-Leach, ed. Ion Stoica (London: Forest, 1991), 125–31.

Crăciunescu, Ioana (b. 1950) Romanian poet. Born in Bucharest, Crăciunescu studied to be an actress at the Institute of Theater and Film from 1969 to 1973. Until she left Romania for Paris in 1989, she was a member of the C. I. Nottara Theater Company in Bucharest and had worked in cabaret and film. Apart from her acting career, Crăciunescu is a talented poet who has published several volumes of verse, beginning with *Scrisori dintr-un cîmp cu maci* (Writings in a Poppy Field, 1977). This was followed by *Duminică absentă* (Missing Sunday, 1980); *Supa de ceapă* (Onion Soup, 1981); *Iarnă clinică* (Clinical Winter, 1983); *Maşinăria cu aburi* (Steam Engines, 1984); and *Caietul cu adnotări* (Notebook with Commentaries, 1988). Crăciunescu is a highly imaginative poet—elusive, given at times to macabre imagery, ironic, even cynical—who seems rather indifferent to the everyday world around her and who conveys a certain worldweariness, as in the small but typical poem "Thursday":

> Maybe in the afternoon
> I'll dress in silky brown
> When I climb high to see the town
> and so look beautiful
> to throw myself down.

In 1981 Crăciunescu was awarded the Bucharest Writers Union Prize.

Translations: Six poems, trans. Fleur Adcock, in *Child of Europe: A New Anthology of East European Poetry,* ed. Michael March (London: Penguin, 1990), 83–88; eleven poems in *Silent Voices: An Anthology* of *Contemporary Romanian Women Poets*, trans. Andrea Deletant and Brenda Walker (London: Forest, 1986), 77–88.

Crăsnaru, Daniela (b. 1950) Romanian poet and short-story writer. One of the most impressive Romanian poets of the 1980s and 1990s, Crăsnaru was born in Craiova, where she studied Romanian and English at Craiova University. Although she made her literary debut in 1967, it was the year of her graduation from the university, 1973, that she published her first collection of poetry, *Lumină cît umbra* (Light Like Shade). She currently lives in Bucharest, where she is an editor at the Eminescu publishing house. After the fall of the regime of Nicolae Ceauşescu, she was elected a member of the new parliament on 2 May 1990 on a slate run by the National Salvation Party, of which she was not formally a member.

In addition to *Lumină cît umbra*, Crăsnaru has published at least eight collections of poetry as well as several children's books and two collections of short stories. Her other books of poetry include *Spaţiul de graţie* (A State of Grace, 1976); *Arcaşii orbi* (Blind Archers, 1978); *Crîngul hipnotic* (The Hypnotic Grove, 1979); *Vînzătorul de indulgenţe* (The Vendor of Indulgences, 1981); *Şaizeci şi nouă de poezii de dragoste* (Sixty-Nine Poems of Love, 1982); *Niagara de plumb* (Niagara of Lead, 1984); *Emisferele de Magdeburg* (The Hemispheres of Magdeburg, 1987); and *Fereastra în zid* (Window on the Wall, 1988). Her short stories are contained in the volumes *Marele premiu* (The Big Prize, 1983) and *Plută răsturnata* (The Capsized Raft, 1990). Crăsnaru's poetry spans a wide gamut of emotions, from lyric tenderness to somber desperation over past disappointments, especially in love, and a growing sense of confinement and entrapment. With time, at least until the overthrow of the Ceauşescu regime, her outlook seemed to turn darker and more cynical. Much admired for her bright and clever imagery—some of the most effective of which uses the stage as a metaphor for human existence—Crăsnaru did not shrink from registering her own hostility toward the censorship and repression of the Ceauşescu dictatorship. However, she did so more by the indirection of metaphor. A number of her published poems make it clear that Crăsnaru had no intention of varnishing reality to appease the literary watchdogs of the Communist Party. But it is in poems that she did not publish in the Ceauşescu era, poems she has called *Letters from Darkness* and that she kept hidden in an aunt's cellar lest they be discovered during a search of her own apartment, that she deals forthrightly with the inescapable, all but hopeless reality of oppression. The mood of *Letters from Darkness* is splendidly captured by a typical poem such as "Love Poem in Captivity":

They listen to everything.
They spy on everything.
They know everything.
I'm afraid of the furniture, the walls, the
    cat purring
on the cold radiator.
I'm afraid of friends, of my own child,
I'm afraid of myself.
On the telephone I talk about the
    weather,
about yesterday's football match.
About nothing.
I'd like to tell you, darling,
that I love you.
But I must be cautious
because who knows what they might
    think I meant by that?

Crăsnaru has won several awards for her work: the Writers Union Prize for poetry in 1979 and 1982, and the prize of the Romanian Academy for 1988, which was presented after the downfall of the Ceauşescu regime in December 1989.

Translations: *Letters from Darkness: Poems by Daniela Crăsnaru,* trans. Fleuer Adcock (Oxford: Oxford University Press, 1991), which is divided into two parts: the first containing poems from the collections *Niagara de plumb* and *Emisferele de Magdeburg,* and the second consisting of poems of a largely political nature that Crăsnaru did not risk trying to publish during the Ceauşescu regime; *Sea-Level Zero,* trans. Adam J. Sorkin with Daniela Crăsnaru and other hands (Rochester, N.Y.: BOA, 1999); ten poems in *An Anthology of Romanian Women Poets,* ed. Adam J. Sorkin and Kurt W. Treptow (New York: East European Monographs, 1994), 97–110; seven poems in *15 Young Romanian Poets: An Anthology of Verse,* trans. and ed. Liliana Ursu (Bucharest: Eminescu, 1982), 9–15; eleven poems in *Silent Voices: An Anthology of Contemporary Romanian Women Poets,* trans. Andrea Deletant and Brenda Walker (London: Forest, 1986), 89–102.

Crnjanski, Miloš (1893–1977) Serbian novelist, poet, essayist, and diplomat. A native of the Vojvodina region, Crnjanski moved to Belgrade after World War I. His career spanned both the literary and the diplomatic. He began writing poetry before the war, but published his first volume of poems, *Lirika Itake* (The Lyre of Ithacus), in 1919. Crnjanski's attraction for the avant-garde was confirmed by the appearance of his poem "Sumatra" in the Zagreb journal *Savremenik* in 1920. The republication of this poem, together with Crnjanski's essay "Objašnjenje 'Sumatre'" ("An Explanation of 'Sumatra'"), in the Belgrade journal *Srpski Književni Glasnik* was regarded as a manifesto of Serbian literary modernism in the post–World War I era. But although his early poetry inclined toward surrealism and expressionism, Crnjanski was unsympathetic toward the procommunist political leanings

of much of the Serbian avant-garde, and he engaged in literary polemics with them from the early 1930s.

Crnjanski began writing prose fiction around the time that his postwar poetry started to appear. Although his collection of stories, *Priče o muškom* (Stories of the Masculine, 1920), was uneven, his first novel, *Dnevnik o Čarnojeviću* (Čarnojević's Diary, 1921), was impressive. Set in Galicia and Kraków, Poland, during World War I, the first-person narrative recounts the disillusionment and alienation experienced by a Serb compelled to fight in the Austrian armies against fellow Slavs. Crnjanski's major work of fiction, the highly regarded novel *Seobe* (*Migrations*), appeared in 1929. This is a fine historical novel about the Serb soldiers of the Slavonian-Danubian Regiment who fought for Maria Theresa of Austria in the eighteenth century, when Serbia was part of the Hapsburg Empire. The focus of the novel is on the leader of the regiment, the proud warrior Vuk Isaković. The toll the campaign against the French in 1744/1745 takes on his spirit and on his family life encapsulates the terrible price paid in misery and rootlessness by Maria Theresa's loyal Serb volunteers. Since most Serbian historical fiction is anchored either in the period of the Turkish domination or during World War I, Crnjanski's novel is especially interesting for its eighteenth-century setting. In a sequel, *Seobe II* (Migrations II, 1962), Pavle Isaković, the son of Vuk, his family, and a large part of the Serbian community immigrate to Russia from the Vojvodina area of the Hapsburg Empire, thus fulfilling a dream of Vuk Isaković. But Russia proves to be a false promised land. The Serbs are treated as little more than pawns in the political struggle between the Romanov and Hapsburg empires. Crnjanski's last novel, *Roman o Londonu* (A Novel of London, 1971), grew out of his diplomatic service. The novel won the coveted Yugoslav NIN Prize in 1972.

Crnjanski's entry into the Yugoslav foreign service as a press attaché began after World War I. He served mostly in Berlin and Rome, his career ending with the German bombing of Belgrade on 6 April 1941. With diplomatic immunity, Crnjanski and his wife made their way to safe haven in England via Lisbon. The years in London were harsh. Although loosely aligned with the Yugoslav government-in-exile, Crnjanski had no regular income, and he and his wife took any jobs they could to scrape by. The despair of these years is reflected in *Roman o Londonu*, which deals with Russian émigrés in England after World War II. The central figure in the novel is Prince Repnin, who commits suicide in 1948, a solution to his misery with which Crnjanski himself flirted. Crnjanski tried to write the novel in English in 1946 and 1947 for commercial reasons, but although he had studied English for many years, his knowledge of the language was not up to the task and he eventually completed it in Serbo-Croatian.

Although he was anxious to return to Yugoslavia after the war, the new communist regime under Marshal Tito regarded Crnjanski as a monarchist and profascist who would be unwelcome in the country. It was only after Tito's break with the Cominform that Crnjanski felt able to return to Yugoslavia in 1965. He remained in Belgrade until his death.

Apart from his fiction, Crnjanski wrote a great deal of expository prose, beginning with *Itaka i komentari* (Ithaca and Commentaries, 1959), a book of essays. *Embahade* (Embassies), a four-part work published in two volumes in 1983, is an account of his diplomatic career in different European capitals. The volume also contains a complete bibliography of his writings. *Politicki spisi: 1918–1945* (Political Writings: 1918–1945) was published in 1989. This was followed in 1990 by a volume of political profiles, *Politicki porteti* (Political Portraits). His press corre-

spondence from his consular positions in Berlin (1936–1938) and Rome (1938–1941) was published in 1991 as *Nova Evropa* (New Europe). Crnjanski's other volumes of nonfiction prose include *Putopisi* (Travelogues 1966), a book of travel writings; *Kod hyperborejaca* (Among the Hyperboreans, 1966), a partly autobiographical account of his stay in Italy; two volumes of essays on different subjects from literature to politics, *Eseji* (Essays, 1966) and *Eseji i prikazi* (Essays and Speeches, 1991); a collection of critical writings, *Pisci kao kritičari posle prvog svetskog rata* (Writers as Critics After World War I, 1975); a collection of interviews with Crnjanski edited by Zoran Avramović and published as *Ispunio sam svoju sudbinu* (I Fulfilled My Destiny, 1992); and *Lament nad Beogradom/Lament pour Belgrade* (Lament for Belgrade, 1936, 1962), a French–Serbian publication.

Crnjanski also had an early interest in the stage and wrote three plays: *Maska* (Mask, 1918, 1923); *Konak: Drama i komedija o ubijstvu kralja Aleksandra Obrenovića i kraljice Drage u pet slika* (Konak: Drama and Comedy About the Murder of King Aleksandar Obrenović and Queen Draga in Five Acts, 1958); and *Tesla*. Aleksandar Obrenović was king of Serbia from 1876 to 1903; his consort, Queen Draga, lived from 1867 to 1903; the subject of Crnjanski's third play, the Serbian scientist Nikola Tesla, was long affiliated with Columbia University after he immigrated to the United States. Crnjanski's three plays were published in a single volume in 1966 under the title *Drame*.

After Crnjanski returned to Yugoslavia in 1965, the previous neglect of him turned into near adulation. He was hailed as one of the leading Serbian writers of the twentieth century, and virtually all his works began appearing in new editions. A volume of prose appeared in 1966 as *Proza* (Prose). This was followed by a collection of various writings published under the title *Lirika. Proza. Eseji* (Poetry, Prose, Essays, 1972) and a volume of collected poems, *Sabrane pesme* (Collected Poems, 1978). The fourteen-volume edition of Crnjanski's works published by Nolit in 1983 is the most complete.

Literature: David Norris, ed., *Miloš Crnjanski and Modern Serbian Literature* (Nottingham, Eng.: Astra, 1988), a collection of articles by different hands; David A. Norris, *The Novels of Miloš Crnjanski: An Approach Through Time* (Nottingham, Eng.: Astra, 1990). Of the now sizable literature on Crnjanski in Serbo-Croatian, the following studies may be mentioned: Radovan Popović, *Život Miloša Crnjanskog* (Belgrade: Prosveta, 1980), a biography; Zoran Avramović, *Politika i književnost u delu Miloša Crnjanskog* (Belgrade: Vreme knjige, 1994), on politics and literature in Crnjanski's works; Radmila Popović, *Crnjanski i London* (Sarajevo: NISRO Oslobodenje, 1990), and Mirjana Popović-Radoić, *Književna radionica izgnanstva: Miloš Crnjanski u Londonu, 1940–1965* (Belgrade: Narodna Biblioteka Srbije, 1993), both studies of Crnjanski's London period; Slavko Leovač, *Romansijer Miloš Crnjanski* (Sarajevo: Svetlost, 1981), on Crnjanski's novels; Novica Petković, *Seobe Miloša Crnjanskog* (Belgrade: Zavod za udzbenika i nastavna sredstva, 1985), on *Migrations*; Novica Petković, *Lirika Miloša Crnjenskog* (Belgrade: Tersit, 1994), and *Lirske epifanije Miloša Crnjanskog* (Belgrade: SKZ, 1996), and Aleksandar Petrov, *Poezija Crnjanskog i srpsko pesništvo* (Belgrade: Nolit, 1998), three studies of Crnjanski's poetry and poetics; Petar Marjanović, *Crnjanski i pozorište* (Novi Sad: Prometej, 1995), a study of Crnjanski and the stage.

Translations: *Migrations,* trans. Michael Henry Heim (New York: Harcourt Brace Jovanovich, 1994); *Lament nad Beogradom/ Lament pour Belgrade,* trans. Slobodan Despot, Collection Classiques slaves (Belgrade: Bureau Central de Presse, 1936, 1962). *Priče o muškom* is available in French as *Recits au masculain,* trans. Vladimir André Cejović and Anne Renoue (Lausanne: L'Age d'homme, 1996).

Csaplár, Vilmos (b. 1947) Hungarian novelist and short-story writer. Csaplár was born in Újpest, now part of Budapest, and began studying law at Eötvös Lóránd University following his graduation from high school. However, after one year he switched to Hungarian language and literature and received a teaching diploma in 1972. But literature soon became his major calling and profession. He began his literary career as a writer of short stories and published his first collection, *Lovagkor* (The Age of Chivalry), in 1971. The sentimentality, lyricism, and play with language in which the volume abounds were subsequently repudiated by Csaplár in favor of a greater detachment and simplicity of style. His first major work after *Lovagkor* was the novel *Két nap, amikor összevesztünk, vagyis a történetírás nehézségei* (Two Days When We Quarreled, or the Difficulties of Historiography, 1972). His next collection of short stories, with a typical Csaplár title, was *Vásárloínk figyelmébe ajánljuk a Zaporoszec 968-as tipusú gépkocsit* (We'd Like to Recommend to Our Customers the Model 968 Zaporozhets Automobile, 1975; translated as "Our Customers' Attention Is Drawn to the Model 968 Zaporozhets Automobile"). Csaplár's talent for humor and satire is amply evidenced in such subsequent works as *A kék szem és a rózsaszinű mellbimbó históriája* (The Story of the Blue Eyes and the Pink Nipples, 1980); *Előtanulmányok a Szép epikus korszakunk című regényhez* (Preliminary Studies for a Novel Entitled Our Beautiful Epic Time, 1982); *A kételkedés útjai: Válogatott novellák* (The Way of Doubt: Selected Stories, 1982); his series of "career stories," consisting of *Pénzt, de sokát! Karriertörtenét* (Money, But a Lot of It! A Career Story, 1987), *Kurva vagyok: Karriertörténet* (I

Am a Whore: Career Story, 1989), and *Zsidó vagyok Magyarországon: Karriertörténet* (I Am a Jew in Hungary: Career Story, 1990); *Vágy a róka vére után* (Desire for the Fox's Blood, 1989); two books on postcommunist Hungary, *Magyarország, te dög* (Hungary, You Bastard!, 1991) and *A demokrácia álarc az ördög ábrázatán* (Democracy in the Devil's Mask, 1992); the autobiographical *Gyermekkor, földi körülmények között* (Childhood amid Earthly Circumstances, 1994) and *Én* (I, 1996); and the somewhat irreverent *Az Isten* (God, 1995).

Translations: "Our Customers' Attention Is Drawn to the Model 968 Zaporozhets Automobile," trans. John Freeman, in *Ocean at the Window: Hungarian Prose and Poetry Since 1945*, ed. Albert Tezla (Minneapolis: University of Minnesota Press, 1980), 416–22.

Cseres, Tibor (1915–1993) Hungarian novelist, short-story writer, and journalist. Born in the Transylvanian village of Gyergyóremete, Cseres attended high schools in Marosvásárhely and Budapest and subsequently trained as an economist in Kolozsvár. He began working as a journalist for a regional newspaper in the Békéscsaba area until called up for military duty before the outbreak of World War II. He served for some four and a half years before deserting, as an officer, in 1944. In 1945/1946, he was back working as a journalist in Békéscsaba, but in 1947 accepted a short-term position as ministerial councillor in Budapest. After existing for several years as a freelance writer, he signed on with the review *Élet és Irodalom* in 1963, and held the position until 1970. In the meantime, Cseres had begun to develop a prolific literary career. He began publishing poetry and short prose fiction in the 1930s, writing mostly on Hungarian village life by drawing on his own background. It was only in the 1950s that Cseres's first novels began to appear, among them *Tűz hódréten* (Fire in the Beaver Field, 1950);

Térdigérő tenger (Kneedeep Sea, 1954); and *Herebáró* (Baron Drone, 1956), the last a popular comic work about the adventures of a Casanova of the Great Hungarian Plains.

In the 1960s, especially after publication of the novel *Hideg napok* (Cold Days, 1964), which was subsequently made into a film and remains the only work of fiction by Cseres to achieve any international recognition, Cseres's interest tended to shift away from village life to World War II and its impact on Hungary and to the ever-contentious issue of Hungarian–Romanian relations—above all, in Transylvania. Between 1960 and 1988, he published over a dozen new books, mostly novels, including *Halálos vétek* (Deadly Sin, 1960); *Pesti háztetők* (Budapest Roofs, 1961); Cold Days; *Fekete rózsa* (Black Rose, 1967); *Bizonytalan század* (The Uncertain Century, 1968); *Játékosok és szeretők* (Gamblers and Lovers, 1970); *Hol a kódex?* (Where Is the File?, 1971), a collection of articles; *Siratóének* (Funeral Song, 1975); *Parázna szobrok: Ikerregény* (Lewd Statues: A Twin Novel, 1979); *Foksányi-szoros* (Focşani Pass, 1985), the title of which refers to the Romanian city of Focşani, about 100 miles northeast of Bucharest and the site of a famous battle between the Germans and the Romanians in World War I; *Igazolatlanul jelen* (Present Unverified, 1985); and *Vízaknai csaták* (The Battles of Vízakna, 1988).

One of his best-known works, *Vízaknai csaták* is an overstuffed two-volume novel set in a small, ethnically mixed Transylvanian salt-mining village during World War I. A combination of adventure epic and historical document, the novel is a fairly dispassionate attempt to trace the roots of the Hungarian–Romanian antagonism in the much disputed territory. Cseres's last novel, *Kentaurok és kentaurnők: Tragiko-szatíra* (Centaurs and Female Centaurs: A Tragico-Satire, 1993), is a curious work about Szabolcs Pető, an economist and highly placed official in the regime of János Kádár who eventually turned against the system and even denounced the invasion of Czechoslovakia in 1968. Although Cseres makes the most of Pető's reputation as a lecher despite his age (he is near seventy in the novel) and his prostate cancer, the novel pursues too many tangents, and at too great length, to make for a coherent whole. Cseres has also published three collections of short stories: *Különböző szerelmek* (Different Loves, 1957); *Ember fia és farkasa* (Man's Child and Enemy, 1967); and *Itt a földön* (Here on Earth Too, 1973). Cseres's strong views about Hungarian claims to Transylvania are evident in *Őseink kertje: Erdély* (The Garden of Our Forefathers: Transylvania, 1990). Even more overtly political is *Vérbosszú Bácskában* (Vendetta in Bácska, 1991; translated as *Titoist Atrocities in Vojvodina, 1944–1945: Serbian Vendetta in Bácska*), about alleged Yugoslav atrocities against Hungarians during World War II. It is Cseres's only larger work available in English. Cseres won several literary awards during his career, among them the Attila József Prize (1951, 1955, 1965); the Kossuth Prize (1975); the Hungarian Trades Union Council Prize (1988); and the Hungarian Art Foundation Prize (1991).

Translations: *Titoist Atrocities in Vojvodina, 1944–1945: Serbian Vendetta in Bácska* (Buffalo, N.Y.: Hunyadi, 1993); "Oh, How High the Sky Is! (The Dreams of a Woman)," trans. László T. András, and one poem, trans. Kenneth McRobbie, in *44 Hungarian Short Stories*, ed. Lajos Illés (Budapest: Corvina, 1979), 419–28. *Hideg napok* is available in French as *Jours glacés*, trans. Anne-Marie de Backer, Philippe Haudiquet, and Georges Kassai (Paris: Gallimard, 1971).

Csoóri, Sándor (b. 1930) Hungarian poet, essayist, and screenwriter. A greatly respected poet, to many the poetic voice of post–World War II Hungary, Csoóri was born in Zámoly, a rural village in western Hungary. He was educated at the presti-

gious Protestant College in Pápa and later briefly studied Russian history and Marxism at the Lenin Institute in Budapest. He worked as a journalist for several newspapers both before and after moving to Budapest, and after 1968 was affiliated with the Budapest film studio MAFILM, mostly as a scriptwriter. In 1988 he became editor in chief of the cultural review *Hitel* and, in 1991, became president of the World Federation of Hungarians. Csoóri's formidable reputation owes much to his strong identification with the destiny of the Hungarian people throughout the turmoil of the period 1945 to 1989. As he writes in one poem,

> I imagine my heart
> as a repository of such heaps of
>   wreckage.
> I'm full of memories of war, exploded
>   bridges.

A moral voice, Csoóri condemned Stalinist repression in his own country and signed the Czech Charter 77 in opposition to the Soviet invasion of 1968. He has also embraced the struggle to preserve human dignity and individuality in the face of relentless depersonalization attributable to the impact of technology and modern civilization. His concerns for justice extend far beyond national boundaries. He has written poems about the war in Vietnam, about miners in France, and about Cuba, which he visited and made the subject of a published journal: *Kubai napló* (Cuban Diary, 1956). Csoóri's poetry is one generally of dark moods, pain, world-weariness, loss, and death, yet it still preserves a measure of hope for the future. A poet of strong imagery, shaped in part by surrealism, Csoóri often finds inspiration in the folk tradition to which he relates easily in light of his peasant origins. His first book of poetry, *Felröppen a madár* (The Bird Takes Wing), appeared in 1954, the year Csoóri won the Attila József Prize for poetry. It was followed by such volumes as *Ördögpille* (Dragonfly, 1957); *Menekülés a magányból* (Escape from Loneliness, 1962); *Második születésem* (My Second Birth, 1968); *Párbeszéd, sötétben* (Dialogue in the Dark, 1973); *A látogató emlékei* (A Visitor's Remembrances, 1977); *Jóslás a te idődről* (Prophecy About Your Time, 1979); *A tizedik este* (The Tenth Evening, 1980); *Iszapeső* (Raining Mud, 1981); *Elmaradt lázálom* (Postponed Nightmare, 1983); *Várakozás a tavaszban* (Waiting for Spring, 1983); *Kezémben zöld ág* (A Green Branch in My Hand, 1985); *A világ emlékművei* (The World's Monuments, 1989); *Nappali hold* (The Day's Moon, 1991); and *Ha volna életem* (If It Were My Life, 1996). Csoóri has also published several volumes of prose, mostly essays addressing concerns he has raised in his poetry as well as on art, folklore, and literature. They include *Tudosítás a toronyból* (Reporting from the Tower, 1963), a book of reportage about collective farms; *Faltól falig* (From Wall to Wall, 1969); *Utazás félálomban* (Journey While Half-Asleep, 1974); *Nomád napló: Novellák, esszék, karcolatok* (Diary of a Nomad: Novellas, Essays, Sketches, 1979); *A félig-bevalott élet* (The Half-Examined Life, 1982); *Készülődés a számadásra* (Drawing Up Accounts, 1987); *Brevárium* (1988); and the two-volume *Tenger és diólevél: Összegyűjtött esszék, naplók, beszédek, 1961–1994* (The Sea and the Walnut Leaf: Collected Essays, Sketches, Talks, 1961–1994, 1994). Of Csoóri's film scripts, two enjoy particular renown: *Tízezer nap* (Ten Thousand Days), which won an award at the Cannes Film Festival in 1964, and *Pergőtűz* (Barrage), on the fate of the Hungarian armies at the Don front during World War II.

Translations: *Barbarian Prayer: Selected Poems*, ed. Mátyás Domokos, trans. by various hands (Budapest: Corvina, 1989); *Memory of Snow*, trans. Nicholas Kolumban (Great Barrington, Mass.: Penmaen, 1983); *Selected Poems of Sándor Csoóri*, trans. Len Roberts (Port Townsend, Wash.: Copper Canyon, 1992); five poems in *The Colonnade of Teeth: Modern Hungarian Poetry*, ed. George Gömöri and George Szirtes (Newcastle upon Tyne: Bloodaxe, 1996), 167–72; nine poems in *The Face of Creation: Contemporary Hungarian Poetry*, trans. Jascha Kessler (Minneapolis: Coffee House, 1988), 4–9; five poems in *Modern Hungarian Poetry*, ed. Miklós Vajda (New York: Columbia University Press, 1977), 233–37; fifteen poems and the prose piece "Approaching Words," trans. by various hands, in *Ocean at the Window: Hungarian Prose and Poetry Since 1945*, ed. Albert Tezla (Minneapolis: University of Minnesota Press, 1980), 282–300; twelve poems in *Turmoil in Hungary*, ed. and trans. Nicholas Kolumban (St. Paul, Minn.: New Rivers, 1982), 18–32.

Csurka, István (b. 1934) Hungarian short-story writer, novelist, playwright, and feuilletonist. Csurka was born in Budapest and educated in Békés, Transylvania, as well as in Budapest. During World War II, he was relocated to Lichting, a village near Munich. His father, who served in the army and was captured by the Americans, eventually took the family back to Békés. In 1952 Csurka began studying at the Academy of Dramatic and Film Art in Budapest. He received his degree in dramaturgy in 1957, subsequently becoming playwright-in-residence at the Vígszínház (Comedy Theater) of Budapest.

Csurka began his literary career as a writer of short stories, publishing his first story, "Nász és pofon" ("Nuptials and a Slap"), in 1954. Two years later, his first volume of stories appeared under the title *Tűzugratás* (Leaping over Fire, 1956). Most of the texts in it depict the skepticism of young people toward the life around them in the early 1950s. Csurka's next collection of stories, *Százötös mellék* (Extension No. 105, 1964), comprises texts written from 1958 to 1964. Again, the volume is pervaded with skepticism and disenchantment, and his leading characters are mostly antiheroes. After *Százötös mellék,* Csurka published such additional collections of stories as *A ló is ember* (A Horse Is Also Human, 1968); *Nász és pofon* (Nuptials and a Slap, 1969); *Kint az életben* (In the Stream of Life, 1972); and *Létezés-technika* (Being and Technology, 1983), an 800-plus–page volume of selected stories and novellas. With few exceptions, Csurka's stories are written in a spare narrative style, some almost entirely in dialogue. In *Hamis tanú* (The False Witness, 1959), his first novel, he drew on his own origins in his portrayal of the social and professional situation of intellectuals of peasant origin. His next novel, *Moór és Gaál* (Moor and Gaal), which appeared in 1965, was later adapted for the stage. It was followed by the two-volume *Házmestersirató* (The Complaining Janitor, 1980) and *A kard* (The Sword, 1983).

As well known for his dramatic writing as for his prose fiction, Csurka published a volume of plays, *Ki lesz a bálanya?* (Who Will Be the Patroness of the Ball?), in 1970. A collection of plays from 1945 to 1974 appeared next in 1980 under the title *Húsz dráma, 1945–1975* (Twenty Plays, 1945–1975). The one-act *Túrógombóc* (Cheese Dumplings, 1980), one of the nine short stage, radio, and television plays in the collection *Amerikai cigaretta* (American Cigarette, 1978), and Csurka's best-known play in English, is typical of his social criticism in its combination of grotesque humor and the absurd. Set in a radio studio, leading intellectuals of the day have been brought together as guests on a talk show to discuss social issues of importance to lowbrows—in this case, the role of stupidity in society. By the time the play is at an end, it is the intellectuals who fare the worst. Csurka has also written several plays for radio performance. The volume *Visszajátszás hangjátékok* (Playback Radio Plays, 1980) contains radio plays by Csurka and other writers. A new collection of Csurka's dramatic works came out in 1999 under the title of an earlier novel, *Házmestersirató* (The Complaining Janitor). Csurka's screenplays have been collected in the volume *Hét tonna dollár* (Seven Tons of Dollars, 1971). One of his films, *Kertes házak utcája* (The Street of Homes with Gardens), won a Gold Palm at the Cannes Film Festival in 1963. Csurka's feuilletons have been collected in the volume *Kettes kolbász* (Cheap Sausage, 1980). His essays, studies, and conversations, mostly on Hungarian and Central European political issues, appear in the volumes *Elfogadhatatlan realitás* (Unacceptable Reality, 1986); *Közép-Európa hó alatt* (Central Europe Under Snow, 1988); *Új magyar önépítés* (New Hungarian Self-Construction, 1991); *Keserű hátország* (Bitter Hinterland, 1993); *Nemzeti összefogás* (National Union, 1996); and *Minden, ami van: Politikai írások és beszédek gyűteménye, 1979–1998* (Everything There Is: Collected Political Writings and Conversations, 1979–1998, 1998).

Although admired as a writer, Csurka has attracted much negative atttention through the years, especially in the 1980s and 1990s, for his ultranationalistic right-wing views. As the leader of the Party for Truth and Life (MIEP), he has attracted a certain following with his antidemocratic, anti-Semitic, and anti-Gypsy views.

Translations: *Cheese Dumplings,* trans. Eugene Brogyányi, in *Drama Contemporary: Hungary,* ed. Eugene Brogyányi (New York: PAJ Publications, 1991), 103–28; *On Location: A Tragicomedy in Two Acts,* trans. Margaret Varga (Budapest: Centre Hongrois de l'I. I. T., 1979), a translation of Csurka's play *Eredeti helyszín;* "Four Students," trans. Elizabeth Szász, in *Present Continuous: Contemporary Hungarian Writing,* ed. István Bart (Budapest: Corvina, 1985), 119–41; "Happening," trans. Nicholas Rand, in *Hungarian Short Stories,* ed. Paul Varnai (Toronto: Exile Editions, 1983), 63–81; "The Two Rheumatics,"

"The Main Wall," "LSD," and "The Passengers," trans. Albert Tezla, in *Ocean at the Window: Hungarian Prose and Poetry Since 1945*, ed. Albert Tezla (Minneapolis: University of Minnesota Press, 1980), 306–33.

Čuić, Stjepan (b. 1945) Croatian novelist and short-story writer. Although the author of a few novels, among them *Orden* (The Order, 1981) and *Tajnoviti ponor* (The Mysterious Precipice, 1995), Čuić is most highly regarded for his stories, most of which are grotesque and occult in nature. His two best collections are *Stalinjova slika i druge priče* (Stalin's Picture and Other Tales, 1975) and *Tridesetogodišnje priče* (Thirty-Year-Old Stories, 1979). Čuić is also the author of two works of nonfiction dealing with contemporary Croatian politics and the wars of the Yugoslav secession of the 1990s: *Abeceda licemjerja* (The Alphabet of Hypocrisy, 1992), on Croatian self-determination, and *Lule mira* (Peace Pipes, 1994), a journalistic work about the Croats in Bosnia-Herzegovina during the conflicts of the 1990s.

Translations: "Crosses," in *Croatian Tales of Fantasy*, trans. Graham McMaster (Zagreb: The Bridge, 1996), 171–79.

Cvenić, Josip (b. 1952) Croatian novelist, short-story writer, and essayist. Cvenić was born in Osijek, where he received his early education. He later earned his university degree in philosophy and sociology in Sarajevo. He made his literary debut in 1976 with a book of poems, *Protumarani zavičaji* (Indolent Hometowns). This was followed by the story collection *Pričanja Heraklitovog kušača i druga pričanja* (Tales of Heraclites' Taster and Other Stories, 1982); the psychological novel *Blank* (1986), which was made into a film three years later; and another collection of stories, *Lektira* (Readings, 1990). Cvenić's most recent novel, *Kralica noći* (Queen of the Night, 2000), is set in the year 1960 and deals mostly with the problem

a young boy has with sexual maturation because of a physical malformation. In 1995 Cvenić was awarded the Ivana Brlić Mažuranić Prize for his children's novel, *Čvrsto drži joy-stick* (Hold the Joy-Stick Steady, 1994). *Udžbenik priča* (A Story Textbook), which came out in 1995, is really a book about childhood for adults. In 1997 Cvenić published a volume of essays, *Ogledanje s krajem stoleća* (A View from the End of the Century), that look back on the recent turmoil in a disintegrating Yugoslavia, and the novel *Kajinov pečat* (The Mark of Cain), which is set in his native Osijek and revives memories of youth in a town destined to know the ravages of strife in the Balkan turmoil of the 1990s.

Czakó, Gábor (b. 1942) Hungarian novelist, short-story writer, playwright, and poet. Czakó was born in the small town of Decs in southern Hungary. After completing secondary school in Szekszárd in 1960, he studied art for a year at Eötvös Lóránd University and then transferred to Pécs, where he earned a degree in law. From the time he graduated in 1965 until 1972, when he became a freelance writer, he was employed mostly as a corporate legal adviser. His first book was the short novel *A szoba* (The Room, 1970), in which he tries to make a connection between an individual's physical environment and the development of character. It was followed by *Emberkert* (Human Garden, 1971), a collection of stories indebted to the classical animal fable, on which Czakó draws in other works as well; *Indulatos jelentések* (Passionate Reports, 1973), a collection of sociological writings; *Megváltó* (The Savior, 1974), a novel; *Csata minden áldott nap* (A Fight Every Blessed Day, 1975), a novel for children; *Iskolavár* (School Fortress, 1976), a novel opposing traditional methods of schooling and vaguely reminiscent of the Austrian writer Robert Musil's *Die Verwirrungen des*

Zöglings Törless (The Trials of Young Tör-less, 1906); *Varkonyi krónika* (The Varkony Chronicle, 1978), a 600-page chronicle; the play *Disznójáték* (*Pigs*, 1978), a farcical polit-ical allegory about a rebellion of power-crazed pigs, which Czáko said he had writ-ten when he was twenty-one and still a stu-dent and before he had ever heard of George Orwell's *Animal Farm*; *Sorrendben* (In Order, 1981), a collection of stories; *Plusz* (Excess, 1982), a novella cycle; *Eufémia* (Eu-phemia, 1983); *Lélek fele* (Half-Hearted, 1986), a novel; *Luca néni föltámadása* (Aun-tie Luca's Resurrection, 1988), a novel; *Teremtő mosolya* (The Creator's Smile, 1988); *Van itthon elég krumpli?* (Are There Enough Potatoes There?, 1989), a collection of plays; *Angyalok* (Angels, 1992), a novel; and the collection . . . *és hetvenhét magyar rémmese: A Szépasszony szalonja, 1989–1995* (. . . and Seventy-Seven Hungarian Ghost Tales: The Beautiful Woman's Drawing Room, 1989–1995, 1996), which Czakó pre-pared with Ferenc Banga. Czakó's collected essays were published in two volumes in 1996, *Világfasírt* (World Hash) and *Mi a helyzet? Gazdaságkor titkai* (What's the Story? Secrets on the Farm, 1996). From 1979 to 1984, Czakó served on the editorial staff of the monthly review *Mozgó világ*.

Translations: *Pigs,* adapted by Judith Sollosy, in *Three Contemporary Hungarian Plays,* ed. Albert Tezla (London: Forest, 1992), 9–53; "The Cat," trans. Georgia Lenart Greist, in *Ocean at the Window: Hungarian Prose and Poetry Since 1945,* ed. Albert Tezla (Minneapolis: University of Minnesota Press, 1980), 381–83.

Czechowski, Heinz (b. 1935) German poet, essayist, and travel writer. Born in Dresden, Czechowski was trained as a commercial artist and worked as a draftsman until 1958 when he entered the Johannes R. Becher In-stitute of Literary Studies in Leipzig. Fom the time he graduated in 1961 until 1965, he served

as an editor at the Mitteldeutscher Verlag in Halle. He was later affiliated with a theater in Magdeburg. Czechowski eventually made Leipzig his home. Like other writers of his generation from the Saxony region (Volker Braun, Reiner Kunze, Sarah Kirsch and Rainer Kirsch, and Karl Mickel), Czechowski had an abiding interest in its culture and landscape and drew on these often in his po-etry and prose. Typical of the latter is his col-lection of reminiscences from the late 1960s to the late 1970s published under the title *Herr Neithardt geht durch die Stadt* (Mr. Neithardt Passes Through the City, 1983). A productive poet, Czechowski has published some fifteen volumes of verse: *Nachmittag eines Liebe-spaares* (Afternoon of a Pair of Lovers, 1962); *Wasserfahrt* (River Trip, 1968); *Schafe und Sterne* (Sheep and Stars, 1974); *Was mich bet-rifft* (What Befalls Me, 1981); *Ich, beispielsweise* (Me, for Example, 1982); *An Freund und Feind* (To Friend and Foe, 1983); *Ich und die Folgen* (Me and the Consequences, 1987); *Kein näheres Zeichen* (No Closer Sign, 1987); *Auf eine im Feuer versunkene Stadt* (On a City Sunk in Fire, 1988), a volume of selected verse; *Sanft gehen wie Tiere die Berge neben dem Fluss* (The Mountains Tread Softly as Animals Along the River, 1989); *Mein Venedig: Gedichte und andere Prosa* (My Venice: Poems and Other Prose, 1989); *Nachtspur: Gedichte und Prosa* (Night Trail: Poems and Prose, 1992); *Wüste Mark Kolmen* (Desert Mark Kolmen, 1997); *Mein Westfälischer Frieden* (My West-phalian Peace, 1998); and *Das offene Geheim-nis: Liebesgedichte* (The Open Secret: Love Lyrics, 1999).

The best single collection of Czechowski's selected verse is *Die Zeit steht still: Aus-gewählte gedichte* (Time Stands Still: Selec-ted Verse), published by Grupello Verlag of Düsseldorf in 2000. It contains poems from 1958 through 1999. Despite the range of his themes from bitter recollections of World War II and its privations to landscape and love lyrics, Czechowski has long cultivated a rather calm, undramatic style, almost prosaic in character, usually unrhymed, and tending toward the laconic. An admirer of such classic German poets as Friedrich Klopstock and Friedrich Hölderlin, to whom he has dedicated several poems and traces of whose style can be found in his own verse, Czechowski was also susceptible to the influence of the avant-garde, especially in his earlier writing. As time went on, Czechowski's outlook, which had been one of a somewhat critical acceptance of reality, became progressively more somber and pessimistic, even taking on tragic accents.

In 1982 Czechowski's edition of a collection of texts by the poet Georg Maurer (1907–1971), with whom he had studied at the Becher Institute, appeared under the title *Was vermag Lyrik: Essays, Reden, Briefe* (What the Lyric Could Do: Essays, Speeches, Correspondence). A collection of his own essays on twentieth-century German literature, *Spruch und Widerspruch* (Dictum and Protest), had appeared in 1974. As a prose writer, apart from his collection *Herr Neithardt geht durch die Stadt* and his essays, Czechowski was the author principally of a travel book, *Von Paris nach Montmartre: Erelebnis einer Stadt* (From Paris to Montmartre: Experience of a City, 1981), a pleasant but unremarkable account of his trip to Paris in 1977 accompanied by his own photographs.

Czechowski has also been well known for his familiarity with Slavic literatures. His dramatization of the Russian writer Mikhail Bulgakov's famous novel, *Master and Margarita,* served as the basis for an opera mounted in Karlsruhe in 1986 and a stage production in Leipzig the same year. Czechowski also translated other Russian authors, such as the poets Anna Akhmatova and Marina Tsvetaeva, as well as the Poles Adam Mickiewicz and Stanisław Wyspiański, and has written poems honoring Vladimir Mayakovsky and Sergei Esenin. In a few poems from 1997 to 1999 ("Hauptbahnhof" ["Central Station"] and "In Kalifornien" ["In California"]), Czechowski recalls the year he spent in the Dutch university town of Limburg and his trip from there to the United States, where he visited Virginia and Washington, D.C., as well as California.

Czekanowicz, Anna (b. 1952) Polish poet. Born in Sopot, on the Baltic Sea, Czekanowicz studied Polish philology at Gdańsk University. She was a member of the Wspólność group of poets in the late 1970s, and made her literary debut in 1976 with a set of poems titled *Ktoś kogo nie ma* (The Someone Absent). Subsequent volumes of poetry include *Więzienie jest tylko we mnie* (Prison Is Only Within Myself, 1978); *Pełni różobłędu* (A Full House of the Roses of Madness, 1980); *Najszczersze kłamstwo* (The Sincerest Lie, 1984); and *Śmierć w powietrzu* (Death in the Air, 1991). A poet of disappointment and depression, Czekanowicz writes often of her fear of loneliness and having no one else to rely on but herself. Although she has written short poems, her preference is clearly for longer works narrated in colloquial idiom. Czekanowicz was another Polish participant in the University of Iowa's International Writing Program, which she makes the subject of a few poems.

Translations: Nine poems in *Young Poets of a New Poland: An Anthology,* trans. Donald Pirie (London: Forest, 1993), 43–57.

Czeszko, Bohdan (b. 1923) Polish novelist, short-story writer, and screenwriter. A leading representative of the post–World War II generation of Polish prose writers, Czeszko was born in Warsaw and finished secondary school in 1939, shortly before the German invasion. In 1942 he joined the Gwardia Ludowa (People's Guard) and, after its formation, became a member of the Związek Walki Młodych (Union of Young Combatants). He then became active in the Resistance, primarily as a military instructor and communist political activist, and subsequently took part in the Warsaw Uprising of 1944. In January 1945, he was made a commander of the Milicja Obywatelska (Civil Militia), afterward serving in the regular Polish army. Wounded in action toward the end of the war, he retired from the army and became an official of the Union of Young Combatants. It was in that capacity that he took part in an organizational conference of the World Federation of Democratic Youth in London in the fall of 1945.

Czeszko made extensive use of his underground and military experiences in much of his fiction, as in his first collection of short stories, *Początek edukacji* (The Beginning of Education, 1949), and in his first novel, *Pokolenie* (The Generation, 1951), for which he was awarded the State Prize, Second Class, in 1952. In his next volume of stories, *Krzewy koralowe* (Coral Reefs, 1953), Czeszko shifted the focus from the end of the armed conflict to the problems facing the members of the Resistance as they assume political power and attempt to organize a new state in the postwar era. Czeszko published another collection of short stories in 1959 under the title *Edukacja niesentymentalna* (Unsentimental Education). The same year, his novel *Przygoda w kolorach* (An Adventure in Color) appeared. It deals with artists and reflects his own training at the State School for the Plastic Arts in Warsaw, from which he graduated in 1947. Upon graduation, Czeszko became a technical editor at the journal *Po prostu* and, from 1947 to 1951, resumed his art studies at the State School for the Plastic Arts. He later served as correspondent for the Communist Party newspaper *Trybunu Ludu* and in 1955 became a member of the editorial board of the journal *Przegląd Kulturalny*. His book about the USSR appeared in 1956 under the title *Moskwa, Wołga, Baku: Z notatnika radzieckiego* (Moscow, Volga, Baku: From a Soviet Notebook). *Tren* (The Train),

Czeszko's second novel, appeared in 1961. A volume of his selected short stories, *Opowiadania wybrane,* was awarded the State Prize, Second Class, in 1964. The following year, Czeszko was elected a delegate to the Sejm (Parliament) and was also honored by the Ministry of Culture and Art for his film scripts. In 1970 he was further honored with the City of Warsaw Prize. Czeszko's other publications include *Inne miejsca* (Other Places, 1966), a book of travel reportage; *Marginalki* (Marginalia, 1971), a collection of feuilletons about books; and *Wióry* (Shavings, 1971), a collection of feuilletons and sketches.

Translations: "Vexations of Power" (from *Krzewy koralowe*), trans. Ilona Ralf Sues, in *Contemporary Polish Short Stories,* selected by Andrzej Kijowski (Warsaw: Polonia, 1960), 129–39.

Dąbrowska, Maria (1889–1965) Polish novelist, short-story writer, and essayist. One of the distinguished Polish writers of the twentieth century, Dąbrowska was born in a village near Kalisz. Her higher education was pursued in Belgium, where she studied natural sciences at Louvain University and then sociology and economics at the New University in Brussels. Although her career spanned the interwar and post–World War II periods, Dąbrowska's major works appeared before the war. She made her literary debut in 1910 as a journalist for the rural press. Her firsthand knowledge of Polish village life and her social activism would endure throughout her long career. After World War I, from 1918 to 1924, Dąbrowska worked as a librarian and an editor for the Ministry of Agriculture and Agricultural Reforms. She thereafter devoted herself primarily to creative writing. Her first volume of stories, *Gałąż czereśni i inne nowele* (The Cherry Tree Branch and Other Novellas), appeared in 1922. In 1933 Dąbrowska received a State Prize for the first volume of her massive four-volume family chronicle, *Noce i dnie* (Nights and Days, 1932–1943). A vast panorama of Polish gentry life in the half century up to World War I built around a single family, this is the work for which Dąbrowska has long been best known and most admired.

Her principal post–World War II publications include several collections of stories, the majority dealing with village life and the changes both positive and negative brought to it by collectivization and industrialization, among them *Ludzie stamtąd* (Folk from Over Yonder, 1945), one of her best collections of stories about rural society; *Znaki życia* (Signs of Life, 1947); *Gwiazda zaranna* (The Morning Star, 1955); *Uśmiech dzieciństwa: Wspomnienia* (The Smile of Childhood: Recollections, 1956); *Na wsi wesele* (A Village Wedding, 1967); *Najdalsza droga* (The Farthest Road, 1968); and *Pielgrzymka do Warszawy* (Pilgrimmage to Warsaw, 1969). Dąbrowska's other works published in her lifetime include a book of travel sketches, *Szkice z podróży* (Travel Sketches, 1956); literary sketches, *Myśli o sprawach i ludziach* (Thoughts About Issues and People, 1956); a collection of essays on Joseph Conrad, *Szkice o Conradzie* (Sketches About Conrad, 1959); and two historical plays, both published in 1957: *Stanisław i Bogumil* (Stanisław and Bogumił), set in eleventh-century Poland, and *Geniusz sierocy* (The Orphaned Genius), about the failure of the Polish king Władysław IV to prevent the Polish–Cossack wars of the seventeenth century. Dąbrowska was also the the author of two posthumously published novels: *Domowe progi* (Domestic Thresholds, 1969) and *Przygody człowieka myślącego* (The Adventures of a Thinking Person, 1970). Two volumes of Dąbrowska's diaries (*Dzienniki*) were published in 1988 and 1996.

Literature: Zbigniew Folejewski, *Maria Dąbrowska* (New York: Twayne, 1967).

Translations: *A Village Wedding and Other Stories* (Warsaw: Polonia, 1957); "A Change Came o'er the Scenes of My Dream" (from *Gwiazda zaranna*), in *Contemporary Polish Short Stories* (Warsaw: Polonia, 1960), 142–54.

Dalchev, Atanas (1904–1978) Bulgarian poet and translator. Born in Salonika, Greece, Dalchev studied philosophy and pedagogy in Sofia. A respected poet, of fairly small output, Dalchev published his first book of poems, *Prozorets* (Window), a volume of only thirty pages, in 1926. The next two years Dalchev spent in Paris attending lectures at the Sorbonne. Prior to the appearance of his major work, *Stihotvoreniia. Fragmenty* (Poems. Fragments), in 1974, Dalchev published five volumes of poetry: *Stihotvoreniia* (Poems, 1928); *Parizh* (Paris, 1930); *Angelut na Shartur* (The Angel of Chartres, 1943); *Stihotvoreniia* (Poems, 1965); and *Balkon* (Balcony, 1972). Dalchev's most persistent theme is the desecration of nature by the spread of modern urban civilization. One of his most characteristic images is that of a lonely, forlorn tree standing in isolation in a jungle of steel and concrete. Denied other possibilities of a livelihood for political reasons between 1947 and 1952, Dalchev turned to translation. He translated extensively from Russian, French, Spanish, and German; a volume of translations by him and Aleksandur Muratov appeared in 1978. Dalchev is remembered most for his collection of aphoristic "fragments" on a wide variety of subjects, which he published together with a collection of poems (hence the title Poems. Fragments) in 1974. An example: "Nothing wastes a writer as much, I feel, as as his sole preoccupation with literature," and "Poetry expires from too much music." A subsequent edition, *Stihotvoreniia. Fragmenti. Misli i vpechatleniia* (Poems. Fragments. Thoughts and Impressions), appeared in 1978. A volume of Dalchev's literary criticism was published posthumously in 1980 under the title *Stranitsi* (Pages). A two-volume edition of his works appeared in 1984.

Translations: Excerpts from *Stihotvoreniia. Fragmenty,* in *The Balkan Range: A Bulgarian Reader,* ed. John Robert Colombo and Nikola Roussanoff (Toronto: Hounslow, 1976), 230–33; four poems, trans. John Balaban, in *Poets of Bulgaria,* ed. William Meredith (Greensboro, N.C.: Unicorn, 1985), 13–16.

Dalos, György (b. 1943) Hungarian novelist, essayist, and poet. Born in Budapest, where he received his early education, Dalos studied Russian language and literature at Moscow State University from 1962 to 1967. In 1968, the year after his return to Hungary, he was brought up on vague charges of "antistate activities," stripped of his membership in the Communist Party, and banned from holding a regular job. He was also kept under regular police surveillance. Earning what living he could as a translator, he eventually joined the democratic opposition in Hungary and, before the collapse of the Hungarian communist regime in 1989, resettled first in Vienna and then in Berlin. Much of his literary work has appeared first in German.

Dalos's first literary work to attract international attention was a kind of sequel to George Orwell's *1984—1985: A Historical Report (Hongkong 2036) from the Hungarian of . . .* (1983). The work appeared in German, in 1982, simply as *1985*. Its publication in Hungary, under the title *1985: Történelmi jelentés* (1985: A Historical Report), came in 1990, after the communists had vacated power. After conducting research at the "Academic Historical Research Institute of Irkutsk, Eurasia," in the third decade of the twenty-first century, the book's historian-narrator then proceeds to chronicle the events of 1985 when Oceania, after the death of Big Brother, was defeated in conflict with the other two superpowers at the time: Eurasia and Eastasia. All that remained of Oceania was Great Britain and Northern Ireland. Dalos's political satire is amusing most of all in its English setting and characters. After *1985*, Dalos published, in German, an account of the democratic opposition in Hungary, *Archipel Gulasch: Die Entstehung der demokratischen Opposition in Ungarn* (The Gulasch Archipelago: The Origin of the Democratic Opposition in Hungary, 1986), and two works of fiction in Hungarian: the story "Hosszú menetelés, rövid tanfolyam: Történet" ("Long March, Short Course: A Story," 1989) and the novel *A körülmetélés* (The Circumcision, 1990). Arguably his best work of fiction, *A körülmetélés* is the witty, humorous, and at times poignant story of a twelve-year-old Hungarian Jewish boy (Robi Singer) whose principal concern in the period shortly before the Hungarian revolution of 1956 is his long delayed and much feared circumcision. Of Jewish background himself, Dalos writes knowingly in his fiction of the internal life of the small Jewish community in post–World War II Hungary. Besides *A körülmetélés,* his other novels include *A kulcsfigura* (The Key Figure, 1995) and *Az istenkereső* (The God Seeker, 1999).

Further attesting to Dalos's impressive productivity in the 1990s are an essay (first published in German) on the role of the writer in postcommunist Eastern Europe, *Vom Propheten zum Produzenten: Zum Rollenwandel der Literaten in Ungarn und Osteuropa* (From Prophets to Producers: On the Role Change of Writers in Hungary and Eastern Europe, 1992), and two books reflecting his intimate knowledge of Russian literature: *Olga Pasternaks letzte Liebe: Fast ein Roman* (Olga Pasternak's Last Love: Almost a Novel, 1999), inspired by the (mostly literary) relationship between the Soviet writer Boris Pasternak (the author of *Doctor Zhivago*) and his cousin Olga Freidenberg, and, in its translated title, *The Guest from the Future: Anna Akhmatova and Isaiah Berlin*. Dalos's most successful book internationally, *The Guest from the Future* recalls the meeting in Moscow in November 1945 between the eminent Russian-born English thinker Sir Isaiah Berlin (then in the British Foreign Service) and the celebrated Russian poet Anna Akhmatova. Dalos writes knowingly of Akhmatova's career and her subsequent repression by the Soviet authorities. Dalos has also edited a series of translations of contemporary Hungarian literature called *Ungarn von Montag bis Freitag* (Hungary from Monday to Friday) for the German publishing house Suhrkamp and an anthology of Hungarian stories under the same title.

Translations: *The Guest from the Future: Anna Akhmatova and Isaiah Berlin*, trans. from the German by Antony Wood (New York: Farrar, Straus and Giroux, 1999); *1985: A Historical Report (Hongkong 2036) from the Hungarian of . . .* , trans. Stuart Hood and Estella Schmid (New York: Pantheon, 1983). *A körülmetélés* is available in German as *Die Beschneidung*, trans. György Dalos and Elsbeth Zylla (Frankfurt am Main: Insel, 1990; Frankfurt am Main: Suhrkamp, 1999).

Damianov, Damian Petrov (1935–1999) Bulgarian poet. A well-liked poet, Damianov was born in Sliven, where he completed high school in 1953. He went on to study Bulgarian language and literature at Sofia University, from which he graduated in 1961. After university, Damianov held several editorial positions at such journals as *Narodna mladezh* and *Plamuk*. His first poems appeared in 1949 in the hometown newspaper, *Slivensko delo*. After his first book of poetry was published in 1958 under

the title *Ako niamashe ogun* (In the Absence of Fire), Damianov produced a new book of verse virtually every year: *Ochakvane* (Expectation, 1960); *Lirika* (Lyrics, 1962); *Poema za shtastieto* (Poem About Luck, 1963); *Pred oltara na sluntseto* (Before the Altar of the Sun, 1964); *Steni* (Walls, 1964); *Predi vsichko liubov* (Love Before Everything, 1965), a dramatic poem; *Kato trevata* (Like the Grass, 1966); *Gimnaziia "Rodina"* ("Fatherland" High School, 1967); *I si otiva liatoto . . .* (And Summer Is Drawing to an End . . . , 1968); *Kolenicha pred tebe . . .* (I Kneel Before You . . . , 1968); *Ti prilichash na moia sulza* (You Resemble My Tear, 1969); *Vchera po sushtoto vreme* (Yesterday at the Same Time, 1971); *Molba kum sveta* (A Request to the World, 1973); *Radostno, tuzhno i veselo* (Happily, Sadly, Gaily, 1974); *Shte ima vrushtane* (There Will Be a Return, 1976); *Da biaha hliab . . .* (If Only I Were Bread . . . , 1977); *Blagosloveno da e neshtoto, koeto!* (May Something, Someone Be Blessed!, 1979; 2nd enl. ed., 1982); *Stigat mi solia i hliaba . . .* (Salt and Bread Suffice Me . . . , 1980); *Tetradka po vsichko* (Notebook for Everything, 1980); *Otvoren krug* (Open Circle, 1983); *Vseki delnik ima krasota* (There Is Beauty in Each and Every Workday, 1985); *Izbrane stihove* (Selected Poems, 1985); *Molitva v polunosht* (Prayer at Midnight, 1986); *Liubovna lirika* (Love Lyrics, 1990); and *Oshte sam zhiv* (I Am Still Alive, 1999).

As a poet who wrote generally well-regarded poetry within the confines of an official literary culture he found no need to challenge, Damianov was comfortable with a straightforward, natural style that made his verse acceptable to a broad spectrum of the reading public. Many of his poems are of a civic and patriotic character, and his sincerity as regards contemporary social, national, and universal human problems comes across as genuine rather than merely Party-mandated. Crippled by polio and confined to a wheelchair for much of his life, Damianov knew hardship and suffering at first hand and emphasized the need for strength of spirit and hope as the surest means to overcome adversity. He also wrote often about love, and these lyrics have remained among his most popular.

Damianov's prose writing embraced literary, social, and travel essays and notes, a book of childhood recollections, and a novel. His essays and travel writings are contained in the collections *Zhivei taka che ... Eseta, silueti, impresii* (Live as Though ... Essays, Silhouettes, Impressions, 1969); *Sbogom, burzam! Proza i ne suvsem* (Goodbye, I'm on My Way! Prose But Not Entirely, 1989); *... I moiata Bulgariia putuva* (... And My Bulgaria Is Traveling: A Literary Chronicle, 1971), in which he airs his views on contemporary Bulgarian society; and *Purvoto ime na shtastieto: Stranitsi ot putni belezhki* (The First Name of Happiness: Pages from Travel Notes, 1976). His childhood recollections appear in *Hvurchiloto se vrushta: Razkazi za edno detstvo* (The Kite Is on Its Way Back: Stories About a Childhood, 1978); *Tavanut: Pochti roman* (That's the Limit: Almost a Novel, 1983) was his sole novel. In 1997 Damianov was honored with the Ivan Vazov Award for his entire body of creative work.

Danailov, Georgi (b. 1936) Bulgarian playwright, novelist, screenwriter, and essayist. Danailov was born in Sofia and finished high school in Pleven in 1954. He then received a degree in chemistry and physics at Sofia University in 1960. He began working as a teacher of chemistry and director of a factory laboratory in Svishtov. From 1963 to 1976, he was engaged as an assistant in organic and general chemistry at the Technical Institute in Sofia. Notwithstanding his subsequent literary career mostly as a dramatist, Danailov maintained a lifelong interest in chemistry and published a number of scholarly papers in the field in Bulgaria and elsewhere. His interest in writing first manifested itself during his school years. In 1960 he published his first texts in the student journal *Narodna mladezh* and in the newspaper *Vecherni novini*. He later contributed popular scientific articles to *Nauka i tehnika, Kosmos, Orbita,* and *Pogled.* Danailov's first play, *Kraiat ostava za vas* (The End Awaits You), premiered in 1975. He wrote another nine plays after that: *Sudiiata i zhultata roza* (The Judge and the Yellow Rose, 1977); *Neseriozna komediia* (An Unserious Comedy, 1979); *Esenta na edin sledovatel* (The Autumn of One Examining Magistrate, 1980); *Dokle e mladost* (So Long as There Is Youth, 1982); *Solunskite suzakliatnitsi* (The Salonica Conspirators, 1983); *Gospodin Balkanski* (Mister Balkan, 1985); *Edna kaloriia nezhnost* (A Single Calorie of Tenderness, 1986); *Kradetsut na troleibusi* (The Bus Thief, 1987); and *Pochivka predi Raia* (Rest Before Eden, 1990).

A popular and successful dramatist and screenwriter, Danailov builds his dramatic plots generally around actual occurrences, some of them of a sensational nature, and characters who seem to stand apart from society but have their own moral principles. Emphasis is mainly on the psychological makeup of his characters, their reasons for behaving as they do, and their mental acuity that enables them to engage in duels of wit. Dialogue is often clever and not without satire and humor. Even a historical play such as *Gospodin Balkanski* follows the same pattern of construction as Danailov's social dramas.

Besides his poetry and plays, Danailov published a book about the murder of Mozart, *Ubiistvoto na Mozart: Razmisli za vuzpitanieto* (The Murder of Mozart: Thoughts for Consideration, 1982); an occasionally witty and self-ironizing but politically predictable ("You mean you're really going back to Bulgaria? That rotten country?") account of a visit to the United States,

Chikago i nazad—sto godini po-kusno: Purva chast (Chicago and Back—A Hundred Years Later: Part One, 1990); a collection of twenty-three "light" essays under the title *Spomeni za gradskiia idiot* (Memoirs of the Town Idiot, 1993) and devoted to such topics as the death of Mozart, the 1987 film festival in Georgia (USSR), Wittgenstein's Vienna, the writer and politics, the contemporary Bulgarian theater, power and psychopathy, and the intrusion of Anglicisms and Americanisms into Bulgarian speech; and a second collection of seven longer essays, mostly on literary and political topics, *Za Zhan-Zhak Ruso i drugi gluposti* (On Jean-Jacques Rousseau and Other Stupidities, 1997). Danailov was also the author of a few texts dealing with Bulgarian literature, among them *Problemite na zhivota—problemi na literaturata: Doklad iznesen pred Vtorata natsionalna konferentsiia na Suiuza na bulgarskite pisateli* (The Problems of Life—Problems of Literature: A Lecture Delivered Before the Second National Conference of the Bulgarian Writers Union, 1970) and *Ot Botev do Botev* (From Botev to Botev, 1982), a collection of articles and lectures devoted to the Bulgarian national poet and revolutionary hero, Hristo Botev (1848–1876).

Danilov, Dragan Jovanović (b. 1960) Serbian poet, novelist, and essayist. An original, in some ways challenging and controversial, writer, Danilov was born in Požega where he was educated through high school and then earned a degree in art history at Belgrade University. His poetry, which often draws on Christian religious themes for inspiration, began appearing in book form in 1990 with the publication of the collection *Euharistija* (Eucharist). This was followed by *Enigma noči* (Enigma of Night, 1991); *Pentagram srca: Ronda, uspavanke, balade, bluzovi* (Pentagram of the Heart: Rondos, Lullabies, Ballads, and Blues, 1992); his highly regarded poetic trilogy consisting of *Kuća Bahove muzike* (The House of Bach's Music, 1993), *Živi pergament* (Living Pergament, 1994), and *Evropa pod snegom* (Europe Under Snow, 1995); and *Pantokreator* (Pantocreator, 1998). By far his major poetic achievement, and his most widely translated work, The House of Bach's Music trilogy is notable for a wide variety of poetic forms and themes, many related to Danilov's interest in music and the performing arts. The trilogy also represents an example of Danilov's idea of an integrated poetic whole woven together of often disparate elements but inspired by a unifying vision. His newest collection of poems, *Alkoholi s juga* (Alcohols from the South, 1999), with the "alcohols" of the title referring to the inspiration of the Mediterranean, was awarded the Oskar Davičo Prize.

In 1996 Danilov published his first novel, the verbally dazzling *Almanah peščanij dina* (Almanac of Sand Dunes), an original type of bildungsroman (a novel about the moral and intellectual upbringing usually of someone young) and further demonstrating his commitment to the integrated work of art. This was followed in 1998 by *Ikonostas na kraju sveta* (Iconostasis at the End of the World), a short novel (termed by the author "a novel cenotaph") inspired by the Bosnian War. It is about a Serb living temporarily in Paris who leaves behind his pregnant girlfriend to return to Serbia, only to get caught up in the fighting in Bosnia. He is captured, witnesses terrible scenes of torture and killing, is eventually released, and reunites with the woman who is now the mother of his child. A philosophical rumination of sorts on the loss of ethical values that made possible the atrocities of the Bosnian War, *Ikonostas na kraju sveta* is a somewhat weak novel. In a short, upbeat epilogue Danilov forecasts a resurrection of the spirit that will make future Bosnias less likely. Apart from the Oskar Davičo Prize, Danilov has received the Meša Selimović, Prosveta, and

Branko Miljković prizes but has declared in interviews that the great number of literary awards being distributed has robbed them virtually of any significance.

Danilov, Nichita (b. 1952) Romanian poet. A native of Iaşi, where he was educated through university, with a degree in economics, Danilov is currently director of the youth theater Luceafărul in Iaşi. His first published volume of poems, *Fîntîni carteziene* (Cartesian Wells, 1980), won the Writers Union Prize. It was followed by *Cîmp negru* (Black Field, 1982); *Arlechini la margina cîmpului* (Harlequins at the Edge of the Field, 1985); *Poezii* (Poems, 1987); and *Deasupra lucrurilor, neamtul* (Above Things, Nothingness, 1990). Danilov is a writer of simple lyrics, many of which convey a sense of desolation and sorrow in life.

Translations: Five poems in *Young Poets of a New Romania: An Anthology,* trans. Brenda Walker with Michaela Celea-Leach, ed. Ion Stoica (London: Forest, 1991), 15–20.

Darvasi, László (b. 1962) Hungarian poet, short-story writer, playwright, and novelist. Born in Törökszentmiklós, Darvasi was trained as a schoolteacher but since 1989 has been cultural editor at the daily *Délmagyarország.* In 1990 he became editor of a literary periodical, *Pompeji,* and since 1993 has been a member of the staff of the literary weekly *Élet és Irodalom.* Darvasi's first published volume was a collection of poems, *Horger Antal Pâriszban* (Antal Horger in Paris, 1991). It was followed the next year by *A portugálok* (The Portuguese), a volume of verse and short prose pieces. Darvasi's first collection of short stories, *A veingaheni rózsabokrok* (The Weinhagen Roses), appeared in 1993. His next book of stories, *A Borgognoni-féle szomorúság* (The Borgognoni Sadness, 1994), was awarded the Book of the Year Prize. The collection *A Kleofás képregény: Históriák, legendák és*

képregények (The Cleophas Comic Book: Tales, Legends, and Picture Stories) appeared in 1995. His most recent books are *Szerelmem, Dumumba elvtársnő* (My Love, Comrade Dumumba, 1998) and *Szerezni egy nőt: Háborús novellák* (Getting a Woman: War Stories, 2000). Darvasi is an intriguing, if disturbing, postmodernist writer with a fondness for the bizarre and macabre. There is no subject, from murder and rape to mother–son incest, that is taboo for him, and he seems to delight in shocking and offending the reader with graphic descriptions of bodily functions. From his very short (one- to two-page) stories to longer works, Darvasi, like other relatively younger contemporary Hungarian writers, seems intent on waging combat against the traditional and expected in literature, and above all against the literary norms prevailing in the period of communist Hungary.

Translations: "The Roses of Weinhagen," trans. Bernard Adams, in *Give or Take a Day: Contemporary Hungarian Short Stories,* ed. Lajos Szakolczy (Budapest: Corvina, 1997), 138–54. A collection of Darvasi's stories is available in German as *Das traurigste Orchester der Welt* (Berlin: Rowohlt, 1995).

Davičo, Oskar (1909–1989) Serbian novelist, poet, essayist, and literary theorist. One of the most prolific post–World War II Yugoslav writers, Davičo was born in Šabac. In 1926 he went to Paris, where he spent the next two years stuying. After his Paris sojourn, he settled in Belgrade and became actively involved in the surrealist movement. With Djordje Kostić and Dušan Matić, he issued the Serbian surrealist manifesto of 1932, "Položaj nadrealizma u društvenom procesu" ("The Position of Surrealism in the Social Process"). The same year, Davičo was imprisoned for alleged communist activity. He was released in 1938. Prior to World War II, he published two collections of poetry, *Pesme* (Poems, 1938) and *Hana* (1939), one of his most highly regarded works. During the war, in 1941, Davičo was interned by the Italians, but with the fall of Italy he was released, whereupon he joined Tito's partisans. After the war, Davičo resumed his literary career, publishing a number of volumes of poems, several novels, literary studies, and books of essays on political and cultural issues. His two novels *Medju Markosovim partizanima* (Among Marko's Partisans, 1947) and *Pesma* (*The Poem*, 1952) grew out of his wartime experiences. *The Poem*, the better of the two and perhaps Davičo's best-known work, is a large novel set in German-occupied Belgrade during World War II, and covering a time span of only thirty-six hours. The repudiation of a poet (who wants to join the partisans) by a morally overzealous young communist sets up a tragic situation in which the poet attempts to vindicate himself in a public denunciation of the occupation and is ultimately freed from German imprisonment in an action that costs the young communist his life.

In 1955 Davičo became the editor of *Delo*, the journal that led the Serbian modernists in their struggle against *Savremenik*, the journal of the realists. He also helped organize the Yugoslav Writers Association in the mid-1960s, but resigned from it in 1965 to protest against its policies.

Davičo's many postwar volumes of poetry include, among others, *Višnja za zidom* (The Cherry Tree Behind the Wall, 1950), which contains some poems written much earlier and a number of texts of a patriotic and also more traditional realistic character; *Čovekov čovek* (A Man's Man, 1953), a long poem on the disparity between revolutionary events and socialist ideals; *Nastanjene oči* (Settled Vision, 1954); *Kairos* (Cairo, 1959); *Tropi* (Tropics, 1959); *Snimci* (Snapshots, 1963); *Trg e M* (e M Square, 1968); *Zavičaji* (Homelands, 1971); *Pročitani jezik* (A Language Read Aloud, 1972); *Izabrana Srbija* (Chosen Serbia, 1972); *Telo telu* (Body

to Body, 1975); *Misterije dana* (Mysteries of the Day, 1979); *Trema smrti: Poema* (The Gates of Death: A Poem, 1982); *Što volim rosu* (Why We Like the Dew, 1984), a collection of his poems edited by Milosav Mirković; *Mali oglasi smrti* (Small Notices of Death, 1986); *Svetlaci neslicni sebi* (Glittering Differences, 1987); *Dvojezična noc* (A Bilingual Night, 1987); and *Mitološki zverinjak smrti* (Mythological Garden of Death, 1987). Beginning with his poetry from the 1960s and 1970s, Davičo seemed anxious to move away from a constraining realism and back to the surrealism with which he obviously felt more comfortable. That became possible in the less doctrinaire literary climate of the time.

In addition to *Medju Markosovim partizanima* and *The Poem*, Davičo was the author of several other novels, among them *Beton i svici* (Concrete and Glowworms, 1958); *Radni naslov beskraja* (The Working Title of Infinity, 1958); *Čisti i prljavi* (The Clean and the Dirty, 1958); *Pre podne* (In the Early Afternoon, 1960); *Ćutnje* (Silence, 1963); *Gladi* (Hungers, 1963); *Tajne* (Secrets, 1964); *Tragovi* (Traces, 1969); *Crno na belo* (White on Black, 1969); *Reći na delu* (Words in Action, 1977); *Gospodar zaborava* (The Sovereign Forgets, 1980); and *Gladni stoliv* (The Hungry, 1983), in which he sought to part company with realism, as he had earlier in his poetry. His collection of stories from 1984, *Nežne priče* (Tender Fables: Stories), further evidenced the inclination toward greater experimentation.

Davičo was no less prolific an essayist, often publishing several volumes in one year. He wrote on many subjects, but his essays on literature and politics are among his best. His major collections of essays include *Notes: Eseji i članci* (Notes: Essays and Articles, 1969); *Novine nevine: Eseji i članci* (An Innocent Journal: Essays and Articles, 1969); *Pristojnosti: Eseji i članci* (Proprieties: Essays and Articles, 1969); *Poezija: Otpori i neotpori*

(Poetry: Resistance and Submission, 1969); *Rituali umiranja jezika* (The Death Rituals of Language, 1972); *Pod-tekst: Podtekst* (Sub-Text: Subtext, 1979); *Pod sećanja* (Beneath Memory, 1981); *Procesi: Eseji i članci* (Trials: Essays and Articles, 1983); and *Polemika i dalje* (Polemics and Beyond, 1986). Two of his prose works are of an autobiographical nature: *Detinjstvo 1958* (Childhood 1958, 1958) and *Po zanimanju samoubica: Roman-sirana autobiografija 1927. i 1928. godine u trećem licu uglavnom* (After Consideration of Suicide: A Fictionalized Autobiography of the Years 1927 and 1928, 1987–1988). In 1971 the composer Mihailo Vukdragović composed a cantata to verses of DaviČo under the title *Srbija: Kantata za solo-bas, recitatora, mešoviti hor i orkestar* (Serbia: Cantata for Solo Bass, Recitative, Mixed Chorus, and Orchestra, 1971).

Literature: Barbara Czapik, *Twórczość po-etycka Oskara Daviča: Poszerzanie świado-mości w awangardowej praktyce poetyckiej* (Katowice: Uniwersytet Śląski, 1987), a good Polish study of Daviča's poetry; Stojan Dordić and Cveta Kotevska, eds., *U potrazi radovi: O književnom delu Oskara Daviča* (Belgrade: Narodna knjiga, 1979), a collection of essays on various facets of Daviča's writings; Radomir Konstantinović, *DaviČo* (Belgrade: Rad, 1980). For a good bibliography of Daviča's work to that year, see Stanka Kostić, ed., *Bibliografja Oskara Daviča* (Belgrade: Prosveta, 1969).

Translations: *The Poem*, trans. Alec Brown (London: Lincolns-Prager, 1959).

David, Filip (b. 1940) Serbian short-story writer. David, who lives in Belgrade, is a writer of modern fantastic prose, some with Jewish themes. His stories are contained in such collections as *Bunar u tamnoj šumi* (The Well in a Dark Forest, 1964); *Zapisi o stvarnom i nestvarnom* (Notes on the Real and the Unreal, 1969); and *Princ vatre: Priče o okultnom* (The Prince of Fire: Tales of the Occult, 1987). His novel, *Hodočasnici neba i zemlje* (Pilgrimages of Heaven and Earth, 1995), is something of a tour de force of the fantastic. Escaping from the Inquisition, a man travels throughout the Mediterranean area and along the way is plunged into a world of magic and mystery where he encounters an astonishing variety of supernatural forces, evil spirits, demons, and ghosts. David's book *Jesmo li čudovišta* (Are We Monsters?, 1997) deals with the Yugoslav wars of 1991 to 1995. In 1998 a collection of correspondence between David and the writer Mirko Kovač was published under the title *Knjiga pisama: 1992–1995* (Book of Letters: 1992–1995).

Translations: "The Prince of Fire," trans. Karolina Udovički, in *The Prince of Fire: An Anthology of Contemporary Serbian Short Stories*, ed. Radmila J. Gorup and Nadežda Obradović (Pittsburgh: University of Pittsburgh Press, 1998), 164–76.

Davidkov, Ivan (1926–1990) Bulgarian poet, novelist, short-story writer, essayist, translator, and painter. A versatile and very talented artist, Davidkov was born in Zhivovtsi in the Mihailovgrad district of northwestern Bulgaria. He finished high school in Berkovitsa in 1944 and then earned a degree in Slavic philology at Sofia University in 1951. In 1958/1959, he spent a year in the Ukraine and Belarus on an exchange agreement. He became particularly fond of Ukrainian literature, from which he later translated extensively and which inspired his third book of verse, *Ukrainetsut s bialata harmonika* (The Ukrainian with the White Harmonica, 1951). Davidkov was affiliated for a number of years in an editorial capacity with such journals as *Septemvriiche, Rodni prostori, Pla-muche*, and *Slaveiche*, and from 1968 to 1986 he was the editor in chief of the major publishing house Bulgarski pisatel. A highly prolific and varied poet, Davidkov published a large number of poetry collections, many of which were intended for children and young readers. The only collection of his poetry in English translation, *Fires of the Sunflower,* includes texts drawn from such major volumes as *Hulmove pod vechernitsata* (Hills Beneath the Evening Star, 1966); *Trakiiski mogili* (Thracian Tumuli, 1968*); Ozarenie* (Illumination, 1970); *Bial kon na prozoretsa. Tants na kiparisite* (White Horse in the Window. Dance of the Cypresses, 1975), which was dedicated to the Greek poet Yanis Ritsos; *Molitvi za dletoto i kamuka* (Prayers for Chisel and Stone, 1977); *Vladeteliat na noshtnite sluntsa* (The Ruler of Nocturnal Suns, 1981); *Oko na ptitsa* (Bird's Eye, 1983); *Korida* (Corrida, 1984); *Otlitaneto na skortsite* (The Departure of the Starlings, 1987); and *Moreto* (The Sea, 1988).

Some of Davidkov's other books of poetry include *Svetlina ot skrezha* (Light from the Frost, 1957); *Dnepur pod moia prozorets teche* (The Dnieper Flows Under My Window, 1960); *Pesni i baladi* (Songs and Ballads, 1965); *Kamenolomna* (Quarry, 1972*); Nazdravitsa za zvezdopada* (Toast to a Shooting Star, 1972); *Stihotvoreniia* (Poems, 1977); *Iskam da ti podaria* (I Want to Make You a Present, 1977); *Melodiia za fleita: Lubovna lirika* (Melody for Flute: Love Lyrics, 1984); *Termopili: 9 stihotvoreniia* (Thermopylae: 9 Poems, 1988), a bibliophile edition in fifty copies; *Kupaneto na nimfite* (The Nymphs' Bath, 1990); and *Mozhe bi sbogom* (Perhaps Goodbye, 1992). Although mostly lyrical in his early poetry, Davidkov subsequently turned to a more philosophical and humanistic view of the world that, while troubled by the ephemerality of life, nonetheless expressed some hope in man's ability to achieve a meaningful existence. Davidkov's abiding dismay at the brevity of life was mitigated by his deeply pantheistic love of nature and the painterly impressionistic landscapes he created in a reflection of his work as a visual artist as well as an imaginative writer. For the most part laconic in

style, Davidkov favored rhyme while experimenting widely in the areas of stanzaic and rhythmic structure. As time went on, his poetry also became more heavily metaphoric and shaped by his intimate knowledge of painting and music.

Apart from his poetry, Davidkov wrote several novels and collections of essays. His novels include *Dalechnite brodove* (Distant Fords, 1967); *Kushei hliab za putnika* (A Morsel of Bread for a Traveler, 1971); *Vecheren razgovor s duzhda* (Evening Conversation with Rain, 1973); *Sbogom, Akropolis!* (Farewell, Acropolis!, 1976); and *Zimnite sunishta na luvovete* (The Lions' Hibernation, 1982). In large measure related thematically to his lyrics, these works eschew conventional chronological narration, move backward and forward in time toward the impressionistic, and clearly contain elements of self-portraiture in major characters whose artistic and intellectual talents set them apart from the rest of society. Typical in this respect is his last novel, *Zimnite sunishta na luvovete,* in which the central figure, Martin Kalinov, is identified as The Translator (recalling Davidkov's own career as a translator), while another prominent character, an older writer, is The Essayist. The entire work pivots on literary and artistic issues and toward the end, in a section entitled "From the Author," recalls youthful recurring dreams involving lions first observed in a circus and echoes of (obviously) Davidkov's own later travels in Algeria and the imapct on his consciousness of the vast expanses of the Sahara.

Davidkov's essays, many of which are quite short and include pieces on his foreign travels, appear in three collections: *Poletut na strelata: Belezhki, nabliudeniia, eseta* (The Flight of the Arrow: Notes, Commentaries, Essays, 1985); *Noshtno violonchelo: Belezhki, nabliudeniia, eseta* (Nocturnal Cello: Notes, Commnentaries, Essays, 1989); and *Kafeneto na klounete: Kniga s eseta, etiudi, nabliudeniia i dnevnik ot 1989* (The Clowns' Coffeehouse: A Book of Essays, Etudes, Observations, and a Diary from 1989, 1995). Although Davidkov's essays address a wide range of topics, some of the most interesting explore the creative process and are often self-analytic. The diary section of his last collection of essays, covering the period from 10 August to 31 December 1989, recounts political events including the forced migration to Turkey of Bulgarian Muslims who refused to Slavicize their names and otherwise adopt Bulgarian ways in a brief period of state-enforced Bulgarian nationalism.

Translations: *Fires of the Sunflower: Poems by Ivan Davidkov,* trans. Ewald Osers (London: Forest, 1988).

Debeljak, Aleš (b. 1961) Slovene poet, critic, essayist, and translator. One of Slovenia's most highly regarded contemporary writers, Debeljak was born in Ljubljana. He received his undergraduate degree in comparative literature and philosophy and a master's in cultural studies from Ljubljana University. In 1988 he left for the United States, and two years later received a doctorate in social thought from Syracuse University. Besides translations of his own poetry in the United States, he has helped disseminate poetry of the former Yugoslavia in English translation. In 1993, for example, he edited the Slovene, Croatian, and Serbian section for *Shifting Borders: East European Poetries of the Eighties* (Rutherford, N.J.: Farleigh Dickinson University Press). He also served as the editor of *Prisoners of Freedom: Contemporary Slovenian Poetry* (Santa Fe, N.M.: Pedernal Press, 1994). Debeljak has held writing fellowships at the Virginia Center for the Creative Arts and at Cambridge University. Apart from five books of published poetry—*Zamenjave, zamenjave* (Exchanges, Exchanges, 1982); *Imena smrti* (The Names of Death, 1985); *Slovar tišine*

(*Dictionary of Silence,* 1987); *Minute strahu: Fotografije s poti* (*Anxious Moments: Photographs in Sweat,* 1990); and *Mesto in otrok* (*The City and the Child,* 1996)—Debeljak has published two books of essays on literature and art, *Melanholične figure* (Figures of Melancholy, 1988) and *Postmoderna sfinga* (Postmodern Sphinx, 1989), and a fine study of modernity, postmodernity, and bourgeois society, *Postmoderna sfinga: Kontinuiteta modernosti in postmodernisti* (The Postmodern Sphinx: The Continuity of Modernism and the Postmodernists, 1989; translated as *Reluctant Modernity: The Institution of Art and Its Historical Forms*). In 1988 Debeljak also edited an anthology of American short stories in Slovenia. He is the author, moreover, of *Somrak idolov* (*Twilight of the Idols: Recollections of a Lost Yugoslavia,* 1994), a small book lamenting the loss of the ethnic and cultural mosaic that had been Yugoslavia and Serb responsibility for its destruction.

As a poet, Debeljak has a strong proclivity for the prose poem (as in *Anxious Moments*), which he fills with unsettling and haunting images, long lines of verse that read like prose, and, thematically, an abiding sense of loneliness, melancholy, and foreboding. He is not, however, a poet of resignation. Silence, and the power of silence over language, are among the dominant motifs of his poetry, as in the collection *Slovar tišine.* A number of his poems reflect his American travels and his affinities with American poetry, which he himself has acknowledged. In 1991 he published *Temno nebo Amerika* (The Dark Cloud of America), in which he discusses American intellectual life and society. Among the several awards Debeljak has received for his work are the prestigious Prešeren Prize in Slovenia (1990); the Hayden Carruth Poetry Prize (1989); the Roscoe Martin Dissertation Prize (1990) at Syracuse University; and the Miriam Lindberg Israel Poetry for Peace

Prize (Tel Aviv). He contributes a regular column to the Slovene cultural fortnightly, *Razgledi,* and to *Literatur und Kritik,* an Austrian literary magazine, and is a contributing editor of *Trafika,* an English-language literary quarterly published in Prague. He currently holds the position of professor and chair of the Department of Cultural Studies at Ljubljana University.

Translations: *Anxious Moments: Poems by Aleš Debeljak,* trans. Christopher Merrill with Aleš Debeljak (Fredonia, N.Y.: White Pine, 1994); *The Chronicle of Melancholy* (Chattanooga, Tenn.: Poetry Miscellany, 1989, 1991); *The City and the Child,* trans. Christopher Merrill and Aleš Debeljak (Buffalo, N.Y.: White Pine, 1999); *Dictionary of Silence,* trans. Sonja Kravanja (Santa Fe, N.M.: Lumen, 1999); *Reluctant Modernity: The Institution of Art and Its Historical Forms* (Lanham, Md.: Rowman & Littlefield, 1998); *Twilight of the Idols: Recollections of a Lost Yugoslavia,* trans. Michael Biggins (Fredonia, N.Y.: White Pine, 1994); "Lonesome Heart and the Failed Community," trans. Erica Johnson Debeljak, in *The Slovenian Essay of the Nineties,* selected by Matevž Kos (Ljubljana: Slovene Writers Association, 2000), 45–61. SOUND RECORDING: A sound recording, dated 25 October 1999, of Debeljak reading his poetry—made at the Farnsworth Room, Lamont Library, Harvard University, and sponsored by the Woodberry Poetry Room—is available.

De Bruyn, Günter. *See* Bruyn, Günter de

Dedaj, Rrahman (b. 1939) Kosovo Albanian poet. A native of Podujeva, Dedaj pursued Albanian studies in Priština, after which he became executive editor of the Rilindja publishing house, the major publisher of Albanian books in Yugoslavia. Dedaj's first collection of poems, *Me sy këngë* (With Eyes of Song), appeared in 1962. It was followed by *Simfonia e fjalës* (Word Symphony, 1968);

Baladë e fshehur (The Hidden Ballad, 1970); *Etje* (Thirst, 1973); *Gjërat që s'preken* (Intangibles, 1980); *Jeta gabon* (Life Errs, 1983); and *Fatkeqësia e urtësi* (The Misfortune of Wisdom, 1987). A poet largely of Romantic and symbolist inclinations, Dedaj has also shown an interest in history and in the literary process itself. *Poezi* (Poetry, 1989), an anthology of poems from Dedaj's previously published volumes, was his first verse collection to be published in Albania proper, although he has been as well known in that country as in Kosovo.

Translations: Five poems in *An Elusive Eagle Soars: Anthology of Modern Albanian Poetry,* ed. and trans. Robert Elsie (London: Forest, 1993), 105–10.

Dekleva, Milan (b. 1946) Slovenian poet, playwright, and essayist. Dekleva was born and educated in Ljubljana, where he graduated from Ljubljana University with a degree in comparative literature and literary theory. He then went into journalism and writes for several newspapers and journals. Dekleva is the author of over a dozen volumes of poetry; several plays, most of which were written for radio, puppet, and children's theater; and a novel. As a poet, he is known especially for his love lyrics, linguistic dexterity, and poems of philosphical content in which the influence of the German philosopher Martin Heidegger (1889–1976) is discernible. The musical qualities of Dekleva's verse are generally attributed to his skills as a jazz musician (he serves as the vice president of the jazz club Gao, which was founded in 1994), a lyricist for popular songs, and a writer of musical comedy. His first published collection of verse, *Mushi mushi,* appeared in 1971 and is a collection of poems in the manner of Japanese haiku. It was followed by *Dopisovanja* (Correspondence, 1978); *Nagovarjanja* (Persuasions, 1979); *Narečje telesa* (Dialect Bodies, 1984); *Zapriseženi prah* (The Oath Powder, 1987); *Odjedanje božjega* (Cloak of Divinity, 1988); *Panični človek* (A Man in Panic, 1990), a collection of short philosophical poems inspired by the ancient Greek philosopher and astronomer Anaximander; *Preseženi človek* (Superlative Man, 1992); *Oko v zraku* (Eye in the Air, 1993); *Kvantaški stihi* (Indecent Poems, 1994); *Šepavi soneti* (Limping Sonnets, 1995); *Jezikava rapsodija* (Language Rhapsody, 1996); *A so kremšnite nevarne* (Even Cream Puffs Are Dangerous, 1996); *Gnezda in katedrale* (Nests and Cathedrals, 1997); and *Reševalec ptic* (The Rescuer of Birds, 1999). Among his theatrical texts, apart from his radio, puppet, and children's plays, is the political cabaret *Igra na vrhu* (Game at the Top, 1993). His short novel, *Pimlico*, appeared in 1998. Dekleva was awarded the Jankov Prize in 1990.

Translations: Five poems, and five of the Anaximander poems (from *Panični človek*), trans. Jože Žohar, Boris A. Novak, Richard Jackson, and Mia Dintinjana, in *The Imagination of Terra Incognita: Slovenian Writing, 1945–1995*, ed. Aleš Debeljak (Fredonia, N.Y.: White Pine, 1997), 249–55; "A Dark Poem, a Screened Poet," trans. Irena Zorko Novak, in *The Slovenian Essay of the Nineties*, selected by Matevž Kos (Ljubljana: Slovene Writers Association, 2000), 93–97.

Déry, Tibor (1894–1977) Hungarian novelist, short-story writer, playwright, and poet. One of the outstanding Hungarian writers of the twentieth century, Déry published his first story in 1917 in the famous avant-garde periodical *Nyugat,* and thereafter a number of poems. In 1919 he joined the Communist Party, but emigrated from Hungary after the defeat of Béla Kun and the so-called Hungarian Republic of Soviets. He spent most of the interwar period out of the country, particularly in Berlin and Vienna. A small edition of his poems from 1921 and 1922 was published in Vienna in 1922 under the title *Ló buza ember* (Horse, Wheat, Man). Most of his creative work appeared in Hungary after World War II. Apart from the novel *Jókedv és buzgalom* (Ambition and Hilarity, 1948)—also the title of an often anthologized short story by him—his first major success came with the novel *A befejezetlen mondat* (Unfinished Sentence, 1949), a realistic panorama of the interwar Hungarian bourgeoisie. This was followed in 1951 by *Felelet* (The Answer), also set in the interwar period and dealing with the working class. However, the attacks on the novel by the Communist Party on ideological grounds set the stage for Déry's later imprisonment (1956–1963). Of the works by him published in the years immediately preceding his imprisonment and during that time, the most important were *Simon Menyhért születés* (The Birth of Simon Menyhért, 1953), a novella; *Hazáról, emberekről: Útijegyzetek* (The Land and the People: Travel Notes, 1954), a book of descriptions of Hungarian towns and cities; *Két emlék* (Two Mementos, 1955); *Út kaparó* (The Path Digger, 1955), a novel; *A ló meg az öregasszony* (The Horse and the Old Woman, 1955), a volume of selected stories; *Niki, egy kutya története* (*Niki: The Story of a Dog*, 1956), his only novel available in English; and two volumes of short stories: *Vidám temetés és más elbeszélések* (The Cheerful Funeral and Other Stories, 1960) and *Szerelem és más elbeszélések* (Love and Other Stories, 1963).

Déry's first important work to appear after his release from prison was *G. A. úr X.-ben* (Mr. G. A. in X, 1964), a widely translated utopian novel. The late 1960s and the 1970s proved very productive for him. His fictionalized biography of St. Ambrose (bishop of Milan, d. 397), *Kiközösítő* (The Excommunicator), appeared in 1966. This was followed by *Az óriáscsecsemő* (The Big Baby, 1967); *Theokritosz Újpesten* (Theocritos in New Pest, 1967); *Szembenézni* (Facing Up, 1968); *Ambrosius* (1968); *A felhőállatok* (Animals in the Clouds, 1970), a selection of verse; *Képzelt riport egy amerikai pop-fesztiválról* (Imaginary Report About an American Rock Festival, 1971), a long-running musical about American hippies; *Alkonyodík, a bárányok elvéreznek* (Night Is Falling, the Sheep Are Bleeding to Death, 1972), a collection of stories; *Kedves bópeer . . . !* (Dear Beaupère . . . , 1973), an ironic novel about old age; *A kéthangú kiáltas: Négy regény* (The Two-Toned Shout: Four Novels, 1975); *Újabb napok hordaléka* (New Days' Deposits, 1975); *Félfülű: Rémtörténet* (Half an Ear: A Blood-Curdler, 1975); and three collections of stories published in 1977 and 1979: *A gyilkos és én: Kisregények* (The Murderer and I, 1977), *Niki* (Niki, 1977), and *Niki és más történetek* (Niki and Other Stories, 1979). His first important autobiographical work, based on his prison experiences, appeared in 1958 under the title *Börtönnapok hordaléká: Önéletrajzi jegyzetek* (Prison Days Deposits: Autobiographical Notes), edited by Ferenc Botka. Déry's very candid autobiography, *Ítélet nincs* (No Verdict), came out in 1969. A volume of his plays was published in 1976 under the title *Színház* (Theater). Of Déry's posthumous publications, the two most interesting are *Botladozás* (Stumbling Along, 1978), a two-volume collection of articles and studies, and *Lia: Korai elbeszélések, 1915–1920* (Lia: Early Stories, 1915–1920, 1996).

Literature: Ferenc Botka, *Déry Tibor és Berlin: A szemtől szembe és forrásvidéke* (Budapest: Argumentum, 1994), a study of Déry's time in Berlin.

Translations: *The Giant, Behind the Brick Wall, Love,* trans. Kathleen Szasz (London: Calder and Boyars, 1966); *Niki: The Story of a Dog,* trans. Edward Hyams (Garden City, N.Y.: Doubleday, 1958); *The Portuguese Princess and Other Stories,* trans. Kathleen Szasz (London: Calder and Boyars, 1967; Chicago: Quadrangle Books, 1968; Evanston, Ill.: Northwestern University Press, 1987);

"Ambition and Hilarity," trans. István Farkas, in *The Kiss: Twentieth Century Hungarian Short Stories,* selected by István Bart (Budapest: Corvina, 1998), 101–16; "The Circus," trans. Elizabeth Csicsery-Rónay, in *Hungarian Short Stories,* ed. Paul Varnai (Toronto: Exile Editions, 1983), 16–32. Déry also wrote the text for a picture book about Lake Balaton, *Lake Balaton* (Budapest: Corvina, 1968). Several of Déry's novels and short-story collections are also available in French and German.

Desnica, Vladan (1905–1967) Croatian novelist and short-story writer. Born in Zadar on the Dalmatian coast, Desnica studied philosophy and law in Zagreb and Paris. Following his graduation from law school, he entered government service. In 1948 he resigned from the Croatian Ministry of Finance in order to become a professional writer. Strongly interested in moral and philosophical issues, Desnica began his literary career as a short-story writer, publishing four collections of stories between 1952 and 1956: *Olupine na suncu* (Derelicts in the Sun, 1952); *Proljeće u Badrovcu* (Springtime at Badrovac, 1955); *Tu, odmah pored nas: Priče o proljeću, o ljubavi, o smrti* (Here, Right Alongside Us: Stories About Spring, Love, and Death, 1956); and *Fratar sa zelenom bradom* (The Friar with the Green Beard, 1959). His first novel, *Proljeća Ivana Galeba* (The Springtimes of Ivan Galeb), appeared in 1960 and was soon hailed as one of the finest Yugoslav literary achievements since World War II. Desnica's second novel, the short *Zimsko ljetovanje* (Winter Vacations), was published in 1966 and has also long been regarded as one his best works. A posthumous collection of his stories was published in 1974 under the title *Pripovijetke* (Stories), and in 1975 a large collection of his essays and other nonfiction writings was issued as *Essays, kritike, pogledi* (Essays, Criticism, Views). Also in 1975, a four-volume edition of his collected works appeared (*Sabrana djela*). A collection of his stories was published in 1990 as *Konac dana* (The Thread of Days).

Translations: "Justice," trans. Jan Dekker, in *Introduction to Yugoslav Literature: An Anthology of Fiction and Poetry*, ed. Branko Mikasinovich, Dragan Milivojević, and Vasa D. Mihailovich (New York: Twayne, 1973), 493–96; "Justice," trans. E. D. Goy, in *New Writing in Yugoslavia*, ed. Bernard Johnson (Harmondsworth: Penguin, 1970), 83–86; "Mr. Pink's Soliloquy," trans. Petar Mijušković, and "The Tale of the Friar with the Green Beard," trans. Olga Humo, in *Death of a Simple Giant and Other Modern Yugoslav Stories*, ed. Branko Lenski (New York: Vanguard, 1965), 271–81, 283–90.

Diaconescu, Ioana (b. 1947) Romanian poet. A native of Bucharest, Diaconescu graduated from high school in her native city in 1965 and received a degree in Romanian language and literature at Bucharest University in 1971. She subsequently worked as a librarian and has regularly collaborated with such journals as *Luceafărul, România literară*, and *Steaua*. Her first poems appeared in the journal *Contemporanul* in 1965. Two years later, she published her first book of poems, *Furăm trandafiri* (Stealing Roses). This was followed by *Jumătate zeu* (A God Almost, 1970); *Adagio* (1973); *Taina* (The Secret, 1976); *Amiaza* (The Afternoon, 1978); *Ceața* (The Mist, 1978); *Poetica* (Poetic Art, 1981); *Vîrtejul și lumea* (The Whirlwind and the World, 1982); *Amintiri neverosimile* (Improbable Memories, 1983); *Dumnealui, destinul* (To Fate, 1984); *Uranus* (1985); and *Herb* (Coat of Arms, 1987). Diaconescu writes mainly about the Romanian countryside, nature in the different seasons, time, love, and humans in relation to nature and time. Hers is a quiet, relaxed, spontaneous poetry with no rough edges.

Translations: Four poems in *15 Young Romanian Poets: An Anthology of Verse*, trans. and ed. Liliana Ursu (Bucharest: Eminescu, 1982), 17–21.

Dichev, Ivailo (b. 1955) Bulgarian novelist, short-story writer, and literary scholar. A representative of contemporary Bulgarian postmodernism, Dichev was born in Sofia. He graduated from high school in 1973, after which he received a degree in English language and literature from Sofia University in 1979. In the 1980s he held editorial positions at the journal *Orbita* and at the Bulgarski pisatel publishing house, and was affiliated with the Union of Bulgarian Translators. He joined the Department of Logic, Ethics, and Aesthetics of Sofia University in 1990 and in 1991 went to the Sorbonne in Paris for advanced study. He received his doctorate in 1992. Between 1987 and 1991, Dichev was a member of the Synthesis group of intellectuals in Sofia who in 1989 published the semi-samizdat collection of essays, *Ars Simulacri*, and in 1992 the collection *Ars Erotica*. Dichev made his debut as a creative writer in 1979, the year he graduated from university, with a collection of short stories titled *Ucha se da placha* (Learning to Cry). It was followed by a volume of novellas, *Zvezden kalendar* (Astral Calendar, 1982); the novel *Identifikatsiia* (Identification, 1987), for which he is perhaps best known; a collection of stories and novellas, *Mig sled kraia na sveta* (A Moment Along the Edge of the Earth, 1988); a book of essays under the title *Granitsi mezhdu men i men* (Boundaries Between Me and Me, 1990); the scholarly study *Erotika na avtorstvoto: Isledvane* (The Erotics of Authorship: Research, 1991); and a volume of *razkazoidi* (narratoids) called *Bukvalizm* (Literalism, 1991).

As the titles of such texts as *Identifikatsiia* and *Granitsi mezhdu men i men* suggest, Dichev is much concerned in his writing with the problem of the definition of the self (i.e., the literary character) in a contemporary environment of collapsing social and moral values. How, in other words, does the individual define himself when everything around him is undergoing a process of relativization? In *Identifikatsiia* he uses the fictional form of the novel to question the very legitimacy of the genre and the various norms, from the social to the linguistic, that have long governed its practice. As Dichev's writing became still more postmodern, he exploded the distinctions among genres and drew more heavily on contemporary philosophical and literary critical theories to develop his views. In his last major published work, *Bukvalizm,* he toys with the notion of the genre of the short story (Bulgarian, *razkaz*) by creating a variant of it that he calls *razkazoid* (narratoid). The book is in fact composed of small sketches subdivided into three sections, "Facts," "Desires," and "Numbers." The section "Desires" contains probably Dichev's best-known essay, "Erotika na komunizma" ("The Eroticism of Communism"), in which he reduces communist dogma to a shambles through humorous sketches about everyday lust and sex. In his essay "Prohozhdane sred metaforite" ("Strolling Through Metaphors"), he also argues that contemporary life, including communism and its eventual collapse, is a literalization of metaphor and gives a number of examples, such as "the sexual revolution, which literally realized the Christian call to love one's neighbor."

Translations: "The Eroticism of Communism," trans. Robert Sturm, in *Description of a Struggle: The Vintage Book of Contemporary Eastern European Writing,* ed. Michael March (New York: Vintage, 1994), 189–201; "The Transparent Book," "Literalisms," "The Post-Paranoid Condition," and "Epitaph for Sacrifice, Epitaph for the Left," in *Post-Theory, Games, and Discursive Resistance: The Bulgarian Case,* ed. Alexander Kiossev (Albany: State University of New York Press, 1995), 1–2, 3–9, 105–18, 119–34.

Dichev, Stefan (b. 1920) Bulgarian novelist. A highly popular writer, Dichev was born in Turnovo. After completing his secondary education in Turnovo, he studied civil engineering in Czechoslovakia in 1939 and graduated from Sofia University in 1943 with a degree in law. He received a doctorate in political science in 1946. In 1948 he was appointed inspector in the Supreme Economic Chamber. Dichev soon became active in editing and publishing. He founded the journal *Kosmos* in 1962 and served as its editor in chief until 1990. From 1967 to 1972, he was director of the Narodna kultura publishing house and one of the founders of the series Svetovna klasika (World Classics). An engrossing storyteller, Dichev's speciality was the historical novel of high adventure dealing with Bulgarian efforts to shake free of Turkish rule in the nineteenth century. The novels are full of local color; faithful in historical detail; blend real and fictitious characters, with the latter coming more to the fore only in his later work; introduce Westerners as well as Bulgarians, Russians, and Turks; and incorporate convincing psychological characterization. His novels include the two-part *Za svobodata* (For Freedom, 1954; rev. ed., 1959, 1964); *Rali* (1960); *Mladostta na Rakovski* (Rakovski's Youth, 1966); *Eskadronut* (The Squadron, 1968); *Putiat kum Sofia* (The Road to Sofia, 1967); *Neulovimiiat* (The Elusive, 1976); *Kreposti* (Citadels, 1976); *V labirinta* (In the Labyrinth, 1977); *Sudbonosnata misiia* (The Fateful Mission, 1978); *Sreshta na silite* (Meeting of Forces, 1978); *Podzemiiata na sen Zhan d'Akr* (The Crypt of Saint-Jean-d'Acre, 1988); and *Zavoevateliat na mirazhite: Roman za Aleksandur Makedonski* (The Fighter of Mirages: A Novel About Alexander of Macedonia, 1993).

Dichev's first major work of fiction, and his most famous, *Za svobodata,* is a huge novel about the Bulgarian national hero, Vasil Levski. It was a great success and indeed secured the place of the historical novel in post–World War II Bulgarian literature besides inspiring a host of imitations. *Rali,* Dichev's only novel to be translated into English, is a picaresque-like adventure tale about a fourteen-year-old boy named Rali, the narrator, who sets out in 1876 to free his brother from a Turkish prison. He succeeds, and at the end of the novel he and his brother are on their way to fight alongside the Russians in the campaign, which has just began against the Turks. One of his last and better novels, *Podzemiiata na sen Zhan d'Akr* follows essentially the same pattern of Dichev's other works of historical fiction except for the greater prominence of invented characters and the protagonists' personal dramas. The novel is about a Bulgarian doctor who lives and works in Istanbul and for whom the Bulgarian liberation struggle is of no consuming interest. But because he had once treated a Bulgarian conspirator, the Turks arrest him and imprison him in the underground prison of Saint-Jean-d'Acre, the ancient Mediterranean port (now in Israel) and the capital of the Crusaders. Before the doctor's escape from prison at the end of the novel, which finds him and other prisoners precariously floating in the Bay of Acre, Dichev weaves a complex tale of political and romantic intrigue complete with natural disasters, a bevy of colorful Occidental characters, and a fairly convincing depiction of the growth of national consciousness of the main figure.

Translations: *Rali,* trans. Margaret Roberts (Harrisburg, Pa.: Stackpole, 1968). *Putiat kum Sofia* is available in German as *Der Weg nach Sofia* (Vienna: Amandus, 1969; Leipzig: List, 1970).

Dilov, Liuben (b. 1927) Bulgarian novelist and short-story writer. Known above all for his fantastic and science-fiction writing, Dilov was born in Cherven Briag and received his early education in Sofia. From 1939 to the end of World War II, he lived with his family in Germany. After his return to Bulgaria, he completed secondary school in Lukovit and in 1954 graduated from Sofia University with a degree in Bulgarian literature. He subsequently held editorial positions at several journals. Although Dilov began publishing short stories in a magazine for children as early as 1937, his literary career began in earnest with the publication in 1953 of a book based on his experiences in Germany during World War II: *Gulubi nad Berlin* (Pigeons over Berlin). Dilov's first novel, *Atomniiat chovek* (The Atomic Man), appeared in 1958 and initiated his long association with the genre of science fiction. His other works in this vein or in that of the fantastic include *Chovekut, koito tursi* (The Seeker, 1964), a collection of science-fiction stories; *Chuzhdiiat chovek* (The Strange Man, 1964); *Mnogoto imena na strakha* (Fear Has Many Names, 1967); *Tezhestta na skafandura* (The Weight of the Space Suit, 1969); *Moiat stranen priiatel—astrononut* (My Strange Friend—the Astronaut, 1971); *Vulshebnata grivna* (The Magic Bracelet, 1972); *Paradoksut na ogledaloto* (The Paradox of the Mirror, 1976); and his two well-known science-fiction novels for young readers: *Zvezdnite prikliucheniia na Numi i Niki* (The Astral Adventures of Numi and Niki, 1980) and *Do raiskata planeta i nazad: Drugite prikliucheniia na Numi i Niki* (To Paradise and Back: The Further Adventures of Numi and Niki, 1983). Of particular interest are Dilov's own views on science-fiction writing contained in the volume *Vpechatleniia ot edna planeta: Zapiski na fantasta* (Impressions from One Planet: Notes of a Science-Fiction Writer, 1990). Of Dilov's sometimes psychologically interesting fiction about contemporary society in which journalists and writers appear prominently, perhaps his best book is the collection of stories published in 1961 under the title *Pochivkata na Boian Darev* (Boian Darev's Vacation). Other works by Dilov include *V edin proleten den* (One Spring Day, 1960); *Pomni tazi prolet* (Remember This Spring, 1964); and *Putiat na vernostta* (The Path of Righteousness, 1967).

Dimić, Moma (b. 1944) Serbian novelist, short-story writer, playwright, essayist, poet, and travel writer. A native of Belgrade, Dimić was educated in local shools and in 1968 received a degree in philosophy from Belgrade University. He currently divides his residence between Sweden and Belgrade. An interesting and diverse writer, Dimić began his career in the 1960s with one of his best works, *Živeo život Tola Manojlović* (Long Live the Life of Tola Manojlović, 1966), a diary-like autobiography narrated by a "man of the people," named Tola Manojlović, going back to his childhood and extending to the post–World War II period. The account moves backward and forward in time (jumping at one point from 1909 to 1946) and spends considerable time chronicling Tola's illnesses (especially tuberculosis) and injuries—all narrated by the various affected parts of his body—and his many stays in the hospital. Separate sections are devoted to his love affairs, his experiences as a factory worker, and his retirement. In dramatic form, as a monodrama, the work was staged in Belgrade in 1967 and, in an English translation by Celia Williams, in London in 1968 by the London Arts Lab Theatre.

Živeo život Tola Manojlović was followed by a volume of poems, *Ciganski krevet* (The Gypsy, 1968); *Antihrist* (The Antichrist, 1970), a collection of prose stories; *Maksim srpski iz doma staraca* (Maxim of Serbia from the Home of the Angel, 1971); *Poznanstvo sa danima malog Maksima* (Getting to Know Little Maxim, 1974), a book of poems that he wrote with V. Parun; *Šumski gradjanin* (The Citizen of the Forest, 1982); *Mala ptica: Roman za poodraslu naročito osetljievu decu* (The Little Bird: A Novel for

Grown-up and Sensitive Children, 1989), a basically symbolic text about man and human existence; and two travel books: *Putnik bez milosti* (Traveler Without Mercy, 1991), devoted mainly to his travels in Rome, Sicily, Jerusalem, Israel and China; and *Pesnik i zemljotres: Vidjenja & putovanja* (The Poet and the Earthquake: Outlooks & Travels, 1978), about the 1963 earthquake in Skopje, Macedonia, and Dimić's travels through Spain, Hungary, Sweden, and the United States, where he visited Broadway; saw performances of Shakespeare in Central Park; made the acquaintance of the authors Henry Miller and Paddy Chayefsky, with whom he seemed to find affinities; and visited Harvard University, where he met South Slavic scholars as well as Professor Albert Lord, an authority on the South Slavic oral epic.

Translations: "Night Under the Kosmaj," trans. Robert Gakovich, in *The Prince of Fire: An Anthology of Serbian Short Stories,* ed. Radmila J. Gorup and Nadežda Obradović (Pittsburgh: University of Pittsburgh Press, 1998), 216–20.

Dimitrova, Blaga (b. 1922) Bulgarian poet and novelist. Widely regarded as Bulgaria's finest contemporary poet, Dimitrova was born in the town of Biala Slatina and raised in Veliko Turnovo, the old capital of Bulgaria. After completing secondary school there in 1941, she studied philology at Sofia University, from which she graduated in 1945. She received her doctorate from the Maxim Gorky Institute of Literature in Moscow in 1951; her dissertation was on "Mayakovsky and Bulgarian Poetry." Dimitrova's literary career began to flower in the 1950s, and before long she had replaced Elisaveta Bagriana as Bulgaria's leading woman poet.

First and foremost a poet, Dimirova has published nearly two dozen volumes of poetry, including *Liliana* (1959); *Do utre* (To

Morning, 1960); *Svetut v shepa* (The World in Hand, 1962); *Ekspeditsiia kum idniia den* (Expedition to the Coming Day, 1964); *Obratno vreme* (Reverse Time, 1967); *Osudeni na liubov* (Sentenced to Love, 1967); *Migove* (Moments, 1968); *Ime* (Name, 1971), a volume of verses from 1950; *Impulsi* (Impulses, 1972); *Gong* (1976); *Zabraneno more* (Forbidden Sea, 1976), a long poem and arguably Dimitrova's most highly regarded work of poetry; *Kak* (How, 1977); *Prostranstva* (Expanses, 1980); *Glas* (Voice, 1985); *Labirint* (Labyrinth, 1987); *Otvud liubovta* (And Then, There's Love, 1987); *Mezhdu* (Among, 1990); *Kliuch* (The Key, 1991); *Noshten dnevnik* (Night Diary, 1992), a collection of poems from 1989 to 1992; *Pomen za topolite* (Celebrating Poplars, 1992); *Do ruba* (To the Edge), a collection of poetry from 1994 and 1995; *Gluharcheta* (Dandelions, 1996); *Cherna kotka v tunela: Zagadki i dogadki* (Black Cat in a Tunnel: Riddles and Guesses, 1996); and *Krilopisi: Pticha-oratoriia* (Quill Jottings: A Bird-Oratory, 1997).

In her poetry, Dimitrova conveys a great sense of personal strength and independence, an unwillingness to make moral compromises, a reverence for freedom and the brave and solitary human gesture, and an unerring understanding of the feminine psyche. Her small poem "Grass" (1974) splendidly encapsulates her political outlook:

I'm not afraid
they'll stamp me flat
Grass stamped flat
soon becomes a path.

Highly intellectual, keen to ironies and paradoxes, Dimitrova has written of the boundaries of life and yet the contact made possible by them. This, in essence, is the subject of perhaps her finest long poem, "Forbidden Sea" (in the collection of the same name), a series of meditations on the Black Sea after she was forbidden to swim following a diagnosis of cancer. The "forbidden sea" is made to serve as a metaphor for other demarcations that create surmountable barriers. The point is also eloquently made in the modest poem "Touch" (1988), in which she writes of her identity as a woman: "I am nailed within a woman's skin—through it I know caress and wound." As a poet with a continuous love affair with the challenges and resources of language, Dimitrova equates words with freedom, and her greatest fear is of an interdiction on words, hence the recurrent image in her poetry of a severed, mutilated, or imprisoned tongue. Toward death, which recurs in a number of her poems, Dimitrova is philosophically distant and essentially unafraid, as evidenced in her moving poems on the deaths of her mother ("Introduction to the Beyond," 1966) and her brother ("In memory . . . ," 1988).

Apart from her more than twenty collections of poetry, Dimitrova has published several novels, among them *Putuvane kum sebe si* (*Journey to Oneself,* 1969); *Lavina* (The Avalanche, 1971), a "novel-poem" that was denounced by the establishment as "existentialist" because it focuses on the body, death, and language; *Otklonenie* (Deviation, 1973), which served as the basis of a prize-winning film; *Litse* (Face, 1990), an anticommunist novel that had once been banned; and *Uraniia* (Urania, 1993). *Journey to Oneself,* Dimitrova's best-known work of prose, is at once autobiographical and political and shares features with her poetry. It is about a young woman (Raina Stamatova) who joins a mostly male construction crew in the Rhodope Mountains as a way of escaping from her past and finding a meaningful place for herself in life. Ashamed of the fact that her father was a royalist officer and uneasy over her privileged lifestyle in Sofia, Raina seeks redemption in the rugged mountains. When her past eventually becomes known, she again resorts to flight, only to realize that her place is back in the mountains among people who value her for herself and do not hold her background against her, and where she has found love. Dimitrova is very much a women's writer sensitive to every facet of the feminine psyche and the differences between men and women. Intellectual and sensual at the same time, she is keenly aware of the ironies of life. Dimitrova cannot resist trying to enter people's minds, to imagine their thought processes.

Earlier in her career, Dimitrova conformed to the demands of literary Stalinism, which she later repudiated when it fell into disfavor. In the late 1960s she became an outspoken critic of the Vietnam War, publishing two books on the conflict: *Strashniia sud: Roman-putepis (za Vietnam)* (A Terrible Judgment: A Novel-Travelogue [On Vietnam], 1968) and *Podzemno nebe: Dnevnik 72* (Underground Heaven: Diary 72, 1972). She has also written many essays on Bulgarian political and cultural topics collected in such volumes as *Predizvikatelstva: Politicheski etiudi* (Provocations: Political Studies, 1991); *Otsam i otvud: Silueti na priiateli* (One Side and the Other: Silhouettes of Friends, 1992); *Hobiada Hobioda Hobimoda* (1992); *Dni cherni i beli: Elisaveta Bagriana. Nabliudeniia i razgovori* (Black and White Days: Elisaveta Bagriana. Observations and Conversations, 1975); and *Mladostta na Bagriana i neinite sputnitsi* (Bagriana's Youth and Her Fellow Travelers, 1993), which was written with Iordan Vasilev. Dimitrova has also translated extensively from such languages as German, French, Polish, Swedish, and Ancient Greek. In 1992 Dimitrova, one of the most respected women of her generation, was elected vice president of Bulgaria.

Translations: *Because the Sea Is Black: Poems of Blaga Dimitrova,* trans. Niko Boris and Heather McHugh (Middletown, Conn.:

Wesleyan University Press, 1989); *Journey to Oneself,* trans. Radost Pridham (London: Cassell, 1969); *The Last Rock Eagle: Selected Poems of Blaga Dimitrova,* trans. Brenda Walker with Vladimir Levchev and Belin Tonchev (London: Forest, 1992); thirteen poems in *The Devil's Dozen: Thirteen Bulgarian Women Poets,* trans. Brenda Walker with Belin Tonchev, in collaboration with Svetoslav Piperov (London: Forest, 1990), 41–58.

Dimov, Dimitur (1909–1966) Bulgarian novelist. A native of Lovech in northern Bulgaria, Dimov was the author of what used to be touted during the communist period in Bulgaria as the most significant Bulgarian novel since World War II: *Tiutiun* (Tobacco, 1951). A sober, richly detailed portrayal of life in the country before and during World War II, the novel was awarded the Dimitrov Prize in 1952. Dimov also wrote three plays that were widely performed in the 1960s: *Zheni s minalo* (Women from the Past), *Vinovniiat* (The Guilty), and *Pochivka v Arko Iris* (The Stop in Arco Iris). The first two deal with the contemporary Bulgarian professional and intellectual class, whereas *Pochivka v Arko Iris* is set in Andalusia during the Spanish Civil War and features the Bulgarian commander of a battalion in the republican army with the Hispanicized name Estanislao Bravo. A staunch supporter throughout his career of the Party line on literature, Dimov wrote in praise of the Bulgarian Writers Union and its role in achieving humanism.

Translations: Excerpt from *Tiutiun,* trans. Grigor Pavlov, in *The Balkan Range: A Bulgarian Reader,* ed. John Robert Colombo and Nikola Roussanoff (Toronto: Hounslow, 1976), 249–54.

Dimov, Leonid (1926–1987) Romanian poet. Born in Ismail, Bessarabia (now in Ukraine), Dimov attended the Saint Sava high school in Bucharest, in whose literary review, *Revista literară*, he published his first poems in 1943. After being dismissed from the Faculty of Letters of Bucharest University in 1945 for political reasons, Dimov enrolled successively in the Institute of Theology, the Faculty of Philosophy, the Faculty of Law, and the Faculty of Biology, but left before completing any degree program. Dimov had joined the Romanian Communist Party in 1944, but was expelled from it in 1950 primarily because of his 1945 university dismissal. During the Stalinist period, the only employment he could find was as an assistant to various translators from Russian, a language he knew fluently as a native of Bessarabia. In 1956 he began contributing to the journals *Tînarul scriitor* and *Gazetă literară*, but was arrested in 1958 on charges of insulting Stalin and spent nearly a year in prison.

Dimov made his real literary debut as a poet only in 1966 with his volume *Versuri* (Poems), although some of his poems had appeared the year before in the journals *Viaţa Românească* and *Ramuri*. He subsequently published several other collections of poems, among them *7 poeme* (Seven Poems, 1968); *Pe malul Styxului* (On the Banks of the Styx, 1968); *Carte de vise* (Book of Dreams, 1969); *Eleusis* (1970); *Semne cereşti* (Heavenly Signs, 1970); *Deschideri* (Openings, 1972); *La capăt* (At the End, 1974); *Litanii pentru Horia* (Litanies for Horia, 1975); *Dialectica vîrstelor* (The Dialectics of the Ages, 1977); *Tinereţe fără bătrîneţe* (Youth Without Old Age, 1978); *Spectacol* (Performance, 1979); and *Veşnica reîntoarcere* (Eternal Return, 1988). Dimov's poetry is characterized by baroque ornateness and inventiveness as well as affinities with surrealism. In the second half of the 1960s and in the 1970s, with his fellow poet Dumitru Ţepeneag, Dimov became actively involved in promoting the onirist movement in Romanian literature, the goal of which was to liberate literature from any and all

ideology. An anthology of their essays, *Momentul oniric* (The Oniric Moment), edited by Corin Braga, was published in Bucharest in 1997 by Cartea Românească. Dimov also translated extensively from French, Italian, and Russian literatures.

Translations: Five poems in *46 Romanian Poets in English*, trans. and ed. Ştefan Avădanei and Don Eulert (Iaşi: Junimea, 1973), 186–90; three poems, including the long "Vedeniile Regelui Pepin" ("King Pepin's Visions"), which Dimov dedicated to the memory of Ion Barbu, in *Romanian Poets: An Anthology of Verse*, trans. and ed. Dan Duţescu (Bucharest: Eminescu, 1982), 146–50.

Dimovska, Milica Mićić (b. 1947) Serbian short-story writer and novelist. Born in Novi Sad, Dimovska graduated from Belgrade University with a degree in world literature and literary theory. She made her literary debut in 1972 with a collection of short stories, *Priče o ženi* (Stories About a Woman), which established both her literary abilities and her strong predilection for women's issues. Her next collection of stories, *Poznanici* (Acquaintances, 1980), won the Karolj Sirman Prize in 1981. In 1987 Dimovska published her first novel, *Utvare* (Ghosts), followed a decade later by a second novel, *Poslednji zanosi MCC* (The Last Raptures of Milica Stojadinović Srpkinja, 1997). A feminist writer in the sense that she draws much of her material from the lives of women, Dimovska is also concerned with matters of faith. Typical in this regard is *Utvare*, in which a woman who is a communist and an atheist, and who works for the state, sees an apparition of the Virgin Mary and then sorts through her life, her communist training, and the death and nonreligious burial of a colleague to try to understand how such an event could be possible. At the end, she joyously rediscovers her Christian faith. The subject of *Poslednji* *zanosi MCC* is the fictionalized life of the Serbian woman poet Milica Stojadinović Srpkinja, in which Dimovska nicely brings to life the atmosphere of the period.

Translations: "Smiles," trans. Biljana Šljivić-Šimšić, in *The Prince of Fire: An Anthology of Contemporary Serbian Short Stories,* ed. Radmila J. Gorup and Nadežda Obradović (Pittsburgh: University of Pittsburgh Press, 1998), 240–45.

Dinescu, Mircea (b. 1950) Romanian poet. A native of Slobozia (about seventy miles east of Bucharest), Dinescu moved to Bucharest as soon as he finished his secondary-school education. Dinescu's first poem, "Destin de familie" ("Family Destiny"), appeared in the journal *Luceafărul* in 1967. He was seventeen at the time. His first published book of poems appeared in 1971 under the title *Invocaţie nimănui* (Invocation to No One). It was followed by *Elegii de cînd eram mai tînăr* (Elegies from When I Was Younger, 1973); *Proprietarul de poduri* (The Owner of Bridges, 1976); *La dispoziţia dumneavoastră* (At Your Disposal, 1979); *Demokraţia naturii* (The Democracy of Nature, 1980); *Teroarea bunului simţ* (The Terror of Good Taste, 1981); *Exil pe o boabă de piper* (*Exile on a Peppercorn,* 1983); *Moartea citeste ziarul* (Death Reads the Newspaper, 1990); *O beţie cu Marx* (An Intoxication with Marx, 1996); and *Pamflete vesele şi triste: 1990–1996* (Pamphlets Happy and Sad: 1990–1996, 1996). From the beginning, Dinescu's poetry has been characterized by bitterness, anger, rebelliousness, and a lack of sentimentality at the plight of contemporary man and his despair of finding a solution. Spiritual beliefs are of little value, and neither is poetry, as he declares in the poem "Şah absurd" ("Absurd Chess") from *Teroarea bunului simţ*:

Sweet innocence
to believe that poetry can improve the
    world.

It's as if throwing a lump of sugar
into a tiger's cage
would start it reading Shakespeare.

Adding greater sharpness to Dinescu's provocativeness is his frequent use of unsual juxtapositions of words and images and his introduction of elements of the surreal and fantastic. As a typical example of his outlook and style, here is his short poem "Teatru ambulant" ("Strolling Theater") from *Democraţia naturii*:

Oh God how I was born
red with rage
crying out in an unknown tongue
full of thunder and the airs of a great
    actor
and how I'll die
trembling and just carrying a tray
full of stage fright before death
like an amateur on a provincial stage
with the prompter suffocated in the box
    of my chest.

Dinescu has for some time been affiliated with the journal *România literară*. In 1989, before the revolution that brought down the regime of Nicolae Ceauşescu, he was dismissed from his editorial postition at *Romanîa literară* because of his dissident political views (primarily in foreign publications) and placed under house arrest for a two-year period. After the revolution, which he played a part in planning, he also took an active role in the organization of a new political structure until the general elections of May 1990. In 1990 he was elected president of the Writers Union, a position he held until 1993.

Translations: *Exile on a Peppercorn: The Poetry of Mircea Dinescu,* trans. Andrea Deletant and Brenda Walker (London: Forest, 1985); seven poems in *15 Young Romanian Poets: An Anthology of Verse,* trans. and ed. Liliana Ursu (Bucharest: Eminescu,

1982), 23–29; nine poems, in versions by Brendan Kennelly, in *When the Tunnels Meet,* ed. John Fairleigh (Newcastle upon Tyne: Bloodaxe, 1996), 65–72.

Dizdar, Mak (real name Mehmed Alija Dizdar; 1917–1971) Bosnian Muslim poet. Widely regarded as the foremost Bosnian poet of the twentieth century, Dizdar was born in the town of Stolac in Herzegovina. He received his early education in Stolac and completed high school in Sarajevo. Dizdar is best known by the pseudonym Mak (poppy), which he adopted when he joined the partisans during World War II. His literary career began in the 1930s when he managed to publish half the poems in his collection *Vidovopoljska noć* (An Enchanted Country Night, 1936); the state prosecutor's office banned sixteen of the poems. The same year Dizdar joined the staff of the paper *Jugoslovenski list.* He thereafter held a number of important editorial posts: *Jugoslovenska pošta* (1939–1940); *Tanjug* (Bosnia-Herzegovina; editor in chief, 1946–1948); *Oslobodjenie* (editor, 1949–1951); *Narodna prosvjeta* (editor in chief, 1951–1959); and *Život* (1964–1971). After *Vidovopoljska noć,* and a substantial hiatus from literature, Dizdar resumed his poetic output with the well-received volume *Plivačica* (The Woman Swimmer, 1954). This was followed by several other books of poetry: *Povratak* (Homecoming, 1958); *Okrutnosti kruga* (Cruelties of a Circle, 1960); *Koljena za Madonu* (Carols for the Madonna, 1963); *Minijature* (Miniatures, 1965); *Ostrva* (Lakes, 1966); *Kameni spavač* (Stone Sleeper, 1966); *Poezija* (Poetry, 1971); *Modra rijeka* (Blue River, 1972); *Pjesme* (Poems, 1972); and *Zapis o vremenu: Izabrane pjesme* (A Text on Time: Collected Poems, 1999). A three-volume edition of his collected works (*Izabrana djela*) was published in Sarajevo in 1981.

Apart from his poetry, Dizdar was active as an editor of and a commentator on medieval and contemporary Bosnian literature. His collection *Panorama savremene bosansko-hercegovačke poezije* (A Panorama of Contemporary Bosnian-Herzegovinian Prose) appeared in 1961. This was followed the same year by a collection of old Bosnian grave inscriptions, *Stari bosanski epitafi* (Old Bosnian Epitaphs), and in 1969 by a collection of old Bosnian texts, *Stari bosanski tekstovi* (Old Bosnian Texts).

As a poet, Dizdar is esteemed above all for *Stone Sleeper.* Originally published in 1966, a posthumous 1973 edition contains extensive revisions made by the author not long before his death. The lavish Serbo-Croatian–English edition of the book, published in Sarajevo in 1999, is based on this revised text. The title, *Stone Sleeper,* alludes to the white limestone tombs of *krstjani* (Christians), followers of the schismatic medieval Bosnian church denounced and persecuted by the Orthodox and Roman Catholic religious establishments as a dualist heresy influenced by the ancient South Slavic Bogomil faith. Bosnian Muslims regard themselves as the direct spiritual and historical descendants of the medieval *krstjani,* whose separatist church survived until it was outlawed by the Bosnian king Stefan Tomaš in an effort to appease the Vatican and win its support in the campaign against the Turks. The tombs, or *stećci,* that dot the Bosnian landscape are inscribed with various enigmatic signs, which were interpreted by Dizdar as the spirit of Bosnia expressed by means of an esoteric symbolism of mixed Christian and Islamic origin. Composed in elegantly simple verses of great variety metrically and stanzaically, *Stone Sleeper* is an admirable work of poetic beauty and spiritual depth.

Translations: *Kameni spavač/Stone Sleeper,* trans. Francis R. Jones (Sarajevo: DID, 1999), a Serbo-Croatian–English edition with illustrations by the Bosnian artist Dževad Hozo. *Kameni spavač* is also available in German as

Der steinerne Schläfer, trans. and ed. Leonore Scheffler (Frankfurt am Main: Peter Lang, 1995), a scholarly edition that contains a somewhat more solid historical and critical apparatus than the English edition and places greater emphasis on the possible Bogomil influence on the Bosnian gravestones.

Djilas, Milovan (1911–1995) Montenegran statesman, political writer, memoirist, novelist, and short-story writer. One of the outstanding political figures and thinkers of the former Yugoslavia, and a close ally of Tito during World War II, Djilas became a member of the Communist Party as early as 1932 after studying law and philosophy in Belgrade, and was jailed from 1933 to 1936 for his opposition to the Yugoslav monarchy. Together with Tito, Djilas organized volunteers to fight on the side of the republic in the Spanish Civil War. He joined Tito's partisans during World War II and after the war rose to high rank in the party and government. His autobiographical *Wartime* (1977) gives a remarkably detailed account of the Yugoslav resistance against the Germans.

Djilas's eventual fall from political grace was occasioned by his progressively more outspoken criticism of the nature of postwar Yugoslav communism. His first salvo against the inequities rampant in the new society was the intellectually impressive *Nova klasa: Analiza komunističkog sistema* (*The New Class: An Analysis of the Communist System,* 1957), which made Djilas a worldwide celebrity and has since become a required text in university courses on communism and postwar Europe. It was followed by two books of a similar nature: *Nesavršeno društvo: I dalje od "nove klase"* (*The Unperfect Society: Farther Away from the "New Class,"* 1970) and the posthumously published *Pad nove klase: Povest o samorazaranju komunizma* (*Fall of the New Class: A History of Communism's Self-Destruction,* 1994). Although widely consid-

ered Tito's logical successor, Djilas supported the Hungarian revolution in 1956, resulting in his imprisonment, which was extended when *The New Class* first appeared in the West. He was released in 1961, but was jailed again from 1962 to 1966. Djilas subsequently published an intellectually substantive book about his various prison experiences under the title *Tajemnica i idea* (*Of Prisons and Ideas,* 1986).

After Tito's death, Djilas published two books about his complex relationship with his old comrade in arms and the guiding figure of postwar Yugoslavia, *Druženije s Titom* (*Friendship with Tito,* 1980) and *Tito: The Story from Inside* (1984). Djilas's open hostility to Soviet attempts to bring Yugoslavia deeper into its orbit is vividly displayed in his illuminating book *Susreti sa Staljinom* (*Conversations with Stalin,* 1962), which details his meetings with Stalin and his impressions of the Soviet dictator.

Apart from his political writings, Djilas was an able storyteller whose fictional texts are set mostly in his native Montenegro. These include, among others, the story collection *Gubavac i druge priče* (*The Leper and Other Stories,* 1964) and the huge historical novel *Crna Gora* (*Montenegro,* 1989). Another collection of stories, translated under the title *The Stone and the Violets,* which was written between 1959 and 1966 when Djilas was imprisoned in Sremska Mitrovica, is set mostly during the two world wars of the twentieth century and is permeated with brutality and sexual passion. The longest story in the collection, "The Brothers and the Girl," is dedicated to the memory of Djilas's younger brother, Milivoj, who died a horrible death at the hands of his captors during World War II. Djilas's other collections of stories include *Sluga božji i druge pripovetke* (The Servant of God and Other Stories, 1994) and *Svetovi i mostovi: Povesti u tri knjige* (Worlds and Bridges: Stories in Three Books, 1997). The closest Djilas came to writing his autobiography are the four books known best and most accessible under their English titles: *Land Without Justice* (1958), covering the years 1911 to 1928; *Memoir of a Revolutionary* (1973); *Parts of a Lifetime* (1975), a valuable anthology of his political and literary writings; and *Wartime.* Djilas was also the author of a fine critical biography of the great Montenegran poet Njegoš: *Njegoš: Pjesnik, vladar, vladika* (*Njegoš: Poet, Prince, Bishop,* 1988).

Literature: Stephen Clissold, *Djilas, the Progress of a Revolutionary* (Hounslow, Eng.: Maurice Temple Smith, 1983); Dennis Reinhartz, *Milovan Djilas: A Revolutionary as a Writer* (Boulder, Colo.: East European Monographs, 1981), both of which are just adequate.

Translations: *Conversations with Stalin* (New York: Harcourt, Brace & World, 1962); *Fall of the New Class: A History of Communism's Self-Destruction,* trans. John Loud, ed. Vasilije Kalezić (New York: Knopf, 1998); *Land Without Justice* (New York: Harcourt, Brace, 1958); *The Leper and Other Stories,* trans. Lovett F. Edwards (New York: Harcourt, Brace & World, 1964); *Memoir of a Revolutionary,* trans. Drenka Willen (New York: Harcourt Brace Jovanovich, 1973); *Montenegro,* trans. Kenneth Johnstone (New York: Harcourt, Brace & World, 1963); *The New Class: An Analysis of the Communist System* (New York: Praeger, 1957); *Njegoš: Poet, Prince, Bishop,* trans. Michael B. Petrovich (New York: Harcourt, Brace & World, 1966); *Of Prisons and Ideas,* trans. Michael Boro Petrovich (San Diego: Harcourt Brace Jovanovich, 1986); *Parts of a Lifetime,* ed. Michael Milenkovitch and Deborah Milenkovitch (New York: Harcourt Brace Jovanovich, 1975); *Rise and Fall* (San Diego: Harcourt Brace Jovanovich, 1985); *The Stone and the Violets,* trans. Lovett F. Edwards (New York: Harcourt Brace Jovanovich, 1972); *Tito: The Story from Inside,* trans. Vasilije Kojic and Richard Hayes (New York: Harcourt Brace Jovanovich, 1980); *Under the Colors,* trans. Lovett F. Edwards (New York: Harcourt Brace Jovanovich, 1971); *The Unperfect Society: Beyond the New Class,* trans. Dorian Cooke (New York: Harcourt, Brace & World, 1969); *Wartime,* trans. Michael B. Petrovich (New York: Harcourt Brace Jovanovich, 1977).

Doinaş, Ştefan Augustin (pseudonym Ştefan Popa; 1922–2002) Romanian poet, essayist, and translator. Doinaş was born in a village in the Arad region and studied first medicine at Cluj-Sibiu University from 1941 to 1944, and then literature and philosophy from 1944 to 1948. He finally received his university degree in 1949. In 1948 he returned to his native village, where he taught Romanian language until 1955. After that, he moved to Bucharest where he became editor of the review *Teatru* and was able to devote most of his time to literature. Doinaş began writing poetry at the age of seventeen, but did not publish his first book of verse until 1964. However, as early as 1947 he was honored with the Eugen Lovinescu Prize for a volume of poems still in manuscript: "Manual de dragoste" ("Manual of Love"). The volume was never published. In 1957 Doinaş's career was interrupted when he was sentenced to a year in jail for political reasons. A few years after his release from prison, he became editor of the literary review *Lumen,* a position he held until 1968 when he moved to the review *Secolul 20,* of which he eventually became editor in chief.

Doinaş's long-delayed first published book of poetry, *Cartea mareelor* (Book of Tides), appeared in 1964. It was followed by such representative volumes as *Omul cu compasul* (The Man with the Compass, 1966); *Seminţia lui Laokoon* (The Tribe of Laocoön, 1967); *Alter ego* (1970); *Ce mi s-a întîmplat cu două cuvinte* (What Happened to Me in Two Words, 1972); *Anotimpul discret* (Season of

Discretion, 1975); *Hesperia* (1980); *Vînătoare cu șoim* (Hunting with Falcons, 1985); *Lamentații* (Lamentations, 1994); and *Aventurile lui Proteu* (The Adventures of Protheus, 1995). Several volumes of his selected verse have also appeared: *Ipostaze* (Hypostases, 1968); *Versuri* (Poems, 1972); *Alfabet poetic* (The Alphabet of Poetry, 1978); and *Foamea de unu* (One Man's Hunger, 1987). Doinaș's extensive critical essays on Romanian and other literatures are contained in such volumes as *Lectura poeziei* (Reading Poetry, 1980) and *Eseuri* (Essays, 1996). His well-regarded translations from French and German poetry were published in 1970 in the volume *Sunete fundamentele* (Fundamental Sounds).

A poet of broad range and rich literary culture, Doinaș is deeply philosophical and frequently draws on classical mythology and thought. Often seeming to yearn for the infinite, he is no stranger to the sensuous. Although he cannot be typecast as to formal preferences, and has written a number of shorter poems, he has tended to favor works of moderate length that seem best suited to his philosophical purposes. Doinaș has won several honors. In 1982 he was named president of the Literary Foundation (Fondul Literar) and, in 1990, corresponding member and then titular member of the Romanian Academy. In 1990 he was also elected honorary director of the journal *Euphorion* and, in 1993, honorary president of the Writers Union. He was awarded the Goethe Prize by the Goethe Institute in Munich in 1982, mainly for his translation of *Faust*.

Translations: *Alibi and Other Poems,* trans. Peter Jay and Virgil Nemoianu (Iowa City: University of Iowa Press, 1975); two poems in *Anthology of Contemporary Romanian Poetry,* ed. and trans. Roy MacGregor-Hastie (London: Peter Owen, 1969), 128–29; six poems in *An Anthology of Contemporary Romanian Poetry,* trans. Andre Deletant and Brenda Walker (London: Forest, 1984), 48–53; five poems in *46 Romanian Poets in English,* trans. Ștefan Avădanei and Don Eulert (Iași: Junimea, 1973), 160–67.

Dončević, Ivan (1909–1982) Croatian novelist and short-story writer. Born into a farming family in the village of Moslavina, which he writes about in his autobiography *Životopis bez svršetka: Kronika iz seljačkog života* (Autobiography Without End: Chronicle of a Farm Life, 1948), Dončević began studying agriculture after finishing secondary school. However, he soon gave it up in order to become a writer. His first success came with his short-story collection *Bezimeni* (Nameless People, 1946), followed in 1948 by the collection *Četiri priče* (Four Stories). Dončević mined the same basic thematic material of *Bezimeni* in such subsequent books of short stories as *Posljednji ciganin, i druge priče o bezimenima* (The Last Gypsy, or Other Stories About Nameless People, 1951) and *Priče o bezimenima* (Stories About Nameless People, 1961). His first novel, *Mirotvorci* (The Peacemakers), appeared in 1953. For many years, Dončević served as director of the Zora publishing house in Zagreb. One of his best works, the fairly short *Sbarač kukaca* (The Insect Collector, 1953), renders much of the local color of Zagreb. His other novels include *Potopljeni svijet* (The Sunken World, 1963) and *Krvoproliće kod Krapine* (Bloodshed at Krapina, 1968).

Translations: "The Insect Collector," trans. Cordia Kveder, in *Death of a Simple Giant and Other Modern Yugoslav Stories,* ed. Branko Lenski (New York: Vanguard, 1965), 246–69.

Donchev, Anton (b. 1930) Bulgarian novelist. A well-known historical novelist, Donchev was born in Burgas. He graduated from high school in Turnovo in 1948 and then studied law at Sofia University, from where he received his degree in 1953. He subsequently worked for the Ministry of Culture (1954–1958); as an editor at Narodna mladezh publishing house, which specializes in literature for younger readers (1961–1964); as a member of the film-script commission of Bulgarian Cinematography (1969–1979); and as an editor and a commentator with Bulgarian TV (1979–1989). In 1989 Donchev began a period of employment with the Sofia Press Agency. Most of his literary career has been taken up with richly detailed, almost documentary fictionalizations of what may be regarded as defining moments in earlier Bulgarian history, and he has long been regarded as one of the masters of Bulgarian historical fiction. His first major text of this type was *Skazanie za vremeto na Samuila, za Samuila i brata mu Aaron, za sinovete im Radomir i Vladislav za seliaka Zhitan i stareishinata Gorazd Mudriia i za mnogi drugi hora, zhiveli predi nas* (Tale of the Time of Tsar Samuil, Concerning Samuil and His Brother Aaron, Their Sons Radomir and Vladislav, the Peasant Zhitan and the Elder Gorazd the Wise, and Many Other People Who Lived Before Us, 1961), which has been reprinted several times. Two of his best-known novels are devoted to the life of Asparuh, khan of Bulgaria from around 664 to around 700: *Skazanie za han . . . Asparuh* (The Legend of Khan Asparuh, 1982–1984) and *Nachaloto na nashata vechnost: Kraiat na skazanieto za han Asparuh, kniaz Slav i zhretsa Teres* (The Beginning of Our Eternity: The End of the Legend About Khan Asparuh, Prince Slav, and the Pagan Priest Teres, 1993). Donchev's major work of fiction, *Vreme razdelno* (*Time of Parting*, 1969), is a historical novel set in the seventeenth century in the period of Bulgarian–Turkish conflict. The forced conversion of a Bulgarian community in the Rhodope Mountains is narrated by a French nobleman who, taken captive by the Turks at the siege of Candia, has learned Bulgarian

and acts as a translator for them, and by an Orthodox priest who leads his people into Islam in order to spare their lives. Rich in detail and exotic coloration, the novel also pleads the case for reconciliation and unity among all Bulgarians, be they Christian or Muslim.

Translations: *Time of Parting*, trans. Marguerite Alexieva (New York: Morrow, 1968).

Dones, Elvira (b. 1960) Albanian novelist and short-story writer. A native of the port city of Durres, Dones studied Albanian and English literatures at Tirana University and subsequently worked in Albanian television and film. She has attracted much favorable attention in recent years for her unvarnished depiction of the plight of young women in Albania and abroad both under the communist regime and in the postcommunist period. Her first novel, *Dashuri e huaj* (A Foreign Love, 1997), explores the emotional and moral ramifications of the defection of an Albanian woman who, on her first trip away from communist Albania, falls in love with a foreigner and decides to abandon her former way of life and family. Like much of Dones's fiction, it is heavily autobiographical. Dones herself fled to Switzerland in 1988 and has lived there ever since. A Foreign Love was followed in 1998 by the novel *Kardigan* (Cardigan), which contrasts the rigidities of Albanian life in the 1970s with the freedoms of a western European society, such as that of Switzerland in the 1990s, and the hardships of adjustment. Dones's reputation in Europe was much enhanced by her third novel, *Yjet nuk vishen kështu* (Stars Don't Dress Like That, 2000), which, like A Foreign Love, was translated into Italian. The novel is a grim look at the "white slave" trade operated by the thriving Albanian Mafia and the procurement of Albanian girls for foreign bordellos. *Yjet nuk vishen kështu* is the first of a novelistic trilogy that also includes *Ditë e* *bardhë e fyer* (The Desolation of Happy Days, 2001) and *Më pas heshtja* (Afterward Silence), which has not yet appeared. Dones is also the author of two collections of short stories, *Lule të gabuar* (Mistaken Flowers, 2000) and *I Love Tom Hanks: Përralla moderne* (I Love Tom Hanks: Modern Tales, 2002).

Translations: *Dashuri i huaj* is available in Italian as *Senza bagagli*, trans. Alba Molla (Lecce: BESA, 1998), and *Yjet nuk vishen kështu* as *Sole bruciato*, trans. Elio Miracco (Milan: Feltrinelli, 2001).

Drakul, Simon (b. 1930) Macedonian novelist, short-story writer, playwright, and historian. Drakul was born in Lazaropole, where he received his early schooling, but was resettled with his family in Ohrid in 1943 during World War II. He began high school there but moved to Skopje after the war and completed secondary school in that city in 1948. He later studied Macedonian language and literature at the Faculty of Philosophy in Skopje. Upon graduation, he found employment as a teacher and journalist and subsequently became director of the Macedonian National Theater. He has also served as secretary of the Macedonian Writers Union. Although he began his career as a poet and has written plays and film scripts, Drakul is known best for his prose. His first collection of stories, *Planinata i dalečinite* (The Mountain and the Distance), appeared in 1953. It was followed by a second collection, *Vitli vo porojot* (Whirlpools in the Flood), in 1956. Two collections of Drakul's selected stories were published in 1966 and again in 1985. Drakul is also the author of several novels: *I svezdite padjaat sami* (The Stars Fall on Their Own, 1957), about the struggle against the enemy in a large city during World War II; *Bela dolina* (The White Valley, 1962), arguably his most popular work, about the problems related to the establishment of farm cooperatives in Macedonian villages; *Roman za selskiot pravednik Zmejko* (A Novel About the Village Righteous Man, Zmejko, 1969), which continues Drakul's preoccupation with the central character (the villager Zmejko) of his previous novel; *Buni* (1979), a huge, ponderous three-part novel about ancient Macedonia and the Bogomil heretics; and the four-part *Ili smrt* (Or Death, 1990). Steeped in Macedonian history, in which he received his doctorate in 1984 and on which he often writes, Drakul builds his stories and novels around Macedonian village life, which he depicts with an unerring eye for detail and invests with a poetic quality but without idealizing it, or around events in Macedonian history. In 1988 he published a biography of the important nineteenth-century Macedonian Orthodox Church leader Anatolij Zografski (d. 1848) under the title *Arhimandrit Anatolij Zografski* (The Archimandrate Anatolij Zografski). A volume of Drakul's dramatic works, *Drami* (Plays), appeared in 1985. His most important play remains *Nemirna Rudina* (Restless Rudina), which consists of three loosely related parts—"Domot od tvojot tatko" ("The Home of Your Father"), "Noć za ljubov" ("A Night for Love"), and "Stolbovi za neboto" ("Pillars to Heaven")—and carries the action from World War II to the social, political, and professional crises of the postwar era.

Translations: "The Big Horse," in *The Big Horse and Other Stories of Modern Macedonia,* ed. Milne Holton (Columbia: University of Missouri Press, 1974), 7–17.

Drakulić, Slavenka (b. 1949) Croatian journalist and novelist. A native of Zagreb, Drakulić has become as well known internationally, especially in the United States, where she spends much time, as she is in her native Croatia. Her celebrity owes much to her brisk and intelligent books of political reportage. *How We Survived Communism and Even Laughed* (1992) is a series of short pieces on Eastern Europe after 1989 written originally in January and February 1990 on assigment for *Ms.* magazine in New York. In light of the extensive coverage worldwide of the collapse of communism in Eastern Europe, Drakulić's intention was to focus on a less well covered dimension of the unfolding situation, the plight of women—the impact on them of the changes taking place and their reactions to them. Her next book of reportage, *Balkan Express: Fragments from the Other Side of the War* (1993), consists of stories about the "less visible side" of the Yugoslav conflicts of the early 1990s. Drakulić wrote the pieces between April 1991 and May 1992, during which she viewed the disintegration of the former Yugoslavia from her home in Zagreb. Her third book of reportage, *Café Europa: Life After Communism* (1996), contains two dozen pieces written between 1992 and 1996. As in *How We Survived Commnism and Even Laughed,* Drakulić's field of vision again expands to take in the whole of Eastern Europe in the aftermath of the collapse of communism. Her pieces deal with such subjects as the apalling condition of public toilets in Bucharest; the surprise return to Yugoslavia of Crown Prince Alexander; the graves of Nicolae and Elena Ceauşescu in Bucharest; reactions to her visit as a Croat to Israel in light of the treatment of the Jews under the fascist puppet regime of Ante Pavelić; and her father's role in World War II.

Like her reportage, Drakulić's fairly short novels are narrated in the first person, by a younger woman, and have an intensely personal character that is easy to read as at least partly autobiographical. *Hologrami strahu* (*Holograms of Fear,* 1992), for example, deals with a presumably successful kidney transplant undergone by the narrator. *The Taste of a Man* is a macabre tale of a brief but extremely passionate love affair between a Polish female graduate student in New York and the young married Brazilian researcher on cannibalism she meets there. Unable to face the inevitability of her lover's return to Brazil, and out of a desire to keep him wholly hers for the rest of her life, the Polish woman murders him and deposits his dismembered remains in different parts of New York, including Kennedy Airport, but not before partaking of some of his flesh. *Mramorna koza* (*Marble Skin,* 1989) is about a tortuous mother–daughter relationship in which the daughter, a sculptor, is unwholesomely obsessed with her mother's body—as if wanting to possess it completely and finding a release of sorts in sculpting it in marble. The illness and approaching death of the mother in *Marble Skin* echoes the medical ambience of *Holograms of Fear,* while the preoccupation with the body, intense sexuality, and blood link *Marble Skin* and *The Taste of a Man.* In her most recent book, the novel *Kao da me nema* (As If I Didn't Exist, 1999; translated as *S.: A Novel About the Balkans*), Drakulić for the first time in her fiction draws inspiration from the Balkan conflicts by depicting the plight of a woman who is raped repeatedly by Serbian soldiers during the Bosnian War and who has to bear an unwanted child in exile. Nothwithstanding the easy readability and lurid morbidity of Drakulić's fiction, it is primarily as a writer of reportage on the tumultous changes in Eastern Europe and the Balkans from 1989 to 1995 that she will most likely be remembered.

Translations: [In this list of translations of Drakulić's works, translators are identified only when so indicated in the English editions of her works. Since Drakulić knows English well enough to write in it, it must be assumed that a work for which no translator's name appears was written in English by Drakulić herself.] *Balkan Express: Fragments from the Other Side of the War,* trans. Marja Solan (London: Hutchinson, 1993; New York: Norton, 1993); *Café Europa: Life After Communism* (London: Abacus, 1996; New York: Norton, 1997); *Holograms of Fear,* trans. Ellen Elias-Barsaić and Slavenka Drakulić (London: Hutchinson, 1992; New York: Norton, 1992); *How We Survived Communism and Even Laughed* (London: Hutchinson, 1992; New York: Norton, 1992); *Marble Skin: A Novel,* trans. from the French by Greg Mosee (London: Hutchinson, 1993; New York: Norton, 1994); *S: A Novel About the Balkans,* trans. Marko Ivić (New York: Penguin, 2000).

Drašković, Vuk (b. 1946) Bosnian Serb novelist. A native of Bosnia-Herzegovina, Drašković is best known for his novel *Nož* (*The Knife,* 1983), which recounts the massacre of an entire Serb family (Jugović) by their Muslim neighbors (Osmanović) on Christmas Day 1942 in a Bosnian village within the Ustaša fascist-controlled Croatian state. Only a boy is spared the slaughter, but is raised as a Muslim with a hatred of Christian Serbs. When he later falls in love with a Serbian girl, he gradually comes to understand the need for tolerance between Bosnian Serbs and Bosnian Muslims, who share a language and an ethnic origin and who have been divided only by religious intolerance. The title refers to the Bosnian Muslim and Croatian Ustaša ritual of kissing a knife as the preferred instrument of death for the Serbs. Drašković was roundly taken to task for the novel on the grounds that at a time when the official emphasis was on national unity and the need to create an all-encompassing Yugoslav identity, depicting Croatian and, especially, Muslim atrocities against the Serbs during World War II was divisive. Drašković answered his critics in *Odgovori* (Rejoinders, 1989), but in a novel published the same year, *Ruski konzul* (The Russian Consul), he demonstrated a similar Serbian nationalism and ethnic intolerance. The focus this time is on the still greater differences separating Serbs and Albanians in Kosovo. Drašković even carried over his main character from *Nož,*

Alija Osmanović (alias Ilja Jugović before his conversion to Islam), who reappears with his original Serb name and is reconverted to Orthodox Christianity. *Ruski konzul* depicts the Kosovo Albanians as fiercely anti-Serb; they flout the law at every opportunity, and their goal in the province is to drive out the Serbs, whether by acts of hostility or by their demographic preponderance and higher birth rate. In considering Drašković's views as demonstrated by *Nož* and *Ruski konzul,* it is easy to forget that he was the leader of an opposition party in the Serbian Parliament (Srpski Pokret Obnove [SPO; Serbian Movement of Renewal]) and figured prominently in the anti-government demonstrations in Belgrade in March 1992. However, he eventually joined the government and became an outspoken supporter of Slobodan Milošević during the Kosovo war of the spring of 1999. Drašković's other novels include *Sudija* (The Judge, 1982; rev. ed., 1987); *Molitva* (Prayer, 1985; rev. ed., 1990); *Timor mortis* (1989); and *Noć djenerala* (Night of the General, 1994), a fictionalized biography of Draža Mihailović (1893–1946), the leader of the Serbian royalist army known as "chetniks" in World War II. In 1989 Drašković also published a book on the political situation in Yugoslavia from 1980 to 1992 and on Serbian–Albanian relations in Kosovo.

Translations: *The Knife,* trans. Milo Yelesiyevich (New York: Serbian Classics, 2000).

Dubarova, Petia (1962–1979) Bulgarian poet and short-story writer. A native of Burgas, on the Black Sea, where she attended an English-language school, Dubarova was an exceptionally promising writer until her suicide at the age of seventeen. Her five books of poems (some including short stories) were published posthumously: *Az i moreto* (The Sea and I, 1980 and 1981); *Poeziia: Stihove i razkazi ot razlichni godini* (Poetry: Poems and Stories from Different

Years, 1984*); Liastovitsa: Stihove i razkazi* (Sparrow: Poems and Stories, 1987); and *Nai-sin'oto vulshebstvo* (The Bluest Magic, 1988). Dubarova's poetry is full of the dreams and visions of youth and combines a keen sensitivity to nature, love, and poetry with a passionate hostility toward everything banal and false. In 1985 the writer Veselin Andreev published *Sonata za Petia Dubarova* (Sonata for Petia Dubarova), a poetic tribute that conveys the greast sense of loss Dubarova's suicide meant to Bulgarian literature.

Translations: Six poems in *Young Poets of a New Bulgaria,* ed. Belin Tonchev (London: Forest, 1990), 1–7.

Dukovski, Dejan (b. 1969) Macedonian playwright. An international literary celebrity at the age of thirty on the basis of such prizewinning plays as *Bure baruta* (The Powder Keg, 1995) and *Mame mu ebankoj prv počna* (Who the Fuck Started All This, 1997), Dukovski was born and educated in Skopje. He graduated from Skopje University with a degree in dramaturgy, which he studied with the playwright and professor Goran Stefanovski. Dukovski subsequently worked for Macedonian TV as a dramatist and in 1993 became an assistant in the department of film and television scriptwriting at the Dramatic Academy in Skopje. In 1994 he spent several months in the United States on a fellowship from the ArtsLink program. Since 1998 he has been a professor at the Dramatic Academy. Before his leap to international fame with *Bure baruta* and *Mame mu ebankoj prv počna,* he was the author of such plays as *Balkanska* (The Balkan Way, 1987); *Balkanski vampir* (Balkan Vampire, 1989); and *Balkan ni mrtev* (Balkan Isn't Dead), 1993)—all on themes inspired by the Balkan troubles. *Bure baruta,* which was written in 1995 and was soon translated into several other European languages and staged widely, was inspired by the Balkan wars of the 1990s,

but does not deal directly with them. Rather, in eleven loosely connected scenes and with a large number of characters set in Belgrade on a single night in 1995, it exposes the mind-set from which the wars emerged through a series of images of senseless rage and violence between individuals. The play won the Grand Prize at the 1996 Rome BITEF theater festival and in the summer of 1997 was adapted into what became an extraordinarily successful film under the title *Cabaret Balkan,* directed by the Paris-based Serb Goran Paskaljević and released as a French-German-Turkish-Macedonian-Yugoslav co-production. The film won prizes in Bitola (Macedonia), Antalya (Turkey), and Haifa (Israel), as well as the FIPRESCI (Association of Film Critics) Award at the Venice Film Festival and the FELIX Prize at the London Film Festival. *Mame mu ebankoj prv počna* won the Grand Prize at BITEF in Belgrade in 1997. That year, the play had its premiere at the Macedonian National Theater in Skopje. It has been described as a modern version of Dante's *Divine Comedy.* Inspired ultimately by the same violence of war and ethnic cleansing as The Powder Keg, it is a metaphysically nihilistic play in which literary and mythological characters are thrown together in hell with masked contemporaries in order to act out a postmodernist morality play in which love and death, eros and thanatos, can no longer be differentiated. Dukosvki has said, with reference to his play, "This war has made us forget how to speak about love. We no longer have a word for it." Directed by Aleksandar Popovski of the Macedonian National Theater in Skopje, *Mame mu ebankoj prv počna* has also been widely performed and was featured at the Bonner Biennale '98 in Bonn, Germany.

Dumbrăveanu, Anghel (b. 1933) Romanian poet, prose writer, novelist, and translator. One of the most prolific and highly regarded Romanian poets to emerge in the 1960s,

Dumbrăveanu was born in Dobroteasa, along the Olt River in southern Romania. Even before graduating in philology from Timişoara University, he began publishing poems in 1952 in such literary reviews as *Scrisul bănăţean*. His literary output has been prodigious and includes fourteen single volumes and collections of poetry, five books of prose, and six volumes of individual and collaborative translations. His first published volume of poetry, *Fluviile visează oceanul* (Rivers Dream of the Ocean), appeared in 1961. It was followed by *Iluminările mării* (Illuminations of the Sea, 1967); *Oase de corăbii* (Bones of Ships, 1968); *Poeme de dragoste* (Love Poems, 1971); *Faţa străină a nopţii* (The Foreign Face of Night, 1971); *Singurătatea amiezii* (The Solitude of Noon, 1973); *Intrarea in cetate* (Entrance into the City, 1980); *Tematica umbrei* (The Subject of Darkness, 1982); and *Curtea retorilor* (The Court of Orators, 1989). An edition containing much of his poetry was published in 1979 under the title *Poeme* (Poems). A Romanian–English edition of selected works appeared in Romania in 1981 as *Cuvinte magice* (*Magic Words*). Another collection of his poems, also containing works of the early 1980s, was published in 1986 under the title *Iarna imperială* (The Imperial Winter). Dumbrăveanu was the recipient of two Writers Union poetry awards and, in 1986, was given the grand prize of the Nichita Stănescu Poetry Festival for his complete oeuvre. He has served as coeditor of the cultural weekly *Orizont* and as president of the regional Timişoara Writers Association, and was a member of the national board of the Romanian Writers Union until the revolution of 1989. In April 1990 he founded a new periodical, *Meridianul Timişoara* (Timişoara Meridian), a monthly magazine of literature and commentary of which he is editor.

Dumbrăveanu's poetry defies pigeonholing. His consistently unrhymed verse of no striking musicality has a certain autumnal quality. The poet's favorite season, autumn, is accompanied by feelings of melancholy, ephemerality, and resignation. Dusk and darkness are often his favorite times of day, the appropriate setting for expressions of solitude and loneliness. Silence is his frequent companion. Similarly, the forlorness and mystery of the sea hold a strong attraction for him. But Dumbrăveanu's poetic landscape is not bereft of other humans. He is celebrator of woman, from whom song was born, and erotic and voluptuous images are a strong and meaningful presence in his poetry. He compares his words to "woman-scented flowers," and the words he writes are a way of "speaking with the humility of silence":

> Cuvintele scrise de mine
> Sînt un fel de-a vorbi
> În umilinţa tăcerii . . .

Communication for Dumbrăveanu is often bound up with a decoding of signs and runes whose meanings, unless grasped, reduce one to silence.

Literature: Adam J. Sorkin, "Introduction," in *Selected Poems of Anghel Dumbrăveanu in Romanian and English: Love and Winter,* trans. Adam J. Sorkin and Irina Grigorescu Pana (Lewiston, N.Y.: Mellen, 1992), iii–xi, which also includes an interview with Dumbrăveanu in an appendix.

Translations: *Cuvinte magic/Magic Words,* trans. Irina Grigorescu (Cluj-Napoca: Dacia, 1981); *Selected Poems of Anghel Dumbrăveanu in Romanian and English: Love and Winter,* trans. Adam J. Sorkin and Irina Grigorescu Pana (Lewiston, N.Y.: Mellen, 1992), both of which are very good Romanian–English editions of Dumbrăveanu's poetry, with critical commentary.

Dumitraşcu, Aurel (1955–1990) Romanian poet. Born in the town of Piatra Neamţ, Dumitraşcu studied French and Romanian at Iaşi University. He made his literary debut in 1976 in the magazine *Luceafărul*. His first book of poetry, *Furtunile memoriei* (Tempests of Memory), which was completed in 1981, won the competition that year for first-time authors held by the Albatros publishing house in Bucharest. But publication of the volume was held up until 1984 because of objections to some of the poems for political reasons. Dumitraşcu died in 1990 of leukemia. The last volume of poetry he published before his untimely death was *Biblioteca din nord* (Library in the North, 1986). Dumitraşcu's favorite form was the short poem in prose. In one, "Poetry won't keep silent," the poet defined his defiant view of poetry: "The poem always resists. First against any form of collectivism, of salvation through the herd. Never in the history of poetry in this space has the poet been more consistently subversive, so that it could well be that all the books of my generation are antitotalitarian."

Translations: Six poems in *Young Poets of a New Romania: An Anthology*, trans. Brenda Walker with Michaela Celea-Leach, ed. Ion Stoica (London: Forest, 1991), 1–7.

Dumitriu, Petru (b. 1924) Romanian novelist, short-story writer, and playwright. One of the most prolific contemporary Romanian writers, Dumitriu was born in Baziaş. After graduating from high school in Tîrgu Jiu in 1941, he studied philosophy at Munich University from 1941 to 1944, when his studies were interrupted by the overthrow of the wartime Romanian government, which Dumitriu experienced firsthand while on a visit home. Although his first short-story collection, *Eurydice: 8 proze* (Eurydice: 8 Stories, 1947), suggested otherwise, he made an easy accommodation with socialist realism and in this vein wrote the Soviet-style potboiler *Drum fără pulbere* (Road Without Dust, 1950), about the building of the Danube–Black Sea Canal. Ideologically similar in form and spirit were his next few novels: *Duşmănie* (Enmity, 1948); *O sută de kilometri* (One Hundred Kilometers, 1949); and *Nopţile de iunie* (*June Nights*, 1950). With the five-part novel *Cronică de familie* (Family Chronicle, 1956), however, he attempted to move toward a middle ground between the official literary style and something more independent.

In 1960 Dumitriu immigrated to West Berlin, where he continued to write and publish in Romanian and French. Of his novels published in Paris in French, two—*Rendez-vous au Jugement dernier* (*Meeting at the Last Judgment*, 1961) and *Incognito* (1962)—were satires on Romanian themes. However, in such works as *L'Extrème Occident* (*The Extreme Occident*) and *Les Initiés* (The Initiated), both published in 1966; *Le Sourire sarde* (*The Sardinian Smile*, 1967); and *L'Homme aux yeux gris* (The Man with the Gray Eyes, 1968), his satire was aimed at Western culture. Dimitriu's other works include *Le Beau Voyage* (The Good Journey, 1969); *Au Dieu inconnu* (*To the Unknown God*, 1979); *Zéro, ou le point de départ* (Zero, or Point of Departure, 1982), a collection of essays; *La Liberté* (Freedom, 1983), a novel; *Mon semblable, mon frère* (My Lookalike, My Brother, 1983), a second book of essays; *Walkie Talkie: Marcher vers Dieu, parler à Dieu* (Walkie Talkie: Walking Toward God, Talking to God, 1983), a third book of essays; *Je n'ai d'autre boneur que Toi* (You Are My Only Good Fortune, 1984), subtitled "An Essay on Modern Devotion"; *La Femme au miroir* (The Woman in the Mirror, 1988), a novel; *Les Amours difficiles* (Difficult Loves, 1989), a collection of short stories and novellas; and *La Moisson* (The Harvest, 1989), another novel. As their titles suggest, several of Dimitriu's books are of a religious nature.

Translations: *The Extreme Occident*, trans. Peter Wiles (New York: Holt, Rinehart and Winston, 1966); *Family Jewels*, trans.

Edward Hyams, in consultation with Princess Anne-Marie Callimachi (New York: Pantheon, 1961); *Incognito,* trans. Norman Denny (New York: Macmillan, 1964); *Meeting at the Last Judgment,* trans. Richard Howard (New York: Pantheon, 1962); *Nights in June* (Bucharest: Book, 1952); *The Prodigals,* trans. Norman Denny (New York: Pantheon, 1962); *The Sardinian Smile,* trans. Peter Green (London: Collins, 1968); *To the Unknown God,* trans. James Kirkup (New York: Seabury, 1982); "The Best-Cared-For Horses," in *The Phantom Church and Other Stories from Romania,* ed. and trans. Georgiana Farnoaga and Sharon King (Pittsburgh: University of Pittsburgh Press, 1996), 35–39, a story originally published in a Romanian literary review in Munich in 1962.

Duraković, Ferida (b. 1957) Bosnian Serb poet. Duraković was born in the village of Olovo and published her first book of poems, *Bal pod maskama* (Masked Ball), in 1977, before she had graduated from Sarajevo University. She has since published another four collections of poems: *Oči koje me gledaju* (Eyes That Keep Watching Me, 1982); *Mala noćna svjetiljka* (A Little Night Lamp, 1989); *Selidba iz lijepog kraja gdje umiru ruže* (A Move from a Lovely Neighborhood Where Roses Die, 1993), a volume of poetry and prose; and *Serce tame: Sarajevo, 1973–1993* (*Heart of Darkness: Sarajevo, 1973–1993,* 1994), its title taken from the Joseph Conrad novel. She was also one of the editors of the English-language *Cultural Institutions and Monuments in Sarajevo* (Budapest, 1995). Duraković has attracted attention both in and out of Bosnia on the strength of her decision to remain in Sarajevo during the Bosnian War of 1992 to 1996 and to try to give voice in her poetry to the devastation to which she bore witness. As secretary of the Bosnian PEN Center in Sarajevo, she also earned universal respect for her courage and dedication in keeping the center open throughout the war. Notwithstanding Duraković's celebrity as a poet of the Bosnian War, her books of poetry from before the war had already established her as a major talent in contemporary Bosnian literature. Her deceptively simple verse is illuminated by striking imagery, often occurring for maximum effect at the very beginning of the poem. An introspective poet, Duraković writes of isolation and solitude; dreams, in particular those of a young girl; her family; her love for her husband; the solace she derives from writing poetry; Slavic mythology; and roses, which appear frequently in her writing. Her sense of perceived affinities with poets who also have lived through cataclysmic times are obvious in her poems on the Russians Anna Akhmatova, Marina Tsvetaeva, and Joseph Brodsky; the Austrian Georg Trakl, who committed suicide during World War I and whom she recalled again during the siege of Sarajevo; and the martyred Spaniard Federico García Lorca. Some of her poems from the Bosnian War are in the form of Japanese haiku in which the stark simplicity and highly compressed style of the form make her fleeting impressions of the horror of the war all the more striking.

In the autumn of 1999, after the English-language publication of *Serce tame: Sarajevo, 1973–1993,* Duraković visited the United States on a speaking and poetry-reading tour. She visited the College of the Holy Cross in Worcester, Massachusetts; the International Center for Ethics, Justice, and Public Life at Brandeis University; and Harvard University. She was also featured on the television program *Nightline.* She had been in the United States in the winter of 1995 for a short stay at the Sitka Center for Art and Ecology in Otis, Oregon. Duraković was the recipient of PEN New England's 1999 Vasyl Stus Freedom-to-Write Award, which honored her decision to keep the Sarajevo PEN Center open during the Bosnian War, and the Hellman-Hammet Grant for Free Expression. She currently lives with her family in Sarajevo.

Translations: *Heart of Darkness*, trans. Amelia Simic and Zoran Mutic, ed. Greg Simon (Fredonia, N.Y.: White Pine, 1999).

Dušek, Dušan (b. 1946) Slovak short-story, film, and television writer, and poet. A native of Gbelce, almost on the Hungarian border not far north of Budapest, Dušek finished elementary school in Piešt'any and graduated from a chemical industrial high school in Bratislava. He went on to earn a degree in chemistry and geology at Comenius University in Bratislava in 1970 and then spent the next two years working as an editor at the newspaper *Smena*. His next job was as an editor of the sports daily *Tip*, and from 1973 to 1979 he was editor of the youth journal *Kamarát*. From 1979 to 1982, he was a professional writer, after which he became a member of the editorial board of the monthly *Slovenské pohl'ady*. He held this position until 1992, when he joined the Faculty of Film and Television of the College of Musical Arts in Bratislava as a specialist in drama and scriptwriting. Dušek made his literary debut as a writer of fiction in 1972 with his collection of short stories *Strecha domu* (The Roof of the House), which draws on his childhood experiences in his native Záhorie region. His omniscient narrator style, to which he has remained consistent for the most part throughout his career, can be characterized as simple, with a preference for short sentences, a fair use of dialogue, and a certain overall naive quality. Dušek's next book, *Oči a zrak* (Eyes and Sight, 1975), is a mixed bag of short stories, humorous poems, and authorial observations and reminiscences. Dušek again returned to his memories of childhood for a series of children's books, which can easily be enjoyed by adults. They include *Najstarši zo všetkých vrabcov* (The Oldest of All the Sparrows, 1976); *Pravdivý pribeh o Pačovi, Pišťáčik* (The True Adventure of Pač, Pišťáčik, 1980); and *Pišťáčik sa ženi* (Pišťáčik Gets Married, 1981). Dušek's next two collections of stories, *Poloha pri srdci* (A Place near the Heart, 1982) and *Kalendár* (Calendar, 1983), share a small-town setting and well-etched human portraits, especially those of older townspeople of different backgrounds. The small-town setting of *Náprstok* (Thimble, 1985), subtitled *Zopár idylických fotografii poštmajstra Emanuela, požičanych zo starého albumu a vydaných vlastným nákladom ako pohl'adnice* (A few idyllic photographs taken by the postmaster Emanuel, borrowed from an old album and published privately as postcards), in this instance serves as a similar framework for a collection of snapshot-like views of the town's inhabitants. The loosely connected stories, linked mainly by the central character of Adam, are set in the early years of the new post–World War I Czechoslovak state and include episodes from the war itself. Dušek's strong interest in sexuality as the driving force of life and the ways by which sexual frustration manifests itself in men and women alike is much in evidence in *Náprstok*, and discernible in other stories as well.

In 1987 Dušek published another three books of stories: *Dvere do kl'učovej dierky* (The Door to the Key-Hole), which deals mostly with the emotional responses of young people maturing and experiencing romance and erotic contacts for the first time; *Babka na rebríku* (Granny on a Ladder), in which generational conflicts and misunderstandings within a family, also noted in previous stories by Dušek, now hold center stage; and *Prášky na spanie* (Sleeping Pills), which, like the subsequent *Rodina z jedného kolena* (A Family from One Knee, 1991), is a volume of Dušek's selected stories. More generally humorous in nature are the stories in such later collections as *Milosrdný čas* (A Time for Mercy, 1992); *Kufor na sny* (Suitcase for Dreams, 1993); and *Teplomer* (Thermometer, 1996). Dušek was also the author of several film and television scripts and a book of poetry, *Dášky* (Draughts, 1990), containing lyrical reflections and dialogues on nature and on the easily overlooked poetry of everyday life.

Dygat, Stanisław (1914–1978) Polish novelist, short-story writer, and essayist. Dygat was born in Warsaw, and after attending secondary schools in Warsaw and Kraków he studied architecture at the Warsaw Polytechnic and philosophy at Warsaw University. He made his debut as a writer in 1938 with the short story "Różowy kajecik" ("The Little Red Notebook") in a newspaper literary supplement. After the German invasion of Poland in September 1939, he was interned by virtue of his French citizenship (he was partly of French background) in a camp for foreigners in Konstanz, near Lake Boden (Bodensee). He managed to return to Warsaw in 1940 and remained there for the duration of the war as an active member of the cultural underground. After the war he lived in Kraków, Łódź, and Wrocław, where he was president of the Wrocław branch of the Writers Union, and again in Warsaw from 1950. In 1952 he began appearing on a regular basis as a satirical feuilletonist in the weekly *Przegląd Kulturalny.* His first major work, and long his most popular one, was the novel *Jezioro Bodeńskie* (Bodensee, 1946), in which his experiences at Bodensee provide a pretext for contrasting his French frivolity and the weighty heroic tradition of Polish Romanticism, with which he also identifies. Dygat subsequently published three more novels: *Pożegnania* (Farewells, 1948), *Podróż* (The Journey, 1958), and *Disneyland* (1965; original title in English; translated as *Cloak of Illusion*); five vol-

umes of short stories: *Pola Elizejskie* (Elysian Fields, 1949), *Słotne wieczory: Opowiadania najkrótsze* (Rainy Evenings: The Shortest Stories, 1957), *Różowy kajecik* (The Little Pink Notebook, 1958), *Pięć minut przed zaśnięciem* (Five Minutes Before Nodding Off, 1960), and *Karnawał* (Carnival, 1968); and two books of feuilletons: *Wiosna i niedźwiedzie* (Spring and Bears, 1953) and *Rozmyślania przy goleniu* (Thoughts While Shaving, 1959). In much of his fiction, Dygat explores the dichotomy between his unromantic characters' romantic dreams of a different, more colorful, more exciting way of life than the drabness of their ordinary existence and the futility of their achieving their goals. A realist with a taste for mockery and self-dramatizaton, Dygat was fond of ripping the mask off illusion and make-believe.

Translations: *Cloak of Illusion,* trans. David Welsh (Cambridge, Mass.: MIT Press, 1969).

Dzhagarov, Georgi (b. 1925) Bulgarian poet, playwright, and political figure. Born in the village of Biala, in the Burgas region, Dzhagarov fought with the partisans in World War II while still in his teens. For a time he was imprisoned by the Germans. After the war, he completed secondary school in Sliven in 1946 and then studied literature at the Gorky Institute in Moscow, from which he graduated in 1951. From 1951 to 1956, he was editor of *Literaturen front;* from 1961 to 1966, dramatic adviser to he National Youth Theater; and from 1966 to 1972, chairman of the Bulgarian Writers Union. In addition to his literary positions, Dzagarov, a dedicated communist, held the prominent office of vice president of the State Council of Bulgaria from 1971 to 1989. Dzhagarov's several books of poems—most of which are of a patriotic, political, or lyrical character, and some of which were inspired by his wartime prison experiences—

include *Stihotvoreniia* (Poems, 1969); *Ponia-koga: Izbrani stihotvoreniia* (Now and Then: Selected Poems, 1975); *Sezoni* (Seasons, 1981); *Izpoved: Stihove i publitsistika* (Confession: Poems and Journalistic Writings, 1984); *Moite pesni* (My Songs, 1985); *V minuti na mulchanie* (In Minutes of Silence, 1985); and *Ptitsi sreshtu viatura* (Birds Meet the Wind, 1985). As a playwright, Dzhagarov is the author of *Vratite se zatvariat* (The Doors Close, 1961); *I utre e den* (Tomorrow Is Also a Day, 1963); *Prokurorut* (*The Public Prosecutor*, 1965; republished 1969, 1975, 1986); and *Tazi malka zemia* (This Small Land, 1975), a work with an ecological theme.

Dzhagarov's literary fame, both in Bulgaria and abroad, rests almost entirely on his political play, *The Public Prosecutor*, which has been widely translated and performed, including in England and the United States. A product of the "thaw" in Bulgarian literature made possible by the April 1956 Plenary Session of the Central Committee of the Bulgarian Communist Party, *The Public Prosecutor* is a taut political drama centered on the tug of war between a relentless younger investigating magistrate and his older colleague, the public prosecutor Marko Voinov, over the criminal indictment of a family friend of Voinov's on dubious charges of antistate activity. Risking grave consequences, the public prosecutor acts in accordance with his conscience and orders his friend released. In 1982 Dzhagarov was honored for his poetry by the French Academy.

Literature: *Koreni v zhivota: Sreshta-razgovor s Georgi Dzhagarov* (1985), a book of interviews with Dzhagarov; Ivan Spasov, *Georgi Dzhagarov: Literaturen-kriticheski profil* (1988), a literary-critical "profile" of the writer.

Translations: *The Public Prosecutor*, trans. Marguerite Alexieva, adapted by C. P. Snow and Pamela Hansford Johnson (London: Peter Owen, 1969); *Poems*, trans. Peter Tempest (Sofia: Sofia Press, 1977); eight poems, trans. by various hands, in *Poets of Bulgaria*, ed. William Meredith (Greensboro, N.C.: Unicorn, 1986), 30–38; two poems, trans. Theodore Weiss, in *Window on the Black Sea: Bulgarian Poetry in Translation*, ed. Richard Harteis, in collaboration with William Meredith (Pittsburgh: Carnegie Mellon University Press, 1992), 124–25.

Eliade, Mircea (1907–1986) Romanian scholar and fiction writer. A native of Bucharest, Eliade was arguably the most prominent Romanian thinker of the twentieth century. After graduating from Bucharest University in 1928, having written a thesis on the philosophy of the Renaissance, Eliade spent the next three years at Calcutta University studying Indian philosophy. When he returned to Romania, he received his doctorate from Bucharest University in 1933 with a dissertation on yoga. Until 1939, he also taught philosophy and the history of religions at the university. From 1940 to 1945, Eliade served as a Romanian cultural attaché, first in London and then in Lisbon. When World War II ended, he did not return to Romania but took up residence as an émigré in Paris. He remained in Paris until 1956, lecturing on philosophy at the Sorbonne as well as other European universities. It was in this period that Eliade established himself as an international authority on religion and myth. In 1956 he accepted a professorship in the history of religions at the University of Chicago and remained there until his retirement in 1983. He was Sewell L. Avery Distinguished Service Professor in the Divinity School and professor on the Committee of Social

Thought. A chair was named for him at the university after he retired. He died in Chicago in 1986.

Eliade's work falls into two main categories: scholarship and fiction writing. His scholarly works, dealing primarily with myth, magic, yoga, shamanism, and the history of religions, include *Alchimie asiatică* (Asiatic Alchemy, 1935); *Yoga: Essai sur les origines de la mystique indienne* (Yoga: A Study of the Origins of Indian Mysticism, 1936); *Metallurgy, Magic and Alchemy* (1938); *Mitul reintegrării* (The Myth of Reintegration, 1942); *Le Mythe de l'éternel retour* (1949; *The Myth of the Eternal Return*, 1954); *Traité d'histoire des religions* (1949; translated as *Patterns in Comparative Religions*, 1958); *Le Chamanisme* (1951; translated as *Shamanism*, 1964); and *Yoga: Immortalité et liberté* (1952; translated as *Yoga: Immortality and Freedom*, 1964). His crowning scholarly achievement was the four-volume *A History of Religious Ideas* (1976–1983).

Eliade's fictional writing began early, and before long he was recognized as an important figure in Romanian modernism on the basis especially of his novels and stories with Indian settings, reflecting his stay in India, and his works of an occult and supernatural character. The most important of Eliade's "Indian" tales is *Maitreyi* (1933; translated as *Bengal Nights*), about the love between a young European and an Indian teenage girl. Also set in India are *Şantier* (Work in Progress, 1935) and the travel book *India* (1991). Eliade's literature of the fantastic includes *Isabel şi apele diavolului* (Isabel and the Devil's Waters, 1930); *Domnişoara Christina* (Miss Christina, 1936); *Şarpele* (The Snake, 1937); the two tales of the occult included in *Secretul Doctorului Honigberger* (The Secret of Dr. Honigberger, 1940; translated as *Two Tales of the Occult*; reprinted as *Two Strange Tales*); and *Noaptea de sanzieni* (Night of Saint John, 1971; translated as *The Forbidden Forest*). His other fictional works

include "Pelerina" ("The Cape," 1975), published in German in 1976 and in Romanian, in the Paris-based émigré journal *Ethos*, in 1982; "Tinereţe fără de tinereţe" ("Youth Without Youth"), published in Romanian, in the Munich-based émigré journal *Revista Scriitorilor Români*, in 1978 and 1979, and in French in 1981; "Nouasprezece trandafiri" ("Nineteen Roses"), published in Romanian as a separate volume brought out by *Ethos* in 1980 and in French in 1982.

Literature: Mac Linscott Ricketts, *Mircea Eliade: The Romanian Roots, 1907–1945*, 2 vols. (Boulder, Colo.: East European Monographs, 1988); Eugen Simion, *Mircea Eliade: A Spirit of Amplitude* (Boulder, Colo.: East European Monographs, 2001); Norman Manea, "Felix Culpa," in *On Clowns: The Dictator and the Artist* (New York: Grove and Weidenfeld, 1992), 91–123, which deals with Eliade's never-repudiated sympathy for Romanian right-wing and anti-Semitic nationalistic thought and the canonization of Eliade in the post-1989 Romanian nationalist press.

Translations: *Bengal Nights*, trans. Catherine Spencer (Chicago: University of Chicago Press, 1994); *Fantastic Tales by Mircea Eliade & Mihau Niculescu*, trans. and ed. Eric Tappe (London: Forest, 1990), which includes two stories by Eliade: "Twelve Thousand Head of Cattle" and "A Great Man," both published originally in *Nuvele* (Madrid: Colecţie Destin, 1963); *The Forbidden Forest*, trans. Mac Linscott Ricketts and Mary Park (Notre Dame, Ind.: Notre Dame University Press, 1978); *Mystic Stories: The Sacred and the Profane*, trans. Ana Cartianu (Bucharest: Minerva, 1982); *Tales of the Sacred and Supernatural* (Philadelphia: Westminster, 1981); *Two Strange Tales* (Boston: Shambhala, 1986); *Two Tales of the Occult*, trans. William Ames Coates (New York: Herder & Herder, 1970); *Youth Without Youth and Other Novellas*, ed. Matei Calinescu, trans. Mac Linscott Ricketts (Columbus: Ohio State University Press, 1988), which also includes "The Cape" and "Nineteen Roses"; "The Captain's Daughter," in *The Phantom Church and Other Stories from Romania*, ed. and trans. Georgiana Farnoaga and Sharon King (Pittsburgh: University of Pittsburgh Press, 1996), 129–47.

Erb, Elke (b. 1938) German poet, essayist, and translator. Dubbed "our flip-out Elke" by her fellow East German writer Volker Braun, Erb is the daughter of the Marxist historian of literature Ewald Erb, who resettled with his family in the newly established German Democratic Republic in 1949. A native of Scherbad, in the Eifel region, she studied German and Slavic literatures at Halle University and later moved to East Berlin. Strongly supported by members of the so-called Saxon school of poetry, notably Sarah Kirsch, Erb was quickly recognized as a leading representative of the young generation of East German poets born between 1934 and 1940. Characteristic of this group was their opposition to the exploitation of poetry for political and didactic aims and their rejection of then prevailing social norms. They aspired instead to what W. Emmerich has described as a "synthesis of the subjective and the social, of poetry and politics, and of an acceptance of provocation." In her earliest books of poetry, *Gutachten* (Expert Opinion, 1976) and *Einer schreit: Nein!* (One Cries, No!, 1976), a collection of very short prose pieces and a few dreamlike poems of virtually no social content, Erb demonstrated great concern for stylistic precision and a talent for irony. Typical of her short pieces, for example, is "Poverty": "I don't have enough things and, anyway, they're the sort that will do only in the worst pinch. If they were of better quality, it'd be all right to have fewer of them. Also, I don't have enough room for my things. Among them, I am one of the things tossed out by

someone who doesn't have enough." Erb's next collection, *Der Faden der Geduld* (The Web of Guilt, 1978), again primarily of very short prose pieces, a number of them carried over from *Einer schreit: Nein!*, contains an epigraph from the Alsa-tian Dada poet Hans (Jean) Arp, whose influence is felt strongly in the little volume. The book also contains a substantial interview with Christa Wolf based on a four-hour tape recording. It was followed by three more books of poems: *Trost: Gedichte und Prosa* (Consolation: Poetry and Prose, 1982), a selection of texts made by Kirsch; *Vexierbild* (Puzzle Picture, 1983), a similar collection of small prose and verse pieces; and *Kastanienallee* (Chestnut Alley, 1987), Erb's most mature volume of verse to that time and especially interesting for the poet's comments on each poem set in smaller type at the bottom of the page or on the facing page. In 1985 Erb and the East German writer Sascha Anderson edited an antiestablishment literary anthology, *Berührung ist nur eine Randerscheinung: Neue Literatur aus der DDR* (Contact Is Just a Peripheral Phenomenon: New Writing from the GDR). Erb's works published since the reunification of the two Germanys include *Winkelzüge* (Shady Tricks, 1991); *Nachts, halb zwei, zu hause* (Night, One Thirty A.M., at Home, 1991), a volume of her selected works; *Unschuld, du Licht meiner Augen* (Innocence, You Light of My Eyes, 1994); and *Der wilde Forst, der tiefe Wald: Auskünfte in Prosa* (The Primitive Forest, the Dense Woods: Information in Prose, 1995), an exceptionally interesting selection of essays, dialogues, and poems published originally between 1989 and 1995, a few of which deal specifically with East German themes (including "DDR und aus: Bemerkungen zu den Angriffen auf Christa Wolf" ["GDR and Beyond: Observations on the Attacks on Christa Wolff"], 1990). Erb has translated from such major Russian writers as Nikolai Gogol, Aleksandr Blok, and Anna Akhmatova, and has rendered into German the thirteenth-century Georgian romance *Vis and Ramin.*

Translations: *Mountains in Berlin,* trans. Rosmarie Waldrop (Providence, R.I.: Burning Deck, 1995), which includes poems from *Gutachten, Der Faden der Geduld,* and *Vexierbild.*

Esterházy, Péter (b. 1950) Hungarian novelist, short-story writer, and essayist. A native of Budapest, and a member of one of Hungary's most illustrious aristocratic families, Esterházy is a hugely popular novelist known for his fondness for literary puzzles, language play, and brashness. He is also one of the most widely translated of contemporary Hungarian writers. Esterházy began publishing prose fiction in 1974, but first attracted serious critical and popular attention with his novel *Termelési-regény* (A Novel of Production, 1979). In no time, he became the acknowledged leader of a group of young writers who came to the fore in the 1970s and were known most for their rejection of then prevalent norms of a literary realism and sociopolitical orientation that were the legacy of socialist realism. *Termelési-regény* set the pattern for much of Esterházy's subsequent writing, with its playfulness, parodic impulses, and subversion of conventional narrative technique. Beginning with the short novel *Függő* (the title can mean "hanging," "suspended," "conditional"), which he published in 1981, Esterházy embarked on the writing of a series of novels of varying length collectively subsumed under the general title *Bevezetés a szépirodalomba* (An Introduction to Literature, 1986) and in which the individual "pieces" represent different aspects of what has been referred to as a kind of "supra-novel" embracing a broad range of historical and philosophical interests and concerned ultimately with the act of literary creation.

Typical of Esterházy's literary gamesmanship is the highly entertaining novel *Tizenhét hattyúk* (Seventeen Swans, 1987), which Esterházy wrote in archaic sixteenth- and seventeenth-century Hungarian and presented to his readers as the autobiography of a young woman of a working-class background named "Lili Csonkai." Only later was it revealed that Esterházy was the author of the tour de force. One of Esterházy's first works to capture public attention after *Termelési-regény* was the novel *Kis magyar pornográfia* (*A Little Hungarian Pornography,* 1984). Structured in a loose, fragmentary manner—which Esterházy carried over into other works—the novel sets out to capture the bleak everyday rhythms of Hungarian communist society in a process of disintegration. The pornography of the title refers to the lies and deceits rife in an oppressed society in which even normal human contact has to be approached with trepidation. A great admirer of the Czech writer Bohumil Hrabal, Esterházy wrote a novel, *Hrabal könyve* (*The Book of Hrabal,* 1990), that is a kind of homage set in 1988, the year before the collapse of communism in Hungary. (Such is Esterházy's admiration for Hrabal that he wrote the story "Want to See Golden Budapest?" after Hrabal's story "Want to See Golden Prague?" for the Czech's seventy-fifth birthday.) The "writer" of *Hrabal könyve,* who resembles Esterházy, and his wife, Anna, are obsessed with Hrabal. While the writer struggles to write about him, his wife dreams about him and holds long imaginary conversations with him. When Hrabal finally appears, it is in a conversation with God (partly in Czech), who is drawn with Esterházy's characteristic irreverence. The Lord, by the way, is a jazz enthusiast who desperately wants to learn to play the saxophone and eventually summons the legendary Charlie Parker for help. Beneath the surface of its playfulness, *Hrabal könyve* is a no-holds-barred indictment of the Hungarian police-state regime in its death throes. Literary play is carried further in *A szív segédigéi* (*Helping Verbs of the Heart*, 1985), a riotous family portrait of sorts occasioned presumably by the death of his mother (one of Esterházy's bigger-than-life characters). All the pages of the short work are bordered in black, and footnote-like commentary appears at the bottom of each page in capitals. *Helping Verbs of the Heart* was followed by a casual, meandering, and fitfully entertaining account of a Danubian journey from Germany to Romania in the company of his distant uncle Roberto under the title *Hahn-Hahn grófnő pillantása* (*The Glance of Countess Hahn-Hahn: Down the Danube*, 1994). Consisting in the main of historical asides and contemporary observations, the work achieves its goal of turning the traditional travel book on its head. Esterházy's next novel, *Egy nő* (*She Loves Me*, 1996), has to be considered one of his very best. Esterházy begins each of the work's nearly 100 brief chapters, some only a few lines long, with a variation on the formula "She loves me, she loves me not"— "She loves me, she hates me" and still different combinations thereof. What follows is the narrator's recounting of different romantic relationships from the frankly sexual to the bizarre as if the purpose of the book were to chronicle the range and ironies of love. Esterházy's other works include, among others, *Fancsikó és Pinta* (Fancsikó and Pinta, 1976), a novel; *Pápai vizeken ne kalózkodj!* (Make Sure You Avoid Papal Waters, Pirate!, 1977), a collection of short fiction; *Ki szavatol a lady biztonságáért?* (Who Guarantees the Lady's Safety?, 1982); *Fuvarosok* (*The Transporters*, 1983), a novella; *Búcsúszimfónia* (Farewell Symphony, 1994), a three-act comedy; and *Egy kék haris* (One Blue Stocking, 1996). His newest publication, *Harmonia caelistis* (Celestial Harmony, 2000), the title referring to a musical composition by a family ancestor, Pál Esterházy (1635–1713), is a more than 700-page book consisting in the main of a grandiose but sui generis history of the author's illustrious family, clearly inspired by his father's passing.

Translations: *The Book of Hrabal*, trans. Judith Sollosy (Budapest: Corvina, 1993; London: Quartet Books, 1993); *The Glance of Countess Hahn-Hahn: Down the Danube*, trans. Richard Aczel (London: Weidenfeld and Nicolson, 1994); *Helping Verbs of the Heart*, trans. Michael Henry Heim (New York: Grove Weidenfeld, 1990); *A Little Hungarian Pornography*, trans. Judith Sollosy (Evanston, Ill.: Northwestern University Press, 1995); *She Loves Me*, trans. Judith Sollosy (Evanston, Ill.: Northwestern University Press, 1997); *The Transporters*, trans. Ferenc Takács, in *A Hungarian Quartet: Four Contemporary Short Novels* (Budapest: Corvina, 1991), 145–63; "The Miraculous Life of Prince Bluebeard," trans. Paula Balo and Martha Cowan, in *The Kiss: Twentieth Century Hungarian Short Stories*, selected by István Bart (Budapest: Corvina, 1998), 408–20.

Fabrio, Nedeljko (b. 1937) Croatian playwright, novelist, short-story writer, critic, and essayist. A native of the Adriatic port city of Split, Fabrio has often drawn on the history of the city and its mixed Slavic and Italian population in his fiction. This is especially true of such well-known novels as *Vježbanje života: Kronisterija* (Practicing Life: A Chronicle History, 1985) and *Berenikina kosa: Familienfuge* (Berenice's Hair: A Family Fugue, 1989). The first traces the destinies of a single Italian family within the context of the history of Rijeka (Italian, Fiume) in the nineteenth and twentieth centuries, until the city was incorporated into Yugoslavia. Fabrio followed a similar narrative pattern in *Berenikina kosa: Familienfuge*. Here 200 years of Split history form the background to the tale of two star-crossed lovers, the last descendants of two antagonistic families—one Italian, and the other Croatian. They become trapped in communist Yugoslavia after returning to their home city clandestinely, and both perish when they try to return to Italy. Fabrio's most recent novel, *Smrt Vronskog: Deveti dio "Ane Karenjine" Lava Nikolajeviča Tolstoja: Romanzetto alla russa* (The Death of Vronsky: The Ninth Chapter of "Anna Karenina": Romanzetto Russian Style, 1994), is an interesting exercise in metafiction in which Tolstoy's character Vronsky, sent to the Serbian–Turkish front in 1877, arrives in the midst of the Serb–Croat war of 1991, particularly the fighting in the city of Vukovar.

A student of theater as well as a dramatist, Fabrio's first published work was his university dissertation, *Odora Talije, Teatar Draga Gervaisa: Književno-kazališni razgovori, materijali i kontroverzije* (Thalia's Robe, the Theater of Drago Gervais: Literary-Theatrical Conversations, Materials, and Controversies, 1963). His first novel, *Labilni položaj* (Condition Unstable), came out in 1969, followed by a volume of his plays, *Drame* (Plays, 1976); another novel, *Lavlja usta* (The Lion's Mouth, 1978); and a book on theater, *Kazalištarije* (Theatricalities, 1987). An active critic and essayist throughout his career, Fabrio has published several books of essays: *Partite za prozu* (Partitas for Prose, 1966); *Apeninski eseji* (Apennine Essays, 1969); *Stavljenje štiva: Eseji i sinteze* (The Disposition of the Text: Essays and Syntheses, 1977); and *Maestro i njegov šegrt: Glazbena kronika, 1986–1993* (The Maestro and His Novice: A Musical Chronicle, 1986–1993, 1997), additionally subtitled *Prilozi bratimstvu duša u hrvatskoj umjetnosti* (Toward a Brotherhood of Souls in Croatian Art).

Translations: "The Infernal Dominican," trans. Graham McMaster, in *Croatian Tales of Fantasy* (Zagreb: The Bridge, 1996), 147–69. *Berenikina kosa: Familienfuge* is available in German as *Das Haar der Berenice*, trans. Klaus Detlef Olaf (Klagenfurt: Wieser, 1992).

Faludy, György (b. 1910) Hungarian poet. Born and educated in Budapest, Faludy first attracted attention in the 1930s with his colorful paraphrases of François Villon's ballads. He was forced to flee Hungary in 1938 because of his leftist and antifascist views. He eventually settled in the United States and served in the American army in the Pacific theater of operations. In 1946 he returned to Hungary, where he worked as a journalist until he was arrested in 1950. He was interned for the next three years in the notorious labor camp at Recsk. A number of his poems are dated from his stay in Recsk. In 1956 Faludy emigrated for the second time and lived in London, Malta, and finally Canada. He returned to Hungary in 1989 after the fall of the communist regime. Some of Faludy's most readable and interesting poems were inspired by his political experiences and the various countries he lived in during his emigrations from Hungary. Faludy is also the author of an autobiography, *My Happy Days in Hell*, which was published in London in 1962.

Translations: *Corpses, Brats, and Cricket Music/Hullák, kamaszok, tücsökzene: Poems by George Faludy*, trans. Robin Skelton, in collaboration with György Faludy (Vancouver: Tanks, 1987), a Hungarian–English edition; *East and West: Selected Poems by George Faludy*, ed. John Robert Colombo, with a profile of the poet by Barbara Amiel (Toronto: Hounslow, 1978); *Karaton: City of Splintered Gods,* trans. Flora Papastavrou (New York: Morrow, 1966); *Learn This Poem of Mine by Heart: Sixty Poems and One Speech by George Faludy,* ed. John Robert

Colombo, trans. John Robert Colombo and other hands (Toronto: Hounslow, 1983); *My Happy Days in Hell,* trans. Kathleen Szasz (London: Deutsch, 1962; Don Mills, Ont.: Totem, 1985); *Selected Poems, 1933–80: George Faludy,* trans. Robin Skelton, in collaboration with György Faludy, with additional translations by other hands (Athens: University of Georgia Press, 1985).

Farkašová, Etela (b. 1943) Slovak scholar of philosophy and short-story writer. Born in Levoča, Farkašová was brought up and educated in Bratislava. After graduating from high school in 1960, she studied mathematics and physics at the Pedagogical Faculty in Trnava and then pursued philosophical and sociological studies at Comenius University in Bratislava. In 1972 she joined the Department of Philosophy and the History of Philosophy at Comenius University, where she has concentrated primarily on epistemology. She was the coauthor of the monograph *Teória poznania* (Theory of Knowledge, 1980, 1987) and in the academic year 1995/1996 was a visiting professor in the Philosophical Institute in Vienna. She is also a member of the Slovak Writers Union. Farkašová has distinguished herself as both a scholar and a creative writer by her deep and abiding interest in women's issues. She was, for example, one of the founders of the Club of Slovak Women Authors, Femina. Her collections of short stories—among them *Reprodukcia času* (Reproduction of Time, 1978), with which she made her literary debut; *Snívanie v tráve* (Dreaming in the Grass, 1983); *Nočne jazvy* (Nocturnal Scars, 1986); and *Unikajúci portét* (The Disappearing Portrait, 1989)—are interesting above all for their sober, rationalistic, and sometimes skeptical view of the problems faced by women in contemporary society and for their philosophical underpinnings. Farkašová has no illusions about the hardships women face and the kinds of choices

they have to make across a broad spectrum of everyday life. A skilled portraitist who spurns photographic verisimilitude in favor of an attempt to grasp the inner world of the individual, Farkašová appeals as a writer to both male and female readers. *Nedeľne fotografie* (Sunday Photographs), which appeared in 1993, consists of two novellas, the first about an old woman who chooses to live out the rest of her life in a pensioners' home where she gradually builds a new life, and the second about the life of a young singer. Farkašová's most recent publications are the story collection *Deň za dňom* (Day After Day, 1997) and *Etudy o bolesti a iné eseje* (Studies in Pain and Other Essays, 1998). She has also written several works for radio as well as essays on cultural subjects.

Fejes, Endre (b. 1923) Hungarian novelist, short-story writer, and playwright. Fejes was born into a working-class family in Budapest, where he was educated through high school. Upon graduation, he was employed mostly as a lathe operator. After World War II, he worked for five years (1945–1949) in the West as a common laborer and as a lathe operator, again in Budapest, from 1949 to 1956. Fejes began publishing in periodicals in 1955. His first book, *A hazudós* (The Liar), a collection of short stories, appeared in 1958. It was awarded a prize by the Central Council of Hungarian Trade Unions in 1958 and has been translated into German. It was with his second novel, *Rozsdatemető* (Cemetery of Rust, 1962; translated as *Generation of Rust*), with its penetrating examination of a petit-bourgeois family, that Fejes won his greatest acclaim. The work was awarded the Attila József Prize in 1963 and was staged that year by the Thália Theater in Budapest. A keen observer of the life of the Hungarian worker, Fejes is particularly good at portraying average people struggling to cope as best they can with life's hardships while trying to suppress rage and frustration. His novel *Jó estét* *nyár, jó estét szerelem* (Good Evening, Summer, Good Evening, Love, 1969) was made into a popular television series and has been performed widely as a musical. In 1966 Fejes published a collection of novellas under the title *Vidám cimborák* (Merry Partners). His collected plays, including the ever popular comedy *Vonó Ignác* (a personal name, literally "Ignatius the Bow"), appeared in 1969 under the title *Színművek* (Plays). In 1975 he published the autobiographical *Szerelemről bolond éjszakán* (Love on a Foolish Night).

Translations: *Generation of Rust,* trans. Sanford J. Greenburger with Teranece Brashear (New York: McGraw-Hill, 1970); "Blue-White Love," trans. Ivan Sanders, in *The Kiss: Twentieth Century Hungarian Short Stories,* selected by István Bart (Budapest: Corvina, 1998), 246–63; "Ignác Vonó," trans. Eszter Molnár, in *Present Continuous: Contemporary Hungarian Writing,* ed. István Bart (Budapest: Corvina, 1985), 110–18.

Ferencz, Győző (b. 1954) Hungarian poet and translator. Born and educated in Budapest, Ferencz studied English and Hungarian at Eötvös Lóránd University, from which he graduated in 1978. Until he received his doctorate in 1982, he taught in a Budapest high school. In 1982 he went to work as an editor at the Europa publishing house, a position he held until 1992. In 1985/1986, he also taught English literature at Eötrös Lóránd University, and in 1993 joined the faculty there on a permanent basis. From 1989 to 1991, he was editor of the *Újhold* yearbook. Ferencz has translated extensively from American and English poetry and was honored for his work with the Graves Prize in 1987 and the Tibor Déry Prize in 1990. His own poetry has been published in such volumes as *Ha nem lenne semmi nyom* (If There Is No Trace of Anything Below, 1981); *Omlásveszély* (Danger of Collapsing, 1989); and *Két ív: Versek és fordítasok* (Two Arches: Poems and Translations, 1993).

Translations: Four poems in *The Colonnade of Teeth: Modern Hungarian Poetry,* ed. George Gömöri and George Szirtes (Newcastle upon Tyne: Bloodaxe, 1996), 247–50.

Ferko, Milan (b. 1929) Slovak poet, novelist, literary scholar, and historian. Ferko is known mostly for his historical novels set in ancient Rome, fifteenth-century England, and ancient Slovakia. He was born in Velký Roven, where he was educated in local schools until attending high school in Nitra and Žilina, graduating in 1949. He then went to work as an editor for the newspaper *Smena* while studying for a law degree at Comenius University in Bratislava. After receiving his degree in 1953, he became editor of the weekly *Kultúrny život.* In 1957 he founded and edited the literary monthy *Mlad'a tvorba,* and in 1960 became editor in chief of *Slovenské pohlady.* He was dismissed from this latter post and expelled from the Slovak Writers Union in 1968/1969 because of the democratic orientation of the journal and its social criticism. From 1970 to 1975, he was employed at the Slovenský spisovatel' publishing house in an editorial capacity. In 1976 he became a full-time writer. After the change of government in 1989, he became one of the leading figures in the new postcommunist Slovak Writers Association as well as head of the art department of the state publishing house, Matica slovenská. Since then, he has served as an official of the Ministry of Culture of the Slovak Republic.

Ferko began his literary career as a poet, publishing such collections as *Zväzácka čest* (The Honor of the League, 1952); *Vit'azná mladost'* (Heroic Youth, 1953); *Husle a pol'nica: Verse, 1954–1955* (The Lyre and the Bugle: Poems, 1954–1955, 1957); *Svet na dlani* (The World in Hand, 1961); and *Rovnováha* (Equilibrium, 1966) as well as over a dozen books of verse and fairy tales for children. His two early novels, *Keby som mal pušku* (If I Had a Gun, 1969) and *Keby som mal dievča*

(If I Had a Girl, 1983), both of which were made into films, drew heavily on his own youth and student years as well as on the impact of World War II and the early postwar period. In the novels *Svadba bez nevesty* (A Wedding Without the Bride, 1979) and its sequel, *Svadba bez ženicha* (A Wedding Without the Groom, 1982), Ferko brings some humor to the subject of the collectivization of agriculture in the Orava region and industrialization in eastern Slovakia.

Ferko's greatest literary successes remain undoubtedly his historical novels. The first of these was *Krádež svätoštefanskej koruny* (The Theft of the Crown of Saint Stephen, 1970), about the relationship between Queen Elizabeth I of England and her chambermaid. This was followed by *Svätopluk* (1975), the first volume of the *Svätopluk* trilogy, which deals with Svatopluk, duke of Moravia (d. 894); the other volumes in the trilogy are *Svätopluk a Metod: Oheň života, oheň skazy* (Svatopluk and Methodius: The Fire of Life, the Fire of Ruin, 1985), about the relations between Svatopluk and Saint Methodius, Apostle of the Slavs (ca. 824–884/885), and *Svätoplukovo dedičstvo* (The Legacy of Svatopluk, 1989). *Jánočík,* a novel about the legendary Slovak Robin Hood, Jánošík, appeared in 1975. In 1980 Ferko published an intriguing novel about the sojourn of the Roman emperor Marcus Aurelius in Slovakia: *Medzi ženou a Rímom* (Between Woman and Rome). *Otváranie studničiek* (The Opening of the Wells, 1988) celebrates the self-sacrificing devotion of Slovak womanhood against the background of historical events in the early years of the twentieth century.

Ferko is also the author of several works dealing with the Slovak language, Slovak independence, Slovak national identity, and Slovak–Hungarian relations, among them *Prvá láska nastorako* (First Love Askew, 1989), a stylistically amusing collection of short pieces on the subject of the richness of the Slovak language; *Stary narod, mladý štát*

(Old Nation, Young State, 1994; translated as *Slovak Republic: Old Nation, Young State*); *Sto slávnych Slovákov* (A Hundred Famous Slovaks, 1995); *Šestdesiat jeden krokov k slovenskej identite: Zvrchované Slovensko* (Sixty-One Steps to Slovak Identity: A Sovereign Slovakia, 1996), a collection of documents of which he was one of three contributors; and *Slováci a maďari: Súbor študii* (Slovaks and Hungarians: A Collection of Studies, 1996), which Ferko edited. As a historian, Ferko wrote *Velkomoravské záhady* (Great Moravian Puzzles, 1990), dealing with the history of Moravia to the year 906.

Translations: *Slovak Republic: Old Nation, Young State,* trans. Martin Styan (Bratislava: Print-Servis, 1998).

Filipčič, Emil (b. 1951) Slovenian novelist, short-story writer, and playwright. Filipčič was born in Belgrade and educated at the Academy of Theater, Radio, Film, and Television in Ljubljana. His career has been mostly that of a freelance artist. Much of his prose and theatrical writing is of a surreal, grotesque, or satirical-parodic character. It is generally light and contemporary. His prose fiction includes the so-called novels *Grein Vaun* (1979); *Kerubini* (Cherubims, 1979), a political satire about authority coauthored with Branko Gradišnik (b. 1951) and originally published under the joint pseudonym Jožef Paganel; *Ervin Kralj* (Erwin Kralj, 1986), this edition also containing the satirical comedies *Altamira* and *Bolna nevesta* (The Sick Bride); *X-100* (1988); *Orangutan* (1992); and *Jesen je* (It's Autumn, 1995), this edition also containing the comedy *Psiha* (Psyche) as well as the novellas *Kuku* (Cuckoo, 1985); *Dobri robotek* (The Good Little Robot, 1993), a child's tale; and *Urugvaj 1930* (Uruguay 1930, 1993). Apart from the comedies *Altamira, Bolna nevesta,* and *Psiha,* Filipčič wrote the satirical and grotesque play *Kegler 6* (1981); the satirical comedy *Ujetniki svobodne* (Free Prisoners, 1982); and the drama *Božanska tragedia*

(The Divine Tragedy, 1989). With Albert Marko Derganc, Filipčič wrote the "comic strip" *Wyatt Earp* (1990) and the radio serial spoof on authority *Butnskala,* which was performed on Radio Študent in 1979 and 1980. Although Filipčič designates some of his prose works as novels, the term is used lightly since the "novels" generally consist of loosely, if at all, related sketches with an interpolated theatrical work. *Jesen je,* for example, is made up of a series of fairly short prose sketches, each titled separately, whose sequence is interrupted by *Psiha,* which is subtitled *Opera— Tragedy-Ballet* and has as its subject the "first Olympic games ever held in Slovenia." Genres, in fact, mean nothing to Filipčič, who plays with the very notion.

Filkova, Fedia (b. 1951) Bulgarian poet and translator. Filkova was born in Iablanitsa and graduated from the German-language high school in Lovech in 1968. She went on to earn a degree in German language and literature at Sofia University in 1972. Apart from her own poetic writing, Filkova has translated extensively from German and from 1986 to 1991 worked as editor and head of the poetry and drama section at the Narodna Kultura publishing house, which is based in Sofia. She has also taught German philology at Sofia University. In 1992 Filkova was appointed cultural attaché to the Bulgarian Embassy in Vienna. Filkova made her debut as a published poet with the collection *Tsvetia s ochite na zheni* (Flowers with the Eyes of Women) in 1982. Her next two volumes, *Nezhen vuzduh* (Tender Air, 1988) and *Risunki v mraka* (Drawings in the Dark, 1990), are composed of cycles of poems dedicated to various Bulgarian and foreign writers, including, for example, Anna Akhmatova and Christa Wolf. Filkova's poetry consists mainly of short pithy lyrics of a reflective nature inspired by love as an existential condition and by human destiny, her view of which inclines toward the tragic.

Translations: Six poems in *Clay and Star: Contemporary Bulgarian Poets,* trans. and ed. Lisa Sapinkopf and Georgi Belev (Minneapolis: Milkweed, 1992), 189–91; two poems, trans. Michael Collier, in *Window on the Black Sea: Bulgarian Poetry in Translation,* ed. Richard Harteis, in collaboration with William Meredith (Pittsburgh: Carnegie Mellon University Press, 1992), 130–31; six poems in *Young Poets of a New Bulgaria: An Anthology,* ed. Belin Tonchev (London: Forest, 1990), 16–21.

Fink, Ida (b. 1921) Polish novelist and short-story writer. Fink was born in Zbaraż, where she received her early education and aspired to a musical career. She was removed to a ghetto during the German occupation in World War II, but managed to escape and spent the remainder of the war years in hiding. In 1957 she immigrated to Israel. Fink is best known as a writer for her moving, sensitive works about the Holocaust. Her first book, *Skrawek czasu* (*A Scrap of Time,* 1983), which won the Anne Frank Prize in 1987, is composed of a series of largely unconnected sketches. It was followed by the novel *Podróż* (*Journey,* 1990), which draws on her experiences in flight from the ghetto and subsequent search for refuge, and *Ślady* (*Traces,* 1996), another collection of stories. Set mostly in eastern Poland, Fink's narratives about everyday life during the Holocaust, with its myriad assaults on body and mind and small triumphs of survival, are presented in a muted, understated manner free of hysterics and hyperbole. If anything, her sensitive, soft-spoken style sets the terrible circumstances she portrays in even bolder relief.

Translations: *Journey,* trans. Joanna Wechsler and Francine Prose (New York: Farrar, Straus and Giroux, 1992; New York: Plume, 1993); *A Scrap of Time and Other Stories,* trans. Madeline Levine and Francine Prose (New York: Pantheon, 1987; Evanston,

Ill.: Northwestern University Press, 1995); *Traces,* trans. Philip Boehm and Francine Prose (New York: Metropolitan Books, 1997).

Fischerová, Daniela (b. 1948) Czech playwright and short-story writer. The daughter of the composer Jan Fischer, Fischerová was born in Prague where she studied dramaturgy and scriptwriting at the film section of the Academy of Performing Arts. After graduating in 1971, she worked for a while as a scriptwriter for film, radio, and television, and in 1973 became an editor at the Orbis publishing house. She left in 1974 to become a freelance writer. Although Fischerová has written children's and puppet plays as well as short stories, her reputation rests primarily on her adult dramas. They include *Hodina mezi psem a vlkem* (The Hour Between Dog and Wolf, 1979; translated as *Dog and Wolf*) and *Princezna T.* (Princess T., 1986). She has also published a collection of short stories under the title *Prst, který se nikdy nedotkne* (The Finger That Will Never Touch, 1996; translated as *Fingers Pointing Somewhere Else*). *Dog and Wolf,* her only play available at present in English, is also arguably her best. It is a fictional account of the trial of the French writer François Villon that addresses the problem—relevant to communist Czechoslovakia—of the conflict between a nonconformist artist and society. The authorities canceled it after four performances, and Fischerová herself was banned from bringing further works to the stage for eight years.

Translations: *Dog and Wolf,* trans. A. G. Brain, in *Czech Plays: Modern Czech Drama,* ed. Barbara Day (London: Nick Hern, 1994), 139–224; *Fingers Pointing Somewhere Else,* trans. Neil Bermel (North Haven, Conn.: Catbird, 2000); "Allskin Dances on Tables," trans. Alexandra Büchler, in *Allskin and Other Tales by Contemporary Czech Women,* ed. Alexandra Büchler (Seattle: Women in

Translation, 1998), 3–15; "Letter for President Eisenhower," trans. Neil Bermel, in *Daylight in Nightclub Inferno: Czech Fiction from the Post-Kundera Generation,* ed. Elena Lappin (North Haven, Conn.: Catbird, 1997), 29–46.

Fischerová, Sylva (b. 1963) Czech poet. Fischerová was born in Prague but was brought up in the Moravian town of Olomouc, where her father, a well-known philosopher and sociologist, had been the first rector of Olomouc University. The objection to his non-Marxist writings by the communist authorities in 1948 made it impossible for him thereafter to publish in Czechoslovakia. From 1983 to 1985 Fischerová, studied at Charles University in Prague where her interests ranged from physics and philosophy to Greek and Latin. She received her doctorate in classical philology in 1991. Her first book of poetry, *Chvění závodních koní* (*The Tremor of Racehorses*), appeared in 1986. Poems by her had been published in such anthologies of young Czech poets as *Zvláštni znamení* (Special Signs) and *Klíčení: Almanach mladé české poezie* (Germinating: An Almanac of Young Czech Poets), both of which came out in 1985. Her second collection of poems, *Velká zrcadla* (Great Mirrors), was published in 1990. A poet of striking if sometimes elusive imagery, yet grounded in the world around her (including contemporary films, whose lead characters or actors occasionally crop up in her lyrics), Fischerová often writes of feminine perceptions and of the perception of women. Imbued with national pride, she has also conveyed in subtle but unmistakable terms her sense of outrage at the Warsaw Pact invasion of Czechoslovakia in 1968.

Translations: *The Tremor of Racehorses: Selected Poems,* trans. Jarmila Milner and Ian Milner (Newcastle upon Tyne: Bloodaxe, 1990).

Flămând, Dinu (b. 1947) Romanian poet and critic. Flămând was born in the Bistriţa-Nasaud district and was educated in local schools as well as in the cities of Braşov and Cluj. After graduating from high school in 1965, he entered Cluj University where he studied Romanian language and literature, receiving his degree in 1970. While at the university, he was a member of the literary circle grouped around the *Echinox* review. From 1968 to 1970, he served as editor of the review and then moved to Bucharest, where he was employed first at the Central Book House (1970–1971) and later as an editor at the Romanian Encyclopedic publishing house (1971–1973). He was subsequently affiliated with such periodicals as *Flacăra* (1973–1974), *Amfiteatru* (1974–1988), and *Secolul 20* (1988–1989). In 1989 he settled in Paris, where he began studying for a doctorate and working for the Romanian Service of Radio France Internationale. Flămând began publishing poems in a variety of reviews and journals in 1966. His first volume of poetry appeared in 1971 under the title *Apeiron,* which alludes to the view of the ancient Greek astronomer and philosopher Anaximander that the basis of the universe could be found in an indefinite, unlimited substance. *Apeiron* was followed by *Poezii* (Poems, 1974); *Altoiuri* (Graftings, 1977); *Stare de asediu* (State of Siege, 1983); *Viaţa de proba* (The Trial Life, 1998), which appeared after more than a decade of the author's exile in France; and *Dincolo* (Over Yonder, 2000). Also in 2000 Flămând published a selection of poems from all his previous volumes under the title *Migraţia pietrelor* (The Migration of Stones).

As *Apeiron* suggests, Flămând's poetry is often bookish and inspired by ancient philosophy and mythology. In other poems, the motivating force is a nostalgia for the past, both remote and that of childhood, and a preoccupation with the dynamics of recollection. Flămând's austerity and bookish-ness, remarked by critics, contrasts with the Dionysian exuberance, acute sensuousness, and expressiveness with which many of his poems are also pervaded. His apparent acceptance of his exile status coupled with the prominence of Romania in his consciousness are in evidence in some of his more recent poetry with Parisian settings—for example, a poem about Romanian Gypsies in the Paris Metro ("Ţsigani români în metro la Paris") or "'Oraşul poeţilor meteci" ("The Legendary City of Poets"), in which he recalls such famous literary exiles in Paris as Czesław Miłosz and Paul Celan and Romanian predecessors from Tristan Tzara to Gherasim Luca and Ion Pillat. Flămând has accommodated his serious interest in literary criticism with a small monograph on the poet George Bacovia (1881–1957), *Introducere în opera lui G. Bacovia* (An Introduction to the Work of G. Bacovia, 1979), in which he situates his subject in a larger context than that of his symbolism, and the study *Intimitatea textului* (The Intimacy of the Text, 1985), in which the emphasis falls heavily on the use of language and expressiveness. With Omar Lara, Flămând has also published an anthology of translations of Latin American poetry, *20 de poeti latinoamericani contemporani* (20 Contemporary Latin American Poets, 1983).

Flămând has participated in the Writers Program of the University of Iowa and has held scholarships from the Italian Ministry of Culture and the Kalouste Gulbenkian Foundation in Portugal. He currently lives in France.

Translations: Six poems in *15 Young Romanian Poets: An Anthology of Verse,* trans. and ed. Liliana Ursu (Bucharest: Eminescu, 1982), 31–36.

Flisar, Evald (b. 1945) Slovenian playwright, travel writer, poet, and novelist. A bilingual writer in Slovenian and English, Flisar was born in the village of Gerlinci, in southeastern Slovenia. He studied comparative literature at Ljubljana University and English language and literarure at Chiswick Polytechnic in London. Flisar has traveled very widely and lived for several years in Australia, the United States, and India. Since 1975 he has divided his time as a freelance writer and editor between London and Ljubljana, and has recently held the position of president of the Slovene Writers Association. Flisar is known most for his travel writings, often set in exotic locales, and for his plays. He began his literary career as a poet with the volume *Symphonia poetica* (Poetic Symphony), which appeared in 1966, but thereafter switched entirely to prose writing. He has published four novels, a pamphlet-like novella, four books of travel writings, five dramas, and four radio and television plays. His novels include *Mrgolenje prahu* (A Swarm of Dust, 1968); *Umiranje u gledalu* (Death in a Mirror, 1969); *Čarovnikov vajenec* (The Sorcerer's Apprentice, 1986); and *Noro živlenje* (Crazy Life, 1989). Flisar's travel books, which have enjoyed considerable popularity, are *Tisoč in ena pot* (A Journey Too Far [literally, A Thousand and One Roads], 1979), of which the novel *Čarovnikov vajenec* is a fictional adaptation; *Južno od severa* (South of North, 1981); *Lov na lovca in druge zgodbe* (Hunt the Hunter and Other Tales, 1984), a collection of short stories; and *Popotnik v kraljestvu senc* (Travels in Shadowlands, 1992). Most of Flisar's travel works are set in India and Southeast Asia.

As a dramatist, Flisar is known most for his tragicomedy *Kostanjeva krona* (The Chestnut Crown, 1972), a dramatization of his novel *Mrgolenje prahu*. It is a sordid tale of youthful alienation, incest, and murder. Two plays have been published in Slovenian–English editions: the tragicomedy *Kaj pa Leonardo?/What About Leonardo?* (1992), about competing approaches to nervous disorders in a mental hospital, and *Tristan in Izolda/Tristan and Iseult* (1994), a

contemporary reading of the medieval tale. *Final Innocence* (1996) is set during the Bosnian War and makes the point that with such searing conflicts it becomes impossible to stand on the sidelines. Flisar won the coveted Prešeren Fund Prize for his plays *Utro bo lepše* (Tomorrow Will Be Better, 1992) and *What About Leonardo?* The latter also won the Grum Award for the best play of the year.

Translations: *Final Innocence,* trans. Evald Flisar, in *Contemporary Slovenian Drama* (Ljubljana: Slovene Writers Association, 1997), 29–68; *Tales of Wandering,* trans. Alan McConnel-Duff and Evald Flisar (Norman, Okla.: Texture, 2001), a collection of short stories based on Flisar's extensive travels; *Tristan in Izolda/Tristan and Iseult: A Play About Love and Death* (Ljubljana: Pergar, 1994; London: Goldhawk, 1994), a Slovenian–English edition; *Kaj pa Leonardo?/What About Leonardo?* (Ljubljana: Ganeš, 1992; London: Goldhawk, 1992), a Slovenian–English edition; "Executioners," trans. Evald Flisar, in *The Imagination of Terra Incognita: Slovenian Writing, 1945–1995,* ed. Aleš Debeljak (Fredonia, N.Y.: White Pine, 1997), 412–23.

Fotev, Meto (Metodija) (b. 1932) Macedonian novelist and short-story writer. Fotev was born in the village of Ljubojno near Lake Prespa, in southwestern Macedonia. He was educated in local schools and at the teachers college in Bitola. In 1954 he moved to Skopje to work as a journalist at *Nova Makedonija,* the daily newspaper, and later at Skopje Radio and TV, where he became a drama editor. He began his career as a writer in 1955 when he started to publish short stories. His two early novels, *Potomcite na Kat* (Kat's Descendants, 1966) and *Selani i vojnici* (Villages and Soldiers, 1969), are rooted in Macedonian life, with which virtually all of Fotev's fiction deals. Both were critically well received and won prizes. They were followed by *Golemite skitači* (The Great Wanderers, 1970) and *Neplodna voda* (Unfruitful Water, 1977).

Translations: "The Witness," in *The Big Horse and Other Stories of Modern Macedonia,* ed. Milne Holton (Columbia: University of Missouri Ptress, 1974), 126–40.

Fries, Rudolf Fritz (b. 1935) German novelist, short-story writer, essayist, and translator. Fries was born in Bilbao, Spain, and moved with his family to Germany in 1942. He studied English and Romance languages at Leipzig University from 1953 to 1958, thereafter earning a living primarily as a translator of Spanish and Latin American literature. He made his literary debut with the novel *Der Weg nach Oobliadooh* (*The Road to Oobliadooh,* 1966), his most intriguing, artistically and politically significant, and controversial work. Its title presumably inspired by a jazz song by the American musician Dizzy Gillespie, the novel operates in several different ways with musical motifs and structures. Music, American jazz in particular, can in fact be regarded as the novel's subtext, signifying freedom from creative restraints and artificially imposed artistic norms. Set in the German Democratic Republic between the summers of 1957 and 1958, a time when "heroic" socialist construction was in the forefront of the East German communist program, the novel traces the adventures of two latter-day East German picaresque heroes: Arlecq, a would-be author of a novel and a translator (who shares features with Fries himself), and his friend Paasch, a heavy drinker and dental student. Disillusioned and bored with the banality of everyday life in East Germany and its repression of the individual spirit, they escape into a world of music (mostly American), movies (mostly American), alcohol, and sex, finally impregnating their girlfriends. At one point they flee to West Berlin, only to be disillusioned by the rampant materialism and commercialism they find there, and return to the GDR. In the final (third) part of the novel, they take refuge in an insane asylum from which Alecq's pregnant lover arranges his discharge and where Paasch, also awaiting fatherhood, will remain until his alcoholism is cured. Despite the "politically correct" redemptive ending of the work, *The Road to Oobliadooh*—in its jazz-patterned structure, its content, and its overt deference to then officially out-of-favor Romanticism (the German writers Jean Paul [Johann Richter] and Novalis [Friedrich von Hardenberg]) and modernism (Proust, Gottfried Benn, Picasso, Gertrude Stein)—is a defiant rejection of the East German ideology and society of the 1950s. Since it was obviously impossible for a work of such nature to be printed in the GDR, the novel first appeared in West Germany in 1966. Its publication in East Germany came only in 1989, in the last days of the communist regime. Perhaps surprisingly, Fries's subsequent works tended to be more conformist in style and outlook. This is apparent in such short-story collections as *Der Fernsehkrieg* (The Television War, 1969) and *See-Stücke* (Sea Pieces, 1973). Fries's second novel, *Das Luft-Schiff: Biographische Nachlässe zu den Fantasien meines Grossvaters* (The Air Ship: Biographical Supplements to My Grandfather's Imagination, 1974), about the unusual adventures of a Don Quixote–type inventor who wants to endow mankind with the ability to fly, received at best mixed reviews. *Das Luft-Schiff* was subsequently made into an experimental film (in the GDR), which ran for only a brief period of time. Of Fries's next two novels, *Alexanders neue Welten: Ein akademischer Kolportageroman aus Berlin* (Alexander's New Worlds: An Academic Sensationalist Novel from Berlin, 1982) and *Verlegung eines mittleren Reiches* (The Transfiguration of a Middle Empire, 1984), the latter—a science-fiction novel about the aftermath of a nuclear catastrophe—is the more successful. Dealing with the narrator's efforts to probe the secret of the life of a "problematic" individual, Alexander's New Worlds is a convulted, difficult work that met with little success. Despite the very long delay in the East German publication of *The Road to Oobliadooh,* Fries's travel outside the GDR was never restricted, and in 1970 he lived for a time as a writer in residence at St. John's University in Collegeville, Minnesota. He was also a member of the GDR Academy of Arts and Sciences and in 1979 was awarded the Heinrich Mann Prize. His post-GDR publications include the novels *Die Väter im Kino* (Fathers in Film, 1990); *Die Nonnen von Bratislava: Ein Staats und Kriminalroman* (The Nuns of Bratislava: A State and Criminal Novel, 1994); and *Der Roncalli-Effekt* (The Roncalli Effect, 1999). He also published a diary under the title *Im Jahr des Hahns* (In the Year of the Rooster, 1996).

Translations: *The Road to Oobliadooh,* trans. Leila Vannewitz (New York: McGraw-Hill, 1968).

Fühmann, Franz (1922–1984) German novelist, short-story writer, poet, and playwright. One of the most formidable of East German writers whose reputation has increased in the years since his death, Fühmann was born in the Czech Sudeten town of Rokytnice (German, Rochlitz). Raised in a bourgeois fascist home environment, he enlisted in the Wehrmacht in 1939, saw action on several fronts in World War II, was captured by the Soviets, and was released in 1949 after a long period of "reeducation" that left him a convinced Marxist and anxious to atone for the evils of the Nazi era. After the establishment of the German Democratic Republic, he became active in journalism and politics. From 1954 to 1963, he was on the governing board of the Kulturbund (League of Culture) and in 1958 became a freelance writer. His first two vol-

umes of poetry, *Die Nelke Nikos Gedichte* (The Nelke Nikos Poem) and the epic-like and autobiographical *Fahrt nach Stalingrad* (The Journey to Stalingrad), were both published in 1953 and brim with praise for the heroic defenders of Stalingrad and postwar socialist construction. Not entirely in the socialist realist mode, *Die Nelke Nikos Gedichte* also contains some lyrics of a more personal nature. Fühmann's breakthrough as a writer of prose fiction came with his novella *Kameraden* (Comrades, 1955), which is based on his own experiences in June 1941 just before the German invasion of the USSR. To a greater extent than *Fahrt nach Stalingrad,* it set the pattern for the autobiographical character of subsequent publications. *Kameraden* was followed by two more novellas of a similar nature: *Kapitulation* (Capitulation, 1958) and *Das Gottesgericht* (The Judgment of the Lord, 1959). Fühmann next published *Kabelkran und blauer Peter* (Cable Crane and the Blue Peter, 1961), a book of reportage about the Warnow shipyards at Warnemünde, the title referring to the German Blue Peter naval flag and the new gantry crane in use in shipyards. *Kabelkran und blauer Peter* was followed by a series of autobiographical prose works recalling his early youth in the Sudetenland, his assimilation of Nazi ideology, and more of his war experiences: *Böhmen am Meer* (Bohemia on the Sea, 1962); the impressive collection of stories *Das Judenauto: Vierzehn Tage aus zwei Jahrzeiten* (The Jew Car: Fourteen Days out of Two Seasons, 1968; also translated as *The Car with the Yellow Star*), Fühmann's first work to be published in the West, and later revised by him under political pressure; the story collections *König Ödipus: Gesammelte Erzählungen* (King Oedipus: Collected Stories, 1966) and *König Ödipus: Erzählungen, 1954–1965* (King Oedipus: Stories, 1954–1965, 1972); and *Der Jongleur im Kino oder Die Insel der Träume: Studien zur bürgerlichen Gesellschaft* (The Juggler in the Cinema, or The Island of Dreams: Studies on Bourgeois Society, 1971). In 1973 Fühmann brought out the well-regarded *22 Tage oder Die Hälfte des Lebens* (*Twenty-two Days, or Half a Lifetime*), a loosely structured diary of a trip to Hungary, mostly Budapest, in which Fühmann comments on virtually every aspect of Hungarian life and culture, of which he was an admirer. Fühmann knew Hungarian and translated poems by Endre Ady (1877–1919), Attila József (1905–1937), Milán Füst (1888–1967), and Miklós Radnóti (1909–1944). Fühmann's other works include collections of short stories, among them *Elite* (1970), *Saiäns Fiktschen* (Science-Fiction, 1981), *Erzählungen, 1955–1975* (Stories, 1955–1975, 1977), *Bagatelle, rundum positiv* (A Mere Trifle, Wholly Positive, 1978), *Geliebte der Morgenröte* (The Lover of the Dawn, 1979), and *Pavlos Papierbuch und andere Erzählungen* (Pablo's Paperback Book and Other Stories, 1982); literary essays in *Erfahrungen und Widersprüche* (Experiences and Contradictions, 1975); books about German and Soviet artists, including the famous Bolshoi Ballet dancer Galina Ulanova (1961), the German expressionist painter and writer Ernst Barlach (1963, 1977), and the Austrian poet and playwright Georg Trakl (1985); and several works based on or inspired by figures in classical Greek mythology (Alcestis, Odysseus, Prometheus). In 1975 Fühmann was one of the contributors to the anthology *Menschen im Krieg: Erzählungen über den 2. Weltkrieg von Autoren aus der Deutschen Demokratischen Republik und der Sowjetunion* (Men in War: Stories About World War II by Authors in the German Democratic Republic and the Soviet Union). One of Fühmann's more interesting posthumous publications is an exchange of correspondence with Christa Wolf under the title *Monsieur, wir finden uns widerig: Briefe, 1968–1984* (Monsieur, Here We Are Again: Letters, 1968–1984, 1995). Fühmann's several literary awards include the Heinrich Mann Prize (1956); the GDR National Prize (1957, 1974); the Johannes R. Becher Prize, 1963); the Lion Feuchtwanger Prize (1972); and the Geschwister Scholol Prize (1982).

Literature: Dennis Tate, *Franz Fühmann Innovation and Authenticity: A Study of His Prose-Writing* (Amsterdam: Rodopi, 1985), the best book on Fühmann in English.

Translations: *The Car with the Yellow Star: Fourteen Days out of Two Decades,* trans. Joan Becker (Berlin: Seven Seas, 1968); *Twenty-two Days, or Half a Lifetime,* trans. Leila Vennewitz (Berlin: Seven Seas, 1980); "The Jew Car," trans. Jan van Heurck, in *The New Sufferings of Young W. and Other Stories from the German Democratic Republic,* ed. Therese Hörnigk and Alexander Stephan (New York: Continuum, 1997), 214–24.

Fuks, Ladislav (1923–1994) Czech novelist and short-story writer. One of the major Czech prose writers of the post–World War II period, Fuks was a native of Prague, where he studied philosophy and psychology. After a period of employment at the State and the Prague National Gallery, he became a freelance writer. Of Jewish origin, Fuks often dealt with Jewish themes in his works, notably the experience of Jews in Czechoslovakia during the German occupation.

His first novel, *Pan Theodor Mundstock* (*Mr. Theodor Mundtsock,* 1963), is a poignant tale of the obsessions, fantasies, and memories of a humble Prague Jew who at the end of the work escapes the horrors of a concentration camp to which he is about to be sent when he is accidentally run down in the street by a German truck. Fuks's next novel, *Spalovač mrtvol* (*The Cremator,* 1967), which was made into a film by Juraj Herz in 1968, is a chilling story about an ethnic German Czech funeral parlor cremator who succumbs to Nazism when the Germans overrun Czechoslovakia and eventually assure him of a prominent role in their plans for the mass extermination of the Jews. When his wife's Jewish background becomes an obstacle to him, he hangs her and subsequently kills and cremates his sixteen-year-old son when he, too, threatens to become a hindrance. Fuks's other novels include *Variace pro temnou strunu* (Variations for a Dark String, 1966), also made into a film by Juraj Herz in 1968, a psychological study of a neurotic young man coming to grips with reality during Hitler's rise to power; *Příběh kriminálního rady* (The Story of the Police Commissioner, 1971), a Kafkaesque detective story; the "humoresque" (although hardly comic) *Nebožtíci na bále* (The Ball of the Dead, 1972), set in the immediate pre–World War I period; *Návrat z žitného pole* (The Return from the Wheat Field, 1974), a commemoration essentially of the communist takeover of Czechoslovakia in February 1948; *Pasáček z doliny* (The Shepherd Boy from the Valley, 1977), set in eastern Slovakia after World War II; *Myši Nátalie Mooshabrové* (Natalia Mooshabrová's Mice, 1977), a complex and not fully successful novel, also in the fantastic-grotesque Kafkaesque mode, about an elderly woman's obsession with a growing mice population she has trouble controlling in the context of a ruthless regime ultimately overthrown at the end in a coup d'état; *Obraz Martina Blaskowitze* (The Picture of Martin Blaskowitz, 1980), dealing with Czech–German relations during the two world wars; and *Vévodkyně a kuchařka* (The Duchess and the Cook, 1983), a huge panorama of turn-of-the-century Vienna.

Some of Fuks's best writing is in the form of short stories included in such collections as *Mí černovlasí bratři* (My Blackhaired Brothers, 1964); *Smrt morčete* (The Death of the Guinea Pig, 1969), his best-known work after *Pan Theodor Mundstock*; and *Cesta do zaslíbené země a jiné povídky* (The

Road to the Promised Land and Other Stories; 2nd enl. ed., 1991). Apart from fiction, Fuks wrote an affectionate biography of the early years of his fellow writer Julius Fučík under the title *Křišťálový pantoflíček: Příběh dětsví a mládí Julia Fučíka* (The Crystal Slipper: The Childhood and Youth of Julius Fučík, 1978) and a book of reminiscences and opinions, *Moje zrcadlo: Vzpomínky, dojmy, ohlédnutí* (My Mirror: Remembrances, Impressions, Views, 1995), for which the author Arnošt Lustig wrote a preface.

Literature: Bohumil Svozil, *Próza obrazná i věcná* (Prague: Alfaprint, 1995), a book of critical essays on Ladislav Fuks, Bohumil Hrabal, and Ota Pavel.

Translations: *The Cremator,* trans. Eva M. Kandler (London: Boyars, 1984); *Mr. Theodor Mundstock,* trans. Iris Urwin (New York: Orion, 1968); "Kchony Sees the World," trans. Alex Zucker, in *This Side of Reality: Modern Czech Writing,* ed. Alexandra Büchler (London: Serpent's Tail, 1996), 1–17.

Füst, Milán (1888–1967) Hungarian poet, novelist, playwright, and critic. A lawyer by training, Füst worked mostly as a schoolteacher until his leftist views forced him into early retirement in reactionary interwar Hungary. A Budapest native, he began his career as a poet as early as 1913 with the publication of his collection *Változtatnod nem lehet* (You Can't Change It). A second volume, *Az elmúlás kórusa* (The Choir of Oblivion), came out in 1920. A selection of his poems was published in 1935 under the title *Válogatott versei* (Selected Poems). Although his poetic output was small, Füst was admired for the stately rhythms of a poetry given over largely to personal expressions of a pessimistic outlook on life, a twilight poetry of old age. Admired also are his translation of Shakespeare's *King Lear* and his two original plays, *Boldogtalanok* (The

Unhappy Ones) and *Negyedik Henrik Király* (King Henry IV, 1931), both of which were produced after 1945. An aesthetician and, after 1947, a professor of aesthetics at Budapest University, Füst wrote several studies in this field. They were collected and published in 1948 under the title *Látomás és indulat a művészetben* (Vision and Passion in Art). Although the author as well of two books of reminiscences, *Emlékezések és tanulmányok* (Reminiscences and Studies, 1956) and *Ez mind én voltam egzykor* (All This I Once Was, 1957), Füst is remembered most as a prose writer for his novel *A feleségem története* (*The Story of My Wife,* 1957), his sole literary work to be translated into other languages.

In the hostile environment of the late 1930s and early 1940s, Füst, who was Jewish, became virtually a recluse in his Budapest home between 1939 and 1942 and devoted most of his time to writing *The Story of My Wife.* The long novel is an intriguing first-person narrative by a burly, self-deprecating, tragicomic Dutch sea captain, Jacob Störr, who professes to be a contented ignoramus but who, as the novel progresses, reveals an impressive knowledge of world literature from Shakespeare to Edgar Lee Masters's *Spoon River Anthology.* At the heart of the novel is the banal subject of a jealous husband, a younger wife he suspects of infidelities, the cat-and-mouse game between them, and the tantalizing quest for elusive truth. The novel is essentially a character study of Captain Störr himself, a man full of contradictions who in the course of uncovering the truth about his wife reveals his own weaknesses and proclivities. A stylistic tour de force in the original, *The Story of My Wife* even in translation well rewards the reader's patience.

Translations: *The Story of My Wife: The Reminiscences of Captain Störr,* trans. Ivan Sanders (New York: PAJ Publications, 1987); "The Youth of Master Konstantin," trans.

John Brown, in *44 Hungarian Short Stories,* ed. Lajos Illés (Budapest: Corvina, 1979), 157–68; nine poems in *In Quest of the "Miracle Stag": The Poetry of Hungary,* ed. Adam Makkai (Chicago: Atlantis-Centaur, 1996), 535–44.

G

Gafiţa, Gabriel (b. 1952) Romanian novelist and short-story writer. The son of the literary critic and historian Mihai Gafiţa (1923–1977), Gafiţa was born and educated through high school in Bucharest. He entered Bucharest University in 1971 and graduated in 1975 with a degree in English and Romance languages and literatures. After a year as a freelance writer (1975–1976), he taught English the following year, and subsequently became an editor at the Kriterion publishing house. He has also been a regular contributor to the Bucharest daily press and to such literary reviews as *România literară, Luceafărul, Steaua, Tribuna, Secolul 20,* and *Amfiteatru,* in which he published his first short story in 1968. His first book, *Moartea măştilor* (The Death of the Masks), a collection of fantastic stories, appeared in 1971. It was followed in 1975 by his first novel, *Lumină pentru cei singuri* (Light for the Lonely), a straightforward realistic narrative about moral problems in academia, Gafiţa's favorite subject and one that served as the basis of his next novel, *Iarna e o altă ţsară* (Winter Is Another Land, 1980), whose title comes from a poem by Archibald MacLeish. In this work, with its secondary-school as opposed to university setting, petty intrigues and jealousies drive a young man from teaching to journalism, whereas his wife (whom he marries after he leaves teaching), also a teacher, suffers a mental breakdown for similar reasons and has to undergo treatment in an odd clinic in the mountains far from Bucharest. Although much of the focus of the novel is on the circumstances of the wife's treatment, Gafiţa does not lose the opportunity to satirize the academic world in Bucharest and in the provinces, as he had in his first novel. Some of his satire is reserved for the working-class milieu of Bucharest, which he portrays as boorish and given to heavy drinking. After *Iarna e o altă ţsară,* Gafiţa's most widely translated text to date, he published two other works—*Martiriu parţial* (Partial Martyrdom, 1991) and *Schiţa de portret pentru un cap de familie* (Portrait Sketch for a Head of the Family, 1995)—before entering the Romanian foreign service. After serving as secretary of state for foreign affairs, in 1998 he became ambassador to Canada, a position he currently holds. Gafiţa has also translated extensively from English, French, and German literatures and art history, and in 1975 was awarded the Union of Communist Youth (UTC) Prize for prose.

Gajtani, Adem (1935–1982) Kosovo Albanian poet, short-story writer, and playwright. A native of Podujevo, Kosovo, Gajtani studied law at Skopje University in Macedonia but, apart from writing poetry, worked as a journalist in Skopje and for some time was affiliated with the paper *Flaka e vëllazërimit.* A poet of delicate lyrics who shuns social issues, Gajtani has published poetry in the collections *Drita në zemër* (The Light in the Heart, 1961); *Dryni i heshtjeve* (The Key of Silence, 1964); *Ti këngë, ti zog i largët* (Thou Song, Thou Distant Bird, 1968), his largest collection of poems; *Amfora e fundosur* (The Sunken Amphora, 1977); *Kuq* (Red, 1978); *Kënga e mjellmës* (Swan Song, 1980); and *Poezi* (Poetry, 1980). Gajtani is also the author of several poetic dramas, among them *As dru as zog, dashurie* (Neither Tree nor Bird—Love, 1972) and *Unaza* (The Ring, 1974), and in 1968 published a collec-

tion of translations from Albanian literature into Macedonian under the title *Pravostoina* (Entitlement). In 1983 Gajtani was awarded the Brothers Miladinov Prize at the Struga Poetry Festival in Macedonia for *Kënga e mjellmës.* His collected works were published in three volumes in 1985 as *Vepra 1–3* (Works 1–3).

Galgóczi, Erszébet (1930–1989) Hungarian novelist, short-story writer, and screenwriter. Born into a peasant family in rural western Hungary, Galgóczi studied screenwriting at the Academy of Dramatic Arts in Budapest from 1950 to 1955. She subsequently worked as a journalist and for a film studio in Budapest. From 1959, she was able to devote herself entirely to her writing. Her first volume of short stories, *Egy kosár hazai* (A Basket from Home), appeared in 1951. She subsequently published several other collections of stories and novellas, among them *Ott is csak hó van* (There Is Only Snow There, 1961); *A vesztes nem te vagy* (Not You Are the Loser, 1976); *Ez a hét még nehéz lesz* (This Week Too Will Be Hard, 1981); *Törvényen kívül és belül* (Outside and Inside the Law, 1980; translated as *Another Love*); *Kettősünnep* (A Twofold Celebration, 1989); and *Mama öltözik* (Mother Is Getting Dressed, 1999). Although long a dedicated member of the Communist Party—reflected, for example, in her book about the socialization of agriculture, *Nádtetős szocialízmus* (Socialism Under Thatched Roofs, 1970)—Galgóczi became more critical of the Party as time went on and attracted attention for the frank way she dealt with political issues in her fiction. She was named general secretary of the Hungarian Writers Union in 1979 but resigned the position eight years later as a protest against the government's reneging on tax reforms for writers. Galgóczi's best-known work is *Another Love,* a readable detective story about a border officer's efforts to uncover the truth behind the apparent defection and fatal shooting of a female journalist well known for her fearless political reporting. What attracted attention to the novel when it first appeared, and to its film version, *Egymásra nézve* (Looking at Each Other, 1982), was its candid treatment of lesbianism—with which Galgóczi personally identified—and its straightforward depiction of Hungarian society in the aftermath of the 1956 uprising. Galgóczi's other novels, which, like a number of her stories, deal with peasant life as well as issues of crime and punishment, include *Félúton* (Half Way, 1961); *Pókháló* (The Cobweb, 1972); *A közös bűn* (The Public Vice, 1976), which Galgóczi and Imre Mihályfi turned into a film script in 1978; and *Vidravas* (The Iron Otter, 1984). Galgóczi's plays and film scripts were collected in *A főügyész felesége* (The Attorney General's Wife, 1974) and *Úszó jégtáblák* (Ice Floes, 1978). A volume of her reportage, *Törvény szövedéke* (The Letter of the Law), was published in 1988. Galgoczi was twice honored with the prestigious Attila József and Kossuth prizes.

Translations: *Another Love*, trans. Ines Rieder and Felice Newman (Pittsburgh: Cleis, 1991); "Below Zero," trans. John Brown, in *44 Hungarian Short Stories*, ed. Lajos Illés (Budapest: Corvina, 1979), 589–628; "Mother Is Dressing," trans. Peter Szente, in *Present Continuous: Contemporary Hungarian Writing*, ed. István Bart (Budapest: Corvina, 1985), 248–60, and in *The Kiss: Twentieth Century Hungarian Short Stories*, selected by István Bart (Budapest: Corvina, 1998), 274–83.

Gáll, István (1931–1982) Hungarian novelist, short-story writer, and poet. A native of the mining town of Tatabánya, Gáll made mining a central theme in his writing. His career began in 1954 with publication of his first volume of poetry, *Garabonciás diák* (The Wandering Scholar). However, it was with

his prose that he achieved his greatest literary success. In his collection of novellas, *Patkánylyuk* (Rat's Hole, 1961), and his volume of short stories, *Kétpárevezős szerelem* (Love with Double Sculls, 1962), he questioned the social and political conditions of the 1950s. His three novels—*Az öreg* (The Old Man, 1975); *A napimádó* (*The Sun Worshiper*, 1970); and *A ménesgazda* (The Stud Farm Boss, 1976)—brought him considerable success and, in 1978, the Kossuth Prize. *A napimádó* and *A ménesgazda,* which was made into a popular film, are arguably his best major works of fiction. In the former, a woman's restless sleep, which inadvertently wakes her husband, serves as the frame for a series of recollections and inner monologues that revive painful memories of the war in Hungary, the Holocaust (Juli, the heroine, is Jewish), and the difficult adjustments to the early postwar communist years. Using the techniques of sociological inquiry, Gáll brings his subject vividly to life in *A ménesgazda*. Gáll was a member of the Board of the Hungarian Writers Association.

Translations: *The Sun Worshiper*, trans. Thomas DeKornfeld (Budapest: Corvina, 1999); "The Great Adventure," trans. J. E. Sollosy, in *Present Continuous: Contemporary Hungarian Writing*, ed. István Bart (Budapest: Corvina, 1985), 310–33.

Gavran, Miro (b. 1961) Croatian novelist, playwright, screenwriter, and librettist. A prolific and widely performed dramatist as well as a novelist, Gavran was born in the village of Gornja Trnava. He studied dramaturgy at the Academy for Theater, Film, and Television in Zagreb and worked at Zagreb's ITD Theater, first as a dramatist (1986–1989) and thereafter as dramatic director (1989–1992). Gavran organized and headed the Modern Croatian Drama project (1990–1992) and the ITD Theater's series "Drama Library." He also founded and edited (1993–1996) the literary magazine *Plima*.

Although a freelance writer since 1990, Gavran has run a school of creative writing, drama, and prose and in 1995 founded the Epilogue Theater in Zagreb, where he is the company's resident dramatist.

Gavran made his literary debut in 1983 as a playwright with the one-act *Kreontova Antigona* (Creon's Antigone), which was produced by Zagreb's Gavella Theater. Since then, he has written some twenty plays, among them *Noć bogova* (Night of the Gods, 1986; 2nd version, 1987); *Ljubavi Georgea Washingtona* (*The Loves of George Washington*, 1989); *Čehov je Tolstoju rekao zbogom* (*Chekhov Says Goodbye to Tolstoy*, 1989); *Kraljevi i konjušari* (*Royalty and Rogues*, 1990), which was performed at the Eugene O'Neill Theater Center Playwright's Conference in 1999; *Muž moje žene* (My Wife's Husband, 1991); *Shakespeare i Elizabeth* (*Shakespeare and Elizabeth*, 1994); *Smrt glumaca* (Death of an Actor, 1994); *Pacijent doktora Freuda* (*Dr. Freud's Patient*, 1994); *Zaboravi Hollywood* (Forget Hollywood, 1996); *Povratak muža mojej žene* (The Return of My Wife's Husband, 1996); *Bit će sve u redu* (Everything Will Be All Right, 1996); *Traži se novi muž* (Wanted—A New Husband, 1996); *Otelo sa otoka Suska* (Othello from the Island of Susak, 1997), a parody of Shakespeare's tragedy; and *Sve o ženama* (All About Women, 1999–2000).

As their titles suggest, Gavran bases some of his plays on the love life of famous personalities, mostly writers. The patient in *Dr. Freud's Patient* is the young Hitler, who has come to Vienna to seek from Freud the solution to his sexual problem. Sexual desire and seduction, real or imagined, are the motors of much of Gavran's playwriting. Another favorite subject of Gavran is the acting profession, which he explores in terms of both the relations between actors and actresses and the mystique of role-playing. A few of his plays are built around the device of the assumption of multiple roles by a single character. The comic and the dramatic usually pair successfully in Gavran's works and, together with their subject matter, explain much of their popularity.

Apart from his adult dramatic works, plays for children, radio plays, and a film script, Gavran is the author such well-received novels as *Zaboravljeni sin* (*Forgotten Son*, 1989); *Kako smo slomali noge* (How We Broke Our Legs, 1995); *Klara* (*Clara*, 1997), a first-person narrative about her life by a young woman that gradually acquires a supernatural dimension; and *Margita ili putovanje u prošli život* (Margita, or A Journey into a Past Life, 1999), also a partly supernatural work in which past and present interweave as a man searches for a woman he loved long ago. Gavran has also published a collection of short stories, *Mali neobični ljudi* (Extraordinary Ordinary People, 1989). His literary awards include the "Central European Time" International Literary Award for the Best Central European Writer of the Year (1999).

Translations: *Clara,* trans. Laura Gudim (Zagreb, 2000); *Forgotten Son or The Angel from Omorina,* trans. Nina H. Kay-Antoljak (Zagreb: Epilog Teatar, 2000); *Four Plays,* trans. Nina H. Kay-Antoljak and Ellen Elias-Bursać (Zagreb: Epilog Teatar, 2000); *Three Plays,* trans. Ellen Elias-Bursać, Graham MacMaster, and Dominic Andreas Varga (Zagreb: Most/The Bridge, 2000).

Georgievski, Taško (b. 1935) Macedonian novelist and short-story writer. Georgievski was born in Krončelovo, a predominantly Slavic village in northern Greece. He went as a refugee to Yugoslavia and in 1946 was settled in Dolneni (near Prilep) before being moved to Gakovo in Vojvodina, that part of eastern Serbia bordering Hungary. In 1951 he took up permanent residence in Macedonia, making his home in Skopje. It was in the Macedonian capital that he went to secondary school and then entered the Faculty of Philosophy. He has worked as a journalist and for Skopje Radio and TV. Georgievski has written both short stories and novels. His first collection of stories, *Nije zad nasipot* (We Behind the Embankment), came out in 1957. It won the Kočo Racin Award. Additional short-story collections followed: *Suvi vetrovi* (Dry Winds, 1964); *Odebrani raskazi* (Selected Short Stories, 1970); and *Kukja pod kaleto* (House Under the Fortress, 1978). *Lugje i volci* (People and Wolves), his first novel, was published in 1960. It was followed by *Dzidovi* (Walls, 1962), which won the 11 October Prize. The short novel *Crno seme* (*Back Seed*), Georgievski's best known work of fiction, appeared in 1966 and was awarded the 13 November Prize of the City of Skopje. It is a poignant story of Macedonian conscripts caught up in the politics of the Greek civil war at the end of World War II. It was followed by the novels *Doždovi* (Rains, 1969); *Zmijski vetar* (Snake Wind, 1969); *Crveniot konj* (The Red Horse, 1975), which won the Kočo Racin and Stole Popov prizes; *Vreme na molčanje* (Time for Silence, 1979); *Ramna zemja* (Flatlands, 1980); *Grob na ridot* (Grave on the Hill, 1988); and the autobiographical *Kajmakjalan* (1992). In 1982 Georgievski also published a book of criticism, *Zemjata na Hristos* (The Land of Christ), and, in 1988, his diaries, *Pločata na životot* (Record of Life). His newest work of fiction, *Isčeznuvanje* (*Disappearance*), appeared in 1998.

Translations: *Black Seed,* trans. Elizabeth Kolupacev Stewart (Five Dock, Australia: Pollitecon, 1996); *Disappearance,* trans. Natasha Papazovska-Lekova (Skopje: Macedonian Academy of Arts and Sciences, 2000).

Gerlach, Harald (b. 1940) German poet, novelist, and playwright. Born in Bunzlau (Polish, Bolesławiec), Silesia, Gerlach went to work as a copy boy at a newspaper after finishing high school in 1958. Long inter-

ested in the stage, he took courses in stage design from 1966 to 1968 and then joined the theater in Frankfurt am Oder. He left it in 1984 in order to devote himself entirely to his literary career. Gerlach made his literary debut in 1969 on the pages of the journal *Neue Deutsche Literatur.* His first book publication was a volume of poems in the series Poesiealbum (Poetry Album, no. 56), published by Neue Leben in 1972. Both in his poetry and subsequently in his prose fiction, Gerlach has distinguished himself by his attempts to link landscape and history. This is evident in his verse collection *Sprung ins Hafermeer* (Leap into the Hafermeer, 1973), which was based on a trip to Silesia. Gerlach also has shown himself sensitive to the historical multiethnic character of his hometown and the Silesian region in general in his collection of short stories *Vermutungen um einen Landstreicher* (Suspicions About a Tramp, 1978). In such other collections of poems as *Mauerstücke* (Pieces of Wall, 1979); *Nachricht aus Grimmelshausen* (Report from Grimmeshausen, 1984); and *Nirgends und zu keiner Stunde* (Nowhere and at No Hour, 1998), Gerlach moved away from the earlier influences of such poets as Johannes Bobrowski and Peter Huchel toward greater abstraction and surrealism. If politics infrequently appears in his verse, Gerlach proved himself a sharp critic of the German Democratic Republic in his prose fiction, as in the novels *Das Graupenhaus* (The Silo, 1976) and *Gehversuche* (Trying to Walk, 1985) and the novella collection *Abschied von Arkadien* (Leavetaking from Arcadia, 1988). In his plays—for example, those in such collections as *Spiele* (Plays, 1983) and *Folgen der Lust: Neue Spiele* (Consequences of Desire: New Plays, 1990)—Gerlach on occasion used remote historical periods (the Renaissance and Enlightenment) to trace the consequences of the past in the present. Gerlach's most recent work, the novel *Rottman's Bilder*

(Rottman's Pictures, 1998), is the story of a talented East German musician (Scheerbarth) whose dream of composing a great opera eludes him and whose doomed romance with a woman after his wife's death takes him to France and the famous cave paintings at Lascaux.

Gerov, Aleksandur (b. 1919) Bulgarian poet and story writer. An exceptionally popular poet, who is also admired for his tales of the fantastic, Gerov was born in Sofia where in 1942 he graduated from Sofia University with a degree in law. In 1944, during World War II, he was arrested for conspiratorial activity and spent nearly a year in prison. After his release, he went to work for Radio Sofia as literary director. From 1953 to 1955, he was a reporter for the cinema journal *Kino-izkustvo* and, in 1963, joined the agricultural journal *Kooperativno selo*. He also became affiliated with the publishing house Bulgarski pisatel and the film journal *Fokus*. Gerov began writing, in prose, at the age of eleven and has had a strong commitment to children's literature throughout his career. Besides collaborating with publishing houses and journals specializing in literature for young readers, Gerov wrote several volumes of verse for children, among them *Dete na prozoretsa* (Children in the Window, 1959) and *Obiknoveni prikliucheniia* (Ordinary Adventures, 1962, 1969). Many of Gerov's poems written during and after the war and contained in such collections as *Nie horata* (We the People, 1942); *Dva miliarda: Stihove* (Two Billion: Poems, 1947); *Nashata sila* (Our Strength, 1953); *Stihotvoreniia* (Longer Poems, 1956); *Nai-hubavoto* (The Very Best, 1958); *Geroi* (Heroes, 1961); and *Stihotvoreniia* (Longer Poems, 1961) reflect his experiences during the war and his tendency toward metaphysical and philosophical speculation expressed often in a childlike manner. His other volumes of mostly lyrical poetry include *Sto megatona* (A Hun-

dred Megatons, 1963); *Priiateli* (Friends, 1965); *Zlatni pantofki* (Golden Slippers, 1966); *Svoboden stih* (Free Verse, 1967); *Liubovna lirika* (Love Lyrics, 1983); *Obrushtenie* (An Appeal, 1983), a collection of longer poems; *Vnezapni stihotvoreniia* (Unexpected Poems, 1986); and *Kniga za Tamara* (Tamara's Book, 1991), a collection of longer poems. A volume of Gerov's selected poems, *Izbrani stihotvoreniia* (Selected Poems), appeared in 1984. Gerov has also published several volumes of stories, among them *Shtastie i neshtastie* (Happiness and Unhappiness, 1963) and *Inzhektsii* (Injections, 1966), consisting of humorous and satirical tales. *Fantastichni noveli* (Fantastic Novellas, 1966) contains one of his best works, the well-regarded "Nespokoino suznanie" ("Uneasy Consciousness"), a first-person narrative of autobiographical character intended as an antidote to the dogmatic realism of Bulgarian literature of the 1960s. The collection also contains "4004 godina" ("4004 Years"), an upbeat tale on the theme of human immortality. A three-volume collection of Gerov's works was published in 1989.

Translations: Ten poems in *Clay and Star: Contemporary Bulgarian Poets,* trans. and ed. Lisa Sapinkopf and Georgi Belev (Minneapolis: Milkweed, 1992), 20–30; three poems, trans. John Balaban, in *Poets of Bulgaria,* ed. William Meredith (Greensboro, N.C.: Unicorn, 1985), 43–45; seven poems, trans. Grace Cavalieri and Maxine Kumin, in *Window on the Black Sea: Bulgarian Poetry in Translation,* ed. Richard Harteis, in collaboration with William Meredith (Pittsburgh: Carnegie Mellon University Press, 1992), 41–47.

Gjata, Fatmir (1922–1989) Albanian novelist and poet. Gjata, one of the leading representatives of Albanian socialist realism, was born in Korçë, where he was educated and later became a schoolteacher. He fought with the partisans during World War II and then studied at the Gorky Institute of World Literature in Moscow. After returning to Albania, he became editor of the literary journal *Nëntori*. Gjata's first novel, *Përmbysja* (The Overthrow, 1954), traces the growth of political consciousness in a peasant boy during the national liberation struggle in Albania during World War II. It was followed by *Këneta* (The Marsh, 1959), a Soviet-inspired account of the draining in 1946 of the swamp of Maliq on the plain of Korçë and of cloak-and-dagger plots to sabotage the project. Rarely rising above the level of state propaganda, the novel has little to recommend it artistically. Interestingly, it was based on the American Military Mission to Albania headed by Harry Fultz, who was forced to leave the country in 1964. Gjata's other works include *Në pragun e jetës* (On the Threshold of Life, 1960), a collection of stories; *Tana* (1969), a novel with a strong folk element that was awarded the Prize of the Republic; *Tregime të zgjedhura* (Selected Stories, 1973); *Kënga e maliherit* (The Song of the Rifle, 1975), a volume of verse; and *Fillim pranvere* (The Beginning of Spring, 1977), a novel. Nine volumes of Gjata's collected works (*Vepra letrare*) were published in 1984.

Translations: *Këneta* is available in French as *Le Marais* (Tirana: Naim Frashëri, 1984).

Gjuzel, Bogomil (b. 1939) Macedonian poet. A major figure in post–World War II Macedonian literature, Gjuzel was born in Čačak and earned a degree in English literature from Skopje University. He also studied in Edinburgh in 1964/1965. Gjuzel has worked as an editor, the drama director of the Dramatic Theater in Skopje, and an official of the Writers Union. His first published book of poetry, *Medovina* (Mead), appeared in 1962. It was followed by *Al-hemiska ruža* (Alchemist Rose, 1963); *Nebo, zemja i sunce* (Sky, Land, and Sun, 1963); and *Mironosci* (The Peacebringers, 1985). In 1972/1973, Gjuzel was a writer in residence at the University of Iowa's International Writers Workshop (see his poem "Flood at the International Writers Workshop"). Gjuzel has drawn the inspiration for much of his poetry from ancient legends and myths, particularly those of his native Macedonia, whose antiquity he celebrates. Like Blaže Koneski, he did his own version of the old Macedonian epic song "Bolen Dojčin" ("Dojčin the Ill"). In general, Gjuzel writes a catastrophist poetry of doom and gloom, of death and suffering, barely relieved by the creative act of writing poems.

Translations: Seven poems in *Contemporary Macedonian Poetry*, ed. and trans. Ewald Osers (London: Forest, 1991), 39–44; two poems, trans. Bogomil Gjuzel and Howard Erskine-Hill, in *New Writing in Yugoslavia*, ed. Bernard Johnson (Harmondsworth: Penguin, 1970), 296–99; eleven poems, including the longish "Dojčin the Ill," "Odysseus in Hell," and excerpts from "Journey to the City of Lengyel," trans. and versions by Carolyn Kizer, Milne Holton, and Arvind Krishna Mehrotra, in *Reading from the Ashes: An Anthology of the Poetry of Modern Macedonia*, ed. Milne Holton and Graham W. Reid (Pittsburgh: University of Pittsburgh Press, 1977), 109–25.

Głowacki, Janusz (b. 1938) Polish playwright, essayist, and short-story writer. The best-known and most widely translated and performed Polish dramatist after Sławomir Mrożek and Tadeusz Różewicz in the postwar period, Głowacki is the author of a dozen plays. He has also written numerous feuilletons and essays on a broad range of subjects from boxing to Shakespeare and is the author as well of a number of short stories. Głowacki's major plays are *Kopciuch* (*Cinders*, 1979); *Polowanie na karaluchy* (*Hunting Cockroaches*, 1986); *Fortynbras się upił* (*Fortinbras Gets Drunk*, 1990); and *Antygona w Nowym Yorku* (Antigone in New York, 1992). *Cinders*, Głowacki's most often produced play after *Antygona w Nowym Yorku*, is a black comedy about the filming of a performance of "Cinderella" by inmates of a girls' reform school near Warsaw that turns gruesome at the end. It was produced at the Royal Court Theatre in London in 1981 and at the Public Theater in New York in 1984. In 1986 it won the prestigious Argentinian Premio Molière. Written during Głowacki's stay in New York, *Hunting Cockroaches* is an absurdist view of the wretched lives of a couple of Polish émigré artists in New York in the post-Solidarity period. The world premiere of the play took place at the Manhattan Theater Club in 1987 in a production directed by Arthur Penn. The play was subsequently staged in more than fifty American theaters as well as in many other countries. A wildly hilarious rereading of Shakespeare in the manner of Alfred Jarry's famously irreverent *Ubu roi* (Ubu the King), *Fortinbras Gets Drunk* was staged at the Fountainhead Theater in Los Angeles in 1990 and at the Timepiece Theatre in London in 1995. By now Głowacki's most celebrated play, the tragicomic Antigone in New York is set in that erstwhile magnet of the homeless in New York City, Tompkins Square Park, and features a group of three homeless people—a Polish émigré, a Russian Jewish émigré artist, and a Puerto Rican girl of the streets—and the bizarre plan to retrieve her dead boyfriend's body from Potter's Field for a "decent" burial in Tompkins Square Park. The play has had a number of foreign productions, including in Australia, Russia, the Republic of China, and South Korea. It was staged in the United States at the Arena Stage in Washington, D.C., in 1993. *Time* magazine included it in its list of the ten best plays performed in the United States in 1993. It also won first prize at the Festival of Contemporary Polish Arts in Wrocław in 1993. Głowacki's other dramatic works include four short plays on male–female relations, each with only two characters—*Spacerek przed snem* (A Walk Before Sleep, 1979); *Zaraz zaśniesz* (You'll Fall Right Asleep, 1980); *Herbata z mlekiem* (Tea with Milk, 1974); and *Choinka strachu* (The Christmas Tree of Fear, 1981)—and the full-length *Cudzołówto ukarane* (Adultery Punished, 1972); *Konfrontacja* (Confrontation, 1973); *Obciach* (Goofball, 1974); and *Mecz* (The Match, 1976), a play with soccer as its theme.

Głowacki's nondramatic writing comprises fiction and nonfiction. Most of his stories are included in six published volumes: *Wirówka nonsensu* (The Separator of Nonsense, 1968); *Nowy taniec la-ba-da* (The New Dance La-Ba-Da, 1970); *Paradis* (Paradise, 1973); *Polowanie na muchy i inne opowiadania* (Hunting Flies and Other Stories, 1974); *Opowiadania wybrane* (Selected Stories, 1978); and *Skrzek. Coraz trudniej kochać: Opowiadania* (Croak and It's Getting Harder to Love: Stories, 1980). His well-known stories "My Sweet Raskolnikow" (1977; original title in English) and "Retro" ("Flashback," 1977) were published separately. Apart from his many feuilletons, originally published in the collections *W nocy gorzej widać* (It's Harder to See at Night, 1972) and *Powrót hrabiego Monte Cristo* (The Return of the Count of Monte Cristo, 1975), Głowacki's major work of prose is *Moc truchleje* (Power Grows Faint, 1981; translated as *Give Us This Day*), a short but vivid personal account of events leading up to the founding of Solidarity, later subtitled "the first novel about the Polish August" when it was republished in 1982 in London. Virtually all of Głowacki's dramatic and prose works have been collected in the volume *Ścieki skrzeki karaluchy: Utwory prawie wszystkie* (Trails, Croaks, Cockroaches: Almost All Works, 1996).

Among the awards Głowacki has received are the American Theatre Critics Association Award (1986); the Drama League of New York Playwriting Award (1987); the Joseph Kesselring Award (1987); the Hollywood Drama-League Critics Award (1987); a John S. Guggenheim Fellowship (1988); a National Endowment for the Arts Playwriting Fellowship (1988); and an award from the Alfred Jurzykowski Foundation of New York (1995).

Translations: *Give Us This Day,* trans. Konrad Brodzinski (London: Deutsch, 1983; New York: St. Martin's Press, 1983); *Hunting Cockroaches and Other Plays,* trans. Janusz Głowacki (Evanston, Ill.: Northwestern University Press, 1990), which contains *Cinders, Hunting Cockroaches,* and *Fortinbras Gets Drunk.*

Goma, Paul (b. 1935) Romanian novelist and short-story writer. The most famous literary dissident of communist Romania and a writer often compared with the Russian Aleksandr Solzhenitsyn, Goma was born in the Bessarabian village of Mana. After the Soviet takeover of Bessarabia in 1940, his family managed to find refuge in Romania. However, his father was arrested by the NKVD and deported to Siberia in 1943. Eventually reunited, the Goma family took up residence in the village of Buia in the Tîrnava Mare district. Most of Goma's early education was in schools in the Sibiu (Transylvania) area. In 1952 he was expelled for political reasons. He finally graduated from a school in Făgăraş (between Sibiu and Braşov) in 1953, after vain attempts at entering schools in Sighişoara and Braşov. After gaining entry to both the Faculty of Philosophy of Bucharest University and the Mihai Eminescu School of Literature, he chose to attend the latter. A natural-born rebel and nonconformist, Goma before long ran afoul

of the authorities and, after the Hungarian uprising of 1956, was imprisoned for two years. Upon his release from the penitentiary in Gherla, he was sentenced to an additional three years of house arrest (1960–1963) in the village of Lăteşti. As a free man, he worked at a variety of odd jobs in Transylvania until he resumed his studies at Bucharest University in 1965. In 1967, however, he left the university in part because of the physical abuse he was made to endure.

Goma made his literary debut in 1966 with a short story published in the review *Luceafărul* with which he collaborated as well as with *Gazetă literară, Viaţa Românească,* and *Ateneu.* In 1968 he published his first volume of stories, *Camera de alături* (The Room Next Door). His novel *Ostinato* (the title refers to a term in musical composition, from the Italian *ostinato* [obstinate]) appeared in Germany in 1971 after having been rejected by Romanian publishers. This set the pattern for most of Goma's subsequent publications until the regime of Nicolae Ceauşescu was driven from power in Romania. *Uşa* (The Door), his next novel, was also published in Germany in 1972. Not long afterward, Goma was again arrested but freed after an intense international campaign on his behalf. He claims to have been beaten in the streets, threatened with death, and made subject to the scrutiny and harassment of the dreaded Securitate. In 1977 Goma was forced to emigrate. He and his family received political asylum in France. Until he could again be published in Romania after the revolution of 1989, all his books of the late 1970s and the 1980s appeared in France and in French. His novel *Gherla* had in fact been published in 1976 first in French by Gallimard of Paris before Goma emigrated; Gherla is a town in the Cluj district and the site of a notorious prison for political prisoners in the Ceauşescu era. *Gherla* was followed by such novels as *Dans le cercle* (Within the Circle,

1977); *Garde inverse* (Reverse Guard, 1979); *Le Tremblement des hommes* (The Trembling of People, 1979); *Chassée-croisé* (Intersection, 1983); *Les Chiens de la mort* (The Dogs of Death, 1981), which details his prison experiences in Pitești in the 1950s; and *Bonifacia* (1986). The autobiographical *Le Calidor*, which appeared in French in 1987, was subsequently published in Romanian under the title *Din Calidor: O copilărie basarabeană* (In Calidor: A Bessarabian Childhood, 1989, 1990; translated as *My Childhood at the Gate of Unrest*) in the Romanian émigré journal *Dialog*, edited by Ion Solacolu.

In its totality, Goma's literary work comprises a persuasive and grimly fascinating exposure of totalitarian inhumanity from which, in his own case, even foreign exile was no guarantee of safe haven. In such later novels as *Bonfacia* and *My Childhood at the Gate of Unrest*, the biographical element dominates as Goma carries his readers back to his Bessarabian childhood and adolescence. Of particular interest for the light they shed on Goma's later life and career are the several sets of diaries, all published in Romania in 1997 and 1998: *Alte jurnale* (Other Journals), which covers his stay in the United States in the fall of 1978 but concentrates primarily on the period 1994 to 1996; *Jurnal I: Jurnal pe sărite* (Journal I: By Leaps and Bounds, 1997); *Jurnal II: Jurnal de căldură mare* (Journal II: Journal of Great Heat, 1997), which covers the period June and July 1989; *Jurnal III: Jurnal de noapte lungă* (Journal of the Long Night, 1997), covering the period September to December 1993; and *Jurnalul unui jurnal 1997* (The Journal of a Journal, 1997), which is devoted just to the year 1997.

Literature: Virgil Tanase, ed., *Dossier Paul Goma: L'Écrivain face au socialisme du silence* (Paris: Editions Albatros, 1977).

Translations: *My Childhood at the Gate of Unrest*, trans. Angela Clark (London: Read-ers International, 1990). Available in French are *Bonifacia,* trans. A. Paruit (Paris: Hachette, 1986); *Le Calidor,* trans. A. Paruit (Paris: Albin Michel, 1987); *La Cellule des libérables* [*Ostinato*], trans. Alain Paruit (Paris: Gallimard, 1971); *Chassé-croisé*, trans. A. Paruit (Paris: Hachette, 1983); *Les Chiens de mort, ou, La Passion selon Pitesti*, trans. A. Paruit (Paris: Hachette, 1981); *Dans le cercle,* trans. Yvonne Krall (Paris: Gallimard, 1977); *Elles étaient quatre . . . ,* trans. Alain Paruit (Paris: Gallimard, 1975); *Garde inverse*, trans. Șerban Cristovici (Paris: Gallimard, 1979); *Gherla*, trans. Șerban Cristovici (Paris: Gallimard, 1976); and *Le Tremblement des hommes: Peut-on vivre en Roumanie aujourd'hui?*, trans. A Paruit (Paris: Seuil, 1979). Available in German are *Ostinato,* trans. Marie-Thérèse Kerschbaumer (Frankfurt am Main: Suhrkamp, 1971), and *Die Tür*, trans. Marie-Thérèse Kerschbaumer (Frankfurt am Main: Suhrkamp, 1972).

Göncz, Árpád (b. 1922) Hungarian playwright, short-story writer, essayist, and translator. On 2 May 1990, Göncz became Hungary's first democratically elected president in four decades. He was born in 1922 in Budapest into a well-off bourgeois family. After his secondary-school education, he studied law at Budapest University from 1938 to 1944. He received his degree in 1944 and shortly thereafter found himself a private in the army. He also served in the Hungarian underground and at one point was wounded in a skirmish with German military police. After World War II, he was hired as an attorney by an agricultural bank in Budapest and continued his earlier collaboration with the Independent Smallholders Party, a left-of-center opposition group. The communist takeover of Hungary in 1948 cost him his job, and he was forced to find work at first as an unskilled laborer in several Budapest factories. He subsequently became involved in soil reclamation and studied agricultural engineering at Gödöllő University. For his role in the Hungarian uprising of 1956, he was sentenced to life imprisonment but served only six and a half years. His first play, the black comedy *Rácsok* (Iron Bars, 1979), about a poet imprisoned because the president of an unnamed republic wants him to admit that he, the president, not the poet, wrote the country's national anthem, drew on the experience of a fellow inmate in the Budapest prison. It was also while he was in prison that Göncz began his study of English, which led eventually to his extraordinary career as a translator of American, Canadian, and English literatures. Once released from prison, Göncz was denied permission to work either as a lawyer or as an agricultural engineer. He turned instead to translation, first technical and then literary, in order to make a living. The American writers whose works he has translated include, among others, James Baldwin, Truman Capote, Willa Cather, William Faulkner, Ernest Hemingway, John Updike, and Thomas Wolfe. He was awarded the Wheatland Prize for his translations from American literature.

As a creative writer, Göncz is the author of a few plays and several short stories. Two of his plays are modern interpretations of ancient Greek dramas: *Magyar Médeia* (Hungarian Medea), a contemporary version of Euripides' play set in socialist Hungary, in which Jason plans to marry the daughter of the head of a coal-hydrogen program; and *Persephone*, which was inspired by Hesiod's Homeric hymn to Demeter. Both *Rácsok* and *Magyar Médeia* were published for the first time in 1979. *Sarusok* (Sandal Makers; translated as *Men of God*), which dates from 1974, is an arresting political allegory dealing with the persecution of Hungarian followers of the Waldensian heresy in the city of Sopon in 1401, but obviously alluding to the post–Mátyás Rákocsi

era in Hungary. A collection of Göncz's plays was published in 1990 under the title *Mérleg: hét drámája* (Scales: Seven Plays). The title refers to the play based on Göncz's story of the same name about a brief encounter of former lovers. Göncz's short stories are available in two volumes: *Találkozások* (Encounters, 1980) and *Hazaérkezés* (Homecoming, 1991), which contains a few of the stories published in the earlier volume. They range thematically from terse vignettes of the horror of World War II to an encounter several hundred years after her burning at the stake between Joan of Arc and Bishop Couchon. Göncz's style is very spare, indeed laconic, but his prose works, like his plays, convey a deep respect for human dignity and a love of life. While certainly well regarded for both his dramatic and his story writing, it may well be that Göncz's most memorable achievement will be judged his large oeuvre of translations from English.

Translations: *Homecoming and Other Stories,* trans. Katharina M. Wilson and Christopher C. Wilson (Budapest: Corvina, 1991); *Plays and Other Writings,* trans. Katharina M. Wilson and Christopher C. Wilson (New York: Garland, 1990); *Voices of Dissent: Two Plays,* trans. Katharina M. Wilson and Christopher C. Wilson (Lewisburg, Pa.: Bucknell University Press, 1989).

Gotovac, Vlado (1930–2000) Croatian poet and political figure. Gotovac was a leading poet of the 1960s and a prominent dissident in communist Yugoslavia as well as a champion for democracy under the authoritarian rule of president Franjo Tudjman (who died in December 1999). He was born in Imotski, in southern Croatia, and received his degree in philosophy from Zagreb University. Gotovac worked mostly as a journalist and as an editor for radio and television, and from 1990 to 1996 headed Matica Hrvatska. He also edited such journals as *Medjutim,*

Razlog, and *Hrvatski tjednik.* Gotovac's first book of poetry, *Pjesme oduvijek* (Poems from Always), appeared in 1956. It was followed by sixteen other volumes: *Opasni prostor* (Dangerous Space, 1961); *Jeka* (Echo, 1961); *I biti opravdan* (And Also to Be Right, 1963); *Osječanje mjesta* (Sensitive Places, 1964); *Čujem oblaka* (I Hear the Clouds, 1965); *Princip djela* (The Principle of the Thing, 1966); *Zatire se zemlja* (The Earth Will Be Exterminated, 1967); *Približavanje* (The Approach, 1968); *Prepjevi po sjećanju* (Translations from Memory, 1968); *Čarobna spilja* (The Enchanted Cave, 1969); *Sporne sandale* (Disputable Sandals, 1970); *Sadržaj vjetra* (Contents of the Wind, 1971); *Zabranjena vječnost* (Forbidden Eternity, 1989); *Isto* (Likewise, 1990); *Crna kazaljka* (The Black Watch-Hand, 1991); and *Čekati sjevernije* (Awaiting the More Northerly, 1995).

Essentially an urban poet despite his rural upbringing, Gotovac wrote a highly philosophical poetry whose main themes were the integrity of the individual and the need to preserve democratic freedoms. His prose works are addressed to social issues, including totalitarianism and, later, the Yugoslav wars of the 1990s. *U svakodnevnom* (In the Daily Routine), which first appeared in 1970, deals with contemporary Yugoslav society. Gotovac's willingness to confront sensitive issues head on—above all, the matter of political rights in Yugoslavia—earned him four years' imprisonment from 1972 to 1976 and an additional two years from 1982 to 1984 on charges of "criminal thinking." He was also prohibited from all forms of public activity for eight years. Gotovac drew on his own prison experiences in such works as *Pisma protiv tiranije* (Letters Against Tyranny, 1981); *Moj slučaj* (My Case, 1989); and, especially, *Zvjezdana kuga: Zatvorski zapisi, 1972–1973* (Star-studded Plague: Prison Notes, 1972–1973, 1995). In 1989 Gotovac founded the Croatian Social-Liberal Party, which lost his country's first multiparty elections, in the spring of 1990, to Tudjman's Croatian Democratic Union. Gotovac's preoccupation with the conflict resulting from the breakup of Yugoslavia led to his participation with other writers in a discourse on Bosnia published under the title *Okovana Bosna: Razgovor* (Bosnia in Chains: A Conversation, 1995) and his editing of the Bosnian Croatian writer Juraj Njavro's book, *Glava dolje ruke na ledja* (Head Down, Hands Behind You, 1992), which deals mainly with the siege of Vukovar.

Translations: Five poems, trans. Michael Scammell, in *New Writing in Yugoslavia,* ed. Bernard Johnson (Harmondsworth: Penguin, 1970), 194–97.

Gradišnik, Brane (b. 1951) Slovenian short-story writer, novelist, and scriptwriter. The son of the writer Janez Gradišnik (b. 1917), Gradišnik was born in Ljubljana, where he studied art history and sociology at Ljubljana University. He subsequently received a master's degree in creative writing at the University of Lancaster in Great Britain. From 1984 to 1989, he served as literary editor at the publishing house Kmečki glas and then accepted the position of assistant to the editor in chief of Radio Slovenia. In 1994 he ran (unsuccessfully) for mayor of Ljubljana and has since been a freelance writer. Gradišnik's stock-in-trade is psychological realism and a postmodernism mixed with elements of the fantastic. He is best known for his short stories and novellas in such collections as *Čas* (Time, 1977); *Zemlja zemlja zemlja* (Earth, Earth, Earth, 1981); and *Mistifikacije* (Mystifications, 1987). His other works include *Mavrična krila* (Wings of Rainbow, 1978), an anthology of well-known tales of the fantastic that he coedited; *Kerubini* (Cherubim, 1979), a satirical novel about political authority, coauthored with Emil Filipčič and published under the joint pseudonym Jožef

Paganel; a novel, *Leta* (Lethe, 1985); the "criminal story" *Nekdo drug* (The Other Man, 1990); and a collection of correspondence under the title *Nekaj drugega* (Nobody Else, 1990). Apart from his several film scripts, he has translated extensively from English, including works by R. Adams, James M. Cain, G. K. Chesterton, James Dickey, Ralph Ellison, A. A. Milne, P. Pearce, Mark Twain, and Kurt Vonnegut.

Translations: "Oeopath," "Mouseday," and "Life Story," trans. Brane Gradišnik, in *The Day Tito Died: Contemporary Slovenian Short Stories* (London: Forest, 1993), 39–77.

Grafenauer, Niko (b. 1940) Slovenian poet and essayist. A leading representative of post–World War II Slovenian poetic modernism, Grafenauer was born and educated in Ljubljana, where he studied comparative literature at the university. Long associated with the review *Nova revija* as its editor in chief and director of its publishing house, Grafenauer published his first book of poetry, *Večer pred praznikom* (The Evening Before the Holiday), in 1962. It was followed by such volumes as *Stiska jezika* (The Hardship of Language, 1965); *Štukature* (Stuccos, 1975); *Pesmi* (Poems, 1979), a selection; *Pesmi* (Poems, 1979), with poems also by Svetlana Makarovič (b. 1939) and Tomaž Šalamun; *Palimpsesti* (Palimpsests, 1984); *Izbrisi* (Erasures, 1989), a collection of elegies; and *Samota* (Solitude, 1990), a selection. Grafenauer is also the author of a number of books of verse for children. Typical of the poets of his generation (those born in the early 1940s), Grafenauer is most admired for the autonomy and self-sufficiency of a poetry in which linguistic and aesthetic concerns far outweigh content. For the most part indifferent to external reality, it is a poetry that becomes an absolute value, obedient only to its own inner directives. Yet a sense of melancholy, darkness, and transience is pervasive in Grafenauer's work, and he has written a few moving poems on Sarajevo during the Bosnian War. Of his six books of criticism, two deal with poetry in a more theoretical way: *Kritika in poetika* (Criticism and Poetics, 1974) and *Izročenost pesmi* (Transmitting the Poem, 1982). His *Tretja beseda* (The Third Word, 1991) is an interesting collection of essays about Slovenian poetry. Grafenauer is also an able translator, mostly from German, and has also written studies of such poets as Hans Magnus Enzensberger, Gottfried Benn, Rainer Maria Rilke, and Friedrich Hölderlin, who clearly influenced the direction his own poetic writing would take.

Translations: Ten poems, including the longer poem "Solitude" (from *Izbrisi*), trans. Jože Lazar, in *The Imagination of Terra Incognita: Slovenian Writing, 1945–1955,* ed. Aleš Debeljak (Fredonia, N.Y.: White Pine, 1997), 230–37; "Poetic Language and Nationality," trans. Marjan Golobič, in *The Slovenian Essay of the Nineties,* selected by Matevž Kos (Ljubljana: Slovene Writers Association, 2000), 31–44.

Gruša, Jiří (b. 1938) Czech poet, novelist, short-story writer, literary critic, and translator. One of the best known of the Czech dissident writers of the 1970s and 1980s, Gruša was born in Pardubice where he received his early education. He studied history and philosophy at Charles University, from which he graduated in 1962. In 1967 he became editor of the weekly *Nové knihy* and, in 1969, editor of the weekly *Zítřek.* He later cofounded and edited the literary magazines *Tvář* and *Sešity.* Gruša made his literary debut with a volume of poetry published in 1962 under the title *Torna* (Knapsack). It was soon followed by two collections of short stories: *Světlá lhůta* (Clear Deadline, 1964) and *Cvičení mučení* (Rehearsal for Torture, 1969). After 1968, he became active in the samizdat movement and especially the Edice Petlice series. He also earned a reputation as a translator of German literature, including works by Paul Celan, Franz Kafka, and Rainer Maria Rilke, among others. Because of his more increasingly overt support of the movement for liberalization and democratization, Gruša was prohibited from further publication. Thus his first work after the ban, *Mimner aneb Hra o smrd'ocha* (Mimner, or A Play About a Stinker), could circulate only in manuscript. His next text, *Dámský gambit* (The Queen's Gambit), was published first in samizdat in 1973 and then in book form in Toronto only in 1979. In 1978 Gruša was taken into custody in connection with his seemingly absurdist political novel *Dotazník aneb modlitba za jedno město a přítele* (*The Questionnaire or Prayer for a Town and a Friend*), which came out in samizdat in 1975 and in book form in Toronto in 1978, and subsequently became the basis of Gruša's international celebrity. After his release, Gruša left Czechoslovakia in 1980. His last literary work to circulate in Czechoslovakia before his departure was the ribald *Dr. Kokeš Mistr Panny* (Doctor Cocker, Virgin Master), published in samizdat in 1980 and in book form in Toronto in 1984.

Gruša received a grant to the Mac Dowell Colony in the United States in 1981, but the Czechoslovak authorities stripped him of his citizenship before his return. He took up residence in West Germany from 1982 to 1990, returning to Czechoslovakia after the fall of the communist government. In October 1990 he became an employee of the Ministry of Foreign Affairs and, in January 1991, extraordinary and plenipotentiary ambassador of the Czechoslovak Republic—and as of 1 January 1993 of the post-Czechoslovak Czech Republic—to the Federal Republic of Germany.

Translations: *Franz Kafka of Prague*, trans. Eric Mossbacher (London: Secker & Warburg, 1983); *The Questionnaire or Prayer for a Town and a Friend*, trans. Peter Kussi (New York: Farrar, Straus and Giroux, 1982); "Uncle Anton's Coat," trans. Milan Pomichalek and Anna Mozga, in *Good-bye, Samizdat: Twenty Years of Czechoslovak Underground Writing*, ed. Marketa Goetz-Stankiewicz (Evanston, Ill.: Northwestern University Press, 1992), 42–46; "Honking Horns" (chapter 1 of *Dr. Kokeš Mistr Panny*), trans. Alex Zucker, in *This Side of Reality: Modern Czech Writing*, ed. Alexandra Büchler (London: Serpent's Tail, 1996), 77–93; "A Bride for Sale: Or the National Opera of the Czechs," trans. Miroslav Rensky; "Salamandra," trans. Peter Kussi; and "The Feuilletons I Promised to Write," trans. Miroslav Rensky, in *The Writing on the Wall: An Anthology of Contemporary Czech Literature*, ed. Antonin Liehm and Peter Kussi (Princeton, N.J.: Kartz-Cohl, 1983), 34–58.

Grynberg, Henryk (b. 1936) Polish novelist, essayist, and poet. Grynberg, who is well known for his writings about Jews in Poland during World War II and about his own experiences during the German occupation and later, was born in Warsaw. After the war, he completed secondary school in Łódż and then went on to study journalism at Warsaw University. He came to the United States in 1967 and in 1971 received a master's degree in Slavic languages and literatures from the University of California at Los Angeles. His works include *Ekipa Antygona* (The Crew of the *Antigone*, 1963); *Święto kameni* (Holiday of the Stones, 1964); *Żydowska wojna* (The Jewish War, 1965); *Zwycięstwo* (*The Victory*, 1969); *Antynostalgia* (Anti-Nostalgia, 1971); *Dzieci Syjonu* (*Children of Zion*, 1994); *Rysuję w pamięci* (I Draw in Memory, 1995); *Szkice rodzinne* (Domestic Sketches, 1990); *Prawda nieartystyczne* (Unartistic Truth, 1984, 1994); *Pomnik pod Potomakiem* (Monument Beneath the Potomac, 1989); *Wiersze z Ameryki* (Poems from America, 1980); *Wśród nieobecnych* (Among the Absent, 1983); *Wiersze wybrane z lat 1964–1983* (Collected Poems from the Years 1964–1983, 1985); *Życie ideologiczne* (Ideological Life, 1975); *Życie osobiste* (Private Life, 1979); *Życie codzienne i artystyczne* (Daily and Artistic Life, 1980); *Kadisz* (Prayer, 1987); *Wróciłem* (I Returned, 1991); and *Pamiętnik Marii Koper* (The Memoirs of Maria Koper, 1993). More recently, Grynberg has published *Memorbuch* (2000) and *Szmuglerzy* (Smugglers, 2001). *Memorbuch* is a biography of the important Polish publisher Adam Bromberg, who left Poland in the wake of the anti-Semitic campaign of 1968. Based in large part on video- and audiocassettes made by Bromberg toward the end of his life, *Memorbuch* presents Bromberg himself as the narrator of the text. In Smugglers, Grynberg relates the true exploits of a Polish boy named Jan Kostański, who arranged food deliveries to the Jewish Ghetto in Warsaw during World War II.

Translations: *California Kaddish*, trans. Malgorzata Smorag (Paris: Ballard, 1991); *Child of the Shadows, Including The Grave* (London: Vallentine Mitchell, 1969); *Children of Zion*, trans. Jacqueline Mitchell (Evanston, Ill.: Northwestern University Press, 1997); *The Victory*, trans. Richard Lourie (Evanston, Ill.: Northwestern University Press, 1993).

Guga, Romulus (1939–1983) Romanian novelist, short-story writer, poet, and playwright. A native of Oradea, Guga studied in the Faculty of Philology of Bucharest University from 1957 to 1964. After a two-year employment at the university in Cluj (1964–1966), he became literary adviser and secretary of the Theater of the State of Tîrgu-Mureş from 1967 to 1971. Thereafter, he served as editor in chief of the review *Vatra* until his death in 1983. Guga made his debut as a poet on the pages of *Steaua* in 1959 and subsequently published two collections of poems of a largely elegaic and melancholic character: *Bărci părăsite* (Abandoned

Ships, 1968) and *Totem* (1970). Guga was destined, however, to make his mark primarily as a novelist interested mainly in politics and the nature of power. His first novel, and possibly his best, was *Nebunul şi floarea* (The Lunatic and the Flower, 1970), a work set in a penitentiary asylum among mysterious and obviously symbolic characters named Jesus, The Fool, The Scholar, His Majesty, and The Philosopher, and reminiscent of Ken Kesey's novel *One Flew over the Cuckoo's Nest*. *Viaţa post-mortem* (Life Postmortem, 1972), Guga's next novel, explores the abuse of power in the period of postwar Romanian Stalinism. *Viaţa post-mortem* was followed by *Sărbători fericite* (Happy Celebrations, 1973), in which the impact of a woman's death on her husband and son is viewed over the course of three days; *Paradisul pentru o mie de ani* (The Thousand Year Paradise, 1974), essentially an analysis of the nature of heroism; and *Adio, Arizona* (Bye-Bye, Arizona, 1974), named for a 1950s Romanian confectionary where young people gather to talk about ideals. Besides his novels, Guga was the author of four plays that, like his novels, have an underlying political character and convey the author's belief that human progress is impossible without freedom: *Speranţa nu moare în zori* (Hope Doesn't Die at Dawn, 1973); *Noaptea cabotinilor* (The Night of the Ham Actors, 1978); *Evul Media întîmplător* (The Fortuitous Middle Ages, 1980); and *Amurgul burghez* (The Twilight of the Philistines, 1982), the last two being arguably his best. Guga was awarded the Writers Union Prize in 1970 and 1977.

Guliashki, Andrei (b. 1914) Bulgarian novelist. Known, above all, for his thrillers about espionage and counter-espionage, Guliashki was born in the village of Rakovitsa, in the Mihailovgrad district of northwestern Bulgaria. After an early education in a French-language commercial college, and graduation (in 1934) from a secondary school in Vratsa, he studied at Sofia University and worked as a bank clerk and a French teacher. In 1944 he became editor in chief of *Literaturen front*. Guliashki was a correspondent for the Dobrudzha newspaper *Rabotnichesko delo* from 1948 to 1952, editor of *Septemvri* from 1952 to 1956, editor in chief of *Plamuk* from 1956 to 1966, and editor in chief of *Suvremenik* from 1972 to 1973. From 1967 to 1969, he was director of the National Theater in Sofia. From 1956 on, he was also an official of the Bulgarian Writers Union.

Guliashki first appeared in print on the pages of student journals as a short-story writer with a taste for the sentimental and romantic. A member of the left-wing Hristo Smirenski circle of writers, he soon developed an interest in social problems and in such plays and novels of the the late 1930s and early 1940s as *Don Kihot ot Silvetsia* (Don Quixote of Silvezia, 1936), *Zheni* (Ladies, 1938), *Smurtna prisuda* (Death Sentence, 1940), and *Novolunie* (New Moon, 1944), he demonstrated a new preference for a broad spectrum of big-city social groups, unusual characters, and striking situations. In the early 1950s, he directed his attention to the contemporary Bulgarian village and turned out a series of novels lauding the achievements of socialism in contrast to the exploitative policies of the prewar fascist ruling class. Works of this type include, above all, the trilogy *MT stantsiia* (MT Station, 1950), *Selo Vedrovo* (The Village of Vedrovo, 1952), and *Zlatnoto runo* (The Golden Fleece, 1958). In *Sedemte dni na nashiia zhivot* (The Seven Days of Our Life, 1969), arguably the best of his novels, Guliashki showed an ability to develop complex psychological characterization in depicting the tension between social and political commitment and personal ambition. It was, however, with his spy novels and detective thrillers—a genre without previous tradition in Bulgarian literature—

that Guliashki really came into his own as a popular writer. The novels of this type are politically predictable in that they "reveal" the anti-Bulgarian and anti–Soviet bloc intrigues of the capitalist West during the Cold War and the nefarious activities in and out of Bulgaria of representatives of the old regime. However, these works are fairly well crafted and entertaining and feature a Bulgarian equivalent of Ian Fleming's James Bond ("007") in the form of detective and counter-espionage officer Avakum Zahov. The novels in this series include *Prikliucheniiata na Avakum Zahov* (The Adventures of Avakum Zahov, 1962); *Sreshtu 007* (Faceoff with 007, 1966); *Poslednoto prikliuchenie na Avakum Zahov* (The Last Adventure of Avakum Zahov, 1976); and the two-volume *Zhivotut i prikliucheniiata na Avakum Zahov* (The Life and Adventures of Avakum Zahov, 1977).

Guliashki's success as a writer of thrillers did not carry over into his historical fiction, and the three-part *Zlatniiat vek* (The Golden Age, 1970–1972), about the reign of Czar Simeon, is one of his weakest works and an insipid specimen of conformist socialist realism. He was more successful, however, in such subsequent novels as *Zavrushtaneto na inzhener Nadin* (The Return of Engineer Nadin, 1972); *Domut s mahagonovo stulbishte: Semeina hronika* (The House with the Mahogany Staircase: A Family Chronicle, 1975); *Trite zhivota na Iosif Dimov* (The Three Lives of Joseph Dimov, 1977); and *Otdelenie za reanimatsiia* (Resuscitation Unit, 1979), in which he raised the question of the cost to society—above all, in moral terms—of environmentally threatening technological advances and the ever-increasing quest for material prosperity. In one of his later novels, *Ubiistvoto na ulitsa "Chekhova"* (The Murder on Chekhov Street, 1985), Guliashki renewed his enthusiasm for the murder mystery genre, in which he had never completely lost interest.

Translations: *Adventure at Midnight*, trans. Georgina Moudrova (Sofia: Sofia Press, 1976); *The Momchilo Affair*, trans. Georgina Moudrova (Sofia: Sofia Press, 1976); *The Zakhov Mission*, trans. Maurice Michael (London: Cassell, 1968).

Gunga, Fahredin (b. 1936) Kosovo Albanian poet. Born in Kosovska Mitrovica, Gunga earned a degree in Albanian studies at Belgrade University and for a number of years was editor in chief of Priština TV. His first book of poetry, *Përshpëritjet e mëngjezit* (Morning Whispers), appeared in 1961. It was followed by *Mallkimet e fjetuna* (Torpid Curses, 1970); *Kepi i Shpresës së Mirë* (The Cape of Good Hope, 1973); *Flaka e fjalës* (The Blazing Word, 1975); *Psalmet e gurta* (Psalms of Stone, 1977); *Nokturno për Orkidenë* (Nocturne for the Orchid, 1981); *Mallkimet e zgjuara* (Awakened Curses, 1985); *Poezi* (Poems, 1986); and *Shtrezet e fatësimit* (Benevolent Frosts, 1990). Gunga also selected and edited an anthology of poetry from Kosovo under the title *Flaka e fjalës: Poezi nga Kosova* (The Blazing Word: Poetry from Kosovo, 1975). The somberness and preoccupation with death so prominent in some of Gunga's early poetry later yielded to a more opaque symbolism and enigmatic but arresting metaphors sometimes characterized as surrealistic.

Gyurkó, László (b. 1930) Hungarian novelist, short-story writer, playwright, and journalist. A talented writer of largely political orientation, Gyurkó was born in Budapest and, with little formal education, began working as an unskilled laborer until he got a job as a clerk. He started writing in the 1950s and by 1956 was ready to offer his stories and criticism to publishers. In 1957 he decided to devote himself entirely to his literary career and in 1961 and 1963, respectively, published his first two works, the novellas *Bűnüsök* (Guilty) and *Csütörtök*

(Thursday), both concerned with ethical and behavioral developments in a socialist society. In 1964, the year he came out with *A negyedik ember* (The Fourth Man), a volume of stories, he became a contributor to *Valóság*. From 1970 to 1981, he held the position of manager first of Budapest's Theater Twenty-Five (Huszonötödik Színház) and then of the Folk Theater (Népszínház). From 1975 to 1981, Gyurkó was a member of the Hungarian parliament. In 1982 he became affiliated with the Folk Art Institute and, from 1986 to 1989, served as editor in chief of the journal *Új Tükör*. Gyurkó's second novel, *Faustus doktor boldogságos pokoljárása* (Doctor Faust's Blessed Descent into Hell, 1979), is a tableau of Hungarian history from the 1950s. It was followed by *A halálugrás* (The Death Dive, 1978), a love story; *A halál árnyéka* (The Shadow of Death, 1981), a crime novel; *A családi regény* (A Family Novel, 1984), a chronicle-like series of stories overflowing with facts; and *Fociország* (The Soccer State, 1987), a quasi-sports medical report on the current state of Hungarian society.

Gyurkó's first play, *Szerelmem, Elektra* (My Love, Electra, 1968), a political drama about the conflict between revolutionary intractability and the sobriety of practical politics, initiated a series of Brechtian plays of political engagement collected in the two volumes *Az égesz élet* (A Whole Life, 1970) and *Utak* (Roads, 1977). Gyurkó has also published several prose works of a political historical nature, the best known of which are *Lenin, október* (Lenin, October, 1967) and *Négyszemközt a forradalommal* (Face to Face with the Revolution, 1970), both dealing with the Russian Revolution of 1917 on the basis primarily of previously unknown documents. In 1982 he also published a book about János Kádár, the Communist Party leader who took over in the aftermath of the Hungarian uprising of 1956, under the title *Arcképvázlat történelmi háttér-*

rel (Portrait with Historical Background). Gyurkó was awarded the Attila József Prize in 1968 and the Kossuth Prize in 1980.

Translations: Excerpt from *A családi regény,* trans. Christina Rozsnyai, in *Present Continuous: Contemporary Hungarian Writing,* ed. István Bart (Budapest: Corvina, 1985), 70–95.

H

Habaj, Ivan (b. 1943) Slovak short-story writer and novelist. Habaj was born in Ur-mince, in south-central Slovakia; received his law degree from Comenius University; and worked subsequently as an attorney and a journalist. He broke into print in the early 1970s with a collection of short stories, *Dolniaci* (Lowlanders, 1972). Other collections followed within a few years: *V tieni moruše* (In the Shadow of the Mulberry Tree, 1973); *Mária* (Mary, 1976); *Príbuzní z Ostrava* (The Relatives from Ostrovo, 1978); *Polné samoty* (Solitudes, 1979); and *7 poviedok* (7 Stories, 1984). Habaj's major work of fiction, the one he is best known for, is the sprawling trilogy *Kolonisti* (Colonists). The first part appeared in 1980; the second, in 1981; and the third, in 1986. Part I takes place mostly in 1938, and parts II and III from 1945 to 1965—that is, from the end of World War II, through the establishment of the communist Czechoslovak regime, to the massive campaign of agricultural collectivization. Although the trilogy has an obvious historical dimension, history itself is not the main focus of the work. Rather, it operates as a backdrop against which Habaj traces the fortunes of several Slovak rural families who move into the Danubian basin region known as Rye (Žitný) Island, between Bratislava and Komárno (main settlement, Dunajská Streda), which was incorporated into the Czechoslovak state created after the breakup of the Austro-Hungarian Empire at the end of World War I. Previously Hungarian, the region long retained a sizable Hungarian and Gypsy population. Ethnic rivalries and animosities are woven into the fabric of the novel, and Habaj makes no effort to conceal his hostility toward Hungarians, Gypsies, and Jews. With the outbreak of World War II, the German occupation of the Czech lands, and the creation of the fascist Slovak republic under Josef Tiso, Rye Island reverts to Hungarian rule and the Slovak farmers migrate into the new Slovak state. With the end of the war in 1945, the region once again becomes part of Czechoslovakia and the families return there. Their migrations, the relationships within and among families, their relations with the other ethnic communities in the region, their efforts to work the land, and their subsequent need to confront the reality of collectivization are Habaj's main concerns in the novel. Although Habaj demonstrated his interest in Slovak history and in history in general as a relentless process of time as early as his first collection of stories in 1972, the tumultous events of the period 1938 to 1965 spanned by *Kolonisti* never becomes dominant in the novel and emphasis falls instead on the human dramas. Rather than regarding *Kolonisti* as a historical novel in the strict sense, it may be best to view it, as critics have suggested, as a rural chronicle in a well-established Slovak literary tradition, with a historical backdrop. Between the second and third parts of *Kolonisti,* Habaj published the novel *Posolstvo detstva* (The Message of Childhood, 1982), which has been all but completely overshadowed by *Kolonisti.*

Habjanović-Djurović, Ljiljana (b. 1953) Serbian novelist. A popular, distinctly feminist writer, Habjanović-Djurović was born in Kruševac, Serbia, where she received her secondary-school education before study-ing economics at Belgrade University. After earning her degree, she worked for the offi-cial Yugoslav travel agency, Putnik, in Bel-grade and then became a journalist for the monthly magazine *Duga*. She has also been closely affiliated with the women's magazine *Žena*. In 1995 she became a full-time writer. Her first book, the short-story collection *Glasovi* (Voices), appeared in 1988. It was followed by the novel *Javna ptica* (Public Bird, 1988), which enjoys the reputation of the first Serbian feminine erotic novel; *Iva* (1994), a romantic novel inspired by the concept of reincarnation in which dream sequences play a pivotal role, and whose main character is a young woman writer; *Ana Marija me nije volela* (*Ana Maria Did Not Love Me*, 1997), which was made into a successful film and television series; *Ženski rodoslov* (*Feminine Genealogy*, 1998), which spans nearly 200 years of Serbian and Mon-tenegran history in tracing the destinies of the female members of a family; and *Paunovo pero* (The Peacock's Plume, 1999). After *Javna ptica*, all of Habjanović-Djurović's novels are heavily autobiograph-ical, intimate, often narrated in the first per-son, and concerned with women and their place in society in Serbia and Montenegro in the nineteenth and twentieth centuries. Although her portraits of women are well drawn and sensitive, men are rarely positive in Habjanović-Djurović's fiction and ap-pear usually as selfish and exploitative to-ward women. Her one major work of non-fiction, *Srbija pred ogledalem* (Serbia Before the Mirror, 1994), consists of a series of pro-files of outstanding Serbian women against the background of the Balkan wars of the 1990s, including such figures as Dana Drašković, the wife of the Serbian demo-cratic opposition leader Vuk Drašković, and Mira Marković, the wife of the deposed Ser-bian president Slobodan Milošević, herself a powerful political personality. Habjanović-

Djurović won Special "Gold Best-Seller" prizes in 1998 for *Ana Maria Did Not Love Me* and *Feminine Genealogy* and a National Library of Serbia prize for *Feminine Geneal-ogy* as the "most read book in Serbian li-braries in 1998."

Translations: *Ana Maria Did Not Love Me* (Belgrade: Narodna Knjiga, 1997); *Femi-nine Genealogy*, trans. Alice Copple Tošić (Belgrade: Narodnja Knjiga, 1998).

Hacks, Peter (b. 1928) German playwright, short-story writer, poet, essayist, and author of children's books. A native of Breslau (now Wrocław, Poland), Hacks settled with his family in Dachau after World War II. After receiving his high-school diploma, he went to Munich where he studied sociology, philosophy, literature, and theater. He re-ceived his doctorate for a dissertation on Beidermeier theater that was published as *Das Theaterstück des Biedermeier, 1815–1840* (Biedermeier Theater Art, 1815–1840, 1951). In 1955, following his political sympathies, Hacks resettled in East Berlin where he be-came affiliated with Bertolt Brecht's Berliner Ensemble Theater. In 1960 he took over the position of literary director of the Berlin Deutsches Theater, but lost it three years later when he came under fire from doctrinaire communists. However, Hacks did an about-face in the 1970s, becoming a staunch defender of official German Demo-cratic Republic policy. Although he has written in several genres, Hacks is best known as a dramatist. His first plays were written under the influence of Brecht's "epic theater" and his Marxist revisionist inter-pretations of history. It was in the spirit of the latter that Hacks wrote *Die Schlacht bei Lobosit* (The Battle at Lobosit, 1954), which is set in the time of the Seven Years' War, and *Der Müller von Sanssouci* (The Miller of Sanssouci, 1958), which deals with Frederick the Great. With such "dialectical comedies" as *Die Sorgen und Macht* (Troubles and Power, 1959) and *Moritz Tassow* (1965), Hacks returned to contemporary GDR issues. Written to promote the goals of socialist realism, the plays nevertheless contain elements of satire directed, above all, at philistinism in the communist state. Both plays were soon removed from stages, and Hacks was denounced in the official media for "anarchistic tendencies." In a form of retreat, Hacks turned in the late 1960s from plays with contemporary settings to works inspired by fairy tales and legends. He rationalized his new "poetic theater" in a series of essays, many of which are included in *Die Massgaben der Kunst: Gesammelte Aufsätze* (The Norms of Art: Collected Essays, 1977; the edition of 1996 covers 1959–1994) and *Essais* (Essays, 1983) as well as in his theoretical study, *Die Poetische: Ansätze zu einer postrevolutionären Dramaturgie* (The Poetic: Essays on a Postrevolutionary Dramaturgy, 1972). The best examples of Hacks's "poetic theater" are the plays *Adam und Ewa* (Adam and Eve, 1976), a comedy with some veiled allusions to problems in the GDR; *Margarete in Aix* (Margaret in Aix, 1974), a comedy based on the life of Margaret of Anjou, the queen consort of Henry VI of England (1430–1482); *Amphitryon* (1968), an adaptation of the Greek myth; and *Omphale* (1970). Hacks's interest in fairy tale, legend, and myth is reflected in his narrative and dramatic contributions to children's literature and in his collections *Historien und Romanzen: Urpoesie, oder, Das scheintote Kind* (Histories and Romances: Primeval Poetry, or The Seemingly Dead Child, 1985) and *Zwei Märchen* (Two Fairy Tales, 1985). Hacks's deep admiration for Goethe led him to write works inspired by Goethe, among them *Pandora* (1981), about the triumph of poetic imagination over the "prose" of mundane reality, and a reworking of a Goethe puppet play, *Das Jahrmarktsfest zu Plundersweilen*. (The Fair in Plunders-

weilen), which he published with the comedy *Rosie traümt* (Rosie Dreams), in 1976. It was also Goethe who inspired the intriguingly structured and humorous monologue *Ein Gespräch im Hause Stein über den abwesenden Herrn von Goethe* (A Conversation in the Stein House About the Absent Herr von Goethe, 1998), by a lady of the Weimar court, Charlotte von Stein, addressed to a life-size model of her husband, concerning her relationship with Goethe. In such plays written after 1975 as *Die Fische* (The Fish, 1975); *Senecas Tod* (Seneca's Death, 1977); and *Musen* (Muses, 1979), Hacks's outlook turned decidedly pessimistic in response to a tightening of cultural policy in the GDR. Of the various editions of Hacks's plays that have appeared in print, the most comprehensive are the three-volume *Ausgewählte Dramen* (Selected Plays) of 1981 and the two-volume collection *Die späten Stücke* (The Late Plays), published in 1996 by Nautilus of Hamburg.

Literature: Thomas Di Napoli, *The Children's Literature of Peter Hacks* (New York: Peter Lang, 1987); Michael Mitchell, *Peter Hacks: Drama for a Socialist Society* (Glasgow: Scottish Papers in Germanic Studies, 1990); Judith R. Scheid, *Enfant Terrible of Contemporary East German Drama: Peter Hacks in His Role as an Adaptor and Innovator* (Bonn: Bouvier, 1977).

Hadži-Tančić, Saša (b. 1948) Serbian novelist, short-story writer, poet, and essayist. A native of Niš, where he has lived for most of his life and whose history he draws on in a number of his works, Hadži-Tančić has made his mark as a short-story writer. He has published some eleven collections of stories, including *Jevrem, sav u smrti* (Jeremiah in the Throes of Death, 1976); *Savršen oblik* (A Perfect Form, 1984); *Silazak u vreme* (Descent into Time, 1987); *Zvezdama povezani* (Linked by Stars, 1990), devoted mainly to Niš's distant past and winner of the Andrić Prize in 1991; *Ivicom, najlepši put* (Along the Edge Is the Best Path, 1990); *Galopirajči vojnik* (Galloping Soldier, 1990); *Skidanje oklona* (Removal of the Armor, 1993); *Ključ za čudnu bravu* (The Key for a Strange Lock, 1994), selected stories; *Hram u koferu* (The Temple in a Suitcase, 1995), which consists of thirty short prose pieces and thirty poems, many on religious themes and death; *Povratak u Nais* (The Return to Nais, 1997), a selection based in part on stories in *Zvezdama povezani*; and *Nebeska gubernija* (The Province of Heaven, 1997), *gubernija* being the Russian word for an administrative district. One of his best collections of stories, *Nebeska gubernija* conjures up the physical and spiritual landscape of such Russian masters as Gogol, Dostoevsky, and Chekhov, as if Hadži-Tančić's aim was to re-create especially the spiritual values of nineteenth-century Russian literature, which, by inference, are sadly lacking in his own country. Hadži-Tančić has also published two novels, *Sveto mesto* (A Holy Place, 1993) and *Crvenilo* (The Color Red, 1995); two books of literary essays under the title *Paralelni svetovi* (Parallel Worlds, 1979, 1989); and three volumes of poetry: *Zapisan svršiće se svet* (Transcribing Ends the World, 1973); *Pejzaž dušom* (Landscape with Soul, 1995); and *Lična smrt* (A Personal Death), a collection of thirty-one very short poems on the theme of death that forms a part of *Hram u koferu*. Hadži-Tančić has also won the Liberation Prize of the City of Niš as well as the Lazar Vuković Prize.

Translations: "Skull Tower," trans. Veselin M. Śćekić, in *The Prince of Fire: An Anthology of Contemporary Serbian Short Stories*, ed. Radmila J. Gorup and Nadežda Obradović (Pittsburgh: University of Pittsburgh Press, 1998), 268–72.

Haiduczek, Werner (b. 1926) German novelist, short-story writer, and playwright. A native of Hindenburg (Polish, Zabrze),

Haiduczek was pressed into military service during World War II at the age of seventeen and subsequently taken prisoner by the Americans and the Soviets. After the war, he studied pedagogy in Halle until 1949 and then held various teaching positions until becoming a freelance writer in 1965. His first book, *Matthes und der Bürgermeister* (Matthew and the Mayor, 1961), reflects Haiduczek's strong interest early in his career in children and youth. As in much of his fiction, he concerns himself with the search for truth and the moral value of an individual's actions. His next novel, *Abschied von der Engeln* (Parting from the Angels, 1968), reflects his own family's deportation from Hindenburg when it was incorporated into Poland after the war, the division of Germany into two states, and the postwar adjustments to two different social and political systems. Haiduczek's abiding concern with moral issues and his negative attitude toward the opportunism he saw rampant in East German society come to the fore in his next novel, *Tod am Meer* (Death at the Seaside, 1977), which is generally regarded as his finest work of fiction. Clearly motivated by his own experiences as a writer in the early years of the East German state, Haiduczek draws several compelling portraits in the novel, beginning with the narrator, a writer named Jablonski. An eminently successful author, a winner of awards, and a member of the Academy of Arts, Jablonski falls seriously ill while on a visit to Bulgaria in 1974 and writes his final work, a intensely personal literary testament and confession that begins with his recollections of the Nazi era but concentrates on the years 1949 to 1953. His narrative paints a disturbing picture of a man whose career rested on a foundation of cynicism, hypocrisy, opportunism (he joined the Communist Party because he was paid 100 marks to do so), and exploitation, especially of women. Although the story of a single individual, it can scarcely be doubted that Haiduczek's protagonist was meant to represent a widespread phenomenon in the German Democratic Republic. Unburdening a deeply troubled conscience in his last work, Jablonski rejects virtually everything he had previously written as "inauthentic." Although *Tod am Meer* was allowed to be published in the GDR, it quickly sold out and was not reprinted. It was available in many libraries only on special request. Apart from children's literature and his adaptations of ancient and foreign fairy tales and myths, Haiduczek has published a collection of his unauthorized texts under the title *Im gewöhnlichen Stalinismus. Meine unerlaubtenten Texte: Tagebücher, Briefe, Essays* (In Everyday Stalinism. My Unauthorized Texts: Diaries, Letters, Essays, 1991) and in 1990 coedited with Stefan Heym the collection *Die sanfte Revolution: Prosa, Lyrik, Protokolle, Erlebnisberichte, Reden* (The Gentle Revolution: Prose, Lyrics, Records, Personal Experiences, Speeches).

Haitov, Nikolai (b. 1919) Bulgarian novelist, short-story writer, essayist, and playwright. Haitov was born in the village of Iavrovo in the Rhodope Mountains, which stretch along southern Bulgaria and northern Greece. At the age of fourteen, he left for Bulgaria's second largest city, Plovdiv, where he worked at various menial jobs. Three years later, he returned to Iavrovo and found employment as a woodsman. This led eventually to the study of forestry at Sofia University and a regular position as a forestry engineer in his native region with the Bulgarian Forestry Commission. He held this position from 1946 to 1954, when he was dismissed on charges of insubordination, which he has vehemently denied, imputing political motives to his dismissal. Two years later, the authorities claimed that a mistake had been made and he was offered his old job back. But by then, Haitov had discovered writing and chose not to look back. His first literary works were the short-story collections *Supernitsi* (Rivals, 1957); *Iskritsi ot ognishteto* (Sparks from the Hearth, 1959); and *Gorski razkazi* (Tales from the Forest, 1965) and two books of essays: *Pisma ot pushtinatsite: Ochertsi, putepisi* (Letters from the Wilderness: Essays and Travels, 1960) and *Shumki ot gabur* (Hornbeam Leaves, 1965). They draw heavily on his intimate knowledge of the Rhodope Mountains. Haitov's enduring love affair with the Rhodope region—its people and its past—in fact dominates much of his literary output and is reflected in such later fictional texts as *Prikliucheniia v gorata* (Adventures in the Mountain, 1970); *Hvurkatoto korito* (The Winged Trough, 1979); *Razkazi i eseta* (Tales and Essays, 1984); and *Gorskiiat duh* (The Spirit of the Mountains, 1995), a collection of stories and essays. Haitov's most popular work of fiction set in the Rhodope Mountains has long been *Divi razkazi* (*Wild Tales*), a collection of robust, earthy tales dealing mostly with the life of the *pomaks* (descendants of Bulgarian converts to Islam). The collection was first published in 1967 and won the 1969 Dimitrov Prize for Literature—Bulgaria's highest literary award under the communists. In 1974 it was voted the most popular work written by a living Bulgarian writer since the end of World War II. It has been translated into many languages, including English.

Besides his short stories, Haitov has written historical studies of his native and other nearby villages in the Rhodopes: *Selo Asenovgradsko* (The Village of Asenovgrad, 1958), published by the Bulgarian Academy of Sciences; *Asenovgrad v minaloto* (Asenovgrad in the Past, 1965); *Selo Monastir, Smoliansko* (The Village of Monastir, Smoliansko, 1965), also published by the Academy of Sciences; and *Minaloto na Iavrovo, Devin, Monastir*

(Iavrovo, Devin, and Monastir in the Past, 1985). These monographs were complemented by a series of "documentary" tales about the Rhodopes' most illustrious brigands and revolutionaries: *Haiduti: Ochertsi* (The Haiduks: Sketches, 1968, 1971, 1985); *Rodopski vlastelini: Istoricheski ochertsi* (Rulers of the Rhodopes: Historical Sketches, 1974), also on the *haiduks*; *Kapitan Petko Voivoda: Istoricheski ocherk* (Captain Petko Voivoda [1844–1900]: Historical Sketch, 1974); *Poslednite migove i grobut na Vasil Levski* (The Last Moments and the Grave of Vasil Levski [1837–1873], 1985); and *Aferata s groba na Vasil Levski* (The Matter of Vasil Levski's Grave, 1997). Bulgarian national history has also been an interest of Haitov. In 1972 he edited a collection of reminiscences and tales from the period 1896 to 1912 by Bulgarian revolutionaries, and in 1973 he wrote the introduction to the memoirs of the revolutionary Panaiot Hitov (1830–1918) and edited a collection of contemporary and other accounts of the Balkan War of 1912/1913.

Notwithstanding his deep attachment to his native Rhodope Mountains, Haitov has traveled extensively throughout the world and has published books based on his travels in Peru, *Peruanski zapisi* (Peruvian Notes, 1975), and Africa, *Afrikanski zapiski* (African Jottings, 1988). A volume of his personal diaries (*Dnevnik*) was published in 1988. Haitov's later essays and journalistic writings, on everything from nature and the environment to literature, are contained in the collections *Publitsistika: Chovek-priroda, ezik-literatura, istoriia, kraeznanie-folklor, razni* (Journalism: Man-Nature, Language-Literature, History, Landscape-Folklore, and Various, 1975); *Istini v sianka: Statii, eseta, interviuta* (Truths in the Shadows: Articles, Essays, Interviews, 1987); and *Vreme za razhvurliane na komuni* (Time for Loosening Up the Commune, 1994). An edition of his collected essays appeared in 1996.

Translations: *Wild Tales*, trans. Michael Holman (London: Peter Owen, 1979).

Hájnoczy, Peter (1942–1981) Hungarian short-story writer, novelist, and playwright. A very promising writer, Hájnoczy, a Budapest native, died in a drowning accident in 1981 at the age of thirty-nine, leaving behind several well-regarded works. Lacking much formal education, he began working as a common laborer from the age of sixteen, but in 1962 received a high-school diploma by correspondence. Although interested in the novel and drama, Hájnoczy achieved his reputation mostly on the basis of his short stories and novellas, which are notable for their modern narrative methods (including the cinematographic) and for the strange and bizarre events that take place in them. His first published book, *A fűtő* (The Stoker, 1975), a collection of stories, was based on his own work experiences. It was followed by *M* (1977), another volume of stories; *A halál kilovagolt Perzsiából* (Death Rode Out from Persia, 1979), a novella; *Jézus menyasszonya* (Jesus's Bride, 1982), a posthumously published collection of short stories, not to be confused with the 1981 novella by the same name; *A parancs* (The Command), an undated novella; and two short plays: *A herceg* (The Prince, 1980) and *Dinamit* (Dynamite, 1981). The best single collection of Hájnoczy's fiction is *Jézus menyasszonya*, which contains, in addition to the title novella, the previously published *A halál kilovagolt Perzsiából* and the "sociography" (*szociográfia*) "Az elkülönítő" ("The Isolation Ward," 1973–1975). It is here especially that Hájnoczy's fondness for film (*Jézus menyasszonya* begins in a movie theater), montage, diary, interview, epistolary techniques, abnormal mental states, and intertextuality comes to the fore. Of particular interest is his obvious familiarity with such American writers as Edgar Allan Poe, Ambrose Bierce, Malcolm

Lowry, F. Scott Fitzgerald, Eugene O'Neill, and Ken Kesey. *Hátrahagyott írások* (Unpublished Writings), a volume of short pieces left behind by Hájnoczy and presumed to date from the mid-1960s to 1981, was published in 1981. A comprehensive posthumous collection of his novellas and other writings (*Kisregények és más írások*) appeared in 1983. In 1980 Hájnoczy was awarded the Milán Füst Prize and the Tokay Prize.

Translations: "The Funeral," trans. Eszter Molnár, in *Ma/Today: An Anthology of Contemporary Hungarian Literature* (Budapest: Corvina, 1987), 169–78; "Mandrake," trans. László T. András, in *Hungarian Short Stories,* ed. Paul Varnai (Toronto: Exile Editions, 1983), 92–105. *A fűtő* is available in French as *Dialogues de ventriloque,* trans. Cécile Mennecier (Nantes: Le Passeur, 1998).

Haliti, Faslli (b. 1935) Albanian poet. Haliti was born in Lushnjë and originally planned to be a painter. He graduated from the Lushnjë high school of art in 1951, but subsequently pursued a program in Albanian language and literature at Tirana University. After graduating, he worked as a literature teacher in Lushnjë until he was compelled for ideological reasons to become a factory worker from 1973 to 1983. During this period, he was forbidden to publish. Haliti published his first volume of poetry, *Sot* (Today), in 1969; it won third place in a national literary competition. His second collection of poems, *Mesazhe fushe* (Field of Messages), appeared only in 1984, after his long enforced absence from the literary scene. Since then, he has published *Edhe shkronjat paskan gojë* (The Alphabet Too Can Speak, 1986); *Motrat* (Sisters, 1988); *S'di të hesht* (Don't Keep Quiet, 1997); *Lamtumirë kapedanët e mi* (Goodbye, My Brave Ones, 1997); and *Mbrapsht* (Amiss, 1998). Haliti is an urbane poet who writes of contemporary social and cultural phenom-

ena, including politics, with a fair degree of skepticism and in a laconic style that often favors lines of no more than a word or two.

Hamiti, Sabri (b. 1950) Kosovo Albanian poet, novelist, essayist, and literary critic. Hamiti was born near Podujevo, Kosovo, and later studied Albanian language and literature in Priština and comparative literature in Zagreb and at the École Pratique des Hautes Études in Paris. His poetry collections include *Njeriu vdes i ri* (A Person Dies Young, 1972); *Faqe e fund* (Bottom of the Page, 1973); *Lind një fjalë* (A Word Is Born, 1986); *Thikë harrimi* (Knife of Oblivion, 1975); *Trungu ilir* (The Illyrian Stock, 1983); *Leja e njohtimit* (Identity Papers, 1985); and *Kaosmos* (Chaosmos, 1990). Hamiti is also the author of two novels, *Njëqind vjet vetmi* (A Hundred Years of Solitude, 1976) and *Faik Konica—jam unë* (I Am Faik Konica, 1994), as well as of several literary studies, including *Variante* (Variants, 1974); *Teksti i dramatizuar* (The Dramatized Text, 1978); *Kritika letrare* (Literary Criticism, 1979), which Hamiti and the critic and political figure Ibrahim Rugova wrote jointly; *Arti i leximit: Sprova për një poetike* (The Art of Reading: An Attempt at a Poetic, 1984); *Letra shqipe* (Albanian Literature, 1996); and *Vetëdija letrare* (Literary Awareness, 1989), which was honored with the Rilindja Prize as best book of the year for its valuable contribution to the study of Albanian literature.

Translations: Three poems in *An Elusive Eagle Soars: Anthology of Modern Albanian Poetry,* ed. and trans. Robert Elsie (London: Forest, 1993), 183–86.

Hamvas, Béla (1897–1968) Hungarian writer and philosopher. An iconoclastic critic and thinker, a disciple of Nietzsche and Kierkegaard, Hamvas became a cult figure in the 1930s. His major pre–World War II publications were *A világválság* (The World Crisis, 1938) and *A láthatatlan történet* (The Invisible Story, 1943). His first postwar publication, the sweeping *Anthologia humana: Ötezer év bölcsessége* (An Anthology of Man: Five Thousand Years of Wisdom), based on a series of lectures, appeared in 1947 and was reprinted in 1989. Also in 1947 he published *Forradalom a művészetben: Absztrakció és szürrealizmus Magyarországon* (Revolution in Art: Abstraction and Surrealism in Hungary). In the 1940s the communists, led by the literary scholar Georg Lukács, carried on a vicious campiagn to discredit Hamvas, accusing him of decadence and other moral and social sins. Until his death, while never abandoning writing, he was forced to earn his way as a manual laborer. With the changes in Hungary's political and cultural life after the fall of communism, a new interest in Hamvas's huge literary output has awakened, leading to the publication of many of his works. Among them are *Szellem és egzistencia: Kilenc tanulmányok* (Spirit and Existence: Nine Studies, 1987) and *Scientia sacra: Az őskori emberiség szellemi hagyománya* (Scienta sacra: The Intellectual Tradition of Prehistoric Mankind, 1988). Most of these volumes consist of essays and tracts arguing for a rejection of materialism and scientism in favor of a celebration of the mystery of faith. Hamvas was also the author of a perplexing two-volume novel, *Karneval* (1985), a kaleidoscope of fantasy, prophecy, and exhortation written in a highly charged, sensuous language and sometimes described as a catalogue of the fate of the twentieth century. A special issue of the journal *Életünk* devoted entirely to his life and work sold out so quickly that its editors reprinted the entire issue.

Hankiss, Ágnes (b. 1950) Hungarian novelist. Hankiss is a native of Budapest, where she graduated from high school in 1968 and from Eötvös Lóránd University in 1973 with a degree in psychology. She taught at the university from 1974 to 1985, when she left to become a full-time writer. Hankiss's first book-length works were professional studies in psychology, such as *A bizalom anatomiája* (The Anatomy of Trust, 1978), a collection of essays, and *Kötéltánc* (Tightrope, 1987), a volume of studies on social psychology from the mid- to late 1980s. The following year, 1988, she published her first novel, the prize-winning *Széphistória* (*A Hungarian Romance*). This is the story of an unconsummated marriage between a nobleman and his wife and her passionate love affair with another man. The sometimes violent romantic triangle mirrors the political and religious turbulence of late-sixteenth- and early-seventeenth-century Hungary, the setting of the work, to which Hankiss devotes nonfictionalized separate chapters. Allusions in these chapters to subsequent events in Hungarian history suggest that for Hankiss deception and betrayal are recurrent patterns in Hungarian history. Since the novel can also be regarded as the story primarily of a young woman's coming of age, of her journey to self-enlightenment, it can be viewed as a feminist work. The "beautiful history" of the original title of Hankiss's novel is thus grimly ironic in that Hungarian history, as seen by the author, is laced with tragedy. In 1992 Hankass was awarded the Attila József Prize.

Translations: *A Hungarian Romance*, trans. Emma Roper-Evans (London: Readers International, 1991).

Hanzlík, Josef (b. 1938) Czech poet. Hanzlík was born in Neratovice, near Prague, and educated at Charles University. A prolific if often disturbing writer, who first appeared in print in the early 1960s, he has published some eleven volumes of poetry. These include *Bludný kámen, 1960–61* (The Stone of Error, 1960–61, 1962); *Lampa* (The Lamp, 1962); *Země za Paříž* (Paris Hinterland, 1963); *Stříbrné oči* (Silver Eyes, 1963); *Černý kolotoč* (Black Carousel, 1964); *Úzkost* (Anguish, 1966); *Potlesk pro Herodesa* (Applause for Herod, 1967); *Krajina Eufórie* (Euphoria Land, 1972); *Požár babylónske věže* (The Fire of the Tower of Babel, 1981); *Ikaros existoval* (Icarus Did Live, 1986); and *Kde je ona hvězda* (Where Is That Star, 1990). Two anthologies of his poems have also appeared: *Láska pod mostem* (Love Beneath the Bridge, 1980) and *Prometheus a Sodoma* (Prometheus and Sodom, 1996). Hanzlík's poetry written before the Soviet invasion of Czechoslovakia in 1968 consists generally of somewhat longer works, written in an almost prosaic narrative style frequently devoid of punctuation, and distinguished by a disquieting strangeness intensified by gruesome images of death and dying, the slaughter of humans and animals, beheadings, and mutilation. The "Variations" cycle from *Úzkost*, for example, is typical. In a number of Hanzlík's poems, such as the monologic "Tartat III" and "Applause for Herod," the political undertones are unmistakable; the poet's target is totalitarian authority. Until the Soviet invasion, Hanzlík had been the poetry editor of *Plamen*, the literary monthly of the Czech Writers Union. The journal was suspended, however, in 1969, and Hanzlík was virtually unable to publish his own poetry in the new political climate. His first postinvasion collection of poems, *Krajina Eufórie*, appeared in 1972. Although violence and grim imagery still appear in his later poetry, and the tone is often one of disillusionment, Hanzlík seems less intent on shocking and repelling. There are poems now of a more lyrical character and a number with their subjects drawn from contemporary events and places—the 1985 Nobel Prize, post–World War II Berlin Alexanderplatz, the explosion of the *Challenger* space shuttle, the town of Karlovy Vary, the annual air show at Letňany airfield, *Star Wars*, and so on. Hanzlík also opens himself more to the world of children in his later poetry, nowhere

more engagingly perhaps than in his long poem "Stamp Collection" (from *Ikaros existoval*), in which world history and especially that of the twentieth century come alive through colorful stamps viewed through the eyes of a child.

Translations: *Selected Poems*, trans. Ewald Osers, Jarmila Milner, and Ian Milner (Newcastle upon Tyne: Bloodaxe, 1993); twenty-four poems in *Three Czech Poets: Vítězslav Nezval, Antonín Bartušek, Jozef Hanzlík*, trans. Ewald Osers and George Theiner (Harmondsworth: Penguin, 1971), 119–58.

Harasymowicz, Jerzy (1933–1999) Polish poet. A native of Puławy in central Poland, and a sometime forester, Harasymowicz is known above all for the rich fairy-tale world he conjures up in his poetry. As Czesław Miłosz writes of him in *The History of Polish Literature* (1969, 1983): "Sometimes tenderly, sometimes cruelly, humorous, always impervious to ratiocinations, he travels through a fairyland of his own." Harasymowicz published his first book, the verse collection *Cuda* (Miracles), in 1956. It was followed by *Powrót do kraju łagodności* (Return to the Land of Gentleness, 1958). Harasymowicz's closeness to individual interpretation of folk religion shaped such collections of poems notable for their religious motifs as *Mit o Świętym Jerzym* (The Myth of Saint George, 1959); *Podsumowanie zieleni* (Summation of Green, 1964); *Pastoralki polskie* (Polish Pastorals, 1964); and *Madonny polskie* (Polish Madonnas, 1969). Long a resident of Kraków, Harasymowicz drew extensively on the art, architecture, history, and lore of the city in such collections as *Wieża melancholii* (The Tower of Melancholy, 1958), which is notable for its brutality, sexuality, and grotesqueness in an important departure from his previous poetry; *Bar na Stanach* (The Bar at the Ponds, 1972); and *Barokowe czasy* (Baroque Times,

1975). His keen interest in and glorification of Polish history, manifest in such collections as *Bar na Stanach* and *Barokowe czasy,* is particularly evident in his collection *Banderia Prutenorum czyli Chorągwie pruskie podniesione roku pańskiego 1410* (Banderia Prutenorum, or Prussian Banners Raised in the Year of Our Lord 1410), which was inspired by the Polish victory over the Prussians in the battle of Grunewald. *Zielnik, czyli wiersze dla wszystkich* (A Herbarium, or Verses for Everyone, 1972) and *Żaglowiec i inne wiersze* (The Sailboat and Other Poems, 1974) consist mostly of poetic miniatures in the style of Japanese haiku.

Translations: One poem, in Polish and English, trans. Sylvester Domański, in *The New Polish Poetry: A Bilingual Collection,* ed. Milne Holton and Paul Vangelisti (Pittsburgh: University of Pittsburgh Press, 1978), 71; five poems, trans. Celina Wieniewska and Adam Czerniawski, in *Polish Writing Today,* ed. Celina Wieniewska (Harmondsworth: Penguin, 1967), 57–60.

Hartwig, Julia (b. 1921) Polish poet and essayist. Widely regarded as the most important woman poet in Poland after Wisława Szymborska, Hartwig was born in Lublin and graduated from Warsaw University with a degree in Polish literature. She published her first poetry in the Lublin journal *Odrodzenie* in 1944. She spent the years 1947 to 1950 in Paris, first on a fellowship and then as an employee of the Polish Embassy. Her fine knowledge of French language and literaure is evident not only in her literary translations but also in her books on the French poets Guillaume Apollinaire (1961) and Gérard de Nerval (1972). Her first published book was a collection of reportage under the title *Z nedalekich stron* (From Nearby Places, 1954). It was followed two years later by her first collection of poetry to appear in print, *Pożegnania*

(Farewells). Hartwig's subsequent volumes of poems include *Wolne ręce* (Free Hands, 1969); *Czuwanie* (Vigilance, 1978); *Chwila postoju* (A Moment's Rest, 1980); *Wybór wierszy* (Selected Poems, 1981); *Poezje wybrane* (Selected Poems, 1983), selected and introduced by Hartwig; *Obcowanie* (Relations, 1987); *Nim opatrzy sę zieleń: Wybór wierszy* (Before the Greenery Changes Color: Selected Verse, 1995); and three volumes in 1999: *Zawsze od nowa: 100 wierszy* (Always Anew: 100 Poems); *Zobaczone* (Forgotten); and *Przemija postać świata* (The Shape of the World Is Changing). Often writing in the first person and addressing her reader directly in conversational style, Hartwig was deeply touched by the ravages of World War II and the injustices of thwarted freedom in postwar communist Poland. She conveys her feelings about her age in easy rhythms that contrast with an element of resignation in her writing, coupled with an acknowledgment of natural beauty that still cannot provide the solace that writing affords her. Hartwig is also the author of a popular children's book, *Wielki pościg* (The Big Race, 1969). Besides French poetry, she has translated such American poets as Robert Bly and Marianne Moore.

Translations: Ten poems in *Polish Poetry of the Last Two Decades of Communist Rule: Spoiling Cannibals' Fun,* ed. and trans. Stanisław Barańczak and Clare Cavanagh (Evanston, Ill.: Northwestern University Press, 1991), 48–53.

Havel, Václav (b. 1936) Czech playwright, essayist, and political activist. A native of Prague, Havel is the most famous of the Czech political dissidents to emerge from the "Prague Spring" of 1968. He was the founder of the human rights movement Charter 77, for which he was sentenced to four and a half years in prison. He was released for reasons of health in 1983. As a measure of the international esteem in which he had come to be held as an artist and a political dissident, Havel was awarded the Erasmus Prize, the highest cultural award in the Netherlands, in 1986. Three years later, Havel became one of the founders of the Civic Forum, the first movement of legal opposition in Czechoslovakia in forty years. In November 1989, he led the "Velvet Revolution," which overthrew the communist regime, and in January 1990 he was elected president of Czechoslovakia. After the division of Czechoslovakia into separate Czech and Slovak states in 1993, Havel also was elected president of the new Czech Republic.

Apart from his extraordinary career as a political dissident of international stature and his subsequent responsibilities as a statesman, Havel is known as a writer above all for his absurdist plays mocking the authoritarianism, intransigence, mindless bureaucracy, and Kafkaesque nightmarishness of communist rule in Czechoslovakia. After working from 1951 to 1955 as an assistant in a chemistry laboratory, he completed his obligatory military service from 1957 to 1959. He began his career as a dramatist in 1962 when he accepted the position of drama director of the Prague avant-garde Balustrade Theater. In the mid-1960s, working with Jan Grossman at the same theater, he wrote such memorable two-act plays as *Zahradní slavnost* (*The Garden Party*, 1963); *Vyrozumění-Protokoly* (*The Memorandum*, 1966); and *Ztížená možnost soustředění* (*The Increased Difficulty of Concentration*, 1968). Because of their patent mockery of life in communist Czechoslovakia, his plays could no longer be published or performed after 1968. This hardly dampened his enthusiasm for playwriting, and in the 1970s and 1980s he turned out a series of one-act plays— *Audience* (1975); *Vernisáž* (*Unveiling*, 1975); *Protest* (1978); and *Chyba* (*Mistake*, 1983)— conceived in the same absurdist vein as his previous works. They were all published abroad. In 1988 Havel wrote *Zítra to spustíme* (Tomorrow We'll Take Care of It) for one of the new avant-garde companies. It premiered in October 1988 in a production celebrating the founding of the Czechoslovak state in 1918.

Literature: Marketa Goetz-Stankiewicz and Phyllis Carey, eds., *Critical Essays on Václav Havel* (New York: Twayne, 1999); Eda Kriseová, *Václav Havel: The Authorized Biography,* trans. Caleb Crain (New York: St. Martin's Press, 1993); Michael Simmons, *The Reluctant President: A Political Life of Václav Havel* (London: Methuen, 1991).

Translations: *The Garden Party and Other Plays,* trans. Vera Blackwell, George Theiner, and Jan Novak (New York: Grove, 1993), which includes, in addition to *The Garden Party, The Memorandum, The Increased Difficulty of Concentration, Audience, Unveiling, Protest,* and *Mistake; The Increased Difficulty of Concentration,* trans. Vera Blackwell (London: Cape, 1972); *Largo desolato: A Play in Seven Scenes,* in a version by Tom Stoppard (New York: Grove, 1987); *Letters to Olga: June 1979–September 1982,* trans. Paul Wilson (New York: Knopf, 1988); *Open Letters: Selected Writings, 1965–1990,* ed. Paul Wilson (New York: Vintage, 1992); *Sorry . . . : Two Plays,* trans. and adapted by Vera Blackwell (London: Eyre Methuen [for the] British Broadcasting Corporation, 1978); *Summer Meditations,* trans. Paul Wilson (New York: Knopf, 1992); *Temptation: A Play in Ten Scenes,* trans. Marie Winn (New York: Grove, 1989); *Tomorrow! A Historical Meditation in Five Acts,* trans. Barbara Day, in *Czech Plays: Modern Czech Drama,* selected and introduced by Barbara Day (London: Nick Hern, 1994), 1–26; *A Word About Words* (New York: Cooper Union, 1992).

Háy, János (b. 1960) Hungarian novelist and poet. Known for his exuberant imagination and stylistic excesses, Háy was born in Vámosmikola. He made his literary debut in 1989 with the volume of poems *Gyalog megyek hozzád sétálóúton* (I'm Coming to You on Foot). His next publication, in 1992, was a small collection of poems and prose texts from 1989 to 1990 under the English title *Welcome in Africa*. Two similar volumes of mixed verse and prose appeared in 1993 and 1995, respectively: *Marlon és Marion* (Marlon and Marion) and *Holdak és napok: 1993–1994* (Moons and Sons: 1993–1994). The work for which Háy is best known, the wildly imaginative *Dzsigerdilen: A szív gyönyörűsége* (Dzhigerdilen: The Beauty of the Heart), about Hungary under Turkish domination, came out in 1996. It was followed by another novel in much the same style, *Xanadu* (1999). Set in late-fifteenth-century Venice, the novel is a rather too elaborate and convoluted story about a Venetian merchant and his seasonal lover set in Piran on the Adriatic in which God and angels put in regular appearances. Háy's most recent publication is the short-story collection *Közötte apának és anyának, fölötte a nagy mindenségnek: Kilenc történet* (Between Fathers and Mothers, Above the Universe: Nine Stories, 2000).

Hein, Christoph (b. 1944) German playwright, novelist, and essayist. A native of Heinzendorf, Silesia, Hein grew up in Bad Düben near Leipzig. Denied the right to a secondary-school education in the German Democratic Republic because he was the son of a Luthern minister, he was sent in 1958 to West Berlin. He returned to the GDR in 1960 and took his qualifying examination to enter a university. After first working at different jobs, he studied philosophy at both Leipzig and Berlin universities. Upon completion of his studies, he became the literary director of the Volksbühne Theater in Berlin, headed at the time by the well-known director B. Besson. Hein made his literary debut in 1980 with a collection of short stories published under the title *Einladung zum Lever Bourgeois* (Invitation to the Lever Bourgeois). This was followed in 1982 by his play collection *Cromwell und andere Stücke* (Cromwell and Other Plays). The other plays in the volume are *Lasalle fragt Herrn Herbert nach Sonja: Die Szene ein Salon* (Lasalle Asks Mr. Herbert About Sonya: The Scene a Salon); *Schlötel oder Was solls?* (Schlötel, or What's the Use?); and *Der Neue Menoza oder Geschichte des kumbanoschen Prinzen Tandi* (The New Menoza, or History of the Kumban Prince Tandi), an adaptation of a play by the early-nineteenth-century German writer J. M. R. Lenz. In 1983 Hein's first big literary hit appeared, *Der fremde Freund* (The Strange Friend; translated as *The Distant Lover*), published in West Germany in 1983 under the title *Drachenblut* (Dragonblood). It is a short engrossing novel narrated by a divorced woman doctor in her late thirties who has inured herself against meaningful relationships of any sort and spends her spare time taking photographs, symbolically, of people-less landscapes. The intensity of its single-focus narrative, which heightens the isolation of the narrator by excluding other perspectives, caught the attention of the reader and catapulted Heim to international fame. Hein's next major work was *Die wahre Geschichte des Ah Q* (The True Story of the Ah Q, 1984), a collection of plays. The title play is Hein's most successful theatrical text. It is absurdist and reminiscent of Samuel Beckett's *Waiting for Godot*, although based on a modern Chinese story, and deals, as do other works by Hein, with the theme of failed revolution. Two other books followed in 1985 and 1986, respectively: *Horns Ende* (Horn's End), a novel, and the play and essay collection *Schlötel oder Was solls?* *Horns Ende* proved to be one of Hein's most controversial works whose publication was long delayed by the censors. In it, four people relate what they remember about a Leipzig University historian named Horn (loosely based on a real person), who hanged himself from a tree in a forest on the outskirts of Leipzig when he could no longer take being harassed for his liberal political and social views. In 1987 Hein made a two-month trip to the United States, where, among other things, he lectured at Amherst College, New York University, Vanderbilt University, the University of Texas, and UCLA. Hein's next literary success, after his American trip, was the novel *Der Tangospieler* (*The Tango Player*, 1989), the story of an apathetic young university history teacher who tries to pick up the threads of his life after being released from nearly two years' imprisonment merely for playing piano accompaniment to a student cabaret political skit for which he had not seen the text. *The Tango Player* completes an informal trilogy begun with *The Distant Lover* and including also *Horns Ende*, in which each novel takes place against the background of a defining moment in the history of the GDR: in *The Distant Lover*, it is the June 1953 uprising in East Berlin; in *Horns Ende*, the Hungarian uprising of 1956; and in *The Tango Player*, the "Prague Spring" of 1968 in Czechoslovakia and its calamitous aftermath. Hein's other works include the comedy *Die Ritter der Tafelrunde* (The Knight of the Round Table, 1989), his last play before the collapse of the GDR; *Das Napoleon-Spiel* (The Napoleon Play, 1993), a difficult novel consisting of two letters to his lawyer by the amoral (and successful) perpetrator of a cold-blooded murder; *Exekution eines Kalbes* (Execution of a Calf, 1994), his second collection of short stories dating from 1977 to 1990; a volume of essays and conversations, *Öffentlich arbeiten: Essais und Gespräche* (Working Publicly: Essays and Conversations, 1987); and another collection of essays, *Als Kind hab ich Stalin gesehen: Essais und Reden* (As a Child I Saw Stalin: Essays and Speeches, 1990), also published the same year, with some changes, as *Die fünfte Grundrechenart: Aufsätze und Reden, 1986–1989* (The Fifth Mathematical Operation: Articles and Speeches, 1986–1989). Hein's literary awards include the Heinrich Mann Prize (1982); the Literature Prize of the Association of German Critics, West Berlin; the literary prize "Der erste Roman" ("The First Novel"), of the New Literary Society of Hamburg (1986); the Lessing Prize, the highest recognition for playwrights in the GDR (1989); the Stefan Andres Prize, from the city of Schweich, West Germany, for *The Tango Player* (1989); and the Erich Fried Prize, Vienna (1990).

Literature: Phillip McKnight, *Understanding Christoph Hein* (Columbia: University of South Carolina Press, 1995); David W. Robinson, *Deconstructing East Germany: Christoph Hein's Literature of Dissent* (Rochester, N.Y.: Camden House, 1999).

Translations: *The Distant Lover,* trans. Krishna Winston (New York: Pantheon, 1989); *The Tango Player,* trans. Philip Boehm (New York: Farrar, Straus and Giroux, 1992); "I Saw Stalin Once When I Was a Child," trans. Jan van Heurck, in *The New Sufferings of Young W. and Other Stories from the German Democratic Republic,* ed. Therese Hörnigk and Alexander Stephan (New York: Continuum, 1997), 274–77.

Hensel, Kerstin (b. 1961) German poet, playwright, short-story writer, and essayist. One of the most impressive women poets to make her debut in the 1980s, Hensel was born in Chemnitz and studied writing at the Johannes R. Becher Institute in Leipzig from 1982 to 1985. She thereafter began working with the Leipzig Theater der Jungen Welt. In 1988 she won an Anna Seghers scholarship from the German Democratic Republic

Academy of Arts and moved to Berlin, where she began her career as a freelance writer. Although she had begun publishing poetry in 1983, she came out with her first book of verse in 1986. It appeared in the series Poesiealbum (Poetry Album, no. 222), published by Neue Leben. The following year, she won first prize in a literary competition sponsored by the journal *Temperamente* for her short story "Kotterba," which subsequently was included in her collection *Hallimasch* (Honey Mushroom, 1989). Incorporating texts from 1984 to 1988, the book is a grotesque portrayal of the impact of fascism on the everyday life of a rural community in the East German past.

A very careful craftswoman who hews to her own path largely unaffected by popular literary trends, Hensel is also the author of *Stillleben mit Zukunft* (Still Life with Future, 1988), one of her strongest collections of verse. It captures the mood of her generation and its general sense of ineffectuality as well as its lack of belief in the future, which in the short title poem is reduced to a mere has-been:

The old crate [i.e., the future]
was spilled out onto the beach
a long time ago
and the sea gnaws on it
day by day
like a bone.

Her subsequent books of poems include *Schlaraffenzucht* (Born to Luxury, 1990); *Auditorium panopticum* (1991); *Gewittefront* (Storm Front) and *Ab tritt Fräulein Jungfer: Liebesgedichte* (The Young Miss Makes Way: Love Lyrics), two collections of verse published in 1991; and *Angestaut: Aus meinem Sudelbuch* (Pent Up: From My Scratch Pad, 1993), a collection of poetry and literary essays in part about women's issues and about such writers as Anna Seghers, Irmtraud Morgner, and Osip Mandelshtam. Some of her more trenchant personal observations about the life around her appear in the five short prose pieces titled "Berliner Abende" ("Berlin Evenings").

Literature: "Kerstin Hensel," in *Literary Intellectuals and the Dissolution of the State: Professionalism and Conformity in the GDR*, ed. Robert von Hallenberg, trans. Kenneth J. Northcott (Chicago: University of Chicago Press, 1996), 208–12.

Herbert, Zbigniew (1924–1998) Polish poet and essayist. One of post–World War II Poland's most gifted and celebrated poets, Herbert was born in Lwów when that city still belonged to Poland (it is now in Ukraine). He claimed the seventeenth-century English poet George Herbert as a distant relation. Herbert began writing poetry during the Nazi occupation of Poland in World War II and the besieged city is a recurrent image in his work. At the end of the war, in which he took part in the resistance movement, Herbert studied economics at the Jagiellonian University in Kraków and then earned a law degree at Nicholas Copernicus University in Toruń. He later received a degree in philosophy from Warsaw University. His refusal to submit to the dictates of the Communist Party in literary matters during the Stalinist period hindered his ability to publish for fifteen years. But it was during this period that he refined his poetic syle, with its characteristic lack of punctuation, its precision and clarity, and its calm restraint. While a modernist in his abandonment of rhyme and meter, Herbert was steeped in classical literature and mythology and drew heavily on them in his verse. His fondness for Shakespeare is also evident in his work.

It was only with the "thaw" in 1956 that Herbert began publishing his poetry. His first three books of poems—*Struna światła* (A String of Light, 1956); *Hermes, pies i gwiazda* (Hermes, a Dog, and a Star, 1957);

and *Studium przedmiotu* (The Study of an Object, 1961)—at once established him as a major new voice in Polish poetry: crystal clear, unpretentious, philosophical, ironic, and deeply humanistic. He subsequently published the collections *Napis* (Inscription, 1969); *Pan Cogito* (*Mr. Cogito,* 1974); *Raport z oblężonego miasta i inne wiersze* (*Report from the Besieged City and Other Poems,* 1983); and *Elegia na odejście* (An Elegy on Leaving, 1990). His last book of poetry appeared in 1997 under the title *Epilog burzy* (Storm's Epilogue). Herbert was poet in residence at the Free University in then West Berlin from 1965 to 1969 and taught at UCLA in the academic year 1970/1971. He was coeditor of the poetry journal *Poezja,* but resigned in protest over its anti-Semitic policies. A morally independent poet, Herbert shunned political or philosophical typecasting.

As a prose writer, Herbert is best remembered for his two books on Western art and culture: *Barbarzyńca w ogrodzie* (*Barbarian in the Garden,* 1962) and *Martwa natura z wędzidłem* (*Still Life with a Bridle,* 1993). *Barbarian in the Garden* is a collection of essays on art, architecture, and history in Western Europe by a deeply appreciative and cultured man of letters who assumes the persona of a barbarian from the Slavic world traveling through the "garden" countries of Western Europe. Among the topics it covers are the remarkable cave paintings in Lascaux, France; the Doric style in Italy; the great cathedrals at Arles and Notre Dame in Paris; *The Last Judgment* in Orvieto; the Albigensian heresy; the poetry of the troubadours; the origins of the Knights Templar; and the paintings of Piero della Francesca. The longest essay in the book is a loving stroll through the art treasures of Siena. Somewhat similar in spirit is *Still Life with a Bridle,* which is devoted wholly to better and lesser known facets of seventeenth-century Dutch art, of which Herbert had an exquisite command reflected in his stories about little known, even obscure, aspects of the period. During his lifetime, Herbert won several awards for his writing: the Jurzykowski Prize (1964); the Austrian Government Prize for European Literature (1965); and the Petrarch Prize (1979).

Literature: Stanislaw Barańczak, *A Fugitive from Utopia: The Poetry of Zbigniew Herbert* (Cambridge, Mass.: Harvard University Press, 1987); Przemysław Czapliński, Piotr Śliwiński, and Ewa Wiegandt, eds., *Czytanie Herberta* (Poznań: WiS, 1995), an excellent collection of articles covering Herbert's complete career.

Translations: POETRY: *Mr. Cogito: Poems,* trans. John Carpenter and Bogdana Carpenter (Hopewell, N.J.: Ecco Press, 1993); *Report from the Besieged City and Other Poems,* trans. John Carpenter and Bogdana Carpenter (New York: Ecco Press, 1985); *Selected Poems,* trans. John Carpenter and Bogdana Carpenter (Oxford: Oxford University Press, 1977); *Selected Poems,* trans. Czesław Miłosz and Dale Scott (Hopewell, N.J.: Ecco Press, 1986). ESSAYS: *Barbarian in the Garden,* trans. Michael March and Jaroslaw Anders (Manchester, Eng.: Carcanet, 1985); *Still Life with a Bridle: Essays and Apocrypha,* trans. John Carpenter and Bogdana Carpenter (Hopewell, N.J.: Ecco Press, 1991).

Herburger, Günter (b. 1932) German novelist, short-story writer, poet, and essayist. A natural rebel whose fiction is filled with disillusioned, antiestablishment young people, Herburger was born in Isny (Allgäu). He left the town before finishing his schooling in order to travel around France, Italy, and Spain, supporting himself by working at a variety of odd jobs. He also for a time studied philosophy and Sanskrit, in which he had long been interested, in Munich and Paris. After returning to Germany, he affiliated with the Group 47 literary circle in 1964 and in 1972 joined the Communist Party.

Herburger's first published work was *Eine gleichmässige Landschaft* (*A Monotonous Landscape*, 1969), a collection of seven short stories exposing those currents beneath the surface of German provincial life that gave rise to boredom, frustration, cynicism, and petty nastiness. Nothwithstanding Herburger's caustic sense of humor, the picture of human relations that emerges is bleak and depressing. His novel *Die Messe* (The Mass, 1969) was the first of several works by Herburger portraying people who rebel against a routinized existence in search of a life of greater meaning. *Jesus in Osaka: Zukunftsroman* (Jesus in Osaka: A Novel About the Future), which appeared in 1970, is a work of fantasy dominated by a messianic-like preacher who offers love and classless brotherhood in place of a spiritually empty mass consumption. Herburger's subsequent work became more extreme in its depiction of capitalist society as a breeding ground of alienation and inequality. Reflecting in part the ideas about "concrete utopias" of the Marxist philosopher Ernst Bloch (1885–1977), Herburger's major, if uneven, novelistic cycle consisting of *Flug ins Herz* (Flight into the Heart, 1977), *Thuja* (1981), and the two-volume *Die Augen der Kämpfer* (The Eyes of the Fighters, 1980, 1983) drew on such different genres as the social and political novel, the adventure tale, and utopian fiction. He was also the author of such inspirational books as *Das Glück: Eine Reise in Nähe und Ferne* (Happiness: A Journey Near and Far, 1994) and *Die Liebe: Eine Reise durch Wohl und Wehe* (Love: A Journey Through Well-being and Woes, 1996). Herburger's other collections of stories include *Die Eroberung der Zitadelle* (The Conquest of the Citadel, 1972) and *Birne kehrt zurück* (Birne Heads Back, 1996), subtitled "New Adventure Tales," a work for children featuring the protagonist of such previous collections as *Birne kann alles* (Birne Can Do Everything, 1971); *Birne kann noch mehr* (Birne Can Do Even More, 1971); and *Birne brennt durch* (Birne Runs Off, 1975). In 1972 he published an anthology of verse, essays, a radio play, a story, and a film script under the title *Die amerikanische Tochter* (The American Daughter), the title of the film script (never produced) in the anthology. Herburger's poems are in the volumes *Ventile* (Valves, 1966); *Training* (1970; original title in English); *Ziele* (Goals, 1977); *Orchidee* (Orchid, 1979); *Makadam* (Macadam, 1982); *Das brennende Haus* (The Burning House, 1984); *Kinderreich Passmoré* (Passmoré, the Children's Kingdom, 1986); and *Im Gebirge* (In the Mountains, 1998). His other prose works include *Capri: Die Geschichte eines Diebs* (Capri: The Story of a Thief, 1984); *Traum und Bahn* (Dream and Path, 1994); and *Elsa* (1999). In 1981 Herburger published a volume of plays under the title *Blick aus dem Paradies* (A View from Paradise), containing *Thuja* and *Zwei Spiele eines Themas* (Two Plays on One Theme). He has also written nearly a dozen radio plays and several film and television scripts.

Literature: Klaus Siblewski, ed., *Der Hörspielautor Günter Herburger: Texte, Daten, Bilder* (Hamburg: Luchterhand, 1991), the only work of a general nature on Herburger. Of particular interest are the pieces by Herburger himself, about his own life, his poetry, the novel, and so on.

Translations: *A Monotonous Landscape: Seven Stories,* trans. Geoffrey Skelton (New York: Harcourt, Brace & World, 1968).

Herling-Grudziński, Gustaw (1919–2000) Polish short-story writer and essayist. A gifted and much admired writer, who lived in Italy after World War II, Herling-Grudziński was born in Kielce, in central Poland. His studies of Polish literature in Warsaw were interrupted by the outbreak of the war and his capture in 1940 by the Soviets in their part of occupied Poland and subsequent imprisonment in a labor camp on the White Sea. He later wrote a harrowing narrative based on his experiences in the Soviet gulag from 1940 to 1942 under the title *Inny świat* (*A World Apart*, 1951). When the English translation appeared in Britain in 1986, it carried an introduction by the distinguished philosopher Bertrand Russell. After his release from Soviet prison, Herling-Grudziński joined the Polish army raised by the London-based government-in-exile and took part in the Allied invasion of Italy. When the war ended, he remained in Italy, settling in Naples.

Other than *A World Apart*, which has been widely translated, Herling-Grudziński is known mostly for his short stories and voluminous diaries, which, until the collapse of communism in Poland, were published mainly by the Paris-based Polish émigré journal *Kultura*. His collections of stories, most of which were reprinted in Poland in the 1990s, include *Szkrzydła ołtarza* (Wings of the Altar, 1960); *Wieża i inne opowiadania* (The Tower and Other Stories, 1988); *Portret wenecki: Trzy opowiadania* (Portrait of Venice: Three Stories, 1995); *Don Ildebrando: Opowiadania* (Don Ildebrando: Stories, 1997); and *Opowiadania zebrane* (Collected Stories, 1999). A few of his best stories—"The Island," "The Tower," and "The Second Coming"—are available in English. All the stories are set in Italy past and present, which Herling-Grudziński knew so well and evoked superbly. Traditional in the sense of having a well-delineated narrative structure, Herling-Grudziński's stories are finely written and engrossing in their often out-of-the-ordinary, if troubling, subject matter.

Herling-Grudziński's diaries were published between 1973 and 1998. Under the collective title *Dziennik pisany nocą* (*The Journal Written at Night*), they comprise six volumes arranged chronologically (the dates in parentheses are those of publication): 1971–1972 (1973, 1995); 1973–1979 (1980, 1995); 1980–1983 (1996); 1984–1988 (1996); 1989–1992 (1997); and 1993–1996 (1998). Dealing with his life and travels in Italy, current events, Polish and world literature (he had a special affinity for Russian literature and wrote about it with much insight), art, philosophy, and intellectual life, Herling-Grudziński's diaries make superb reading and have been widely praised. Another, less well known diary relates, as its title indicates, his experiences and observations on a trip to Burma: *Podróż do Burmy: Dziennik* (Journey to Burma: A Diary, 1999). Herling-Grudziński also published a volume each of essays and sketches: *Godzina cieni: Eseje* (Hour of Shade: Essays, 1997) and *Wyścia z milczenia: Szkice* (Exits from Silence: Sketches, 1998). While his fictional skills enjoy an enviable reputation, Herling-Grudziński will undoubtedly be most remembered as the author *of A World Apart* and *The Journal Written at Night*.

Translations: *The Island: Three Tales,* trans. Ronald Strom (Cleveland: World, 1967; New York: Viking, 1993); *Volcano and Miracle: A Selection from "The Journal Written at Night,"* trans. Ronald Strom (New York: Viking, 1996); *A World Apart*, trans. Joseph Marek (London: Heinemann, 1951); *A World Apart*, trans. Andrzej Ciozkosz [Joseph Marek] (New York: Arbor House, 1986).

Hermlin, Stephan (real name Rudolf Leder; b. 1915) German novelist, short-story writer, essayist, and poet. Born in Chemnitz (later Karl-Marx-Stadt), of a well-to-do Jewish family, Hermlin worked as a printer in Berlin for three years after Hitler came to power. But his early affiliation with the communists (he joined the Communist Youth Organization at the age of sixteen) and his antifascist underground activities compelled him to leave Germany in 1936. He spent the next few years in Egypt, Palestine, England,

Spain (where he fought on the side of the republic in the Civil War), and France, where he joined the Resistance. In 1944/1945, he was interned in Switzerland, and returned to Germany in 1945. He worked for the Hessian Broadcasting Company in Frankfurt but in 1947 resettled in East Germany, where he promptly joined the Socialist Unity Party. He soon became a prominent member of the literary community. He also moved rapidly up the ranks of the literary bureaucracy, becoming vice chairman of the Writers Union and secretary of the poetry section of the Academy of Arts. Firm in his Marxist beliefs, Hermlin interpreted communism in a way that enabled him to lend vigorous support, for example, to the East German poetic avant-garde and to oppose the politics of cultural repression on the part of the Party. Accused of "decadence," he was forced to give up his official posts in 1963. But as a measure of the esteem in which he was widely held, he was chosen vice president of the International PEN Club in 1975.

Hermlin made his literary debut with the hugely successful volume of poems *Zwölf Balladen von den Grossen Städten* (Twelve Big City Ballads, 1945), in which an apocalyptic view of life is offset by the utopian vision of a world free of hatred and fear. A similar hopeful tone also pervades his next publication, *Die Zeit der Gemeinsamkeit* (The Time Together, 1949; translated as *City on a Hill*). This is a collection of four World War II stories, the best of which is "The Time Together," which deals with the Warsaw Ghetto Uprising in 1943 and underlines the need for Jewish–Christian solidarity. Here, as in his previous poetry and in subsequent works, Hermlin clings loyally to a belief in the rightness of communism and Soviet leadership (the defects of which Hermlin generally ignores) in the great ongoing antifascist struggle. Much of Hermlin's later writing is essayistic and memoiristic, contained in such volumes as

Begegnungen, 1954–1959 (Meetings, 1954–1959, 1960); *Kassberg* (1965); *Corneliusbrücke* (The Cornelius Bridge, 1968); *Mein Friede* (My Peace, 1975); *Lektüre, 1960–1971* (Readings, 1960–1971, 1973); *Abendlicht* (1983; translated as *Evening Light*); *Äusserungen, 1944–1982* (Comments, 1944–1982, 1983); *In einer dunklen Welt* (In a Dark World, 1993); and *In den Kämpfen dieser Zeit* (In the Struggles of Our Time, 1995). The most important of these works by far is *Evening Light*, a small finely written book of personal reminiscences of his youth in Berlin in the 1930s, his discovery of Marxism and entry into the Communist Party, the growing rise of National Socialism, and his participation in the struggle against fascism. Some of Hermlin's best shorter works— "Der Leutnant Yorck von Wartenburg" ("Lieutenant Yorck from Wartenburg," 1944); "Die Zeit der Einsamkeit" ("The Time Alone," 1948); "Arkadien" ("Arcadias," 1949); and "Die Zeit der Gemeinsamkeit" ("The Time Together," 1949)—are included in the collection *Arkadien* (Arcadias), which appeared in 1983.

Literature: Silvia Schlenstedt, *Stephan Hermlin: Sein Leben und Werk* (Berlin: Das europäische Buch, 1985).

Translations: *Evening Light*, trans. Paul F. Dvorak (San Francisco: Fjord, 1983); "My Peace," trans. Jan van Heurck, in *The New Sorrows of Young W. and Other Stories from the German Democratic Republic*, ed. Therese Hörnigk and Alexander Stephan (New York: Continuum, 1997), 239–45.

Heym, Stefan (real name Helmut Flieg; 1913–2001) German novelist and essayist. A talented and provocative writer, with a passion for politics that permeates virtually all his writing, Heym enjoys a reputation that rests in part on his bold defiance of the East German communist bureaucracy. Born in Chemnitz of Jewish background, Heym immigrated to Prague when Hitler became chancellor in 1933. He remained in Czecho-slovakia for two years and then left for the United States, eventually becoming an American citizen. Until he joined the army in 1943, he was employed principally as the editor in chief of the German-language antifascist weekly *Deutsches Volksecho*. During World War II, Heym saw action on the western front. When the war ended, he stayed in Munich to edit newspapers published by the occupation powers. However, he was charged with procommunist sympathies and recalled to the United States in 1945. Outspoken in his opposition to the American participation in the Korean War and the witch-hunting anticommunist crusade of Senator Joseph McCarthy, Heym sent the Bronze Medal he had earned during the war directly to President Eisenhower as a form of protest. Shortly thereafter, he defected to the German Democratic Republic. Although he was well received by the communist authorities, Heym soon earned their disfavor by being as critical of their regime as he had been of conservative politics in the United States. His bold and fearless criticism of East German social and cultural repression soon earned him the reputation of the enfant terrible of East German literature.

Heym's literary career began during his residence in America. Written originally in English, his first three books were published in the United States: *Hostages* (1942), a dark picture of life in German-occupied Prague, which became a best-seller and was made into a film; *The Crusaders* (1948), which is about American soldiers in Europe, but expresses fears for the future of American democracy because of the growing power of the military–industrial complex; and *Goldsborough* (1953), a sociopolitical novel based on the famous Pennsylvania miners' strike.

Heym's first work written in the GDR, *Fünf Tage im Juni* (Five Days in June), immediately signaled the collision course he

was on with the communist regime. The subject of the novel is the strike by workers in East Berlin in June 1953 that finally had to be suppressed by Soviet tanks. A ban in 1959 prohibiting publication of the novel remained in effect for thirty years. It was only in 1989 that an East German edition of the novel appeared. In a precedent for much of Heym's subsequent literary activity in the GDR, a manuscript of *Fünf Tage im Juni* was smuggled to West Germany and published in 1974.

Heym's progressively more strident criticism of the GDR, which included a public argument in 1956 with Communist Party boss Walter Ulbricht, over the development of cultural life in the GDR, earned him the wrath of the authorities. However, Heym remained a staunch supporter of socialism and gave no serious thought to leaving the GDR. For this reason, as well as his growing international reputation, the authorities expressed their displeasure primarily in an outright ban on further publication of his works in the GDR. At the risk of even sterner measures to muzzle him, Heym circumvented the ban by smuggling his works to West Germany, where they were published and added further luster to his reputation as a writer and rebel.

Heym's most provocative work was the novel *Collin*. Published in the West in 1978, it uses the morally compromised career of the writer Hans Collin to unmask the East German secret police. The novel is composed in the form of the memoirs written in feverish haste by the dying Collin. Enraged over the publication of the novel, the GDR fined Heym for allegedly violating foreign currency regulations and denounced him as a traitor and an American (even though Heym had given up his American passport when he became a citizen of the GDR).

Of Heym's subsequent novels, *Schwarzenberg* (1984) and *Radek* (1995), the former is the more interesting. In it Heym depicts the six-week life of a tiny autonomous republic that arose on a small area of German territory at the end of World War II and in which an exemplary democratic socialism (in implied contrast to the undemocratic socialism of the GDR) was practiced. The novel was partly based on fact, since the Schwarzenberg District in the Erz Mountains was administratively restructured in such a way that none of the Allied armies assumed jurisdiction over it. Heym was also the author of a few historical and biblical novels. Two of them are drawn from episodes in German history: *Die Papiere des Andreas Lenz* (The Papers of Andreas Lenz, 1963; translated as *The Lenz Papers*) addresses certain events in the German "Spring of Nations" in 1848; *Lassalle* (1969) is based on the career of Ferdinand Lassalle, one of the early theorists of socialism. In *König David Bericht* (*The King David Report*, 1974), an intriguing retelling of the biblical story, Ethan the Scribe discovers a very different side to King David, whose panegyric history King Solomon has commissioned him to write. *Ahasver* (Ahasuerus, 1981; translated as *The Wandering Jew*) is a largely autobiographical work in which a fallen angel, embodying the spirit of the eternal revolutionary, roams the world in an attempt to rectify the mistakes of creation. In 1994 Heym became the oldest member elected to the German parliament.

Literature: Peter Hutchinson, *Stefan Heym: The Perpetual Dissident* (Cambridge: Cambridge University Press, 1992).

Translations: *The King David Report* (New York: Putnam, 1973; Evanston, Ill.: Northwestern University Press, 1997); *The Lenz Papers* (London: Cassell, 1964); *Uncertain Friend: A Biographical Novel* (London: Cassell, 1969); *The Wandering Jew* (New York: Holt, Rinehart and Winston, 1984).

Hieng, Andrej (b. 1925) Slovenian playwright, short-story writer, and novelist. Born in Ljubljana, where he received his secondary-school education, Hieng studied directing at the Academy of Performing Arts in the capital. He began his career as a director in 1951 and has stayed active in the theater. It was also in the 1950s that Hieng began his literary career, specializing at first in stories of a psychological and psychoanalytical character in which a basically realistic style occasionally accommodates elements of expressionism. His first published collection of stories, *Usodni rob* (Edge of Destiny, 1954), was an undertaking with his fellow writers Lojze Kovačič (b. 1928) and Franček Bohanec (b. 1923). After the appearance of his second book of stories, *Planota* (Plateau, 1961), Hieng turned to the writing of novels as well as plays for the stage, radio, and television. His five novels are *Gozd in pečina* (Forest and Cave, 1966); *Orfeum* (Orpheum, 1972); *Čarodej* (The Magician, 1976); *Obnebje metuljev* (Horizon of Butterflies, 1980); and the novel for which he is best known, *Čudežni Feliks* (Magical Feliks, 1993), a suggestive epic portrait of conditions in Slovenia before the outbreak of World War II built around the quest for his roots of the eponymous main protagonist, a boy of Jewish origin.

Some of Hieng's best dramatic work was written for radio and television, including three plays with Spanish settings and dealing especially with the lives of such rebellious painters as El Greco and Francisco Goya: *Burleska o Grku* (A Burlesque About El Greco, 1969), a television play; *Cortesova vrnitev* (The Return of Cortés, 1969), a radio drama about the Spanish conquistador; and *Gluhi mož na meji* (The Deaf Man on the Border, 1969), a television play about Goya. *Osvajalec* (The Conqueror, 1971), a tragicomedy about the conquistadores written for the theater, continued Hieng's interest in Spanish subjects, the novelty of which in the Slovenian cultural milieu of the time did much to enhance the appeal of these works. Hieng's fascination with the lives of out-of-the-mainstream artists, reflected in his "Spanish" plays, led him to the mentally ill Slovenian painter Jožef Petkovški (1861–1898). In the television drama *Nori malar* (The Mad Painter, 1979), Hieng exposes the coldness and venality of the "normal" artistic milieu, to which Petkovški was incapable of relating. Hieng's other dramatic works are *Lažna Ivana* (False Ivana, 1973), a romantic comedy; *Izgubljeni sin* (The Prodigal Son, 1976), a melodrama; *Večer ženinov* (The Bridegrooms' Evening, 1979), subtitled "A Play with a Masquerade"; and *Zakladi gospe Berte* (The Treasures of Mrs. Bertha, 1983). *Izgubljeni sin, Večer ženinov,* and the earlier television drama *Spominska plošča* (The Commemorative Plaque) are generally regarded as forming a cycle of melodramas dealing with a Slovenian petite bourgeoisie still living in the past.

Translations: "The Fatal Boundary," trans. Mia Dintinjana, in *The Imagination of Terra Incognita: Slovenian Writing, 1945–1995,* ed. Aleš Debeljak (Fredonia, N.Y.: White Pine, 1997), 332–50.

Hilbig, Wolfgang (b. 1941) German poet, novelist, and short-story writer. Hilbig was born in Meuselwitz, near Leipzig, where he studied to be a turner. After his obligatory military service, he worked as a manual laborer in different cities. In 1967 he was recruited into the Leipzig Circle of Writing Workers (Zirkel schreibender Arbeiter), a proletarian literary organization, but left the following year because some of the poetry he wrote at the time was not deemed representative of the workers' outlook. The brutal suppression of the "Prague Spring" in 1968 plunged Hilbig into a deep personal crisis, which such literary friends as Siegmar Faust and Gert Neumann tried to help him overcome, to little avail. Hilbig returned home in 1970 and worked as a fireman. In 1985 he left the German Democratic Republic on a visa and resettled permanently in West Germany.

A literary autodidact, Hilbig made his debut as a poet in 1978 with the publication of some of his poems in Wilfried Ahrens's anthology *Hilferufe von drüben* (A Call for Help from Over There). After the book's release, he was briefly jailed and fined for "currency violations." Shortly thereafter, the journal *L '76* published several of his poems accompanied by a literary portrait of Hilbig by Faust. This and other public-relations efforts on his behalf facilitated Hilbig's release from jail. He thereafter returned to East Berlin, where he continued working as a fireman. Hilbig's first published volume of poems was *abwesenheit* (absence), which was published to very favorable reviews in West Germany in 1979 and for which he had to pay another East German "currency violations" fine. The poems in the collection owe much to the inspiration of German late Romanticism as well as to Poe, Baudelaire, and Kafka. Hilbig worked comfortably in a variety of meters and poetic forms, revealing himself at times as a bold experimenter. In 1979 he became a freelance writer in East Berlin and Leipzig. Four years later, in 1983, a selection of Hilbig's poetry and prose under the title *Stimme, Stimme* (Voices, Voices) became his first book to be published in the GDR. Once resettled in West Germany, Hilbig published the following works: *Der Brief: Drei Erzählungen* (The Letter: Three Stories, 1985); *die versprengung* (the dispersal, 1986); *Die Territorien der Seele* (The Territories of the Soul, 1986); *Die Weiber* (The Women, 1987), a curious first-person narrative combining a personal language crisis, sexuality, and a dream-inspired search for women the narrator believes are disappearing from his town; *Eine Übertragung* (A Broadcast, 1989); *Die Angst vor Beethoven* (Fear of Beethoven, 1990); *Über den Tonfall: Drei Prosastücke* (On Intonation: Three Prose Pieces, 1990); *Alte Abdeckerei* (Old Junk, 1991), a long story; *Das Meer in Sachsen: Prosa und Gedichte* (The Sea in Saxony:

Prose and Poetry, 1991); *Zwischen den Paradiesen: Prosa, Lyrik* (Between Paradises: Prose, Lyrics, 1992), a good selection of Hilbig's prose and poetry; *Aufbrüche* (Outbreaks, 1992); *Er, nicht ich* (He, Not I, 1992); *Grünes grünes Grab* (Green, Green Grave, 1993), a collection of stories; *ICH* (I, 1993), an intriguing novel about literature and morality involving a protagonist who is an East German writer and a Stasi, or State Security, informer; *Die Arbeit an den Öfen* (Working in the Flames, 1994), a collection of stories about firefighting; *Die Kunde von den Bäumen* (The News from the Trees, 1994); and *Das Provizorium* (The Temporary Measure, 2000). In 1995, during the summer semester, Hilbig gave four lectures on aesthetics at the Johann Wolfgang Goethe University in Frankfurt am Main that were subsequently published under the title *Abriss der Kritik: Poetikvorlesungen* (The Frankfurt Poetics Lectures: An Outline). Hilbig's literary prizes include the Brothers Grimm Prize of the City of Hanau (1983); the Patrons' Prize of the Berlin Academy of Arts (1985); the Kranichsteiner Prize, for *Die Weiber* (1987); the Ingeborg Bachmann Prize, for an excerpt from *Eine Übertragung* (1989); the Brandenburg Literary Prize, for *ICH* (1993); and the Bremer Literature Prize, for *ICH* (1994).

Literature: The best general introduction to Hilbig is Uwe Wittstock, ed., *Wolfgang Hilbig: Materialen zu Leben und Werk* (Frankfurt am Main: Fischer, 1994), which includes public speeches and other pieces by Hilbig as well as analyses of his major works.

Translations: Five poems, trans. Agnes Stein, in *Child of Europe: A New Anthology of East European Poetry,* ed. Michael March (London: Penguin, 1990), 55–60.

Hłasko, Marek (1934–1969) Polish novelist and short-story writer. A native of Warsaw, Hłasko was widely regarded in his time as the "angry young man" of Polish literature. He was also likened to the American film actor James Dean and the writers of the Beat Generation. At the age of sixteen, he interrupted his schooling in order to work as a cab driver, the first of several jobs he held that gave him ample opportunity to familiarize himself with the seamier side of contemporary Polish urban life that became his stock-in-trade as a writer. His literary career was launched in 1954 with publication of the story "Baza Sokołowska" ("The Sokołowska Station"), which drew on his experiences as a cab driver. In 1956 he published a collection of stories under the title *Pierwszy krok w chmurach* (First Step in the Clouds), which was honored with a Publishers' Prize. The work that brought Hłasko international attention was the short novel *Ósmy dzień tygodnia* (*The Eighth Day of the Week,* 1957), which was translated into fifteen languages and subsequently made into a film shown at the Cannes Film Festival in 1958. The Polish thaw of October 1956 had run its course by 1958, and Hłasko's next two novels were denied permission for publication. Undeterred, Hłasko went to France in February 1958 and arranged for *Cmentarze* (Cemeteries; translated as *The Graveyard*) and *Następnego do raju* (Next to Heaven) to be published by the Paris-based Polish émigré publishing house Instytut Literacki. His outspoken contempt for communism in public interviews abroad resulted in the denial by the Polish authorities of his request for an extension of his passport and the demand that he return at once to Poland. Hłasko refused and, indeed, never returned to Poland. After traveling around Europe for a while, he left for Israel. He remained there until 1961, earning his living as a common laborer. Four novels and two novellas were inspired by his experiences in Israel: *Wszyscy byli odwróceni* (They Were All Turned Away, 1964); *Brudne czyny* (Dirty Deeds, 1964); *Drugie zabicie psa* (Killing the Dog a Second Time, 1965; translated as *Killing the Second Dog*); and *Nawrócony w*

Jaffie (Converted in Jaffa, 1966). The two novellas were *W dzień jego śmierci* (The Day of His Death, 1963) and *Opowiem wam o Esther* (I'll Tell You About Esther, 1966). In 1961 Hłasko married the German actress Sonia Ziemann, who had appeared in the German–Polish coproduction of Hłasko's novel *The Eighth Day of the Week* and moved with her to West Germany. In 1966 and 1967, he published two more novels, *Piękni dwudziestoletni* (Pretty Twenty-Year Olds) and *Sowa córka piekarza* (Sowa, the Baker's Daughter). After separating from his wife, Hłasko immigrated to the United States, where he qualified for a pilot's license and completed his last novel, *Palcie ryż każdego dnia* (Chew Your Nails Every Day, 1985). Hłasko died of an overdose of sleeping pills in Wiesbaden, Germany, in June 1969 before a planned return trip to Israel.

Literature: Zyta Kwiecińska, *Opowiem Wam o Marku* (Wrocław: Wydawnictwo Dolnośląskie, 1991), a popular biography of Hłasko.

Translations: *The Eighth Day of the Week,* trans. Nobert Guterman (New York: Dutton, 1958; Westport, Conn.: Greenwood, 1975; Evanston, Ill.: Northwestern University Press, 1994); *The Graveyard,* trans. Norbert Guterman (New York: Dutton, 1959); *Killing the Second Dog,* trans. Tomasz Mirkowicz (New York: Cane Hill, 1990).

Hodrová, Daniela (b. 1946) Czech literary scholar and novelist. Hodrová was born in Prague, where she studied Russian and Czech at Charles University, and then French and comparative literature. Her doctoral dissertation was on the beginnings of the novel in Old Russian literature. Hodrová has impressive credentials as a literary scholar and has also attracted much attention as a novelist. She was a contributor to a book of essays on Czech literature from 1945 to 1970 published in 1992 and is the author of four monographs on the typology of lit-

erary genres in the novel (1989); literary typology (1994), a study dealing mainly with space and time in literature; initiations in literature (1993); and architecture in literature (1997). Her first effort as a novelist was the impressive trilogy *Trýznivé město* (The Suffering City), which consists of *Podobojí* (Ultraquists, 1991), *Kukly* (Chrysalises, 1991), and *Théta* (Theta, 1992). Her second novel was *Perunův den* (Perun's Day, 1994).

An intellectual writer whose professional expertise as a literary scholar is much in evidence in her fiction, Hodrová tends toward the postmodern and intertextual. *Théta,* arguably her best work of fiction, is a novel about the narrator, who may or may not be the author but a fictionalized young woman writer trying to come to grips with the death of her father, a prominent actor. In rediscovering his identity, she also sets about recapturing her own past. The structure of the novel is complex, however, as situations and characters are in constant flux and boundaries shift or dissolve. As in much of her fiction, Hodrová has an abiding interest in the literary process itself, how a novel becomes written, so her creative writing can be viewed as an extension of her theoretical investigations.

Translations: Excerpts from *Théta,* trans. Tatiana Firkušný and Veronique Firkušný-Callegari, in *Allskin and Other Tales by Contemporary Czech Women,* ed. Alexandra Büchler (Seattle: Women in Translation, 1998), 50–71; excerpts from *Perunův den,* trans. Tatiana Firkušný and Veronique Firkušný-Callegari, in *Daylight in Nightclub Inferno: Czech Fiction from the Post-Kundera Generation,* selected by Elena Lappin (North Haven, Conn.: Catbird, 1997), 191–202. *Théta* is available in German as *Theta: Cittá dolente III,* trans. Susanna Roth (Zurich: Ammann, 1998).

Holka, Peter (b. 1950) Slovak novelist and short-story writer. A popular and prolific writer, Holka was born in the small town of Považská Bystrica and, after working at a variety of odd jobs, finally became a journalist affiliated with several newspapers and reviews. He is currently editor in chief of the newspaper *Pravda*. Although he has published a collection of short stories, *Škára (do trinastej komnaty)* (The Crack [into the Thirteenth Room], 1994), Holka is primarily a writer of (generally) short novels. They include *Ústie Riečok* (1983); *Leto na furmanskom koni* (Summer on a Carter's Horse, 1986); *Prekážka v džínsach* (Impediment in Jeans, 1990); *Piráti z Marka Twaina* (Pirates out of Mark Twain, 1992); *Normálny cvok* (An Ordinary Crackpot, 1993); *Neha* (Tenderness, 1995); and *Sen o sne* (A Dream About Dream, 1998). A facile storyteller rooted in contemporary society, Holka often deals with transition in life and personal loss. Drawing on his own background, his male protagonists are usually journalists or writers. In *Ústie Riečok* (the title derives from the name of a small out-of-the-way town), his leading character is a reporter whose assignment to write about the provincial town convinces him of the need to leave his paper despite a more prestigious position offered him there. The main interest in the work is its inside view of a socialist-era newspaper. Drug use and its toll are the subjects of *Normálny cvok,* in which a man fights for the life of the woman he loves who is a drug addict. The effectiveness of the novel owes much to Holka's nonjudgmental and unsentimental treatment of the drug problem in a postcommunist Eastern European country. Arguably his best work of fiction is *Neha,* a warm study of the impact of the death of his wife on a writer and his young son. Committed to writing a novel about hope and patience based on his own loss, the writer comes to understand the void left in his son's life by the untimely death of his mother. *Sen o sne* consists of a series of seven dreams built around places associated with the narrator's missing daughter, Paula. In the last dream, set in Paris, the narrator draws a parallel between his own quest in Paris and that of the American Beat writer Jack Kerouac, who once returned there in search of his own roots. In 1992 Holka published a book of biographical conversations with his fellow Slovak writer Vladimír Mináč, under the title *V košeli zo žih'lavy* (In a Hair Shirt, 1992). His most recent work is the short novel *Nezabudnutelná vôňa zrelej pšenice* (The Unforgettable Smell of Ripe Wheat), which appeared in 1999.

Holub, Miroslav (1924–1998) Czech poet and scientist. One of the most highly esteemed Czech—and European—men of letters of the twentieth century, Holub is as much respected for his contributions to science as to poetry. Among his best-known works on disease and immunology available in English are *Immunology of Nude Mice* (1989); *The Dimension of the Present Moment: Essays* (1990); and *Shedding Life: Disease, Politics, and Other Human Conditions* (1997). The last book, a collection of essays on a wide variety of topics including "Kidneys and History" and "Red Noodles, or, About Uselessness," reflects his range of concerns as well as his profound interest in humanity, its well-being, and its environment. Holub was born in Plzeň and educated in a classic grammar school in his native city. He began studying medicine at Charles University in Prague, but his studies were interrupted by World War II when he was forced to work on the railroads during the German occupation. He completed his medical studies in 1953 and began his career first as a clinical pathologist at the main Prague hospital and then as a research immunologist at the Microbiological Institute of the Czechoslovak Academy of Sciences in Prague and later at the Institute for Clinical and Experimental Medicine. He received his doctorate in 1958. At his death, he held the position of chief research immunologist at the last institution. In 1956/1957, Holub was visiting investigator at the Department of Immunology, Public Health Research Institute of the City of New York. He also collaborated in 1968/1969 with the Max-Planck-Institut für Immunbiologie in Freiburg, Germany. From 1952 to 1969, he edited the popular scientific magazine *Vesmír*.

As a creative writer, Holub was the author of seventeen volumes of verse and five books of essays or prose sketches. His books of poetry are *Denní služba* (Day Duty, 1958); *Achilles a želva* (Achilles and the Tortoise, 1960); *Slabikář* (Primer, 1961); *Jdi a otevři dveře* (Go and Open the Door, 1962); *Kam teče krev* (Where the Blood Flows, 1963); *Zcela nesoustavná zoologie* (Totally Unsystematic Zooology, 1963); *Tak zvané srdce* (The So-Called Heart, 1963); *Anamnéza* (Anamnesis, 1964), a selection of poems published in 1958 to 1963 and new works; *Ačkoli* (*Although*, 1969); *Beton: Verše z New Yorku a z Prahy* (Concrete: Poems from New York and Prague, 1970); *Naopak* (On the Contrary, 1982); *Interferon, čili o divadle* (Interferon, or On Theater, 1986), which contains short dramatic sketches in addition to poems; *Sagitální řez* (Sagittal Section, 1988); *Maxwellův démon, čili o tvořivosti* (Maxwell's Demon, or On Creativity, 1988); *Ne, patrně ne: Zcela malá knížka nadávek, zákazů, odkazů apod* (No, Obviously No: A Quite Small Book of Imprecations, Injunctions, Rejections, and So On, 1989); *Syndrom mizející plíce* (Vanishing Lung Syndrome, 1990); and *Ono se letělo: Suita z rodného města* (1994; translated as *Supposed to Fly: A Sequence from Pilsen*). Among his major collections of prose, apart from his many scientific and popular works on medicine and health, are two books of travel pieces based on his tours of the United States between 1951 and 1980—*Anděl na kolečkách: Poloreportáž z USA* (Angel on

Wheels: Polo Reportage from the USA, 1964) and *Žít v New Yorku* (Living in New York, 1969)—and *K principu rolničky* (*The Jingle Bell Principle*, 1987), a collection of highly entertaining and shrewdly perceptive "essaylets" on a wide variety of subjects from the technical to the literary that were originally newspaper "Column Articles" subtitled "Notes and Objections, maximum length 43 lines."

Holub's poetry defies facile characterization. Addressing an extraordinary range of topics, from the most mundane to the loftiest, it is notable especially for its simplicity of expression, its remarkable wit and irony, its wry observations of human society, and its introduction of the scientific and medical in unexpected contexts. Holub's collection *Interferon, čili o divadle*, in which immunology and theatrical representation are treated as related metaphors, is typical in this respect. Concrete political events rarely find direct expression in his poetry, although reflections of the impact of World War II are discernible in his first published book of poems, *Denní služba*, and his first collection after the Soviet invasion of Czechoslovakia in 1968, *Although*, contains a poem in honor of the young martyr Jan Palach ("The Prague of Jan Palach"). Whimsy, fable, and allegory were the principal means by which Holub sought to circumvent censorship during the rigid Stalinist repression of the 1950s. After the events of 1968, he was unable to publish in Czechoslovakia until 1982, and publication abroad, in translation, was not without risk. Of particular interest in Holub's later poetry are his poems inspired by puppet theater under the title "The Merry Adventures of the Puppets" as well as the puppet-theater motifs in other poems and his short dramatic sketches collectively titled "Endgames." The last are reminiscent of the cabaret-style playlets in the Polish writer Konstanty Ildefons Gałczyński's "Theater of the Green

Goose." Both cycles are included in Interferon, or On Theater. One of the best introductions to the world of Holub's wit, humor, and subtextual subtlety, the "puppet poems" arose out of the poet's feeling for fantasy and whimsy as well as for the indigenous Czech folk tradition.

Among Holub's many expressed thoughts on poetry, perhaps the most revealing are these, from the collection *Although*: "Certainly a poem is only a game./Certainly a poem exists only at the moment of origin and at the moment of reading. And at best in the shadow play of memory./ . . . But in its aimlessness, in its desperate commitment to the word, in its primal order of birth and rebirth, a poem remains the most general guarantee that we can still do something against emptiness, that we haven't given in but are giving ourselves to something."

Translations: *Although,* trans. Ian Milner and Jarmila Milner (London: Cape, 1971); *The Dimension of the Present Moment: Essays,* ed. David Young (London: Faber and Faber, 1990); *The Fly,* trans. Ewald Osers (Newcastle upon Tyne: Bloodaxe, 1987); *Intensive Care: Selected and New Poems* (Oberlin, Ohio: Oberlin College Press, 1996); *The Jingle Bell Principle,* trans. James Naughton (Newcastle upon Tyne: Bloodaxe, 1992); *Notes of a Clay Pigeon,* trans. Jarmila Milner and Ian Milner (London: Secker & Warburg, 1977); *On the Contrary and Other Poems,* trans. Ewald Osers (Newcastle upon Tyne: Bloodaxe, 1984); *Poems Before and After: Collected English Translations,* trans. Ian Milner, Jarmila Milner, Ewald Osers, and George Theiner (Newcastle upon Tyne: Bloodaxe, 1990); *The Rampage,* trans. David Young, Dana Hábová, and Rebekah Bloyd (London: Faber and Faber, 1997); *Sagittal Section: Poems New and Selected,* trans. Stuart Friebert and Dana Hábová (Oberlin, Ohio: Oberlin College Press, 1980); *Selected Poems,* trans. Ian Milner and George Theiner (Harmondsworth: Penguin, 1967); *Supposed to Fly: A Sequence from Pilsen,* trans. Ewald Osers (Newcastle upon Tyne, Bloodaxe, 1996); *Vanishing Lung Syndrome* (Oberlin, Ohio: Oberlin College Press, 1990). SOUND RECORDING: Sound recordings of poetry and other readings by Holub during his visits to the United States are available: *Poetry Reading* (New York: Academy of American Poets, 1979); *Poetry Reading* (Cambridge, Mass.: Woodberry Poetry Room, Harvard University, 1982); *Poetry and Science* (Cambridge, Mass.: Woodberry Poetry Room, Harvard University, 1982); *Poetry Reading* (Cambridge, Mass.: Woodberry Poetry Room, Harvard University, 1991).

Höntsch, Ursula (b. 1934) German novelist and journalist. Höntsch was born in Frankenstein, Lower Silesia, but resettled in Saxony in 1945 after World War II when most of the German population of Silesia was compelled to leave after the area was ceded to Poland. In 1952 she moved to Potsdam, where she studied commerce before earning a degree in journalism at Berlin's Humboldt University in 1964. From 1968 to 1973, she pursued graduate studies in history. The book with which she made her relatively late literary debut in 1985, *Wir, Flüchtlingskinder* (We, The Children of Refugees), proved such a huge success that by 1991 six editions had been published. Although intended as a novel based on her own experiences as the child of Germans expelled from Silesia, the work drew heavily on Höntsch's training as a journalist and has a distinctly journalistic character. What enhanced interest in it, apart from the novelty of the naive and unbiased perspective of a child, was the fact that in the German Democratic Republic at the time, writing on the subject of the German expulsion from Silesia was a virtual taboo in light of the East German policy of developing close relations with the neighboring communist state of Poland. Höntsch pursued the same theme in her next book, *Wir sind keine Kinder mehr* (We Are No Longer Children, 1990), which is devoted to the subsequent fate of her heroine, Marianna Hönow, in the GDR. However, the work lacks the feeling of authenticity and the unique point of view of the first book, and comes across as a not entirely successful attempt to eschew journalistic techniques in favor of a more literary narrative. In 1992 Höntsch edited a Silesian reader titled *Mir bleibt mein Lied: Schlesisches Lesebuch* (My Song Remains with Me: A Silesian Reader) and in 1993 published a somewhat similarly designed reader, *Was ist des Deutschen Vaterland: Ein deutsch–deutsches Lesebuch* (What Is the German's Fatherland: A German–German Reader). This is a large collection of writings on Germany: its history, culture, and politics from the World War II period to the fall of the GDR and the reunification of the two German states, by a wide variety of German writers. Höntsch edited the book with Olav Münzberg (b. 1938), a fellow Silesian. In their preface to the book, the editors point out that it was begun in East Germany in 1990 and finished in a reunited Germany.

Horák, Jozef (1907–1974) Slovak novelist. Horák made his literary debut with a wartime historical novel, *Zlaté Mesto* (The Golden City, 1942), a sprawling work to which he published a sequel in 1968 under the title *Smrť kráča k Zlátnemu mestu* (Death on Its Way to the Golden City). His next publication was the story collection *Zahmlený návrat* (The Beclouded Return, 1946), which was faulted for anachronistic traditionalism. The following year, however, Horák came out with the novel generally considered his most important work of prose fiction, *Hory mlčia* (The Mountain Forests Are Silent, 1947), a lyricized depiction of the growth of Slovak resistance to the Germans, culminating in the Slovak National Uprising of July 1944. It was followed by other novels set among the Slovak mining communities he knew so well in terms of his own background: *Šachty* (Shafts, 1953); *Rudniki* (Miners, 1954); *Horou pieseň šumí . . . : Román o živote Jozefa Dekreta Matejovie* (A Song Rustles Through the Woods . . . : A Novel About the Life of Jozef Dekret Matejová, 1956); *Pionerske srdce* (Pioneer Heart, 1957); *Šašovský hradný pán* (The Castle Jester, 1973); and *Volanie lesa* (The Woods Call, 1977). After his first collection of short stories, *Zahmlený návrat*, Horák published another four: *Povesti* (Stories, 1969); *Návraty* (Homecomings, 1973); *Sestry-blízence* (Sisters-Neighbors, 1981); and *Povesti spod Sitna* (Stories from Sitno, 1987). He was also the author of a collection of essays, *Na baňu klopajú . . . : Rozprávky* (They're Rapping Against the Mine . . . : Essays, 1954). Although his novels and stories about Slovak miners have considerable local color and a certain sociocultural interest, Horák will best be remembered for his novel of the Slovak resistance during World War II: *Hory mlčia*.

Hrabal, Bohumil (1914–1996) Czech novelist, short-story writer, poet, and screenwriter. Born in Brno-Židenice, Hrabal studied law at Charles University in Prague from 1934 to 1939. He obtained his doctorate after World War II, in 1946. Although he began his literary career with small romantic poems, several of which first appeared in the Nymburk *Občanské listy* in 1937 to 1939, he became a full-time writer only in 1963. Before then, he worked at a wide variety of jobs, including in the Polda steelworks (1949–1954), as a packer in a paper-collecting plant (1954–1959), and as a stagehand in a theater. His manual labor experiences are reflected in stories, for example, in the collection *Inzerát na dům, ve kterém už nechci bydlet* (An Advertisement for the

House I Don't Want to Live in Anymore, 1965), which originally was to have been published in 1959 under the title *Skřivánci na niti* (Skylarks on a String), but was banned. His first real poem, *Krásná Poldi* (Beautiful Poldi, 1950), was later reworked as prose. Hrabal also wrote the film script for the internationally celebrated Czech film about World War II, *Ostře sledované vlaky* (*Closely Watched Trains*), which was published as a novella in 1965.

Although previously critical of the communist regime for its cultural policies, Hrabal aroused considerable controversy when he recanted his dissidence during a television appearance. However, his ideological about-face again permitted works by him to be published by the state publishing houses (albeit in censored form). At the same time, he published the uncensored versions of his works in samizdat. *Skřivánek na niti* (Lark on a String), a collection of stories originally scheduled for publication in 1959, was delayed for political reasons but brought out in 1963 under a new title, *Perlička na dně* (Pearl on the Bottom). It was followed chronologically by one of his best-known collections of stories, *Pábitelé* (loosely translated as The Crazies, 1964), which gives ample evidence of Hrabal's fondness for the eccentric and grotesque and his great skill with language. Most of Hrabal's subsequent works were first published in samizdat editions. They include *Taneční hodiny pro starší a pokročilé* (*Dancing Lessons for the Advanced of Age*), which Hrabal wrote in 1946 but which went through extensive revisions before appearing in print in 1964; *Postřižiny* (Croppings), published in samizdat in 1970; *Obsluhoval jsem anglického krále* (*I Served the King of England*), published in samizdat in 1971 and in book form in Cologne in 1980; *Nežny barbar* (The Gentle Barbarian), published in samizdat in 1974; *Automat svět* (Automaton World, 1974; translated as *The Death of Mr. Baltisberger*), a collection of

two dozen short stories, including such favorites as "A Prague Nativity," "The Death of Mr. Baltisberger," and "The World Cafeteria"; *Městečko, kde se zastavil čas* (*The Little Town Where Time Stopped*), published in samizdat in 1974 and in book form in Innsbruck in 1978, a first-person reminiscence about his family in a small town during World War II; *Příliš hlučná samota* (*Too Loud a Solitude*, 1976); *Proluky* (Vacant Sites), published in samizdat in 1985 and in book form in Toronto and Cologne in 1986; *Pražská ironie* (Prague Irony), published in samizdat in 1986; *Životopis trochu jinak* (Autobiography, a Little Different), published in samizdat in 1986; *Svatby v domě: Dívčí románek* (Weddings in the House: A Girls' Novel), published in samizdat and in book form in Toronto in 1987; and *Vita nuova*, published in samizdat and in book form in Toronto in 1987.

One of his earliest works, *Dancing Lessons for the Advanced of Age* typifies Hrabal's earthiness and robust humor. It is narrated in the first person—a favorite Hrabal technique—by a shoemaker who reminisces about World War I and, especially, about his relations with women through the years. *Too Loud a Solitude* is also a first-person narration, this time by a man named Hanta, who for thirty-five years has worked a big compressing machine in a basement full of flies and rats. A heavy beer drinker, Hanta is also a thinker with a great reverence for books. At a certain point he concocts a private joke: he will sanctify every bale he makes either by plastering the outside with some artistic reproduction or by concealing inside it an open volume of Kant, Erasmus, or another of his favorite authors. Later in the novel, he visits a new compacting plant and sees how indifferent workers pulp whole printings of books. To Hanta, a lover of books, it is tantamount to the end of life. The obvious allegorical nature of the story is inescapable.

Another Hrabal favorite is *I Served the King of England*, a tragicomic, picaresque allegory of twentieth-century Czech history as lived and narrated by a short hotel busboy-become-waiter, Dítě ("child"), at the Golden Prague hotel in the 1930s. The novel is full of irony, with each hotel Dítě works in representing a different phase of Czech history. During World War II, the pragmatic Dítě shifts his allegiance to the Germans and marries a German woman who bears him a brain-dead child. When the communists come to power, he loses the big hotel he has built in fulfillment of his dreams.

A collection of Hrabal's essays was published in 1970 under the title *Domácí úkoly* (Homework), and in 1979 a volume of his early prose fiction from 1944 to 1953 was issued as *Tři teskné grotesky* (Three Wistful Grotesques).

Literature: Monika Zgustlová, *V rajské zahradě trpkých plodů: O životě a díle Bohumila Hrabala* (Prague: Mladá fronta, 1997), a good popularized Czech survey of Hrabal's life and career broken up into a large number of small segments; George Gibian, "The Haircutting and I Waited on the King of England: Two Recent Works by Bohumil Hrabal," in *Czech Literature Since 1956: A Symposium*, ed. William E. Harkins and Paul I. Trensky (New York: Bohemica, 1980), 74–90.

Translations: *Closely Watched Trains: A Film* (New York: Simon and Schuster, 1971); *Dancing Lessons for the Advanced of Age*, trans. Michael Henry Heim (New York: Harcourt Brace Jovanovich, 1995); *The Death of Mr. Baltisberger*, trans. Michael Henry Heim (Garden City, N.Y.: Doubleday, 1975); *I Served the King of England*, trans. Paul Wilson (San Diego: Harcourt Brace Jovanovich, 1989); *The Little Town Where Time Stood Still*, trans. James Naughton (London: Abacus, 1993), which also contains Naughton's translation of "Cutting It Short" (1976); *Too Loud a Solitude* (San Diego: Harcourt Brace Jovanovich, 1990); *Total Fears:*

Letters to Dubenka, trans. James Naughton (Prague: Twisted Spoon, 1998).

Hristov, Boris (b. 1945) Bulgarian poet and prose writer. Perhaps the best known of the generation of poets who emerged in the 1970s and 1980s, Hristov made his literary debut in the collection *Trimi mladi poeti: Parush Parushev, Ekaterina Tomova, Boris Hristov* (Three Young Poets: Parush Parushev, Ekaterina Tomova, Boris Hristov, 1975). He subsequently published four separate volumes of verse, notable especially for his indifference to ideology and his flair for metaphor: *Cherna kutiia* (The Black Box, 1988); *Krilete na vestitelia* (*The Wings of the Messenger*, 1991); *Dumi & grafiti* (*Words & Graphite*, 1991), with Iana Levieva; and *Vecheren trompet; Chesten krust* (Evening Trumpet; The Upright Cross, 2000). Hristov has also published a volume of stories, *Sliapoto kuche* (The Mole, 1990), and the novel *Smurtni petna* (Dead Spots, 1990), both of which are experimental in nature and blur the boundaries between poetry and prose. Much of Hristov's literary activity is represented by his editorship of several anthologies of Bulgarian literature. In 1974 he published an anthology of Bulgarian lyrics from Khristo Botev to Aleksandur Vutimski; in 1994, an anthology of Bulgarian folk lyrics; and in 1995, an anthology of Bulgarian folk and oral literature and an anthology of Bulgarian stories from Ivan Vazov to Emilian Stanev. The year 1995 also saw the publication of a book by him on the political trial of the revolutionary Traicho Kostov (1897–1949). Like many other Eastern European writers, Hristov participated in the International Writers Forum in Iowa. He has also given lectures and readings in the United States and in a number of European cities.

Translations: *The Wings of the Messenger*, trans. Roland Flint, Betty Grinberg, and Lyubomir Nicolov (Sofia: Petrikov, 1991), a Bulgarian–English edition; *Words &*

Graphite, trans. Betty Grinberg and Roland Flint (Varna: Andina, 1991); *Words on Words,* trans. Betty Grinberg, Roland Flint, and Lyubomir Nicolov (Sofia: Petrikov, 1992), a Bulgarian–English edition of *Dumi vurhu drugi dumi;* four poems, trans. Roland Flint, in *Poets of Bulgaria,* ed. William Meredith (Greensboro, N.C.: Unicorn, 1985), 52–55; six poems, trans. Robert Pinsky and William Jay Smith, in *Window on the Black Sea: Bulgarian Poetry in Translation,* ed. Richard Harteis, in collaboration with William Meredith (Pittsburgh: Carnegie Mellon University Press, 1992), 33–40.

Hristozov, Nikolai (b. 1931) Bulgarian poet, novelist, and essayist. Hristozov was born in Dimitrovgrad, graduated from secondary school in Haskovo in 1948, and then studied Bulgarian literature at Sofia University, receiving his degree in 1953. He taught Bulgarian literature in Sofia for two years (1952–1954) before assuming a series of editorial positions: editor of the literary section of Radio Sofia (1954–1964; editor in chief, 1964–1967); assistant editor in chief of the journal *Obzor* (1967–1972); assistant editor in chief of the journal, *Septemvri* (1972–1984); editor in chief of *Obzor* (from 1988). From 1979 to 1984, Hristozov served also as assistant chairman of the Bulgarian Writers Union. Hristozov established his literary reputation initially and primarily as a lyrical poet of broad humanistic concerns—the fate of humanity and the planet, environmental concerns, the need for love, universal justice, and national pride. He was always a politically correct poet under the communist regime, not challenging established canons, promoting the appropriate international issues as well as the Party's official literary platform. Hristozov has published ten books of poetry: *Purvi pesni* (First Poems, 1958); *Znamenata ne tezhat* (The Banners Are Not Heavy, 1965); *Devetnadeset pesni za Tsvetan Zangov i edna za nas* (Nineteen Poems for Tsvetan Zangov and One for Us, 1966); *Bdenie* (The Vigil, 1969); *Tretata planeta* (The Third Planet, 1971); *Raneno mulchanie* (Wounded Silence, 1975); *Bitka za migove* (The Battle for Seconds, 1976); *Granitsite na optimizma* (The Boundaries of Optimism, 1978), a volume of selected lyrics; *Sniag v gnezdoto* (Snow in the Nest, 1981); and *Zemia bez vuzdukh* (The Earth Without Air, 1989). Hristozov's prose comprises mainly a series of documentary novels built around key junctures and personalities in Bulgarian history and meant to serve as universal exemplars. These books include *Dulgut da zhiveesh* (The Duty to Live, 1967); *Po diriata na bezsledno izcheznalite* (On the Trail of the Missing, 1972), an oft-reprinted book; and *Garnizonnoto strelbishte* (The Garrison Shooting Range, 1983). In his administrative position at the Writers Union, Hristozov was one of the editors of such Party-sponsored conferences and subsequent publications as *Suvremennata tema i literaturniiat protses: Materiali ot tretata natsionalna konferentsiia na suiuza na bulgarskite pisateli, 28–29 Noembri 1974 g.* (Contemporary Theme and Literary Process: Materials from the Third National Conference of the Bulgarian Writers Union, 28–29 November 1974) and *Narod, rodina, partiia: Poetichna kniga* (Nation, Fatherland, Party: A Book of Poetry, 1981), which were published by the Party publishing house.

Translations: Three poems, trans. William Meredith, in *Poets of Bulgaria,* ed. William Meredith (Greensboro, N.C.: Unicorn, 1985), 48–50; three poems, trans. William Meredith, in *Window on the Black Sea: Bulgarian Poetry in Translation,* ed. Richard Harteis, in collaboration with William Meredith (Pittsburgh: Carnegie Mellon University Press, 1992), 132–34.

Hrúz, Pavel (b. 1941) Slovak novelist. Hrúz was born in Banska Bystrica and studied at the electrotechnical faculty in Bratislava. He has long been employed as a technician in the constructiuon industry in his hometown. Hrúz made his literary debut with *Dokumenty o výhľadoch* (Documents About Outlooks) in 1966. This was followed two years later by his book *Okultizmus* (Occultism), actually a collection of fourteen short stories called "seances" that are mostly in a lighter vein and intended to illustrate various facets of occult experience, including telepathy, telekinesis, clairvoyance, second sight, and hyperamnesia. After *Okultizmus*, Hrúz published nothing for over twenty years, but returned to print in 1990 with his generally well received but in some ways puzzling novel *Chliev a hry* (Stable and Games). Intended doubtless as a revelation of the power and influence of the communist regime and its absurdities, the text tends to deflect attention away from its theme to its composition. The book is divided into four sections. In the first, a footnote extends for the entire twenty-seven pages of the section. In the second, lines in italics alternate with underlined passages in italics. The text of the third section is broken up by interpolated passages in boldface, all in capitals, while other lines of the text appear just in boldface. And in the fourth part, a number of lines of what appear to be computer-programming text are interspersed throughout the chapter. In his most recent work, *Bystrica . . . tom* (Bystrica . . . Back Then, 2000), Hrúz uses anecdotes, little stories, and dialogue to pay homage to the past of his native town.

Huchel, Peter Helmut (1903–1981) German poet, radio scriptwriter, and editor. Born in Berlin the son of an official in the Prussian Ministry of Religious Affairs, Huchel became best known for his exquisite lyric poetry and for his editorship of *Sinn und Form,* the most famous and respected literary journal in the history of the German Democratic Republic. Wounded during the Kapp Putsch of 1920, Huchel shared hospital quarters with ordinary workers, conversations with whom played a decisive role in his early acceptance of communism. After receiving his high-school diploma in 1923, he briefly studied literature and philosophy in Berlin, Vienna, and Freiburg. He published his first poetry in 1924 in the journal *Die Kunstblätter* and then for a time collaborated with *Literarische Welt.* He next became a writer for Radio Berlin, which broadcast nineteen of his radio plays between 1933 and 1940. At first regarded favorably by Nazi literary critics, Huchel nevertheless withdrew from publication his first volume of poems, *Der Knabenteich* (The Boy's Pond, 1933), lest its celebration of youth and his native landscape lend itself to interpretation in terms of Nazi ideology. Huchel was mobilized in 1940, served on the eastern front, and was captured by the Soviets in 1945. However, he was released that year and entrusted with the responsibility of setting up an editorial board for the transmission of radio plays in East Berlin. In 1948 Huchel published a collection of verse under the title *Gedichte* (Poems), which included seventeen texts from his earlier *Der Knabenteich* and other poems of diametrically opposite character. Thanks to the intervention of the influential literary figure Johannes R. Becher, Huchel was offered the editorship of *Sinn und Form* in 1949. Under Huchel's direction, the journal gained international prestige. But because of his opening up the pages of the journal to avantgarde and experimental writers—despite *Sinn und Form*'s outward Marxist orthodoxy—Huchel ran afoul of the authorities and was dismissed from his position in late 1962. After nine years of "inner exile," during which it was impossible for him to publish anything in the GDR, Huchel was allowed to immigrate to West Germany in 1972.

Even before he left the GDR, Huchel had begun publishing in West Germany. His poetry collections *Chausseen* (Highways, 1963) and *Die Sternenreuse: Gedichte, 1925–1947* (The Star Trap: Poems, 1925–1947, 1967) had basically a retrospective character. In such later volumes of poetry as *Gezählte Tage* (Numbered Days, 1972); *Der Tod des Budners* (The Death of Budner, 1976); *Unbewohnbar die Trauer* (You Can't Get Used to Sorrow, 1978), published in Saint Gall, Switzerland; and *Die neunte Stunde* (The Ninth Hour, 1979), the influence of Johannes Bobrowski and a "landscapist" such as Heinz Czechowski is discernible. Several poets wrote poems in Huchel's honor, among them Wolf Biermann, Stephan Hermlin, Günter Kunert, and Reiner Kunze. A two-volume edition of Huchel's collected works, edited by the Huchel specialist Axel Vieregg, was published by Suhrkamp of Frankfurt am Main in 1984.

Literature: Stephen Parker, *Peter Huchel: A Literary Life in Twentieth-Century Germany* (Bern: Peter Lang, 1998); Uwe Schoor, *Das geheime Journal der Nation: Die Zeitschrift "Sinn und Form": Chefredakteur, Peter Huchel, 1949–1962* (Berlin: Peter Lang, 1992).

Translations: *The Garden of Theophrastus and Other Poems,* trans. Michael Hamburger (Manchester, Eng.: New Carcanet, 1983; Dublin: Raven Arts, 1983), a German–English edition; *Selected Poems,* trans. Michael Hamburger (Cheadle, Eng.: Carcanet, 1974).

Huelle, Paweł (b. 1957) Polish novelist, short-story writer, and critic. A native of the port city of Gdańsk, which forms the background of most of his writing, Huelle, a one-time journalist for Solidarity, made his literary debut with the novel *Waiser Dawidek* (1987; translated as *Who Was David Weiser?*). The novel won the prestigious Kościelski Prize and has been translated into several languages. Huelle's first collection of short stories appeared under the title *Opowiadania na czas przeprowadzki* (Stories

for a Stroll, 1991; translated as *The Moving House*). A gifted writer of considerable imaginative power, Huelle inhabits the domain of the unusual, mysterious, and puzzling, with overtones of the magical and supernatural. In *Who Was David Weiser?* the nature and significance of his titular character is strange and elusive.

A frail young Jewish boy in an otherwise overwhelmingly Polish landscape, he is rescued from a beating by a bunch of twelve-year-old boys by a local Polish girl named Elka, a fascinating character who radiates sex appeal. She introduces the boys to David's seemingly magical powers, including levitation. A crack shot obsessed with demolition, David has a hoard of salvaged Russian and German weapons. His would-be tormentors now see him in an entirely different light. Toward the end of the novel, in a series of mishaps, an explosion apparently set off by David wounds the narrator, who in a subsequent interrogation is at a loss to explain it and the disappearance without a trace of David and Elka. Set in 1957 (the year of Huelle's birth), *Who Was David Weiser?* paints a vivid, if grim, picture of Gdańsk in the early years of postwar communist reconstruction, focusing mainly on its more squalid sides. With the wholesale destruction of the once enormous Jewish community of Poland in World War II, Huelle's David Weiser may represent the "magical Jew" of postwar Polish literature, a purely artistic construct freed from the anchors of social reality.

The seven stories in *The Moving House* are linked by the narrator, who grows from childhood to young manhood as the sequence progresses, and by recurring members of his family. Although the stories appear at first rooted in everyday reality, they move seamlessly into the realm of the surreal, driven by the youthful narrator's great inquisitiveness and vivid imagination. In perhaps the most intriguing of the stories,

"Snails, Puddles, Rain," the narrator, as a boy, goes on expeditions with his unemployed father, a ship engineer, to catch snails for profit. They find their most abundant supply of snails in local cemeteries where the snails appeared to stick out their horns ahead of them to catch the voices of the dead. In the story's eerie climax, father and son witness the spectacle of hundreds of snails marching up a hill at twilight in a vain ritualistic effort to scale the slippery sides of a gigantic stone at the top. Underlying Huelle's stories as well as *Who Was David Weiser?* is a perceptible yearning to know the past, specifically in this case that of Danzig/Gdańsk, to reassemble it as best one can from the fragments left by the ravages of war and dislocation that turned Poland into the "moving house" of Huelle's title. Huelle's most recent publication is *mercedes-benz: z listów do hrabala* (Mercedes-Benz: From Letters to Hrabal, 2001), a humorous, nostalgic, essentially autobiographical tale about the narrator's deflating experience trying to learn how to drive a car in the early 1990s and his recollections of the fate of his grandfathers' Citroën and Mercedes. The work is conceived in the form of a long letter to the Czech writer Bohumil Hrabal, who once wrote a short story on the subject of his own experiences with a motorcycle.

Translations: *The Moving House*, trans. Michael Kandel (New York: Harcourt Brace Jovanovich, 1995); *Who Was David Weiser?*, trans. Michael Kandel (New York: Harcourt Brace Jovanovich, 1992); "Mina," trans. Antonia Lloyd-Jones, in *Description of a Struggle: The Vintage Book of Contemporary Eastern European Writing*, ed. Michael March (New York: Vintage, 1994), 65–79.

Hykisch, Anton (b. 1932) Slovak novelist and short-story writer. Hykisch's first prose work was *Sen vchádza do stanice* (Dream Pulls into the Station, 1961), which takes place on a single night at a railroad station when the probable derailing of a train in unusual circumstances is halted by young people who represent the collective "hero" of the novel. Similarly, a young engineer working in a transportation company in Hykisch's next novel, *Krok do neznáma* (A Step into the Unknown, 1963), learns the hard way to distinguish principle from practice. Hykisch's interest in young people is also reflected in a middling collection of short stories, *Stretol som t'a* (I Met You, 1963), in which the device of the internal monologue is used to explore the problems of the young in work and love. Love is also at the center of his once popular novel *Nad'a* (Nadia, 1964), about the romance between a young female economist and a librarian. Three slight works followed *Nad'a* before the publication of Hykisch's acknowledged masterpiece, *Čas majstrov* (The Age of the Masters, 1977): *Námestie v Mähringu* (A Place in Mähring, 1965), about a Slovak gymnast who tries and fails to immigrate to the West but is later able to travel there and confront the disparity between his youthful illusions and reality; *Kanada nie je "kanada"* (Canada Is Not "Canada," 1968), a work of reportage about the Montreal World's Fair; and *Volanty do niebies* (Steering Wheels to Heaven, 1975), on the subject of racing cars and their drivers. *Čas majstrov*, the work that made Hykisch's reputation, is an impressive two-volume historical novel about a late-fifteenth- and early-sixteenth-century painter who lived in the Upper Hungarian mining towns and signed himself MS. The novel's sociopolitical dimension develops out of a rebellion of exploited miners and the painter's embrace of their cause. After *Čas majstrov*, Hykisch returned to the subject of young people and their problems in two novels with the same female protagonist: *Vzt'ahy* (Relationships, 1978) and *Túžba* (Desire, 1980). The "heroine" of the works is a young engineer, Magda Šimečková, who embodies Hykisch's views of the communist-style liberated Slovak woman. In 1984 Hykisch published his second major historical novel, *Milujte královnú!* (Love the Queen!, 1984). It is set during the reign of Maria Theresa and, while focused primarily on the empress, succeeds in situating her in a broad social, economic, and political context that brings eighteenth-century Central Europe to life. Hykisch's interest in the genre of science fiction comes through clearly in such subsequent works as the collection of stories and novellas *Dobre utajený mozog* (A Well-Concealed Brain, 1979), in which the focus is mainly on the problem of humans in a technologically overdeveloped society; *Atómové leto* (Atomic Summer, 1988); and *Obrana tajomstiev* (In Defense of Secrets, 1990).

I

Ieronim, Ioana (real name Ioana Brânduş; b. 1947) Romanian poet and translator. One of the more impressive Romanian poets to emerge in the late 1970s and early 1980s, Ieronim was born in Rîsnov, where she graduated from high school in 1965. She then studied English and Romanian literatures at Bucharest University, from which she received her degree in 1970. After 1975 she was employed for several years as an editor for foreign encyclopedias at the Scientific and Encyclopedic Publishing House in Bucharest. She served as cultural attaché to the Romanian Embassy in Washington, D.C., from 1992 to 1996, and is currently program director of the Fulbright Commission for Romanian–U.S. Exchanges. Ieronim made her debut as a poet on the pages of *Luceafărul* in 1972 and came out with her first volume of poetry, *Vară timpurie* (Early Summer), in 1979. This was followed by *Proiecte de mitologie* (Plans for a

Mythology, 1981); *Cortina* (The Curtain, 1983); *Egloga* (Eclogue, 1984); *Poeme* (Poems, 1986); and *Luni dimineaţa* (Monday Morning, 1987). Ieronim's delicate, subtly nuanced poetry is a world of small things, seemingly prosaic and insignificant. In 1992 Ieronim published what some consider to be her most important work, the unrhetorical but poignant *Triumful paparudei* (*Fool's Triumph*), a large collection of prose poems representing an autobiographical recollection of childhood in a Transylvanian Saxon (German) community and the destruction of that community following the communist takeover of Romania. An active translator, Ieronim has published well-regarded translations of works by Joseph Conrad, the Danish writer Nils Peteresen, and the Dutch writer Simon Vestdijk. She has also published an excellent translation into Romanian of *Alien Candor: Selected Poems, 1970–1996* (*Candoare străină: Poeme alese, 1970–1996*, 1997) by the Romanian-American writer Andrei Codrescu (b. 1946), who has lived in the United States since 1966 and writes almost exclusively in English. Ieronim received the *Luceafărul* Prize for her poetry in 1975.

Translations: *The Triumph of the Water Witch*, trans. Adam J. Sorkin with Ioana Ieronim (Newcastle upon Tyne: Bloodaxe, 2000), which is also available as *Triumful paparudei/Fool's Triumph*, trans. Georgiana Gălaţeănu-Fârnoaga and Sharon King (Piteşti: Paralela 45, 2000), a Romanian–English edition.

Ilica, Carolina (b. 1951) Romanian poet and translator. Ilica was born in the village of Vîrfurile, in the Arad district. She graduated from high school in Arad in 1971 and then studied philosophy at Bucharest University, from which she earned her degree in 1975. She published her first poems in the Arad daily, *Flacăra Roşie,* in 1966 and won the Nicolae Labiş Poetry Prize in 1968. Her first volume of poetry, *Neîmblînzită ca o stea lactee* (As Untamed as a Milky Way), appeared in 1974 and was awarded the debut prize of the Eminescu publishing house. Two other collections of poems followed in 1975 and 1977: *Cu împrumut mireasma tinereţii* (The Perfume of Youth on Loan) and *Dogoarea şi flacăra* (The Heat and the Flame). In 1982 and 1985, two volumes with the same title, *Tirania visului* (The Tyranny of the Dream), appeared, one in verse and the other in poetic prose. Another collection of poetry, *Ephemeris*, came out in 1987. Ilica writes mostly about love and relations between the sexes in a highly sensual and erotic way. Her poetry, which at times approaches the delicacy of the Pre-Raphaelites, is likened by some critics to that of Emily Dickinson. Ilica explores the whole range of amorous experience from the heights of ecstasy to the depths of despair. Melancholy, world-weariness, and hints of depression come to the fore in her more recent volume, *Ephemeris*. In collaboration with others, Ilica has also translated extensively from modern South Slavic literatures, principally Macedonian, and from Armenian. In 1981 she was one of the editors and translators of an anthology of classical and modern Armenian poetry.

Translations: Five poems in *15 Young Romanian Poets: An Anthology of Verse*, trans. and ed. Liliana Ursu (Bucharest: Eminescu, 1982), 43–50; seven poems in *Silent Voices: An Anthology of Contemporary Romanian Women Poets*, trans. Andrea Deletant and Brenda Walker (London: Forest, 1986), 103–10.

Ilkov, Ani (b. 1957) Bulgarian poet. Born in Ruzhintsi, about thirty miles south of Vidin in the northwestern corner of Bulgaria, Ilkov graduated from the English-language school in Vidin in 1975 and from Sofia University in 1984 with a degree in Bulgarian literature. From 1987 to 1990, he did postgraduate work in the field of folklore and literature, with an emphasis on the development of Bulgarian comic literature in the period 1800 to 1910. In 1990/1991, Ilkov was an editor at the newspaper *Demokratsiia* and, from 1991 to 1993, at *Literaturen vestnik*. In 1991 he was appointed an assistant professor in Bulgarian literature at Sofia University. Since 1992 Ilkov has been a member of the executive board of the Independent Literary Society and, in 1995/1996, served as deputy chairman of the Bulgarian Writers Association. Ilkov is the author of three collections of poems: *Polia i mostove* (Fields and Bridges, 1990); *Izvorut na groznohubavite: Pesni i umotvoreniia* (The Source of the Frightfully Beautiful People: Songs and Brainchildren, 1994); and *Etimologiki/Etymologies* (1996), a small volume of poems in Bulgarian with English translations. Ilkov is a highly fanciful, clever, and challenging poet inclined toward the surreal. In one poem, he imagines himself the tiny leaf of a male carnation perched on the edge of a female vase; in another, warm, living flowers thirst for rain and poetry; two blooming roses in a field become a lion's eyes and a lion's mane; robots and ships float above him and salute him. From "Triangular Lovers," a typical short poem:

> We are appalled by space
> unless we can fill it with objects.
> We are frightened by time
> unless we can dress it in events.
> Such geometeric nudity is persecuting
>   us
> as if
> a couple of triangles mate
> and give birth to a square.

Translations: *Etimologiki/Etymologiea* (Plovdiv: Zhanet-45, 1996), a small Bulgarian–English edition; eight poems in *Clay and Star: Contemporary Bulgarian Poets*, trans. and ed. Lisa Sapinkopf and Georgi Belev (Minneapolis: Milkweed, 1992), 215–23.

Illés, Endre (b. 1902) Hungarian short-story writer, essayist, and playwright. Although he had planned to pursue a medical career, Illés was strongly attracted to literature and became a well-known critic in the 1930s. Before long, he joined the staff of the literary journal *Nyugat*. Highly respected for the polish of his essay writing, Illés won no less a reputation for his many short stories, which are characterized by brevity, dramatic tension, and a keen interest in psychological motivation. His first volume of short stories, *Zsuzsa* (Susan), appeared in 1942. The most complete collection of his stories was published in 1966 under the title *100 történet* (100 Stories). Other collections by him include *Kettős kör* (Concentric Circles, 1962); *Szakadékok* (Precipices, 1969); *Szigorlat* (The Exam, 1969); *Örvények között* (Amid Whirlpools, 1975); and *Hamisjátékosok* (The Swindlers, 1975). A collection of plays was published in 1967 under the title *Színház* (Theater). A subsequent collection appeared in 1981 as *Kulisszák nélkül* (Without Backdrops). His essays have been collected in such volumes as *Krétarajzok* (Chalk Drawings, 1957); *Gellérthegyi éjszakák* (Gellért Hill Nights, 1965); *Írók, színészek, dilettánsok* (Writers, Actors, and Dilettantes, 1968); *Árnyékrajzok* (Shadow Pictures, 1972); and *Hármas könyv* (Tripartitum, 1971). A good representative collection of Illés's essays was published in 1979 under the title *Mestereim, barátaim, szerelmeim* (My Teachers, Friends, and Lovers). Illés has served as director of the important Budapest publishing house Szépirodalmi Könyvkiadó and was the recipient of a Kossuth Prize.

Translations: "Fear," trans. Rudolf Bilek, in *44 Hungarian Short Stories,* ed. Lajos Illés (Budapest: Corvina, 1979), 289–307; "Room 212," trans. Etelka Láczay, in *Present Continuous: Contemporary Hungarian Writing,* ed. István Bart (Budapest: Corvina, 1985), 156–63.

Illyés, Gyula (1902–1983) Hungarian poet, playwright, and prose writer. One of the finest of twentieth-century Hungarian poets, Illyés was born in Rácegrespuszta, in western Hungary. After his early schooling, he served in the army of the Hungarian Republic of Soviets under Béla Kun in 1919 and, after its suppression, sought refuge in France, where he lived from 1921 to 1926. His first volume of poems appeared in 1928, two years after his return to Hungary. In the 1930s Illyés was one of a number of writers and sociologists who took part in the village research movement, which produced a series of studies detailing the wretched conditions then prevailing in the countryside. Illyés's own contribution, the highly regarded *Puszták népe* (*The People of the Puszta,* 1936), was part autobiography, part sociology, and part literature. In 1962 Illyés published a sequel, *Ebéd a kastélyban* (Luncheon at the Mansion), the focus of which was the transformation of the *puszta* (the Hungarian plain) since his childhood. Before World War II, Illyés also became editor of the two most successful literary reviews of the period, *Nyugat* and *Magyar Csillag,* its successor.

Illyés's first post–World War II collection of poems was *Szembenézve* (Face to Face, 1947). A number of mostly retrospective volumes followed: *Illyés Gyula válogattot versei* (Gyula Illyés: Selected Poems, 1952); *Nem volt elég* (It Was Not Enough, 1962), selected poems; *A költő felel* (The Poet Replies, 1962), selected poems; *Poharaim* (My Drinking Glasses, 1967), collected poems; *Abbahagyott versek* (Unfinished Poems, 1971); *Haza a magasban: Összegyűjtött versek, 1920–1945* (In the High Country: Collected Poems, 1920–1945); *Teremteni: Összegyűjtött versek, 1946–1968* (To Create: Collected Poems, 1946–1968, 1973); *Minden lehet* (Anything Possible, 1973), a collection of new poems; *Konok kikelet* (Stubborn Spring, 1981), collected poems; *Szemben a támadással: Összegyűjtött versek, 1969–1981*

(Facing the Attack: Collected Poems, 1969–1981, 1984); and *Év: Versek 1944 szeptember–1945 szeptember* (A Year: Poems, September 1944–September 1945, 1985).

A traditional and accessible poet who was as much at home in longer as in shorter poems, Illyés wrote often of the countryside he knew so well from his own youth, of the poverty there, and yet the pleasure of the closeness to nature. In a number of his poems, the *puszta*, for all its poverty, is contrasted with the monotony, pretensions, and smugness of the more prosperous urban life, which Illyés often portrayed with humor and sarcasm. One of his most powerful poems, "One Sentence on Tyranny," which addresses tyranny in any form, first appeared during the Hungarian uprising of 1956.

A dramatist as well as a poet, Illyés published at least three collections of plays, including *Másokért egyedül* (Alone for Others, 1963); *Drámák* (Plays, 1969); and *Újabb drámák* (New Plays, 1974). An enthusiast of historical drama, Illyés wrote one of his better plays, *A tiszták* (The Pure Ones), about the suppression of the medieval Cathar heresy in southern France. Apart from his verse and dramatic works, Illyés published two volumes of collected essays; two volumes of translations; a volume of travel notes on France—*Franciaországi változatok* (Varieties of France, 1947)—a book about the Hungarian Romantic poet Petőfi Sándor (*Sándor Petőfi*, 1963), which has been translated into English; and several novels: *Hunok Parisban* (The Huns in Paris, 1946); *Két férfi* (Two Men, 1950); *Kharon ladikján vagy az öregedés tünetei: Esszé-regény* (The Barge of Charon or Signs of Growing Old: An Essay-Novel, 1969); *Beatrice apródjai* (Beatrice's Pages, 1979); and *Szentlélek karavánja* (Caravan of the Holy Spirit, 1987).

Literature: Thomas Kabdebo and Paul Tabori, eds., *A Tribute to Gyula Illyés* (Washington, D.C.: Occidental, 1968).

Translations: *The People of the Puszta*, trans. G. F. Cushing (Budapest: Corvina, 1967, 1979); *Sándor Petőfi*, trans. G. F. Cushing (Budapest: Corvina, 1973); *Selected Poems*, trans. and ed. Thomas Kabdebo and Paul Tabori (London: Chatto and Windus, 1971); *What Have You Almost Forgotten: Selected Poems of Gyula Illyés*, trans. William Jay Smith et al., ed. William Jay Smith (Willimantic, Conn.: Curbstone, 1999); nineteen poems, including a few longer texts, trans. William Jay Smith, Charles Tomlinson, and Daniel Hoffman, in *Modern Hungarian Poetry*, ed. Miklós Vajda (New York: Columbia University Press, 1977), 14–40.

Isaeva, Liudmila (1926–1991) Bulgarian poet. A native of the town of Provadiia, Isaeva completed high school and the Pedagogical Institute in Shumen in 1944 and 1948, respectively. After participating in the grand projects of the construction of the industrial city of Dimitrovgrad in 1947 and the Koprinka Dam in 1948/1949, she went to work with Radio Sofia from 1949 to 1955, and from 1964 to 1990 edited the poetry section of the Bulgarski pisatel publishing house. She committed suicide in 1991. A rather widely translated poet, Isaeva's published volumes of poetry include *Surtseto govori* (The Heart Speaks, 1957); *Istina* (Truth, 1967); *Ne pozvoliavaite sveta da ostariava* (Don't Let the World Grow Old, 1970); *Surtsevina* (The Very Core, 1975); *Izpoved* (Confession, 1976); *Stihotvoreniia* (Poems, 1978); *Sudba* (Fate, 1979); and *Chuvstva* (Feelings, 1986). She was also the author of *Lirichna biografiia* (Lyrical Biography, 1963) and *Pisma ot bialata kushta* (Letters from the White House, 1984), whose title refers to a hospital. Isaeva's is a very personal and often very feminine lyric poetry—many poems are narrated in the first person, and a number of them have the word "feminine" in the title. She has written about love, hurt, vulnerability, a woman's dignity, poetry as an escape from petty everyday trials, the good and bad in her own century (e.g., "XX vek" ["The Twentieth Century"] in *Chuvstva*), her discomfort with a society dominated by technology, her own sense of isolation and resignation, her nostalgia for Bulgaria when traveling, and her yearning for better understanding among people. Isaeva's poems are for the most part simple and straightforward in expression, usually short, with short lines, and often rhymed. Several of her poems have Russian and Polish themes based on her travels ("S dushteria mi v muzeia na Pushkin, ili maluk razgovor za slavata" ["With My Daughter in the Pushkin Museum, or a Short Conversation About Fame"], "Balada za Shopen" ["A Ballad About Chopin"], and "Tolstoiv Iasna poliana" ["Tolstoy in Yasnaya Polyana"] in *Chuvstva*).

Translations: Eight poems in *The Devil's Dozen: Thirteen Bulgarian Women Poets*, trans. Brenda Walker with Belin Tonchev, in collaboration with Svetoslav Piperov (London: Forest, 1990), 61–69.

Ivanov, Binio (1939–1998) Bulgarian poet. A compelling, if at times obscure, poet, Ivanov was born in the village of Barakovo, in the Rila Mountains, and was educated at the Industrial Institute in Sofia, from which he graduated in 1965. He worked in industry in Kiustendil, where he first broke into print. Ivanov published his first book of poetry, *Do drugata treva* (Until the New Grass), in 1973. His next book, *Nad poleto, sred nebeto* (Above the Field, Amid the Heavens), came out in 1979, followed by *Naviarno vechno* (Presumably Eternal, 1980); *Prirodi* (Still Lifes, 1985); *Puteshestvieto na babinite ochila* (The Journey of Granny's Spectacles, 1985), a volume of poems for children; *Stihotvoreniia* (Poems, 1989); *Si iskam zhivota* (I Want to Live, 1993); and *Chasut na uchastta* (The

Hour of Fate, 1998). A political dissident uncompromising in his hostility to the totalitarian system, Ivanov was a strikingly original poet. Whatever his subject, he possessed an uncanny ability to craft unusual metaphors. But the nature of his imagery and his tendency toward abstraction and experimentation—at times built around motifs borrowed from the folklore tradition—make him often a difficult poet despite the frequent ordinariness of his material.

Translations: Seven poems in *Clay and Star: Contemporary Bulgarian Poets,* trans. and ed. Lisa Sapinkopf and Georgi Belev (Minneapolis: Milkweed, 1992), 107–18.

Ivanova, Mirela (b. 1964) Bulgarian poet. Ivanova was born in Sofia, where she graduated from high school in 1981 with a strong background in German language. She earned a degree in Bulgarian literature from Plovdiv University in 1985. In 1987 she began working with *Literaturen front* and in 1988 became editor of the journal *Ikar*. Ivanova has published four volumes of verse: *Kameni krile* (Wings of Stone, 1985); *Samotna igra* (A Lonely Game, 1990); *Shepoti* (Whispers, 1990); and *Pamet za podrobnosti* (A Memory for Details, 1992). A lyrical poet with a keen sense of womanhood, its strengths and fragilities, whose themes are mostly endangered love, friendship, and loneliness, Ivanova conveys deep emotions in a calm and disciplined manner.

Translations: Five poems, trans. Josephine Jacobsen, in *Window on the Black Sea: Bulgarian Poetry in Translation,* ed. Richard Harteis, in collaboration with William Meredith (Pittsburgh: Carnegie Mellon University Press, 1992), 135–41.

Ivanovski, Srbo (b. 1928) Macedonian poet, short-story writer, and novelist. A native of Štip, in eastern Macedonia, Ivanovski graduated from Saints Cyril and Methodius University in Skope with a degree in the history of Yugoslav literature and the Macedonian language. He subsequently went to work for Skopje Radio and TV, where he has held several positions. Ivanovski has published nearly a dozen collections of poetry, which like his prose fiction reflect an intimacy with nature and a keen knowledge of rural Macedonian traditions: *Lirika* (Lyrics, 1950); *Želbi i megji: Lirska poema* (Desires and Boundaries: A Lyrical Poem, 1950); *Sredbi i razdelbi* (Meetings and Partings, 1953); *Beli krikovi* (White Screams, 1956); *Madjepsan patnik* (The Enchanted Traveler, 1966); *Sproti bregot* (Facing the Shore, 1967); *Pena od planinata* (Mountain Foam, 1971); *Bosi peperugi* (Barefoot Butterflies, 1987); *Gorčliv koren* (Bitter Root, 1994); *Celust na vremeto* (The Jaw of Time, 1996); and *Prsten na vremeto* (The Ring of Time, 1998). After bringing out a collection of stories in 1955 under the title *Žena na prozorecot* (The Woman in the Window, 1956), Ivanovski concentrated on the novel for the next several years, publishing such works as *Osameni* (The Lonely Ones) and *Martin Nunata*, both of which appeared in 1979; *Leonida trča okrvaven* (Leonida Runs Bleeding, 1980); *Dodeka go čekavme Andreja* (While Waiting for Andrea, 1990); *Mesto megju živite* (A Place Among the Living, 1990), a revised version of *Osameni* with a new title; *Balada za isčeznatite* (Ballad for Those Who Disappeared, 1995); and *Nepodobniot* (The Unsuitable One, 1997). In 1982 Ivanovski published his second collection of stories, *Koga tetin Klimente setase nad gradot* (When Uncle Clement Walked over the Town, 1982). Ivanovski's fiction brims with the earthy lore and mores of the Macedonian folk but shuns sentimentalism in favor of realistic depictions of hardship and loss. Some of his most interesting narratives are drawn from the lives of itinerant Macedonian craftsmen and other workers who wander far from home in search of work. Ivanovski's literary awards include the 13 November and Stale Popov prizes of Macedonia and the Branko Miljković Prize from Serbia.

Translations: "The Shirt," in *The Big Horse and Other Stories of Modern Macedonia,* ed. Milne Holton (Columbia: University of Missouri Press, 1974), 141–45; "The Ballad of a Fellow Without His Love," trans. A. Lenarčić, in *Introduction to Yugoslav Literature: An Anthology of Fiction and Poetry,* ed. Branko Mikasinovich, Dragan Milivojević, and Vasa D. Mihailovich (New York: Twayne, 1973), 626; "The City on My Palms," trans. Vasa D. Mihailovich, *Macedonian Review* 11 (1981): 84.

Ivasiuc, Alexandru (1933–1977) Romanian novelist. A major novelist of the 1960s and 1970s, Ivasiuc, the son of the geologist Leon Ivasiuc, was born in Sighetul Marmației and attended schools in Bucharest. From 1951 to 1956, he studied first philosophy and then medicine at Bucharest University, but was prevented from completing his degree program when he was arrested for organizing a meeting of medical-school students to protest the Soviet invasion of Hungary. He was sentenced to five years in prison. After his release and a period of required residence at the detention center of Bărăgan, he eventually settled in Bucharest, where he was employed as a chemist. From 1963 to 1968, he worked as a translator for the American Embassy in Bucharest. Ivasiuc published his first stories in *Gazeta literară* in 1964. Comfortable in English, he also published an essay on Faulkner and one on American prose. Ivasiuc's first novel, *Vestibul* (The Lobby), an intriguing psychological study of the central character, the much troubled Dr. Ilea, appeared in 1967 and won the award for prose of the Writers Union. His second novel, *Interval* (Interval), in essence a dark and turbulent family chronicle, came out in 1968 and won the award for prose of the review *România liter-*

ară. The same year, Ivasiuc and his wife, the journalist Tita Chiuper-Ivasiuc, were awarded a Ford Foundation grant to participate in the International Writing Program of the University of Iowa in Iowa City. While in the United States, Ivasiuc gave lectures on Romanian literature at Columbia University and at the University of California at Berkeley. He also stopped off in Great Britain and lectured at Oxford University on his return trip home. Back in Romania in 1968, Ivasiuc became editor in chief of the Cartea Româneasca publishing house and secretary of the Writers Union.

In 1969 Ivasiuc published the novel *Cunoaștere de noapte* (Night Exploration), about a bureaucrat whose terminal illness forces him to reevaluate his life, and the following year the novel *Păsările* (The Birds), in which a love affair collides with the fortunes of a family. One of his most effective works, the novella *Corn de vînătoare* (Hunting Horn), appeared in 1972. Set in a richly atmospheric sixteenth-century Transylvania, its main theme of the consolidation of power through political violence has obvious contemporary resonances. The principal character, Mihai, a kind of Eastern philosopher vexed by the vanity and transience of all "fine things," is nonetheless an expert stage manager of local history. During a hunt, he arranges for the massacre of the deposed princely family in order to consolidate his new master's rule of the khanate of Mara (northern Transylvania). After the murder, Mihai passes through moments of Macbethian anxiety, which only reconfirm his political cynicism. The story set the tone and method for much later Romanian political fiction. Ivasiuc subsequently published two volumes of essays, *Radicalitate și valoare* (Radicalism and Value, 1972) and *Pro domo* (Pro Domo, 1974), and three novels: *Apă* (Water, 1973), about revolution and perhaps Ivasiuc's weakest work; *Iluminari* (Illuminations, 1975), arguably Ivasiuc's best

novel in which an opportunistic scholar, years after achieving his career goals, has a sudden revelation of his own mediocrity and wants to free himself from further compromises; and *Racul* (The Crawfish, 1976), a political novel with an invented South American setting that, like *Corn de vînătoare,* deals with the nature of power.

Iwaszkiewicz, Jarosław (1894–1980) Polish novelist, poet, short-story writer, and essayist. One of the most formidable presences in twentieth-century Polish literature, and all but unknown in English, Iwaszkiewicz was born in Kalnik in Ukraine. Although he moved to Warsaw in 1918, the Ukrainian landscape and history left a deep impression on him and recur in his writings. From 1912 to 1918, Iwaszkiewicz studied law at Kiev University and music at the local conservatory. His love of music remained with him throughout his life and expressed itself in books and stories with musical subjects and themes. Iwaszkiewicz made his literary debut as a poet in 1915 on the pages of the Kiev monthly *Pióro* and collaborated with the Studya theater of Stanisława Wysocka (about which he published a book in 1963). After he resettled in Warsaw, he became one of the founders of the very important Skamander group of poets, who dominated the Polish poetic landscape in the 1920s. His first book of poetry, *Oktostychy* (Octostichs), appeared in 1919. It was followed by *Ucieczka do Bagdadu* (Escape to Baghdad, written 1916–1918); *Legendy i Demeter* (Legends and Demeter, written 1917–1918); and *Dionizje* (Dionysiacs, 1922). From 1920 to 1923, Iwaszkiewicz was director of the literary section of *Kurier Polski,* and from 1923 to 1925 served as marshal of the Polish parliament. When his term of office expired, he entered the diplomatic service and for the next twelve years held positions in the Polish embassies in Copenhagen and Brussels; he then became a press official in the Ministry of Foreign Affairs. During the German occupation in World War II, he was active in underground cultural life and when the war ended became editor in chief of the bimonthly *Życie Literackie* in Poznań. In 1947/1948, he was editor in chief of the weekly *Nowiny Literackie* in Warsaw, and in 1954 took on his most significant editorship, that of the monthly *Twórczość*, for many years the most important literary journal in Poland. For a number of years, Iwaszkiewicz was head of the Polish Writers Union, and in 1952 was elected a delegate to Parliament. His major writings before World War II, apart from his poetry, include *Hilary, syn buchaltera* (Hilary, Son of a Bookkeeper, 1923), which is essentially autobiographical; *Księżyc wschodzi* (The Moon Rises, 1924); *Czerwone tarcze* (Red Shields, 1934), a diffuse but entertaining novel about a Polish medieval prince and crusader who travels throughout Europe and the Middle East, enjoys extraordinary adventures, and upon his return home loses his throne; *Lato w Nohant* (Summer in Nohant, 1936), a three-act comedy based on the relationship between George Sand and Frédéric Chopin; and *Maskarada* (Masquerade, 1938), which was inspired by the final episode in the life of Pushkin.

After World War II, Iwaszkiewicz continued his active literary career, publishing a large number of works in different genres. Apart from many new editions of his prewar poetry and prose fiction, his major fictional undertaking was the three-part novel *Sława i chwała* (Glory and Vainglory, 1956, 1958, 1962), in which he traces the destinies of several decades of Polish intelligentsia in times of war and social upheaval. Iwaszkiewicz's major work of poetry in the postwar period was *Ody olimpijskie* (Olympic Odes, 1948), written in honor of the Olympic Games held in London in 1948. It was honored with a prize in 1948 and won a prize at the Games. Iwaszkiewicz also pub-

lished several collections of stories, one of the best of which was *Nowa miłość i inne opowiadania* (A New Love and Other Stories, 1946). This contains for the first time two of his best prose texts, "Bitwa na równinie Sedgemoor" ("Battle on the Plain of Sedgemoor," written 1942) and "Matka Joanna z Aniołów" ("Mother Joan of the Angels," written 1943), one of his most widely translated works, about the nuns of a seventeenth-century French convent (Loudun) who were possessed by the devil (the same subject of Aldous Huxley's later *The Devils of Loudun*). An indefatigable traveler throughout his life, Iwaszkiewicz was one of the foremost Polish travel writers of the twentieth century, and this aspect of his work has commanded possibly the greatest attention among Polish scholars. Italy inspired the stories in *Nowele włoskie* (Italian Tales, 1947), for which Iwaszkiewicz was awarded the Odrodzenie literary prize in 1947, and *Podróże do Włoch* (Italian Travels, 1977). Sicily, which held a strong appeal for him, was the subject of *Książka o Sycylii: Wspomnienia i szkice* (A Book About Sicily: Reminiscences and Sketches, 1956). In 1978 Iwaszkiewicz also published a book of poems under the title *Śpiewnik włoski* (Italian Songbook). An extended trip through South America provided the inspiration for *Listy z podróży do Ameryki Południowej* (Letters from a Journey to South America, 1954). The book is particularly interesting for its glimpses into the life of Polish émigré communities in South America that Iwaszkiewicz visited. Lest he ignore his own country, Iwaszkiewicz also published a travel book about Poland, *Podróże do Polski* (Travels in Poland, 1977).

A talented musician and a keen student of music and musicians, Iwaszkiewicz wrote several books on musical subjects, including two on the Polish composer Karol Szymanowski (1882–1937), with whom he collaborated on several occasions in the

1920s: *Spotkania z Szymanowskim* (Meetings with Szymanowski, 1947) and *"Harnasie" Karola Szymanowskiego* (The "Harnasie" [Ballet-Pantomime] of Karol Szymanowski, 1964); *Chopin* (1949), a monograph that has been translated into several languages; *Jan Sebastian Bach* (1951), a biographical sketch; *Pisma muzyczne* (Writings on Music, 1958); and *Muzyka wieczorem* (Music in the Evening, 1980). Iwaszkiewicz is also the author of several books about literature. They include five collections of reviews: *Cztery szkice literackie* (Four Literary Sketches, 1953); *Rozmowy o książki* (Conversations About Books, 1961); *Rozmowy o książkach* (Conversations About Books, 1968), covering the years 1961 to 1966; *Ludzie i książki* (People and Books, 1971, 1983); and *Szkice o literaturze skandynawskiej* (Sketches on Scandinavian Literature, 1977). He also wrote two books on the theater: *Teatr Polski w Warszawie, 1938–1939* (The Teatr Polski in Warsaw, 1938–1939, 1971) and *Teatralia* (On Theater, 1983). In 1957 he published a volume of his memoirs, *Książka moich wspomnień* (The Book of My Memories; reprinted 1975). In 1991 an important diary-like collection of notes, covering the World War II period, appeared under the title *Notatki, 1939–1945* (Notes, 1939–1945) in a volume edited by Andrzej Zawada.

Translations: *Gathering Time: Five Modern Polish Elegies/Iwaszkiewicz . . . [et al.]*, trans. Andrzej Busza and Bogdan Czaykowski (Mission, B.C.: C. and J. Elsted at Barbarian Press, 1983); *Mr. Balzac's Wedding*, trans. Doris Ronowicz, *Dialog* [special issue] (1970): 40–56; *Summer in Nohant*, trans. Celina Wieniewska (London, before 1942); "The Badger," trans. Ilona Ralf Sues, in *Contemporary Polish Short Stories*, selected by Andrzej Kijowski (Warsaw: Polonia, 1960), 171–77. SOUND RECORDING: A sound recording, dated "between 1950 and 1969," of Iwaszkiewicz reading his poetry is available at the Woodberry Poetry Room, Harvard University.

J

Jančar, Drago (b. 1948) Slovene novelist, short-story writer, playwright, and essayist. Widely regarded as the most accomplished contemporary Slovenian prose writer and dramatist, Jančar was born in the city of Maribor. He studied law and worked as a journalist and playwright. In 1974 he was jailed on a charge of disseminating "enemy" propaganda and was sentenced to a year in prison, but was released after serving for three months. He fulfilled his obligatory military service in southern Serbia and then for the next three years devoted himself wholly to developing his career as a writer. In 1979/1980, he held the position of literary director of the Virba Film Studio in Ljubljana, after which he became editor and secretary of the Matica slovenska publishing house. In 1985 he received a Fulbright Fellowship for study and travel in the United States. His experiences in the United States, mostly in New Orleans, and his thought-provoking contrast of European and American cultures, form the subject of his novel *Posmehljivo poželenje* (*Mocking Desire*, 1992). After his stay in the United States, Jančar held a Bavarian state stipend for writers in Munich (1989) and in 1992 was a guest of the Austrian Writers Association in Vienna. From 1987 to 1991, Jančar was president of the Slovenian PEN Center and has served as editor at the Slovenian Literary Society in Ljubljana. He is currently an editor of *Nova Revija*, a cultural journal closely identified with the Slovenian dissident movement in the early 1980s.

A writer who frequently uses satire, the absurd, and allegory to expose and mock the evils of totalitarian government, Jančar began his literary career with a collection of stories under the title *Romanje gospoda Houžvičke* (The Pilgrimage of Mr. Houžvička, 1971). He subsequently published another four collections of short prose fiction: *O bledem hudodelcu* (About a Pale Criminal, 1978), dealing mostly with the theme of the individual versus the state in a totalitarian regime; *Smrt Pri Mariji Snežni* (Death at Mary of the Snows, 1985); *Pogled angela* (The Look of an Angel, 1992); and *Augsburg in druge resnične pripovedi* (Augsburg and Other True Stories, 1994), satirical and ironic pieces for the most part inspired by the Balkan wars of the 1990s. His novels include *Petintrideset stopinj* (Thirty-five Degrees, 1974), a satirical account of a single day in the life of an activist student; *Galjot* (Galley-Slave, 1978), a political allegory about an individual threatened by the power of the state; *Severni sij* (*Northern Lights*, 1984), about the ethnic tensions and growing irrationality in Maribor on the eve of World War II, as experienced by a stranger in town who apparently has no reason to be there; and the aforementioned *Mocking Desire*. *Zvenenje v glavi* (Ringing in the Head, 1998) is a picaresque work about an adventurer whose greatest claim to fame is the Livada prisoners' revolt he incited on the occasion of the broadcast of a basketball game between the United States and Yugoslavia. It is based, in fact, on Jančar's seven-month incarceration in 1997 on the charge of political espionage. In his newest novel, *Katarina, pav in jezuit* (Katarina, the Peacock, and the Jesuit, 2000), which won the Kresnik Prize for Best Slovenian Novel of the Year, Jančar follows the intertwined fates of the three principal characters: thirty-year-old Katarina, with a taste for adventure; Simon Lovrenc, a vain officer (the "peacock") who pursues her romantically but who eventually enters the Society of Jesus (Jesuits); and a Jesuit missionary in Paraguay. The historical novel (set in the eighteenth century) cuts a wide geographic swath as it moves from Cologne, Germany, to South America and back.

Jančar has had an active career as a dramatist, writing plays for the theater, television, and radio. His best plays for the theater are *Veliki briljantni valček* (The Great Brilliant Waltz, 1985); *Zalezujoč Godota* (*Stakeout at Godot's*, 1989); and *Halštat* (Hallstatt, 1994). The setting for *Veliki briljantni valček* is a quasi-mental hospital, "somewhere in the East," officially known as the Freedom Makes Free Institute. There the agents of a totalitarian political system transform patients into citizens who have been "purged" of their hidden antisocial tendencies. *Zalezujoč Godota,* which was performed by the 7 Stages Theater in Atlanta, Georgia, in 1998, is an absurdist take-off on Samuel Beckett's *Waiting for Godot* and features two policemen who are keeping a watch out for a character named Godot who will, of course, never appear. *Halštat* is a somewhat ribald play about a tramp who seeks shelter among a group of male and female archaeologists uncovering relics of the ancient Celts from the so-called Hallstatt period, but which turn out to be from World War II.

As an essayist, Jančar has written mostly about the Yugoslav situation before and after the dissolution of the state, the Balkan wars of the 1990s, nationalism, and Slovenia's place in European politics and culture. His major collections of essays are *Sproti* (Making Ends Meet, 1984); *Terra incognita* (1989); *Poročilo iz devete dežele* (Report from Wonderland, 1991); *Razbiti vrč* (The Broken Jug, 1992); *Disput* (Dispute, 1992), a dialogue with the Polish democratic leader and later foreign minister Adam Michnik; *Egiptovski lonci mesa* (Egyptian Pots of Meat, 1995); and *Ura evropske resnice za Slovenijo* (The Hour of European Truth for Slovenia, 1997). His most recent collection, *Prikazen iz*

Ravenske (The Ghost of Ravenska, 1998), comprises five essays, including one on Emperor Maximilian in Mexico and one on James Joyce. Jančar's works have been translated into several languages, and his plays have been produced in Austria, Hungary, and the United Sates. In 1993 Jančar was awarded the Prešeren Prize and in 1994 the European Prize for Short Fiction.

Literature: *Ka se nasanjano, bomo spali nasprej: Pogovori* (1997), a book of interviews with Jančar.

Translations: *Mocking Desire*, trans. Michael Biggins (Evanston, Ill.: Northwestern University Press, 1998); *Northern Lights*, trans. Michael Biggins (Evanston, Ill.: Northwestern University Press, 2000); *Stakeout at Godot's: A Drama in Two Acts*, trans. Ann Ceh, American adaptation by Peter Perhonis (Washington, D.C.: Scena, 1997); "Death at Mary-of-the Snows," "The Jump off the Liburnia," and "Ultima Creatura," in *The Day Tito Died: Contemporary Slovenian Short Stories* (London: Forest, 1993), 5–36; "Memories of Yugoslavia," trans. Anna Čeh, and "Augsburg," trans. Alasdair Mackinnon, in *The Imagination of Terra Incognita: Slovenian Writing, 1945–1995,* ed. Aleš Debeljak (Fredonia, N.Y.: White Pine, 1997), 110–38; "Reflecting on Poland," trans. Allen McConnell Duff, in *The Slovenian Essay of the Nineties,* selected by Matevž Kos (Ljubljana: Slovene Writers Association, 2000); "Augsburg," trans. Alasdair MacKinnon, in *Storm Out of Yugoslavia,* ed. Joanna Labon (London: Carcanet, 1994), 74–86.

Janevski, Slavko (1920–2000) Macedonian poet, novelist, and short-story writer. One of Macedonia's most celebrated and prolific contemporary writers, Janevski was born in Skopje and attended the College of Technology there before the outbreak of World War II. He joined the partisans and came to play an active role in their literary program. His first published book of poems, most of which were written during the war, appeared in 1945 under the title *Krvava niža* (The Bloody String, 1945). Other collections of verse soon followed: *Pruga na mladosta* (The Track of Youth, 1947), which he composed with the poet Aco Šopov; *Pesme* (Poems, 1948); *Egejski barutna bajka* (The Aegean Gunpowder Tale, 1950); *Lirika* (Lyrics, 1951); *Leb i kamen* (Bread and Stone, 1957); *Evangelie po Itar Pejo* (The Gospel According to Pejo the Sly, 1966); *Kainavelija* (The Tale of Cain, 1968); *Okovano jabolko* (The Chained Apple, 1978); *Astropeus* (1979); *Zmejovi za igra* (Kites for Playing, 1983); and *Pejsi šumi* (Dogs' Forests, 1988). Several volumes of Janevski's selected verse have also been published: *Gluvi komandi* (Deaf Commands, 1966); *Najgolemiot kontinent* (The Biggest Continent, 1968); *Vojnik dva metra v zemja* (The Soldier Six Feet Under the Ground, 1969); *Tančarka na dlanka* (The Dancer on the Palm, 1976); *Pesme* (Poems, 1987); *Zabraneta odaja* (The Forbidden Room, 1988); and *Orac medgy skeleti* (Sower Among Skeletons, 1992), edited by the poet Sande Stojčevski. Janevski's poetry is distinguished by its lyricism; its attachment to the world of nature, especially the sea; its indebtedness to the Macedonian folk tradition and reverence for ancient Macedonia; and its imaginative accommodation of the Turkish dimension of Macedonian culture, with its exoticism balanced by the recollection of Slav–Turk conflict. Janevski often adopts the persona of a Macedonian bandit singer embodied in the figure of Pejo the Sly.

Janevski was also the author of a substantial number of novels. Those that have had the greatest resonance are *Selo zad sedumte jaseni* (A Village Beyond the Seven Ash Trees, 1952), which enjoys the distinction of being the first novel in modern Macedonian, and *Čudotvorci* (*The Miracle Workers*, 1988), a tale about Turkish assaults on a Macedonian Slav village in 1719 and the subsequent fate of the village, written in the style of an old chronicle and permeated with lore and legend. *The Miracle Workers* is one of the texts in Janevski's octology, which traces life in the village of Kukulino from 700 to 2096 and also includes *Tvrdoglavi* (The Stubborn Ones, 1969); *Legionite na Sveti Adofonis* (The Legions of Saint Adofonis, 1984); *Kučesko raspetie* (A Heavy Cross, 1984); *Čekajki čuma* (Waiting for the Plague, 1984); *Devet Kerubinovi vekovi* (Nine Centuries of Cherubim, 1986; translated as *The Nine Centuries of Kerubin*); *Rulet so sedum brojki* (Roulette with Seven Numbers, 1989); and *Kontinent kukolino* (The Kukulino Continent, 1996). Janevski's other novels are *Dve Marije* (The Two Marias, 1956); *I bol i bes* (Both Pain and Rage, 1964); and *Stebla* (Tree Trunks, 1965).

The most important collections of Janevski's short stories are *Ulica* (The Street, 1946), a story; *Klonovi i lugje* (Clowns and People, 1956); *Omarnini* (Sultry Days, 1972); *Kovčeg* (The Chest, 1976); and *Zad tajnata vrata* (Behind the Secret Gate, 1993). His other writings include *Gorčlivi legendi* (Bitter Legends, 1962), a travel book about Asia; *Temni kazuvanja* (Dark Tales, 1962), a volume of Macedonian tales edited by Janevski, with Meto Jovanovski and Kiril Kamilov; and *Skopje* (1964), a picture book about the Macedonian capital with text in Macedonian, English, French, German, Russian, and Spanish. Janevski was a member of the Macedonian Academy of Sciences and Arts, the Macedonian Writers Association, and the Macedonian PEN Center. He won many important Yugoslav and Macedonian literary prizes.

Literature: Georgi Stardelov, *Kerubin's Tribe*, trans. Snezana Necovska (Skopje: Detska Radost, 1998); Miodrag Drugovac, *Kniga za Janevski* (Skopje: Makedonska Kniga, 1971); Miodrag Drugovac, ed., *Slavko Janevski vo kniževnata kritika* (Skopje: Naša Kniga, 1976); Hristo Georgievski, *Dve Mar-*

ije Slavka Janevskog (Belgrade: Zavod za udzbenike i nastavna sredstva, 1982), a Serbian study of Janesvki's novel *Dve Marije*; Zlatko Kramaric, *Romanite na Slavko Janevski* (Skopje: Makedonska Kniga, 1987); Radivoje Pesić, *Slavko Janevski* (Belgrade: Rad, 1968), an introductory Serbian study; Georgi Stardelov, *Experimentum Macedonicum* (Skopje: Makedonska Kniga, 1983).

Translations: *The Bandit Wind,* trans. Charles Simic (Takoma Park, Md.: Dryad, 1991), a well-done Macedonian–English edition of selected poems; *The Miracle Workers,* trans. Zoran Ančevski and David Bowen (Skopje: Detska Radost, 1994); *The Nine Centuries of Kerubin,* trans. Snezana Nikolovska-Necovska (Skopje: Detska radost, 1997); *Paletata na prokletstvoto/The Palette of Damnation* (Skopje: Misla, 1995), a small Macedonian–English edition of poems.

Janković, Sava (b. 1923) Serbian novelist. Apart from a volume of poems, *Putevima i prostorima* (Along Roads and Expanses, 1994), Janković is known primarily as the author of the tetralogy *Na prelomu* (Turning Point), published between 1994 and 1998. This massive work deals with World War II in Serbia, with the focus mainly on the fighting between the royalist Draža Mihailović's chetniks and Tito's communist partisans. The ultimate victory of the partisans, aided by the Allies, is seen through the eyes of a young student named Slobodan Spasojević.

Janovic, Vladimír (real name Vladimír Pičman; b. 1935) Czech poet. One of the more impressive Czech poets of the post–World War II period, Janovic was born in Prague where he graduated from high school in 1953. He then studied mathematics at the Faculty of Natural Sciences of Brno University from 1953 to 1958. Upon receiving his degree, he taught for the next two years in secondary schools in Moravia and then became an assistant in mathematics at the College of Agriculture and Forestry in Brno. In 1961/1962, he served as the literary editor of the Brno scientific journal *Československý rozhlas.* From 1962 to 1965, Janovic devoted himself entirely to his literary career as a journalist and freelance writer, resettling permanently in Prague in 1965. For the next several years, he held a variety of editorial positions—at the publishing houses Odeon and Svoboda, the journal *Plamen,* and the review *Literární noviny* —while composing poetry. It was while working as an editor at Svoboda that Janovic founded and edited the poetry magazine *Syrinx* (1967–1970). From 1970 to 1972, he returned to freelance writing and, from 1973 to 1988, held the editorship of the poetry section of the Československý spisovatel publishing house. After a year's sabbatical, he joined the editorial staff of the journal *Literární měsíčník.* In 1990 Janovic resumed his earlier career as a secondary-school teacher, instructing in mathematics and English in Prague. He also intensified his activity as a translator and promoter of Italian literature and worked diligently to expand Czech and Italian literary contacts. From 1991 to 1993, he headed and also taught in the program of Italian-language courses offered by the Czechoslovak-Italian Association.

Janovic began writing poetry while still in high school and published his first texts in the early 1960s in local Brno newspapers and magazines. His first book of poems, *Zatmění ráje* (Black-out of Paradise), appeared in 1968. He subsequently published another eight volumes of poetry: *Romulův nářek* (Romulus's Lamentation, 1970); *Plást hlíny* (Honeycomb of Clay, 1975); *Báseň o sněžné levitaci* (Poem About a Snowy Levitation, 1978); *Jarmark v mlze* (Fair in the Mist, 1981); *Všechna tvoje těla* (All Your Bodies, 1983), a volume of selected poems; *Dům tragického básníka* (*The House of the Tragic Poet,* 1984), the work for which he is arguably best known; *Ohňová abeceda* (Burning Alphabet, 1984), another volume of selected poems; and *Most alchymistů* (The Bridge of the Alchemists, 1989), an emotional biography of the author from boyhood to manhood. Janovic ranges in his lyric poetry from an abiding sense of loneliness and futility to a more positive outlook on life to striking eroticism. His fondness for a highly expressive Baroque-inspired metaphorical style was already demonstrated in his second book of poems, *Romulův nářek.*

Janovic's most impressive achievements are his two longer epic-like poems: Poem About a Snowy Levitation and *The House of the Tragic Poet.* The rondel "Leningrad" in the volume *Plást hlíny* became the point of departure for the twelve-canto Poem About a Snowy Levitation. Inspired by the "white nights" for which Leningrad (now again St. Petersburg) is famous, Poem About a Snowy Levitation is a celebration of the mystique of Peter the Great's capital that does justice to its literary heritage as well as to its tumultous history in the twentieth century—from the Revolution of 1917 to the German siege in World War II. *The House of the Tragic Poet,* Janovic's only work available in English, is a witty evocation of ancient Pompeii a few days before the city was buried under volcanic ash following the eruption of Mount Vesuvius. Janovic's inspiration for his "lyrical-epic" was a visit to Pompeii and his fascination with a colored mosaic from the city depicting the chorodidascalus, or tragic poet, and producer directing a rehearsal of a satyr play to be performed by six young men. An imaginative reconstruction in verse form of Pompeiian life on the eve of the great disaster that destroyed the city, *The House of the Tragic Poet* is archaeologically faithful yet entertaining reading, especially for Janovic's contemporary touches and ribaldry.

Translations: *The House of the Tragic Poet,* trans. Ewald Osers (Newcastle upon Tyne: Bloodaxe, 1988).

Jaroš, Peter (b. 1940) Slovak novelist and short-story writer. Born in Hybe, and later a full-time resident of Bratislava, Jaroš graduated from the Faculty of Philosophy of Comenius University in Bratislava in 1962. Following his studies, he worked as an editor at such cultural journals as *Kulturný život* and *Mladá tvorba,* as a dramatic adviser to the Slovak film studio in Koliba, and then as a freelance writer. From 1992 to 1994, he served as a delegate to the parliament of the Slovak Republic and is currently art director of the Trigon film production company, of which he is cofounder.

Jaroš's literary career began in 1958 with the publication of short stories in literary journals such as *Mladá tvorba.* His first published book was the novella *Popoludnie na terase* (Afternoon on the Terrace, 1963), in which the monologue form is used to explore the interaction of employees at a Bratislava publishing house in the course of a single day. It was followed in 1964 by the short novel *Urob mi more* (Make Me a Sea), in which a student's work in a mine during a holiday period serves as the basis for wide-ranging ruminations on labor, life, love, and so on. Although Jaroš's next novel, *Zdesenie* (Dismay, 1965), followed *Urob mi more* by only a year, it marked a change in literary direction. In his two first novels, Jaroš dealt with concrete social milieus and everyday reality, but in a style marked by a certain willingness to experiment with narrative structure. This inclination toward experimentation came much more to the fore in *Zdesenie* and such subsequent novels as *Vahy* (The Scales, 1966) and *Putovanie k nehybnosti* (The Road to Immobility, 1967), which reflect Jaroš's awareness of the contemporary French "anti-novel."

The same year in which *Putovanie k nehybnosti* appeared, Jaroš published a collection of short stories under the title *Menuet* (Minuet) that seemed to herald a turning away from experimentation in favor of a new interest in his native region and the past of his own family. Although more outwardly traditional in style, the stories in *Menuet* and in the subsequent collections *Návrat so sochou* (Return with a Statue, 1969), *Krvaviny* (Bloody Tales, 1970), *Až do belneš psa* (Till You Catch Up with the Dog, 1971), and *Pradeno* (Skein, 1974), and the novel *Trojúsmevový miláčuk* (The Lover with the Three Smiles, 1973), contain elements of the grotesque, absurd, and fantastic, attesting to their author's unwillingness to completely part company with techniques of modernist storytelling. After a hiatus of a few years, Jaroš returned to prose writing with a new collection of thirteen stories, *Télo v herbári* (Body in the Herbarium, 1979), in which his principal concern is the contradictory nature of human relations, especially in terms of the relationship between a husband and a wife. A year after he published *Télo v herbári,* Jaroš's most acclaimed work appeared: the novel *Tisícročná včela* (The Millennial Bee). It is an epic-style family novel spanning three generations and set in the second half of the nineteenth and the beginning of the twentieth centuries. Slovak history is likened to a millennial beehive, as exemplified in the Pichanda family of farmers and bricklayers through whom Jaroš elevates a culture of toil to the level of a sui generis Slovak national philosophy. In its sequel, *Nemé ucho, hluché oko* (Deaf Ear, Deaf Eye, 1984), Jaroš carries the action into the period immediately following the establishment of the new Czechoslovak state in 1918.

Between *Tisícročná včela* and *Nemé ucho, hluché oko,* Jaroš returned to the genre of the short story with his collection *Parádny výlet* (The Dandies' Excursion, 1982), which is notable, above all, for its inclination toward the bizarre and fantastic. Jaroš's next novel, *Laský hmat* (A Touch of Love, 1988), is a sharp critical commentary on the lifestyles of urban intellectuals. Similarly acerbic in nature is the novel *Psy sa ženia* (The Dogs Are Marrying, 1990), in which the visit of a writer to a small town to collect material for a new book serves as a lever for the exposure of insincerity and falsehood in human relations in a changing society. In essence also a social critique is the novel *Milodar slučka* (The Gift Noose), which came out a year after *Psy sa ženia*. Jaroš's most recent novel, which further evidences his taste for the bizarre and even macabre, *Lady Dracula Alias Báthory Story* (1998; original title in English), is based on the life of the vampirish Hungarian countess Erszébet (Elizabeth) Báthory (1560–1614). Jaroš's most recently published collection of short stories, *Grimasy* (Grimaces, 1996), contains twenty stories from such previous collections as *Menuet, Návrat so sochou, Krvaviny, Pradeno, Télo v herbári,* and *Parádny výlet*. It also includes a new version of the story "Záchranca" (The Deliverer, from *Télo v herbári*) and a new, previously unpublished story, "Lono a pentagram" ("The Womb and the Pentagram").

Jašík, Rudolf (1919–1960) Slovak poet, novelist, and short-story writer. Jašík began his career as a poet in the surrealist style and later turned to prose. His first published book, the novel *Na brehu priezračnej reiky* (On the Shores of the Pellucid River, 1956), was based on his own youth in the town of Kysúc. In this typical socialist realist work about the rise of social consciousness among workers, Jašík to some extent offsets the obvious ideological underpinnings with a lyrical evocation of the town's natural setting. This lyrical element weakens in his second novel, *Námestie sv. Alžbety* (St. Elizabeth Square, 1958), in which the ill-fated romance between a poor Christian boy and a

Jewish girl is used to dramatize the growing tensions in a small Slovak town in the early years of the fascist state. Jašík's next novel, the huge and overly ambitious *Mŕtvi nespievaju* (The Dead Do Not Sing, 1961)— part of a projected trilogy that never materialized—extends the themes of *Námestie sv. Alžbety* by undertaking a broad canvas of Slovakia during World War II, including the fate of Slovak troops on the eastern front. Two of Jašík's novels, *Černe a biele kruhy* (Black and White Rings, 1961) and *Povest' o bielych kameňoch* (The Tale of the White Stones, 1961), were published posthumously.

Jastrun, Tomasz (b. 1950) Polish poet and essayist. The son of the poet Mieczyslaw Jastrun (1903–1983), Jastrun was born in Warsaw and educated at Warsaw University, where he studied Polish literature. He made his literary debut in 1978 with a small volume of poems under the title *Bez usprawiedliwienia* (Without Justification). His next book of poetry, *Promienie Błędnego koła* (Rays of the Errant Circle), was honored by the Robert Graves Foundation in 1980. That was the year when the Solidarity union was born of the strike in the Gdańsk shipyards. Jastrun was present at the time, threw his wholehearted support to the movement, and from then on became closely identified as a poet with Solidarity and its aspirations. He also wrote poems in opposition to the martial law imposed on Poland in December 1981. As a result of such dissident activities, it was impossible for Jastrun to publish his poetry with the state publishing houses until the mid-1980s, and he turned instead to the underground press and to foreign outlets. In 1983 Jastrun published in Berlin a sixty-one-page pamphlet, *Zapiski z Błędnego koła* (Notes from the Errant Circle), dealing with Solidarity and political prisoners in Poland in the early 1980s. Also in 1983 or 1984 (the exact date of publication is uncertain), his *Biała łąka:*

Dziennik poetycki 9 listopada–23 grudnia 1982 (White Meadow: A Poetic Diary from 9 November to 23 December 1982), an account in verse of martial law, was published by a Solidarity underground press. Not long afterward, *Na skrzyżowaniu Azji i Europy* (*On the Crossroads of Asia and Europe*), his only collection of poems and essays available in English translation, won the prize of the Interim National Commission of Solidarity. Jastrun's last underground publication, *Życie Anny Walentynowicz* (The Life of Anna Walentynowicz), about one of the "heroines" of the Solidarity movement, appeared in 1985. The same year, Jastrun returned to mainstream publishing with two collections of verse: the retrospective *Czas pamięci i zapomnienia: Wiersze z różnych lat* (A Time to Remember and to Forget: Poems from Various Years) and *Kropla, kropla* (Drop by Drop). Another volume of selected verse, which also included some new poems, appeared in 1988 under the title *Węzeł polski: Wiersze stare i nowe* (The Polish Knot: Old and New Verses). In 1989 Jastrun published a new book of verse, *Obok siebie* (Beside Myself), as well as *W złotej klatce: Notatnik amerykański* (In the Gilded Cage: An American Notebook). Brought out by a Berlin publisher, it was based on his travels in the United States. His book of essays, *Z ukosa* (Askance), was published under the pseudonym Smecz by the Polish émigré Instytut Literacki (Literary Institute) in Paris. Jastrun's most recent collection of verse, *Wiersze* (Poems), appeared in 1997 and contains mostly previously published poems. From 1981 to 1988, Jastrun was editor in chief of the literary monthly *Wezwanie*, of which he was a cofounder. His literary awards also include the Kościelski Foundation Award (1986); the award of Polish Independent Journalists; and the *Kultura* (Paris) award (1990). From 1990 to 1994, Jastrun served as director of the Polish Institute in Stockholm and was the cultural attaché to the Polish Embassy in Stockholm. From 1994 to 1996, he conducted

the cultural magazine *Pegaz* on Polish television and has collaborated with several leading Polish daily newspapers and monthly journals. In both his Solidarity period and his subsequent poetry, which is mostly personal in nature, Jastrun has inclined to small forms and a simple everyday style. As he declares in the poem "Ziarna" ("Grains"):

I don't like long poems . . .
A short poem is a sign of our times
A grain waiting for its day.

Three typical short poems are "Deszcz" ("Rain"):

He didn't love her for so many years
But now suddenly
Like a morning rain
Love penetrated him
When he caught sight of her slippers
Left by mistake on the balcony
Damp after a lonely night.

"Zgaszony" ("Extinguished"):

He lit up
She extinguished him
With a single look
Of her green eyes.
And she left
With his face on her shoulders
Cleaved by the scorn of a braid.

and "Współczesny rycerz" ("A Contemporary Knight"):

I ride a sad mare
And hum sad songs
I ride a sad mare
Don Quixote
Who read Cervantes.

Translations: *On the Crossroads of Asia and Europe,* trans. Daniel Bourne (Anchorage: Salmon Run, 1999).

Jebeleanu, Eugen (1911–1991) Romanian poet. One of the outstanding Romanian men of letters of the twentieth century, Jebeleanu was born in Cîmpina where he attended elementary school. He graduated from high school in Braşov in 1922 and five years later published his first poems in the literary review *Viaţa literară*. His first book of poetry, *Schituri cu soare* (Monasteries with Sun), appeared in 1929, the same year in which Jebeleanu moved to Bucharest and began studying law at Bucharest University. Although he published another volume of poems, *Inimi sub sabii* (Hearts Under Swords) in 1934, Jebeleanu's principal literary activity in the 1930s was as a journalist closely allied with the left-wing press. After the war, he threw his support solidly behind the new communist leadership and became an ardent propagandist on behalf of socialist realism. Most of his post–World War II poetry deals with the struggle against fascism, the Romanian revolutionary tradition going back to 1848, and championing the ideology of the new regime. Notwithstanding his political engagement, Jebeleanu managed to rise poetically above the level of a verse pamphleteer. His postwar volumes of poetry include *Ceea ce nu se uită* (What Cannot Be Forgotten, 1945); *Scutul pacii* (The Shield of Peace, 1949); *Poeme de pace şi de luptă* (Poems of Peace and War, 1950); *În satul lui Sahia* (In the Village of Sahi, 1952); *Bălcescu* (1952); and *Cîntecele pădurii tinere* (Songs of the Young Forest, 1953). The long poem *Bălcescu* was written in honor of the distinguished Romanian historian and patriot Nicolae Bălcescu. Jebeleanu first achieved international recognition with his collection of humanitarian poems about the atomic bombing of Hiroshima: *Surîsul Hiroşimei* (The Smile of Hiroshima, 1958). After an "oratorio" in celebration of the liberation at the end of World War II, *Oratoriul Eliberării* (The Oratorio of Lberation, 1959), and a volume of selected verse, *Poezii*

şi poeme (Poems, 1961), Jebeleanu published one of his most highly regarded collections of poems, *Lidice, Cîntece împotriva morţii* (Lidice, Songs Against Death, 1963). In the same spirit of universal humanism as *Surîsul Hiroşimei*, his new collection was inspired by a postwar visit to the site of the Czech town of Lidice, which together with all its inhabitants was totally destroyed by the Germans during World War II in a act of revenge. Jebeleanu's other publications include *Din veacul XX* (From the Twentieth Century, 1956), a collection of journalistic texts; *Poeme, 1944–1964* (Poems, 1944–1964, 1964); *Elegie pentru floarea secerată* (Elegies for the Cut Flower, 1966), one of his most important collections of lyrics and a break from his previous engaged poetry; *Hanibul* (Hannibal, 1972), a volume of poems; and *Deaspura zilei* (Beyond the Day, 1981), a book of "jottings" on a variety of subjects.

Translations: Three poems, including "Lidice," in *Anthology of Contemporary Romanian Poetry,* ed. Roy MacGregor-Hastie (London: Peter Owen, 1969), 105–8; five poems, including excerpts from *Surîsul Hiroşimei,* trans. Andrei Bantaş, in *Like Diamonds in Coal Asleep: Selections from Twentieth Century Romanian Poetry,* ed. Andrei Bantaş (Bucharest: Minerva, 1985), 220–29.

Jentzsch, Bernd (b. 1940) German poet, short-story writer, essayist, and author and publisher of children's books. After graduating from high school in his native Plauen and completing his obligatory military service, Jentzsch studied German language and literature as well as art history at Leipzig University in Jena from 1960 to 1965. Upon graduation, he moved to Berlin where until 1974 he worked as an editor at the Neues Leben publishing house. In this capacity, Jentzsch played an important role in East German literature through his sponsoring of the Poesiealbum (Poetry Album) series, which carried the works primarily of younger writers. In all, 121 numbers of Poesiealbum appeared under Jentzsch's editorship. After the Wolf Biermann episode in 1976, Jentzsch, who was in Switzerland at the time, did not return to the German Democratic Republic and, moreover, issued a strong denunciation of the treatment of Biermann that outraged the East German authorities. While in Switzerland, in 1977, Jentzsch collaborated with other writers in publishing an anthology of twentieth-century Swiss lyrics from the four linguistic regions of the country: *Schweizer Lyrik des zwanzigsten Jahrhunderts: Gedichte aus 4 Sprachregionen*. In 1986 Jentzsch took up permanent residence in West Germany, where he continued his literary career and became actively involved in publishing.

Jentzsch made his literary debut in 1961 with the poetry collection *Alphabet des Morgens* (Morning Alphabet), which met with a mixed reception. In 1971 he published both an anthology of the works of young East German poets of the postwar decade under the title *Ich nenn euch mein Problem: Gedichte der Nachgeborenen. 46 junge, in der DDR lebende Poeten der Jahrgänge 1945–1954* (I Call You My Problem: Poems of the Postwar Generation. 46 Young Poets living in the GDR in the Decade 1945–1954) and an anthology of German writers of Anacreaontic poetry, *Lauter Lust, wohin das Auge gafft: Deutsche Poeten in der Manier Anakreont* (Pure Pleasure, Wherever the Eye Rests: German Poets in the Style of Anacreaon). Jentzsch continued his activities as an editor throughout the 1970s. In 1972 he brought out *Wort Mensch: Ein Bild vom Menschen in deutschsprachigen Gedichten aus drei Jahrhunderten* (Word, Man: The Image of Man in Three Centuries of German-Language Poems); in 1974, in collaboration with Silva Schlenstedt and Heinrich Olschowsky, he published the collection *Welt im sozialistischen Gedicht: Poeten, Methoden und internationale Tendenzen im Gespräch* (The World in the Socialist Poem: Poets, Methods, and International Tendencies in Conversation); in 1974 and 1975, he issued two collections of the poetry of Barthold Hinrich Brockes (1680–1747); and in 1979 he published his edition of poetry and other writings by Max Hermann-Neisse (1886–1941). Jentzsch's next original publications after *Alphabet des Morgens* were the critically better received *Jungfer im Grünen* (Maiden in Green, 1973), a sparely written short-story collection notable for its blending of realistic and fantastic elements, and the pessimistic volume of verse *Die Henker des Lebenstraums* (The Executioner of the Dream of Life). This was followed in 1975 by his provocative collection of verse *Ratsch und Ade! Sieben jugendfreie Erzählungen, mit einem "Nach-Ratsch"* (Up Yours, I'm Splitting! Seven Youth-Free Stories, with a Postcript of Sorts), which was published in Munich. In 1978 came a new volume of poems, *Quartiermachen* (Setting Up Quarters), which also first appeared in Munich. The following year, 1979, Jentzsch edited three works in which Germany's Nazi past and immediate postwar political division are viewed through the witness of poetry: *Tod ist ein Meister aus Deutschland: Deportation und Vernichtung in poetischen Zeugnissen* (Death Is a Master from Germany: Deportation and Extermination in the Accounts of Poets); *Ich sah das Dunkel schon von ferne kommen: Erniedrigung und Vertreibung in poetischen Zeugnissen* (I Saw the Darkness Coming from the Distance: Humiliation and Expulsion in the Accounts of Poets); *Ich sah aus Deutschlands Asche keinen Phönix steigen: Rückkehr und Hoffnung in poetischen Zeugnissen* (I Saw No Phoenix Arising from Germany's Ashes: Return and Hope in the Accounts of Poets). In 1984 Jentzsch published an edition of the poems of Rudolf Leonhard (1889–1953) under the title *Prolog zu jeder kommenden Revolution* (Prologue to Every Coming Revolution), followed the same year by a biographical essay on Leonhard with documents and a bibliography titled *Rudolf Leonhard, "Gedichteträumer"* (Rudolf Leonhard, "Dreamer of Poems"). Jentzsch's book about the political persecution of writers, drawing in part on his own experiences, *Schreiben als strafbare Handlung: Fälle* (Writing as Punishable Activity: Instances), appeared in 1985. In 1992 and 1993, respectively, he published a new collection of his own selected poetry, *Alte Lust, sich aufzubäumen: Lesebuch* (The Old Desire to Kick Up My Heels: A Reader), and a volume of his writings and archives from 1954 to 1992 under the title *Flöze* (Strata).

Translations: Three poems, in German and English, trans. Michael Hamburger and Christopher Levenson, in *East German Poetry: An Anthology,* ed. Michael Hamburger (New York: Dutton, 1973), 210–13.

Jesih, Milan (b. 1950) Slovenian poet and playwright. A popular poet and playwright who has written plays for the stage, radio, television, and children's theater, Jesih was born and educated in Ljubljana. He studied comparative literature at Ljubljana University, after which he became for a time a member of the avant-garde literary-performance group known as Pupilija Ferkeverk, of which the playwright and theater director Dušan Jovanovič was cofounder. Jesih took part in several of the theater's experimental productions, and its style of performance clearly influenced his own playwriting. Jesih made his debut as a poet in 1972 with the collection *Uran v urinu, gospodar* (Uranium in Urine, Master). This was followed by several other volumes of poems: *Legende* (Legends, 1974); *Kobalt* (Cobalt, 1976); *Volfram* (Wolfram, 1980); *Usta* (Mouth, 1985); *Soneti* (Sonnets, 1989); *Soneti drugi* (Sonnets II, 1993); *Jambi* (Iambs, 2000); and *Verzi: Izbrane pesmi* (Verses: Selected Poems, 2001), a collection of Jesih's poetry written over thirty years. *Soneti* won the Jenkov Prize as the most pop-

ular book of poetry of the 1980s and was critically hailed as the best postmodernist collection of Slovene poetry. A master of language, Jesih has demonstrated with his sonnets an ability to move beyond the avant-garde experimentalism of his early poetry to an impressive postmodernist accommodation of the rigid discipline of the sonnet form. In his other poetry, he often balances melancholy rooted in a sense of futility and hopelessness with irony, satire, and a sense of play. Although as adept at short laconic poems with lines of one or two words (as in *Usta*) as he is with the sonnet, Jesih does very well with longer poems with long prosaic lines, affording freer rein to his narrative skill (*Kobalt* and *Volfram*). After coauthoring such avant-garde experimental plays as *Žlahtna plesen Pupilije Ferkeverk* (The Noble Mold of Pupilija Ferkeverk, staged 1969) and *Pupilija, papa Pupilo pa Pupilčki* (Pupilija, Papa Pupilo, and the Little Pupil, 1969), Jesih progressed to mostly satirical plays, the best of which are *Grenki sadeži pravice* (The Bitter Fruits of Justice, staged 1974); *Vzpon, padec in ponovni vzpon zanesenega ekonomista* (The Ascent, Descent, and Ascent Again of an Enthusiastic Economist, staged 1974), a "morality play"; *Brucka ali obdobje prilagajanja* (The Frosh or the Era of Accommodation, staged 1976); *Pravopisna komisija* (The Commission on Orthography, staged 1985); *Afrika* (Africa, staged 1986), a parody; *Ptiči* (The Birds, staged 1987), a satire based on Aristophanes' comedy; *En sam dotik* (Just One Touch, staged 1990), a "drama"; *Kronan norjec* (Kronan the Fool, staged 1990), subtitled a "Childish Puppet Play"; and *Cesarjeva nova oblačila* (The Emperor's New Clothes, staged 1993). A few of Jesih's plays were adapted for television, radio, and puppet-theater performance; he also wrote a number of original plays for television, radio, and the puppet theater. Apart from his poetry and dramatic writing, Jesih has earned a formidable reputation as a translator, mostly of drama and including many plays by Shakespeare, Chekhov, Gogol, and Mikhail Bulgakov. In 1986 he won both the Prešeren Foundation Prize and the Slovenian National Book Award.

Literature: Peter Kolšek, "Podobar in podoba," in *Verzi: Izbrane pesmi* (Ljubljana: Mladinska knjiga, 2001), 203–26.

Translations: Excerpts from *Volfram*, trans. Sonja Kravanja, in *The Imagination of Terra Incognita: Slovenian Writing, 1945–1995*, ed. Aleš Debeljak (Fredonia, N.Y.: White Pine, 1997), 257–63.

Johanides, Ján (b. 1934) Slovak novelist and short-story writer. One of the most important post–World War II Slovak writers, Johanides was born in Dolny Kubin, where he was educated through high school. He later studied history, aesthetics, and art history at Comenius University in Bratislava, but was expelled in his junior year for political reasons. He then worked for a while as a psychologist in the Tesla factory in Nižna na Orave, as a reader at the Slovak Writers Union in Bratislava, as a "cultural worker" at the Municipal House of Culture and Enlightenment in Bratislava, and, in the 1980s, as an employee of the Commission of Art Criticism and Film Documentation. In 1972 he settled in the town of Šala. Johanides's main themes are the behavior of the Slovaks during World War II, with particular attention to their attitude toward and treatment of Jews; the moral cost of materialism and the craving for affluence in postwar Slovak society; and the mores of the Slovak lower classes. His first published work was *Súkromie* (Privacy, 1963), a collection of five stories of particular interest for the author's depiction of the passive collaboration of the Slovaks in the deportation of the Jews. However, it was over twenty years later that Johanides wrote his major work about the war, *Slony v Mauthausene* (Elephants in

Mauthausen, 1985), in which the mindless brutality of World War II and the German concentration camps is recalled by survivors of the Mauthausen camp, chief among them a Dutchman of lesser nobility whose children reflect the ahistorical pursuit of bourgeois self-gratification of the postwar period. Of particular interest in the novel is Johanides's straightforward depiction of a bizarre moral relativism in the Slovak treatment of Jews during the war.

Johanides's serious concerns about indifference toward and neglect of the environment are reflected in several of his novels, among them *Podstata kameňolomu* (The Essence of the Stone Quarry, 1966); *Nie* (No, 1966), in which the central landscape is a garbage dump, the obvious symbol of an affluent society's moral refuse; and *Niepriznané vrany* (Unacknowledged Crows, 1978), about a huge chemical plant in a small city that a writer wants to make the subject of a book until his focus shifts more to the attitudes of the townspeople toward the plant, their work, and the surrounding environment. Other texts by Johanides motivated by his loathing for the greed of postwar society include *Balada o vkladnej knižke* (Ballad of a Savings Book, 1979); *Marek koniar a uhorský pápež* (Marek, Master of Horse, and the Hungarian Pope, 1983); and *Pochovávanie brata* (Burying My Brother, 1987).

In some of his later fiction, Johanides took aim squarely at the Slovak lower classes whose narrow-mindedness and potential for cruelty apalled him. His intention with the novel *Najsmutnejšia oravská balada* (The Saddest Orava Ballad, 1988), for example, was to "convey the soul of old Orava" as he came to know it in the people who lived there in recent decades and who experienced the changes the town underwent during this period. In one bizarre episode during World War II, the townspeople's respect for lawyers is such that they will do nothing to harm the one Jewish lawyer in the town. However, they make him watch as they put his wife in a barrel into which they have driven nails and then roll the barrel down a hill. The lawyer suffers a heart attack during the scene and dies. Johanides's other novels on the broad theme of the Slovak lower classes include *Previest' cez most* (The Passage over the Bridge, 1991); *Kocúr a zimný človek* (The Tomcat and the Cold Man, 1994); *Identita v kríze* (Identity in Crisis, 1996); and *Nositel čarodějného jednorožce* (The Bearer of the Magic Unicorn, 1997).

Translations: "Memorial to Don Giovanni," trans. James Naughton, in *Description of a Struggle: The Vintage Book of Contemporary East European Writing,* ed. Michael March (New York: Vintage, 1994), 162–68; "The Myth of the Magic Unicorn," trans. George Theiner, in *New Writing in Czechoslovakia,* ed. George Theiner (Baltimore: Penguin, 1969), 171–80.

Joho, Wolfgang (b. 1908) German novelist, short-story writer, and literary critic. A native of Karlsruhe, Joho was educated at Freiburg, Heidelberg, and Berlin universities where he studied medicine, philosophy, history, and political science. A member of the German Communist Party since 1929, he was arrested on charges of conspiracy against the state in 1937 and imprisoned until 1941. During the war, he was pressed into service in a penal colony and saw action in Greece in 1943. He was eventually captured by the British and interned in a prisoner of war camp in 1945/1946. After the war and the establishment of the German Democratic Republic, he became especially active first as an editor at the journal *Sonntag* (1947–1954) and then as editor in chief of the prominent literary publishing house Neue Deutsche Literatur.

Although Joho began his literary career as a critic and journalist from the time he entered the Communist Party, his first book, a collection of short stories under the title *Die Hirtenflöte* (The Shepherd's Flute), did not appear until 1948. Joho's main focus in the stories is on the social maturation of the urban intelligentsia and their eventual embrace of the workers' cause. *Die Hirtenflöte* was followed in 1949 by the novella *Die Verwandlungen des Doktor Brad* (The Transformations of Dr. Brad) and the novel *Jeanne Peyrouton. Zwischen Bonn und Bodensee* (Jeanne Peyrouton. Between Bonn and Bodensee), a book based on his personal observations about social conditions in West Germany, appeared in 1954. Joho followed the same pattern of the ideological travel work in *Korea trocknet die Tränen: Ein Reisebericht* (Korea Dries Her Eyes: A Travel Report, 1959), a pro–North Korean propaganda piece. Other works by him from the 1950s and early 1960s include *Wandlungen: Fünf Erzählungen* (Changes: Five Stories, 1955); *Die Wendemarke* (The Turning Point, 1957); and *Die Zeit trägt einen roten Stern* (Time Bears a Red Star, 1962). As Joho moved into the later 1960s and the 1970s, his writing became more concerned with contrasting the different value systems of the West and the East, often within the framework of family and generational conflicts. This is especially true of such works as *Aufstand der Träumer* (The Revolt of Dreams, 1966); *Klassentreffen: Geschichte einer Reise* (Class Reunion: The Story of a Journey, 1968); *Eine Rose für Katharina* (A Rose for Catherine, 1970); *Die Kastanie* (The Chestnut, 1970), arguably his best work of fiction, in which the principal character shares important features with the author himself; *Begegnung und Bündnis* (Encounter and Alliance, 1972); *Es gibt keinen Erbarmen* (There Is No Mercy, 1972); *Der Sohn: Nachrichten aus der Bender-Welt* (Son: Reports from Bender's World, 1974); and *Der Weg aus der Einsamkeit: Geschichte einer Familie* (The Road out of Loneliness: A Family History, 1981). In 1991 Joho published *Abberufung:*

Beginn eines Tagebuches (Recall: Starting a Diary, 1991), his first autobiographical work.

Jókai, Anna (b. 1932) Hungarian novelist and short-story writer. One of the most popular post–World War II Hungarian writers, Jókai was born and educated in Budapest, where she earned a degree in Hungarian studies at Eötvös Lóránd University in 1961. She then embarked on her long career as a Budapest schoolteacher. Attracted to literature, she began writing around 1965 and published her first novel, *4447*, in 1968. Other works followed in rapid succession: *Kötél nélkül* (Without Rope, 1969), a collection of short stories; *Tartozik és követel* (Assets and Liabilities, 1970), a novel; *A labda* (The Ball, 1971), a novella and short stories; *Napok* (Days, 1972), a novel; *Szeretteink, szerelmeink* (Our Loves, Our Lovers, 1973), a collection of short stories); a dramatization of *Tartozik és követel* (1973); *Mindhalálig* (Until Death, 1974), a novel; *A reimsi angyal* (The Angel at Reims, 1975), a collection of short stories; *A feladat* (The Task, 1977), a novel; *Panasz leírása* (A Complaint About Writing, 1980); *Jákob lajtorjája* (Jacob's Ladder, 1982), a novel; *Szegény sudár Anna* (Poor Thin Anna, 1989); *Mi ez az álom?* (What Is This Dream?, 1990); *A töve és a gallya* (By Stem and Stalk, 1991) and *Az ifjú halász és a tó* (The Young Fisherman and the Lake, 1992), novellas; *Három* (Three, 1995), a novel; and *Pèrc-emberkék dáridója* (Little Minute Men's Orgy, 1996). Her latest novel, *Ne féljetek* (Don't Be Afraid, 1998), follows the basic pattern of her most ambitious previous work of fiction, *Napok*. In the earlier text, Jokai traces the life of a central male figure from the 1930s through the early 1970s as a way of exploring the impact on ordinary Hungarians of the vast changes the country went through in some of its most tumultuous decades. In *Ne féljetek* she follows four characters—two past lovers and their present partners—through the period

1977 to 1997. In this instance, apart from again situating the lives of her characters within the larger historical frame of Hungary's transition from communism to the postcommunist era, she places a special emphasis on how individuals prepare for inevitable death. Jókai's most recent publication, *Mennyből az ember* (Man Is from Heaven, 2000), is a collection of lectures, critical studies, essays, and philosophical ruminations reflective of the author's wide range of interests—from anthroposophy to pop culture. Jokai was awarded the Attila József Prize in 1970 and the Central Council of Hungarian Trade Unions Prize in 1974.

Translations: "The Angel at Reims," trans. Georgia Lenart Greist, in *Ocean at the Window: Hungarian Prose and Poetry Since 1945*, ed. Albert Tezla (Minneapolis: University of Minnesota Press, 1980), 339–44.

Jovanovič, Dušan (b. 1939) Slovenian playwright. Slovenia's best known contemporary dramatist, Jovanovič was born in Belgrade but has lived in Slovenia since 1951. He studied French and English languages and literatures at Ljubljana University and then theater directing at the Academy of Theater Arts in Ljubljana. Jovanovič has had a long and distinguished career in Ljubljana theater and throughout the former Yugoslavia. In 1963 he founded the student theater ŠAG (Študentsko aktualno gledališče); in 1969 he was one of the founders and then director of the Pupilija Ferkeverk Theater; and in 1970 he cofounded the GLEJ Experimental Theater. He also served as artistic director of the Slovensko mladinsko gledališče (Slovenian Youth Theater). Apart from his directorial work, Jovanovič has been a prolific, highly imaginative, and provocative dramatic writer always experimenting with new means of theatrical expression and deeply interested in problems of language. His plays include *Znamke, nakar še Emilija* (Postage Stamps and Then Emily, 1968;

staged 1969), an absurd situational comedy; *Norci* (Madmen, 1970; staged 1971), a play about revolution that recalls the works of the British playwright John Osborne and the British "angry young man" generation; *Igrajte tumor v glavi in onesnaženje zraka* (*Act a Brain Tumor and Air Pollution*, 1972; staged 1976), a wildly abusurdist play about theater in which actors in a certain theater demand the freedom to do experimental drama and lock out those members of the organization who want to stick to traditional fare and methods; *Življenje podeželskih plejbojev po drugi svetovni vojni ali tuje hočemo, svojega ne damo* (The Life of Provincial Playboys After World War II, or Three Cuckolds, staged 1972), an erotic comedy in the style of the Italian commedia dell'arte; *Žrtve mode bum bum* (Victims of the Boom Boom Fashion, staged 1975), a "scenario for theatrical presentation"; *Generacije* (Generations, staged 1977), a satirical comedy about the relationship between culture and politics; *Osvoboditev Skopja* (The Liberation of Skopje, staged 1978) and *Karamazovi* (The Brothers Karamazovs, staged 1980), both dealing with questions of political determinism in Yugoslavia during and after World War II; *Vojaška skrivnost* (The Military Secret, staged 1983), a "zoolinguistic miracle" set in contemporary Slovenia with animal and human characters used to explore the state of mind and the state of language in a society approaching its end; *Viktor ali dan mladosti* (Victor or Youth Day, staged 1989), a variation on Roger Vitrac's *Victor ou les enfants au pouvoir*; *Jasnovidka ali dan mrtvih* (The Soothsayer, or the Day of the Dead, 1988; staged 1989), a farcical political satire; *Zid, jezero* (The Wall, the Lake, staged 1989), a "whole evening's one-acter" about the disintegration of a marriage through jealousy and suspicion; *Don Juan na psu* (Don Juan in Agony, 1990), based on Jovanovič's 1969 novel, a grotesque black comedy intended as a kind

of ironic epilogue to the former Yugoslavia; *Antigona* (Antigone, staged 1993), which resonates with memories of the brief Slovenian war of independence in 1991; *Uganke korajže* (The Puzzle of Courage, staged 1994), which relates the depression of an actress playing the lead character in Bertolt Brecht's *Mother Courage* to the experiences of a character who has lost her sons in the Balkan wars; and *Kdo to poje Sizifa* (*Who's Singing Sisyphus?*), mainly a performance production about a madcap opera based on the torments of Sisyphus. *Antigona, Uganke korajže,* and *Kdo to poje Sizifa* were published in 1997 in a single volume under the title *Balkanska trilogija* (Balkan Trilogy). The best single edition of Jovanovič's plays is *Zid, jezero in druge igre* (The Wall, the Lake and Other Plays, 1991); it contains six of the playwright's most popular works. Jovanovič's plays have been widely staged, including in the United States, and his reputation is international.

Translations: *Act a Brain Tumour and Air Pollution,* trans. Lesley Soule, *Studies in Theatre Production,* supp. 1 (1994/1995); *The Puzzle of Courage,* trans. Lesley Wade Soule, in *Contemporary Slovenian Drama* (Ljubljana: Slovenian Writers Association, 1997), 153– 91, which also contains synopses of two other plays by Jovanovič: *Osvoboditev Skopja* and *Zid, jezero; Who's Singing Sisyphus? A Musical Drama in Three Parts,* trans. Lesley Wade Soule, *Studies in Theatre Production,* supp. 3 (1997); "What Does That Make Me? A Sketch for My Autobiography," trans. Tamara Soban, in *The Slovenian Essay of the Nineties,* selected by Matevž Kos (Ljubljana: Slovene Writers Association, 2000).

Jovanovski, Meto (b. 1928) Macedonian novelist and short-story writer. A native of Brajčino, a village near the Macedonian–Greek border, Jovanovski was educated at the Teachers College in Skopje. He subsequently spent several years as a teacher in a school near his native village and elsewhere in Macedonia. He later went to work for the major Skopje publishing house, Makedonska Kniga, and served as editor of such well-known literary journals as *Sovremenost* and *Kulturen život*. He has also worked for Radio Skopje as director for foreign programming and has been president of the Macedonian PEN Center.

Jovanovski's literary career began with the publication of short stories in 1951, but it was only in 1956 that his first collection of stories, *Jadreš*, appeared. His subsequent volumes of stories include *Hajka na peperutki* (Chasing Butterflies, 1957); *Nateznati dzvezdi* (Stretched Stars, 2nd ed., 1969); *Meni na mojata mesečina* (Change of My Moon, 1959); and *Patot do osamata* (The Road to Loneliness, 1978). Jovanovski was also one of three authors (the others were Kiril Kamilov and Slavko Janevski) who contributed a story to the collection *Temni kazuvanja* (Dark Punishments, 1962, 1967). Besides his short stories, Jovanovski has written several novels: *Zemja i tegoba* (Land and Toil, 1964); *Slana vo cutot na bademite* (Frost in the Almond Tree Blossom, 1965); *Svedoči* (To Bear Witness, 1971); *Prvite čovekovi umiranja* (The First Men of Death, 1971); *Budoletinki* (Cousins, 1973); *Orlovata dolina* (Valley of the Eagles, 1979); and *Krstopat kon spokojot* (Transgressing the Peace, 1987). In 1979/1980, Jovanovski was named an Honorary Fellow in Writing at the University of Iowa and later published an informal and entertaining account of his travels in the United States (as well as Europe and Israel) under the title *Klučevite na Manhatan: Zapisi od zapadnite predeli* (The Keys to Manhattan: Notes from the Western Lands, 1983). An edition of selected stories by Jovanovski appeared in 1985 under the title *Izbor* (Selected Tales). His satirical political work *Balkanska kniga na umrenite, ili, Osloboduvanje preku zboruvanje* (The Balkan Book of the Dead, or, Emancipation Through Talking) came out in 1992.

Although deeply rooted in Macedonian history and culture, which is more immediately evident in some works than others, Jovanovski's wry humor, wit, irony, and keen eye for the grotesque have a universal appeal. His style tends toward the simple, even the laconic, and his subjects range from World War I and the Balkan wars to the post–World War II communist era. The short novel *Cousins* and the stories collected in *Faceless Men and Other Macedonian Stories* are representative of his style and outlook and serve as a good introduction to his writing for the foreign reader until other works are translated.

Translations: *Cousins*, trans. Sylvia Wallace Holton and Meto Jovanovski (San Francisco: Mercury House, 1987); *Faceless Men and Other Macedonian Stories*, trans. Jeffrey Folks, Milne Holton, and Charles Simic (London: Forest, 1992); "The Man in the Blue Suit," in *The Big Horse and Other Stories of Modern Macedonia*, ed. Milne Holton (Columbia: University of Missouri Press, 1974), 18–24.

Juhász, Ferenc (b. 1928) Hungarian poet. Widely regarded as among the foremost poets of his generation, and compared at times with Walt Whitman, Juhász was born into a working-class family of peasant origin in the village of Bia, near Budapest. He pursued a higher education at Budapest University from 1948 to 1951 as a member of the People's College movement, but left without a degree. From 1951 until his retirement, he worked for the Budapest publishing house Szépirodalmi Könyvkiadó and later served as editor of the influential periodical *Új Írás* until it ceased publication in 1990. His first poems appeared in 1947, and his first book of poetry, *Szárnyas csikó* (Winged Colt), containing poems written between 1946 and 1949, came out in 1949.

The following year, he was awarded the Kossuth Prize for *Apám* (My Father, 1950), a long narrative poem commemorating his father, who died in 1950 after years of serious lung illness. By 1957 he had published nine volumes of poems, among them *A Sántha család* (The Sántha Family, 1950); *Új versek* (New Poems, 1951); *Óda repüléshez* (Ode to Flying, 1953); *A nap és a hold elrablása* (Laying Hold of the Sun and the Moon, 1954); *A tékozló ország* (The Profligate Country, 1954), an epic about the downfall of György Dózsa, the leader of the peasant revolution of 1514; *A virágok hatalma* (The Power of Flowers, 1956), in which he tries to find greater meaning for humanity by informing it with a cosmic dimension; and *A tenyészet országa* (The Breeding Country, 1957), a collection of verses from 1946 to 1956.

Increasing cultural repression and official criticism brought on severe depression in 1957, and Juhász was hospitalized in 1958. His recovery, which began only in 1962, was attributed by him to the writing of his long poem "József Attila sírjánál" ("At the Grave of Attila József") in 1962. It was published in *Új Írás* and touched off serious debate. Juhász's first book in nine years, the verse collection *Harc a fehér báránnyal* (Battling the White Lamb), appeared in 1965. It contains his most celebrated single work, the long poem "A szarvassá változott fiú kiáltozása a titkok kapujából" ("The Boy Changed into a Stag Clamors at the Gate of Secrets," 1955), usually referred to just as "The Boy Changed into a Stag." About a boy turned into a stag who can no longer heed his mother's anguished calls for him to come back to her, the poem is a symbolic rejection of the city and of modern urban culture, and a fervent plea to return to the land, to the roots of the native culture. The British poet W. H. Auden deeply admired the work, and the literary scholar George Steiner lauds it in his book *After Babel* as

the best long poem ever written. The year in which *Harc a fehér báránnyal* appeared also brought a selected edition of Juhász's poems from 1946 to 1964 under the title *Virágzó világfa* (The Flowering World Tree, 1965). It was followed by *Éjszaka képei* (Images of the Night, 1961), in which the poet voices his anguish over the atomic, hydrogen, and neutron bombs and their threat to the earth; *Anyám* (My Mother) and *A szent tűzözön regéi* (Legends of the Holy Flood of Fire), both from 1969; *A halottak eposza* (The Epic of the Dead) and *A halottak királya* (The King of the Dead), both from 1971; *A megváltó aranykard* (The Redeeming Gold Sword, 1973); *Három éposz* (Three Epics, 1975); *A halott feketerigó* (The Dead Blackbird, 1985); and *A föld alatti liliom* (The Undeground Lily, 1991). In these later mostly "lyrical" epic poems—some of them extremely long—Juhász grapples with the most basic questions of life and death as he seeks to find meaning in life that would allow the acceptance of death, with which Juhász became obsessed as time went on. Juhász was awarded a second Kossuth Prize in 1973. A large two-volume edition of his poetry, containing texts dating from 1946 to 1970, was published under the general title *A mindenség szerelme* (Love for the Universe). The first volume, *A szarvassá változott fiú* (The Boy Changed into a Stag), appeared in 1971; the second, *A titkok kapuja* (The Gate of Secrets), came out in 1972.

Literature: Kenneth McRobbie, "Introduction" and "Brief Confessions About Myself," in Ferenc Juhász, *The Boy Changed into a Stag: Selected Poems, 1949–1967*, trans. Kenneth McRobbie and Ilona Duczynska (Toronto: Oxford University Press, 1970), 8–19, 21–32.

Translations: *The Boy Changed into a Stag: Selected Poems, 1949–1967*, trans. Kenneth McRobbie and Ilona Duczynska (Toronto: Oxford University Press, 1970), which is the best collection of Juhász's poetry in English and contains, in addition to "The Boy Changed into a Stag," such other long poems as "Four Voices: Non-Maledictory, in Lament and Supplication," "Images of the Night," "The Power of Flowers," and "The Grave of Attila József." There is also a fair selection of Juhász's poems as well as poems by Sándor Weöres in *Selected Poems,* trans. David Wevill (Harmondsworth: Penguin, 1970). A complete translation, by David Wevill, of "The Boy Changed into a Stag Clamors at the Gate of Secrets" also appears in *In Quest of the "Miracle Stag": The Poetry of Hungary,* ed. Adam Makkai (Chicago: Atlantis-Centaur, 1996), 853–64. SOUND RECORDING: Sound recordings, dated 1977, of Juhász reading his poetry in Hungarian and of Juhász, Amy Károlyi, István Vas, and Sándor Weöres reading their poetry, recorded as *An Evening of Hungarian Poetry,* are available at the Recorded Sound Reference Center, Library of Congress.

Jurewicz, Aleksander (b. 1952) Polish poet and story writer. A native of the village of Lida in what used to be Soviet Belarus, Jurewicz and his family resettled in Poland in 1957. He has been a prolific poet, as evidenced by such volumes as *Sen który na pewno nie był miłością* (A Dream that Was Certainly Not Love, 1974); *Po drugiej stronie* (On the Other Side, 1978); *Nie strzelajcie do Beatlesów* (Don't Shoot at the Beatles, 1983); and *Jak gołębie gnane burzą* (Like Doves Chased by the Storm, 1990). Jurewicz is also the author two novellas, *W środku nocy* (In the Middle of the Night, 1980) and *Lida* (1990), about the village of his birth, and a short novel narrated in the first person, *Pan Bóg nie słyszy głuchych* (The Lord Does Not Hear the Deaf, 1995), dealing mostly with his own family. Jurewicz is a poet of loneliness who conveys a sense of lost youth, of being burned out and unsure about how to move into the future. The uprootedness he

experienced in his own life is reflected in the poems about Lida, from which he was wrenched in his youth and of which he now has only fading memories.

Translations: Eight poems in *Young Poets of a New Poland: An Anthology,* trans. Donald Pirie (London: Forest, 1993), 29–41.

Kadare, Elena (b. 1943) Albanian novelist and short-story writer. The wife of the distinguished Albanian novelist Ismail Kadare, Kadare enjoys the reputation of being the first woman writer to publish a novel in Albania. She received her early education in her native town of Fier before going on to secondary school in Elbasan. She subsequently studied at Tirana University, after which she worked as a journalist and an editor. Her first major publication was the collection of short stories *Shuajë dritën Vera!* (Turn Off the Light, Vera!, 1965). This was followed in 1970 by her first novel and the basis of her literary fame, *Një lindje e vështirë* (A Difficult Birth). Kadare's second book of short stories, *Nusja dhe shtetrrethimi* (The Bride and the State of Siege), appeared in 1978, followed in 1981 by the novel *Bashkëshortët* (The Spouses). Kadare's fiction deals mainly with the second-class-citizen status of women in traditional Albanian society and the changes being achieved in the post–World War II society shaped by the communists.

Translations: *Një lindje e vështirë* is available in French as *Une Femme de Tirana,* trans. Jusuf Vrioni and Anne-Marie Autissier (Paris: Stock, 1995).

Kadare, Ismail (b. 1936) Albanian novelist. The most celebrated Albanian author of the twentieth century, Kadare was born and raised in the picturesque mountain city of Gjirokastër, the birthplace as well of the Albanian communist dictator Enver Hoxha. He studied at the Faculty of History and Philology at Tirana University and at the Gorky Institute of World Literature in Moscow. He remained in Moscow until 1960, when relations between Albania and the Soviet Union cooled. Although Kadare immigrated to Paris in 1990 and has long been critical of the severity of communist rule in Albania, he had a good working relationship with Hoxha and enjoyed privileges denied other writers. This did not endear him to fellow Albanian authors and explains his malice toward them, particularly in his émigré writings.

Kadare began his literary career in the 1950s with such volumes of poetry as *Frymëzimet djaloshare* (Youthful Inspiration, 1954); *Ëndërrimet* (Dreams, 1957); and *Shekulli im* (My Century, 1961), which attracted readers for their diversity and originality. It is, however, as a novelist that Kadare has had his greatest impact as a writer.

His first novel, *Gjenerali i ushtrisë së vdekur* (*The General of the Dead Army*), takes place in the aftermath of World War II and the Italian occupation of Albania. A satire aimed at ridiculous notions of patriotism, the work was first published in 1963 but had to be revised in 1967 because of official discontent with the partly favorable treatment of the central figure of an Italian general who returns to Albania to recover the remains of Italian soldiers defeated and disgraced during the war. The novel became immensely popular and was very widely translated. Kadare encountered even more trouble with censorship over his next novel, *Përbindëshi* (The Monster), a curious reworking of the Trojan horse legend with political implications. It was first published in 1965 in the official Tirana literary journal, *Nëntori*, but was soon suppressed; it was republished in a revised version only in 1990

and 1991. But Kadare was not one to be intimidated by censorship. *Dasma* (*The Wedding*), which came out in 1967, is in essence a mockery of Albanian socialist realism. *Kështjella* (The Fortress, 1970) at first appears to be a historical novel about the Turkish siege of an unnamed Albanian fortress defended by the Albanian national hero, Skenderbeg (1405–1468). But Skenderbeg in fact never appears in the work, which can easily be read both as an allusion to the tensions between little Albania and the powerful Soviet Union in the 1960s and as a debunking of the most pervasive of Albanian national myths. *Kronikë në gur* (*Chronicle in Stone*, 1971) is largely autobiographical and is based on Kadare's experiences as a young boy in his native Gjirokastër, under enemy occupation during World War II. Kadare's next novel, the less successful *Nëntori i një kryeqyteti* (November in a Capital City, 1973), revised in 1989/1990 to expunge requisite procommunist propaganda in the original edition, has a World War II setting but was inspired by the Albanian purge of 1973 to 1975. Also political in content is *Dimri i madh* (The Great Winter), which Kadare wrote in the period 1971 to 1976 and which reflects Albania's rift with the Soviet Union in 1961. The original edition of the novel appeared in 1973 as *Dimri i vetmise së madhe* (The Winter of the Great Solitude), but had to be rewritten because of the sensitive nature of its subject; it was finally reprinted in 1977.

Dimri i madh was followed in 1978 by three more novels: *Le Crepuscule des dieux de la steppe* (The Twilight of the Steppe Gods), an autobiographical novel, available only in French, describing Kadare's years as a student in the Soviet Union; *Pashallëqet e mëdha* (The Big Pashaluks), a parody of a historical novel based on the career of the ruthless "Lion of Janina" (Ali Pasha Tepelena, 1740–1822); and, the best of the three, *Ura me tri harqe* (*The Three-Arched*

Bridge), which takes place in the Albanian Middle Ages. Kadare published another five novels in the 1980s. *Prilli i thyer* (*Broken April*, 1980) is set in the 1930s and revolves around the ancient Albanian tradition of the blood feud (the Canon of Lek Dukagjini). *Kush e solli Doruntine?* (Who Brought Back Doruntine?, 1980; translated as *Doruntine*, 1980) is an atmospheric and intriguing novel based on the Albanian folk legend of Constantine and his sister Doruntine, known also as Garentine. *Nata me hënë* (A Moonlit Night, 1985) was banned a few months after publication for its frank depiction of the status of women in the patriarchal and intolerant Albanian society of Kadare's own time. *Dosja H.* (*The File on H.*, 1981) is about two Irish-born scholars looking for the roots of the *Iliad* and *Odyssey* and the true identity of their author (the "H." of the title). Published in Albania during the dark days of the Hoxha dictatorship, the novel brims with an almost offensive nationalism as Kadare sets out to prove that the Albanians preceded the Greeks on the Balkan peninsula and can lay rightful claim to some of the territory of their neighbors.

In *Nëpunësi i pallatit të ëndrrave* (The Official of the Palace of Dreams, 1981), first published in Albania and immediately banned, Kadare's subject is again totalitarianism, but the setting is a fictional United Ottoman States, where his protagonist, a bureaucratic functionary named Mark-Alem, works in a secret-police-like agency (the "Palace of Dreams") dedicated to stifling opposition to a totalitarian state by controlling people's dreams. A revised version of the novel appeared in 1996 under the title *Pallati i ëndrrave* (*The Palace of Dreams*). *Koncert në fund të dimrit* (*The Concert*, 1988) is a long novel dealing with the dissolution of the once close relations between Albania and China in the 1970s. Much of the action takes place in China, which Kadare knew firsthand from his visits there as a member of official Albanian writers' delegations, and introduces Mao Zedong and Zhou Enlai as characters. Cut off from the rest of Europe, the Soviet Union, and then China, Albania becomes isolated in a world of its own imagining. Kadare's satire not only exposes the absurdist geopolitical situation of Albania, but also aims barbs at the arrogant backwardness of the Chinese, who for a time grotesquely remain Albania's sole link to the outside world. Among Kadare's other writings of the 1980s were *Autobiografia e popullit në vargje* (*The Autobiography of the People in Verse*, 1980), an interesting but nationally biased essay on Albanian folk poetry and its antiquity, and *Eskili, ky humbës i madh* (Aeschylus, or the Eternal Loser, 1988), on the ancient Greek dramatist. Kadare's interest in Greece, both classical and modern, is manifest in his translations of the *Orestia* into Albanian and of modern Greek poetry for his *Antologji e poezisë greke* (Anthology of Greek Poetry, 1986).

Kadare's literary productivity continued unabated in the 1990s. *Ftesë në studio* (Invitation to the Studio, 1990) was Kadare's last publication in Albania before he left for France in 1990. It contains a selection of thirty-two poems, verse translations from several languages (including Chinese and Russian), and personal reflections on a broad variety of subjects from literature to current events. Several of his pieces amount to a caustic settling of scores with other easily identified Albanian writers. Kadare's next work, *Pesha e kryqit* (The Weight of the Cross, 1991), was originally designed as an appendix to *Ftesë në studio*, which is why both works were published as a single volume in French translation under the title *Invitation à l'atelier de l'écrivain suivi de Le Poids de la croix* (Invitation to the Writer's Studio, Followed by The Weight of the Cross). *Nga një dhjetor në tjetrin: Kronikë, këmbim letrash, persiatje* (From One December to the Next: Chronicle, Correspondence,

Reflections), which appeared in 1991 simultaneously in Paris with its French translation, *Printemps albanaises: Chronique, lettres, réflexions* (Albanian Spring: Chronicle, Letters, Reflections; translated as *Albanian Spring: The Anatomy of Tyranny*), is a sequel to *Ftesë në studio* and together with that work and *Pesha e kryqit* forms a kind of trilogy of a distinctly autobiographical character that provides many insights into Kadare and his world. It is a personal chronicle of events covering the transitional period in Kadare's life, from December 1989 to December 1990, and written in much the same tone and spirit. In 1995 Kadare published *Piramida* (*The Pyramid*), an allegorical novel set in Egypt in the twenty-sixth century B.C. during the building of the Great Pyramid under Pharaoh Cheops. In Kadare's view, the grandiose project is nothing more than a cynical means of instilling dread in the populace and crushing any will to oppose the pharaoh's totalitarianism. The parallels between ancient Egypt during the reign of Cheops and post–World War II Albania in the time of Hoxha are easily discerned. Kadare's most recent publications are the novella *Tri këngë zie për Kosovën* (Three Sad Songs for Kosovo, 1998; translated as *Three Elegies for Kosovo*) and the novel *Lulet e ftohta të marsit* (Cold Flowers of March, 2000). In *Three Elegies for Kosovo*, the Turkish victory over the Serbs, the Bosnians, and their Christian Albanian allies on the Plain of Kosovo in June 1389 serves as the historical background for a lament for the subsequent disunity and enmity among the Balkan peoples, culminating in the ravaging of the predominantly Albanian province during the Serbian campaign of "ethnic cleansing" of 1999. Cold Flowers of March is closely related to *Broken April* (which, unlike the more recent novel, is set in the 1930s) and has as its subject the resurgence of the traditional blood feud in postcommunist Albania.

Kadare's short stories and novellas were published in three collections: *Emblema e dikurshme* (Signs of the Past, 1977); *Gjakftohtësia* (Cold-bloodedness, 1980); and *Koha e shkrimeve* (Epoch of Writings, 1986). *Kush e solli Doruntine?*, *Pallati i ëndrrave*, and *Prilli i thyer* originally appeared in these collections, which also contain such well-regarded stories as "Sjellësi i fatkeqësisë ("The Bearer of Ill Tidings," also known as "The Caravan of Veils"); "Viti i mbrapshtë" ("The Dark Year"), set in 1914 when World War I broke out; and "Krushqit janë të ngrirë" ("The Wedding Procession Turned to Ice"), about events in Kosovo as seen through the eyes of a surgeon in Priština.

Literature: No full-length study of Kadare in English has yet appeared. There are, however, several helpful works in French: Alain Bosquet, *Les Trente Premières Années* (Paris: Grasset, 1993); Eric Faye, *Ismail Kadare: Promethee porte-feu* (Paris: Corti, 1991); Michel Metais, ed., *Ismail Kadare et la nouvelle poésie albanaise: Choix, traduction et présentation de textes de Ismail Kadare, Dritero Agolli, Fatos Arapi, et Natasha Lako* (Paris: Oswald, 1973); Ismail Kadare, *Entretiens avec Eric Faye* (Paris: Corti, 1991); Anne-Marie Mitchell, *Un Rhapsode albanais: Ismail Kadare* (Marseille: Le Temps parallele, 1990); Fabien Terpan, *Ismail Kadare* (Paris: Editions universitaires, 1992); and Alexandre Zotos, *De Scanderberg à Ismail Kadare: Propos d'histoire et de littérature albanaises* (Saint-Etienne: Publications de l'Université de Saint-Etienne, 1997). The principal Albanian studies are Shaip Beqiri, *Sfida e gjeniut: Kadare, ekzili, Kosova* (Priština: Gjon Buzuku, 1991); Tefik Caushi, *Universi letrar i Kadaresë* (Tirana: Evropa, 1993), and *Kadare: Fjalor i personazheve* (Tirana: Enciklopedike, 1995); and Injac Zamputi, *Eksursion në dy vepra te Kadaresë* (Tirana: Dituria, 1993). In the absence of major studies in English, the reader knowing only English is well served by the material on Kadare in Robert Elsie, *History of Albanian Literature*, 2 vols. (Boulder, Colo.: East European Monographs, 1995), and *Studies in Modern Albanian Literature and Culture* (Boulder, Colo.: East European Monographs, 1996).

Translations: *Albanian Spring: The Anatomy of Tyranny*, trans. from the French by Emile Capouya (London: Saqi, 1995); *The Autobiography of the People in Verse* (Tirana: 8 Nëntori, 1987); *Broken April* (New York: New Amsterdam, 1990); *Chronicle in Stone* (London: Serpent's Tail, 1987); *The Concert*, trans. from the French of Jusuf Vrioni by Barbara Bray (New York: Morrow, 1994); *Doruntine*, trans. from the French of Jusuf Vrioni by Jon Rothschild (New York: New Amsterdam, 1988); *The File on H.*, trans. from the French of Jusuf Vrioni by Barbara Bray (London: Harvill, 1997); *The File on H.*, trans. from the French of Jusuf Vrioni by David Bellos (New York: Arcade, 1998); *The General of the Dead Army*, trans. from the French by Derek Coltman (London: Allen, 1971; New York: Grossman, 1972); *The Palace of Dreams*, trans. from the French of Jusuf Vrioni by Barbara Bray (New York: Arcade, 1996); *The Pyramid*, trans. from the French of Jusuf Vrioni by David Bellos (New York: Vintage, 1998); *Three Elegies for Kosovo*, trans. Peter Constantine (London: Harvill, 2000); *The Three-Arched Bridge*, trans. John Hodgson (New York: Arcade, 1997); *The Wedding*, trans. Ali Cungu (Tirana: Naim Frashëri, 1968). *Lulet e ftohta të marsit* is available in French as *Froides fleurs d'avril*, trans. Jusuf Vrioni (Paris: Fayard, 2000).

Kahlau, Heinz (b. 1931) German poet, screenwriter, and television scriptwriter. A popular writer in his time, Kahlau was born in Drewitz (today part of Potsdam) and, before launching a literary career, was trained as a tractor driver. A loyal supporter of the German Democratic Republic, Kahlau be-

came an active member of and later a functionary in the FDJ (Free German Youth) organization. In 1953 Kahlau began a close association, as a theatrical writer, with Bertolt Brecht, who was a formative influence on him. His early poetry was written in the "agitprop" style—for example, the collection *Maisschule: Ein Agitprop-Programm* (Corn School: An Agitprop Program, 1959), with music by Wolfgang Lesser. Kahlau's first collection of verse, *Hoffnung lebt in den Zweigen des Caiba* (Hope Lives in the Branches of the Caiba), had in fact appeared in 1954. Beginning with his post-agitprop poetry, Kahlau settled into the style with which he became identified: a keen observation of daily life in order to understand and reveal social dynamics, concreteness, an absence of emotion, and a tendency toward the laconic and at times even aphoristic. Kahlau expressed his ideas on poetry, the writing of verse, and his own habits as an artist in his pleasantly readable book *Der Vers. Der Reim. Die Zeile: Wie ich Gedichte schreibe* (Verse, Rhyme, Line: How I Write Poetry, 1974).

Kahlau became a freelance writer in 1956. His collections of poetry after *Maisschule: Ein Agitprop-Programm* include *Fluss der Dinge: Gedichte aus 10. Jahren* (The Flow of Things: Poems from Ten Years, 1965); *Poesiealbum 21* (Poetry Album 21, 1969); *Berlin aus meiner Bildermappe: Einundziebzig Gedichte zu Zeichnungen von Heinrich Zille* (Berlin from My Picture Collection: 71 Poems for Heinrich Zille's Drawings, 1969); *Balladen* (Ballads, 1971); *Du: Liebesgedichte, 1954–1979* (You: Love Lyrics, 1954–1979, 1971); *Flugbrett für Engel* (Flight Deck for Angels, 1974); *Fluss der Dinge: Kantate für Soli, Chor, Sprecher und Orchester* (The Flow of Things: Cantata for Soloist, Chorus, Speaker, and Orchestra, 1979); *Lob des Sisyphus: Gedichte aus einem viertel Jahrhundert* (In Praise of Sisyphus: A Quarter Century of Poems, 1980); *Bögen: Aus-*

gewählte Gedichte, 1950–1980 (Arcs: Selected Poems, 1950–1980, 1982); *Fundsachen* (Articles Found, 1984); *Querholz: Sinn- und Unsinngedichte* (Crossbar: Sense and Nonsense Poems, 1989); and *Zweisam: Liebesgedichte* (Together: Love Lyrics, 1999). Kahlau had a particular liking for love lyrics, which he wrote with a light, deft touch. They remain among his most popular poems. Kahlau was a longtime member (1979–1991) of the GDR Writers Association in Berlin. By his own confession, he also actively collaborated with the East German secret police (Stasi) from 1956 to 1963. Kahlau has been the recipient of several literary awards, among them the Arts Prize of the FDJ, the Heinrich Greif Prize, and the Heinrich Heine Prize, all awarded in 1963.

Translations: Three poems, in German and English, trans. Michael Hamburger et al., in *East German Poetry: An Anthology*, ed. Michael Hamburger (New York: Dutton, 1973), 112–15.

Kaleb, Vjekoslav (1905–1966) Croatian novelist, essayist, short-story writer, and screenwriter. Intimately identified as a literary figure with his native Dalmatia, Kaleb was born in the town of Tijesno, near Šibenik, on the Dalmatian coast. After his early education in Tijesno (1912–1918), he studied at a school for future teachers in Zadar, but moved to Belgrade when Zadar was occupied by Italian troops in 1922. After a year at a similar institution in Belgrade, Kaleb transferred to a school in Šibenik from which he graduated in 1924. He remained in Šibenik for several years, working as a teacher and cultivating his literary career. His first book of short stories, *Na kamenju* (On Stone, 1940), which effectively evokes the life of the Dalmatian peasants, proved a considerable success and led to an appointment in Zagreb at the Department of Education. From 1941 to 1943, Kaleb also studied at the Higher Pedagogical Institute in the Croatian capital. In 1942 he published his second collection of stories, *Izvan stvari* (Outside of Things). It, too, was a success. Both collections were republished several times as *Novele* (Novellas, 1946, 1947); *Pripovijetke* (Stories, 1951); and *Ogledalo* (The Mirror, 1962). In an expanded version, they formed a part of the six-volume edition of Kaleb's collected works (*Odabrane djela*), issued in 1969. Although affection clearly motivated Kaleb's literary attraction for the Dalmatian peasant, he had no illusions about the world of his characters and did not flinch from portraying their darker side, their ignorance, jealousies, and capacity even for murder. There is an undeniable bleakness to his view.

In 1942, the same year that Kaleb's second volume of stories appeared, he published the patently autobiographical *U stakleniku* (In the Glasshouse), the reminiscences of a young teacher whose own harsh schooling made him withdrawn and introspective. During World War II, Kaleb joined Tito's partisans, in 1943 moving to Otočac and eventually to Livno and the Dalmatian islands of Hvar and Vis. In January 1944 he and other partisans were evacuated to Egypt, from where Kaleb returned to Zagreb in 1945. After the war, he became the editor of the journal *Republika*, a position he held from 1945 to 1950. He also edited the newspaper *Književne novine*. He later became secretary of the important Matica hrvatska publishing house and artistic director of the Jadran Film Company. In 1956 Kaleb was elected president of the Union of Croatian Writers.

Apart from his short stories, Kaleb's reputation rests mainly on his war fiction. His first effort in this vein was a collection of stories under the title *Brigada* (Brigade, 1945). But the Soviet-style socialist realism then virtually mandatory in Yugoslavia compromised the literary quality of the writing. Kaleb came into his own, however, with his novel *Divota prašine* (*Glorious*

Dust, 1945). It is a stark, unsentimental account of the effort by two partisans—one identified as the Boy, the other as the Naked Man—to rejoin their unit from which they have been separated. It has long been Kaleb's best work of fiction and the only one well represented in foreign translation.

Translations: *Glorious Dust*, trans. Zora G. Depolo (London: Lincolns-Prager, 1960).

Kamondy, László (real name László Tóth; 1928–1972) Hungarian short-story writer, novelist, and playwright. A native of Balatonmagyaród, Kamondy received a degree in teaching from Eötvös Lóránd University and then taught in a trade school. He subsequently was employed for nine years as a reader for the Szépirodalmi publishing house in Budapest. Kamondy made his debut as a writer with the short story "Verekedők" ("Brawlers"), which was published in *Csillag* in 1954. His first collection of stories, *Fekete galambok* (Black Pigeons), appeared in 1957 and confirmed Kamondy's resistance to the schematic formulas of the socialist realism of the 1950s and his cultivation of psychological analysis. His novel, *Apostolok utóda* (The Apostles' Successor, 1960), was followed by several collections of short stories and novellas: *Megdézsmált örömök* (Decimated Joys, 1964), a collection of his short stories from 1953 to 1963; *Ádám apja* (Adam's Father, 1968); *Feltételes vallomás* (Conditional Confession, 1969); and *Szerelmes házastársak* (Married Lovers, 1973). Kamondy published his first play, *Szerelmesek fája* (Lover's Tree), in 1960. This was followed by other dramatic works, including *Vád és varázslat* (Prosecution and Witchcraft, 1963) and *Lány az aszfalton* (Girl on the Street) and *Szöktetés albérletbe avagy a szemérmes ateisták* (Elopement in a Rented Room or The Bashful Atheists), both dating from 1965.

Translations: "The Student and the Woman," trans. Judit Házi, in *Hungarian Short Stories* (Toronto: Exile Editions, 1983), 163–80.

Kanov, Liubomir (b. 1944) Bulgarian psychiatrist and short-story writer. One of the better-known literary émigrés of the 1980s, Kanov was born in Bankia, near Sofia, and was trained as a medical doctor at Sofia University. He worked as a psychiatrist in Lom, Kurilo, and Sofia until his arrest by the Bulgarian State Security on 3 March 1977 on charges of disseminating "counterrevolutionary propaganda" and planning to flee to the West. He was imprisoned in Starozagorsk Prison, following which he worked for several years as a general physician and psychiatrist in hospitals in Kurilo and Karlukovo. He continued to be held under surveillance until 1984, when he succeeded in immigrating to Canada. He subsequently worked part time in a psychiatric clinic in Texas, and beginning in the summer of 1989, as a psychiatrist in New York. His stories were published in the Most series and in such literary journals as *Vek 21, Literaturen forum,* and *Literaturen vestnik.* Kanov's only published book is *Chovekut kukuvitsa* (The Cuckoo Man, 1991), a collection of thirteen stories. Although written in emigration, they clearly grew out of and reflect Bulgarian society and culture of the 1970s and 1980s; a few were conceived while Kanov was in prison. The work of an original storyteller, Kanov's stories are an intriguing blend of the absurd and the grotesque, the mythological and the historical, with elements of parody. Among the best stories in the collection are "Logofago," "Diavolska karutsa" ("The Devil's Wagon"), and "Apokalipsis togava" ("Apocalypse Then").

Kant, Hermann (b. 1926) German novelist, short-story writer, and journalist. Born in Hamburg, Kant was trained as an electrician and saw military service toward the end of World War II. He spent three years (1945–1948) in a Polish prisoner-of-war camp. From 1949 to 1952, he studied at the Workers and Peasants Faculty of Ernst-Moritz-Arndt University in Greifswald, after which he pursued Germanic studies at Humboldt University in Berlin. It was in his Humboldt period that Kant's talent for journalism blossomed. He became editor in chief of the student journal *tua res,* for which he wrote political satire. He also contributed articles in the same vein to *Neue Deutschland.* In 1959 he became a freelance writer with permanent residence in Berlin. As his literary career developed, Kant also became prominent in the administration of the East German Writers Union. He was elected a member of the board of the union in 1963, its vice president in 1969, and in 1978 its president, a position he held until 1990. In 1969 Kant was also elected a member of the Academy of Arts of the German Democratic Republic.

Kant began his career as a writer of fiction with the publication in 1962 of a collection of stories titled *Ein bischen Südsee* (A Bit of the South Seas). The title refers to an aquarium of ornamental fish maintained by a Hamburg street cleaner whose life is followed from the prewar to the postwar period. *Ein bischen Südsee* was followed by arguably his best novel, *Aula* (The Lecture Hall), in 1965. Kant published two other novels in the 1970s: *Das Impressum* (The Imprint, 1972) and *Der Aufenhalt* (The Stop, 1976). A second collection of stories, *Eine Übertretung* (A Transgression), appeared in 1972, preceded by a volume of reportage, *In Stockholm* (In Stockholm), based on his travels and observations in Sweden, in 1971. Although often cavalierly dismissed as an ideological hack, a literary stooge of the East German regime, Kant was a talented writer capable of real literary achievement. This is evident above all in *Aula,* which became one of the most widely read

and controversial works of fiction in the history of the GDR. Strongly autobiographical, like most of his fiction, *Aula* replaces a traditional protagonist with a collective entity, in this case a Workers and Peasants University established during the development stage of the GDR for the purpose of training young workers for eventual positions of leadership in the new state. The point of departure for the novel is the invitation to a former WPU student and electrician-turned-journalist to deliver a commemorative address on the occasion of the closing of his alma mater. But the address does not take place, replaced instead by the novel *Aula,* a texturally rich interweaving of a variety of heterogeneous elements drawn from and collectively representing a commentary on the state-building period of the GDR (the late 1940s), the purpose of which is to awaken and keep alive a historical consciousness.

The dissolution of the East German state opened access to a host of privileged state documents and archives, including those of the secret police (Stasi). This development has dealt a crippling blow to Kant's reputation insofar as unimpeachable documentation has revealed that he was a Stasi agent, codenamed I. M. "Martin." This documentation was published in 1995 by the literary scholar and journalist Karl Corvino in his book *Die Akte Kant: IM "Martin," die Stasi und die Literatur in Ost und West* (The Kant File: I. M. "Martin," the Stasi, and Literature in East and West).

Literature: "Hermann Kant," in *Literary Intellectuals and the Dissolution of the State: Professionalism and Conformity in the GDR,* ed. Robert von Hallberg, trans. Kenneth J. Northcott (Chicago: University of Chicago Press, 1996), 143–54; Karl Corvino, ed., *Die Akte Kant: IM "Martin," die Stasi und die Literatur in Ost und West* (Reinbek bei Hamburg: Rowohlt, 1995); Leonore Krenzlin, *Hermann Kant: Leben und Werk* (Berlin: Das europäische Buch,

1979); Theodor Langenbruch, *Dialectical Humor in Kant's Novel "Die Aula": A Study in Contemporary East German Literature* (Bonn: Bouvier, 1975).

Translations: "For the Files," trans. Jan van Heurck, in *The New Sufferings of Young W. and Other Stories from the German Democratic Republic,* ed. Therese Hörnigk and Alexander Stephan (New York: Continuum, 1997), 270–73.

Kantorowicz, Alfred (real name Helmuth Campe; 1899–1979) German literary critic, journalist, and biographer. A decorated World War I veteran, Kantorowicz studied law and German language and literature in his native Berlin, Erlangen, and other universities from 1919 to 1923. A Jew long interested in Jewish issues, he wrote his doctor of jurisprudence dissertation on the international legal bases of a national Jewish homeland in Palestine. Between 1924 and 1933, Kantorowicz worked as a correspondent and drama and literary critic for a variety of newspapers and journals. In 1931 he joined the Communist Party. When the Nazis came to power in 1933, he fled Germany and sought exile in France, where he became active in German exile causes. He served in the International Brigades in the Spanish Civil War (1936–1938). Before immigrating to the United States in 1941, after the fall of France, he was briefly incarcerated in a concentration camp in France but managed to escape. He returned to Germany in 1947, settled in East Berlin, and edited and published the widely read and respected journal *Ost und West.* The journal was closed in 1949. Between 1950 and 1956, Kantorowicz was professor of contemporary German literature and director of the Institute for German Studies at Humboldt University in East Berlin. He also served as custodian of the Heinrich Mann archive at the Academy of Arts, where he assumed responsibility for the publication of Mann's works; he served additionally as custodian of the Thomas Mann archive at the Academy of Sciences. When Kantorowicz refused to sign a petition condemning the Hungarian uprising of 1956, he was stripped of his professorship at Humboldt University. He left East Germany in 1957 and settled first in Munich and later in Hamburg. But his resettlement in West Germany was initially marred by a hostile reception because of his activities while in the German Democratic Republic.

Although he published two plays, *Erlangen* and *Die Verbündeten* (The Allies), in 1929 and 1950, respectively, and excerpts from his novel *Der Sohn des Bürgers* (The Mayor's Son) appeared in *Ost und West* from 1947 to 1949, Kantorowicz has largely been forgotten as a fiction writer. His autobiographical works, however, are highly regarded and collectively represent his most important literary achievement. Kantorowicz's memoirs in the form of diaries are bound up with some of the momentous political events of the twentieth century. *Spanisches Tagebuch* (Spanish Diary, 1948) is an account of Kantorowicz's experiences during the Spanish Civil War; in the two-volume *Deutsches Tagebuch* (German Diary, 1959, 1961), he chronicles the betrayal of his hopes and disillusionment in the GDR; arguably the best of his memoirs, *Exil in Frankreich: Merkwürdigkeiten und Denkwürdigkeiten* (Exile in France: Curiosities and Memorable Events, 1971) covers the period from Kantorowicz's immigration to France after the Nazis came to power in Germany to his arrival in New York in June 1941.

During his five-and-a-half-year stay in New York, Kantorowicz worked first as a journalist and then as a broadcaster for the Columbia Broadcasting System, devoting most of his energies to the plight of German writers under the Nazis. The summers he spent at the writers' colony of Yadoo in Saratoga Springs, New York, brought him in touch with several American writers who became good friends, among them Truman Capote, Malcolm Cowley, Langston Hughes, Carson McCullers, and Katherine Anne Porter. The best overview of Kantorowicz's experiences in Germany and abroad from 1933 to 1966 is his own anthology-like *Im 2. Drittel unseres Jahrhunderts: Illusionen, Irrtümer, Widersprüche, Einsichten, Voraussichten* (In the Second Third of Our Century: Illusions, Errors, Contradictions, Insights, Foresights, 1967). This is a compilation of articles and lectures, most of which had been published separately at different times; they cover Kantorowicz's exile in France (1933–1940) and the United States (1941–1946), his experiences in East Berlin after his return to Germany (1947–1957), and his break with the GDR and resettlement in West Germany (1957–1966). The final two sections of the book contain Kantorowicz's reflections on the Spanish Civil War and German exile literature from 1933 to 1945.

Literature: For the most complete bibliography of Kantorowicz's publications, see Jürgen Rühle, ed., *Alfred Kantorowicz* (Hamburg: Hans Christian Verlag, 1969).

Kantůrková, Eva (b. 1930) Czech novelist, short-story writer, and essayist. A native of Prague, the daughter of the communist journalist Jiří Síla (1911–1960), and the wife of the journalist Jiří Kantůrkov (b. 1932), Kantůrková graduated from high school in 1951 and then studied philosophy and history at Charles University. After earning her degree in 1956, she worked for roughly the next ten years mostly as an editor before devoting herself full time to writing in 1967. Her family background notwithstanding, Kantůrková soon became an opponent of the Czechoslovak communist regime (for which she did time in prison) and a visible and vocal spokeswoman for a liberal and democratic Czechoslovakia. Consequently, the majority of her works were published originally in Edice Petlice editions. Although Kantůrková has published several novels and two collections of novellas, she has had more of an impact with her documentary writing, memoirs, and essays and feuilletons. Her views are best set forth in such publications as *Fejetony, 1976–1979* (Feuilletons, 1976–1979, 1979), an Edice Petlice edition; *Eseje* (Essays, 1983), an underground publication, a photocopy of which Palach Press of London published in 1986; *Pekařovské studie* (Pekař Studies), a collection of articles on the fiftieth anniversary of the death of the historian Josef Pekař, author of a history of the interwar Czechoslovak Republic, for which Kantůrková wrote the commentary, published first in an underground edition in 1987 and then in Prague in 1995; *Jan Hus: Příspěvek k narodní identitě* (Jan Hus: A Contribution to the National Identity, 1988, 1991), an underground publication; *Památník* (Diary, 1994), a book of essays about fellow writers and other personalities, the most of interesting of which is the one on Karel Steigerwald since it is here that Kantůrková recalls her travels through the United States with such other Czech literary luminaries as Ivan Klíma, Arnošt Lustig, and Josef Škvorecký; *Valivý čas promĕn* (The Fast Time of Changes, 1995), a collection of thirty-one short pieces from 1977 to 1989, some of them feuilletons, dealing mostly with literature and politics, and an essay on Kantůrková by František Kautman in place of an afterword (several of the pieces are addressed to specific individuals such as Josef Zvěřin, Jiří Hajek, and Dominik Tatarka on their seventieth birthdays, and Václav Černý on his seventy-fifth); *Na národa roli dĕdičné* (On the Hereditary Role of the Nation), a twenty-nine-page underground publication; and *Záznamy pamĕti* (Records of Memory, 1997), a book of reminiscences about writers and political figures. She is also the author of a book of essays on Václav

Maria Havel (1897–1979), Karel Sabina (1813–1877), and Thomas Mann (1875–1955).

Her novels and novellas, most of which appeared originally as underground publications, include *Černá hvězda* (Black Star, written 1974), published first as an Edice Petlice edition in 1978 and then in the Index series in Cologne, Germany, in 1982; *Sen o zlu* (A Dream About Evil, 1978), an Edice Petlice edition; *Pán věže* (Lord of the Tower, 1979), an Edice Petlice edition; *Zahrada dětství jménem Eden* (The Garden of Childhood Named Eden, 1997); *Pozůstalost Pána Abela* (Mr. Abel's Legacy, 1977), published in the Index series; *Člověk v závěsu* (The Man in Suspension), a collection of novellas published first as an Edice Petlice edition in 1977 and then in the Index series in 1988; and *Krabička se šperky* (The Jewelry Box, 1992), a volume of five psychological novellas.

The two works that form the basis of Kantůrková's reputation as a dissident writer are *Dvanáct rozhovorů* (Twelve Conversations, 1980) and *Přítelkyně z domu smutku* (*My Companions in the Bleak House*, 1987). Originally an underground publication, *Dvanáct rozhovorů* consists of a series of conversations with twelve women whose husbands were imprisoned for political reasons. A similar publication, devoted specifically to such women dissenters as Olga Havlová, Maria Rut Křížková, and Elzbieta Ledererová, was published in the Index series in 1980 under the title *Sešly jsme se v této knize* (We Came Together in This Book). *My Companions in the Bleak House* is a vivid reminiscence about Kantůrková's one-year incarceration in the infamous Ruzyně Prison on the outskirts of Prague on a charge of sedition and of the women inmates whom she met there.

Translations: *My Companions in the Bleak House* (Woodstock, N.Y.: Overlook, 1987); "On the Ethics of Palach's Deed," trans. Milan Pomichalek and Anna Mozga,

in *Good-bye, Samizdat: Twenty Years of Czechoslovak Underground Writing*, ed. Marketa Goetz-Stankiewicz (Evanston, Ill.: Northwestern University Press, 1992), 174–80. *Dvanáct rozhovorů* is available in German as *Verbotene Bürger: Die Frauen der Charta 77*, trans. Marianne Pasetti-Svoboda (Munich: Langen Müller, 1982).

Kapor, Momo (b. 1937) Serbian novelist, short-story writer, poet, travel writer, and painter. A talented, prolific, and popular artist, Kapor was born in Sarajevo, where as a child he experienced the horror of World War II at first hand. A bomb struck his home, killing his mother and nearly burying him in rubble. The trauma of these events was exacerbated by subsequent impoverishment, which he eventually overcame, and in more recent times by the siege of his native Sarajevo during the Yugoslav wars of the 1990s of which he was a witness. Discovering his talent for painting, Kapor studied at the Academy of Visual Arts, from which he graduated in 1961. He has exhibited widely in Yugoslavia and abroad, including in such American cities as New York and Boston. He is also known for his illustrations of his own literary works as well as those of other authors. Kapor made his literary debut in 1972 with the novel *Beleške jedne Ane* (Notes of a Certain Ana), which in its light touch, everyday casualness, and appeal to younger readers set the tone for much of his fiction. A sequel to it was published in 1975 as *Hej, nisam ti to pričala: Nove beleške jedne Ane* (Hey, I Didn't Tell You That: New Notes of a Certain Ana). Kapor's other novels along the same lines of what is sometimes referred to as "jeans-fiction" include *Ada* (1977); *Zoe* (1978); *Od sedam do tri* (Seven Till Three, 1980); *Una: Ljubavni roman* (Una: A Novel of Love, 1981); and *Knjiga žalbi* (The Book of Complaints, 1984). In light of his troubled background and difficult road to success,

Momor's autobiographical *Provincijalac* (The Provincial, 1976) is one of his more interesting books. Also much indebted to his personal experiences are the novels that make up his well-regarded "Sarajevo trilogy"—*Poslednji let za Sarajevo* (The Last Flight to Sarajevo, 1995); *Hronika izgubljenog grada* (Chronicle of the Lost Town, 1997); and *Čuvar adrese* (The Address Guard, 2000)—which collectively represent a record of the brutal destruction of the city during the Bosnian War and the author's vivid recollections of its past. *Želena čoja Montenegra* (The Green Cloth of Montenegro, 1992) was conceived in a similar spirit of nostalgia.

Apart from his novels, Kapor has been a prolific short-story writer and has published at least a dozen collections of stories, a few of them with war themes: *I druge priče* (And Other Stories, 1973); *Lanjski snegovi* (Last Year's Snows, 1977); *Foliranti* (Phonies, 1977); *Skitam i pričam* (I Roam and Talk, 1979); *101 priča* (101 Stories, 1980); *Off: Vrlo kratke priče* (Off: Very Short Stories, 1983); *Blokada 011* (Blockade 011, 1988); *Istok-Zapad-011* (East-West-011, 1989); *Halo, Beograd* (Hello, Belgrade, 1991); *Dama skitnica i off* (Lady Vagabond and Off, 1992); and *Najbolje godine i druge priče* (The Greatest Years and Other Stories) and *Smrt ne boli: Priče iz poslednjeg rata* (Death Doesn't Hurt: Stories from the Last War), both published in 1997. In 1998 Kapor brought out a book of personal recollections about his career as painter and illustrator under the title *Uspomene jednog crtaca* (Recollections of One Sketcher). *Lep dan za umiranje* (A Lovely Day to Die, 1999), one of his newest books, reflects his abiding interest in the Yugoslav wars of the 1990s and the extreme Serbian nationalism for which he has been criticized in some quarters.

Translations: "The Gift," trans. Anita Lekić, in *The Prince of Fire: An Anthology of Serbian Short Stories,* ed. Radmila J. Gorup and Nadežda Obradović (Pittsburgh: University of Pittsburgh Press, 1998), 132–35. *Želena čoja Montenegra* is available in French as *Le Tapis vert du Montenegro,* trans. Ruža Jelić (Lausanne: L'Age d'homme, 1994).

Kapuściński, Ryszard (b. 1932) Polish journalist. Born in Pińsk, which was incorporated into the USSR after World War II, Kapuściński became an international literary celebrity by virtue of his lively and engrossing books of foreign reportage. After studying Polish history at Warsaw University, he began his career in journalism as a domestic reporter and later as a foreign correspondent for the Polish Press Agency (until 1981). Kapuściński's books, which reflect his strong attraction to the Third World, popular revolutionary movements, and civil wars, include *Cesarz* (Emperor, 1978; translated as *The Emperor: Downfall of an Autocrat*), about the downfall in 1974 of the last emperor of Ethiopia, Haile Selassie I (1892–1975), which when it first appeared in Poland was widely interpreted as a political allegory aimed at Edward Gierek, the first secretary of the United Workers Party (communist) from 1970 until his removal in disgrace in 1980; *Szachinszach* (*Shah of Shahs*, 1982), covering the downfall of the last shah of Iran, Mohammed Reza Pahlavi (1919–1980); *Jeszcze dzień życia* (*Another Day of Life*, 1986), on the revolution in Angola in the late 1960s and 1970s; *Wojna futbolowa* (*The Soccer War*, 1978), about a war between Honduras and San Salvador (the title piece of the collection) as well as upheavals in Ghana, Nigeria, Mozambique, the Congo, and Algeria; and *Imperium* (1993), which chronicles the final years of the Soviet Union.

Kapuściński's style draws heavily on interviews with people close to the events, quoted accounts, and personal observations. Seemingly thriving on danger, Kapuściński writes with a keen eye for the quirky, absurd, and morbid. His particular attraction to Africa is evident in such other books set on that continent as *Czarne gwiazdy* (Black Stars, 1963); *Gdyby cała Afryka* (If All Africa, 1969); and *Heban* (Ebony, 2001; translated as *The Shadow of the Sun*). Kapuściński's immensely readable books have been translated the world over, and he is regarded as one of the most respected of contemporary writers of reportage. His ninety-page booklet *Dlaczego zginął Karl von Spreti* (Why Karl von Spreti Died, 1970) deals with the kidnapping and death of Count von Spreti, the German ambassador to Guatemala at the time. In *Kirgiz schodzi z koni* (The Kirghiz Dismounts His Horse) and *Chrystus z karabinem na ramieniu* (Christ with a Rifle over His Shoulder), both published in 1988, he turns his attention to conflicts and social conditions in the Near East and Central Asia, regions he knows well from personal experience. Kapuściński has also published a book of "occasional" stories based on his adventures in the "bush" under the title *Busz po polsku* (The Bush Polish Style, 1962) and a series of books of essays on reportage and his own career beginning with the very short *Notes* (1986) and continuing with the three-part *Lapidarium* (1990), *Lapidarium II* (1996), and *Lapidarium III* (1997).

Translations: *Another Day of Life*, trans. William R. Brand and Katarzyna Mroczkowska-Brand (New York: Harcourt Brace Jovanovich, 1986, 1988); *Another Day of Life* [with updated material], trans. Klara Glowczewska (New York: Vintage, 2001); *The Emperor: Downfall of an Autocrat*, trans. William R. Brand and Katarzyna Mroczkowska-Brand (San Diego: Harcourt Brace Jovanovich, 1983, 1984); *Imperium*, trans. Klara Glowczewska (New York: Knopf, 1994); *The Shadow of the Sun*, trans. Klara Glowczewska (New York: Knopf, 2001); *Shah of Shahs*, trans. William

R. Brand and Katarzyna Mroczkowska-Brand (San Diego: Harcourt Brace Jovanovich, 1985, 1986); *The Soccer War*, trans. William Brand (New York: Viking Penguin, 1990; New York: Knopf, 1990, 1991; New York: Vintage, 1992).

Karahasan, Dževad (b. 1953) Bosnian Muslim novelist and theater critic. Born in Duvno, now Tomislavgrad, Bosnia, Karahasan moved to Sarajevo in 1972. He graduated from Sarajevo University in 1976 with a degree in literature and drama, and in 1986 received his doctorate. Karahasan taught drama at Sarajevo University and in 1992 became dean of the Academy of Theatrical Arts there. He was also the editor in chief of *Izraz*, a journal of literature and criticism. Karahasan attracted considerable attention with his book dealing with the siege of Sarajevo during the Bosnian War of 1991 to 1995: *Dnevnik selidbe* (Diary of an Exodus, 1994; translated as *Sarajevo: Exodus of a City*). In February 1993, determined to publish *Sarajevo: Exodus of a City* in the West, Karahasan escaped the besieged city at great personal risk. After leaving Bosnia, he and his wife settled in Salzburg, Austria. Karahasan's major work of fiction is the novel *Istočni divan* (The Oriental Divan, 1989), which scored an immediate success. It was honored as the best Yugoslav novel of the year. Set in Baghdad (the "new center of the world") in the eighth century, *Istočni divan* is a colorful mosaic of history, literature, and fable united in a historical novel that has as its leading figures such great protagonists of medieval Islamic culture as the writer al-Muqaffa, the mystic al-Hallag, and the philosopher al-Tauhidi. Other works by Karahasan include *Dosadna razmatranja* (Annoying Speculations, 1997), on ontology in literature, perception, and the Yugoslav war of 1991; *Misionari: Dvije komedije* (Missionaries: Two Comedies, 1989); a study of philology under the title *O jeziku i strahu* (On Language and Fear, 1987); and the novel *Šahrijarov prsten* (The Šahrijar Ring, 1994).

Translations: *Sarajevo: Exodus of a City*, trans. Slobodan Drakulić, with an afterword by Slavenka Drakulić (New York: Kodansha International, 1994); "Sarajevo: Portrait of an Inward City," trans. Celia Hawkesworth, in *Storm Out of Yugoslavia*, ed. Joanna Labon (London: Carcanet, 1994), 89–103. *Istočni divan* is available in German as *Der östliche Divan* (Klagenfurt: Wieser Verlag, 1993) and, in a superior translation, in Italian as *Il divino orientale*, trans. Nicole Janigro (Milan: Saggiatore, 1997).

Karaliichev, Angel (1902–1972) Bulgarian short-story writer. Among the most prolific and popular twentieth-century Bulgarian writers of short fiction and fairy tales, Karaliichev was born in Strazhitsa in northern Bulgaria. He completed his schooling in Veliko Turnovo in 1921 and went on to study chemistry at Sofia University. Karaliichev began publishing prose fiction in the 1920s, beginning with a short-story collection on rural themes: *Ruzh* (Rice, 1925). *Zhultitsi* (Wise Guys), a second collection of short stories, appeared in 1926 and was soon followed by *Krilatiiat iunak* (The Winged Hero, 1927), a fairy tale; *Imane* (Property, 1927), a collection of stories; *Bogorodichna sulza* (Our Lady's Tear, 1928), a book of fairy tales; *Chestit chovek* (The Honest Man, 1929); *Prikazen svet* (Imagined World, 2nd ed., 1930); *Luzhoven svet* (Treacherous World, 1932; 3rd rev. ed., 1941, under the title *Rosenskiiat kamen most* [The Rosenski Stone Bridge]); *Prikaznik: Sbornik ot narodni i khudozhestveni prikazi* (Stotryteller: A Collection of Popular and Literary Tales, 1933), a school text coauthored with N. Monev; and *Sreburna rukoika: Putopisi, nastroeniia, razkazi* (The Silver Handle: Travels, Moods, Stories, 1935). During World War II, Karaliichev published several collec-

tions of patriotic and historical stories and domestic travel books, among them *Ptichka ot glina* (The Clay Pigeon, 1941) and *Zemiata na Bulgarite: Putepisi* (The Land of the Bulgarians: Travelogues, 1941). His embrace of postwar Bulgarian communism is manifest in such books as *Naroden zakrilnik* (Protector of the Nation, 1954); *Razkazi* (Stories, 1958); *Iunachni Bulgari* (Bulgarian Heroes, 1959); and *Lokomotivut na istoriiata* (The Locomotive of History, 1965), stories and sketches on Bulgarian historical themes. Constant throughout Karaliichev's career was an interest in the Bulgarian fairy tale and legend, as keen as his devotion to Bulgarian history. In 1963 he published *Prikazki vulshebni i za zhivotni* (Magical and Animal Fairy Tales), another collection of fairy tales. He followed this in 1964 with *Gostencheta krilati* (Winged Guests), and in 1967 with *Vihrusha* (Whirlwind), a collection of stories and legends that he edited. Karaliichev's nonfiction is limited mainly to two books: a commemorative collection of articles on the Bulgarian national liberation movement, *Osvobozhdenieto, 1877–1878: Osemdeset godini* (The Liberation, 1877–1878: Eighty Years, 1958), edited by Karaliichev, Zdravko Srebrov, and Ivan Krustev; and the personal and partly autobiographical miscellany *Spodeleno: Razmisli, nastroeniia, statii, retsenzii, otzivi, pisma* (Shared: Reflections, Moods, Articles, Reviews, Comments, Letters, 1972).

Literature: Stefan Kolarov, *Angel Karaliichev: Literaturno-kriticheski ocherk* (Sofia: Bulgarski pisatel, 1976), and *Maister na lirichnata proza: Angel Karaliichev* (Sofia: Nauka i izkustvo, 1983). For a biography of Karaliichev, apart from his own *Spomeni* (Memoirs, 1967), see Simeon Sultanov, *Sudbata na edin prikaznik* (Sofia: Bulgarski pisatel, 1985).

Translations: *The World of Tales*, trans. Lyudmila Dimitrova, Zora Takova, and Elena Mladenova, ed. Marguerite

Alexieva (Sofia: Foreign Languages Press, 1965); "The Little Coin," in *The Balkan Range: A Bulgarian Reader,* ed. John Robert Colombo and Nikola Roussanoff (Toronto: Hounslow, 1976), 212–18.

Karaslavov, Georgi (1904–1980) Bulgarian short-story writer and novelist. Prolific, widely translated, and a loyal communist throughout his career, Karaslavov was a native of Purvomai, not far east of the industrial city of Plovdiv. He completed secondary school in his native town and then enrolled in the Telegraph and Mail Institute in Sofia. He also studied at teachers colleges in Harmanli (1923) and Kazanluk (1924–1925). An early member of the Communist Party of Bulgaria, Karaslavov participated in the September uprising of 1923. After it was crushed, he returned to his native town in order to complete his teacher training and to begin his career, but he was denied a teaching position because of his communist affiliations. From 1925 to 1928, he studied agronomy at Sofia University, but was expelled on the grounds that he had been one of the organizers of a student antigovernment strike. He then left the country to continue his studies at Charles University in Prague from 1929 to 1930. He eventually received his degree in agronomy from Sofia University in 1930.

During World War II, Karaslavov worked in the political sector of the army and, after the war, from 1947 to 1949, served as director of the Ivan Vazov National Theater in Sofia. He subsequently became editor in chief of the journal *Septemvri* and, from 1958 to 1962, chief secretary and then president of the Bulgarian Writers Union. In 1961 he was elected a member of the Bulgarian Academy. He also served as a delegate to the Narodno Subranie (parliament) from 1950 to 1962 and then was a member of its presidium.

Karaslavov's first volume of short stories, *Ulichnitsi* (Guttersnipes, 1926), depicts the life of street urchins in big-city slums. As virtually all of Karaslavov's works, the emphasis is on sociopolitical conflicts and their ideological resonance. *Kavalut plache* (The Kaval [Wooden Flute] Is Wailing), a second collection of short stories, dealing with the September uprising of 1923, appeared in 1928. Karaslavov's first novel, *Sporzhilov* (1931), is essentially a book of reportage based on Karaslavov's own experiences as a construction worker in the Prague suburb of the title. It was followed by *Na post* (Man Your Station, 1932), a book of short stories; *Selkor* (The Village Correspondent, 1933), one of his most successful novels, although because of it he was jailed for a short period on political grounds; *Na dva fronta* (On Two Fronts, 1934) and *Imot* (The Estate, 1936), both short-story collections; and *Tatul* (The Thornapple, 1938), a novel.

In 1942 Karaslavov published his immensely successful novel *Snaha* (Daughter-in-Law, 1942). The work went through over twenty editions and was made into a film in 1951. Like *Tatul,* it is in the well-worn tradition of Bulgarian rural prose. In 1944 Karaslavov turned out two more collections of short stories, *Sega mu e vremeto* (The Time Is Now Ripe) and *Vrag* (The Enemy). In the postwar years of 1945 and 1946, respectively, he published two collections of political feuilletons, *Ratai na reaktsiiata* (Farmhands of Reaction) and *Borba za demokratsiia* (The Struggle for Democracy), which further enhanced his standing with the new communist regime. *Tango* (1946), a popular novella reprinted several times and dramatized in 1967, was aimed at the intolerance of the privileged classes and the harsh repression of any opposition in the interwar period. It remains Karaslavov's most widely translated work of fiction. His next publications were *Ot Liditse do Banska Bistritsa* (From Lidice to Banska Bystrica, 1951), a travel book about Czechoslovakia; *Prevuzhodstvoto na sotsialisticheskata kultura*

(The Superiority of Socialist Culture, 1951), a political text; *V geroichna Koreia* (In Heroic Korea, 1952), a propaganda piece in praise of North Korea during the Korean War; and *Obiknoveni hora* (Ordinary People), a novel in six parts published between 1952 and 1975 covering historical events in Bulgaria from World War I to 1944. Although the work is well regarded, Karaslavov's fondness for documentary accuracy is compromised to some extent by the lack of psychological persuasiveness in character depiction.

The first edition of Karaslavov's collected works was published in ten volumes from 1956 to 1958. This was followed by *Novi putishta* (New Roads, 1959), a collection of novellas and stories; *Blizki i poznati: Misli i spomeni* (Friends and Acquaintances: Thoughts and Recollections, 1968), essentially a book of memoirs; and two works of historical and political character: *Kniga za Smirnenski i Vaptsarov* (A Book in Honor of Smirnenski and Vapstarov, 1971), dedicated to two heroes of the Bulgarian liberation movement on whom Karaslavov had previously published books—a biography of Hristo Smirnenski (1949) and *Sreshti i razgovory s Nikola Vapstarov* (Meetings and Conversations with Nikola Vaptsarov, 1961)—and *Sreshti i razgovori s Georgi Dimitrov* (Meetings and Conversations with Georgi Dimitrov, 1971). A collection of Karaslavov's plays was published in 1972, followed in 1976 by his selected story collection *Kavali sviriiat: Triptih* (The Wood Flutes Sing: A Triptych) and in 1978/1979 by a new eleven-volume edition of his complete works. Although not well known outside Bulgaria despite translations of a few of his works, Karaslavov has long been regarded as one of the most formidable Bulgarian writers of the twentieth century.

Literature: V. Andreev, *Georgii Karaslavov: Kritiko-biograficheskii ocherk* (Leningrad: Khudozhestvennaia literatura, 1972), in Russian.

Translations: *Tango and Other Stories*, trans. M. Todorov (Sofia: Sofia Press, 1972).

Kardos, György (b. 1925) Hungarian novelist. A Jew, Kardos was deported to Yugoslavia during World War II and after the war immigrated to Israel. He returned to Hungary in 1951 and settled in Budapest. His first novel, *Avraham Bogatir hét napja* (Seven Days in the Life of Abraham Bogatir, 1969), takes place in Palestine during World War II and traces the complexities of nation building. The theme is explored further in his novels *Hová tűntek a katonák?* (Where Have All the Soldiers Gone?, 1971) and *A történet vége* (The End of the Story, 1977). Kardos is also the author of a rock musical, *Villon és a többiek* (Villon and the Others), which premiered in 1976 at the Attila József Theater in Budapest. After a sixteen-year hiatus, Kardos returned to print with a new novel, *Jutalomjáték* (Benefit Performance, 1993). The work takes place on a single day in 1951 and draws on Kardos's own extensive theatrical experiences to depict in a humorous and compassionate way the dreary goings-on when a shabby provincial theater sets out to do a benefit performance of a typical Stalin-era Soviet play. In 1978 Kardos won the Attila József Prize for his novelistic trilogy: *Avraham Bogatir hét napja, Hová tűntek a katonák?*, and *A történet vége*.

Translations: "The First Lines," trans. Judit Házi, in *Present Continuous: Contemporary Hungarian Writing*, ed. István Bart (Budapest: Corvina, 1985), 44–57; "You Must Like Théophile Gautier," trans. Paul Aston, in *Hungarian Short Stories,* ed. Paul Varnai (Toronto: Exile Editions, 1983), 125–34.

Karinthy, Ferenc (1921–1992) Hungarian, novelist, short-story writer, and playwright. The son of the well-known writer Frigyes Karinthy (1887–1938), Karinthy was born and educated in Budapest. He received a doctorate in philology from Budapest University. His first novel, *Don Juan éjszakája* (The Night of Don Juan), appeared in 1943. It was followed by two novels, both autobiographical: *Invokáció* (Invocation, 1946), mostly a recollection of his father, and *Kentaur* (Centaur, 1947), about his university years. The two-volume *Budapesti tavasz* (*Spring Comes to Budapest*, 1955), his most popular novel, is about the siege of Budapest during World War II and his only major work translated into several languages, including English. It was subsequently made into a film. His other novels include *Leányfalu és vidéke* (Leányfalu and Its Environs, 1973); *Végtelen szőnyeg* (The Endless Carpet, 1974); *Harminchárom* (Thirty-three, 1977); *Mi van a Dunában?* (What's on the Danube?, 1980); *Magnóliakert* (The Magnolia Garden, 1982); *X utolsó kalandja* (X: The Last Adventure, 1983); *Zenebona* (Hullabaloo, 1986); and *Szkizofrénia: Man Overboard* (Schizophrenia: Man Overboard, 1988; original subtitle in English). A collection of two novels was published in 1973 under the title *Ősbemutató* (World Premiere).

Karinthy was also a prolific writer of short stories and novellas and published several collections in his lifetime, among them *Gyönyörű élet* (Beautiful Life, 1949); *Irodalmi történetek* (Literary Stories, 1956); *A ferencvárosi szellem* (The Ghost of Ferencváros, 1959); *Kék-zöld Florida* (Green-Blue Florida, 1962); *Hátország* (The Home Front, 1965); *Víz fölött, víz alatt* (Above and Beneath the Water, 1966); *Három huszár* (Three Hussars, 1971); *Hosszú weekend* (The Long Weekend, 1981); *Mélyvízi hal* (Deep Water Fish, 1982); and *Utolsó cigaretta, utolsó ítélet* (The Last Cigarette, the Last Judgment, 1983), the last two being novella collections. *Szabad rablás* (Permissable Robbery), a volume of sketches, came out in 1983. As a playwright, Karinthy is best

known for *Ezer év* (A Thousand Years, 1956); *Steinway Grand* (1967), which is listed in translation in the Samuel French drama text series (undated); *Dunakanyar* (The Danube Bend, 1967); and *Gellérthegyi álmok* (Dreams on Gellért Hill, 1970). Apart from his early autobiographical novels, Karinthy also published three volumes of diaries: *Alvilági napló* (Infernal Diary, 1979); *Óvilág és Újvilág* (The Old World and the New World, 1985); and *Napló* (A Diary, 1993). His other volumes of nonfiction include *Hazai tudósítások* (Home Reports, 1954); *Pesten és Budán* (In Pest and Buda, 1972); *Körvadászat: Riportok, beszélgetések* (The Hunting Circle: Reports and Conversations, 1984); and *Staféta* (Relay, 1991).

Literature: Károly Szalay, *Karinthy Ferenc alkotásai és vallomásai* (Budapest: Szepirodalmi Könyvkiadó, 1979), a biography.

Translations: *Spring Comes to Budapest,* trans. István Farkas (Budapest: Corvina, 1964); "The Birthday of Emil Dukich," trans. Károly Ravasz, in *Hungarian Short Stories* (Toronto: Exile Editions, 1983), 143–62; "Requiem," trans. J. E. Sollosy, in *Present Continuous: Contemporary Hungarian Writing,* ed. István Bart (Budapest: Corvina, 1985), 164–80.

Kárpáti, Péter (b. 1961) Hungarian playwright. Kárpáti was born in Budapest and graduated from the Academy of Dramatic Arts in 1983. He has worked as dramatic adviser at several theaters and currently holds the position of literary director of the Új (New) Theater in Budapest. Kárpáti is the author of eight plays, a few of which have been widely performed and are available in the published collections *Halhatatlan háború: Három színdarab* (Immortal War: Three Plays, 1992) and *Világvevő: Öt színdarab* (All-Wave-Band Receiver: Five Plays, 1999). They include *Szingapúr* (Singapore) and *Végallomás* (Terminal), both produced in 1988; *Halhatatlan háború* (Immortal War, staged 1990); *Az út végén a folyó* (The River at the End of the Road, 1990); *Akárki* (Anyone; translated as *Everywoman*, staged 1993); *Országalma* (The Golden Orb, 1995); and *Tótferi* (2000). Arguably the best of these are the last three. *Országalma* is a historical play about the Hungarian Gypsies based on an old Gypsy fairy tale and clearly motivated by Kárpáti's desire to overcome prejudice against Gypsies by making their culture better known. *Everywoman* is a modern version, with touches of the absurd, of the medieval play *Everyman* set in modern Budapest and depicting the final day in the life of a middle-aged woman who learns she has cancer and then tries to set her affairs in order before dying. It is the only play by Kárpáti currently available in English. *Tótferi*, which is named for the central character—a failed savior figure—is a folkish version, with heavy use of dialect, of the myth of Creation in the style of a medieval mystery play.

Translations: *Everywoman*, in a version by Jack Bradley, verse passages by Tony Curtis, in *Hungarian Plays: New Drama from Hungary*, selected and introduced by László Upor (London: Nick Hern, 1996), 175–242.

Karpowicz, Tymoteusz (pseudonym Tadeusz Lirmian; b. 1921) Polish poet and playwright. Karpowicz was born in the village of Zielona, in the Wilno region (now Lithuania). Because of the disruptions in his life caused by World War II, he received his high-school diploma only in 1949. He subsequently studied Polish literature at Warsaw University, graduating in 1954. Karpowicz made his literary debut (as Tadeusz Lirmian) in 1941 as a journalist for the Wilno newspaper *Prawda Wileńska*. After World War II, he became editor of Radio Poland in Szczecin, a position he held until 1949. From 1953 to 1958, he was an assistant lecturer in the history of Polish literature at Wrocław University. In 1956 he became chairman of the Wrocław branch of the Polish Writers Union. He also became a member of the editorial board of the journal *Nowe Sygnały* and then of the journal *Odra*, both located in Wrocław. Until 1969 he was also assistant editor in chief of the monthly *Poezija*.

Karpowicz's first book of poetry, *Żywe wymiary* (Live Dimensions), appeared in 1948. The same year, he also published a book of stories about the Baltic region, based on his experiences in Szczecin: *Opowieści pomorskie* (Pomeranian Stories). His next collection of poems, *Gorzkie źródła* (Bitter Springs), which established him as one of the freshest new talents in Polish postwar poetry, appeared in 1957, followed in 1958 by the collection *Kamienna muzyka* (Stone Music). Karpowicz was honored for his poetry in 1958 with the Prize of the City of Wrocław. He published four more volumes of poetry in the 1960s, before turning to dramatic writing: *Znaki równania* (Equation Signs, 1960); *W imię znaczenia* (In the Name of Meaning, 1962), which was honored at the Bydgoszcz "Spring of Poetry" as the year's best book of poetry; *Trudny las* (A Difficult Forest, 1964); and a volume of selected poems (*Wiersze wybrane*, 1969). Karpowicz's poems are carefully crafted and generally laconic; they are often haunting and surreal in their imagery. Deeply moral in his outlook, his concern with contemporary social and political issues reflects a broad philosophical background.

Karpowicz's plays began appearing first in the drama journal *Dialog* in 1958. Eventually, his fourteen short plays were published in 1975 in the single volume *Dramaty zebrane* (Collected Plays), which includes *Wracamy późno do domu* (We Return Home Late); *Wszędzie są studnie* (There Are Wells All Over the Place); *Dziwny pasażer* (The Strange Passenger); *Zielone rękawice* (Green Gloves); *Przerwa w podróży* (Interrupted Journey); *Kiedy ktoś zapuka* (When Someone Knocks); *Jego Mała Dziewczynka* (His Little Girl); *Czterych nocnych stróżów* (Four

Nightwatchmen); *Człowiek z absolutnym węchem* (A Man with a Perfect Sense of Smell); *Zakup z dostawą na miejsce* (Purchase with Immediate Delivery); *Charon od świtu do świtu* (Charon from Dawn to Dawn); *Przyjdź jak najprędzej* (Come as Fast as Possible); *Noc jest tylko wygnanym dniem* (Night Is Just Exiled Day); and *Mam piękną kolekcję noży, czyli pogrzeb przyjaciela* (I Have a Fine Collection of Knives, or The Burial of a Friend). Karpowicz's plays are short and either have a specific contemporary Polish content or deal with universal problems, hence his preference in such texts for generic characters (director, secretary, passenger, fisherman, and so on). Much of the humor of the plays derives from the grotesque situations in which Karpowicz places his characters.

Karpowicz's last book of poetry, published in 1972—the year before he left Poland for the United States—is titled *Odwrócone światło* (Reversed Light). It is a large collection notable for its linguistic experimentation, which was only rarely evident in his previous poetic writing. *Odwrócone światło* was the last poetry Karpowicz published. Deeply interested in the theory of poetry, in 1975 he brought out a study of the poetry of Bolesław Leśmian (1878–1937) under the title *Poezja niemożliwa: Modele Leśmianowskiej wyobraźni* (Impossible Poetry: Models of Leśmian's Imagination). In 1978 Karpowicz became professor of Polish language and literature at the University of Illinois, Chicago Circle. He has since retired and currently holds the title of professor emeritus.

Literature: Tomasz Tabako, "The Return of the Forester: On Reading Tymoteusz Karpowicz," *Chicago Review* 46, nos. 3–4 (2000): 68–73.

Translations: Four poems in *The Burning Forest: Modern Polish Poetry,* trans. and ed. Adam Czerniawski (Newcastle upon Tyne: Bloodaxe, 1988), 86–87; two poems,

trans. Małgorzata Sady and Bożena Bialik, in *The New Polish Poetry: A Bilingual Collection,* ed. Milne Holton and Paul Vangelisti (Pittsburgh: University of Pittsburgh Press, 1978), 20–23; five poems, trans. Adam Czerniawski, in *Polish Writing Today,* ed. Celina Wieniewska (Harmondsworth: Penguin, 1967), 54–60.

Kaštelan, Lada (b. 1961) Croatian playwright. A native of Zagreb, Kaštelan graduated from Zagreb University with a degree in classical philology in 1983. She subsequently studied drama at the Academy of Dramatic Arts. In 1984 Kaštelan became part-time dramatic director of the Croatian National Theater in Zagreb; she became permanent dramatic director in 1987. Her first published book, *Hrana za ptice* (Played for the Birds), a volume of poems, appeared in 1978. She thereafter directed her attention to dramatic writing. In 1997 three of Kaštelan's most popular plays and a television drama were published together as *Četiri drame* (Four Plays), which includes *A tek se vjenčali* (They Were Just Recently Married, 1983); *Posljednja karika* (The Last Link, 1994), which won the Dubravka Dujšin Prize in 1994 and the Gavella Prize for best production at the Marulić Festival in 1995; *Giga i njezini* (Giga and Her Family, 1995), based on the novel *Giga Barićeva* by Milan Begović and awarded the prestigious Marin Držić Prize of the Croatian Ministry of Culture as the best dramatic text of 1995; and *Adagio* (1987), written for television. Her other television and film scenarios include *Requiem za Borisa* (Requiem for Boris, 1990); *Sestre* (Sisters, 1991); and *Krhotine* (Fragments, 1992). She has also written the radio plays *Izložba* (The Exhibition, 1981) and *Pljusak* (Downpour, 1986). An able classical scholar, Kaštelan has also made a reputation with her translations and adaptations of classical Greek drama. Her volume *Pred vratima Hada* (Before the Gates of Hades), which consists primarily of adaptations of Euripides, appeared in 1993.

Kaštelan is very much a woman's writer in that her plays explore facets of the male–female relationship mostly through the prism of the feminine psyche. Her first play, the one-act *A tek se vjenčali,* unfolds in the compartment of a train headed for Zagreb containing four passengers: two live and two dead. The live characters, who meet for the first time on the train, are Branko, a soldier on leave from Ljubljana, Slovenia, and Ana, a psychiatrist living in Switzerland. The dead passengers are Lidija, the woman Branko once loved, and Petar, her husband who killed both her and himself the day before the action of the play begins. As he dozes, Branko has recurrent troubling dreams about his failed relationship with Lidija that Ana, who gradually becomes interested in him, tries to help him deal with. Lidija and Petar, who of course remain invisible to and unheard by the other couple, comment on the dialogue between Branko and Ana and put their own interpretation on the events that culminated in the murder and suicide. The most interesting aspect of the play is the reconstruction of past events through Branko's dreams and the comments on them by Lidija and Petar. *Posljednja karika* is an absurdist play about three women, representing three generations, who come together to celebrate their common birthday. Generically named (She, Mother, Granny), the women at first appear to be related, but it soon becomes obvious that they are not and may be only projections of the play's central character, She, a woman in her middle thirties who has never married and hungers for love and a family. Much of the absurdist humor in the play is generated by the dialogue between the other women and their male companions (Mother's Lover and Granny's Husband) until at the end of the play She's Lover appears. After tense moments between She and her lover over his relationship with another woman, he commits himself to She and the play ends on a hopeful note. Through the other characters of the play, Kaštelan underscores her belief, however, in the near impossibility of gratifying permanent relationships between men and women.

Kawalec, Julian (b. 1916) Polish novelist and short-story writer. Kawalec was born in a village near Tarnobrzeg, where he was educated in local schools. He subsequently studied Polish literature at the Jagiellonian University in Kraków. During the German occupation of Poland in World War II, he lived almost the entire time in his native village. After the war, he became a journalist affiliated with the Peasant Party. His affinity for rural life and his particular interest in the moral fallout of the breakdown of traditional village values are reflected in his fiction. Although among the more interesting writers on rural themes in post–World War II Poland, Kawalec faced critical objections to his convoluted style, which some attributed to the influence, among others, of Faulkner. His first published book, a collection of short stories under the title *Ścieżki wśród ulic* (Paths Through the Streets), appeared in 1957. He eventually turned out another five volumes of short stories: *Blizny* (Scars, 1960); *Zwalony wiąż* (The Felled Elm, 1962); *Czarne światło* (Black Light) and *Marsz weselny* (The Wedding March), both from 1965; and *Szukam domu* (I'm Searching for Home, 1968). Kawalec's first novel, *Ziemi przypisany* (Bound to the Land), appeared in 1962. It was followed by three other novels: *W słońcu* (In the Sun, 1963); *Tańczący jastrząb* (The Dancing Hawk, 1964); and *Wezwanie* (The Summons, 1968). His most recent works are *Ukraść brata. Oset* (Stealing Brother. Thistle, 1985) and *W gąszczu bram* (In the Thicket of the Gates, 1989).

Literature: Bogusław S. Kunda, *Julian Kawalec* (Warsaw: Państwowy Instytut Wydawniczy, 1984), a small but useful introduction to Kawalec and his literary work; Anna Marzec, *Proza Juliana Kawalca* (Warsaw: Wydawnictwa Szkolne i Pedagogiczne, 1983); Aleksander Wilkoń, ed., *Julian Kawalec: Zbiór recenzji i szkiców o twórczości pisarza* (Warsaw: Ludowa Spółdzielnia Wydawnicza, 1981), a collection of reviews and articles.

Kerim, Usin (1927–1983) Bulgarian poet. Of Gypsy background, Kerim was born and educated through high school in Teteven, some sixty miles northeast of Sofia. After participating from 1947 to 1949 in the brigade construction movement, he worked as a woodcutter in the Triavna Mountains from 1949 to 1951 and in the state mining enterprise in Madzharovo for the next two years. From 1954 to 1956, he was employed as a correspondent with *Otechestven front* for the Sliven district and thereafter held several editorial positions. His early poems began appearing in *Narodna mladezh* and a variety of other periodicals from 1948. Kerim's first book of poetry, *Pesni ot katuna* (Songs from a Gypsy Camp), appeared in 1955 and was followed by *Ochite goriat* (Burning Eyes, 1959); *Pod siniia shatur* (Beneath the Blue Tent 1968); *Zaiu baiu i oracha: Prikazka v stihove* (Brer Rabbit and the Plowman: A Tale in Verse, 1969): *Surtseto mi* (This Heart of Mine, 1978); *S bashtin glas* (With Father's Voice, 1978); and *Kato prashen skitnik se zavrushtam* (I Return as a Wretched Vagabond, 1978). Kerim was a rather joyous poet who wrote for the most part in simple, conventional meters and found much to celebrate in his Gypsy origins, love, the memories of his parents, the freedom of the open road, and the camaraderie of the workplace. He also wrote the usual communist-era obligatory poems on the Party, Prime Minister Georgi Dimitrov, and the successes of national industrialization.

Translations: Five poems, trans. William Matthews, in *Window on the Black Sea: Bulgarian Poetry in Translation,* ed. Richard Harteis, in collaboration with William Meredith (Pittsburgh: Carnegie Mellon University Press, 1992), 142–48.

Kertész, Ákos (b. 1932) Hungarian novelist, short-story writer, and playwright. Kertész was born in Budapest, where he graduated from evening high school in 1950 and then was employed as a metalworker for the next ten years. He studied in the Faculty of Philosophy at Eötvös Lóránd University from 1961 to 1966, subsequently devoting himself entirely to his writing. In 1958 he published his first volume of short stories under the title *Hétköznapok szerelme* (Weekday Love). Since the 1970s, he has published mostly novels, the best known being *Makra* (1976) and *Családi ház manzarddal* (House with a Garret, 1982). *Makra,* named for the young man at the center of the novel (Ferenc Makra) and set in the time of the Hungarian uprising of 1956, deals with the ennui with conformist ideology experienced by younger people, particularly artists, in contemporary Hungarian society and their restless desire for the freedom to achieve self-realization. After ten years of respectable success as a designer of metal objects, and what would appear to be a good family life, Makra becomes dissatisfied with his existence and the disparity between reality and his dreams and commits suicide. The novel was taken as a commentary on the breakdown of society in the most somber period of post–World War II Hungarian history. A collection of Kertész's short novels and novellas appeared in 1984 as *A vílag rendje* (The Order of the World), the title derived from one of the three novellas in the book. In 1987 *Makra* and *Családi ház manzarddal* were issued in a single volume with the novel *Sikátor* (Alley). Kertész's plays, especially *Özvegyek* (The Widows), have been widely performed. He is the winner of the Attila József Prize.

Translations: "Snapshot," trans. Georgia Greist, in *Present Continuous: Contemporary Hungarian Writing,* ed. István Bart (Budapest: Corvina, 1985), 344–51. *Makra* is available in German as *Die verschenkte Leben des Ferenc Makra,* trans. Jörg Buschmann (Berlin: Volk und Welt, 1975).

Kertész, Imre (b. 1929) Hungarian novelist. A native of Budapest, Kertész is best known for two works related to the Holocaust and obviously based on personal experiences: *Sorstalanság* (*Fateless,* 1975) and *Kaddis a meg nem született gyermekért* (*Kaddish for a Child Not Born,* 1990). Narrated in the first person by a fifteen-year-old Hungarian Jewish boy, *Fateless* follows the young narrator from his roundup in Budapest in 1944 and assignment to a work camp through his experiences in such concentration camps as Auschwitz and Buchenwald until his liberation by American troops and his return to Budapest after the war. The privations of the camps and the conditions on the freight trains that carry the prisoners are recounted in a bland, matter-of-fact, naive style appropriate to the age of the narrator, who only slowly perceives the true reality and larger dimensions of what is going on around him. Although the novel is well detailed, the emphasis is less on the horrors of the camps, few of which are described, than on the perceptions of the narrator, who is neither emotional nor self-pitying. The novelty of *Fateless,* given its grim subject, is the tendency of the narrator to see things in the best possible light, which carries over into the immediate postwar period when he declares that when asked about the "terrors of the camps" he will respond that for him "the happiness there will always be the most memorable experience, perhaps." By happiness, he means contacts with other inmates of different nationalities, the beauties of na-

ture he is able to savor every now and then, the ability to adapt to camp food, the occasional human treatment shown him, and the preservation of a certain youthful innocence. A shorter work, *Kaddish for a Child Not Born* is a touching and disturbing account of the impact of the narrator's concentration camp experiences on his marriage. Because of what he experienced as a Jew, and his deeply rooted fear that Jews might again become victims of persecution, he refuses to allow his wife to become pregnant, thereby destroying his marriage. His wife remarries a Christian and has two children whom the narrator eventually meets and is afterward pained by the knowledge that they could just as well have been his. Beautifully written in the form of a philosophically tinged personal narrative unbroken into chapters and only rarely into paragraphs in the original, *Kaddish for a Child Not Born* illuminates the deeper consequences of the Holocaust among those for whom even survival brought little peace.

Translations: *Fateless,* trans. Christopher C. Wilson and Katharina M. Wilson (Evanston, Ill.: Northwestern University Press, 1992); *Kaddish for a Child Not Born,* trans. Christopher C. Wilson and Katharina M. Wilson (Evanston, Ill.: Northwestern University Press, 1997).

Kipphardt, Heinar (1922–1982) German playwright, novelist, short-story writer, and poet. Internationally renowned for his docudrama about the American nuclear physicist J. Robert Oppenheimer, *In der Sache J. Robert Oppenheimer* (*In the Matter of J. Robert Oppenheimer,* 1964), Kipphardt was born in Heidersdorf (Polish, Gościejowice), Lower Silesia. After completing his early schooling in nearby Gnadenfrei (Polish, Pilawa Górna), he went to high school in Krefeld, in the Rhineland, where his family moved after his father's release from the Buchenwald concentration camp in 1937. His father, Heinrich, had first been imprisoned in a concentration camp near Breslau in 1933 because of his activities as a Social Democrat. Determined to become a doctor, Kipphardt began studying medicine in Bonn and later in Cologne and Düsseldorf. His studies were interrupted by World War II when he was drafted into the army and sent to the Russian front. He tried to resume his medical studies in Breslau in late 1944, but the invading Russian army necessitated a change of plans. Eventually deserting the army in January 1945, Kipphardt found his way to Düsseldorf, where he continued his studies. In 1949 he accepted an assistantship in the psychiatric department of the Charité, the renowned Berlin University clinic. By 1950, out of political conviction, he had resettled in East Berlin, finished his medical training there, and received his degree from Düsseldorf in December 1950. Kipphardt later turned his war experiences into literary material in "Der Hund des Generals" ("The General's Dog," 1960) and "Der Deserteur" ("The Deserter," 1977) as well as in his plays Der Hund des Generals (1963), a dramatization of his story; Joel Brand: Die Geschichte eines Geschäfts (Joel Brand: The Story of a Trade, 1965); and Bruder Eichmann (Brother Eichmann, 1983).

Long attracted to imaginative writing, Kipphardt had the chance to give up a medical career for a literary one when he accepted a position at the famed Deutsches Theater in Berlin, which was located near the Charité. In time, Kipphardt became the theater's chief dramatic adviser. His first play, Entscheidung (Decision), dealing with German–Russian relations before, during, and after World War II, had its premiere in 1952. It was followed by the better written and more successful satirical comedy Shakespeare dringend gesucht (Shakespeare Urgently Sought, 1953), which had to do with theater conditions in the new German Democratic Republic and for which

Kipphardt won the National Prize of the GDR, Third Class, and Der Aufstieg des Alois Piontek: Eine tragikomische Farce (The Rise of Alois Piontek: A Tragicomical Farce, 1954; staged 1956), a satire aimed at the West German "economic miracle." Kipphardt's next play, Die Stühle des Herrn Szmil (Mr. Szmil's Chairs, 1957–1958), originally titled "Esel schreien im Dunkel" ("Donkeys Bray in the Dark") and loosely based on the comico-satirical novel The Twelve Chairs by the Soviet authors Ilya Ilf and Yevgeny Petrov, had a harder time reaching the stage. The authorities found it objectionable in some respects, and its premiere took place only in 1961 and in Wuppertsal, West Germany.

Kipphardt's reputation, nationally and internationally, catapulted with the dramatic texts for which he is best known, the docudramas Der Hund des Generals, which consists of a trial (in this case fictional) of a German general accused of deliberately causing the deaths of a large number of his subordinates; In the Matter of J. Robert Oppenheimer; Joel Brand: Die Geschichte eines Geschäfts, which deals with the true-to-life German proposal in Budapest 1944 that the Allies trade them 10,000 trucks for the lives of 1 million Jews; and Bruder Eichmann, about the Adolf Eichmann trial in Jerusalem. These are by and large fact-based plays of weighty political and moral content. In the most widely known of them, In the Matter of J. Robert Oppenheimer, the withholding of a government security clearance from the famed atomic bomb scientist is motivated by his alleged deliberate retardation of the development of the hydrogen bomb out of communist sympathies. Although much is made of the anticommunist hysteria in the United States during the time of Senator Joseph McCarthy, Kipphardt's play is much less a propaganda piece than a serious inquiry into the moral responsibility of the scientist capable of developing weapons of mass destruction. Does he place his talents entirely in the hands of his government, or does he have a responsibility toward humankind as well? Kipphardt's obvious support of the right of the individual to hold and express views contrary to those of his government without having his loyalty questioned applied to the GDR as well as to the United States. Much of the considerable success of *In the Matter of J. Robert Oppenheimer* lay in Kipphardt's blending of invented elements and documentary material. Oppenheimer himself objected to the play strenuously, charging Kipphardt with transforming what he regarded as a farce into a tragedy. Kipphardt's best-known prose text, apart from his plays, is the intriguing novel *März* (1976), a fictional biography of the schizophrenic poet Alexander März that also probes the social implications of his long confinement in mental hospitals.

After mounting attacks on his work by orthodox communist critics and in the wake of the uprisings in Poland and Hungary in 1956, Kipphardt decided to leave the GDR. He and his family resettled in West Germany in 1959, and he eventually took up residence in Munich and in 1970 became the chief dramatic adviser of the Munich Kammerspeiele theater. His contract was not renewed at the end of August 1971, however, because of the enormous furor kicked up over his staging in April 1971 of Wolf Biermann's play *Der Dra-dra*. No longer tied professionally to Munich and anxious to devote himself full time to his writing, Kipphardt resettled in the small town of Angelsbruck in the spring of 1972.

Literature: Adolf Stock, ed., *Heinar Kipphardt mit Selbstzeugnissen und Bilddokumenten* (Reinbek bei Hamburg: Rowohlt, 1987), a good short overview of Kipphardt's life and career.

Translations: *In the Matter of J. Robert Oppenheimer*, trans. Ruth Speirs (New York: Hill and Wang, 1968).

Kirsch, Rainer (b. 1934) German poet, playwright, short-story writer, essayist, and translator. Born in Döbeln, Saxony, where he received his early education through high school, Kirsch studied history and literature at the universities of Halle and Jena, but in 1956 was expelled on political grounds and pressed into labor first in a chemistry plant and then as a farmer. From 1963 to 1965, he was enrolled at the Johannes R. Becher Institute of Literature. From 1961 he was a freelance writer in the Halle/Salle region. Kirsch's literary activity falls into five areas: poetry; dramatic writing; essays; children's literature; and adaptations of foreign, mostly Russian, poetry and plays. Although a dedicated communist, Kirsch addressed himself as a writer to those contradictions in East German society that impeded the development of a true socialist state and led to conflicts between the individual and the collective. His views were considered provocative and suspect, and Kirsch was prohibited from publishing his poetry in the GDR throughout the 1960s. His play *Heinrich Schlaghands Höllenfahrt* (Heinrich Schlaghand's Ascension, 1973), in which he takes issue with simplistic notions of socialism, served as the pretext for his expulsion from the Socialist Unity Party (communist). Relentless in his challenge to the official ideology of the East German state, which he believed actually undermined true socialism, he published a volume of poetry in 1978 under the title *Auszog das Fürchten zu lernen* (Don't Be Afraid to Learn), which is imbued with his social and ethical views. His other books of poetry include *Kunst in Mark Brandeburg* (Art in the Mark of Brandenburg), which appeared in Munich in 1989, and *Anna Karenina oder die Nacht am Moorbusch nebst einem tiefgründigen Gespräch* (Anna Karenina, or The Night in the Moors Together with a Profound Conversation, 1991).

Apart from *Heinrich Schlaghands Höllenfahrt*, Kirsch is the author of the plays

Der Soldat und das Feuerzeug (The Soldier and the Lighter, 1967) and *Das Feurzeug* (The Lighter, 1967). He has also done stage adaptations and translations of a number of foreign plays. Kirsch's essays and other non-fiction were collected in the volumes *Kopien nach Originalen* (Copies from Originals, 1974); *Das Wort und seine Strahlung* (The Word and Its Radiance, 1976); and *Amt des Dichters: Aufsätze, Rezensionen, Notizen, 1964–1978* (The Poet's Office: Essays, Reviews, Notes, 1964–1978, 1979). Kirsch has also written a number of children's books and has published adaptations of poems by the Russian poets Sergei Esenin, Anna Akhmatova, and Osip Mandelshtam, as well as of works by Keats and Georgian poets. In 1990 Kirsch succeeded Hermann Kant as head of the East German Writers Union.

Literature: "Rainer Kirsch," in *Literary Intellectuals and the Dissolution of the State: Professionalism and Conformity in the GDR*, ed. Robert von Hallberg, trans. Kenneth J. Northcott (Chicago: University of Chicago Press, 1996), 155–62.

Kirsch, Sarah (real name Ingrid Bernstein; b. 1935) German poet and short-story writer. One of the most highly regarded poets to come out of East Germany, Kirsch was born in Limlingerode, in the South Harz region. She adopted the first name Sarah as a protest against German anti-Semitism before, during, and after World War II. Kirsch studied biology and, from 1963 to 1965, took writing courses at the Johannes R. Becher Institute of Literature in Leipzig. The impetus to her literary career owed much to her marriage (1958–1968) to the poet and essayist Rainer Kirsch, with whom she wrote her first book of poetry, *Gespräch mit dem Saurier* (Conversation with the Sauropod, 1965). In this collection, as well as in her next two volumes of poetry published under her own name, *Landaufenthalt* (A Stay in the Coun-

try, 1967) and *Zaubersprüche* (Magic Spells, 1973; translated as *Conjurations*), her interest was heavily in the realm of nature described in a strikingly simple style without benefit of metaphor. Through her observations of nature, Kirsch leads her reader to contemplate issues both universal and contemporary, such as the Holocaust, the division of Germany, and the war in Vietnam. Kirsch never abandoned her attachment to nature and landscape, despite the prominence of other concerns in her subsequent poetry. Her volumes *Erdreich* (Soil, 1982); *Katzenleben* (*Catslives*, 1984); and *Schneewarme* (Snow Warmth, 1989), which were published after she had resettled in West Germany, were inspired by the north German countryside, especially in winter. Notwithstanding Kirsch's previous inclination toward the introspective and subjective, the breakup of her marriage to Rainer Kirsch intensified these tendencies in her writing. The profound impact of her divorce led her to a new concentration on the crises of her own life and on her own emotional turmoil. Kirsch's poetry henceforth became intensely private and autobiographical, as she sought ways of expressing and resolving her own inner conflicts. A sense of anguish, hurt, and desolation coupled with rage at a hostile fate and a passionate desire to reclaim what had been lost inform, to various degrees, the poems in *Zaubersprüche* and in such later volumes as *Rückenwind* (Tail Wind, 1976); *Erlkönigs Tochter* (The Erl King's Daughter, 1992); and *Bodenlos* (Bottomless, 1996).

Although no outspoken critic of the East German regime on the order of Wolf Biermann, Kirsch had strong feelings about the artist's right to creative autonomy and made her position known mainly through her spiritually independent and introspective poetry. Although much admired as a poet, she was chastised for her passivity and resignation at the Sixth Writers Congress of the

GDR in 1969. It was, however, only after the Biermann affair that Kirsch resolved to quit the GDR and settle in West Germany, which she did in 1977. Since moving to the West, Kirsch has been able to satisfy a fondness for travel, as manifest in such volumes as *Catslives*; *Drachensteigen* (Dragon Paths, 1979), which grew out of a year's stay in Italy; *La Pagerie* (1980), a small book of travel impressions inspired by the landscapes of Provence in the form of very short prose fragments; and Soil, which also incorporates poems inspired by a visit to the United States. Rediscovering the world of nature and foreign landscapes has had a calming effect on the intense passion and tangled emotions of Kirsch's previous private and poetic world.

Apart from her poetry, Kirsch has written several books of prose. They include the journalistic *Die Pantherfrau: Fünf unfrisierte Erzählungen aus dem Kassetten-Recorder* (*The Panther Woman: Five Ungroomed Stories from the Cassette Recorder*, 1973), a collection of minimally edited interviews with five women from different walks of life in the GDR; *Die ungeheuren berghohen Wellen auf See: Erzählungen* (The Enormous Mountain-High Waves at Sea, 1973), a collection of seven stories written between 1968 and 1972 and also dealing primarily with the status of women in East Germany; *Irrstern* (Comet, 1986); *Allerlei-Rauh: Eine Chronik* (Allerlei-Rauh: A Chronicle, 1988); *Schwingrasen* (Grassland, 1991); *Spreu* (Chaff, 1991); and *Das Simple Leben* (The Simple Life, 1994). The last five volumes consist in the main of often complex personal reflections and reminiscences from Kirsch's West German period; except for *Allerlei-Rauh* (whose title derives from a well-known fairy tale by the Brothers Grimm), which is one continuous narrative, they are mostly in the form of small prose pieces of a random, disparate nature. *Spreu* is a verbally and visually playful diary of

reading tours undertaken by Kirsch on the urging of her publisher between May 1988 and December 1990. Kirsch also contributed to *Meine Träume fallen in die Welt: Ein Else Lasker-Schuler Almanach* (My Tears Fall on the World: An Else Lasker-Schuler Almanac, 1995), the commemorative volume in honor of the German Jewish poet Else Lasker-Schuler (1869–1945).

Kirsch has won a number of awards for her writing: the Kunstpreis der Stadt Halle (1965); the Heinrich Heine Prize of the GDR (1973); the Petrarca Prize (1976); the Austrian State Prize and Kritikerpreis (1981); the Roswitha-Gedenkenmedaille of the town of Bad Gandersheim (1983); the Friedrich Hölderlin Prize in Bad Homburg (1984); the Weinpreis der Literatur (1986); the Kunstpreis des Landes Schleswig-Holstein and the Stadtschreiber-Literaturpreis of the city of Mainz (1988); the Kulturpreis der Konrad-Adenauer-Stiftung (1993); the Georg-Büchner Prize (1996); and the Annette-von-Droste-Hülshoff Prize (1997). In 1996 Kirsch was appointed to the Brothers Grimm Professorship at Kassel University.

Literature: Mererid Hopwood and David Basker, eds., *Sarah Kirsch* (Cardiff: University of Wales Press, 1997), the best work on Kirsch in English and contains interesting material on Kirsch's two visits to Swansea, Wales, in 1989 and 1994. Major German studies include Christine Cosentino, *"Ein Spiegel mit mir darin": Sarah Kirschs Lyrik* (Tübingen: Francke, 1990); *Sarah Kirsch: Begleitheft zur Ausstellung* (Frankfurt am Main: Stadt- und Universitätsbibliothek, 1996–1997), the catalogue of an exhibition devoted to Sarah Kirsch, with good pictures and a chronology; Barbara Mabee, *Die Poetik von Sarah Kirsch: Erinnerungsarbeit und Geschichtsbewusstein* (Amsterdam: Atlanta, 1989); Hans Wagener, *Sarah Kirsch* (Berlin: Colloquium, 1989), the best general introduction to Kirsch in German; and *Sarah Kirsch: Texte, Dokumente, Materialen* (Baden-Baden: Elster, 1955), a useful source book. There is also some material on Kirsch in English in *Three Contemporary German Poets: Wolf Biermann, Sarah Kirsch, Rainer Kunze,* ed. Peter J. Graves (Leicester: Leicester University Press, 1985), 17–20, 31–32 (bibliography).

Translations: *Catslives: Sarah Kirsch's Katzenleben,* trans. and ed. Marina Roscher and Charles Fishman (Lubbock: Texas Tech University Press, 1991); *Conjurations,* trans. Wayne E. Kvam (Athens: Ohio University Press, 1985); *The Panther Woman: Five Tales from the Cassette Recorder,* trans. Marion Faber (Lincoln: University of Nebraska Press, 1989); *Poems,* in versions by Jack Hirschman (Santa Cruz, Calif.: Alcatraz, 1983); *Winter Music: Selected Poems,* trans. Margitt Lehbert (London: Anvil, 1994); "A Remarkable Example of Determination in a Woman," trans. Jan van Heurck, in *The New Sufferings of Young W. and Other Stories from the German Democratic Republic,* ed. Therese Hörnigk and Alexander Stephan (New York: Continuum, 1997), 190–201.

Kiš, Danilo (1935–1989) Serbian novelist, short-story writer, and essayist. The most cosmopolitan and innovative Yugoslav writer of the post–World War II period, Kiš was a native of Subotica, on the border between Serbia and Hungary. His father was a Hungarian Jew who died in Auschwitz, and his mother, a Serbian Orthodox Christian from Montenegro. Kiš spent much of his youth in Hungary and Montenegro. He was educated at Belgrade University, where he earned his degree in comparative literature in 1958. His literary debut came in 1962 with two prose works: *Mansarda* (The Attic), about the torment of juvenile love, and *Psalam 44* (Psalm 44), dealing with a young Jewish girl who survives the Holocaust. After he ran afoul of the Yugoslav Writers Union because of the publication in 1976 of *Grobnica za Borisa Davidovića* (*A Tomb for Boris Davidovich*), Kiš spent increasingly more time in France, where he had studied. Although he never considered himself a political exile, Kiš lived virtually the last ten years of his life in Paris, where he died on 15 October 1989. Fluent in French, he taught Serbo-Croatian and lectured on Yugoslav literature at the universities of Strasbourg, Bordeaux, and Lille. He also won recognition for his translations from French, English, Russian, and Hungarian poetry.

Kiš's major works after *Mansarda* and *Psalam 44* include a family triptych: *Rani jadi* (Early Sorrows, 1968), a book of stories; *Bašta, pepeo* (*Garden, Ashes,* 1965), a novel; and *Peščenik* (*Hourglass,* 1972), a narratively complex and demanding novel inspired by his father's life and death. Also important are *A Tomb for Boris Davidovich,* a collection of linked stories on the fate of several characters (mostly Eastern European and Russian Jews) who in various ways become victims of Stalinist terror; *Čas anatomije* (The Anatomy Lesson, 1978), a collection of polemical essays; *Enciklopedija mrtvih* (*The Encyclopedia of the Dead,* 1983), a book of fact-based unrelated stories on the theme of death set in different places and times; and three collections of essays on art and literature, all published in 1990: *Gorki talog iskustva* (The Bitter Harvest of Art), *Život, literatura* (Life and Literature), and *Homo Poeticus* (1990).

The best-known work in Kis's family trilogy is *Garden, Ashes,* a stunning fictionalized reminiscence, mostly of his father, that is clearly influenced by the Polish Jewish writer Bruno Schulz's phantasmagoric *Cinnamon Shops* (1934). Kiš carried his obsession with his father, and his demise during World War II, into *Hourglass,* the most complex and experimental of the three works that make up the family triptych.

The unequivocal anti-Stalinism of *A Tomb for Boris Davidovich* earned Kiš the enmity of the Yugoslav Writers Union, which mounted a campaign of defamation against him by accusing him of plagiarism. Kiš went on a counteroffensive in *Čas anatomije*, in which he took aim at nationalism as well as totalitarianism. It was in this work that he declared: "Nationalism is the ideology of banality. It is a totalitarian ideology."

Kiš's broad literary interests, and his acknowledged affinities with such writers as Jorge Luis Borges and Bruno Schulz, form much of the subject matter of *Homo Poeticus*. The interview section of the book is of particular interest for Kiš's comments on his own works and his attitude toward Jews, Jewishness, and the Holocaust.

Kiš's literary achievements were honored on several occasions. He won the Yugoslav NIN and Goran prizes in 1973 and 1977, respectively. In 1980 he was awarded the Golden Eagle of the City of Nice. Previous winners of the award were the English writer Graham Greene and the South African Nadine Gordimer. In 1989 he was postumously awarded the PEN/Bruno Schulz Prize, which was established in honor of writers underrecognized in the United States and named for the Polish author who was much admired by Kiš.

Literature: There are no book-length studies of Kiš in English. Some critical material on him can be found in M. D. Birnbaum and R. Trager-Verchovsky, eds., *History, Another Text: Essays on the Fiction of Kazimierz Brandys, Danilo Kiš, György Konrád and Christa Wolf* (Ann Arbor: University of Michigan Press, 1988). Of books on Kiš in Serbo-Croatian, the best are Petar Pijanović, *Proza Danila Kiša* (Priština: Jedinstvo, 1992), a general study of Kiš's prose, and Jovan Delić, *Književni pogledi Danila Kiša: Ka poetici kišove proze* (Belgrade: Prosveta, 1994), a study of the poetics of Kiš's prose.

Translations: *The Encyclopedia of the Dead*, trans. Michael Henry Heim (New York: Farrar, Straus and Giroux, 1989; New York: Penguin, 1991); *Garden, Ashes*, trans. William J. Hannaher (New York: Harcourt Brace Jovanovich, 1975); *Homo Poeticus: Essays and Interviews*, trans. by various hands, ed., with an introduction, by Susan Sontag (New York: Farrar, Straus and Giroux, 1995), which comprises selections from *Čas anatomije* and *Homo Poeticus*; *Hourglass*, trans. Ralph Mannheim (New York: Farrar, Straus and Giroux, 1990); *A Tomb for Boris Davidovich*, trans. Duška Mikić-Mitchell, with an introduction by Joseph Brodsky (New York: Harcourt Brace Jovanovich, 1978; New York: Penguin, 1980); "The Lute and the Scar," trans. Paul M. Foster, in *The Prince of Fire: An Anthology of Contemporary Serbian Short Stories*, ed. Radmila J. Gorup and Nadežda Obradović (Pittsburgh: University of Pittsburgh Press, 1998), 120–30; "A Man with No Country," trans. Christina Pribićević-Zorić, in *Storm Out of Yugoslavia*, ed. Joanna Labon (London: Carcanet, 1994), 178–89, Kiš's last piece, unpublished in his lifetime, and based on the life of the Hungarian-born Austrian playwright Ödön von Horváth (1901–1938).

Kiss, Anna (b. 1939) Hungarian poet. Kiss was born in Gyula and was raised in Zsadány, in the Békés district along the Romanian border. After finishing her secondary education in local schools, she attended the Debrecen Medical School while working as an auxiliary nurse. However, she gave up her medical studies after two and a half years and, intent on becoming a teacher, earned a degree in Hungarian and Russian at the Szeged Teachers College. In 1963 she began working as a full-time teacher in Budapest. Kiss made her literary debut with a collection of poems under the title *Fabábú* (Wooden Puppet, 1971), the title operating as a metaphor for Kiss's sense of her own existence at the time. Her feeling of closeness with the earth and her own peasant origins as well as with the landscape of her childhood is reflected in much of her verse writing. So, too, is an acceptance of life's hardships, which she has strengthed herself against by means of her poetry and a kind of personal mythological realm in which she sometimes appears amid a variety of ghosts and goblins. After *Fabábú*, Kiss published five more collections of poetry: *Feketegyűrű* (Black Ring, 1974); *Kísértenek* (Hauntings, 1976); *Vilagok* (Worlds, 1978), which includes plays and poems; *Tükörképek* (Mirror Images, 1983); and *A viszony* (The Relationship, 1983). Kiss has also published two plays in verse: *A két ökör* (The Two Oxen, 1976) and *A vár* (The Fortress, 1976). Although her early poetry shows the strong influence of the folk song and ballad, with the volume *Tükörképek* she moved into prose poems.

Translations: Two longer poems in *The Face of Creation: Contemporary Hungarian Poetry*, trans. Jascha Kessler et al. (Minneapolis: Coffee House, 1988), 64–71; five poems, trans. Enikő Molnár Basa and Robert Austerlitz, in *Ocean at the Window: Hungarian Prose and Poetry Since 1945*, ed. Albert Tezla (Minneapolis: University of Minnesota Press, 1980), 369–72.

Kjulavkova, Katica (b. 1951) Macedonian poet and literary scholar. A well-known literary scholar and professor at Saints Cyril and Methodius University in Skopje as well as a poet, Kjulavkova has concentrated her studies primarily on poetic language and the Macedonian poetic tradition. *Figurativniot govor i makedonskata poezija* (Figures of Speech and Macedonian Poetry, 1984) was her first published scholarly study and was followed by such related works as *Pothod i ishod* (Norm and Deviation, 1987), which supports theoretical discussions of poetic metaphor, models, and themes with analyses of specific works by Macedonian authors; *Odliki na lirikata* (Reflections of the Lyric, 1989), a sophisticated and wide-ranging study of the emotive and figurative in lyric poetry; and *Kopnez po sistem* (I Long for a System, 1992). Her original poetic writing is contained in the volumes *Našiot soglasnik* (Our Agreement, 1981), which was issued with a laudatory afterword by her fellow Macedonian poet Gane Todorovski; *Nova pot* (New Path, 1984); and *Žedbi* (Thirsts, 1989). Eschewing the folkloric and patriarchal currents in Macedonian poetry, Kjulavkova's writing is elegant, urbane, often sensuous and erotic, and learned, reflecting a great breadth of literary culture both modern and classical. She seasons her poetry with allusions to James Joyce, Jorge Luis Borges, Marguerite Yourcenar, Franz Kafka, and others; writes of dreams, myth, metaphysics, and the occult sciences; yet can find inspiration in everyday personal experience. In July 1997 she was invited on a visit by the Maison des écrivains étrangères et des traducteurs de Saint-Nazaire. The visit led to the publication in 1998 of a small French–Macedonian collection of her poetry.

Translations: *Via lasciva*, trans. Harita Wybrands (Saint-Nazaire: M.E.E.T., 1998), a French–Macedonian edition of seventeen poems; seven poems in *Contemporary Macedonian Poetry*, ed. and trans. Ewsald Osers (London: Forest, 1991), 179–87.

Klíma, Ivan (b. 1931) Czech novelist, short-story writer, playwright, and essayist. One of the most celebrated twentieth-century Czech writers, Klíma was born in Prague where he was educated and where, at Charles University, he pursued a program of Czech studies. During World War II, he was confined for three years to the Terezín (Theresienstadt) concentration camp as a Jew. After several years' experience as a publishing house editor after the war, he eventually took over the editorship of the prestigious literary journal *Literární listy*. Although he denounced the Soviet invasion of

Czechoslovakia in 1968, he was still able to accept a visiting lectureship in Czech at the University of Michigan for the academic year 1969/1970. When he returned to Prague, he was forbidden to publish, with the result that until the overthrow of communism in Czechoslovakia all his works were published either underground or in foreign countries, primarily England and Canada.

Klíma made his literary debut in 1960 with a book of reportage about eastern Slovakia, *Mezi třemi hranicemi* (Between Three Borders). The same year, he also published a collection of short stories, *Bezvadný den* (The Perfect Day), which owes much to the influence of the celebrated Czech writer Karel Čapek (1890–1938), whom Klíma greatly admired and whose reputation he tried to rehabilitate in his book *Karel Čapek* (1962) at a time when this was politically incorrect. In his first novel, *Hodina ticha* (The Quiet Hour, 1963), Klíma returned to the eastern Slovak setting of *Mezi třemi hranicemi* in a work brimming with enthusiasm for socialist construction and reminiscent of Ivan Olbracht's (1882–1952) pre–World War II works about Subcarpathian Rus. His next collection of stories, *Milenci na jednu noc* (Lovers for a Night, 1964), was the first of a series of story collections and novels in which love and sex, marriage and adultery, are viewed from different angles and always wryly, ironically, and with gentle humor. After *Milenci na jednu noc*, Klíma brought out *Milenci na jeden den* (*Lovers for a Day*, 1970), but part of the edition was confiscated and destroyed; *Moje první lásky* (*My First Loves*, 1985); *Láska a smetí* (*Love and Garbage*, 1986); *Milostné rozhovory* (Conversations About Love, 1995); and *Poslední stupeň důvernosti* (The Last Degree of Intimacy, 1996; translated as *The Ultimate Intimacy*). In this last work, a stunning novel, Klíma anticipates the problems of adjustment and readjustment in a postcommunist

Czechoslovakia full of uncertainties. The novel traces the impact of an adulterous affair on the lives of those around a wayward Protestant minister in the context of the rapidly changing contemporary Czech society. From the point of view of narrative structure, the novel is particularly interesting for Klíma's use of omniscient author narration alternating with epistolary exchanges and excerpts from the minister's diary. Klíma's other novels include *Lod, jménem Naděje* (1969; translated as *A Ship Named Hope*); *Má veselá jitra* (*My Merry Mornings*, 1979); *Soudce z milosti* (A Judge out of Love, 1986; translated as *Judge on Trial*), which an advertisement in the *New York Times* touted as "the book that is likely to survive as the key version of the late twentieth-century Eastern European political novel"; *Čekání na tmu, čekání na světlo* (*Waiting for the Dark, Waiting for the Light*, 1993); and *Jak daleko je slunce* (How Far the Sun, 1995).

Klíma's essays, most dealing with politics and in many instances originally published in samizdat form or abroad, appear in such collections as *Už se blíží meče: K prameni inspirace Franze Kafky* (The Swords Are Approaching: On the Source of Franz Kafka's Inspiration, 1985) and *Užse blíží meče: Eseje, fejetony, rozhovory* (The Swords Are Approaching: Essays, Feuilletons, and Conversations, 1990). Possibly the best, and most accessible, introduction to Klíma the thinker and essayist is *The Spirit of Prague and Other Essays* (1994), a collection of personal and political essays that tell us as much about Klíma as about his beloved city of Prague from the German occupation during World War II to the Soviet invasion of Czechoslovakia in 1968. The essays were culled for translation from published Czech collections.

If his dramatic writings have had to take a back seat to his prose fiction and essays, Klíma nonetheless has a number of plays to his credit. These include both longer, usually two-act plays, and several one-acters: *Zámek* (The Castle, 1964); *Porota: Hra o 2 dílech* (The Jury: A Play in Two Acts, 1968); *Mistr* (The Master, 1967); *Pokoj pro dva a jiné hry* (A Room for Two and Other Plays, 1973); *Hry: Hra o dvou dejstvich* (*Games: A Play in Two Acts*, 1973); and *Ministr a anděl* (The Minister and the Angel, 1990). He has also written such one-acters as *Klára a dva páni* (Klára and the Two Men, 1968); *Cukrárna Myriam* (The Pastry Shop Myriam, 1968); *Ženich pro Marcelu* (A Bridegroom for Marcela, 1969); *Pokoj pro dva* (A Double Room, 1970); and *Thunder and Lightning* (1972).

Translations: *Between Security and Insecurity* (New York: Thames and Hudson, 1999); *Games,* trans. Jan Drabek, in *Drama Contemporary: Czechoslovakia,* ed. Marketa Goetz-Stankiewicz (New York: PAJ Publications, 1985); *Games,* trans. Barbara Day, in *Czech Plays: Modern Czech Drama,* selected and introduced by Barbara Day (London: Nick Hern, 1994), 27–93; *Judge on Trial,* trans. A. G. Brain (New York: Knopf, 1993); *Love and Garbage,* trans. Ewald Osers (London: Chatto & Windus, 1991; New York: Knopf, 1993); *Lovers for a Day,* trans. Gerald Turner (New York: Grove, 1999); *My First Loves,* trans. Ewald Osers (London: Chatto & Windus, 1986; New York: Harper & Row, 1988); *My Golden Trades,* trans. Paul Wilson (London: Granta, 1992; New York: Scribner, 1994); *My Merry Mornings: Stories from Prague,* trans. George Theiner (London: Readers International, 1985); *A Ship Named Hope: Two Novels,* trans. Edith Pargeter (London: Gollancz, 1970); *The Spirit of Prague and Other Essays,* trans. Paul Wilson (New York: Granta, 1994); *A Summer Affair,* trans. Ewald Osers (London: Chatto & Windus, 1987); *The Ultimate Intimacy,* trans. A. G. Brain (London: Granta, 1997); *Waiting for the Dark, Waiting for the Light,* trans. Paul Wilson (New York: Penguin, 1994; New York: Grove, 1995). SOUND RECORDING: A sound recording, dated 1990, of Klíma reading from his book *Láska a smetí* is available at the Recorded Sound Reference Center, Library of Congress.

Kocbek, Edvard (1904–1981) Slovenian poet, short-story writer, and essayist. Widely regarded as one of the most important Slovenian writers of the twentieth century, Kocbek was born in the village of Sv. Jurij ob Ščavnici (after 1953, Videm ob Ščavnici). From 1916 to 1925, he attended secondary schools in Maribor and Ptuj. Strongly attracted to the religious life, Kocbek began seminary studies but gave them up in 1927 in order to pursue Romance philology at Ljubljana University. He received his diploma in 1930. His literary career developed in the context of collaboration with Slovenian Catholic reviews and journals such as the Catholic youth magazine *Križa,* where he served as editor and where his first works were published, and *Dom in svet,* in which his first cycle of poems, "Jesenske pesmi" ("Autumn Poems") appeared in 1931. The same year, a French government fellowship enabled him to spend time in Paris and Lyons. Kocbek's first published book of poetry appeared in 1934 under the title *Zemlja* (The Land). It was followed by seven more collections of poetry, similarly informed with his Christian worldview: *Groza* (Dread, 1963), for which Kocbek won the Prešeren Prize in 1964; *Poročilo* (The Report, 1969); *Žerjavica* (Embers, 1974); *Zbrane pesmi* (Collected Poems, 1977), consisting of two volumes—*Pentagram,* containing Kocbek's partisan poems from April 1941 to May 1942, and *Nevesta v črnem* (The Bride Wore Black)—published first in this collection; and *Rane pesmi* (Early Poems) and *Kamen skala* (The Rocky Cliff), both published posthumously in 1991.

Apart from his poetry, Kocbek wrote extensively in prose beginning in the late 1920s. His first book-length prose publication was the travel book *Krogi navznoter* (The Inner Circles, 1934). The bulk of Kocbek's prose appeared in the postwar period and falls into two major categories. The first consists of writings of a religiophilosophical nature and includes such publications as *Eros in seksus* (Eros and Sex, 1970), in which he addresses the religious aspects of sex; *Svoboda in nujnost* (Freedom and Necessity, 1974), a collection of philosophical, theological, political, and autobiographical writings covering the period 1928 to 1972; and *Sodobni misleci* (Contemporary Thinkers, 1981), which is devoted to such (predominantly Catholic) twentieth-century thinkers and writers as Karl Barth, Albert Camus, Teilhard de Chardin, Graham Greene, Theodore Haecker, Emmanuel Mounier, Charles Péguy, and Simone Weil. Kocbek's second major body of prose writing consists in the main of diaries chronicling his experiences and observations as a partisan (whose ranks he joined in 1942) during World War II. They include *Tovarišija: Dnevniski zapiski od 17 maja 1942 do 1 maja 1943* (Comradeship: Diary Notes from 17 May 1942 to 1 May 1943, 1949); *Slovensko poslanstvo: Dnevnik s poti v Jajce 1943* (The Slovenian Mission: Diary En Route in Jajka 1943, 1964); *Pred viharjem* (Before the Storm, 1980), which includes fragments of diaries from the years 1938, 1940, 1941, and 1942; and *Listina: Dnevniski zapiski od 3 maja do 2 decembra 1943* (Document: Diary Notes from 3 May to 2 December 1943, 1967). During the war, from November 1941 to June 1942, Kocbek also edited the political and cultural journal *Osvobodilna fronta*. Apart from their factual content, the diaries are especially interesting for Kocbek's reconciliation of Christianity and communism. His postwar diaries (all published posthumously)—*Dnevnik, 1951–1952* (Diary, 1951–1952, 1986) and *Dnevnik* (Diary, 1991)—similarly advance the belief that there is a dialectical relationship between a Marxist-inspired social revolution and metaphysical salvation. Kocbek's most

controversial literary work proved to be *Strah in pogum* (Fear and Courage, 1951), a collection of four novellas inspired by the wartime partisan struggle. What provoked the controversy surrounding the book were the moral and ethical questions (above all, the Christian attitude toward killing) raised by Kocbek, which for many Yugoslavs seemed to be motivated by the desire to strip the partisan war of some of its mythic glory. So hostile was the reaction to *Strah in pogum* that Kocbek was virtually ostracized from Yugoslav literary and public life for nearly a decade. Kocbek busied himself during this dark period in his life with extensive translation from French and German literatures.

Literature: *Edvard Kocbek: Poezija, kultura, politika* (Ljublana: Komunist, 1988), a collection of sixteen articles (in Slovenian) covering a broad spectrum of Kocbek's writings and views; Joanna Sławińska, *Poetycka kosmogonia Edvarda Kocbeka* (Kraków: Universitas, 1993), a Polish study concentrating mostly on the philosophical content of Kocbek's poetry; Andrej Inkret, "Pričevanje o brezumni slasti in o zadnji grozi," the afterword to Edvard Kocbek, *Strah in pogum: Štiri novele* (Ljublana; Mladinska knjiga, 1984), 341–93. This edition of *Strah in pogum* also contains a very useful chronology of Kocbek's life (394–409).

Translations: *Embers in the House of Night: Selected Poems of Edvard Kocbek*, trans. Sonja Kravanja (Santa Fe, N.M.: Lumen, 1999).

Koehler, Krzysztof (b. 1963) Polish poet. Koehler belongs to the "barbarian" group of poets who publish in the Kraków quarterly *bruLion*. His first collection of verse, *Wiersze* (Poems), appeared in 1990. It was followed by *Partyzant prawdy* (A Partisan of Truth), a slim volume of verse published in 1996, and by the retrospective volume *Na krańcu długiego pola i inne wiersze z lat, 1988–1998*

(At the Edge of a Long Field and Other Poems from 1988 to 1998) in 1998. A poet attracted to death who wonders if he may be a "partisan of truth"—without making clear what truth he has in mind—Koehler often draws his imagery from classical antique and Christian sources as well as from nature and specific locales (Kraków, Wilanów). Although Christian imagery appears often in his poetry, Koehler seems unable or unwilling to find inspiration in religious faith as such, pondering instead his own disconnectedness in a world that often seems bereft of meaning.

Translations: "OHarism," trans. W. Martin, *Chicago Review* 46, nos. 3–4 (2000): 280–81; seven poems in *Young Poets of a New Poland*, trans. Donald Pirie (London: Forest, 1993), 183–92.

Kohlhaase, Wolfgang (b. 1931) German short-story and screenwriter. Kohlhaase was born in Berlin and after a secondary-school education began working as a journalist for youth newspapers and for the East German DEFA film studio. He became well known for such feature films as *Berlin—Ecke Schönhauser* (Berlin—Schönhauser Corner, 1957); *Ich war neunzehn* (I Was Nineteen, 1968); *Mama, ich lebe* (Mama, I'm Alive, 1977); *Solo Sunny* (1980; original title in English); and *Der Aufenthalt* (The Stopover, 1983), which was based on the novel of the same name by Herman Kant. Kohlhaase's favorite themes in his films are the problems of children and young people and a reckoning with the German National Socialist past, within the limits, of course, permitted by the political realities of the German Democratic Republic. In his prose fiction, Kohlhaase often portrays ordinary people trying to preserve their individuality despite the extreme conformist pressures surrounding them in GDR society. He is a keen observer of social mores and a good storyteller, with a sense of humor. His most suc-

cessful collection of short stories, which first brought him to the serious attention of West German readers, is *Silvester mit Balzac und andere Erzählungen* (New Year's Eve with Balzac and Other Stories, 1977). The story from which the collection derives its title is typical of Kohlhaase. Beneath the gaiety of a multinational New Year's holiday party in Budapest, to which the narrator has come on a short vacation from East Berlin, lie the melancholy of an unsatisfying separation from his wife, for whom he still cares, and the evaporation of his brief romance with a Hungarian woman he knows from before. The shoddy New Year's Eve betrayal of the hostess of the party by her callous husband further underlines Kohlhaase's preoccupation with the hardships of male–female relationships.

Translations: "Suffer the Little Children . . . ," trans. Jan van Heurck, in *The New Sufferings of Young W. and Other Stories from the German Democratic Republic*, ed. Therese Hörnigk and Alexander Stephan (New York: Continuum, 1997), 69–82.

Kohout, Pavel (b. 1928) Czech playwright, novelist, and screenwriter. A prominent post–World War II dramatist closely identified with the prodemocratic movement, Kohout was born in Prague where he was educated through high school. Even before his graduation in 1947, he became active in youth organizations and upon graduation began working for the youth magazine *Československý rozhlas*. At the same time, he undertook studies in comparative literature, aesthetics, and theater at Charles University but never completed a degree program. From 1949 to 1950, he served as the second cultural attaché of the Czechoslovak Embassy in Moscow. After returning to Czechoslovakia, he accepted the editorship of the journal *Dikobraz* from 1951 to 1952. He thereafter completed his military service (1952–1954) and until 1955 edited the cultural section of the army publication *Československý voják*. This affiliation, together with his continued involvement in youth organizations, provided Kohout with the opportunity to travel extensively not only throughout Europe but also to China and Mongolia. For several months in 1956, he was a reporter and commentator with the domestic political section of Czechoslovak TV, after which he became a full-time writer.

Kohout's theatrical career began in the 1960s when from 1963 to 1966 he worked as dramatic adviser to the famous Divadlo na Vinohradech (Theater in the Vineyards). This ended when he resigned his membership on the governing board of the Czechoslovak Writers Union over disagreement with its cultural and political orientation. His speech at the Fourth Congress of the union in 1967 earned him the same kind of disciplinary measures as were applied to such other literary progressives as Ivan Klíma, Antonín Liehm, and Ludvik Vaculík. Kohout's very active role in the "Prague Spring" of 1968 and his collaboration in the drafting of Charter 77 resulted in his being dismissed from the Party and the Czech Writers Union. Although he was permitted to accept an invitation in 1979 to visit Austria as a guest director and playwright, neither he nor his wife was allowed to return to Czechoslovakia and they were stripped of their citizienship. Kohout remained in Vienna, writing his more recent works originally in German. He returned to Prague only in 1989 after the change of regime.

Kohout began his literary career as a poet as early as 1945 and subsequently published several collections of poems. In the 1970s and 1980s, he also became an active contributor of stories, essays, and feuilletons to samizdat and foreign publications. However, it was primarily as a playwright that he achieved international celebrity. Arguably his best-known play abroad, *Ubohý vrah*

(*Poor Murderer*, 1972), based on a story by the Russian writer Leonid Andreev, was successfully performed, for example, in New York in the 1976/1977 Broadway season. Set in St. Petersburg, Russia, in 1900, the play features an intriguing play-within-a-play staged in a mental institution by a Russian actor who has gone mad in the role of Hamlet. *Poor Murderer* also exemplifies Kohout's success in dramatizing literary texts by foreign as well as Czech authors. Besides *Poor Murderer*, his play *Ruleta* (Roulette, 1976), first published in German, is based on another story by Andreev. *Válka z mloky* (The War with the Newts, 1963) and *Josef Švejk* (The Good Soldier Schweik, 1966) are based on two well-known works by the prominent twentieth-century Czech writer Karel Čapek. *Třetí sestra* (The Third Sister, 1960), ultimately indebted to Chekhov's *Three Sisters*, is built on the contrast among three sisters, the oldest of whom, Libuše, is an avowed communist. When the sisters discover a notebook of their dead mother, a prostitute, they also find clues to the identity of their father and set out to find him. Kohout also wrote stage versions of Jules Verne's *Around the World in Eighty Days* (*Cesta kolem světa za 80 dní*, 1962) and a few of Shakespeare's plays.

Kohout's many wholly original plays include, among others, *Dobrá píseň* (The Good Song, 1952), written in verse; *Zářijové noci* (September Nights, 1956), with its military setting; *Říkali mi soudruhu* (They Called Me Comrade, 1961); *Taková láska* (Such a Love, 1957), one of his most popular plays; *Sbohem, smutku!* (Goodbye, Sadness, 1958); and *August, August, August* (1967). Generally viewed at the time as a political allegory, and considered one of Kohout's finest plays, *August, August, August* is set in a circus milieu and features a clown (August) whose greatest dream is to transcend his lowly stature by performing with a set of beautiful white horses. But when the time comes for the fulfillment of his dream, the sadistic Director sets loose wild beasts that tear the hapless clown to pieces. Kohout's next several dramatic works appeared first in either samizdat or foreign (primarily German) editions, among them a collection of three short plays under the title *Život v tichém domě* (Life in a Quiet House, 1974); *Aksál* (1969; published in German as *Evol*); *Válka ve třetím poschodí* (1960; War on the Third Floor, published in German as *Krieg im dritten Stock*); *Pech pod střechou* (1974; Bad Luck Under the Roof, published in German as *Pech unter dem Dach*); *Požár v suterénu* (1974; Fire in the Basement, published in German as *Brand im Souterain*); and *Hodina tance a lásky* (The Hour of Dance and Love, 1989), which first appeared in West Germany.

Although active throughout his career as a playwright and stage director, Kohout began devoting more of his energy to prose writing in the late 1960s. Most of his prose works have a political character and are addressed to the suppression of democratic freedoms in Czechoslovakia and the efforts by the communist regime to quash efforts at reform. *Z deníku kontrarevolucionáře* (From the Diary of a Counterrevolutionary, 1969; published in German as *Aus dem Tagebuch eines Kontrrevolutionärs*) is a kind of collage of diary notes and supplemental material covering the period from the 1940s to the Soviet-led invasion of Czechoslovakia in 1968. *Kde je zakopán pes* (Where the Dog Lies Buried), which was eventually published in 1987, is usually described as a "memoir novel in which Kohout, drawing obviously on his own experiences, traces the evolution of a dissident and his growing conflicts with the authorities and the police." Employing the arsenal of the absurd and grotesque, so well developed in Czech antiestablishment writing under the communists, Kohout

made the so-called normalization after 1969 (in the wake of the armed suppression of the "Prague Spring") the subject of *Bílá kniha o kauze Adam Juráček* (The White Book About the Adam Juráček Case), which in 1970 was published in an expanded German edition as *Das Weissbuch in Sachen Adam Juráček*. Similar in spirit are *Katyně* (The Hangwoman, 1978; published in German as *Die Henkerin*), an absurdist work about a school for executioners, and *Nápady svaté Kláry* (The Fancies of Saint Clara, 1980; published in German as *Die Einfälle der Heilighen Klara*), which deals with the fate of a young girl who tells fortunes in the improbable setting of a communist society.

Kohout's last major work was the novel *Hvězdná hodina vrahů* (The Stellar Hour of Murderers, 1998; translated as *The Widow Killer*), a suspenseful thriller with allegorical undertones set in the final months of the German occupation of Prague. A mad killer and would-be avenger carries out a series of gruesome ritual slayings of German and Czech widows, beginning with the widow of a German general who turned against Hitler. Of particular interest in the novel, which develops an intriguing role reversal between the Germans and Czechs as victimizers and victims, is the relationship between a Czech detective and a German police official who works in the Prague Gestapo.

Literature: Marketa Goetz-Stankiewicz, *The Silenced Theatre: Czech Playwrights Without a Stage* (Toronto: University of Toronto Press, 1979); Paul I. Trensky, *Czech Drama Since World War II* (White Plains, N.Y.: Sharpe, 1978).

Translations: *Fire in the Basement*, trans. Peter Stenberg and Marketa Goetz-Stankiewicz, in *Drama Contemporary: Czechoslovakia*, ed. Marketa Goetz-Stankiewicz (New York: PAJ Publications, 1985), 91–126; *The Hangwoman*, trans. Káča

Poláčková-Henley (New York: Putnam, 1981); *Permit,* trans. Jan Drabek; *Morass,* trans. Vera Pech; and *Safari,* trans. from the German by Anna Mozga, in *The Vaněk Plays,* trans. Marketa Goetz-Stankiewicz (Vancouver: University of British Columbia Press, 1987); *Poor Murderer,* trans. Herbert Berghof and Laurence Luckinbill (New York: Viking, 1977; New York: Penguin, 1977); *The Widow Killer,* trans. Neil Bernel (New York: St. Martin's Press, 1998).

Kolbe, Uwe (b. 1957) German poet. Kolbe was born and educated in Berlin and remained in East Germany until 1987, when he was given a long-term visa that allowed him to live in West Germany. A freelance writer since 1976, he made his literary debut that year with poems published in the journal *Sinn und Form.* He thereafter published three volumes of verse while still living in East Germany: *Hineingeboren* (Inbred, 1979); *Abschiede und andere Liebesgedichte* (Departures and Other Love Poems, 1979); and *Bornholm II* (1986). His first collection of poems published in the West after he resettled in Hamburg was *Nicht wirklich platonisch* (Not Really Platonic, 1994). Kolbe studied at the Johannes R. Becher Institute of Literature in Leipzig in 1980/1981 and from 1983 to 1987 edited the well-known journal *Mikado oder Der Kaiser ist nackt.* His first publication after his departure from East Germany was a domestic German travel book under the title *Vaterlandkanal: Ein Fartenbuch* (Fatherland Canal: A Travel Book, 1990). Of particular interest in Kolbe's writing is his intense preoccupation with the degradation of language in the public sphere in communist East Germany, attributable to the cultural politics of the state. However, he was equally opposed to some of the strategies employed especially by younger East German writers to engage the language of power critically or even subversively, regarding this as a compromise.

Instead, he advocated the avoidance of any and all dialogue with the official culture and its language and the search for an alternative, or even silence.

Kolozsvári-Grandpierre, Emil (1907–1992) Hungarian novelist and short-story writer. A formidable presence in twentieth-century Hungarian literature, Kolozsvári-Grandpierre wrote most of his works after World War II. Kolozsvári was born in Kolozsvár (now Cluj, Romania) of partly French background. After graduating from high school in Kolozsvár, in 1924 he moved with his family to Budapest, where he attended Budapest University without, however, graduating. Instead, he set out to learn the textile business at a school in Colmar, France. After returning to Hungary in 1928, he reentered Budapest University and studied French, Italian, and philosophy, writing a doctoral dissertation on the Italian playwright Luigi Pirandello. Failing to get a teaching job, he went to work first for the Bureau of Statistics, then the School of Applied Arts and Crafts, and finally the Institute for Minority Studies where he specialized in Transylvanian affairs.

Kolozsvári made his literary debut in 1931 with the novel *A rosta* (The Sieve). This set the pattern for his three other novels published before the outbreak of World War II dealing mostly with the Hungarian middle class of the period, whom he tended to view ironically and to portray at times in a grotesque manner accentuated by his interest in offbeat characters: *Dr. Csibraky szerelmei* (The Loves of Dr. Csibraky, 1935); *A nagy ember* (The Great Man, 1936); and *Az alvajárók* (The Sleepwalkers, 1938). Until he was drafted into military service in World War II, he managed to publish two more works: *A sárgavirágos leány* (The Yellow-Flowered Maiden, 1940), an attempt by Kolozsvári to tell a tale in a dreamlike surreal style, and the autobiographical *Tegnap*

(Yesterday, 1942), perhaps his best-known prewar work (and one of his best), in which he set out to expose so-called middle-class values as phony and harmful.

Kolozsvári was taken prisoner by the Soviets and was released at war's end. Upon his return to Hungary, he was employed mainly in editorial positions at major literary journals (*Új Íras, Kortárs,* and *Jelenkor*) and publishing houses (Hungária, Magvető, and Szépiródalmi) as well as at Hungarian Radio. His first postwar publication was the autobiographical novel *Szabadság* (Freedom, 1945), in which the period of his adolescence is recalled in an intellectual yet sentimental manner. It was followed by *Lelki finomságok* (Mental Standards, 1947), a collection of short stories; *A mérlegen* (On the Scales, 1950), a novel; *A csillagszemű* (Starry-Eyed), a historical piscaresque novel; *Elmés mulatságok* (Witty Amsements, 1955), a collection of anecdotes; *A törökfejes kopja* (The Turk's Head Copy, 1955), a novel; *A tisztesség keresztje* (The Honor of the Cross, 1957), short stories; *A boldogtalanság művészete* (The Art of Being Unhappy, 1958), a novel; *Párbeszéd a sorssal* (Dialogue with Destiny, 1962), a novel; *Keresztben az úton* (At the Crossroads, 1964), a novel; *Eljegyzés mai módra* (Today's Betrothal Customs, 1966), short stories; *Arcok napfényben* (Faces in Daylight, 1967), short stories; *Változatok hegedűre* (Violin Variations, 1967); *Eljegyzés mai módra* (Betrothal à la Mode, 1966), short stories; *Nők apróban* (Women in Miniature, 1970), a novel; and *Változó felhőzet* (Changing Clouds, 1977), short stories. In these postwar novels and stories alike, Kolozsvári demonstrates no less keen an awareness of the outlook and behavior of the society that was emerging in Hungary after the war as he had in his fiction about the middle-class intelligentsia and office workers in the prewar period. Writing in a comfortable, easy style he was able to convey revealing nuances of character while re-

lating character to the social and economic reality of the time.

In the 1970s and 1980s, Kolozsvári embarked on a series of satirically oriented family history novels intended to mirror contemporary urban society, mainly the intelligentsia. They include *Az utolsó hullám* (The Last Wave, 1973); *Táguló múlt* (The Expanding Past, 1975); *A szerencse mostohafia* (The Stepson's Luck, 1976); *Hullámtörűk* (Breakwaters, 1978*); Béklyók és barátok: Önéletrajzi regény* (Fetters and Friends: An Autobiographical Novel, 1979); *Árnyak az alagútban* (Shadows in the Tunnel, 1981); *Egy házasság előtörténete* (A True Story of a Marriage, 1983); *Emberi környezet: Családregény* (A Man's Surroundings: A Family Novel, 1986); and *Egy potenciavadász följegyzései az összeomlás után* (A Potency Hunter's Notetaking After the Downfall, 1989), a later novel in Kolozsvári's career that reaffirmed his wry sense of humor, especially with regard to irony in male–female relationships.

Kolozsvári was also the author of a number of essays and literary studies throughout his career. They appeared in such collections as *Az értelem dicsérete* (In Praise of Intellect, 1948); *Legendák nyomában* (On the Trail of Legends, 1959); *Utazás a valóság körül* (Voyage Around Reality, 1969); *Herder árnyékában: Cikkek, tanulmányok* (In Herder's Shadow: Articles and Studies, 1979); *Eretnek esszék* (Heretical Essays, 1984); and *A beton virágai* (Concrete Flowers, 1988). In 1980 Kolozsvári published *A szeplős Veronika: Kisregények, novellák, szatirák, tükörcserépek* (Freckled Veronica: Short Novels, Novellas, Satires, Mirror Tiles), a large collection of quite varied texts including such typically light Kolozsvári fare as the novella from which the title takes its name and such stories as "A szexbomba" ("The Sex Bomb") and "Tánc a boldogság körül" ("Dance About Happiness"). His last work was the posthumously published *Polgári sze-*

relem (Civil Love, 2000), a collection of ten mostly previously published stories. As a translator, Kolozsvári rendered into Hungarian such diverse writers as Voltaire, Anatole France, Casanova, Massimo Bontempelli, Samuel Beckett, and Sean O'Casey. His literary awards included the Baumgarten (1944), Attila József (1964, 1975), and Kossuth (1980) prizes.

Translations: "Conditioned Reflex," trans. László T. András, in *44 Hungarian Short Stories,* ed. Lajos Illés (Budapest: Corvina, 1979), 351–60.

Koneski, Blaže (1921–1993) Macedonian poet, short-story and essay writer, critic, translator, and scholar. An outstanding authority on the Macedonian language, Koneski was born in the village of Nebregovo, near Prilep. He studied philology at Skopje University and, after working as a lector at the Macedonian National Theater, in 1946 became professor of Macedonian literature at the university. Koneski's great contribution to Macedonian culture was as a scholar of the language after its establishment as an independent literary language in 1945. It was Koneski who codified literary Macedonian with a series of pioneering texts, including *Gramatika na makedonskiot literaturen jazik* (A Grammar of the Macedonian Literary Language, 1952–1954); *Istorija na makedonskiot jazik* (A History of the Macedonian Language, 1965); *Jazikot na makedonskata narodna poezija* (The Language of Macedonian Folk Poetry, 1971); *Od istorijata na jazikot na slovenskata pismenost vo Makedonija* (On the History of the Language of Slavic Literature in Macedonia, 1975); and *Makedonski mesta i iminja* (Macedonian Places and Names, 1991). In 1961 he also published a history of Macedonian literature, *Makedonska književnost,* and edited a dictionary of the Macedonian language that was published in three volumes in 1961, 1965, and 1966. Koneski's collection of and commentary on the Macedonian folk-song tradition—beginning with *Zbirka na makedonski narodni pesni* (Collection of Macedonian Folk Songs) of 1947—was also of inestimable value to the campaign to provide the new literary language with the proper underpinnings.

Apart from his scholarly work, Koneski wrote a great deal of lyric poetry that is highly regarded both for its variety thematically and metrically and for its depth. Of particular interest is his use of the Macedonian oral tradition and the folklore and literature of other Slavic cultures. Koneski's first collection of poems, published in 1948 under the title *Zemjata i ljubovta* (Land and Love), was followed by *Vezilka* (The Embroideress, 1955); *Pesni* (Poems, 1963); *Sterna* (The Sterna, 1966); *Prepevi* (Poetic Renditions, 1967); *Reke* (Rivers, 1968); Zapisi (Notes, 1974); *Prosta i stroga makedonska pesna* (A Simple and Strict Macedonian Song, 1978); *Stari i novi pesni* (Old and New Poems, 1979); *Pesni, raskazi, zlaten venec* (Poems, Stories, and the Golden Wreath, 1981); *Češmite* (The Water Fountains, 1984); *Poslanie* (Epistle, 1987); *Zlatovrv* (Gold-tipped, 1989); *Seizmograf* (Seismograph, 1989); *Nebeska reka* (Heavenly River, 1991); and *Crn oven* (Black Ram, 1993).

Although more prolific a poet than a writer of prose fiction, Koneski was interested in the genre of the short story and in 1955 published a collection of his stories in the well-received volume *Lojze* (Vineyard); in 1966 a new edition of the collection augmented by poems in prose was published as *Lojze i pesni vo proza* (Vineyard and Prose Poems). Besides his poetry, short stories, and scholarly studies, Koneski wrote essays on literature and other cultural topics, as in the collections *Jazični temi* (Barbarian Themes, 1981), devoted to early Slavic and Macedonian subjects; *Za literaturata i kulturata* (On Literature and Culture, 1981); *Ogledi i besedi* (Speeches and Essays, 1978);

and *Likovi i temi* (Images and Themes, 1987). His diary, spanning many years, was published in 1988 under the title *Dnevnik po mnogu godini* (A Diary of Many Years). Koneski received many honors for his scholarly and literary work. In 1946 he became president of the Macedonian Academy of Arts and Sciences. He was also a corresponding member of the Yugoslav Academy of Arts and Sciences as well as of the Serbian and Slovene academies. Both the University of Chicago and the Jagiellonian University in Kraków, Poland, bestowed honorary doctorates on him. For his poetry, he won the Macedonian AVNOJ and Njegoš prizes as well as the "Zlaten Venec" ("Golden Wreath") of the Struga Poetry Evenings festival. Koneski's complete works were published in seven volumes in 1981 under the title *Izbrani dela vo sedum knigi* (Collected Works in Seven Volumes).

Literature: Cane Andreevski, *Razgovori so Koneski* (Skopje: Kultura, 1991); Milorad R. Blećić, *Blaže Koneski: Portret pesnika* (Belgrade: Novo Delo, 1987); Radomir Ivanović, *Poetika Blaža Koneskog* (Belgrade: Partizanska knjiga, 1982); Slobodan Micković, *Poetskite idei na Koneski* (Skopje: Naša Kniga, 1986); Georgi Stardelov, *Odzemanje na silata: Poezijata na Blaže Koneski* (Skopje: Misla, 1990). Andreevski's and Blećić's books are more interesting for the nonspecialist in that the former consists of conversations with Koneski and the latter is a biography.

Translations: *About the Macedonian Language,* ed. Todor Dimitrevski, Blaže Koneski, and Trajko Stamatoski (Skopje: Krste Misirkov Institute of the Macedonian Language, 1978); *A Historical Phonology of the Macedonian Language,* trans. Victor A. Friedman (Heidelberg: Winter, 1983); *The Macedonian Language in the Development of the Slavonic Literary Languages,* trans. Ivanka Koviloska-Poposka and Graham W. Reid (Skopje: Kultura, 1968); *Macedonian Na-* *tional Treasures,* ed. Blaže Koneski et al. (Skopje: Makedonska Kniga, 1989); *Pesni/Poems,* trans. Andrew Harvey and Anne Pennington (Skopje: Makedonska Kniga, 1981), a Macedonian–English edition; *Towards the Macedonian Renaissance: Macedonian Text-Books of the Nineteenth Century,* trans. Ivanka Koviloska (Skopje: Institute of National History, 1961); nine poems in *Contemporary Macedonian Poetry,* ed. and trans. Ewald Osers (London: Forest, 1991), 11–21; seven poems, trans. by various hands, in *Reading the Ashes: An Anthology of the Poetry of Modern Macedonia,* ed. Milne Holton and Graham W. Reid (Pittsburgh: University of Pittsburgh Press, 1977), 3–11. SOUND RECORDING: A sound recording of Koneski reading his poetry at Harvard University is available as *Blaže Koneski: Poetry Reading* (Cambridge, Mass.: Woodberry Poetry Room, Harvard University, 1961).

Kongoli, Fatos (b. 1944) Albanian novelist and journalist. Kongoli was born in Elbasan, in central Albania, and was trained as a mathematician. After a three-year period of study in China, he returned to Albania, completed his studies in mathematics, and began a career as a teacher in that field. Strongly attracted to literature, he eventually moved to Tirana and became active in publishing. He served as an editor of the literary journal *Drita* and after 1977 was affiliated with the important publishing house Naim Frashëri. His first work, the novel *Ne të tre* (The Three of Us, 1985), has been overshadowed by the first two volumes of a four-novel cycle: *I humburi* (The Lost, 1992) and *Kufoma* (The Cadaver, 1994). The latter was awarded the most prestigious Albanian literary prize the year of its publication. In *I humburi,* Kongoli follows the career of a young man, Thesar Lumi, who in March 1991 changes his mind at the last moment and decides against joining the many Albanians fleeing to Italy by boat. Relying on his wiles, he eventually gains entry into the university and from there into the small circle of the powerful who rule Albania. Kongoli's real subject, however, is the corruption and degradation of Albanian daily life in the 1960s and 1970s, the period of his own youth. A strong novel, written in a lively syle felicitously yoking interior monologue, dialogue, and narration, *I humburi* remains one of the most important novels to come out of Albania in the 1990s. In *Kufoma*, Kongoli again uses a single character, Festim Gurabardhi, an employee of a publishing house (a world Kongoli himself knew well), to expose the inner rot of the last years of Albanian communism. Kongoli's latest novel, *Dragoi i fildishtë* (The Ivory Dragon, 1999), has as its subject the life of an Albanian student in China against the background of the Albanian–Chinese alliance of the 1960s and 1970s. It also draws on Kongoli's own experiences in China earlier in his career.

Translations: *I humburi* is available in French as *Le Paumé,* trans. Christiane Montécot and Edmond Tupja (Paris: Rivages, 1997); *Kufoma* as *L'Ombre de l'autre,* trans. Edmond Tupja (Paris: Rivages, 1998); and *Dragoi i fildishtë* as *Le Dragon d'ivoire,* trans. Edmond Tupja (Paris: Rivages, 2000).

Königsdorf, Helga (b. 1938) German short-story writer, essayist, and novelist. A feminist writer much admired for her interweaving of science and fiction, Königsdorf was born in Gera. She studied mathematics and physics at the universities of Jena and Berlin and received her degree in 1961. She then joined the Institute for Higher Mathematics of the Academy of Sciences in East Berlin, where she received her doctorate in 1963. In 1974 she became a full professor. Although Königsdorf continued her scientific research and publication under the name Bunke until 1990, she began her career as a writer of fiction in the mid-1970s. She published her first volume of short stories in 1979 under the title *Meine ungehörigen Träume* (My Improper Tears). Decidedly feminist in character, and reflecting the academic milieu she knows so well, the stories collectively imply a protest against the social system of the German Democratic Republic, which is responsible, in Königsdorf's opinion, for the emotional alienation of women. In this work, as elsewhere in her fiction, she dramatizes the price women pay for independence. Königsdorf, however, is anything but a schematic writer, and the issues and characters as she draws them are hardly simple. In her subsequent works of fiction—*Die Lauf der Dinge* (The Progress of Life, 1982); *Respektloser Umgang* (Bad Company, 1986); *Lichtverhältnisse* (Light Conditions, 1988); *Die geschlossenen Türen am Abend* (The Closed Doors in the Evening, 1989), a collection of stories; *Ungelegener Befund: Erzählung* (Inconvenient Findings: A Story, 1990); and *Ein sehr exakter Schein: Satiren und Geschichten aus dem Gebiet der Wissenschaft* (A Very Exact Phenomenon: Satires and Tales from the Field of Science, 1990)—Königsdorf demonstrated a flair for the ironic and grotesque and the ability to put her training as a scientist to good use in her imaginative writing. In one of her best works, *Respektloser Umgang,* she introduced the figure of the real-life woman nuclear physicist Lise Meitner, who was forced to leave Germany in 1938 because she was a Jew, to address the question of scientific responsibility. Also interesting for its documentary basis is *Ungelegener Befund: Erzählung,* a novella in epistolary form that moves from 1987 back to the late 1930s and the war years and exposes the easy accommodation to totalitarianism of the scientific community.

From 1989 to 1991, Königsdorf was a member of the governing board of the East German branch of PEN. Although not a political activist as such, Königsdorf welcomed the upheaval of 1989, the tearing down of the Berlin Wall, and the collapse of the GDR. Several of her works from the late 1980s and early 1990s pivot on these events and their meaning, among them *1989, oder, Ein Moment Schönheit: Eine Collage aus Briefen, Gedichten, Texten* (1989, or, A Moment of Beauty: A Collage of Letters, Poems, and Texts, 1990); *Adieu DDR: Protokolle einer Abschieds* (Adieu to the GDR: Report of a Departure, 1990); *Aus dem Dilemma eine Chance machen: Reden und Aufsätze* (Making a Chance of the Dilemma: Speeches and Essays, 1991); *Gleich neben Afrika* (Right Next to Africa, 1992); and *Über die unverzügliche Rettung der Welt* (On the Immediate Salvation of the World, 1994), a collection of short essays from the late 1980s and early 1990s on science, the ability of people to shape their destiny for the better, and internal German issues. In *Unterwegs nach Deutschland: Über die Schwierigkeit, ein Volk zu sein: Protokolle eines Aubruchs* (Under Way for Germany. On the Difficulty of Being a Nation: Transcript of a Leavetaking), published in 1995, she addresses the problems of German reunification and resultant social and political issues. *Die Entsorgung der Grossmutter* (Disposing of Granny), her first novel, appeared in 1997. Königsdorf was the recipient of the Heinrich Heine Prize in 1985.

Translations: "Property Damage," trans. Jan van Heurck, in *The New Sufferings of Young W. and Other Stories from the German Democratic Republic*, ed. Therese Hörnigk and Alexander Stephan (New York: Continuum, 1997), 138–41; "The Surefire Tip," trans. Dorothy Rosenberg, in *Daughters of Eve: Women's Writing from the German Democratic Republic*, trans. and ed. Nancy Lukens and Dorothy Rosenberg (Lincoln: University of Nebraska Press, 1993), 141–50.

Konrád, György (b. 1933) Hungarian novelist and essayist. A native of Budapest, Konrád, of Jewish origin, barely missed being sent to Auschwitz, as he tells us in the "Self-Introduction" to *Ujjászületés melankóliája* (The Melancholy of Rebirth, 1991). Although he was expelled several times from Eötvös Lóránd University, he was permitted to graduate in 1956. He became a staff member of a new magazine, a voice of "critical thought" as he calls it, but the Hungarian uprising of 1956 broke out on the day the first issue was to have appeared, 23 October. After the uprising was suppressed by the Soviets, Konrád, by then a married man with a family, chose to remain in Hungary. He eventually found employment as a social worker, a position he held for seven years. In 1965 he was given the position of urban sociologist by an institute of town planning, but lost it in 1973 as a result of pressure from the secret police. He was subsequently banned from all employment for the next sixteen years, until 1989 and the collapse of communism in Hungary.

Konrád was thirty-six by the time his first novel, *A látogató* (The Case Worker, 1969), was published. The work drew heavily on Konrád's own experiences as a social worker and at once catapulted its author to literary fame. Although condemned in Hungary for its stark realism and its exposure of the seamier side of contemporary Hungarian society, the novel was widely translated and enjoyed critical acclaim. Konrád recalls in his introduction to *The Melancholy of Rebirth* that for the first time he received respectable royalties for *The Case Worker*, which came in handy after his subsequent arrest with Iván Szelényi, with whom he had written a study on socialism and the intelligentsia. However, before they could microfilm the manuscript, which analyzed the vicissitudes of power wielded by intellectuals as a class, the authorities ordered it destroyed. The authors managed to save two carbon copies, which made publication in the West possible. An English translation under the title *The Intellectuals on the Road to Class Power* (*Az értelmiség útja az osztályhatalomhoz*), appeared in 1979.

Konrád's next novel, *Városalapító* (*The City Builder*), was rejected by publishers in Hungary as too bleak. It, too, first appeared in the West. A censored version was eventually published in Hungary in 1977. That was the last book Konrád was able to publish in Hungary. Because of his continued defiance of the authorities' demands that he exercise self-censorship along the lines they indicated, he was placed under a total ban. For the next twelve years, he published only with the underground samizdat press. His next two novels, *Cinkos* (*The Loser*) and *Kerti mulatság* (*A Feast in the Garden*), first appeared in samizdat editions. He also published three collections of essays in samizdat editions. One of these, *Antipolitika* (*Antipolitics*), was a critique of the "Yalta system" and what Konrád perceived to be its disastrous consequences for Eastern Europe. Konrád concludes the introduction to *The Melancholy of Rebirth* by pointing out that when communism began to collapse in Hungary in 1989—and "before the bottom fell out of the publishing industry"—five of his books appeared in Budapest at the same time.

The Loser is a grim first-person narrative by a Hungarian Jewish intellectual who fought in World War II against the Russians and then joined them, threw his lot in with the communists in the new postwar regime, and lived through the 1956 Hungarian uprising. Profoundly disillusioned and cynical about the totalitarian system he had served as a party functionary and at whose hands he had himself suffered terribly, his life a shambles, he allows himself to be confined to an insane asylum at the age of fifty-five. But in an irony worthy of Kafka and the twentieth-century Polish avant-garde dramatist Stanisław Ignacy Witkiewicz ("Witkacy"), he is in a sense relieved to be behind the walls of the institution, believing that they protect him from the truly insane world on the outside: "A former communist, I became an antipolitician. I am no longer interested in power, nor in counterpower." In *A Feast in the Garden,* largely an experimental, nonlinear novel, Konrád traces the fortunes of his family, friends, and neighbors through the calamities of two world wars, the Holocaust, Hungary's harsh communist era, and, finally, exposure to American society. Although strongest in those parts of the work dealing with the Holocaust, the novel is weakened by Konrád's stepping in and out of the central character, an eleven-year-old boy clearly patterned on himself. Weakness and strength also coexist in Konrád's last published novel, *Kőóra* (*Stonedial,* 1995). In this work, a Hungarian Jewish exile (Dragoman), now a famous writer, returns to the city of his youth and looks up old friends and acquaintances. The visits are a collective springboard for revisiting the tragedy of the Jews of Hungary during World War II and the ill-fated Hungarian uprising of 1956 and Dragoman's accidental responsibility for the execution of six fellow protestors. The novel is full of strange accidents and deaths for which Dragoman seems to bear some responsibility and which suggest that past and present, like the tragic and comic in life, are intertwined. As is often the case in Konrád, the novel, for all its intellectual weight, is marred by long-windedness, sprawling narrative structure, and his tendency to use characters and incidents to deliver a wide assortment of political and philosophical judgments. That Konrád also wants his readers to understand that he himelf is the model for his character Dragoman is obvious from the name of the international business consortium, Darnok ("Konrád" spelled backward), that hires a detective to spy on Dragoman, and from the name of Dragoman's hometown, Kandor (an anagram of "Konrád").

Konrád followed his fictional writing on Jewish themes with a book of essays, *Láthatatlan hang: Zsidó tárgyú elmélkedések* (*The Invisible Voice: Meditations on Jewish Themes,* 1997). A prolific essayist, Konrád's other volumes of essays, articles, and related writings include *Európa köldökén: Esszék, 1979–1989* (In the Heart of Europe: Essays, 1979–1989, 1990); *Várakozás: esszék, cikkek, naplórészletek* (Expectation: Essays, Articles, Diary Fragments, 1995); *Átramló leltár: Elmélkedések* (Horsepower Inventory: Meditations, 1996); and *Útrakészen: Egy berlini műteremben: Esszék, cikkek, tanulmányok* (In a Berlin Studio: Essays, Articles, Studies, 1999).

Translations: *Antipolitics: An Essay,* trans. Richard E. Allen (San Diego: Harcourt Brace Jovanovich, 1984); *The Case Worker,* trans. Paul Aston (New York: Harcourt Brace Jovanovich, 1974); *The City Builder,* trans. Ivan Sanders (New York: Harcourt Brace Jovanovich, 1977); *A Feast in the Garden,* trans. Imre Goldstein (New York: Harcourt Brace Jovanovich, 1992); *The Intellectuals on the Road to Class Power,* trans. Andrew Arato and Richard E. Allen (New York: Harcourt Brace Jovanovich, 1979); *The Invisible Voice: Meditations on Jewish Themes,* trans. Peter Reich (San Diego: Harcourt, 2000); *The Loser,* trans. Ivan Sanders (San Diego: Harcourt Brace Jovanovich, 1982); *The Melancholy of Rebirth: Essays from Post-Communist Central Europe, 1989–1994,* trans. Michael Henry Heim (San Diego: Harcourt Brace Jovanovich, 1995); *Stonedial,* trans. Ivan Sanders (New York: Harcourt, 2000).

Konstantinović, Radomir (b. 1928) Serbian novelist, poet, playwright, and philosopher. An extraordinarily prolific and varied writer, much respected among Serbian liberals for his stand against nationalism, Konstantinović began his literary career in 1951 with the collection of poems *Kuća bez krova* (House Without a Roof, 1951). Four novels followed in the next several years: *Daj nam danas* (Give Us This Day, 1954); *Mišolovka* (Mousetrap, 1956); *Čisti i prljavi* (The Clean and the Dirty, 1958); and *Izlazak* (*Exitus,* 1960), yet another fictional treatment of the biblical Judas and the only work by Konstantinović available in English. The novels are noteworthy for their merging of Konstantinović's interests in both ethical problems and formal experimentation. Two subsequent prose works, *Ahasfer ili traktat o pivskoj flaši* (Ahasuerus or Treatise on a Battle of Beer, 1964) and *Pentagram: Beleške iz hotelske sobe* (Pentagram: Notes from a Hotel Room, 1966), follow essentially the same pattern of the philosophical and literary experimental. *Filosofija palanka* (Small-Town Philosophy), which appeared in 1969, deals specifically with Serbian culture, which Konstantinović explores in terms of the ideological consciousness of a small-town mentality.

Apart from his poems and novels, Konstantinović wrote plays, mostly dating from the late 1950s and 1960s. They include *Saobraćajna nesreća* (Traffic Accident, 1958); *Euridika* (Eurydice, 1959); *Veliki Emanuel* (Emmanuel the Great, 1961); *Ikarov let* (Flight of Icarus, 1963); *Liptonov čaj* (Lipton Tea, 1964); and *Obična, oh, kokoška* (Ordinary, ah, Chicken, 1966). Konstantinović's most recent work, *Dekartova smrt* (The Death of Descartes, 1996), is one of his most intellectually provocative. By means of a strained and complex father–son relationship, Konstantinović engages in a broad philosophical inquiry into the relative merits of Cartesian rationalism, represented by the authoritarian father figure, and Montaigne-like skepticism, represented by the rebellious son. Played out in a variety of locales, mostly along the Adriatic, and with a cast of characters running from Jesus Christ to Adolf Hitler, *Dekartova smrt* is an intriguing work that defies typological pigeonholing.

Konstantinović's twin passions of philosophy and literary creativity are nowhere so brilliantly on display as in his eight-volume *Biće i jezik u iskustvu pesnika srpske kulture 20. veka* (Being and Language in the Experience of a Poet of Twentieth-Century Serbian Culture, 1983), in a sense his crowning literary achievement. A political activist who foresaw the ethnic strife that exploded so horrifically into the Bosnian War, Konstantinović was the founder of the Belgrade Circle, an antiwar and antifascist association of Serbian intellectuals.

Translations: *Exitus: A Novel*, trans. E. D. Goy (London: Calder and Boyars, 1965).

Konwicki, Tadeusz (b. 1926) Polish novelist. One of the best-known Polish prose writers of the post–World War II period, Konwicki was born in a small town near Wilno. Like Czesław Miłosz, Konwicki had a deep attachment to the Lithuanian region of his origins and returned to it in several of his literary works. During World War II, Konwicki saw action against the Germans as a member of an Armia Krajowa (Home Army) unit and against the Soviets when in late 1944 and 1945 they set about liquidating Home Army units in Lithuania preparatory to their absorption of the area into the USSR. After the war, Konwicki studied Polish literature at the Jagiellonian University in Kraków and became affiliated with such cultural journals as *Odrodzenie* and *Nowa Kultura*. He also became involved in film as both a director and a scriptwriter. Konwicki's first novel, *Rojsty* (Marshes), was written as early as 1948, but because of its treatment of the partisan combat in Lithuania during the war was withheld from publication until 1956. After he joined the Communist Party in 1950, Konwicki turned out a few ideologically correct works such as *Przy budowie* (Alongside Construction, 1950) and *Władza* (Power, 1956). He soon abandoned socialist realism and Party-pleasing writing and turned in other directions. In 1966 he left the Party and in the 1970s threw his lot in with the new democratic opposition.

Beginning with his novel *Z oblężonego miasta* (From a Besieged City, 1956), Konwicki began exploring the complex interaction of wartime experiences and postwar realities. Past and present intertwine in a disturbing, almost unreal way, above all in the novel that established Konwicki's fame: the dense, symbolic *Sennik współczesny* (A Dreambook for Our Time, 1963). A former partisan fighter returns to a remote village where during the war he was ordered to execute an apparent traitor but did not do so, and where rumor has it the man is now living. Paweł, the narrator, seeks desperately to rid himself of the baggage of the past by returning to it as if in a dream and reconstructing those incidents that haunted him after the war. The strangeness of the novel is effected by a series of factors: the setting of the village in a valley soon to be flooded by water needed for a new electric plant, thereby lending urgency to Paweł's quest; the odd mixture of characters meant to represent a wide variety of Polish wartime and postwar experiences; the presence in the village of a curious religious sect; and the fragmentary way the past coheres to finally illuminate Paweł's spiritual crisis. In Konwicki's next novel, *Kompleks polski* (The Polish Complex)—written in 1976, and published first by an underground press in 1979 and then by an official press in 1989—he explored various facets of "the Polish complex" with respect to Polish–Russian relations in the past and present (Russian and then Soviet domination over a once more powerful and more Western-oriented Poland) and Western attitudes toward Poland. *The Polish Complex* was followed by the related novel *Mała apokalipsa* (A Minor Apocalypse, 1979), first published underground after Konwicki became involved with the democratic KOR (Committee for the Defense of Workers) organization. The novel paints a hyperbolized catastrophic picture of Soviet-dominated Poland at the end of the twentieth century as a country in which all values have been corrupted, the land has been ruined by environmental and ecological disasters, and people so broken spiritually and morally by years of abuse of power and corruption are incapable of bringing about any change.

As if seeking relief from the bleak, oppressive present of a Poland brought to ruin by communism, Konwicki revisited his happier Lithuanian past and youth in such works as *Dziura w niebie* (A Hole in the Heavens, 1959); *Zwierzoczłekoupiór* (1969; translated as *The Anthropos-Spectre-Beast*); *Kronika wypadków miłosnych* (A Chronicle of Love Affairs, 1974), which was made into a film by the famous Polish director Andrzej Wajda; and the lyrical and nostalgic *Bohin* (1987; translated as *Bohin Manor*), a recollection of his grandmother set on a gentry estate in Lithuania at the end of the nineteenth century and in some ways reminiscent of Czesław Miłosz's *Dolina Issy* (*The Issa Valley*). These works were followed by the novelistic *Kalendarz i klepsydra* (Calendar and Hourglass, 1976); *Nowy Świat i okolice* (*New World Avenue and Vicinity*, 1990), a book of reminiscences and reflections named for a main Warsaw thoroughfare; *Wschody i zachody słońca* (*Moonrise, Moonset*, 1982), first published by an underground press—a highly personal book of recollections of his relations with other writers and artists; ruminations on the Polish national character, Polish–Russian relations, and World War II and its immediate aftermath in Poland; and pervaded with Konwicki's profound loathing for the communist system—*Wniebowstąpienie* (The Assumption into Heaven, 1967); and *Nic albo nic* (Nothing or Nothing, 1971).

Translations: *The Anthropos-Spectre-Beast*, trans. George Korwin-Rodziszewski and Audry Korwin-Rodziszewski (New York: Oxford University Press, 1977); *Bohin Manor*, trans. Richard Lourie (New York: Farrar, Straus and Giroux, 1990); *A Dreambook for Our Time*, trans. David Welsh (Cambridge, Mass.: MIT Press, 1969); *A Minor Apocalypse*, trans. Richard Lourie (New York: Farrar, Straus and Giroux, 1983); *Moonrise, Moonset*, trans. Richard Lourie (New York: Farrar, Straus and Giroux, 1987); *New World Avenue and Vicinity*, trans. Walter Arndt (New York: Farrar, Straus and Giroux, 1991); *The Polish Complex*, trans. Richard Lourie (New York: Farrar, Straus and Giroux, 1982).

Koreshi, Vath (b. 1936) Albanian novelist, short-story writer, journalist, and screenwriter. A native of Lushnjë, Koreshi is widely respected for the honesty and sincerity of his writing and his ability to maintain his artistic integrity within the limits previously imposed by the communist regime. After graduating from the Polytechnic in Tirana, he held a variety of jobs before earning his university degree in the Faculty of History and Philology at Tirana University. Apart from his creative writing, he has been a journalist for *Zëri i Rinisë* and a screenwriter for Albanian Film Studios. After the fall of communism in Albania, he was invited to become director of the "Art Magazine" of the Ministry of Culture. As a novelist, Koreshi has published *Dy të shtunat e Suzanës* (Suzanna's Two Saturdays, 1971), recounting the wedding of a young couple; *Mars* (March, 1975), an industrial novel; *Mali mbi kënetë* (The Mountain Above the Marsh, 1977), set in the 1930s and depicting the birth of a peasant uprising against the "sellout" of Albania to Italy by King Zog; and *Rrugë per larg* (Distant Road, 1985). His major volumes of stories include *Kur zunë shirat e vjeshtës* (As the Autumn Rains Began, 1964); *Toka nën hijen e shtëpive* (The Land in the Shadow of Houses, 1968);

Ndërrimi i qiejve (Change of Heavens, 1972); *Dasma e Sakos* (Sako's Wedding, 1980), the title story of which was made into a film; *Balada e Kurbinit* (The Ballad of Kurbini, 1987); *Haxhiu i Frakullës, Dasma e Sakos* (Pilgrim from Frakula and Sako's Wedding, 1989), a collection of new and older stories; and *Konomea* (1999), a collection of three longer stories from 1996: "Konomea," a historical tale in which a young girl recalls the circumstances of her murder by drowning; "Kajamak," a piece about filmmaking in the form of a series of conversations with the film director "F. F."; and "Shtëpia Bethoven" ("The House of Beethoven"), the shortest of the stories. In 1997 Koreshi won the Velija Cultural Foundation Prize for his novel *Ulku dhe Uilli* (Wolf and Willy, 1996).

Translations: *Mali mbi kënetë* is available in French as *Le Mont sur le marais,* trans. Vedat Kokona, with a short foreword by Ismail Kadare (Paris: Écriture, 1998).

Kornis, Mihály (b. 1949) Hungarian playwright and short-story writer. A native of Budapest, Kornis is one of post–World War II Hungary's most prominent men of the theater. He was trained as a stage director and was affiliated with some of Budapest's best-known stages both as a director and as a dramatist. He has also taught playwriting at the Academy of Theater and Cinematography, from which he graduated. Kornis's solid literary reputation was established in the early 1980s when his first volume of short stories, *Végre élsz* (You're Alive at Last, 1980), appeared and when his acclaimed and controversial play *Halleluja* (1979), a black comedy ironically subtitled "a play about love," was first staged in 1981. Kornis's stock-in-trade is a grotesque nonrepresentational style, in which the dead and the living often intermingle, used effectively in social satire aimed principally at the emptiness and inequities of Hungarian life under communism. His treatment of the bureau-

cracy in his plays and stories is merciless. In one of his stories, "fastidious apparatchiks" use their tongues or small tweezers to gather up dust and dirt from the floors of their office building "between eight in the morning and four-thirty in the afternoon" so that later they can gulp them down at their convenience. In *Kozma* (1986), one of Kornis's best and boldest plays, an enigmatic stranger (Kozma), a kind of avenging angel, confronts three callous women who are sunbathing and drinking in a resort on Lake Balaton reserved for the well-connected. Set in Hungary in 1980, the play is an unsparing satire on the privileges of the profoundly corrupt bureaucracy and their indifference to the rest of society, here represented by a bus full of corpses from all walks of life who haunt the play from begining to end. The best edition of Kornis's plays is *Drámák* (1999). It includes, in addition to *Halleluja* and *Kozma, Körmagyar* (named after an old Hungarian ballroom dance); *Bűntetések* (Punishments), a hallucinatory Kafkesque play; and *A Kádár-Beszéd* (Kádár Talking) and *Kádárné Balladája* (Mr. Kádár's Ballad), both dealing with the post-1956 regime of János Kádár. In 1989, Kornis published a book of prose, essays, and criticism under the title *A félelem dicsérete* (In Praise of Fear). His second book of short stories, *Napkönyv: Történetünk hőse* (Daybook: Stories of Our Heroes), came out in 1994.

Translations: *Kozma,* trans. Eugene Brogyányi, in *Drama Contemporary: Hungary,* ed. Eugene Brogyányi (New York: PAJ Publications, 1991), 201–47; *Kozma,* in *A Mirror to the Cage: Three Contemporary Hungarian Plays,* ed. and trans. Clara Györgyey (Fayetteville: University of Arkansas Press, 1983), 187–245; "Father Wins," trans. Thomas J. Dekornfeld, in *The Kiss: Twentieth Century Hungarian Short Sories,* selected by István Bart (Budapest: Corvina, 1998), 397–408; "Morning," trans. Judith Sollosy, in *Give or Take a Day: Contemporary Hungar-*

ian Short Stories, ed. Lajos Szakolczay (Budapest: Corvina, 1997), 105–10.

Korudzhiev, Dimitur (b. 1941) Bulgarian novelist, playwright, and essayist. Korudzhiev, a popular writer, was born and educated in Sofia. He graduated from Sofia University in 1966 with a degree in Bulgarian language and literature. From 1966 to 1989 he held editorships at such journals as *Trud* (1966–1972), *Narodna kultura* (1972–1974), *Plamuk* (1974–1976), and *Bulgarski pisatel* (1976–1989). Since 1989 he has been affiliated with *Suvremennik.* His first published book was the collection of stories *Shte mine vreme* (Time Will Pass, 1972), which set the pattern for his writing down to the late 1970s of fairly plotless, psychologically oriented stories about ordinary people in everyday situations. *Shte mine vreme* was followed by the novel *Koridori v duzhda* (Passageways in the Rain, 1974); *Tozi chudesen ritm* (This Splendid Rhythm, 1974), a book of sketches; *Noshtnata ulitsa* (The Night Street, 1975), a collection of stories; and *Ostrov ot tishina* (Island of Silence, 1976), a book of stories and novellas. Beginning with his novel *Podozrenieto* (Suspect, 1978), Korudzhiev became more introspective, "mystical," and philosophical. This trend continued through such subsequent works as *Nevidimiiat svat* (The Invisible World, 1978), an impressive collection of stories about dreams and the subconscious; *Migut predi zdrachavane* (The Moment Before Dusk, 1981), a collection of stories and novellas; his best-selling novel, *Gradinata s kosovete: Iz spomenite na vechniia rednik* (The Garden of Blackbirds: From the Memoirs of an Eternal Private, 1984), which deals with the effects of physical sickness on personal psychology and morality; *Domut na Alma: Shvedskie zapiski* (The Home on Alma: Notes from Sweden, 1986); *Kushta pod naem* (House for Rent, 1988), a novel; and *Deset godini po-kusno* (Ten Years Later, 1992). Korudzhiev used these fictional texts to advance his ideas on such issues as the need for people to live in harmony with themselves and the world, without which all the advances in technology and material well-being would ultimately lose meaning. He believed that a spiritually shaped system of values combining morality and humility was the main requisite for achieving inner and universal harmony as well as true freedom. These and related ideas cohere with particular vigor in the 103-page *Deset godini po-kusno*, a sequel to *Gradinata s kosovete: Iz spomenite na vechniia rednik* motivated by personal loss (the deaths of his and his wife's parents) and his own experience with major surgery, all in a relatively short period of time. Drawing on ancient philosophers and modern thinkers and writers, and with wide-ranging, freewheeling commentary on everything from Michael Jackson to Swiss banks, Korudzhiev decries materialism and a way of life that threatens even the survival of the planet. His essayistic writings dealing with these and related issues as well as with postcommunist Bulgarian democracy are contained in the volumes *Bolkata, kogato e prekrasna: Estetichni fragmenti* (The Pleasant Pain: Aesthetic Fragments, 1989) and *Pusnete slunchevata svetlina: 77 eseta ot v. "Demokratsiia"* (Let the Sunlight Shine: 77 Essays from "Democracy," 1991). Korudzhiev has also written several books for children and two plays, *Omag'osaniiat krug* (The Enchanted Circle) and *Staiata* (The Room), both produced in Sofia between 1979 and 1981.

Koš, Erih (b. 1913) Bosnian Serb novelist and short-story writer. A native of Sarajevo, Koš graduated from the Law Faculty of Belgrade University in 1935, saw service with the partisans during World War II, and spent some time in England immediately afterward as a diplomat. His stories, most of which are concerned with his early Bosnian background, appear in the collections *U vatri* (In the Flame, 1947); *Tri hronike* (Three Chronicles, 1949); *Zapisi o mladim ljudima* (Notes on Young People, 1950); *Vreme, ratno* (Wartime, 1952); *Najlepše godine* (The Best Years, 1955); *Kao vuci* (Like Wolves, 1958); *Prvo lice jednine* (First-Person Singular, 1963); *Na autobuskoj stanici* (At the Bust Stop, 1974); *Izlet u Paragvaj* (A Trip to Paraguay, 1983); *Bosanske priče* (Bosnian Tales, 1984); and *Nove i stare bosanske priče* (New and Old Bosnian Tales, 1996). Most of the stories in *Bosanske priče* and *Nove i stare bosanske priče* are set in the period of Turkish rule over Bosnia. Koš has also published nine novels, including *Čudnovata povest o kitu velikom, takodje zvanom Veliki Mak* (The Marvelous Tale of the Great Whale, Also Known as Big Mac, 1956); *Il tifo* (Typhoid, 1958); *Novosadski pokol* (The Butcher of Novi Sad, 1961); *Sneg i led* (Snow and Ice, 1961); *Imena* (*Names,* 1964); *Mreže* (Nets, 1967); *Dosije Hrabak* (1971); and *U potrazi za Mesijom* (On the Trail of the Messiah, 1978). Koš has also published some four volumes of essays: *Taj prokleti zanat spisateljski* (This Damned Writer's Craft, 1965); *Zašto da ne* (Why Not, 1971); *Pripovetka i pripovedanje* (Narrative and Narration, 1980); and *Satira i satiričari* (Satire and Satirists, 1985). His most recent novel, *Pisac govora* (The Speechwriter, 1989), is a rather entertaining, ironic novel about the trials and tribulations of a man whom World War II propels into the career of a professional speechwriter. It reflects the strong interest in language manifest elsewhere in Koš's writing—for example, *Names.* Koš won the Yugoslav Writers Union Prize for his novel *Čudnovata povest o kitu velikom, takodje zvanom Veliki Mak*; the October Prize of the City of Belgrade for *Prvo lice jednine*; and the NIN Prize for his novel *Mreže.*

Translations: *Names,* trans. Lovett F. Edwards (New York: Harcourt, Brace & World, 1966); "The Man Who Knew Where the North Was and Where the South," trans. Mary Stanfield-Popović, in *New Writing in Yugoslavia,* ed. Bernard Johnson (Harmondsworth: Penguin, 1970), 15–48.

Kosmač, Ciril (1910–1980) Slovenian novelist and short-story writer. Kosmač was born on Slovenian ethnic lands controlled by Italy between the two world wars. In 1929, while still in high school, he was arrested by the Italian authorities because of his membership in a Slovene nationalist organization. He spent several months in prisons in Goriza, Rome, and Trieste. Shortly after his release, he escaped to Yugoslavia, where he lived for several years in Ljubljana as a freelance writer before going to Paris in 1938 on a French scholarship. When the Germans occupied Paris in 1940, he left for Marseille and eventually arrived in London by way of Spain and Portugal. In 1944, via Bari, he was able to join Tito's partisans, in whose ranks he became editor of a Slovenian newspaper. His literary reputation was established by his short-story collection *Sreća in kruh* (Happiness and Bread), which appeared in 1946 and included works written before World War II. His greatest success in the novel came with *Pomladni dan* (*A Day in Spring,* 1953), which was published in England in 1959 and deals with a writer's return home after fifteen years in exile. Stylistically, the novel marks a departure from Kosmač's previous preference for social realism. Kosmač's other prose works include three collections of short stories, *Iz moje doline* (From My Valley, 1958); *V gaju življenja* (In the Grove of Life, 1972); and *Sreča in lepota* (Happiness and Beauty, 1973), and the novellas *Balada o trobenti in oblaku* (The Ballad of a Trumpet and a Cloud, 1968) and *Tantadruj* (1980). A four-volume edition of Kosmač's selected works (*Izbrano delo*) was published in 1964, and a three-volume edition in 1970.

Translations: *A Day in Spring,* trans. Fanny S. Copeland (London: Lincolns-Prager, 1959); "Luck" and "Death of a Simple

Giant," trans. Cordia Kveder, in *Death of a Simple Giant and Other Modern Yugoslav Stories,* ed. Branko Lenski (New York: Vanguard, 1965), 118–35, 137–88.

Kosta, Koça (b. 1940) Albanian novelist and short-story writer. Born in Gjirokastër, Kosta graduated from Tirana University and subsequently became a schoolteacher. Although he has published two novels, *Buka e një stine me borë* (The Bread of a Snowy Season, 1979) and *Ata të dy e të tjerë: Novelë—e thyer* (The Two of Them and Others: A Novella in Pieces, 1994), the latter issued in part in 1986 but then banned for alleged gay content, Kosta is known mostly as a writer of short stories and sketches. They include the collections *Shënime përmes shiut* (Notes in the Rain, 1968); *Unë dhe komiti* (The Outlaw and I, 1969); *Krismë midis gurgullimash* (Crash amid the Gurglings, 1969); *Bisedë në mesnatë* (Discussion at Midnight, 1971); *Dademadhja* (The Grandmother, 1976); *Era e udhëve* (The Road Wind, 1982); and *Tregime të zgjedhura* (Selected Stories, 1985).

Kostov, Vladimir (b. 1932) Macedonian novelist, short-story writer, essayist, and political commentator. A native of Bitola, which was captured by Bulgaria in World War II, Kostov completed his schooling in his native town and later received his degree in Yugoslav literature in Skopje. He then returned to Bitola to join the faculty of the Teacher Training College there. As his literary career began to develop in the 1960s, Kostov demonstrated an interest in political writing that he continued to cultivate even while turning increasingly to fiction. One of his first printed works was an anti-NATO diatribe published by the Bulgarian Communist Party under the title *Chetirite cherni mesetsa na NATO* (Four Black Months of NATO, 1966). This was followed in 1968 by *Evropeiskite sotsialisticheski strani: Faktor na mira i sigurnostta na kontinenta* (The Euro-

pean Socialist Countries: A Factor for Peace and Security on the Continent). Despite its support for Kostov as an apparently trustworthy communist writer throughout the 1960s and 1970s, Bulgaria would eventually become the principal target of Kostov's political writing. Notwithstanding his publications in support of the official ideology, Kostov proved with his first two novels, *Lica so maski* (Faces with Masks, 1967) and *Svadbata na Mara* (Mara's Wedding, 1968), that he cared little for realism and inclined toward the experimental. This remained true for the most part of such subsequent fictional texts as his first collection of short stories, *Igra* (The Game, 1969); his third novel, *Nov um* (A New Mind, 1970); another book of stories, *Ah, bre!* (Well Now!, 1970); the novel *Učitelot* (The Teacher, 1976); and *Grešniot Zaharija* (Zaharia's Sin, 1986), a collection of four novellas. In 1983, with his wife, Nataliia, Kostov published (in Paris, with an émigré Bulgarian publisher) a book about the situation in Bulgaria—which had by now become the focus of most of his political interest—under the title *Tsotsializmut v Bulgariia opit za ravnosmetka: Repliki i belezhki po aktualni vuprosi* (Socialism in Bulgaria: An Attempt at a Balance Sheet: Retorts and Notes on Current Issues). Because of the book's provocative nature, Kostov also chose to publish in Paris, and in French, *Le Parapluie bulgare* (The Bulgarian Umbrella, 1986), his account of the assassination of the Bulgarian dissident writer Georgi Markov. In the aftermath of the downfall of communism in Bulgaria and Eastern Europe in general, Kostov delivered his own prognoses for the future of the region in the form of his book *Nakude vurvim: Shte nadigraem li zliia zhrebli?* (Where Are We Headed? Will We Overplay a Bad Hand?, 1994). Kostov's interest in literary criticism had already manifested itself in 1983 in his collection of essays *Maski* (Masks). In 1994, the same year in which *Nakude vurvim: Shte nadigraem li zliia zhrebli?* appeared, he came out with the more personal and revealing *Lichno mnenie: Niakoi statii, komentari i interviuta mezhdu liatoto na 1991 i zimata na 1994* (Personal Opinion: Some Articles, Commentaries, and Interviews from Summer 1991 to Winter 1994).

Translations: *The Bulgarian Umbrella: The Soviet Direction and Operations of the Bulgarian Secret Service in Europe*, trans. Ben Reynolds (New York: St. Martin's Press, 1988); "The Game," in *The Big Horse and Other Stories of Modern Macedonia*, ed. Milne Holton (Columbia: University of Missouri Press, 1974), 198–232.

Kovač, Mirko (b. 1938) Serbian novelist, short-story writer, and essayist. Well known for his outspoken criticism of the Serbian government during the Yugoslav wars of the 1990s, Kovač was born in Petrovići, near Bileća, Montenegro. His first major work, *Gubilište* (The Scaffold, 1962), was followed by *Moja sestra Elida* (My Sister Elida, 1965); *Rane Luke Meštrevića ili povest rasula* (The Wounds of Luka Meštrević or a Tale of Decadence, 1971; enl. ed., 1980); and one of his most popular works, *Životopis Malvine Trifković* (The Story of Malvina Trifković, 1976). *Vrata od utrobe* (The Door to the Womb), a novel Kovač published in 1978, won the annual award of the National Library of Serbia in 1979 as the book read by the greatest number of people in the previous year. Kovač subsequently published *Uvod u drugi život* (Introduction to the Next World, 1983); *Nebesne zaručnici* (Heavenly Betrothal, 1987); and the novel *Krystalne rešetke* (Crystal Bars, 1995), which he began writing in 1987. His most recent work of fiction is *Rastrešan život: Novi roman* (A Shattered Life: A New Novel, 1996).

Possibly his best-known work of fiction, *Životopis Malvine Trifković* reflects Kovač's anxieties over Serb–Croat relations. Cast in the form of a series of short manuscripts by various players in the drama of Malvina Trifković, and set in the early twentieth century, the novel recounts Malvina's enrollment in a Serbian religious school by her pious Orthodox parents and her subsequent fall from grace. Malvina's apparent lesbian tendencies lead to a too close relationship with another girl, the girl's suicide, and Malvina's flight. She runs off with a Croatian Catholic, whom she eventually weds but later divorces in part because of her extremely close relationship with her husband's sister, the only member of the family who shows her any kindness. When the sister dies in childbirth after a relationship with a man she never identifies, Malvina rears the child, a girl, as her own and in the Serbian Orthodox faith, as her sister-in-law had wished. The daughter, also named Malvina, later meets and marries a young man, and they live happily together. Later, their slain, badly mutilated bodies are discovered in their house in Trebinje, which once belonged to Malvina Trifković's sister-in-law. A cross cut in the belly of the young Malvina, and the mutilation of the couple's sexual organs, suggest a religious motive behind the killings. The novel ends with the mystery unsolved.

Persona non grata at home because of his denunciation of the politics of Slobodan Milošević, Kovač in 1992 went into voluntary exile on the island of Rovinj, in Istria on the western coast of Croatia. Further alienating himself from his fellow Serbs, he also became a Croatian citizen. In 1993 he was awarded the Kurt Tucholsky Memorial Award for exiled authors. A frequent writer of articles on Yugoslav, Serbian, and Croatian politics, Kovač is also the author of a book of essays on contemporary European issues, *Evropske truleži drugi eseji* (European Corruption and Other Essays, 1986, 1994, 1997), and a critical look at mass ideology and nationalist sentimentality titled *Cvjetanje mase* (The Blossoming of the Mass, 1997).

Literature: For insights into Kovač and his world, a good source is the correspondence between him and his fellow Serbian writer Filip David: *Filip David, Mirko Kovač, Knjiga pisama, 1992–1995* (Split: Feral Tribune, 1998).

Translations: "Farewell to Mother" (from *Krystalne rešetke*), trans. Christina Pribićević-Zorić, in *Storm Out of Yugoslavia*, ed. Joanna Labon (London: Carcanet, 1994), 152–76; "The Other Side of Our Eyes," trans. Alice Copple-Tošić, in *The Prince of Fire: An Anthology of Contemporary Serbian Short Stories*, ed. Radmila J. Gorup and Nadežda Obradović (Pittsburgh: University of Pittsburgh Press, 1998), 144–49; "Uncle Donato's Death," trans. Michael Scammell, in *New Writing in Yugoslavia*, ed. Bernard Johnson (Harmondsworth: Penguin, 1970), 215–30. Kovač is better represented in German and French: *Moja sestra Elida* is available in German as *Meine Schwester Elida*, trans. Peter Urban (Frankfurt am Main: Suhrkamp, 1967), and *Životopis Malvine Trifković* in French as *La Vie de Malvina Trifković*, trans. Pascale Delpech (Paris: Payot & Rivages, 1994).

Kovič, Kajetan (b. 1931) Slovenian novelist and poet. A native of Maribor, Kovič graduated from Ljubljana University with a degree in comparative literature. His first published poems appeared in 1953 in the volume *Pesmi štirih* (Poems of Four) together with texts by Ciril Zlobec (b. 1925), Tone Pavček (b. 1928), and Janez Menart (b. 1929). Kovič's subsequent books of poetry include *Przgodnji dan* (Too Early Day, 1956); *Korenine vetra* (Roots of the Wind, 1961); *Improvizacije* (Improvisations, 1963); *Ogenjvoda* (Fire-Water, 1965); *Mala čitanka* (A Little Reader, 1973), a collection of prose poems; *Labrador* (1976); *Dežele* (Lands, 1988), a selection of previously published and new poems; *Poletje* (Summer, 1990); and *Sibirski ciklus in druge pesmi raznih let*

(The Siberian Cycle and Other Poems from Different Years, 1992). Kovič is also the author of three novels, *Ne bog ne žival* (Neither God nor Animal, 1965); *Tekma ali kako je arhitekt Nikolaj preživel konec tedna* (The Match, or How the Architect Nikolai Survived the Weekend, 1970); and *Pot v Trento* (The Road to Trento, 1994), as well as a volume of stories, *Iskanje Katarine* (Looking for Catherine, 1978). Kovič's fiction for young readers and poetry for children is widely read, and he enjoys an admirable reputation as a translator of such poets as Paul Eluard, Boris Pasternak, Georg Trakl, and Rainer Maria Rilke, and of the German works of the classical Slovenian poet France Prešeren (1800–1849) into Slovenian. As a poet, Kovič displays an exquisite sense of nature tinged with melancholy and oscillates between a sense of existential dread and a vitalistic embrace of the world. Although he shuns overt political concerns, some of his poems clearly allude to the oppression of the individual in a totalitarian society. In 1978 Kovič was awarded the Prešeren Prize for lifetime achievement.

Translations: Eleven poems, trans. Tom Ložar, in *The Imagination of Terra Incognita: Slovenian Writing, 1945–1995*, ed. Aleš Debeljak (Fredonia, N.Y.: White Pine, 1997), 212–19; four poems, trans. Veno Taufer and Michael Scammell, in *New Writing in Yugoslavia*, ed. Bernard Johnson (Harmondsworth: Penguin, 1970), 231–35.

Kozak, Primož (1929–1981) Slovenian playwright and essayist. The son of the writer Ferdo Kozak (1894–1957), Kozak was born in Ljubljana where, after finishing the classical high school, he studied philosophy at Ljubljana University, from which he received his degree in 1955. The following year, he earned a degree in dramaturgy from Ljubljana's Academy of Performing Arts. He held the position of dramatic adviser at Triglav Film from 1956 to 1959 and then worked as an assistant at the Literary Institute of the Slovenian Academy of Arts and Sciences from 1965 to 1972. In 1972 he began teaching dramatic writing at the Academy for Stage, Radio, Film, and TV in Ljubljana, and in 1977 received his doctorate in dramatrurgy. Although he wrote the scripts for several films and contributed to such important periodicals of the time as *Beseda, Revija 57,* and *Perspektive,* Kozak was first and foremost a dramatist. He made his debut as a playwright with the World War II political drama *Afera* (*An Affair*), which with the plays *Dialogi* (Dialogues) and *Kongres* (Congress) was published as a trilogy in 1969. Kozak was not a hugely prolific dramatist and operated within a fairly narrow thematic range. His specialty was the political play set either among the Yugoslav partisans during World War II or in some other revolutionary setting. What interested Kozak, above all, was the dialectic between romantic, idealistic revolutionaries who are well intentioned but impractical, and hardheaded, seemingly emotionless planners and organizers capable of formulating plans and seeing them through to a successful conclusion. Perhaps his best-known revolutionary play is *Legenda o sv. Che* (The Legend of Saint Che, 1969), based on the life of the famous South American revolutionary Che Guevara. Kozak was especially good at crisp realistic dialogue, and his plays have been likened by some Slovenian critics to those of the French existentialist philosopher Jean-Paul Sartre. *Dialogi,* which has an unspecified Eastern European setting, dramatizes his conviction—already conveyed in *Afera*—that intellectuals are ill-equipped to effectively wield political power. After *Legenda o sv. Che,* Kozak wrote two more plays: *Direktor* (The Director, 1975) and *Ptički brez gnezda* (Birds Outside the Nest, 1977), actually a dramatization of a novel by Fran Milčinski (1867–1932). Kozak's major work as an essay-

ist was his collection *Peter Klepec v Ameriki* (Peter Klepec in America, 1971), a harsh commentary on contemporary civilization as viewed by a Slovenian. Kozak may have been inspired to write the book by his stay in the United States as a guest of the International Writing Program at the University of Iowa.

Translations: *An Affair,* trans. Elliott Anderson and Tomaž Salamun, in *Five Modern Yugoslav Plays,* ed. Branko Mikasinovich (New York: Cyrco, 1977), 87–145.

Kozioł, Urszula (b. 1935) Polish poet, novelist, and essayist. A talented and respected poet and prose writer, Kozioł was born in the village of Rakówka, near Biłgoraj. She has long been identified with the city of Wrocław, where she studied Polish literature at the university and long served as editor of the poetry section of the Wrocław literary monthly *Odra.* She also taught for a number of years in local schools. Kozioł's first poems appeared in the periodical press in 1954; her first published volume of poetry, *Gumowe klocki* (Rubber Toy Blocks), came out in 1957. It was followed by *W rytmie korzeni* (In the Rhythm of the Source, 1962) and *Smuga promień* (Trail of Beams, 1965). In 1965 Kozioł was awarded the Literary Prize of the City of Wrocław and the Broniewski Prize for Poetry. The next year, *Smuga promień* won the Piętak Prize. Her subsequent books of poetry include *Lista obecności* (Attendance Record, 1967); *Poezje wybrane* (Selected Poems, 1969), selected and introduced by Koziol herself; *W rytmie słońca* (In the Rhythm of the Sun, 1974); *Wybór wierszy* (Selected Poems, 1976); *Wielka pauza* (The Big Pause, 1995); *W płynnym stanie* (In a State of Flux, 1998); and *Stany nieoczywistości* (States of Unclarity, 1999).

A poet of sincerity and accessibility, Kozioł writes, among other things, of the loneliness of the poetic imperative, of the impossibility of suppressing truth, and of the need for circumspection in communist society. She generally shuns overt political topics, preferring to deal with them by indirection and inference. Of Kozioł's major novels, *Postoje pamięci* (Stations of Memory, 1965); *Noli me tangere* (1984); and *Postoje słowa* (Stations of the Word, 1994), *Postoje pamięci* is the most successful. Undoubtedly autobiographical in essence, the novel views life in a Polish village before, during, and after World War II through the eyes of the central character, the very young daughter of a local schoolteacher. Although Kozioł is a fine portraitist of Polish village life, the most memorable parts of *Postoje pamięci* are those dealing with life under the German occupation, the fate of the local Jews, and her heroine's love for a schoolmate who is of German descent. The novel closes in the immediate postwar period when Mirka, the main figure, is a high-school student in a provincial town. Kozioł is also the author of a collections of feuilletons under the title *Z poczekalni: Wybór felietonów oraz Osobnego sny i przypowieści* (From the Waiting Room: Selected Feuilletons Together with Dreams and Stories of a Private Person, 1978).

Literature: Jacek Łukasiewicz, *Kozioł* (Warsaw: Agence des Auteurs et Czytelnik, 1981), a very short biography translated into French from the Polish original.

Translations: *Poems,* trans. Regina Grol-Propczyk (New York: Host, 1989), a Polish–English edition; three poems in *Polish Poetry of the Last Two Decades of Communist Rule: Spoiling Cannibals' Fun,* ed. and trans. Stanisław Barańczak and Clare Cavanagh (Evanston, Ill.: Northwestern University Press, 1991), 128–29; five poems, trans. Celina Wieniewska, in *Polish Writing Today,* ed. Celina Wieniewska (Harmondsworth: Penguin, 1967), 61–62.

Krall, Hanna (b. 1937) Polish journalist and fiction writer. A Warsaw native, Krall lost her entire family in the Majdanek concentration camp during World War II. She survived thanks to the efforts at hiding her on the part of a large number of Poles. After the war, Krall studied journalism at Warsaw University and from 1955 to 1966 worked for the popular Warsaw daily *Życie Warszawy.* She then moved to the influential weekly *Polityka.* She was the paper's Moscow correspondent from 1966 to 1969—a period she described in her book *Na wschód od Arbatu* (East of Arbat, 1972). She later served on the editorial staff of *Polityka* from 1970 to the imposition of martial law in 1981. Krall made her literary reputation primarily with her books of reportage. The best known of them, and widely translated, is *Zdążyć przed Panem Bogiem* (1977; translated as *Shielding the Flame: An Intimate Conversation with Dr. Marek Edelman, the Last Surviving Leader of the Warsaw Ghetto Uprising* and as *To Outwit God*). The book, which in its original form was a long article published in a literary journal, won high praise and has appeared in over two dozen editions. It also did much to catapult Edelman into national and international prominence. *Shielding the Flame* is not a series of interviews, but a compilation of recollections by Edelman from his years in the Warsaw Ghetto and the subsequent uprising in 1943 interwoven with fragments from his postwar career as a medical doctor and reminiscences of him by patients and colleagues. Other volumes of reportage by Krall include *Trudności ze wstawaniem* (Trouble Getting Up, 1990) and *Dowody na istnienie* (Proof of Existence, 1995).

As a writer of fiction, Krall is widely known for her patently autobiographical short novel *Sublokatorka* (*The Subtenant*), which was first published in Paris mainly because of its glimpses of the Soviet and Polish communist campaign against the Polish nationalist Home Army during World War II, the Warsaw Uprising of 1944, the suppression of dissent in Poland, the malevolent role of the Soviet Union in Polish political life, the anti-Semitic campaign of 1968, the birth of Solidarity, and the declaration of martial law in December 1981. The work is narrated in the first person by the author, who speculates on the whereabouts of her father, an army officer, who was missing after World War II. Krall's other novels include the very short *Okna* (Windows, 1987); *Hipnoza* (Hypnosis, 1989), which won the German Critics' Prize; *Taniec na cudzym weselu* (Dancing at Someone Else's Wedding, 1993); *Co się stało z naszą bajką* (What Happened to Our Fairy Tale, 1994); and *Tam nie ma już żadnej rzeki* (There Is No River There Anymore, 1998), for which she was awarded the Jan Karski-Pola Nireńska Prize in 2000.

Translations: *Shielding the Flame: An Intimate Conversation with Dr. Marek Edelman, the Last Surviving Leader of the Warsaw Ghetto Uprising*, trans. Joanna Stasinska and Lawrence Wechsler (New York: Holt, 1986); *The Subtenant*, trans. Jarosław Anders [and] *To Outwit God*, trans. Joanna Stasinska Wechsler and Lawrence Weschler (Evanston, Ill.: Northwestern University Press, 1992); "The One from Hamburg," trans. Wiesiek Powaga, *Chicago Review* 46, nos. 3–4 (2000): 131–38; "A Tale for Hollywood," trans. Basia Plebanek, in *The Eagle and the Crow: Modern Polish Short Stories*, ed. Teresa Halikowska and George Hyde (London: Serpent's Tail, 1996), 149–82. *Hipnoza* is available in German as *Hypnoze*, trans. Roswitha Matwin-Buschmann (Frankfurt am Main: Neue Kritik, 1997).

Krasznahorkai, László (b. 1954) Hungarian novelist and short-story writer. A relatively younger writer who has already attracted much attention, in and out of Hungary, Krasznahorkai was born in Gyula. He worked for a number of years as an editor until 1984, when he became a freelance writer. Given to flamboyant dress and with a penchant for reclusiveness, especially in re-

cent years, Krasznahorkai has published four novels, a book of short stories, and an account of a solitary trip to China, via Siberia, in the 1980s. A ponderous, convoluted, bizarre, yet sometimes spellbinding postmodern writer who commands an impressive knowledge of science and technology, Krasznahorkai is fond of painting dreamlike and surreal pictures of small-town Hungarian life as mired in drabness, stagnation, and decay. This pattern was established with his first novel, *Sátántangó* (Satan Tango, 1986), which was made into a successful seven-hour film, and extended impressively to his subsequent collection of stories under the title *Kegyelmi viszonyok: Halálnovellák* (Relations of Grace: Tales of Death, 1986) and his next novel, *Az ellenállás melankóliája* (*The Melancholy of Resistance*, 1989). The eight stories in *Kegyelmi viszonyok: Halálnovellák* are built around wretched human creatures who appear at some point to achieve grace, only to suffer a reversal of fortune that ends in their death or suicide. One of the best stories, "Herman, a vadőr" ("Herman, the Gamekeeper"), is about a former gamekeeper and renowned trapper whose sudden compassion for an animal in a trap changes his outlook and values and leads him to the opposite extreme, of setting traps for humans until he himself is hunted down and killed. *The Melancholy of Resistance*, Krasznahorkai's only major work so far to appear in English, is a dense narrative divided into chapters but not paragraphs about the bizarre events that occur after a circus featuring what it advertises as the largest whale in the world arrives in an out-of-the-way Hungarian town reminiscent of the settings of Krasznahorkai's previous works. Since *The Melancholy of Resistance*, Krasznahorkai has published two more novels, *Az urgai fogoly* (The Prisoner of Urga, 1992) and *Háború és háború* (War and War, 1999). The more interesting of the two, and different from Krasznahorkai's previous writing, *Az urgai fogoly* describes several unusual experiences of the narrator on a trip to China, especially the extraordinary impression made on him by a young actress in an opera in Beijing, and all framed by an arduous train trip between Urga (Ulan Bator), the capital of Mongolia, and Beijing.

Translations: *The Melancholy of Resistance,* trans. George Szirtes (London: Quartet, 1998); "Dumb to the Deaf," trans. Eszter Molnár, *Hungarian Quarterly* 41 (2000): 49–55; "Getting Away from Bogdanovich" and "The Last Boat," in *Thy Kingdom Come: 19 Short Stories by 11 Hungarian Authors,* ed. Peter Doherty, Gyöngyi Köteles, and Zsófia Bán, trans. Eszter Molnár (Budapest: Palatinus, 1998). *Kegyelmi viszonyok: Halálnovellák* is available in German as *Gnadenverhältnisse,* trans. Hans Skirecki and Juliane Brandt (Berlin: Literarisches Colloquium Berlin, 1988).

Kratochvil, Jiří (b. 1940) Czech novelist, short-story writer, playwright, and essayist. A native of Brno, where he still lives, Kratochvil graduated from high school in Brno in 1957 and then pursued a program of Czech and Russian studies at Brno University. After earning his degree in 1965, he taught school in Dobruška and worked as a librarian. Kratochvil ran afoul of the authorities with his first collection of short stories, *Případ s Chatnoirem* (The Chat Noir Case, 1971), which was withdrawn from distribution not long after its publication. Kratochvil was also banned from further publishing. He eventually returned to the literary scene with a generally well received trilogy of novels: *Medvědí roman* (A Bear Novel), published in samizdat in 1988 and in print in 1990, a complex Orwellian antiutopian work with a number of autobiographical elements; *Uprostřed nocí zpěv* (Song in the Middle of the Night, 1992), a Jekyll and Hyde–type novel full of bizarre situations about a man's search for his true

identity and reflecting Kratochvil's familiarity with the literature of magic realism and the postmodern movement in general; and *Avion* (1995), another exercise in the fantastic also combining autobiographical elements. These were followed in 1997 by his "carnival novel," *Nesmrtelný příběh aneb Život Soni Trocké-Sammlerové* (An Immortal Tale, or, The Life of Sonia Trocká-Sammlerová), about a girl picked up by an airship when she was five years old and, under hypnosis, given a message for the twenty-first century; in 1999 by *Noční tango, aneb, Román jednoho léta z konce století* (Nocturnal Tango, or, A Novel About a Single Year at the End of the Century), for which he received the Jaroslav Seifert Prize; and in 2000 by *Truchlivý Bůh* (Mournful God), a novel divided into twenty-three small chapters identified just by number and narrated by the author, who works in a bookshop and is pessimistic about the future of books as he peppers his narration with references to the likes of Bernard Malamud, Julia Roberts, Alfred Hitchcock, and Roman Polanski. He has also published two collections of short stories, *Orfeus z Kénigu* (The Orpheus of Kénig, 1994), Kénig being a part of Brno, and *Má lásko, Postmoderno* (Postmodern, My Love, 1994), and a volume of nine short radio plays titled *Slepecká cvičení* (Exercise for the Blind, 1997). Kratochvil is the author as well of two books of essays on literature and culture: *Kultura jako katarze* (Culture as Catharsis, 1994) and *Vyznání příběhovosti* (The Calling of Narration, 2000), a collection of essays from the late 1960s to the 1990s in which he addresses such topics as the metanovel, postmodernism, and the literature of carnival. A highly imaginative writer, often witty and humorous, Kratochvil has had a strong attraction to magic realism, with its elements of the bizarre and fantastic, and a fondness for play and mystification. He particularly enjoys undermining the concept of storytelling itself by having a narrator begin a story, only to interrupt it and tell the reader that it has all been invented.

Translations: "The Orpheus of Kénig" (from *Orfeus z Kénigu*), trans. Alexandra Büchler, in *This Side of Reality: Modern Czech Writing,* ed. Alexandra Büchler (London: Serpent's Tail, 1996), 129–39; "The Story of King Candaules" (from *Orfeus z Kénigu*), trans. Jonathan Bolton, in *Daylight in Nighclub Inferno: Czech Fiction from the Post-Kundera Generation,* selected by Elena Lappin (North Haven, Conn.: Catbird, 1997), 103–46.

Kravos, Marko (b. 1943) Slovenian poet, novelist, short-story writer, and essayist. Kravos was born in Montecalvo Irpino, in southern Italy. He is fluent in both Slovenian and Italian. After World War II, he and his family resettled in Trieste, where he received his early education through secondary school. In 1969 he graduated from Ljubljana University with a degree in Slavic languages and literatures. Trieste subsequently became his permanent home, and he has made the city the subject of several works, particularly the recent autobiographical collection of sketches *Kratki čas: Trst iz žabje perspektive* (A Short Time: Trieste from the Frog's Perspective, 1999). He was employed for over twenty years as a book editor and has taught Slovenian in the Faculty of Humanities of Trieste University. He became a freelance writer in 1993.

Kravos has published some thirteen collections of poems: *Štirinajst* (Fourteen, 1967); *Pesem* (Poems, 1969); *Trikotno jadro* (The Triangular Sail, 1972); *Obute in bose* (Shoed and Barefoot, 1976); *Paralele* (Parallels, 1977); *Tretje oko* (The Third Eye, 1979), for which he won the coveted Prešeren Prize; *Napisi in nadpisi* (Epigrams and Epitaphs, 1984); *V znamenju škržata* (In the Sign of the Cicadas, 1985); *Sredozemlje* (The Mediterranean, 1986), one of his most popular books of poems, which has been pub-

lished in five languages; *Ko so nageljni dišali* (When the Carnations Bloomed, 1988); *Obzorje in sled* (Horizon and Trail, 1992); *Sredi zemlje: Sredozemlje* (In the Middle of the Earth: The Mediterranean, 1993), a selection of his poems; and *Krompir na sercu* (Potato on the Heart, 1996). A collection of Kravos's poems from 1966 to 1991 in Italian translation (by various hands) was published by Campanotto of Udine in 1994 under the title *Il richiamo del cuculo* (The Call of the Cuckoo).

Kravos is highly attentive to the rituals of contemporary life and has written poems on the routine of the everyday, work, study, love, marriage, the family, and the city—above all, Trieste. Writing in general and poetry in particular become for him a way out of isolation and a means of establishing relations and communication with others. His penchant for "cosmic" reflection on human destiny and nature is counterbalanced by a constant tendency toward irony and self-irony. Restlessness, solitude, silence, the search for a way to come to grips with the complex human dynamic, and a fascination with the myth of the sea are leitmotifs of his lyrical writing. Kravos operates with a broad range of subjects. He has written poems on wine; the call of the other world; the Hotel Astoria in St. Petersburg, where the Russian poet Sergei Esenin (one of his favorites) committed suicide; returning from war; and the American folk singer Bob Dylan, whose song "Lay Lady Lay" causes him to think of the thighs of a woman he saw in the porno magazine *Lui*. Kravos is a member of the Slovenian PEN Club and the Association of Slovenian Writers in Ljubljana.

Kriseová, Eda (b. 1940) Czech novelist, short-story writer, and journalist. A native of Prague, Kriseová studied at the Prague Institute of Journalism from 1958 to 1962, after which she became editor of the weekly *Mladý svět* and, briefly, the editor of

Listy. Kriseová has traveled very widely, including to the Middle and Far East, and in 1966 won the Julius Fučík Prize for her reportage. Two years later, she published a travel book about Japan that became an immediate success: *Já ponsko: Putování bez fraku* (I and Japan: Traveling Without an Evening Dress, 1968). The Warsaw Pact invasion of Czechoslovakia in 1968 ended her journalism career. She turned instead to the writing of short stories and novels that circulated in either samizdat or Edice Petlice editions. They include *Pompejanka* (The Woman from Pompeii, written 1976–1977 [published in 1979 by Edice Petlice and in 1990 in Czechoslovakia]); *Sluneční hodiny* (The Sundial, written 1978 [published in 1979 by Edice Petlice]), where for the first time Kriseová writes about her experiences observing patients in a mental hospital; and *Ryby raky* (Fish and Fowl, written 1978–1981 [published in 1983 by Edice Petlice and in 1991 in Czechoslovakia]), a very personal account of her trip to Israel and problems of readjustment, especially in her marital life, after her return home.

Kriseová's most notable work of fiction is a sensitive, typically quite personal, and highly readable collection of tales about the inmates of a mental hospital somewhere in Bohemia under the title *Křížová cesta kočárového kočího* (The Passion of the Carriage Driver, 1979), published by Edice Petlice. Kriseová won the Egon Hostovský Prize for the book in 1979. Since then, she has written mostly collections of short stories, among them *Prázdniny s bosonožkou* (Holidays with the Barefoot Fairy, written 1981 [published in 1984 by Edice Petlice and in 1985 in London]), which features the two young girls who figure as well in Kriseová's *Terézka a Majda na horách* (Terezka and Majda in the Mountains, 1988), published in England; *Klíční kůstka netopýra a jiné povídky* (The Bat's Collarbone and Other Stories, 1994), a collection of three novel-las—the first (and longest), from which the title of the collection is derived, written in 1972; the second, "Bratři" ("Brothers"), dating from 1985; and the third, "Milost" ("Love"), written in 1993—*Sedm lásek* (Seven Loves, 1985), published by Edice Petlice; *Arboretum, 1980–1985* (1987), a collection of eight stories pubished by Index of Cologne; *Co se stalo . . . 1981–1987* (What Happened . . . 1981–1987 [published in 1988 by Edice Petlice and in 1991 by Sixty-Eight Publishers]), a book of short tales thematically related to *Křížová cesta kočárového kočího* and to the earlier *Sluneční hodiny,* and in which she juxtaposes her experiences among patients in a mental hospital ("In the Asylum") with her encounters with people on the outside during a summer stay in the Czech mountains ("In the Mountains"). In 1997 Kriseová published the novel *Kočičí životy* (Cat's Lives), a somber work that follows the lives of mostly the female members of a Czech family from largely Polish and Ukrainian Wolhynia from 1908 to the early 1990s. The turbulent history of this multiethnic region, peopled before World War II primarily by Poles, Ukrainians, and Jews, forms an integral part of the novel, carrying the reader through World War I, the Polish-Soviet War of 1920, World War II, the postwar communist era, the Warsaw Pact invasion of Czechoslovakia in 1968, and the "Velvet Revolution" of 1989 and its aftermath. Kriseová worked on the novel in the artists' colony of Schöppingen, in northern Westphalia, after receiving a six-month stipend from the Ministry of Culture of the German federal state of Rhineland-Westphalia. Kriseová's latest novel is *Perchta z Rožemberka aneb Bílá Pani* (Perchta of Rožmberk, or The White Lady, 2001), a novel about a dynastic marriage set in the fifteenth century. Kriseová is also widely known as the author of an authorized biography of Václav Havel: *Václav Havel: Životopis* (*Václav Havel: A Biography*, 1991).

Translations: *Václav Havel: The Authorized Biography,* trans. Caleb Crain (New York: St. Martin's Press, 1993); "A Knight of the Cross" and "Our Small Town," trans. Suzanne Rappaport, in *The Writing on the Wall: An Anthology of Contemporary Czech Literature,* ed. Antonin Liehm and Peter Kussi (Princeton, N.J.: Karz-Cohl, 1983), 134–51, 152–65; "The Martyr of Love," trans. Alexandra Büchler, in *Allskin and Other Tales by Contemporary Czech Women,* ed. Alexandra Büchler (Seattle: Women in Translation, 1998), 150–58; "Morning in Church," trans. Milan Pomichalek and Anna Mozga, in *Good-bye, Samizdat: Twenty Years of Czechoslovak Underground Writing,* ed. Marketa Goetz-Stankiewicz (Evanston, Ill.: Northwestern University Press, 1992), 88–94; "The Unborn" (from *Arboretum, 1980–1985*), trans. James Naughton, in *Description of a Struggle: The Vintage Book of Contemporary Eastern European Writing,* ed. Michael March (New York: Vintage, 1994), 119–33. *Křížová cesta kočárového kočího* is available in German as *Der Kreuzweg des Karossenkutschers: Geschichten aus einem Irrenhaus,* trans. Susanna Roth (Cologne: Bund-Verlag, 1985).

Kruczkowski, Leon (1900–1962) Polish playwright and novelist. A native of Kraków, where he studied chemistry and worked as a professional chemist in the cement and petroleum industries, Kruczkowski is best remembered as the author of the controversial best-seller *Kordian i cham* (Kordian and the Peasant, 1932), a Marxist revisionist account in fictional form of the anti-Russian November uprising of 1830. Kruczkowski's first published work, it is based on the diary of a peasant named Kazimierz Deczyński (1800–1838), who participated in the uprising. Two more, generally weaker, novels followed within a few years, *Pawie pióra* (Peacock Feathers, 1935), which also addresses the November 1830 uprising, and *Sidła* (The

Trap, 1937), a drab social novel about white-collar unemployment. Staunchly antifascist, in 1938 Kruczkowski published his first play, an anti-Nazi work, under the title *Przygoda z Vaterlandem* (An Adventure with Vaterland). The same year, Kruczkowski, a socialist activist, spent several months in Belgium studying the lives of Polish émigré miners. An officer in the Polish army, Kruczkowski took part in the September 1939 campaign against the invading Germans, but was captured and spent five years in a prisoner-of-war camp in Germany. After the war, Kruczkowski resumed his literary career while becoming active politically. In 1945 he became a member of the National Council of State and in 1947 was elected a delegate to the Legislative Commission of the Polish parliament. It was also in 1947 that he was decorated with the Commander's Cross of the Order of Polonia Restituta. From 1949 to 1956, he served as president of the Polish Writers Union. Apart from the State Prize for Art, First Degree, awarded him in 1950, Kruczkowski received the international prize "For the Preservation of Peace Among Nations" in 1953 for his active participation in the communist-sponsored World Peace Movement. From 1952 to 1956, Kruczkowski was a delegate to parliament and head of the parliamentary Commission of Enlightenment, Science, and Culture. In 1954 he became a member of the Central Committee of the Polish United Workers Party (communist). Two years later, he was named a corresponding member of the German Academy of Fine Arts. Of the several plays Kruczkowski wrote, his most famous were *Pierwszy dzień wolności* (The First Day of Freedom, 1949), arguably his best dramatic work, about the problem of trying to rebuild a normal life after war and years of occupation; *Juliusz i Ethel* (Julius and Ethel, 1954), a political drama about the Rosenberg spy case in the United States; and *Niemcy* (Germans, 1961), which stirred controversy because of its balanced treatment of a German family. The most complete collection of Kruczkowski's plays was published in 1962 under the title *Dramaty* (Dramatic Works).

Literature: Zenona Muczanka, *Leon Kruczkowski* (Warsaw: Iskra, 1976), a fair general introduction; Roman Szydłowski, *Dramaturgia Leona Kruczkowskiego* (Kraków: Wydawnictwo Literackie, 1972), a study of Kruczkowski's plays.

Translations: *Niemcy* is available in Spanish as *Los alemanes,* trans. Maria Różycka and Carmen Dorronsoro (Mexico City: Colección Teatro Contemporaneo, 1953), and *Pierszy dzień wolności* in German as *Erste Tag der Freiheit,* trans. Viktor Mika, *Theater Heute* 2, no. 7 (1962).

Krynicki, Ryszard (b. 1943) Polish poet. An important poet closely identified with the dissident movement in Poland and a representative of the new wave of young poets who came to prominence after 1968, Krynicki was born in Sankt Valentin, Austria, and later studied Polish literature at Poznań University. He subsequently made Kraków his home. His first book of poetry, *Pęd pogoni, pęd ucieczki* (Haste of Pursuit, Haste of Flight), appeared in 1968 and was soon followed by *Akt urodzenia* (Act of Birth, 1969) and *Organizm zbiorowy: Wiersze i przekłady* (Collective Organism: Poems and Translations, 1975). Notwithstanding the grim view of contemporary reality presented in these works and attributable to Krynicki's political and metaphysical beliefs, it was his overt protest in 1975 against projected changes in the Polish constitution that led to his being forbidden to publish between the years 1976 and 1980. His next collection of poems, *Nasze życie rośnie* (Our Life Grows), was published first in Paris in 1978 by the Instytut Literacki and then in Poland in 1981. But even when the prohibition on Krynicki was lifted, he sought to preserve his integrity by publishing his next

few works independently. *Niewiele więcej* (Not Much More) was published in two private illustrated editions in 1981 and 1985; *Jeżeli w jakimś kraju* (If in Some Country) was distributed independently in typescript with illustrations by Jerzy Piotrowicz in 1982; and *Wiersze, głosy* (Poems, Voices) was published independently with illustrations by Zbylut Grzywacz in 1985 and 1987. *Niepodlegli miłości: Wybrane wiersze i przekłady* (Independent Loves: Selected Poems and Translations) was published first by the small house Nowa in 1988 and then by another small press, CiS, in 1996.

Niepodlegli miłości: Wybrane wiersze i przekłady was Krynicki's most comprehensive collection of poetry. Now a bibliographic rarity, the volume has, however, been superseded by *Magnetyczny punkt* (The Magnetic Point, 1996), the most thorough collection of Krynicki's poetry yet to appear. A fascinatingly independent and original poet, whose poetic style has ranged from Baroque excess to almost ascetic simplicity, Krynicki has demonstrated a particular predilection in his later poetry for brevity and pithiness. Many of his poems are very short, no more than a few lines, at times aphoristic in style with ironic twists at the end, as in "Najbiedniejszym tej ziemi" ("The Poorest on Earth"):

The poorest on earth
aren't spared hard work
even dying.

Or as in "Tak" ("Yes"):

Yes, I survived.
Now I face an equally
serious task: to board a streetcar, and
    head home.

In a number of his poems, irony appears in a political context, as in "Podobno" ("Most Likely"):

Similarly, in the Political Bureau
Only liberals are now ruling.
They're still lacking the strong hands to
    introduce that liberalism into life at
    large.

Or as in "Nie musi"("Doesn't have to . . . "):

In order to explain many crimes
the Ministry of Internal Affairs
doesn't have to look too far.

Krynicki often plays with words and images, as in "Biała plama" ("White Stain"), dedicated to the memory of the Polish futurist poet Bruno Jasieński, in which the page is blank. Apart from Jasieński and his fellow futurist writer Tadeusz Peiper, Krynicki has dedicated poems to such other well-known Polish figures as the poet Stanisław Barańczak and his wife, Anna; the poet Zbigniew Herbert and his fictitious Pan (Mr.) Cogito; and the Polish Solidarity leader Adam Michnik. In a verse dialogue with his former verse, "Chorągiew nadrealizmu" ("The Banner of Surrealism"), Krynicki signals his break with surrealism, declaring

Not everything we expect from
    surrealism
is capable of fulfillment.

In a note at the end of the collection *Magnetyczny punkt*, Krynicki tells us that the volume recalls the selection of his verse and translations published in 1988 by the Niezależna Oficyna Wydawnicza (Independent Publishing House) as *Niepodlegli nicości* (Independent Nothings). But the two books are not exactly identical. He originally wanted to publish *Magnetyczny punkt* under the title "N. N." or "n. n." The new volume also contains a few poems deleted from the original edition by the censors; a poem by the Israeli poet Yehuda Amichai that Krynicki translated in June 1988 at the Po-

etry International festival in Rotterdam, at which Amichai was present; and one poem that was supposed to appear in the thirteenth number of *Solidarność Wielkopolska* but was lost along with an entire archive of the journal in a special police-unit assault on the administrative headquarters of "S" District in Poznań on 13 December 1981.

Translations: *Citizen R. K. Does Not Live: Poems of Ryszard Krynicki*, selected and introduced by Stanisław Barańczak, ed. Robert A. Davies and John M. Gogol (Forest Grove, Ore.: Mr. Cogito, 1985).

Kukorelly, Endre (b. 1951) Hungarian poet and short-story writer. A native of Budapest, Kukorelly studied history and library science at Eötvös Lóránd University from 1975 to 1981 and then worked as a correspondent and an editor for various literary and cultural journals, including *Új Könyvék, Négy Évszak,* and *Újhold.* He is now head of the literary section of the weekly *Magyar Narancs* and the Hungarian edition of *Lettre internationale.* As a poet, Kukorelly's closeness to and yet independence of the avantgarde is manifest in the anthology that he and László Császár put out in 1989: *Szó gettó* (Word Ghetto). This independence, especially toward poetic language, was amply in evidence in such preceding and subsequent volumes of poetry as *A valóság édessége* (The Sweetness of Truth, 1984); *Manière* (1986); *Én senkivel sem üldögélek* (I Don't Hang Around with Anybody, 1989); *Azt mondja aki él* (So Says He Who Lives, 1993); and *Egy gyógynövény-kert* (A Garden of Herbal Plants, 1993), in which Kukorelly carries his deliberate disregard of grammar and punctuation to a new high (or low), although poems with specific Budapest settings are often effective. The poet's love affair with his native city, clearly reflected in *Egy gyógynövény-kert,* is very much in evidence in *Budapest—Papírváros* (Budapest, City of Paper, 1994), an essay illustrated with photographs by Károly Gink. Although he published another volume of poems in 1998, *H. Ö. L. D. E. R. L. I. N.*, the title of which points to the German poet who was the principal inspiration for the collection, Kukorelly became more extensively involved in prose writing in the 1990s. Apart from *Budapest—Papírváros*, he published another two books of essays, *Napos terület* (A Sunny Spot, 1994) and *Kedvenc* (The Favorite, 1998); a book mostly of stories under the title *Mintha már túl sokáig állna* (As If He Would Remain for a Long Time After, 1995); the memoiristic *A memória-part* (The Memory Box, 1999); and, in 2000, a withering satire on the decline of the former Soviet Union under the title *Rom, a Szovjetónió története* (Ruin: The Story of the Soviet Union), whose title in Hungarian contains a pun, since the word for "union," *unió*, is changed to the mocking *ónió*. Covering events from February 1987 to April 2000, and drawing on his own experiences, Kukorelly focuses on the obsolete nature of the Soviet system and reserves some of his sharpest barbs for Hungarian literary fellow travelers. In 1984 Kukorelly won the Hungarian literary prize for the best first book of poetry for *A valóság édessége*, and in 1993 he was awarded the coveted Attila József Prize.

Translations: *A memória-part* is available in German as *Die Gedächtnisküste,* trans. Andrea Seidler (Graz: Droschl, 1997), and a collection of stories as *Die Rede und die Regel: Erzählungen,* trans. Hans Skirecki (Frankfurt am Main: Suhrhamp, 1999).

Kulavkova, Katica. *See* Kjulavkova, Katica

Kuncewiczowa, Maria (1897–1989) Polish novelist, short-story writer, and essayist. One of the outstanding women writers of twentieth-century Poland, and well represented in English translation, Kuncewiczowa was born in Samara, Russia, the descendant of political exiles. She studied French literature in Nancy, France, and Polish literature in Kraków and Warsaw. She also prepared for an operatic career at the Warsaw Conservatory and in fact sang at the conservatories of Warsaw and Paris. Her career as a writer spans both halves of the twentieth century, with major literary works appearing both before and after World War II. Her first important publication was the rather antibourgeois novel *Pzymierze z dzieckiem* (A Pact with a Child, 1927), which deals with the gap between a young artist's aspirations and reality and is striking for its withering assault on the institution of motherhood. Although actually written in 1922, her next novel, *Twarz mężczyźni* (A Man's Face), appeared in 1928. Set within an intelligentsia household, the milieu Kuncewiczowa knew best, it is in essence a series of psychological studies of a woman reaching erotic maturity. In 1933 Kuncewiczowa published the much acclaimed *Dwa księżyce* (Two Moons), an affectionate book of short stories about the quaint Renaissance town of Kazimierz on the Vistula, where she and her husband long had a residence. The town was famous as a popular artists' colony and was well known for its large prewar Orthodox Jewish population.

Kuncewiczowa's major breakthrough as a novelist came in 1935 with *Cudzoziemka* (*The Stranger*), an autobiographical, psychologically penetrating novel about the "strangeness" that Polish exiles brought up in Russia experienced after their return to their homeland. It was awarded the Prize of the City of Warsaw in 1937. In 1936 Kuncewiczowa published an account of her travels through the Middle East under the title *Miasto Heroda* (The City of Herod). Of particular interest in the work is her description of the Polish Jews she met who had settled in Palestine. The year after *Miasto Heroda*, Kuncewiczowa's *Dnie powszednie państwa Kowalskich* (The Everyday Life of the Kowalski Family) and *Kowalscy się odnaleźli* (The Kowalskis Are

Back Again), the story of an average Warsaw family, became the first radio serial in Europe. In the work, Kuncewiczowa assumes the persona of an amateur detective who follows her characters around the streets of Warsaw. Her post–World War II serial, *Rodzina Matysiaków* (The Matysiak Family), was constructed along similar lines.

Kuncewiczowa left Poland not long after the German invasion in 1939, settling for a time in Paris and then moving to London, where she lived from 1940 to 1955. She subsequently immigrated to the United States, in 1960 becoming a professor of Polish literature at the University of Chicago. During the war, Kuncewiczowa worked tirelessly on behalf of the Polish cause and to make her native land better known in the West. Toward that end, she published two very small works in English on Polish literature and culture: *Polish Millstones* (1942) and *Modern Polish Prose* (1945). Once established in her position at the University of Chicago, Kuncewiczowa continued her work on behalf of Polish culture by publishing a large anthology in English containing a number of texts from Polish literary and other sources under the title *The Modern Polish Mind: An Anthology* (1962).

Although some of Kuncewiczowa's best works date from the war years and the postwar period, only one, and that just in part, was written in Poland. The first of her novels to appear during the war was *Klucze* (The Keys, 1943), which was published in a Polish edition in London. A hybrid text consisting of elements of reportage, essay, poetry, and the novel, it covers the period from 1939 to 1943 and documents the flight across Europe of so many Polish refugees, including Kuncewiczowa herself. *Zmowa nieobecnych* (The Conspiracy of the Absent, 1946), which spans the period from the outbreak of World War II to 1944, is set in Poland and England and deals with the resistance

movement in Poland and its links with Polish communities in the West—above all, England. *Leśnik* (The Forester, 1952), arguably the best of Kuncewiczowa's psychological novels, is a historical novel set in the Polish countryside during and after the Polish anti-Russian uprising of January 1863.

Gaj oliwny (The Olive Grove), which followed *The Forester* in 1961, is one of Kuncewiczowa's rare works with no connection to anything Polish. It was based on a real-life event that attracted much publicity at the time, the senseless murder of the renowned British scientist Sir Jack Drummond and his family in the south of France in 1952. The novel grew out of Kuncewiczowa's interest in the clash of different cultures—in this instance, the irrational xenophobia of a French peasant. *Tristan* (1946), which was first published in Poland in 1967, was Kuncewiczowa's best postwar work of fiction. She wrote it partly in her residence in Kazimierz. A modern retelling of the medieval Celtic myth, Tristan has been transformed into a young Polish refugee burdened with the sufferings his people endured in World War II; Isolde, whom he meets and falls in love with in England, has become the Irish girl Kathleen. Although Kuncewiczowa published several books of essays and travel accounts, her most popular work of nonfiction has long been *Fantomy* (Phantoms, 1971), a volume of memoirs. A fine stylist and a master of psychological portraiture, Kuncewiczowa can be read with interest even by readers with no specific interest in Poland.

Literature: Alicja Szałagan, *Maria Kuncewiczowa: Monografia dokumentacyjna, 1895–1989* (Warsaw: Instytut Badań Literackich, 1995), a good documentary monograph.

Translations: *The Conspiracy of the Absent*, trans. Maurice Michael and Harry Stevens (New York: Roy, 1950); *The Forester*, trans. H. C. Stevens (London: Hutchinson, 1954); *The Keys: A Journey Through Europe at War* (London: Hutchinson, 1945); *The Modern Polish Mind: An Anthology* (Boston: Little, Brown, 1962); *The Olive Grove* (New York: Walker, 1963); *Polish Millstones,* trans. Stephen Garry (London: King & Staples, 1942); *The Stranger* (New York: Fischer, 1945); *Tristan* (New York: Braziller, 1974).

Kunchev, Nikolai (b. 1936) Bulgarian poet and translator. A native of the village of Biala voda in the Pleven district, Kunchev completed high school in Svishtov in 1955 and then studied Bulgarian literature at Sofia University from 1959 to 1961. Virtually throughout his career, he has been a freelance writer. Kunchev began publishing poems in the periodical *Narodna mladezh* in 1957. His first collection of poetry, *Prusutsvie* (A Presence), appeared in 1965, but because of his lack of ideological commitment, bold use of language, and elusive imagery, he was faulted by establishment critics for his opaqueness. After the publication in 1968 of his second book of poems, *Kolkoto sinapeno zurno* (So Many Mustard Seeds), he could earn his living only by publishing books for children (of which he has written several) and translations mainly from French and Georgian literatures. Kunchev reentered the literary mainstream with his collection of poems *Chudesii* (Wondrous Things, 1973). It was followed by *Ohliuvata kushta* (The House of Snails, 1978); *Poslanie ot peshehodets* (Greeting from a Pedestrian, 1980); *Kukuriak: Humoristichna lirika* (Hellebore: Humorous Lyics, 1981); *Oslaniam se na maraniata* (I Depend on the Heat, 1981); *Noshten pazach na zorata* (Night Watchman of the Dawn, 1983); *Vulni na veroiatnostta* (Waves of Probability, 1985); *Redom s vsichki migove* (Together with Every Moment, 1986); *Vremeto razdadeno na vsichki* (The Time Given to Everyone, 1989); *Sus sluntse na surtseto* (With Sun for the Heart, 1989); *V gorata ima niakoi* (There's Somebody in the Woods, 1990); *I mezhduochieto da progleda* (Let the Third Eye See,

Too, 1992); *Otpechatutsi ot prustite na ieti* (The Yeti's Fingerprints, 1992); *V bialoto pro-stranstvo na bezkraia* (In the White Expanse of Infinity, 1994); *Pod shatura na zhretsa* (Beneath the High Priest's Tent, 1996), a large collection of poems in prose; and *Galaktizirane na praznotata* (The Galactizing of Emptiness, 1996). Kunchev is an intriguing and original writer who often expresses a delight in life along with a sense of the mystery of existence. However, his highly metaphorical style and unusual imagery make him anything but an "easy" poet.

Literature: Svetlozar Igov, *Poeziiata na Nikolai Kunchev* (Sofia: Pero, 1990), a short introductory essay on Kunchev's poetry.

Translations: *Anthology,* trans. by various hands (Sofia: Ab, 1999), a Bulgarian–English–French–German edition; *Journey of the Sinner,* trans. Yordan Kosturkov (Sofia: Citizen Society, 2000), a Bulgarian–English–French anthology; seven poems in *Clay and Star: Contemporary Bulgarian Poets,* trans. and ed. Lisa Sapinkof and Georgi Belev (Minneapolis: Milkweed, 1992), 99–105; two poems, trans. John Balaban, in *Poets of Bulgaria,* ed. William Meredith (Greensboro, N.C.: Unicorn, 1985), 56–57; nine poems, trans. Lucille Clifton and Theodore Weiss, in *Window on the Black Sea: Bulgarian Poetry in Translation,* ed. Richard Harteis, in collaboration with William Meredith (Pittsburgh: Carnegie Mellon University Press, 1992), 54–62. A collection of Kunchev's poetry is available as *Pred stenata na straha/Vor der Wand der Angst: Gedichte* (Sofia: Ango Boi, 1996), a Bulgarian–German edition.

Kundera, Milan (b. 1929) Czech novelist, short-story writer, and playwright. One of the most highly regarded Czech authors of the post–World War II period, Kundera, who was born in Brno, ran afoul of the communist authorities at an early age. Although he became a member of the Czech Communist

Party shortly after the war, he was expelled from it after the communists took power in Czechoslovakia in February 1948. Before settling on a career in literature and film, he earned his way as a laborer and a jazz musician. His musical talent ran in the family; Kundera's mother was a well-known pianist. Not unexpectedly, musical motifs appear in several of his works. Kundera eventually became a professor at the Prague Institute for Advanced Cinematographic Studies, which produced several of the most compelling Czech films of the postwar period.

Kundera's first novel, *Žert* (*The Joke*), was completed in 1965 and published in Czechoslovakia in 1967, a year before the Soviet invasion of the country. It at once established him as one of the most gifted writers of the day, and at the same time adumbrated his future difficulties with the communist authorities. Like most of his fiction, *The Joke* is a deft combination of wry humor, irony, political candor, and unabashed sex. Essentially a tale of a love affair turned sour, it was taken primarily as a negative picture of communist rule in Czechoslovakia. It was followed by one of his most popular works, *Směšné lásky* (*Laughable Loves*, 1965; enl. ed., 1981), which was published in Czechoslovakia not long after *The Joke*. *Laughable Loves* is a collection of highly entertaining stories all built around the game of sex. It was the last work by Kundera that the communists in Czechoslovakia permitted to be published.

Already suspect before the Soviet invasion in 1968 on the basis of *The Joke* and *Laughable Loves*, Kundera was one of the first literary victims of the repression that came in the wake of the suppression of the "Prague Spring." He was removed from his position at the Institute for Cinematographic Studies in 1970, was prohibited from further publication, and suffered the indignity of seeing all his books removed from public libraries in Czechoslovakia.

Kundera was allowed to leave Czechoslovakia in 1975; he eventually settled in Paris after lecturing for a few years at the University of Rennes. In light of the ban on publication of his works in his own country, Kundera had actually begun publishing in French translation before his emigration from Czechoslovakia. *Život je jinde* (*Life Is Elsewhere*), his first book after *Laughable Loves*, was published in French in 1973 before a Czech edition appeared in Toronto in 1969. The novel won the Prix Médicis for the best foreign novel published in France that year. *Life Is Elsewhere* was followed by *The Farewell Party*, which first appeared in French translation in 1976 as *Le Valse aux adieux*. Spanning a period of just five days, it features a philandering jazz trumpeter of renown (Klíma) who suddenly has to deal with an unwanted pregnancy resulting from a one-night stand in a famous resort spa. *Kniha smíchu a zapomnění* (*The Book of Laughter and Forgetting*), first published in French in 1979 as *Le Livre du rire et de l'oubli*, was Kundera's next book; it is a loosely constructed novel similar in style and humor to *Laughable Loves*. *Nesnesitelná lehkost bytí* (*The Unbearable Lightness of Being*, 1985), which appeared in English translation in 1984, extends Kundera's unquenchable interest in human sexuality and the dialectics of the male–female relationship. It traces the erotic and emotional intricacies in the relations of two couples: a compulsively womanizing doctor who falls in love with and marries a woman but is unable to change his sexual ways, and his artist mistress and her other married lover. Interwoven with the erotic play and foibles of the four principals is an unsparing view of the inanity of communist repression in Czechoslovakia during and after the Soviet invasion of 1968.

Literature: Maria Němcová Banerjee, *Terminal Paradox: The Novels of Milan Kundera* (New York: Grove Weidenfeld, 1990); John O'Brien, *Milan Kundera and Feminism:*

Dangerous Intersections (New York: St. Martin's Press, 1995); Peter Petro, ed., *Critical Essays on Milan Kundera* (New York: Hall, 1999); Antonin J. Liehm, "Milan Kundera: Czech Writer," in *Czech Literature Since 1956: A Symposium,* ed. William E. Harkins and Paul I. Trensky (New York: Bohemica, 1980), 40–55; Peter Kussi, "Kundera's Novel and the Search for Fatherhood," in *Czech Literature Since 1956: A Symposium,* ed. William E. Harkins and Paul I. Trensky (New York: Bohemica, 1980), 56–61.

Translations: *The Book of Laughter and Forgetting,* trans. Michael Henry Heim (New York: Knopf, 1980); *The Farewell Party,* trans. Peter Kussi (New York: Knopf, 1976); *Ignorance,* trans. Linda Asher (New York: HarperCollins, 2002); *Jacques and His Master: An Homage to Diderot in Three Acts,* trans. Michael Henry Heim, in *Drama Contemporary: Czechoslovakia,* ed. Marketa Goetz-Stankiewicz (New York: PAJ Publications, 1985); *The Joke* (New York: HarperCollins, 1992), the definitive version, fully revised by Kundera; *Laughable Loves,* trans. Suzanne Rappaport (New York: Knopf, 1974; New York: Penguin, 1975); *Life Is Elsewhere,* trans. Peter Kussi (New York: Knopf, 1974; New York: Penguin, 1986); *The Unbearable Lightness of Being,* trans. Michael Henry Heim (New York: Harper & Row, 1984; New York: Harper Perennial, 1991).

Kunert, Günter (b. 1929) German poet and essayist. One of the most respected and prolific post–World War II German poets, Kunert was born in Berlin. But because his mother was Jewish, he was denied schooling and for that reason later declared unfit for military service. After World War II, from 1946 to 1948, he studied graphics at the College of Applied Art in Berlin. It was during this period that he began to write poetry. His first published book of poems, spare of ornamentation and idealistic in outlook, issued with the blessings of Johannes R. Becher, was *Wegschilder und Mauerinschriften* (Signposts and Graffiti, 1950). The volume created an immediate sensation, not the least for Kunert's acknowledged indebtedness to such German poets as Heinrich Heine, Kurt Tucholsky, and Joachim Ringelnatz, and the Americans Edgar Lee Masters and Carl Sandburg. This was followed by such other volumes of poetry as *Unter diesem Himmel* (Beneath This Heaven, 1955); *Tagwerke* (Day's Labor, 1961); *Das kreuzbrave Liederbuch* (The Well-Behaved Song Book, 1961); *Der ungebetene Gast* (The Uninvited Guest, 1965); and *Warnung vor Spiegeln* (Watch Out for Mirrors, 1970). In 1967 Kunert published his sole novel, *Im Namen der Hüte* (In the Name of the Hat).

Although expected of a writer at the time, Kunert showed no interest in conforming to the principles of socialist realism despite his ideological commitment to the new political order. He was vehemently attacked for this, but showed no reticence in responding to it with the full force of his convictions. Clearly reflecting the impact on his consciousness of the war and the stigma he was made to feel because of his partly Jewish origin, Kunert's poetry is littered with the debris of war and the anxiety and uncertainty bred by war. Even as he yearns for peace, tranquillity, even silence, content to catch the sounds of the city outside without necessarily wanting to be a part of it, he has few illusions and conveys a deep sense of pessimism about the workings of history. Many of Kunert's poems are short and written in short lines of unrhymed verse in fairly unadorned style. Much the same outlook on life as his poetry informs Kunert's books of short prose, which are notable for their verbal conciseness and Kunert's impressive skill as an essayist. Those published before he resettled in West Germany in 1979 include *Die Beerdigung findet in aller Stille statt* (The Funeral Takes Place in Silence, 1968); *Ortsangaben* (Place

Names, 1971); *Die geheime Bibliothek* (The Secret Library, 1973); and *Warum Schreiben? Notizien zur Literatur* (Why Write? Notes on Literature, 1976). A number of Kunert's essays are addressed to poetry and imaginative writing in general. *Camera obscura*, which appeared in 1978 and anticipates some of his subsequent prose writing in the West, is a collection of stories, philosophical miniatures, and travel notes.

In 1952, a year after he joined the East German Communist Party, Kunert became a collaborator of the journal *Eulenspiegel*, which had published some of his poems in 1948 and 1949. He also wrote for film, radio, and television. In 1962 Kunert won the Heinrich Mann prize of the German Democratic Republic Academy of Arts, and in 1973 the Johannes R. Becher Prize for lyric poetry. In 1972 he was appointed visiting associate professor at the University of Texas in Austin. His experiences in the United States form the subject of his volume *Der andere Planet: Ansichten von Amerika* (The Other Planet: Postcards from America, 1975). In 1975, the year in which he published one of his best books of poems, *Das kleine Aber: Gedichte* (The Small But: Poems), Kunert was invited to be writer in residence at the University of Warwick, England. His stay in England is described in *Ein englisches Tagebuch* (An English Diary, 1978). After his return to Germany, Kunert was elected a member of the West Berlin Academy of Arts. He has also served as a juror for the Books Abroad/Neustadt Prize. As a result of his signing a petition in the Wolf Biermann case, he was stripped of his membership in the Communist Party in 1977. Kunert immigrated to West Germany in 1979.

Kunert's extraordinary creativity continued unabated after his resettlement in West Germany. He published another six books of poems in the 1980s and 1990s: *Abtötungsverfahren* (Method of Destruction, 1980); *Stillleben* (Still Life, 1983); *Berlin beizeiten* (Berlin

in Good Time, 1987); *Ich Du Er Sie Es* (I You He She It, 1988); *Fremd daheim* (Strange at Home, 1990); and *Mein Golem: Gedichte* (My Golem: Poems, 1996). His later prose works include mostly collections of essays, such as *Die Schreie der Fledermäuse: Geschichten, Gedichte, Aufsätze* (The Screams of Bats: Stories, Poems, Essays, 1979); *Verspätete Monologe* (Belated Monologues, 1981); *Diesseits des Erinnerens: Aufsätze* (This Side of Memory: Essays, 1982); *Leben und Schreiben* (Living and Writing, 1983); *Die letzten Indianer Europas: Essay* (Europe's Last Indians: An Essay, 1983); *Zurück ins Paradies* (Back to Paradise, 1984); *Vor der Sintflut: Das Gedicht als Arche Noah* (Before the Deluge: The Poem as Noah's Ark, 1985); *Auf Abwegen und andere Verirrungen* (On Errors and Other Aberrations, 1988); and *Der Sturz vom Sockel: Feststellungen und Widersprüche* (The Fall from the Pedestal: Perceptions and Contradictions, 1992). *Erwachsenenspiele: Erinnerungen* (Games for Grownups: Memoirs), a very readable and interesting book of memoirs, came out in 1997.

Translations: Twenty poems, in German and English, trans. Michael Hamburger, Christopher Levenson, and Christopher Middleton, in *East German Poetry: An Anthology,* ed. Michael Hamburger (New York: Dutton, 1973), 88–109; "Love Story—Made in the GDR," trans. Jan van Heurck, in *The New Sufferings of Young W. and Other Stories from the German Democratic Republic,* ed. Therese Hörnigk and Alexander Stephan (New York: Continuum, 1997), 162–71.

Kunze, Reiner (b. 1933) German poet and prose writer. Kunze was born in Oelsnitz, the son of a miner. He studied philosophy and journalism at Leipzig University, subsequently working at a variety of jobs before becoming a freelance writer in 1962. His literary career began with the publication of his first book of poetry, *Sensible Wege* (Sensible Ways), in 1969. This was followed by a second volume of verse, *Zimmerlautstärke* (Household Noise Level, 1972; translated as *With the Volume Turned Down*); a prose work, *Die wunderbaren Jahre* (The Wonderful Years, 1976); a book of interviews under the title *In Deutschland zuhaus, Funk- und Fernseh Interviews, 1977–1983* (At Home in Germany: Radio and Television Interviews, 1977–1983, 1984); a third volume of poetry, *eines jeden einziges leben* (each and every life, 1986); an essay, *Die weisse Gedicht* (The White Poem, 1989); a documentary report, *Deckname "Lyrik"* (Code Name "Lyric," 1990); another volume of interviews, *Begehrte, unbequeme Freiheit* (Desired Uncomfortable Freedom, 1993); and a diary under the title *Am Sonnenhang: Tagebuch eines Jahres* (At Sundown: Diary of a Year, 1993). All of Kunze's work after 1977 was published in the West. He was expelled from the East German Writers Union in 1976 and immigrated to West Germany in 1977. Kunze was awarded the German Prize for Children's Books (1971); the Georg Büchner Prize (1977); the Georg Trakl Prize (1977); the Geschwister Scholl Prize (1981); the Federal Order of Merit (1984); and the Hanns Martin Schleyer Prize (1990–1991).

Literature: "Reiner Kunze," in *Literary Intellectuals and the Dissolution of the State: Professionalism and Conformity in the GDR*, ed. Robert von Hallberg, trans. Kenneth J. Northcott (Chicago: University of Chicago Press, 1996), 227–35. Translations: *Three Contemporary German Poets: Wolf Biermann, Sarah Kirsch, Reiner Kunze*, ed. Peter J. Graves (Leicester: Leicester University Press, 1985); twenty poems, in German and English, trans. Gordon Brotherston, Gisela Brotherston, and Michael Hamburger, in *East German Poetry: An Anthology*, ed. Michael Hamburger (New York: Dutton, 1973), 118–49; "My Friend, a Poet of Love," trans. Jan van Heurck, in *The New Suffer-*

ings of Young W. and Other Stories from the German Democratic Republic, ed. Therese Hörnigk and Alexander Stephan (New York: Continuum, 1997), 149.

Kurucz, Gyula (b. 1944) Hungarian novelist and short-story writer. A native of Nyíregyháza, Kurucz graduated from high school in Sárospatak in 1962 and then pursued a program of German studies at Debrecen University. After receiving his degree in 1968, he settled in Budapest and worked variously as a German-language teacher, a literary and dramatic adviser, an instructor in education, an interpreter, and a translator. In 1980 he became editor in chief of the trilingual journal *Hungarian Book Review*, a position he held until 1990, although a scholarship enabled him to spend the period 1988 to 1990 in Berlin. In 1987 Kurucz was one of the founders of the Hungarian Democratic Forum opposition party, and in 1991 he was named director of the Hungarian cultural center (Haus Ungarn) in Berlin. His first success as a creative writer came with his novel *Nohát meséljünk . . .* (Let's Tell Stories . . . , 1970). This was followed by several more novels: *A mákszem hölgy* (Lady Poppy Seed, 1974); *A ködfaragó* (The Fog Cutter, 1976); *Négy csend közt a hallgatás* (The Silence amid Four Stillnesses, 1977); *Kicsi nagyvilág* (Small Big World, 1978); *Összezárva* (Lockup, 1978); *Léggömbhuszárok* (Balloon Hussars, 1981); *Lukács evangéliuma* (The Gospel of Luke, 1986); *A veszett ember* (The Wild Man, 1984); and *Lassú visszavonulás* (Slow Withdrawal, 1990) as well as a volume of short stories, *Szeretek, tehát voltam* (I Love, Therefore I Have Been, 1981). Most of Kurucz's writing presents true-to-life pictures of workers and village people in the harsh circumstances of the postwar years; in some of his later works, he also addresses the moral dilemmas faced by intellectuals in their search for greater independence in the period 1960 to 1980. Although essentially a realist in style and narrative mode, Kurucz has occasionally experimented with allegory and symbolism.

Apart from his fiction writing, Kurucz has devoted much time and energy to promoting Hungarian culture in Germany and in demonstrating the proper place of Hungary and other Eastern European nations in Western culture. In 1992, with Hildegarde Groschl, he published in Hamburg an anthology of contemporary Hungarian fiction in German, *Ungarische Erzähler der Gegenwart* (Contemporary Hungarian Writers); in 1985 he and Laszló Sorenyi issued a collection of essays on European influences on Hungarian literature under the Latin title *Hungaria litterara, Europae filia* (Literary Hungary, a Branch of Europe); and in 1994 he edited a collection of papers on Eastern Europe and the European idea, *Nationalismus, Identität, Europaertum: Wortmeldungen aus acht Ländern* (Nationalism, Identity, Europeanism: Verbal Reports from Eight Countries). Kurucz was also the editor of *Das Tor zur deutschen Einheit: Grenzdurchbruch Sopron 19. August 1989* (The Gate to German Unity: Border Breakthrough, Sopron, 19 August 1989), a collection of papers delivered at a conference in Sopron, Hungary, commemorating the tenth anniversary of the 19 August 1989 "Pan-European Picnic" on the Hungarian–Austrian border near Sopron when some 150 East Germans broke through a border gate and crossed into Austria. The event was widely regarded as anticipating the tearing down of the Berlin Wall and the collapse of the German Democratic Republic.

Translations: "Showdown," trans. J. E. Sollosy, in *Present Continuous: Contemporary Hungarian Writing*, ed. István Bart (Budapest: Corvina, 1985), 352–91.

Kuśniewicz, Andrzej (1904–1993) Polish novelist and poet. Kuśniewicz was born in the village of Kowenice in the Sambor district of pre–World War II southeastern Poland. He attended secondary school in Sambor and fought with the French Resistance during World War II. After the war, he served as the Polish consul general in France. His first published literary work, a volume of poetry titled *Słowa o nienawiści* (Words About Hatred), appeared in 1955. Kuśniewicz was fifty-two years old at the time. *Słowa o nienawiści* was followed by three additional volumes of poetry: *Diabłu ogarek* (The Devil's Soot, 1959); *Czas prywatny* (Private Time, 1962); and *Piraterie* (Pirateerings, 1975). Kuśniewicz is best known in Poland and internationally as a novelist. His eleven published novels include *Eroica* (1963); *W drodze do Koryntu* (On the Way to Corinth, 1964); *Król obojga Sycylii* (*The King of the Two Sicilies*, 1970), which won the Seguier Prize for the most outstanding foreign novel published in France that year; *Strefy* (Zones, 1971); *Stan nieważkości* (State of Insignificance, 1973); *Trzecie królestwo* (The Third Kingdom, 1975); *Lekcja martwego języka* (Lesson of a Dead Language, 1977), which was made into a film in 1979 by Janusz Majewski; *Moja historia literatury* (My History of Literature, 1980); *Witraż* (Stained Glass, 1980); *Mieszaniny obyczajowe* (A Hodgepodge of Customs, 1985); and *Nawrócenie* (Conversion, 1987). Kuśniewicz has twice been awarded the National Prize for Literature in Poland. In *The King of the Two Sicilies*, arguably Kuśniewicz's masterpiece, the disintegration of the Hapsburg Empire in its twilight years is viewed through the prism of an effete and decadent young officer in the Austro-Hungarian army involved in an incestuous relationship with his sister.

Literature: Wacław Sadkowski, *Kuśniewicz*, trans. Joanna Infeld-Sosnowska (Warsaw: Authors Agency, 1974), a brochure on Kuśniewicz in English; Mieczysław Dąbrowski, *Nierzeczywista rzeczywistość: Twórczość Andrzeja Kuśniewicza na tle epoki* (Warsaw: Wydział Polonysttiki Uniwersytetu Warszawskiego, 1987); *Puzzle pamięci: Z Andrzejem*

*Kuśniewiczem w marcu i kwietniu 1991 roz-
mawiała Grażyna Szcześniak* (Kraków: Eu-
reka, 1992), an interesting book of interviews
with Kuśniewicz conducted by Grażyna
Szcześniak.

Translations: *The King of the Two Sicilies,*
trans. Celina Wieniewska (New York: Harcourt Brace Jovanovich, 1980). *Strefy* is
available in French as *Constellations: Les
signes du zodiaque,* trans. Christophe
Jezewski and François Xavier Jaujard (Paris:
Laffont, 1993).

Labiş, Nicolae (1935–1956) Romanian poet.
A gifted and exceptionally promising lyric
poet before his untimely death in a tram accident, Labiş was born in the village of
Văleni in the Baia district. He attended a
local school until his family took refuge in
the Suceava area of southern Romania during World War II. After attending secondary
schools in Fălticeni and Iaşi, he was enrolled
in the Mihai Eminescu Literary Institute in
Bucharest from 1952 to 1954. This was followed by studies at the Philological Faculty
of Bucharest University, but Labiş left the
university after two years. Until his death,
Labiş worked professionally as an editor for
such prominent journals as *Contemporanul*
and *Gazeta literară.* He also became a regular contributor to *Viaţa românească* and
Iaşul nou. Although he began publishing
poetry at the age of fifteen, primarily in the
journal of the Eminescu Literary Institute,
of which he was editor, Labiş's first volume
of poems, *Primele iubiri* (First Loves), appeared only in 1956, the year of his death.
Drawing heavily on the experiences of his
own village childhood and youth in the collection, and of the growing impact of war
and privation, Labiş struck chords of lyric

sensitivity and emotional intensity that infused new life into the contemporary Romanian lyric. Two other books of poetry,
Lupta cu inerţia (The Struggle with Inertia)
and *Albatrosul ucis* (The Slain Albatross),
were published posthumously in 1958 and
1966, respectively. Throughout his poetry,
Labiş reveals a sensitive spirit, attuned to the
beauties of nature, coupled with a sense of
human needs. The most up-to-date edition
of Labiş's poetry was published in 1989
under the editorship of Gheorghe Tomozei.

Literature: Gheorghe Tomozei, *Umele
poetului Labiş* (Bucharest: Sport-Turism,
1985); *Nicolae Labiş: Album memorial*
(Bucharest: Secolul 20, 1987).

Translations: Seven poems, including a
complete translation of "The Death of the
Doe," one of Labiş's best poems, in *46 Romanian Poets in English,* trans. and ed. Ştefan
Avădanei and Don Eulert (Iaşi: Junimea,
1973), 234–41. *Primele iubiri* is available as
Primele iubiri/Premières amours, trans. Aurel
George Boeşteanu (Bucharest: Eminescu,
1974), a Romanian–French edition.

Laço, Teodor (b. 1936) Albanian novelist,
short-story writer, and playwright. A native
of the village of Dardhë in the Korçë region
of southeastern Albania, Laço came to
prominence as a writer with his novel *Tokë e
ashpër* (Rough Land, 1971), about agricultural collectivization, a favorite subject of
socialist realism. His second novel, *Përball-
imi* (Resistance, 1980; translated as *The Face-
Up*), deals with a somewhat related subject,
the emergency measures taken by the government in the winter of 1949 to ensure adequate grain supplies to cities at a time of
growing bread shortages. The quotas demanded of peasants as food suppliers, and
the rigorous execution of the policy, provoked widespread unrest and resistance. Although the mandatory positive hero of socialist realism here is personified in a
younger Party district official whose no-

nonsense approach to problems earns him respect, the novel does bring to life the issue of adequate grain supply and of opposition and hoarding by kulaks (better-off peasants), and features a number of realistic characterizations. With his next two novels, *Lëndina e lotëve* (The Meadow of Tears, 1978) and *Korbat mbi mermer* (Crows on the Marble, 1981), Laço left contemporary Albania for the 1930s and the hardships faced by Albanians forced to emigrate from their country at the time. However, in *Të gjithë lumenjtë rrjedhin* (All the Rivers Flow, 1987) he returned to the typical Soviet-style socialist realist work about a great construction project—in this case, the Sobora reservoir and dam—that, despite numerous obstacles, is finally completed, thereby vindicating the positive hero, a young hydraulics engineer. Among Laço's other novels are *Pushimet e kolonelit* (The Colonel's Vacation, 1990), a political satire set in the time of King Zog, and *Vit i hidhur* (The Bitter Year, 1995).

Laço is also the author of several volumes of short stories, which tend to be more highly regarded than his novels and plays and are often built around a single dominant character. A number of them are also set in the days of the Albanian struggle against the Germans in World War II and in a few instances introduce the figures of Albanian collaborationists. Some stories shed light on the isolated life of Albanian immigrants to the United States and their nostalgia for their homeland. Others deal with Albanian immigrants who return to Albania after World War II and the establishment of a communist government. Laço's collections of short stories include *Era e tokës* (Wind and Earth, 1965); *Rruga e bardhë* (The White Road, 1967); *Tregime* (Stories, 1971); *Tregime të zgjedhura* (Selected Stories, 1974); *Portar e dashurisë* (The Gates of Love, 1980); *Një ditë dhe një jetë* (A Day and a Life, 1983); *Një dimër tjetër* (Another Winter, 1986); *Zemërimi i një njeriu të urtë* (The

Wrath of a Wise Man, 1990); and *Mozaik dashurish* (Mosaic of Love, 1998). Laço's dramatic works, for the most part social and political plays, include *Duke gdhirë viti 1945* (At the Dawn of the Year 1945, 1975); *Katër drama* (Four Plays, 1979); *Ditë dhe njerëz: Pas heshtjes* (Day and Man: After the Silence, 1983); *Një nuse për Stasin: Shi në plazh* (A Bride for Stasin: Rain at the Beach, 1985); and *Qyteti i akuzuar: Një det helmi* (The Town Stands Accused: A Sea of Poison, 1996). In 1998 a volume of Laço's political and literary essays from 1997 and 1998 appeared under the title *Kohë për të kujtuar, kohë për të harruar: Shënime politike e letrare, 1997–1998* (A Time to Remember, a Time to Forget: Political and Literary Notes, 1997–1998).

Translations: *The Face-Up* (Tirana: 8 Nëntori, 1980); *A Lyrical Tale in Winter,* trans. Ronald Taylor (Tirana: 8 Nëntori, 1988); "The Pain of a Distant Winter," trans. Robert Elsie, in *Description of a Struggle: The Vintage Book of Contemporary Eastern European Writing,* ed. Michael March (New York: Vintage, 1994), 267–73.

Lako, Natasha (b. 1948) Albanian poet and novelist. An outstanding representative of the first generation of Albanian women writers, Lako was born in Korçë, in southeastern Albania. She studied journalism at Tirana University. After the appearance in 1972 of her first book of poetry, *Marsi brënda nësh* (March Within Us), Lako published the novel *Stinët e jetës* (The Seasons of Life) in 1977 and then returned to poetry with such volumes as *E para fjalë e botës* (The World's First Word, 1979); *Këmisha e pranverës* (The Spring Shirt, 1984); *Yllësiand e fjalëve* (Constellation of Words, 1986); *Këmbë dhe duar* (Foot and Hands, 1998); and *Natyre e getë* (Quiet Nature, 1990). In recent years, Lako has been actively involved in promoting Albanian cinematography and currently holds the position of director of the Albanian

Central Film Archive in Tirana. In 2000 she published an article on Albanian film in the second volume of part III of the collective *Storia del cinema mondiale* (History of World Cinema), issued by the Italian publisher Einaudi.

Translations: Eight poems in *An Elusive Eagle Soars: Anthology of Modern Albanian Poetry,* ed. and trans. Robert Elsie (London: Forest, 1993), 151–59.

Lalić, Ivan V. (b. 1931) Serbian poet, critic, and translator. Widely acknowledged as arguably the leading living poet of the former Yugoslavia, Lalić was born in Belgrade, but finished secondary school in Zagreb where he also went on to university to study law. His wife, Branka, is a Croatian, and it was in Zagreb that he published his first volumes of poetry. Lalić eventually returned to Belgrade. To date, Lalić has published some fourteen volumes of poetry: *Bivši devčak* (Once a Boy, 1955); *Vetrovito proleće* (Windy Spring, 1956); *Velika vrata mora* (The Great Gates of the Sea, 1958); *Melisa* (Melissa, 1959); *Argonauti i druge pesme* (The Argonauts and Other Poems, 1961); *Vreme, vatre, vrtovi* (Times, Fires, Gardens, 1961); *Čin* (Act, 1963); *Krug* (Circle, 1968); *Izabrane i nove pesme* (Collected and New Poems, 1969); *Smetnje na vezama* (*Fading Contact,* 1975); *Strašna mera* (*The Passionate Measure,* 1984), which won the important Branko Miljković literary award in 1984; *Pesme* (Poems, 1987); *Vizantija* (Byzantium, 1988); and *Pismo* (Script, 1992). The selection of the poems included in *Izabrane i nove pesme* (Collected and New Poems, 1969) was made by Lalić himself, who regards this as the definitive collection of his early verse.

Lalić is a superb as well as productive poet. He has operated with a variety of verse forms and is a master of brilliantly inventive metaphors and similes. Although his range of interests is broad, from classical antiquity to contemporary subjects, certain recurring elements can be noted. A native Serb with important ties to Croatia, Lalić is equally respectful of the Orthodox Christian and Eastern traditions of Serbia and the Roman Catholic and Western traditions of Croatia. Thus a number of his poems are addressed to other Serbian writers (the talented poet Branko Miljković, who hanged himself at age twenty-seven in 1961, and the interwar poet Rastko Petrović) and associated with prominent events in Serbian history: the fortress of Smederevo; the medieval monastery of Resava, or Manasija, Kosovo; the Kalamegdan fortress; the feudal principality of Raška; Sarajevo and the assassination of Archduke Franz Ferdinand of Austria in 1914. Lalić's fascination with Byzantium, with whose history that of the South Slavs is closely intertwined, has been especially productive, as evidenced in the resplendent series of poems on Byzantine topics. But Lalić can with equal facility devote a poetic cycle to the lovely city of Dubrovnik, the gem of Croatia's Dalmatian litoral. A man of cosmopolitan culture, Lalić has also written a number of poems on aspects of classical mythology and civilization and on cultural monuments and landscapes in Italy (Rome, Ravenna, Venice), Austria (Vienna), and Germany (Wittenberg). His strong attraction to Venice, in particular, is natural in light of the ties of history binding Venice and the Byzantine world.

Lalić's obvious love of the sea—the Adriatic, the Mediterranean, the Tyrhennian ("a scented rag of blue/Torn apart by the thousand hooves of the sinewed air")—is reflected in his many poems with maritime motifs. Lalić is an extraordinarily visual poet, and the sea is never static in his poetry, but is alive and vibrant with shimmering colors. The sea also has a metaphoric significance to the poet in that sailing it is likened to the journey of man on earth in which the act of sailing itself matters far more than the end, the destination. There is hardly a season of the year or an aspect of nature that is not represented in Lalić's poetic canon, and his lyric celebration of nature is an extraordinary canvas of color and light. Having lived through the horrors of World War II in his native Yugoslavia, Lalić is no stranger to death. Its presence in his poetry is prominent—for example, in his touching "My Mother's Memorial"; "A Poet's Grave," about the death of the poet Rastko Petrović; and "Requiem," which is dedicated to "The seven hundred from the church in Glina," a reference to the massacre of Orthodox Serbs in the church in Glina in 1941 carried out by members of the Croatian fascist military organization known as the Ustaša.

As a translator of foreign poetry, Lalić has been strongly attracted to the Germans Friedrich Hölderlin and Rainer Maria Rilke, the Americans Walt Whitman and T. S. Eliot, and the Frenchman Charles Baudelaire.

Literature: Although he is well represented in translation, especially into English, there is as yet no monograph on Lalić. Probably the best introduction to his work in English is Francis R. Jones's introductions to his two volumes of translations, *The Passionate Measure* (London: Anvil, 1989) and *A Rusty Needle* (London: Anvil, 1996), and Charles Simic's introduction to his book of translations, *Roll Call of Mirrors: Selected Poems of Ivan Lalić* (Middletown, Conn.: Wesleyan University Press, 1988).

Translations: *Fading Contact,* trans. Francis R. Jones (London: Anvil, 1997); *Fire Gardens: Selected Poems, 1956–1969,* trans. Charles Simic and C. W. Truesdale (New York: New Rivers Press, 1970); *Last Quarter: Poems from The Passionate Measure* trans. Francis R. Jones (London: Anvil, 1987); *The Passionate Measure,* trans. Francis R. Jones (London: Anvil, 1989); *Roll Call of Mirrors: Selected Poems of Ivan Lalić,* trans. Charles Simic (Middletown, Conn.: Wesleyan University Press, 1988); *A Rusty Needle,* trans. Francis R. Jones (London: Anvil, 1996); *Works of Love: Selected Poems of Ivan V. Lalić,* trans. Francis R. Jones (London: Anvil, 1981).

Lalić, Mihailo (b. 1914) Serbian novelist and short-story writer. A native of Trepča, Montenegro, Lalić studied law at Belgrade University. He became a communist in his university years and fought as a partisan in World War II. After the war, he was professionally active as a journalist and an editor. He began his literary career in 1948 with a book of short stories under the title *Izvidnica* (Reconaissance Patrol). However, his reputation rests mainly on a series of novels depicting various aspects of World War II in Yugoslavia. They include *Svadba* (The Wedding, 1950); *Zlo proljeće* (The Evil Spring, 1953); *Raskid* (The Break, 1955); *Hajka* (The Chase, 1960); and *Lelejska gora* (*The Wailing Mountain,* 1957). Widely acknowledged as the best of the series, *The Wailing Mountain* is a first-person narrative by a partisan who is being hunted down by anticommunist royalist chetniks in the Montenegran mountains. In the absence of military conflict in the novel, Lalić's principal concern is with the relations between the partisan and various people, mostly villagers, he encounters on his way and his ability to survive amid the strange but magnificent nature all around him.

Translations: *The Wailing Mountain,* trans. Drenka Willen (New York: Harcourt, Brace & World, 1965); "The Shepherdess," trans. Zora Depolo, in *Death of a Simple Giant and Other Modern Yugoslav Stories,* ed. Branko Lenski (New York: Vanguard, 1965), 189–200.

Lange-Müller, Katja (b. 1951) German short-story writer. A native of Berlin, where she spent the first six years of her life in an orphanage and was educated through high school, Lange-Müller worked for a while as a printer and technical editor for the *Berliner Zeitung.* She then studied for two years in an art school before working for five years as a nurse's aid in Berlin hospitals, including a psychiatric clinic. She draws frequently on her hospital experiences in her writing. Lange-Müller left her nurse's practice to study at the Johannes R. Becher Institute for Literature from 1979 to 1982. The next year she spent in Mongolia on a research fellowship, working at times with the sick in Ulan Bator. After her return to Berlin, she was employed briefly as a literary editor before immigrating to West Berlin in 1984. Lange-Müller began her literary career as a short-story writer, publishing her work in several journals and anthologies. Her two published books of stories, *Wehleid: wie im Leben* (Self-pity: As in Life, 1986), for which she won the Ingeborg Bachmann Prize that year, and *Kaspar Hauser: Die Feigheit vorm Freund* (Kaspar Hauser: Cowardice in the Face of a Friend, 1988), first appeared in West German editions. In the former she addresses such isues as illness, loneliness, and death, obviously based on her own experiences, whereas in the latter she deals with all-German social and political issues. A definite tendency toward the experimental in Lange-Müller's writing shows up in her use of free association and, sometimes, unusual word combinations.

Literature: "Katja Lange-Müller," in *Literary Intellectuals and the Dissolution of the State: Professionalism and Conformity in the GDR,* ed. Robert von Hallberg, trans. Kenneth J. Northcott (Chicago: University of Chicago Press, 1996), 236–48.

Translations: "Sometimes Death Comes in Slippers," trans. Dorothy Rosenberg, in *Daughters of Eve: Women's Writing from the German Democratic Republic,* trans. and ed. Nancy Lukens and Dorothy Rosenberg

(Lincoln: University of Nebraska Press, 1993), 295–302.

Lars, Krystyna (b. 1950) Polish poet. A native of Ełk, Lars studied Polish literature at Gdańsk University and became closely affiliated with the poets of the Wolność (Freedom) group. Besides contributing to such local magazines as *Literaria, Punkt,* and *Autograf,* she cofounded and later edited the Gdaśnk quarterly *Tytuł.* Her first volume of poetry was published in 1981 under the title *Ja, Gustaw* (I, Gustav). It was followed by *Chirurgia mystyczna* (Mystical Surgery, 1985) and *Kraina pamiątek* (The Land of Souvenirs, 1991). A poet of striking and freely associated, often surreal, images, many involving weapons (especially knives) and hinting at violence, Lars finds her subjects in a grim urban landscape of menacing characters, hotels, public baths, restrooms, and so on. There is in her poetry a great sense of danger and loneliness and the vulnerability of women in particular.

Translations: Ten poems in *Young Poets of a New Poland: An Anthology,* trans. Donald Pirie (London: Forest, 1993), 1–14.

Lebedinski, Slavko (1939–2000) Serbian short-story writer and novelist. Lebedinski was born in Moscow, but after 1945 lived in Belgrade, where he received almost all his education. His writing reflects a long-standing romance with the Serbian capital and its people. He knew its bright and dark sides and drew much of the inspiration for his writing from it. His first collection of stories, *Poznanik Isak Belj* (My Friend Isak Belj), was published in 1971 and was followed by two subsequent collections, *Baldahin* (Baldachin, 1977) and *Slatka gugutka* (Sweet Turtledove, 1984), which are also predominantly narrated in the first person. *Kasni orasni* (Late Walnuts, 1977), his first novel, was a critical success and was followed in 1999 by *Jevrejska perika* (The

Jewish Wig), for which he won the Oskar Davičo and Prosvetina awards. Admired especially for his great skill at rendering the everyday speech of ordinary Belgrade city dwellers—from young lovers to coffeehouse denizens—viewed in realistic situations, Lebedinski often found his material in the city's tougher neighborhoods and depicted both the violence there and the widespread sense of hopelessness under the communist system.

Translations: "Sweet Turtledove," trans. Amanda Blasko, in *The Prince of Fire: An Anthology of Contemporary Serbian Short Stories,* ed. Radmila J. Gorup and Nadežda Obradović (Pittsburgh: University of Pittsburgh Press, 1998), 152–62.

Lem, Stanisław (b. 1921) Polish novelist and short-story writer. An internationally celebrated master of science fiction, Lem was born in Lwów (now Lviv, Ukraine). He pursued a medical degree at the Jagiellonian University in Kraków and was able to continue his studies during World War II. He also worked for a while as an automobile mechanic. When the war was over, Lem remained in Kraków where he made his literary debut in 1946 as a poet. His first work of science fiction, and one of his best, *Astronauci* (The Astronauts), appeared in 1951. It was followed in 1954 by a collection of short stories under the title *Sezam in inne opowiadania* (Sesame and Other Stories). A gifted and extraordinarily prolific writer whose science fiction combines humor and impressive scientific and technical knowledge, Lem thereafter turned out a large body of work, much of which has appeared in translation. His fiction after *Sezam in inne opowiadania* includes (all novels unless otherwise indicated) *Obłok Magellana* (The Magellan Nebula, 1955); *Czas nieutracony* (Time Not Lost, 1955); *Dialogi* (Dialogues, 1957), a collection of sketches; *Dzienniki gwiazdowe* (*The Star Diaries,* 1957); *Eden* (1959); *Śledztwo* (The Investigation, 1959); *Inwazja z Aldebarana* (Invasion from Aldebaran, 1959), a collection of stories; *Powrót z gwiazd* (*Return from the Stars,* 1961); *Pamiętnik znaleziony w wannie* (*Memoirs Found in a Bathtub,* 1961); *Księga robotów* (The Book of the Robots, 1961), a collection of stories; *Solaris* (1961); *Noc księżycowa* (Lunar Night, 1963), a collection of stories and television scripts; *Bajki robotów* (Tales of Robots, 1964), a collection of stories; *Niezwyciężony i inne opowiadania* (*Invincible and Other Stories,* 1964); *Cyberiada* (*Cyberiad,* 1965), a collection of stories; *Polowania* (Hunts, 1965), a collection of stories; *Ratujmy Kosmos i inne opowiadania* (Let's Save the Cosmos and Other Stories, 1966); *Wysoki Zamek* (*Highcastle,* 1966), an autobiographical work about Lem's childhood and youth in Kraków, its title alluding to the former royal castle on Wawel Hill; *Głos Pana* (*His Master's Voice,* 1968); *Opowieści o pilocie Pirxie* (Tales of the Pilot Pirx, 1968), a collection of stories; *Opowiadania* (Stories, 1969); *Doskonała próżnia* (*A Perfect Vacuum,* 1971); *Katar* (Catarrh, 1976; translated as *The Chain of Chance*); *Kongres futurologiczny* (*The Futurological Congress,* 1978); *Szpital przemienienia* (Hospital of the Transfiguration) and *Wizja lokalna* (Local Vision), both published in 1982; and *Bomba megabitowa* (The Megabyte Bomb, 1999). Lem has also published several volumes of essays and monographs, among them *Wejście na orbitę* (The Entry into Orbit, 1962), a collection of sketches and feuilletons; *Summa techhnologiae* (1964), a collection of sketches; *Filozofia przypadku: Literatura w świetle empirii* (A Philosophy of Chance: Literature in Light of Empiricism, 1968), a study; the two-volume *Fantastyka i futurologia* (The Fantastic and Futurology, 1970), a monograph; *Rozprawy i szkice* (Essays and Sketches, 1975); and *Dziury w całym* (Holes in the Cosmos) and *Ogólna teoria dziur* (A General Theory of Holes), both published in 1997. In 1957 Lem was awarded the Literary Prize of the City of Kraków for *Czas nieutracony* and in 1965 the Literary Prize, Second Class, of the Ministry of Culture and Art for his complete body of work.

Literature: Richard E. Ziegfeld, *Stanislaw Lem* (New York: Ungar, 1985), an introductory monograph; Peter Swirski, ed., *Stanislaw Lem Reader* (Evanston, Ill.: Northwestern University Press, 1997), a useful overview of Lem's work, including interviews with him.

Translations: *The Chain of Chance*, trans. Louis Iribarne (New York: Harcourt Brace Jovanovich, 1978); *Cosmic Carnival of Stanislaw Lem: An Anthology of Entertaining Stories by the Modern Master of Science Fiction*, ed. Michael Kandel (New York: Continuum, 1981); *The Cyberiad: Fables for the Cybernetic Age,* trans. Michael Kandel (London: Secker & Warburg, 1974); *Eden,* trans. Marc E. Heine (San Diego: Harcourt Brace Jovanovich, 1989); *Fiasco,* trans. Michael Kandel (London: Deutsch, 1987); *The Futurological Congress: From the Memoirs of Ijon Tichy,* trans. Michael Kandel (New York: Seabury, 1974); *Highcastle: A Remembrance,* trans. Michael Kandel (New York: Harcourt Brace Jovanovich, 1995); *His Master's Voice,* trans. Michael Kandel (San Diego: Harcourt Brace Jovanovich, 1983); *Hospital of the Transfiguration,* trans. William Brand (San Diego: Harcourt Brace Jovanovich, 1988); *Imaginary Magnitude,* trans. Marc E. Heine (San Diego: Harcourt Brace Jovanovich, 1984); *The Investigation,* trans. Adele Milch (New York: Seabury, 1974); *The Invincible: Science Fiction* (New York: Seabury, 1973); *Memoirs Found in a Bathtub,* trans. Michael Kandel and Christine Rose (New York: Seabury, 1976); *Memoirs of a Space Traveler: Further Reminiscences of Ijon Tichy,* trans. Joel Stern and Maria Swiecicka-Ziemianek (New York: Harcourt Brace Jovanovich, 1982); *Microworlds: Writings on Science Fiction and Fantasy,* trans. Franz Rottensteiner (San Diego: Har-

court Brace Jovanovich, 1984); *More Tales of Pirx the Pilot,* trans. Louis Iribarne and Michael Kandel (San Diego: Harcourt Brace Jovanovich, 1983); *Mortal Engines,* trans. Michael Kandel (New York: Seabury, 1977); *One Human Minute,* trans. Catherine S. Leach (San Diego: Harcourt Brace Jovanovich, 1985); *Peace on Earth,* trans. Elinor Ford with Michael Kandel (New York: Harcourt Brace Jovanovich, 1994); *A Perfect Vacuum,* trans. Michael Kandel (New York: Harcourt Brace Jovanovich, 1979); *Return from the Stars,* trans. Barbara Marszal and Frank Simpson (New York: Harcourt Brace Jovanovich, 1980); *Solaris,* trans. from the French by Joanna Kilmartin and Steve Cox (New York: Walker, 1970); *Stanislaw Lem Reader,* ed. Peter Swirski (Evanston, Ill.: Northwestern University Press, 1997); *The Star Diaries,* trans. Michael Kandel (New York: Seabury, 1976); *Tales of Pirx the Pilot,* trans. Louis Iribarne (New York: Seabury, 1979); "Reflections on My Life," trans. Franz Rottensteiner, in *Four Decades of Polish Essays,* ed. Jan Kott (Evanston, Ill.: Northwestern University Press, 1990), 270–90.

Lenčo, Ján (b. 1933) Slovak novelist and short-story writer. Lenčo is best known for historical novels with ancient settings, such as *Zlaté rúno* (The Golden Fleece, 1979); *Odyseus, bronz a krv* (Odysseus, Bronze and Blood, 1982); and *Kleopatrin mienec* (Cleopatra's Lover, 2000). Lenčo's novels with contemporary settings include the short work *Druhý semester* (Second Semester, 1977), about a young woman soon to leave academia and anxious to make her way in life without the need to prove herself to others, and the novella *Roky v kine Úsmev* (The Years in the Smile Movie House), an amusing novella about what happens in a provincial movie theater after a change of managers. In Lenčo's later book of very short stories, *Nebezpečná Šeherezáda* (Dangerous Sheherezade, 1993), the narrator brings together a group of tales united by the common themes of humans' unquenchable thirst for adventure and need for ideals. The stories range from the title work, with its *A Thousand and One Nights* setting, to one about a world traveler whose primary purpose in visiting foreign lands is to collect stones and then meticulously catalogue them. Lenčo demonstrated his versatility as a writer with his publication as well of a volume of forty-one short science-fiction stories under the title *Socha z Venuše* (The Statue of Venus, 1988). As in most of Lenčo's fiction, the characteristic lightness of style is achieved through the use of narration in the first person, extensive dialogue, and everyday language. This lightness of touch is an important ingredient in the tongue-in-cheek humor of much of his writing.

Lengyel, József (1896–1975) Hungarian novelist, short-story writer, essayist, and playwright. Lengyel began his career during World War I as a poet in the expressionist style. A staunch communist throughout his life, he was one of the founding fathers of the Hungarian Communist Party. However, after the defeat of Béla Kun's Hungarian Republic of Soviets in 1919, he was compelled to leave the country. He lived in Austria, Germany, and the Soviet Union. In 1938 he was arrested, held in prison for several years on false charges, and then deported to Siberia. His release came only in 1953; he returned to Hungary two years later. A number of his short stories deal with the victims of the Stalinist-era trials and draw heavily on his own experiences. Lengyel's novels include *Visegrádi utca* (Visegrádi Street, 1932), a historical novel about the Hungarian Republic of Soviets written in the form of the expressionist montage; *Prenn Ferenc hányatott élete* (Ferenc Prenn's Troubled Life, 1959; translated as *Prenn Drifting*); *Ujra a kezdet* (*The Judge's Chair*, 1964); *Hídépítők* (*The Bridge Builders*,

1966), about the three men who built the famous Chain Bridge in Budapest: Count István Széchenyi, Thierney William Clark, and Adam Clark; *Isten ostora* (The Scourge of God, 1972), about the life of the Hungarian king Attila; and *Szembesítés* (Confrontation, 1973). Lengyel's two major collections of short stories, *Igézo* (The Spell, 1961; translated as *From Beginning to End. The Spell*) and *Elévült tartozás* (*Acta Sanctorum*, 1964), contain two of Lengyel's better known works: "Elejétöl végig" ("From Beginning to End") and "Igézo" ("The Spell"). Lengyel was also the author of a few novels with biblical and classical settings, such as *Ézsau mondja* (So Says Esau, 1969); *Levelek Arisztophanészhez* (Letters to Aristophanes, 1972); and *Argonidész hajói* (Ships of Argonides, 1973).

Translations: *Acta Sanctorum and Other Tales*, trans. Ilona Duczynska (London: Peter Owen, 1970); *The Bridge Builders* (Budapest: Corvina, 1979); *Confrontation*, trans. Anna Novotny (London: Peter Owen, 1973); *From Beginning to End. The Spell*, trans. Ilona Duczynska (London: Peter Owen, 1965); *The Judge's Chair*, trans. Ilona Duczynska (London: Peter Owen, 1968); *Prenn Drifting*, trans. Ilona Duczynska (London: Peter Owen, 1966); "The Forget-Me-Not," trans. Judith Elliott, in *44 Hungarian Short Stories*, ed. Lajos Illés (Budapest: Corvina, 1979), 227–39.

Lengyel, Péter (b. 1939) Hungarian novelist and short-story writer. A native of Budapest, Lengyel tells us that he never knew his father, who died in 1943 while a Soviet prisoner of war. His first three years after the war were spent in an orphanage, following which he grew up on the streets of the city that became his home. He wrote his first story after the suppression of the Hungarian uprising of 1956 and while he was preparing for his high-school graduation examination. The story is about two young Hungarian runaways who take refuge in Paris. At Budapest University, Lengyel studied Italian and Spanish literatures. His first literary success was his widely translated science-fiction novel *Ogg második bolygója* (The Second Planet of the Sun Ogg, 1969). He subsequently published another novel, *Cseréptörés* (Smashing to Smithereens, 1978), and a book of stories, *Rondó* (1982), before his next major success, the huge three-tiered novel *Macskakő* (*Cobblestone*, 1988). The greatest part of the novel is devoted to the daring theft of a famous jewel intended for the imperial family and the intricate police work involved in tracking down the thieves across Europe and Turkey. The work is set in turn-of-the-century Budapest, whose atmosphere the author captures with some flair. In the other tiers of the novel, the author discusses himself as the author of the novel living in present-day Budapest and, less successfully, the origins of the Hungarian people going back to early humans. After *Cobblestone*, Lengyel published another two novels, *Holnapelött* (Before Tomorrow, 1992) and *Mellékszereplök* (Secondary Charactetrs, 1993). He also wrote a whirlwind guide to Budapest called *A város, egy nap* (The City, in One Day, 1992). Lengyel is also known as an able translator who has rendered texts by such diverse writers as Luigi Pirandello and Ernest Hemingway into Hungarian.

Translations: *Cobblestone*, trans. John Bátki (London: Readers International, 1993); "Rising Sun," trans. Oliver A. I. Botar, in *The Penguin World Omnibus of Science Fiction*, ed. Samuel J. Lundwall and Brian W. Aldiss (Harmondsworth: Penguin, 1986).

Levchev, Liubomir (b. 1935) Bulgarian poet, novelist, critic, and memoirist. A native of Troian, Levchev is regarded as one of the foremost Bulgarian poets of the twentieth century, notwithstanding his impeccable communist credentials. He has held such positions as president of the Union of Bulgarian Writers, vice president of the Committe for Culture, and member of the Central Committee of the Bulgarian Communist Party. Levchev's ouput as a poet has been prodgious. Between 1960 and 1996, twenty-eight books of his poetry have been published: *Zavinagi* (For Ever and Ever, 1960); *No predi da ostareia* (Before I Go Out of Date, 1964); *Pristrastiia* (Prejudices, 1966); *Observatoriia* (Observatories, 1967); *Retsital* (Recital, 1968); *Stihotvoreniia* (Poems, 1970); *Strelbishte* (The Shooting Gallery, 1971); *Poemi* (Poems, 1972); *Zvezdoput: Poema s mnogo obrushteniia* (Starway: A Poem with Many Revolutions, 1973); *Svoboda* (Freedom, 1975); *Izhod* (Exit, 1976); *Sledliubov* (Love's Aftermath, 1980); *Luk* (Onions, 1983); *Robotnicheska kruv* (Workers' Blood, 1984); *Baven marsh i drugi stihotvoreniia* (Slow March and Other Poems, 1973); *Samosud: Stihotvoreniia iz deset knigi* (Self-Judgment: Poems from Ten Books, 1975); *Pozdrav kum ogunya* (Salute to Fire, 1978); *Zaklinanie* (Incantation, 1980); *Zaklinaniia* (Incantations, 1981); *Poemi* (Poems, 1981); *Samosud 83: Stihotvoreniia iz chetirinadeset knigi* (Self-Judgment 83: Poems from Fourteen Books, 1983); *Poeziia* (Poetry, 1985), two volumes; *Metronom* (Metronome, 1986); *Sedmata smurt* (The Seventh Death, 1989); *Ritsaria, smurtta i diavola* (The Knight, Death, and the Devil, 1992); *Ovtud, i drugi stihotvoreniia* (Beyond, and Other Poems, 1994); *Bezlunen kalendar: Izbrani stihove, 1955–1995* (Moonless Calendar: Selected Poems, 1955–1995, 1995); and *Nebesen sriv* (Sky Break, 1996). Levchev has also published several volumes of prose, among them *Poeticheskoto izkustvo* (The Art of Poetry, 1986), a study of poetics; a book about the hero in socialist realist literature, *Vreme za geroi* (A Time for Heroes, 1980); a mediocre novel, *Ubii Bulgarina!* (Kill the Bulgarian!, 1988); and a book of memoirs under the title *Ti si sledvashtiiat* (You're Next, 1998). Subtitled "A Novel of Recollections," it reads easily and is particularly interesting in those sections devoted to Levchev's foreign travels (Latin America, for example) and his meetings with foreign communist bigwigs and writers of compatible political persuasion, among them the American Marxist activist Angela Davis, whom Levchev met in Bulgaria along with other representatives of the Black Panther Party of the late 1960s.

Literature: Liuben Georgiev, *Liubomir Levchev* (Sofia: Bulgarski Pisatel, 1985), the only monograph on Levchev in Bulgarian.

Translations: *The Left-Handed One: Poems by Lyubomir Levchev,* trans. John Robert Colombo and Nikola Roussanoff (Toronto: Hounslow, 1977); *The Mysterious Man: Poems by Lyubomir Levchev,* trans. Vladimir Phillipov (Chicago: Ohio University Press, 1980); *Sky Break/Nebesen sriv,* trans. Chtiliana Halatcheva-Rousseva, adapted by Pamela Bond and Niles Bond (Pueblo, Colo.: Passeggiata, 1997), an English–Bulgarian edition; *Stolen Fire: Selected Poems by Lyubomir Levchev,* trans. Ewald Osers (London: Forest/UNESCO, 1986); six poems in *Poets of Bulgaria,* ed. William Meredith (Greensboro, N.C.: Unicorn, 1985), 58–65; eight poems in *Window on the Black Sea: Bulgarian Poetry in Translation,* ed. Richard Harteis, in collaboration with William Meredith (Pittsburgh: Carnegie Mellon University Press, 1992), 63–79.

Levchev, Vladimir (pseudonym Vladimir Liubomirov; b. 1957) Bulgarian poet. A native of Sofia, Levchev graduated from the English-language high school in Sofia and then studied art history at the Bulgarian Academy of Fine and Applied Arts, from which he received his degree in 1982. He was editor of the literary review *Poeziia* from 1982 to 1990 and was on the editorial staff of the Narodna Kultura publishing house. In the autumn of 1989, he was dismissed from

Narodna kultura because of his political activities, which also involved his editorship of the illegal literary and political almanac *Glas.* After the fall of communism in Bulgaria, he was able to resume his former position. Since 1990 he has been in charge of the cultural section of the periodical *Demokratsia* and assistant editor in chief of *Literaturen vestnik.* Levchev has also been a member of the executive committee of Ecoglasnost and the Bulgarian Independent Literary Society. He made his literary debut in 1972 with verse published in *Narodna mladezh* and *Rodna reč* (under the pseudonym Vladimir Liubomirov). His first published book of poetry was *Aritmii* (Arythmias, 1977), followed by *16 stihotvoreniia* (16 Poems, 1981); *Koi sunuva moia zhivot* (Who Dreams My Life, 1983); *Niakoi den* (One of These Days, 1983); *Tsvetia, gradove i moreta* (Flowers, Cities, and the Sea, 1986); and *Peizazh na neizvesten maistor* (Landscape of an Unknown Master, 1987). In a highly metaphorical style, Levchev's poetry addresses universal questions of human existence as well as concrete contemporary social issues. He has also translated such English-language poets as Keats, T. S. Eliot, and Allen Ginsberg.

Translations: Six poems in *Young Poets of a New Bulgaria: An Anthology,* ed. Belin Tonchev (London: Forest, 1990), 72–81; one poem, trans. Carolyn Forché, in *Window on the Black Sea: Bulgarian Poetry in Translation,* ed. Richard Harteis, in collaboration with William Meredith (Pittsburgh: Carnegie Mellon University Press, 1992), 152–53.

Liebmann, Irina (b. 1943) German short-story writer, novelist, playwright, and journalist. Liebmann was born in Moscow and received her early education in Halle. In 1961 she enrolled in Leipzig University, where she eventually earned her degree in Sinology. She immigrated to West Berlin in 1988. From

1965 to 1975, she served as developing nations editor for the foreign affairs journal *Deutsche Aussenpolitik,* and from 1975 (the year in which she became a freelance writer) to 1979 she contributed articles to the *Wochenpost.* Although her first efforts as a creative writer took the form of radio plays, a few of which served as the basis of regular dramatic works, her breakthrough came with the volume of stories *Berliner Mietshaus* (Berlin Apartment House, 1981), in which she paints a realistic picture of everyday life in a closed society such as the German Democratic Republic. Equally successful was her novel of a love affair in divided Berlin, *Mitten im Krieg* (In the Middle of War, 1989). In 1990 her plays were published under the title *Quatschfresser* (Trash Hound). The novels *In Berlin* (In Berlin) and *Wie Gras bis zu Tischen hoch: Ein Spaziergang im Scheunenviertel* (Like Grass as High as a Table: A Stroll in the Scheunen District) followed in 1994 and 1995, respectively. Liebmann was awarded the Aspekte Prize for Literature, the Bremen Prize for Literature, and the Ernst Willner Prize, all in 1987.

Translations: "Sibylle N.," trans. Jan van Heurck, in *The New Sufferings of Young W. and Other Stories from the German Democratic Republic,* ed. Therese Hörnigk and Alexander Stephan (New York: Continuum, 1997), 202–4.

Linhartová, Věra (b. 1938) Czech fiction writer and art historian. A native of Brno in Moravia, Linhartová has lived in France since 1968 and holds the position of curator of Oriental art at the Musée Guimet in Paris. She made her literary debut in 1964 with the novel *Meziprůzkum nejblíž uplynulého* (Intersurvey of the Nearest Past), a work as baffling to critics as it was to readers at the time, the very antithesis of the realistic novel—to say nothing of socialist realism. *Prostor k rozlišení* (Space for Differentiation, 1964); *Rosprav o zdviži* (Discourse on

the Elevator, 1965); *Přestořeč* (Despite Speech, 1966); and *Dům daleko* (Home Far, 1968) are works that brilliantly question narrative conventions and the possibilities of language. Linhartová has been writing in French since 1970, and her published work includes *Twor* and *Portraits carnivores.* She is also the author and editor of studies and theoretical works in the field of art history: *Dada et suurealisme au Japon* (1987), which she edited and translated; *Sur un fond blanc: Écrits japonais sur la peinture du IXe au XIXe siècle* (1996); and *Tàpies,* trans. from the French by Anne Engel (New York: Abrams, 1972).

Translations: "The Road to the Mountains," trans. Ewald Osers, in *This Side of Reality: Modern Czech Writing,* ed. Alexandra Büchler (London: Serpent's Tail, 1996), 18–24.

Lipska, Ewa (b. 1945) Polish poet. A widely known and respected poet of the first post–World War II generation of Polish writers, Lipska was born and educated in Kraków. Although she studied at the Kraków Academy of Fine Arts, poetry remained her true calling. Her first published volume of poems, *Wiersze* (Poems), appeared in 1967. It was followed by four more numerically titled volumes: *Drugi zbiór wierszy* (Second Collection of Poems, 1970); *Trzeci zbiór wierszy* (Third Collection of Poems, 1972); *Czwarty zbiór wierszy* (Fourth Collection of Poems, 1974); and *Piąty zbiór wierszy* (Fifth Collection of Poems, 1979). She subsequently published such additional volumes as *Dom spokojnej młodości* (The House of Quiet Youth, 1978); *Żywa śmierć* (Living Death, 1979); and *Nie o śmierć tutaj chodzi, lecz o biały kordonek* (It's Not About Death Here, but a White Piece of Thread, 1982). In 1985 the underground Warsaw Independent Poets and Artists Publishing House published her collection *Przechowalnia ciemności* (Storeroom of

Darkness). An anthology of her poetry appeared in 1986 under the title *Utwory wybrane* (Selected Poems), and in 1990 she came out with *Strefa ograniczonego postoju* (Short-term Parking Area). In both her short and her longer poems, Lipska conveys a skepticism and even cynicism born of growing disillusionment with the communist-dominated postwar society. In "Instruction Manual" (1990), for example, she writes:

I'm trying to get the country started.
I study the instruction manual carefully.
I turn the nation to the left.
I turn the nation to the right.
But the country doesn't work.

She is keenly aware of her membership in the postwar generation and its vain search for values in a society often perceived as lacking any. Hence her envy, by no means unique, of those who experienced the war. Distrust of language is a recurrent sentiment in her poetry; in one poem she declares that language "like all living things/is ripe for cruelty and treason." Images of death and suicide—in part attributable to her own fight against cancer—pair with those of impermanence and uncertainty. A disarmingly informal poet who uses language sparingly, Lipska often writes in the first person and can combine wit with striking visual images. In 1970 she became poetry editor of the important Kraków publishing house Wydawnictwo Literackie. She later cofounded the literary monthly *Pismo* and edited it from 1981 to 1983. Her literary awards include the Kościelski Fund Award (Geneva, 1973) and the Robert Graves PEN Club Award (1979). She spent the academic year 1975/1976 in the United States on invitation from the International Writing Program of the University of Iowa. Of the poems she wrote based on her experiences in the United States, one of the best is "New

York the Highjacked City" (1982). Her most recent publication is the slim volume of poems *1999*, consisting of just twenty poems intended as a fitting summing up of and farewell to the twentieth century.

Translations: *Poet? Criminal? Madman? Poems by Ewa Lipska,* trans. Barbara Plebanek and Tony Howard (London: Forest, 1991).

Lipski, Leo (real name Lep Lipschuetz; b. 1917) Polish short-story writer. Lipski was born in Zurich, but was raised and educated in Kraków. After completing secondary school, he studied psychology and philosophy at the Jagiellonian University in Kraków. He began his literary career as a poet and prose writer before World War II, publishing in such literary journals as *Kuźnia Młodych, Nasz Wyraz,* and *Pion.* When the Germans launched their invasion of Poland on 1 September 1939, Lipski fled east and found refuge in Lwów. However, like many other Poles living in Soviet-occupied eastern Poland, he was arrested in 1940 and sent to a forced-labor camp. After he managed to escape, he joined the Polish army of General Władysław Anders, which re-formed in the Middle East. But severe illness contracted during the army's stay in Iran made him unfit for military service. He eventually settled permanently in Tel Aviv, where, in 1943, his health took a decisive turn for the worse when he suffered a paralyzing stroke. Although his protracted illnesses curtailed Lipski's literary activity, his small output is now highly regarded for his effective use of the grotesque in his two major works: the short-story collection *Dzień i noc* (Day and Night, 1957), consisting of just fifty-six pages in the original, and the seventy-nine-page novella *Piotruś: Apokryf* (Pete: Apocrypha, 1960). The stories in *Dzień i noc* present a harrowing picture of life in a Soviet gulag. Equally rooted in Lipski's own experiences, *Piotruś:*

Apokryf, which has an Israeli setting, is the story of a lonely, handicapped man who has nothing to look forward to except physical decay and death. Lipski is also the author of an unfinished novel, "Niespokojni" ("The Restless"), about the coming of age of a bright but troubled young man. Until 1988, when an underground press in Lublin brought out an edition of his collected stories, Lipski was little known in Poland. All his works had appeared in such émigré Polish journals as *Kultura* in Paris and *Wiadomości* in London. In 1991 the same Lublin publisher also issued a larger (150 pages) collection of his stories under the title *Śmierć i dziewczyna* (Death and the Maiden). *Paryż ze złota* (Golden Paris), a sizable collection of previously unpublished texts, was published in Poland in 2002.

Lipuš, Florjan (pseudonym Boro Kostanek; b. 1937) Slovenian short-story writer, novelist, and playwright. Lipuš is the most distinguished representative of the Slovenian literary community in Austria and is always reckoned in the ranks of contemporary Slovenian writers. He was born in the Austrian town of Lobnig (Slovenian, Lobnik), in Carinthia province, and was raised by a grandmother after his mother was transported to the Ravensbrück concentration camp and killed there, and his father returned late from military service and internment as a prisoner of war. After graduating from parochial school in Tanzenberg in 1958, Lipuš decided on a career in the clergy and entered the theological seminary in Klagenfurt, but left it in 1962. After a variety of jobs, he completed teachers college in 1966 and thereafter worked for a number of years as a teacher and subsequently a headmaster in an elementary school in Lepeň. Since 1985 he has been the principal of the bilingual (German–Slovenian) elementary school in St. Philippen (Slovenian, Šentlipš) in Carinthia. In 1960 Lipuš, with

Erik Prunc and Karel Smolle, founded the Carinthian Slovenian literary review *Mladje;* he served as its editor in chief in 1980/1981.

Lipuš's literary output consists mainly of novels, short stories, and one major play. *Mrtvo oznanilo* (Death Notice), a dramatic allegory about the Slovenian community in Carinthia, was produced in 1962. Lipuš's novels are *Zmote dijaka Tjaža* (The Mistakes of the High-School Student Tjaž, 1972), which in German translation by the well-known Austrian dramatist (of Slovenian origin) Peter Handke, with Helga Mracnikar, has become Lipuš's most celebrated work; *Odstranitev moje vasi* (The Elimination of My Village, 1983); *Jalov pelin* (Barren Wormwood, 1985); *Prošnji dan* (Petition Day, 1987); *Srčne pege* (Spotted Hearts, 1991); and *Stesnitev: Neogibni, a sumljivi opravki z zmedo* (Stesnitev: Unavoidable, but Suspicious Dealings with Chaos, 1995). His collections of short stories include *Črtice mimogrede* (Vignettes by the Way, 1964), published under the pen name Boro Kostanek; *Zgodbe o čuših* (Stories About Owls, 1973); *Škorenj* (The High Boot 1976); and *Izjava* (A Declaration, 1978).

Clearly Lipuš's major work to date, *Zmote dijaka Tjaža* draws heavily on his own experiences as a parochial school and later theological seminary student. Rebelling against the strictness and stifling atmosphere of the Catholic religious school system, Tjaž is expelled from school and home, cannot adjust to the new freedom he finds himself in, and commits suicide. The novel is not Lipuš's only settling of accounts with the authoritarianism of the Roman Catholic Church. His historical novel, *Stesnitev: Neogibni, a sumljivi opravki z zmedo,* which is set in the village of Kapla in southern Carinthia in the year 1670, also takes issue with certain rural religious and other traditions. Strange happenings are invested with portentous meanings by the superstitious townspeople and a clairvoyant's vision, and culminate in the torture, hanging, and dungeon starvation of two brothers accused of murder. Death is also prominent in Lipuš's other novels. *Jalov pelin* tells the story of a traveler who has returned after a long absence to his native town because of the death of his father. As the death vigil in the funeral home evolves into a carnal celebration, the traveler is overcome with memories of the past and instead of paying his last respects to his deceased parent seeks out the places of his childhood and then departs. In *Srčne pege*, a teacher of classical languages retires to the place of his birth and works half time in a museum in order to supplement his pension. At the funeral of a poet he knew, he runs into his youthful love—from whom he was forced to separate by her parents. But she is again taken from him when she suffers a fatal heart attack.

Lipuš's literary awards include the Book Prize of the Austrian Ministry of Education and Art (1981); the Novel Prize of the Austrian Ministry of Education and Art (1982); the Vienna Literar-Mechana Prize (1987); and the Literary Prize of Carinthia Province (1995). In 1985 Lipuš was elected a corresponding member of the Slovenian Academy of Arts and Sciences.

Translations: "The Day of the Country Wake," trans. Dušanka Zabukovec, in *The Imagination of Terra Incognita: Slovenian Writing, 1945–1995*, ed. Aleš Debeljak (Fredonia, N.Y.: White Pine, 1997), 401–10. *Jalov pelin* is available in German as *Die Verweigerung der Wehmut* (Salzburg: Residenz, 1989); *Srčne pege* as *Herzflecken* (Klagenfurt: Wieser, 2000); *Stesnitev: Neogibni, a sumljivi opravki z zmedo* as *Verdächtiger Umgang mit dem Chaos* (Klagenfurt: Wieser, 1997); and *Zmote dijaka Tjaža* as *Der Zögling Tjaz* (Salzburg: Residenz, 1981).

Loest, Erich (pseudonyms Hans Walldorf and Waldemar Nass; b. 1926) German novelist, short-story writer, journalist, and playwright. A native of Mittweida, Saxony, Loest was called to military service while still in school. He served mostly in Slovakia. After the war and work for a time at odd jobs, he finally received his secondary-school diploma and immediately signed on as a correspondent with the *Leipziger Volkszeitung*. His membership in the Socialist Unity Party (communist) in 1947 proved to no avail when his first novel, *Jungen, die übrig bleiben* (Young People Left Behind, 1950), was harshly reviewed in the *Tagliche Rundschau* (the organ of the Soviet military administration) and he was dismissed from his job. Nevertheless, in 1952 he was elected head of the Leipzig branch of the Writers Union. Loest got into trouble again because of his analysis of the workers' uprising on 17 June 1953, but the furor soon diminished. In 1955/1956, he attended the Johannes R. Becher Institute of Literature in Leipzig. Loest's opposition to the Stalinist "cult of personality" and dogmatism in East German cultural life resulted in his arrest in 1957 on charges of having organized "counterrevolutionary groups." He was given a seven-year prison sentence. After his release, he was taken back into the Writers Union, but he left it in 1979 after signing a letter condemning censorship. Loest quit the German Democratic Republic for good in 1981 after receiving an exit visa.

Loest made his literary debut in 1950 with a collection of stories under the title *Nacht über dem See* (Night at Sea), which, like much of his fiction deals, with the trauma experienced by young people raised in the spirit of Nazi ideology in the aftermath of World War II and the downfull of the Hitler regime. This concern is manifest as well in his autobiography, *Durch die Erde ein Riss* (A Tear in the Earth, 1981), in which he also addresses the matter of cultural repression in the GDR. Elsewhere in his fiction, Loest writes about everyday life under socialism, as in *Es geht seinen Gang oder Mühen in unserer Ebene* (It Takes Its Course, or Trouble on Our Level, 1978), the title drawn from a well-known poem by Bertolt Brecht. Once he left the GDR and especially after the tearing down of the Berlin Wall and the reunification of the Germanys, Loest published several books of a largely autobiographical character focusing, in particular, on literary censorship in the GDR, his prison experiences, and his trials and tribulations at the hands of the East German secret police, the Stasi. They include such works as *Der vierte Zensor: Vom Enstehen und Sterben eines Romans in der DDR* (The Fourth Censor: The Emergence and Death of a Novel in the GDR, 1984), about his experiences with the censors over his book *Es geht seinen Gang oder Mühen in unserer Ebene*; *Der Zorn des Schafes: Aus meinen Tagewerk* (It Takes Its Course . . . ; The Anger of the Simpleton: From My Day's Work, 1990); *Die Stasi war mein Eckermann oder: Mein Leben mit der Wanze* (The Stasi Were My Eckermann, or My Life with the Bedbug, 1991), consisting mostly of state and secret-police files about his case; *Heute kommt Westbesuch* (Today We Have a Visitor from the West, 1992), a short work made up of monologues by two former citizens of the GDR who look back on their life under the communist regime that now seems senseless to them; and *Als wir in den Westen kamen: Gedanken eines literarischen Grenzgängers* (When We Came West: Thoughts of a Literary Border Crosser, 1997), a collection of fifty short pieces on a wide variety of subjects, many of interest to historians of the GDR. Closely identified with the history and culture of his native Saxony, Loest based his cynical novel *Völkerschlachtdenkmal* (The Monument to the Battle of Nations, 1984) on Leipzig's sesquicentennial, the origins of the monument in the Napoleonic Wars (when Saxony and Prussia were enemies), and on subsequent Saxon–Prussian relations. The novel is narrated by a man who has been arrested on suspicion of wanting to blow up the monument and whose narrative sweeps from Napoleonic times to the post–World War II communist era. Loest's biography in novel form of the ever-popular writer Karl May, *Swallow, mein wackerer Mustang* (Swallow, My Trusty Mustang, 1980), was well received. So, too, were his travel writings contained in two collections: *Geordnete Rückzüge: Reisefeuilettons* (Orderly Retreats: Travel Feuilletons, 1984) and *Saison in Key West: Reisebilder* (The Season in Key West: Travel Pictures, 1986). Loest is also the author of a number of detective novels published pseudonymously, among them *Pistole mit sechzehn* (The 16-Round Pistol, 1984); *Ein Sachse in Osnabrück* (A Saxon in Osnabrück, 1986); and *Froschkonzert* (String Concert, 1987).

Translations: *The Monument,* trans. Ian Mitchell (London: Secker & Warburg, 1984); "I Have Never Drunk Champagne," trans. Jan van Heurck, in *The New Sufferings of Young W. and Other Stories from the German Democratic Republic,* ed. Therese Hörnigk and Alexander Stephan (New York: Continuum, 1997), 278–91.

Londo, Bardhyl (b. 1948) Albanian poet. Londo was born in the village of Lipë, near Përmet, in the southern interior of Albania. He studied Albanian language and literature at Tirana University, taught school for a number of years in the Përmet district, and then worked for the Tirana literary and cultural journal *Drita*. He began his literary career in 1975 with the publication of a book of poems under the title *Krisma dhe trëndafila* (Shots and Roses). This was followed by *Hapa në rrugë* (Steps in the Street, 1981); *Emrin e ka dashuri* (They Call It Love, 1984); *Si ta qetësoj detin* (How Can I Calm the Sea, 1988); *Vetëm Itaka* (Only Ithaca, 1989); *Kur perënditë ndaluan vetvrajsen* (When the Gods Forbid Suicide,

1995); and *Eksodi i yjeve* (Exodus of the Stars, 1996). *Vetëm Itaka,* which was published in Priština, Kosovo, is a selection of poems drawn from Londo's three previously published collections. In one of the five cycles into which *Vetëm Itaka* is divided—"Vdekja e kish harruar" ("Death Had Forgotten Him")—Londo pays homage to such predecessor Albanian poets as Andon Zako Çajupi (1866–1930), a poet and playwright who lived in Egypt; Ndre Mjeda; Naim Frashëri; Migjeni (acronym of Millosh Gjergi Nikolla; 1911–1938); and Lasgush Poradeci (1899–1987). A poet of melodious, regular verse, Londo writes generally about the feelings evoked in him by everyday experiences. The major exception is the cycle of poems inspired by ancient Ithaca, wherein ancient and contemporary images commingle and Ithaca emerges as an eternal symbol of humanity. In 1988 Londo won the Migjeni Prize for his collection *Si ta qetësoj detin.* He is also the former chairman of the Albanian League of Writers and Artists.

Translations: Thirteen poems in *An Elusive Eagle Soars: Anthology of Modern Albanian Poetry,* ed. and trans. Robert Elsie (London: Forest, 1993), 162–75.

Longinović, Tomislav (b. 1955) Serbian novelist and literary scholar. Long an expatriate in the United States, where he currently holds the position of associate professor of Slavic languages and literatures at the University of Wisconsin in Madison, Longinović settled in the United States after participating in the International Writing Program of the University of Iowa. He received his bachelor's degree in psychology from Belgrade University and his doctorate in comparative literature from the University of Iowa in 1990. Longinović's reputation as a Serbian author rests primarily on his novel *Minut ćutanja: 36 oblika iste mladosti* (A Moment of Silence: 36 Forms of the Same Youth). He began writing it in the late 1970s as a group portrait of disaffected, alienated Serbian youth, many of whom finally emigrate, as did Longinović himself when it became obvious to him that he had little chance of publishing his novel in Yugoslavia. It was only in 1997 that *Minut ćutanja: 36 oblika iste mladosti* was published in Serbia in Longinović's translation from his own English. His most recent major publication in Serbian is a book about the United States published under the title *Sama Amerika* (Just America).

Works in English: *Borderline Culture: The Politics of Identity in Four Twentieth-Century Slavic Novels* (Fayetteville: University of Arkansas Press, 1993).

Lustig, Arnošt (b. 1926) Czech novelist and short-story writer. A native of Prague, Lustig was sixteen when, as a Jew, he was deported to the Theresienstadt concentration camp. In 1944 he was transferred to Auschwitz and then Buchenwald. It was while he was on a death transport to Dachau in the spring of 1945 that he managed to escape during an American air raid and hide in Prague until the end of the war. From 1945 to 1948, he studied journalism at Charles University and worked for Radio Prague, which assigned him to cover the Arab–Jewish war of 1948 when the state of Israel was declared. After returning to Czechoslovakia, he worked in radio, film, and the press. A volume of his reportage was published in 1961 under the title *První stanice štěstí: Reportáže* (The First Station of Happiness). The Soviet invasion of Czechoslovakia in 1968 occurred while Lustig was in Italy. In protest, he decided to remain abroad. In 1970 he immigrated to the United States after a year each in Israel and Zagreb, Yugoslavia. After a summer as a guest of the International Writing Program at the University of Iowa, he moved to Washington, D.C., where he had been offered a teaching position in literature and film at American University.

Lustig's literary career was shaped by his personal experience of the wartime death camps, and most of his writing deals in one way or another with the plight of the Jews during World War II. Often his leading characters are young women whose compassionate and understanding portrayal is a hallmark of his style. His first books of stories—*Noc a naděje* (*Night and Hope*, 1957); *Démanty noci* (*Diamonds of the Night*, 1958); and *Ulice ztracených bratří* (*The Street of Lost Brothers*, 1959)—laid the groundwork for such later works as his compelling short novel *Tma nemá stín* (*Darkness Casts No Shadow*, 1976), about two Jewish children who survive the Holocaust by hiding in the woods; *Nemilovaná: Z deníku sedmnáctileté Perly Sch.* (*The Unloved: From the Diary of Perla S.*, 1979), a poignant tale in diary form of five months in the life of an adolescent prostitute in the Theresienstadt concentration camp; and *Modlitba pro Kateřinu Horovitzovou* (*A Prayer for Katarina Horovitzova*, 1964), about the gassing of a small group of Jews with American passports, caught in Italy in 1943, among them the beautiful young dancer Katerina Horovitzova, who moments from her death yanks the gun from the holster of one of her tormentors and shoots two German officers. The novel, which won the Clement Gottwald State Prize in 1967, has been called by Josef Škvorecký "perhaps the finest short novel to have come out of Bohemia about the suffering of the innocent." In *Neslušné sny* (*Indecent Dreams*, early 1960s), a collection of three novellas set in Prague during the German occupation, Lustig not only shifts the focus from the death camps to the squalor of occupied Prague not long before the liberation, but brings non-Jewish heroines to the fore. The three novellas that make up *Indecent Dreams*—"Blue Day," "The Girl with the Scar," and "Indecent Dreams"—pivot in different ways on the motif of vengeance. In "Blue Day" (one of Lustig's best shorter works), a provincial German prostitute finds herself in the ironic position of being asked for shelter by a haughty Nazi military judge on the eve of the German surrender; in "The Girl with the Scar," his unlikely heroine is an orphaned Czech schoolgirl who summons the courage to murder a German noncommissioned officer who has taken a fancy to her; in "Indecent Dreams," German deserters meet a swift death while Czech women prove as adept as men in exacting revenge on the remaining Germans.

Despite the grim context of most of his novels, novellas, and short stories, Lustig is anything but a depressing writer. Unsentimental and free of self-pity, his emphasis is on the triumph of the human spirit in the terrifying conditions of the camps and on the efforts of the inmates to enjoy whatever moments of normality they can for however long they can. In *The Unloved: From the Diary of Perla S.*, for example, the young prostitute finds refuge from the horrors around her in dreams and fantasy and in recalling normal aspects of life in conversations with two other adolescent inmates. Lustig's nonjudgmental fascination with prostitutes would reemerge in two later works with postwar settings: *Tanga: Dívka z Hamburgu* (Tanga: A Hamburg Girl) and *Colette: Dívka z Antverp* (Colette: An Antwerp Girl), both published in 1992. Several of Lustig's works from the 1960s also address postwar themes: *Dita Saxová* (1962); *Noc a den* (Night and Day, 1962); *Nikoho neponížíš* (Nobody Can Be Humiliated, 1963); *Bílé břízy na podzim* (White Birches in Autumn, 1966), which is openly critical of the politics of the Czech regime at the time; *Hořká vůně mandlí* (The Bitter Scent of Almonds, 1968); and *Miláček* (The Lover), about a Czech Jew's divided loyalties during the Arab–Israeli war of 1968. The last was originally published in Prague in 1969, but part of the print run was destroyed by order of the authorities; a new edition came out in Toronto in 1973. The best of these works by far is *Dita Saxová*. It is a finely crafted, and poignant, novel about the emotional and erotic problems a lovely nineteen-year-old Jewish survivor of the concentration camps experiences in trying to reconcile the horrors she has lived through and the need to create a semblance of normal existence in the postwar world. Lustig's more recent writings include the novels *Dům vracené ozvěny* (*House of Returned Echoes,* 1994); *Kamarádi* (Comrades, 1995); *Porgess* (1995); and *Propast* (The Chasm, 1996). Publication of a collected edition of his works was begun in Prague in 1995. That Lustig's lasting literary fame will rest on his remarkable writings about the Holocaust is evident in their now being published under the collective title *Children of the Holocaust.*

Literature: The only monograph on Lustig is the short Czech study by Aleš Haman, *Arnošt Lustig* (Jinočany: H + H, 1995).

Translations: *Children of the Holocaust: Selections,* trans. Jeanne Němcová and George Theiner (Evanston, Ill.: Northwestern University Press, 1995); *Darkness Casts No Shadows,* trans. Jeanne Němcová (Washington, D.C.: Inscape, 1976); *Diamonds of the Night,* trans. Jeanne Němcová (Washington, D.C.: Inscape, 1978); *Dita Sax,* trans. George Theiner (London: Hutchinson, 1966); *Dita Saxova,* trans. Jeanne Němcová (New York: Harper & Row, 1979; Evanston, Ill.: Northwestern University Press, 1993); *House of Returned Echoes,* trans. Josef Lustig (Evanston, Ill.: Northwestern University Press, 2001); *Indecent Dreams: Selections,* trans. by various hands (Evanston, Ill.: Northwestern University Press, 1988); *Night and Hope,* trans. George Theiner (Washington, D.C.: Inscape, 1976); *A Prayer for Katarina Horovitzova,* trans. Jeanne Němcová (New York: Harper & Row, 1973); *The Street of Lost Brothers,* trans. by various hands (Evanston, Ill.: Northwestern University Press, 1990); *The Unloved: From the Diary of Perla S.,* trans. Vera Kalina-Levine (New York: Arbor House, 1986; Evanston, Ill.: Northwestern University Press, 1996).

Madej, Bogdan (b. 1934) Polish novelist and short-story writer. Madej is a highly respected writer whose fictional exposures of the reality of life in communist Poland and anti-Soviet hostility made it impossible for him to publish his works in Poland in the 1970s. He was born in the village of Mikaszewicze, in the Polesie region of eastern Poland, and was raised in the city of Grodno until the Soviet invasion in 1940, when his family resettled in German-occupied Poland. He lived subsequently in Białystok, Rzeszów, and Chełm, and finally took up residence in Lublin. Although he began publishing in the periodical press as early as 1958, Madej came out with his first book of short stories, *Młodzi dorośli ludzie* (Young Grownups) in 1964. It was followed by the novels *Uczta* (The Feast, 1965) and *Konstelacja* (Constellation, 1968). His next book, the grotesque and absurdist novel about everyday life under communism *Piękne kalalie albo dojrzewanie miłości* (A Fine Mess, or Suspicion of Love, 1974), was denied publication in Poland and was brought out in Paris by the Polish émigré publishing house Instytut Literacki. Although his reputation as a writer was steadily growing, the first work that brought Madej literary fame was *Maść na szczury* (Ointment for Rats, 1977), a collection of satirical short stories mostly dealing with the compromises that people have to make just to get by in People's Poland. It, too, was first published in Paris, where it proved immensely popular among Polish émigrés and was eventually reprinted several times in Poland. Arguably the best story in the collection, "Kurs na lewo" ("Left Course"), was, like other works by Madej, eventually made into a film.

After the appearance in the underground press of his condemnatory historical-political essay *Polska w orbicie Związku Radzieckiego* (Poland in the Orbit of the Soviet Union, 1978), Madej found it virtually impossible to pursue a public literary career and published nothing for the next twenty years. It was only in 1997, after the collapse of the Polish communist regime, that he reappeared in print with *Półtraktat o lewitacji* (A Semi-Treatise on Levitation), a collection of seven stories of an autobiographical character ranging from a childhood episode to disturbing pictures of corruption and an ever-present and oppressive bureaucracy in post–World War II and postcommunist Poland. Despite the obvious cynicism and skepticism, Madej is at his best as a satirist whose sense of humor allows him to "levitate" above the mess he describes. In 1998 Madej was awarded the Kościelski Foundation Prize.

Madžunkov, Mitko (b. 1943) Macedonian short-story writer, playwright, and novelist. Madžunkov made his literary debut in 1970 with the short-story collection *Čudna sredba* (Strange Meeting). He published a second collection, *Ubi govorljivog psa* (Kill the Talkative Dog), in 1972 before taking a temporary leave from the genre to devote himself to novel writing. His first novel, *Nad troskotot oblaci* (Clouds over the Weed), came out in 1974 and was followed by *Kula na ridot* (The Tower on the Hill, 1981); *Mirisot na zemjata* (The Smell of the Earth, 1984); and *Kon dragata zemja* (Toward the Other World,1993). Madžunkov returned to

the short story with his collection *Megjata na svetot* (The Edge of the World), which appeared in 1985. Another collection of short stories, *Paradoksalen son* (Paradoxical Dream), was published in 1987. In his short stories and novels, Madžunkov conjures a world of the mysterious, frightening, and fantastic. In 1996 he published the dramatic trilogy *Večna igra* (Eternal Game), consisting of *Golemiot smok* (The Big Grass Snake), *Senkata* (The Shadow), and *Pusta zemja* (Wasteland). Folkish in style and local in interest, the trilogy charts the course of strange events after the Big Grass Snake appears in the town of Strumitsa in 1963, as recounted in *Golemiot smok*. *Senkata* is also set in Strumitsa, but in the 1980s. However, the action of *Pusta zemja* takes place "in eternity."

Translations: "The House of Lunatics" and "The Purge," trans. Milena Mitrovska and Michael Black, in *Antologija na makedonskiot postmodernistički raskaz/Anthology of the Macedonian Postmodern Short Story,* ed. Savo Cvetanovski (Skopje: Naša Kniga, 1990), 42–45, 46–55, a Macedonian–English-edition.

Mahmutefendić, Sead (b. 1949) Bosnian Muslim novelist, essayist, and journalist. A native of Sarajevo, Mahmutefendić studied language and literature at Sarajevo University and then taught Croatian and Latin at a school in Rijeka, Croatia. A member of the Croatian Writers Association, he is well known as a columnist for several daily newspapers and as a writer of philosophical, anthropological, and theological essays, some of which have been broadcast on radio. Mahmutefendić published his first book, *Knjiga opsjena i privida* (The Book of Illusions and Visions), in 1991. It was soon followed by *Kelvinova nula* (Zero on the Kelvin Scale, 1993); *Knjiga sna i nespokoja* (The Book of Dream and Anxiety, 1994); *Ribe i jednooki Jack* (Fish and One-eyed

Jack, 1995); *Memorandum za rekonkvistu* (A Memorandum for Reconquest, 1995); *Centrifugalni gradjani* (Centrifugal Citizens, 1996); and *Zezanje Salke Pirije* (Making Merry with Salko Pirija, 1997). Mahmutefendić is a writer of catastrophic events whose outlook on life, shaped by these events, tends toward the cataclysmic. In consequence, his expository writing and fiction are characterized by a relativization of values and extensive use of irony (including self-irony) and the grotesque. His most recent works, the novels *Centrifugalni gradjani* and *Zezanje Salke Pirije*, are set in a provincial Bosnian town and indirectly trace the rise and collapse of communism from the late 1940s to the late 1980s. In essence a family novel, the multi-narrative *Centrifugalni gradjani* explores the impact of the protracted death from cancer of Lejla Kajtaz on her husband, Osman, and their son, Zulfikar. In the wake of her death, Zulfikar launches into a stream-of-consciousness confessional that becomes progressively more linguistically exuberant and grotesque and consumes the last 60 pages of the 180-page novel. *Zezanje Salke Pirije* is another multinarrative postmodern novel that begins in the 1950s and recounts the legend of an American Indian named Bull-Who-Has-No-Peace and is in reality a young Serb named Salko Pirija who is fascinated with American cowboys and Indians and who commits suicide at the age of twenty-eight. Certainly on one level, the novel can be viewed as a takeoff on the European (and especially Eastern European) fascination with American popular culture.

Maj, Bronisław (b. 1953) Polish poet, essayist, and literary critic. A native of Kraków, where he studied Polish literature at the Jagiellonian University, Maj worked as a scriptwriter and an actor for the KTO Theater. He was also in charge of the arts section of the local bi-weekly, *Student*, which was shut down during the period of martial law. In 1983 he and Jerzy Pilch organized the journal *Na Głos* (Out Loud), which consisted of recorded readings of poetry and prose, lectures, and interviews. The audio journal eventually evolved into a highly regarded printed quarterly. As a poet, Maj has published several volumes of verse: *Wiersze* (Poems, 1980); *Taka wolność* (That Kind of Freedom, 1981); *Wspólne powietrze* (The Air We Share, 1981); *Zmęczenie* (Fatigue, 1986); and *Zagłada świętego miasta* (The Annihilation of the Holy City, 1986), which was published by a Polish émigré press in London. Maj's most recent published work is *Kronika wydarzeń artystycznych, kulturalnych, towarzystkich i innych* (A Chronicle of Artistic, Cultural, Social, and Other Events, 1997), a collection of clever feuilletons that originally appeared in the Kraków paper *Gazeta Wyborcza* in the fall of 1993. In her preface to the Polish edition, the Nobel Prize–winning poet Wisława Szymborska has kind words for the collection and remarks that the greatest Polish feuilletonist, the poet and prose writer Antoni Słonimski, would look approvingly on Maj as one of his pupils.

Translations: Seven poems in *Polish Poetry of the Last Two Decades of Communist Rule: Spoiling Cannibals' Fun,* ed. and trans. Stanisław Barańczak and Clare Cavanagh (Evanston, Ill.: Northwestern University Press, 1991), 178–82; fourteen poems in *Young Poets of a New Poland: An Anthology,* trans. Donald Pirie (London: Forest, 1993), 60–74.

Mălăncioiu, Ileana (b. 1940) Romanian poet. A highly regarded and productive poet, Mălăncioiu was born in the village of Godeni, in the Argeş region. She studied philosophy at Bucharest University, from which she graduated in 1968. Seven years later, she received her doctorate with a dissertation on the tragic. Mălăncioiu made her literary debut as a poet in 1965 in the journal *Luceafărul.* Her first book of poems, *Pasărea tăiată*

(The Slaughtered Bird), was published in 1967. It was followed by *Către Îeronim* (Toward Hieronymous, 1970), for which she received an award from the review *Argeş*. Nine more volumes of Mălăncioiu's poetry were published between 1971 and 1996: *Inime reginei* (Heart of the Queen, 1971); *Poezii* (Poems, 1973); *Crini pentru domnişoara mireasă* (Lilies for the Bride, 1973), which was honored by the Romanian Academy; *Ardere de tot* (Everything Afire, 1976); *Peste zona interzisă* (Across the Forbidden Zone, 1979), which won the Writers Union Prize; *Soră mea de dincolo* (My Sister from Beyond, 1980); *Linia vieţii* (Life Line, 1982), which won the Prize of the Association of Bucharest Writers; *Urcarea muntelui* (Climbing the Mountain, 1985; rev. and enl. ed., 1992), for which Mălăncioiu won her second Writers Union Prize; and *Poezii* (Poems, 1996). In 1992 a new edition of *Ardere de tot*, containing poems from all her previously published collections as well as unpublished poems from the period 1982 to 1991, was published. Her volume *Soră mea de dincolo* was also reissued in 1992 and was awarded the "Urmaşii Văcăreştilor" ("Descendants of the Cowherds") Prize for the most beautiful book of poetry. Apart from her poetry writing, Mălăncioiu has held various editorial positions at Romanian TV, the Animafilm studio, and the literary journals *Argeş* and *Viaţa Românească*, and currently writes a regular column, "Cronica melancoliei" ("Chronicle of Melancholy"), for *România literară*. A formally conservative poet, Mălăncioiu writes in a consistently personal vein with recurring motifs of loneliness, resignation, melancholy, and the wintry and funereal.

Translations: *Peste zona interzisă/Across the Forbidden Zone*, trans. Dan Duţescu (Bucharest: Eminescu, 1985), a Romanian–English edition of 124 poems.

Maleski, Vlado (1919–1984) Macedonian novelist and short-story writer. Acknowledged as the author of the Macedonian national anthem in 1943 or 1944, Maleski was born in Struga. After receiving his early education in Albania, he attended high school in the Macedonian city of Bitola. In 1939 he entered the Faculty of Law of Belgrade University, but his studies were interrupted by the outbreak of World War II. He joined the Macedonian resistance movement, and in the postwar period served in the diplomatic corps. His literary career began with the publication in 1950 of his first collection of short stories, *Gjurgjina alova* (George's Crimson). This set the pattern for much of his subsequent fiction, which deals with the war. Maleski was the author of several collections of short stories and/or novellas, three novels, and a book of essays. His books of shorter fiction include *Branuvanja* (Groundswells, 1953); *Vojnata, lugje, vojnata* (The War, People, the War, 1967), a collection of six novellas from the period 1945 to 1954; *Sinovi* (Sons, 1969), its title derived from one of the texts in *Vojnata, lugje, vojnata*; *Kazuvania* (Tales, 1976); and the posthumously published collection *Selenkata od Kopačka* (The Girl from Kopačka, 1988). Maleski's first novel, *Ona što beše nebo* (That Was Heaven, 1958), like most of his stories, was inspired by World War II. His second novel, *Razboj* (Loom, 1969), widely acclaimed as one of the best Macedonian novels of the postwar period, is deeply rooted in the history and life of his native Struga. It was also to Struga and the Struga region that the impressive compilation *Struga i Strusko: Istorija, stopanstvo, kultura, umetnost, obrazovanje, zdravstvo, fizicka kultura* (Struga and Strusko: History, Economy, Culture, Art, Education, Health, Physical Culture, 1970), which Maleski edited, was devoted. His last published novel was *Zapisi za Ezerko Drimski* (Notes on Little Lake Drim, 1980). An edition of Maleski's collected works in five volumes was published in Skopje in 1976, the year in which

Maleski published a book of essays and polemics under the title *Razgledi* (Views), based on his experiences as an editor of the literary journal of the same name.

Translations: "Dipithon," in *The Big Horse and Other Stories of Modern Macedonia,* ed. Milne Holton (Columbia: University of Missouri Press, 1974), 25–42.

Mandič, Slobodan (b. 1947) Serbian novelist and short-story writer. Mandič is a talented writer whose subjects are drawn mostly from rural life but who departs from the familiar conventions of the genre. His desire to strike out on new paths is manifest in his two collections of short stories, *Za vremenom kiša* (In the Rainy Season, 1977) and *Petoljetka* (The Five-Year Plan, 1985), and in his four novels: *Vreme očeva* (The Time of Fathers, 1987); *Hronika napuštenih kuča* (The Chronicle of the Abandoned Houses, 1988); *Kolonisti* (The Colonists, 1996); and *Kairos* (Cairos: God of Instantaneous Happiness, 1998). Arguably the best of Mandič's novels, *Vreme očeva* captures the frustrations and general sense of purposelessness of educated young people of rural background caught up in the turmoil of the revolutionary year 1968. Written in colloquial style, with the curious feature of explanatory footnotes, the novel emphasizes the generational conflict as fathers fail to understand the student demonstrations of the time. *Kairos,* Mandič's most recent work, offers valuable insights into the social and moral impact of collectivization on a rural Yugoslav community after World War II but gives way to the bizarre story of the narrator's love life. When his penis is cut off by a woman with whom he has had a brief affair, he drives the woman he truly loves to leave him after he expresses doubt that the child she is carrying is his. However, in Mandič's world, all's well that ends well. The lover's member is reattached and functions normally, his beloved returns to him, they marry, and he finally finds happiness in the context of family life complete with children.

Mándy, Iván (b. 1916) Hungarian novelist, short-story writer, and playwright. One of contemporary Hungary's most esteemed and popular writers, Mándy, a native of Budapest, has made the bleak world of lower-middle-class Budapest—with its urban decay, forlorn shabbiness, and odd characters—the focus of most of his works, beginning with his first collection of stories, published in 1943. Although lacking higher education (he did not even finish high school), Mándy honed his literary skills by writing sports pieces for various journals and plays for radio, sometimes under pseudonyms. His first big success as a writer came in 1948 with the novel *Francia kulcs* (The Spanner), which deals with much the same bleak world as his early stories. It was also in 1948 that he won the prestigious Baumgartner Prize for his novel *A huszonegy-dik utca* (The Twenty-first Street). His next novel, *A pálya szélén* (At the Edge of the Field, 1963), reflects Mándy's interest in sports, especially soccer, and his ability to look beyond the game to the broader social context and the everyday misery and emptiness of people for whom sports contests offer a brief diversion. Mándy's subsequent novels include *A locsolókocsi* (The Water Wagon, 1965); *Egy ember álma* (A Man's Dream, 1972); *Mi az, öreg?* (What's Up, Old Boy?, 1972); *Bútorok* (Pieces of Furniture, 1980); *Átkelés* (The Crossing, 1983); and *Strandok, uszodák* (Baths and Swimming Pools, 1984).

Fascinated by film, the potential value of film for literary technique, and the romantic world conjured up by films of the past, Mándy also wrote a trio of novels with films and filmmakers as their subjects: *Régi idők mozija* (Those Good Old Movies, 1967); *Zsámboky mozija* (Zsámboky's Cinema, 1975); and *Álom a színházról* (A Dream About the Theater, 1977). The last work was made into a television opera by István Lang in 1986. Mándy has written a large number of short stories and novellas published in such collections as *Az ördög konyhája* (The Devil's Kitchen, 1965); *Séta a ház körül* (A Walk Around the House, 1966); *Egyérintő* (One Crack, 1969); *Mi van Veráual?* (How Are Things with Vera?, 1970); *Tribünök árnyéka* (The Tribunes' Shadow, 1974); *Fél hat felé* (Around Half Past Five, 1974); *Lány az uszodából* (The Girl from the Swimming Pool, 1977); *Tájak, az én tájaim* (Lands, My Lands, 1981); *Magukra maradtak* (Left Behind, 1986); *Huzatban* (In the Draft, 1992); and *Légyvádasz* (The Fly Hunter, 1996). His one play, *Mélyvíz* (Deep Water, 1961), is a musical about a pair of starcrossed lovers. *Előadók, társszerzők* (Lectures, Fellow Authors), a bold work dealing candidly with the moral and creative dilemmas of the Eastern European writer in the repressive 1950s, appeared in 1970. In 1969 Mándy was awarded the Attila József Prize.

Translations: *Fabulya's Wives and Other Stories,* trans. John Bátki (Budapest: Corvina, 1999); *On the Balcony,* trans. Albert Tezla (Budapest: Corvina, 1988), a collection of stories. *A pálya szélén* is available in German as *Am Rande des Spielfeldes* (Stuttgart: Verlangsanst, 1971). SOUND RECORDING: A sound recording is available of István Lang's television opera based on Mándy's *Álom a színházról* (New York: Hungaraton, 1986).

Manea, Norman (b. 1936) Romanian novelist, short-story writer, and essayist. A native of Bukovina and of Jewish origin, Manea first experienced imprisonment and privation beginning at the age of five when he spent five years in a Ukrainian internment camp in the aftermath of the Soviet takeover of Bessarabia in 1940. By the time he immigrated to the United States in 1986, Manea was already an established writer on the basis of such works as the novels *Captivi* (Captives, 1970); *Atrium* (1974); and *Cartea fiului* (The Boy's Book, 1976) and the title novella in the collection

Zilele și jocul (Happy Times, 1977; translated as *Compulsory Happiness*). The literary and political circumstances that prompted his emigration are recounted in a collection of essays written between 1988 and 1991, *Despre clovni: dictatorul și artistul* (On Clowns: The Dictator and the Artist, 1992). Manea's literary reputation rests mainly on works published in English in the United States after his emigration from Romania. Apart from his essays, they include the novel *Plicul negru* (*The Black Envelope,* 1986); *Compulsory Happiness;* and a collection of fifteen haunting stories under the title *Octombrie oră opt* (*October, Eight O'Clock,* 1981). Set in Bucharest in the 1980s, and suffused with the mood of malaise and paranoia endemic to communist Romania, *The Black Envelope* is an almost surreal tale of a disgraced professor's attempt to solve the mystery of his father's death some forty years earlier. The novellas in the ironically titled *Compulsory Happiness* share the theme of the grotesque nightmarishness of life in the Romania of Nicolae Ceaușescu. The first, and best, of the four novellas, "The Interrogation," details the unspeakable mental and physical brutality with which agents of the Securitate (Secret Police) pursue the interrogation of a woman prisoner. In "A Window on the Working Class" and "The Trenchcoat," trivial things assume huge significance in a deeply paranoid state obsessed with security and burdened with a mindless bureaucracy. The longest of the stories, "Composite Biography," was originally published in Romania in 1981 while the Ceaușescu regime was still in power. The careers of a loyal Party member and a group of his co-workers in a bank are examined through the looking glass of an "Institute of Futurology." The essays in *On Clowns: The Dictator and the Artist* provide compelling insights especially into the workings of the cultural establishment under the Ceaușescu regime. *Ani de ucenicie ai lui August Prostul* (Auguste the Fool's Apprenticeship Years, 1979), however, is a humorous collection of fragmentary selections from one of the Romanian cultural periodicals from the period 1949 to 1965, intended to expose the banal policies of the literary establishment under the communist regime. Manea is now a professor of literature at Bard College in Annandale-on-Hudson, New York.

Literature: Must reading is Manea's own detailed account of his problems with the censors over his novel *The Black Envelope* in "Censor's Report," in *On Clowns: The Dictator and the Artist* (New York: Grove Weidenfeld, 1992), 69–85.

Translations: *The Black Envelope,* trans. Patrick Camiller (New York: Farrar, Straus and Giroux, 1995); *Compulsory Happiness,* trans. Linda Coverdale (New York: Farrar, Straus and Giroux, 1992); *October, Eight O'Clock,* trans. Cornelia Golna, Anselm Hollo, Mara Soceanu Vamos, Max Bleyleben, Marguerite Dorian, and Elliott B. Urdan (New York: Grove Weidenfeld, 1992); *On Clowns: The Dictator and the Artist* (New York: Grove Weidenfeld, 1992).

Mantov, Dimitur (b. 1930) Bulgarian novelist, short-story writer, and screenwriter. One of contemporary Bulgaria's major historical novelists, Mantov was born in the village of Bosilkovtsi, in the Ruse region. He completed his secondary-school education in Polski Trumbesh and subsequently graduated from Sofia University in 1952 with a degree in law. While a student, he edited several youth journals in which he also published his first literary efforts. In addition to his later professional work as a lawyer and journalist, Mantov held several editorial and administrative positions with such publishing houses as Narodna mladezh (1964–1969), OF (1970–1972), and Knigoizdavane (1973–1975), and was the editor in chief of the Center for Literary Information of the Bulgarian Writers Union (1976–1990). As a writer, Mantov is known above all for his contributions to the development of the Bulgarian historical novel. Of his more than two dozen books, almost all of them historical novels, the best known remains *Ludite glavi* (The Wild Ones, 1972), about the Bulgarian uprising of April 1876. This forms part of his family chronicle *Pradedi i pravnutsi* (Grandfathers and Grandsons, 1990), which also includes *Haidushka kruv* (A Brigand's Blood, 1969); *Zla zemia* (Bad Land, 1970); *Zubato sluntse* (The Jagged Sun, 1975); *Cherven kalendar* (Red Calendar, 1976); and *Kamenno gnezdo* (The Stone Nest, 1980). Other well-known historical works of fiction by Mantov are *Ivan Asen II* (1960); *Svishtov* (1962); *Pencho Slaveikov: Poslednite dni na poeta* (Pencho Slaveikov: The Poet's Last Days, 1967); *Kaloian, tsar na bulgarite* (Kaloian, Czar of the Bulgarians, 1969); *Ivan Asen II: Tsar i samodurets* (Ivan Asen II: Czar and Autocrat, 1970); *Han Krum* (Khan Krum, 1973); *Albigoiska legenda* (The Albigensian Legend, 1974); *Kniaz Boris I* (Prince Boris I, 1978); *Tsar Simeon* (1979); *Tsar Petrovo vreme* (In the Time of Czar Peter, 1981); *Iuzhnabulgarska hronika: Mai–dekemvri 1885* (A South Bulgarian Chronicle: May to December 1885, 1984); *Via mala* (1985); *Haidut Velko* (Velko the Brigand, 1985); *Putiat na poteriata* (The Path of the Search Party, 1988); and *Aleko Konstantinov* (1989). Over the span of his productive literary career, Mantov progressed from narratives of a colorful but essentially superficial and descriptive character to more expressive novels with greater psychological verisimilitude. He also has written historical works for young readers as well as documentary and historical film scripts.

Translations: Excerpt from *Ludite glavi,* in *The Balkan Range: A Bulgarian Reader,* ed. John Robert Colombo and Nikola Roussanoff (Toronto: Hounslow, 1976), 304–9.

Marin, Mariana (real name Mariana Pintilie; b. 1956) Romanian poet. One of the more outstanding of the younger poets who made their literary debuts in the 1980s,

Marin was born in Bucharest where, upon completing secondary school, she studied Romanian literature at Bucharest University. After her graduation, she taught grade school for ten years and worked as a librarian. Her first published collection of poems appeared in 1981 under the title *Un război de o sută de ani* (A War of One Hundred Years). It was awarded the Romanian Writers Union Prize for a first book. Her subsequent collections include *Cinci* (Five, 1983), actually a collective undertaking with the poets Romulus Bucur, Ion Bogdan Lefter, Bogdan Ghiu, and Alexandru Mușina; *Aripa secretă* (The Secret Room, 1986); and *Atelierele* (Ateliers, 1990). *Aripa secretă* is particularly interesting in that it alludes to the ultimately betrayed hiding place of the German Jewish girl Anne Frank in German-occupied Amsterdam. In a familiar ploy by Eastern European writers to circumvent censorship in the darker days of communism, Marin metaphorically suggests through another time and place of repression the existing situation at home. She conducts, as it were, a dialogue with Anne Frank, whose fears and dreams she both shares and chronicles. In this as well as in her other books of poetry, Marin is a somber, pessimistic poet with a keen feeling for the multiplicity of the horrors and betrayals of the life around her and the presence of death. She can at times also be difficult in terms of imagery that does not readily yield meaning. At a time when it was still difficult for Marin to publish in Romania, a French–Romanian edition of her poetry appeared in Paris in 1990 under the title *Carrefour des grandes routes commerciales*. She took a prominent role in the revolution of 1989, after which she worked for the oppositionist literary magazine *Contrapunct*. She has since been dividing her time between Paris and Bucharest.

Translations: Ten poems, trans. Adam J. Sorkin with Mia Nazarie and Angela Jianu, in *An Anthology of Romanian Women Poets*, ed. Adam J. Sorkin and Kurt W. Treptow (New York: East European Monographs, 1994), 127–37; seven poems in *Young Poets of a New Romania: An Anthology*, trans. Brenda Walker with Michaela Celea-Leach, ed. Ion Stoica (London: Forest, 1991), 54–60.

Marinescu, Angela (b. 1941) Romanian poet. A native of Arad, Marinescu studied medicine at Cluj University and then received a degree in psychology from Bucharest University in 1971. She has worked as an editor at *Luceafărul* and is now with *Vatra*. Marinescu made her literary debut as a poet with the volume *Sânge alabastru* (Blue Blood, 1969). This was followed by *Ceară* (Beeswax, 1971); *Poezii* (Poems, 1974); *Poeme albe* (White Poems, 1978); *Structura nopții* (The Structure of Night, 1979); *Blindajul final* (The Final Armoring, 1981); *Var* (Lime, 1989), a volume of selected poems; and *Parcul* (The Park, 1991). Although she was awarded the Writers Union Prize in 1980 for *Structura nopții*, she refused it as a form of political protest. Freely alternating between very short and longer poems and lines of verse, Marinescu is a writer of somber moods, abandonment, loneliness, and hints of violence; she is given to disturbing images of blood and death, attracted and repelled by night and darkness—"black" (*negru*) being one of her favorite adjectives.

Translations: Seven poems in *Silent Voices: An Anthology of Contemporary Romanian Women Poets*, trans. Andrea Deletant and Brenda Walker (London: Forest, 1986), 123–30.

Marinković, Ranko (b. 1914) Croatian short-story writer, playwright, and novelist. A native of the island of Vis, where he was educated as well as in Split and Zagreb, Marinković began his career as a writer before World War II, while a student at Zagreb University from 1931 to 1935. His first book, *Proza* (Prose), was published in 1948 at a time when Marinković held the position of dramatic director of the Croatian National Theater in Zagreb. However, he gained recognition only in 1953 with the publication of his short-story collection *Ruke* (Hands), which has been reprinted several times. The work won the award of the Federation of Writers of Yugoslavia for 1953. Marinković's other major collection of stories, *Pod balkonom* (Under the Balcony), was published in 1982. Apart from his short stories and the novels *Kiklop* (Cyclops, 1971); *Zajednicka kupka: Što da se priča* (The Communal Cup: What's to Tell, 1982), described as an "antinovel"; and *Never More: Roman fuga* (Never More: A Novel Fugue, 1993; original title in English), Marinković is well known as a dramatist on the strength of such plays as *Albatros* (Albatross); *Glorija* (Gloria); *Politeia ili inspektorove spletke* (Politeia, or Inspectorial Intrigues); and *Pustinja* (Desert). *Gloria*, written in 1955, was first published in 1966. All three came out in a single volume under the title *Tri drame* (Three Plays) in 1977. In 1988 they appeared in a collection with a fourth play, *Desert*, titled *Glorija i druge drame* (Gloria and Other Plays). Arguably Marinković's best dramatic work, *Gloria* is based on an interesting juxtaposition of the circus and the church. A beautiful former circus dancer (Gloria) becomes a nun (Sister Magdalene) and is cynically used by priests to take the place of a statue of the Virgin Mary in a cathedral and, by appearing to have some human qualities (moving her eyes, shedding tears), to convince the congregation that she is a miraculous presence. But a foredoomed love develops between Gloria and the priest who exploits and humiliates her, but cannot bring himself to confess his true feelings for her. She returns to the circus and at the end of the play, with the priest in the audience, falls to her death during a dangerous acrobatic act, an obvious suicide. Apart from his plays, Marinković, who was long affiliated with the Academy of Drama in Zagreb, has written extensively on drama and theater. *Geste i grimase* (Gestures and Grimaces), a collection of essays and criticism on various aspects of drama, was published in 1979. In 1986 Marinković published a book of essays on drama, theater, and film under the title *Nevesele oči klauna* (The Clown's Sad Eyes).

Translations: *Gloria*, trans. David Mladinov and Roberta Reeder, in *Five Modern Yugoslav Plays*, ed. Branko Mikasinovich (New York: Cyrco, 1977), 148–266; excerpts from *Kiklop*, trans. Maria Malby, in *Introduction to Yugoslav Literature: An Anthology of Fiction and Poetry*, ed. Branko Mikasinovich, Dragan Milivojević, and Vasa D. Mihailovich (New York: Twayne, 1973), 434–43; "Badges of Rank," trans. Svetozar Brkić, in *New Writing in Yugoslavia*, ed. Bernard Johnson (Harmondsworth: Penguin, 1970), 49–68; "The Hands," trans. Petar Mijušković, in *Introduction to Yugoslav Literature: An Anthology of Fiction and Poetry*, ed. Branko Mikasinovich, Dragan Milivojević, and Vasa D. Mihailovich (New York: Twayne, 1973), 425–33; "The Hands," trans. Petar Mijušković, and "Ashes," trans. Zora Depolo, in *Death of a Simple Giant and Other Modern Yugoslav Stories*, ed. Branko Lenski (New York: Vanguard, 1965), 209–20, 221–46.

Marko, Petro (1913–1991) Albanian novelist and poet. Known mostly for his prose, Marko, long an ardent communist, came to literary prominence first in 1958 with the publication of his antifascist novel *Hasta la vista* (1958; original title in Spanish), which drew heavily on his experiences during the Spanish Civil War of 1936 to 1938. The novel, a kind of second-rate Albanian *Farewell to Arms* with its Albanian hero Gori and its Spanish heroine Anita, is interesting primarily for the light it sheds on the participation of Albanians in the fighting on the side of the republic. Marko's next novel, *Qyteti i fundit* (The Last City, 1960), also has a war theme but this time focuses on the end of the Italian occupation of Albania in World War II. Surrealist in style, in contrast to the straight action prose of *Hasta la vista*, *Qyteti i fundit* became Marko's major work and has been reprinted several times, as recently as 2000. He subsequently published another five novels: *Shpella e piratëve* (The Cave of Pirates, 1964); *Stina e armëve* (The Season for Arms, 1966); *Urata dhia dhe perëndia* (The Priest, the Goat, and God, 1967); *Të thjeshtët* (The Plain Ones, 1984); and *Nata e Ustikës* (Ustica Night, 1989), based on his wartime internment with many other Balkan prisoners on the isolated island of Ustica in the Tyrrhenian Sea north of Sicily. He was also the author of the autobiographical *Intervistë me vetveten: Retë dhe gurët* (An Interview with Myself: Clouds and Stones, 2000).

Markov, Georgi (1929–1978) Bulgarian novelist, playwright, and screenwriter. A well-regarded representative of the "April Generation," Markov became internationally known as the result of his murder by Bulgarian secret agents on Waterloo Bridge in London on 7 September 1978. Much of the notoriety of the case stemmed from the device used to commit the murder, a poison pellet fired from a weapon disguised as an umbrella. A graduate in chemical engineering of Sofia's Polytechnic, which he attended from 1947 to 1952, Markov worked for the next seven years in a metallurgy plant, for a time heading it. He made his literary debut in the late 1950s, first with the story collection *Tsezieva nosht* (Cesium Night, 1957), followed by the science-fiction novel *Pobeditelite na Aiaks* (The Conquerors of Ajax), 1959). He published two more collections of stories and novellas in 1961, *Anketa* (Advertisement) and *Mezhdu noshta i denia* (Between Night and Day), and then in 1962 came out with the novel that made him an overnight success, *Muzhe* (The Men, 1962, 1990). Taking advantage of the thaw permitted under Khrushchev in the USSR, Markov wrote one of the first literary works openly critical of contemporary Bulgarian society. However, he did so in such a way that individuals, with human failing, and not the Communist Party, were portrayed as the culprits, a line the Party itself was promoting. The novel won the Writers Union Prize as the best Bulgarian novel of the year.

Markov subsequently went on to enhance his prestige and popularity as the author of a popular television series about a fictional communist partisan who later becomes an intelligence agent named Major Deianov. But then he suffered a series of reversals when his plays *Da se provresh pod dugata* (Let's Go Under the Rainbow, 1966) and *Komunisti* (Communists, 1969), both dealing with World War II and the communist assumption of power in 1944, and his satirical comedy *Az biah toi* (The Man Who Was Me, 1969) were either closed after several performances or banned from production. It was soon after that that Markov defected and sought, and received, political asylum in Great Britain. During the 1970s, he worked for the Bulgarian section of the BBC in London and then for Radio Free Europe in Munich. He became especially well known for his series of radio essays, later published, about Bulgaria under communism, *Zadochni reportazhi za Bulgaria* (Reports in Absence from Bulgaria). In 1970 he also wrote a play in English, *The Archangel Michael*, which won an award at the Edinburgh Festival in 1974. So incensed were the Bulgarian authorities over his broadcasts from London and Munich that (as it was later established) Markov was secretly condemned in 1972 for "anticommunist and anti-Bulgarian propaganda." His brazen murder, which became an international incident, was proof to many of the lengths the communists would go to eliminate a declared enemy. *Zadochni reportazhi za Bulgaria* was first published in book form in Bulgarian in two volumes in Zurich in 1980 and 1981. It appeared in Bulgaria just a few months after the sweeping political changes of November 1989 and became an instant best-seller. It was followed by the publication in 1991 of *Kogato chasovnitsite sa spreli: Novi zadochni reportazhi za Bulgaria* (When the Clock Stopped: New Reports in Absence from Bulgaria), a second volume of Markov's broadcast essays. In 1989/1990, an official investigation was launched into the circumstances surrounding Markov's murder, and in 1991 he was awarded a posthumous prize for his literary work.

Translations: *The Truth That Killed,* trans. Liliana Brisby, with an introduction by Annabel Markov (London: Weidenfeld and Nicolson, 1983).

Markov, Mladen (b. 1934) Serbian novelist and short-story writer. A native of the village of Samoš in the Banat region (which figures often in his fiction), Markov attended high school in nearby Panchevo but had to leave before graduating because of illness. He spent the next five years in the hospital, after which he worked at a variety of odd jobs in the Panchevo area. It was during this period that he discovered his literary calling and published his first story, "Dobrovoljci" ("Volunteers"). It won second prize in an anonymous contest sponsored by the newspaper *Narodna armija.* The notable writers Ivo Andrić, Dobrica Ćosić, and Erih Koš were members of the selection committee. In 1955 the Sarajevo newspaper *Narodna prosvetja* announced an anonymous all-Yugoslav novel competition. Markov's *Hronika o zaboravljenom selu* (Chronicle of a Forgotten Village) was among the finalists and was printed in 1956. The following year, his novel *Ravnica* (The Plain), which was based on "Volun-

teers," was again selected for publication in the same competition. Markov subsequently entered yet another novel, *Metrovka* (The Folding Measure), in the same competition. Set in Vojvodina in the period of post–World War II Soviet-style collectivization, the novel depicts the hardships inflicted on peasants by the policy of compulsory grain requisitioning. At the very beginning, Markov explains that the title is taken from the Russian name for the device used to measure unripe wheat in order to determine the quantity of grain to be requisitioned from the individual peasant. *Metrovka* was intended to be the first part of a trilogy about village life in the Serbian Banat region during and soon after World War II. Although the novel was purchased for publication under its original title, "Večiti san mračni sveče" ("Eternal Dream, Gloomy Saints"), a reference to the peasants' patron saints, it was not immediately published due to the closing, for financial reasons, of the sponsoring newspaper, *Narodna prosvjeta.* After other similar setbacks, the novel, now carrying its new title, *Metrovka,* was finally brought out in 1972 by the Slova ljubve publishing house.

Markov, who worked as a journalist for over thirteen years, went on to publish several more novellas, short-story collections, and novels. Most deal with World War II: *Likvidacija: Povest o smrti* (The Liquidation: A Tale of Death, 1972), which recounts the grim internment of Yugoslav prisoners of war in German-occupied Norway; *Šta sa otadjbinom* (What Is Happening with the Homeland, 1972), set during World War II; *Banatski voz* (The Banat Train, 1973), a tense World War II story set in the Banat region of Serbia during the Hungarian occupation; *Žablji skok* (Frog's Leap, 1974); *Srednje zvono* (The Middle Bell, 1979); *Za odmor radnog naroda: Tri povesti* (For the Leisure of Working People: Three Novellas, 1978), consisting of the title story, "Šta sada, profesore?"

("What Now, Professor?"), and "Likvidacija: Povest o smrti" ("Liquidation: A Tale of Death"); and *Starci na selu* (Old People in the Country, 1986), for which he was awarded the Andrić Prize in 1986. He also wrote another two novels after *Metrovka*: *Isterivanje Boga* (Wringing the Soul, 1984) and *Pseče groblje* (The Dog Cemetery, 1990).

Translations: "The Banat Train," trans. Vasa D. Mihailovich, in *The Prince of Fire: An Anthology of Contemporary Serbian Short Stories,* ed. Radmila J. Gorup and Nadežda Obradović (Pittsburgh: University of Pittsburgh Press, 1998), 104–9.

Marsall, László (b. 1933) Hungarian poet. Marsall was born in Szeged, where he received his early education before his family moved to Budapest. He experienced war at first hand in the capital and resumed his secondary-school education only in 1949. Three years later, he entered Budapest University where he studied mathematics and physics. An indifferent student who had already begun creative writing, Marsall quit university after three years in order to devote himself entirely to his writing. In 1957, however, he accepted an appointment with Hungarian Radio, with which he has long been affiliated. His first volume of poetry, *Vízjelek* (Watermarks), appeared in 1970. It was followed by *Szerelem alfapont* (Alpha Point of Love, 1977); *Portáncfigurák* (Dance Figures in Dust, 1980); *Egy világ mintája* (A Model for the World, 1987); and *Negyvenegy öregek* (Forty-One Old Men, 1988). A two-volume edition of his selected poems was published in Budapest in 1987 and 1988. A sensual poet, at times startlingly sexual, often inclined toward the surrealistic, Marsall is also fond of images of a disturbing grotesqueness. In 1984 he was awarded the Attila József Prize.

Translations: Three poems in *The Colonnade of Teeth: Modern Hungarian Poetry,* ed. George Gömöri and George Szirtes (Newcastle upon Tyne: Bloodaxe, 1996), 173–76; three poems in *Ocean at the Window: Hungarian Prose and Poetry Since 1945,* ed. Albert Tezla (Minneapolis: University of Minnesota Press, 1980), 347–51.

Martínek, Lubomír (b. 1954) Czech novelist. Martínek was born in České Budějovice, but was taken to Prague by his mother in 1955 after his father's death. He was educated in Prague and earned his university degree in industrial engineering in 1974. After his compulsory military service and a short period of employment, which included work as a stagehand at the celebrated Prague theater Divadlo Na zábradlí (Theater on the Balustrade), he immigrated to Paris in 1979. In addition to holding a variety of odd jobs in France, he took university courses in art history and psychology. Ship travel soon became a passion of Martínek's, and he covered much of Europe as well as other continents by boat. His first book, *Představení* (Introductions), was not allowed to be published in Czechoslovakia and was brought out in Cologne, Germany, in 1986 by the émigré publishing house Index. Although most of Martínek's subsequent fiction was written after he left Czechoslovakia, his works have been printed in his native land since the early 1990s. His second novel, written between September 1985 and April 1986, was *Linka č.2 (Porte Dauphine–Nation)* (Line 2 [Porte Dauphine–Nation], 1992). In fragmentary style, it follows a single rider, Jonáš, as he reads film posters and comments on sights along the Paris Métro route Porte Dauphine–Nation. It was followed by the "fragment" *Persona non grata,* which was published first in Paris in 1988 and then in Bratislava, Slovakia, in 1993. *Sine loco—sine anno* (Without Place, Without Year; original title in Latin); *Palubní nocturnal* (On Deck Nocturnal); and *Errata,* a loosely related trilogy, appeared next in 1990 in the Czech émigré journal *Svědectví* in Paris. *Mys dobré* *beznaděje* (Cape of No Hope) and *Nomad's Land* (original title in English), both of which were published in 1994, are, like much of Martínek's writing, clearly based on personal experiences. They capture the political émigré's appreciation of freedom and, at the same time, his sense of rootlessness and drift.

Márton, László (b. 1959) Hungarian novelist, short-story writer, playwright, and essayist. A native of Budapest, Márton studied literature, sociology, and German at Eötvös Lóránd University. He worked for several years as editor at Helikon Publishers. His first volume of short stories appeared in 1984 under the title *Nagy-budapesti Rémöldözés* (The Great Budapest Monster Chase) and consists of three loosely interrelated novellas and seven stories of different lengths. The collection is notable for Márton's playful experimentalism, intertextuality within the Hungarian literary context, and use of pastiche. *Nagy-budapesti Rém-öldözés* was followed in 1986 by *Lepkék a kalapon* (Butterfiles on the Hat), a collection of three plays, and *Menedék* (The Refuge), a novel. In 1994 Márton was awarded the Book of the Year Prize. His most recent novel, *Jacob Wunschwitz igaz története* (The True Story of Jacob Wunschwitz, 1997), is set in seventeenth-century Germany, in the town of Guben on the Neisse River. It is an overly complex but nevertheless interesting chronicle-like narrative about how an innocent man becomes embroiled though chance in a conflict that eventually costs him his life. Márton has translated works by German Romantic writers, including Heinrich von Kleist's well-known novella *Michael Kohlhaas,* which was clearly the model for *Jacob Wunschwitz igaz története.*

Translations: "Meditation on a Great Big Zero," trans. Bernard Adams, in *Give or Take a Day: Contemporary Hungarian Short Sto-* ries, ed. Lajos Szakolczay (Budapest: Corvina, 1997), 155–86.

Matevski, Mateja (b. 1929) Macedonian poet, translator, and critic. A gifted and widely translated poet, Matevski was born in Istanbul, but shortly after his birth moved with his family to Gostivar, Macedonia. He graduated from the Faculty of Philosophy in Skopje and later studied modern French drama at the Sorbonne in Paris. For several years, he served as editor of the journals *Mlada Literatura* and *Razgledi,* later becoming a professor in the Faculty of Drama at Skopje University. He also became a member of the Academy of Arts and Sciences of Macedonia and president of the Macedonian PEN Center. When his first book of poetry, *Doždovi* (Rains), appeared in 1956, it was obvious that a new sensibility had appeared in Macedonian poetry. The older, more conservative folk-oriented tradition had aleady been challenged, and the search for a new poetic discourse begun with such post–World War II writers as Slavko Janevski, Blaže Koneski, and Aco Šopov was now carried to new heights. By means of a highly symbolic and metaphoric style rich in ambiguity and indirection, Matevski, in *Doždovi* as well as in his successive books of poetry, conveyed a dark, pessimistic view of human life coupled with an ardent desire to understand the meaning of existence. Skeptical of great human constructs, emblems of the futility of power, and the "sterility of hate," Matevski becomes obsessed with time in all its permutations—the subject of many of his poems—and mines a rich vein of nature imagery in his need for respite from existential struggle. His sense of spritual communication with the sea is thought by some to reflect the influence of the Spanish poet Juan Ramón Jiménez, whom Matevski translated. After *Doždovi,* Matevski published another eight volumes of poems: *Ramnodenica* (Equinox, 1963); *Perunika* (Iris, 1976); *Krug*

(The Circle, 1977); *Lipa* (The Linden Tree, 1980); *Ragjanje na tragedijata* (The Birth of Tragedy, 1985); *Oddalečuvanje* (Distancing, 1990); *Crna kula* (*The Black Tower*, 1992), his sole volume of poetry available in English and one of his best; and *Zavevanje* (Permeation, 1996). Two of these stand apart from Matevski's usual thematics and his cosmopolitanism. In *Perunika*, Matevski explores his own poetic development in the context of Macedonian poetic tradition, but tries to find an accommodation between folk traditionalism and a contemporary European sensibility shaped in part by such French modernists as Paul Valéry, to whom Matevski is especially close. In *Ragjanje na tragedijata*, he embarks on a related inquiry by considering poetic thought in different cultures, beginning with the ancient Egyptians and including the Aztecs. Besides Matevski's nine books of poetry, eight volumes of selected poems by him have also been published: *Praznična romansa* (Holiday Romance, 1966); *Zalez* (Sunset, 1969); *Mokjta na svetulkata* (The Power of the Firefly, 1979); *Poezia—Poésie—Poetry* (1985), in Macedonian, French, and English; *Podgotovki za patuvanje* (Traveling Preparations, 1987); *Poezija* (Poetry, 1987); *Maski* (Masks, 1992); and *Letot na crvenata ptica* (The Flight of the Red Bird, 1995). Matevski has also written extensively on Macedonian literature and culture, most notably in his book of essays *Od tradicijata kon idninata* (From Tradition Toward the Future, 1987).

Matevski has been honored many times for his poetry and for his translations from Albanian, French, Italian, Russian, Slovenian, and Spanish. Apart from such Macedonian distinctions as the 11 October Prize, the Brothers Miladinov Prize (twice) at the Struga Poetry Evenings, the Kočo Racin Prize, and the Grigor Prličev Prize (for translation), he has received the Blaise Cendrars Prize, presented annually at Yverdon, Switzerland; the Italian Premio Mediterraneo; the Spanish Fernando Rielo Prize; the Slovenian Županičeva Listina Prize; the Croatian Goranov Vijenac Prize; and the grand prize ("The Lilac") of the first Days of Balkan Poetry festival held in Istanbul in 1996 and organized by the Union of Turkish Writers. Matevski has also been decorated with the French Legion of Honor and Art and Literature medals.

Literature: The best critical study of Matevski is in Macedonian: Blaže Kitanov, *Od pejzažot kon čovekot: Niz poetskiot svet i izraz na Mateja Matevski* (Skopje: Makedonska Kniga, 1985).

Translations: *The Black Tower*, trans. Zoran Ančevski and Ewald Osers (Skopje: Detska Radost, 1996); *Footprints of the Wind: Selected Poems*, trans. Ewald Osers (London: Forest, 1988); six poems in *Contemporary Macedonian Poetry*, ed. and trans. Ewald Osers (London: Forest, 1991), 39–46; nine poems, including a short excerpt from "Ramnodenica," trans. by various hands, in *Reading the Ashes: An Anthology of the Poetry of Modern Macedonia*, ed. Milne Holton and Graham W. Reid (Pittsburgh: University of Pittsburgh Press, 1977), 57–67.

Mehmedinović, Semezdin (b. 1960) Bosnian Muslim short-story writer, poet, and screenwriter. One of the most prominent members of the Bosnian Muslim literary community, Mehmedinović is a native of the village of Kiseljak, near Tuzla. He moved to Sarajevo, where he received a degree in comparative literature and library science and, after completing compulsory military service, became very active in Sarajevo's cultural life. He served, for example, as editor of the journal *Valter* until it fell victim to censorship. Mehmedinović's first book, *Modrac*, a collection of poems, was published in 1984 and won the Trebinje Award for a first book of poetry. His second book, *Emigrant*, appeared in 1990. The following year, he became one of the founders of the journal *Phantom of Liberty,* three issues of which came out in Sarajevo before the war and three during the siege. He wrote the script for and codirected with Benjamin Filipović the film *Mizaldo* (Leaving-Am-I, or The End of Theater), which was shown at the Berlin Film Festival in 1994 and was awarded first prize at the Mediterranean film festival in Rome in 1995. Also in 1995 an expanded version of *Sarajevo Blues* was published in Zagreb. *Sarajevo Blues* (original title in English) was first published at the end of 1992 by the Durieux publishing house of Zagreb, Croatia, and was the first book in the Biblioteka egzil-abc series, issued in Ljubljana, Slovenia, which provided a forum for Bosnian writers and translators under siege or living in exile. It consists of small essays, prose vignettes, and poems born of the terrible ordeal of Sarajevo during the Bosnian war of 1992. Mehmedinović and his family left Bosnia for the United States as political refugees in 1996.

Translations: *Sarajevo Blues,* trans. Ammiel Alcalay (San Francisco: City Lights, 1998).

Mekuli, Esad (1916–1993) Albanian poet and translator. One of the most respected Albanian-language poets and intellectuals of the twentieth century, Mekuli was born in Plava, Montenegro, where he received his early schooling. He attended high schools in Peć, Prizren, and Sarajevo and then went on to Belgrade University, where he earned a degree in veterinary medicine. After World War II, he became the first editor of the Kosovo newspaper *Rilindja* and the founder and long-standing managing editor of the literary review *Jeta e re.* Mekuli, who began writing poems before the war and publishing them in newspapers and magazines throughout Yugoslavia, brought out his first volume of poetry, *Për ty* (For You), in 1955. This was followed by the later collections *Dita e re* (A New Day, 1966); *Avša ada* (Avša Island, 1971);

Vjersha (Poems, 1973); and *Brigjet* (Coasts, 1981). As a poet, Mekuli celebrated his Albanian origins, the land, and the Albanians' love of freedom and the price they have had to pay throughout their history to achieve and preserve it. Some of his best poems were inspired by the rugged nature of his homeland and the nearby sea and its coasts. Fluent as well in Serbo-Croatian, Mekuli also published six collections of poetry in that language: *Na putu* (On the Road, 1964); *Glasovi vremena* (Voices of Time, 1974); *Izmedju voljeti i mrziti* (Between Loving and Hating, 1970); *Avša ada* (Avša Island, 1975); *Pjesme* (Poems, 1981); and *Pjesme* (Selected Poems, 1984). Throughout his career, Meguli was an indefatigable translator from the Yugoslav literatures into Albanian and of a number of Albanian writers into Serbo-Croatian. In recognition of his achievements as poet and translator and as a bridge between the Slav cultures of Albania and the former Yugoslavia, he was made a member of the learned academies of virtually all the republics of the former Yugoslavia as well as of the Acadedmy of Arts and Sciences of Kosovo. He was also the recipient of several literary awards and other distinctions.

Translations: Three poems in *An Elusive Eagle Soars: Anthology of Modern Albanian Poetry,* ed. and trans. Robert Elsie (London: Forest, 1993), 27–30.

Mensching, Steffen (b. 1958) German poet. A native of East Berlin, Mensching studied at the Johannes R. Becher Institute of Literature after graduating from secondary school in 1977. He received his diploma the following year. He then worked for a time with Radio Berlin International and the journal *Temperamente,* and from 1979 to 1988, when the troupe broke up after often being banned from performing by the authorities, he wrote and performed for Hanz-Eckardt Wenzel's "Karls Enkel" satirical cabaret. Mensching first appeared in print as a poet in 1979 in the

Poesiealbum series (no. 146). His first published book of poems, *Erinnerung an eine Milchglassscheibe* (Recollection of a Pane of Frosted Glass), came out in 1983. Unlike the renegade poets of the Prenzlauer Berg Connection, Mensching tended to shun experimentation and the poetics of expressionism and the avant-garde in favor of the proletarian-revolutionary tradition. He had no illusions, however, about socialism and its rhetoric and boldly contrasted the stated ideals with the reality—above all, of private experience. However, he was also critical of West German materialism. Mensching's poetic writing turned more obviously cynical in such later collections as *Tuchfühlung* (Close Contact, 1986) and *Berliner Elegien* (Berlin Elegies, 1989). Mensching's first major prose text was *Die Stadt: Eine Beichte* (The City: A Confession, 1989), which is based on a trip he took to Paris. It was followed in 1990 by the literary hoax *Pygmalion*, subtitled *ein verloren geglaubter dubioser Kolportage-Roman aus dem späten 8oer Jahren entschlüsselt und herausgegeben von Stefan Mensching* (a believed lost dubious trashy novel from the '80s decoded and published by Stefan Mensching) and presented as the work of a friend who sent Mensching the manuscript in the form of a packet of diskettes from Mexico in May 1990 before committing suicide.

Mészöly, Miklós (b. 1921) Hungarian novelist, short-story writer, and playwright. A native of the village of Szekszárd in the Hungarian wine-growing country, Mészöly led a checkered existence until settling down as a student of law and political science at Budapest University. After his early education in local schools, most of his time was spent pursuing such disparate sports as tennis and shot put, hunting, and living a hedonistic life to the full. After receiving his law degree in 1943, he practiced law until called up into the military. He saw action with the Germans on the Russian front, made his way back to

Hungary by a ruse, was found out, was sent back to the front, and wound up a prisoner of war in Serbia. After the war, he abandoned the law in favor of a variety of doomed money-making ventures (including the purchase and editorship of a provincial weekly) and odd jobs. Although he had begun publishing short stories in the antifascist Pécs journal *Sorsunk* in the early 1940s, it was only with the publication in 1948 of his first collection of stories, *Vadvizek* (Floodwater), that he began attracting serious attention as a writer. In 1949 Mészöly settled in Budapest, where he worked briefly with the journals *Rádió* and *Válasz* until the latter closed over internal political rifts. Mészöly himself fell victim to the rigid Stalinism of the 1950s and was barred from further publication. He found an outlet as a script editor for the Budapest Puppet Theater and published only children's stories until 1957. That year, he was able to rejoin the Hungarian literary mainstream with his new collection of stories, *Sötét jelek* (Dark Signs), which comprised works written between 1945 and 1956. However, it was only with publication of his novel *Az atléta halála* (Death of an Athlete, 1966), which features a monomaniacal long-distance runner and drew on his own experiences as an amateur athlete, that his literary stock began to rise. The novel is typical of many of Mészöly's stories in its extreme concentration and the absence of anything extraneous, including "background." His next novel, *Film* (A Movie, 1976), met with a mixed reception largely over its use of the device of a film team following and "shooting" an elderly couple as they take their usual walk through the city, of which they themselves are a part, to capture the atmosphere of a half-century of Hungarian life. Narrated in the first-person plural—the film team as a collective entity—the novel achieves the complete objectivity Mészöly sought. In 1968 Mészöly had already replied to the detractors of his unorthodox and un-Marxist storytelling techniques in his biblical novel, *Saulus* (Saul), in which Saul's conversion is revealed through carefully assembled, mosaic-like fragments of Saul's inner life rather than by means of linear external action.

Mészöly's strong preference for shorter fictional forms, and his skill at the genre, is evident in such collections of short stories and novellas as *Jelentés öt egérről* (Report on Five Mice, 1967), containing stories from the period 1957 to 1964; *Magasiskola* (The Perfect Example, 1967), a short novel; *Pontos történetek útközben* (Precise Stories En Route, 1970); *Alakulások* (Evolvings, 1975), a collection of novellas, short stories, and sketches, several of which had been published in separate editions; *Megbocsátás* (*Forgiveness*, 1984), one of his more compelling collection of stories, about the family of a small-town municipal clerk from early summer to Christmas in the immediate post–World War I period; *Merre a csillag jár* (Where Stars Wander, 1985); and *Volt egyszer egy Közép-Európa* (*Once There Was a Central Europe*, 1989), which includes essays as well as short fiction.

As an essayist on literary theory and aesthetics with a comfortable knowledge of the visual arts, including film and foreign literatures, Mészöly is at his best in such collections as *Tágasság iskolája* (The Discipline of Distance, 1977) and *A pille magánya* (The Loneliness of the Moth, 1989). Recognition came slowly largely because of critical indifference or even hostility to his formal experimentation, which Hungarian critics have related to the French *nouveau roman* or American postmodernism. However, Mészöly's experimentation tends toward the sparse and is not designed to call attention to itself. The novella *Forgiveness* typifies Mészöly's style. Working with conventional material in Hungarian literature, Mészöly transforms the ordinary into the strange by developing odd relationships and introducing an element of enigma by means of an unsolved murder and other strange happenings. In much of Mészöly's fiction, the mysterious, unrelated, and random are hallmarks of a sometimes complex but often fascinating narrative technique. Mészöly's views on life, literature, his own writing, and the politics of East Central Europe are vividly conveyed in a series of interviews with him conducted by László Szigeti and published in 1999 under the title *Párbeszédkísérlet* (Trial Dialogues).

Translations: *Once There Was a Central Europe: Selected Short Stories and Other Writings*, trans. Albert Tezla (Budapest: Corvina, 1997), the best collection of Mészöly's writings in English; *Forgiveness*, trans. John Bátki, in *A Hungarian Quartet: Four Contemporary Short Novels* (Budapest: Corvina, 1991), 89–145; "Report on Five Mice," trans. Janos Fogarasi, in *Hungarian Short Stories*, ed. Paul Varnai (Toronto: Exile Editions, 1983), 8–15.

Mićić-Dimovska, Milica. *See* Dimovska, Milica Mićić

Mickel, Karl (b. 1935) German poet, playwright, and essayist. A native of Dresden, Mickel studied economic history in Berlin, served as editor of the journal *Junge Kunst*, taught economic history from 1965 to 1970 at the Institute of Economics in East Berlin, and then affiliated with Bertolt Brecht's Berliner Ensemble. He began his literary career as a poet with two well-known volumes of verse, *Lobverse und Beschimpfungen* (Poems of Praise and Insults, 1963) and *Vita nova mea—Mein neues Leben* (*Vita nova—My New Life*, 1966). In *Lobverse und Beschimpfungen*, the praise is enthusiastically bestowed on the countries of the socialist bloc for their preservation of world peace, whereas the insults are hurled at the capitalist West, particularly West Germany, for its threat to peace. The *Vita nova mea* collection also contains two essays, one devoted to the German poet Friedrich Klopstock—whom Mickel admired, as opposed, for example, to a post-Romantic like Rainer Maria Rilke—and the other a discussion of the reception of the literary text before, in fact, the subject was taken up in a serious way by theorists. His third collection of poems, *Eisenzeit* (The Iron Age), appeared in 1975.

As a dramatist, Mickel is the author of *Nausikaa* (Nausicaa, 1968); the libretto for the opera *Einstein* (1972), with music by Paul Dessau; and *Celestina* (1974), Mickel's greatest theatrical success, a dramatization of the prose drama by the late-fifteenth-century Spanish writer Fernando de Rojas. Both *Einstein* and *Nausikaa* were published in a single volume in 1974 with the subtitle *Die Schrecken des Humanismus in zwei Stücken* (The Dreads of Humanism in Two Plays). *Nausikaa* is a takeoff on the episode in the *Odyssey* when the shipwrecked Odysseus is washed ashore in the land of Alcinous, the king of the Phaecians. Mickel emphasizes Euryalos's envy over Odysseus's friendship with King Alcinous's daughter, Nausicaa, and his plan to get rid of him. *Einstein* is an antiwar, anti–atomic bomb drama enlivened with the introduction of Casanova, Galileo, Giordano, and da Vinci as characters along with Nazis, American GIs, and the German folk comic figure Hans Wurst.

Mickel's best essays, collected in the volume *Gelehrtenrepublik: Aufsätze und Studien. Essay* (The Republic of the Learned: Essays and Studies. An Essay, 1976), are devoted mainly to his communist and untraditional views on such German writers as Klopstock, Ewald von Kleist, Schiller, and Goethe. The volume also includes imaginary dialogues between Karl Marx and his father, Paul Feuerbach and Martin Luther, and Marx and Friedrich Engels. With Adolf Endler, Mickel published in 1966 what proved to be a controversial anthology of East German poetry since 1945 under the title *In diesem besseren Land: Gedichte der Deutschen Demokratischen Republik seit 1945* (In This Better Land: Poetry of the German Democratic Republic Since 1945). The controversy turned in part on the emphasis on poems in which an outlook on life is expressed through descriptions of landscape.

Literature: "Karl Mickel," in *Literary Intellectuals and the Dissolution of the State: Professionalism and Conformity in the GDR*, ed. Robert von Hallberg, trans. Kenneth J. Northcott (Chicago: University of Chicago Press, 1996), 164–69.

Translations: "The Well-Groomed Head," trans. Ruth Mead and Matthew Mead, and "Lament and Laughter," trans. Michael Hamburger (both from *Vita mea nova*), in German and English, in *East German Poetry: An Anthology*, ed. Michael Hamburger (New York: Dutton, 1973), 158–61.

Mihailović, Dragoslav (b. 1930) Serbian novelist and short-story writer. A native of Ćuprija, Mihailović belongs to the generation of Yugoslav writers who came to the fore in the 1960s. After secondary school, he enrolled in 1949 in the Faculty of Philosophy at Belgrade University to study Yugoslav literature and the Serbo-Croatian language. His studies, however, were interrupted by a serious bout of tuberculosis early in 1950; arrest and imprisonment, including in the notorious Goli otok camp for political prisoners, until the spring of 1952; and obligatory military service in 1952 and 1953. He finally received his university degree in 1957. His first book of short stories, *Frede, laku noć* (Good Night, Fred), was published in 1967 and draws on the author's own experiences in the Goli otok camp. Mihailović was sent to the camp following Yugoslavia's break with the USSR when many people suspected of Soviet sympathies became political detainees. These experiences, as well as teen violence in Belgrade in the late 1940s and early 1950s—which Mihailović also deals with—could be written about openly only in the 1960s. In 1990 Mihailović published a long documentary based on his experience in the camp under the title *Goli otok*. Mihailović's best-known work, the novel *Kad su cvetale tikve* (*When Pumpkins Blossomed*, 1968), deals with the life of a Yugoslav expatriate and former boxer who is married to a Swede and living in Sweden. The novel draws on Mihailović's own experiences as a boxer. It was adapted for stage performance but was withdrawn after fewer than a dozen performances, presumably because of objections on the part of Marshal Tito. *When Pumpkins Blossomed* has been widely translated. *Petrijin venac* (Petrija's Wreath), Mihailović's second novel, appeared in 1975. *Lov na stenice* (Hunt for Bedbugs), a collection of short stories written in the first-person singular and published in 1993, also has prison camp life as its principal theme. In two of the stories in his most recent collection, *Jalova jesen* (Barren Autumn, 2000)—"Najbolji prijatelj" ("The Best Friend") and "Parionicar, general i islednik" ("The Steam Bath Warden, the General, and the Investigator")—Mihailović returns to the subject of his imprisonment in Goli otok. Mihailović received the October Prize of the City of Belgrade in 1967 for *Frede, laku noć*, and the Andrić Prize in 1976 for *Petrijin venac*. He was made a corresponding member of the Serbian Academy of Arts and Sciences in May 1981.

Literature: The best bibliography of works by and on Mihailović appears in Dragoslav Mihailović, *Frede, laku noć* (Belgrade: Prosveta, 1984), 185–241, the first volume of Mihailović's short stories.

Translations: *When Pumpkins Blossomed*, trans. Drenka Willen (New York: Harcourt Brace Jovanovich, 1971); "Catch a Falling Star," trans. Henry R. Cooper Jr. and Gordana B. Todorović, in *The Prince of Fire: An Anthology of Contemporary Short Stories*, ed. Radmila J. Gorup and Nadežda Obradović (Pittsburgh: University of Pittsburgh Press, 1998), 72–81.

Mihaiu, Virgil (b. 1951) Romanian poet. A native of Cluj-Napoca, Mihaiu graduated from the Faculty of Philology of Cluj University in 1974. His professional career has been divided between his writing of poetry and his editorial work with several cultural magazines, among them *Echinox* (1971–1983) and, since 1990, *Steaua* and *Criterion*. He has also served as a member of the editorial staff of the International Jazz Federation's *Jazz Forum*, which is published in Warsaw. Mihaiu's prize-winning first volume of poetry, *Legea conservării adolescenței* (Law for the Conservation of Adolescence), appeared in 1977. It was followed by *Sighişoara, Suedia şi alte stari de spirit* (Sighişoara, Sweden, and Other States of Mind, 1980); *Indicaţiuni pentru balerina din respiraţie* (Directions for the Ballerina out of Breath, 1981); and *Poeme* (Poems, 1986). Many of his poems revolve around everyday, ordinary experiences and occurrences. His most recent volume of poems, *Paradis pierdut în memorie* (Paradise Lost in Memories), appeared in 1993.

Translations: Four poems in *Young Poets of a New Romania: An Anthology*, trans. Brenda Walker with Michaela Celea-Leach, ed. Ion Stoica (London: Forest, 1991), 117–23.

Mihalić, Slavko (b. 1928) Croatian poet and playwright. One of the finest and most respected contemporary Croatian poets, Mihalić was born in Karlovac, the son of a popular local actress and the novelist Stjepan Mihalić. After his secondary education in Karlovac, in 1947 Mihalić moved to Zagreb, where he joined the Croatian editorial office of the recently founded newspaper *Borba*. But he resigned in 1952 in protest against the stifling political atmosphere at the paper and enrolled in courses in Croatian language and literature at Zagreb University. It was there that he became chief editor of the student literary magazine *Tribuna*. In 1953 Mihalić printed his first poems in the then leading literary magazine of the younger generation, *Krugovi*. His first book of verse, *Komorna muzika* (Chamber Music), consisting of only twelve poems, was published in 1954 by a small printing company (Lykos) in Lika, his wife's hometown. The book's title alluded to Mihalić's early interest in music when he attended the Karlovac Music School. His subsequent collections of poems include *Put u nepostojanje* (Road to Non-Being, 1956); *Početak zaborava* (The Beginning of Oblivion, 1957); *Darežljivo progonstvo* (The Generous Exile, 1959); *Godišnja doba* (The Seasons, 1961); *Ljubav za stvarnu zemlju* (Love for the Real Land, 1964); *Jezero* (The Lake, 1965); *Prognana balada* (The Exiled Ballad, 1965); *Izabrane pjesme* (Selected Poems, 1966); *Posljednja večera* (The Last Supper, 1969); *Vrt crnih jabuka* (*Orchard of Black Apples*, 1972); *Krčma na uglu* (The Inn at the Corner, 1974); *Klopka za uspomene* (Trap for Memories, 1977), a collection of his own favorite poems; *Pohvala praznom džepu* (In Praise of an Empty Pocket, 1981), which in 1982 won the Tin Ujević Prize awarded by the Writers Association; *Tihe lomače* (Quiet Stakes, 1985); *Iskorak* (A Step Out, 1987); *Mozartova čarobna kočija* (Mozart's Magic Coach, 1990); *Ispitivanje tišine* (The Exploration of Silence, 1990); *Zavodnička šuma* (The Seductive Woods, 1992), which won the annual Nazor Prize and is rare among Mihalić's collections for its poems in prose; *Baršumasta žena* (A Velvety Woman, 1993); and *Petrica Kerempuh* (2nd ed., 1994), whose title refers to the Croatian Till Eugenspiegel and which won the Ivana Brlić Mažuranić Prize. Several editions of Mihalić's collected poetry (*Izabrane pjesme*) have been published: in 1966, 1980, 1982, 1988, and 1990. A selection of his poems under the title *Atlantida*

(*Atlantis*) appeared in 1982. The most recent edition of his collected poems, *Sabrane pjesme* (Collected Poems), came out in 1998. An active promoter of Croatian poetry, Mihalić in 1959 edited an anthology of Yugoslav revolutionary poetry, also published in Lika, and, with Ivan Kušan, published a French-language anthology of Croatian poetry: *La Poésie croate: Des origines à nos jours* (Paris: Seghers, 1972). In 1966 Mihalić was elected secretary of the Writers Association.

A poet of remarkable inventiveness, full of surprises, and with an uncanny ability for yoking the sublime and the mundane, Mihalić writes often of death and dying, of the ravages of war, and of man's existential dilemma. But his poetry is anything but bleak. While eloquently voicing the traumas of existence, it also celebrates the immense resources of the human spirit. Concise, very sparing of metaphors, firmly anchored in reality, Mihalić's poems explore the loftiest of human aspirations and the deepest depths of human misery and yet with equal brilliance often make simple things their subjects. As a poet who has himself known repression, Mihalić has never shrunk from conveying his utter contempt for totalitarianism and his fervent belief in the need to resist it. Universal in his appeal, Mihalić is at the same time very much a Croatian poet, steeped in his country's history and culture, which he has always freely acknowledged.

Literature: By far the best material on Mihalić in English is "Dossier: Slavko Mihalić," *Bridge Literary Magazine, the Journal of the Association of Croatian Writers* 1, no. 2 (1998): 2–129.

Translations: *Atlantis: Selected Poems, 1953–1982*, trans. Charles Simic and Peter Kastmiler (Greenfield Center, N.Y.: Greenfield Review Press, 1983); *Black Apples: Selected Poems, 1954–1987*, trans. Bernard Johnson (Toronto: Exile Editions, 1989);

Orchard of Black Apples: Selected Poems, 1954–1990, trans. Bernard Johnson (Zagreb: Erasmus, 1994); *Selected Poems, 1953–1982*, trans. Charles Simic and Peter Kastmiler (Greenfield Center, N.Y.: Greenfield Review Press, 1993). SOUND RECORDING: A sound recording, dated 1996, of Charles Simic reading Mihalić's poetry is in the Woodberry Poetry Room, Harvard University.

Mikeln, Miloš (b. 1930) Slovenian playwright, poet, and prose writer. A native of Celje, Mikeln graduated from high school in Ljubljana and then earned a degree in comparative literature at Ljubljana University. He also studied stage directing at the Academy of Performing Arts. In his professional career, he has worked as a journalist, the editor of a Ljubljana daily, the editor of the journal *Naši razgledi*, a freelance writer, director of the Ljubljana City Theater, director of the Cankar foundation, and again a freelance writer. From 1981 to 1987, he served as president of the Slovenian PEN Center and in 1985 took the lead in establishing the Writers for Peace Committee-International PEN. Mikeln served for ten years as chairman of the committee, which is still resident in the Slovenian capital. A prolific writer in several genres, Mikeln is well known as a satirist and playwright who has written a number of works for the stage, radio, and cabaret. Apart from a comedy such as *Golobje miru* (Doves of Peace, 1960), some of his best-known theater pieces are the cabaret satires *Inventura 65* (Inventory 65, 1966); *2 × 2 = 5* (1968); and *Zaradi inventure odprto* (Closed for Inventory, 1976) and the political drama *Stalinovi zdravniki* (Stalin's Doctors, 1972). His prose satires include the popular works *Kako se je naša dolina privadila svobodi: Pretežno vesela zgodba iz prvega leta po veliki vojni* (How Our Valley Won Its Freedom: A Mostly Merry Tale from the First Year After the Great War, 1973); *Zgaga vojvodine Kranjske: Humorske in satire* (The Prob-

lem of the Duchy of Carniola: Humoresques and Satires, 1985); *Adolfa Hitlerja tretja svetovna vojna in kratki kurz vladanja za začetnike* (Adolf Hitler's Third World War and a Short Course on Ruling for Beginners, 1980); *Stalin: Življenska pot samodržca* (Stalin: Biography of a Tyrant, 1985); *Slovenija* (Slovenia, 1995); and *Malo zgodovinsko berilo: Najkrajša zgodovina Slovencev, posebno novejše in najnovejše dobe* (A Small Historical Reader: The Shortest History of the Slovenians, Especially of the Newer and the Newest Periods, 1991). Mikeln's major work of prose fiction is *Veliki voz* (The Great Bear, 1992), a sweeping historical novel set in the twentieth century about two Slovenian families divided by politics. Mikeln won the Novel of the Year Award for it.

Translations: Chapter from *Petrijin venac*, trans. Martin Creegan, in *The Imagination of Terra Incognita: Slovenian Writing, 1945–1995*, ed. Aleš Debeljak (Fredonia, N.Y.: White Pine, 1997), 374–92.

Miljkovič, Branko (1934–1961) Serbian poet. A highly promising young poet, Miljković became a legendary figure, occasionally compared with Sylvia Plath, as a result of his suicide in Zagreb in February 1961. Miljković was born in Niš and studied philosophy at Belgrade University. His first poems appeared in the journals *Delo* and *Mladost* in 1953 and attracted immediate attention for their polish and striking imagery. Miljković truly came into his own in the late 1950s and early 1960s with such collections of poetry as *Uzalud je budim* (I Wake Her in Vain, 1959); *Smrču protiv smrti* (Death Against Death, 1959), with Branimir Šćepanović; *Poreklo nade* (The Origin of Hope, 1960); *Vatra i ništa* (Fire and Nothing, 1960); and *Krv koja svetli* (Blood That Shines, 1961). Eloquent and elegant, Miljković's poetry often conjures images of darkness, suffering, evil, and death. His attitude toward poetry seems conflicted. In one poem he opines that

everyone will write poetry
the truth will be in every word
in a place where the poem is most
  beautiful
the one who first started to sing
will withdraw so that others may
  continue.

In another poem "singing" (i.e., writing poetry) and dying are equated:

Life is deadly but has a way of
  surmounting death.
A fatal illness will be named after me.
We've suffered so much. Now the
  domesticated hell
Sings. Let the heart not hesitate,
To sing and to die is the same thing.

Interestingly, and sadly, a week before committing suicide, Miljkovič renounced all poetry in a letter to a Zagreb periodical. Several collections of Miljkovič's poems have been published posthumously, among them *Pesme* (Poems, 1965); *Dok budeš pevao* (So Long as You Sing, 1981); *Poezija Branka Miljkovića* (The Poetry of Branko Miljkovič, 1988), edited by Saša Hadži Tančić; and *Prejaka reč* (The Powerful Word, 1992). A four-volume edition of Miljkovič's collected works (*Sabrana dela*) was published in Niš in 1972. A volume of his translations (*Prevodi*) from the poetry of the French symbolists and the Russian poet Osip Mandelshtam also appeared in 1972. Of the tributes to Miljkovič after his death, one of the most moving, "Spring Liturgy for Branjko Miljković," was written by the Serbian poet Ivan K. Lalić.

Literature: Živorad Petrović, ed., *Branko Miljković—njim samim, ili, Pesnik, umesto da kaže, biva kazan* (Niš: Narodni Muzej Niš, 1985), a substantial catalogue of a Miljković exhibition held at the National Museum in Niš; Petar Djadjić, *Branko Miljković ili neukrotiva reč* (Niš: Prosveta,

1994), a short study of Miljković's poetry by someone who knew him well.

Translations: Eleven poems in *The Horse Has Six Legs,* ed. and trans. Charles Simic (St. Paul, Minn.: Graywolf, 1992), 83–93; five poems, trans. Bernard Johnson, in *New Writing in Yugoslavia,* ed. Bernard Johnson (Harmondsworth: Penguin, 1970), 240–42. A collection of Miljković's poetry is available in French as *Eloge du feu,* trans. Zorica Terzic (Paris: Transition, 1998).

Miłosz, Czesław (b. 1911) Polish poet, novelist, and essayist. Winner of the Nobel Prize in Literature in 1980 and the best-known Polish poet of the twentieth century, Miłosz was born in Szetejnie (Lithuanian, Šetainiai), Lithuania. Although a writer in the Polish language throughout his long career, Miłosz has always felt a deep attachment to the Lithuanian landscape of his childhood and youth and evokes it in several of his works—above all, *Dolina Issy* (The Issa Valley, 1955) and *Rodzinna Europa* (Native Europe, 1959; translated as *Native Realm*). Miłosz studied law at Wilno University and published his first volume of poetry in 1930. The following year he founded Żegary, one of the more important groups of Polish poets in the interwar period. Before the outbreak of World War II, Miłosz published two books of poems, *Poemat o czasie zastygłym* (A Poem on Frozen Time, 1933) and *Trzy zimy* (Three Winters, 1936), both in the vein of "catastrophism." During the war, the poet lived mainly in Warsaw, where he was active in underground publishing. In 1942 the Polish underground press published an anthology of poems by various authors that Miłosz edited under the title *Pieśń niepodległa: Poezja polska czasu wojny* (The Invincible Song: Polish Poetry During the War). With the end of the war, Miłosz entered the diplomatic service of the new communist government. He served for a few years as cultural attaché in the Polish Embassy in Washington, D.C., and was then posted to the Polish Embassy in Paris in a similar capacity. It was in 1951, while still in Polish government service in Paris, that Miłosz requested, and was granted, political asylum by the French authorities. He remained in Paris for nearly ten years, living as a freelance writer and publishing with the important Polish émigré publishing house Instytut Literacki, located in the French capital. His life was anything but easy, especially in view of his lack of acceptance among the many anticommunist Polish émigrés in Paris at the time who viewed Miłosz with suspicion, notwithstanding his defection. As if to establish his anticommunist credentials, Miłosz published two works of a patently political nature in Paris in the 1950s that won him international celebrity. One was *Zniewolony umysł* (*The Captive Mind*, 1953), an analysis of the compromises that artists and intellectuals make in a communist state for the sake of their careers based on certain well-known individuals in Poland who serve as paradigms and are easily recognized beneath their fictitious names in the book. The other was *Zdobycie władzy* (*The Seizure of Power*, 1953; also translated as *The Usurpers*), an almost melodramatic novel of intrigue about the Soviet-backed communist takeover of Poland after World War II for which Miłosz was awarded the French Prix Littéraire. Before leaving France for the United States in 1961 to accept a professorship of Slavic literatures at the University of California at Berkeley, Miłosz published several other works: *Światło dzienne* (The Light of Day, 1953), a collection of poetry; *Traktat poetycki* (A Treatise on Poetry, 1957); and the aforementioned *Native Realm*, the closest he has come to writing an autobiography and especially interesting for its vivid evocation of his youth in Wilno and the interwar years in Poland in general.

Since he settled in the United States, Miłosz's reputation as both a poet and an essayist has grown steadily, culminating in his Nobel Prize in Literature in 1980, and his literary output has been prodigious. Besides publishing such volumes of poetry as *Gucio zaczarowany* (Bobo's Metamorphosis, 1965); *Wiersze* (Poems, 1967); *Miasto bez imienia* (City Without a Name, 1969); *Prywatne obowiązki* (Private Obligations, 1972); *Gdzie wschodzi słońce i kędy zapada* (Where the Sun Rises and Sets, 1974); *Lud da siłę swojemu poecie: Wiersze i eseje* (The People Give Power to Their Poet: Poems and Essays, 1981); *Osobny zeszyt* (The Separate Notebooks, 1984); *Świat/The World: A Sequence of Twenty Poems in Polish* (1989); and *Na brzegu rzeki* (On the Bank of a River, 1994), Miłosz has been very active in translating his own poetry either by himself or in collaboration with American poets, particularly Robert Hass. Thus the number of collections of poetry by Miłosz published in English translation has surpassed those in Polish since the 1960s. Until his works began being published in Poland after he won the Nobel Prize in 1980 and, above all, since the downfall of the Polish communist regime, the best collection of his poetry in Polish was *Utwory poetyckie* (Poetic Works) (Ann Arbor: Michigan Slavic Publications, 1976).

Apart from disseminating his poetry by means of his own translations or through collaborative efforts with others, Miłosz has promoted the cause of Polish poetry in the English-speaking world through his anthology *Postwar Polish Poetry* (1965), edited and translated by Miłosz himself, and his books of translations of such important poets as Zbigniew Herbert, Anna Świrszczyńska (pseudonym Anna Swir), and Aleksander Wat. Arguably his most spectacular feat of translation has been from the biblical Hebrew of the complete book of Psalms, translated into Polish as *Księga psalmów* (The Book of Psalms, 1982), and for which he was awarded the Zygmunt Hertz Literary Award. The same year, Miłosz also published his translation, from Hebrew and Greek, of the megillah (the biblical narrative of the book of Esther) under the title *Księgi pięciu megilot* (The Books of the Five Megillot). In 1992 he edited and translated a book of Japanese haiku and in 1994 served as editor of the international anthology of poetry *A Book of Luminous Things.*

In the near decade that Miłosz was in Paris following his defection from the Polish diplomatic service, his major literary works were in prose: *The Captive Mind* and *The Seizure of Power.* This interest in prose writing did not diminish after his resettlement in the United States; if anything, it grew—above all, in the area of essay writing. With the exception of *The History of Polish Literature* (1969), almost all of Miłosz's prose publications since the 1970s have been collections of essays on an extraordinarily wide range of topics, from his impressions of the youth scene in Berkeley, California, in the 1960s to Russian and Polish literatures, Catholic and Protestant mysticism, the dilemmas of modern civilization, and much else. His principal books of essays include *Ziemia Ulro* (*The Land of Ulro,* 1977); *The Emperor of the Earth: Modes of Eccentric Vision* (1977); *Widzenia nad Zatoką San Francisco* (*Visions from San Francisco Bay,* 1982); *The Witness of Poetry* (1983), which comprises the Norton Lectures that Miłosz delivered at Harvard University and published in 1983 in Polish (with the Instytut Literacki in Paris) as *Świadectwo poezji: Sześć wykładów o dotkliwościach naszego wieku; Zaczynając od moich ulic* (*Beginning with My Streets,* 1985); and *Rok myśliwego* (*A Year of the Hunter,* 1994), one of his most engaging works, a far-ranging diary running from 1 August 1987 to 31 July 1988 and touching on a wide variety of personal, literary, philosophical, and historical topics. Of particular interest is the greater light the book sheds on the 1950s in Paris when Miłosz became a political defector and the circumstances in

which he wrote *The Captive Mind* and *The Seizure of Power.* Milosz's most recent collections of prose writings are the related volumes *Abecadło Miłosza* (*Miłosz's ABC's,* 1997) and *Inne abecadło* (Another ABC Book, 1998). The "ABC's" consist of alphabetized entries, usually one or two pages long, some of a general and thematic nature and others addressed to more particular topics from Walt Whitman to childhood friends from Wilno. Many of the entries deal with little-known personalities from Miłosz's past and are motivated by his belief that nobody deserves to be forgotten.

Apart from the Nobel Prize in Literature (1980), Miłosz's other literary awards include the Martin Kister Literary Award (London, 1968); the Alfred Jurzykowski Foundation Award (New York, 1960); the Neustadt International Prize for literature (1978); and the Berkeley Citation of the University of California at Berkeley (1978). He has also received honorary degrees from the University of Michigan (1977) and New York University (1981).

Literature: Ewa Czarnecka and Aleksander Fiut, *Conversations with Czeslaw Milosz,* trans. Richard Lourie (San Diego: Harcourt Brace Jovanovich, 1987); Donald Davie, *Czeslaw Milosz and the Insufficiency of Lyric* (Knoxville: University of Tennessee Press, 1986); Aleksander Fiut, *The Eternal Moment: The Poetry of Czeslaw Milosz,* trans. Theodosia S. Robertson (Berkeley: University of California Press, 1990); Leonard Nathan and Arthur Quinn, *The Poet's Work: An Introduction to Czeslaw Milosz* (Cambridge, Mass.: Harvard University Press, 1991).

Translations: POETRY: *Bells in Winter,* trans. Czesław Miłosz and Lillian Vallee (New York: Ecco Press, 1978); *The Collected Poems, 1931–1987* (New York: Ecco Press, 1988); *Facing the River: New Poems,* trans. Czesław Miłosz and Robert Hass (Hopewell, N.J.: Ecco Press, 1995); *A Portrait with a Cat* (Tucson, Ariz.: Chax, 1987); *Provinces,* trans. Czesław Miłosz and Robert Hass (New York: Ecco Press, 1991); *Roadside Dog,* trans. Czesław Miłosz and Robert Hass (New York: Ecco Press, 1998); *Selected Poems,* trans. by various hands, with an introduction by Kenneth Rexroth (New York: Seabury, 1973); *Selected Poems,* rev. ed. (New York: Ecco Press, 1980); *The Separate Notebooks,* trans. Robert Hass and Robert Pinsky, with Czesław Miłosz and Renata Gorczyńskı (New York: Ecco Press, 1984); *Świat/The World: A Sequence of Twenty Poems in Polish,* trans. Czesław Miłosz, with an introduction by Helen Vendler and a portrait of the poet in dry-point engraving by Jim Dine (San Francisco: Arion, 1989); *Unattainable Earth,* trans. Czesław Miłosz and Robert Hass (New York: Ecco Press, 1986). PROSE FICTION: *Native Realm: A Search for Self-Definition,* trans. Catherine S. Leach (Garden City, N.Y.: Doubleday, 1968); *The Seizure of Power,* trans. Celina Wieniewska (New York: Criterion, 1955; New York: Farrar, Straus and Giroux, 1982). ESSAYS: *Beginning with My Streets: Essays and Reflections,* trans. Madeline G. Levine (New York: Farrar, Straus and Giroux, 1991); *The Captive Mind,* trans. Jane Zielonko (New York: Vintage, 1981); *The Emperor of the Earth: Modes of Eccentric Vision* (Berkeley: University of California Press, 1977); *The Land of Ulro,* trans. Louis Iribarne (New York: Farrar, Straus and Giroux, 1984); *Milosz's ABC's,* trans. Madeline G. Levine (New York: Farrar, Straus and Giroux, 2001); *Visions from San Francisco Bay,* trans. Richard Lourie (New York: Farrar, Straus and Giroux, 1982); *A Year of the Hunter,* trans. Madeline Levine (New York: Farrar, Straus and Giroux, 1994). LECTURES: *Nobel Lecture* (New York: Farrar, Straus and Giroux, 1980); *The Witness of Poetry* (Cambridge, Mass.: Harvard University Press, 1983). SOUND RECORDING: A sound recording, dated 2 April 1997, is available of Miłosz reading his poetry in the Montpelier Room, Library of Congress. MUSIC: Roman Palester, *Trzy wiersze Czesława Miłosza: Na sopran i 12 instrumentów* (Three Poems by Czesław Miłosz for Soprano and 12 Instruments) (Kraków: Polskie Wydawnictwo Muzyczne, 1993). CORRESPONDENCE: Robert Faggen, ed., *Striving Towards Being: The Letters of Thomas Merton and Czesław Miłosz* (New York: Farrar, Straus and Giroux, 1997), a collection of correspondence between Miłosz and the noted Catholic mystic and writer Thomas Merton (1915–1968).

Mináč, Vladimir (1922–1996) Slovak novelist and essayist. A major Slovak prose writer of the post–World War II period, Mináč was born in the village of Klenovca, where he received his early schooling. He graduated from high school in nearby Rimavska Sobota in 1940, subsequently studying the Slovak and German languages and literatures at Comenius University in Bratislava. An active participant in the Slovak National Uprising, he was taken prisoner by the Germans toward the end of 1944 and imprisoned first in Mauthausen and then in Dachau concentration camps. During his obligatory military service after the war, he became editor of the daily *Bojovnik,* the name of which was later changed to *Obrana ľudu.* He remained in this position until 1949, when he became secretary of the Slovak section of the Czechoslovak Writers Union. He was also editor of the weekly *Kultúrny život.* In 1951 he became the head of the screenwriting section of Czechoslovak State Film and then editor in chief of *Kultúrny život.* In 1955 he became editor in chief of *Slovensk'e pohľady.* From 1956 to 1974, Mináč devoted himself wholly to writing. In 1974 he became the head of Matica slovenska publishing house, a position he held until 1990. From 1990 to 1992, he served as a delegate to the Slovak Federal Assembly.

Mináč's first major publication was the novel *Smrt' chodí po horách* (Death Walks the Mountains, 1948), which deals with the antifascist resistance in Slovakia during World War II and drew on his own experiences. His next novel, *Včera a zajtra* (Yesterday and Tomorrow, 1949), was an attempt to develop a sense of the new postwar society. Before the appearance of the work of fiction for which he is best known, the trilogy *Generácia* (Generation), Mináč published the industrial novel *Modré vlny* (Blue Waves, 1951) and the short-story collection *Na rozhraní* (At the Crossroads, 1954). The first volume of *Generácia*, *Dlhý čas čakania* (A Long Time of Waiting), appeared in 1958. It was followed by the second volume, *Živí a mrtvi* (The Living and the Dead) in 1959, and the third and last volume, *Zvony zvonia na deň* (Bells Ring in the Day), in 1961. The trilogy as a whole is an ambitious, if artistically flawed, attempt to construct a sweeping panorama of Slovak society during the years of World War II, the Slovak National Uprising, and the early postwar period. As if exhausted by the effort involved in the writing of *Generácia*, Mináč published only four more books of fiction, all in the 1960s: the short-story collection *Tmavý kút* (Dark Corner, 1960); *Nikdy nie si sama* (You Are Never Alone, 1962), which consists of two novellas; *Záznamy* (Entries, 1963); and his satirical novel, *Výrobca šťastia* (The Happiness Manufacturer, 1964), which takes aim at vestiges of petit-bourgeois attitudes and behavior in the new postwar Slovak society.

Mináč subsequently turned his energies mostly to essays as well as critical and polemical texts that appeared, after his earlier volume *Čas a knihy* (Time and Books, 1962), in such collections as *Paradoxy* (Paradoxes, 1966); *Súvislosti* (Connections, 1976); *Texty kontexty* (Texts, Contexts, 1982); *Sub tegmine* (1992); and *Návraty z prevratu* (Returns from the Revolution, 1993). The last two collections deal with more recent Slovak political developments. Many of Mináč's more resonant essays have to do with the fate of the Slovak nation historically and the place of Slovakia in European civilization. In the volume *Portréty* (Portraits, 1982), he brought together a number of small essays in the form of portraits of cultural, political, and literary personalities in contemporary and past Slovak history. *Spomienky na SNP* (Recollections of the Slovak National Uprising), which appeared in 1994 with photographs by Karol Kállay, is a valuable addition to the substantial body of publications on the uprising.

Translations: *Zvony zvonia na deň* is available in German as *Glocken läuten den Tag ein*, trans. Gustav Just (Berlin: Verlag der Nation, 1974).

Mishev, Georgi (b. 1935) Bulgarian novelist and short-story writer. A native of the village of Ioglav, in the Lovech district, Mishev graduated from veterinary school in Lovech in 1953 and then earned a degree in journalism at Sofia University in 1958. He was a provincial correspondent for the paper *Septemvriiche* from 1958 to 1967, an editor at the Narodna mladezh publishing house from 1967 to 1970, and an editor and a scriptwriter for Bulgarian film from 1971 to 1983. In 1988 he was a member of the Committee for the Defense of Ruse—an organization composed mostly of intellectuals intent on publicizing the horrific pollution of the city of Ruse near the Romanian border—for which he was expelled from the Bulgarian Communist Party. In 1989/1990, he served as a deputy in the Bulgarian parliament. Identified mostly with the rural theme in postwar Bulgarian literature, Mishev has taken a keen interest in the impact on village and town of the sweeping social and economic changes brought about by farm collectivization, which, in turn, caused the migration of peasants into cities and the new industrial plants. Mishev is a keen observer of the life around him and has brought a great sense of realism to his writing, from his use of language to his analysis of behavioral patterns. His most important novels and collections of stories include *Sineokiiat ribar: Razkazi za V. Levski* (The Blue-Eyed Fisherman: Stories About V. Levski, 1958); *Osumski razkazi* (Tales of Osum, 1963), a collection of stories set in Mishev's native Osum River valley, which he writes about in other works as well; *Adamiti* (The Adams, 1966), a collection of stories; *Matriarhat* (The Matriarch, 1967), a novella that possibly is Mishev's best piece of fiction; *Dobre oblecheni muzhe: Prosti provintsialni razkazi* (Well-Dressed Men: Simple Provincial Tales, 1967); *Esenen panair* (Fall Fair, 1976), a collection of stories; *Otdalechavane* (Alienation, 1973), a novel; *Vilna zona* (The Summer House District, 1976), a novel about exurbia, Bulgarian-style; *Proizvedeno v provintsiiata* (Made in the Provinces, 1980), a collection of novellas; *Bozainitsi* (Mammals, 1982), a collection of stories; *Pupna vruv: Dve povesti* (Umbilical Cord: Two Short Novels, 1982); *Selianinut s koleleto* (The Peasant with the Bicycle, 1985), a volume of selected prose; *Dami kaniat* (The Ladies Invite, 1986), a novel; *Selo krai dvorets: Kusi razkazi* (The Village near the Court: Short Stories, 1998); and *Chetivo za misleshti trustiki* (A Reader for Thinking Reeds, 1991–1992), a collection of stories. Mishev's film scripts were published in 1978 under the title *Kinostsenarii* (Film Scenarios). He is also highly regarded for his prose fiction for children and young readers.

Mitana, Dušan Krist (b. 1946) Slovak novelist, short-story writer, and poet. One of the more provocative contemporary Slovak writers, Mitana, who was born in Moravský Lieskový, made his debut in 1970 with the novel *Psie dni* (Dog Days), which freely experiments with genres and features the typical Mitana lead character, who is in conflict with himself as well as with his surroundings and life in general. This pattern obtains as well in his next work, the novella

Patagónia (Patagonia, 1972). Two years after this appeared, Mitana became a freelance writer. His sense of the mysterious, irrational, and even mystical order of the world pervades his collection of short stories *Nočné správy* (Nocturnal Matters), which came out in 1976. Mitana's fascination with crime and punishment, with detection and the seemingly inexplicable, is reflected in one of his best works, *Koniec hry* (The End of the Game, 1984), a novel about the killing of a Slovak by Hungarian nationalists in which the clever murderer constructs a game as a means of concealment of his crime. Disappearance, search, and mystery, intertwined at times with the absurd and philosophical, are also at the core of Mitana's short-story collection *Na prahu* (On the Threshold, 1987) and his most intriguing text, the self-mocking and parodistic postmodernist experimental novel *Hľadanie strateného autora* (The Search for a Missing Author, 1991), in which an author named Tomáš Eliáš, who published under the pseudonym Dušan Mitana, has disappeared. Mitana's other works include the novels *Slovenský poker* (Slovak Poker, 1993) and *Môj rodný cintorín: Pamäti* (My Family Cemetery: Memories, 2000), a book of recollections of his rural family background and his fledgling literary efforts; two volumes of meditative lyrics, *Krutohry* (Tongue Twisters, 1991) and *Maranatha* (1995); and *Prievan* (Draft, 1995), a collection of short prose pieces.

Literature: The best book on Mitana, in Slovak, is Milan Rešutik, ed., *Pocity pouličného nasinca: Rozhovory a úvahy Dušana Mitanu* (Bratislava: Dilema, 1998), consisting mainly of interviews with Mitana.

Translations: "On the Threshold" (from *Na prahu*), trans. James Naughton, in *Description of a Struggle: The Vintage Book of Contemporary Eastern European Writing*, ed. Michael March (New York: Vintage, 1994), 169–74.

Mňačko, Ladislav (1919–1994) Slovak novelist and journalist. Mňačko was born in the village of Valašské Klobouky, on the Moravian–Slovak border, but moved with his family to Martin, in central Slovakia, in 1920. Although ethnically Czech, Mňačko always regarded himself as a Slovak and wrote exclusively in that language. His strong communist sympathies, with which he eventually parted in the wake of the Soviet-led Warsaw Pact invasion of Czechoslovakia in 1968, were already well developed in the late 1930s, a period described in his collection of short stories *Marxova ulica* (Marx Street, 1957). During World War II, he took an active part in the Slovak partisan movement and was badly wounded at Jihlava. In October 1945, he became a member of the Communist Party and the same year published the play *Partyzaní* (Partisans), based on his wartime experiences. It was also in 1945 that Mňačko began his career as a journalist (for which he had no formal training), working for the Communist Party newspaper *Rudé Pravo*. He held this position until 1948, the time of the communist coup in Czechoslovakia, when he went to the Middle East to cover the founding of the state of Israel and the first Israeli–Arab war. After his return from Israel, he worked as editor of the Slovak Party newspaper *Pravda* until 1953. During this period, he had a chance to visit Albania and in 1950 published a book of reportage about his trip, *Albánska reportáž* (Report from Albania, 1950). Mňačko subsequently published several other books of reportage, among them *Dobrodružstvo vo Vietname* (Adventure in Vietnam, 1954), based on his first trip to Vietnam; *Daleko je do Whampoa* (It's a Long Way to Whampoa, 1958), on his impressions of China; *Co nebolo v novinách* (What Wasn't in the Papers, 1958), a domestic political commentary; *Výstavba Slovenska, 1945–1960* (The Building of Slovakia, 1945–1960, 1960), an illustrated travel book about Slovakia; *U-2 se nevracia* (The U-2s Won't Return, 1960), on the American spy plane incident; *Já, Adolf Eichmann* (I, Adolf Eichmann, 1961), on the Adolf Eichmann trial in Jerusalem, which Mňačko covered; *Oneskorené reportáže* (Delayed Reportage, 1963); *Dlhá, biela, prerušovaná čiara* (The Long, White, Broken Line, 1965), based on a trip to West Germany; and *Rozprával ten kapitán* (So Reported This Captain, 1965), a report on the Danubian floods. Mňačko's second play, *Mosty na východ* (Bridges to the East, 1952), about the development of heavy industry in Slovakia, was similar in spirit to his reportage.

Mňačko's first novel, *Smrt' sa volá Engelchen* (*Death Is Called Engelchen*), was an immediate success on publication in late 1959. Narrated in the first person by a badly wounded Russian partisan fighter after the events, it describes the bloody fighting in Moravia toward the end of the Slovak National Uprising of 1944. Predictable in its optimism and the eventual recovery of the narrator, the novel's effectiveness comes from its exciting action and its most outstanding character—a Jewish woman who sleeps with German officers in order to get information from them for the partisans and ultimately commits suicide after the war. Mňačko did less well with his second novel, *Nočný rozhovor* (Nocturnal Conversation, 1966), which became overshadowed because of the scandal beginning to break out over his next, and most famous, novel, *Ako chutí moc* (*The Taste of Power*), which was published first in German in Vienna and Munich in 1967 and then in Slovakia in 1968. Like virtually every work by Mňačko, *Nočný rozhovor* is a first-person narrative, this time about a Slav man and a German woman who are thrown together by chance in a Dresden hotel after the war and recall the grim wartime experiences that in a sense bind them both to the city that was laid waste by Allied firebomb raids. *The Taste of Power* changed the course of Mňačko's life. His only major work not written in the first person, it recounts the rise and fall of a Czechoslovak political figure and former partisan and revolutionary activist whose ever-growing lust for power corrupts his idealism, destroys his marriage and family life, and hastens his death. The reaction among Party and state officialdom was so negative that Mňačko immediately responded with a protest of his own in the form of a trip to Israel to register his discontent with Czechoslovakia's anti-Israeli policy during the Six-Day War in the Middle East. Mňačko was stripped of his citizenship and expelled from the Writers Union. He remained in Israel until, during the liberal "Prague Spring" of 1968, his citizenship was returned and he was invited back into the Writers Union. He returned in mid-May 1968. However, fearing for his safety in the wake of the Warsaw Pact invasion of Czechoslovakia on the night of 20 August 1968, Mňačko fled the country six days later. In Austria, on the first leg of his flight, from 1 to 20 September 1968, he wrote his impressions of the invasion of Czechoslovakia. The text was originally published in German as *Die siebente Nacht: Erkenntnis und Anklage eines Kommunisten* (*The Seventh Night: Perception and Indictment by One Communist*, 1968). From Austria, Mňačko went to Italy for a while, but returned to Austria and established permanent residence there. In December 1969 he was expelled from the Slovak Writers Union; in June 1971 his books were placed under a ban throughout Czechoslovakia; and shortly thereafter he became a nonperson in Czechoslovak literary history. His relations with other Czech and Slovak émigrés were also strained because of their resentment that he had remained a communist for so long and because he paraded as a Slovak while he was in fact an ethnic Czech. After *The Seventh Night*, Mňačko published three more novels, two exclusively in German and one simultaneously in Slovak and German. *Der Vorgang* (The Proceedings, 1970), a crime novel involving the director of a large chemical plant, appeared only in German. *Súdruh Münchhausen* (Comrade Münchhausen, 1972), which appeared in German and Slovak editions, is an entertaining account of a visit to communist Czechoslovakia by an illegitimate descendant of the illustrious Baron Münchhausen, who hopes to redress the skewed image of Eastern Europe presented by his famous literary forebear. *Der Gigant* (The Giant, 1972), which was published only in German, is a science-fiction novel set on a mysterious island of eternal love.

Literature: The best works on Mňačko in any language are Suzanne L. Auer, *Vom sozialistischen Realismus zu Kritizismus und Satire: Ladislav Mňačkos Romanwerk* (Bern: Peter Lang, 1989), and *Ladislav Mňačko: Eine Bibliographie* (Munich: Otto Sagner, 1989).

Translations: *Death Is Called Engelchen*, trans. George Theiner (Prague: Artia, 1961); *The Seventh Night* (New York: Dutton, 1969); *The Taste of Power,* trans. Paul Stevenson (New York: Praeger, 1967). Several of Mňačko's works are available in German: *Die Aggressoren: Von der Schuld und Unschuld der Schwachen* (The Aggressors: On the Guilt and Innocence of the Weak) (Vienna: Molden, 1968), a pro-Palestinian, anti-Israeli description of travel in Israel; *Hanoi-Report: Vietnam leidet und siegt* (Hanoi Report: Vietnam Suffers and Triumphs) (Hamburg: Holsten, 1972), a strongly pro–North Vietnamese account of the Vietnam War, with photographs; *Jenseits von Intourist: Satirische Reportagen* (Beyond Intourist: Satirical Reportage) (Munich: Lange-Müller, 1979), a book of satirical reportage about the USSR; *Die Nacht von Dresden* (Dresden's Night), trans. Erich Bertleff (Vienna: Molden, 1969); and *Der Vorgang* (The Proceedings) (Munich: Kindler, 1970).

Moldova, György (b. 1934) Hungarian novelist, short-story writer, and screenwriter. An extraordinarily prolific author, Moldova was born in Budapest, where he studied dramaturgy at the Academy of Dramatic and Film Arts. An irreverent cynic who made no secret of his contempt for the communist regime in Hungary, Moldova was able to make a living for several years only by working in factories, in construction, and as a miner. His first volume of short stories, *Az idegen bajnok* (The Foreign Champion), appeared in 1963. Several of his works deal with the Stalinist era of the 1950s, among them *Magányos pavilon* (The Solitary Pavilion, 1966); *Az elátkozott hivatal* (The Cursed Bureau, 1967); *Malom a pokolban* (Flour Mill in Hell, 1968); *Gázlámpák alatt: Elbeszélésciklus* (Under the Gas Lamps: A Story Cycle, 1968); *Tetovált kereszt* (The Tattooed Cross, 1969); *Tisztelet komlónak* (Honor to Hops, 1971); and *A változásokőrei* (The Guards of Change, 1972). One of his best novels set in the period 1956 to 1960, *Sötét angyal* (*Dark Angel*, 1971), recounts the adventures of a boy who participates in the Hungarian uprising of 1956, is arrested for subversive activities after the uprising is crushed, is sent to a reform school, has an erotic affair with an older woman who is the matron of the establishment and mistress of its director, and then tries to make a life for himself after his release. It was followed by *Negyven prédikátor* (Forty Preachers, 1973), a historical novel set in the time of the Counter-Reformation and one of Moldova's best-known works. *A szent Imre-induló* (Saint Emery March), which came out in 1975, is an autobiographical novel about the survival of the Budapest ghetto and relates to *Dark Angel* in terms of the troubled romance of that novel's central figure with a Jewish girl whose mother forbids their relationship because he is a Christian.

Moldova's other prose fiction includes *Titkos záradék* (The Secret Codicil, 1973); *Ferencvárosi koktél: H. Kovács történeteiből* (A Ferencváros Cocktail: From the Records of H. Kovács, 1974); *Mandarin, a híres vagány* (Mandarin, the Famous Tough Guy, 1976); *Akar velem beszélgetni? Kisregények* (Who Wants to Chat with Me? Novellas, 1977); *Akit a mozdony füstje megcsapott* (Once You've Caught a Wiff of Engine Smoke, 1977); *Magányos pavilon: Az elbocsátott légió* (The Solitary Pavilion: The Discharged Legion, 1981); *A napló* (Diary, 1983); *Puskás-ügy* (The Way of the Gun, 1984); *Méhednek gyümölcse* (Fruit of Your Womb, 1986); *Árnyék az égen* (A Shadow in the Sky, 1987); *Ésszel fél az ember* (The Man with Half a Mind, 1987); *Életem rövid: Kerüld a nőket!/Cirkuszi történet: Boldog vagy?, H. Barta Lajos* (My Short Life: Stay Clear of Women!/The History of Circus: Are You Happy?, H. Barta Lajos, 1987); *Lopni tudni kell* (You've Got to Know How to Steal, 1989); *Törvény szolgája és egyéb történetek* (Domestic Law and Other Stories, 1990); *Utolsó határ* (The Last Frontier, 1990); *Néma súgó* (The Mute Prompter, 1991); *Félelem kapuja* (Gate of Fear, 1992); *Magyarország szennybemenetele* (Hungary's Dirty March, 1995); *Akit a múzsa fenéken csókolt* (Whom Necessity Kissed on the Butt, 1996); *Ideális hadifogoly* (Prisoner of War, 1996); *Rövid élet titka* (The Short Life of a Secret, 1997); and *Mint falu bolond pappal: Régi és új aforizmák* (Like a Village with a Mad Priest: Old and New Aphorisms, 1997). Moldova has also won acclaim as a satirist, especially on the strength of *Kámfor akció: Szatírák* (Camphor Action: Satires, 1996); *Beszélő disznó: Szatírák* (The Talking Pig: Satires, 1978); *Magyar atom* (The Hungarian Atom, 1979), a collection of humorous writings; *Abortusz-szigetek: Szatírák, történetek* (Abortion Isles: Satires and Stories, 1989); *Bal oroszlán: Humoreszkek és szomoreszkek* (The Lions' Ball: Humoresques and Lachrymesques, 1992); and *Hitler Magyarországon: Titkos záradék* (Hitler in Hungary: The Secret Codicil, 1992).

Moldova also has to his credit several books of reportage addressed to various aspects of contemporary Hungarian society and industry and well regarded for their sociographic detail. They include *Rongy és arany: Riportok* (Rags and Gold: Reportage, 1967); *Hajósok éneke: Válogatott riportok* (Sailor's Song: Selected Reportage, 1971); *Az Őrség panasza* (Complaints of the Őrség Region, 1974); *A szent tehén: Riport a textiliparról* (The Sacred Law: Report on the Textile Industry, 1980); *A pénz szaga: Riport a kamionsofőrökről* (The Saga of Money: Report on Truck Drivers, 1986); *Bűn az élet: Riport a rendőrökről* (The Crime Life: Report on the Police, 1988); *Jog zsoldosai: Riport az ügyvédekről* (The Law of Mercenaries: Report on Lawyers, 1994); and *Ég a duna! Riport a Bős-Nagymarosi Vízlépcsőről* (The Danube Ablaze! Report on the Bős-Nagymaros Dam, 1998). A trip to Israel provided the inspiration for a book of reportage about that country under the title *Ki ölte meg a Holt-tengert? Riport Izraelről* (Who Killed the Dead Sea? Report from Israel, 1988).

Translations: *Dark Angel*, trans. Ursula McLean (Budapest: Corvina, 1967); "Pater Fabricius," trans. J. E. Sollosy, in *Present Continuous: Contemporary Hungarian Writing*, ed. István Bart (Budapest: Corvina, 1985), 142–54; "The Sixth Book of Moses," trans. Thomas Morry and Marietta Morry, in *Hungarian Short Stories*, ed. Paul Varnai (Toronto: Exile Editions, 1983), 48–62. *Gumikutya* is available in French as *Chiens de caoutchouc*, trans. Georges Kassa (Paris: Éditions des Autres, 1978), and *Magányos pavilon* in German as *Einsame Pavillon*, trans. Éva Vajda (Munich: Desch, 1970).

Morgner, Irmtraud (1933–1990) German novelist and short-story writer. Morgner was born into an uneducated proletarian family in Chemnitz (renamed Karl-Marx-Stadt after the German Democratic Republic was established). She studied German language and literature in Leipzig from 1952 to 1956, following which she worked for two years for the journal *Neue deutsche Literatur*, which was published by the GDR Writers Association in Berlin. After 1958 she became a freelance writer, with her permanent residence in Berlin. Her first literary work, the story "Das Signal steht auf Fahrt" ("The Signal Is at Go," 1959), was put out by the big East German publishing house Aufbau Verlag, which published all of Morgner's works with the exception of *Gauklerlegende* (A Mountebank Legend, 1971). Her first novel, *Ein Haus am Rander der Stadt* (A House on the Edge of Town), appeared in 1962. *Notturno*, which appeared in 1964, was one of the earliest specimens of East German socialist realism; Morgner later repudiated it.

Morgner's literary reputation really began in earnest with the publication in 1968 of her short novel *Hochzeit in Konstantinopel* (Wedding in Constantinople), which appeared in a West German edition in 1969. Its combination of biographical elements, eroticism, keen interest in women's issues, and the style of fable and legend became Morgner's literary trademark. It was soon followed by two works of similar character: *Gauklerlegende*, subtitled *Eine Spielfraungeschichte* (A Minstrel's Story), and *Die wundersamen Reisen Gustavs des Weltfahrers: Lügenhafter Roman mit Kommentarien* (The Extraordinary Journeys of Gustav the World Traveler: A Liar's Novel with Commentaries, 1972). Although the latter novel draws heavily on Morgner's family background as well as on the Baron Münchhausen tradition of the hyperbolic liar, Morgner herself stated that the central theme of the work was the "entry of woman into history."

The two monumental works of fiction for which Morgner is now most remembered, *Leben und Abenteuer der Trobadora Beatriz nach Zeugnissen ihrer Spielfrau Laura: Roman in dreizehn Büchern und sieben Intermezzos* (The Life and Adventures of the Troubador Beatrice as Chronicled by Her Minstrel Laura: A Novel in Thirteen Books and Seven Intermezzos) and *Amanda: Ein Hexenroman* (Amanda: A Witches' Novel) appeared in 1974 and 1983, respectively. The most original feature of the hugely entertaining novels is Morgner's mix of various disparate elements—epic structure; a pseudo-utopian fable style; interviews with contemporary figures; the war in Vietnam; and the pairing of the troubador, Beatrice, and Laura Salman, a present-day German language and literature scholar, construction worker, railcar operator, and minstrel—for the purpose of addressing contemporary East German social conditions, especially the place of women in society and what Morgner regarded as their subsidiary status. In so doing, she struck a blow against so-called bourgeois feminism as well as "patriarchal socialism." Comparable in some respects to the Russian writer Mikhail Bulgakov's magesterial *Master and Margarita,* the novels are built around the appearance in contemporary East Berlin of a Provençal female troubadour who, after awakening from a sleep of centuries, commits herself to the "liberation" of women in the German communist state. The novels, which were enthusiastically received in West Germany, have a rich erotic dimension consonant with the author's belief that women must be freed above all from their traditional biological and social roles.

After her death, three of Morgner's unpublished works were issued: *Der Schöne und das Tier: Eine Liebesgeschichte* (The Handsome Fellow and the Beast: A Love Story, 1991), a slight text of some thirty pages that might have been planned as a part of *Das heroische Testament: Rumba auf einen Herbst* (The Heroic Testament: An Autumn Rumba, 1992), a formally interesting work that was to have been published in 1964 but ran afoul of the censors and was withheld from print, although much of it was subsequently incorporated into *Leben und Abenteuer der Trobadora Beatriz,* and *Das heroische Testament: Roman in Fragmenten* (The Heroic Testament: A Novel in Fragments, 1998), which Morgner had planned as the third part of a trilogy consisting of *Leben und Abenteuer der Trobadora Beatriz* and *Amanda: Ein Hexenroman.* In 1975 Morgner was awarded the Heinrich Mann Prize of the Academy of Arts of the GDR; in 1977, the GDR National Prize; in 1985, the Hroswitha von Gandersheim Prize; and in 1989, the Literary Prize for Grotesque Humor of the City of Kessel. She was the first woman ever to receive the last award, which, because of Morgner's grave illness at the time, was awarded in absentia. During the fall of 1984, Morgner and her fellow East German writer Helga Schütz gave readings at several universities on a trip through the United States.

Literature: The best introduction to Morgner is *Irmtraud Morgner: Texte, Daten, Bilder* (Frankfurt am Main: Luchterhand, 1990). Also valuable are Stephanie Hanel's small study, *Literarischer Widerstand zwischen Phantastischem und Alltäglichem: Das Romanwerk Irmtraud Morgners* (Pfaffenweiler: Centaurus, 1995); Biddy Martin, "Socialist Patriarchy and the Limits of Reform: A Reading of Irmtraud Morgner's *Life and Adventures of Troubadora Beatriz as Chronicled by Her Minstrel Laura,*" *Studies in Twentieth Century Literature* 5, no. 1 (1980): 59–74, and in *Modernism and Postmodernism in Contemporary German Literature*; and Angelika Bammer, "Women's Place in the GDR: Irmtraud Morgner's *Leben und Abenteuer der Trobadora Beatriz nach Zeugnissen ihrer Spielfrau Laura,*" *Alternative Futures: The Journal of Utopian Studies* 3, no. 1 (1980): 13–25.

Translations: "White Easter," trans. Jan van Heurck, in *The New Sufferings of Young W. and Other Stories from the German Democratic Republic,* ed. Therese Hörnigk and

Alexander Stephan (New York: Continuum, 1997), 177–83.

Mrożek, Sławomir (b. 1930) Polish short-story writer and playwright. An outstanding humorist and one of the leading representatives of the theater of the absurd in Poland, Mrożek was born near Kraków. After studying architecture and painting, he began his career as a cartoonist and as the author of short humorous pieces for newspapers and periodicals. His stock-in-trade as a humorist is a wonderful sense of the absurd and grotesque, especially with respect to the workings of the bureaucracy in a communist society and the helplessness of its citizens, although few of his works have specifically Polish locales. His first published collection of stories appeared in 1958 under the title *Słoń* (*The Elephant*). This was followed by such additional collections as *Wesele w Atomicach* (A Wedding in Atomtown, 1959); *Ucieczka na południe* (Escape to the South, 1961); *Deszcz* (Rain, 1962); and *Opowiadania* (Stories, 1964). Mrożek's first play, *Policja* (*The Police*), an absurdist spoof of the self-perpetuating nature of the police apparatus in a totalitarian state, appeared the same year as *The Elephant*. It was followed soon by the one-act plays *Na pełnym morzu* (*Out at Sea*); *Striptease* (original title in English); *Męczeństwo Piotra Ohey'a* (*The Martyrdom of Peter Ohey*); *Karol* (translated as *Charlie*); *Zabawa* (*The Party*); *Czarowna noc* (*Enchanted Night*); and *Profeci* (*The Prophets*) and by the two-act *Drugie danie* (*The Second Course*). The first collected edition of Mrożek's plays, *Utwory sceniczne* (Dramatic Works), was issued in 1963. Arguably his best work for the stage, the widely performed and translated three-act *Tango* (1965) is a wry commentary on the nature of power in a totalitarian society, the failure of the intelligentsia to lead effectively, and the delicate balance between the need for tradition and the need for the right to rebel against it.

The unmistakable satirical thrust of Mrożek's stories and plays, compounded by his strenuous objection to Poland's participation in the Soviet-led Warsaw Pact invasion of Czechoslovakia in 1968, led to his self-exile to the West, mainly Paris, in 1969. His subsequent support of the Solidarity movement and denunciation of the imposition of martial law in 1981 further alienated him from communist Poland. A small underground collection of his "denunciations" (*Donosy*) appeared in 1983; a more complete collection of his stories and "denunciations" from the emergence of Solidarity and the erosion of communist power in Poland in 1989 appeared in 1994 under the title *Opowiadania i donosy: 1980–1989* (Stories and Denunciations: 1980–1989).

Until the political transformation in Poland after 1989, virtually all of Mrożek's subsequent literary works had to be published abroad. His first postexile collection of stories, *Dwa listy i inne opowiadania* (Two Letters and Other Stories), containing seven short and longer stories from the 1960s, was published by the Polish émigré publishing house Instytut Literacki in Paris in 1970. A volume of his stories from the 1950s, *Opowiadania, 1953–1959* (Stories, 1953–1959), appeared in Poland in 1998. A collection of new stories from the early 1990s, *Opowiadania, 1990–1993* (Stories, 1990–1993), came out in 1994. Two plays postdating *Tango*, *Vatzlav* and *Ambasador* (Ambassador), were published in a single edition by the Instytut Literacki in 1982. Mrożek's cartoons, illustrations, and other drawings have also been published in book form, beginning with *Rysunki* (Drawings), in 1982. A collection covering the 1960s, *Przez okulary: 1965–1968* (Through Eyeglasses: 1965–1968), appeared in 1999. A new collection of Mrożek's plays (*Teatr*) was published in 1995, and a twelve-volume edition of his collected works (*Dzieła zebrane*) began appearing in 1994.

Literature: Halina Stephan, *Transcending the Absurd: Drama and Prose of Sławomir Mrożek* (Amsterdam: Rodopi, 1997), a translation of the author's 1996 Polish study, *Mrożek*. There are also a few good Polish studies on Mrożek: Jan Błoński, *Wszystkie sztuki Sławomira Mrożka* (Kraków: Wydawnictwo Literackie, 1995); Małgorzata Sugiera, *Dramaturgia Sławomira Mrożka*, 2nd ed. (Kraków: Universitas, 1997); and Jacek Zakowski, *Co dalej panie Mrożek?* (Warsaw: Iskry, 1999), a biography.

Translations: *The Elephant*, trans. Konrad Syrop (London: Macdonald, 1962; New York: Grove, 1963, 1984; Westport, Conn.: Greenwood, 1975); *Six Plays*, trans. Nicholas Bethell (London: Cape, 1967), which includes *The Police, The Martyrdom of Peter Ohey, Out at Sea, Charlie, The Party*, and *Enchanted Night; Striptease, Repeat Performance, and The Prophets: Three Plays by Sławomir Mrożek*, trans. Lola Gruenthal, Teresa Dzieduszycka, and Ralph Mannheim (New York: Grove, 1972); *Striptease; Tango; Vatzlav: Three Plays* (New York: Grove, 1981); *Tango*, trans. Nicholas Bethell, adapted by Tom Stoppard (London: Cape, 1968); *Tango*, trans. Ralph Mannheim and Teresa Dzieduszcycka (New York: Grove, 1968); *The Ugupu Bird*, trans. Konrad Syrop (London: Macdonald, 1968); *Vatzlav: A Play in 77 Scenes*, trans. Ralph Mannheim (New York: Grove, 1970; London: Cape, 1972).

Müller, Heiner (1929–1995) German playwright. A native of Eppendorf in Saxony, Müller, arguably the best-known (and most problemmatic) East German dramatist after Bertolt Brecht, attended elementary and secondary school in Waren (Mecklenburg), to which his family moved in 1938. From 1939 to the end of World War II, he was a compulsory member of the Hitler Youth. In 1947 his father became mayor of Frankenberg (Saxony) in the Soviet Occupation Zone, subsequently the German Democratic Republic. When his family moved to the West as the result of a political scandal, Müller chose to remain in the GDR. Between 1953 and 1955, he was employed by the East German Writers Union. His first play, *Der Lohndrücker* (The Scab, 1956), had its premiere in Leipzig in 1958. It was followed in 1957 by *Die Korrektur* (The Correction), which itself had to be "corrected" to satisfy Party criticism. With his wife, Inge (a poet, writer of children's literature, and later collaborator on his plays), Müller received the Heinrich Mann Prize in 1959. Two years later, Müller incurred the wrath of the authorities with his play *Die Umsiedlerin* (The Resettler), which was forced to close shortly after its opening. Müller himself was expelled from the East German Writers Union. A similar fate befell Müller's next play, *Der Bau* (The Construction Site, 1965), when in 1965 its premiere was canceled after it was attacked by the Central Committee of the GDR Communist Party. It was finally permitted a premiere, in East Berlin, in 1980. A long-delayed East German production also befell his play *Philoktet* (*Philoctetes*, 1964), which had its premiere in Munich in 1968 but was kept from East German stages until 1977. In 1966 Inge Müller committed suicide. The following year, 1967, Müller's second play on a classical subject after *Philoktet*, *Ödipus Tyrann* (Oedipus Rex), became his first play to be produced in West Germany (in Bochum). Another "classical" play, *Der Horatier* (*The Horatian*, 1968), premiered in West Berlin in 1973. In 1975, *Mauser* (1970), one of Müller's best-known plays and one that was never produced in the GDR, had its premiere in Austin, Texas. It was the first production of a play by him in the United States. Repeating the pattern of his other plays, which had their premieres in the West years before they were permitted to be staged in the GDR, *Germania Tod in Berlin* (Germania Death in Berlin, 1971), was staged first in Munich in

1978 and in the GDR only much later. Müller's version of *Macbeth* (1972) was severely attacked by the philosopher Wolfgang Harich.

Müller continued to be extraordinarily prolific in the 1970s and 1980s. Between 1972 and 1987, he wrote twelve more plays: *Zement* (Cement, 1972; premiere 1973, Berlin); *Die Schlacht* (*The Battle*, 1974; premiere 1975, Berlin), one of his best plays; *Leben Gundlings Friedrich von Preussen Lessings Schlaf Traum Schrei* (Gundling's Life Frederick of Prussia Lessing's Sleep Dream Scream, 1976; premiere 1979, Frankfurt am Main), another of Müller's most successful plays; *Hamletmaschine* (*Hamletmachine*, 1977; premiere 1979, Paris), Müller's most famous play; *Untergang des Egoisten Fatzer* (Downfall of the Egoist Fatzer, 1978; premiere 1978, Hamburg); *Der Auftrag* (The Mission, 1979; premiere 1980, East Berlin); *Quartett* (Quartet, 1980; premiere 1982, Bochum); *Verkommens Ufer Medeamaterial Landschaft mit Argonauten* (Despoiled Shore Mediamaterial Landscape with Argonauts, 1982; premiere 1983, Bochum); *Bildbeschreibung* (Description of a Picture, 1984; premiere 1983, Graz, Austria); *Anatomie Titus Fall of Rome* (Anatomy of Titus Fall of Rome, 1985; premiere 1985, Bochum); and *Wolokolamsker Chaussee* (Volokolamsk Highway), a five-part work completed in 1987. Müller's last play, *Mommsens Blok* (Mommsen's Block), was completed in 1992. Müller was also active as a director of his own plays and those of others. In 1982 he codirected *Macbeth* in East Berlin; in 1987, a revival of *Der Lohndrücker* in East Berlin; in 1989/1990, *Hamletmaschine* in East Berlin around the time of the fall of the Berlin Wall; in 1991, *Mauser* in Berlin; in 1993, a production of Wagner's *Tristan and Isolde* at the Bayreuther Festspielhaus; in 1994, his own *Quartett* in Berlin; and in 1995, the year of his death from cancer, Brecht's *The Resistible Rise of Arturo Ui* at the Berliner Ensemble, of which

Müller had become sole artistic director that year. The awards Müller received for his playwrighting include, after the Heinrich Mann Prize of 1959, the Lessing prize (1975); the GDR National Prize, First Class (1986); the Kleist Prize (1990); and the European Theater Prize (1991). In 1990 Müller was named president of the East German Academy of Arts. Müller made his first of several trips to the United States in 1975 in order to accept a teaching residency at the University of Texas in Austin. He returned to the United States the following year. In 1994 he went to California to convalesce after an operation for cancer in Munich. Müller's autobiography, *Krieg ohne Schlacht* (War Without Battle), was published in 1992. But in 1993 his reputation was tarnished by revelations that he had had contacts with the East German secret police (Stasi) going back as far as 1978.

Literature: Jonathan Kalb, *The Theater of Heiner Müller* (Cambridge: Cambridge University Press, 1998), the best study of Müller in English.

Translations: *The Battle: Plays, Prose, Poems by Heiner Müller*, ed. and trans. Carl Weber (New York: PAJ Publications, 1989); *Cement*, trans. Helen Fehervary, Sue-Ellen Case, and Marc Silberman, *New German Critique* 16, suppl. (1979): 7–64; *Explosion of Memory: Writings by Heiner Müller*, ed. and trans. Carl Weber (New York: PAJ Publications, 1989); *Hamletmachine and Other Texts for the Stage*, ed. and trans. Carl Weber (New York: PAJ Publications, 1984); *The Horatian*, trans. Marc Silberman, Helen Fehervary, and Guntram Weber, *Minnesota Review*, n.s., 6 (1976): 40–50; *Mauser*, trans. Helen Fehervary and Marc Silberman, *New German Critique* 8 (1976): 122–49; *Philoctetes*, trans. Oscar Mandel with Maria Kelsen Feder, in Oscar Mandel, *Philoctetes and the Fall of Troy* (Lincoln: University of Nebraska Press, 1981), 215–50; *The Slaughter*, trans. and ed. Marc von Henning (London: Faber and Faber, 1995).

Müller, Herta (b. 1953) Romanian German novelist. A native of the Timis region of Romania, Müller pursued German and Romanian studies at the university in Timişoara from 1973 to 1976. She began her literary career, writing exclusively in German, a few years later. Her first book, *Niederungen* (Lowlands, 1984; translated as *Nadirs*), is a collection of mostly autobiographical stories based on her childhood in the Romanian countryside in which reality and the fantastic are skillfully blended in order to convey the nightmarishness of life in the Romania of Nicolae Ceauşescu. It was followed by her first work to attract international attention, *Der Mensch ist ein grosser Fasan auf der Welt* (Man Is a Great Peacock in the World, 1986; translated as *The Passport*). A member of Romania's dwindling ethnic-German community, Müller immigrated to Germany in 1987 and established residence in Hamburg. Prior to her emigration, her situation had become precarious because of her refusal to work clandestinely for the Romanian secret police. This also cost her the teaching position she held at the time. Her three major novels, all written in German—*The Passport*; *Reisende auf einem Bein* (*Traveling on One Leg*, 1992); and *Herztier* (Hearteater, 1993; translated as *The Land of Green Plums*)—draw extensively on her own experiences both before she left Romania and after her resettlement in Germany. *The Passport* paints an almost surreal and anything but flattering picture of a German village in Romania from which most of its inhabitants are immigrating to Germany. *Traveling on One Leg* traces the profound sense of isolation of a young German woman who immigrates to Germany and feels as alien in her new home as she did in her native Romania. *The Land of Green Plums* is a bleak account of the crushing of the spirits of a group of young Romanian students who leave their impoverished native villages to study at the university in Bucharest, only to confront the inescapable brutality of the Ceauşescu regime. Müller is highly regarded as a writer for the poetic qualities of her language and the tension she creates between the bleakness of her subjects and the outward simplicity of a primitivist narrative style. She has received many literary awards in her career: the Aspekte Prize (1984); the Förderpreis des Brenner Literaturpreises (1985); the Rauriser Prize (1985); the Ricarda-Huch Prize (1988); and the International IMPAC Dublin Literary Award (1998).

Translations: *The Land of Green Plums*, trans. Michael Hofmann (Evanston, Ill.: Northwestern University Press, 1998); *Nadirs*, trans. Sieglinde Lug (Lincoln: University of Nebraska Press, 1999); *The Passport*, trans. Martin Chalmers (London: Serpent's Tail, 1989); *Traveling on One Leg*, trans. Valentina Glajar and André Lefevere (Evanston, Ill.: Northwestern University Press, 1998).

Murín, Gustáv (b. 1959) Slovak scientist, short-story writer, and essayist. A prolific and multifaceted writer, Murín was born in Bratislava and received his early schooling in Bratislava and Baghdad (1967–1970). He graduated from high school in Bratislava and then studied biology and cytology at Comenius University, receiving his doctorate in natural sciences in 1983. He currently holds the position of scientific researcher in the Department of Cellular Biology at Comenius University. While still a student, as early as 1978, Murín began publishing articles on the preservation of the animal environment as well as those of a cultural nature and short stories in newspapers and journals. He has over 440 articles to his credit. Murín published his first book, the journalistic *Případ pohřbeného hřbitova* (The Case of the Buried Cemetery), in 1989. Rooted in Murín's ecological concerns, the book pleads the case for the preservation of an important Bratislava cemetery threatened with liquidation. The following year, Murín came out with a volume of eleven science-fiction stories titled *Návraty zo svetla* (Returns from the Light) in which he demonstrates his feeling for both the humorous and the erotic. Murín's growing interest in sexual issues, especially the sexual problems of the young, comes to the fore in several works, beginning with *Leto praje milencom* (Summer Favors Lovers, 1990), a collection of fourteen short stories. This was followed by *Pud kontra kultúra* (Instinct versus Culture, 1994), a book of essays examining the role of sex and sexuality in human history. In *Orgazmodrómy* (Orgasmodromes, 1997), he addresses such matters as AIDS and orgasm within the context of sex in everyday life and as promoted via the media.

Murín's environmental concerns, with respect to both humans and animals, form the subject of such books as *Náhradný koniec sveta* (Alternate End of the World, 1992), in which he considers the place of humanity in this world and the next; *Ako se máš* (How Do You Do, 1998), his best work of fiction to date, which is set in the recent past; and *Zvieratá, ja a iné* (Animals, I, and Others, 1998), a collection of short stories in which Murín questions a number of commonly held assumptions about the relationship between humans and animals. Murín is also the author of several radio and television plays. He has also traveled widely in the United States and given readings and lectures in such cities as Cedar Rapids and Iowa City, Iowa (1995), during a three-month affiliation with the International Writing Program of the University of Iowa; Norfolk, Virginia (1995); and Norman, Oklahoma (1998). He has also been the editor of the Slovak edition of *Playboy* (1994) and editor of *Central Europe—Now!*, the almanac of young writers from Central and Eastern Europe (1995).

Translations: "The Best Chest in the West," "Culture Shock," and "Crossing Borders," *Euphorion* (Romania) 1 (1997); "The Day in My Hometown," *Short Story International*, no. 115 (1997); "On the Road with Wild Horses,"*Autumn Leaves* (1996); "Program of the Glory," *Short Story International*, no. 62 (1996); "Searching for Paradise," *Art Panorama* (Romania) 6 (1988); "Virus as a Principle," *Slovak Literary Review* 1 (1997); "Well-Organized Hopelessness," *River Oak Review* (1996).

Musiał, Grzegorz (b. 1952) Polish poet and novelist. A native of Bydgoszcz, Musiał studied medicine at the Medical Academy in Gdańsk, where he also grew close to the Wolność (Freedom) group and the literary scholar Maria Janion, at Gdańsk University. Although he began publishing poems in the 1970s, his first published book of poetry, *Rewia* (Revue), appeared in 1978. Subsequent volumes of poetry include *Kosmopolites* (Cosmopolites, 1980); *Listy do brata* (Letters to My Brother, 1983); *Przypadkowi świadkowie zdarzeń* (Chance Witnesses to Events, 1986); *Berliner Tagebuch* (Berlin Diary, 1989); and *Smak popiołu* (The Taste of Ashes, 1992). He is also the author of three semiautobiographical novels—*Stan płynny* (Fluid State, 1982); *W ptaszarni* (In the Aviary, 1989); and *Al fine* (1997)—and has translated into Polish all the poems of Allen Ginsburg. One of the more interesting poets of the Gdańsk group of the 1980s and 1990s, in 1988 Musiał participated in the International Writing Program at the University of Iowa, which he made the subject of a few of his poems as well as a prose account under the title *Dziennik z Iowa* (Iowa Diary, 2000). His poetry often conveys a greater sense of World War II, with its horrors, and the political repression in Poland and East Europe as a whole in the communist era. There are also allusions in his poems to other contemporary European and American writers, such as Günter Grass, Allen Ginsburg, and Jack Kerouac, toward whom he feels affinities. Musiał's very readable and interesting book about the United States, *Dziennik z Iowa*, is arguably one of the best books on the subject by a Polish writer.

Translations: *Poems of Grzegorz Musiał: Berliner Tagebuch and Taste of Ash,* trans. Lia Purpura (Madison, N.J.: Fairleigh Dickinson University Press, 1998).

Muşina, Alexandru (b. 1954) Romanian poet and essayist. Muşina was born in Sibiu, Transylvania, and graduated from the Faculty of Philology of Bucharest University in 1978. While there, he was a member of the well-known Cenaclul de luni (Monday Literary Circle), conducted by the literary critic Nicolae Manolescu (b. 1939) until its closing by the authorities. He was also a member of the literary circles 19 (1981–1985), Alternative (1987–1988), and Interval (from 1990). From 1978 to 1988, he taught French at a school in Buzău; from 1988 to 1990, he worked as a florist; and in 1990/1991, he edited the literary review *In-terval*. He currently holds the position of lecturer in comparative literature at the Transylvania University in Braşov. A lively, witty, entertaining, very contemporary, and casual poet, fond of long prosaic lines of verse, Muşina published his first book of poems, *Cinci* (Five), in 1982 with his fellow poets Romulus Bucur (b. 1956), Ion Bogdan Lefter (b. 1957), Bogdan Ghiu (b. 1958), and Mariana Marin (b. 1956). Subsequent collections of his poetry include *Strada castelului 104* (104 Castle Street, 1984); *Lucrurile pe care le-am văzut* (Things I Have Seen, 1992); *Aleea Mimozei* (Mimosa Alley, 1993); *Tomografia şi alte explorări* (Tomography and Other Explorations, 1994); and *Tea* (1998).

Muşina has also been an active anthologist and literary scholar. In 1993 he published an anthology of the poetry of the 1980s generation and, with Bucur, an anthology of modern poets on poetry (1997).

He is also the author of three books of literary essays: *Unde se află poezia?* (Where Does Poetry Lie?, 1996); *Paradigma poeziei moderne* (The Paradigm of Modern Poetry, 1996); and *Eseu asupra poeziei moderne* (Essay on Modern Poetry, 1997). In 1984 he was awarded the Writers Union Prize; in 1993 and again in 1996, the Poesis Prize; and in 1994, the Association of Professional Writers of Romania (ASPRO) Prize.

Translations: Seven poems, trans. Adam J. Sorkin and Radu Surdulescu, in *Romanian Poets of the '80s and '90s,* ed. Andrei Bodiu, Romulus Bucur, and Georgeta Moarcăs (Piteşti: Paralela 45, 1999), 105–13.

Mustafaj, Besnik (b. 1958) Albanian novelist, poet, essayist, and screenwriter. One of the most important literary figures of postcommunist Albania, Mustafaj was born in Bajram Curri and educated at Tirana University. He began his literary career with a volume of poems, *Motive të gëzuara* (Happy Motives, 1978). A second volume, *Fytyrë burri* (A Man's Face), appeared in 1987. Since then, Mustafaj has devoted himself almost entirely to prose. His first novel was the short *Vera pa kthim* (Summer of No Return, 1989). It was followed by *Vapa* (Scorcher, 1993); *Një saga e vogël* (A Small Prison Saga, 1994); *Daullja prej letre* (The Paper Drum, 1996); and *Boshi* (The Abyss, 1998). Mustafaj has also published a theatrical work under the title *Doruntine, motra-bije* (Doruntine, Daughter-Sister, 1997), subtitled "A Tale for the Opera and Dramatic Theater," and two books of nonfiction: *Midis krimeve dhe mirazheve: Ese* (Between Crimes and Mirages: Essays, 1991, 1999), on the precarious situation of the Albanians in Kosovo and the historic animosity between Albanians and Serbs, and *Fletorja rezervat: Shënime jashtë valixhes diplomatikë* (Reserved Pages: Notes Outside the Diplomatic Pouch, 1995), an account of his experiences in

Paris as his country's ambassador to France, a position Mustafaj held from 1992 to 1997.

Most of Mustafaj's work reflects his ardent opposition to the Enver Hoxha regime in Albania. The terror of repression is strikingly vivid in such novels as *Një saga e vogël* and *Boshi*. A novelistic triptych, *Një saga e vogël* develops the image of Albania as a political prison from Ottoman times through the Hoxha era. The three parts of the novel recount the grim prison experiences of various members of a single family who for one reason or another have been victimized by the oppressive machinery of the state—above all, in the time of King Zog in the interwar period and then by post–World War II communists. In the most poignant part of the work (the second), the eagerly anticipated first conjugal visit permitted a prisoner and his wife becomes a nightmare of physical and psychic impotence. The absurd and grotesque come to the fore in the third part when the old jailer of the prison, faced with an absence of prisoners after the fall of the dictatorship, loses his mind and fills cells with rocks to overcome the void he feels. He is, in fact, the father of the prisoner's wife in the second part. She believes that she became pregnant after the conjugal visit with her husband, but gives birth instead to a rock. *Boshi* also has the quality of a combination of fable and allegory. While on an assignment about chromium miners, a young woman photojournalist uncovers the grim evidence of a cave in. She thereafter becomes a "nonperson." Her parents, employer, and former fiancé refuse to acknowledge her existence when she attempts to resume her previous routine in Tirana. She returns to the small town near the scene of the mine, hoping to be helped by an agricultural engineer she met there and with whom she had an affair. But when he retraces her steps in Tirana, he runs into the same wall of denial. Upon his return to the town and the same hotel where he left Ana B., she is nowhere to be found and everyone denies that they ever had a guest by that name.

Translations: *Boshi* is available in French as *Le Vide,* trans. Elisabeth Chabuel (Paris: Albin Michel, 1999); *Daullja prej letre* as *Le Tambour de papier,* trans. Elisabeth Chabuel (Arles: Actes Sud, 1996); *Doruntine, motra-bije* as *Doruntine, fille-soeur: Une histoire pour opéra et théâtre dramatique,* trans. Elisabeth Chabuel (Arles: Acts Sud, 1997); *Fletorja rezervat: Shënime jashtë valixhes diplomatikë* as *Pages réservées: Un albanais à Paris,* trans. Elisabeth Chabuel et al. (Paris: Grasset, 1996); *Midis krimeve dhe mirazheve: Ese* as *Entre crimes et mirages, l'Albanie,* trans. Elisabeth Chabuel (Arles: Actes Sud, 1992); *Një saga e vogël* as *Petite Saga carcérale,* trans. Elisabeth Chabuel (Arles: Actes Sud, 1994); *Vapa* as *Les Cigales de la canicule,* trans. Christiane Montecot (Arles: Actes Sud, 1993); *Vera pa kthim* as *Un été sans retour,* trans. Christiane Montécot (Arles: Actes Sud, 1992). *Midis krimeve dhe mirazheve: Ese* is available in German as *Albanien: Zwischen Verbrechen und Schein,* trans. Joachim Röhm (Frankfurt: Frankfurter Verlagsanstalt, 1997), and *Një saga e vogël* as *Kleine Saga aus dem Kerker,* trans, Joachim Röhm (Frankfurt: Frankfurter Verlagsanstalt, 1997).

Mutafchieva, Vera (b. 1929) Bulgarian historian and novelist. The daughter of the historian Petur Mutafchiev, Mutafchieva was born in Sofia, where she earned a degree in history at Sofia University in 1951. Both before and after the defense of her doctoral dissertation in 1978, she held a variety of academic positions in Balkan and Oriental studies at both Sofia University and the Bulgarian Academy of Sciences. From 1978 to 1980, she was director of the Center for Ancient Languages and Cultures of the Committee of Culture; from 1980 to 1982, the head of the Bulgarian Research Center in

Austria; and from 1982 to 1986, secretary of the Bulgarian Writers Union. In 1992 she became affiliated with the Institute of History, where her principal field of research has been agrarian relations during the Ottoman Middle Ages.

Mutafchieva has had a prolific literary career as a historian of Bulgaria and Ottoman Turkey and as a writer of fiction known best for her richly detailed and colorful novels about ancient Byzantium and nineteenth-century Bulgaria and Ottoman Turkey. Her novels include, among others, *Povest za dobroto i zloto* (The Tale of Good and Gold, 1963); *Letopis na smutnoto vreme* (Chronicle of a Sad Age, 1965–1966), on Rumelia and the reign of the Turkish sultan Selim III (1789–1807); *Sluchaiat Dzhem* (The Case of Cem, 1967), about Prince Cem, son of Mehmed II, sultan of the Turks (1459–1495); *Poslednite Shishmanovtsi* (The Last Shishmanovs, 1969); *Ritsariat* (The Knight, 1970); *Belot na dve rutse* (Belote for Two Hands, 1973), belote being a card game; *Alkiviad Malki* (Alcibiades the Young, 1975); *Alkiviad Velki* (Alcibiades the Great, 1976); *Suedinenieto pravi silata* (Strength Through Union, 1985), a novel based on the Serbo-Bulgarian war of 1885; and *Azm, Anna Komina* (I, Anna Komina, 1991), about the Byzantine empress. *Bombite* (The Bombs), which Mutafchieva published in 1985, is an autobiographical novel based on her experiences during World War II.

As a historian, Mutafchieva has written such works as *Kniga za Sofroni* (A Book About Sofroni, 1978), about the influential eighteenth-century Bulgarian church figure Sofroni Vrachanski, bishop of Vratsa; *Rumeliiski delnitsi i praznitsi ot XVIII v.* (Rumelian Workdays and Holidays in the Eighteenth Century, 1978); and *Obraz nevuzmozhen: Mladostta na Rakovski* (Impossible Model: The Youth of Rakovski, 1983), on the early years of the nineteenth-century revolutionary Georgi Stoikov Rakovski. In

1994 Mutafchieva published a travel book, *Beliia sviat* (The White World). It was followed in 1995 by a collection of journalistic writings, *Reaktsi* (Reactions), and in 1997 by a biography of her father, *Razgadavaiki bashta si: Opit za biografiia na Petur Mutafchiev* (Unraveling the Mystery of Your Own Father: A Biography of Petur Mutafchiev).

Translations: *Agrarian Relations in the Ottoman Empire in the Fifteenth and Sixteenth Centuries* (Boulder, Colo.: East European Monographs, 1988); *Bulgaria's Past* (Sofia: Sofia Press, 1969), with Nikolai Todorov.

Nádas, Péter (b. 1942) Hungarian novelist, essayist, and playwright. A native of Budapest, Nádas studied chemistry, photography, and journalism; worked for several newspapers and journals; and spent a year with the Kisfaludy Theater in Győr. He first began publishing in 1965 and became a full-time writer in 1969. His first major novel, *Egy családregény vége* (The End of a Family Novel, 1977), is a muddled, fitfully interesting work about a family with Jewish and Christian roots, a grandfather who lives on the memories of the past, and a boy's growing awareness of his father's betrayal during the dark days of Stalinist repression. In 1986 Nádas published the work for which he is best known and will long be remembered: *Emlékiratok könyve* (A Book of Memoirs). The novel was kept from publication for several years by the Hungarian censors not only for its expansive eroticism, but also for its ideological implications. A huge, multilayered work, the very size of which makes a statement about Nádas's belief in the viability of the genre, *A Book of Memoirs* is structured around three separate but related memoirs narrated in the first person. The main story is about an unnamed Hungarian writer who during a stay in East Germany in the 1970s (the atmosphere of which Nádas superbly evokes) enters into a psychologically intricate relationship with an aging actress (Thea) and a young man (Melchior Thoenissen), with whom she is also in love. Interwoven into the writer's personal chronicle are sections of a novel he is composing about a fin-de-siècle German novelist named Thomas Thoenissen, who seems to have been modeled on Thomas Mann. Both writers, the author of one of the memoirs and his fictional creation, Thomas Thoenissen, are prone to incestuous longings, and both become involved in bisexual triangles. The novel is heavy with sexuality, sensuality, and an intense preoccupation with the body that takes up considerable space in the text and slows its pace to a crawl. Nádas, however, moves effortlessly from the present into successive strata of the past and in so doing—within the context of a dense, provocative, and at times exasperating novel—splendidly evokes the Central and Eastern Europe of the post–World War II era and the impact of political events on the human psyche. At the end of the work, the main narrator's childhood friend and homosexual lover (Krisztian), who is now living in the West, inherits his friend's manuscripts after his death and completes them by describing his last years and offering his, Krisztian's, own perspective on their relationship. This then becomes the third memoir of the novel. Of Nádas's more recent fiction, the best work is the short novel *A fotográfia szép története* (*A Lovely Tale of Photography*, 1999), in part a reflection of the author's own experiences as a photojournalist and an intriguing blend of the visual and literary in a story about a female photographer with a strange illness who is put in a sanatorium and has to view life from a different perspective than through the lens of her camera.

Nádas's other prose fiction includes a volume of novellas, *Leírás* (Describing, 1979); three volumes of theatrical stories, *Egy próbanapló utolsó lapjai* (The Last Page of a Rehearsal Diary, 1980), *Szinter* (The Stage, 1982), and *Ünnepi színjátékok* (Festive Plays, 1986); *Évkönyv: Ezerkilencszáznyolc-vanhét-ezerkilencszáaznyolcvannyolc* (Yearbook: Nineteen Hundred Eighty Seven-Nineteen Hundred Eighty Eight, 1989), a month-by-month account of a year in the life of a writer living in the countryside with recollections of events back in Budapest; and *Talált cetli és más elegyes írások* (The Discovered Note and Other Writings, 1992). Besides his fiction, Nádas is an accomplished essayist and critic whose pieces appear in such collections as *Játéktér* (Games, 1988; reprinted, 1995, as *Esszék* [Essays]) and *Kritikák* (Critiques), a volume of critical writings from the periods 1973 to 1982 and 1990 to 1999, mostly on Hungarian writers although two deal with the Polish writers Stanisław Ignacy Witkiewicz and Miron Białoszewski. He was also the author of a quirky but witty philosophy of love titled *Az égi és a földi szerelemről* (On Celestial and the Earthy Love, 1991). A volume of his plays was published in 1996 as *Drámák* and contains *Protokoll* (Protocol, 1966); *Takarítás* (Tidying Up, 1977); *Találkozás* (The Encounter, 1979); and *Temetés* (The Funeral, 1980). *Vonulás: Két filmnovella* (Moving: Two Film Novellas) appeared in 1995. Nádas has received several literary awards: the Prize for Hungarian Art (1989); the Austrian State Prize for European Literature (1991); and the Vilenica International Prize for Literature (1998).

Translations: *A Book of Memoirs*, trans. Ivan Sanders with Imre Goldstein (New York: Farrar, Straus and Giroux, 1997); *The End of a Family Story*, trans. Imre Goldstein (New York: Farrar, Straus and

Giroux, 1998); *A Lovely Tale of Photography*, trans. Imre Goldstein (New York: Farrar, Straus and Giroux, 1999); "August" (from *Évkönyv*), trans. Ivan Sanders, in *Give or Take a Day: Contemporary Hungarian Short Stories*, ed. Lajos Szakolczay (Budapest: Corvina, 1997), 111–37; "Family Portrait Against a Purple Sunset," trans. Judith Sollosy, in *The Kiss: Twentieth Century Hungarian Short Stories*, selected by István Bart (Budapest: Corvina, 1998), 330–40. *Takarítás* is available in French as *Menage: Comedia perpetua*, trans. Ibolya Virag and Jean-Pierre Thibaudat (Paris: Editions Theatrales, 1996).

Nagy, Ágnes Nemes (1922–1991) Hungarian poet and translator. Widely acknowledged as one of the finest poets to emerge in Hungary after World War II, Nagy was born in Budapest. After receiving her degree in Hungarian and Latin at Budapest University, she worked for several years on the staff of an educational magazine and as a secondary-school teacher before devoting herself wholly to writing in 1958. She was associated with the postwar literary review *Újhold* until its suppression in 1948. Nagy's first book of poetry, *Kettős világban* (Two Worlds), appeared in 1946 and was honored with the Baumgartner Prize. She published another two volumes of poems in 1967, *Szárazvillám* (Heat Lightning) and *Napforduló* (Solstice), and then a collected edition of her poems under the title *A lovak és az angyalok* (The Horses and the Angels, 1969), for which she was awarded the Attila József Prize. Long identified with the impersonality of a poetry of objects, Nagy was no less versatile at concretizing the abstract and philosophical. In 1975 a collection of her essays, *64 hattyú* (64 Swans), was published, and in 1983 Nagy was awarded the Kossuth Prize for her poetry. In the late 1970s she and her husband, the critic Béla Balázs, spent several months at the University of Iowa as guests of the International Writing Program. She translated extensively from French, German, and English.

Translations: *Ágnes Nemes Nagy on Poetry: A Hungarian Perspective*, ed. Győzo Ferencz and John Hobbs, trans. Mónika Hámori (Lewiston, N.Y.: Mellen, 1998), an excellent collection of Nagy's essays on poetry; *Selected Poems*, trans. Bruce Berlind (Iowa: University of Iowa Press, 1980); *Between*, trans. Hugh Maxton (Budapest: Corvina, 1989); nine poems in *The Colonnade of Teeth: Modern Hungarian Poetry*, ed. George Gömöri and George Szirtes (Newcastle upon Tyne: Bloodaxe, 1996), 128–36; thirteen poems and an excerpt from "Interview," in *Ocean at the Window: Hungarian Prose and Poetry Since 1945*, ed. Albert Tezla (Minneapolis: University of Minnesota Press, 1980), 150–80.

Nagy, András (b. 1956) Hungarian playwright, novelist, short-story writer, and screenwriter. A native of Budapest, and a graduate of Eötvös Lóránd University, Nagy worked for a number of years as a lecturer at the university and as an editor before turning full time to writing. His first published work was a collection of short stories titled *Toron, 1867* (Toron, 1867, 1978). He subsequently turned to the novel and in 1980 published *Savonarola*, a large novel based on the life of the martyred Italian political and church reformer Girolamo Savonarola (1452–1498). Two years later, his short biography of Savonarola appeared under the title *Savonarola: Kísérlet* (Savonarola: An Experiment). Nagy's next major publication was a fictionalized account of the personal relationship between the Hungarian Marxist literary critic György Lukács and Irma Seidler: *Kedves Lukács: Lukács György és Seidler Irma* (Dear Lukács: György Lukács and Irma Seidler, 1984). As a playwright, Nagy has written at least a dozen plays, several of which, like some of his prose fiction, are built around the lives of historical figures and most of which abandon traditional dramatic structures. His first play, *Báthory Erzsébet* (1984), for example, features the legendary Transylvanian countess Erzsébet (Elizabeth) Báthory. *Kierkegaard Budapesten: A Kierkegaard-hét elöadásai* (Kierkegaard in Budapest: The Kierkegaard Week Performances; translated as *The Seducer's Diary*), Nagy's only play available in English, is a drama of tormented love and spiritual quest whose principal character is modeled on the Danish philosopher Søren Kierkegaard. The play's premiere was held in Budapest in 1992 as the finale of an International Kierkegaard Conference. *Alma* (1991) is a one-woman play about Alma Mahler, the wife of the composer Gustav Mahler and later of the Austrian writer Franz Werfel. Nagy has also drawn inspiration from classical Russian literature. One of his plays, *Anna Karenina Pályaudvar* (The "Anna Karenina" Railway Station), is based on Tolstoy's novel *Anna Karenina*; *Mi hárman* (The Three of Us, 1991) is an adaptation of Chekhov's *The Three Sisters*. His most recent work, on the Don Juan theme, appeared in 1997 under the title *Az sevillai, a kővendég és a szédelgő* (The Sevilleian, the Stone Guest, and the Swindler). Nagy's plays have been published in the two collections *Biberach és a többiek: Színművek* (Biberach and the Rest: Plays) and *Az sevillai, a kővendég és a szédelgő: Színművek* (The Sevilleian, the Stone Guest, and the Swindler: Plays), both published in 1997. Nagy is also the author of a study of the grotesque, *Kis szörnyestétika* (A Small Aesthetics of the Grotesque, 1993), and a book of essays on three outstanding figures in whom he has long been interested, *Főbenjárás: Kierkegaard, Mahler, Lukács* (Trailblazers: Kierkegaard, Mahler, Lukács, 1998).

Translations: *The Seducer's Diary*, in a version by Julian Garner, in *Hungarian Plays: New Drama from Hungary,* selected and introduced by László Upor (London: Nick Hern, 1996), 3–76.

Nagy, László (1925–1978) Hungarian poet and translator. A native of Felsőiszkáz, in western Hungary, Nagy moved to Budapest in 1946 to study graphic arts but soon entered a newly established "people's college," where he studied philosophy and Russian. It was during this time that he determined to become a poet instead of a painter. His first poems appeared in the December 1947 issue of the journal *Valóság*. In 1949 he published his first book of poetry, *Tűnj el fájás* (Vanish, Pain), in which he wholeheartedly embraced the new socialist economic plans for Hungary. Stylistically, the poems in *Tűnj el fájás* already demonstrate Nagy's effective blend of folk and modernistic elements. From 1949 to 1952, Nagy lived in Bulgaria on a writer's fellowship and studied and translated Bulgarian folk poetry. His disillusionment with conditions in Hungary after his return is reflected in a number of poems that were published for the first time in 1953. From 1953 to 1956, Nagy was on the staff of the children's magazine *Kisdobos,* and from 1959 he worked as picture editor for the weekly *Élét és Irodalom*. Although he did not participate in the 1956 uprising, the pessimism of much of his poetry of the 1950s made it impossible for him to publish anything but translations between 1957 and 1965. His best work is to be found in his collections *Deres majális* (Frosty Fair in May, 1957), which contains poems written from 1944 to 1956, including the splendid long poem "A vasárnap gyönyöre" ("Pleasuring Sunday"), a celebration of life's simpler pleasures; *Himnusz minden időben* (A Hymn for All Seasons, 1965); and *Versben bújdosó* (Hiding in Verse, 1973). Many of Nagy's finest poems deal with love; arguably the best of them, "A forró szél imádata" ("Love of the Scorching Wind"), was dedicated to his wife, the poet Margit Szécsi. A four-volume collection of Nagy's work was published in 1975 under the title *Versek es versfordítások* (Poems and Poetry Translations). Besides his translations from Balkan literatures, Nagy translated works by Federico García Lorca, Dylan Thomas, and the Polish poet Zbigniew Herbert. His last collection of poems, *Jönnek a harangok értem* (The Bells Are Calling for Me), was published posthumously in 1978. Nagy's literary awards include the Attila József Prize (1950, 1953, 1955); the Kossuth Prize (1966); and the Golden Laurel of the International Poetry Festival held in Struga, Yugoslavia, in 1968.

Translations: *Love of the Scorching Wind: Selected Poems, 1953–1971*, trans. Tony Conner and Kenneth McRobbie (London: Oxford University Press, 1973); five poems in *The Colonnade of Teeth: Modern Hungarian Poetry*, ed. George Gömöri and George Szirtes (Newcastle upon Tyne: Bloodaxe, 1996), 137–45; six poems in *The Face of Creation: Contemporary Hungarian Poetry*, trans. Jascha Kessler (Minneapolis: Coffee House, 1988), 80–100; eleven poems in *In Quest of the "Miracle Stag": The Poetry of Hungary*, ed. Adam Makkai (Chicago: Atlantis-Centaur, 1996), 827–36; eleven poems in *Modern Hungarian Poetry*, ed. Miklós Vajda (New York: Columbia University Press), 168–87; thirteen selections, both verse and prose, in *Ocean at the Window: Hungarian Prose and Poetry Since 1945*, ed. Albert Tezla (Minneapolis: University of Minnesota Press, 1980), 187–213; three poems in *Turmoil in Hungary*, ed. and trans. Nicholas Kolumban (St. Paul, Minn.: New Rivers, 1982), 158–61.

Nałkowska, Zofia (1885–1954) Polish novelist, short-story writer, and playwright. A major novelist of the interwar period, Nałkowska composed most of her works in the first half of the twentieth century. The daughter of the well-known scholar and journalist Wacław Nałkowski, she was born in Warsaw where she studied philosophy, history, geography, economics, and linguistics in a secret "flying university" operated to provide university education in Polish, which was not permitted at the time by the authorities of the Russian partition. Raised in a liberal tradition, and with a strong interest in women's issues, Nałkowska made her literary debut in 1898 as a poet with a few poems published in a weekly. Her first novel, *Kobiety* (*Women*), which was translated into English, appeared in 1906. Pretentious and shallow, it was surpassed by such subsequent novels as *Narcyza* (Narcissus, 1910); *Romans Teresy Hennert* (The Romance of Teresa Hennert, 1923); *Dom nad łąkami* (House in the Meadows, 1925); *Niedobra miłość: Romans prowincialny* (An Unwise Love: A Provincial Romance, 1928), which demonstrates a keen knowledge of feminine psychology; and, above all, *Granica* (The Boundary, 1936), which went through a number of post–World War II editions. A well-crafted novel of social analysis, *Granica* deals in large part with the intelligentsia and addresses the network of boundary lines imposed by the social order that inhibits an individual's self-realization.

Before the war, Nałkowska was active in women's and other social organizations and in 1933 was elected a member of the Polish Academy of Literature. During the German occupation, she lived in Warsaw and participated in underground literary activities. After the war, she joined the editorial staff of the influential literary weekly *Kuźnica*. She was also elected a deputy to the Diet. A member of the Commission for the Investigation of Nazi Crimes, in 1946 Nałkowska published a small collection of stories based on her findings under the title *Medaliony* (*Medallions*). Simple and eloquent, the little pieces in this collection represent her major contribution to postwar Polish literature. Other postwar works by Nałkowska include the political novel *Węzły życia* (The Knots of Life, 1948); the autobiographical *Mój ojciec* (My Father, 1953); and, of greater interest, her posthumously published diaries, *Dzienniki czasu wojny* (Wartime Diaries, 1970) and *Dzienniki* (Diaries, 1975). Nałkowska was honored many times in her lifetime for her literary achievements as well as for her social and political contributions.

Literature: Ewa Kraskowska, *Zofia Nałkowska* (Poznań: Rebis, 1999).

Translations: *Kobiety/Women: A Novel of Polish Life* (New York: Putnam, 1920); *Medallions,* trans. Diana Kuprel (Evanston, Ill.: Northwestern University Press, 2000).

Naum, Gellu (b. 1915) Romanian poet, novelist, and playwright. A native of Bucharest, where he was educated through university, and the son of André Naum, a poet of local reputation and a war hero, Naum was one of the leading figures in pre– and post–World War II Romanian surrealism. He belonged to the circle of surrealists that included the painters Victor Brauner and Jacques Hérold and the writers Paul Păun, Gherasim Luca (real name Zollmann Locker), and Virgil Teodorescu. Naum made his literary debut in 1936 with the nine-poem collection *Drumețul incendiar* (The Incendiary Voyager), which was published in the Bucharest Surrealist Collection. The poems were accompanied by drawings by Brauner. His second volume of poetry, also published in the Surrealist Collection, appeared the following year. It contained ten poems under the title *Libertatea de a dormi pe o frunte* (The Freedon to Sleep on One's Forehead) and included a drawing by Brauner. Naum's last publication before the outbreak of war was the twelve-poem collection *Vasco da Gama,* which appeared in the Surrealist Collection in 1940 accompanied by a drawing by Hérold. Naum served in the Romanian army from 1941 to 1943, first as an enlisted man and then as an officer in the cavalry corps. He was retired from active service in November 1943 because of ill health and spent a long period of convales-

cence with his family. It was during this time that he compiled a collection of thirty-six "automatic" poems under the title *Culoarul somnului* (The Corridor of Sleep). It appeared, with a portrait of Naum by Brauner, in the Surrealist Collection in September 1944 when Bucharest was already under Allied and Soviet occupation. In 1945 Naum published his first collection of prose, *Medium,* some of which had been written in 1940 and 1941 before the outbreak of hostilities. The work consists of a hallucinatory biographical account of the poet's meanderings around Bucharest after his return from Paris in the early autumn of 1940. It was in this context that he had a premonition that he would meet the woman predestined for him. He in fact met her, in 1943, during the war. Her name was Lydgia Alexandrescu, and she later became Naum's second wife and the inspiration of his major prose work, the essentially autobiographical surrealist novel *Zenobia* (1985). In recognition of their union, Naum added a second "l" (in honor of Lydgia) to his first name, which was originally spelled Gelu.

Two other collections of Naum's prose appeared in 1945 and 1946: *Teribilul interzis* (The Frightful Prohibition), which contains four stories plus fragments of an unfinished play written during the war and boasts a frontispiece by Păun, and *Castelul orbilor* (The Castle of the Blind), actually a long poem in prose. The year 1946 also brought a joint work by Naum and Teodorescu titled *Spectrul longevității. 122 de cadavre* (The Specter of Longevity. 122 Cadavers), a collection of "automatic" texts and games generated during an evening at Tedorescu's.

The regrouping of the Bucharest surrealists after the war was heralded by their grand exhibition at the Cretulescu Gallery in January 1945. From 7 to 28 January and from 20 February to 11 March, a separate surrealist show was held elsewhere in Bucharest by a rival group headed by Gherasim Luca and Dolfi Trost. Dissension between the two groups, especially over the matter of theory, became acrimonious and erupted in heated polemics. Naum and his fellow surrealists Păun and Teodorescu went on the attack with their manifesto *Critica mizeriei* (The Criticism of Poverty, 1945), a violent attack on Romanian criticism and the Romanian avant-garde of the 1930s that appeared in the Surrealist Collection. A counterattack by the Luca–Trost faction, *Dialectique de la dialectique* (The Dialectic of Dialectics), was also published in 1945. A further source of friction, which found Naum at odds with a few of his own colleagues, was the creation in 1946 of a collection of surrealist texts in French under the title *Infranoir* (Infra-Black). Naum strenuously objected to the fact that the entire work was to be in French and wanted no part of the project. *Infranoir* was nevertheless published in 1947 in the form of a manifesto signed by all five members of the group and subtitled *Préliminaires à une intervention surthaumaturgique dans la conquête du désirable* (Prelimaries to a Surthaumaturgical Intervention in the Conquest of the Desirable). The manifesto had been preceded in the autumn of 1946 by an exhibition under the same name at a Bucharest gallery. Two additional manifestos, in French, to which Naum contributed also appeared in 1947: *Éloge de Malombre* (Elegy of Malombra) and *Le Sable nocturne* (The Sands of Night). Both were later included in Marin Mincu's *Avangarda literară românească* (The Romanian Literary Avant-Garde, 1983); The Sands of Night was also published in Paris in 1947 in *Le Surréalisme en 1947*.

The frenzied literary activity of 1947 was, in retrospect, the swan song of Romanian surrealism. The encroachments of censorship kept pace with the ominous political developments of 1947 when with the forced abdication of King Mihai I nothing stood in the way of the complete communist takeover of the country in 1948. After the publication of their two short manifestos in 1947, the group of five disbanded, its members going their separate ways.

Until he was able to publish his own kind of poetry again in the late 1960s, Naum kept himself alive as a writer through such collections of poems in the officially sanctioned realistic style as *Filonul* (The Lode, 1952) and *Tabăra din munți* (The Camp in the Mountains, 1953); translations, mainly from the French; and children's literature, beginning with the story *Așa-i Sanda* (Here's Sanda) in 1956. This was followed in 1959 by *Cartea cu Apolodor* (The Adventures of Apollodore) and in 1964 by *A doua carte cu Apolodor* (The Second Book of Apollodore). The Apollodore books were reprinted many times and won Naum the Prize for Children's Literature of the Romanian Writers Union in 1958. Transformed into a puppet play, the Apollodore stories were also honored at the International Puppet Festival in Warsaw in 1962.

Poeme despre tinerețea noastră (Poems of Our Youth), which drew on Naum's own early years and can be related to his children's literature, appeared in 1960. The book contained drawings by the artist Jules Perahim, who had illustrated all of Naum's children's books. With the gradual easing of censorship, Naum was able to publish weightier books of poetry. *Soarele calm* (The Calm Sun), a small collection of twelve poems, appeared in 1961. But the work that truly marked Naum's return to active publishing was *Athanor* (1968), an important collection of ninety-two poems in six cycles containing mostly texts written during the long years when Naum was prohibited from publication. The year 1968 also brought with it a boost to Naum's international reputation. The French poet Alain Bosquet, whom Naum had met on his previous sojourns in Paris, included seven of Naum's poems in his *L'Anthologie de la poésie roumaine* (Anthology of Romanian Poetry). Another poem, translated by André Fleury, appeared in the January 1968 issue of *Nouvelle Revue française. Athanor* was followed in 1970 by *Poeme alese* (Selected Poems), which was based on previous collections; the volume contains a portrait of Naum by Brauner. Several other volumes of poetry appeared from 1971 to 1990: *Copacul animal* (The Animal Tree, 1971); *Tatăl meu obosit* (*My Tired Father*, 1972), a collage-like collection of largely disconnected very short prose fragments, some apparently autobiographical, some scientific, drawn from a wide range of sources and having nothing to do with Naum's father; *Poeme alese* (Selected Poems, 1974), a second collection of mostly previously published poems; *Descrierea turnului* (The Description of the Tower, 1975), actually two editions of basically the same collection of poems, the longer edition being a noncommercial publication and the other, published by a state publishing house with certain texts deleted because of the censor's objections; *Partea cealaltă* (The Other Shore, 1980); and *Malul albastru* (The Blue River Bank, 1990). A collection of prose and various fragments appeared in 1970 under the title *Poetizați, poetizați ...* (Poeticize! Poeticize!). Arguably Naum's best-known prose work, the novel *Zenobia* was published in Bucharest in 1985.

Naum's theatrical writing began in earnest in 1962, the year he wrote *Poate Eleonora* (Eleanor, Perhaps). *Insula* (The Island), a takeoff on the story of Robinson Crusoe, came next in 1963, followed in 1966 by *Ceasornicăria Taus* (Taus the Watchmaker), first published in 1972 in the Italian journal *Il Drama*. All three plays were published in a collection of Naum's plays issued in Bucharest in 1979. Naum has also adapted Diderot's novel *Le Neveu de Rameu* (Rameau's Nephew) and Beckett's *Waiting for Godot* for the Romanian stage.

In addition to his awards for children's literature and a puppet play, Naum won the Translation Prize of the Writers Union in 1968; the Poetry Prize of the Writers Union in 1975; and a special award for his complete literary activity by the Writers Union in 1986.

As Naum's political and material circumstances improved beginning in the late 1950s and 1960s, he was again able to travel to foreign countries, which he did extensively. Although his favorite port of call was Paris, where he had spent the most time abroad before World War II and where he maintained contact with the French surrealists, he eagerly took advantage of the opportunity to visit the United States. On an invitation by a relative in America, and with financial support from the cultural affairs office of the American Embassy in Bucharest, Naum and his wife, Lydgia, spent the period from 28 December 1982 to 4 March 1983 in the United States. They visited New York, Washington, D.C., Virginia Beach, San Francisco, and Berkeley, where Naum gave readings of his poems at the University of California with simultaneous translation into English by a member of the Berkeley faculty.

Literature: Rémy Laville, *Gellu Naum: Poète roumain prisonnier au château des aveugles* (Paris: Éditions L'Harmattan, 1994), a popularly written biography of Naum intended primarily for a French audience and thin on critical analysis of Naum's works.

Translations: *My Tired Father: Pohem*, trans. James Brook (Copenhagen: Green Integer, 1999); *Zenobia*, trans. James Brook and Sasha Vlad (Evanston, Ill.: Northwestern University Press, 1995); five poems in *46 Romanian Poets in English*, trans. Ştefan Avădanei and Don Eulert (Iaşi: Junimea, 1973), 144–48.

Neagu, Fănuș (b. 1932) Romanian novelist, short-story writer, and playwright. Neagu was born in the district of Gradiştea de-jos, where he attended primary school from 1939 to 1944. In 1948 he completed his studies at the military secondary school in Iaşi. He prepared for a teaching career in Bucharest and Galaţi and in 1953 became a teacher of Romanian language and literature in Largu. In 1954 he was appointed editor of the national youth newspaper *Scînteia Tineretului.* Before entering Bucharest University, Neagu was among the first graduates of the Mihai Eminescu School of Literature. Neagu's extensive work as a newspaper and journal editor included affiliation with such journals as *Luceafărul* and *Amfiteatru.* He made his debut as a writer of fiction with the story "Duşman cu lumea" ("The World Is My Enemy," 1954), which was first published in the journal *Tînărul scriitor* (The Young Writer). His first collection of stories, *Ningea în Bărăgan* (It Was Snowing in the Bărăgan), appeared in 1959. Neagu's Romantic treatment of the peasant landscape in his early works as well as his narrative technique recall the style of his eminent predecessor Mihai Sadoveanu. For the atmospherics of the Danubian area and its Balkan picturesqueness, Neagu was clearly indebted to the Romanian writer Panait Istratis (1884–1935). Neagu's typical blend of the realistic and the fantastic shows up well in such subsequent collections of stories as *Somnul de la amiază* (The Afternoon Nap, 1960) and *Dincolo de nisipuri* (Beyond the Sands, 1962). His first novel, *Îngerul a strigat* (The Angel Has Shouted), was published in 1968. This was followed in 1976 by his second novel, *Frumoşii nebuni ai marilor oraşe* (The Handsome Madmen of the Big City), subtitled *Fals tratat despre iubire* (A False Treatise on Love).

Neagu was also the author of a few plays. In collaboration with Vintilă Ornaru, he wrote *Apostolii* (The Apostles, 1966) and, by himself, the absurdist and parable-like *Echipa de zgomote* (The Smell Factory, 1971).

Neagu was honored several times for his literary achievements. He won the Writers Union Prize for his short-story collection *Cantonul părăsit* (The Abandoned Station Attendant's House, 1964) and the same award for the novel *Îngerul a strigat* (1968). His collection of fairy tales, *Caii albi din oraşul Bucureşti* (The White Horses of Bucharest, 1967), was awarded the Prize of the Central Committee of the Communist Youth Association.

Translations: "Beyond the Sands," in *The Phantom Church and Other Stories from Romania,* trans. and ed. Georgiana Farnoaga and Sharon King (Pittsburgh: University of Pittsburgh Press, 1996), 18–23; excerpts from *Ningea în Bărăgan,* in *Introduction to Rumanian Literature,* ed. Jacob Steinberg (New York: Twayne, 1966), 408–27.

Nedelciu, Mircea (1950–1999) Romanian novelist and short-story writer. One of the best writers to emerge from the generation of the 1980s, Nedelciu was born in the village of Fundulea, in the Ilfov district. After graduating from local schools, he went on to study philology at Bucharest University, from which he received his degree in 1973. He published his first book, the short-story collection *Aventuri într-o curte interioară* (Adventures in a Courtyard), in 1979. It was followed by *Efectul de ecou controlat* (The Controlled Echo Effect, 1981), a collection of short fiction; *Amendment la instinctul proprietăţii* (Amendment to the Instinct of Ownership, 1983); *Zmeura de cîmpie* (Wild Raspberry, 1984), a novel; *Tratament fabulatoriu* (Fabling Treatment, 1986; 2nd ed., 1996), a novel; *Şi ieri va fi o zi* (Yesterday Will Be Another Day, 1989), short stories; *Femeia în roşu* (Lady in Red, 1990; 2nd ed., 1997), a novel written with Adriana Babeţi and Mircea Mihăieş; and *Povestea poveştilor generaţiei '80* (The Story of the Stories of the '80s Generation, 1998), a novel that is said to have been written in November 1988 during a single night. In 1999, before his death, he collected all his short fiction in a large book to which he gave the title of his first collection, *Aventuri într-o curte interioară*.

In 1990 Nedelciu began working as secretary of the Romanian Writers Union. He also became editor of the review *Contrapunct* and was president of the Euromedia Cultural Association. After the regime of Nicolae Ceauşescu was overthrown in December 1989, Nedelciu was the principal founder of the independent Association of Professional Writers of Romania (ASPRO). In 1991 Nedelciu was diagnosed with cancer and was invited to France for an operation, with the support and financial aid of French writers. The operation was to have taken place in 1995, but Nedelciu's visa expired and he had to return to Romania and request a new one. The visa was late in coming, but he eventually returned to France and was operated on in 1997. The surgery was of limited success, and Nedelciu died on 14 July 1999. Not long after Nedelciu's death, a previously planned premiere of Catalina Buzoianu's adaptation of his novel *Femeia în roşu* at the National Theater in Timişoara took on the semblance of an homage to the respected writer.

While a member of the Junimea student literary club at Bucharest University directed by the critic and professor Ovid S. Crohmălniceanu, Nedelciu formulated a so-called textualist school of writing, which in effect created a shared proprietary relationship among the author, the text, and the reader. As his prose fiction amply demonstrates, this took the form mainly of textual interpolations and footnotes on how the text was generated as well as suggestions as to how readers might choose to read and "perceive" it. Nedelciu frequently addresses his readers directly, explaining his approach to the narrative and sharing with them the different possible perspectives on an event.

A previously unpublished heavily autobiographical short novel by Nedelciu, *Zodia scafandului* (Sign of the Frogman), believed to have been written between 1988 and 1992 and dated 1996 (possibly the date of a revised version of the text) was published posthumously in 2000.

Nedelciu won the Writers Union Prize in 1979 for *Aventuri într-o curte interioară* and the Ion Creanga Prize of the Romanian Academy. In 1991 *Femeia în roşu* was awarded the Writers Union Prize. Nedelciu was also honored by the Association of Professional Writers of Romania for his last book, *Povestea poveştilor generaţiei '80*.

Translations: "Forbidden Story" (from *Amendment la instinctul proprietăţii*), in *The Phantom Church and Other Stories from Romania*, ed. and trans. Georgiana Farnoaga and Sharon King (Pittsburgh: University of Pittsburgh Press, 1996), 53–61.

Nedelcovici, Bujor (b. 1936) Romanian novelist. A native of Bîrlad, Nedelcovici moved with his family to the city of Ploeşti while he was still a child. It was there that he received his elementary- and secondary-school education. In 1958 he earned a degree in law at Bucharest University and briefly practiced his profession. This was interrupted when, for the next twelve years, he was pressed into work on a hydroelectric station and other construction jobs. Nedelcovici made his literary debut in 1970 with his novel *Ultimii* (The Last), a kind of parable on the theme of the individual and history. Together with two successive novels, *Fără vîsle* (Without Oars, 1972) and *Noaptea* (Nighttime, 1974), it forms the *Moştenitorii* (The Heirs) cycle. When it appeared, *Noaptea* was widely acclaimed and won the prize of the Bucharest Writers Association. Nedelcovici's next novel was *Grădina Icoanei* (Garden of the Icon, 1977). His fifth novel, *Zile de nisip* (Days of Sand, 1979), a "police novel," was honored by the Writers Association and later made into a movie. The three novels *Fără vîsle, Noaptea,* and *Grădina Icoanei* were reissued as a trilogy under the title *Somnul vameşului* (The Publican's Sleep), which Nedelcovici himself described as a "mosaic novel" or a "sketch in motion" rather than a "family chronicle." His next work, *Al doilea mesager* (The Second Messenger, 1985), an anti-utopian novel usually compared with those of Aldous Huxley and George Orwell, was denied permission by the censors for publication in Romania. However, it was published in Paris by the house of Albin Michel and won the Prix de la Liberté of the French PEN Club. The original Romanian version appeared for the first time in 1991 and was awarded the Romanian-American Academy of Arts and Sciences Prize the following year. Under the title *Somnul insulei* (Dream of the Island), it was made into a film directed by Mircea Veroiu and premiered at the Festival of Arcachon in France. It was shown on Romanian television in 1995. Although Nedelcovici had held the position of editor in chief of *Almanah literar* of the prose section of the Bucharest Writers Association since 1982, in 1987 he fell subject to political repression and was forced to emigrate. He sought refuge in France, where by then he enjoyed a certain name recognition. In 1990 he was elected "chevalier" of the Order of Arts and Letters and made a member of the editorial board of the review *Esprit.* Nedelcovici's status as a writer in France was further solidified in 1991/1992 when he became a titular member of the Society of Authors and Dramatic Composers and the Society of French Men of Letters. In 1998 the Eminescu publishing house in Bucharest brought out Nedelcovici's richly detailed and quite interesting diary of his exile under the title *Jurnal infidel: Pagini din exil, 1987–1993* (Disloyal Journal: Pages from Exile, 1987–1993). Of equal interest is the companion volume, *Aici şi acum* (Here and Now, 1996), which consists of a number of short articles published in various journals, texts of broadcasts over the BBC, and interviews arranged in this order: Paris (1987–1995), Bucharest (1970–1987), and film chronicles from Paris (1987–1992).

With the downfall of the regime of Nicolae Ceauşescu, Nedelcovici was again able to publish in Romania. His first book to appear in his native country after his exile to France was *Îmblînzitorul de lupi* (The Tamer of Wolves, 1991), a strange, unquieting work about an émigré Romanian journalist who disappears and the efforts of his wife and son to discover his whereabouts. Intended to convey the sense of unreality and mysteriousness of the life of an exile, it was issued in French translation in 1994. In 1992 the Dramatic Theater of Baia Mare staged Nedelcovici's play *Noaptea de solstiţiu* (Night of the Solstice). The same year, his volume of stories *Oratoriu pentru imprudenţa* (Oratory for Imprudence) was published. Nedelcovici's French publisher, Éditions Actes Sud, also brought out his novel *Le Matin d'un miracle* (The Morning of a Miracle) in 1992. Set in an unspecified land, probably Romania, the work traces the efforts by a woman to heal herself after a great but destructive passion. The Romanian version, *Dimineaţa unui miracol,* was published in 1993 and was honored by the Writers Union. In 1994/1995, Nedelcovici visited the United States and delivered a series of lectures in California (Los Angeles, San Diego, Riverside, and Pasadena). In 1997 he published *Provocatorul* (The Provocateur), an entertaining, in some ways parodic novel about a torrid love affair between Céline, a student of film and a scenarist, and Guy, a former journalist become actor who is also a jazz pianist. The work is wholly French in tone, set in France, with French characters, peppered with lines and even paragraphs in French, and motivated by Nedelcovici's desire to understand French society after living in it for ten years as a political exile.

Translations: *Al doilea mesager* is available in French as *Le Second Messager,* trans. Alain Paruit (Paris: Albin Michel, 1985); *Dimineaţa unui miracol* as *Le Matin d'un miracle,* trans. Alain Paruit (Arles: Actes Sud, 1992); *Îmblînzitorul de lupi* as *Le Dompteur de loups,* trans. Alain Paruit (Arles: Actes Sud, 1994); and *Zile de nisip* as *Crime de sable,* trans. Alain Paruit (Paris: Albin Michel, 1989).

Németh, Ákos (b. 1964) Hungarian playwright. Németh was born in Székesfehérvár, not far southwest of Budapest, and graduated from Eötvös Lóránd University with a degree in history and literature. He wrote his first play, *Lili Hofberg,* at the age of twenty-two; it was produced in 1990. Németh has since written five other plays: *A Heidler-színház utolsó napjai* (The Last Days of the Heidler Theater, 1987), a sequel to *Lili Hofberg; Vörös bál* (Red Ball, 1989); *Müller táncosai* (*Müller's Dancers*), first produced in 1992; *Júlia és a hadnagya* (Julia and Her Lieutenant), first produced in 1993; and *Anita* (1994). There are three distinct foci in Németh's plays: earlier twentieth-century Hungarian history, as in *Vörös bál,* which deals with the short-lived communist revolution in Hungary in 1919, and *A Heidler-színház utolsó napjai;* the maddening complexities of male–female relationships, especially as in *Júlia és a hadnagya,* a dark love story involving a discharged army officer and a stripper, and *Anita;* and theater as sociopolitical allegory, as in *Lili Hofberg, A Heidler-színház utolsó napjai,* and *Müller's Dancers.* Set in Austria in 1933, the year Hitler became chancellor of Germany, *Lili Hofberg* examines the usual petty intrigues in a theatrical company against the background of a changing, increasingly more menacing political climate. The allusions to the traumas of postcommunist change in Hungary are unmistakable in *Müller's Dancers,* which deals with the painful ad-

justments a theater company's anything but flatteringly portrayed dancers must make, in both their careers and their private lives, when the company's famous director deserts them after many years. Németh's attraction to the sordid and even criminal is evident in *Müller's Dancers* as much as in *Júlia és a hadnagya.* His most recent play, *Haszonvágy* (Lust for Profit), appeared in 1999.

Translations: *Müller's Dancers,* in a version by Daniel Mornin from a translation by Pálma Melis and László Upor, in *Hungarian Plays: New Drama from Hungary,* selected and introduced by László Upor (London: Nick Hern, 1996), 123–74.

Neumann, Gert (real name Gert Härtl; b. 1942) German novelist. Born in Lidzbark, Warmia, Poland, Neumann was trained as a tractor operator and locksmith and, after obligatory military service, worked at various jobs. When he developed an interest in writing, he enrolled in the Johannes R. Becher Literary Institute in Leipzig, but was expelled from it for the expression of views incompatible with official doctrine. He was also dismissed from the Communist Party, which he had joined in 1960, and banned from publication. He subsequently became involved in the editing and publishing of several unofficial journals, among them *Anschlag* (1986–1988) and *Zweite Person* (1987–1988). Since he was prohibited from publishing in the German Democratic Republic, and in fact was treated as a nonperson by being omitted from official literary histories, Neumann turned to West German publishers and brought out his first book, *Die Schuld der Worte* (The Guilt of Words, 1979), with the venerable firm of Fischer of Frankfurt am Main. From the beginning, it was obvious that Neumann's stock-in-trade was to be an uncompromisingly experimental form of prose writing at odds with the tenets of the

Party that governed creative writing. In his next book, *Elf Uhr* (Eleven O'Clock, 1981), which was similarly published outside the GDR, Neumann further alienated the authorities by depicting a Leipzig department store as the model for East German society. Relentless in his effort to shape a highly individual means of expression, Neumann drew inspiration from Kafka and Joyce as well as from the works of the French thinkers Jacques Lacan and Gilles Deleuze and contemporary linguistic theory. His next novel, *Die Klandestinität der Kesselreiniger: Ein Versuch des Sprechens* (The Clandestineness of the Pot Cleaners: A Way of Speaking, 1989), extended the hermeticism of his language by eschewing traditional norms of grammar. Neumann's other publications include the privately printed *Die Stimme des Schweigens* (The Voice of Silence, 1987) and *Anschlag* (The Poster, 1999). Neumann was permitted to leave the GDR in 1989.

Neutsch, Erik (b. 1931) German novelist, short-story writer, playwright, journalist, and poet. Neutsch was born in Schönebeck. He joined the Socialist Unity Party in 1949 and, from 1953 to 1956, studied journalism in Leipzig, thereafter becoming the culture editor of the journal *Freiheit*. In 1960 he became a freelance writer. Neutsch began his literary career with a collection of short stories titled *Bitterfelde Geschichten* (The Bitterfeld Stories, 1961). The title of the collection is symptomatic of Neutsch's general literary orientation—that advocated by the Bitterfeld conferences of the first half of the 1960s. These meetings sought to develop a new relationship between artists and workers by calling for artists to support the creative efforts of workers and to learn at first hand about workers and their outlook by taking jobs in industry. Neutsch's first novel, *Spur der Steine* (Trace of Stone, 1964), was a further exemplification of the Bitterfeld ide-

ology. The novel proved popular, went through a large number of editions, and was made into a film in 1966. Neutsch's second novel, *Auf der Suche nach Gatt* (In Search of Gatt, 1973), was considered a negative response to Christa Wolf's highly controversial *The Quest for Christa T.* Motivated by the desire to create a kind of East German socialist epic work depicting the fate of his own generation, Neutsch undertook the writing of an extraordinarily ambitious six-part novel under the title *Friede im Osten* (Peace in the East). Four volumes were published between 1974 and 1989: *Am Fluss* (At the River, 1974); *Frühling mit Gewalt* (Springtime with a Vengeance, 1978); *Wenn Feuer erlöschen* (When the Fires Go Out, 1985); and *Nahe der Grenze* (Near the Border, 1987). The last volume was withdrawn from publication in 1990 by Neutsch himself because of its false picture of the Warsaw Pact invasion of Czechoslovakia in 1968. Neutsch's other works include the novels *Claus und Claudia: Nach neueren Dokumentation* (Claus and Claudia: Based on Newer Documentation, 1989) and *Totschlag* (Death Blow, 1994); *Haut oder Hemd: Schauspiel und Dokumentation* (Skin or Shirt: A Play and Documentation, 1981), a four-act play "in the Halle Version revised according to the Cottbus production"; and several collections of short stories and other works of prose fiction: *Zweite Begegnung und andere Geschichten* (Second Meeting and Other Stories, 1961); *Heldenberichte: Erzählungen und Kurz Prosa* (Reports of Heroes: Stories and Other Short Prose, 1976); *Tage unseres Lebens: Geschichten* (Days of Our Lives: Stories, 1979); *Forster in Paris: Erzählung* (Forster in Paris: A Tale, 1981), which was reissued in 1994 with the addition of three essays; and *Hirt: Erzählung* (The Innkeeper: A Tale, 1978). Neutsch is also the author of a book of essays titled *Fast die Wahrheit: Ansichten zu Kunst und Literatur* (Almost the Truth: Views on Art and

Literature, 1979). Neutsch was awarded the GDR National Prize in 1964 and the Heinrich Mann Prize in 1971.

Translations: "Hartholz," trans. Jan van Heurck, in *The New Sufferings of Young W. and Other Stories from the German Democratic Republic,* ed. Therese Hörnigk and Alexander Stephan (New York: Continuum, 1997), 104–20.

Nikolov, Liubomir (b. 1954) Bulgarian poet. Born in the village of Kiriaevo, in the Vidin region of northwestern Bulgaria, Nikolov completed high school in Kula and then studied journalism at Sofia University, from which he graduated in 1979. In 1980 he began working as an editor at *Literaturen front* and in 1984 participated in the International Writing Program at the University of Iowa. His first published book of poems, *Povikani ot prliva* (Called by the Tides), appeared in 1981 and was followed by three other collections: *Putnik* (Traveler, 1987); *Piiano sluntse* (The Tipsy Sun, 1991); and *Garvan* (Raven, 1995). With Hristo Tsachev and Marko Malamov, Nikolov wrote a book on the Rodopa combine in Stara Zagora, *Kombinat "Rodopa" Stara Zagora* (1985), and in 1992 wrote the text for a picture book titled *Ognena pustiniia* (The Fiery Desert). Nikolov's poetry draws much of its inspiration from village life and the world of nature. Trees, flowers, animals, and insects abound. Although he celebrates the joy of family life, Nikolov also expresses a yearning to be free of the senses and often alludes to the harshness of life and to death, the mystery of which fascinates him. It is, however, the delicate nature images that stand out most prominently in his generally short poems. Nikolov has a good knowledge of English and has published translations of works by British and American poets. His anthology of contemporary American poetry appeared in 1989 under the title *Pir vsled tainata vecheria* (Banquet During the Last Supper). In January 1990, Nikolov was chosen Poet of the Month for the BBC's Radio Three.

Translations: *Pagan: Poems by Lyubomir Nikolov,* trans. Roland Flint and Viara Tcholakova (Pittsburgh: Carnegie Mellon University Press, 1992).

Nikolov, Nino (b. 1933) Bulgarian poet, essayist, and translator. Born in Troian, Nikolov finished high school in Sofia in 1950 and then studied journalism and Hungarian language and literature at Budapest University, from which he graduated in 1955. He pursued graduate studies in aesthetics in Budapest from 1956 to 1959 and international relations in Moscow from 1960 to 1962. Nikolov began working as a Hungarian translator for the Bulgarian Committee for Cultural Relations with Foreign Countries in 1956; in 1960 he was employed by the Ministry of Internal Affairs, and in 1963 by the Ministry of Foreign Affairs. After founding the Information Center for Translation of the Bulgarian Writers Union, he served as its director from 1963 to 1966. From 1966 to 1969, he headed the foreign section of the periodical *Literaturen front.* In 1970 he became director of the Bulgarian Cultural Center in Budapest, a position he held until 1972 and again from 1984 to 1989. From 1972 to 1974, he was vice chairman of the Congress for Friendship and Cultural Relations with Foreign Countries and, from 1974 to 1984, a leading official of the Writers Union. He held the position of editor in chief of *Literaturen front* in 1989/1990 and, in 1990, was named an honorary lecturer in Hungarian language and literature at Sofia University.

Although he has published journalistic articles and essays, Nikolov is above all a poet. His publications include the following volumes of poetry: *Spodeleni minuti* (Shared Minutes, 1959); *Svetlini krai relsite* (Lights Along the Tracks, 1967); *Godinite ne si prilichat* (The Years Do Not Resemble Each

Other, 1967); *Vsiako zavrushtane e mulchalivo* (Every Homecoming Is Silent, 1972); *Bezsunie* (Insomnia, 1974); *Prisustvieto na moreto* (The Presence of the Sea, 1975); *I otrazheniiata na dalechiia briag* (Reflections of a Distant Shore, 1976); *Stihotvoreniia* (Poems, 1977); *Stihotvoreniia od petdesette godini* (Poems from the 1950s, 1977); *Liato, chetvurtuk* (Summer, Thursday, 1978); *Poemi* (Poems, 1979); *Dokato stupkite se razminavat: Liricheski poemi* (Until Our Paths Cross: Lyric Poems, 1982); *Kato duh* (Like Spirit, 1983); *Sled Kolumb* (After Columbus, 1983); *Nikulden: Izbrana lirika* (Saint Nicholas's Day: Selected Lyrics, 1983); *Krasi mira v bialo: Liubovna lirika* (Paint the World White: Love Lyrics, 1983); and *Pusteiat klonite: Osmostishiia* (The Branches Wither: Octets, 1989).

A careful craftsman with a keen eye for apparently insignificant details, Nikolov has written on a wide variety of subjects from the national to the universal, including his visits to England, Vietnam, and the USSR, among others. In a number of poems, he expresses a certain sense of impermanence, of passing and separation, and of the worthiness of the struggle for human dignity. Unhappy over conditions in Bulgaria in the 1960s, he withdrew from a public literary career for several years and returned to it only in the late 1960s and 1970s. Apart from his many translations from both classical and modern Hungarian literature, Nikolov has translated several Russian and English-language poets, including Robinson Jeffers and Dylan Thomas. In 1992 he completed his twenty-year project of translating the Finnish national epic, the *Kalevala,* into Bulgarian. In recognition of his achievement, in 1993 he was awarded Finland's Order of the Golden Lion. Nikolov has been a guest in the University of Iowa's International Writing Program.

Translations: Three poems, trans. May Swenson and Richard Harteis, in *Poets of Bulgaria,* ed. William Meredith (Greensboro, N.C.: Unicorn, 1985), 69–71.

Nikolova, Olivera (b. 1936) Macedonian novelist and playwright. Nikolova was born and educated in Skopje, where she has long been a resident. Her writing deals mostly with the life of the modern, urbanized Macedonian woman. Her first published novel was *Den za letuvanje* (A Day for a Holiday, 1964). After a long hiatus, she reappeared on the literary scene with the novel *Tesna vrata* (Narrow Doors, 1983), followed in 1989 by *Domašni zadači* (Domestic Chores). *Trombot* (1997), a change of pace for Nikolova, is crime novel set in the world of sports. *Srebrenoto jabolko: Dramski tekstovi* (The Silver Apple: Dramatic Texts), a collection of plays for stage and radio, came next in 1998.

Translations: "Saturday Evening," in *The Big Horse and Other Stories of Modern Macedonia,* ed. Milne Holton (Columbia: University of Missouri Press, 1974), 183–90.

Njatin, Lela B. (b. 1963) Slovenian novelist, critic, and screenwriter. Born in Ljubljana, Njatin (a pen name) studied comparative literature and philosophy at Ljubljana University. In 1988 she published her first novel, *Nestrpnost* (Intolerance). As a critic, she contributed the interview section on E. H. Gombrich to John Hutchinson's *Antony Gormley/John Hutchinson, E. H. Gombrich/Lela B. Njatin* (London: Phaidon, 1995). She has also edited a book of interviews with members of the young Slovenian literary generation of the 1980s under the title *Začasno bivališče: Portreti mlade književne generacije 80-ih let* (Temporary Residence: Portraits of the Young Literary Generation of the '80s, 1990).

Translations: "The Dead Perpetually Dream the Truth (Wings of Desire over Ljubljana)," "Intolerance (A Fragment)," and "Intolerance (Another Fragment)," trans. Anna Čeh, and "Why Do These Black Worms Fly Just Everywhere I Am Myself Only Accidentally," trans. Krištof Jacek

Kozak, in *The Day Tito Died: Contemporary Slovenian Short Stories* (London: Forest, 1993), 104–16.

Noll, Dieter (b. 1927) German novelist, poet, and journalist. A native of Riesa, Noll was pressed into military service in 1945 and was taken prisoner by the Americans. After the war, he finished his secondary schooling and in 1946 became a member of the Communist Party. He then went on to Jena University, where he studied philosophy, art history, and German literature. In 1950 he settled in Berlin, where he worked as a journalist for the journal *Aufbau*. He became a freelance writer in 1956. Noll's literary reputation rested initially on his two books of reportage: *Neues vom lieben närrischen Nest: Erlebnisse eines jungen Mannes in der Zeiss-Stadt Jena* (News from the Dear Mad Nest: The Experiences of a Young Man in Jena, the City of Zeiss, 1950) and *Die Dame Perlon und andere Reportagen* (The Lady Perlon and Other Reportage, 1953). As a writer of fiction, his major effort was the two-volume bildungsroman (educational novel) *Die Abenteuer des Werner Holt: Roman einer Jugend* (The Adventures of Werner Holt: A Novel of Youth, 1960) and *Die Abenteuer des Werner Holt: Roman einer Heimkehr* (The Adventures of Werner Holt: The Novel of a Homecoming, 1963). The work enjoyed considerable success, was widely translated, and was made into a film in 1964. Arguably the first volume is the more effective in its gritty portrait of the shattered illusions of those Germans who went off to war from 1943 to 1945 with exaggerated notions of heroism instilled in them by Nazi ideology. Noll planned to continue the story of Werner Holt and his generation in successive volumes, but only a second volume was published, carrying the story up to the year 1946. Noll's other works include the novel *Kippenberg* (1979), a rather good, if in basic respects formulaic, "industrial novel" about tensions and intrigue in an institute of biological research narrated in the first person by the doctor and chemist Joachim Kibbenberg, and a collection of poems spanning twenty years published in 1985 under the title *In Liebe leben: Gedichte, 1962–1982* (Living in Love: Poems, 1962–1982). In 1979 Noll published an open letter to Erich Honecker, then head of the Communist Party of the German Democratic Republic, which resulted in the expulsion from the Writers Union of such fellow writers as Stefan Heym, Joachim Seyppel, and Rolf Schneider.

Novak, Boris A. (b. 1953) Slovenian poet and playwright. One of the more interesting Slovenian writers to emerge in the 1970s and 1980s, Novak was born in Belgrade where he was educated through high school. He then went on to Ljubljana University, where he earned a degree in comparative literature and philosophy. After graduating, he worked as dramatic adviser to the Ljubljana Drama Theater and as editor at the *Kurirček* review. His subsequent affiliation as editor with the influential and prestigious *Nova Revija* brought him into conflict with the communist authorities when in 1987 the special fifty-seventh number of the review took up the matter of Slovenian independence. The government began a campaign against the literary community and threatened the review itself with closure. Novak wrote about the entire matter in the sixty-ninth and seventieth issues of *Nova Revija* in 1988. After the dust settled from the affair, Novak became editor in charge of the children's literature section at the Slovenian State Publishing House (DZS) in Ljubljana and, in 1991, chairman of the Slovenian PEN Center. In 1991 he visited the University of Tennessee (Chattanooga) for a semester as a lecturer on poetry. Three years later, he was named chairman of the International Peace Committee of PEN.

Novak's very active literary career has assumed many forms. Apart from the poetry for which he is best known, he has written a large number of poems and, especially, plays for children; published his own translations of the poetry of Mallarmé and Valéry, with commentaries; edited or coedited over a dozen literary anthologies; recorded musical and literary tapes; and published a scholarly study (based on his doctoral dissertation) on the reception in Slovenian poetry of poetic forms borrowed from Romance languages. Novak published his first volume of poetry in 1977 under the title *Stihožitje* (Verse Hagiography). It was followed by *Hči spomina* (Daughter of Memory, 1981); *1001 stih* (1001 Verses, 1983); *Kronanje* (Coronation, 1984); *Vrtnar tišine* (Gardener of Silence, 1990), a Slovene–English edition of his selected poems; *Stihija* (Elements, 1991); and *Mojster nespečnosti* (Master of Insomnia, 1995).

Novak's poetry is often about poetry—the generation of the poetic text, the shape and form of verse, the language of the poem. He delights in the acoustical aspect of language, its potential for play, and he explores the notion of the poem as a moment of silence before the storm. His fondness for children is reflected not only in the many works he has written for children, but in the impact of the world of the child and the vision of the child on his own creativity. Novak's dramatic texts not written exclusively for children's or puppet theater include *Spati v barvi* (Sleeping in Color, 1975) and *Manifest tišine* (Manifesto of Silence, 1976), both staged by the Nomenklatura student experimental theater of Ljubljana, and the 1988 dramatic diptych *Vojaki zgodovine* (Soldiers of History) and *Hiša iz kart* (House of Cards). Novak's activities as an editor have been particularly concentrated on his fellow Slovenian poet and playwright Dane Zajc. In 1984 he brought out an anthology of Zajc's poetry under the title *Kepa pepla* (A Lump of Ashes); in 1990 he edited a five-volume edi-

tion of Zajc's works; and in 1995 he also edited and contributed to *Interpretacje 4*, a collection of essays on Zajc.

Novak, Slobodan (b. 1924) Croatian poet, novelist, short-story writer, playwright, and critic. A major figure in post–World War II Croatian literature, Novak was born in Split, but was raised on the nearby island of Rab by his maternal aunt after his mother's death at an early age. When his education was interrupted by the Italian occupation of the Dalmatian coast, he studied privately and completed his secondary education in 1943. He then joined the partisans, was wounded, and was hospitalized for a time in Allied medical facilities in southern Italy. After the war, he entered the Faculty of Philosophy of Zagreb University, from which he eventually received his degree. His active career as an editor and a journalist began when, as a university student, he and some friends established and edited the literary journal *Izvor*. He then went on to found and edit another literary journal, *Krugovi*. Novak worked for a time in Split as drama director of the Split Theater. He was also a member of the Split literary magazine *Mogućnosti*. After that, he was long affiliated with the Zora publishing house in Zagreb.

Novak published his first literary works in war newspapers from 1943 to 1945 as well as in *Studentski list* in Zagreb. His first book publications were the verse collections *Glasnice u oluji* (Harbingers in the Storm, 1950) and *Iza lukobrana* (Behind the Breakwater, 1953). They were followed by a volume of novellas and short stories titled *Tvrdi grad* (Unyielding City, 1961); the novel *Mirisi, zlato i tamjan* (*Gold, Frankincense, and Myrrh*, 1968); three radio plays produced by Radio Zagreb in 1961, 1966, and 1968; and a substantial number of critical articles in various newspapers and journals.

Gold, Frankincense, and Myrrh, Novak's best and most honored work, was awarded the Matica Hrvatska Prize, the NIN Prize, the Croatian State Prize, and the Vladimir Nazor Prize. The novel is primarily a character study of a cranky aged aristocrat of Italian background, Madonna, and the couple who take care of her as she nears death, presumably on the Adriatic island of Rab. The pace is slow, the detail abundant, and a message of sorts introduced near the end in a didactic and obvious way about the old world represented by Madonna that had to go and the widespread disillusionment engendered by the insufficiencies of the new communist society.

Translations: *Gold, Frankincense, and Myrrh*, trans. Celia Hawkesworth (Zagreb: Most/The Bridge, 1991).

Nowakowski, Marek (b. 1935) Polish short-story writer. Until the declaration of martial law in Poland on 13 December 1981, Nowakowski, a Warsaw native and graduate in law of Warsaw University, was known primarily as a remarkably prolific writer of short stories collectively representing a kind of chronicle of everyday Polish life under communism. Nowakowski was an active supporter of Solidarity and after the imposition of martial law wrote one of the most compelling accounts of that time of turmoil in Poland under the title *Raport o stanie wojennym* (Report on Martial Law; translated as *The Canary and Other Tales of Martial Law*). Because of the nature of the book, it could not be printed in Poland and was originally published in two volumes in Paris in 1982 and 1983. It consists of a series of "snapshots" depicting everyday life in Poland in the first weeks of martial law in a true-to-life gritty style. *Raport o stanie wojennym* was widely translated and catapulted Nowakowski to international fame.

Prior to his celebrity, Nowakowski was known mostly for his stories of sharp-eyed social observation, particularly with respect to the tougher fringe element in Warsaw and its surroundings. They appear in such collections as *Ten stary złodziej* (This Old Thief, 1958); *Benek Kwaciarz* (Benek the Flower Peddlar, 1961); *Silna gorączka* (High Fever, 1963); *Trampolina* (The Trampoline, 1964); *Zapis* (Legacy, 1965); *Marynarska ballada* (A Sailor's Ballad, 1966); *Gonitwa* (The Chase, 1967); *Przystań* (The Harbor, 1969); *Opowiadania wybrane* (Selected Stories, 1969); *Mizerykordia* (Misericordia, 1971); *Układ zamknięty* (A Settled Deal, 1972); *Zdarzenie w miasteczku* (Happening in a Small Town, 1972); *Śmierć żówia* (The Death of a Turtle, 1973); *Gdzie jest droga na Walnę?* (Where Is the Road to Walna?, 1974); *Sielanka* (Idyll, 1974), a volume of selected stories; *Książę nocy* (The Prince of Night, 1978); *Chłopak z gołębiem na głowie* (The Boy with a Pigeon on His Head, 1979); and *Tutaj całować nie wolno* (No Kissing Here), which was published in the Polish community in Chicago in 1979.

After *Raport o stanie wojennym* Nowakowski published a few other books based on or otherwise related to the period of Solidarity and martial law, and they, too, first appeared in Paris (or, in one instance, in Chicago). They include *Notatki z codzienności: Grudzień 1982–Lipiec 1983* (Everyday Notes: December 1982–July 1983, 1983); *Życiorys Tadeusza Nawalanego, czyli Solidarność ma głos* (The Biography of Tadeusz Nawalany, or Solidarity Has the Floor, 1983), a radio play; *Dwa dni z aniołem* (Two Days with an Angel, 1984); *Osiem dni w ojczyźnie* (Eight Days in the Fatherland, 1985); "Grisza, ja tiebie skażu" ("Listen Here, Grisha," 1986); *Kto to zrobił?* (Who Did It?, 1987), published in Chicago; and *Karnawał i post* (Carnival and Fast, 1988).

After the victory of Solidarity, leading to free elections and the collapse of communism, Nowakowski turned his penetrating gaze and literary inventiveness to the social changes in Poland in the wake of the "transformation." These form the subject of such collections of stories as *Portret artysty z czasu dojrzałości* (Portrait of the Artist as an Adult, 1989); *Wilk podchodza ze wszystkich stron* (The Wolf Is Coming from All Sides, 1990); *Homo polonicus* (Polish Man, 1992; original title in Latin); *Grecki bożek* (The Little Greek God, 1993); *Rachunek* (Reckoning, 1984); *Powidoki: Chłopcy z tamtych lat* (Snapshots: The Boys of Yesteryear, 1995); *Powidok 2: Wspomnij ten domek na Gęsiowce?* (Snapshot 2: Remember the House in Gęsiowka?, 1996); *Fortuna liliputa* (1997); *Reda* (Roads, 1998); *Tapeta i inne opowiadania* (Wallpaper and Other Stories, 1996); *Strzały w motelu George* (Shots in Hotel George, 1997); and *Powidoki 3: Warszawiak pilnie poszukiwany* (Snapshots 3: A Varsovian Eagerly Searched For, 1998). A good collection of Nowakowski's stories was published in 1995 under the title *Od Benka Kwiaciarza do Księcia Nocy: Opowiadania wybrane* (From Benek the Flower Peddlar to the Prince of Night: Selected Stories).

Translations: *The Canary and Other Tales of Martial Law,* trans. Krystyna Bronkowska (Garden City, N.Y.: Dial, 1984); "The Slob," trans. Andrzej Czartoryski, in *Polish Writing Today,* ed. Celina Wieniewska (Harmondsworth: Penguin, 1967), 160–75. Two collections of Nowakowski's stories are available in German as *Die schragen Fürsten,* trans. Rolf Fieguth (Berlin: Henssel, 1967), and *Karpfen für die Miliz: Satiren und Nachrichten* (Munich: Hanser, 1983).

O

Ognjenović, Vida (b. 1941) Serbian playwright, short-story writer, novelist, essayist, and translator. A highly regarded writer of prose fiction and plays, Ognjenović was born near Nikšić, in Montenegro, but grew up and was educated in Serbia. After studying world literature and then directing at Belgrade University, she undertook postgraduate studies at the Sorbonne in Paris and completed them at the University of Minnesota in the United States. She has held several teaching positions in drama and theater, including at the Faculty of Dramatic Arts in Belgrade and at the University of California at Los Angeles. She has also been the director and permanent dramatic adviser of the National Theater in Belgrade. Apart from her extensive work as a director, Ognjenović has written several plays as well as studies on drama and theater. Her plays include *Prosidba od Čehova kako bi je izvodili ludaci u Šarantonu* (Chekhov's *The Proposal* as It Might Have Been Performed by the Madmen of Charanton, 1971), first published in Minneapolis; *Mileva Ajnštajn* (Mileva Einstein, 1972); *Maj nejm iz Mitar* (My Name Is Mitar, 1983); *Kako zasmejati gospodara* (How to Make the Master Laugh, 1985); *Kanjoš Macedonović* (1989); *Je li bilo kneževe večere?* (Did the Prince's Dinner Ever Take Place?, 1990); and *Devojka modre kose* (The Girl with the Dark-Blue Hair, 1993). Two of her most popular works for the stage, *Maj nejm iz Mitar* and *Je li bilo kneževe večere?*, were published in a single volume under the title *Melanholične drame* (Melancholic Dramas) in 1991. *Maj nejm iz Mitar* is a lightweight play about Serb emigrants to the United States aboard the *Dante* on its way from Kotor to New York in 1910; *Je li bilo kneževe večere?*, on the contrary, is a political-historical drama about patriotic Serbs wanting to continue the tradition of honoring the battle of Kosovo and their pragmatic opponents pushing for a pro-Austro-Hungarian policy as in the best interests of the Serbian nation. Ognjenović's two major studies on drama and theater are *Strah od scenske rasprave* (Fear of Stage Debate, 1980) and *Shakspiromanija* (Shakespeareomania, 1980). After her long involvement in dramatic writing and stage production, Ognjenović branched out into prose fiction in the mid-1990s. Within the space of two years, she had published two well-received collections of short stories, *Otrovno mleko maslačka* (The Poisonous Milk of Dandelions, 1995) and *Stari sat* (The Old Watch, 1996), with a few of the best stories dealing with writers, and her quite successful novel, *Kuća mrtvih mirisa* (*The House of Dead Scents*, 1995). As a writer of prose fiction, Ognjenović is a good, rather traditional storyteller with a wide range of interests and a certain predilection for foreign locales and characters.

Translations: *The House of Dead Scents*, trans. Mirka Janković (Belgrade: Dereta, 1998); "The Duel," trans. Paul M. Foster, in *The Prince of Fire: An Anthology of Contemporary Serbian Short Stories*, ed. Radmila J. Gorup and Nadežda Obradović (Pittsburgh: University of Pittsburgh Press, 1998), 178–92.

Olujić, Grozdana (b. 1934) Serbian novelist and short-story and fairy-tale writer. Born in Erdevik, Vojvodina, and educated at Belgrade University, where she majored in English language and literature, Olujić published her first novel, *Izlet u nebo* (*An Excursion to the Sky*), in 1957. It won the Narodna Prosvjeta Prize and was adapted for both film and stage. *An Excursion to the Sky* is a depressing tale of a cynical, "existentialist," and promiscuous young woman during World War II in German-occupied Belgrade who attends university but sees nothing in life worth any real commitment. When she finds herself pregnant, she prefers not to keep the child, but decides to have it after she marries its probable father, a young medical student suffering from tuberculosis with whom she lives briefly before he dies in a freak accident at the end. *Glasam za ljubav* (I Vote for Love, 1963), Olujić's second novel, like *An Excursion to the Sky* and her

other works of fiction, deals with contemporary youth, their joys and sorrows, their conflicts with themselves and with others, which she depicts with understanding and compassion. It was well received and won awards for best short novel in both Yugoslavia and Germany. Like *An Excursion to the Sky*, it was made into a film. Olujić's other novels include *Ne budi zaspale pse* (Let Sleeping Dogs Lie, 1964) and *Divlje seme* (Wild Seed, 1967). Besides a book of short stories published in 1958 under the title *Africka ljubičica* (African Violet), Olujić has written a number of fairy tales collected in three volumes: *Sedefna ruža* (Mother-of-Pearl Rose, 1979; translated as *Rose of Mother-of-Pearl: A Fairy Tale*), her only major work, other than *An Excursion to the Sky*, available in English translation; *Nebeska ruka* (The Heavenly Hand, 1984); and *Zvezdane lutalice* (The Starry Wanderers, 1987). Olujić has won several awards for her works for children. Besides her fictional writing, Olujić translated and edited an anthology of contemporary Indian poetry (1980) and has published translations of plays by Arnold Wesker and Saul Bellow, among others. In 1991 she came out with a book of interviews with various Serbian writers under the title *Pisci u sebi* (Authors About Themselves).

Translations: *An Exursion to the Sky*, trans. Kenneth Johnstone (New York: Dutton, 1961); *Rose of Mother-of-Pearl: A Fairy Tale*, trans. Grozdana Olujić and Jascha Kessler (West Branch, Iowa: Toothpaste Press, 1983); "The African Violet," trans. Christina Pribićević-Zorić, in *The Prince of Fire: An Anthology of Contemporary Serbian Short Stories*, ed. Radmila J. Gorup and Nadežda Obradović (Pittsburgh: University of Pittsburgh Press, 1998), 112–18.

Oravecz, Imre (b. 1943) Hungarian poet. A native of the village of Szajla, in northeastern Hungary, Oravecz graduated from Kossuth

Lajos University in Debrecen with a degree in Hungarian and German language and literature. He also did graduate work in linguistics at the University of Illinois, Chicago Circle. He has been a visiting fellow at the University of Iowa and a Fulbright lecturer at the University of California, Santa Barbara. His books of poetry include *Héj* (Skin, 1972); *Egy földterület növénytakarójának változása* (Changes in the Vegetation of a Landscape, 1979); *Máshogy mindenki más* (Otherwise We're Not the Same, 1979); *A hopik könyve* (The Book of the Hopi, 1982); and *1972. szeptember* (September 1972, 1988; translated as *When You Became She*), the work that really established his literary reputation. *When You Became She* is a compelling romantic-erotic account of the ups and downs, the passionate encounters and betrayals, and the final end of a love affair and marriage between a foreigner, "He," and a (presumably) East European, "She," recounted in the first person by both (this gleaned only from the context), in a series of ninety-five prose poems. Oravecz's most recent publication is *Halászóember* (Fishing Man, 1998), an almost whimsical and sly poetic autobiography. Several of the poems allude to his stays in the United States.

Translations: *When You Became She*, trans. Bruce Berlind (Riverside, Calif.: Xenos, 1993).

Orbán, Ottó (b. 1936) Hungarian poet and translator. One of the more refreshing and unpredictable contemporary Hungarian poets, Orbán, a Budapest native, was raised in a war orphanage after the death of his father in a concentration camp. He studied Hungarian and English literatures at Eötvös Lóránd University but never received a degree, opting instead for the career of a freelance writer. In 1981 he joined the staff of the Budapest literary review *Kortárs*. A down-to-earth, very contemporary poet with few illusions but no despair, Orbán confronts life as it is with wit and brashness and in a style bordering on the prosaic and everyday. His first book of poetry, *Szegénynek lenni* (To Be Poor), appeared in 1974. It was followed by *Távlat a történethez* (Perspective on the Story, 1976); *Helyzetünk az óceánon* (Our Bearings at Sea, 1983), a collection of prose poems structured as a "novel in poems"; *Szép nyári nap* (A Lovely Summer Day, 1984); *A mesterségről* (On the Profession, 1984); *Honnan jön a költő?* (Whence Comes the Poet?, 1980); *Összegyűjtött versek* (Collected Poetry, 1986); *A fényes cáfolat* (The Brilliant Denial, 1987); *Egyik oldaláról a másikra fordul: Él* (He Turns from One Side to the Other: He Is Alive, 1992), in which he expresses his disenchantment with postmodernism and what he regards as its indifference to poetry; *Cédula a romokon: Esszék és egyéb arcátlanságok* (The Tornup Index Card: Essays and Other Impertinences, 1994); and *Kocsmában méláz a vén kalóz: Új versek, 1993–1994* (The Old Pirate Muses in the Tavern: New Poems, 1993–1994, 1995). Orbán has also been a tireless translator from such languages as English, French, German, Spanish, and Russian. His many translations from English include works by T. S. Elliot, Robert Lowell, and poets of the American Beat Generation. He has visited the United States several times and taught at the University of Minnesota as a guest professor in 1987/1988. Orbán has received both the Attila József and Kossuth prizes.

Translations: *The Blood of the Walsungs: Selected Poems,* ed. George Szirtes (Budapest: Corvina, 1993; Newcastle upon Tyne: Bloodaxe, 1993); *The Journey of Barbarus,* trans. Bruce Berlind (Pueblo, Colo.: Passeggiata, 1997); six poems in *The Colonnade of Teeth: Modern Hungarian Poetry,* ed. George Gömöri and George Szirtes (Newcastle upon Tyne: Bloodaxe, 1996), 187–92; four poems in *The Face of Creation: Contemporary Hungarian Poetry,* trans. Jascha Kessler (Minneapolis: Coffee House,

1988), 105–9; six poems in *Modern Hungarian Poetry*, ed. Miklós Vajda (New York: Columbia University Press, 1977), 251–57; nine poems in *Turmoil in Hungary*, ed. and trans. Nicholas Kolumban (St. Paul, Minn.: New Rivers, 1982), 174–86.

Ördögh, Szilveszter (b. 1948) Hungarian novelist, short-story writer, playwright, and essayist. A native of Szeged, where he was educated through high school, Ördögh studied humanities at Eötvös Lóránd University from 1968 to 1973. His first published work, a volume of short stories titled *A csikó* (The Foal), appeared in 1973. It was followed by the biblical novel *Koponyák hegye* (Golgotha, 1976) and a play on a classical theme, *Kapuk Thébában* (Gates in Thebes, 1978), which was performed by the theater of Kecskemét. His subsequent prose fiction included three novels—*Bizony nem haltok meg* (Of Course You Won't Die, 1979); *Lázár békéje* (The Peace of Lazarus, 1985); and *Koponyaüreg* (The Empty Skull, 1994)—and two more collections of stories: *Változatok megváltásra* (Variations of Redemption, 1982) and *Dobol a hó* (The Snow Beats the Drum, 1991). A book of literary studies on the text and the reader appeared in 1993 under the title *A könyv is olvas engem* (The Book Also Reads Me).

Translations: "The Elephant," trans. John Freeman, in *Ocean at the Window: Hungarian Prose and Poetry Since 1945*, ed. Albert Tezla (Minneapolis: University of Minnesota Press, 1980), 423–29; "Sea with Gulls," trans. Richard L. Aczel, in *Present Continuous: Contemporary Hungarian Writing*, ed. István Bart (Budapest: Corvina, 1985), 233–47.

Örkény, István (1912–1979) Hungarian novelist, short-story writer, essayist, and playwright. One of twentieth-century Hungary's most distinguished writers, Örkény remains post–World War II Hungary's best-known playwright. After receiving a diploma in pharmacy, he went on to graduate from the Technical University in Budapest. His literary career began with the publication of a volume of short stories, *Tengertánc* (Sea Dance), in 1941. Örkény was taken prisoner during World War II. Not long after his return home, he wrote the play *Voronyezs* (Voronezh) and a sociographical work called *Lágerek népe* (People of the Camps). His personal confession, *Emlékezők: Amíg idejutottunk* (Remembrances: Until We Got This Far), was published in 1946. At the beginning of the 1960s, he entered a new phase of his career with the publication of such short novels as *Macskajáték* (Catsplay, 1963); *Tóték* (*The Toth Family*, 1964); and *Rózsakiállitás* (*The Flower Show*, 1977). Dramatizations of Catsplay and *The Toth Family* have been performed throughout the world, including the United States, with much success. Of his fifteen plays, at least three—*Tóték*, *Macskajáték*, and *Kulcskeresők* (Keysearchers)—have proved especially popular in theaters in Hungary and elsewhere. *Pisti a vérzivatarban* (*Stevie in the Bloodbath*, written 1969; staged 1979), one of his most popular plays, is a wildly absurdist drama in two parts in which the experiences of the Hungarian and East European Everyman, Stevie, and his three alter egos encapsulate the horrors and ambiguities of the twentieth century, with its wars, Holocaust, atomic bomb, and great social and political upheavals. Örkény's volume of short stories *Egyperces novellák* (*One Minute Stories*) appeared in 1968. Witty, ironic, sometimes poignant, Örkény's little stories are drawn from everyday life as well as from his experiences in World War II. So popular did his "one-minute stories" become that Örkény continued writing them until the end of his life. The prominence in these stories, as elsewhere in Örkény's works, of a kind of dark irony and a sense of absurdity was rooted in his experiences as a Jew who had to serve in a forced-labor battalion during World War II and, after he was captured by the Russians, was put in a Soviet prisoner-of-war camp for four more years. Örkény also was punished for his participation in the Hungarian uprising of 1956 and was a frequent target of public abuse and humiliation. Örkény was awarded both the Attila József and Kossuth prizes for his writing. In addition, he served as a member of the secretariat of the Hungarian Writers Association.

Translations: *The Flower Show. The Toth Family,* trans. Michael Henry Heim and Clara Gyorgyey (New York: New Directions, 1982); *One Minute Stories,* trans. Judith Sollosy (Budapest: Corvina, 1995), a collection compiled from *Egyperces novellák* (One Minute Stories, 1977), *Egyperces novellák* (One Minute Stories, 1984), *Visszanézve* (1985), and *Búcsú* (Parting, 1989); *Stevie in the Bloodbath: A Grotesque Play in Two Parts,* in *A Mirror to the Cage: Three Contemporary Hungarian Plays,* ed. and trans. Clara Györgyey (Fayetteville: University of Arkansas Press, 1993), 19–100.

Otčenášek, Jan (1924–1979) Czech novelist. Otčenášek threw his lot in with the communists during World War II and became a prominent representative of socialist realism after the war. He was a member of the Czechoslovak Writers Union in the 1950s and, from 1956 to 1959, held the position of first secretary of the organization. Although a staunch supporter of the official literary culture for most of his career, Otčenášek is generally well regarded as a writer. His first novel, *Plným krokem: Příběh lidí a ohňů* (At Full Speed: A Story of Men and Fires, 1952), which deals perhaps too openly with problems in an industrial plant, was not well received. He did better with *Občan Brych* (Citizen Brych, 1955), a rather prolix novel about the communist takeover of Czechoslovakia in 1948. While not uninteresting reading, the novel follows the standard Party line of portraying the takeover as a victory of the

working class over a bourgeoisie intent on reviving capitalism. Otčenášek's best-received work was *Romeo, Julie a tma* (*Romeo and Juliet and the Darkness,* 1958), a poignant novella about the romance of a Czech Christian soldier and a Jewish girl during World War II. *Kulhavý Orfeus* (Lame Orpheus), which came out in 1964, is a largely autobiographical novel about the naive efforts of a group of boys to organize underground units during the last phase of the war. Otčenášek's next novella, *Mladík z povolání: Poznámky k jisté situaci* (A Young Man by Profession: Observations on a Certain Condition, 1968), took readers by surprise both because of its subject—the erotic adventures of an aging man—and because of its evidence of a gradual loosening of the grip of socialist realism on Otčenášek. This trend continued into his next novel, *Když v ráji pršelo* (When It Rained in Paradise, 1972), a lyrical account of the flight of a young couple from modern urban civilization into the countryside. Otčenášek's last novel, *Pokušení Katarina* (Katarina's Temptation), was unfinished at his death and was posthumously published in 1985. It, too, suggests the author's progressive departure from the tenets of socialist realism.

Translations: *Romeo and Juliet and the Darkness* (Prague: Artia, 1960). *Když v ráji pršelo* is available in German as *Als es im Paradies regnete,* trans. Gustag Just (Berlin: Volk und Welt, 1975), and in French as *Quand il pleuvait au paradis,* trans. and adapted by Yvette Joye (Paris: Éditeurs français réunis, 1975); *Kulhavý Orfeus* as *Der hinkende Orpheus,* trans. Ilse Seehase (Berlin: Verlag der Nation, 1968); and *Plným krokem: Příběh lidí a ohňů* as *Auch dieser Ton muss klingen,* trans. Rudolf Pabel (Berlin: Volk und Welt, 1956).

Ottlik, Géza (1912–1990) Hungarian novelist, short-story writer, and essayist. A native of Budapest, Ottlik abandoned his previous interest in physics and mathematics for literature. He began his career as a writer with a number of short stories published in literary magazines in the 1930s and collected in 1941 in the volume *Hamisjátékosok* (Swindlers). After the war, he concentrated mainly on reviewing books, writing essays, drama criticism, and translating plays for various Budapest theaters. During the Stalinist era of the late 1940s and early 1950s, Ottlik was barred from publishing his own works, was condemned for his "bourgeois" values, and had to make a living primarily as a translator. Nevertheless, he was able to retain his position as secretary of the largely inactive Hungarian PEN Club from 1954 to 1957.

Ottlik's return to active participation in Hungarian literary life came with the publication of his short-story collection *Hajnali háztetők* (Rooftops at Dawn) in 1957 and the work for which he is best known, the novel *Iskola a határon* (*School at the Frontier*), in 1959. A talented prose writer with a broad literary horizon, he subsequently published a collection of short stories under the title *Minden megvan* (Nothing's Lost, 1968; enl. ed., 1996); *Próza* (Prose, 1980), a collection of short fiction, essays, and reviews dealing, for example, with Hungarian literature from 1945 to 1947, the theater, and "the novel and reality" (1960–1979), and including an interview with the novelist Péter Lengyel; and *A valencia rejtély* (The Valency Enigma, 1989), a collection of three longer stories, the most interesting of which, "Hajónapló" ("Logbook"), is available in English.

Ottlik's only longer fictional work, *School at the Frontier*, is a highly detailed, thinly veiled autobiographical novel about young cadets in a Hungarian military academy in a frontier town in the 1920s. The work begins in 1957, moves back briefly to the war year of 1944, and finally reconstructs the past largely through an unpublished manuscript written by the most unruly of the cadets,

Gabor Medve, and delivered to the narrator after Medve's death.

Literature: Ferencz Győző, "The Strategy of Silence: Géza Ottlik's Posthumous Novel," *Hungarian Quarterly* 34 (1993): 21–24.

Translations: *School at the Frontier*, trans. Kathleen Szasz (New York: Harcourt, Brace & World, 1966); excerpt from "Buda," trans. Eszter Molnár, *Hungarian Quarterly* 34 (1993): 25–33; "Logbook," trans. John Bátki, in *A Hungarian Quartet: Four Contemporary Short Novels* (Budapest: Corvina, 1991), 7–42; "Nothing's Lost," trans. Eszter Molnár, in *The Kiss: Twentieth Century Hungarian Short Stories*, selected by István Bart (Budapest: Corvina, 1988), 160–92.

P

Pahor, Boris (b. 1913) Slovenian novelist, short-story writer, essayist, and diarist. One of the major Slovenian prose writers of the post–World War II period, Pahor was born in Trieste, Italy, and was a student at Bologna University when he was pressed into Italian military service. He served in North Africa but after the Italian capitulation of 1943 was imprisoned in German concentration camps until the end of the war. He completed his university education in 1947 and for a time lived as a freelance writer before accepting an academic appointment in Trieste. He had begun publishing fiction before World War II in the illegal press and in various journals and reviews. Two themes have long dominated his writing: the tenuous situation of Slovenian culture in Trieste—which he deals with in such novels as *Mesto v zalivu* (City on the Gulf, 1955); *Parnik trobi nji* (The Steamship Signals Us, 1964); and *V labirintu* (In the Labyrinth, 1984) and in the story collection *Kres v pristanu* (Bonfire in Port, 1959)—and his concentration camp experi-

ences during World War II, especially as recalled in *Nekropola* (Necropolis, 1967; translated as *Pilgrim Among the Shadows*), a personal reminiscence that is his only major
work translated into English. Pahor has also
published books based on, or inspired by, his
experiences and travel in North Africa:
Nomadi bez oaze: Afriška kronika (Nomads
Without an Oasis: An African Chronicle,
1956) and *Skarabej v srcu: Ladijski dnevnik*
(Scarab in the Heart: A Log Book, 1970). An
indefatigable diarist, Pahor has published
several volumes of his diaries covering the
years 1974 to 1992: *Ta ocean strašno odprt:
Dnevniški zapiski od julija 1974 do februarja
1976* (This Ocean Frightfully Open: Diaries
from July 1974 to February 1976, 1989);
*Žlahtne transverzale: Dnevniški zapiski,
1975–1985* (Noble Transversals: Diaries,
1975–1985, 1991); *Napoved nove plovbe:
Dnevniški zapiski, 1986–1989* (A New Sailing
Forecast: Diaries, 1986–1989, 1992); and
Slovenska svatba: Dnevniški zapisi, 1990–1992
(A Slovenian Wedding: Diary Entries,
1990–1992, 1995). His other works of fiction
include the novels *Vila ob jezeru* (The Villa
on the Lake, 1955); *Onkraj pekle so ljudje* (Beyond Hell There Are People, 1958); *Zatemn-
itev* (Darkness, 1975); and *Zibelka sveta* (The
Cradle of the World, 1999) and the story collections *Na sipini* (On the Sandbank, 1960);
Grmada v pristanu (The Pyre at Port, 1972);
and *Varno naročje* (Safe Haven, 1974). Pahor's
major collections of essays and polemics
consist of *Svobodna polemika* (Free Polemics,
1952); *Odisej ob jamboru: Glose in polemičke
zapiski* (Odyssey Along the Mast: Glosses and
Polemical Notes, 1969); *Edvard Kočbek: Priče-
valec našega časa* (Edvard Kočbek: Storyteller
of Our Time, 1975), a book about the Slovenian writer Edvard Kočbek written with Alojz
Rebula; and *Tržaški mozaik: Izbor občasnih
zapiskov* (Triestine Mosaic: A Selection of Periodical Writings, 1983), covering the period
from the autumn of 1979 to the autumn of
1981. Kočbek's correspondence with Pahor

from 1940 to 1980 was published in 1984
under the title *Peščena ura: Pisma Borisu Pa-
horju, 1940–1980* (The Hourglass: Letters to
Boris Pahor, 1940–1980).

Literature: Probably the most useful
book on Pahor is Marija Pirevec and Vera
Ban Tuta, eds., *Pahorjev zbornik: Spomini,
pogledi, gradivo* (Trieste: Narodna in študij-
ska knjižnica v Trstu, 1993), a fine Slovenian
collection of letters, reminiscences, critical
pieces, and similar materials by fellow writers and friends issued on the occasion of
Pahor's eightieth birthday that contains a
complete bibliography of Pahor's works and
literature on him.

Translations: *Pilgrim Among the Shadows*, trans. Michael Biggins (New York: Harcourt Brace Jovanovich, 1995).

Panitz, Eberhard (b. 1932) German novelist,
short-story writer, and screenwriter. A prolific and popular author, several of whose
works were made into films, Panitz was
born and educated through high school in
Dresden. From 1949 to 1953, he studied German language and literature and pedagogy
at Leipzig University, after which he worked
as an editor at various publishing houses.
Strongly attracted to documentary writing,
Panitz made his literary debut in 1955 with
the biographical story *Käte*, about Käte
Niederkirchner, who was sentenced to death
because of her participation in an anti-Nazi
resistance organization during World War
II. This proved the first of several works by
Panitz in which his lead character or characters are strong, independent women striving
in one way or another for self-realization.
Possibly his most popular text in this regard
was the novel *Die sieben Affären der Doña
Juanita* (The Seven Affairs of Doña Juanita,
1973), which was made into a movie in 1973
and became the subject of an opera by
J. U. Günther in 1981. Essentially along similar lines are *Unter den Bäumen regnet es
zweimal* (It Rains Twice Under the Trees,

1969), an industrial novel in which the main protagonist is a female chemical engineer and which was made into a film in 1972 under the title *Der Dritte* (The Third One); *Die unheilige Sophia* (Impious Sophie, 1974); *Die Moral der Nixe: Eine Sommergeschichte* (The Moral of the Nymph: A Summer Tale, 2nd ed., 1978), a modern story of a water sprite; and the novellas *Absage an Viktoria* (The Disowning of Victoria, 1975) and *Viktorias Tod* (Victoria's Death, 1985). After *Käte,* Panitz wrote the novel *Die Feuer sinken* (The Fires Are Abating, 1960), based on his own recollections of the Anglo-American fire bombing of Dresden in 1945. *Cristobal und die Insel* (Christopher Columbus and the Island), which was published in 1963 and focused on the role of ordinary people in the making of the Cuban revolution, drew on Panitz's travels in Cuba in 1961. Latin America was also the background for *Der Weg zum Rio Grande* (The Road to the Rio Grande, 1973), a biographical story, similar in nature to *Käte,* about the revolutionary Tamara Bunke, who fought alongside Che Guevara in Cuba and Bolivia. Panitz's interest in Che Guevara remained high even after the dissolution of the German Democratic Republic; in 1997 he brought out a biographical sketch of Guevara, *Comandante Che.* Panitz also visited Vietnam in the 1970s and published an account of his journey under the title *Gesichter Vietnams* (Faces of Vietnam, 1978).

Panitz's novels from the late 1970s and 1980s pursued directions different from those of his earlier prose fiction. The first two were autobiographical: *Meines Vaters Strassenbahn: Eine Erzählung* (My Father's Streetcar: A Story, 1979), which drew on Panitz's memories of his father, who in fact was a streetcar conductor, and *Mein lieber Onkel Hans: Fünf Kapitel eines königlichen Lebens* (My Dear Uncle Hans: Five Chapters of a Royal Life, 1982). Panitz's next novel, *Eiszeit: Eine unwirkliche Geschichte* (The Ice

Age: A Unlikely Story, 1983), about the residents of an East German hotel who survive an atomic explosion, was little more than an antinuclear admonishment typical of the period. His last works before the collapse of the GDR were the crime novel *Phosphorblume* (The Phosphorus Flower, 1986) and *Leben für Leben: Roman einer Familie* (Life for Life: The Novel of a Family, 1987).

After the reintegration of the two Germanys, Panitz's writing took on a more obvious political character. He was now more forthcoming about his discomfort with certain policies of the former East German state, and he sought to take stock of the transformation of German life in light of reunification. Such works include *Mein Chef ist ein Wessi: Gedächtnisprotokolle* (My Boss Is a "Westie": A Report from Memory, 1992); *Das Lächeln des Herrn O: Hundert Geschichten zur Zeit* (The Smile of Mr. O: A Hundred Timely Stories, 1994); *Ossiland ist abgebrannt* (Ossiland [East Germany] Has Been Destroyed, 1994), with Klaus Huhn; and *Verhör im Café* (Interrogation in a Cafe, 1996), which is in the form of an extended conversation between the narrator and "the man from W." about East and West German issues and Panitz's own life and career. Most of these politically oriented texts of the 1990s were put out by Spotless Verlag, a small publishing house operated in Berlin by Panitz and Huhn. Panitz's newest book, *Die grüne Aue des alten Fritz: Merkwürdigkeiten des 250 jährigen Grunaus im Osten Berlins* (The Green Pasture of the Old Fritz: Curiosities in the 250-Year-Old Grunau in Berlin East, 1999), is a fresh look at aspects of the sixteenth-century Prussian chronicle of Simon Grunau. Panitz's literary awards include the Erich Weinert Medal (1967); the Heinrich Greif Prize (1971); the Literary Prize of the DFD (1973); and the Goethe Prize (1982).

Pantić, Mihajlo (b. 1957) Serbian short-story writer, essayist, and literary critic. Pantić was born and educated in Belgrade and still lives there. His literary career began in 1984 with a collection of short stories, *Hronika sobe* (Chronicle of the Room). He subsequently published another three volumes of stories: *Vonder u Berlinu* (Wonder in Berlin, 1987); *Ne mogu da se setim jedne rečenice* (I Cannot Remember a Single Sentence, 1993), a selection of previously published and new pieces, mostly short essays (some less than a page long), several of the most interesting of which deal with film; and *Novobeogradske priče* (New Belgrade Stories, 1994), a volume of nineteen short stories with contemporary Belgrade settings. A year after his first book of stories appeared, Pantić gave clear evidence of his interest in and talent for essayistic and critical writing with a collection of essays on the genre of the short story, *Iskušenja sažetosti* (Temptations of Conciseness, 1985). Although he continued writing and publishing short stories, Pantić turned more increasingly to critical and theoretical writing about Serbian and other literatures of the former Yugoslavia as well as to the publication of literary anthologies. Besides *Iskušenja sažetosti,* his critical texts and anthologies include *Aleksandrijski sindrom* (Alexandrian Syndrome, 1987), a collection of essays and critical writings on contemporary Serbian and Croatian prose; *Protiv sistematičnosti* (Against Systematicization, 1988), a collection of critical texts from the period 1980 to 1988; *Šum Vavilona* (Murmur in Babylon, 1988), a critical-poetic anthology of young Serbian poetry; *Pesnici, pisci & ostala menažerija* (Poets, Writers, and the Rest of the Menagerie, 1992), subtitled *LP-priče* (LP-Stories), a collection of short prose pieces about literature, some with allusions to such other contemporary Yugoslav writers as Ivo Andrić and David Albahari (in one, Pantić humorously juxtaposes his own way of writing stories and Albahari's); *Novi prilozi za savremenu srpsku poeziju* (Toward a New Theory of Contemporary Serbian Poetry, 1994); and *Antologija srpske pripovetke, 1945–1996* (An Anthology of Serbian Short Stories, 1945–1996, 1997), a valuable collection of thirty-six stories beginning with Ivo Andrić and ending with Goran Petrović. In 1992 Pantić, in collaboration with Slobodan Zubanović, published a collection of interviews and essays under the title *Deset pesama, deset razgovora* (Ten Poems, Ten Conversations). Pantić has been the editor of such prominent Serbian literary journals as *Književne novine* and *Književna reč*. In 1985 he was awarded the Milan Bogdanović Prize.

Translations: "The Morning After (Remake)," trans. Snežana Dabić, in *The Prince of Fire: An Anthology of Contemporary Serbian Short Stories,* ed. Radmila J. Gorup and Nadežda Obradović (Pittsburgh: University of Pittsburgh Press, 1998), 334–42.

Papenfuss-Gorek, Bert (b. 1956) German poet. A native of Reuterstadt Stavenhagen, Papenfuss-Gorek (or just Papenfuss, as he prefers it) completed his early schooling in Greifswald and, from 1972 to 1975, studied to be an electrician. He subsequently worked professionally as a theatrical lighting technician. In 1976 he moved to East Berlin, where he further nurtured his creative interests—composing poems during punk-rock concerts, according to anecdotal reports. By 1980 he was spending most of his time writing poetry and drew close to the Prenzlauer Berg group. Inventive, anarchic, playful, irreverent—especially with respect to German orthography and typography, clichés, and GDR officialese—outspoken and raw in his treatment of sex, Papenfuss has drawn inspiration from such disparate sources as ancient Celtic mythology and the punk culture of his own time. He also has composed poems in English. His first printed poems appeared in the journal *Temperamente* in 1977. In 1979 he published his first independent work, *W. E. L. F.*, under his own imprint. It was followed by such other collections of poems as *harte zarte hertsn* (hard tender hearts, 1984); *harm: arkdichtung 77* (harm: arkpoem 77, 1985); *die freiheit der meere* (the freedom of the sea, 1986); *silent rooms* (1987; original title in English); *urlogik im dialekte* (original logic in dialect, 1988); and *der blutspur* (the blood trace, 1989). The catalogue of an exhibit of works by the artist Helge Leiberg—*Helge Leiberg: Bilder, Galerie Bodo Niemann. 4. Juni–2. Juli 1988* (Helge Leiberg: Paintings, Bodo Niemann Gallery. 4 June–2 July 1988, 1988)—included texts by Papenfuss and Sascha Anderson. The same year, the first retrospective collection of Papenfuss's poems from 1973 to 1986 appeared under the title *dreizehntanz* (thirty-dance), thereby enabling him to bring together in a single volume a number of poems scattered among various journals and anthologies. This was the first of several such collections: *till: gedichte, 1973 bis 1976* (till: poems, 1973 to 1976, 1993); *naif: gedichte, 1973 bis 1976* (primitive: poems, 1973 to 1976, 1993); *TrakTat zum Aber: Gedichte, 1981 bis 1984* (TreaTise on But: Poems, 1981 to 1984, 1996); and *hetze: gedichte, 1994 bis 1998* (slapdash: poems, 1994 to 1998, 1998). Subsequent volumes of Papenfuss's poems include: *Tiske* (Exit [spelled backward], 1990), a typical Papenfuss play with words but not insignificant for a text written in the last year of the GDR; *Vorwärts im Zorn usw* (Forward in Anger and So On, 1990); *SoJa* (YeahYeah, 1990), with thirty drawings by Wolfram Adalbert Scheffler; *Led Saudaus: Notdichtung, Karrendichtung* (Damned Unwed Slut: Emergency and Cart Poems, 1991); *Nunft: FKK/IM endart. novemberklub: Gedichte mit Graphiken der Gruppe Endart und einer CD des Novemberklub* (Nunft: FKK/IM: Poems, with Graphics by the Endart Group and a CD of the November Club, 1992); *Mors ex nihilo: Zeichnungen von Jörg Immendorf* (Death from Nothing: Drawings by Jörg Immen-

dorf, 1994); *routine in die romantik des alltags* (the romanticism of the everyday, 1995), with illustrations by Helge Leiberg; and *SBZ: Land und Leute* (SBZ: Land and People, 1996), with drawings by Silka Teichert.

Literature: "Bert Papenfuss-Gorek," in *Literary Intellectuals and the Dissolution of the State: Professionalism and Conformity in the GDR*, ed. Robert von Hallenberg, trans. Kenneth J. Northcott (Chicago: University of Chicago Press, 1996), 273–83.

Páral, Vladimír (b. 1932) Czech novelist. In his first novel, really novella, *Veletrh splněných praní* (The Fair of Fulfilled Desires, 1964), Prague-born Páral deals with the subject of much of his writing—the routinization and modernization of social life. In his second novel, *Soukromá vichřice* (Private Whirlwind, 1966), the repetition of phrases and whole scenes, which runs throughout the work, textually reinforces the same theme. Páral's vision turns bleaker in *Milenci a vrazi* (Lovers and Murderers, 1969), in which modern urban society is presented in a wholly negative light. *Profesionalní žena* (Professional Woman, 1971; translated as *The Four Sonyas*) demonstrates Páral's lighter side and his capacity for humor. The novel is a fantasy about a modern Cinderella in a socialist society. *Mladý muž a bílá velryba* (The Young Man and the White Whale, 1973) is a curious combination of a novel about a man capable of real love (as opposed to the loveless erotic adventures most of Páral's characters pursue) and the heroism of ordinary workers in the socialist state who work long hours without additional compensation. *Katapult* (Catapult), which was written originally in 1967, is Páral's principal claim to literary fame. Alternately comic and serious, the novel is about a thirtyish chemical engineer, Jacek Jost, who has an unexpected experience on a commuter train that he hopes will change his life. A married man and father who can no longer abide what he regards as his drearily predictable suburban existence, Jost is thrown into the lap of an unfamiliar young woman when his train comes to a sudden stop. He winds up having an affair with the woman, and this sets the precedent for a series of subsequent affairs he has with different women, in different towns, along his train route. Desperate to change his life, to be catapulted into a new life, the possibility for which is represented by each of his lovers, Jost is thwarted at each critical junction by his indecisiveness. The efforts of the neurotic and ambivalent Jost to get fired or to get his wife to divorce him end in failure.

Literature: William E. Harkins, "Vladimír Páral's Novel *Catapult*," in *Czech Literature Since 1956: A Symposium*, ed. William E. Harkins and Paul I. Trensky (New York: Bohemica, 1980), 62–73.

Translations: *Catapult: A Timetable of Rail, Sea, and Air Ways to Paradise*, trans. William Harkins (Highland Park, N.J.: Catbird, 1989, 1992); *The Four Sonyas*, trans. William Harkins (North Haven, Conn.: Catbird, 1993).

Paraschivescu, Miron Radu (1911–1971) Romanian journalist, poet, and painter. Well known for his humanitarian and antifascist views before and during World War II, Paraschivescu became a staunch supporter of the communist regime in Romania after the war. He had begun writing poetry in the 1920s, and his early texts were gathered in the volume *Primele* (Firsts), which covers the period 1926 to 1932. This was followed by *Laude și alte poeme* (Eulogies and Other Poems, 1953); *Declarația patetică* (Declaration of Pathos, 1963), a collection of poems from 1934 to 1948; and *Versul liber* (Free Verse, 1965), a collection of poems from 1931 to 1964. A later edition of *Declarația patetică* included addenda in the form of other poems from the early and late 1960s, among

them a somewhat long poem in praise of the American singer Ella Fitzgerald ("Ella Fitzgerald," 1966); a poem decrying war and guerrilla fighting in such places as Vietnam, the Dominican Republic, Kashmir, and Cyprus ("Colind" ["Christmas Carol"], 1966); and one inspired by the civil war in Biafra, Africa ("Greva generală" ["General Strike"], 1968). As a poet, Paraschivescu is perhaps known best for his collection *Cîntice țigănești* (Gypsy Songs, 1941), which recalls the Gypsy poetry of the Spanish poet Federico García Lorca. A volume of selected poems from *Declarația patetică* and *Laude și alte poeme* appeared in 1971, the year of Paraschivescu's death, under the title *Poeme* (Poems). Paraschivescu's verse forms are as varied as his subject matter. He wrote generally rhymed short and long poems, but had a definite predilection for longer poems and long lines of verse capable of accommodating his need to express himself expansively. His longer poems read almost like poems in prose. Besides his poetry, Paraschivescu was the author of three plays, which he prepared for publication in 1961, but they remained unprinted until 1975 when they were included in the fourth volume of his collected works. The plays are *Asta-i ciudat!* (That's What I Call Strange!); *În marginea vieții* (In the Margin of Life); and *Irezistibulul Bolivar* (The Irresistible Bolivar). Paraschivescu also left behind fragments of a rhymed version of *Hamlet* titled *Hamlet meu* (My Hamlet). The four-volume edition of his collected works, *Scrieri* (Works), was published between 1969 and 1976.

Parnicki, Teodor (1908–1988) Polish novelist. A prolific and highly imaginative historical novelist, Parnicki was born in Germany, to a Russian father and a Polish Jewish mother. He lived in Russia until uprooted by the revolution of 1917 and, like many others fleeing the Bolshevik seizure of power, resettled in Harbin, Manchuria. It was there that he completed secondary school and published an article on Henryk Sienkiewicz and Alexandre Dumas (pére) in a Polish newspaper, *Dziennik Polski*. After his move to Poland, he settled in Lwów and studied Polish, English, and Asian literatures at Lwów University. He also worked for the newspaper *Kurier Lwowski*. His first book, *Czan-Tso-Lin*, with an Oriental setting, appeared in 1932. During World War II, Parnicki was deported to the USSR and briefly imprisoned. In 1941 he was able to leave for Teheran and Jerusalem, and then lived for a while in England and Mexico, where in 1944/1945 he served as the cultural attaché of the Polish Embassy.

Parnicki's fame as a novelist rests on a series of historical novels rich in incident and atmosphere covering much of the ancient world, West and East, as well as early Poland. His first real success came with the novel *Aecjusz ostatni rzymianin* (Aesius, the Last Roman, 1937), set in Rome in the fifth century when the glory of ancient Rome was already becoming a thing of the past. In 1966 Parnicki published a sequel to the novel under the title *Śmierć Aecjusza* (The Death of Aesius). His next major novel was *Srebrne orły* (Silver Eagles, 1944–1945), published in Jerusalem. It traces the formation of the Polish state at the turn of the tenth and eleventh centuries when it grew strong enough to successfully challenge the Holy Roman Empire in battle. Typical of his style, Parnicki viewed developments in Poland against the broad background of far-reaching changes occurring throughout the early medieval world.

Parnicki demonstrated his considerable skill at handling dense plot structures in one of his most fanciful works, *Koniec "Zgody Narodów"* (The End of the *Covenant of Nations*), published first in Paris in 1955 and then in Poland in 1957. Set in the second century B.C. in Bactria, a Hellenistic state in Asia between India and the Seleucid Em-

pire, the novel deals with the attempt to take over the state by an official of the security police. The *Covenant of Nations* is actually a ship outfitted with all sorts of advanced technological wizardry.

Attracted to characters of mixed ethnic and racial backgrounds—a reflection of his own origins—Parnicki often situated them in intricate tales of adventure and politics covering a wide swath of history and geography. One of the best examples of this type of fiction is the novel *Słowo i ciało* (The Word and the Flesh, 1959), in which the narrator, a man of Persian–Greek origin detained by the Romans in early-third-century Alexandria, composes a book combining esoteric knowledge, dreams, and reminiscences of the women in his life that moves throughout the entire ancient world, including Asia. In his next novel, *Twarz księżyca* (The Face of the Moon, 1961), set at the turn of the third and fourth centuries A.D., Parnicki tells the story of Mitroania, the daughter of the king of Choresm, near the Caspian Sea. The novel takes place in Choresm, Illyria, and Rome. *Tylko Beatrycze* (Only Beatrice), which followed *Twarz księżyca* in 1962, is one of Parnicki's most highly regarded works. It has a purely Polish setting and is based on a fire that leveled a Cistercian monastery in the year 1309. Built largely around the trial of the arsonist, a Cistercian monk of Polish–Tartar origins, the novel consists principally of dialogue and written confessions. Apart from its psychological dimension, the novel addresses philosophical issues related to Scholasticism. Parnicki claims in the preface that he spent five years studying the period in which the event occurred.

In 1962 Parnicki published the first part of another major novel, *Nowa baśń* (The New Fairy Tale). A book of great imagination, it is set in the eleventh and twelfth centuries and, like other works by Parnicki, takes in a great deal of geography from ancient Novgorod to

Ireland. Parnicki drew heavily for it on medieval literature and chronicles as well as Celtic and Scandinavian tales. Like much of his fiction, which was written during the period he lived in Mexico, it also reflects Parnicki's interest in and knowledge of ancient Mexican culture and mythology. Published in six volumes between 1962 and 1970, *Nowa baśń* consists of *Robotnicy wezwani o jedenastej* (Workers Summoned at Eleven, 1962); *Czas siania i czas zbierania* (A Time for Sowing and a Time for Reaping, 1963); *Labirynt* (Labyrinth, 1964); *Gliniane dzbany* (Clay Pots, 1966); *Wylęgarnia dziwów* (The Hatchery of Wonders, 1968); and *Palec zagrożenia* (The Threatening Finger, 1970).

While still working on *Nowa baśń*, Parnicki managed to publish two other historical novels in the 1960s: *I u możnych dziwny* (The Powerful Too Are Strange, 1965), which is set in the seventeenth century, and *Koła na piasku* (Wheels in the Sand, 1966), dealing with the rise and fall of Hellenistic culture in Asia and set in 160 B.C. In 1968 and 1969, respectively, Parnicki brought out two novels about Cleopatra: *Zabij Kleopatrę* (Kill Cleopatra), in which he shares with readers his bizarre views of history, and *Inne życie Kleopatry* (Cleopatra's Other Life). The Cleopatra works were followed by several other novels: *Tożsamość* (Identity, 1970); *Muza dalekich podróży* (The Muse of Distant Journeys, 1970); *Przeobrażenie* (Transformation, 1973); *Staliśmy jak dwa sny* (We Stood Like Two Dreams, 1973); and *Sam wyjdę bezbronny* (I Myself Will Leave Unarmed, 1976), a "historical-fantastic novel in three parts." *Rodowód literacki* (Literary Origin), which appeared in 1974, is interesting for Parnicki's biographical information and artistic comments, whereas *Historia w literaturę przekuwana* (History Reforged into Literature, 1980), one of his last published works, is a transcript of a series of lectures delivered at Warsaw University in 1972 and 1973.

Literature: Wacław Sadkowski, *Parnicki: Wprowadzenie w twórczość powieściopisarska* (Warsaw: Agencja Autorska, 1970), a good short introduction to Parnicki's novels; Jacek Łukasiewicz, ed., *Świat Parnickiego: Materiały z konferencji* (Wrocław: Towarzystwo Polonistyki Wrocławskiej, 1999), papers from the most recent scholarly conference on Parnicki.

Partljić, Tone (b. 1940) Slovenian novelist, short-story writer, and playwright. Partljić was born in Maribor and educated at the Higher Pedagogical Institute. He worked for several years as a teacher before becoming artistic director in theaters in Maribor and Ljubljana. From 1983 to 1987, he held the position of chairman of the Slovenian Writers Association. As a writer, Partljić is an able satirist in a lighter vein who has specialized in short stories, novels, and plays about contemporary Slovenian life. His collections of stories include *Ne glej za pticami* (Don't Look Out for the Pigeons, 1967); *Jalovost* (Sterility, 1971); *Volk na madridskih ulicah* (A Wolf in the Streets of Madrid, 1974); *Hotel sem prijeti sonce: Otroške spominske črtice* (I Wanted to Grasp the Sun: Childhood Memory Sketches, 1981); *Na svidenje nad zvezdami: Novelistična zbirka in komedija* (To Meeting Above the Stars: A Novella Collection and a Comedy, 1982); *Pepsi ili provincialni donjuan* (Pepsi, or A Provincial Don Juan, 1986); *Kulturne humoreski, prosim* (Cultural Humoresques, If You Please, 1988); *Slišal sem, kako trava raste: Otroške spominske črtice* (I Heard the Grass Grow: Childhood Memory Sketches, 1990); and *Goool! Predvolilne humoreske* (Goool! Pre-Election Humoresques, 1992). Similar in spirit and style to his stories, Partljić's three novels are *Prelest, prelesti* (Charm, Charms, 1990); *Mala* (Little Girl, 1992); and *Pri Mariji Snežni zvoni* (The Bells of Mary of the Snows, 1994). As a dramatist, Partljić is the author of several plays, mostly satirical comedies: *Ribe na plitvni* (Fish in the Shallows, 1968); *Naj poje čuk* (Let the Screech-Owl Sing, 1971); *Ščuke pa ni* (There Isn't Any Pike, 1973); *O, ne, ščuke pa ne* (Oh No, We Don't Want a Pike, 1976); *Ščuk ni, ščuke ne: Združeni prejšnji dve)* (There Isn't Any Pike and We Don't Want It Either: The Previous Two Joined, 1977); *Oskubite jastreba* (Pluck the Vulture, 1977); a satirical paraphrase of the great Slovenian writer Ivan Cankar's (1876–1918) well-known work, *Hlapci* (Farmhands, 1910); *Nekoč in danes* (Once Upon a Time and Today, 1979); *Za koga naj še molim* (Let's Pray for Someone, 1980); *Starec za plotom: Elegija v prozi* (The Old Man Behind the Fence: An Elegy in Prose, 1995); *Moj ata, socialistični kulak* (My Dad, a Socialist Kulak, 1983); *Justifikacija* (Justification, 1986); and *Štajerc v Ljubljani* (A Styrian in Ljubljana, 1995).

Páskándi, Géza (1933–1995) Hungarian playwright, poet, short-story writer, and essayist. A well-regarded poet and dramatist, Páskándi was born in Szatmár, Transylvania (now Satu Mare, Romania), and graduated from Cluj University. He began his career as a poet, and his first book of poems, *Piros madar* (Red Bird), appeared in 1957. Before he had a chance to publish another book, Páskándi, as a Hungarian living in what was now Romania, fell victim to the antiminority policies of the regime of Gheorghe Gheorghiu-Dej and spent time in prison. He resurfaced as a writer in the mid-1960s, his new book of poems, *Holdbumeráng* (Moon Boomerang), appearing in 1967. A thoughtful poet who often comes across as light and humorous, Páskándi reached his zenith in the important collection *Tű foka* (Eye of the Needle, 1972). This gave ample evidence of a greater willingness to experiment with every important facet of poetry writing, from verse form to imagery, without sacrificing his easy humor and wit. After *Tű foka*, Páskándi's next most important

collection of poems was the retrospective *Nagy dilettantissimo: Új versek, 1973–1985* (The Big Dilettantissimo: New Verses, 1973–1985, 1989).

Although he had published a collection of short stories in 1968, *Üvegek* (Bottles), Páskándi soon turned to writing plays, most of them humorous, and established a solid reputation as one of contemporary Hungary's more intriguing dramatists. His first collection of plays appeared in 1970 under the title *Eb olykor emeli lábát: Párbeszédek, színjátékok* (A Dog Sometimes Raises a Leg: Dialogues and Plays). It was followed by *A vegytisztító becsülete* (The Dry Cleaners' Honor, 1973) and *Vendégség: Tornyot választok* (A Gathering: I Choose a Tower, 1973; translated as *Sojourn*), his only play available in English, a rather static historical parable about religious controversy set in Transylvania during the Reformation and pivoting on the figure of Ferenc Dávid, the leader of Unitarian anti-Trinitarianism. Páskándi's other plays have appeared in such volumes as *Páskándi Géza színművei* (Plays by Géza Páskándi, 1974); *Színművek* (Plays, 1975); *Papírrepülő eltérítése* (The Highjacking of a Paper Pilot, 1976); *Sárikás anyós: Humoros párbeszédek, színjátékok* (Sárikás, Mother-in-Law: Humorous Dialogues and Plays, 1979); *Erdélyi triptichon: Püspökdrámák* (Transylvanian Triptych: The Bishop's Plays, 1984); *Szörnyszülött* (Monsters, 1985); *Páskándi Géza színművei* (Plays of Géza Páskándi, 1985); *Páskándi Géza drámái* (Dramatic Works of Géza Páskándi, 1987); *Lélekharang: Dráma két részben* (The Deathknell: A Drama in Two Parts, 1989); *Kalauz nélkül: humoros párbeszédek, színjátékok* (Without Conductor: Humor-ous Dialogues and Plays, 1989); and *Medvebőrben* (In Bearskin, 1994), another collection of his plays.

In 1989 Páskándi published a novel, *Sírrablók* (Grave Robbers), and in 1995 the collection *Esszék, előadások, levelek: Az ab-*

szurd és az Isten (Essays, Lectures, Letters: The Absurd and God). Often characterized as a dramatist in the spirit of the theater of the absurd, Páskándi addresses the matter of absurdist theater in his essays and shows where such pigeonholing of his own playwriting is not wholly accurate. After his rehabilitation following imprisonment, Páskándi became editor in chief of the Bucharest-based Hungarian-language publishing house Kritérion and in 1974, after resettling in Budapest, the poetry editor of the journal Kortárs. He was awarded the Attila József Prize in 1977 and the Kossuth Prize in 1993.

Translations: Sojourn, trans. Gabriel John Brogyányi, in Drama Contemporary: Hungary, ed. Eugene Brogyányi (New York: PAJ Publications, 1991), 65–101; four poems in In Quest of the "Miracle Stag": The Poetry of Hungary, ed. Adam Makkai (Chicago: Atlantis-Centaur, 1996), 848–52.

Paskov, Viktor (b. 1949) Bulgarian novelist, poet, and musician. Paskov was born in Sofia, where he completed secondary school before studying at the Leipzig Conservatory. An accomplished musician, he has played with jazz bands, composed, sung opera, and been a music critic in Germany. From 1980 to 1987, he served as the literary and musical editor of the Sofia Press Agency, and in 1987 he became editor and film adviser at the Boian feature film studios. Paskov began publishing poems and short stories in various periodicals in 1964 but then concentrated on the writing of novels and novellas, among them Nevrustni ubiistva (Infant Murders, 1986); Balada za Georg Henih (A Ballad for Georg Henig, 1987); Tsii Kuk (1991); Germaniia—mrusna prikazka (Germany: A Dirty Story, 1993), which was based to a great extent on Paskov's own experiences in Germany, where he lived for several years; and Aliluia (Hallelujah, 2001), a collection of seven previously published novellas. Paskov is best known for A Ballad for Georg Henig, a poignant work about the fate of a real Czech master violin maker named Georg Henig, who settled in Bulgaria, and his impact on the narrator of the novel and his family. Paskov's love of the world of music, his preoccupation with the survival of the spirit in the face of social and moral squalor, his use of expressive language, and his application of musical form to literary structure come together here more effectively than in any other work by him.

Translations: A Ballad for Georg Henig, trans. Robert Sturm (London: Peter Owen, 1990); "Big Business," trans. Lyubomir Nikolov and Roland Flint, in Description of a Struggle: The Vintage Book of Contemporary Eastern European Writing, ed. Michael March (New York: Vintage, 1994), 202–19.

Păunescu, Adrian (b. 1943) Romanian poet and journalist. One of the most popular poets of his generation, Păunescu was born in Copăceni, the son of a teacher. He began publishing poems at the age of seventeen. From 1963 to 1968, he pursued a degree in Romanian studies at Bucharest University, during which time he was affiliated with the student paper Amfiteatru. In 1967/1968, he was deputy editor in chief of the literary magazine Romania literară and, from 1969 to 1972, a member of the editorial staff of the journal Luceafărul. In 1973 he became editor in chief of the political journal Flacăra. However, he was dismissed from his position at the journal following the collapse of spectator stands at the rock concert he organized in Ploiești, where poems dedicated to Nicolae Ceaușescu were performed to rock music.

Păunescu's first volume of poetry, Ultrasentimente (Ultra Sentiments), appeared in 1965 and at once evidenced the intensity, provocativeness, and rebelliousness for which he has long been admired, especially by younger readers. Ultrasentimente was followed by *Mieii primi* (The Newborn Lamb, 1966), which is notable for its greater self-restraint; its embrace of patriotism and nationalism, with which Păunescu has also been identified; and its nostalgia for the Romanian rural past. Subsequent volumes of poetry such as *Fîntîna somnambulă* (The Sleepwalking Well), which won the poetry prize of the Writers Union in 1968; *Istoria unei secunde* (History of a Second, 1971); and *Repetabila povară* (Repeatable Burden, 1974) continued Păunescu's consideration of the cost involved in the technological and social modernization of a largely rural population. This nostalgia for the past, and his embrace of the peasant, have caused Romanian critics to situate Păunescu, to some extent, in the tradition of patriotic poetry of such pre–World War II Romanian writers as Octavian Goga (1881–1938) and Aron Cotruş (1891–1961). In *Pămîntul deocamdată* (The Earth Until Now, 1976), a collection of sonnets, Păunescu deals with similar, and unconventional, thematic material within the rigors of a traditional form, which he approaches with his customary bravado. *Manifest pentru sănătatea pămîntului* (Manifesto for the Health of the Earth), a collection of poems published in 1980, marks a certain return to the activism of his poetry of the 1960s. During the Romanian revolution of December 1989, Păunescu sought refuge in the American Embassy, to which he had gone with a briefcase full of jewels. After dropping out of sight for a while, he returned to public life, publishing poetry designed to demonstrate his hostility to the Ceauşescu regime. A volume of his alleged previously censored poetry appeared in 1989 under the title *Poezii cenzurate: 22 august 1968–22 decembrie 1987*. It was put out by the Editura Păunescu, Păunescu's own publishing house. Păunescu's distaste for socialism is expressed in no uncertain terms. In the title poem of the collection, however, he also reveals a nationalistic patriotism when he expresses his belief that had Romania's World War II fascist leader, Marshal Ion Antonescu, been tried by an impartial tribunal he would have to have been "unreservedly" declared a hero and a martyr, "at least after reading the Ribbentrop–Molotov pact."

Păunescu's prose writing falls into three categories represented by three collections: fantastic stories, as in *Cărţile poştale ale morţii* (Postcards of Death, 1970); journalistic essays, largely of a political character, as in *Sub semnul întrebării* (Under the Sign of a Question, 1971); and *Lumea ca lume* (The World as World, 1973), a collection of articles and interviews with writers, prominent cultural figures, and politicians. Some of his other writings include *Drept cooperatist* (Cooperative Farmer Law, 1974, 1980), with his wife, Daniela; *De la barca la viena şi înapoi: Desene de A. A. Păunescu* (By Boat to Vienna and Back: Drawings by A. A. Păunescu, 1981), a travel book; and such newer collections of poetry as *Iubiţi-vă pe tunuri* (Make Love, Not War, 1981); *Locuri comune: 202 poezii noi* (Commonplaces: 202 New Poems, 1986); *Între-adevăr: Noi poezii noi* (Indeed: All New Poems, 1988); and *Sînt un om liber* (I Am a Free Man, 1989).

Translations: One poem in *Anthology of Contemporary Romanian Poetry,* ed. and trans. Roy MacGregor-Hastie (London: Peter Owen, 1969), 163–65; six poems in *46 Romanian Poets in English,* trans. Ştefan Avădanei and Don Eulert (Iaşi: Junimea, 1973), 320–26; one poem in *Modern Romanian Poetry,* ed. Nicholas Catanoy (Oakville, Ont.: Mosaic Press/Valley Editions, 1977), 21.

Pavel, Ota (real name Ota Popper; 1930–1973) Czech sportswriter and short-story writer. A native of Prague, Pavel became the sole support of his mother, a non-Jew, when in 1944 his father, who was Jewish, and his two brothers were sent to different German concentration camps. He worked mostly as a coal miner. After the war, he completed his education and from 1949 to 1956 was affiliated with Radio Prague as a sports correspondent. He was also a staff member of the sports magazine *Stadion,* where his first literary work appeared in 1949. Pavel traveled throughout Europe and the United States as a sports correspondent; his career ended, however, when he suffered a mental collapse in 1964 on a trip to Innsbruck, Austria, with the Czech Olympic team. Despite extensive treatment for what was diagnosed as a manic-depressive psychotic condition, he never fully recovered and was retired with a disability pension in 1966. His death in 1973 has been described as having occurred in "mysterious circumstances."

Pavel's first publication, an underground edition, was *Běh Prahou: Jak tatínek byl a zase nebyl komunistou* (The Prague Race: How Daddy Was and Was Not a Communist, 1972). His first book to appear in print was a collection of three longer stories: *Fialový poustevník* (The Purple Hermit Crab); *Smrt krásných srnců* (The Death of the Red Deer); and *Jak jsem potkal ryby* (How I Came to Know Fish), his only work to be translated into English. The volume was reprinted in 1995 under the title *Fialový poustevník. Mám rád tu řeku* (I Like This River), a novella of under 100 pages, appeared posthumously in 1989, as did a book about climbing titled *Výstup na Eiger* (The Ascent of the Eiger). Two more of Pavel's "daddy" novellas came out in 1990 and 1994, respectively: *Tatínkova loď naděje* (Daddy's Ship of Hope) and *Jak šel táta Afrikou* (How Dad Traveled Around Africa). Three collections of short stories were also published posthumously: *Zlatí úhoři* (The Golden Eels, 1985); *Omyl a jiné povídky* (The Error and Other Stories, 1995); and *Olympijské hry a jiné povídky* (Olympic Games and Other Stories, 1996). Pavel's stories, as in the compilation in English *How I Came to Know Fish,* are often like miniature paintings in the primitive syle: simple in manner, charming in their calcu-

lated naivete. His affection for nature and for animal life is genuine and much in evidence. The angler would find his stories on fishing delightful. His father (the "daddy" of his works) appears frequently as a character in his stories, and it is from a few of those in *How I Came to Know Fish* that we learn of his fate during the German occupation.

Literature: Jan Šimon Fiala, ed., *Slzy na stoncích trávy* (Prague: NTC Interpress, 1991), a modest collection of writings about Pavel by friends and associates.

Translations: *How I Came to Know Fish,* trans. Jindriska Badal and Robert McDowell (New York: New Directions, 1990).

Pavić, Milorad (b. 1929) Serbian novelist. Born in Belgrade, where he still lives, Pavić is a specialist on the Baroque and teaches courses on that period as well as on the eighteenth and nineteenth centuries at Belgade University. As a scholar, he has published a number of books on older Serbian literatures, among them a history of Serbian Baroque literature (1970) and a history of Serbian classicism and pre-Romanticism (1979). As a writer of fiction, Pavić is known primarily for his intricate, puzzle-like novel *Hazarski rečnik: Roman-leksikon u 100,000 reči* (*Dictionary of the Khazars: A Lexicon Novel in 100,000 Words,* 1984), which has been translated into twenty-four languages. It won the prestigious Yugoslav NIN Prize as the best novel in Serbo-Croatian in 1984 and was hailed as the best-received work of fiction published in Serbia in the decade 1982 to 1992. Ostensibly a 1980s reconstruction and updating of a book of the same name from 1691, which was, in turn, a reconstruction of the lost "dictionary" of the ancient Khazar people, the entire novel is composed in the form of a great puzzle. Alphabetized entries out of chronological order and cross-referencing symbols invite readers to use the book as they would, for example, a dictionary. It can be picked up and read at any arbitrary point, read from left to right or right to left, and even read "diagonally." There is one major division—into three separately alphabetized books divided along religious lines (Christian, Islamic, and Hebrew), prefaced by preliminary notes and followed by appendixes that contain the bulk of the narrative. The story itself is divided into three periods in time, each with its own set of three characters. It was published in male and female editions, different only by seventeen lines, since according to Pavić masculine and feminine stories cannot have the same ending. The work has sometimes been compared with Umberto Eco's *The Name of the Rose* and Patrick Suskind's *Perfume*. Pavić pursued a similar game-playing technique in such subsequent novels as *Predeo slikan čajem* (*Landscape Painted with Tea*, 1990) and *Unutrašnja strana vetra ili roman o Kheri i Leandru* (*The Inner Side of the Wind, or The Novel of Hero and Leander*, 1991). *Landscape Painted with Tea* is another large novel, this time in the form of a crossword puzzle woven out of the life and papers of the successful Serbian architect Atanas Razin (alias Atanas Svilar), who settles in Los Angeles but eventually sells his engineering and pharmaceuticals company and moves to North Carolina. Along the way, Pavić provides instructions on how to solve the puzzle and discusses his novel with his readers. *The Inner Side of the Wind, or The Novel of Hero and Leander*, a new reading of the ancient tale of Hero and Leander, includes both a male and a female version within the same volume (unlike *Dictionary of the Khazars*). Not only are both versions accommodated within the same volume, but the book can be opened from one side or the other with identical title pages and with one of the versions printed upside down from the other. The reader thus can start with whichever version he or she prefers. Hero's story is some twenty pages shorter than Leander's. The combined stories transpose the

ancient tale to ancient and modern Serbia. The story of Heroena Bukur (the Hero of the "female" book) is set in twentieth-century Yugoslavia and culminates in the violent death of the heroine. The narrative is anything but linear. It incorporates direct authorial intervention at one point as well as a story-within-a-story by Heroena, covertly inserted into translations she makes of such French authors as Anatole France and Pierre Loti, copies of which she sends to her brother with the interpolated passages indicated in lipstick. In Leander's story, Leander is the nickname given a young Serb by a Russian teacher of Latin in Belgrade's Serbian–Latin school when his class is assigned the reading of a Latin translation of the original Greek *Love and Death of Hero and Leander*. The story itself takes place during the seventeenth-century wars between the Serbs and the Turks and, like that of Hero, culminates in the violent death of the male protagonist. Pavić's most recent novel is *Poslednja ljubav u Carigradu* (*Last Love in Constantinople*, 1998), subtitled *A Tarot Novel for Divination*. The book, which is divided into a "special key" and twenty-one additional "keys" corresponding to Tarot cards, comes equipped with illustrations of the various cards, instructions on how to lay out the cards, an explanation of the use of the book for divination, and a section called "The Keys of the Great Secret for Ladies of Both Sexes."

Pavić has also published several collections of stories and reminiscences, among them *Ruski hrt* (The Russian Greyhound, 1979); *Konji Svetoga Marka* (The Horses of Saint Mark, 1989); and *Stakleni puž: Priče sa interneta* (The Glass Snail: Stories from the Internet, 1998). *Ruski hrt* contains nineteen separate personal reminiscences, some set in Belgrade in 1944 at the time of the Soviet capture of the city. *Konji Svetoga Marka* comprises thirteen stories of an esoteric character set in different places (from Mexico to Constantinople) and historical periods, and with a mixture of historical and fictional personages. Throughout the collection, Pavić develops a fascinating system of correspondences between events in different places and times. A game of chess begun, for example, in 1970 can be transformed into a bloody Serbian–Tukish battle in 1389; the rivalry of two Serbian pre-Romantic poets is reproduced a century and a half later; and a moon rock on exhibit in New York, Moscow, Belgrade, London, and elsewhere recalls for the author an ancient South Slavic Bogomil legend. In this way, Pavić suggests that even banal everyday events are subject to the same ineffable laws and are charged with the same sense as great historical episodes. A few of the stories incorporate the type of quasi-cabbalistic numerology familiar from Pavić's previous works. In *Stakleni puž*, Pavić adopts the persona of an Internet author. The three stories in the collection are presented as printouts from their own Web sites. And after an author's epilogue in which he writes about himself as a third party, he offers his own www. address: khazaro.com. Pavić has also written a short history of Belgrade, which was published in a well-illustrated edition in Serbo-Croatian and English in 1990.

Pavić's well-known fondness for literary game-playing has carried over as well into his dramatic writing. The best example of this is his play *Zauvek i dan više* (1993; translated as *Forever and a Day: A Theatre Menu*). With a restaurant menu as his model, Pavić offers his readers, viewers, or theater directors a choice of starters, main courses, and deserts, and recommends his own preference for a 3 + 1 + 3 structure. The main course and deserts concentrate on the otherworldly romance between a pair of lovers in seventeenth-century Istanbul.

Literature: Andrew Wachtel, "Postmodernism as Nightmare: Milorad Pavić's Literary Demolition of Yugoslavia," *Slavic and East European Journal* 41, no. 4 (1997): 627–44. This is an interesting, rather persuasive political interpretation of Pavić's *Dictionary of the Khazars* in light of the ethnic and religious conflicts in the former Yugoslavia in the 1990s.

Translations: *Dictionary of the Khazars: A Lexicon Novel in 100,000 Words*, trans. Christina Pribićević-Zorić (New York: Knopf, 1988); *Forever and a Day: A Theatre Menu* (Belgrade: Dereta, 1997); *The Inner Side of the Wind, or The Novel of Hero and Leander*, trans. Christina Pribićević-Zorić (New York: Knopf, 1993); *Landscape Painted with Tea*, trans. Christina Pribićević-Zorić (New York: Knopf, 1990); *Last Love in Constantinople: A Tarot Novel for Divination*, trans. Christina Pribichevich-Zorić (Chester Springs, Pa.: Dufour, 1998); *A Short History of Belgrade*, trans. Christina Pribićević-Zorić, with photographs by Miodrag Djordjević (Belgrade: Prosveta, 1990).

Pavličić, Pavao (b. 1946) Croatian novelist and short-story writer. A prolific and highly contemporary Croatian writer, Pavličić was born and educated through high school in Vukovar. He earned a degree in Croatian literature at Zagreb University, where he currently teaches, specializing in old Croatian literature. His contributions to the study of Croatian literature include books on Croatian Baroque literature (1979), literary genealogy (1983), verse in drama and drama in verse (1985), the poetics of mannerism (1988), verse and meaning (1993), the Baroque style in Dubrovnik (1995), and the modern Croatian lyric (1999). Other literary studies by Pavličić include *Sedam interpretacija* (Seven Interpretations, 1986); *Škola pisanja* (The School of Writing, 1994); and *Studije o Osmanu* (Studies About Osman, 1996). In light of the destruction of his native city of Vukovar by the Serbs in late February and early March 1992, during the Bosnian War, Pavličić has sought to preserve the memory of the once handsome city as it has been. His *Dunav: p.s. 1991, vukarske razgled-nice* (The Danube: p.s. 1991, Picture Post-cards of Vukovar, 1992) and *Vodič po Vuko-varu* (A Guide to Vukovar, 1997) were conceived in this spirit. He also wrote the text for a picture book about Zagreb: *Zag-rebački trgovi* (Zagreb Squares, 1998).

Pavličić began his literary career as a writer of criminal stories, the first collection of which, *Dobri duh Zagrebu* (The Good Air of Zagreb), came out in 1976. It was fol-lowed a year later by his *kriminalistički roman* (criminal novel) *Plava ruža* (The Blue Rose) and in 1978 by the murder mys-tery *Stroj za maglu* (The Fog Machine). In 1990 Pavličić published a book about the genre of the murder mystery under the title *Sve što znam o krimiću* (All I Know About the Murder Mystery, 1990). After his crime fiction, Pavličić produced a steady stream of novels from 1982 to 1999: *Umjetni orao* (The Artificial Eagle, 1979); *Slobodni pad* (Free Fall, 1982); *Večernji akt* (Evening Nude, 1982); *Eter* (Ether, 1983); *Dunav* (Danube, 1983); *Kraj mandata* (End of a Term of Of-fice, 1984); *Čelični mjesec* (Moon of Steel, 1985); *Skandal na simpoziji* (Scandal at a Symposium, 1985); *Trg slobode* (Freedom Square, 1986); *Krasopis* (Calligraphy, 1987); *Koraljna vrata* (The Coral Gate, 1990); *Pro-lazna soba* (The Temporary Room, 1992); *Rakova djeca* (Every Which Way, 1992); *Rupa na nebu* (Hole in the Sky, 1992); *Nevi-dljivo pismo* (The Invisible Letter, 1993); *Sapudl* (1995); *Diksilend* (Dixieland, 1995); *Kruh i mast* (Bread and Lard, 1996); *Pokora* (Repentance, 1998); *Numerus clausus* (1998); and *Nepovrat* (Irretrievable, 1999). His witty *Rukoljub: Pisma slavnim ženama* (Hand-kissing: Letters to Famous Women), came out in 1995. Pavličić is also the author of three books of feuilletons: *Zagrebački odrezak* (Zagreb Snipping, 1985); *Inventura* (Inventory, 1989); and *Svoj svome* (To Each His Own, 1992). His *Leksikon uzaludnih znanja* (Lexicon of Futile Knowledge),

which was published in 1995, also consists of feuilletons that appeared mostly in the newspaper *Slobodna Dalmacija* from the autumn of 1992 to the summer of 1994 but, in contrast to his previous collections of feuilletons, was conceived as a self-contained whole. *Kako preživjeti mladost* (How to Survive Youth), a book by Pavličić about his school years in the form of eight separate first-person narratives, each under the name of its narrator, with the last "Ja" ("I"), appeared in 1997.

Translations: *Lament over Europe,* trans. Nikolina Jovanović (Zagreb: Croatian Writ-ers Association 1994). *Krasopis* is available in French as *La Calligraphie,* trans. Ljiljana Huibner-Fuzellier (Paris: Griot, 1995).

Pavlov, Konstantin (b. 1933) Bulgarian poet and screenwriter. One of the more impor-tant Bulgarian poets and film writers of the second half of the twentieth century, Pavlov also earned a reputation as an outspoken critic of literary regimentation and repres-sion under the communists. He was born in the village of Vitoshko, in the Sofia region, and attended high school in Sofia. By the time he graduated in 1952, he had become the Bulgarian national champion in sprint-ing. From 1952 to 1957, he studied law at Sofia University, after which he held a series of ed-itorial positions at Radio Sofia (1957–1959), the Bulgarski pisatel state publishing house (1961–1962, 1964–1965), *Literaturen front* (1963), and Multifilm Studios (1965–1966). From 1973 to 1991, he was a consulant as well as an editor at Bulgarian Cinematog-raphy and, in 1992, became chief artistic di-rector for Channel I of Bulgarian National TV. Despite this record of employment, Pavlov was no stranger to joblessness and of-ficial surveillance because of his indepen-dence and caustic writings. The period of partial democratization that followed the death of Stalin began unraveling in the 1960s, and poets of the "April" (1956) generation like Pavlov began receiving harsh criticism from official censors for their deviations from prescribed literary norms and increasing pressure to toe the line in their writing. Pavlov's inclination toward the humorous, parodic, and satirical are already evident in the poems and epigrams he first published in 1947 in the journal *Septemvriiche,* and even more so in his first published collection of poems, *Satiri* (Satires, 1960). His ironies and innuendoes aimed at the totalitarian system were all the more effective for their liberal dose of the absurd and grotesque. It was, however, Pavlov's second book of poems, *Stihove* (Poems, 1965), that brought him the greatest political grief. One of the poems in the collection in particular, "Five Old Men," was interpreted as a mockery of the members of the Politburo of the Central Committee of the Communist Party. Long uncomfortable with Pavlov's independence and critical attitude toward authority, the establishment critics and Party literary overseers moved against him. Besides attacks on his writing and person, he was forbidden to publish anything for nearly twenty years. During this period, he found himself frequently without a job. When Pavlov resumed his literary career in 1983, his first publication was an anthology of his poems and film scenarios under the title *Stari neshta* (Old Stuff, 1983). This was followed by *Poiaviavane* (Appearance, 1989); *Agoniio sladka* (Sweet Agony, 1991); *Ubiistvo na spiasht chovek* (The Suicide of a Sleeping Man, 1992); and *Otdavna . . .* (Way Back When . . . , 1998), a collection of poems from the early 1980s. That Pavlov's pungent wit had not been dulled by the years of enforced absence from print is evident from such typical poems in *Otdavna . . .* as

> Government slogan: Before we feed
>   Man,
> we have to feed the System.
> And the System is fed with Men.

and

> Such was the age—
> we killed . . .
> Who makes the age?
> The Murderers . . .
> Hoorah!
> Long live the age!
> Hoorah!
> Long live the murderers!

In 1992 Pavlov was awarded a prize for his poetry by the International Academy of Art in Paris.

Translations: Seven poems in *Window on the Black Sea: Bulgarian Poetry in Translation,* ed. Richard Harteis, in collaboration with William Meredith (Pittsburgh: Carnegie Mellon University Press, 1992), 80–90.

Pavlović, Miodrag (b. 1928) Serbian poet, literary critic, playwright, and stage director. A native of Novi Sad, Pavlović studied medicine in Belgrade and has lived most of his life in the Serbian capital. After the controversial reception of his first book of poetry, *87 pesama* (87 Poems, 1952), Pavlović practiced medicine for a while, but then decided to devote himself entirely to literature. Although *87 pesama* appeared at a time when the arts in Yugoslavia were beginning to distance themselves from political controls, Pavlovic's break with traditionalism aroused the ire of some critics who were hostile to the modernism and surrealism coming to the fore in Yugoslav poetry in the 1950s. But the enthusiasm of his younger contemporaries helped Pavlović withstand the torrent of criticism from traditionalists and other readers who were baffled by the poet's seeming indifference to the great trauma through which the nation had recently passed. Yet despite its rationalism and cerebral aspect, as well as Pavlović's frequent surreal imagery, his poetry was neither untouched by nor unresponsive to the calamities of World War II and the Holocaust. Images of violence, death, and an abiding sense of fear pervade his early writing.

Pavlović's works published after *87 pesama* include eleven volumes of poetry: *Stub sećanja* (The Pillar of Memory, 1953); *Oktave* (Octaves, 1957); *Mleko iskoni* (Primeval Milk, 1962); *Velika Skitiia* (Great Scythia, 1969); *Nova Skitiia* (The New Scythia, 1970); *Svetli i tamni praznici* (Light and Dark Holy Days, 1971); *Zavetine* (Vows, 1976); *Pesme o detinjstvu i ratovima* (Poems About Childhood and War, 1992); *Ulazak u Kremonu* (Entering Cremona, 2nd ed., 1995); *Izabrane i nove pesme: 1946–1996* (Selected and New Poems: 1946–1996, 1996); and *Srbija do kraja veka: Izabrane pesme, 1969/1989* (Serbia to the End of the Century: Selected Poems, 1969/1989, 1997). He has also written a book of short stories, *Most bez obale* (Bridge Without Shores, 1965); three plays, *Igre bezimenih* (The Dance of the Nameless, 1963); *Koraci u drogoj sobi* (Steps in the Other Room, 1958); and *Put u neizvesnost* (The Road to the Unknown, 1958); and several books of essays on Serbian and other poetry, including *Rokovi poezije* (The Terms of Poetry, 1958); *Eseji o srpskim pesnicima* (Essays on Serbian Poetry, 1992); and *Poetika žrtvenog obreda* (The Poetics of the Sacrificial Rite, 1987), a study of myth and ritual in literature.

Among Pavlović's most interesting works, and the best represented in translation, are his closely linked books of poetry *Mleko iskoni, Velika Skitiia, Nova Skitiia,* and *Svetli i tamni praznici.* The volumes draw heavily on Greek mythology (Primeval Milk) and Byzantine and medieval Serbian history (Great Scythia and The New Scythia); mythological and folk elements commingle with those of the New Testament in Light and Dark Holy Days, which celebrates the birth of Christ and the advent of Christianity. Pavlović views myths as the repository of humans' collective experience, and in his essay "Myth and Poetry" (1971) describes their significance for poetry as the "grammar of poetic thought, the grammar of imagination." Pavlović's ideas on antiquity and myth owed much to the rich tradition of the Serbian folk song and epic, which scholars such as Albert Lord of Harvard University proposed in his now classic *The Singer of Tales* as the direct lineal descendants of the *Iliad* and *Odyssey.* In historical terms, the Serbs have long felt a close kinship with ancient Greece through their belief that had it not been for the Turkish victory at Kosovo in 1389, the great medieval Serbian kingdom of Emperor Dušan was destined to incorporate and thus succeed Byzantium. Many of the "Scythia" poems relate the events of the battle of Kosovo, which is still alive in the collective Serbian consciousness; the subsequent Turkish conquest of Constantinople in 1453; and the surrender of the last Serbian fortress, at Smederevo, in 1459. Pavlović's keen interest in the Serbian oral tradition and folk literature is evident not only in his poetry, but also in his anthology of Serbian folk-lyric poetry published in 1982 and in two books of essays on old and folk Serbian poetry: *Ogledi o narodnoj i staroj srpskoj poeziji* (Views on Old Serbian and Folk Poetry, 1993) and *Obredno i govorno delo: Ogledi sa srpskim predanjem* (Ceremonial and Oral Literature: Views of the Serbian Tradition, 1986). He has also published a book on ancient Slavdom under the title *Knjiga staroslavna* (The Ancient Slavic Book, 1989) and another on narratives from the Lake Vskrsnje region, *Bitni ljudi: Priče sa Vskrsnjeg ostrva* (Essential People: Tales from Lake Vskrsnje, 1995). In 1961 Pavlović coauthored the text accompanying a picture book on Lake Ohrid in Macedonia. He has also edited a bilingual (Macedonian and Serbo-Croatian) collection of poems by the Macedonian poet Petre Andreevski (1977), and in 1966 published a volume of his own translations of the Albanian poet Eros Sequi (b. 1912).

Literature: Zlata Kočić, *Rtanjska svetila: Ogled poeziji Miodraga Pavlovića* (Niš: Prosveta, 1996); Časlav Dordjević, *Pesnikovo svevidece oko: Eseji o pesniku Miodraga Pavlovića* (Belgrade: Prosveta, 1997).

Translations: *The Conqueror of Constantinople* (St. Paul, Minn.: New Rivers, 1976); *The Slavs Beneath Parnassus: Selected Poems*, trans. Bernard Johnson (London: Angel, 1985; St. Paul, Minn.: New Rivers, 1985); two poems in *The Horse Has Six Legs: An Anthology of Serbian Poetry*, ed. and trans. Charles Simic (St. Paul, Minn.: Graywolf, 1992), 77–80; seven poems, trans. Anne Pennington, in *New Writing in Yugoslavia*, ed. Bernard Johnson (Harmondsworth: Penguin, 1970), 289–95.

Pavlović, Živojin (b. 1933) Serbian novelist, short-story writer, essayist, and film director. An extraordinarily prolific, imaginative, provocative even outrageous writer, equally renowned for his fiction, prose, and films, Pavlović was born in Šabac and studied painting at the Serbian Academy of Applied Arts. He made his literary debut in the early 1960s, around the time that he brought out his first films. His first collection of short stories was *Krivudava reka* (The Curving River, 1963). It was followed by such other story collections as *Dve večeri u jesen* (Two Evenings Toward Autumn, 1970), which won the Isadora Sekulić Prize; *Cigansko groblje* (The Gypsy Cemetery, 1972); *Vetar u suvoj travi* (The Wind in the Dry Grass, 1976); *Ubijao sam bikove* (I Killed the Bulls, 1985); *Kriške vremena* (Slices of Time, 1993); *Ljubav* (Love, 1998); and *Blato* (Mud, 1999). Pavlović has been even more prolific as a novelist. Beginning with *Lutke* (Dolls, 1965), he has published some fourteen novels, including *Kain i Avelj: Alegorija* (Cain and Abel: An Allegory, 1969), a mystico-

fantastic reading of the career of the Serbian revolutionary Slobodan Antić that was based on the scenario of Pavlović's 1964 film *Neprijatelj* (The Enemy); *Zadah tela* (The Odor of the Body, 1982); *Zid smrti* (The Wall of Death, 1985), which won the NIN Prize for novel of the year; *Trag divljači* (Hunting Game, 1985); *Neprijatelj* (The Enemy, 1986), revised edition of *Kain i Avelj: Alegorija*; *Oni više ne postoje* (They Exist No More, 1987); *Raslo mi je badem drvo* (My Almond Tree, 1988); *Vašar na svetog arkandjela* (Fair on Saint Archangel's Day, 1990); *Lutke na bunjištu* (Dolls on the Garbage Heap, 1991); *Lapot* (Wild Wind, 1992), which won the NIN Prize for novel of the year; *Biljna krv* (The Blood of Plants, 1995); and *Dolap* (Symmetry, 1997).

Much of Pavlović's fiction is set in eastern Serbia and recounts older Serbian ways and customs through family histories unfolded by representatives of different generations. What he depicts can be harsh and offensive, as, in *Lapot*, the killing of the elderly and infirm to rid a community of its useless members; but cruelty, inhumanity, and often the shocking are partially offset by a lyrical and poetic style particularly sensitive to nature and Pavlović's skill with language.

Apart from his fiction, Pavlović has published several other volumes of prose, among them three books of essays, mostly on film and other arts: *Djavoli film* (Devilish Film, 1969), *O odvratnom* (On the Repulsive, 1972), and *Balkanski džez* (Balkan Jazz, 1989); a collection of articles about film in the schools, *Film u školskim klupama* (Film in School Benches, 1964); a book of criticism, *Davne godine* (Past Years, 1997); a few collections of "conversations," *Jezgro napetosti* (The Essence of Tension, 1990) and *Ludilo u ogledalu* (Madness in the Mirror, 1992), a volume of epistolary prose written with Goran Milašinović; a diary, *Ispljuvak pun krvi* (Sputum Full of Blood), which was first published in 1984 but suppressed in

1990; a miscellany called *Otkucaji* (Raps, 1998), containing a large assortment of very small pieces, aphorisms, poems, conversations, and anecdotes on everything from four lists of writers, painters, and film and theater people he worshiped in the period 1944 to 1994 ("Komedija idolatrije" ["Comedy of Idolatry"]) to a paragraph on "Prostitution and the Porno Film" ("Prostitucija i porno film"); and a small volume of "notes" (*beleške*) under the title *Flogiston* (1989).

Pavlović's fame as a film director rests primarily on such films as *Budjenje pacova* (The Rat's Awakening, 1967); *Kak budem mrtav i beo* (When I'm Dead and White, 1968); the ideologically controversial *Zaseda* (The Ambush, 1969), which was not permitted to be exported; and *Crveno klasje* (Red Grain Stalks, 1970). In the early 1970s, Pavlović began teaching at Belgrade's Film School, but because of the controversial nature and notoriety of some of his films was accused of negativism and exerting a bad influence on the young and was soon banned from the classroom. He returned to filmmaking with *Let mrtve ptice* (The Flight of the Dead Bird, 1973); *Hajka* (The Chase, 1973); and, based on his novels, *Zadah tela* (The Odor of the Body, 1983) and *Dezerter* (Deserter, 1992).

Translations: "First Love," trans. Bernard Johnson, in *New Writing in Yugoslavia,* ed. Bernard Johnson (Harmondsworth: Penguin, 1970), 162–67; "The Question," trans. Stephen M. Dickey, in *The Prince of Fire: An Anthology of Contemporary Serbian Short Stories,* ed. Radmila J. Gorup and Nadežda Obradović (Pittsburgh: University of Pittsburgh Press, 1998), 92–102.

Pavlovski, Božin (b. 1942) Macedonian short-story writer and novelist. A native of the village of Žvan, near Bitola, Pavlovski attended school in Bitola and later graduated from Skopje University. He began his career as a journalist, later becoming director of the Misla publishing house in Skopje. Pavlovski made his literary debut in 1964 with the novel *Igra sa ljubov* (The Game of Love, 1964). It was followed in 1967 by the short-story collection *Fantasti* (The Fantasts) and in 1967 and 1968 by arguably his most important work of fiction, the two-volume novel *Miladin od Kina* (Miladin from China), which deals with the rootless and disoriented "little" people in modern Skopje. In 1969 Pavlovski's novel *Ludisti* (Madmen) appeared, with an introduction by the Macedonian writer Vlada Urošević titled "Božin Pavlovski ili nemirot na selenjata"("Božin Pavlovski, or The Restlessness of Migration"), in which Urošević discusses the role of migration and its social and psychological impact in Pavlovski's works. After publishing a collection of selected stories (*Odbrani raskazi*) in 1970, Pavlovski came out the following year with *Makedoncite zad Ekvatorot* (Macedonians Beyond the Equator), about Macedonian immigrants to Australia. He returned thereafter to novel writing, producing five new works over the next several years: *Duva* (It's Windy, 1973); *Vest Aust* (News Australia, 1977); *Crveniot hipokrit: Roman za nemokjta i mokjta* (The Red Hypocrite: A Novel About Weakness and Power, 1987); *Utkini sosedi: Pofalba na prirodata* (The Ducks' Neighbors: In Praise of Nature, 3rd ed., 1987); and *Bolesta na korenot* (Sickness of the Root, 1988).

Translations: "Border Incident," in *The Big Horse and Other Stories of Modern Macedonia,* ed. Milne Holton (Columbia: University of Missouri Press, 1974), 146–60.

Pekárková, Iva (b. 1963) Czech novelist. Pekárková was born in Prague, where she studied microbiology at Charles University after completing high school. However, she immigrated to the United States in 1986 before receiving her degree. She lived in New York for nearly a decade before returning to Prague in 1996. Her literary reputation rests principally on her first two novels: *Péra a pe-rutě* (Plumes and Pinions, 1989; translated as *Truck Stop Rainbows*), first published in Czech by Sixty-Eight Publishers in Toronto, and *Kulatý svět* (*The World Is Round*, 1993). The novels are closely related and, although not so designated, *The World Is Round* is really a sequel to *Truck Stop Rainbows*. Clearly the stronger of the two works, *Truck Stop Rainbows* is a bittersweet look into the restless devil-may-care life of a twenty-something university student of psychology who is at the same time a passionate street photographer dedicated to capturing on film the countless examples of environmental pollution, neglect, and decay attributable to years of communist indifference. Whenever she can, the heroine of the novel hitchhikes her way across Czechoslovakia and neighboring countries in the Eastern bloc, photographing wherever she goes and sleeping with almost every truck driver who picks her up. Although not a prostitute, she accepts gifts and, on occasion, money and makes amusing distinctions between the Czecho-slovak drivers she runs into on the northern route and the foreign drivers she travels part of the way with on the international southern route. An amoral yet good-hearted, altruistic young woman, Pekárková's protagonist loses no opportunity to make caustic comments on the communist system in Czecho-slovakia. In this sense, the novel, apart from its focus on the outlook and behavior of a young Czech woman who has no illusions about the society she lives in or about herself, is a brutally honest and depressing picture of life in one of the more repressive communist regimes of the postwar period. Also narrated in the first person, *The World Is Round* follows the flight to the West presumably of the lead character in *Truck Stop Rainbows*. Although the heroine eventually receives permission to immigrate to the United States, where she marries and has a child, nothing of her life in America forms a part of the

novel. Instead, Pekárková throws the entire emphasis on the degrading and raunchy life of refugees from throughout the former Eastern bloc who are thrown together in a detention camp in Austria (and based on Pekárková's own ten-month stay in the Traiskirchen camp). The sexual dimension of *Truck Stop Rainbows* is enlarged and rendered even more graphic in *The World Is Round*, in which communal sex and brutal gang rapes are everyday occurrences. In her most recent novel, *Dej mi ty prachy* (*Gimme the Money*, 1996), Pekárková traces her expatriate heroine's life in New York, where she marries an African immigrant, primarily at first for a green card permitting her to work as a taxi driver. Pekárková has also published stories and sketches she wrote in English in such diverse publications as the *New York Times* and *Penthouse*.

Translations: *Gimme the Money*, trans. Raymond Johnston (London: Serpent's Tail, 2001); *Truck Stop Rainbows*, trans. David Powelstock (New York: Farrar, Straus and Giroux, 1992); *The World Is Round*, trans. David Powelstock (New York: Farrar, Straus and Giroux, 1994); "Talibe" (excerpt from *Dej mi ty prachy*), trans. Iva Pekárková and Alexandra Büchler, in *Allskin and Other Tales by Contemporary Czech Women*, ed. Alexandra Büchler (Seattle: Women in Translation, 1998), 125–49.

Pekić, Borislav (1930–1993) Serbian novelist. Born in Titograd, Montenegro, Pekić was accused in 1948 of having organized a student conspiracy against the state and was sentenced to fifteen years at hard labor. He was pardoned in 1954. Ten years later, he won a major Yugoslav literary prize for his biblical novel *Vreme čuda* (*The Time of Miracles*, 1964). One of Yugoslavia's most acclaimed writers, he lived in England from 1971 until his death.

Before his resettlement in England, Pekić had published his two major novels: *The*

Time of Miracles and *Hodočašće Arsenija Njegovana* (The Pilgrimage of Arsenije Njegovan, 1970; translated as *The Houses of Belgrade*). His long residence in England proved extraordinarily productive. His works from this period include several novels: *Uspenje i sunovrat Ikara Gubelkijana* (The Rise and Fall of Icarus Gubelkian, 1975); *Zlato runo: Fantazmagorija* (The Golden Fleece: A Phantasmagoria, 1978); *Basnilo: Žanr roman* (Basnilo: A Genre Novel, 1983); the two-volume *Atlantida: Epos* (Atlantida: An Epic, 1988); *Novi Jerusalim: Gotska hronika* (The New Jerusalem: A Gothic Chronicle, 1988); *Graditelji* (The Builders, 1995), a collection of novellas; and *Odbrana i poslednji dani* (Defense and Last Days, 1977). He also wrote two books of memoirs, *Godine koje su pojeli skakavci: Uspomene iz zatvora ili antropopeja (1948–1954)* (The Years the Locusts Consumed: A Prison Memoir or Anthropopeia [1948–1954], 1987), about his years in prison, and *Skinuto sa trake: Dnevničke zabeleške i razmišljanja, 1954–1983* (Stripped of My Stripes: Daily Notes and Thoughts, 1954–1983, 1996), consisting of personal reflections from his postprison years; *Poslednja pisma iz tudine* (Last Writings from Abroad, 1991), a book on English and Yugoslav politics; *Sentimentalna povest Britanskog carstva* (A Sentimental Novel of the British Monarchy, 1993); and works of a political nature, among them *Kako upokojiti vampira* (How to Appease a Vampire, 1977), about World War II, and *Odmor od istorije* (A Vacation from History, 1992), a collection of essays on Yugoslav and Serbian politics in 1945 and 1992, edited by Radoslav Bratić.

The Time of Miracles, the biblical novel that established Pekić's career, is divided into two main parts, the first describing various miracles of Christ and the second recounting various deaths, the longest and most compelling of which, "Death at Hinnom," records the hanging of Judas. Pekić's second major novel and arguably his finest work of fiction, the offbeat *Houses of Belgrade,* has a contemporary setting. Told from the perspective of a finicky, misanthropic, and reclusive builder of homes in Belgrade, Arsenije Njegovan, it explores the impact of the disorder of social and political upheaval on the mind of a master builder for whom order is everything and who cannot abide the threatened impermanence of his structures. The Belgrade student riots of 1968 recall earlier turmoil experienced by Njegovan—Serbia's participation in World War II and, especially, the riots in Belgrade just before the German attack on the city in 1941. For Njegovan, the houses he has built are more important than people; in fact, they substitute for people and are all identified by women's names. The events of past and present narrated by Njegovan are framed by the drawing up of his last will and testament and his death at the end of the novel. In a postscript, Pekić asserts in a literary fiction that, as the cousin of Njegovan's wife and the "self-appointed" chronicler of the Njegovan–Turjaški clan, he became the editor of the late Arsenije Njegovan's manuscript.

Literature: Radomir Baturan, *Romani Borislava Pekića* (Nikšić: NIO Univerzitetska riječ, 1989); Petar Pijanović, *Poetika romana Borislava Pekića* (Belgrade: Prosveta, 1991); Svetislav Jovanov, *Piknik na Golgoti: Svetska književnost Borislava Pekića* (Belgrade: Vreme knjige, 1994); Božo Koprivića, ed., *Vreme reči* (Belgrade: BIGZ, 1993), interviews with Pekić.

Translations: *The Houses of Belgrade,* trans. Bernard Johnson (New York: Harcourt Brace Jovanovich, 1978; Evanston, Ill.: Northwestern University Press, 1994); *The Time of Miracles: A Legend,* trans. Lovett F. Edwards (New York: Harcourt Brace Jovanovich, 1976); *The Time of Miracles: A Legend,* trans. Bernard Johnson (Evanston, Ill.: Northwestern University Press, 1994);

"Megalos Mastoras and His Work, 1347 A.D.," trans. Stephen M. Dickey and Bogdan Rakić, in *The Prince of Fire: An Anthology of Contemporary Serbian Short Stories,* ed. Radmila J. Gorup and Nadežda Obradović (Pittsburgh: University of Pittsburgh Press, 1998), 18–53.

Peniev, Penio (1930–1949) Bulgarian poet. A native of the village of Dobromirka, Peniev became a cult hero among many Bulgarian youths after he committed suicide in 1949. He had lived in Dimitrovgrad, where he was employed as a factory worker. A number of his poems are in the robust, agitational style of the twentieth-century Russian poet Vladimir Mayakovsky.

Translations: One poem, in a version by Roy MacGregor-Hastie, in *Modern Bulgarian Poetry,* comp. Bozhidar Bozhilov (Sofia: Sofia Press, 1976), 154–57, a Bulgarian–English edition.

Petkova, Vania (b. 1944) Bulgarian poet. A native of Sofia, Petkova graduated from high school there in 1962 and then received a degree in Slavic philology at Sofia University in 1967. She worked as an editor for the journal *Slaveiche* from 1966 to 1968 and then joined the Bulgarian Embassy in Khartoum, Sudan, from 1969 to 1970 as a correspondent and translator. After returning to Bulgaria in 1970, she worked for the next three years for the foreign division of *Literaturen front.* In 1974/1975, she studied Spanish at the José Martí Institute for Foreign Languages in Havana, Cuba. From 1979 to 1980, she was the editor in charge of the poetry section of the journal *Suvremennik.* Petkova made her literary debut in 1965 with a volume of poems under the title *Soleni vetrove* (Winds of Salt) and from the outset of her career came to be regarded as controversial writer by virtue of her antitraditional attitudes and the unabashed eroticism of much of her writing. Undeterred by negative and even hostile criticism, she continued to champion the right to freely express a woman's nature based on her own experiences and outlook, and not to be bound in writing about the erotic aspect of love by conventional morality. After *Soleni vetrove,* Petkova published another fourteen collections of poems: *Kurshumi v piasuka* (Bullets in the Sand, 1967); *Privlichane* (Attraction, 1967); *Greshnitsa* (The Sinful Woman, 1968); *Predskazanie* (Prediction, 1970); *Chernata gulubitsa* (The Black Dove, 1972); *Kestenova liubov* (Chestnut Love, 1973); *Obratna reka* (River of Return, 1976); *Obet za mulchane* (Pledge of Silence, 1979); *Siniiata kniga* (The Blue Book, 1980); *Triptih* (Triptych, 1980); *Tsiganski romans* (Gypsy Romance, 1984); *Grum* (Thunder, 1984); *Zemetresenie* (Earthquake, 1988); and *Proshtavane* (Parting, 1989). Her stay in Cuba in the mid-1970s yielded the strongly pro-Cuban volume *Venseremos: Lirichna eseta za Kuba, streshti s izvestni latinoamerikanski pisateli i revolutsioneri* (*Venceremos* [Spanish, We Shall Conquer]: A Lyrical Essay About Cuba. Meetings with Famous Latin American Writers and Revolutionaries, 1980). A gifted linguist, Petkova also has translated from Arabic, Armenian, Russian, Serbian, and French, and in 1968 edited an anthology, in Bulgarian, of contemporary Arabic poetry.

Translations: Eight poems in *The Devil's Dozen: Thirteen Bulgarian Women Poets,* trans. Brenda Walker with Belin Tonchev, in collaboration with Svetoslav Piperov (London: Forest, 1990), 165–74.

Petković, Radoslav (b. 1953) Serbian novelist, short-story writer, and essayist. A highly imaginative, often intriguing writer, with a strong interest in history, Petković first attracted attention with his novel *Put u Dvigrad* (Journey to Dvigrad, 1973). It was followed by a second novel, *Senke na zidu* (Shadows on the Wall, 1985), and a collection of short stories, *Izvestaj o kugi* (Report on the Plague, 1989). *Senke na zidu* is particularly interesting for its breezy history of motion pictures within the framework of a fictional narrative about the strange disappearance of a Serbian movie-theater owner and the suspicion that he was in fact killed by one of his employees, Emil Wedekind, and Wedekind's émigré Russian wife. The history of film is conveyed by chapters with such titles as "Pictures Painted with Brilliance (1876–1904)," "Moving Pictures (1904–1910)," "An Age of Comedy and Horror (1910–1920)," and "On the Road to the Spoken Film (1920–1927)."

Petković's most highly regarded literary work to date is the novel *Sudbina i komentari* (Destiny and Comments, 1993), which was awarded the Meša Selimović Prize and the NIN Prize and was named best book of the year by the literary critics of the Belgrade daily newspapers *Politika* and *Borba*. The novel, which at first glance resembles a work of historical fiction and includes a fair amount of information about the Serbs themselves, covers a span of some 300 years and is divided into four unequal parts, each possessing its own stylistic character. Parts I and II deal principally with the adventures of a Russian imperial naval officer named Pavel Volkov, who happens to be of Serbian origin (Pavel Volkov is the Russianized form of Pavle Vuković) and becomes involved in spy intrigue aimed at thwarting Napoleon's plans to seize Trieste and parts of Dalmatia in 1806. In Part III, Pavel Volkov reappears in the twentieth century as Pavle Vuković, whose diaries and notes—in large measure devoted to his relationship with a Hungarian fellow historian (Marta Kovacs) whom he meets at a conference in Dubrovnik and which later lead him to Budapest—become the prism through which the Yugoslav–Soviet break of 1948 and the Hungarian uprising of 1956 are viewed. Vuković, as we learn from a note by

his daughter, ended his days in the monastery of Krusedol in Fruška Gora as a monk named Spiridon. The much shorter Part IV ("Summa") is set in the seventeenth century and is built around the figure of Count Djordje Branković, a distant relative of the Vuković family who claims also to be a descendant of Djordje Branković, the "despot of Illyria," and thus the heir to the Serbian throne. Fearing his ambitions, the Austrians confine him to a small Czech town, where he dies in 1711. Largely a historical novel that shifts fairly seamlessly three-quarters of the way through from the Napoleonic period into such major post–World War II political events as the Yugoslav–Soviet break and the Hungarian uprising, *Sudbina i komentari* seems at the core to have been motivated by a desire to project the traumas of Serbian rootlessness and emigration. Viewed as a postmodern text, the novel, as a work of fictional history, treats the past in such a way as to suggest the impossibility of achieving true historical truth. This is underscored as well in the many interpolated discussions of the author with his reader about the novel he is trying to write and in the obvious personal dimension of the later parts of the work set in 1948 and 1956.

The same year that *Sudbina i komentari* appeared, Petković published *Zapisi iz godine jagoda* (Notes from the Year of the Strawberry, 1993), a digressive narrative of long sentences and paragraphs that takes the reader through the four seasons of a year in the life of an artist named Vidak. The focus is mainly on Vidak's inner life, his fantasies and dreams (of being an alchemist, for example), and on his relations with the two people closest to him, a friend whose portrait he paints and his girlfriend. *Zapisi iz godine jagoda* was followed in 1995 by *Ogledi o mački* (On Cats), a book of mildly entertaining essays about cats in history and lore, ranging from the ancient Egyptians to

T. S. Eliot, Doris Lessing, and Stephen King, and in 1998 by his new collection of stories, *Čovek koji živeo u snovima* (The Man Who Lived in Dreams). Characterized by an air of strangeness common to much of Petković's work, the stories range from biblical to contemporary times and begin with a free version of the Epistle to the Romans and Nero's burning of Rome. Petković's concerns, manifest elsewhere in his writing, are with choice and death, the incomprehensibility of time, and the reality of dream.

Translations: "The Plague Report" (excerpt from *Izvestaj o kugi*), trans. Paul M. Foster, in *The Prince of Fire: An Anthology of Contemporary Serbian Short Stories,* ed. Radmila J. Gorup and Nadežda Obradović (Pittsburgh: University of Pittsburgh Press, 1998), 316–23. *Čovek koji živeo u snovima* is available in French as *L'Homme que vivait dans les rêves,* trans. Alain Cappon (Paris: Gaïa, 1999); *Izvestaj o kugi* as *Communication sur la peste,* trans. Alain Cappon (Larbey: Gaïa, 1992); *Senke na zidu* as *Des ombres sur la mur,* trans. Alain Cappon (Paris: Gaïa, 1996); and *Sudbina i komentari* as *Destin et commentaires,* trans. Alain Cappon (Paris: Gaïa, 1994).

Petlevski, Sibila (b. 1964) Croatian poet. The daughter of the painter Ordan Petlevski, Petlevski was born and educated in Zagreb. A talented and sophisticated poet with a strong interest in the visual arts, she published her first major book of poetry, *Skok s mjesta* (Standing Jump), in 1990. It includes the earlier collection "Kristal" ("Crystal"), which originally appeared in a portfolio with prints by the artist Nevenka Arbanas. In 1993 Petlevski came out with *Sto aleksandrijskih epigrama* (One Hundred Alexandrian Epigrams), an impressive modern rendering of the classical elegiac distich, reflective of the poet's erudition. An active participant in forums and colloquiums on the future of an independent postcommunist Croatia, Petlevski

edited the 1994 publication *Velika Europa—Mali narodi* (Big Europe, Small Nations), a collection of texts based on presentations at an international conference held in Zagreb in early November 1992 on the subject of the book's title. Petlevski's largest, most varied, and most impressive volume of poetry, *Francuska suita* (French Suite), appeared in 1996. Since then, Petlevski has been building an international reputation. She was a featured poet in the Munich literary journal *Literatur* in 1999 and, the same year, was a guest at the prestigious Munich artists colony, the Villa Waldberta. In May 2000 she also participated in the Sixteenth International Festival of Poetry in Barcelona.

Petrescu, Camil (1894–1957) Romanian novelist, playwright, essayist, and poet. A native of Bucharest, Petrescu was raised by servants after the deaths of his parents the year of his birth. In extreme hardship, he completed secondary school in Bucharest and later studied at the Faculty of Literature and Philosophy of Bucharest University. In 1917 he volunteered for the army and was wounded in action in World War I. After his release from military service, he completed his studies in 1919 and then began working as a teacher of Romanian in a German–Hungarian school in Timişoara. It was here that he also began his journalistic activity. After Timişoara, he returned to Bucharest and a series of editorial jobs with several journals and newspapers. From 1934 to 1947, he was editor of the prestigious literary journal *Revista Fundaţiilor Regale,* and from 1939 also held the post of director of the National Theater. In recognition of the esteem in which he was held in post–World War II Romania, Petrescu was elected a member of the Romanian Academy in 1948.

Petrescu began his career as a poet in 1923 with a volume of poems titled *Versuri. Ideia. Ciclul morţii* (Verses. The Idea. The Cycle of Death). Two other volumes followed in 1931 and 1957. Largely a poet in the confessional mode, Petrescu exerted considerable influence on Romanian poets of the younger generation. However, he is most remembered as a novelist on the strength of such works as *Ultima noapte de dragoste, prima zia de război* (The Last Night of Love, the First Day of War, 1930); *Patul lui Procust* (Procust's Bed, 1933); and, above all, the trilogy *Un om între oameni* (A Man Among Men, 1955–1957), which is based on the life of the outstanding nineteenth-century Romanian historian Nicolae Bălcescu (1819–1852), the leader of the 1848 revolution in Wallachia. Petrescu's play *Bălcescu* (1949) deals with the same figure. Petrescu wrote other plays on historical subjects—for example, *Danton* (1931), one of his best dramatic works, set in the time of the French Revolution, and *Caragiale în vremea lui* (Caragiale in His Time, 1957), about the major Romanian playwright Ion Luca Caragiale (1852–1912). Two other well-known plays, *Jocul ielelor* (Tha Dance of the Elves, 1918) and *Act venețian* (Venetian Act, 1919), are dramas of ideas of essentially antibourgeois character. A gifted and productive essayist, Petrescu was especially well known in the interwar period for such volumes as *Teze și antiteze* (Theses and Antitheses, 1933), on aesthetics and philosophy; *Estetica teatrului* (The Aesthetics of Theater, 1937); and an introduction to Edmund Husserl's phenomenology published in 1938. Five volumes of essays and related writings have been published posthumously: *Opinii și atitudini* (Opinions and Attitudes, 1962); *Maxime și reflecții* (Maxims and Reflections, 1975); *Note zilnice, 1927–1940* (Daily Notes, 1927–1940, 1974); a collection of essays on writing, *Din laboratorul de creație al scriitorului* (From the Writer's Worskop, 1979); and a book on theater, *Comentarii și delimitarie în teatru* (Commentaries and Delimitations in the Theater, 1983). A three-volume collected edition of his plays was published in 1973. Six volumes of his collected works have been published since 1973.

Translations: Excerpts from *Un om între oameni*, in *Introduction to Rumanian Literature*, ed. Jacob Steinberg (New York: Twayne, 1966), 246–60. *Patul lui Procust* is available in French as *Le Lit de Procuste*, trans. Ion Herdan (Bucharest: Minerva, 1984).

Petrescu, Razvăn (b. 1956) Romanian short-story writer and playwright. Petrescu was born in Berești, in the Galați district, where he received most of his early schooling. In 1982 he graduated from the Faculty of General Medicine at Bucharest University. Although he has remained close to medicine throughout his career, Petrescu's growing interest in creative writing while at university resulted in his inclusion in the anthology of short stories *Debut '86*, published by the large state publisher, Cartea Romanească. He also became a literary editor first at the student review *Amfiteatru* and then at *Cuvântul*, before moving on to the Litera publishing house. Since 1995 he has been the head of the medical section of All Group publishers. In 1989 Peterescu came out with his own first collection of short stories, *Grâdina de vară* (The Summer Garden), for which he won the Liviu Rebreanu Prize. He subsequently published another two collections of stories, *Eclipsa* (The Eclipse, 1993) and *Într-o după-amiază de vineri* (On a Friday Afternoon, 1997). He has also published two books of plays, *Farsa* (The Trick, 1994), which won the Dramatists Union Prize, and *Primăvara la bufet* (Spring at the Tavern, 1995). Petrescu's works are built mostly around strange and bizarre happenings, somewhat in the manner of the novels of Stephen King. Although not a writer of medical thrillers as such, his writing often reflects his training as a physician. Petrescu is a member of the Writers Union and the Association of Medical Writers of Romania.

Translations: "Diary of an Apartment Dweller (February–June 1990)," in *The Phantom Church and Other Stories from Romania*, trans. and ed. Georgiana Farnoaga and Sharon King (Pittsburgh: University of Pittsburgh Press, 1996), 221–25.

Petreu, Marta (real name Rodică Marta Crișan; b. 1955) Romanian poet and essayist. Born in Jucu, Cluj, Petreu graduated from Cluj University in 1980 with a degree in philosophy and received her doctorate from Bucharest University in 1992. She taught in a Cluj high school from 1980 to 1990. Apart from her creative writing, she has worked as an editor for various newspapers and magazines, including *România literară* in Bucharest and *Steaua* in Cluj. In December 1990, after the overthrow of the regime of Nicolae Ceaușescu, she became editor in chief of *Apostrof*, a new monthly literary journal that she had established. The same year, she also joined the department of philosophy of Cluj University. Petreu's first book of poetry, *Aduceți verbele* (Bring Verbs, 1981), won a Writers Union prize. Three more volumes of poetry followed: *Dimineața tinerelor doamne* (The Morning of Young Women, 1983); *Loc psihic* (A Psychic Place, 1991); and *Poeme nerușinate* (Impudent Verses, 1998). Favoring a casual contemporary idiom and lines of varying length of a distinctly prosaic character, Petreu writes about loneliness and pain, about the private anguish of being a woman, and about the hardship and pleasure of writing poetry. A strikingly original poet, she blunts any self-pity or moroseness with cleverness, wit, and irony. Petreu is also the author of two collections of essays, *Teze neterminate* (Unfinished Theses, 1991) and *Jocurile manierismului logic* (Games of Logical Mannerism. 1995). Petreu was awarded the Writers Union Prize in 1981 and again in 1987, and the George Bacovia Prize in 1984.

Translations: Five poems, trans. Liviu Bleoca, in *An Anthology of Romanian Women Poets*, ed. Adam J. Sorkin and Kurt W. Treptow (New York: East European Monographs, 1994), 118–23; five poems in *Young Poets of a New Romania: An Anthology*, trans. Brenda Walker with Michaela Celea-Leach, ed. Ion Stoia (London: Forest, 1991), 20–26.

Petri, György (b. 1943) Hungarian poet. Petri is best known for his courageous defiance of the communist regime, as evidenced in poetry that is highly critical both of Hungarian internal politics and of policies of the former Eastern bloc. His willingness to articulate a widely held disillusionment and malaise is conveyed directly in one of his earliest poems, "By an Unknown Poet from Eastern Europe, 1955," which is included in his first published collection of poems, *Magyarázatok M. számára* (Explanations for M., 1971). He has lambasted the Warsaw Pact invasion of Czechoslovakia in 1968, the Stalinist regime of Mátyás Rákosi and Ernő Gerő in Hungary, the execution in 1958 of the reform-minded Imre Nagy (prime minister, 1953–1955; prime minister of the revolutionary government, October–November 1956), and the trampling of human rights and individual freedom of expression under the communist regimes in general. He also expressed views on the rise of Solidarity in Poland. Petri's first two volumes of poems—*Magyarázatok M. számára* and *Körülírt zuhanás* (Circumscribed Fall, 1974)—were published by the state publishing house, a fact explained only by the relative relaxation of censorship in Hungary at the time. Although his first books brought him celebrity and the privileges that went with literary fame in Eastern Europe in the communist period, Petri turned his back on all that and from 1982 on began publishing only with unofficial samizdat publishers. His first samizdat collections of poetry were *Örökhétfő* (*Eternal Monday*, 1982) and *Azt hiszik . . .*

(They Think So . . . , 1985). Petri's poetry since the fall of communism in Hungary has become both more private and broader in scope when addressing issues of public concern.

Translations: *Eternal Monday: New and Selected Poems*, trans. Clive Wilmer and George Gömöri (Newcastle upon Tyne: Bloodaxe, 1999); *Night Song of the Personal Shadows: Selected Poems*, trans. Clive Wilmer and George Gömöri (Newcastle upon Tyne: Bloodaxe, 1991).

Petrov, Aleksandar (b. 1938) Serbian poet, essayist, and literary scholar. Of Russian parentage, Petrov was born in Niš and was educated in Belgrade. He received his undergraduate degree from Belgrade University in 1961, with a major in Yugoslav and world literatures. He received his master's degree, also from Belgrade, in 1967 and his doctorate from Zagreb University, where he wrote his dissertation on the poetry of Miloš Crnjanski and the evolution of Serbian poetry. From 1965 to 1996, he was affiliated with the Institute of Literature and Art in Belgrade, heading a project on the history of Serbian literary periodicals. He became a member of the Serbian Writers Association in 1964 and of PEN in 1965. He served as a member of the presidium of the Writers Association in 1983/1984 and as chairman in 1986 to 1988. From 1985 to 1988 Petrov was also a member of the presidium of the Yugoslav Writers Union and in 1987 served as its chairman.

Petrov's poetry, which is distinguished by its lyric delicacy, has appeared in such collections as *Sazdanac* (Builder, 1971); *Brus* (Whetstone, 1978); *Slovenska škola* (Slavic School, 1985); and *Poslednje Kosovo* (The Last Kosovo, 1988). A number of his poems have Russian subjects (one, for example, on the poet Marina Tsvetaeva and another on the fate of Russian Yiddish writers). Others are about his family, accessible poetry (of

which he has long been an advocate), and such American universities he has visited on his travels as Ohio State and Harvard. Petrov was the recipient of the Isidora Sekulić Prize in 1971.

Even before he began publishing poetry, Petrov established a reputation as a prolific literary scholar. His study of the Serbian writer Mihailo Lalič appeared in 1967 and was followed by *U prostoru proze: Ogledi o prirodi proznog izraza* (In the Space of Prose: Studies in the Nature of Prosaic Expression, 1968), which examines texts by such Yugoslav writers as Ivo Andrić, Veljko Petrović, Miloš Crnjanski, Miroslav Krleža, Oskar Davičo, and Mihailo Lalić; a book on the poetry of Miloš Crnjanski and the Serbian poetic tradition (1971, 1988); *Radanje moderne književnosti: Roman* (The Florescence of Modern Literature: The Novel, 1975); an edition of the poems of the Slovenian poet Jože Udovič (1977); an edition of poems by the Serbian poet Ante Popovski (1977); a book of essays and studies on modern poetry under the title *Krila i vazduh* (Wings and Air, 1983); and *Poezija danas* (Poetry Today, 1980), a volume of essays on contemporary Serbian poetry. Petrov also edited *Prilozi za istoriju srpske književne periodike: Spomenica Dragisi Vitoseviću* (Addenda to a History of the Serbian Literary Periodical: The *Spomenica* of Dragisa Vitosević, 1990) and *Srpski modernizam: Glasnici, glasila, sudije* (Serbian Modernism: Writers, Texts, Judgments, 1996). He also edited a two-volume, bilingual edition of Russian poetry from the seventeenth century to the present (1977). Petrov has been a visiting professor in universities throughout Europe, Asia, and the United States, and in 1993 accepted a professorship at the University of Pittsburgh. He has since played an important role in Serbian-American literary activities.

Translations: *A Book for Bhopal: 13 Poets from Belgrade*, ed. and trans. Aleksandar

Petrov (Belgrade: Serbian Writers Association, 1985); *Lady in an Empty Dress,* trans. Richard Burns (London: Forest, 1990); *Manje poznati Dučić/The Less Well Known Dučić* (Pittsburgh: Signature, 1994), a study of the Serbian poet and diplomat Jovan Dučić (1871–1943), including a selection of his verse in Serbian and English, translated by Petrov; *New Serbian Poetry/La Nouvelle Poésie serbe,* trans. Aleksandar Petrov (Belgrade: Relations, 1980); *The Poet's Space and Time* (Taipei: Tamkang University, 1994), an English–Chinese edition; *Sochi, Eroticism, Siberia,* trans. Aleksandar Petrov (Chattanooga: University of Tennessee Press, 1992).

Petrov, Ivailo (real name Prodan Petrov Kiuchukov; b. 1923) Bulgarian novelist and short-story writer. A native of Bdinsti, in the Varna district, Petrov graduated from secondary school in Dobrich in 1942. After World War II, in which he participated only toward the end, he tried his hand at business in Varna for a year (1946–1947), thereafter studying law for a year in Sofia, and subsequently accepting a position at Radio Sofia in 1949. In 1953 he began a long period of work as an editor for the Bulgarski Pisatel publishing house (1953–1966) and for such journals as *Plamuk* (1966–1967) and *Literaturen front* (1968–1971). From 1973 to 1983, he served as an adviser on church properties to the Bulgarian Council of State. Petrov began his literary career with the publication in 1953 of a collection of stories titled *Krushtenie* (Baptism), which, like his later short novel *Na chuzhda zemia* (On Alien Soil, 1962), draws on his experiences during the war and focuses primarily on the ordinary soldier. His real breakthrough as a writer came with the novel *Nonkinata liubov* (Nonka's Love, 1956). The work deals with the impact on a young peasant woman of the transformation of Bulgarian rural society brought on by the forces of collectiviza-

tion, industrialization, and the flight of peasants from the village into the city in search of employment. Although his approach to the village would later change, at this stage in his writing Petrov followed the familiar pattern of Bulgarian literature by portraying rural life in a lyrical, idealized way. *Nonkinata liubov* was followed by Petrov's second novel, *Murtvo vulnenie* (Dead Emotion, 1963), and by his second collection of short stories, *Malki iliuzii* (Small Illusions, 1963; 2nd, enl. ed., 1968). He subsequently published another eleven collections of stories and novellas: *Zelenata shapka* (The Green Cap, 1965); the first volume of *Oburkani zapiski* (Confused Notes, 1971); *Predi da se rodia i sled tova* (Before I Was Born and Afterward, 1973); *Luzhlivi hora* (Lying People, 1973); *Liubov po pladne* (Love at Noon, 1976); *Esenni razkazi* (Autumn Tales, 1978); *Bozhi raboti* (Divine Matters, 1979), a parody of biblical motifs; *Nai-dobriiat grazhdanin na Republikata* (The Foremost Citizen of the Republic, 1980), a parody this time of totalitarianism; *Tri sreshti* (Three Meetings, 1981); *Tsvetut na mechtite* (The Flower of Dreams, 1989); and the second volume of *Oburkani zapiski* (1989). Arguably the most notable of Petrov's story collections is *Predi da se rodia i sled tova,* principally because of the author's change in outlook toward the Bulgarian village. Not only does Petrov no longer idealize and poeticize the village, but he highlights its material and spiritual poverty and even makes light of the nostalgic treatment of it common in Bulgarian literature in the 1960s. Two of Petrov's most important works appeared in the 1980s and early 1990s: *Haika za vultsi* (Hunting Wolves, 1982), an unvarnished picture of the brutality with which the collectivization of Bulgarian agriculture was carried out in the late 1940s and 1950s, and *Prisuda smurt* (Death Sentence, 1991), which alludes to the de facto coup d'état of 9 September 1944 by the communist-controlled Fatherland Front. His most recent novel is *Baronovi* (Barons, 1997). It was followed in 1999 by the third volume of *Oburkani zapsiki,* under the title *O voliata bozhiia* (By God's Will), a collection of fourteen casual pieces, narrated in the first person, the longest and perhaps best of which, "Granitsata" ("The Border"), recalls three of the author's illegal border crossings into neighboring Romania, Yugoslavia, and Hungary during World War II.

Literature: Stoian Iliev, *Ivailo Petrov i negovite geroi* (Sofia: Narodna prosveta, 1990), a standard treatment of Petrov's literary heroes.

Translations: "The Death of a Knight" (from *Predi da se rodia i sled tova*), in *The Balkan Range: A Bulgarian Reader,* ed. John Robert Colombo and Nikola Roussanoff (Toronto: Hounslow, 1976), 300–302. *Predi da se rodia i sled tova* is available in French as *Avant ma naissance et aprés,* trans. Marie Urinat (Lausanne: L'Age de homme, 1994).

Petrov, Valeri (real name Valeri Nisim Mevorah, has also used the pseudonym Asen Rakovski; b. 1920) Bulgarian poet, playwright, screenwriter, and translator. One of the most popular post–World War II Bulgarian poets, Petrov was born and educated in Sofia where he graduated in medicine from Sofia University in 1944. He served as a correspondent during World War II, but already had begun attracting attention as a poet in his student years, appearing for the first time in print in 1936. Most of the works published by Petrov before World War II appeared under the pseudonym Asen Rakovski. One of the founders of the periodical *Sturshel,* Petrov served as its editor from 1945 to 1962 and then as assistant editor in chief and a member of its editorial board. From 1947 to 1950, Petrov was the Bulgarian press attaché in Rome. He later worked as a film editor (1955–1968, 1977–1980), and in 1961–1962 was affiliated with the Bulgarski pisatel publishing house. After the collapse of the communist regime in Bulgaria in 1989, Petrov was elected a deputy to the Great National Assembly and served in that capacity in 1990/1991.

During the war, in 1944, Petrov published *Naroden sud: Horovodna agitka* (The Nation's Court: A Ring-Dance Propaganda Piece). His first postwar collection of poems, *Stihotvoreniia* (Poems, 1949), contained texts written in the period 1940 to 1948, one of Petrov's most fruitful periods as a poet. The collection *Dnite, koito zhiveem* (The Days We Live In) followed in 1952. *Tam na zapad* (There in the West), a collection of poems of a political nature, appeared in 1954. Petrov's subsequent volumes of poems include *V mekata esen* (To the Gentle Autumn, 1961); *Poemi* (Poems, 1962); *Poemi* (Poems, 1966); *Duzhd vali—sluntse gree* (Rain Pours, Sun Burns, 1967); *Kato poglednesh nazad* (As You Look Back, 1969), selected longer and shorter poems; *Na smiah* (To Laughter, 1970), a volume of satirical verse; *Poeziia* (Poetry, 1973), another volume of selected verse; *Stihotvoreniia i poemi* (Longer and Shorter Poems, 1977); *Poeziia* (Poems, 1984); and *Satirichni poemi* (Satirical Poems, 1988). Both a two-volume collection of Petrov's selected works (*Izbrani proizvedeniia v dva toma*) and a volume of his longer and shorter poems (*Stihotvoreniia i poemi*) were published in 1980. The most recent edition of his longer poems (*Stihotvoreniia*) appeared in 1994. In 1996 an anthology of Petrov's poems from 1940 to 1989 appeared under the title *Zhivot v stihove* (Life in Poetry). His most recent book of poetry, *Raztvoren prozorets* (The Wide Open Window), appeared in 1998. A very readable and accessible poet, at home in short as well as very long poems, Petrov has worked comfortably with a variety of rhymes and stanzaic patterns. He has written on everything from childhood memories to the horrors of World War II and is especially admired for his wit, satire, sense of humor, and generally upbeat view of life.

Apart from his poetry, Petrov has published two travel books, *Kniga za Kitai* (A Book About China, 1958) and *Afrikanski belezhnik* (African Diary, 1965), based on personal experiences; a lyrical play, *Kogato rozite tantsuvat* (When the Roses Dance, 1965); a puppet play, *Biala prikazka* (A White Tale, 1977); and several fairy tales for young readers and adults such as *Kopche za sun: Prikazna povest* (Button of Sleep: A Fairy Tale, 1978); *Meko kazano* (To Put It Mildly, 1980; translated as *Tales*); *Puk: Prikazka* (Crack! A Tale, 1983); *Pet prikazki* (Five Stories, 1986); and *Neveroiatnite prikliucheniia na Sin Diado* (The Unbelievable Adventures of Sin Diado, 1992). With Hristo Ganev and the poet Radoi Petrov, Petrov also composed the satirical show *Improvizatsiia* (Improvisation) in 1962. Two volumes of Petrov's plays, film scripts, and stories were published in 1990 under the title *Piesi, kinostsenarii, prikazki* (Plays, Film Scripts, and Stories). Petrov is also highly regarded for his translations of the plays of Shakespeare. His Bulgarian versions of the comedies appeared in two volumes in 1970 and 1971, followed in 1973 and 1974 by two volumes of his translations of the tragedies.

Translations: *Tales,* trans. Christine Bartlet (Sofia: Sviat, 1986); two poems, in versions by Roy MacGregor-Hastie, in *Modern Bulgarian Poetry,* comp. Bozhidar Bozhilov (Sofia: Sofia Press, 1976), 108–11, a Bulgarian–English edition; four poems, trans. Richard Wilbur, in *Window on the Black Sea: Bulgarian Poetry in Translation,* ed. Richard Harteis, in collaboration with William Meredith (Pittsburgh: Carnegie Mellon University Press, 1992), 91–94.

Petrović, Miomir (b. 1972) Serbian novelist and playwright. A native of Belgrade, Petrović studied at the Academy of Dramatic Arts in Belgrade and works actively in the theater. He has published several plays, among them *Vagabund u gradskom vrtu* (Vagabond

in a City Park, 1995); *Argivski incident* (Argiv's Incident, 1996); *Demijurg* (Demiurge, 1997); *Appendix* (1997); and *Metastaziranje duše* (Metastasis of the Soul, 1998). He is also the author of three antiwar novels: *Sakačenje romana* (Mutilation of a Novel, 1997); *Pankration* (Pancratium, 1998); and *Samoučitelj* (The Autodidact, 2000). Arguably the most powerful of these is *Pankration*. It is a grim tale of a Serbian photographer, Kovač, who became a murderer during the war in Bosnia and subsequently lost his sight, possibly by his own hand. His story is narrated to another photographer, Novak, by yet another blind man who knows Kovač and his terminally ill wife. The novel creates suspense concerning undeveloped war films taken by Kovač and milks obvious symbolism from the motifs of blindness—at one point, a rapist has his eyes gouged out—and the camera lens as an extension of the human eye. So horrible are the images of war seen by the eye and recorded on film that they can be forever shut out only through blindness.

Pietrass, Richard (b. 1946) German poet. Pietrass, whose family had been resettled in Germany from Poland, was born in Lichtenstein, Saxony. After graduating from high school in 1965, he trained as a miner, but eventually studied clinical psychology at Humboldt University in Berlin from 1968 to 1972. He had worked as a male nurse for a year and then performed his obligatory two-year period of military service (1966–1968). From 1975 to 1980, Pietrass served as an editor at the Neues Leben publishing house and until 1978 also edited the poetry section of the journal *Temperamente*. From 1977 to 1979, he was publisher of the important poetry series Poesiealbum, having succeeded Bernd Jentzsch. It was in this series (no. 82) in 1974 that Pietrass had made his literary debut with a volume of poems. He subsequently published another six books of verse: *Notausgang* (Emergency Exit, 1980); *Freiheitsmuseum* (The Freedom Museum, 1982), with seven collages by Martin Hoffmann; *Spielball* (Game Ball, 1987), with five photographs by Richard Pietrass; *Was mir zum Glück fehlt* (What I'm Happily Lacking, 1989); *Ostkreuz* (The Eastern Cross, 1990); and *Weltkind* (Child of the World, 1990). Although conservative with respect to traditional rhyme and meter, Pietrass has demonstrated an inclination toward linguistic experimentation in a manner reminiscent to some extent of that of the Russian futurists. He is also known for his laconic style as well as for his irony and sarcasm. In common with other German writers of the generation born after World War II, Pietrass has carried less of a burden of the war, and German guilt, into his writing. However, he never aligned himself with the oppositional outlook of the Penzlauer Berg group.

Literature: "Richard Pietrass," in *Literary Intellectuals and the Dissolution of the State: Professionalism and Conformity in the GDR,* ed. Robert von Hallberg, trans. Kenneth J. Northcott (Chicago: University of Chicago Press, 1996), 180–85.

Pilch, Jerzy (b. 1952) Polish novelist and essayist. One of the wittiest and most provocative observers of the postcommunist Polish political and social scene, Pilch was born in the Silesian town of Wisła. He studied Polish philology at the Jagiellonian University in Kraków and subsequently began his literary career as a writer of fiction. His first published book was the short-story collection *Wyznania twórcy pokątnej literatury erotycznej* (Confessions of a Writer of Clandestine Erotic Literature, 1988). Anticipating problems with the censors, Pilch chose to publish the book with a Polish émigré publishing house in London. The volume won the prestigious Kościeleski Foundation Prize. It was followed in 1993 by the novel *Spis cudzołożnic: Proza podróżna* (The Whores' Conspiracy: Travel Prose), which was also published in London, a satirical view of Poland in the 1980s and a putdown of Catholic and communist morality. It was soon made into a highly successful film that was one of the highlights of Polish cinema in the 1994/1995 season. Pilch's next novel, *Inne rozkosze* (Other Pleasures, 1995; translated as *His Current Woman*), is the hilarious account of what happens when the current paramour of a philandering veterinarian attempts to move in with him and his family.

After joining the editorial staff of the influental Kraków Catholic paper *Tygodnik Powszechny,* Pilch began publishing weekly feuilletons that soon became widely read and admired for their witty and ironic commentary on contemporary Poland. The first published collection of his feuilletons from 1984 to 1993 appeared in 1994 under the title *Rozpacz z powodu utraty firmanki* (Despair as the Result of Losing a Carriage). This humorous and, at the same time, grotesque chronicle of changes in the Polish mentality since 1989 was followed by another two collections of feuilletons, *Monolog z lisiej jamy* (Monologue from the Wolves' Den, 1996) and *Tezy o głupocie, piciu i umieraniu* (Theses on Stupidity, Drinking, and Dying, 1997), published in London; and the novel *Tysiąc spokojnych miast* (Thousands of Peaceful Cities, 1997), also published in London, about how his father and a certain Mr. Trąba set out to assassinate Władysław Gomułka, then first secretary of the Communist Party of Poland. Pilch's newest book, *Pod mocnym aniołem* (Under a Mighty Angel, 2000), whose title refers to a favorite pub of the author, is a lighthearted recounting of Pilch's long struggle with alcohol problems.

Translations: *His Current Woman,* trans. Bill Johnston (Evanston, Ill.: Northwestern University Press, 2002); "The Register of

Adulteresses," trans. Jarosław Anders, in *Description of a Struggle: The Vintage Book of Contemporary Eastern European Writing*, ed. Michael March (New York: Vintage, 1994), 60–64.

Pilinszky, János (1921–1981) Hungarian poet and prose writer. Hungary's most highly regarded post–World War II poet, Pilinszky was a native of Budapest. He began his literary career in 1938 when his first poem appeared in the journal *Élet*. Although a contributor to other leading journals, Pilinszky became closely identified with the liberal Catholic monthly *Vigilia* (founded in 1935) and the prestigious periodical *Csillag*. Called up for military service only in 1944, Pilinszky served on the western front and with his own eyes saw the remnants of the German concentration camps and the terrifying destruction of German cities. The war and the Holocaust left a lasting impression on the poet. Christian religious imagery and a sense of isolation and desolation pervade his first published collection of poems, *Trapéz és korlát* (Trapeze and Parallel Bars, 1946). The war and the mass extermination of the Jews are addressed more directly in poems in his next collection, *Harmadnapon* (On the Third Day, 1959), and in the dramatic "oratorio" "KZ-oratórium" ("Concentration Camp Oratorio"), included in *Nagyvárosi ikonok: Összegyűjtött versek, 1940–1970* (Metropolitan Icons: Collected Poems, 1940–1970, 1970, 1971). The effect of such poems as "Harbach 1944," "Francia fogoly" ("French Prisoner"), "Egy KZ-láger falára" ("On a Concentration Camp Wall"), "Ravensbrücki passió" ("Ravensbrück Passion"), and the particularly impressive "Apokrif" ("Apocrypha") is generated as much by Pilinszky's spare, understated style as by the personal nature of the impressions. His poem "Frankfurt" (also in *Harmadnapon*), with its grim description of the war-ravaged city, was similarly based on firsthand experience. At war's end, a serious illness brought Pilinszky to an internment camp in Frankfurt operated by the United Nations Relief and Rehabilitation Agency.

Back in Budapest in November 1945, Pilinszky resumed his career as a poet. But even though recognition was swift in coming, his strong Catholic ties and the elusiveness of many of his poems earned him the disfavor of the communist authorities. Between 1949 and 1956, the year of the Hungarian uprising, he was banned from publishing poetry. Never a prolific poet, often writing no more than a few poems a year, Pilinszky did not published his first new collection of poetry, *Harmadnapon*, containing only thirty-three works, until 1959. This was followed by the film script *Rekviem* in 1964 and four subsequent collections of poems: the aforementioned *Nagyvárosi ikonok: Összegyujtött versek, 1940–1970*; *Szálkák* (Splinters, 1972); *Végkifejlet: Versek és színművek* (Denouement: Poems and Plays, 1974); and *Kráter: Összegyűjtött és új versek* (Crater: Collected and New Poems, 1976, 1981). Pilinszky also wrote a great deal of occasional prose, most of it collected in two volumes under the title *A mélypont ünnepélye* (Celebration of Nadir, 1984). His most intriguing work of prose is *Beszélgetések Sheryl Suttonnal* (Conversations with Sheryl Sutton, 1977). It consists of a mostly imaginary interview, and dialogue, with an American actress who was performing with Robert Wilson's company in *Deafman Glance* in Paris in 1973. Pilinszky was in the French capital at the time and saw *Deafman Glance* before running across Sheryl Sutton in a Paris café. They had several other meetings, which provided Pilinszky with the raw material from which he developed what he calls his "Novel of a Dialogue." Inclined toward an unsure fascination with silence in his later poetry, Pilinszky projects a similar interest onto his construct of Sutton. Indeed, it is this aspect of Wilson's *Deafman Glance* that attracted him the most. Pilinszky's conversations with Sutton and his remarks about *Deafman Glance* are primarily a pretext for an informal chat by the poet about his own views on art and language and his affinities with Dostoevsky and the French Catholic philosopher Simone Weil.

Pilinszky began traveling extensively throughout the West in the late 1940s. As his reputation grew, he became sought after as a participant in international poetry festivals. He visited England in 1969, 1972, 1976, and 1980, the first two occasions in conjunction with the Poetry International held in London. Of the English poets he met, he developed a lasting friendship with Ted Hughes, who, in collaboration with János Csokits, became Pilinszky's first translator into English. In 1972 Pilinszky also lectured at the Sorbonne on the invitation of the French Catholic existentialist philosopher Gabriel Marcel, and in 1975 at Columbia University.

Literature: The only full-length biography of Pilinszky is Tibor Tüskés, *Pilinszky János alkotásai és vallomásai tükrében* (Budapest: Szépirodalmi, 1986).

Translations: *Conversations with Sheryl Sutton,* trans. Peter Jay and Eva Major (Manchester, Eng.: Carcanet, 1992); *Crater: Poems, 1974–5,* trans. Peter Jay (London: Anvil, 1978); *The Desert of Love: Selected Poems,* trans. János Csokits and Ted Hughes (London: Anvil, 1989); *János Pilinszky: Selected Poems,* trans. Ted Hughes and János Csokits (Manchester, Eng.: Carcanet, 1976), which contains selections mostly from *Trapéz és korlát, Harmadnapon, Rekviem, Nagyvárosi ikonok, Szálkák,* and *Végkifejlet: Versek és színművek; Metropolitan Icons: Selected Poems by János Pilinszky in Hungarian and in English,* ed. and trans. Emery George (Lewiston, N.Y.: Mellen, 1995), which contains selections from *Trapéz és korlát, Harmadnapon, Nagyvárosi ikonok, Szálkák, Végkifejlet: Versek és színművek,* and *Kráter.*

The best edition of Pilinszky's poetry in English, *Metropolitan Icons* contains fine translations as well as the original Hungarian texts, a good introduction, extensive explanatory notes, and a valuable bibliography. MUSIC: Istvan Lang, *In Memoriam N. N.: Cantata to Poems by János Pilinszky* (London: Boosey & Hawkes, 1973); György Kurtag, *Dal Pilinszky János verseire: Vier Lieder auf Gedichte von János Pilinszky,* trans. G. Engl / *Four Songs Composed to János Pilinszky's Poems,* trans. L. T. Andras (Vienna: Universal Edition, 1979).

Pipa, Arshi (b. 1920) Albanian poet, novelist, literary scholar, and political writer. Pipa studied in Florence, Italy, and later taught Italian in various schools. His first volume of verse, *Lundertare* (Seamen), was published in 1944. During the war, he edited the review *Kritika letrare*; after the liberation of Albania, he joined the editorial board of *Bota e re,* the organ of the League of Albanian Writers. Soon out of favor with the communist regime because of his views concerning freedom of expression, Pipa became a political prisoner from 1946 to 1956. He eventually escaped to Yugoslavia, from where he immigrated to the United States. In 1959 he published in Rome a nine-part verse account of his years of captivity under the title *Libri i burgut* (The Prison Book). While in prison in 1955, he wrote the epic-like *Rusha* (1968), a Romeo and Juliet tale of love and vendetta between Albanians and Serbs in the second half of the fourteenth century. The Albanian Juliet is Rusha, who falls in love with and secretly becomes engaged to a Serbian Romeo, Melisdrav.

As a literary scholar, Pipa published a study of the influence of Dante on the Italian poet Eugenio Montale (1896–1981), *Montale and Dante,* and has made major contributions to the knowledge of Albanian literature and culture in English. They include the "Trilogia Albanica"—*Albanian Folk Verse: Structure and Genre* (1978); *Hieronymus de Rada* (1978), about the Italo-Albanian writer Girolamo De Rada (1814–1903); and *Albanian Literature: Social Perspectives* (1978)—as well as *The Politics of Language in Socialist Albania* (1989) and *Contemporary Albanian Literature* (1991). Pipa has also been an ardent champion of Albanian democracy and the rights of the Albanian population of Kosovo. His major political studies are *Zhvillimi politik i shtetit shqiptar, 1912–1962* (Albanian Political and National Development, 1912–1962, 1962); *Studies on Kosova* (1984); and *Albanian Stalinism: Ideo-Political Aspects* (1990).

Pištalo, Vladimir (b. 1960) Bosnian Serb short-story writer and novelist. A native of Sarajevo, Pištalo graduated with a law degree but began writing at an early age and publishing in the avant-garde literary journals *Književna reč* and *Student*. He has published seven collections of stories and one novel. His literary debut came in 1986 when in a single year he published three collections of stories: *Slikovnica* (The Picture Book); *Manifesti* (Manifestos); and *Noći* (Nights). They were followed by another collection of stories, *Kraj veka* (The End of the World, 1990); *Corto Maltese* (1990), a novella; *Vitraž u sećanju* (Stained-Glass Memories, 1994), a volume of stories, six of which have American settings and are grouped under the general title "Amerika"; and *Priče iz celog sveta* (Stories from the Entire World, 1997), a collection of stories by émigrés from various countries, including the United States. His novel *Aleksandrida* (Alexandriad), which is based on the life of Alexander the Great, came out in 1999. Pištalo immigrated to the United States in the wake of the Yugoslav wars of the 1990s and currently teaches American history at the University of New Hampshire, where he is a doctoral candidate in history.

Translations: "Man Without a Face," trans. Charles Simic with Vladimir Pištalo, in *The Prince of Fire: An Anthology of Contemporary Serbian Short Stories,* ed. Radmila J. Gorup and Nadežda Obradović (Pittsburgh: University of Pittsburgh Press, 1998), 368–71.

Plenzdorf, Ulrich (b. 1934) German novelist, short-story writer, playwright, and screenwriter. Plenzdorf was born in Berlin-Kreuzberg into a communist workers' family that was imprisoned under Hitler. After briefly studying philosophy, he became a stagehand, served in the military, attended the Babelsberg Film Academy from 1959 to 1961, and then worked as a screenwriter and dramatic adviser for DEFA, the German Democratic Republic's state-run film company. His film scripts include *Mir nach, Canaillen!* (Follow Me, Rabble!, 1964); *Karla* (Carla, 1965); and *Die Legende von Paul und Paula* (The Legend of Paul and Paula, 1972), which was not distributed following the Eleventh Plenum of the Central Committee of the Socialist Unity Party, which stepped up censorship of artists. Plenzdorf eventually became a freelance writer. His first major literary work, and the one that made him famous, was the novella *Die neuen Leiden des jungen W.* (The New Sufferings of Young W., 1972). Originally written in 1968/1969, the novella caused problems with the censors, and Plenzdorf had to shelve it. When it first appeared in *Sinn und Form,* it attracted considerable attention within the cultural community. But when the play based on it reached the stage, it became an overnight sensation and came to be regarded as emblematic of the GDR cultural thaw between 1971 and 1976. The fairly short (a little over sixty pages) prose work tells the story of a latter-day Werther in the form of an alienated young East German boy who becomes a dropout and winds up accidentally electrocuting himself. Much of the narration is in the first person by Edgar Wibeau (the new Werther), who tells his own story from beyond the grave. Goethe's *Sorrows of Young Werther* becomes (like Salinger's *Catcher in the Rye*) one of Edgar's favorite books, and he comes to closely identifying himself with Goethe's tragic hero, the more so in view of his own doomed romance with a married woman. Despite official misgivings about Plenzdorf's portrait of an alienated young East German who cannot seem to fit in anywhere, he was awarded the Heinrich Mann Prize by the Academy of Arts and Sciences in 1973. The novella was also made into a film in West Germany in 1976. Plenzdorf's other literary works include *Legende vom Glück ohne Ende* (The Legend of Endless Happiness, 1979), a novel; *Ein Tag, länger als ein Leben* (One Day Longer than a Life, 1986), a play; *Freiheitsberaubung* (Stealing Freedom, 1988), also a play; and *Das andere Leben des Herrn Kreins* (The Other Life of Mr. Kreins, 1995), a collection of short stories. Plenzdorf was also awarded the Heinrich Greif Prize in 1971 and again in 1973; the Ingeborg Bachmann Prize in 1978; and the Adolf Grimme Prize in 1995.

Translations: "The New Sufferings of Young W.," trans. Kenneth P. Wilcox, in *The New Sufferings of Young W. and Other Stories from the German Democratic Republic*, ed. Therese Hörnigk and Alexander Stephan (New York: Continuum, 1997), 1–68.

Podrimja, Ali (b. 1942) Kosovo Albanian poet. The most impressive Albanian poet to emerge in Kosovo, Yugoslavia, during the Albanian "renaissance" of 1966 to 1981, Podrimja was born in Gjakovë. After completing secondary school in Gjakovë, he pursued Albanian studies at Priština University. Despite the early death of his parents and financial hardship, Podrimja made his literary debut in 1961 while still in secondary school with his first book of poems, *Thirrje* (The Calls). He subsequently pub-

lished another fifteen volumes of poetry: *Shamija e përshëndetjeve* (The Handkerchiefs of Greeting, 1963); *Dhimbë e bukur* (Sweet Pain, 1967); *Loja nën dieli* (Games Beneath the Sun, 1967); *Sampo* (Sampo, 1969); *Fjalë të rilindura* (Words Come Back to Haunt You, 1970); *Torzo* (Torso, 1971); *Folja* (The Verb, 1973); *Credo* (Credo, 1976); *Poezi* (Poems, 1978); *Sampo 2* (Sampo 2, 1980); *Drejtpeshimi* (Equilibrium, 1981); *Lum Lumi* (Happy Lumi, 1982), which Podrimja dedicated to his deceased son, Lumi; *Fund i gëzuar* (Happy Ending, 1988); *Zari* (Spheres, 1990); and *Buzëqeshje në kafaz* (The Smile in the Cage, 1993).

Much of Podrimja's poetry is elegaic, occasioned by the early deaths of his parents, his sister, and, in the blow that had the greatest impact on him, his son. In simple but eloquent verse, the poet bemoans his fate, the pain he experiences, and the ominous (symbolic) howling of the wolf that seems to dog his footsteps, in a borrowing from Albanian lore. Apart from his own poetic output, Podrimja actively promoted Albanian literature in Yugoslavia before its disintegration. With Yugoslav translators, he published an anthology of contemporary Albanian poetry in Yugoslavia under the title *Bez glagola* (Without the Word) in 1978. And in 1984 the Rilindja publishing house in Priština brought out a collection of Albanian poetry from Yugoslavia edited by Podrimja. Two volumes of his own translations were published in Serbo-Croatian in 1972 and 1989, respectively. A Macedonian–Albanian edition of his poetry was published in Skopje in 1968 under the title *Lili dhe lirija jonë/Lili i našata sloboda* (Lili and Our Freedom). Podrimja has also been translated into Polish; a volume of his poems, translated by Mazllum Saneja under the title *Żyć* (To Live), appeared in 1993. Since the Kosovo campaign of the summer of 1999, Podrimja has been living in Cologne, Germany. In late 1999 and early

2000, he was a guest at the Villa Waldberta, the artists' colony in Munich.

Translations: Thirteen poems in *An Elusive Eagle Soars: Anthology of Modern Albanian Poetry*, ed. and trans. Robert Elsie (London: Forest, 1993), 111–25. *Buzëqeshje në kafaz* is available as *Ali Podrimja, Buzëqeshje në kafaz/Das Lächeln im Käfig*, trans. Hans-Joachim Lanksch (Klagenfurt: Wieser, 1993), an Albanian–German edition.

Podsiadło, Jacek (b. 1964) Polish poet. A prolific and talented young poet, Podsiadło was born in Opole. His major work to date consists of two large collections, both published in 1998 and both titled *Wiersze zebrane* (Collected Poems), containing all his previously published poems. The first volume brings together texts published in journals from 1984 to 1996 and in such separate small volumes as *Nieszczęście doskonałe* (Perfect Unhappiness, 1987); *Hej!* (Hey!, 1987); *Wah-Wah* (1988); *Odmowa współudziału* (Rejection of Cooperation, 1989); *Tak* (So, 1989); *Kompot z orangutana* (Compote of Orangutan, 1989); *Sobą po mapie* (A Self-Guided Tour of the Globe, 1989); *Można jeszcze na mnie polować* (You Can Still Hunt Me, 1989); and *W lunaparkach smutny, w lunaparkach śmiszny* (Sad and Funny in Amusement Parks, 1990). The second volume contains texts published in journals from 1994 to 1998 and in the collections *Nie wiem* (I Don't Know, 1989); *Arytmia* (Arythmia, 1993); *Języki ognia* (Tongues of Fire, 1994); *Dobra ziemia dla murarzy* (Good Ground for Bricklayers, 1994); *Duma maszynisty: Dziesiątki zielonych rąk* (A Machinist's Pride: Dozens of Golden Hands, 1995); *Królowa kolorów* (Queen of Colors, 1995); *To All the Whales I'd Love Before* (1996; original title in English); *Niczyje, boskie* (Nobody's but God's, 1998); and *Zielone oczy zmrużyć czas* (It's Time to Blink Green Eyes, 1998). In 1999 Podsiadło brought out a slim volume of verse and short prose texts dating from 1995 under the title *Cisówka* (The Hideaway), and in 2000 a volume of sixty of his poems edited by his friend Paweł Marcinkiewicz appeared under the title *I ja pobiegłem w tę mgłę* (And I Too Ran Off into the Fog). In his short but perceptive introduction to the volume, Marcinkiewicz characterizes Podsiadło as "one of the most important poets of the generation of the transition [i.e., from communism to capitalism]." The tenor of much of Podsiadło's poetry—humorous, brash, deliberately provocative, irreverent, and self-mocking—can be appreciated from this excerpt from "Jadąc do siebie" ("Riding to Myself") in the first volume of *Wiersze zebrane*:

The thought of publishing all my previously printed poems in a single volume arose above all from the unhealthy desire to be able to satisfy the question inferred by the title of the short preface ("Oto cały ja" ["Here's All of Me"]). My exceptional interest in myself, which for years has impelled me to write, also directed me to collect all my scattered works inter alia in order to renounce the luxury of failures favoring the author whose ouput is read just in fragments. . . . When all is said and done, poetry has to be a provider of emotions, and some of my poems from my youthful texts are truly emotionally unsuccessful. But they are in fact harmful only to very inexperienced youths. Both volumes appear in a form that allows them—with the exercise of just a little good will—to be carried in a pocket or knapsack. That's not an accident. These poems lend themselves as well to reading in a luxurious rocking chair, on condition that all the rockers be first sawed off.

Translations: Three poems, trans. Elżbieta Wójcik-Leese and W. Martin, *Chicago Review* 46, nos. 3–4 (2000): 274–75.

Połkowski, Jan (b. 1953) Polish poet. One of the more talented Polish poets to emerge in the 1980s, Połkowski was born in Kraków, where he studied Polish literature at the Jagiellonian University. An active participant in the Solidarity movement in the 1970s and 1980s, the experience of which has shaped many of his poems, he was editor of the clandestine samizdat publishing house kos (Kraków Student Publications) and founded the independent publishing group ABC. When martial law was declared, he was interned on 13 December 1981 but released after the declaration of amnesty. He continued his work in the underground as editor of the leading underground journal of the time, *Arka,* which became legal in 1989 and has since steadily grown. Połkowski is also the editor of the conservative daily *Czas,* which is published in Kraków. His first poems appeared in the underground quarterly *Zapis* in 1978, and his subsequent volumes came out only in samizdat editions. They include *To nie jest poezija* (That's Not Poetry, 1980); *Oddychaj głęboko* (Breathe Deeply, 1981); *Ogień: Z notatek 1982–1983* (Fire: From My Notebooks, 1982–1983, 1983); and *Drzewa* (Trees, 1987). A volume of his poems was published in London in 1986 by the Polish émigré publishing house Puls. The first selected anthology of his work under the title *Elegie z tymowskich gór i inne wiersze* (Elegies from the Tymowo Fields and Other Poems), was published by the Catholic publishing house Znak in Kraków in 1990.

Translations: Seven poems in *Polish Poetry of the Last Two Decades of Communist Rule: Spoiling Cannibals' Fun,* ed. and trans. Stanisław Barańczak and Clare Cavanagh (Evanston, Ill.: Northwestern University Press, 1991), 175–77; ten poems in *Young Poets of a New Poland: An Anthology,* trans. Donald Pirie (London: Forest, 1993), 74–87.

Ponická, Hana (b. 1922) Slovak memoirist, translator, and author of children's books.

Not a great deal is known about Ponická. She was born in Halič and was married to two prominent Slovak poets: Štefan Žarý (b. 1918) and Ján Kostra (1910–1975). As a writer, Ponická became known mostly as the author of several books for children and as a translator from French (Baudelaire, Simone de Beauvoir, Gauguin, Saint-Exupéry), Italian (Alberto Moravia, Cesare Zavattini, Italo Calvino), and Hungarian, which she learned from her mother, an ethnic Hungarian. In 1959 she published a lyrical memoir, *Ábelovský dom* (The House in Ábelova), about her relationship with the well-known editor and translator Zora Jesenská, whom she had met in Martin when she lived there from 1938 to 1940. From 1941 to 1943, Ponická studied in Bratislava, where she grew close to the expressionist artist Janko Novák (1921–1944) and the Bratislava literary and intellectual avant-garde of the time. Ponická began her career as a writer of children's stories in 1953; in 1955 she also published a modest volume of short stories for young readers under the title *Háluzky* (Branches). However, her place in post–World War II Slovak literature was defined by her book *Lukavicke zápisky* (Lukavica Notes, 1989), a 456-page account of how she became a literary nonperson in 1977 after her defiant refusal to sign a denunciation of the Charter 77 movement and her even more provocative stand against official repression of the literary community at the Third Congress of Slovak Writers in Bratislava on 3 March 1977. The efforts to get her to change her views and, especially, to explain how the text of her address to the Writers Union found its way into the 4 May 1977 edition of the French newspaper *Le Monde,* the campaign against her, her expulsion from the Writers Union, and other forms of harassment against her are all vividly retold in *Lukavicke zápisky.* Because of its contents, the book obviously could not be published in Czechoslovakia at the time; it was issued by Sixty-Eight Publishers in Toronto in 1989.

Pop, Augustin (1952–1998) Romanian poet, essayist, and translator. Born in Panticeu, in the Cluj district, Pop studied Romanian and Italian at Cluj University, from which he graduated in 1976. After working for a few years as an editor at the magazine *Echinox*, he left to become a researcher at the Institute of Linguistics and Literary History in Cluj. His work in this area concentrated on the leading nineteenth-century Romanian poet Mihai Eminescu (1850–1889) and yielded such scholarly publications as *Contributii documentare la biografia lui Mihai Eminescu* (Documentary Contributions to the Biography of Mihai Eminescu, 1962); *Noi contribuții documentare la biografia lui Mihai Eminescu* (New Documentary Contributions to the Biography of Mihai Eminescu, 1969); *Întregiri documentare la biografii lui Eminescu* (Documentary Addenda to the Biography of Eminescu, 1983); and *Caleidoscop emenescian* (An Eminescu Kaleidoscope, 1987). In 1985 Pop also published a work on the poet Nicolae Labiș.

Pop's first book of poetry, *Ceea ce fulgerul amîna* (What Lightning Postpones), appeared in 1981. It was followed by his second collection of poems, *Apropierea* (Nearness), in 1990, the year in which Pop became a member of the Writers Union. Also in 1990 *Apropierea* was awarded the prize of the poetry magazine *Poesis*. Strongly committed to the cause of democratic reform in Romania, in 1983 Pop traveled to Gdańsk, Poland, where he met Lech Wałęsa, then director of Solidarity, and presented him with a copy of *Ceea ce fulgerul amîna*. In December 1989, during the revolution in Romania, he read some of his anticommunist poems from the collection *Libertățile dictatoriale* (Dictatorial Freedom) in the main square in Cluj. Humorous, colloquial, ironic in his political verse, Pop was one of Romania's most readable and entertaining contemporary poets.

Translations: Five poems in *Young Poets of a New Romania: An Anthology*, trans. Brenda Walker with Michaela Celea-Leach, ed. Ion Stoica (London: Forest, 1991), 67–73.

Popa, Vasko (1922–1991) Serbian poet. The most original, and esteemed, poet of post–World War II Yugoslavia, Popa was born in the village of Grebenac, on the Yugoslav–Romanian border. He was of Serbian–Romanian background. His early schooling in Vršac, not far from his place of birth, was followed by his move to Belgrade in 1940 to study Romance languages and literatures. With the outbreak of the war, he continued his education in Bucharest and Vienna. In 1949 he received his degree in French from Belgrade University. An early member of the Communist Party of Yugoslavia (1944), Popa began his career as a journalist for Radio Belgrade (1948–1951) and as an editor for the prestigious literary journal *Književne novine*. From 1951 to 1953 he served as secretary-general of the Society for Yugoslav-French Cultural Cooperation. In 1954 he joined the major Belgrade publishing house Nolit as an editor, a position he held for twenty-five years.

A slow, precise, and methodical writer, Popa produced a relatively small body of verse, but one highly prized both in his own country and abroad for its originality and elegant simplicity. His first collection, *Kora* (Bark), which contains poems written between 1943 and 1951, appeared in 1951, and at once established Popa as a poet willing to part from the familiar and conventional. His was truly a spectacularly new voice in Serbian (and Yugoslav) poetry and one that expressed itself entirely in free verse. What struck critics and readers alike at the time was the absence of people in Popa's poetry and the prominence of inanimate objects (ashtray, hat stand, tablecloth), which he animates in unusual images of distinct surrealist referentiality. Animals, fruits, flowers, and vegetables appear similarly. *Kora* was followed by seven other volumes of verse:

Nepočin-polje (*Unrest Field*, 1956); *Spredno nebo* (*Secondary Heaven*, 1968); *Uspravna zemlja* (*Earth Erect*, 1972); *Vučj so* (Wolf Salt), *Živo meso* (Raw Flesh), and *Kuća nasred druma* (*The House on the Highroad*), all published in 1975; and *Rez* (The Cut, 1981). Nolit published the first edition of his collected works, containing his first seven volumes, in 1980. The definitive version of his collected works appeared in 1988 under the title *Pesme* (Poems).

Popa's later volumes—*Earth Erect* (poems from 1951 to 1971), Wolf Salt (poems from 1972 to 1975), Raw Flesh (poems from 1972 to 1975), and *The House on the Highroad* (poems from 1950 to 1975)—differ from the preceding in two noteworthy respects. Although generally spurning nationalist themes, Popa devoted the entire cycle of small poems in Raw Flesh to a review of salient moments in Serbian history from ancient times to the present. Wolf Salt is similarly Serbian in inspiration, but substitutes the mythic for the historical, the wolf imagery referring to the Serbs. Both Raw Flesh and *The House on the Highroad* contain poems of an autobiographical and personal nature, which were absent in Popa's previous collections of verse.

Literature: There are two respectable studies of Popa's poetry in English: Ronelle Alexander, *The Structure of Vasko Popa's Poetry* (Columbus, Ohio: Slavica, 1985), a Serbo-Croatian translation of which was published in Belgrade in 1996, and Anita Lekić, *The Quest for Roots: The Poetry of Vasko Popa* (New York: Peter Lang, 1993), which is especially useful for the number of Popa's poems cited in the original Serbo-Croatian and parallel English translations. For a good German study of Popa, see Vasna Cedilko, *Studien zur Poetik Vasko Popas* (Wiesbaden: Harrassowitz, 1987). A newer Serbian interpretation is Miodrag Petrović, *Univerzum Vaska Pope* (Niš: Prosveta, 1995).

Translations: *Earth Erect,* trans. Anne Pennington (London: Anvil, 1972; Iowa City: University of Iowa Press, 1973); *The Golden Apple: A Round of Stories, Songs, Spells, Proverbs, and Riddles,* trans. Andrew Harvey and Anne Pennington (London: Anvil, 1980), an anthology of Serbian folklore; *Homage to the Lone Wolf: Selected Poems by Vasko Popa, 1955–1975,* trans. Charles Simic (Oberlin, Ohio: Oberlin College Press, 1979); *Homage to the Lone Wolf: Selected Poems by Vasko Popa,* trans. Charles Simic (Oberlin, Ohio: Oberlin College Press, 1987), a slightly revised version of the earlier edition; *Vasko Popa: Collected Poems,* trans. Anne Pennington and Francis R. Jones, with an introduction by Ted Hughes (London: Anvil, 1997), the best collection of Popa's poetry in English, this is an amplified version of *Vasko Popa: Collected Poems, 1943–1976,* trans. Anne Pennington (New York: Persea, 1978), which contains the first six books of Popa's poetry complete, with selections from the seventh, *The House on the Highroad; Unrest Field* and *Secondary Heaven,* in *Vasko Popa: Selected Poems,* trans. Anne Pennington (New York: Penguin, 1969), 41–64, 65–95; excerpts from *Rez,* trans. Anne Pennington and Francis Jones, in *Poetry World No. 2* (London: Anvil, 1986); nineteen poems in *The Horse Has Six Legs: An Anthology of Serbian Poetry,* trans. Charles Simic (St. Paul, Minn.: Graywolf, 1992), 55–75; eleven poems (from *Mala kutija* [*The Little Box*]), in *The Little Box,* trans. Charles Simic (Washington, D.C.: Charioteer, 1970), a 350-copy edition of poems published in a definitive edition in 1984 by the journal *Savremenik.*

Popescu, Adrian (b. 1947) Romanian poet. A native of Cluj-Napoca, Popescu studied philology there and worked as an editor of the literary review *Steaua.* While still a student, he started the review *Echinox,* to which other younger poets at the time, among them Ion Mircea and and Dinu Flămînd, contributed and which he edited until 1971. Since then, he has been the editor of *Steaua*. Popescu's published volumes of verse include *Umbra* (The Shadow, 1971); *Focul și sărbătoarea* (The Fire and the Feast, 1975); *Câmpiile magnetice* (The Magnetic Fields, 1976); *Curtea medicilor* (Physicians' Headquarters, 1979); *Suburbiile cerului* (The Suburbs of Heaven, 1982); *Proba cu polen* (The Pollen Test, 1984); *Vocea interioară* (The Inner Voice, 1987); *Călătoria continuă* (The Journey Without End, 1989); and *Spuma și stânca* (The Foam and the Rock, 1991). Defining himself as a "naturist," Popescu has an abiding fondness for and curiosity about nature and natural phenomena, whose smallest nuances excite his inventiveness as a poet. Popescu has translated from old Italian poetry and is interested in such writers as Ezra Pound, Paul Celan, and Rainer Maria Rilke. Liliana Ursu, who has translated Popescu into English, tells us that he adores old books, miniatures, and Renaissance painting, a fascination reflected in his poetry.

Translations: Three poems in *15 Young Romanian Poets: An Anthology of Verse*, trans. and ed. Liliana Ursu (Bucharest: Eminescu, 1982), 69–74.

Popescu, Dumitru Radu (b. 1935) Romanian novelist, short-story writer, playwright, and essayist. An outstanding and prolific writer, Popescu was born in Păușa (Bihor), Transylvania. He spent part of his childhood in the small village of Oltenia, in southwestern Romania, which he made the setting of several works. After completing secondary school in Oradea, he studied medicine for three years at Cluj University before switching to the Faculty of Philology. Popescu remained in Cluj after receiving his degree and worked first as editor of the review *Steaua* and then as editor in chief of the literary-cultural journal *Tribuna*. He made his debut as a writer in 1958 with a volume of stories in the tradition of Romanian rural prose under the title *Fuga* (Flight). A year later, he published his first novel, *Zilele săptămîni* (The Days of the Week), which, like his subsequent novel *Vara oltenilor* (The Summer of the Oltenians, 1964), deals with the impact of radical economic, political, and social changes on the villagers of the Oltenia region. From 1962 to 1967, Popescu returned to the genre of the short story with such collections as *Umbrela de soare* (The Sun Umbrella, 1962); *Fata de la miazăzi* (The Girl from the South, 1964); *Somnul pămîntului* (The Dream of the Earth, 1965); and *Dor* (Nostalgia, 1966). Although well regarded for his early novels, short stories, and the novella *Duios Anastasia trecea* (Gently Anastasia Was Passing By, 1967), a retelling of the Antigone legend, Popescu's fame rests principally on the epic cycle of interlocking political novels and novellas that he began publishing in 1969 and to which he gave the collective title *F*. The works that make up the cycle (which was not originally conceived as such) include, after *F* (1969), *Cei doi din dreptul Țebei sau Cu fața la pădure* (The Two from Tebea, or Facing the Forest, 1973); *Vînătoarea regală* (*The Royal Hunt*, 1973); *O bere pentru calul meu* (A Beer for My Horse, 1974); *Împăratul norilor* (The Emperor of the Clouds, 1976); *Ploile de dincolo de vreme* (The Rains from Beyond Time, 1976); and *Viața și opera lui Tiron B.* (The Life and Work of Tiron B., 1980).

The Royal Hunt, the only novel in the cycle to be translated into English, is, together with *F* itself, the best of the group. Set in the village of Pătîrlage in a mythical Danubian county sometimes compared with William Faulkner's Yoknapatawpha County, and in part both allegory and parable, the cycle as a whole assumes the proportions of an indictment of the ruthless means employed by the new Romanian communist regime to achieve the collectivization of agriculture in the "dark days" of the 1950s. The revelations of terrible wrongdoing are uncovered in the course of a relentless investigation into the mysterious disappearance years earlier of his father by the young prosecutor Tică Dinarinţu. Although the mosaic structure of the *F* cycle makes for inconsistencies and contradictions in chronology and narrative logic, the work as a whole is a compelling, often chilling inquiry into the subversion of a traditional way of life at the hands of Communist Party functionaries who brook no opposition to the realization of their goals. In the most allegorical of the novels, *The Royal Hunt,* the mystery of the disappearance of Dinarinţu's father and the sacrifice of another dissenter, Dănilă, take on a more grotesque aspect as a real or an imagined epidemic of rabies results in mass hysteria in the end, creating a terrifying image of fenzied men and the dogs being slaughtered by them wholesale seemingly merging into a single species. Popescu's subsequent novels include *9* (1982); *Rezervaţia de pelicane* (The Pelican Reservation, 1983); *Moară de pulbere* (The Powder Mill, 1984); and *Truman Capote şi Nicolae Ţic* (Truman Capote and Nicolae Ţic, 1995).

Popescu's dramatic writing is set in the period of World War II and the decade of the 1950s and explores issues with which he deals in his novels. The exceptions to this pattern are *Baladă pentru nouă cerbi* (Ballad for Nine Stags), which is based on a Romanian folk ballad, and *Două ore de pace* (Two Hours of Peace), which takes place during the Romanian war of liberation of 1877. Popescu's first work for the stage was *Vara imposibilei iubiri* (The Summer of Impossible Love, 1966). The major published collections of his plays are *Aceşti îngere trişti* (These Sad Angels, 1970); *Teatru* (Theater, 1974); and the two-volume *Teatru (1985–1987).* However, not all of Popescu's plays have been published, and some can be found only in the periodicals where they

first appeared. In general, his dramatic style is permeated with elements of the absurd, grotesque, and fantastic to a greater extent than his prose writings and relates to the theater of the absurd of Eugène Ionesco, Bertolt Brecht, Friedrich Dürrenmatt, and Samuel Beckett.

An erstwhile member of the Central Committee of the Romanian Communist Party, Popescu also served as president of the Romanian Writers Union from 1981 to 1989. He was thrice the recipient of the Writers Union Prize: in 1964 for *Vara oltenilor;* in 1969 for *F;* and in 1973 for *The Royal Hunt.* The Writers Union also honored him on several occasions for his dramatic writing, and in 1978 he received the prize for journalism and reportage for his volume of essays *Virgule* (Commas).

Literature: The handiest general work on Popescu is Andreea Vladescu Lupu, ed., *Dumitru Radu Popescu: Antologie, prefaţă, notă asupra ediţiei, cronologie şi bibliografie* (Bucharest: Eminescu, 1987). The only piece on him in English is Radica Boţoman, "Between Myth and Reality: The Novels of D. R. Popescu," *Dialogue* 9 (1982): 9–24.

Translation: *The Royal Hunt,* trans. J. E. Cottrell and M. Bogdan (Columbus: Ohio State University Press, 1985); "The Tin Can" (from *Fuga*), in *The Phantom Church and Other Stories from Romania,* ed. and trans. Georgiana Farnoaga and Sharon King (Pittsburgh: University of Pittsburgh Press, 1996), 40–47. A collection of some of Popescu's plays is available in Russian as *Faiansovyj grom iz letnogo sada* (Moscow: Raduga, 1986).

Popescu, Petru (b. 1944) Romanian novelist, short-story writer, poet, journalist, and filmmaker. Popescu was born in Bucharest and graduated with a degree in English from the Foreign Languages Institute of Bucharest University. Before leaving Romania in 1973 and settling first in London and then in California, he had made a reputation as a successful filmmaker and journalist and as a controversial novelist beginning with his first novel, *Prins* (Captive, 1969), a bold political allegory that scarcely conceals an indictment of the nature of communist rule in Romania. His second novel, *Dulce ca mierea e glonțul patriei* (Sweet as Honey Is My Homeland's Bullet, 1971), also aroused controversy for raising questions about Romania's stand toward the Soviet Union at a time when Nicolae Ceaușescu was forging an independent foreign policy. The "most rebellious" of his books, as he himself describes it, was the novel *Sfîrșitul bahic* (Bacchic End, 1973; translated as *Burial of the Vine*). In it, a young man is expelled from the Communist Party for some trivial reason and out of desperation takes a job as a clerk in a Jewish cemetery, where he is befriended by four body washers. Through his affair with the wife of an old schoolmate, both painters and staunch Party members, and both invested with unflattering features of Ceaușescu and his wife, Elena, Popescu exposes the hedonism and immorality of the communist elite. The book somehow passed the censors but was roundly attacked by "official" critics. Popescu's last work published in Romania was a best-selling historical allegory set in the period of the Ottoman Turkish occupation of Romania. Popescu first left Romania for the United States after he received an invitation from the International Writing Program of the University of Iowa. When it was over, he returned briefly to Europe before deciding to defect. He settled in Los Angeles, where he attended the American Film Institute. Apart from his career as a filmmaker in the United States (he directed *Death of an Angel* in 1986), Popescu has published several novels written in English, the best known of which are *Amazon Beaming* (1991), based on the chance discovery of the Mayoruna "cat people" of the Amazon rain forest by famed National Geographic pho-

tographer Loren MacIntyre, and the thematically related *Almost Adam* (1996), in which a paleoanthropologist comes across two species of hominids believed long extinct in a deserted region of Kenya. In his next book, *The Return* (1997), Popecsu described his life in Romania and the United States and his return to Romania after the downfall of the Ceaușescu regime. With Peter Jay, Popescu also translated poems by the Romanian poet Nichita Stanescu. They were published by the International Writing Program of the University of Iowa in 1974 under the title *The Still Unborn About the Dead: Selected poems/Nichita Stanescu.*

Translations: *Burial of the Vine*, trans. Carol Telford, Peter Jay, and Petru Popescu (London: Barrie and Jenkins, 1975).

Works in English: *Almost Adam: A Novel* (New York: Morrow, 1996); *Amazon Beaming* (New York: Viking, 1991); *In Hot Blood* (New York: Fawcett, 1989); *The Return* (New York: Grove, 1997).

Popescu, Simona (b. 1965) Romanian poet. Popescu was born in the village of Codlea, near Brașov, and, after completing secondary school in Brașov, graduated from the Faculty of Letters of Bucharest University in 1987. She subsequently became an assistant in the same faculty. Her first book of poetry, *Xilofonul și alte poeme* (The Xylophone and Other Poems), appeared in 1990. It was followed by two other collections of poems, *Pauza de respirație* (Breathing Pause, 1991) and *Juventus* (1994), and a long, seventy-three-page poem titled *Noapte sau zi* (Night or Day, 1998). Popescu's casually written, intimate, musing poetry conveys ambivalence toward the world around her, a certain perception of the senselessness of existence, loneliness yet self-reliance, and solace in pursuits of the mind and in poetry. Popescu has also published two volumes of prose: *Exuvil* (Exuvia, 1997), a novel, and *Volubilis* (1999), a book of essays. Popescu's literary awards include the *Calende* literary review and *Poesis* prizes (1980); the *Poesis* Poetry Prize (1994); and the Association of Professional Writers of Romania (ASPRO) Prose Prize (1997).

Translations: Five poems, trans. Cosana Nicolae, in *Romaniann Poets of the '80s and '90s,* ed. Andrei Bodiu, Romulus Bucur, and Georgeta Moarcăş (Piteşti: Paralela 45, 1999), 277–84.

Popova, Nadia (b. 1952) Bulgarian poet. A native of Sofia, Popova graduated from the Gorky Institute of World Literature in Moscow in 1974. For the next fifteen years, she worked for Radio Sofia as an editor and in 1989 joined the staff of the periodical *Panorama.* She has published her poems in a variety of journals and periodicals, and in 1981 came out with her first book of poetry, *Liniia na zhivota: Lyrika* (Life Line: Lyrics). Her next volume of lyrics, *Novolunie* (New Moon), appeared in 1987. In 1981 she won the Vladimir Bashev Literary Prize for the best first volume of poetry. In a direct, outwardly simple, sometimes dialogic style, Popova writes about the vulnerability of women, her own individuality, alienation, a yearning for communication and mutual understanding with her beloved, art as opposed to everyday life, and hope in the possibility of truth in human relations. Popova has also translated from Russian literature.

Translations: Five poems, trans. Belin Tonchev, in *Young Poets of a New Bulgaria: An Anthology,* ed. Belin Tonchev (London: Forest, 1990), 96–100.

Popovici, Titus (real name Titus Viorel; b. 1930) Romanian short-story writer, novelist, and playwright. A native of Oradea, where he received his early education, Povovici studied at the Faculty of Philology of Bucharest University. In 1953 he became an inspector in the Ministry of Art and, in the 1960s, a member of the Central Committee of the Romanian Communist Party. Popovici made an unspectacular literary debut in 1951 with a collection of stories written with Francisc Munteanu and published under the title *Mecanicul şi alţi oameni de azi* (The Mechanic and Other People of Today). A second collection of stories, *Povestiri* (Stories), followed in 1955. Popovici's real reputation as a writer rests mainly on two novels, *Străinul* (*The Stranger,* 1955) and *Setea* (Thirst, 1958), both set in his native Transylvania during and immediately after World War II. A work of broader scope, *The Stranger* depicts Romanian society during the war years down to the Romanian uprising against the Germans on 23 August 1944. In *Setea,* Popovici's last novel, the focus is on the impact of Romanian communist agrarian reform on a Transylvanian village in 1945. The rather weak novella *Moartea lui Ipus* (Ipus's Death), in essence a social satire of a fantastic-grotesque character, appeared in 1970. As a playwright, Popovici is best known for *Passacaglia* (1960), about a talented young pianist obsessed with his own talent whose dangerous flirtation with fascism and the Nazis has disastrous results. As elsewhere in Popovici's fiction, a faulty sense of the collective leads to fascism; only the communists can point the way to a socially responsible and upright future. Following a trip to Cuba, Popovici published a book of feature articles about that country under the title *Însemnări din Cuba: Cuba, teritoriu liber al Americii* (Notes on Cuba: Cuba, a Free Territory of America, 1970). Popovici is also the author of such film scripts as *Pădurea spînzuraţilor* (The Forest of the Hanged, 1965); *Dacii* (The Dacians, 1967); *Columnă* (The Column, 1968); and *Mihai Viteazul* (Michael the Brave, 1969).

Translations: *The Stranger,* trans. Lazar Marinescu (Bucharest: Meridians, 1962); excerpts from *Setea,* in *Introduction to Rumanian Literature,* ed. Jacob Steinberg (New York: Twayne, 1966), 343–79.

Popovski, Ante (b. 1931) Macedonian poet, essayist, and translator. A highly respected poet, well represented in other languages, Popovski was born in Lazaropole, near Debar. After completing his primary- and secondary-school education in Bitola, he earned a degree in medicine at Saints Cyril and Methodius University in Skopje. Popovski began writing poetry at an early age and published his first book of poems, *Odblesoci* (Reflections), in 1955. It was followed by *Vardar* (The Vardar, 1958); *Triptihon* (Triptych, 1966); *Nepokor* (Persistence, 1964); *Makovi* (Poppies, 1969); *Kamena* (Of Stone, 1972); *Tajnopis* (*Arcanum*, 1975); *Ognjena* (Of Fire, 1978); *Ljubopis* (Of Love, 1980); *Rodopis* (Genealogy, 1981); *Sina pesna* (Blue Poem, 1985); *Koren edinak* (The Solitary Root, 1985); *Nenaslovena* (Untitled, 1988); *Tišina* (Silence, 1994); and *Providenija* (Providence, 1995). An intensely philosophical poet, at home generally in shorter verse forms and an understated idiom, free of bombast and rhetoric, Popovski addresses such issues as humanity's place in the universe, the fragility and transience of human existence, and the meaning, or lack of meaning, of life. His images and ideas are drawn from many sources, both ancient and modern, pagan and Christian. The undeniable catastrophic and apocalyptic dimension in his poetry is rooted in the bitter history of the Macedonian people, of which Popovski is ever keenly aware. As he writes in one poem:

> Dear God,
> in this short-lived age
> only the sorrow in the soul of my people
> seems to have no end

or as he laments in "Letters of Blood":

> Even if we went back to begin
>   everything anew,
> outran knowledge and ignorance.

> history and anti-history,
> went back to where
> nothing existed:
> not stars, nor form, nor voice, nor God
> once more it would all be in vain:
> the sword would again be forged first:
> The memories of our descendants
> would again be written
> in its letters of blood!

In universalizing the experience of the Macedonian struggle, however, he rises far above the parochial level. Popovski's deep interest in Macedonian culture is also reflected in his book *Glas od damninata: Kon poetikata na makedonskite srednovekovni crkovni zapisi* (Voice from the Bygone Past: Toward a Poetics of Medieval Macedonian Church Scripts, 1985). Among the foreign poets Popovski has translated into Macedonian are Eugenio Montale, Yehuda Amichai, Ivan B. Lalić, and Arthur Lundquist. He has also edited anthologies of Yiddish and Russian poetry. Popovski has received the Nostro Vivajo Prize (1970); the 11 October Prize; the Kočo Racin Prize; and the Brothers Miladinov Prize (twice) at the Struga Poetry Evenings Festival. Popovski was a member of the Executive Council of the Socialist Republic of Macedonia before independence and served as director-general of the Nova Makedonija (New Macedonia) publishing house.

Translations: *Arcanum* (Palermo: La Meridiana, 1994); *Arcanum II*, trans. Zoran Ančevski, David Bowen, and Dragi Mihajlovski (Skopje: Detska Radost, 1996); twelve poems in *Contemporary Macedonian Poetry*, ed. and trans. Ewald Osers (London: Forest, 1991), 57–68; poems, trans. Zoran Ančevski, David Bowen, and Dragi Mihajlovski, *Macedonian Review* 26, no. 3 (1996): 104–12.

Poświatowska, Halina (1935–1967) Polish poet. The stature of Poświatowska, one of most talented young women poets of post–World War II Poland, has risen considerably since her untimely death at the age of thirty-two. She was born in Częstochowa, where her early education was mostly at home. She graduated from the Jagiellonian University in Kraków with a degree in history and later studied at Smith College in Northampton, Massachusetts. She made her debut as a poet in the literary press in 1956, when expectations for reform were high following the Poznań disturbances of October of that year. Her first book of poems, *Hymn bałochwalczy* (Idolatrous Hymn, 1958), was followed by two more in her lifetime: *Dzień dzisiejszy* (This Very Day, 1963) and *Oda do rąk* (An Ode to Hands, 1966). Her fourth book of poetry, *Jeszcze jedne wspomnienie* (One More Recollection), appeared in 1968, a year after her death. Her poems from 1956 to 1958 and from 1958 to 1962 have been incorporated into the first volume of the fine three-volume edition of her works published by the Wydawnictwo Literackie in Kraków in 1997.

Opowieść dla przyjaciela (Tale for a Friend), which appeared in 1966, is a prose account, partly in diary form, mostly of her trip to the United States in 1958 for a heart operation. Her stay in the United States inspired several poems, including one dedicated to the Beat poet Lawrence Ferlinghetti. There has been speculation concerning the addressee of *Opowieść dla przyjaciela*, with some believing that the "friend" of the title was her second husband, Jan Adamski, a writer and actor who had been married to the poet Anna Świrszczyńska.

Poświatowska's sensitive, and sensuous, poetry conveys an abiding awareness of the fragility of life, her own life in particular, and of death, toward which she assumes an attitude of acceptance. Her poetry is also frequently erotic and expresses as well an interest in women, although not necessarily in terms of lesbian attraction. She wrote

poems, for example, on the death of Marilyn Monroe, on black women, and on women living on the margins of society whom she met in the United States. Her poetry could also be autoerotic in the sense of expressing pleasure in and satisfaction with her own body, which she enjoyed viewing through the eyes of a lover. As she wrote in the poem "Lustro" ("Mirror"): "jestem zaczadzona pięknem mojego ciała" ("I am asphyxiated with the beauty of my own body"). The considerable interest in Poświatowska since her death is reflected in the various editions of her poetry published in 1976, 1979, and 1992 and in the two-volume edition of 1997. A collection of her previously unknown or forgotten poems appeared in 1993, and in 1998 a small volume of poems under the title *Jestem Julia* (I Am Julia) appeared. A collection of her letters and a volume of her prose were published in 1998. The Polish composer Tadeusz Baird wrote five songs for mezzo-sporano and sixteen instruments based on poems by Poświatowska. The composition, with German translations of Poświatowska's poems by Maria Kurecka, was published in 1969 by Hansen of London.

Potrč, Ivan (1913–1993) Slovenian novelist, short-story writer, and playwright. Potrč was born in a village near Ptuj where he completed his secondary schooling. As a young man, he was politically active and briefly imprisoned as a communist. During World War II, he was in a German concentration camp but escaped in 1943 and joined the partisans. Potrč began his literary career before the war, publishing the novella *Sin* (Son) in 1937. After the war, he worked as a journalist and then as an editor with the Mladinska knjiga publishing house in Ljubljana until his retirement. His first postwar publication was the story collection *Kočarji* (The Cottagers, 1946), which continued the style of socialist realism typical of most of

Potrč's writing. It was followed by the novella *Svet na Kajžarju* (The World in Shantyville, 1948); the novel *Na kmetih* (Among Peasants, 1959; translated as *The Land and the Flesh*); the novella *Zločin* (The Crime, 1955); the novel *Srečanje* (The Meeting, 1962); a volume of selected stories, *Nesmilečno življenje* (A Life Without Pity, 1965); the story collection *Onkraj zarje* (Beyond the Dawn, 1966); two collections of stories, each published with *Na kmetih*: *Na verne duše* (To Righteous Souls, 1973) and *Imel sem ljubi dve* (I Had Two Lives, 1976); another collection of stories, *Ko smo se ženili* (We Who Got Married, 1983); and the novel *Tesnoba* (Anxiety, 1991). Without doubt, Potrč is best known as the author of *The Land and the Flesh*. This naturalistic novel is an engrossing tale of lust and unbridled passion. It takes the form of a lengthy confessional by a young peasant whom the narrator meets in prison and who tells him about the events that led up to his sordid affairs, first with the older wife of a dying neighbor and then with one of her two daughters. Both women become pregnant and bear children. When the affair with the older woman eventually palls and the peasant feels himself caught in a trap from which there is no escape, he strangles her, for which he is arrested and sent to prison. In his dramatic works, as in his prose fiction, Potrč found his material mainly in the milieu of Slovenian peasant families in the Styrian region. His major dramatic work is a trilogy dealing with a single such family in the prewar, war, and postwar periods: *Kreflova kmetija* (The Krefli Homestead, 1947); *Lacko in Krefli* (Lacko and Krefli, 1949); and *Krefli* (The Krefli, 1953).

Translations: *The Land and the Flesh*, trans. H. Leeming (London: Peter Owen, 1969).

Preda, Marin (1922–1981) Romanian novelist and short-story writer. Arguably the most representative writer of postwar Romanian literature, Preda wrote works celebrated for their links with the prewar Romanian literary tradition and their author's refusal to submit to Soviet-imposed models. His importance as a writer was established by his first novel, *Moromeţii* (The Moromete Family, 1955; translated as *The Morometes*), a monumental antitraditionalist work about a Romanian peasant family and its attachment to the land. His three novellas of the 1950s—*Desfăşurarea* (The Unfolding, 1952; translated as *In a Village: A Story*); *Ferestre întunecate* (Windows in Darkness, 1956); and *Îndrăzneala* (Daring, 1959)—explore the upheaval of Romanian village life in the wake of the imposition of a socialist system of agriculture. These works were followed by several political novels set against the background of Romania in the Stalinist 1950s: *Risipitorii* (The Squanderers, 1962); *Intrusul* (The Intruder, 1968); and, above all, *Cel mai iubit dintre pămînteni* (The Most Beloved Man on Earth, 1980), widely regarded as one of the best Romanian novels of the postwar era, not the least because novel writing itself is one of the issues that Preda addresses in the work. Preda's other novels are *Friguri* (Fever, 1963), a minor achievement notable mostly for its Far Eastern setting and the theme of the struggle for national and social liberation; *Marele singuratic* (The Great Loner, 1972); and *Delirul* (Frenzy, 1975), two uneven works of a historical-political character. In 1971 Preda published a book of essays under the title *Imposibila întoarcere* (Impossible Return) and in 1977 an autobiographical novel titled *Viaţa ca o pradă* (Life as a Prey). His best collection of short stories, *Albastra zare a morţii* (The Blue Horizon of Death), appeared in 1982.

Literature: Marieta Popescu, *Marin Preda* (Bucharest: Recif, 1995), a modest introductory study; Eugen Simeon, "Marin Preda and the Ways of Realism," in *Romanian Essayists of Today*, trans. Anda

Teodorescu and Andrei Bantaş (Bucharest: Minerva, 1979), 279–305; Marcel Cornis-Pope, "Marin Preda and the New Poetics of Contemporary Political Fiction," in *The Unfinished Battles: Romanian Postmodernism Before and After 1989* (Iaşi: Polirom, 1996), 158–71.

Translations: *In a Village: A Story,* trans. Lazar Marinescu (Bucharest: Book, 1955); *The Morometes* (Bucharest: Foreign Languages Publishing House, 1957); excerpts from *Îndrăzneala,* in *Introduction to Rumanian Literature,* ed. Jacob Steinberg (New York: Twayne, 1966), 298–313; "The Horse," trans. Fred Nadaban and John W. Rathbun, in *Cu bilet circular/With Circular Ticket: Romanian Short Stories,* ed. Mircea Zaciu, with notes by Sever Trifu (Cluj-Napoca: Dacia, 1983), 292–303, a Romanian–English edition. *Albastra zare a morţii* is available in French as *L'Horizon bleu de la mort: Recits* (Bucharest: Cartea Românească, 1982); *Intrusul* as *L'Intrus,* trans. Maria Ivanescu (Bucharest: Minerva, 1982); and *Marele singuratic* as *Marele singuratic,* trans. Claude B. Levenson (Paris: Grasset, 1975).

Prifti, Naum (b. 1932) Albanian short-story writer and playwright. One of Albania's most popular short-story writers, Prifti was born in the village of Rehovë, in the Korçë district. He studied medicine at the Polytechnic in Tirana and was employed as a medical assistant both there and in Korçë. But his interest in writing became so great that he gave up medicine in order to return to Tirana and study literature at the university. Before becoming a freelance writer, he was affiliated for some time with the satirical journal *Hosteni,* as well as with the periodical *Ylli.* His first collection of short stories, *Tregime të fshatit* (Village Stories, 1956), was followed by such other collections as *Lëkura e ujkut* (The Wolf's Hide, 1958), which contains short stories and humorous sketches; *Çezma e floririt* (The Golden Fountain, 1960), widely recognized as one of his best volumes; *Një pushkë në shumë* (One Rifle More, 1966); *Litar i zjarrtë* (Burning Rope, 1970); *Tre vetë kapërcejnë malin* (Three People Cross the Mountain, 1972), a selection of stories made by the noted Albanian writer Azem Shkreli; *Njerëz të kësaj toke* (People of this Land, 1975); *Njëqind vjet* (A Hundred Years, 1983); and *Erë mali, erë fushe* (Mountain Wind, Meadow Wind, 1985).

Prifti's stories clearly reflect his dedication to the cause of a modernized Albanian society and his familiarity with Albanian legend and lore, from which he has often drawn inspiration. Essentially didactic and often sentimental, Prifti is also known for the humor of many of his stories, including those in his early collection, *Lëkura e ujkut,* where much of the focus is on less savory elements in Albanian society. As a playwright, Prifti has written both comedies and dramas. Of folkish humor, a comedy such as *Dasmë pa nuse* (Wedding Without a Bride, 1969) is typical. His dramas—among them *Mulliri i Kostë Bardhit* (The Mill of Kostë Bardhi, 1971); *Rrethimi i bardhë* (The White Siege, 1973); *Me pushkë e me penë* (By Gun and by Pen) and *Plumbat e shkronjave* (Lead Type), both of which date from 1978; and *Zani partizani* (Partisan Legends, 1981)—generally have World War II themes. Although *Mulliri i Kostë Bardhit,* a play about the partisans, was well received, *Rrethimi i bardhë* was condemned for its "negative" qualities at the Fourth Plenary Session of the Albanian Communist Party in 1973. Prifti also made World War II in Albania the setting of one of his more popular novels, *Cikua dhe Beni* (Cikua and Beni, 1964; translated as *Tseeko and Benny: A Novelette*), about the wartime adventures of two provincial boys.

Translations: *The Golden Fountain: Short Stories,* trans. Peter R. Prifti (Shkodër: Camaj-Pipa, 1998); *Tseeko and Benny: A*

Novelette, trans. Peter Prifti (Tirana: 8 Nëntori, 1988).

Procházková, Lenka (b. 1951) Czech short-story writer, poet, and playwright. The daughter of the writer Jan Procházka (1929–1971), who played an active role in the movement to liberalize Czech culture in the 1960s and in the "Prague Spring" of 1968, Procházková was born in Prague, where she was educated through university. She received her degree in journalism from Charles University in 1975. Punished because of her father's activities, she was denied permission to work in her chosen profession and earned her living as a cleaning woman through the 1970s and 1980s. What poems and stories she published in periodicals during this period appeared under pseudonyms. She was also unable to publish any of her more substantial works officially until 1989, which means that virtually all of them first appeared in underground and/or foreign editions. Procházková is very much a woman's writer in that her writing is devoted mainly to exploring the social and personal world of the mostly younger Czech woman within the context of the pressures and limitations created by the repressive conditions prevailing in the country through much of the communist period. She is particularly attentive to the issue of a woman's emotional life and the special problems of single motherhood in a communist society, the subject, for example, of her partly autobiographical novel *Oční kapky* (Eye Drops, 1982), published first in Toronto in 1987 and then in Brno in 1991. Her first collection of stories, *Tři povídky* (Three Stories), appeared in 1980 and was followed by the novel *Růžová dáma* (The Pink Lady, 1980), published in Cologne in 1982; *Oční kapky*; and the short-story collections *Přijeď ochutnat* (Come Have a Taste, 1981), published in Cologne in 1982, and *Hlídač holubů* (The Guard of the Pigeons,

1987). The first books that Procházková was able to publish directly in Czechoslovakia were the novel *Smolná kniha* (The Black Book, 1989), presented as a work of fiction by Pavla Sukovká, the heroine of *Oční kapky,* in which she recounts her later life with a dissident writer and the police harassment to which they were subjected, and the short-story collection *Zvrhlé dny* (Perverse Days, 1995).

Translations: "Come Have a Taste," trans. Milan Pomichalek and Anna Mozga, in *Good-bye, Samizdat: Twenty Years of Czechoslovak Underground Writing,* ed. Marketa Goetz-Stankiewicz (Evanston, Ill.: Northwestern University Press, 1992), 69–87; "The Good New Times," trans. Alexandra Büchler, in *Allskin and Other Tales by Contemporary Czech Women,* ed. Alexandra Büchler (Seattle: Women in Translation, 1998), 159–66.

Puškáš, Jozef (b. 1951) Slovak novelist and short-story writer. A native of Michalovcie, where he completed secondary school, Puškáš went to Bratislava to study film and television writing at the Advanced School of Musical Studies. After graduating, he worked in the creative-writing section of the Smena publishing house and became cultural editor of the daily *Pravda* and then editor in chief of the cultural-political Sunday supplement of *Nové slovo.* He currently works for the monthly *Duel.* Puškáš 's literary career began with the publication of two books of short stories: *Hra na život a na smrť* (The Game of Life and Death, 1972), dealing in the main with the feelings of endangerment of an individual in contemporary society, which Puškáš views as overly technologized; and *Utešené sklamania* (Delightful Disappointments, 1977), again focused on the impact on the individual of social and other pressures and for which Puškáš won the annual prize of the big Slovenský spisovateľ state publishing house. In 1979 he also won the Smena

Award for his three-part novel *Priznanie* (Confession), a mercilessly critical self-analysis by a contemporary intellectual, and in 1980, the Rudolf Jašík Prize for the novel *Štvrtý rozmer* (The Fourth Dimension), arguably his best work of fiction. Dealing with the life of a young married couple from a big city in the early years of their marriage, the novel was made into a film in 1983 based on Puškáš's own script. Puškaš's other works include the novel *Záhrada (V piatom období roka)* (The Garden [In the Fifth Season], 1984), a broad look at Slovak generational conflict before the political changes of the late 1980s and early 1990s; *Sny, deti, milenky* (Dreams, Children, Mistresses, 1985), a collection of six stories examining family relations in terms of marital, parental, and romantic problems; the novel *Smrt' v jeseni* (Death in Autumn, 1990), Puškáš's first work of fiction set in the period of the transition from a communist to a postcommunist system; and *Vreckový labyrint* (Pocket Labyrinth, 1992), a volume of short stories collectively representing an attempt to understand the direction of contemporary society. Since the mid-1990s, Puškáš has directed much of his energy into writing scripts for video films and television programs.

Putík, Jaroslav (b. 1923) Czech journalist, novelist, and short-story writer. Putík was born in Most but grew up in Neratovice, on the outskirts of Prague. During the German occupation of Czechoslovakia in World War II, he joined the communist Resistance and entered an underground youth workers' movement. He was arrested in 1942 and imprisoned eventually in Dachau. After the war, he held the position of district secretary of the communist youth organization ČSM in Ústí nad Labem. From 1946 to 1949, Putík studied journalism at the Institute of Political and Social Sciences in Prague. After that, until 1952, he was affiliated with the Prague newspaper *Lídové noviny*. When the paper was shut down, Putík was employed as editor of the important literary weekly *Literární noviny* from 1953 to 1959, later shifting to the cultural journals *Tvorba* and *Kulturní tvorba*. In the late 1950s, he began publishing reportage based on his many trips abroad. In the early 1960s, he made his debut as a writer of short stories and novels in which he assumes the role of a social critic. These works include *Zed'* (The Wall, 1962); *Indicie* (Indices, 1963); *Dálky* (Distances, 2nd ed., 1964); *Pozvání k soudu: Kniha zpovědi* (Summoned to the Bar: A Book of Confessions, 1964), a collection of stories; and *Smrtelná neděle* (Fatal Sunday, 1967). He won his first literary prize in 1968 and from 1968 to 1970 served as managing editor of the liberal cultural journal *Orientace*. However, the journal was forced to close down in the wake of the suppression of the "Prague Spring," and Putík was prohibited from further publication. Until the downfall of the communist regime, his only outlets for his writing were samizdat and Czech exile publishers. His major work, the novel *Muž s břitvou* (The Man with the Razor), was published outside Czechoslovakia in 1984. A warm, generally entertaining first-person narrative, it views ordinary Czech society from the late 1930s to postwar communism from the perspective of the narrator's uncle, a small-town barber, who spends his last days on an ocean beach in the company of "a conspicuously dark young woman." The novel was much admired for Putík's keen but gentle analysis of a disenchanted generation and was honored with a Czech émigré literary prize. It was followed by several other works in the late 1980s and early 1990s: *Volný let voliérou* (Flying Free in an Aviary), published first by Edice Petlice in 1988 and then in Czechoslovakia in 1990, an ironic novel about how a disparate group of people hope to change their humdrum lives in a freedomless society by joining an expedition to Mount Kilimanjaro, which they ultimately are unable to go on; *Odchod ze zámku* (Leaving the Castle, 1991), an essentially political work about the changes in Czechoslovakia after the fall of communism; *Odysea po česku* (A Czech-style Odyssey, 1992); *Proměny mladého muže* (Transformations of a Young Man, 1992); and *Plyšový pes* (The Plush Dog, 1996), a novel.

Translations: *Svědomí: Případ profesora Oppenheimera* (Conscience: The Case of Professor Oppenheimer, 2nd ed., 1960), on the American nuclear physicist J. Robert Oppenheimer (1904–1967), is available in German as *Der Fall Oppenheimer,* 2nd rev. ed., trans. Ben Budar (Bautzen: Domowina, 1961), and "Pozváni k soudu" as "Ladung vor Gericht," trans. Franz Peter Kunzel, in *Prag erzählt,* ed. Peter Sacher (Frankfurt am Main: Fischer, 1997), 178–86.

Q

Qosja, Rexhep (b. 1936) Kosovo Albanian novelist, short-story writer, and essayist. A native of Priština, Kosovo, Qosja was a professor of Albanian and comparative literature at least until the massive depopulation of the city and NATO bombing of it during the Kosovo war of April and May 1999. He made his mark early as a scholar of Albanian language and literature with such publications as an anthology of Albanian poetry, *Antologjia e lirikës shqipe* (1970); a two-volume history of Romanticism in Albania, *Historia e letërsisë shqipe: Romantizmi* (1984); two volumes of literary essays, *Epizode letrare* (Literary Episodes, 1967) and *Kritika letrare* (Literary Criticism, 1969); a book on nineteenth-century Albanian literature, *Dialogje më shkrimtaret* (1979); one on twentieth-century Albanian literature, *Shkrimtare dhe periudha* (1975); two studies of Albanian philology, *Nocione te rija albanologjike* (1983) *and Panteoni i rralluar:*

Studime, kritika, ese (1988); and a book on society and culture, *Anatomia e kulturës* (The Anatomy of Culture, 1976). He has also written extensively on the plight of the Albanian nation, notably *Çështja shqiptare* (The Albanian Question, 1995), as well as two books on the situation of Albanians in Yugoslavia: *Nezaštićena sudbina: O Albancima u Jugoslaviji danas* (Defenseless Destiny: The Albanians in Yugoslavia Today, 1990), in Serbo-Croatian, and *Populli i ndaluar* (The Forbidden People, 1992).

Apart from a collection of three plays, *Mite te zhveshura* (Naked Myths, 1978), Qosja's major fictional work is the novel *Vdekja më vjen prej syve të tillë* (Death Comes to Me from Eyes Such as These, 1974). Consisting of thirteen stories that "can also be a novel" (as the subtitle informs), the work weaves a rich tapestry of everyday Kosovo Albanian life in the town of Vajazan against the background of the political currents of the late 1950s and 1960s. Its central character is a local writer named Xhezair Gjika, who is working on a novel set in the Middle Ages and through which Kosovo history and legend blend with a colorful cast of characters in the present. Although the novel was written in the aftermath of Tito's alleviation in 1966 of the campaign of harassment of the Kosovo Albanians, Qosja all but prophesies a future resumption of active hostilities against the Kosovars. This indeed happened in the spring of 1981, with a worse deterioration of the situation after 1989 when Slobodan Milošević came to power in Serbia.

Translations: *Çështja shqiptare* is available in French as *La Question albanaise,* trans. Christian Gut (Paris: Fayard, 1995); *Vdekja më vjen prej syve të tillë* in French as *La Mort me vient de ces yeux-là,* trans. Christian Gut (Paris: Gallimard, 1994), and in German as *In solchen Augen liegt der Tod,* trans. Joachim Röhm, with an afterword by Ismail Kadare (Innsbruck: Haymon-Verlag, 1995).

R

Radichkov, Iordan (b. 1929) Bulgarian novelist and short-story writer. One of the most prolific and highly regarded writers of prose fiction in post–World War II Bulgaria, Radichkov was born in the now no longer existing village of Kalimanitsa, in the Mihailovgrad district in northwestern Bulgaria. After an early education in the village school, he graduated from high school in Berkovitsa in 1947. However, he was prevented from continuing his education by a severe case of tuberculosis, for which he had to be confined for some time to a sanatorium in Iskrets, near Sofia, before being able to return home. Radichkov began his career first as a correspondent for the youth periodical *Narodna mladezh* in 1951. From 1952 to 1954, he served as an editor at the same periodical. In 1954 he left *Narodna mladezh* to join the editorial staff of the newspaper *Vecherni novinii*, a position he held until 1960. After spending the next two years as a member of the Script Commission of Bulgarian Cinematography, he became an editor and a member of the editorial board of *Literaturen front*. This lasted until 1969. From 1973 to 1986, Radichkov was an adviser to the Bulgarian Council of State on the development of spiritual values in society. For the next three years (1986–1989), he was the assistant head of the Bulgarian Writers Union.

Radichkov's early stories appeared in such newspapers as *Narodna mladezh* and *Literaturen front*. His first collection of stories was published in 1959 under the title *Surtseto bie za horata* (The Heart Beats for the People). Here, as in subsequent collections of stories, he took a particular interest in rural Bulgaria and, especially, the dislocations and irrevocable transformation of village life as a result of the massive program of collectivization. A number of his stories are set in the fictional village of Cherkaski, which resembles his own native village. Obviously emotionally attached to the traditional folkways, yet cognizant of the inevitability of change under the postwar communist regime, Radichkov developed an engaging and colorful style, partly indebted to folklore, often poetic in its imagery, and lyrical. His writing can demonstrate an admirable inventiveness, a sense of humor, and a tongue-in-cheek blend of the mundane with touches of fantasy. After *Surtseto bie za horata*, Radichkov brought out another five collections of stories in much the same style: *Prosti rutse* (Rough Hands, 1961); *Oburnato nebe* (The Overturned Sky, 1962); *Planinsko tsvete* (The Mountain Flower, 1964); *Sharena cherga* (A Multicolored Rug, 1964); and *Goreshto pladne* (Hot Noon, 1964). Beginning with his next collection, *Svirepo nastroenie* (A Fierce Temper, 1965), Radichkov demonstrated a growing willingness to move away from the style of his earlier stories and to experiment with less traditional narrative structures. Many of the stories of the 1960s and 1970s, for example, use techniques of the absurd and grotesque (on which, in fact, a German study has been published). This is especially true of such collections as *Vodolei* (The Water Carrier, 1967); *Pliava i zurno* (Chaff and Grain, 1972); and *Kak taka?* (How Come?, 1974). The healing power of nature as a means of overcoming the common urban problem of alienation was also addressed by Radichkov in some of the stories and novellas in the collections *Koziata brada* (The Goat's Beard, 1967) and *Spomeni za kone* (Memories of Horses, 1975). Radichkov's other collections of short fiction include *Viaturut na spokoistvieto* (The Wind of Tranquillity, 1967); *Nie, vrabchetata* (We the Sparrows, 1968); *Choveshka proza* (Prose for People, 1971); *Nezhnata spirala* (The Tender Spiral, 1983); *Po vodata* (Along the Water, 1983); *Skakalets* (Grasshopper, 1984); *Verbliud* (Camel, 1984);

Tenekienoto petle (The Tin-plated Cockerel, 1985); *Akustichnoto gurne* (The Acoustical Jar, 1996); and, his most recent book, *Umivane litseto na Bogoroditsa* (Washing the Virgin Mary's Face, 1998). A collection of his short stories and novels, *Avtostradata* (The Highway), was published in 1999 in honor of Radichkov's seventieth birthday.

Radichkov wrote several novels along more or less the same lines as his shorter prose fiction of the 1960s and 1970s: *Kozheniiat pupesh* (The Leather Musk Melon, 1969); *Baruten bukvar* (Gunpowder Primer, 1969); *Ianuari* (January, 1978); *Prashka* (The Ribbon) and *Vsichki i nikoi* (Everybody and Nobody), both dating from 1979; *Luda treva* (Wild Grass, 1981); *Izpadnali ot karutsata na Boga* (They Fell from the Wagon of God, 1984); and *Noev kovcheg* (Noah's Ark, 1988). Although in essence a travelogue, *Neosvetenite dvorove* (Unlit Yards, 1966), subtitled a "Novel-travel Book," straddles the genres of travel book and novel and has for some time been regarded as one Radichkov's best works. In an interesting oscillation between present and past, reality and dream, and North and South, the "novel-travel book" carries its readers from Sweden to the vastness of Siberia.

In 1973 Radichkov was awarded the International Prize for Fantastic Literature by the Polish Ministry of Culture, and in 1976 he won the Special Prize of the European Friends of the Fantastic.

Literature: Dorothee Gelhard, *Absurdes in Jordan Radičkovs "Lazarica": Versuch einer tiefenpsychologischen Deutung* (Wiesbaden: Harrassowitz, 1995), a study of the absurd in *Lazaritsa*; Encho Mutafov, *Iordan Radichkov* (Sofia: Bulgarski pisatel, 1986), an introductory monograph; Dimitur Staikov, *Teaturut na Iordan Radichkov* (Sofia: Sveti Klimat Okhridski, 1993), a study of Radichkov's plays.

Translations: *Hot Noon*, trans. Peter Tempest (Sofia: Sofia Press, n.d.); *January,* trans. Bogdan Athanassov (Sofia: Press and Information Centre of the Committee of Culture, 1982).

Radinska, Valentina (b. 1951) Bulgarian poet and translator. A native of Sliven, Radinska graduated from high school in Sliven in 1969 and then studied Bulgarian literature at Sofia University for the next two years. After that, she continued her literary studies in Moscow and graduated from the Gorky Institute of World Literature in 1976. From 1978 to 1979, she worked as an editor at *Narodna mladezh* before joining the Bulgarian Feature Film Studio, also as an editor. Radinska's published poetry is contained in the volumes *Kum men vurvi chovek* (A Man Walks Toward Me, 1977); *Noshtna kniga* (Night Book, 1983); *Ne* (No, 1989); *Chistilishte* (Purgatory, 1992); and *Vsichko* (Everything, 1995). Radinska writes in a very personal vein about the hardship of writing poetry, about the power of truth, and about the tensions between the individual and his or her surroundings. Many of her poems have nocturnal settings in which night and darkness comfort and disturb at the same time. Her collection *Ne* clearly establishes her emotional and intellectual distance from a totalitarian system. Radinska has translated extensively from Russian literature, including works by Anna Akhmatova, Marina Tsvetaeva, and Bella Akhmadulina.

Translations: Two poems, trans. Belin Tonchev, in *Young Poets of a New Bulgaria: An Anthology,* ed. Belin Tonchev (London: Forest, 1990), 101–3; one poem, trans. Michael Collier, in *Window on the Black Sea: Bulgarian Poetry in Translation,* ed. Richard Harteis, in collaboration with William Meredith (Pittsburgh: Carnegie Mellon University Press, 1992), 162.

Radoev, Ivan (b. 1927) Bulgarian poet, playwright, and short-story writer. An important poet and dramatist after World War II,

Radoev was born in Pordim, where he had his early schooling. After graduating from high school in Pleven in 1946, he worked in construction brigades in Bulgaria and Czechoslovakia in 1947 and 1948. He subsequently studied law and then Bulgarian language and literature at Sofia University. From 1955 to 1957, he was an editor at such papers as *Sturshel, Rodni krile,* and *Bulgarski voin.* Radoev began writing and publishing poems in various newspapers just before World War II. Prior to the appearance of his first volume of poetry, *Shumiat znamenata* (The Banners Rustle), in 1951, most of his poems from the late 1940s revolved around his participation in the big construction projects of the time and were carried by such papers as *Vedrina, Narodna mladezh, Literaturen biuletin,* and *Literaturen front.* The poems in *Shumiat znamenata* are similar in nature and, like those inspired also by nature and village life, are youthfully exuberant, fresh, and unpretentious. Notwithstanding the favorable reception of his first book of poetry, Radoev found himself under attack following the publication in *Literaturen front* in 1952 of a series of love poems, which he had written after 1944. Because the poems deviated from the norms of socialist realism, they were denounced by Marxist critics as sexual and morally decadent. As the tempo of villification increased, Radoev found it harder to remain in Sofia and took up residence in Sliven and then in Burgas, on the Black Sea. His next major collection of verse, *Stihotvoreniia* (Poems), came out in 1958 and marked a transition from the passionate love lyrics of the *Literaturen front* series to a more reflective, skeptical, and ironic poetic writing. Radoev published another work of poetry, *Baladichna poema* (A Balladic Poem), in 1960, before declaring a personal moratorium on the further writing of poetry for the next fifteen years. The continuing attacks against him had taken their toll, and he decided to set poetry aside indefinitely and turn his attention to drama.

Radoev's first play, *Svetut e maluk* (The World Is Small), subtitled a "Novella in Four Acts," was published in 1962. It is a love story about two young people in the uncertain social and political conditions of the period. It was followed the next year by *Odiseia: Luzha v 2 chasti* (The Odyssey: A Lie in Two Acts, 1963). As he began to become better known for his playwriting and interest in the stage, Radoev was offered the position of dramatic director of the National Opera in Sofia. He accepted and remained in that capacity from 1963 to 1968. During that period, he wrote the six-act play *Goliamoto zavurshtvane* (The Big Conclusion, 1965). In 1969 Radoev became editor in chief of Bulgarian TV, and from 1970 to 1972 was artistic director of the Sulza i smiah (Tears and Laughter) Theater. From 1972 to 1986, he held a similar position at the Sofia Theater, and from 1986 to 1990 was the artistic director of the theater in Pernik. Radoev's other plays include a collection of one-acters under the title *Nie ne sme umoreni* (We're Not Tired, 1969) and consisting of "Avtostop" ("Hitchhike"), "Petrol" ("Gas"), "Dzhudo" ("Judo"), and "Romeo i Zhulieta" ("Romeo and Juliet"); *Morskoto ravnishte* (Sea Level, 1970); *Cherveno i kafiavo* (Black and Brown, 1972); *Izbrani piesi* (Collected Plays, 1977); *Chovekoiadkata* (The Man Eater, 1979); *Goliamoto kuche na malkiia Ivancho* (The Big Dog for Little Ivancho, 1981); *Bivolut* (The Water Buffalo, 1981); *Sun* (Night Dream, 1987), a "dramatic comedy"; *Dramatichni komedii* (Dramatic Comedies, 1987); and *Taralezh* (Hedgehog, 1988), a contemporary domestic "dramatic comedy" about the unexpected visit to a rather ordinary family by a rookie journalist. Radoev's combination of contemporary Bulgarian settings and a light, humorous touch proved the right formula for successful playwriting and did much to establish his reputation.

In 1975, after a hiatus of fifteen years, Radoev resumed the publication of poetry. His first new collection was *Edin bial list* (One Blank Sheet), arguably his best book of poetry, its title referring to the period of his silence. The poetry in it differs from his preceding verse by its greater use of metaphor and abstractness as well as by its tendency toward the absurd and grotesque, as in such poems as "Balada za istoricheskiia materializum" ("Ballad for Historical Materialism") and "Balada za dialekticheskiia materializum" ("Ballad for Dialectical Materialism"). *Edin bial list* was followed by several other volumes: the new–old anthology *Stihotvoreniia i poemi* (Short and Long Poems, 1978); *Greshni sunishta: Stihotvoreniia i poemi* (Sinful Suns: Short and Long Poems, 1987); *Pesuchinki-zhivotinki* (Grains of Sand, Little Creatures, 1990); *Bialo potuvane* (White Submergence, 1992); *Da bude liubov* (Long Live Love, 1993); *Rakiia za boga* (A Toast to God, 1994); *Religii* (Religions, 1994), a small collection whose title poem is borrowed from the 1992 collection *Bialo potuvane* and that includes—besides newer poems about solitude, the passing of time, and a certain longing for easier faith—poems of a generally reflective nature from the 1960s and 1970s, especially the longest, "Zhenite, koito sliazat prez poleto" ("Women Who Crawl Across the Field," 1960), which appeared originally in *Edin bial list*; and another fairly large volume of selected poems, *Svurzvane* (Connections, 1997), illustrated with photographs.

Translations: Five poems in *Clay and Star: Contemporary Bulgarian Poetry,* trans. and ed. Lisa Sapinkopf and Georgi Belev (Minneapolis: Milkweed, 1992), 55–61; five poems, trans. Daniel Hoffman, in *Window on the Black Sea: Bulgarian Poetry in Translation,* ed. Richard Harteis, in collaboration with William Meredith (Pittsburgh: Carnegie Mellon University Press, 1992), 95–101.

Radulović, Jovan (b. 1951) Serbian short-story writer, novelist, and playwright. An interesting and colorful writer, Radulović was born in Polače, near the city of Knin, not far from the Bosnian border in western Croatia. This region of Serbian and Bosnian Dalmatia figures in much of his writing. After attending local schools, Radulović subsequently received a degree in Serbo-Croatian language and Yugoslav literature from Belgrade University. His first important publication was a collection of short stories titled *Ilinštak* (The Month of July, 1978). The book was awarded the October Prize of the City of Belgrade but was retracted two days afterward by order of the Belgrade town council, apparently for political reasons. Radulović's next publication was a second collection of stories, *Golubnjača* (The Pigeon's Abyss, 1980), followed in 1983 by a dramatized version of the title story. The prose collection won a literary prize in Zagreb; the stage version was produced, to much acclaim, at a festival of small and experimental theaters in Nova Gorica. Radulović's first novel, *Braća po materi* (Half Brothers), came out in 1986 and was made into a successful film as well as a television series. The film version of the novel was honored at an international film festival in Prague. The novel deals with two brothers, twenty years apart in age, born to the same mother but with different fathers. The younger brother (Veselin) has been convicted of a senseless murder. The older brother addresses eight letters to him intended primarily to acquaint the younger brother with the other side of the family history and events with which he is presumably unfamiliar. The narrative parts of the book, each with its own heading, relate events in Veselin's life leading up to the murder and vignettes of Serbian life in Dalmatia reflective of the long-standing Serb–Croat animosity in the region. The novel concludes with a strange twist as the narrator (the older brother) declares that he has no younger brother, that he has in fact written no letters, and that the whole story has been invented.

In 1988 Radulović published a collection of three novellas under the title *Dalje ot oltara* (Far from the Altar). The collection, which won won the prestigious Andrić Prize as well as the Isidora Sekulić Prize, contains "Dalje ot altara" ("Far from the Altar"), a story about moral wrongdoing among monks; "Sa obe strane" ("From Both Sides"), about the family of Gavrilo Princip, the assassin of the Austrian archduke Franz Ferdinand and his wife in Sarajevo in 1914; and "Linea Grimani" ("The Grimani Line"), the best story in the collection, about the fate of a greedy innkeeper on the old Italian–Bosnian border .

Radulović's second novel, *Prošao život* (Life Has Passed Away, 1997), is a quasi-epistolary work initiated by the deceased Dalmatian Serb schoolteacher Pojka Močivuna and continued by other members of her circle now resident in various cemeteries in Dalmatia. The "letters," really reminiscences, range from Hapsburg imperial times to the present and shed light on the hardships experienced by the Serbs of Dalmatia and their efforts to preserve their native culture. Radulović's interest in Serbian Dalmatian history is also much in evidence in his book *Po srpskoj Dalmaciji* (Through Serbian Dalmatia, 1995), a collection spanning two decades of fairly short historical and other pieces, some on what he terms "Dalmatian Kosovo"; previously published interviews with Radulović about his works and views; and correspondence related to his literary awards.

As a playwright, Radulović is known best for *Učitelj Dositej* (The Teacher Dositej, 1990). The play is based on the real-life story of the well-known Serbian enlightener Dositej Obradovič, who appears in the work as a younger monk and teacher anxious to travel to the great libraries in Greece, Russia, and elsewhere to further his knowledge and for whom local ignorance and superstition have become oppressive. In 1993 a collection of Radulović's dramatic works appeared under the title *Drame* (Plays). Radulović works and lives in Belgrade, where he has been affiliated with the BIGZ publishing house. Apart from the Andrić and Sekulić prizes, he has been awarded the October Prize of the City of Belgrade, the Joakim Vujič Prize for Drama, and the Braća Micić Prize.

Translations: "Linea Grimani," trans. Višeslav Simić, in *The Prince of Fire: An Anthology of Contemporary Serbian Short Stories,* ed. Radmila J. Gorup and Nadežda Obradović (Pittsburgh: University of Pittsburgh Press, 1998), 286–98.

Rainov, Bogomil (b. 1919) Bulgarian novelist, short-story writer, poet, playwright, art historian, and essayist. One of the most prolific and varied contemporary Bulgarian writers, Rainov is the son of the novelist Nikola Rainov (1889–1954). He was born in Sofia, where he received his early education and graduated from high school in 1938. He earned a degree in philosophy from Sofia University in 1943. A communist loyalist throughout his career, Rainov participated in the antifascist opposition in Bulgaria in the late years of World War II. After the war, from 1944 to 1946, he was affiliated with the workers' journal *Rabotnichesko delo,* Radio Sofia, and Radio Motherland (operated by the Ministry of War). He has been assistant editor in chief of *Sturshel* (1947–1953), editor in chief of the art journal *Hudozhnik* (1949–1950), assistant editor in chief of *Septemvri* (1950–1953), editor in chief of the art magazine *Izkustvo,* and assistant editor in chief (1960–1963) and then editor in chief (1966–1970) of *Literaturen front.* Rainov also found time to pursue an academic career and in 1954 became professor of aesthetics at the Higher Institute of Art in Sofia, a position he held until 1986. From 1953 to 1960, he also served as the cultural attaché to the Bulgarian Embassy in Paris.

Known mostly for his prose fiction, Rainov in fact made his literary debut with a volume of poems, *Stihove* (Poems), published in 1940, and continued to publish poetry throughout his career. A second volume, *Stihotvoreniia* (Poems), appeared in 1941. The lyrical poem *Liuboven kalendar* (Love Diary) came out in 1942 and was followed in 1944 by an encomium to Stalin. A similarly politically motivated collection of poems in honor of the Five-Year Plan came out in 1951 under the title *Stihove za piatiletka* (Poems for the Five-Year Plan). Rainov's other books of poetry include *Stihove* (Poems, 1962); *Gradski vetrove* (City Winds, 1969), a volume of selected poems; *Kraiat na putia: Stihove* (The Edge of the Road: Poems, 1988); and *Stupki po piasuka: Stihove* (Tracks in the Sand: Poems, 1989), a collection of fifty years of poetry (1936–1986).

Rainov's first published work of prose was the journalistic novel *Putuvane delnika* (Journey into the Workday, 1945), a collection of sociologically oriented glimpses of everyday life in Sofia constructed along the lines of montage. It was followed in the late 1940s and early 1950s by several books of art criticism and aesthetics, including an attack on Western art under the title *Protiv izkustvoto na imperializma* (Against the Art of Imperialism, 1951). This pattern of shifting from poetry to expository prose to fiction and back again would continue throughout Rainov's career. His first purely fictional published book was a collection of stories, *Chovekut ot ugula* (The Man at the Corner, 1958). The collection as a whole contains the elements of much of Rainov's subsequent fiction: an emphasis on the psychology of his characters; a growing tendency toward the development of plot out of the behavior of an individual, often a loner type,

placed in out-of-the-ordinary situations; a certain cosmopolitanism achieved through foreign (generally Western) settings; an ideologically rooted social and moral contrast between East and West, to the obvious disadvantage of the latter; and a well-paced narrative style. Rainov's subsequent collections of stories and novellas include *Duzhdovna vecher* (The Rainy Evening, 1961), a collection of novellas; *Kakto samo nie umirame* (If We But Survive, 1961), a novella; *Noshtni bulevardi* (Nocturnal Boulevards, 1963), a collection of three novellas; *Sinite tsvetia: Izbrani razkazi* (Blue Flowers: Selected Stories, 1967); *Moiata nepoznata: Izbrani razkazi i povesti* (My Unknown: Selected Stories and Tales, 1969); *V siankata na grada: Razkazi* (In the Shadow of the City: Stories, 1973); *Razkazi i povesti* (Stories and Tales, 1978); and *Iungfrau i izbrani noveli* (Jungfrau and Other Novellas, 1986).

Rainov published a large number of novels—sometimes three in a single year—much along the lines of his shorter fiction. Certainly to be reckoned among the best of these are *Inspekorut u noshtata* (*The Inspector in the Dark*, 1964), the first of a series of detective novels that also includes *Gospodin Nikoi* (Mr. Nobody, 1967) and *Tri sreshti s inspektora* (Three Encounters with the Inspector, 1970), in which the crime-fiction genre is used as a prism through which to view contemporary society; *Putishta za nikude* (*Roads to Nowhere*, 1966), a partly autobiographical and philosophical work written in the wake of the denunciations of the Stalinist "cult of personality"; *Niama nishto po-hubavo ot loshoto vreme* (There's Nothing Better than Bad Weather, 1967), a brisk novel about international economic espionage set in Venice and Amsterdam; *Chernite lebedi* (Black Swans, 1977), a psychologically interesting work about a ballerina who works to master her profession despite a perception of a lack of innate talent; and *Tozi stranen zanaiat* (This

Strange Profession, 1976), an autobiographical novel about Rainov himself as a writer and the first of an autobiographical series that includes the novellas *Tiutiuneviiat chovek* (The Tobacco Colored Man, 1976), *Putiat za Santa Krus* (The Trip to Santa Cruz, 1976), and *Elegiia za murtvite dni* (Elegy for a Dead Day, 1976), essentially a book of remembrances of his father, as well as the novel *Tretiiat put* (The Third Way, 1977). Also of interest are such novels as *Brazilska melodiia* (Brazilian Melody, 1966) and *Taifuni s nezhni imena* (Typhoons with Tender Names, 1977), which typify Rainov's fondness for the combination of intrigue and exotic settings. His most recently published novel, *Chenge vtora upotreba* (Secondhand Snoop, 2000), falls into the pattern of Rainov's detective fiction. Although he also wrote a few plays, Rainov's dramatic writing is the least significant aspect of his literary output.

Some of Rainov's other works on art, society, and literature include a monograph (1962) on the French artist Théophile Alexandre Steinlen (1859–1923); a "lecture" on the freedom of the artist in the bourgeois world (1966); a monograph on mass culture (1974); a study of Degas, Cézanne, and Van Gogh (1982); a two-part collection of literary-essays under the title *Tainata* (The Secret, 1984); and a book on African sculpture. A growing interest in theosophy led to his book on Helena Blavatsky: *Tainoto uchenie: Nachalo i razvitie na teosofiiata* (The Secret Learning: The Beginning and Evolution of Theosophy, 1991).

Rainov was well traveled and generally wove his experiences into his fiction. However, early in his career, in 1952, he brought out a book of travel notes based on trips to Israel, the Soviet Union, and Hungary: *Putni belezhki ot Izrael, SSSR i Ungariia*. A certain interest in Israel is reflected as well in his politically motivated *Putishtata na tsionizma* (The Paths of Zionism), which

appeared in 1969, a year after the Six-Day War in the Middle East that triggered widespread anti-Israeli denunciations throughout the communist world.

Literature: Svetlozar Igov, *Bogomil Rainov* (Sofia: Bulgarski pisatel, 1986), a fair general introduction.

Translations: *The Absurdities of an Investigation* (Sofia: Sofia Press, 1984), about the assassination attempt on Pope John Paul II in 1981 by Mehmet Ali Agca; *Inspector in the Dark and Other Stories*, trans. Theodora Athanassova and Nevena Geliazkova (Sofia: Foreign Languages Press, 1967); *Roads to Nowhere*, trans. Teodorova Atanassova (Sofia: Sofia Press, 1968), a collection of six of Rainov's best-known shorter works, the longest of which is the novella from which the collection derives its name; three poems, in versions by Roy MacGregor-Hastie, in *Modern Bulgarian Poetry*, comp. Bozhidar Bozhilov (Sofia: Sofia Press, 1976), 86–91, a Bulgarian–English edition.

Rákos, Sándor (b. 1921) Hungarian poet. A major post–World War II poet, Rákos was born in the town of Kálmánháza, in northeastern Hungary. Although he studied economics for two years (1942–1944) after graduating from high school, he never earned a degree, opting instead to try to make a career in journalism. He held a variety of editorial positions in the 1940s, including, as of 1949, at the large Szépirodalmi Könyvkiadó publishing house in Budapest. However, by 1952 Rákos had decided to devote himself entirely to his writing. Although he had been writing poetry in the late 1930s, he made his publishing debut in 1949 with the volume *Az eb válaszol* (The Dog Answers Back), which with its preoccupation with youthful restlessness and rebelliousness underscores the problems of postwar adjustment, particularly among the young. It was followed by the similarly oriented collection *Férfikor* (Manhood, 1952). In 1962 Rákos brought out a volume of selected poems from the period 1939 to 1961 titled *Fák, viharban* (Trees in the Storm). An inclination toward the ancient past and exotic peoples and cultures, as if refuges from the harsh realities of postwar life in communist Hungary, already began manifesting itself in Rákos's career as early as the late 1950s. In 1960, for example, he published a translation of the ancient Mesopotamian epic *Gilgamesh* and followed it up with a book of antiquity-inspired verse titled *Agyagtáblák üzenete* (The Message of the Terra-cotta Tablets, 1963). In 1976 he published a volume of folk poems from the South Sea islands: *Táncol a hullámsapkás tenger* (The Sea Dances to the Rhythm of the Waves, 1976). The enthusiasm for space and distance carried over into such subsequent volumes of Rákos's poetry as *Táguló körök* (Widening Circles, 1965) and *Az emlék jelene* (The Present of Memory, 1973). Arguably Rákos's most interesting collection of verse inspired by antiquity was his interpretation, rather than translation, of the *Carmina* (Songs) by the Roman poet Catullus (84–54 B.C.). Titled *Catullusi játékok* (*Catullan Games*) in Hungarian, the poems represent Rákos's attempt to enter into the spirit of the Catullus of the *Carmina* and to re-create the virtual Catullus, with whom he has identified psychologically in his own poetry. Justifiably, *Catullan Games* remains Rákos's only collection of poems translated into English. The poet as a fabricator of masks and the donning of a mask as a gesture of defiance against death, which appears in *Catullan Games,* reappear elsewhere in Rákos's poetry, as in the 1980s collections *Többedmagam* (I Myself and the Rest, 1986) and *Szólítások* (Summonings, 1988). Other major works by Rákos include the verse collection *Társasmonológ* (Joint Monologue, 1982); a collection of essays, studies, and other writings titled *Két vers között* (Between Two Verses, 1990; and *A*

csörte (The Bout, 1991), a volume of poems whose title sheds light on its contents—the poet's wrestling with older age and taking stock of his life. Rákos has won several important literary awards, including the Attila József Prize (1958, 1963, 1975); the Milán Füst Prize (1981); the Tibor Déry Prize (1988); and the Art Foundation Great Prize (1990).

Translations: *Catullan Games,* trans. Jascha Kessler with Maria Kőrösy (Marlboro, Vt.: Marlboro, 1989); three poems, trans. Alan Dixon and Daniel Hoffman, in *Modern Hungarian Poetry,* ed. Miklós Vajda (New York: Columbia University Press, 1977), 139–41.

Rakovszky, Zsuzsa (b. 1950) Hungarian poet. Born in Sopron, where she also received her early education, Rakovszky went on to Eötvös Lóránd University, from which she graduated in Hungarian and English in 1975. Following several years of work as a librarian and reader for the Helikon publishing house, she became a freelance poet and translator in 1986. Her first book of poetry appeared in 1981 under the title *Jóslatok és határidők* (Prophecies and Deadlines). Her second volume, *Tovább egy házzal* (One House Later, 1987), achieved still greater resonance. *Fehér-fekete* (White-Black), her third book of poetry, appeared in 1991 after the collapse of communism in Hungary. Her most recent collection of poems, *Egyirányú utca: Új versek, 1994–1997* (One-Way Street: New Poems, 1994–1997), was published in 1998. Rakovszky is an intellectual poet who often finds her material in the experiences and artifacts of everyday urban life, which she manages to infuse with a certain elusive sense of mystery. Her poems are constructed with much precision and formal discipline, but their tone overall is informal and even colloquial. In many, run-on verse and the absence of punctuation create the rhythm of almost breathless rapidity. Very much at home in English (she spent a year in London and in 1990 was a guest of the University of Iowa's International Writing Program), Rakovszky has translated several English and American poets and is sometimes likened to Sylvia Plath, Robert Lowell and Carol Ann Duffy. Rakovszky has won the (Robert) Graves and Déry prizes, and in 1998 was awarded the prestigious Attila József Prize.

Literature: George Szirtes, "Translating Zsuzsa Rakovszky," *Hungarian Quarterly* 39 (1998): 31–44.

Translations: *New Life,* trans. George Szirtes (Oxford: Oxford University Press, 1994).

Ralin, Radoi (real name Dimitur Stefanov Stoianov; b. 1923) Bulgarian poet, short-story writer, novelist, essayist, and screenwriter. Ralin was born in Sliven, where he received his early education. He later studied law at Sofia University. During World War II, he served as a war correspondent and continued in journalism after the war. His first book-length publication, *Voinishka tetradka* (War Notebook, 1955), was in fact based on his wartime experiences. As a writer, Ralin is known best for his wide-ranging satire and humor, which make up the overwhelming bulk of his published work, as is evident in most cases from their titles and subtitles: *Strogo poveritelno: Humoristichni stihotvoreniia i razkazi* (Strictly Confidential: Humorous Poems and Stories, 1956); *Istoriia s luv: Humoristichni razkazi* (Story with a Lion: Humorous Stories, 1958); *Vtoro razhdane: Humoristichni razkazi* (Second Childbirth: Humorous Stories, 1959); *Nepredvideni chuvstva* (Unforeseen Feelings, 1959); *Bezopasni igli: Epigrami* (Harmless Needles: Epigrams, 1960); *Halosni patroni: Humoristichni razkazi i epigrami* (Lame-brained Patrons: Humorous Stories and Epigrams, 1962); *Vnimatelni feiletoni* (Thoughtful Feuil-

letons, 1963); *Ispravlennaia oshibka: Feiletoni* (Corrected Error: Feuilletons, 1963); *Lirika* (Lyrics, 1965); *Lichen kontakt: Satiricheski stihove* (Personal Contact: Satirical Verse, 1965); *Molia, zapoviadaite! Epigrami* (Please, Help Yourself! Epigrams, 1966); *Duhut i vtoroto shishe: Feiletoni i epigrami* (The Spirit and the Second Bottle: Feuilletons and Epigrams, 1967); *Liuti chushki: Narodni epigrami* (Hot Peppers: Folk Epigrams, 1968); *Esenni kupini* (Autumn Blackberries, 1972); *Obstoiatelstva: Predishni i po predishni stihove, 1940–1968* (Circumstances: Previous and Earlier Poems, 1940–1968, 1973); *Vsichko mi govori: Stihotvoreniia* (Everything Talks to Me: Poems, 1975); *Hliab i portokali* (Bread and Oranges, 1975); *Niama nachin, Hamlete! Humoristichni razkazi* (There's No Way Out, Hamlet! Humorous Stories, 1978); *Apostrofi* (Apostrophes, 1980); *Harakteri horski: Satirichni eseta* (Other Personalities: Satirical Essays, 1980); *Shte doide leto: Lirichna povest* (Summer Will Come: A Lyrical Novel, 1981); *Voina i mir v tri stranitsi: Feiletoni i paraboli* (War and Peace in Three Pages: Feuilletons and Parabolas, 1982); *Epigrami v ramki* (Epigrams in Frames, 1983); *Stihotvoreniia* (Poems, 1984); *Izbrani tvorbi v dva toma* (Selected Works in Two Volumes, 1984); *Diavolska teritoriia: Satirichni eseta i epigrami* (The Devil's Territory: Satirical Essays and Epigrams, 1986); *Ezopiida: Basni* (The Aesopiad: Fables, 1987); *Kadrovikut Teofrast: Satirichni eseta* (Personnel Department Head Theophrastus: Satirical Essays, 1987); *Usmivkite na Pancho Vladigerov* (The Smiles of Pancho Vladigerov, 1987); *Posleden ponedelnik: Stihotvoreniia* (Last Monday: Poems, 1988); *Koilo—galena treva: Lirika* (Spoiled Grass: Lyrics, 1989); *Samorasliatsi: Aforizmi* (Wildings: Aphorisms, 1989); *Suvremenna prikazka za zlatnata ribka: Prikazka za vsichki vuzrasti* (A Contemporary Tale About the Golden Fish: A Fairy Tale for All Ages, 1990); *Zlatnoto runo: Opera za pevtsi bez glas* (The Golden Fleece: An Opera for Singers Without Voices, 1990); *Eskimoski plazh purzalki stalaktiti stalagmiti snezhni topki i s* (Eskimo Beach Toboggan Slides Stalactites Stalagmites Snowballs and So On, 1993); *Az sum Levski: Kinoroman* (I Am Levski: A Cine Novel, 1994); *Utesheniiata na Vasil Chertovenski: Roman v anekdoti* (Vasil Chertovenski's Consolation: A Novel in Anecdotes, 1994); and *Ehoto na usmivkata* (The Echo of Laughter, 1997). His last publication, *Profesiia za spomen* (Profession for Remembrance, 1998), is a book of memoirs.

Translations: Five poems in *Clay and Star: Contemporary Bulgarian Poets,* trans. and ed. Lisa Sapinkopf and Georgi Belev (Minneapolis: Milkweed, 1992), 40–46; two poems, in versions by Roy MacGregor-Hastie, in *Modern Bulgarian Poetry,* comp. Bozhidar Bozhilov (Sofia: Sofia Press, 1976), 132–35, a Bulgarian–English edition; nine poems, trans. Grace Cavalieri, Lawrence Ferlinghetti, and Robert Eberhart, in *Window on the Black Sea: Bulgarian Poetry in Translation,* ed. Richard Harteis, in collaboration with William Meredith (Pittsburgh: Carnegie Mellon University Press, 1992), 102–12.

Raos, Ivan (1921–1987) Croatian short-story writer, novelist, and playwright. A prolific and versatile writer strongly involved in the promotion of tourism in Croatia and Yugoslavia in the 1960s and 1970s, Raos was born in Medov Dolac. He graduated from high school in Split and then studied law at Zagreb University. He began his literary career in the 1950s as a playwright and short-story writer. With few exceptions, his plays are in the lighter vein or ironic—for example, *Bango-Bango* (1954), a "burlesque"; *Kako je New York dočekao Krista* (How New York Greeted Christ, 1956), a "sad play"; and *Autodafe moga oca* (My Father's Auto-da-fe, 1957), a "heroic tragedy." It was also in the 1950s that Raos published three one-act plays, each-consisting of three short "tales":

Tri ratne priče (Three War Stories, 1955); *Tri egzotične priče* (Three Exotic Tales, 1956); and *Tri groteske* (Three Grotesques, 1959). A volume of his collected plays appeared in 1970 under the title *Nemojte nam kosti pretresati* (Don't You Strip Our Bones). Raos's short stories also began appearing in the 1950s. *Gaudamada* (Unusual Tales), in the vein of the fantastic, came out in 1956. *Partija preferansa i druge neobične priče* (A Game of Preference and Other Unusual Tales) followed in 1965. The three-novella collection *Na početku kraj* (At the Beginning the End) appeared in 1969, and the major collection *60 pripovijedaka* (60 Stories) was published in 1980. *Vječno žalosni smijeh* (Eternally Sorrowful Laughter), a trilogy of longer stories, dates from 1965. Raos's best-known novels, a few reflective of his interest in national history and legend, include *Izabrat ćes gore* (You'll Choose Worse, 1964); *Prosjači & sinovi* (Beggars and Sons, 1971); *Župnik na kamenu* (The Parish Priest on the Stone, 1975); *Kraljičin vitez: Roman iz doba kraljice Jelena* (The Queen's Knight: A Novel from the Time of Queen Jelena, 1976); and *Gastarbajteri* (Guest Workers, 1982), about Yugoslav workers in Western Europe. In 1962 he published an autobiographical work under the title *Žalosni Gospin vrt: Kronika mego djéčastva* (The Sad Garden of Lady's Slippers: A Chronicle of My Youth). Raos is especially well known for his introductions to picture books extolling the natural beauties of Croatia and Yugoslavia. Those in English include *Beauties of Yugoslavia* (1966); *Sunny Adriatic* (1966); *Blue Adriatic* (1968); *City of Zagreb* (1968); *Adriatic Tourist Guide* (1969); *Zagreb and Its Surroundings: Tourist Guide* (1970); and *Croatia* (1974).

Translations: "A Game of Preference," trans. Graham McMaster, in *Croatian Tales of Fantasy* (Zagreb: The Bridge, 1996), 109–20.

Rathenow, Lutz (b. 1952) German poet and playwright. Rathenow was born in Jena, where he graduated from secondary school and studied German literature at Jena University from 1973 to 1977. After dismissal from the university on political grounds, he was employed as a transport worker until he moved to East Berlin in late 1977. Once in the capital, he spent most of his time writing unproduced plays for his own theater. He was prohibited from traveling abroad, but was unwilling to emigrate from the German Democratic Republic. A strongly activist poet, yet one given to dreams, Rathenow believed that he should remain in East Germany in order to have some hand in shaping it along new directions. He made his literary debut in 1980 with a book of short stories, *Mit dem Schlimmsten wurde schon gerechnet* (The Worst Ones Have Already Been Dealt With), in which he vents his hostility toward authoritarianism and the impediments to individual happiness imposed in such an environment. The contest between the individual and the state is an unequal one, and Rathenow's outlook is bleak. His perception of the absurdities of the system also inclines him toward elements of the fantastic and grotesque in his writing. Given its subject matter, the book could not be published in the GDR and made its first appearance in West Germany. Rathenow's first book of poetry, *Zangengeburt* (Forceps Delivery, 1982), which contains a mixture of rhymed and unrhymed texts along with prose poems from the period 1972 to 1982, is filled with similarly disturbing images, more intense in their impact because of his often laconic, direct style. Like his first collection of short stories, *Zangengeburt* was first published in West Germany, its publication in the GDR delayed until 1989. Rathenow's play texts are contained in the collections *Boden 411: Stücke zum Lesen und Texte zum Spielen* (Floor 411: Plays for Reading and Texts for Playing), first published in Munich in 1984, with echoes of the theater of the absurd,

both West and East European, and *Die lautere Bosheit: Satiren, Faststücke, Prosa* (The More Honorable Malice: Satires, Carnival Plays, Prose, 1992). His other books, written both before and after the downfall of the GDR, include *Ostberlin: Die andere Seite einer Stadt in Texten und Bildern* (East Berlin: The Other Side of a City in Texts and Pictures, 1984), published in Munich; *Zärtlich kreist die Faust* (Tenderly the Fist Revolves, 1988); *Revolt der Sinnlichkeit? Kunst in der DDR* (Revolt of Sensuality? Art in the GDR, 1989); *Verirrte Sterne oder Wenn alles wieder mal ganz anders kommt* (Mad Stars or If Everything Again Turns Out Otherwise, 1994); *Sisyphos* (Sisyphus, 1995), a collection of stories; and *Der Wettlauf mit dem Licht: Letzte Gedichte aus einem Jahrhundert* (The Race with Light: Last Poems of a Century, 1999).

Translations: Five poems, trans. Agnes Stein, in *Child of Europe: A New Anthology of East European Poetry*, ed. Michael March (London: Penguin, 1990), 61–66.

Rebula, Alojz (b. 1924) Slovenian novelist, short-story writer, playwright, diarist, and essayist. A leading representative of the Slovenian literary community in Trieste, Rebula was born in San Pelagio, near Trieste. After a secondary-school education in Slovenian schools in Trieste province, he received a degree in classical philology from Ljubljana University in 1949. He was thereafter employed for a number of years as a teacher and cultural activist in the Trieste Slovenian community. In 1960 he received his doctorate in Rome with a dissertation on Dante's *Divine Comedy* in Slavic translations. As a writer, Rebula has expressed his interests in ancient history; Roman Catholicism; Slovenehood, particularly in the case of the Trieste Slovenians; and, in a general sense, Mediterranean humanism. His first major publications, especially the short-story collection *Vinograd rimske cesarice in* *zgodnje novele* (The Vineyard of the Roman Empress and Early Stories, 1956), demonstrated the enthusiasm for fictionalized ancient Roman history and philosophical reflection that would characterize several of his subsequent books—above all, the novel long considered his masterpiece, *V Sibilinem vetru* (In the Sibylline Wind, 1968), which is set in the period of Marcus Aurelius. His later novels *Jutri čez Jordan* (Tomorrow the Jordan, 1988); *Maranatha, ali, Leto 999* (Maranatha, or, The Year 999, 1996); and *Pričevalci vstajenja* (Witnesses to the Resurrection, 1999), were written in a similar vein.

An ardent Catholic deeply interested in the place of Christianity and the Roman Catholic Church in the modern world, Rebula was also the author of such prose texts as *Krščanska avantura* (The Christian Adventure, 1970); *Lik Sinu Človekovega* (The Form of the Son of Man, 1972), about the character of Jesus Christ; *Jacques Maritain: Človek in mislec* (Jacques Matritain: Man and Thinker, 1981), about the renowned French Catholic philosopher; *Pastir prihodnosti: Lik Antona Martina Slomška* (The Pastor of the Future: A Portrait of Anton Martin Slomšek, 1992), a biography of a leading nineteenth-century Slovenian Catholic clergyman, Anton Martin Slomšek (1800–1862); *Pogovor v vinogradu: Alojz Rebula se pogovarja s nadškofom Alojzijem Šuštarjem ob njegovi petinsedemdesetletnici* (Conversation in the Vineyard: Alojz Rebula Converses with Archbishop Alojz Šuštarj on the Occasion of His Seventy-Fifth Birthday, 1995); and *Koraki apostolskih sandal: Dnevnik s sinode evropskih skofov v Rimu (28. november–14. december 1991)* (Steps of the Apostolic Sandals: A Diary of the Synod of European Bishops in Rome [28 November–14 December 1991], 1993). Rebula's fondness for the diary form, demonstrated in *Koraki apostolskih sandal,* is much in evidence in his literary canon. Two of his works

based on travel in the United States in the 1970s and 1980s are in diary form: *Oblaki Michigana: Ameriški dnevnik od 22. julija do 19. avgusta 1975* (The Clouds of Michigan: An American Diary from 22 July to 19 August 1975, 1985) and *Vrt bogov: Koloradski dnevnik* (The Summit of the Gods: A Colorado Diary, 1986). He previously had published a diary covering the period 20 October 1962 to 29 December 1964 under the title *Gorje zelenemu drevesu: Dnevnik . . .* (Woe to the Green Tree: A Diary, 1971). In 2000 Rebula published a new diary covering the years 1982 to 1985: *Ko proti jutru gre: Dnevnik, 1982–1985* (When You Oppose Tomorrow: A Diary, 1982–1985).

Rebula's major work of fiction with a contemporary setting is the obviously autobiographical novel *Senčni ples* (Dance in the Shade, 1960). Through the central character of a philosophically inclined writer and teacher of Slovenian in Trieste, it explores the clash of two cultures—in this case, the Italian and the Slovenian. Rebula's most recent work is a novel celebrating ten years of the independence of the Slovene state: *Jutranjice za Slovenijo: Roman o deseti obletnici slovenske državne osamosvojitve* (Morning Stars for Slovenia: A Novel About the Tenth Anniversary of Slovenian State Independence, 2000).

Translations: *Jutri čez Jordan* is available in French as *Demain, le Jourdain,* trans. Zdenka Simec (Paris: Cerf, 1997), and *V Sibilinem vetru* in Italian as *Nel vento della Sibilla* (Trieste: Editoriale stampa triestina, 1992).

Reimann, Brigitte (1933–1973) German novelist and short-story writer. Reimann was born in Burg, near Magdeburg. After graduating from secondary school and working at odd jobs for several years, she was accepted in 1953, the year of her marriage, into the study group of Young Writers of the East German Writers Association. After recovering from a miscarriage and a failed suicide attempt in 1954, Reimann advanced in her literary career over the next two years. Her first story, *Der Tod der schönen Helena* (The Death of the Beautiful Helena), appeared in 1955, followed by the story *Die Frau am Pranger* (The Woman in the Pillory) in 1956, the year she was admitted into the Writers Association. After divorce and remarriage (she would divorce and remarry two more times, in 1964 and 1970/1971), Reimann, an idealist who was full of enthusiasm for socialist reconstruction, moved in 1960 to Hoyerswerda, the site of the huge "Black Pump" construction project. She remained there until she contracted cancer and resettled in Neubrandenberg in 1968 after treatment in Berlin. In the period Reimann was at Hoyerswerda, she published several smaller works, among them *Das Geständnis* (The Confession, 1960); *Ankunft im Alltag* (Weekday Arrival, 1961); *Die Geschwister* (The Siblings, 1963); and the radio plays *Ein Mann steht vor der Tür* (A Man Is at the Door, 1960) and *Sieben Scheffel Salz* (Seven Bushels of Salt, 1960), which she wrote with her husband, Siegfried Pitschmann. In 1961 Reimann and Pitschmann received the Literary Prize of the Free German Federation of Trade Unions. *Die Frau am Pranger* was awarded the Literary Prize of the Free German Federation of Trade Unions in 1962. In 1963 Reimann was elected to the board of directors of the Writers Union and a member of the Youth Commission of the Central Committee of the ruling Socialist Unity Party. As a member of the Central Council of the Free German Youth organization, she made a trip to Siberia in 1964, which was the subject of a book of reportage titled *Das grüne Licht der Steppen: Tagebuch einer Sibirienreise* (The Green Light of the Steppes: Diary of a Siberian Journey, 1965). In 1965 Reimann was also awarded the Heinrich Mann Prize of the Academy of Arts of the GDR and the

Carl Blechen Prize of the Cottbus District Council for Art, Literature, and Artistic Folk Creativity. It was in Neubrandenberg, after leaving Hoyerswerda, that Reimann undertook her only important literary work, *Franciszka Linkerhand* (1974). An ambitious novel of skepticism and cynicism based on her own experiences and disillusionment, Reimann was still working on it when death claimed her at the age of forty. It was published, unfinished, in 1974. Since her death, several collections of her diaries and correspondence, which shed considerable light on her life and outlook, have been published. They include *Die geliebte, die verfluchte Hoffnung: Tagebücher und Briefe* (The Beloved and Damned Hope: Diaries and Letters, 1984); *Sei gegrüsst und lebe: Eine Freundschaft in Briefen, 1964–1973* (Greetings and Be Well: A Friendship in Letters, 1964–1973, 1993), a correspondence between Reimann and Christa Wolf; *Briefwechsel* (Correspondence, 1994), an exchange of letters between Reimann and the East German architect Hermann Henselmann (b. 1905); *Aber wir schaffen es, verlass dich drauf: Briefe an eine Freundin im Westen* (We'll Make Out All Right; Just Look Out for Yourself: Letters to a Friend in the West, 1995); *Ich bedaure nichts* (I Regret Nothing, 1997); and *Alles schmeckt nach Abschied: Tagebücher, 1964–1970* (Everything Tastes of Parting: Diaries, 1964–1970, 1998)

Renn, Ludwig (real name Arnold Friedrich Vieth von Golssenau; 1889–1979) German novelist and author of children's books. Born in Dresden, Renn served as an officer in World War I, after which he studied law, economics, and history at the universities of Göttingen, Munich, and Vienna. With his studies behind him, he traveled extensively on foot in southern Europe and the Middle East. He joined the Communist Party of Germany in 1928 and until 1932 was secretary of the Union of Proletarian-

Revolutionary Writers. He also edited the journals *Linkskurve* and *Aufbruch.* In the wake of the burning of the Reichstag in 1933, Renn was sentenced to two and a half years in prison but managed to escape to Switzerland. Like other German antifascists and communists, Renn took part in the Spanish Civil War on the side of the republic. With the defeat of the republic and the outbreak of World War II, Renn immigrated to Mexico and remained there until 1947. When he returned to Germany, he settled in his native Dresden, where he occupied himself primarily with literary matters.

Virtually all of Renn's works for adult audiences are autobiographical, including the novel that first brought him literary fame, *Krieg* (War, 1927). The novel bears a close kinship with similar works about World War I by Ernst Jünger, Erich Maria Remarque, and Arnold Zweig. Renn's first postwar novel, *Nachkrieg* (After the War, 1930), is a true-to-life picture of the social, economic, and political turmoil in Germany in the 1920s. Although he published a few novels after the establishment of the German Democratic Republic—*Der Neger Nobi* (Nobi the Black, 1955) and *Krieg ohne Schlacht* (War Without Battle, 1957)— Renn's more interesting post–World War II works were his personal accounts of service in the Spanish Civil War and his long exile in Mexico. Although *In Spanischen Krieg* (In the Spanish War, 1968) is less vivid and somewhat less detailed than Alfred Kantorowicz's diary-style *Spanisches Kriegstagebuch* (Diary of the War in Spain, 1966), it still sheds much light on the activities of the International Brigades. *In Mexiko* (In Mexico, 1979) is a collection of short pieces about various facets of Renn's life as a German exile in Mexico during and after World War II. As such, it complements the writings of Anna Seghers, Egon Erwin Kisch, and Bodo Uhse, and further illuminates the political attitudes and cultural activities of this remarkable group of German writers-in-exile during the war. Of particular interest in Renn's book is his account of efforts to return to Europe, and Germany, after the war. Unlike most of his fellow exiles in Mexico City, Renn wandered farther afield and accepted an invitation to lecture on modern European history at Morelia University in the state of Michoacán. Renn's encounters with other Europeans and a few North Americans at the university and his sometimes unusual experiences there are described in *Morelia: Eine Universitätsstadt in Mexiko* (Morelia: A University City in Mexico). This small book was first published in 1968, together with Renn's longer narrative of his participation in the Spanish Civil War.

Richterová, Sylvie (b. 1945) Czech short-story writer, poet, literary scholar, and translator. A native of Brno, Richterová graduated from Charles University in Prague where she earned her doctorate in French and Italian. Richterová settled in Italy in 1971 and is now a professor of Czech literature at Viterbo University. She earned a second doctorate in Italy with a dissertation on her fellow Czech writer Věra Linhartová and has translated several Czech writers into Italian. As a scholar, Richterová has focused mainly on questions of literary theory as related to Czech literature. She has published two collections of critical essays, *Slova a ticho* (Words and Silence, 1986) and *Ticho a smích* (Silence and Laughter, 1997). Richterová made her fiction debut with the short-story collection *Návraty a jiné ztráty* (Returns and Other Losses), which first appeared in Toronto in 1978. Virtually all of her works were originally published abroad, being reprinted in Czechoslovakia and the Czech Republic beginning only in 1991. Richterová's next collection of stories, *Místopis* (Topography, 1981), and *Návraty a jiné ztráty* were republished, with a third volume of stories,

Slabikář otcovského jazyka (Primer of the Father Tongue), in 1991. Richterová is also the author of the novels *Rozptýlené podoby* (Dispersed Images, 1993; translated as *Fragments and Likenesses*) and *Druhé loučení* (The Second Parting, 1994) and has published a collection of poems, *Neviditelné jistoty* (Invisible Certainties, 1995). Richterová's works published in Italian and French have appeared under the name Sylvie Richter. Richterová's fiction, often dealing with relations between the sexes, is interesting above all for her narrative strategies involving multiple points of view and direct contact with her reader about her narrative. Although she has written on humor and demonstrates a talent for humorous storytelling in *Místopis,* much of Richterová's fiction tends toward the strange and unusual.

Translations: "Fear Trip," trans. Michael Henry Heim, in *This Side of Reality: Modern Czech Writing,* ed. Alexandra Büchler (London: Serpent's Tail, 1996), 94–110; "Fragments and Likenesses" (from *Rozptýlené podoby*), trans. Alexandra Büchler, in *Allskin and Other Tales by Contemporary Czech Women,* ed. Alexandra Büchler (Seattle: Women in Translation, 1998), 209–23.

Ristović, Aleksandar (1933–1994) Serbian poet and essayist. One of the finest Serbian poets of the twentieth century, Ristović was born in the town of Čačak, some 100 miles south of Belgrade. After completing secondary school in his hometown, he studied Serbian literature at Belgrade University, thereafter returning to Čačak to teach Serbian language and literature. Later he worked as an editor of children's books for a Belgrade publisher. Risković's first book of poems, *Sunce jedne sezone* (The Sun of One Season), appeared in 1959. It was followed by another fourteen volumes of verse: *Ime prirode* (The Name of Nature, 1962); *Venčanja* (Nuptials, 1966); *Tekstovi* (Texts, 1969); *Trčeći pod drvećem: Istorija dečačkih*

ljubavi (Scampering Under Trees: The Story of a Boy's Love, 1970); *Pisma sanjalici* (Letters of a Daydreamer, 1972); *O putovanju i smrti* (On Travel and Death, 1976); *Ta poezija* (This Poetry, 1979); *Ulog na senke* (A Deposit on Shadows, 1981); *Dnevne i nocne slike* (Day and Night Pictures, 1984); *Slepa kuća i vidovity* (The Mole and the Clairvoyants, 1985); *Lak kao pero* (Light as a Feather, 1988); *Platno* (The Canvas, 1989); *Praznik lude* (Fool's Holiday, 1990); and *Hladna trava* (Cold Grass, 1994). A posthumous collection of selected poems by Ristović appreared in 1995 under the title *Mirisi i glasovi: Izabrane pesme* (Scents and Sounds: Selected Poems).

Ristović was a very inventive, very earthy poet who wrote in many verse forms, including the poem in prose. His poetry is accessible, readable, witty, whimsical, at times grotesque, scatological, and irreverent. Although his range of interests was not broad, it could be unusual. He wrote poems to pigs, whose tastes he says he shares while elsewhere lamenting their fate at the hands of a butcher. A series of poems is dedicated to the lavatory and related bodily functions; another is narrated by whores. Rats, bats, and insects appear frequently in his verse. Clergy and religiosity are often treated irreverently, and the poet, although interested in death in a number of poems, is not morbid about it. For example, he writes in "Image":

The doctor is with the dying man.
He is helping him urinate in a pot
    decorated with dirty pictures.

The boy sent to the principal's office
    hesitates at the door.
Inside he heard the cries of love.
The prioress is naked

in the wooden tub.
Next to it, a pig and a black rooster.

and in "The essential":

> I was not allowed to live my life,
> so I pretended to be dead
> and interested solely in things
> a dead man could be interested in:
> petrified reptiles,
> museum bric-a-brac,
> fake evidence passed off as truth.

and in "The graves of poets":

> My wife is reading a book of great poets.
> While we lie tucked in bed under the
>   same lamp,
> I imagine their graves in various places;
>   the grave of Walt Whiman with
>   branches, flowers, leaves,
> the American flag and empty beer cans
> left by a party of young people.
> . . . The tomb of T. S. Eliot, cut severely
> out of stone and marble, has a young
>   woman
> hanging around at all hours,
> uncomprehending and a bit daffy.

Translations: *Aleksandar Riskovic Devil's Lunch: Selected Poems,* trans. Charles Simic (London: Faber and Faber, 1999); *Some Other Wine and Light: Selected Poems by Aleksandar Ristović,* trans. Charles Simic (Washington, D.C.: Charioteer, 1989). SOUND RECORDING: A sound recording, made in 1996, of Charles Simic reading Ristović's poetry is available in the Woodberry Poetry Room, Harvard University.

Roman, Radu Anton (b. 1948) Romanian novelist, poet, and journalist. A native of Făgăraş, about midway between Sibiu and Braşov in Transylvania, Roman was educated in local schools before studying law and journalism at Bucharest University. His major work is the novel *Zile de pescuit* (Fishing Days), which appeared in 1985. The innocuous title of the book virtually guaran-

teed its easy passage through the censorship process. However, once its contents became known—the harsh lives of the inhabitants of the remote and ecologically fragile Danube delta, which became seriously threatened by Nicolae Ceauşescu's agricultural policies and which was also known as the Romanian "gulag"—Roman was stripped of his employment as a journalist. "Medical reasons" was the official explanation. For the next five years, the writer was supported largely by friends and the little he could earn by fishing, a lifelong passion amply reflected in his novel. After the collapse of the Ceauşescu regime, Roman was able to resume his career as a journalist. He also has been active in the Romanian environmental movement.

Translations: *Zile de pescuit* is available in French as *Des poissons sur le sable,* trans. Odile Cagnat and René Cagnat (Montricher: Noir sur blanc, 1997).

Rosenlöcher, Thomas (b. 1947) German poet and diarist. A native of Dresden, in which much of his poetry is sited, Rosenlöcher made his debut as a poet with the collection *Ich lag im Garten bei Kleinzschachwitz* (I Was Lying in the Kleinzschachwitz Garden, 1982). It was followed in 1998 by his second collection, *Schneebier* (Snow Beer). In short and long lyrics, with an absence of rhyme, and in a prosaic style, Rosenlöcher writes of the stillness of snow-covered scenery, the Elbe River and its banks, the sea and woods, the division of Germany, the drabness of the East German urban–industrial landscape, travel to France and Holland, his disillusionment with communism, and his hopes and anxieties. Rosenlöcher's skeptical attitude toward life, combined at times with a gift for the ironic and comic, show up particularly well in his diary of the last days of the German Democratic Republic, *Die verkauften Pflastersteine: Dresdener Tagebuch* (The Sold

Cobble Stones: A Dresden Diary, 1990), a compelling yet informal account of the period from 8 September 1989 to the first free elections on 18 March 1990. For both this work and his preceding poetry, Rosenlöcher was awarded in 1990 a prestigious Hugo Ball Fellowship. Since the collapse of the GDR, he has published two collections of poetry that still move much within the orbit of his previous poetic writing: *Die Dresdner Kunstaubung* (The Dresden Art Exhibition, 1996) and *Ich sitze in Sachsen und schau in den Schnee: 77 Gedichte* (I Sit in Saxony and Look at the Snow: 77 Poems, 1998).

Rosić, Tiodor (b. 1950) Serbian poet, short-story writer, and literary theorist. Rosić was born in Ušća, where he received his early schooling before eventually earning a degree in Serbo-Croatian language and Yugoslav literature at Belgrade University. He begextan his literary career as a poet with the publication of such collections of verse as *Leptir* (Butterfly, 1977); *Leteča kola* (Flying Wheels, 1970), a longer poem; *Izveštaj specijaliste* (Report of a Specialist, 1987); and *Odbrana od vlasti* (Removed from Power, 1991), a book of poems reflecting the turmoil in Serbia during the Balkan wars of the 1990s and the waning of communism. *Odbrana od vlasti* closes with a prayer that God bless his "sinful nation."

As a writer of prose fiction, Rosić has published the short-story collection *Jarac koji se ne da uzjahati* (A Goat Who Wouldn't Be Mounted, 1987) and the novel *Pseća koža* (A Dog's Skin, 1990). In stories and novel alike, Rosić is particularly fond of turning the seemingly ordinary into the eerie and inexplicable, leaving his readers with an unsettling sense of mystery. A serious and highly intelligent literary theorist with his primary interest in poetry, Rosić is the author of *Poezija i pamćenje: Pesnički iskaz u savremenoj srpskoj poeziji* (Poetry and Recollection: The Poetic in Contemporary Serbian Poetry, 1988), a collection of separate essays from 1980 to 1987, and *O pesničkom tekstu* (On the Poetic Text, 1989). In his theoretical writing, Rosić differentiates the poetic text from the literary text, addresses the syntactic and rhythmic components of the poetic text, and rejects the notion of the poetic text without a corresponding social function. Rosić is also well known for his collections of fairy tales for children and adults alike, especially *Dolina jorgovana* (Valley of Lilacs, 1995), a book of ancient Serbian fairy tales. Rosić has for some time been employed as an editor at the Belgrade publishing house BIGZ and is a recipient of the Miloš Crnjanski Prize.

Translations: "The Yellow Dog," trans. Veselin M. Šćekić, in *The Prince of Fire: An Anthology of Contemporary Serbian Short Stories*, ed. Radmila J. Gorup and Nadežda Obradović (Pittsburgh: University of Pittsburgh Press, 1998), 274–76.

Rožanc, Marjan (1930–1990) Slovenian novelist, short-story writer, and essayist. Rožanc was born in the village of Slapi; four years later, his family settled in Ljubljana. After early training as a graphic artist, he worked for a while as a lithographer in Ljubljana and Maribor print shops before turning to freelance writing. He later became prominent as an official in various Slovenian sports organizations. Rožanc's outspoken criticism of the Yugoslav regime cost him three and a half years in prison (1951–1954) in Belgrade on a charge of disseminating hostile propaganda. His experiences as a political prisoner left a lasting impression on him and are reflected in his writings in various ways. As a writer of fiction, Rožanc is best known for his Kafkaesque novel *Slepo oko gospoda Janka* (The Blind Eye of Mister Janko, 1972); *Ljubezen* (Love, 1979), arguably his best novel (and later made into a film), a first-person account of a boy's life in Italian-occupied Ljubljana during World War II;

and the heavily autobiographical novels *Roman o knjigah* (Novel About Books, 1983) and *Sentimentalni časi* (Sentimental Times, 1985). His other major works of fiction include the novels *Hudodelci* (Criminals, 1981), which is also partly autobiographical and follows the career of a post–World War II rebel and criminal named Peter Bardon; *Metulj* (The Butterfly, 1981), the last in Rožanc's autobiographical cycle and a sequel to *Hudodelci*; *Markov evangelij 1/8* (The Gospel of Mark 1:8, 1985); *Labodova pesem* (Swan Song, 1988); *Lectio divina* (Divine Reading, 1988; original title in Latin); *Indijanska zima* (Indian Winter, 1989); and *Umor* (The Murder, 1990), purportedly a translation by Rožanc from the French about the mysterious murder of a young Croatian painter named Josip Lhotko in Paris in 1918. Besides novels, Rožanc has published several collections of short stories: *Mrtvi in vsi ostali* (The Dead and All the Others, 1959); *Zračna puška* (The Air Rifle, 1971); *Vstajenje mesa* (Resurrection of the Flesh, 1980); *Zelena jama* (The Green Grotto, 1993), a volume of selected stories; and *Pravljica* (Fairy Tale, 1985), a novella. Rožanc has also written a few plays of a social critical nature, especially *Topla greda* (Hotbed, 1989), for which he has sometimes been compared with the English playwright John Osborne of the "angry young man" generation. Much of Rožanc's formidable reputation as a writer rests on his essays, which address a wide range of issues, as exemplified in such collections as *Demon Iva Daneva* (The Demon of Ivo Danev, 1969); *Iz mesi in krvi: Eseji o slovenskih mitih* (Of Flesh and Blood: Essays on Slovenian Myths, 1981); *Evropa: Eseji in legende* (Europe: Essays and Legends, 1987); and *Svoboda in narod* (Freedom and Country, 1989). An edition of Rožanc's selected essays from the late 1960s through the early 1990s—most having to do with religio-philosophical issues and Slovenian history, politics, and culture—appeared in 1995 under the title *O svobodi in bogu* (On Freedom and God). In 1991 Rožanc was awarded the Prešeren Prize. His home in the village of Karst is today the venue for the Best Essay of the Year Award established in his honor.

Translations: "An Essay on Protestantism and the Slovenians" and "The Neoplatonic Cosmos," trans. Erica Johnson Debeljak, in *The Imagination of Terra Incognita: Slovenian Writing, 1945–1995*, ed. Aleš Debeljak (Fredonia, N.Y.: White Pine, 1997), 80-102; "Indignation over the Eternal City," trans. Allen McConnell Duff, in *The Slovenian Essay of the Nineties*, selected by Matevž Kos (Ljubljana: Slovene Writers Association, 2000), 17–29.

Różewicz, Tadeusz (b. 1921) Polish poet, playwright, and short-story writer. Born in Radomsko, Różewicz was educated in local schools but left the Radomsko high school in 1938, two years before taking his graduation examination. During World War II, he served in the Polish underground Armia Krajowa (Home Army), where he got his first real start as a writer by editing his unit's newsletter and putting out a mimeographed collection of poems and prose sketches under the title *Echa leśne* (Forest Echoes). In 1945 he settled in Częstochowa, where he began contributing to local newspapers. The same year he moved to Kraków, passed his high-school graduation examination, and began studying art history at the Jagiellonian University. His first published collection of poems was *Czerwona rękawiczka* (The Red Glove, 1946), followed the same year by *W łyżce wody* (In a Tablespoon of Water), a collection of poetry and prose. However, it was Różewicz's volume of poems *Niepokój* (Anxiety, 1947) that first attracted serious attention to him as a writer. In some ways enigmatic and very private, Rożewicz had made a point in his writing of blurring the boundaries between verse and prose and of creating dramatic texts that resist production. His outlook greatly shaped by the experiences of World War II, Różewicz has made it clear that in the aftermath of the horrors of war old forms and traditions were no longer viable and new structures had to be created more in accord with the times. This meant by and large eschewing the "beautiful" in art and often turning language on itself. Różewicz was also becoming known for his opposition to the official literary policy of socialist realism, which condemned formal experimentation, even though he himself had serious reservations about the cultivation of the new for its own sake. Several other volumes of poems appeared soon after *Niepokój: Pięć poematów* (Five Poems, 1950); *Czas, który idzie* (The Time that's Coming, 1951); *Wiersze i obrazy* (Poems and Pictures, 1952); *Wybór wierszy* (Selected Poems, 1953); *Równina* (The Plain, 1954); *Poemat otwarty: Wiersze i poemat* (An Open Poem: Verses and a Poem, 1956); *Poezje zebrane* (Collected Poems, 1957); *Formy* (Forms, 1958); *Rozmowa z księciem* (Conversation with a Prince, 1960); *Głos anonima* (The Voice of an Anonymous Person, 1961); *Niepokój: Wybór wierszy z lat 1945–1961* (Anxiety: Selected Poems from 1945–1961, 1963); and *Twarz* (Countenance, 1964).

Apart from his repudiation of tradition in light of the nightmarish destruction of World War II, Różewicz raised questions about the relevance, meaning, and even viability of imaginative literature, especially poetry, in the contemporary postwar world. In 1963 he published *Tarcza z pajęczyny* (The Cobweb Shield), in which he rejected the distinction between poetry and prose, and in his 1967 article "Sezon poetycki—jesień 1966" ("The Poetry Season, Autumn 1966"), first published in the journal *Poezja* in February 1967, he went so far as to declare the death of poetry because the war negated the rationale for its continued cultivation. Writing about his views of art and poetry in 1965 in "Do źródeł ("To the Sources"), Różewicz had declared: "In 1945, a few months after the end of World War II and the German occupation, such terms as 'aesthetic response,' 'artistic response,' seemed laughable and suspect to me. Later, in August, the first atomic bomb was dropped. . . . My conviction as to the death of the old 'aesthetic response' still forms the basis of my work as a writer." However, *Poezja*, the same journal that had carried a denunciation of him for his views by his one-time mentor, the poet Julian Przyboś, later devoted a double issue (May–June 1982) to Różewicz's poetry.

Known as much for his dramatic writing as for his poetry, Różewicz wrote his first play, *Będą się bili* (They Will Fight), in 1948. It was followed by *Ujawnienie* (Coming Out, 1949–1950); *Do piachu . . .* (Dead and Buried), a prose work that he began writing in 1948 but revised as a play in 1955; *Kartoteka* (*The Card Index*, written 1959), arguably his most effective dramatic statement about the impact of the war on his generation of Poles, the original censored version of which was published in 1960, with the complete text appearing for the first time in 1972; *Grupa Laookona* (*The Laocoön Group*, 1961), inspired by Różewicz's first trip to Italy in 1960; *Świadkowie albo nasza mała stabilizacja* (*Witnesses, or Our Small Stabilization*, 1962), a putdown of the reemergence of petit-bourgeois values in the postwar Polish socialist society; *Śmieszny staruszek* (*The Funny Old Man*, written 1963; published 1964); *Akt przerywany* (*The Interrupted Act*, written 1963); *Wyszedł z domu* (He Left Home, 1964); *Stara kobieta wysiaduje* (*The Old Woman Broods*, 1968); *Na czworakach* (On All Fours, 1971); and *Białe małżeństwo* (White Marriage, written 1973; published 1974; translated as *Marriage Blanc*), a play censured for its licentiousness by Stefan Cardinal Wyszyński on 9 May 1976. The title refers to a chaste or unconsumated marriage. Set on a turn-of-the-century Polish country estate in a provincial backwater in the Austro-Hungarian Empire, the play combines sexual repression, eroticism, and sexuality. By 1981 the play had had 500 performances in Warsaw and 600 in Wrocław, to which Różewicz and his wife had moved in 1968. His other plays include *Pułapka* (*The Trap*, written 1981; published 1982), a highly imaginative work about Franz Kafka's inner life reflecting Różewicz's long interest in the writer, and *Pogrzeb po polsku* (A Funeral Polish Style, written 1964; published 1971). The first edition of Różewicz's collected plays appeared in 1966 as *Utwory dramatyczne* (Dramatic Works). He has also published two books of plays and other writings about the drama and theater: *Przygotowanie do wieczoru autorskiego: Szkice i sztuki teatralne* (Preparation for an Author's Evening: Sketches and Theatrical Works, 1961) and *Teatr niekonsekwencji: Dramaty i szkice o teatrze* (Theater of Inconsequence: Plays and Sketches About the Theater, 1970).

Różewicz's prose fiction, mostly humorous and satirical in nature, is contained in such collections of stories and novellas as *Uśmiechy: Satyry i humoresky* (Smiles: Satires and Humoresques) and *Opadły liście z drzew* (Fallen Leaves from Trees), both published in 1955; *Przerwany egzamin* (The Interrupted Examination, 1960); *Wycieczka do muzeum* (A Trip to the Museum, 1966); and *Śmierć w starych dekoracjach* (Death in Old Decorations, 1970).

In 1975 Różewicz made his first trip to the United States to attend the American premiere of *Marriage Blanc* in Port Jefferson, New York. He subsequently made a second trip for the production of *The Hunger Artist Departs* in Buffalo, New York. Różewicz's honors include: the Polish State Prize (1955, 1966); the Ministry of Culture literary prize (1962); a literary prize from the Alfred Jurzykowski Foundation in New York City (1965); and the Austrian State Prize for contributions to European literature (1983). In 1982 he was elected a member of the Bavarian Academy of the Arts. Also in 1982 Różewicz was awarded the Juliusz Słowacki Prize (Poland) but declined it on political grounds. In October 1991 he was granted an honorary doctorate by Wrocław University.

Literature: Halina Filipowicz, *A Laboratory of Pure Forms: The Plays of Tadeusz Różewicz* (New York: Greenwood, 1991).

Translations: PLAYS: *Birth Rate*, trans. Daniel Gerould, in *Twentieth-Century Polish Avant-Garde Drama: Plays, Scenarios, Critical Documents*, ed. Daniel Gerould (Ithaca, N.Y.: Cornell University Press, 1977); *The Card Index and Other Plays*, trans. Adam Czerniawski (New York: Grove, 1969); *Marriage Blanc and The Hunger Artist Departs*, trans. Adam Czerniawski (London: Boyars, 1983); *Reading the Apocalypse in Bed: Selected Plays and Short Pieces*, trans. Adam Czerniawski, Barbara Plebanek, and Tony Howard (London: Boyars, 1998); *The Trap*, trans. Adam Czerniawski (Amsterdam: Harwood, 1997); *The Witnesses and Other Plays*, trans. Adam Czerniawski (London: Calder and Boyars, 1970). POETRY: *Conversation with the Prince and Other Poems*, trans. Adam Czerniawski (London: Anvil, 1982); *Faces of Anxiety*, trans. Adam Czerniawski (London: Rapp and Whiting, 1969); *Forms in Relief and Other Works*, trans. Richard Sokoloski (New York: Legas, 1994), a Polish–English edition; *4 Contemporary Polish Poets: Różewicz, Sliwonik, Grochowiak, Harasymowicz*, trans. Victor Contoski (New York: Quixote, 1967); *recycling*, trans. Barbara Plebanek and Tony Howard (Todmorden, Eng.: Arc, 2001); *Selected Poems*, trans. Adam Czerniawski (Harmondsworth: Penguin, 1976); *The Survivor and Other Poems*, trans. Magnus J. Krynski and Robert A. Maguire (Princeton, N.J.: Princeton University Press, 1976); *They Came to See a Poet*, trans. Adam Czerniawski (London: Anvil, 1991); *Unease*, trans. Victor Contoski (St. Paul, Minn.: New Rivers, 1980).

Rrahmani, Zejnullah (b. 1952) Kosovo Albanian novelist. A native of Ballovci, in northern Kosovo, Rrahmani is best known for novels embodying the ethos and aspirations of the Kosovar Albanians. Resistance to oppression—above all, that of the Serbs—and the will to preserve the Kosovar identity as a nation are Rrahmani's principal themes in such novels as *Zanoret e humbura* (The Lost Vowels, 1974); *Udhëtimi i një pikë-uji* (The Journey of a Drop of Water, 1976), a retelling of a fable; *E bukura e dheut* (The Earthly Beauty, 1977), based on an Albanian folktale; *Sheshi i unazës* (Ring Square, 1978); and *Udhëtimi arbdhetar* (loosely translated as The Albanian National Journey, 1993), another inquiry into the essence of Albanianism. A fine stylist with a penchant for the fantastic and mythical, Rrahmani was dean of Priština University, where he taught literature and literary theory, until the institution was closed by the Serbian military in 1992. Rrahmani's last novel, *Udhëtimi arbdhetar,* was published in 1992 by the Rilindja Press, the leading Albanian-language publishing house in Kosovo. The company's operations were shut down in the early 1990s in the Serbian purge of Albanian culture in Kosovo even before the ethnic-cleansing campaign of the summer of 1999. Since the defeat of that campaign in Kosovo, Rrahmani has been exceptionally prolific, publishing two more novels, *Jusufi* (2000) and *Romani për Kosovën* (A Novel About Kosovo, 2000), and such literary studies as *Arti i poëzise* (The Art of Poetry, 2001); *Teoritë letrare klasike* (Classical Literary Theories, 2001); and *Si të shkruhet disertacioni* (How to Write a Dissertation, 2001).

Rudnicki, Adolf (1912–1992) Polish novelist and short-story writer. Rudnicki was born in Żabno, Galicia, where he received a traditional Jewish heder education before attending a Polish secondary school and a trade school. He then went to work as a bank clerk. Rudnicki had already established a firm literary reputation before World War II with such works as *Szczury* (Rats, 1932), an intense psychological novel; *Żołnierze* (Soldiers, 1933), based on his own recently completed military service; *Niekochana* (Unloved, 1937), about the torments of unrequited love experienced by a young woman; and the long story "Lato" ("Summer," 1938). Rudnicki saw action in World War II and was captured by the Germans, but managed to escape to Lwów (now Lviv, Ukraine) in the Soviet-occupied zone of the country. While there, he contributed to *Nowe Widnokręgi,* a communist literary monthly published in Lwów. After the German attack on the Soviet Union, he returned to Warsaw in 1942 and became active in the literary underground; during this time, he lived outside the Warsaw Ghetto on false papers. He took part in the Warsaw Uprising of 1944. After the war, he became a member of the important Kuźnica (Forge) literary group in the city of Łódź, returning to Warsaw in 1949. Between 1953 and 1968, he was a regular contributor to the weekly *Świat.*

Rudnicki's major postwar literary work constituted a chronicle of the tragic fate in Poland of the Jewish community. It was a grand project to which Rudnicki dedicated himself with passion and deep moral commitment. It was also a way to make up for what he regarded as his misdirected works of the 1930s. The first works in his Holocaust cycle, collectively titled *Epoka pieców* (The Epoch of Crematoria), were the short-story collections *Szekspir* (Shakespeare, 1948) and *Ucieczka z Jasnej Polany* (Flight from Yasnaya Polana, 1949). They were followed in 1952 by a major collection of stories under the title *Żywe i martwe morze* (*The Dead and the Living Sea*). The volume was enlarged for new editions in 1955 and 1956 and was further revised for a new edition in 1957. The stories in

The Dead and the Living Sea deal mostly with the fate of the Polish Jews during the German occupation. The last work in The Epoch of Crematoria cycle, *Kupiec łódzki* (The Merchant of Łódź, 1963), is a fictionalized biography of Chaim Rumkowski, the chairman of the Jewish Council during the days of the Łódź ghetto.

Beginning with the multivolume *Niebieskie kartki* (Blue Pages), the first volume of which appeared in 1954, Rudnicki moved away from the Holocaust to writing of a highly personal character, usually in the form of diary notes that are often indistinguishable from fiction. One of Rudnicki's most impressive literary achievements, the *Niebieskie kartki* cycle includes such works as *Ślepe lustro tych lat* (The Blind Mirror of Those Years, 1956); *Prześwity* (Dawns, 1957); and *Obraz z kotem i psem* (A Picture with Cat and Dog, 1962). Before the publication of the last volume of the cycle, Rudnicki had returned to fiction writing and published several collections of stories, among them *Krowa* (The Cow, 1959); *Narzeczony Beaty* (Beata's Fiancé, 1961); *Pył miłosny* (Dust of Love, 1964); *Weiss wpada do morza* (Weiss Falls into the Sea, 1965); and *Rogaty warszawiak* (The Haughty Varsovian, 1982). Rudnicki was awarded state literary prizes in 1955 and 1956. In 1968, during the "anti-Zionist" campaign in Poland, he moved to France but remained there only until the mid-1970s. Rudnicki's last works—among them *Sto lat temu umarł Dostojewski* (Dostoevsky Died a Hundred Years Ago, 1984); *Krakowskie Przedmieście pełne deserów* (Krakowskie Przedmieście Full of Deserts, 1986), named for a main street in Warsaw; and *Teatr zawsze grany* (The Theater that Never Closes, 1987)—represent a curious mix of literary criticism and sometimes highly idiosyncratic personal observations.

Translations: *Ascent to Heaven*, trans. H. C. Stevens (London: Dobson, 1951; New York: Roy, 1951); *The Dead and the Living Sea and Other Stories*, trans. Jadwiga Zwolska (Warsaw: Polonia, 1957); *Lest We Forget*, ed., with an introduction, by Adolf Rudnicki (Warsaw: Polonia, 1955); "Easter" (from *Szekspir*), trans. Jadwiga Zwolska, in *Contemporary Polish Short Stories*, selected by Andrzej Kijowski (Warsaw: Polonia, 1960), 254–64.

Rúfus, Milan (b. 1928) Slovak poet. A native of the village of Závažná Poruba, Rúfus attended the local elementary school, after which he graduated from the high school in Liptovský Mikuláš in 1948. From 1948 to 1952, he studied Slovak literature and history at Comenius University in Bratislava, where he became an instructor in Slovak and Czech literatures after completing his graduate studies. He spent the academic year 1971/1972 as a guest lecturer at Naples University in Italy. Rúfus's first poems appeared in such journals as *Prameň*, *Nový rod*, *Mladá tvorba*, and *Borba*. They were later gathered and published in two volumes: *Chlapec* (A Lad, 1966) and *Chlapec maľuje dúhu* (A Lad Paints a Rainbow, 1974). Rúfus's first book of poetry appeared in 1956 under the title *Až dozrieme* (Until We Mature) and already demonstrated the sense of social responsibility and feeling for Slovak folk culture that would deepen as time went on. *Až dozrieme* was followed by such collections as: *Zvony* (Bells, 1968); *Ľudia v horách* (People in the Mountains, 1969), which owed something to the inspiration of the Slovak photographer Martin Martinček; *Stôl chudobných* (Table of the Poor, 1972); *Kolíska* (Cradles, 1972), accompanied by photographs by Martinček; *Kolíska spieva deťom* (The Cradle Sings to Children, 1974); and *Hora* (The Mountain, 1978), also with photographs by Martinček.

Rúfus's fondness for the Slovak folk tradition as well as the folk-inspired tales of Pavol Dobšinský led him to compose poetic versions of a number of these works, as in his triptych *Kniha rozprávok* (A Book of

Stories, 1975); *Sobotné večery* (Saturday Evenings, 1979); and the much later *Tiché papradie* (Silent Ferns, 1990). Between the second and third parts of the triptych, Rúfus published his meditative *Óda na radost* (Ode to Happiness, 1981), a poetic consideration of the meaning of life, art, and the creative instinct.

Rúfus's highly developed social consciousness and love for his people inform as well such works for children as *Rozpravočka veselá ostań ešte s nami* (Stay Longer with Us, Merry Storyteller, 1985); *Lupienky z jabloní* (Stolen Apples, 1993); and *Studnička* (The Little Well, 1993).

Rúfus has written essays and held literary conversations throughout his career. In his volume *Dve osudové* (Two Destinies, 1991), he brought together the essays contained in his earlier *Štyri epištoly k ľudom* (Four Epistles to People, 1968) and the poetic text *Murárska balada* (A Mason's Ballad), which deals with the art of the poem itself. Other books of essays by Rúfus include *Človek, čas a tvorba* (Man, Time, and Creation, 1968); *O literatúre* (On Literature, 1974); and *Epištoly staré a nové* (Old and New Epistles, 1996). In 1998 Rúfus also published the first volume of a collection of conversations/interviews from the period 1965 to 1991 under the title *Rozhovory so sebou a s tebou* (Conversations with Myself and with You). The book is especially interesting, and valuable, for the light it sheds on the development of Rúfus's ideas as an artist and a thinker from the 1960s.

Several editions of Rúfus's selected poems have been published since the late 1960s: *Triptych* (1969); *Básne* (Poems, 1972, 1975); and *A čo je báseň* (What Really Is a Poem, 1978). Rúfus has also been an active translator of poetry and drama. Apart from his translations from Czech and Russian, he has translated Henryk Ibsen's *Peer Gynt* (1966) and in 1988 brought out a selection of poems by the Cuban poet José Martí. His translations of the Psalms and Jeremiah appeared in 1991 and 1998, respectively. Rúfus's more recent collections of poems, *Neskorý autoportrét* (Late Self-Portrait, 1992); *Čitanie z údelu* (Reading by Lot, 1996); and *Palmy o nevinnej* (Psalms of Innocence, 1998), are by and large autobiographical, reflective, and philosophical.

Rupchev, Georgi (b. 1957) Bulgarian poet and translator. Born and educated in Sofia, Rupchev graduated from Sofia University in 1982 with a degree in Bulgarian literature. His first book of poetry, *Umoreni ot chudoto* (Tired by the Marvel, 1982), won the Vladimir Bashev literary award for a best first volume. Rupchev's second volume, *Smiana na noshtiata strazha* (Change of the Night Guard), appeared in 1987 and was followed by two other volumes: *Smurtta na Tibalt* (The Death of Tibalt, 1989) and *Silite na noshtta* (The Powers of the Night, 1991). Rupchev's poetry is written in an everyday urban idiom—the city is a frequent setting in his works—and conveys a vague sense of peril as well as a deep cynicism about the conditions in which his generation reached maturity and his generation's lack of illusions and faith. Some of his poems appeared in the first numbers of the samizdat almanacs *Most* and *Glas*. Rupchev has also translated extensively from contemporary Russian and American poetry, works by Robert Penn Warren and Lawrence Ferlinghetti, among others.

Translations: Five poems in *Clay and Star: Contemporary Bulgarian Poets,* trans. and ed. Lisa Sapinkopf and Georgi Belev (Minneapolis: Milkweed, 1992), 204–8; two poems, trans. Belin Tonchev, in *Young Poets of a New Bulgaria,* ed. Belin Tonchev (London: Forest, 1990), 105–11.

Rupel, Dimitrij (b. 1946) Slovenian novelist, essayist, playwright, sociologist, and political figure. A native of Ljubljana, Rupel graduated from Ljublana University in sociology and received a doctorate in that discipline from Brandeis University in Waltham, Massachusetts. Apart from his more than thirty books of fiction, essays, and sociological studies, Rupel has been a frequent contributor to Slovenian and foreign journals and reviews, and has written for theater, radio, and television. He was the editor in chief of *Nova Revija* in 1987 when it published the controversial fifty-seventh number, which was one of the harbingers of anticommunist opposition in Slovenia. He was also a founder of the Slovenian Democratic Association (SDZ) and later its president. Rupel has held a full professorship in sociology at Ljubljana University since 1992 and on several occasions has lectured in the United States.

Although he began his literary career with such collections of short stories as *Na pol poti do obzorja* (Half Way to the Horizon, 1968) and *Bele sobe* (White Rooms, 1970), and has written several novels, some of them of a parodic-satirical nature reflecting the Yugoslav and Slovenian political and cultural scene, Rupel is best known as a political writer, literary historian, and sociologist of art and culture. His novels include *Tajnik šeste internacionale* (The Secret of the Sixth International, 1971); *Čaj in puške ob štirih* (Tea and Guns at Four, 1972); *Čas v njej rabelj hudi: Ali, kako strašno kaznujejo slovenske pisatelje: Znanstveno-literarno-fantastični roman* (Time Is a Stern Executioner, or How Terribly Slovenian Writers Are Punished: A Literary-Science-Fiction Novel, 1974); *Hi kvadrát* (Hi Square, 1975); *Družinska zveza* (Family Connection, 1977); *Odloženi* (The Postponed, 1980); *Maks: Roman o maksizmu ali boj med večino in veličino* (Max: A Novel About Maxism, or The Struggle Between the Majority and Greatness, 1983); *Povabljeni, pozableni* (Invited, Forgotten, 1985); and *Levji delež* (The Lion's Share, 1989). Rupel's political writings deal by and large with the independence move-

ment in Slovenia, Slovenian political culture since becoming independent, and Slovenia's place in Europe. They include *Slovensko kot politično prepričanje* (Slovenia as Political Conviction, 1992); *Skrivnost države: Spomini na domače in zunanje zadeve, 1989–1992* (The Secret of Power: Recollections of Domestic and Foreign Affairs, 1989–1992, 1992); *Slovenski pot do samostojnosti in priznanja* (The Slovenian Road to Independence and Recognition, 1992); *Odčarana Slovenija* (Awakened Slovenia, 1993); *Čas politike* (A Time of Politics, 1994), an interesting review of Slovenian political history through the centuries, with particular emphasis on developments nationally and internationally since the establishment of an independent Slovenian state in 1991; *Edinost, sreča, sprava* (Unity, Happiness, Reconciliation, 1996); and *Svoboda proti državi* (Freedom Against the State, 1998). Rupel was also one of the contributors to a collection of essays on political culture under the title *Slovenski smer* (The Slovenian Way, 1996). His book *Slovenski intelektualci: Od vojaške do civilne družbe* (Slovenian Intellectuals: From Military to Civilian Society, 1989) deals with Slovenian intellectutal life after 1945, whereas in *Svobodne besede od Prešerna do Cankara* (Ideas on Freedom from Prešeren to Cankar, 1976) he examines Slovenian literature as a harbinger and an incentive of national liberation in the second half of the nineteenth century. In the field of literary scholarship, Rupel is the author of a book of reviews titled *Branje* (Defenses, 1973), a study of the Slovenian writer Oton Župančič (1878–1949); a collection of essays, *Prijazno življenje* (A Nice Life, 1979); *Besede in dejanja: Od moderne do (post)modernizma: Literarnosocioloski eseji* (Chats and Acts: From the Modern to [Post]Modernism, 1981); *Literarna sociologija* (Literary Sociology, 1982); *Besede božje in božanske* (On God and Divinity, 1987); *Poskusi z resničnostjo* (Experiments with Salvation, 1982), on nineteenth- and twentieth-century Slovenian literary history; his edition of the 1951/1952 volume of the writer Edvard Kočbek's diaries (1986); *Zakaj je svet narobe? Perešna knjiga za težke čase* (Why Is the World Upside Down? A Handbook for Hard Times, 1987); and *Slovenske slovesnosti in vsakdanjosti, 1888–1988* (Slovenian Letters and Everyday Life, 1888–1988, 1990). As a professional sociologist, Rupel, in collaboration with Lidija Herek, also edited the volume *Alienation and Participation in Culture*, written in English, a collection of papers originally delivered at the International Conference on the Sociology of Art (1984), sponsored by the Research Institute of the Faculty of Sociology, Political Science, and Journalism of the Edvard Kardelj University. From 1990 to January 1993, Rupel held the position of first Minister of Foreign Affairs of independent Slovenia. He has served as as a delegate to the Slovenian parliament, and in 1994 was elected mayor of the city of Ljubljana.

Literature: Janko Lorenci, *Dimitrij Rupel* (Ljubljana: Partizanska knjiga, 1990), a Slovenian book of interviews with Rupel.

Rymkiewicz, Jarosław Marek (b. 1935) Polish poet, playwright, and essayist. Rymkiewicz was born in Warsaw and studied Polish literature at Łódź University, from which he eventually received a doctorate. He began his literary career in the mid-1950s and published his first book of poetry, *Konwencje* (Conventions), in 1957. His subsequent volumes of poetry include *Człowiek z głową jastrzębia* (The Man with the Falcon's Head, 1960), which received an award from the weekly *Nowa Kultura*; *Metafyzyka* (Metaphysics, 1963); *Animula* (1964); and *Anatomia* (Anatomy, 1970). Rymkiewicz also wrote several plays that never achieved more than moderate success, among them *Odys w Berdyczowie*

(Odysseus in Berdiczów); *Księżniczka na opak* (The Princess All Awry); and *Król Mięsopust* (King Carnival).

Rymkiewicz is now best known internationally for *Umschlagsplatz* (1988; translated as *The Final Station: Umschlagsplatz*), originally published by the Instytut Literacki in Paris, a penetrating and provocative narrative focused on the complex attitudes of the Poles toward the Holocaust. The German word *Umschlagplatz* was used for the area of the Warsaw Ghetto where Jews were assembled for deportation to the concentration camps. A non-Jew, Rymkiewicz became obsessed with the fate of the Jews in Poland and set out to reconstruct the Umschlagplatz as it existed during the German occupation. This then became the springboard for his probe of Polish–Jewish relations before, during, and after the war, and his assessment of Polish attitudes toward the once huge Jewish community of Poland. Rymkiewicz had addressed the matter of Polish–Jewish relations in his novel *Rozmowy polskie latem roku 1983* (Polish Conversations in the Summer of 1983, 1984). Written when the rise of Solidarity and the imposition of martial law in 1981 were fresh memories, Rymkiewicz's novel acquires additional interest for its ruminations on Polish history, past and present, and its evident pessimism and paranoia concerning the future of the country.

Translations: *The Final Station: Umschlagsplatz*, trans. Nina Taylor (New York: Farrar, Straus and Giroux, 1994); three poems, trans. Adam Czerniawski, in *Polish Writing Today*, ed. Celina Wieniewska (Harmondsworth: Penguin, 1967), 28–30

Šalamun, Tomaž (b. 1941) Slovenian poet. Šalamun was born in Zagreb, Croatia, but fled with his family to Ljubljana, Slovenia, when his father, a pediatrician, learned that the pro-Nazi Croatian Ustaša regime intended to take him into custody for his leftist political views. The future poet spent his early years in the town of Koper (Italian, Capodistria), near Trieste. He eventually earned a degree in art history at Ljubljana University, after which he worked as an assistant curator at the Moderna Galerija, Slovenia's modern-art museum. Šalamun was also a conceptual artist and was affiliated with the avant-garde group known as OHO, which exhibited widely, including at the Museum of Modern Art in New York in 1970. *Poker,* Šalamun's first book of poetry, was originally published in a samizdat edition in 1966 because of his fallout with the communist authorities when he was named editor of *Perspektive,* the leading Slovene cultural and political journal. Although he was arrested and threatened with a long prison term, he was released after five days as a result of international pressure. Šalamun followed *Poker* with some two dozen volumes of poetry: *Namen pelerine* (The Use of a Cloak, 1968); *Romanje za Maruško* (Pilgrimage for Maruška, 1971); *Bela Itaka* (White Ithaka 1972); *Amerika* (America, 1973); *Arena* (1973); *Sokol* (Falcon, 1974); *Imre* (Turbines, 1975); *Druidi* (Druids, 1975); *Praznik* (Celebration, 1976); *Zvezde* (Stars, 1977); *Metoda angela* (Angel's Method, 1978); *Po sledeh divjadi* (Tracking Wild Game, 1979); *Maske* (Masks, 1980); *Balada za Metko Krašovec* (Ballad for Metka Krašovec, 1981); *Analogije svetlobe* (Analogies of Light, 1982); *Glas* (The Voice, 1983); *Sonet o mleku* (Sonnet About Milk, 1984); *Soy Realidad* (I Am Reality, 1985; original title in Spanish); *Ljubljanska pomlad* (Ljubljana Spring, 1986); *Mera časa* (The Measure of Time, 1987); *Živa rana, živi sok* (Living Wound, Living Juice, 1988); *Otrok in jelen* (The Child and the Deer, 1990); and *Ambra* (Ambergris, 1995).

Apart from his fame in Slovenia, where he has won several prominent literary prizes, among them the Prešeren Fund Prize, he is widely known abroad, including in the United States, which he has visited on several occasions. He held a fellowship to the International Writing Program at the University of Iowa, had residencies at the writing colonies of Yaddo and McDowell, was granted a visiting Fulbright Fellowship to Columbia University, and won a Pushcart Prize. He also served as Slovenian cultural attaché in the United States.

Šalamun's poetry is rich and varied and defies easy categorization. Much of his writing is in the surreal style of strange, elusive, disconnected imagery not readily grasped intellectually. Some of the images are repellant and disturbing. Poetry, its power, its destructive potential in a positive sense, is a recurrent theme. As he writes in the poem "Clumsy Guys" from the collection *Po sledeh divjadi*: "Poetry is a sacred machine, the lackey of / an unknown deity who kills as if by conveyer belt." In "The Fish," from *Glas,* he declares:

> I slide headfirst into people's
> mouths and kill and give birth,
> kill and give birth, because I write.

His defiance, as a poet, in the face of complacency is forcefully, and characteristically, presented in a poem such as "To the Deaf Ones," from *Soy Realidad*:

> I've grown weary of our vapid skies,
> Leg touching leg, lips to lips, all dead,
> What is this power preventing a
>   flowering?
> A gulag in toadies' heads, spreading like
>   cancer?
> I carry God in my heart, give Him away
> like water to people dying of thirst . . .
> no longer feeeling fear.
> I refuse to be free
> everywhere else, and fall into a soulless
>   black

void only in my native land.
I'm not a cynic, I'm a poet, a prophet.

But an almost self-mocking playfulness directed at himself (and members of his immediate family) is also characteristic of Šalamun's style—for example, "I Have a Horse" in the collection *Romanje za Maruško*; "Who's Who" in *Bela Itaka*; and "History" and "20 September 1972" in *Arena*. Although rarely an overtly political writer, Šalamun does at times allude to the political situation in his own country in poems conveying poignant pleas for freedom and human worth—for example, "1/1/73" in the collection *Imre*, and "My Tribe" in *Mera časa*. In "Walled in Alive," in the collection *Otrok in jelen*, his mockery of communists is blatant. Šalamun's visits to the United States are reflected in poems in which he tries to grapple with the immensity of New York, such as "My First Time in New York City" in the collection *Praznik*. Virtually every foreign city and country Šalamun ever visited occasioned at least a single poem. Mexico, however, seems to have made a particularly strong impression on him, as is evident by the number of poems with Mexican motifs and his *Soy Realidad* collection.

Translations: *A Ballad for Metka Krašovec*, trans. Michael Biggins (Prague: Twisted Spoon, 2001); *Feast*, ed. Charles Simic (New York: Harcourt, 2000); *The Four Questions of Melancholy: New and Selected Poems*, ed. Christopher Merrill (Fredonia, N.Y.: White Pine, 1997), which contains selections from all of Šalamun's books of poetry; *The Selected Poems of Tomaž Šalamun*, ed. Charles Simic (New York: Ecco Press, 1988).

Salivarová, Zdena (b. 1933) Czech novelist. The wife of the novelist Josef Škvorecký, Salivarová is a former actress who began her career as a singer in the state folklore en-semble. She later performed in the Prague cabaret theaters Laterna Magica and Paravan. After graduating from the Eliška Krásnohorská girl's high school in Prague in 1952, she studied at the Prague Film School and acted in several films in the 1960s before turning to a literary career. Her first book, a triptych of novellas titled *Pánská jízda* (A Gentleman's Foray), appeared in 1968. All her subsequent works were published in Canada after she and Škvorecký immigrated there in 1969. Salivarová had been preceded as an émigré by her father, Josef (1902–1969), a book dealer and publisher who was briefly imprisoned after the communists took power in Czechoslovakia in 1949 and immigrated to the United States in 1950 following his release. Once Salivarová and Škvorecký were settled in Toronto, it was on her urging that in 1971 they founded the émigré publishing house known as Sixty-Eight Publishers (or 68 Publishers), which specialized in the works of writers who were banned in Czechoslovakia or who were forced to emigrate. By the time it ceased operations in 1993, Sixty-Eight Publishers had turned out 227 books by mainly Czech émigré and samizdat writers.

Salivarová's first novel to be published in emigration was the patently autobiographical *Honzlová: Protestsong* (1972, 1976, 1991; translated as *Summer in Prague*). Long banned in Czechoslovakia, it was widely acclaimed elsewhere. Narrated in a seemingly lighthearted manner by a young woman who belongs to a folklore chorus that is permitted to travel abroad, the novel paints a depressing picture of the breakdown of human relations in totalitarian Czechoslovakia dominated by a Stalinist bureaucracy and secret police. At the end of the work, a sympathetic police agent furnishes the heroine with a passport, enabling her to leave for France and freedom. Salivarová has since published two more novels: *Nebe, peklo, ráj: Love Story* (Heaven, Hell, Paradise: Love

Story, 1976, 1991; translated as *Ashes, Ashes, All Fall Down*), about the romance between a Latvian athlete and a Czech girl, and *Hnůj země* (Manure of the Earth, 1994), a diverting and revealing novel in letters about the Czech émigré intelligentsia based obviously on her own experiences. Salivarová was awarded the Czech Order of the White Lion, Third Class, in 1990 for her contributions to Czech culture and literature, and in 1992 was given an honorary doctorate by the University of Toronto.

Translations: *Ashes, Ashes, All Fall Down*, trans. Jan Drábek (Toronto: Larkwood, 1987); *Summer in Prague*, trans. Marie Winn (New York: Harper & Row, 1973).

Samokovlija, Isak (1889–1955) Bosnian short-story writer. A native of Gorazde, a small town on the banks of the Drina River, Samokovlija belonged to the large Sephardic Jewish community of pre–World War II Sarajevo. He and his family settled in Sarajevo after he completed primary school. In 1910 he went to Vienna to study medicine, supported by a scholarship from the La Benevolencia Sephardic Jewish cultural and educational foundation. He graduated in 1917 and, when World War I ended, returned to Bosnia, working as a doctor first in Gorazde and then, beginning in 1925, in Sarajevo, which became his permanent home. Although he did not discontinue his practice of medicine until after World War II, Samokovlija took an early interest in literature, manifested when he became a coeditor of the journal of the Jewish community in Sarajevo. His first short story appeared in this journal in 1927. Two years later, his first collection of short stories was published under the title *Od proljeća do proljeća* (From Spring to Spring). The book was very well received, as was Samokovlija's second volume of stories, published in Belgrade in 1936.

Samokovlija survived the Ustaša regime, which had incorporated Bosnia into the Nazi puppet Independent State of Croatia, and resumed his literary career soon after World War II. In 1946 he published a volume of stories under the title *Nosac Samuel* (Samuel, the Porter). This was followed by two more volumes of stories: *Tragom života* (On Trial for Life, 1948) and *Salomunovo slovo* (Solomon's Word, 1949). A novel based on the life of the Jews of Sarajevo was never finished; only fragments survive. Twelve years after his death in 1955, the Svjetlost publishing house of Sarajevo brought out his collected works (*Sabrana djela*) in three volumes. A five-volume edition of his works was published in Sarajevo in 1989 by the Svjetlost and Veselin Masleša publishing houses. In 1997, a new edition of his Jewish stories appeared as *Jevrejske priče* (Jewish Tales).

Samokovlija's literary reputation rests on his stories about the now-extinct Sephardic Jewish community of Bosnia, most of which was located in Sarajevo. Notwithstanding his successful medical and literary careers, Samokovlija, himself of modest background, chose to focus only on the poorest stratum of Sarajevo's Jewish *mahala* (quarter), the term derived from Arabic through Turkish and once in wide use in Bosnia. It was a world he knew intimately and one that he portrays with a keen eye for detail and with obvious warmth. The appeal of the stories, especially to non-Jewish readers, lay in their color and exotic quality. Avoiding the sentimental, Samokovlija brought vividly to life the mores and rituals of the poor Sephardic Jews whose linguistic mix of Serbo-Croatian, Turkish, Hebrew, and Ladino (a Spanish derivative brought from Spain by the Sephardic Jews after their expulsion during the Inquisition) enriches the fabric of Samokovlija's narratives. The comic and tragic coexist easily in the stories, especially those devoted to the fate of Jewish women who fall in love with Christian or Muslim men and those written after World

War II in which Samokovlija atttempted to come to grips with the devastation of the Sephardic Jewish community at the hands of the Germans and their Croatian collaborators. Deeply troubled by the lack of resistance and the resignation with which so many Jews went to their deaths during the war, Samokovlija sought in his postwar stories to highlight instances of Jewish resistance and bravery. In a number of these stories, he abandons the omniscient narrator of the prewar stories in favor of an internal narrator named Dakova (the nickname of David Bararon), an acquaintance of the omniscient narrator who shares his wartime experiences with him.

Translations: *Tales of Old Sarajevo*, trans. Celia Hawkesworth and Christina Pribićević-Zorić, ed. Zdenko Lešić, with an introduction by Ivo Andrić (London: Vallentine Mitchell, 1997), which contains the only information on Samokovlija in English, in Andrić's introduction and Lešić's essay.

Şandru, Mircea Florian (b. 1949) Romanian poet. After studying engineering and philosophy at Bucharest University, Şandru discovered his true calling in literature and began working as an editor for *Amfiteatru* soon after earning his degree. As a poet, he is known above all for his fascination with city life and urban culture in the high-tech age. This is reflected in the very titles of his collections of poems: *Elegie pentru puterea oraşului* (Elegy for the Power of the City, 1974); *Luminile oraşului* (The Lights of the City, 1975); *Melancolia* (Melancholy, 1977); *Maşina de scris* (The Typewriter, 1981); *Flacăra de magnezii* (The Magnesium Flame, 1980); *Trupuri pe ecranul de radar* (Bodies on the Radar Screen, 1982); *Viaţa în infraroşu* (Life in Infrared, 1985); *Oraşe suprapuse* (Superposed Towns, 1986); and *Legătură de sînge* (Blood Tie, 1989). Şandru has traveled extensively in Europe and America, and his experiences and obervations have also provided material for his poetry.

Translations: Seven poems in *15 Young Romanian Poets: An Anthology of Verse*, trans. and ed. Liliana Ursu (Bucharest: Eminescu, 1982), 75–79.

Sánta, Ferenc (b. 1927) Hungarian novelist and short-story writer. A native of Braşov (Hungarian, Brassó), Transylvania, where he was born into a poor peasant family, Sánta had a rebellious streak that manifested itself at an early age and resulted in his being expelled from schools in Cluj (Hungarian, Koloszvár) and Debrecen, effectively ending his formal education at a young age. In 1951 he moved to Budapest, where he worked mainly as a laborer in order to support a new and growing family. Notwithstanding his difficult economic conditions, Sánta found time to pursue his interest in storytelling and in 1954 published his first story, "Sokan voltunk" ("There Were Too Many of Us"), which was much praised for its departure from socialist realism. Sánta's first collection of stories, *Téli virágzás* (Winter Flowering), appeared two years later. It deals mostly with the life of the peasants in his native Transylvania and recalls especially his own childhood. With time, Sánta's outlook would encompass a wider range of subjects. In 1958 he accepted the position of librarian of the Hungarian Academy's Institute of Literary Studies. He published a second collection of short stories in 1961 under the title *Farkasok a küszöbön* (Wolves on the Threshold) and, in 1963, the work for which he is perhaps best known: the novel *Az ötödik pecsét* (*The Fifth Seal*). Depicting the instability in Hungary near the end of World War II, the novel was later made into a successful film. *Húsz óra* (Twenty-Four Hours, 1964), another hugely popular novel by Sánta, reflects the impact of the Hungarian uprising of 1956. It won a prize at the Moscow Film Festival in 1964. In 1965 Sánta gave up his librarian's post in order to become a full-time writer. His next novel was *Az áruló* (The Traitor, 1966), a kind of political allegory about revolution set in the time of the Hussite wars of the fifteenth century. It was adapted for the stage under the title *Éjszaka* (Night). *Isten a szekéren* (*God in the Wagon*), another collection of Sánta's stories, appeared in 1970. It was followed in 1982 by the collection *Kicsik és nagyok* (The Small and the Big). Sánta is a Kossuth Prize winner.

Translations: *The Fifth Seal,* trans. Albert Tezla (Budapest: Corvina, 1963, 1986); *God in the Wagon: Ten Short Stories,* trans. Albert Tezla (Budapest: Corvina, 1985).

Sarkadi, Imre (1921–1961) Hungarian playwright, novelist, and short-story writer. Sarkadi's unimely death, an apparent suicide on the part of a writer who liked flirting with death, cut short a promising literary career, which began in 1946. His much admired short stories—collected in the volumes *Gál János útja* (The Path of János Gál, 1950); *Royi* (Scribblings, 1951); *Tanyasi dúvad* (A Brute on the Farm, 1953); and *A gyáva* (*The Coward*, 1961)—often deal with the social transformation of the peasantry or conflicts between provincial and urban life. Cynicism and grim irony are typical of his style. When his attention shifted from peasant life to the intelligentsia, his treatment of the latter focused on moral and spiritual bankruptcy. Moral cowardice, especially among women, is often masked by an exterior toughness and senseless acts of bravado. Sarkadi demonstrated a very real ability to conceptualize the issues of greatest concern to him in such plays as *Út a tanyákról* (Road from the Farm, 1952) and *Szeptember* (September, 1955). The film *Körhinta* (The Merry-Go-Round, 1954), which was based on his short story "In the Well," won a prize at the Cannes Film Festival in 1954. *Elveszett paradicsom* (Paradise Lost, 1962) was written originally for the stage. In 1974 a collected edition of Sarkadi's plays was published under the title *Dramak*; a second expanded edition, with the same title, appeared in 1983. Other works by Sarkadi include *Párbeszéd az idő dolgairól* (Conversation About the Weather, 1987) and the short-story collection *Pokolraszállás* (Flying to Hell, 1984). Sarkadi was a recipient of the coveted Kossuth Prize.

Literature: György Somlyó, "The Solution of the Insoluble: About Imre Sarkadi," in Imre Sarkadi, *The Coward and Other Stories,* trans. by various hands (Budapest: Corvina, 1967), 135–48.

Translations: *The Coward and Other Stories,* trans. by various hands (Budapest: Corvina, 1967); "The Deserter," trans. József Hatvany, in *44 Hungarian Short Stories,* ed. Lajos Illés (Budapest: Corvina, 1979), 511–22.

Savić, Milislav (b. 1945) Serbian novelist and short-story writer. Savić's literary career began in the late 1960s when his first collection of short stories, *Bugarska baraka* (The Bulgarian Barracks, 1969), appeared. He then turned to the novel, publishing *Ljubavi Andrije Kurandića* (The Loves of Andrija Kurandić) in 1972. Savić did not publish another novel until the mid-1980s. In 1977 he turned out two more collections of short stories: *Ujak naše varoši* (The Uncle of Our Town) and *Mladići iz Raške* (The Boys from Raška; translated as *Midnight Train from Raška and Other Stories*). With *Topola na terasi* (The Poplar on the Terrace, 1985), Savić resumed novel writing on a full scale. *Ćup komitskog vojvode* (The Jug of the Guerrilla Leader) appeared in 1990, and the highly acclaimed *Hleb i strah* (*Bread and Fear*) in 1991. Much of Savić's fiction views the social and economic development of post–World War II Yugoslavia through the prism of a small Serbian town identified with the author's boyhood. Besides his novels and stories, Savič has written literary studies, among them *Ustanička proza* (Revolutionary Prose, 1985), on the Serbian insurrection of 1804 to 1813 in literature; *Fusnota* (The Footnote, 1995); and *Ožiljci tišine* (Scars of Silence, 1997), dealing with such writers as Ivo Andrić and Miloš Crnjanski. In 1993 he also published a collection of translations of contemporary Italian short stories. Savić has taught at several universities in the United States and Europe.

Translations: *Bread and Fear* (Belgrade: Dereta/Prosveta, 1996); *Midnight Train from Raška and Other Stories,* trans. Randall A. Major (Belgrade: Dereta, 1998); "The Locksmith Was Better," trans. Vidosava Janković, in *The Prince of Fire: An Anthology of Contemporary Serbian Short Stories,* ed. Radmila J. Gorup and Nadežda Obradović (Pittsburgh: University of Pittsburgh, 1998), 222–28.

Šćepanović, Branimir (b. 1937) Serbian novelist, short-story writer, and film, television, and radio scriptwriter. Šćepanović was born in Podgorica, Montenegro, and studied at Belgrade University. He began his literary career as a journalist and publishing house editor. Apart from his two collections of short stories, *Pre istine* (Before the Truth, 1961) and *Smrt gospodina Goluže* (The Death of Mr. Goluža, 1977), Šćepanović is the author of three novels: *Sramno leto* (The Shameful Summer, 1965); *Usta puna zemlje* (*Mouth Full of Earth,* 1974); and *Iskupljenje* (Redemption, 1980). His fame rests largely on *Mouth Full of Earth.* The narrative is constructed along parallel lines that coverge only in terms of the action. On one line, the omniscient author traces the train ride from Belgrade of a man with an incurable disease who is destined to die soon and is returning to the mountains of his native Montenegro to take his own life there, in a mood of serene composure. At a certain point, he im-

pulsively leaves the stuffy train and begins making his way through an unfamiliar wilderness where he comes across two campers whose observations, told in the first-person plural, make up the short novel's second parallel line. When the man from the train sees the campers, he decides not to have contact with them and begins moving away. What follows is a senseless, relentless hunt that begins in idle curiosity and rapidly turns into an obsession afflicting not only the two campers, but other people they meet in the wilderness who join them in their frenzied pursuit. The more the stranger tries to elude them in order to have his final time on earth to himself, the more inflamed their passions become. His pursuers whip themselves into a rage as they read the worst into the stranger's flight from them. Racing after him, rifles on the ready, they are like hunters after big game. When they at last catch up with him, they find his magnificent unclad body stretched across the rock onto which he had obviously flung himself, blood oozing from his smiling mouth, which is partially full of earth. The mystery that torments the stranger's pursuers at the end of the work is the mystery of life, for which Šćepanović offers no answers. The spareness of *Mouth Full of Earth,* its novel structure, and Šćepanović's limpid prose style make a memorable impression.

Translations: *Mouth Full of Earth,* trans. Lovett Fielding Edwards (Nantucket, Mass.: Longship, 1979); "The Scream," trans. Christina Pribićević-Zorić, in *The Prince of Fire: An Anthology of Contemporary Serbian Short Stories,* ed. Radmila J. Gorup and Nadežda Obradović (Pittsburgh: University of Pittsburgh Press, 1998), 138–42.

Schädlich, Hans Joachim (b. 1935) German short-story writer. Schädlich was born in Reichenbach im Vogtland, where he received his early education. He studied German language and literature at the universities of Berlin and Leipzig and in 1960 received his doctorate. From 1959 to 1976, he was employed by the Academy of Sciences of the German Democratic Republic. It was during this period that he began to publish scholarly works in the field of linguistics and to write fiction. His dissertation on the phonology of East Vogtland German appeared in 1966 and was followed in 1973 by another book on linguistics. It was around 1969 that he started writing short stories, but hardly any of them appeared in the GDR. Schädlich's protest against Wolf Biermann's loss of citizenship cost him his job and forced him to earn a living as a freelance translator. Although he was barred from publishing his own works in the GDR, his book *Versuchte Nähe* (1977; translated as *Approximation*), which was published by the West German company Rowohlt Verlag, attracted much favorable attention at the Frankfurt Book Fair. Consisting of twenty-five short texts written between 1969 and 1976, the book spoofs various negative aspects of daily life in the GDR, including the political. Humorous and witty, Schädlich is also a devastating satirist. Of particular interest in the book is Schädlich's use of his linguistic training to mimic different styles and in general to use language as a device of satire. Indeed, the use and abuse of language for political ends is a central concern of the collection. Not long after the publication of *Approximation*, Schädlich received permission to emigrate from the GDR and resettle in West Germany. His next book, a collection of ten stories titled *Irgend etwas irgendwie* (Somewhere Something Somehow), appeared in 1984 and evidences the author's difficulties in adjusting to a new society. In 1985 Schädlich published *Mechanik* (The Mechanic), which is based on extensive research into the subject of euthanasia under the Nazis. *Tallover,* which came out in 1986, is a fictional biography of a secret agent who lived for 136 years (1819–1955) and began his career in Prussia in 1842. Despite political changes through the years, the spy, as conceived by Schädlich, remains a constant of the police state. In two subsequent books, *Der Sprachabschneider* (The Language Artist, 1980) and *Ostwestberlin* (East-West Berlin, 1987), a collection of stories, Schädlich further demonstrates his deep interest in language. His two latest novels, *Schott*, an absurdist comic novel named for its central character, and *Trivialroman* (A Trivial Novel), appeared in 1992 and 1998, respectively. Schädlich is also the author of several books on politics and society, among them *Deutsche im deutschen Exil?* (Germans in German Exile?, 1988); *Über Dreck, Politik und Literatur: Aufsätze, Reden, Gespräche, Kurzprosa* (On Trash, Politics, and Literature: Essays, Speeches, Conversations, and Short Prose Pieces, 1992); and *Vertrauen und Verrat* (Trust and Treachery, 1997).

Literature: "Hans Joachim Schädlich," in *Literary Intellectuals and the Dissolution of the State: Professionalism and Conformity in the GDR*, ed. Robert von Hallberg, trans. Kenneth J. Northcott (Chicago: University of Chicago Press, 1996), 213–26.

Translations: *Approximation,* trans. Richard Winston and Clara Winston (New York: Harcourt Brace Jovanovich, 1980).

Schedlinski, Rainer (b. 1956) German poet, essayist, and editor. Schedlinski was born in Magdeburg. Prior to becoming a freelance writer in 1982, he worked at a variety of jobs. He is also known to have been recruited by the East German security service (Stasi) in 1974, 1979, and 1985, which is the more interesting in light of the fact that his brother lived in West Germany and assisted people who were fleeing from the German Democratic Republic. Over a period of several years, Schedlinski underwent psychiatric treatment and in 1982 attempted suicide. His literary career began to develop after he settled in Berlin in 1984 and established contact with the Prenzlauer Berg group. From 1986 to 1989, he edited the journal *ariadnefabrik,* whose purpose was to provide a theoretical framework for the group's literary practice. It was subsequently revealed that the journal had been supported by funds provided by the Stasi. In 1990 Schedlinski became director of the Galrev publishing house in Berlin, but was removed from the position for a period of time in 1992 after he acknowledged publicly that he had collaborated with the Stasi. In 1991, in fact, the year Sascha Anderson was exposed as a Stasi informer, Schedlinski was also revealed to have been one.

Schedlinski's major collections of poems include *die rationen des ja und das nein* (the rationales of yes and no, 1988) and *die män-ner/der frauen* (the men/of the women, 1991). In 1990 he published two collections of essays of a socially critical nature: *inn-enansichten der letzten bilder* (interior views of the last pictures) and *die arroganz der ohnmacht: aufsätze und zeitungsbeiträge, 1989 und 1990* (the arrogance of weakness: essays and newspaper articles, 1989 and 1990). Schedlinski's poetry and essays are imbued with the spirit of disaffected youth and young artists in the GDR, especially in the wake of the Wolf Biermann affair. His eschewal of content and social relevance in general is a negation of a society toward which he, like other members of his group, felt unrelated. Their deliberate act of self-marginalization was compounded by an esoteric style of writing that both mocked conventions, especially linguistic, and impeded communication with what they tended to dismiss as an unsympathetic public.

Literature: "Rainer Schedlinski," in *Literary Intellectuals and the Dissolution of the State: Professionalism and Conformity in the GDR,* ed. Robert von Hallberg, trans. Kenneth J. Northcott (Chicago: University of Chicago Press, 1996), 265–72.

Schlesinger, Klaus (b. 1937) German novelist, journalist, and radio, film, and television scriptwriter. A native of Berlin, Schlesinger studied chemistry and worked for various laboratories. From 1963 to 1969, when he devoted himself entirely to creative writing, Schlesinger worked as a journalist and an editor. The novel with which he made his literary debut in 1971, *Michael,* caused something of a sensation because of its break with sanctioned socialist realist forms of narration through the use of a centrally important inner monologue within a first-person narrative and its less simplistic approach to the matter of responsibility for Germany's Nazi past. Built around the quest by the narrator, Michael Berger, for his own father, who may have been a war criminal, the novel leads more to the heart of the matter as to who Michael himself really is and what he represents. After *Michael,* Schlesinger published two quite different but interesting works. The first, *Hotel oder Hospital* (Hotel or Hospital, 1972), was published in Switzerland in 1974 under the title *Südstadtkrankenhaus Rostock* (Rostock South City Hospital). It is a book of reportage based on interviews with patients that, despite its outward manner of factual accuracy, probes deeply beneath the surface to reveal people's inner conflicts and the mechanisms by which they try to conceal them from others. In his short ironic novel *Alte Filme* (Old Films), which came out in 1975, Schlesinger took as his subject a man's mid-life crisis, which is alleviated by a sexual adventure when his wife is away for a weekend on a professional matter. The title of the novel derives from the fondness of the main character (Kotte) for watching old films on television and his discovery that an elderly woman who shares the apartment he and his wife live in was once an actress and played in a film he is watching. Contrasting present and past, Kotte views the elderly woman as an object lesson in human mortality. This is what prompts his act of rebellion in his wife's absence and becomes the remedy to his personal crisis.

Although he was never an overt opponent or critic of the East German communist regime and in fact was able to live for a long time in West Germany while retaining his GDR passport, Shlesinger was expelled from the Writers Union in 1979 for having signed a letter critical of the official cultural policy. In 1980 he resettled permanently in West Berlin. Schlesinger's deep fondness for Berlin, East and West, is reflected in several of his works, among them *Berliner Traum: Fünf Geschichten* (Berlin Dream: Five Stories, 1977) and *Leben im Winter* (Life in Winter, 1980). Set in East Berlin, *Leben im Winter,* one of Schlesinger's best works inspired by Berlin and its people, uses the occasion of a grandmother's seventieth birthday party, which brings guests together from both sides of the Berlin Wall, to make the point that only in dreams can the individual nurture hopes for a better future. *Matulla und Busch* (Matulla and Busch), which followed *Leben im Winter* in 1984, has a wholly West German setting, suggesting Schlesinger's transition from an East to a West German writer. Since the collapse of the GDR and the reunification of Germany, Schlesinger has written about this transition in such works as *Fliegender Wechsel: Eine persönliche Chronik* (Flying Change: A Personal Chronicle, 1990) and *Von der Schwierigkeit, Westler zu werden* (On the Difficulty of Becoming a Westener, 1998). His most recent works of fiction are the novels *Die Sache mit Randow* (The Randow Matter, 1996) and *Trug* (Deception, 2000).

Schneider, Rolf (b. 1932) German novelist, short-story and travel writer, essayist, and playwright. A popular and at times controversial writer in both East and West Germany, Schneider was born and educated through high school in Chemnitz. He then pursued a course of German studies at Halle University, from which he graduated in 1955. For the next three years, he worked with the East German Aufbau publishing house and then became a freelance writer. He made his literary debut in 1958 with a book of literary parodies, *Aus zweiter Hand* (Second Hand), based on the works of such writers as Gottfried Benn, Bertolt Brecht, Ernst Jünger, Franz Kafka, and Georg Rilke. Schneider's first collection of short stories, *Brücken und Gitter* (Bridges and Bars, 1965), was intended to reveal the dark side of the capitalist way of life by extensive use of black humor, irony, and the art of the grotesque. Although it became one of Schneider's best-known works, the collection was faulted by some critics for a lack of originality. No less controversial was Schneider's first novel, *Der Tod des Nibelungen* (The Death of the Nibelungen, 1970), the fictional biography of a sculptor who lives through the Wilhelmine period and the Weimar Republic, and achieves success for the first time only under the Nazis. With a number of references to West German politics at the time, *Der Tod des Nibelungen* is based on the 131-question form that the Americans required former National Socialists to fill out as part of the process of denazification at the end of World War II. Some critics have pointed out certain similarities to Thomas Mann's *Doctor Faustus,* whereas others have characterized Schneider's novel as a travesty of Ernst von Salmon's hugely popular autobiographical novel *Die Fragebogen* (The Questionnaire, 1951). Schneider also attracted attention with his book *Die Reise nach Jarosław* (The Journey to Jarosław, 1974), which takes a critical view of some aspects of East German society while holding forth the example of neighboring Poland as a land of greater freedom and better human relations. In his next two works, *Von Paris nach Frankreich: Reisenotizen* (From Paris to Frankfurt: Travel Notes, 1975), another example of Schneider's fondness for the travel genre, and *Die Abenteuer des Herakles: Nach* *alten Sagen neu erzählt* (The Adventures of Heracles: Newly Told from Old Legends, 1978), Schneider for the time being steered clear of controversy. It caught up with him, however, in his next book, *November* (1979), which he chose to publish first in West Germany, the GDR edition appearing only in 1990. Clearly one of Schneider's most interesting books, the work is obviously based on the forced expatriation of the writer and popular singer Wolf Biermann from the GDR in November 1976 and the widespread protest it engendered, despite Schneider's disclaimer that he had not intended to write a documentary novel. Although Schneider was one of the original signatories of the letter protesting Biermann's expulsion, he was criticized in some quarters for exploiting the affair for his own purposes.

After *November*, Schneider returned to the travel genre in *Die Reise zu Richard Wagner* (The Journey to Richard Wagner, 1989) and, several years later, in *Tucholskys Berlin: Eine Bildreise* (Tucholsky's Berlin: A Journey in Pictures, 1997). The latter text also demonstrates Schneider's interest in urban and landscape description, reflected in such postreunification works as *Berliner Wege: Wanderungen, Geschichte und Geschichten* (Berlin Paths: Wanderings, History, Stories, 1992); *Kleine Geschichte des Landes Mecklenburg-Vorpommern* (A Small History of the Mecklenburg–Pre-Pomeranian Region, 1993); *Fischland, Darss, Zingst: Der Reisebegleiter* (Fischland, Darss, Zingst: The Travel Companion, 1993); *Thuringen: Der Reisebegleiter* (Thuringia: The Travel Companion, 1993); *Potsdam: Garnison und Arkadien* (Potsdam: Garrison and Arcadia, 1994); and *Leben in Wien* (Life in Vienna, 1994).

The tearing down of the Berlin Wall, the collapse of the East German state, and the reunification of Germany form the subjects of two works by Schneider from the early 1990s: *Frühling im Herbst: Notizen vom Untergang der DDR* (Spring in Autumn: Notes

from the Downfall of the GDR, 1991) and *Volk ohne Trauer: Notizen nach dem Untergang der DDR* (A People Without Grief: Notes After the Downfall of the GDR, 1992). In *Der rote Stern stirbt leise: Abzug der Russen aus Deutschland* (The Red Star Dies Slowly: Withdrawal of the Russians from Germany, 1995), he took aim at the slow withdrawal of Soviet troops from the former GDR. Also in 1995 he published an account of the German market economy from the perspective of a former East German, under the title *Die Sprache des Geldes: Reisen durch die Marktgesellschaft* (The Language of the Stock Exchange: Travels Through the Market Economy). Other works by Schneider include *Nekrolog: Unernste Geschichten* (Necrology: Unserious Stories, 1973); *Pilzomelett und andere Nekrologe* (Pilzomelett and Other Necrologies, 1974); *Versuch über den Schrecken: Erzählungen* A Study of Fear: Stories, 1995); and *Unerwartete Veränderung: Erzählungen* (Unexpected Transformation: Stories, 1980), four collections of stories in the spirit of the grotesque and macabre; *Die problematisierte Wirklichkeit. Leben und Werk Robert Musils: Versuch einer Interpretation* (Problematized Reality. The Life and Work of Robert Musil: An Attempt at an Interpretation, 1975), a study of the Austrian writer; *Das Glück* (Good Fortune, 1976); *Annäherungen & Ankunft* (Approximations and Arrival, 1982); *Kapellmeister Levi: Eine Novelle* (Choirmaster Levi: A Novella, 1989); and *Jede Seele auf Erden* (Every Soul on Earth, 1990). Schneider's many plays for stage and radio appear in such collections as *Stücke: Dramatiker der Deutschen Demokratischen Republik* (Plays: Dramatists of the German Democratic Republic, 1970); *Stimmen danach: Hörspiele* (Hearing Voices: Radio Plays, 1970); and *Marienbader Intrigen: 6 Hörspiele* (Marienbad Intrigues: 6 Radio Plays, 1985). Schneider also published a study of German drama in the immediate postwar period under the title *Theater in einem besiegten Land: Dramaturgie der deutschen Nachkriegszeit, 1945–1949* (Theater in a Conquered Land: Postwar German Drama, 1945–1949, 1980). Further demonstrating his versatility, Schneider wrote the text for a book about East German grafitti, *Ostdeutsche Graffiti* (East German Graffiti), published in 1994.

Translations: *Bridges and Bars,* trans. Michael Bullock (New York: Viking, 1967); *Deep Waters,* trans. John Paet (Berlin: Seven Seas, 1968); *November,* trans. Michael Bullock (New York: Knopf, 1981).

Schreyer, Wolfgang (b. 1927) German novelist and radio and television scriptwriter. Known above all for his spy and criminal novels, Schreyer was born in Magdeburg, where he was educated through middle school. Before he could continue his education, he was pressed into military service during World War II. After he returned from a prisoner-of-war camp in 1946, he became a pharmacist, but gave up this profession for a literary career in 1952. That was when he published his first novel, *Grossgarage Südwest* (Big Garage Southwest), a mystery novel and one of the first East German works of fiction about West German saboteurs. Schreyer elaborated a theory of the novel of fact (*Tatsachenroman*), in which fiction and journalism are combined and which was exemplified by his next major work, *Unternehmen Thunderstorm* (Operation Thunderstorm, 1954). This is a novel about the Warsaw Uprising of 1944 based in part on Schreyer's own wartime experiences and intended to reveal the English plan to thwart the USSR and the Polish People's Army and return Poland to capitalism. Subsequent novels of a similar combination of fiction and political journalism frequently have Central American locales, as do *Tempel des Satans* (Temple of Satan, 1960), one of Schreyer's most popular books; *Aufstand des Sisyphos: Eine caribische Chronik* (The Re-volt of Sisyphus: A Caribbean Chronicle, 1969); *Der Reporter* (The Reporter, 1980), a novel about the Dominican Republic set in 1961; *Dominikanische Tragödie* (Dominican Tragedy, 1980); and *Eiskalt in Paradies* (Ice Cold in Paradise, 1982). Schreyer's other criminal novels include *Die fünf Leben des Dr. Gundlach* (The Five Lives of Dr. Gundlach, 1982); *Preludio II* (Prelude II, 1988); *Die Beute* (The Loot, 1989); *Nebel: Kriminalroman* (Fog: A Mystery Novel, 1991); and *Das Quartett: Kriminalroman* (The Quartet: A Mystery Novel, 1994). Schreyer's sole collection of stories, *Die Entführung* (The Kidnapping), appeared in 1982. It contains three tales: "Alaskafuchse" ("Alaska Fox"), "Die Entführung" ("The Kidnapping"), and "Die Durststrecke" ("The Lean Years").

Schuder, Rosemarie (real name Rosemarie Hirsch; b. 1928) German novelist and essayist. Admired above all for her historical fiction, Schuder was born in Jena. After graduating from high school, she began working primarily as a journalist. She made her literary debut with the novel *Der Sohn der Hexe* (The Witch's Son, 1957), about the scientist Johannes Keppler. From the beginning, it was clear that Schuder was a talented writer of historical fiction. Besides a fidelity to historical reality, Schuder sought to make her narratives relevant to the contemporary reader by painting a broad social canvas and inviting the reader to draw connections between the past being portrayed and the present. *Der Sohn der Hexe* was followed by *Der Gefesselte* (The Fettered, 1962) and *Die zerschlagene Madonna* (The Smashed Madonna, 1965). As a writer of historical novels, Schuder is perhaps best known for her cycle about the lives of great physicians of the sixteenth century: *Paracelsus und Der Garten der Lüste* (Paracelsus and the Garden of Desire, 1972); *Agrippa und das Schiff der Zufriedenen* (Agrippa and the Ship of the Satisfied, 1977); and *Serveto vor Pilatus*

(Serveto Before Pilate, 1982). In 1988 Schuder and her husband, the writer Rudolf Hirsch, published a collection of essays on anti-Semitism in German history under the title *Der gelbe Fleck: Wurzeln und Wirkungen des Judenhasses in der deutschen Geschichte* (The Yellow Spot: Roots and Effects of Jew Hatred in German History). Schuder is an authority on the Dutch artist Hieronymus Bosch and has published two books on him.

Schütz, Helga (b. 1937) German novelist and screenwriter. Along with Christa Wolf, Brigitte Reimann, Irmtraud Morgner, Gerti Tetzner, and Maxie Wander, Schütz is one of the foremost East German feminist writers to have emerged in the 1970s. A native of Falkenhein, Silesia (now Poland), Schütz moved to Dresden in 1944. She studied gardening and from 1955 to 1958 was enrolled in the new Workers and Farmers School in Potsdam. Her interests subsequently turned to film, however, and from 1958 to 1962 she studied drama at the Film School in Potsdam, where she earned her degree as a film dramatist. She then went to work as a scriptwriter for documentaries and short feature films for the DEFA studios. After turning out a number of film scripts, Schütz made her literary debut in 1970 with the well-received *Vorgeschichte oder schöne Gegend Probstein* (Prehistory, or Scenic Probstein), which deals with the appearance of fascism in daily life and among ordinary people. After three successive volumes of stories and novellas—*Die Erdbeben bei Sangerhausen und andere Geschichten* (The Earthquake near Sangerhausen and Other Stories, 1972); *Festbeleuchtung* (Festive Illumination, 1974); and *Jette in Dresden* (Jette in Dresden, 1977)—Schütz published one of her most probing dissections of East German social behavior: *Julia oder Erziehung zum Chorgesang* (Julia, or An Education in Choral Singing, 1980). *Martin Luther: Eine Erzählung für den Film* (Martin Luther: A

Film Story, 1983) came next, followed by arguably Schütz's most popular work of fiction, *In Annas Namen* (In Anna's Name, 1986). Alternating between the third and the first person, the novel traces a woman's search for identity, from her discovery as a four-month-old in an abandoned truck during the heavy bombing of Dresden in February 1945 to a near-fatal automobile accident (or perhaps suicide attempt) in which she is delivered of a premature infant while still unconscious. Schütz's post–GDR publications include *Heimat Süsse Heimat: Zeit-Rechnungen in Kasachstan* (Homeland Sweet Homeland: Keeping Time in Kazakhstan, 1992), essentially a book of reportage about a trip to the fomer Soviet Central Asian republic, and the novel *Vom Glanz der Elbe* (By the Light of the Elbe, 1995). Schütz was awarded the Heinrich Greif Prize in 1969; the Heinrich Mann Prize in 1973; the Theodor Fontane Prize in 1974; and the ZDF (television) Prize in Literature in 1991, the year in which she was also named Resident Writer of the City of Mainz.

Translations: "The Earthquake at Sangerhausen," trans. Jan van Heurck, in *The New Sufferings of Young W. and Other Stories from the German Democratic Republic,* ed. Therese Hörnigk and Alexander Stephan (New York: Continuum, 1997), 142–48; "In Anna's Name," trans. Dorothy Rosenberg, in *Daughters of Eve: Women's Writing from the German Democratic Republic,* ed. and trans. Nancy Lukens and Dorothy Rosenberg (Lincoln: University of Nebraska Press, 1993), 103–9.

Schwartz, Gheorghe (b. 1945) Romanian novelist and short-story writer. A native of Lugoj, in the Arad district in western Romania near the Hungarian border, Schwartz received his early education in local schools before studying philosophy at the Babeş-Bolyai University in Cluj. He subsequently earned his doctorate in political science.

Schwartz has held several administrative positions, among them chief adviser to the inspectorate for culture of the city of Arad (1990–1993) and cultural attaché of the Romanian Embassy in Bonn, Germany, in 1992 and 1993. In 1992 he taught journalism at Vest University in Arad and since 1994 has anchored a television program in Arad. Schwartz made his literary debut in 1972 with the novel *Martorul* (The Witness). Since then, he has published eleven other novels: *Pietrele* (Stones, 1978); *A treia zi* (The Third Day, 1980); *Spitalul* (The Hospital, 1981); *Efectul P* (The P Factor, 1983); *Om și lege* (Man and Law, 1987); *Cei o suta: Anabasis* (The Hundred: Anabasis, 1988); *Cochilia* (Shells, 1992); *Cei o suta: Ecce homo* (The Hundred: Ecce homo, 1993); a fictionalized account of the trial of Alfred Dreyfus under the title *Procesul: O dramă evreiască* (The Trial: A Jewish Drama, 1996); *Oul de aur* (The Golden Egg, 1998), for which he won the Writers Union prize for prose; and *Mâna albă* (The White Hand, 2000). Undoubtedly Schwartz's major accomplishment to date is the vast ongoing cycle of historical novels that so far comprises *Cei o suta: Anabasis, Cei o suta ecce homo, Oul de aur,* and *Mâna albă,* which, when completed, will range in time from ancient Babylonia to the twentieth century. Rich in historical detail and color, with well-crafted individual portraits, the novels address the historical process itself and can be read on more than one level. Schwartz is also the author of three collections of short stories: *Ucenicul vrăjitor* (The Apprentice Sorcerer, 1976) and *Castelul albastru* (The Blue Castle, 1986), both in the rich tradition of Romanian fantastic literature, and *Maximele-minimele* (The Big and the Small, 1984), a collection of small humorous sketches from everyday life.

Šegedin, Petar (b. 1909) Croatian novelist, short-story and travel writer, and essayist. A formidable presence in twentieth-century Croatian literature, Šegedin was born on the Adriatic island of Korčula. He received his early education both there and in Dubrovnik and eventually graduated from the Pedagogical Institute and the Faculty of Philosophy of Zagreb University. He subsequently worked as a secondary-school teacher, a secretary at the Matica hrvatska publishing house, a lexicographer, and, from 1956 to 1960, the cultural attaché to the Yugoslav Embassy in Paris. In 1964 he was elected a full member of the Yugoslav Academy of Arts and Sciences. Šegedin made his literary debut in 1946 with the novel *Djeca božja* (God's Children), which has been characterized as a "pillar of Croatian modernism." His second novel, *Osamljenici* (The Lonely), appeared in 1947. He eventually published another three novels: *Crni smiješak* (The Dark Smile, 1969); *Getsemanski vrtovi* (The Gates of Gethsemene, 1983); and *Vjetar* (The Wind, 1986), about the adventurous life of one Kazimir Barač, who commits suicide at the end. His first book of travel writings, *Na putu* (On the Road), came out in 1953 and was followed by another collection, *Susreti* (Encounters), in 1962. Šegedin is also the author of several collections of novellas and short stories, among them *Mrtve more* (The Dead Sea, 1954); *Na istom putu* (On the Same Road, 1963); *Orfej u maloj baštei* (Orpheus in the Little Garden, 1964); *Sveti vrag* (The Holy Enemy, 1966); *Izvještaj iz pokrajine* (Report from the Provinces, 1969); *Tišina* (Silence, 1983); *Licem u lice* (Face to Face, 1987); and *Svijetle noći* (Pale Nights, 1993), which is notable for a darker, more pessimistic attitude toward life in comparison with the more positive stance of his previous fiction. As an essayist, Šegedin published his first collection, *Eseji* (Essays), in 1956. A second collection, *Riječ o riječi* (A Word About the Word), came out in 1971. *Svi smo odgovorni* (We Are All Responsible), subtitled "A Sociopolitical

Essay," appeared in 1971. *U carstvu ponesenih duša* (In the Kingdom of Exalted Spirits), which was published in Zagreb in a Croatian–French edition in 1993, is an attempt to overcome French misunderstandings of the Croatians during the Yugoslav wars of the 1990s. The work arose from Šegedin's experiences as cultural attaché to the Yugoslav Embassy in Paris. Also in 1993 Šegedin published *Franfurtski dnevnik ili priča o pobožnom pustolovu* (Frankfurt Diary, or The Tale of a Pious Adventurer). The work was written in 1972 and covers the period from 17 July to mid-September of that year. Of particular interest in *Franfurtski dnevnik* is Šegedin's coverage of the massacre of the Israeli athletes at the Munich Olympics. Šegedin's most recent work, *Nema spasa od života ili Doktor Zero nasuprot pravom čovjeku* (There's No Salvation from Life, or Doctor Zero on the Rights of Man, 1997), is also essentially political in character. Obviously inspired by the newly established independence of Croatia, it considers the struggle for existence of small nations in today's world and, in particular, the issue of nationalism.

Seghers, Anna (real name Netty Reiling; 1900–1983) German novelist and short-story writer. One of the most prominent and influential writers in the German Democratic Republic, Seghers was born in Mainz and was educated at the universities of Cologne and Heidelberg, from where she graduated in 1924. The same year, her first literary work, the tale "Die Toten auf der Insel Djal" ("The Dead on Djal Island"), a kind of ghost story that she subtitled "A Dutch Saga," appeared in a Christmas supplement of the *Frankfurter Zeitung*. In 1925 she married a fellow student, Laszlo Radvanyi, with whom she shared radical leftist views, and settled in Berlin. Her story "Aufstand der Fischer von St. Barbara" ("The Revolt of the Fishermen of Saint Barbara")

won the Kleist Prize in 1928; Erwin Piscator made the story into a film in 1931. It was also in 1928 that Seghers became a member of the German Communist Party and the Association of Proletarian-Revolutionary Writers. Her first collection of stories, *Auf dem Wege auf amerikanischen Bottschaft und andere Erzählungen* (On Route to the American Embassy and Other Stories) appeared in 1930, the year she visited the USSR for the first time. Her novel *Die Gefährten* (The Companions), which was based on the suppression of the short-lived Hungarian Republic of Soviets of 1919, came out in 1932.

When Hitler became German chancellor, Seghers and her family immigrated to France via Switzerland. Her next novel, *Der Kopflohn* (The Price on His Head), about the successful inroads of the Nazis in German peasant villages in the early 1930s, appeared in Amsterdam in 1933. Two years later *Der Weg durch den Februar* (The Way Through February), a novel based on the workers' uprising in Vienna in 1934, was published by the exile press Éditions du Carrefour. Shortly after the collapse of France in World War II, Seghers and her two children set out for the unoccupied southern part of the country, taking up temporary residence first in Pamiers and then in Marseille. In March 1941, after being denied entry into the United States, she traveled to Mexico by way of Martinique, Santo Domingo, and New York. Mexico City was to be their home for the next five and a half years.

In 1939 Seghers completed her most celebrated work, the novel *Das siebte Kreuz* (*The Seventh Cross*). It appeared in German and Spanish in Mexico City in 1942 and, the same year, in English in New York. It enjoyed considerable success in the United States and became a Book-of-the-Month Club selection. Perhaps Seghers's finest work, *The Seventh Cross* is a compelling novel built around the adventures of a German escapee from a Nazi concentration camp. It was made into a film in 1944 with Spencer Tracy in the lead role of the escapee, Georg Heisler. Seghers's next novel, *Transit,* which she had completed in 1943, was based on her own harrowing, and aborted, flight from Paris just before the German entry into the city in June 1940. The novel was published first in Spanish and English translations in 1944 and then in German in 1948. It was made into a movie in 1991.

With few exceptions, Seghers's postwar works generally fall below the level of her prewar writings. Once she returned to Germany in 1947 and established residence in East Berlin, she became increasingly active in GDR literary politics, often in the role of a mediator between a rigorous state aesthetic policy and recalcitrant writers. Her own writings from the 1950s and 1960s tend toward political and social didacticism. This is evident in such works as her short-story collections *Die Linie* (The Line, 1950) and *Die Kinder* (The Children, 1951), and in such ambitious and unabashedly pro-Soviet, pro-communist, and "anti-imperialist" novels as *Die Toten bleiben jung* (*The Dead Stay Young,* 1949) and its sequels, *Die Entscheidung* (The Decision, 1959) and *Der Vertrauen* (Trust, 1968). Her better writing from the postwar period appears for the most part in her shorter fiction, in particular two volumes of stories dealing with the nineteenth-century revolutionary upheavals in the Caribbean islands: *Die Hochzeit von Haiti und andere Erzählungen* (The Wedding on Haiti and Other Stories, 1949) and *Das Licht auf dem Galgen* (The Light on the Gallows, 1960). One of her more unusual later works, *Sonderbare Begegnungen* (Unusual Meetings, 1973), consists of three stories with elements of the fantastic, the last a fictional meeting in a Prague coffeehouse of such historical masters of the genre of the fantastic as Nikolai Gogol, E. T. A. Hoffmann, and Franz Kafka. Through their literary discussions, Seghers advances her own views of art and society and a distinctly utopian-visionary outlook on life.

Seghers won a number of awards in her lifetime: the National Prize of the GDR in 1951 and 1959; the International Stalin Peace Prize in 1952; the Order of Karl Marx in 1965; and an honorary doctorate from Jena University in 1965. In 1975 she was named an honorary citizen of East Berlin, and in 1981 an honorary citizen of the city of Mainz. In 1978 she was elected honorary president of the GDR Writers Union.

Literature: Lowell A. Bangerter, *The Bourgeois Proletarian: A Study of Anna Seghers* (Bonn: Bouvier Verlag Herbert Grundmann, 1980), a fair introduction to Seghers's work; Kathleen J. La Bahn, *Anna Seghers' Exile Literature: The Mexican Years (1941–1947)* (New York: Peter Lang, 1986); Andreas Schrade, *Anna Seghers* (Stuttgart: Metzler, 1993), the best critical study of Seghers in any language; Christiane Zehl Romero, *Anna Seghers* (Reinbek bei Hamburg: Rowohlt, 1993), a handy well-illustrated "life and work" in the Rororo series; Frank Wagner, Ursula Emmerich, and Ruth Radvanyi, eds., *Anna Seghers: Eine Biographie in Bildern* (Berlin: Aufbau-Verlag, 1994), one of the best books on Seghers, this biography in photographs accompanied by excerpts from Seghers's writings includes a chronology of her life and works and a short essay by Christa Wolf; Christa Wolf, "If at First You Don't Succeed . . . ," in *The Author's Dimension: Selected Essays,* ed. Alexander Stephan, trans. Jan van Heurck (New York: Farrar, Straus and Giroux, 1993), 125–30, and "A Visit to Anna Seghers," in *The Reader and the Writer: Essays, Sketches, Memories,* trans. Joan Becker (New York: International, 1977), 138–43.

Translations: *The Dead Stay Young* (Boston: Little, Brown, 1950); *The Revolt of the Fishermen,* trans. Margaret Goldsmith (New York: Longmans, Green, 1930); *The*

Seventh Cross, trans. James A. Galston (Boston: Little, Brown, 1942); *Transit,* trans. James A. Galston (Boston: Little, Brown, 1944).

Seifert, Jaroslav (1901–1986) Czech poet. Seifert was the winner of the Nobel Prize in Literature in 1984, the first Czech writer ever so honored. One of the greatest Czech poets of the twentieth century, he was born in the Prague working-class district of Žižkov. In 1938 he moved to the suburb of Břevnov, where he would live for the rest of his life. After graduating from secondary school, he became a journalist and by 1930 held the position of editor in chief of *Nová scéna,* a theater monthly. Throughout the 1930s and 1940s, he continued to write for daily newspapers, including *Práce.* Seifert joined the Communist Party at an early age, full of enthusiasm for the Soviet Union. But he broke with the Party after a trip to the USSR and in 1929 became a member of the Socialist Democratic Party.

It was while he was earning his living as a journalist that Seifert began to write poetry. He published nearly thirty volumes of poems in his lifetime, beginning with *Bojiště dne* (Battlefield of the Day, 1921). It was followed by *Město v slzách: první verše* (*City in Tears: Early Poems,* 1921); *Samá láska* (*Sheer Love,* 1923); *Na vlnách TSF* (*On the Waves of TSF,* 1925), TSF referring to *télégraphie sans fil* (wireless telegraphy); and *Slavík zpívá špatně* (*The Nightingale Sings Poorly,* 1926). In this early period, Seifert's poetry was mostly light in the sense of being conversational, lyrical, playful and witty, often strongly sensual and erotic. Seifert wrote also of his love of Prague both as a city and as a symbol of Czechoslovakia. Because of the important role played by sound in Seifert's poetry and the nexus between sound and meaning, his poetry of the 1920s and 1930s especially does not lend itself easily to translation.

In keeping with Seifert's communist political affiliation at the time—besides Party membership, he was a contributor to the communist paper *Rudé právo*—a number of the poems in these first collections have a proletarian character. Inclined also toward the experimentalism of the 1920s, Seifert, for example, used different typefaces in *Na vlnách TSF.* One of his infrequent prose texts of this period, the heavily autobiographical *Hvězdy nad Rajskou zahradou* (The Stars Above Paradise, 1929), is of particular interest for the light it sheds on Seifert's affiliations within the Czech art community in the 1920s. His last major work before the outbreak of World War II, *Zhasněte světla* (Put Out the Lights, 1938), was a reaction to Hitler's takeover of Bohemia and Moravia and to the creation of the Nazi puppet state of Slovakia

During the German occupation of Czechoslovakia, Seifert wrote mostly on patriotic themes. However, in the postwar period he was criticized as disloyal, bourgeois, capitalist, escapist, and a betrayer of his class. Taking advantage of the thaw of 1956, he, in turn, criticized the government's cultural policies. Nevertheless, in 1966 he was honored with the title National Artist. The following year he again incurred the wrath of communist officialdom when he became a signatory to Charter 77 and subsequently wrote in his poem "And Now Goodbye": "I believe that seeking beautiful words / Is better than killing and murdering." He added more fuel to the fire in 1968—the year of the Soviet-led invasion of Czechoslovakia—when, on television, he read a statement by the Writers Union (of which he was acting chairman in 1968 and chairman in 1969/1970) chastising the Warsaw Pact countries for "grossly distorted and unsubstantiated attacks from abroad aimed at the ranks of the Czechoslovak writers." Later, the office of censorship banned publication of the statement.

Seifert's major postwar volumes of poetry include *Halleyova kometa* (Halley's Comet, 1967); *Odlévání zvonů* (*The Casting of Bells,* 1967); *Deštník z Piccadilly* (*An Umbrella from Piccadilly,* 1979); *Všecky krásy světa: Příběhy a vzpomínky* (All the Beauties of the World: Experiences and Recollections, 1981), published by Index in Cologne; and *Býti básníkem* (To Be a Poet, 1983). When illness prevented Seifert from going to Stockholm to receive his Nobel Prize, the Czechoslovak government refused to give an exit permit to his son-in-law and secretary, Daribor Plichta, to accept the prize on his behalf. Seifert had previously received Czechoslovak state prizes in 1936, 1955, and 1968. Sixty-Eight Publishers, the Czech émigré publishing house in Toronto, published his memoirs in Czech in September 1981. Some of the memoirs appeared in the 1983 issue of *Cross Currents,* a yearbook of Central European culture, published by the Department of Slavic Languages at the University of Michigan.

Literature: Zdeněk Pešat, *Jaroslav Seifert* (Prague: Československý spisovatel, 1991), a respectable introductory monograph.

Translations: *The Casting of Bells,* trans. Paul Jagasich and Tom O'Grady (Iowa City: Spirit that Moves Us Press, 1983); *Dressed in Light,* trans. Paul Jagasich and Tom O'Grady (New York: Dolphin-Moon, 1990); *The Early Poetry of Jaroslav Seifert: City in Tears, Sheer Love, On the Waves of TSF,* and *The Nightingale Sings Poorly,* trans. Dana Loewy (Evanston, Ill.: Northwestern University Press, 1977); *Morový sloup/The Plague Monument,* trans. Lyn Coffin (N.p.: SVU, 1980), a Czech–English edition; *Mozart in Prague: Thirteen Rondels,* trans. Paul Jagasich and Tom O'Grady (Iowa City: Spirit that Moves Us Press, 1985); *The Plague Monument,* trans. Ewald Osers (London: Terra Nova, 1979); *The Selected Poetry of Jaroslav Seifert,* ed. George Gibian, trans. Ewald Osers (London: Deutsch, 1986); *An Umbrella from Piccadilly,* trans. Ewald Osers (London: Magazine Editions, 1983); *A Wreath of Sonnets/ Věnec sonetů,* trans. J. K. Klement and Eva Stucke (Toronto: Lakewood Books/ Sixty-Eight Publishers, 1987), an English–Czech edition.

Selenić, Slobodan (1933–1995) Serbian novelist, playwright, and essayist. One of the most important writers of his generation, Selenić was born in Zagreb, Croatia. He later became a member of the Serbian Academy of Arts and Sciences and a professor at the Conservatory of Dramatic Art in Belgrade. Selenić was the author of seven novels, beginning with *Memoari Pere Bogalja* (Memoirs of Pera the Cripple, 1968), which won the October Prize in 1969. His second novel was the very popular *Prijatelji sa Kosančićevog Venca 7* (Friends from 7 Kosančić's Crown St., 1980). The novel deals with the complex, possibly allegorical, relationship that develops over time between the decadent, communist-hating son of a once prominent Serbian family (Vladan Hadžislavković) and a poor Kosovo Albanian orphan (Istref) who moves to Belgrade, eventually becomes an engineer, and emerges as the dominant member of the odd pair. Set in the 1970s, the novel is built around a manuscript describing Belgrade just after World War II sent to Istref by Hadžislavković. As Istref becomes more worldly and draws away from his Serbian friend, Hadžislavković tries to keep him close by steeping himself in Albanian culture. The final break is precipitated by the apparently homosexual Serb's discovery of Istref's intimate relations with a woman. *Prijatelji sa Kosančićevog Venca 7* brought Selenić the NIN Prize in 1981. It was followed by the novels *Pismo glava* (Heads/ Tails, 1982); *Očevi i oci* (Fathers and Forefathers, 1981); and *Timor mortis* (1989), which paints a grim picture of the Croatian massacres of Serbs during World War II as part of a longer history of Croatian aggression against the Serbs. Selenić was awarded the

Meša Selimović Prize for it. Selenić's last novel, *Ubistvo s predumišljajem* (*Premeditated Murder*, 1993), was also inspired in part by the latest chapter in the history of Serb–Croat conflict. Set against the fighting of the early 1990s, *Premeditated Murder* effectively juxtaposes scenes from the student antigovernment demonstrations in Belgrade in late 1992, protesting Serbia's role in the disintegration of Yugoslavia, and scenes from Belgrade during the last days of the German occupation and the communist takeover in 1944/1945. These events are set within an interesting multiple narrative frame built around the attempt by Jelena Panić, a brash aspiring writer and drama student in Belgrade, to reconstruct the story of the relationship between her grandmother (also called Jelena) and her "great-uncle" Jovan, whom she never knew. From Jovan's diaries and letters, which she discovers—and which are presented as narrated by Jovan—Jelena learns that her grandmother was raised from infancy by her stepfather, Stavra, and his son Jovan with whom she eventually developed an intense sexual relationship that she broke off after three years. When the communists arrest Stavra as an alleged German collaborator, Jelena has a romance with a security officer named Krsman Jakšić, with whom she works at the Tanjug news agency and who promises to help him. Bitter and resentful toward the communists whom he regards as boors, and jealous of Jelena's relationship with Jakšić, Jovan eventually murders him and then commits suicide, leaving behind his "confession" about his own love affair with his "sister." With the end of her narrative about her grandmother, Jelena's attention is rudely jolted back to the present and the Serb–Croat war. Her boyfriend has gone off to join the fighting and is reported dead in Krajina. Jelena eventually discovers his shattered body and, after arranging for its burial, resolves to leave war-torn Yugoslavia to join her mother in New Zealand. The last part of the novel, re-counting the death of Jelena's boyfriend and subsequent events, is told by a new narrator, the editor to whom Jelena entrusts the manuscript about her grandmother and who gives it the title "Premeditated Murder."

Apart from his fictional and dramatic writing, Selenić was a serious scholar of drama and published three volumes of essays: *Avangardna drama* (Avant-garde Drama, 1964); *Angažman u dramskoj formi* (Engaged Drama, 1965); and *Dramski pravci XX veka* (Trends in Twentieth-Century Drama, 1971), as well as an anthology of contemporary Serbian drama under the title *Antologija srpske drame* (An Anthology of Contemporary Serbian Drama, 1977).

Translations: *Premeditated Murder*, trans. Jelena Petrović (London: Harvill, 1996), which lists fourteen other texts by Selenić in English translation, although *Premeditated Murder* seems to be the only one ever published.

Šeligo, Rudi (b. 1935) Slovenian playwright, short-story writer, and novelist. A well-regarded writer and political activist, Šeligo was born in Rijeka (now in Croatia). After graduating from Ljubljana University with a degree in psychology and philosophy, he worked for several years as a lecturer in statistics. In 1987, after assuming the position of president of the Slovene Writers Association, he became increasingly engaged in politics and was a founding member of the Slovene Democratic Union. After Slovenia's independence, he was elected a parliamentary deputy in the first democratic elections in 1990. Three years later, Šeligo resumed his literary activity on a full-time basis.

Šeligo began his career as a writer of short stories and novels. His first novel, *Stolp* (The Tower), appeared in 1966. It was followed by one of his best-known prose texts, the short novel *Triptih Agate Schwarzkobler* (The Triptych of Agatha Schwarzkobler) and by the story *Kamen* (The Stone), both published in 1968; *Ali naj te z listjem posujem?* (Shall I Sprinkle You with Leaves?, 1971), a short novel; *Poganstvo* (Paganism, 1973), a collection of longer stories; *Rahel stik* (Light Contact, 1976), Šeligo's only full-length novel; and *Molčanja* (Silences, 1986) and *Zunaj sije februar* (Outside, February Is Shining, 1995), both collections of short stories. Šeligo is most admired as a writer of plays, nine of which have been published: *Kdor skak, tisti hlap* (He Who Leaps, Vanishes, 1972); *Čarobnica iz Gornje Davče* (The Witch from Zgornja Davča, 1977); *Lepa Vida* (Beautiful Vida, 1978); *Svatba* (*The Wedding,* 1981); *Ana* (Anna) and *Svetloba in seme* (Light and Seed), both published and staged in 1984; *Slovenska savna* (Slovene Sauna, 1987); *Volčji čas ljubezni* (The Wolf-Time of Love, 1988), which, like his play *Ana,* is a sharp critique of totalitarianism; and *Razveza ali Sveta sarmatska kri* (Divorce, or The Holy Sarmatian Blood, 1994), a political allegory about the dissolution of Yugoslavia. Besides his playwriting, Šeligo published a book on the poetics of theater, *Identifikacija in katarza v nekaterih poetikah drame* (Identification and Catharsis in Some Poetics of Drama), in 1987. As testimony to his importance as a political thinker and activist, a collection of his speeches was published in 1991 under the title *Prehajanja: Izjave, protesti in nagovori* (Transitions: Speeches, Protests, and Discussions). Šeligo's most recent work, a book of memoirs titled *Demoni slavja: Uslišani spomin* (The Demons of Celebration: Heard Memory), appeared in 1997.

Translations: *The Wedding,* trans. Sonja Kravanja, in *Contemporary Slovenian Drama* (Ljubljana: Slovene Writers Association, 1997), 303–59, which also includes summaries of *Lepa Vida* and *Ana.*

Selimović, Meša (1910–1982) Bosnian Muslim novelist. Born in Tuzla, Bosnia, Selimović is justifiably regarded as one of the finest writers in Serbo-Croatian of the twentieth century. In the 1930s he attended Belgrade University, where he concentrated on the Serbo-Croatian language and Yugoslav literatures. During World War II, Selimović was captured by the Croatian Ustaša and imprisoned from September 1942 to January 1943. He managed to escape and join Tito's partisan Yugoslav Army of National Liberation.

Selimović's national and international fame rests principally on his novel *Derviš i smrt* (*Death and the Dervish,* 1966). It was inspired in part by the 1944 court-martial and execution of his brother, Šefkija Selimović, a partisan officer like himself. The novel is set in the late period of Ottoman rule over Bosnia but alludes to the Yugoslavia of Selimović's own time. Using a stream-of-consciousness technique, Selimović weaves an intriguing tale of murky power politics as Ahmed Nuruddin, the head of an order of dervishes in Sarajevo, tries to free his brother who has been arrested and is later killed by the local power structure for no valid reasons. In the misguided belief that he can change the repressive and arbitrary system from within, Nuruddin eventually becomes a part of it, reaches high office, but in the end is devoured by the system to which his brother fell victim. Selimović won instant fame for his celebrated and widely translated novel. He was made a member of the Serbian Academy of Arts and Sciences and the Academy of Arts and Sciences of Bosnia and Herzegovina, and was awarded honorary doctorates by the universities of Belgrade and Sarajevo. He also won the Njegoš Prize for his literary work in general and for *Death and the Dervish* in particular on 10 October 1969, and was a candidate for the Nobel Prize in Literature.

Tišine (Silences, 1961), which antedates *Death and the Dervish* by five years, recreates the historical atmosphere of the period immediately following World War II. It pivots on the troubles experienced by a former soldier as he tries to adapt to the sweeping social changes he encounters in postwar Yugoslavia. A war veteran (Ahmet Šabo) also figures in *Trvava* (*The Fortress*, 1970), but the setting this time is aftermath of the battle of Khotin in the late seventeenth century and the veteran is a Bosnian Muslim who fought in the Ottoman Turkish army against the Russians. Narrated in the first person, the long novel chronicles the hardships of Šabo's life in Sarajevo after the war, various intrigues in the town, and conflicts with the religious hierarchy that brooks no questioning of its authority (symbolized by the fortress that stands on a hill overlooking the town). *Ostrvo* (The Island, 1974), Selimović's most compelling novel after *Death and the Dervish*, is the life story of a retired couple who lived on the mainland but now reside on a remote island. The alienation of the husband and wife from each other, and their lack of mutual understanding, encapsulates the condition of the other residents on the island. Richly metaphoric in structure, the novel consists of nineteen chapters that can almost stand alone as separate stories. As Selimović manipulates his central characters, especially the husband, Ivan Marić, through different situations and relationships on the island, the novel progressively assumes the character of a philosophical rumination on the human condition, an aspect virtually of all his fiction. Although Selimović is compassionate, lightly ironic, and not overtly condemnatory, the picture he presents in *Ostrvo* is bleak. Besides alienation and isolation, there are pettiness and greed, insensitivity and ignorance; the island is a microcosm of human society. In a few of the best chapters dealing with animals, Selimović is masterful in his depiction of the thoughtlessness and inhumanity of people toward animals.

Apart from his fiction, Selimović published a volume of essays, *Eseji i ogledi* (Essays and Views, 1966); a book about the nineteenth-century Serbian linguistic reformer Vuk Stefanović Karadžić, *Za i protiv Vuka* (For and Against Vuk, 1967); a collection of miscellaneous writings under the title *Pisci, mišljenja, razgovori* (Writers, Thoughts, Conversations, 1970); and a book of memoirs, *Sjećanja* (Reminiscences, 1976).

Literature: Razija Lagumdžija, ed., *Kritičari o Meši Selimoviću: Sa autobiografijom* (Sarajevo: Svjetlost, 1973), and *Mesina vjecita uznemirenost: Sjećanja, svjedocenja, kazivanja* (Sarajevo: "Oslobenje public," 1991), two good source books on Selimović; Miodrag Petrović, *Roman Meše Selimovića* (Niš : Gradina, 1981), a study of Selimović's novels; Radovan Popović, *Život Meše Selimovića* (Belgrade: Beogradski izdavackograficki zavod, 1988), a biography.

Translations: *Death and the Dervish*, trans. Bogdan Rakić and Stephen M. Dickey (Evanston, Ill.: Northwestern University Pres, 1996); *The Fortress*, trans. E. D. Goy and Jasna Levinger (Evanston, Ill.: Northwestern University Press, 1999).

Sevov, Kolio (1933–1991) Bulgarian poet and prose writer. A native of the village of Cherna Mogila, Sevov graduated from high school in nearby Harmanli in 1951, after which, strongly attracted to the sea, he enlisted in the Bulgarian merchant marine, in whose service he spent several years. He subsequently studied at the Institute of Bibliography in Sofia in 1958. Sevov then settled in the Black Sea city of Varna and became very active in its cultural life. He was secretary of the Varna branch of the Bulgarian Writers Union and served as editor in chief of the literary quarterly *Prostori*. Sevov's poetry appears in such collections as *Kotvite se vdigat* (Anchors Are Raised, 1961); *Moriashki vuzel* (The Seaman's Knot, 1964); *V sredata na liatoto* (In the Middle of Summer, 1969); *Po visokoto bilo* (Along the High Crest, 1971); *Golemiiat den* (The Big Day, 1972); *Industrialen peyzazh* (Industrial Landscape, 1974); *Esenno more* (Autumn Sea, 1976); *Mezhdu dva prazdniki* (Between Two Holidays, 1979); *Nasreshtii vetrove* (Oncoming Winds, 1980); *Obrok* (The Vow, 1981); *Aysbergi* (Icebergs, 1982); and *Nepredvideno vreme* (An Unforeseen Time, 1989). As the titles of the collections indicate, a great many of Sevov's poems reflect his love for the sea and his experiences in the merchant marine. His enthusiasm for national industrial development is the subject of the volume *Industrialen peyzazh*. Beginning especially in the 1970s, Sevov's poetry also manifested his interest in the ancient Thracian past of Bulgaria and a personal spiritual identification with Thracian legendary figures. Besides his poetry, Sevov wrote essays, film scripts, and interviews with foreign writers. They appear in such volumes as *Moite stranstvuvaniia: Eseistichni putepisi* (My Wanderings: Travel Essays, 1978); *Pod edno nebo: Eseistichni razgovori* (Under One Sky: Essayistic Conversations, 1979); and *Chuzhdi grehove: Dokumentalni ochertsi* (Others' Sins: Documentary Sketches, 1980). His historical novel, *Gradishteto* (Ancient Ruins), appeared in 1982.

Translations: Four poems, trans. John Balaban, in *Poets of Bulgaria*, ed. William Meredith (Greensboro, N.C.: Unicorn, 1985), 72–75; one poem, trans. Henry Taylor, in *Window on the Black Sea: Bulgarian Poetry in Translation*, ed. Richard Harteis, in collaboration with William Meredith (Pittsburgh: Carnegie Mellon University Press, 1992), 165.

Seyppel, Joachim (b. 1919) German novelist, essayist, and journalist. Born in Berlin, Seyppel studied German language and literature, theater, art history, and philosophy in Berlin, Lausanne, and Rostock from 1939 to 1943. Not long after receiving his degree, he was called up for military service, but eventually proved a disciplinary problem and in 1945 was sentenced to imprisonment for nine months and subsequent assignment to the front. In May 1945 he was captured by the Soviets but was released and permitted to return to Germany in the autumn. After returning to Berlin, he began working as a university teacher and journalist. In 1949 he received a fellowship to Harvard University and left Germany for the United States. From 1950 to 1961, when he returned to West Berlin to become a freelance writer and journalist, he taught at several American universities. In 1973 he resettled in East Berlin, motivated by both his desire to be near the woman who later became his wife, Tatiana Rilsky, and the announcement by East German leader Erich Honecker of a more liberal cultural policy. The political "honeymoon" did not last long, however, largely because of Seyppel's protest over the Wolf Biermann affair. His East German publisher, Aufbau-Verlag, rejected his novel *Die Wohnmaschine* (The Housing Machine) because of Seyppel's criticism in it of living conditions in East Berlin; it was eventually published in 1991. *Hinten, weit in der Türkei* (Deep Inside Turkey, 1979), a travel book Seyppel wrote with Rilsky, was accepted by Buchverlag der Morgen, and an edition of 10,000 copies was printed. But before it could be distributed, the entire edition was trashed. By June 1979 Seyppel's relations with the authorities had degenerated to the point where—along with several other writers—he was dismissed from the Writers Union. Nevertheless, a month later he received a three-year entry-and-exit visa that permitted him to spend time in Hamburg. But it was while he was in Hamburg in 1971 that he was informed of the loss of his East German citizenship. Seyppel's trials with the authorities leading up to his expulsion from the Writers Union became the subject of his documentary *Protokoll eines Tribunals* (Proceedings of a Tribunal, 1991). In 1982 he also published *Ich bin ein kaputter Typ: Bericht über Autoren in der DDR* (I'm a Bum: Report on Writers in the GDR), a book about his life in the GDR; the *kaputter Typ* (bum) in the title alludes to the language of a public denunciation of Seyppel and other liberal writers by the East German poet and political stooge Dieter Noll. After Seyppel had resettled in West Germany, he published in 1994 an extensive collection of micro-essays about literary life in East Berlin and contemporary German literature in general under the title *Trottoir & Asphalt: Erinnerungen an Literatur in Berlin, 1945–1990* (Sidewalk and Asphalt: Recollections of Literature in Berlin, 1945–1990).

A highly prolific author, Seyppel had made his literary debut in 1947 with his novel *Flugsand der Tage* (Quicksand of Days). However, it was only with *Torso Conny der Grosse: 21 romantische Tatsachenberichte vom Schelm der keiner war* (Torso Conny the Great: 21 Romantic Reports by the Rogue Who Really Wasn't One, 1969), conceived as a kind of reply to Günter Grass's *The Tin Drum*, that he began attracting serious attention as a writer. An inveterate traveler, Seyppel drew on his own experiences in such works as *Abendlandfahrt* (Journey to the East, 1963); *Columbus Bluejeans oder Der Reich der falschen Bilder* (Columbus Bluejeans, or The Realm of False Images, 1965), in essence an American travel book; *Ein Yankee in der Mark: Wanderung nach Fontane* (A Yankee in Brandenburg: In the Footsteps of Fontane, 1970); and *Hinten, weit in der Türkei.* In 1990 he returned to the Brandenburg setting for his novel *Die Streusandbüchse* (The Sand Box). Long interested in the Mann brothers, Thomas and Heinrich, Seyppel wrote a book about the departure for the United States of Heinrich and Nelly Mann titled *Abschied von Europa:* *Die Geschichte von Heinrich und Nelly Mann, dargestellt durch Peter Aschenback und Georgiewa Mühlenhaupt* (Departure from Europe: The Story of Heinrich and Nelly Mann as Told by Peter Aschenback and Georgieva Mühlenhaupt, 1975). Seyppel's own long stay in the United States is reflected not only in his fiction but also in works of a scholarly character, such as *Dekadenz oder Fortschritt: Eine Studie amerikanischer Geshichtsphilosophie* (Decadence or Progress: A Study of the American Philosophy of History, 1951) and, in English, *Schwenkfeld: Knight of Faith. A Study in the History of Religion* (1961). Seyppel also wrote small monographs on William Faulkner and T. S. Eliot for the West German Köpfe des 20. Jahrhunderts (Heads of the Twentieth Century) series and translated James Baldwin's *Amen Corner.*

Shabani, Resul (b. 1944) Macedonian Albanian poet, novelist, short-story writer, and playwright. One of the foremost contemporary Albanian writers in Macedonia, Shabani was born in Kališta, in the Struga district. After graduating from high school in Struga, he studied Albanian language and literature in Skopje and Priština. He subsequently became a journalist affiliated primarily with the large Albanian publishing company and newspaper in Skopje, *Flaka e vëllazërimit.* He is a member of the Macedonian Writers Association and the Macedonian PEN Center. Fluent in Macedonian as well as his native Albanian, Shabani has published translations of major Macedonian Slav writers, including Kočo Racin, Blaže Koneski, and Dimitar Solev. A prolific and urbane writer who has cultivated poetry, prose fiction, and drama, Shabani began his literary career with the publication in 1974 of a collection of short stories, *Liqeni* (The Lake); the volume was reprinted in 1989. The "lake" of the title refers to Lake Ohrid, which serves as the setting of other works by Shabani and is bound up with his childhood, functioning in fact as a metaphor for idyllic but lost childhood. *Peshq* (Fish), Shabani's first book of poems, came out in 1975. It was followed by *Shën* (Holy, 1978), a second collection of short stories; *Hamlet me plis të zi* (Hamlet in a Black Skullcap, 1978), poems; *Anija e vjetër* (The Old Boat, 1982), a volume of two plays and Shabani's first published stage works; *Ora e liqenit* (The Hour of the Lake, 1983; published in Macedonian 1997), poems; *Dashuria e kapitenit* (The Captain's Love, 1983, 1990), Shabani's first novel; *Kashta e kumtrit* (The Straw Godfather, 1985), a play; *Ujë përshkruesi i fushës* (Water and Field, 1986), poems; *Fani vjen vetëm* (Fani Is Coming Alone, 1987), a collection of three plays; and *Oh, Amerika* (Oh, America, 1989; published in Macedonian 1992); *Qerpik i lagur* (A Moist Eyelash, 1994), a volume of two dozen short stories; *Uji i zemrës* (The Water of the Heart, 1997), a book of poems in Albanian and Romanian; *Mëkat i trilluar* (Make-Believe Sin, 1996), selected poems; *Miris na duvata* (Scent of the Wind, 1998), selected poems in Macedonian; and *Shtatë drama* (Seven Plays, 1999). Although Shabani has written a number of poetic, prose, and dramatic texts about Lake Ohrid, Kalishta, and Struga, and the memories these locales hold for him, he cannot be typecast as a local or even regional writer. Sophisticated, self-assured, seemingly distant from the political clamor of the time, Shabani has found inspiration in a wide variety of sources—from classical antiquity to contemporary Albanian life in Skopje—and writes in an easy, fluent style with deft touches of humor and irony.

Shehu, Bashkim (b. 1955) Albanian novelist and short-story writer. The son of the notorious and much feared general and later prime minister Mehmet Shehu (1913–1981), Shehu was born and educated in Tirana. He began his career as a screenwriter with Albanian film studios and in 1977 published his first literary work, *Një kohë tjetër: Novelë e tregime* (Another Age: Novellas and Short Stories). Although born into privilege, Bashkim suffered a serious reversal of fortune after his father's probable murder on 17 December 1981. He was forced to spend the next eight years in a concentration camp and then a year and a half in political internment. Shehu moved to Budapest in 1992 and the following year published his fascinating autobiography in France, as *L'Automne de la peur* (Autumn of Fear), and in 1994 in Albanian under the title *Vjeshta e ankthit*. Shehu subsequently returned to Tirana to resume his career as a writer. His most recent works of fiction are the novels *Rrugëtimi i mbramë i Ago Ymerit* (The Last Journey of Ago Ymeri, 1995) and *Gostia* (The Dinner Party, 1996). *Rrugëtimi i mbramë i Ago Ymerit* is the more interesting of the two. Ago Ymeri is the hero of an Albanian folk ballad who is allowed to return from the underworld for a single day. This forms a dimension of Shehu's novel in which the leader of a totalitarian state, now Prince of the Underworld, sets out to destroy an intellectual, Viktor Dragoti, who appears one day in a remote Albanian village and is rumored to be a man killed several years earlier while trying to swim to freedom. The novel is clearly intended as an inside look at the machinery of totalitarian persecution implicitly likened to a half century of Stalinist rule in Albania. In 1998 Shehu also published *Rrëfim ndaj një varri të zbrazët: Ëndërr autobiografike* (Confession by an Empty Grave: An Autobiographical Dream), a followup to his autobiography.

Translations: *Rrugëtimi i mbramë i Ago Ymerit* is available in French as *Le Dernier Voyage d'Ago Umeri*, trans. Anne-Marie Autissier (Paris: L'Esprit des péninsules, 1995), and *Vjeshta e ankthit* as *L'Automne de la peur*, trans. Isabelle Joudrain-Musa (Paris: Fayard, 1993).

Shkreli, Azem (1938–1997) Kosovo Albanian poet and novelist. A much respected Kosovo writer, Shkreli was born in Rugova, near Peć. He began his literary career while still a student with his poetry collection *Bulëzat* (Buds, 1961). His first novel, *Karvani i bardhë* (The White Caravan), also appeared in 1961 and won a prize. His second poetry collection, *Engljut e rrugëve* (Angels of the Streets), came out in 1963. Shkreli subsequently graduated from the Faculty of Philosophy of Priština University with a degree in Albanian language and literature. He was chairman of the Kosovo Writers Association, director of the Kosovo National Theater, and head of Kosovo Film in Priština. A poet of deep attachment to his Kosovo homeland, whose turmoil he wrote about with bitterness and irony, Shkreli published such volumes of poetry as *E di një fjalë prej guri* (I Know One Word of Stone, 1969); *Nga bibla e heshtjes* (From the Bible, Silence, 1973); *Vjersha* (Poems, 1977); *Pagëzimi i fjalës* (Baptism by Words, 1981); and *Ploje e mbrame* (The Final Slaughter, 1994). Shkreli was also the author of a collection of stories, *Sytë e Evës* (Eve's Eyes, 1965), and a play, *Fosilet* (Fossils, 1968), and was a contributor to the picture book *My Albania, Ground Zero*, edited by Bob Brewer and published in New York in 1992. An anthology of Shkreli's writings was published in 1974 under the title *Lotët e maleve* (Mountains of Tears). Shkreli was the recipient of the December Prize of SAP Kosovo; the NIP Rilindja Prize; and, posthumously in 1997, the Golden Pen Award.

Translations: *E di një fjalë prej guri* is available in German as *Ich weiss ein Wort von Stein*, trans. Hans-Joachim Lanksch (Klagenfurt: Wieser, 1993).

Sidran, Abdulah (b. 1944) Bosnian Muslim poet, short-story writer, and screenwriter. Sidran was born in Sarajevo, where he was educated through university. Until the outbreak of the war in Bosnia in April 1992, he worked as chief dramatic adviser for Bosnia-Herzegovina Radio. Sidran's works began appearing in 1965 in various local journals and other periodicals. His first major publication was the poetry collection *Šahbaza* (Chessboard, 1970), a reflection of Sidran's serious interest in chess, which crops up in other works as well. *Šahbaza* was followed by another ten volumes of verse: *Potukač* (The Vagabond, 1971), actually a small volume of poems and prose named for the last piece in the collection; *Kost i meso* (Bone and Flesh, 1976); *Sarajevska zbirka* (The Sarajevo Collection, 1979); *Sječas li se Doli Bel* (Do You Remember Doli Bel, 1982); *Otac na službenom putu* (Father on a Business Trip, 1985); *Sarajevska zbirka i nove pjesme* (The Sarajevo Collection and New Poems, 1987); *Bolest od duše* (The Ailing Soul, 1988); *Sarajevski tabut* (The Sarajevo Bier, 1993), for which Sidran received the Liberty Award of the French PEN Center; *Zašto tone Venecija* (Why Venice Is Sinking, 1996); and *Slijepac pjeva svome gradu* (*The Blindman Sings to His City*, 1997), a collection of poems from 1975 to 1985. Sidran also wrote the text for an illustrated book on the Bosnian War, with photographs by Zoran Filipović, published in France in 1994, by the Ministry of Culture, Department of International Affairs, under the title *Sarajevo*. Sidran's earlier poems of personal loneliness, of feelings of desolation and the tenuous shelter of love, as well as his poems on Sarajevo in *The Blindman Sings to His City*, in a sense anticipate those anguished and poignant poems written in response to the siege of Sarajevo during the Bosnian War, which the poet sees as the eternal conflict between the principles of good and evil. Sidran has won several awards for his writing, among them the City of Sarajevo Award for Career Achievement; the annual award of the Bosnia-Herzegovina Writers Association; and the annual award of the Svjetlost publishing house. He is also a member of the Bosnia-Herzegovina Academy of Sciences.

Translations: *The Blindman Sings to His City,* trans. Dubravka Dostal (Sarajevo: Medjunarodni centar za mir, 1997), a Serbo-Croatian–English edition with five separate groups of poems: "Seven Poems Under the Siege (1992–1996)," "Nine Old Poems (1965–1975)," "What We Are the Sum Of (1970–1975)," "The Blindman Sings to His City (1975–1985)," and "Three Poems" ("A Dispute About God," "A Walk with Stevan," and "The Nightmare"). *Sarajevski tabut* is available in French as *Je suis une île au coeur du monde: Poemes,* trans. Mireille Robin (Saint-Paul: La Nuee blue, 1995), and as *Sarajevski tabut/La bara di Sarajevo,* trans. Silvio Ferrrari (Trieste: Edizioni E, 1995), a Serbo-Croatian–Italian edition that in 1996 was awarded the Premio letterario of the Fondazione Laboratorio Mediterraneo.

Šikula, Vincent (b. 1936) Slovak novelist. A major figure in post–World War II Slovak prose fiction, Šikula was born in the village of Dubova, near Modra. He received his early education in Modra and Nitra and, after studying for a while in a teachers college in Hudobna, transferred to the State Conservatory in Bratislava, from which he graduated in 1959 with a degree in French horn. For the next two years, he worked as an organist in Ivanka on the Danube and then served for three years as a teacher in the village school in Modra, where he himself had studied. After a two-year creative fellowship, he became editor of the literary review *Romboid,* following which he received another fellowship for an extended period of independent activity. From 1969 to 1973, Šikula was the artistic director of the Slovak Film School. In 1973 he accepted the editorship for original fiction at the Slovenský spisovateľ publishing house in Bratislava, a position he held until his retirement in 1993.

Šikula made his literary debut in 1964 with a collection of short stories titled *Na koncertoch sa netlieska* (No Applause at the Concerts). Later that year, he came out with his second collection, *Možno si postavím bungalow* (Maybe I'll Build a Bungalow). The stories in both collections pivot on a central figure's search for a place in life. Šikula's previous writing was generally related to World War II, an interest he did not abandon in his later fiction. In *Možno si postavím bungalow,* for example, his main focus is on how men from different walks of life returning home from the military cope with the problem of reentering society. The stories were in fact based on actual experiences. Although he would pursue similar themes in his third collection of stories and novellas, *Horská robota* (Mountain Labor, 1968), Šikula shifted gears in two works published in 1966, directing his attention now to social-psychological issues. In *S Rozarkou* (With Rozarka), his subject is a mentally incapacitated girl who has somehow preserved a child's view of the world that enables her to cope with life in her own way; in *Nebýva na každom vŕšku hostinec* (There's Not an Inn on Every Hill), socially marginal characters—above all, a group of beggars—are shown to possess often considerable inner strength, which endows their lives with meaning and even beauty.

Beginning in 1976, Šikula started publishing arguably his most important work of fiction, the so-called *Majstri* (Master Carpenters) trilogy: the novels *Majstri* (1976); *Muškát* (The Geranium, 1977); and *Vilma* (Wilma, 1979). The subject of the trilogy is the Slovak National Uprising during World War II, which Šikula views from the unique perspective of an artisan's family living in western Slovakia, where very little military action in fact occurred. The time frame of the trilogy extends into the early postwar years. In between the second and third volumes, Šikula published the novel *Vlha* (The

Golden Oriole, 1978). In it, the marriage between an ordinary couple, a laborer named Jano and his wife, Filomena (Fila), who had been left an orphan early in life because of the loss of her family in World War I, serves as the prism through which Šikula views the changes in Slovak plebian life through two world wars. Noteworthy in the novel are Šikula's affection for nature and environmental concerns—a growing interest shared with other Slovak writers at the time—and his characteristic fondness for digressions, commentaries, and other textual interpolations addressed to a variety of issues.

Liesky (Hazels), which came out in 1980, is autobiographical and draws on Šikula's experiences as a village organist. *Vojak* (The Soldier, 1981), Šikula's next novel, is about a crippled war veteran. *Matej* (Matthew), which followed in 1983, is an interestingly structured account of the fate of a nineteenth-century blind cultural activist named Matej Hrebend. Also in 1983 Šikula published *Nokturna* (Nocturne), a large collection of short essays on a wide variety of subjects, including his own works, especially the *Majstri* trilogy. In his next three collections of short stories and novellas—*Heroické etudy pre kone* (Heroic Etudes for a Horse, 1987); *Pastierska kapsička* (A Shepherd's Sack, 1990); and *Pôstny menuet* (Minuet for a Fast, 1994)—Šikula wrote essentially about the villages he knew from childhood and the people who inhabited them. *Ornament* (Ornament, 1991) and its sequel, *Veterná ružica* (A Windy Rosette, 1995), portray the life of small-town Slovak intelligentsia in the 1950s through the story of the disintegrating marriage of Matej Hóza, a secondary-school teacher, and his wife, Eva. In his recent slight novel, *Anjel Gabriela* (Angel Gabriela, 2000), Šikula writes about carefree young people in and out of school, on vacation travels in the Czech and Slovak lands, and the rude awakening to the adult world of the central character, Gabriela,

when she is raped by two casual acquaintances. As a poet, Šikula is represented by two volumes of verse: *Z domu na kopci* (From the House on the Hill, 1983) and *Zo zanedbanej záhrady* (From a Neglected Garden, 1993).

Šimečka, Martin M. (b. 1957) Slovak novelist. Although ethnically Czech and fluent in Czech as well as Slovak, Šimečka decided to become a Slovak writer and now occupies a place of distinction in Slovak literature. He also became a dissident and for most of the 1980s played a prominent role in the Czechoslovak literary underground, participating in the creation of a series of small magazines and publishing fiction and essays in samizdat or abroad. In 1989 he helped found the publishing house Archa, where he subsequently served as editor in chief. He has been chairman of the Slovak branch of PEN since 1992. Although he has published two other novels—*Džin* (1988), actually a collection of three novellas, and *Záujem* (Concern, 1997)—Šimečka's literary reputation was made primarily by his fine novel *Žabí rok* (*The Year of the Frog*). Narrated in the first person, the novel is set in the Czechoslovakia of the early 1980s. It follows the fortunes of Milan, a young intellectual denied entrance to a university because of his father's political activities and imprisonment. Instead, he takes a job in the neurosurgical department of a hospital cleaning up after operations (described in graphic detail). Milan's two great loves in life are long-distance running, which he avidly pursues in Bratislava and in the country, and his lovely girlfriend, Tania, with whom he has a fulfilling romantic relationship that brings him the happiness denied him elsewhere in society. Because of Šimečka's activities as a dissident, as well as its content and tenor, *The Year of the Frog* first became available in the Czechoslovak literary underground in 1983 and in book form in 1985, when it was published by the Czech émigré house Index, located at the time in Cologne, Germany. When it appeared in English translation, it was named winner of the *Los Angeles Times* First Fiction Award.

Translations: *The Year of the Frog,* trans. Peter Petro (Baton Rouge: Louisiana State University Press, 1993; New York: Simon and Schuster, 1996); "On Uncertain Reality and the Possibility of an Agreement," trans. Milan Pomichalek and Anna Mozga, in *Good-bye, Samizdat: Twenty Years of Czechoslovak Underground Writing,* ed. Marketa Goetz-Stankiewicz (Evanston, Ill.: Northwestern University Press, 1992), 240–45; "The Stoneaters," trans. Paul Wilson, in *The Writing on the Wall: An Anthology of Contemporary Czech Literature,* ed. Antonin Liehm and Peter Kussi (Princeton, N.J.: Karz-Cohl, 1983), 173–75.

Simić, Goran (b. 1952) Bosnian Serb poet, essayist, and playwright. A founding member of the Bosnia-Herzegovina branch of PEN, Simić was well known as a writer and an editor in Bosnia before he and his family immigrated to Canada after the siege of Sarajevo from 1992 to 1996 during the Bosnian War. Besides his published collections of poems—*Tačka do kruga ili put* (Full Stop Before the Beat or Time, 1976); *Vertigo* (1977); *Mandragora* (1982); *Korak u mrak* (A Step into the Dark, 1987); *Palčić* (The Wren, 1998); *Dugonja* (A Lanky Man, 1998); and *Biberœ* (Peppers, 1998)—Simić was admired for his children's plays, which were staged by Bosnian puppet theaters. Perhaps his best known of them, *Bajka o Sarajevu* (A Sarajevan Fairy Tale), first was produced by the Young People's Theater of Sarajevo and later toured Germany and Switzerland. Simić's international fame rests on a cycle of poems written during the siege of Sarajevo and published in English as *Sprinting from the Graveyard.* A vivid, if unsettling, record in poetic form of the horrendous destruc-

tion of one of the former Yugoslavia's most vibrant and culturally important cities, *Sprinting from the Graveyard* has been widely translated, although an edition of the poems in the original does not yet seem to have appeared. Simić is also the author of the libretto for the operetta *Europe,* with music by Nigel Osborne; the work was performed in Sarajevo in February 1995.

Translations: *Peace and War: Poems* (Toronto: Sutherland, 1998); *Sarajevo Sorrow,* trans. Amela Simić (Sarajevo: Medjunarodni Centar za Mir, 1995); *Sprinting from the Graveyard,* in versions by David Harsent (Oxford: Oxford University Press, 1997).

Simionescu, Mircea Horia (b. 1928) Romanian novelist and short-story writer. One of the most intriguing experimenters and innovators in Romanian prose fiction in the period since the end of World War II, Simionescu was born in Tîrgoviște, where he was educated through high school. He entered Bucharest University in 1948 but left after two years to become a journalist, working first for the Communist Party newspaper *Scînteia.* He eventually resumed his studies while still working as a journalist and completed his degree in 1964. Simionescu began his career as a creative writer in 1969 with the first of a four-part putdown of socialist realism as well as traditional Romanian literary genres under the title *Ingeniosul bine temperat, I* (The Well-Tempered Innovator, 1969), subtitled *Dicționarul onomastic* (A Dictionary of Names). Subsequent volumes included *Ingeniosul bine temperat, II: Bibliografia generală* (The Well-Tempered Innovator: A General Bibliography, 1970); *Breviarul: Historia calamitatum* (The Breviary: History of a Calamity, 1980); and *Toxicologia, sau, Dincolo de bine și dincoace de rău* (Toxicology, or, Beyond Good and on the Side of Evil, 1983). The first volume is essentially a parodic dictionary of biographies of fictitious people, ending with the letter *I*. The second volume is a grandiose bibliography of invented writers and literary works. After the second volume, the literary climate in Romania changed for the worse, following the relative liberalization engendered by the invasion of Czechoslovakia in 1968 (which the Romanians protested), and Simionescu thought it best to suspend for the time being further publication of his Well-Tempered Innovator. In between the second and third parts of the work, he published a collection of stories, *Dupâ 1900 pe la amiazâ* (After 1900, in the Afternoon, 1974), which was awarded the Writers Union Prize; an imaginative spoof of the travel genre under the title *Răpirea lui Ganymede* (Ganymede's Abduction, 1975); *Jumătate plus unu: Alt dicţionar onomastic* (Half Plus One: Another Dictionary of Names, 1976), a less successful continuation of the first parts of The Well-Tempered Innovator, which nevertheless won the prestigious Ion Creangă Prize of the Romanian Academy; *Nesfîrşitele primejdii* (The Endless Dangers, 1978), a novel within a novel that comments on the form of the novel in general; and *Învăţături pentru Delfin* (Teachings for the Dolphin, 1979), an entertaining romp whose aim is to put down detective fiction by exposing its stereotypicalities and banalities.

Simionescu published the third part of The Well-Tempered Innovator in 1980, but only under the title *Breviarul: Historia calamitatum* in order to head off possible suppression of the work at a time of growing concern about a renewal of less tolerant censorship. Abounding in references to the previous parts of the work and replete with commentaries and footnotes, *Breviarul: Historia calamitatum* is a pseudo-scholarly text with animals, insects, and birds as the principal characters vaguely reminiscent in form of the Russian writer Vladimir Nabokov's *Pale Fire*. After *Breviarul: Historia calamitatum*, Simionescu published a collection of short stories, *Banchetul* (The Banquet, 1982), and a volume of travel notes, *Ulise şi umbra* (Ulysses and the Shadows, 1982). The following year, 1983, the fourth and last part of The Well-Tempered Innovator appeared under the title *Toxicologia, sau, Dincolo de bine şi dincoace de rău*. No less convoluted and fantastic than its predecessor, *Toxicologia* is a parody of the autobiographical genre. With reference to the interwar avant-garde Romanian writer Urmuz (Demetru Demetrescu-Buzău), some critics have dubbed Simionescu's major work the "Urmuz tetralogy," describing it as a "heroic-comic epic, a satire and a panorama of the errors of this century, from which through an ample inventory of types and cliches, a world finally emerges ... sick with inertia and stereotypicality."

After the appearance of the fourth part of his tetralogy and before the fall of the regime of Nicolae Ceauşescu, Simionescu published the rather weak novel *Redingota* (The Riding Coat, 1984); *Licitaţia* (The Auction, 1985), a dense novel in which the narrator returns from the next world in order to write a novel he hopes will earn enough money at an auction so that his debts can be retired; the memoiristic *Trei oglinzi* (Three Mirrors, 1987), in which Simionescu recalls his adolescence; and *Asediul locului comun* (The Siege of the Commonplace, 1988), about a group of writers who sequester themselves in a castle to plan a magazine and wind up writing Simionescu-type works. With the fall of communism, Simionescu produced a volume of short fiction of a largely fantastic character, *Îngerul cu şorţ de bucătărie* (The Angel in an Apron, 1992) and his last work of fiction, the well-received novel *Paltonul de vară* (The Warm Summer Coat, 1996), another excursion into the realm of fantasy but more generally accessible than the volumes in The Well-Tempered Innovator cycle. In 1998

Simionescu published a journal of the years 1963 to 1971 under the title *Febra: File de journal, 1963–1971* (Fever: Pages of a Journal, 1963–1971).

Translations: Excerpts from *Ingeniosul bine temperat, I: Dicţionarul onomastic,* in *The Phantom Church and Other Stories from Romania,* ed. and trans. Georgiana Farnoaga and Sharon King (Pittsburgh: University of Pittsburgh Press, 1996), 74–83.

Škvorecký, Josef (b. 1924) Czech novelist and story writer. One of the outstanding Czech writers of the post–World War II period, Škvorecký was born in the northern Bohemian town of Náchod, where he was educated through high school. After graduation in 1943, he went to work in the Zimmerman and Schilling Metalworks in Náchod and nearby Nové Město during the German occupation. This period, from 1943 to the end of the war in 1945, would subsequently provide the inspiration for several of Škvorecký's best works. After the war, Škvorecký enrolled in Charles University in Prague with the idea of studying medicine, but after the first semester switched to the Faculty of Philosophy where he studied English and philosophy. He graduated in 1949 and two years later received his doctorate for a dissertation on Thomas Paine. Škvorecký had begun studying English in 1938, and by the time he wrote his dissertation had a very good command of English as well of American literature, in which he took a particular interest. In 1948 Škvorecký was awarded first prize for fiction in a Charles University literary contest for his short-story collection *Nové canterburské povídky* (The New Canterbury Tales). It was around that time that he also became a part of a Prague underground circle of writers that included, among others, Bohumil Hrabal and Věra Linhartová.

Škvorecký began his literary career in earnest with his first novel, *Zbabělci* (*The Cowards*), which he wrote in 1948/1949 and which was published for the first time only in 1958. Constructed in the form of a first-person chronicle covering a single week in 1945—from Friday, 4 May, to Friday, 11 May—the work was banned not long after its publication because of official displeasure with the irreverence of its youthful hero, Danny Smiřický, and his friends and its apparent mockery of the Red Army. It was also around this time that Škvorecký wrote the novel "Nylonový věk" ("The Nylon Age"), about the love life of a Charles University student in the late 1940s. But the work was never published, and the manuscript was eventually lost. However, in 1950 he wrote a similarly titled novel, *Konec nylonového věku* (The End of the Nylon Age), about a dance sponsored by the American Institute of Prague in February 1949, and in 1992 published a fragment of the original novel. *Konec nylonového věku* was rejected for publication by the censors in 1956 and remained unpublished until 1967. Škoverecký's next work was *Tankový prapor* (Tank Battalion; translated as *The Republic of Whores*). It was based on his obligatory military service from 1951 to 1953, but remained unpublished until 1969 when a French edition came out in Paris. The Czech original was published in 1980 by the Toronto-based Czech émigré press Sixty-Eight Publishers. After fulfilling his military service, Škvorecký worked for three years in the Czechoslovak Publishing House of Fiction (later Odeon Publishers) and was also editor of the bimonthly *Světová literatura.*

When *The Cowards* was finally published in 1958, the ban on the novel and the public controversy that followed cost Škvorecký his position as editor in chief of *Světová literatura.* For the next several years, he kept himself alive as a writer mostly by translating American literature and by publishing a series of murder mysteries that he wrote with Jan Zábrana—*Vražda pro štěstí* (Murder for Luck, 1962); *Vražda se zárukou* (Murder Guaranteed, 1964); and *Vražda v zastoupení* (Murder by Proxy, 1967)—and a children's book, *Tánja a dva pistolníci* (Tanya and the Two Gunmen, 1966), which was made into a successful film in 1967. In 1964 Škvorecý published the short-story collection *Sedmiramenný svícen* (The Menorah) and, with Lubomír Dorůžka, an anthology devoted to jazz and famous jazz musicians under the title *Tvář jazzu* (The Face of Jazz). After another short-story collection, *Ze života lepší společnosti* (From the Life of High Society, 1965), and a book of criticism, *Nápady čtenáře detektivek* (Ideas of a Detective-Fiction Reader, 1965), Škvorecký published the first of his popular "Lieutenant Borůvka" detective novels, *Smutek poručíka Borůvky* (The Sadness of Lieutenant Borůvky, 1966).

By 1967 the political climate in Czechoslovakia had changed enough to permit the Writers Union to present Škvorecký with its award for the year's best fiction on the basis of the publication of The End of the Nylon Age. The same year also saw the appearance of the short-story collection *Babylónský příběh* (A Babylonian Story) and *Jazzová inspirace* (Inspired by Jazz), an anthology of Czech and American poems inspired by jazz, which he edited with Lubomir Dorůžka. The Soviet-led Warsaw Pact invasion of Czechoslovakia in 1968 came as a rude awakening to Škvorecký—as, indeed, it did to most Czechs—and he made the decision to emigrate. On 31 January 1969 he and his wife—the singer, actress, and writer Zdena Salivarová—left Czechoslovakia for good and settled in Toronto. In 1972 the two of them founded Sixty-Eight Publishers, which became the principal publishing house for émigré, exile, and underground Czech writers. Škvorecký himself also eventually became a professor in the Department of English at Erindale College, the University of Toronto, where he has taught

American literature, creative writing, and film.

Škvorecký's books fared poorly in Czechoslovakia after his and Salivarová's departure. *The Republic of Whores* was finally published in Prague in 1969, but by the following year government authorities had destroyed the plates for the book. This was also the fate of the second edition of Škvorecký's novel *Lvíče* (Lion Cub; translated as *Miss Silver's Past*), a murder mystery set inside a state publishing house in Prague and involving an editor who, while selecting manuscripts worthy of publication without offending the political powers, tries to maintain a delicate balancing act between his girlfriend and Lenka Silver, a young woman with whom he becomes obsessed and who commits an act of murder to avenge a wrong going back to World War II. Škvorecký's next two books were early Sixty-Eight Publishers publications: *Mirákl* (*The Miracle Game*, 1972), about the Stalinist 1950s and the "Prague Spring," and *Hříchy pro pátera Knoxe: Detektivní divertimento* (*Sins for Father Knox: A Detective Divertimento*, 1973), an entertaining detective novel based on the life of Ronald Arbuthnot Knox (1888–1957), a Protestant convert to Catholicism who became a priest, wrote detective fiction under an assumed name, and stirred the world of Sherlock Holmes enthusiasts by publishing an essay on Holmes as a historical figure. The year 1975 brought publication of *The Swell Season* and *Konec poručíka Borůvky* (*The End of Lieutenant Borůvky*). They were followed by *Příběh inženýra lidských duší* (*The Engineer of Human Souls*, 1977), another Danny Smiřický novel contrasting the Czech and Canadian years of the main character. It was also in 1977 that *The Bass Saxophone*, the first book of Škvorecký's fiction to be published in translation in Canada, appeared. In 1981, the year after Škvorecký was awarded the Neustadt Prize by the University of Oklahoma, the last of the "Lieutenant Borůvka" novels appeared: *Návrat poručíka Borůvky* (*The Return of Lieutenant Borůvka*). Škvorecký's subsequent publications include *Scherzo capriccioso* (translated as *Dvorak in Love*, 1983); *O americké literatuře* (On American Literature, 1987); *Talkin' Moscow Blues: Essays About Literature, Politics, Movies, and Jazz* (1988); *Hlas z Ameriky* (A Voice from America, 1990); and *Nevěsta z Texasu* (*The Bride of Texas*, 1992), published by Sixty-Eight Publishers, a large book of fictionalized history about General William Tecumseh Sherman and the American Civil War and the Czechs who took part in it. In 1990 Škorecký and Salivarová returned to Prague, where President Václav Havel awarded them the order of the White Lion, Czechoslovakia's highest award for foreigners (since the writer and his wife had already become Canadian citizens).

Literature: Sam Solecki, ed., *The Achievemnent of Josef Škvorecký* (Toronto: University of Toronto Press, 1987), a generally good collection of articles covering most of Škvorecký's major texts. There are two major bibliographies of Škvorecký's works: Jana Kalish, *Josef Škvorecký: A Checklist* (Toronto: University of Toronto Library, 1986), and Ilja Matouš, *Bibliografie Josefa Škvoreckého*, 3 vols. (Prague: Společnost Josefa Škvoreckého, 1990, 1992, 1993).

Translations: *The Bass Saxophone*, trans. Káča Poláčková-Henley (Toronto: Anson-Cartwright, 1977); *The Bride of Texas: A Romantic Tale from the Real World*, trans. Kaca Polackova Henley (Toronto: Knopf, 1995); *The Cowards*, trans. Jeanne Nemcová (New York: Ecco Press, 1980); *Dvorak in Love*, trans. Paul Wilson (Toronto: Lester & Orpen Dennys, 1986); *The End of Lieutenant Boruvka*, trans. Paul Wilson (Toronto: Lester & Orpen Dennys, 1989); *The Engineer of Human Souls*, trans. Paul Wilson (Toronto: Lester & Orpen Dennys, 1984); *The Miracle Game*, trans. Paul Wilson (Toronto: Lester & Orpen Dennys, 1990); *Miss Silver's Past*, trans. Peter Kussi (New York: Ecco Press, 1985); *The Mournful Demeanor of Lieutenant Boruvka*, trans. Rosemary Kavan, Káča Poláčková, and George Theiner (Toronto: Lester & Orpen Dennys, 1987); *The Republic of Whores*, trans. Paul Wilson (Toronto: Knopf, 1993); *The Return of Lieutenant Boruvka*, trans. Paul Wilson (Toronto: Lester & Orpen Dennys, 1990); *Sins for Father Knox*, trans. Káča Poláčková-Henley (New York: Norton, 1988); *The Swell Season: A Text on the Most Important Things in Life*, trans. Paul Wilson (Toronto: Lester & Orpen Dennys, 1982; London: Chatto & Windus, 1983); *The Tenor Saxophonist's Story*, trans. Caleb Crain, Káča Poláčková-Henley, and Peter Kussi (Hopewell, N.J.: Ecco Press, 1996.

Works in English: *When Eve Was Naked: Stories of a Life's Journey* (New York: Farrar, Straus and Giroux, 2002).

Slamnig, Ivan (1930–1992) Croatian poet, novelist, short-story writer, playwright, translator, and literary scholar. Slamnig was born in Metković, where he received his early schooling. He graduated from Zagreb University in 1955 and later joined the faculty as a professor. As a literary scholar, Slamnig, in collaboration with the poet Antun Šoljan, translated and edited a volume of American lyrics in 1952; in 1956 he published an anthology of contemporary English poetry; in 1961, a similar book of contemporary Nordic poetry; in 1959, an anthology of Croatian poetry from earliest times to the end of the nineteenth century; in 1964, an anthology of seventeenth-century Croatian poetry; in 1965, a study of the imagination, *Disciplina mašte* (The Discipline of Fantasy); in 1970 he edited the plays of the Croatian Renaissance writer Marcus Marullus (1450–1524); and in 1979 he published another anthology of Croatian poetry, from A. Kačić-Miošić to A. G.

Matoš. Drawing on his own extensive experience as a translator from English, Russian, Swedish, and Italian literatures, mainly poetry, he also published a study of the translation of poetry under the title *Stih i prijevod* (Verse and Translation, 1986).

Slamnig's creative writing embraced poetry, prose, and plays. From 1956 to 1990, he published eleven volumes of original poems and two editions of selected and collected works: *Odran* (Early Morning, 1956); *Aleja poslije svečanosti* (Avenue After Festivities, 1956); *Narfonska siesta* (Narfon Siesta, 1963); *Monografija* (Monograph, 1965); *Limb* (Limbo, 1968); *Analecta* (Analectics, 1971); *Pjesme* (Poems, 1973); *Dronta* (1981); *Izabrane djela* (Selected Works, 1983); *Relativno naopako* (Relatively Inside Out, 1987); *Sed scholae* (Latin: And Not to Mention School, 1987); *Tajna* (A Secret, 1988); and *Sabrane pjesme* (Collected Poems, 1990). Slamnig wrote on a wide variety of subjects—from a well-known poem in which he imagines the thoughts of Christopher Columbus aboard ship to one about Matthew, Mark, and Luke writing their gospels. An exceptionally accessible poet, Slamnig wrote in a lucid, unpretentious manner, yet had a fine feeling for language and enjoyed a certain semantic playfulness. His appeal lies above all in the cleverness and freshness of his ideas and his way of expressing them. Slamnig's prose fiction, which is less interesting than his poetry, includes the novella *Neprijatelj* (The Enemy, 1959); the novel *Bolja polovica hrabrosti* (The Better Side of Courage, 1972); and a volume of short stories published in 1992, the year of his death, with an afterword by the writer Pavao Pavličić.

A collection of Slamnig's eleven radio plays, *Firentinski capriccio* (Florentine Capriccio), was published in 1986, followed, in 1990, by a volume of his plays edited by Antun Šoljan.

Translations: Five poems, trans. Ivan V. Lalić and Bernard Johnson, in *New Writ-ing in Yugoslavia*, ed. Bernard Johnson (Harmondsworth: Penguin, 1970), 139–42.

Slaviček, Milivoj (b. 1929) Croatian poet. Slaviček was born in the town of Čakovec in northern Croatia. He attended secondary school in Zagreb and in 1954 graduated from the Faculty of Philosophy of Zagreb University. He became thereafter a permanent resident of the capital. Although he has held editorial positions with several literary journals and has contributed frequently to newspapers, his career has been mainly that of a freelance writer. During the 1950s, Slaviček chose to pursue his own path in the face of imposed socialist realism and earned a reputation for his willingness to dissent. He later wrote that a poet had to dissent. With such major poets as Ivan Slamnig and Antun Šoljan, Slaviček became affiliated with the liberal journal *Krugovi*. In the 1960s and 1970s, he served as vice president and president of the Croatian Association of Writers. A prolific poet, Slaviček is the author of some sixteen volumes of verse: *Zaustavljena pregršt* (Intercepted Armful, 1954); *Daleka pokrajina* (The Distant Province, 1957); *Modro veče* (Blue Evening, 1959); *Predak* (Ancestor, 1963); *Noćni autobus ili naredni dio cjeline* (The Night Bus, or The Next Part of the Whole, 1964); *Izmedju* (In Between, 1965); *Soneti, pjesme o ljubavi i ostale pjesme* (Sonnets, Love Poems, and Other Verse, 1967); *Purpurna, pepeljara, naime to i to* (Purple, Ashtray, That Is to Say, This and That, 1969); *Poglavlje* (A Chapter, 1970); *Naslov što ga nikada neću zaboraviti* (A Title I Shall Never Forget, 1974); *Otvoreno radi (eventualnog) uredjenja* (Open for [Eventual] Regulation, 1978); *Pjesme neke buduće knjige* (Poems of Some Future Book, 1979); *Trinaesti pejzaž* (The Thirteenth Landscape, 1981); *Teror/Terror* (1981); *Sjajne svakodnevice* (The Luster of the Everyday, 1987); and *Nastanjen uvijek* (In Continuous Residence, 1990). An edition of his collected poems (*Izabrane pjesme*) was published in 1987. Slaviček's poetry addresses virtually every aspect of everyday life. He is truly a poet of the everyday, and the prosaic rhythm and diction of his verse are wholly appropriate to his outlook. Reading Slaviček, one has a sense of concentric circles of confinement—from personal living quarters to streets to cities and social conditions. The effect is that of relentless, oppressive sameness yielding to alienation. But what spares Slaviček's bleakness is a refreshing novelty of image and an undeniable irony. Slaviček's good knowledge of English has opened him to the influence of such writers as Ernest Hemingway, F. Scott Fitzgerald, and T. S. Eliot. Anxious to make Croatian poetry better known to the Anglophone reader, in 1965 Slaviček edited and published the English-language anthology *A Collection of Modern Croatian Verse: 49 Poets.*

Translations: *Silent Doors: Selected Poems,* trans. Branko Gorjup and Jeannette Lynes (Toronto: Exile Editions, 1988).

Slavov, Atanas (b. 1930) Bulgarian poet, screenwriter, novelist, literary scholar, and art historian. Known to the reader of English primarily as the author of the literary-political study *The Thaw in Bulgarian Literature* (1981; published, 1994, in Bulgarian as *Bulgarska literatura na razmraziavaneto*) and his memoirs, *With the Precision of Bats* (1986), which eventually was published in Bulgaria in 1992 as *S tochnostta na prilepi,* Slavov was born in Sliven. He attended the American elementary school in Sofia until it was closed in 1941. During World War II, Slavov and his family were evacuated from Sofia to Sliven. They were able to return to the capital in 1944, and it was after that that Slavov could complete high school and then receive a degree in English language and literature at Sofia University in 1953. From 1953 to 1965, he worked mainly as a teacher of Rus-

sian in courses organized by the Bulgarian-Soviet Friendship Committe and as a librarian at the National Library in Sofia. From 1961 to 1971, he was also engaged as a teacher of English language and literature at Sofia University. In 1965 he defended his doctoral dissertation, "The Functions of Rhythm in Poetic Language," at the Literary Institute of the Bulgarian Academy of Sciences. From 1966 to 1976, he worked at the academy's Institute of Art Criticism and took a particular interest in Bulgarian applied art, on which he later published. He also conducted research in the fields of folklore and art theory. It was in conjunction with his work at the Bulgarian Academy of Sciences that Slavov visited New York in 1975/1976. Following that visit, he left Bulgaria and settled in the United States after a brief period of residence in London. He earned his living as a broadcaster for Radio Free Europe and the BBC. While in the United States, he became affiliated with the Woodrow Wilson Center in Washington, D.C., as an Eastern European cultural specialist. He also taught Bulgarian at the Department of State from 1980 to 1983 and from 1983 to 1990 was employed as an editor, a script writer, and a broadcaster for the Voice of America.

While in emigration Slavov wrote his memoirs, which first aired in fifty-two weekly broadcasts (1978–1979) in Bulgarian over the Voice of America. They were later published in Bulgarian under the title *S treva obrasli* (Grown Over with Grass, 1983) by Peev & Popov, the Bulgarian émigré press in Paris, appearing three years later as *With the Precision of Bats* and, in 1992, in Bulgaria as *S tochnostta na prilepi.* It was awarded the Legerete International Writers Union Book Prize as the best autobiography of 1986. It was not long after his Voice of America broadcasts that Slavov published his literary-political study *The Thaw in Bulgarian Literature.* His poetic activity in emigration is contained in such collections as

Pornografska poema (Pornographic Poem, 1968); *Mr. Lampedusa Has Vanished* (1982); and *The Dough of America Is Rising in Me* (1986). In 1988 he published the grotesuqe parody *Handling Vegetables* under the pseudonym Al Santana. In the United States, Slavov was also active in a number of associations for the promotion of Bulgarian and Slavic studies. He was, moreover, a member of the American PEN Club and the American branch of the Pen Club of Writers in Emigration.

Slavov began his literary career as a poet with his first poems appearing in the periodical *Literaturni novini*. However, the communist leader, Todor Zhivkov, publicly rebuked them in a speech delivered on 15 April 1963. This marked the beginning of Slavov's disenchantment with the communist regime and inclined him toward scholarly writing as well as science fiction and the literature of the fantastic. His next book was an innocuous cultural history of his native city, *Sliven: Gradut na suknoto i baruta* (Sliven: The City of Cloth and Gunpowder, 1962). *Zheravna,* the study of the cultural and social development of the village for which the book is named, appeared in 1965. Slavov also published two works of science fiction in 1965: *Faktorut "X"* (The "X" Factor) and *Po goliamata spirala* (Along the Big Spiral). His interest in the fantastic was also strong, as evidenced by the collection *Nova bulgarska fantastika '91* (New Bulgarian Fantastic Literature '91), which he and Aleksandur Karapanchev brought out in 1991, and his own novel *Psihoprogrami raniiat* (Psycho-Programs Wound, 1992). Slavov's research in art criticism and history resulted in such publications as *Durvorezbite na Rozhenskiia manastir* (The Wood Carvings in the Rozhenski Monastery, 1968); *Medni sudove* (Copper Pots, 1975); and *Traditsii i perspektivi v bulgarskoto prilozhno izkustvo* (Traditions and Perspectives in Bulgarian Applied Art,

1975). Representing Slavov's interest in literary scholarship and problems of versification were such texts as *V siankata na Fordoviia mit* (In the Shadow of the Ford Myth, 1963), on the "outsider" in American literature; an outline of Bulgarian versification, which was published in Polish by the Polish Academy of Sciences in 1973; and a book in Polish on comparative Slavic metrics that he coauthored.

Slavov is also the author of a number of film scripts, especially for animated films, a few of which were honored at international film festivals. While still in Bulgaria, Slavov translated works by such English-language authors as Shawn O'Casey, Graham Greene, Charles Dickens, William Saroyan, and Carl Sandburg.

Translations: One poem, trans. Carolyn Forché, in *Window on the Black Sea: Bulgarian Poetry in Translation,* ed. Richard Harteis, in collaboration with William Meredith (Pittsburgh: Carnegie Mellon University Press, 1992), 166–67.

Sloboda, Rudolf (1938–1995) Slovak novelist, short-story writer, and poet. One of the more important renovators of Slovak prose in the 1960s, Sloboda had little higher education and was employed mainly as a mine and factory worker until going into editing and films, before eventually becoming a freelance writer. He made his literary debut in 1965 with the novel *Narcis* (Narcissus), which set the pattern for much of his subsequent writing with its obvious erudition and moral concerns; its reflective, essayistic style full of long monologues; and its predilection for unique "outsider" characters. Typical is Urban Chromý, the central figure in *Narcis.* A prince and the heir to a throne, he believes in the logic of the organization of the world, which he tries, elusively, to penetrate by means of philosophical study, Catholic theology, and the stimuli of literature and existential experience. At one point, he becomes a volunteer worker in the Ostrava ironworks in a reflection of Sloboda's own experiences. *Narcis* was followed by the novel *Britva* (The Razor, 1967), which is built around the crisis in a male–female relationship brought on, as usual in Sloboda, by the characters themselves. Sloboda shifted gears into a lighter vein in his first collection of short stories, *Uhorský rok* (The Hungarian Year, 1968); his "memoiristic" *Romaneto Don Juan* (1971); and his second collection of short stories, *Hlboký mier* (The Deep Peace, 1976). He returned to his typical lead figure and especially the type weighed down with the gravest problems in his novella *Šedé ruže* (Gray Roses, 1969) and in his novel of an intimate affair, *Hudba* (Music, 1977), which reflects a period in his younger life when he was a student at the Bratislava Conservatory in 1957/1958. In his next novel, *Vernost* (Loyalty, 1979), he again addressed the crisis in a male–female relationship. This interest carried over as well into the aptly titled novel *Rozum* (Mind, 1982), the literary event of the decade when it first appeared and an important work in Sloboda's canon in that it brings together his ideas on life and art, especially filmmaking. Central to Sloboda's outlook are his doubts concerning the individual's ability to order his or her own life according to principles of reason. *Druhý človek* (Another), which preceded *Rozum* in 1981, is regarded by many as Sloboda's finest work of fiction, in which, as in other texts, he probes the wide gap between an ideal and everyday life that makes the ideal unattainable.

In other works of the 1980s and 1990s— such as *Dni radosti* (Days of Joy, 1982); *Stratený raj* (Paradise Lost, 1983); his short-story collection *Panský flám* (Men's Night Out, 1986), which contains "Biely pes" ("The White Dog"), his only work available in English; the two-part novel cycle *Uršuľa* (Ursula, 1987) and *Rubato* (Rubato, 1990); *Krv* (Blood, 1991); *Útek z rodnej obce* (Flight from Home, 1992); *Jeseň* (Autumn, 1994); *Herečky* (Actresses, 1995); and *Pamäti* (Memories, 1996)—Sloboda made a gradual shift from the absurdity characteristic of much of his previous writing toward greater realism. He also retreated from his previous fondness for long monologues in favor of greater dialogue. A weaker rather didactic work, *Stratený raj*, for example, features an alcoholic (another of Sloboda's "outsider" types) and is set largely in the rehabilitation center of a mental hospital. More impressive are *Uršuľa* and *Rubato*, which are narrated by the character Ursula, a woman suspected of the murder of her illegitimate son and one of Sloboda's more compelling female portraits. Much of Sloboda's fiction, including such works as *Romaneto Don Juan, Rozum, Útek z rodnej obce, Jeseň, Herečky, Pamäti*, and of course *Pokus o autoportet* (Attempt at Self-Portrait, 1988), has an autobiographical character. Often, the autobiographical is little more than a quasi-fictional frame for the airing of Sloboda's views on a wide variety of issues from the philosophical to the religious. This is carried almost to an extreme in *Jeseň*, in which family recollections are little more than a line on which are hung the author's rationalistic views on Judaism, Christianity, Islam, the Old Testament (particularly the book of Ruth), the figure of Jesus, Catholicism and Protestantism, Jehova's Witnesses, dialectical materialism, and feminism. Conversant with a great body of literature, Sloboda frequently alludes to such figures as Hegel, Marx and Engels, Dostoevsky, Thoreau, Unamuno, Wittgenstein, and Salman Rushdie. Sloboda was also the author of a volume of poems under the title *Večerná otázka vtákovi* (The Evening Question of the Birds, 1977) and several works for young readers.

Translation: "The White Dog," trans. James Naughton, in *Description of a Struggle: The Vintage Book of Contemporary East-*

ern European Writing, ed. Michael March (New York: Vintage, 1994), 175–86.

Solev, Dimitar (b. 1930) Macedonian short-story writer and novelist. A native of Skopje, Solev entered journalism after graduating from the Faculty of Philosophy in Skopje in 1955. A prominent critic and editor (he was editor in chief of the periodical *Razgledi* for ten years), he has published several volumes of short stories, novels, and literary studies of such Macedonian writers as Vasil Antevski (1904–1942) and Kočo Racin (1909–1943). He also published an anthology of Macedonian poetry and prose (1961); a book on the contemporary Macedonian story (1965); and a study of contemporary literary criticism and Marxism (1965). Solev published his first collection of short stories in 1956 under the title *Okopneto snegovi* (The Melted Snows). It was followed by, among others, *Po rekata i sproti nea* (By River and Upstream, 1960); *Zima na slobodata* (The Winter of Freedom, 1968), one of his best collections; *Odbrani raskazi* (Selected Stories, 1970, 1981); and *Polžavi* (Snails, 1975). Solev's prose fiction, stories and novels alike, often explores the psychological ramifications of recollections of childhood interlaced with images of World War II. Although he has written several novels—including *Zora zad agolot* (Sunrise Around the Corner, 1967); *Quo vadis scriptor* (Whither Goest Thou, Writer, 1971; original title in Latin); *Crno ogledalo* (The Black Mirror, 1985); and *Ludo lato* (Crazy Summer, 1988)—he has long been most admired for *Kratkata prolet na Mono Samonikov* (The Short Summer of Mono Samonikov, 1964). This is a compelling psychological novel about a journalist who is strangely ill at ease with himself and the world as he grapples with a guilt complex rooted in events that took place during the war. Solev is also the author of a diary, *Pod usvitenost: Dnevničen zapis* (On the Griddle: A Diary,

1957), and two books of a political nature: *Odumiranje na državata* (The Dying Away of the State, 1990) and *Promena na sistemot* (Changing the System, 1993). His most recent work of fiction, the novel *Mrtva trka* (A Lifeless Race), appeared in 1998.

Translations: "The Round Trip of a Shadow," in *The Big Horse and Other Stories of Modern Macedonia,* ed. Milne Holton (Columbia: University of Missouri Press, 1974), 79–91.

Šoljan, Antun (1932–1993) Croatian poet, short-story writer, novelist, playwright, critic, and translator. A writer whose stature has grown with time as much for his literary skills as for his relentless support of the creative integrity of the artist in the face of communist repression, Šoljan was born in Belgrade but grew up in Zagreb, where he studied English and German at Zagreb University. Although he published several volumes of poems—among them *Na rubu svijeta* (On the Edge of the World, 1956); *Izvan fokusa* (Out of Focus, 1957); *Poezija* (Poems, 1967); *Gezela i druge pjesme* (Gezela and Other Poems, 1970); and *Izabrane pjesme: 1950–1975* (Collected Poems: 1950–1975, 1976)—Šoljan is best known as a writer of short stories and novellas. His first short-story collection was *Specijalni izaslanici* (Special Envoys, 1957). It was followed by *Izdajice* (Traitors, 1961), a cycle of closely woven short stories issued as a novel about a small group of young people, including the narrator, whose complex relations with one another and with others provide the dynamics of the collection; the short novel *Kratki izlet* (*A Brief Excursion,* 1965); the short-story collections *Deset kratkih priča za moju generaciju* (Ten Short Stories for My Generation, 1966) and *Obiteljska večera i druge priče* (A Family Supper and Other Stories, 1975); the unflinching political novel *Luka* (The Port, 1974), a fairly rare type of work during this period; and the short novel *Drugi ljudi* *na mjesecu: Pustolovna priča* (*The Other People on the Moon: An Adventure Story,* 1978).

An able storyteller especially adept at character portrayal, Šoljan often invested ordinary events with an air of mystery and philosophical suggestiveness. This is especially true of arguably his best (and most widely translated) work of fiction, *A Brief Excursion,* the story of a lighthearted search for medieval frescoes in Istria that eventually turns dark, mysterious, and multilayered in its possible meanings. It first appeared in a Zagreb journal in 1965, was then published in the Belgrade journal *Prosveta,* but was withheld from book publication in Zagreb until 1987 because it was regarded as an antisocialist allegory. Šoljan's reputation as a dissident was enhanced by his speech on the fiftieth anniversary of the death of the Croatian poet Antun Gustav Matoš and his support, while he was president of the Croatian PEN (1970–1973), of Croatian writers who were arrested for their participation in the anticommunist, prosecessionist demonstrations of 1971. Apart from his playwriting, represented by such collections as *Devet drame* (Nine Plays, 1970) and *Hrvatski Joyce i druge igre* (The Croatian Joyce and Other Plays, 1989), Šoljan was very active as a translator of American and English literatures, translating the works of such writers as Shakespeare, George Orwell, Lewis Carroll, F. Scott Fitzgerald, Ernest Hemingway, and Norman Mailer. He also published, in 1964, an anthology of the 100 greatest works of world literature; in 1966, an anthology of Croatian poetry from the fourteenth century to the present; and in 1972, a collection of feuilletons mostly on social and political themes under the title *Zanovijetanje iz zamke: Deset godina podlistaka* (A Troublemaker out of the Trap: Ten Years of Feuilletons). The year before his death, his book of essays, *Prošlo nesvršeno vrijeme* (An Unfinished Time Has Passed), was published. A four-volume collection of Šoljan's collected works (*Izabrane djela*) was brought out in 1991.

Translations: *Bard: A Play,* trans. Bernard Johnson (Zagreb: Most/The Bridge, 1992); *A Brief Excursion and Other Stories,* trans. Ellen Elias-Bursać (Evanston, Ill.: Northwestern University Press, 1999); *The Other People on the Moon: An Adventure Story,* trans. Graham McMaster (Zagreb: Društvo hrvatskih književnika, 1994); *Thousand Islands of the Adriatic,* trans. K. Kveder (Belgrade: Jugoslavia, 1965); "Ship in a Bottle," in *Croatian Tales of Fantasy,* trans. Graham McMaster (Zagreb: The Bridge, 1996), 121–30.

Somlyó, György (b. 1920) Hungarian poet, essayist, and novelist. The son of the poet Zoltán Somlyó (1882–1937), Somlyó was born in Balatonboglár. After completing studies primarily in French and philosophy at Budapest University and the Sorbonne in Paris, he held editorial positions at various periodicals and was editor of *Arion: Nemzetközi költői almanach/Almanach International de Poésie* (Arion: An International Poetry Almanach), the multilingual poetry yearbook published by Corvina Press in Budapest. He was also for a time director of the literature section of Radio Hungary. His first book of poems, *Seregszemle* (Review of the Troops), appeared in 1950 and was followed by such collections of verse as *Vallomás a békéről* (Evidence from Peace, 1953); *Tó fölött, ég alatt* (Over the Lake, Beneath the Sky, 1962); *Tó fölött, ég alatt* (Over the Lake, Beneath the Sky, 1965); *Mesék a mese ellen: Költemények prózában* (Fairy Tales Against the Fairy Tale: Poems in Prose, 1967); *Épp ez* (Just This, 1976); *A mesék könyve* (A Book of Fairy Tales, 1976); *A mesék második könyve* (A Second Book of Fairy Tales, 1971); *Árnyjáték* (Shadow Play, 1977); *Ami rajtam túl van: Válogatott versek, 1937–1986* (That Which Is Behind Me: Selected Poems, 1937–1986, 1988); and *Összegyűjtött versek* (Selected

Poems, 1990). As a poet, Somlyó writes admiringly of naturalness and artlessness, yet freely experiments especially with stanzaic structure. Well trained in philosophy, and a philosophically oriented poet who accepts the inexorable movement of human life toward its end, he begs God in one poem: "Lead us not into neurosis but deliver us from the daily catastrophes of vegetative life and consciousness." Somlyó is arguably even better known for his studies of poetry than for his own writing in verse. He is the author of two well-regarded books on the poet and novelist Milán Füst (1888–1967): *Füst Milán: Emlékezés és tanulmány* (Milán Füst: A Reminiscence and Study, 1969) and the expanded version, *Füst Milán, vagy, A lesütöttszemű ember: Emlékezés és tanulmány* (Milán Füst, or The Man with the Downcast Eyes: A Reminiscence and Study, 1993). Somlyó's other books on twentieth-century Hungarian poetry and literature include *Kérdés és felelet: Tanulmányok* (Question and Answer: Studies, 1949); *Hármastükör* (Triple Mirror, 1970), a three-part volume of selected writings; *Költészet vérszerződése* (Poetry's Blood Contract, 1977); *Másutt: Tanulmányok* (Elsewhere: Studies, 1979); *Philoktétész sebe: Bevezetés a modern költészetbe* (Philoctetes' Wound: An Introduction to Modern Poetry, 1980), in which he suggests that the modern poet is a descendant of the lonely outcast on the island of Lemnos whose hideous serpent-inflicted wound caused him to wail terribly from pain; *Megíratlan könyvek: Tanulmányok* (On Unwritten Books: Studies, 1982); *Részletek egy megírhatatlan versesregényből* (Excerpts from an Unwritable Book of Verse, 1983); and *A költészet ötödik évada: Tanulmányok, 1981–1987* (The Fifth Season of Poetry: Studies, 1981–1987, 1988). Somlyó is also the author of two novels, *Rámpa* (The Ramp, 1984) and *Párizsi kettős* (Parisian Double, 1990), and two volumes of writings of a mostly personal nature, *Szerelőszőnyeg: Vis-*

szaemlékezések, esszék, úti jegyzetek (The Carpet Fitter: Recollections, Essays, Travel Notes, 1980) and *Nem titok* (It's No Secret, 1992). Somlyó was a four-time recipient of the Attila József Prize (1951, 1952, 1954, 1966) and won the Tibor Déry Prize in 1987 and the Lajos Kassák Prize in 1992. In 1992 he became a founding member of the Széchenyi Academy of Literature and Art.

Translations: Four poems in *The Face of Creation,* trans. Jascha Kessler (Minneapolis: Coffee House, 1988), 137–41; three poems in *Modern Hungarian Poetry,* ed. Miklós Vajda (New York: Columbia University Press, 1977), 136–39. A collection of Somlyó's poetry is available in French as *Contrefables: Poemes,* trans. Guillevic (Paris: Gallimard, 1974).

Sommer, Piotr (b. 1948) Polish poet and translator. A native of Wałbrzych, Sommer graduated from Warsaw University in 1973. In 1976 he became editor of the world-literature magazine *Literatura na świecie,* and has also contributed to the magazines *Res Publica* and *Tygodnik Literacki.* From 1987 to 1989, he was writer in residence and visiting professor at several American colleges and universities, among them Amherst, Mount Holyoke, Wesleyan, and the University of Nebraska. He has published five volumes of poems: *W krześle* (In the Armchair, 1977); *Pamiątki po nas* (The Things We're Remembered By, 1980); *Kolejny świat* (A Later World, 1983); *Czynnik lyriczny* (The Lyrical Element, 1986); and *Czynik lyriczny i inne wiersze* (The Lyrical Element and Other Poems, 1988). Sommer is also well known as a translator of American, English, and Anglo-Irish poetry. He published an anthology of British poetry in 1983 and a book of interviews with British poets in 1985. His collection of translations of poems by Frank O'Hara appeared in 1987. Sommer's own poetry, occasionally in prose, tends toward brevity, casualness of idiom and style, use of commonplace motifs, and an outlook shaped by whimsy and undemonstrative humor and irony, as in these small examples, from "Talkativeness":

> But the citizen should be honest
> and tell everything —
> after all, the phones have been
>   reconnected
> so that he could communicate with
>   friends
> or whoever he wants,
> and it would be highly immoral
> and, frankly speaking, quite unfair
> to ring a friend
> and not tell him everything
> and in addition
> to hint
> that one knows much more.

and "Grammar":

> What was, one should speak of in the
>   past tense,
> what isn't, in some other tongue.

and "Two Gestures":

> A woman drags herself from bed.
> You know, I think I ought to make
>   myself some dinner
> But she doesn't have time
> and dies between
> two gestures: her mother's
> and her child's, never discovering
> who, or whose she was
> more.

Translations: *Things to Translate,* trans. Piotr Sommer, Ed Adams, John Ashbery, Douglas Dunn, D. J. Enright, Michael Kasper, Charles Mignon, and Elżbieta Volkmer (Newcastle upon Tyne: Bloodaxe, 1991); five poems in *Polish Poetry of the Last Two Decades of Communist Rule: Spoiling Cannibals' Fun,* ed. and trans. Stanisław Barańczak and Clare Cavanagh (Evanston, Ill.: Northwestern University Press, 1991), 170–72.

Šopov, Aco (1923–1982) Macedonian poet and translator. One of the foremost poets of postwar Macedonia, Šopov was born in Štip. After World War II, in which he participated as a partisan, he earned a degree in Yugoslav studies at the Faculty of Philosophy in Skopje. In time, he became a leading figure in Macedonian cultural and political life and served in the diplomatic corps as Yugoslav ambassador to several African countries. He was also elected to the Macedonian Academy of Arts and Sciences. *Pesni* (Poems), which appeared in 1944 (in Belgrade), was the first volume of postwar Macedonian poetry and launched Šopov's prolific career. It was followed by three books of poems similarly devoted to patriotic and revolutionary themes inspired by World War II: *Pruga na mladosta* (The Track of Youth, 1947), which he wrote with his fellow poet Slavko Janevski; *Na Gramos* (On the Gramos, 1950), devoted to the Macedonian and Greek civil war of 1945 to 1949; and *So naši race* (With Our Own Hands, 1950). Beginning with *Stihovi na makata i radosta* (Verses of Sorrow and Joy, 1951), Šopov's poetic writing turned more subjective, introspective, and philosophical, for which it was criticized in some quarters for an apparent spurning of social and political concerns. Resigned to the reality and inescapability of death, yet balancing melancholy and resignation with love, beauty, humor, and an elemental sense of affinity with tempestuous nature, Šopov continued undeterred along the same lines in such subsequent books of poems as *Slej se so tišinata* (Merge with Silence, 1955); *Vetrot nosi ubavo vreme* (The Wind Is Bringing Good Weather, 1957), arguably his finest collection; *Nebidnina* (Non-Being, 1963); *Ragjanje na zborot* (The Creation of Words, 1966); *Predvečerje* (Dusk, 1966); *Zlaten krug na* *vremeto* (The Golden Ring of Time, 1969); *Gledač vo pepelta* (Reading the Ashes, 1970); *Pesna na crnata žena* (Poem to the Black Woman, 1976), which was inspired by Šopov's diplomatic service in Africa; and *Drvo na ridot* (A Tree on the Hill, 1980). *Jus-univerzum* (Yus-Universum, 1968), "Yus" referring to the trademark "Yugoslav Standard," is a volume of satirical verses sparing little in contemporary Yugoslav society and further evidencing Šopov's creative independence. A prolific and respected translator from English, French, German, Serbo-Croatian, and Russian, Šopov translated works by Shakespeare, Corneille, Rostand, Ivan Krylov, and Miroslav Krleža. A five-volume edition of Šopov's collected works was published in Skopje in 1976.

Translations: Three poems in *Contemporary Macedonian Poetry,* trans. Ewald Osers (London: Forest, 1991), 23–27; two poems in *Introduction to Yugoslav Literature: An Anthology of Fiction and Poetry,* ed. Branko Mikasinovich, Dragan Milivojević, and Vasa D. Mihailovich (New York: Twayne, 1973), 624–25; twelve poems, trans. by various hands, in *Reading the Ashes: An Anthology of the Poetry of Modern Macedonia,* ed. Milne Holton and Graham W. Reid (Pittsburgh: University of Pittsburgh Press, 1977), 21–29; eight poems, trans. by various hands, in *The Song Beyond Songs: Anthology of Contemporary Macedonian Poetry,* ed. Venko Andonovski (Prilep: Stremež, 1997), 63–79.

Sorescu, Marin (1936–1996) Romanian poet, playwright, and essayist. Sorescu was born into a peasant family in the town of Bulzeşti, in the Dolj region. After graduating from the Faculty of Philosophy of Iaşi University in 1960, he became editor of the journal *Viaţa studenţească* and the Bucharest culture and literature journal *Luceafărul.* He also worked at the Bucharest film studio Animafilm. Sorescu eventually became a free-

lance writer. An outstanding representative of the Romanian lyric poets who came to the fore in the 1960s, Sorescu attracted considerable attention, and notoriety, with his first book of poetry, *Singur printre poeţi* (Alone Among the Poets, 1964), a collection of parodies aimed at antiquated modes of poetic expression and poetic clichés. *Poeme* (Poems, 1965), which came a year later, deals mostly with ethical concerns, but continues in part the parodic-polemic thrust of *Singur printre poeţi* (as in the poem "Shakespeare"). In *Mortea ceasului* (The Death of the Clock, 1966), one of Sorescu's most accomplished collections of poems, wit, humor, irony, and the use of maxims all serve the poet well as he attempts for the first time to confront the larger questions of human existence, among them the need to reassert authority over the machines of our own creation. These questions are also viewed through the eyes of the child in his very popular *Unde fugim de-acasă?* (Where Do We Run Away?), which also appeared in 1966. The book provided Sorescu with a further opportunity to engage in wordplay and rhymes. Sorescu's many books of poetry also include *Tinereţea lui Don Quijote* (*Don Quixote's Tender Years,* 1968; also translated as *The Youth of Don Quixote*); *O aripă şi un picior. Despre cum eram să zbor* (A Wing and a Leg. How I Nearly Flew Away, 1970); *Tuşiţi* (Cough!, 1970); *Suflete, bun la toate* (Soul, Good for Everything, 1972); the three-volume *La lilieci* (On the Lilac Bush, 1973, 1977, 1980); *Unghi* (Angle, 1970); *Astfel* (And So, 1973); *Starea de destin* (The State of Fate), *Descîntoteca* (The Magic Spell Gallery), and *Norii* (Clouds), all published in 1976; *Sărbători itinerante* (Itinerant Feasts, 1978); *Ceramică* (Ceramics, 1979); *Fîntîni în mare* (Fountains in the Sea, 1982); *Drumul* (The Journey, 1984); *Apă via, apă moartă* (Living Water, Dead Water, 1987); *Ecuatorul şi polii* (The Equator and the Poles, 1989); and *Poezii alese de cenzură* (Censored Poems, 1991). The great appeal of

Sorescu's poetry lies in its intelligence, wit, and essential simplicity of expression. Delightful in the reading, his poems often linger long in the memory both for their lightness and for the underlying seriousness of Sorescu's concerns.

In addition to his poetry, Sorescu wrote essays and plays. His essays are collected in two volumes, *Teoria sferelor de influență* (Theory of Spheres of Influence, 1969) and *Insomnii: Microeseuri* (Insomnia: Micro-Essays, 1971), the latter consisting of aphoristic-like reflections on a wide range of topics—from personal experiences to aesthetic questions. As a playwright, Sorescu's major work remains the trilogy *Setea muntelui de sare* (*The Thirst of the Salt Mountains*, 1974). In each of the plays, which consist of little more than an extended monologue by the principal character addressed to himself or herself, a solitary individual faced with his or her own destiny in the cosmos yearns for belief that there is something beyond death that gives life meaning. The first part of the trilogy is *Iona* (*Jonah*, 1968), which has often been regarded as a reply of sorts to both Samuel Beckett's *Waiting for Godot* and Eugène Ionesco's *The King Is Dying*. In the second play, *Paracliserul* (*The Verger*, 1970), the last verger in the last cathedral ever built, apparently seeking an epiphany, keeps on lighting candles throughout the cathedral until the fire consumes him. The third play of the trilogy, *Matca* (*The Matrix*, 1976), is based in part on the floods in Romania in 1970. During the rains, a woman gives birth to her child at the same time as her father is dying in an adjacent room. As the waters close in on her, her sole thought is to raise her baby above her head in an effort to save the new life. Sorescu is also well known for his historical drama *A treia țeapă* (The Third Stake, 1972; translated as *Vlad Dracula the Impaler*). Set in mid-fifteenth-century Wallachia, the play has an obvious relevance to Romania in the years of Nicolae Ceaușescu's

regime. Sorescu's other plays include *Pluta Meduzei* (The Raft of the Medusa) and *Există nervi* (There are Nerves), both of which date from 1968, and *Răceală* (Cold, 1976). The first two are closely related in that *Pluta Meduzei*, which takes place in an anonymous world with anonymous characters, parodies the positivistic worldview, whereas *Există nervi* ridicules the notion that a perfect society can be achieved by a high level of technology and civilization.

Sorescu visited the United States in 1971/1972 and West Berlin in 1973/1974. He also traveled extensively throughout Europe, both East and West. In 1965 he won the prize for lyric poetry of the Romanian Writers Union and the prize for theater of the same organization in 1968 and again in 1974. The Romanian Academy awarded him a separate prize specifically for his play *Iona*. He also won the Italian "Napoli ospide" Prize for poetry in 1969, and the international prize Le Muze of the Academia delle Muze, Florence, Italy, in 1978. In 1983 he was elected a corresponding member of the Mallarmé Academy in Paris, and in December of that year he received the International Poetry Prize "Fernando Riello" in Madrid. In 1991 he was awarded the prize of the Romanian Writers Union and the Herder Prize (Austria) for his entire work. The following year, he was made a member of the Romanian Academy. From 1993 to 1995, Sorescu served as Romanian minister of culture.

Literature: Mihaela Andreescu, *Marin Sorescu: Instantaneu critic* (Bucharest: Albatros, 1983); Marian Popescu, *Chei pentru labirint: Eseu despre teatrul lui Marin Sorescu și D. R. Popescu* (Bucharest: Cartea Românească, 1986).

Translations: *The Biggest Egg in the World,* in versions by Seamus Heaney, Ted Hughes, Michael Hamburger, et al. (Newcastle upon Tyne: Bloodaxe, 1987); *The Crossing,* trans. Ioana Russell-Gebbett and

John Hartley Williams (Newcastle upon Tyne: Bloodaxe, 1998); *Don Quixote's Tender Years,* trans. Stavros Deligiorgis (Iowa City: Corycian, 1979); *Hands Behind My Back: Selected Poems,* trans. Gabriela Dragnea, Stuart Friebert, and Adriana Varga (Oberlin, Ohio: Oberlin College Press, 1991); *Let's Talk About the Weather: Selected Poems of Marin Sorescu,* trans. Andrea Deletant and Brenda Walker, with an introduction by Jon Silkin (London: Forest, 1985, 1987); *Marin Sorescu: Selected Poems,* trans. Michael Hamburger (Newcastle upon Tyne: Bloodaxe, 1983); *Rame/Frames: Twenty-Five Poems by Marin Sorescu,* trans. Roy MacGregor-Hastie (Bucharest: Eminescu, 1972), a Romanian–English edition; *The Thirst of the Salt Mountain: Three Plays by Marin Sorescu,* trans. Andrea Deletant and Brenda Walker (London: Forest, 1985, 1990), which includes *Jonah, The Verger,* and *The Matrix,* together with eleven poems in translation in an appendix; *This Hour,* trans. Michael Hamburger (Durango, Colo.: Logbridge-Rhodes, 1982); *Vlad Dracula, the Impaler: A Play by Marin Sorescu,* trans. Dennis Deletant (London: Forest, 1987); *The Youth of Don Quixote,* in versions by John F. Deane (Dublin: Dedalus, 1987); poems in *An Anthology of Contemporary Romanian Poetry,* trans. Andrea Deletant and Brenda Walker (London: Forest, 1984), 54–78; *Anthology of Contemporary Romanian Poetry,* ed. and trans. Roy MacGregor-Hastie (London: Peter Owen, 1969), 155–57; *46 Romanian Poets in English,* trans. Ştefan Avădanei and Don Eulert (Iaşi: Junimea, 1973), 242–53; *Modern Romanian Poetry,* ed. Nicholas Catanoy (Oakville, Ont.: Mosaic Press/Valley Editions, 1977), 20, 52, 80, 100.

Spahiu, Xhevahir (b. 1945) Albanian poet. One of the leading poets of contemporary Albania, with an international reputation, Spahiu was born in Skrapar in the southern part of the country. His first book of poems,

Mëngjes sirenash (Siren Morning), appeared in 1970, and was followed by *Vdekje perëndive* (Death to the Gods, 1977); *Agime shqiptare* (Albanian Dawns, 1981); *Nesër jam aty* (I'll Be There Tomorrow, 1986); *Tek rrënja e fjalëve* (To the Roots of Words, 1988); *Poezia shqipe* (Albanian Poetry, 1990); *Kohë e krisur* (A Crackpot Age, 1991); *Ferrparajsa* (The Paradise of Hell, 1994); and *Pezull* (Suspended in Air, 1996). A poet generally of short poems and outward simplicity, Spahiu writes of history, of Albania, of love, and of ordinary objects that suddenly acquire an air of unreality and mystery. Whatever his subject, his writing conveys an often remarked intensity heightened by the effective use of repeated short lines of verse alternating with longer lines. Spahiu currently holds the position of chairman of the Albanian League of Artists and Writers.

Translations: Seven poems in *An Elusive Eagle Soars: Anthology of Modern Albanian Poetry,* ed. and trans. Robert Elsie (London: Forest, 1993), 128–34.

Spiró, György (b. 1946) Hungarian novelist, playwright, poet, essayist, and literary scholar. A widely known and prolific writer, Spiró grew up and was educated in Budapest. He entered Eötvös Lóránd University in 1970 and pursued studies in Slavic languages and literatures. In 1981, after previous employment as a journalist and an editor and the year in which he became a doctoral candidate, Spiró was appointed an associate professor at the university. Spiró began his literary career in 1974 with largely political allegorical poetry in such volumes as *Keringő* (Waltz, 1974) and *História* (History, 1977). Similarly political in nature is his most successful novel and the one he himself regards as his best, *Az ikszék* (The X's, 1981). It is based on the career of the late-eighteenth- and early-nineteenth-century Polish actor and stage director Wojciech Bogusławski. Well versed in Slavic literatures, Spiró has on occasion sought inspiration among or has written on Slavic authors, particularly Polish. The same year in which *Az ikszék* was published, he came out with a biography of the distinguished Croatian writer Miroslav Krleža (1893–1981). His very successful play *Az imposztor* (*The Impostor*, written 1982) is yet another political allegory based on an episode in *Az ikszék*. In it, Bogusławski adroitly, and successfully, turns a rehearsal of *Tartuffe* in Vilna, in the Russian part of then partitioned Poland, into a protest against the czar. Continuing his interest in Polish (and Slavic) theater, Spiró in 1986 published a study (actually his university dissertation) on Eastern European drama with particular emphasis on the late-nineteenth- and early-twentieth-century Polish dramatist Stanisław Wyspiański: *A közép-kelet-európai dráma: A felvilágosodástól Wyspiański szintéziseig* (East Central European Drama: A Synthesis from the Enlightenment to Wyspiański).

One of Spiró's best-known and most highly regarded plays, *Csirkefej* (*Chicken Head*, 1987), is a sordid yet poignant picture of lower-class Hungarian urban society in the 1980s that assumes the aspect of a commentary on contemporary society in general. It could easily have been inspired by the Russian dramatist Maxim Gorky's *The Lower Depths*. In his later play, *Honderű*, Spiró trains his sights on the twentieth century as a whole. The title refers to the French-derived *honte de rue* (shame of the street) and is used by the characters in the play pejoratively to indicate something they dislike or deem idiotic. But it functions like a double-edged sword in that it is the characters themselves—all members of the bourgeoisie—who in their derogation of the age and their own anachronistic ways are the butt of Spiró's putdown. The straightforward, old-fashioned style of the play becomes an integral part of the mockery. In 1987 a collection of Spiró's plays was pub-lished under the title *A békecsászár* (The Emperor of Peace). In March of that year, Spiró raised a ruckus among so-called populist writers when his short poem "Here They Come," in which he warns of the dangers of a revival of anti-Semitism in Hungary, appeared in the journal *Mozgó Világ*. Spiró's other works include the novels *Magániktató* (Private Files, 1985); *Álmodtam neked* (I Dreamed for You, 1987); and *A jövevény* (The Newcomer, 1990) and a collection of essays and other writings titled *Kanásztánc: Válogatott esszék, vallomások, publicisztikák* (The Swineherd's Dance: Selected Essays, Confessions, and Journalism, 1992).

Translations: *Chicken Head*, trans. Eugene Brogyányi, in *Drama Contemporary: Hungary*, ed. Eugene Brogyányi (New York: PAJ Publications, 1991), 129–200; *The Impostor*, ed. and trans. Clara Györgyey, in *A Mirror to the Cage: Three Contemporary Hungarian Plays* (Fayetteville: University of Arkansas Press, 1993), 103–84; *The Impostor*, trans. Judith Sollosy, in *Three Contemporary Hungarian Plays*, ed. Albert Tezla (London: Forest, 1992; Budapest: Corvina, 1992), 147–238; "With My Father at the Game," trans. László Jakabfy, in *The Kiss: Twentieth Century Hungarian Short Stories*, selected by István Bart (Budapest: Corvina, 1998), 340–55.

Srbljanović, Biljana (b. 1970) Serbian playwright. Acclaimed as Serbia's leading young playwright, Srbljanović won several honors for her first work for the theater, *Beogradska trilogija* (Belgrade Trilogy, written 1996), which was widely performed throughout Europe. Set against the background of the Balkan wars of the 1990s, the play focuses on the moral choices facing the characters as they try to come to grips with the difficult consequences of their actions or inactions. The trilogy is composed of stories about three young people who flee Serbia to avoid military service and wind up as outsiders in

Prague, Sydney, and Los Angeles, spending New Year's Eve lamenting what (and whom) they have lost as they struggle to create new lives. Srbljanović's second play, the farcical psychodrama *Porodične priče* (Family Stories), which made its North American debut as a student production at the Yale University School of Drama in April 2000, focuses mainly on one character's parents as they try to prevent him from either leaving Serbia or staying and becoming a politically engaged citizen. Apart from its absurdist touches, the play features a pivotal dream sequence in which three actors speak not as actors playing roles but as themselves. As critics have pointed out, the play has Bertolt Brecht's fingerprints all over it. *Porodične priče* was translated into German for Germany's leading stage magazine, *Theater Heute*, in January 1999. *Beogradska trilogija* and *Porodične priče* were published for the first time in Serbian in a single volume in 2000. Srbljanović's third play, *Pad* (The Fall), a bitter sarcastic spoof, is a mythological play laced with Serbian legends and indebted to Umberto Eco's essay on the roots of fascism. Srbljanović is also the author of a diary of the seventy-eight-day NATO bombing of Serbia that appeared in *Der Spiegel*, *La Repubblica*, and the *Guardian*. *Supermarket*, her most autobiographical play, had its premiere at the Vienna festival in 2001. Set in a small provincial town in Austria or East Germany, it deals with a high-school principal who has spent the decade since the fall of the Berlin Wall fabricating his own past by pretending to be a dissident attacking the old regime. However, no one cares when, in the end, he reveals that it was all make-believe. Srbljanović, who has protested the beatings of demonstrating Serb students, was awarded the Ernst Toller Prize in 1999.

Stachura, Edward (1937–1979) Polish poet and short-story writer. An idol among younger readers after his suicide in 1979, Stachura was born in Charvein, France, the son of Polish emigrants, and was taken back to Poland at the age of eleven. A prolific and accomplished writer of broad literary culture, he was the author of several collections of short stories and other prose writings, one volume of poetry and two longer poetic works, two novels, a volume of songs, and translations from French and Spanish. Restless, nonconformist, possessed of a great appetite for life coupled with an obsession with the total destructiveness of death, Stachura preferred to live as a vagabond because of the freedom it afforded him, and traveled extensively in France, Mexico, Norway, and the Middle East. His passions and anxieties—all reflected in his poetry and prose—eventually led to serious psychological disorders and culminated in his suicide at the age of forty-two, at a time when he was beginning to achieve real popularity as a writer, especially among young readers. Stachura's first published book was the short-story collection *Jeden dzień* (One Day, 1962). The year before, he had received the Young Writers Prize of the City of Warsaw for poems published in literary periodicals. After *Jeden dzień* Stachura alternated between prose and poetry, publishing his first collection of poems, *Dużo ognia* (Much Fire), in 1963. His second book of poems, *Falując na wietrze* (Twisting in the Wind), came out in 1966 and was followed in 1968 by two longer poetic texts, *Po ogrodzie niech hula szarańcza* (Let the Locusts Hop Around the Garden), for which he was awarded the Piętak Prize in 1969, and *Przystępuję do ciebie* (I'm Coming to You), in which every poem begins with the words of the title. His first novel, *Cała jaskrawość* (Sheer Ostentation), appeared in 1969, and for his second, *Siekierezada albo zima leśnych ludzi* (The Axe-iad, or the Winter of the Forest People, 1971), whose title is untranslatable since *siekierezada* is a combination of Polish *siekiera* (ax) and Scheherezade, he won his second Piętak Prize in 1972. A collection of Stachura's songs, *Piosenki* (Songs), was published in 1973. A very eclectic and in some ways eccentric volume of his prose writings that brought together his travel experiences, ideas about literature, attitude toward various Polish and foreign writers, and thoughts about the world at large appeared in 1975 under the title *Wszystko jest poezja* (Everything Is Poetry) and subtitled *Opowieść—rzeka* (A Narration-River). It is arguably the best introduction to Stachura's vision of the world and his most engaging work. Stachura's last collection of short stories came out in 1977 and bore the title *Się*, the term used to form the reflexive of verbs in Polish and possibly translatable as "Self." Stachura's last work, *List do pozostałych* (A Letter to Those Remaining Behind, 1979), can be viewed as a poetic brief of sorts setting forth his case against the world in compelling terms. After his death, in response to the growing Stachura cult, a volume of his selected poetry, *Wybór wierszy* (Selected Verse), was published in 1982. The same year, the big state publishing house in Warsaw, Czytelnik, brought out a four-volume edition of Stachura's collected works under the general title *Poezja i proza* (Poetry and Prose). A book of quasi-philosophical character setting forth Stachura's views on detachment, independence, self-sufficiency, life as poetry and poetry as life, and so on appeared in 1985 as *Fabula rasa: Rzecz o egoizmie* (Fabula rasa: On Egoism, 1985)

Stade, Martin (b. 1931) German novelist, short-story writer, and screenwriter. A native of Haarhausen, near Arnstadt, Stade trained as a mechanic, worked as a Communist Party activist until 1959, and then became a manual laborer until devoting himself wholly to writing in 1969. In 1971/1972, he was enrolled in the Johannes R. Becher Institute of Literature in Leipzig but was expelled before completing his studies. He

later made his expulsion the basis of his story "Die Exmatrikulation" ("The Ex-Matriculation"), which appeared only in West Germany in 1979. Stade's growing antiestablishment attitude worsened as time went on. As one of eight signatories of a letter to Party boss Erich Honecker in 1979 protesting the expulsion of the writer Stefan Heym from the German Democratic Republic, Stade was dismissed from the East German Writers Union. Stade's literary debut came in 1971 with *Meister von Sanssouci* (The Master of Sanssouci), a historical novel, the genre that, to a considerable extent, became the basis of his reputation. The novel, on which he had the guidance of Claus Back, draws a contrast between the imperious and obstinate Prussian ruler Friedrich II (the Great) and the young and talented architect G. W. von Knobelsdorf, who embellished the design of the Sanssouci Palace in Potsdam. As in his other historical fiction, Stade was keenly interested in the nature of relations between artists and intellectuals and political authority. He explored the same theme, from different angles, in such subsequent historical novels as *Der König und sein Narr* (The King and His Jester, 1975), in which he develops the portrait of a corrupt intellectual at the court of Friedrich Wilhem I who, as he is about to die, reviews his life from its peak when he was president of the Academy of Sciences to his fall to the status of court jester; *Der närrische Krieg* (The Foolish War, 1981); and two novels based on the life of Bach, *Junge Bach* (Young Bach, 1985) and *Zwischen Schlehdorn und Paradies: Der junge Bach* (Between Schlehdorn and Paradise: The Young Bach, 1990). In his short stories, a genre he also favored, Stade chose his subjects mostly from rural life. His first published story, "Vetters fröhliche Fuhren: Erzählung" ("Cousin's Happy Fares: A Story"), appeared in 1973. The following year, he came out with the more important, if controversial, collection *Der himmelblaue Zeppelin* (The Sky-Blue Zeppelin, 1974), in essence a portrait of a Thuringian village struggling to cope with the sweeping agricultural changes then under way. The collection had only a middling success, mostly because some critics took exception to the way Stade potrayed the older generation. After *Der himmelblaue Zeppelin*, Stade published another four volumes of stories: *Siebzehn schöne Fische: Erzählungen* (Seventeen Nice Fish: Stories, 1976); *Die scharf beobachtenden Stare und andere Erzählungen* (The Keenly Observed Starlings and Other Stories, 1982); *Präsentkorb: Gesammelte Erzählungen vom Lande* (The Gift Hamper: Collected Stories from the Countryside, 1983); and *Windsucher und andere Dorfgeschichten* (Windfinder and Other Village Stories, 1984). In 1995, with his fellow East German writers Ulrich Plenzdorf and Klaus Schlesinger, Stade published the obviously political post-GDR collection *Berliner Geschichten: Operativer Schwerpunkt Selbstverlag: Eine Autoren-Anthologie: Wie sie entstanden und von der Stasi verhindert wurde* (Berlin Stories: The Operative Center of Gravity Self-Publishing House: An Authors' Anthology and How It Arose and Was Blocked by the Stasi).

Stanca, Dan (b. 1952) Romanian novelist, short-story writer, essayist, and poet. A prolific and respected writer, Stanca was born and educated in Bucharest. After receiving his degree in literature from Bucharest University, he worked as an editor for several literary reviews and journals before joining the cultural department of *România literară* and becoming a regular contributor to the newspaper *România liberă*. Stanca published his first work of fiction, the novel *Vântul sau țipătul altuia* (The Wind, or The Scream of Another Woman), in 1992. It was followed by such novels as *Aripile arhangelului Mihail* (The Wings of the Archangel Michael, 1996); *Apocalips amânat*

(Apocalypse Postponed, 1997), for which he won the Writers Union Prize in 1998 as well as the Literary Prize of the Flacăra Foundation; *Morminte străvezii* (Transparent Graves, 1999); *Ultimul om* (The Last Man, 1999); and *Domnul clipei* (The Master of the Moment, 2000). Stanca is also the author of a collection of short stories titled *Cer iertare* (Forgiving Sky, 1997) and several books of essays: *Contemplatorul solitar* (The Solitary Thinker, 1997); *Ultima biserică* (The Last Church, 1997); *Ritualul nopții* (Nocturnal Ritual, 1998); *Muntele viu* (The Living Mountains, 1998); and *Veninul metafizic* (The Metaphysical Poison, 1998).

Stancu, Zaharia (1902–1974) Romanian novelist, short-story writer, and poet. Born into a peasant family in the village of Salcia in the Teleorman district, on the Danubian plain, Stancu was educated locally before earning his degree in 1932 in literature and philosophy at Bucharest University. He began his literary career as a journalist affiliated with such left-wing publications as *Adevărul literar și artistic* and soon became known for his strong antifascist views. From 1932 to 1938, Stancu edited the journal *Azi*, which had an affiliation with the Romanian Communist Party. In 1937 he edited the daily newspaper *Lumea românească*. Both publications were closed by the censors, in 1938 and 1940. The same fate befell the journal *Revista română*, which Stancu began editing in 1941. During World War II, Stancu was incarcerated along with other left-wing Romanian writers and intellectuals in the labor camp in Tîrgu Jiu. In 1944, after his release, he joined the Communist Party. Two years later, he began a long association with the National Theater in Bucharest as its director; in 1947 he became president of the Romanian Writers Union, a position he held again in 1966, 1968, and 1972. In 1948 and again in 1960, he was elected a member of parliament and, in 1955, a member of the

Romanian Academy. Apart from his journalistic writing, Stancu had a strong interest
in poetry and prose fiction. His first book of
poetry appeared in 1927 under the title
Poeme simple (Simple Poems). It was honored by the prize of the Association of Romanian Writers, and Stancu was invited to
join the influential journal *Gîndirea*. It was
followed by such other collections of verse
as *Albe* (Whitenings, 1937); *Clopotul de aur*
(The Golden Bell, 1939); *Pomul roşu* (The
Red Tree, 1940); *Iarba fiarelor* (The Magic
Herb, 1941); *Anii de fum* (Years of Smoke,
1944); and, after a long hiatus from poetry,
Cîntec şoptit (Whispered Song, 1970); *Sabia
timpului* (The Sword of Time, 1972);
Cîntecul lebedei (Swan Song, 1974); and
Poeme cu lună (Poems with Moon, 1974),
the collections from the 1970s reflecting the
writer's deteriorating health and sense of
approaching death. A two-volume set of his
collected poems (*Poezii*) appeared in 1971.

Although respected as a poet of wit and a
bittersweet attitude toward life, Stancu
gained both national and international
fame as a result of his enormous novelistic
ouput. In terms of reception, his first two
novels, *Taifunul* (Typhoon, 1937) and
Oameni cu joben (Men in Top Hats, 1941),
were completely overshadowed by his greatest literary success, *Desculţ* (Barefoot, 1948).
Departing from the idyllic and sentimental
tradition of Romanian village literature,
Stancu aimed for an unflinchingly realistic
depiction of the struggle for survival of the
poorest stratum of the peasantry in the first
half of the twentieth century. Drawing on
his own firsthand knowledge of peasant life,
he developed the character of the village
youth, Darie, Stancu's alter ego and a type of
picaresque figure, who serves as both narrator and hero not only in *Desculţ* but in subsequent novels spun out of it. They include
Dulăii (Hounds, 1952); the five-volume *Răd-
ăcinile sînt amare* (The Roots Are Bitter,
1958–1959); *Clopote şi struguri* (Bells and

Grapes, 1960); *Printre stele* (Under Stars,
1960); *Carul de foc* (The Chariot of Fire,
1960); *Jocul cu moartea* (*A Gamble with
Death,* 1962); *Pădurea nebună* (The Crazy
Forest, 1963); *Ce mult te-am iubit* (How
Much I Loved You, 1968), focused mainly on
the death of Darie's mother; and the three-
volume *Vîntul şi ploaia* (The Wind and the
Rain, 1969). Collectively, the "Darie" novels
represent a sweeping epic-lyrical panorama
of Romanian peasant and small-town life
from the early twentieth century until after
World War II. *A Gamble with Death,* one of
the best of the novels and one of only two
works by Stancu available in English, is set
in German- and Austrian-occupied Romania during World War I and depicts the picaresque-like wanderings of Darie and a former diplomat called "Ambassador" across
Bulgaria and Macedonia after they escape
from a German forced-labor battalion. Before eventually making their way back to
Bucharest, they experience the full horror of
war in the Balkans. *Şatra* (Gypsy Encamp-
ment, 1968) is an exception to the general
pattern of Stancu's novels in that it deals
only with Romania's Gypsies and addresses
their persecution under the regime of Ion
Antonescu. Stancu's journalistic writings
were published in such collections as *Zile de
lagăr* (Camp Days, 1946), an account of his
incarceration in Tîrgu Jiu; *Secolul omului de
jos* (The Century of the Underground Man,
1946); *Călătorind prin U. R. S. S.* (Traveling
Through the USSR, 1950), a Soviet travel
book; the two-volume *Însemnarile şi am-
intirile unui ziarist* (Notes and Recollections
of a Journalist), which consists of *Sarea e
dulce* (The Salt Is Sweet, 1955) and *Cefe de
taur* (Bullneck, 1956); *Pentru oameni acestui
pămînt* (For the People of This Earth, 1971);
and *Triumful raţiunii* (The Triumph of Reason, 1973). These books address a wide range
of issues from the artistic to the political
and reflect the author's deep sense of social
justice and liberal outlook. During his life-

time, Stancu published several collections of longer and shorter stories, among them *Brazdă îngustă şi adîncă* (Narrow and Deep Funnel, 1949); *Pentru viaţa* (For Life, 1951); *Primii paşi* (First Steps, 1951); *Florile pămîntului* (The Flowers of Earth, 1954); *Iarbă* (Grass, 1957); and *Darie povestind copiilor* (Darie Tells the Children, 1960). In 1974, the year of Stancu's death, a collection of his novellas and stories was published under the title *Uruma: Nuvele şi povestiri* (Uruma: Novellas and Stories). The posthumous publication *Viaţa, poezie, proza . . . Confesiunile lui Darie* (Life, Poetry, Prose: Darie's Confessions, 1975) is a good introduction to Stancu's thoughts about his own career and literature in general. The style is casual and very readable, and makes a strong point of Stancu's attachment to his peasant origins. Stancu was a prolific translator and rendered into Romanian works by such diverse writers as D. H. Lawrence, William C. Morrow, Jack Lindsay, Knut Hamsun, André Kédros, Guido da Verona, and the Russians A. S. Griboedov, Maxim Gorky, and Sergei Esenin. Among the other honors Stancu received during his career were the State Prize (1954), an award for his book of poetry *Cîntec şoptit* (1971), and the International Herder Prize (1971). It was also in 1971 that he was named Hero of Labor.

Literature: Sultana Craia, *Aventura memoriei* (Bucharest: Eminescu, 1983); Ovidiu Ghidirmic, *Zaharia Stancu, sau Interogaţiane sfîrşita* (Craiova: Scrisul Romanesc, 1977).

Translations: *A Gamble with Death,* trans. Richard A. Hillard (London: Peter Owen, 1969); *Hounds* (Bucharest: Book, 1954); four poems in *Anthology of Contemporary Romanian Poetry,* ed. and trans. Roy MacGregor-Hastie (London: Peter Owen, 1969), 83–88; "Lilac Time," in *Introduction to Rumanian Literature,* ed. Jacob Steinberg (New York: Twayne, 1966), 261–70. *Ce mult te-am iubit* is available in French as *Combien je t'ai aimee,* trans. Leon Negruzzi (Paris: Albin Michel, 1972).

Stănescu, Nichita (1933–1983) Romanian poet and essayist. A native of Ploieşti, Stănescu is widely acclaimed as the foremost Romanian poet of the second half of the twentieth century. Born and educated in Bucharest, he received his degree from the Faculty of Philology of Bucharest University in 1957. The same year, he published three poems in the journal *Tribuna* and began collaborating with *Gazeta literară.* From 1957 to 1960, he worked first as a proofreader and then as an editor at *Gazeta literară.* In 1960 he made his literary debut with his first volume of poems, *Sensul iubirii* (The Sense of Love), which despite the obvious signs of the poet's talent still evidences the conformist pressures of socialist realism. In his next three books of poetry—*O viziune a sentimentelor* (A Vision of Feelings, 1964), for which he won the Poetry Prize of the Writers Union; *Dreptul la timp* (The Right to Time, 1965); and *11 elegii* (11 Elegies, 1966)— it was clear that Stănescu had overcome the limitations of *Sensul iubirii* and was rapidly evolving into a poet of considerable depth and stylistic range. Pervaded with metaphysical doubt, the appropriately named *11 elegii* evidence Stănescu's inability to bring about the transformation of the world through feeling and vision, toward which he strove in his two preceeding books. His first anthology, *Alfa,* which contains the previously unpublished "Obiecte cosmice" ("Cosmic Objects"), appeared in 1967 and was followed almost immediately by two further volumes: *Oul şi sferă* (The Egg and the Sphere, 1967) and *Roşu vertical* (Vertical Red, 1967). *Laus Ptolemaei* (Praise of Ptolemy), which Stănescu himself edited, appeared the following year. In 1969 his very important collection of verse, *Necuvintele* (Unwords), appeared and won for Stănescu his second Poetry Prize of the Writers

Union. Representing a resignation of sorts, the poems in this collection acknowledge the poet's failure to define essence through language, hence his attempt to create a poetry of "unwords" (*necuvintele*). *Un pămînt numit România* (A Land Named Romania) appeared in 1969, a year when Stănescu was able to travel extensively in Europe, visiting, among other countries, France, Italy, and Finland. Stănescu's second anthology, *Poezii* (Poetry), appeared in 1970, as did his new volume of poetry, *În dulcele stil clasic* (In the Sweet Classic Style). By now, Stănescu's own poems had begun appearing in other languages, especially the popular *11 elegii*. *Necuvintele* appeared in Serbo-Croatian translation in 1971. Other foreign translations of Stănescu's poetry would follow in due course. Stănescu first came to the attention of the West when he read his poetry at the Poetry International Festival in London in 1971. The first collection of his poems in English appeared in London in 1975. In 1972 Stănescu published his first volume of essays, *Cartea de recitire* (A Book for Reading); it won the Writers Union Prize that year. Two more volumes of poetry also appeared in 1972: *Măreţia frigului* (The Greatness of Cold) and *Belgradul în cinci prieteni* (Five Friends in Belgrade). *Clar de inimă* (Pure of Heart), a third anthology, this time consisting of love poems, came out in 1973. The following year, Stănescu's first collection of poems in English translation appeared under the title *The Still Unborn About the Dead*. In 1975 Stănescu was honored with his first international literary prize, the Herder (Vienna). In a gesture worthy of a poet, Stănescu spent his prize money on white flowers and lilies for all the women of Vienna's Romanian community and black tulips that he strewed along the street in Vienna where the Romanian national poet, Mihai Eminescu, had once lived. Stănescu's new anthology, *Starea poeziei* (The State of Poetry, 1975), enjoyed a warm critical reception. *Epica magna,* which he did in collaboration with the artist Sorin Dumitrescu and which appeared after a three-year hiatus in 1978, generated a certain controversy over the volume's playful tone and graphics. Nevertheless, it won the Mihai Eminescu Prize of the Romanian Academy. The poet's prolific output hardly diminished in the few years before his untimely death brought on by increasingly severe bouts of hepatitis; four new volumes appeared between 1979 and 1982: *Operele imperfecte* (Imperfect Works, 1979), a book of poems marked by greater discontinuousness of style; *Respirări* (Breathing, 1982), a collection of essays and other writings; *Noduri şi semne* (Knots and Signs, 1982), a new, very restrained anthology of his poerty that won the Yugoslav Struga Poetry Evenings Prize; and *Antimetafizică* (Antimetaphysics, 1985), another volume of poems. The posthumously published *Fiziologia poeziei: Proză şi versuri, 1957–1983* (Physiology of Poetry: Prose and Poems, 1957–1983, 1990) is especially valuable for Stănescu's prose pieces on his own writing as well as on that of other writers, both Romanian and foreign, from Dante to Walt Whitman. Stănescu was twice proposed for the Nobel Prize in Literature, in 1979 and 1980. Before he died in 1983, his fiftieth birthday was the occasion for widespread celebration in Romania's artistic community, with a number of publications honoring his contribution to Romanian literature.

Literature: Sanda Anghelescu, ed. *Nichita Stănescu* (Bucharest: Eminescu, 1983), a good collection of articles on Stănescu by fellow Romanian writers and critics as well as by several of his foreign translators. The volume, which was published in conjunction with the celebrations of Stănescu's fiftieth birthday, was in print at the time of his death in 1983. It includes a useful chronology of Stănescu's life and career and a bibliography.

Translations: *Ask the Circle to Forgive You: Selected Poems, 1964–1979,* trans. Mark Irwin and Mariana Carpinian (Cleveland: Globe, 1983); *Bas-Relief with Heroes: Selected Poems, 1960–1982,* trans. Thomas C. Carlson and Vasile Poenaru (Memphis, Tenn.: Memphis State University Press, 1988); *The Still Unborn About the Dead,* trans. Petru Popescu and Peter Jay (Iowa City: International Writing Program, University of Iowa, 1974; London: Anvil, 1975); thirteen poems in *An Anthology of Contemporary Romanian Poetry,* trans. Andrea Deletant and Brenda Walker (London: Forest, 1984), 79–92.

Stanev, Emiliian (real name Nikola Stoianov Stanev; 1907–1979) Bulgarian novelist and short-story writer. A native of Veliko Turnovo, Stanev first studied painting at the Academy of Fine Arts in Sofia. After making his literary debut in 1931, he published several collections of short stories in the 1930s that established his reputation as one of the contemporary Bulgarian masters of the genre. Among these collections were *Primamlivi bliasychi* (Luring Gleams, 1938); *Mechtatel* (The Dreamer, 1939); *Sami* (Alone, 1940); *Vylchi noshti* (Nights of the Wolves, 1943); *Izbrani razkazi i povesti* (Selected Short Stories and Tales, 1959); *Stranitsi za podviga* (Pages About Valor, 1975); and *Iunski den* (A Day in June, 2nd ed., 1979). Stanev made the transition from short to longer forms of fiction in the second half of the 1940s. Two of his best-known works, the novella *V tiha vecher* (On a Quiet Evening, 1947) and his most celebrated work, the novel *Kradetsut na praskovi* (*The Peach Thief,* 1948), as well as the historical romance *Ivan Kondarev* (1958), about the September uprising of 1923 and for which Stanev won the Dimitrov Prize, were written after the war. Stanev's literary work was paralleled by his editorial responsibilities at such leading journals as *Zlatorog, Izkustvo i kritika, Bulgarska misul, Lovets,* and *Literaturen zhivot.* From 1950 to 1955, he was in charge of the fiction section of *Literaturen zhivot.* A collection of his stories and novels appeared in 1965. The novels *Turnovskata tsaritsa* (The Empress of Turnovo) and *The Peach Thief* were published in 1973 in a volume containing as well the stories "Vulkut" ("The Wolf") and "Skot Reinolds i nepostizhimoto" ("Reynolds the Beast and the Unattainable").

Two thematic foci dominate Stanev's fiction: the description of provincial life, of poor petit-bourgeois life, from which it is almost impossible to extricate oneself, and the keen observations of nature and the animal world. Two of his last works were *Legenda za Sibin, preslavskiia kniaz* (The Legend of Sibin, Prince of Preslav, 1974), set in the ancient Second Bulgarian Kingdom and dealing with the dilemma of a ruler attached neither to the Orthodox Christianity of his time nor to the anti-Orthodox Bogomil heresy, and *Antikhrist* (The Antichrist, 1970). His collected works were published in seven volumes in 1981.

Translations: *Over Hill and Dale,* trans. Todor Kirov (Sofia: Foreign Languages Press, 1965); *The Peach Thief and Other Bulgarian Stories,* trans. Radost Pridham and Jean Morris (London: Cassell, 1968), which also contains Dimitur Talev's "The Last Journey," E. Pelin's "Land," and Pavel Vezhinov's "My Father"; *Stranger and Other Stories,* trans. Marguerita Alexieva and Zdravko Stankov (Sofia: Foreign Languages Press, 1967); *Wildlife Heroes and Villains: Personality Portraits of Creatures Great and Small,* trans. Marguerite P. Alexieva (Harrisburg, Pa.: Stackpole Books, 1969).

Stefanova, Liliana (b. 1929) Bulgarian poet and prose writer. One of the most prominent women writers of post–World War II Bulgarian literature, Stefanova was born in Sofia. She graduated from high school in her native city in 1947 and from the Gorky Institute of Literature in Moscow in 1954. From 1957 to 1964, she worked as an editor for *Literaturen front*; from 1964 to 1967, as assistant editor in chief of the journal *Septemvri*; and from 1967 to 1988, as editor in chief of *Obzor*. In 1988/1989, she was the editor in chief of *Literaturen front*. Widely traveled throughout her career, Stefanova participated in the International Writing Program at the University of Iowa in 1980 and attended writers' forums in Tokyo, New York, London, Paris, and Brussels.

A prolific poet, Stefanova has published some thirty books of verse, including *Kogato sme na dvadeset godini* (When We Are Twenty, 1956); *Ne si otivai, den!* (Don't Leave, Day!, 1965); *Obich i muka* (Love and Torture, 1967); *Glas od budeshteto* (The Voice from the Future, 1969); *Sluntseto me tseluna* (The Sun Kisses Me, 1970); *Iuzhen briag* (Southern Shore, 1972); *Parola* (Password, 1973); *Ognena orbita* (Fiery Orbit, 1974); *Nepozvolena skorost* (Forbidden Haste, 1976); *Magnitno pole* (Magnetic Field, 1978); *Lirika* (Lyrics, 1979), a book of selected verse; *Sled polunosht* (After Midnight, 1982); *Shepot i vik* (Whisper and Shout, 1984); *Vliubena, kakto niakoga* (In Love as Never Before, 1985); *Dushite ni sa zaedno: Liubovna lirika* (The Souls Are Not Together: Love Lyrics, 1986); *Bolka na glas* (The Ache of the Voice, 1987); *Nepovtorimoto* (The Unequaled, 1989); and *Obichah-obicham* (I Did Love, I Do Love, 1989). Simply structured, often terse, Stefanova's poems address feminine attitudes and concerns within the broader context of life in general. The love experience in its many manifestations lies at the core of much of her verse. She is particularly sensitive to the ironies and mysteries of male–female relationships and expresses the need for magic in life to make it worth living. Her poems are usually written in the first person and often contain striking images, such as "Why do we sometimes look like an airport with all flights canceled."

Apart from her abundant poetic canon, Stefanova has written a great deal of prose. Several works are descriptions of travel, beginning in the 1950s with books about Moscow (1952), Uzbekistan (1955), and the Caucasus (1957). More interesting are the books she published based on her travels in the United States, Japan, and Mexico: *Edna esen v Amerika* (A Fall in America, 1964); *Vulkanite na Meksiko dimiat* (The Volcanoes in Mexico Are Smoking, 1969); and *Iaponiia bez kimono i vetrilo* (Japan Without Kimono and Fan, 1973). Her essays and journalistic writings, some of which address the impact of technology on the modern consciousness, appear in such collections as *Sreshti: Besedi sus suvetski pisateli* (Encounters: Conversations with Soviet Writers, 1963); *Vreme i dulg: Eseta, etiudi, statii* (Time and Duty: Essays, Etudes, Articles, 1971); *Pisha—znachi, obicham: Eseta, statii* (I'm Writing, Which Means I'm in Love: Essays, Articles, 1976); *Vreme, harakter, lichnost: Eseta* (Time, Character, Personality: Essays, 1978); *Ne duet, a dvuboi: Publitsistika* (Not a Duet, But a Duel: Journalistic Writings, 1981); and *Moliv, opasno podostren* (A Pencil, Dangerously Sharp, 1988). Stefanova has long been a prominent figure in Bulgaria. For many years president of the Bulgarian PEN Club, she also served as deputy minister of education from 1980 to 1984.

Translations: Seven poems in *The Devil's Dozen: Thirteen Bulgarian Women Poets*, trans. Brenda Walker with Belin Tonchev, in collaboration with Svetoslav Piperov (London: Forest, 1990), 87–96; three poems (adapted) in *Poets of Bulgaria*, ed. William Meredith (Greensboro, N.C.: Unicorn, 1985), 76–79.

Stefanovski, Goran (b. 1952) Macedonian playwright. Stefanovski was born in the town of Bitola and was educated at Skopje University, where he majored in English language and literature. He subsequently studied drama at the Academy of Theater in Belgrade. Apart from his professional career as a dramatist, Stefanovski taught English literature at Skopje University from 1977 to 1986. He spent the academic year 1979/1980 at Manchester University in England, working on a doctoral dissertation on contemporary English drama and the plays of Edward Bond. He was a participant in the International Writing Program in Iowa City in the fall of 1984, and in 1990, as the recipient of a Fulbright Fellowship, he returned to the United States, where he lectured on drama and theater at Brown University, Harvard University, UCLA, and the University of Missouri. After returning to Macedonia, he became professor and head of the Department of Drama at the Faculty of Dramatic Arts at Skopje University, a position he held until 1998. Since then, he has been teaching at Christ Church College and the University of Kent in Canterbury, England, and is visiting professor at the Dramatiska Institutet in Stockholm.

Stefanovski's plays include *Jane Zadrogaz* (1974); *Bachanalia* (1979); *Divo meso* (Wild Flesh, 1979); *Let vo mesto* (Flying in Place, 1981); *Hi-Fi* (1982); *Duplo dno* (The False Bottom, 1984); *Tetovirani duši* (Tattooed Souls, 1987); *Crna rupa* (The Black Hole, 1987); *Long-Plej* (Long-Play, 1988), a "rock-and-roll mystery"; *Kula Vavilonska* (The Tower of Babylon, 1989); and *Černodrinski se vraća doma* (Chernodrinski Heads Home, 1991). In the wake of the Bosnian War, Stefanovski wrote, in English, his play *Sarajevo: Tales from a City*. It was performed at the London International Theatre Festival at the Riverside Studios. The work was also staged widely throughout Europe. His next play, *Brecht in Hollywood*, was produced at the Moving Theatre in London in April 1994. The lead roles were played by Vanessa Redgrave and Ekkhard Schall, the legendary actor from Bertolt Brecht's Berliner Ensemble. *Brecht in Hollywood* is about the flight from Hitler's Germany of Brecht and Helena Weigel and their arrival in Los Angeles in 1941. A play about artists in exile, it draws sharp contrasts between California's wealth and the misery of war-torn Europe, between Brecht's idea of theater and the rewards and punishments of working for the Hollywood dream factory.

Translations: *Hi-Fi and The False Bottom,* with an introduction by James McKinley (Kansas City, Mo.: BkMk Press, 1985); *Sarajevo: Tales from a City,* in *Storm Out of Yugoslavia,* ed. Joanna Labon (London: Carcanet, 1994), 211–68.

Ştefoi, Elena (b. 1954) Romanian poet. Ştefoi was born in Boroaia, in the Suceava district, and graduated from secondary school in Fălticeni in 1973 and from Bucharest University, where she attended the Faculty of Philosophy, in 1980. Her first published book, a volume of poems titled *Linea de plutire* (Water Line), appeared in 1983 and was awarded the Writers Union Prize for the best debut volume that year. Ştefoi subsequently published four other volumes of verse: *Repetiţie zilnică* (Daily Rehearsal, 1985); *Schiţe şi povestiri* (Sketches and Stories, 1989); *Cîteva amănunte* (A Few Details, 1990); and *Alinierea la start* (Alignment for a Start, 1996). A bold poet keenly aware of political realities yet unafraid to buck the mainstream in the way she writes poetry as well as in her outlook, Stefoi nonetheless often communicates a certain sense of fear concerning forces in the world around her. As she writes in one poem,

> Now and then, death or impotence or
> the voice of the neighbors swathe
> my beliefs in barbed wire and then it
> takes entire seasons
> to nurse them back to life.

Although she promises to indulge her sense of reality "as I would a baby," and to spoil it, she has at times felt that "I am struggling in a mass grave where / there's room for not even one word more." Yet a defiance tinged with optimism pervades a number of poems, for, as she declares, "Few things are learned through fear." Ştefoi has served as editor of *Contrapunct*, a weekly magazine put out by the Writers Union, and, more recently, of *Dilema*, a leading postcommunist cultural journal published by the Romanian Cultural Foundation. Interested in political matters and able after the downfall of the regime of Nicolae Ceauşescu to actively pursue that interest, Ştefoi has involved herself, for example, in minority affairs in Romania and in 1997 published a series of interviews she conducted with György Frunda (b. 1951), the head of the Hungarian community in Romania. The Association of Hungarian Journalists in Romania awarded the book, *Drept minoritar, spaime naţionale* (Minority Law, National Fears), a prize in 1997. Ştefoi has participated in a number international seminars and symposia on literary, cultural, and political issues, including in Chicago (1993) and New York (1999).

Translations: Five poems, trans. Rodica Albu, in *An Anthology of Romanian Women Poets*, ed. Adam J. Sorkin and Kurt W. Treptow (New York: East European Monographs, 1994), 112–16; six poems, trans. Oana Lungescu, in *Child of Europe: A New Anthology of East European Poetry*, ed. Michael March (London: Penguin, 1990), 102–8; five poems in *Young Poets of a New Romania: An Anthology*, trans. Brenda Walker with Michaela Celea-Leach, ed. Ion Stoica (London: Forest, 1991), 88–92.

Stevanović, Vidosav (b. 1942) Serbian novelist, short-story writer, poet, playwright, and critic. Stevanović is a prominent Serbian writer who fled Yugoslavia with his family at the outset of the Serb–Croat war of 1991 and sought refuge first in Macedonia and then in Greece. In 1995 he was able to settle in France as a political exile. Stevanović was born in the village of Cvetojevac, near Kragujevac, where he received his early education. He graduated from high school in Kragujevac, and then studied at Belgrade University. He began his literary career with the publication in 1967 of a collection of poems titled *Trublje* (Trumpets). Soon thereafter, he directed his energies more to prose fiction and drama. In 1969 he published his first collection of short stories, *Refuz mrtvak* (Refuz the Dead Man). It was followed by the novels *Nišči* (The Wretched, 1971) and *Konstantin Gorča* (1975); the short-story collections *Periferijski zmajevi* (Suburban Dragons, 1978) and *Carski rez* (The Caesarean Section, 1984); and the novels *Testament: Roman u 52 bdenja* (Testament: A Novel in 52 Vigils, 1986), an apocalyptic journey through the hell of an imaginery Balkan country called Kao for which Stevanović was awarded the prestigious NIN Prize in 1986; *Ljubavni krug* (Love Circle, 1988); *Sneg u Atini* (The Snows of Athens, 1992); and *Ostrvo Balkan* (The Balkan Island, 1993), which, like *Sneg u Atini*, draws on his experiences in Greece. His best-known work, and the one to attract the most international attention after *Testament: Roman u 52 bdenja*, is the essentially allegorical novelistic trilogy consisting of *Sneg u Atini*, *Ostrvo Balkan*, and *Hristos i psi* (Christ and Dogs, 1994). It portrays the horrors of the wars against Croatia and Bosnia in vivid and nightmarish terms and, like his first major work of protest, *Testament: Roman u 52 bdenja*, aims squarely, if at times obliquely, at the anachronism and cost of Serbian nationalism. Combining biblical, fantastic, and grotesque elements (trafficking, for example, in organs from fresh corpses on the battlefield) and made up of a number of first-person narratives, the trilogy attracted considerable attenion when first published in France in 1993 in two volumes: *La Neige et les chiens* (Snow and Dogs) and *Christos et les chienes* (Christ and Dogs). His most recent book, *Samo isto* (The Same Thing), appeared in 1999.

In 1988, three years before he fled Yugoslavia, Stevanović's protests against Slobodan Milošević resulted in his being expelled from the League of Communists and excluded from all public functions. He also lost his position at the publishing house Prosveta, where he had managed to promote the publication of dissident works from elsewhere in Eastern Europe. Stevanović further isolated himself from the Milošević government by his establishment of the elitist oppositional Belgrade Circle. When Stevanović's near-native city of Kragujevac voted out the socialists in local elections in early 1997 and the opposition coalition, Zajedno, took over the administration of the city, Stevanović was invited to accept the position of director of the "liberated" TV Kragujevac. But attempts by the authorities in Belgrade to take over the television station led to a nasty fracas involving local residents and police from Belgrade and mass protests, with Stevanović again in the thick of things. Stevanović was awarded the Isidora Sekulić Prize in 1969, the Mladost Prize in 1970, and the Milan Rakić prize in 1972.

Translations: "D. S.," trans. Bogdan Rakić, in *The Prince of Fire: An Anthology of Serbian Short Stories,* ed. Radmila J. Gorup and Nadežda Obradović (Pittsburgh: University of Pittsburgh Press, 1998), 194–200. *Periferijski zmajevi* is available in French as *Les Loulous de banlieue* (Lausanne: L'Age d'homme, 1971); *Samo isto* as *La Même Chose,* trans. Mauricette Begić and Nicole Dizdarevic (Paris: Mercure de France, 1999); *Sneg u Atini, Ostrvo Balkan,* and *Hristos i psi* as *La Neige et les chiens* and *Christos et les chienes* (Paris: Belfond, 1993); and *Testament: Roman u 52 bdenja* as *Prélude à la guerre,* trans. Mauricette Begić and Nicole

Dizdarević (Paris: Mercure de France, 1996). *La Neige et les chiens* is available in German as *Schnee und schwarze Hunde,* trans. Ivan Ivanji (Munich: Europaverlag, 1995).

Stoev, Gencho (b. 1925) Bulgarian novelist, short-story wtiter, and poet. Stoev was born in Harmanli and graduated from high school there in 1945, after which he received a degree in philosophy from Sofia University in 1951. After high school, he worked for nearly a year with the Harmanli district committee of the Union of Working Youth. Apart from his literary career, Stoev held several editorial positions at *Narodna mladezh* (1948–1949, 1952), *Literaturen front* (1950–1951, 1965–1967), the Party Publishing House (1956–1961), and the publishing house Bulgarski pisatel (1968). In 1946 Stoev began publishing poems in the youth journal *Mladezhka iskra,* subsequently contributing poetry, short stories, and documentary texts to several other periodicals, among them a series of articles for *Literaturen front* on the everyday life of workers. They were published in book form for the first time in 1953 under the title *Istinski hora: Ochertsi* (Real People: Sketches). Notwithstanding Stoev's credentials, he was officially reproached by the communist authorities in 1954 for ideological indifference. In consequence, he ceased publishing for the next decade. His novel *Losh den* (A Bad Day, 1965; 2nd ed., 1971) and the stories in the collection *Kato lastovitsi* (Like Swallows, 1970), both of which are set in a workers' milieu, draw heavily on the experiences of that period. In a departure from his previous preoccupation with the contemporary Bulgarian working class, Stoev also published a major historical novel, *Tsenata na zlatoto* (The Price of Gold), in 1965. It was awarded an all-Balkan literary prize by the Inter-Balkan Book Center in Salonica, Greece, in 1997. The work depicts the defense and fall of Perushtitsa during the

April 1876 uprising against the Turks. In 1976 Stoev published *Zavrushtane* (The Return), a sequel to *Tsenata na zlatoto,* which carries the story of Giurga Hadzhivraneva and his heroic family into the period of the Bulgarian liberation of 1878. *Dosietata* (The Dossier), which appeared in 1990 and won first prize in a competition for a novel on a contemporary theme, follows the fortunes of the same family into the late years of World War II, the antifascist resistance of 1944, and the immediate postwar period, with its difficult transition to a communist system. Three years before the publication of *Zavrushtane,* in 1973, Stoev published the novel *Tsikloput* (The Cyclops), about a submarine captain's tensions between his sense of obligation to mankind in the atomic age and the loneliness and emotional tumult in his private life. The short novel *Mnogo visoka terasa* (Many High Terraces) appeared in 1998 but was written in 1982. In an afterword to the 1998 edition, Stoev discusses the problems involved in bringing the book to press and recalls the hardships he experienced with the publication of The Cyclops. He mentions that even the general staff of the Bulgarian army became involved in a purely aesthetic dispute over the "vicious hostility" to which the book was subjected and which he claims he still cannot completely understand. Stoev's most recent publications include *Dalechno, hubavo i chisto* (Distant, Lovely, and Pure, 2000), a collection of light, contemporary stories, and *Prokoba i sluntse* (Omen and Sun, 2000), a small volume of very short pieces dealing with a wide variety of topics from Bulgarian literary figures to the NATO campaign against the Serbs in Kosovo in 1999. All the mini-essays were previously published between 1954 and 2000. A two-volume edition of Stoev's collected works appeared in 1985.

Stoianov, Anastas (b. 1931) Bulgarian poet. Stoianov was born in the village of Zhivovtsi. He graduated from high school in Mihailovgrad in 1950 and then earned a degree in Slavic philology at Sofia University in 1955. He subsequently held a number of editorial positions at *Septemvriiche* (1959–1965); the Narodna mladezh publishing house, where he was managing editor (1965–1966, 1969–1972); *Plamuk,* where he was editor in chief (1972–1974); and *Plamuche,* where he was also editor in chief (1974–1979). From 1966 to 1969, Stoianov served as secretary of the Bulgarian Writers Union. Stoianov's early poetry, which began appearing in the journal *Narodna mladezh,* was in the spirit and style of the civic poetry of the day, with its strong social orientation. With his first published book of love lyrics, *Purva liubov: Lirika* (First Love: Lyrics, 1955), his style became more lyrical and intimate, a trend that continued into his subsequent poetic writing. His books of poetry after *Purva liubov: Lirika* include *Maiska vielitsa: Lirika* (A Blizzard in May: Lyrics, 1961); *Esenni makove: Poemi* (Fall Poppies: Poems, 1963); *Malko e da te obicham: Poema* (It's Not Enough that I Love You: A Poem, 1964); *Posveshtenie: Stihove* (Dedication: Lyrics, 1964); *Narichaite me vechnost ili mig: Antologiia na makovete. Stihove i poemi* (Call Me Eternity or Moment: An Anthology of Poppies. Lyrics and Poems, 1966); *Kladenchovi ochi* (Eyes Like a Well, 1967); *Tantsut na Shiva: Neizprateni pisma ot Indiia* (The Dance of Shiva: Unposted Letters from India, 1970); *Uloveni sunishta* (Captured Dreams, 1970); *Ocharovanie: Lirika* (Enchantment: Lyrics, 1974); *Skitaniia: Pisma ot Indiia* (Wanderings: Letters from India, 1974); *Kipurskite kiparisi* (Cyprian Cypresses, 1974); *Proletio preobrazhenie: Stihotvoreniia* (Vernal Transfiguration: Poems, 1975); *Izbrani stihotvoreniia* (Selected Poems, 1975); *Na greshnata zemia: Lirika, soneti, stihotvoreniia v proza* (On the Sinful Land: Lyrics, Sonnets, Poems in Prose, 1978); *Zhertveno tsvete: Liubovni elegii, epichni pesni, strofi* (Sacrificial

Flower: Love Elegies, Epic Songs, Stanzas, 1981); *Poveche ot liubov: Poema v dnevnitsi i molitvi* (More than Love: A Poem in Diaries and Prayers, 1982); *Tursete bulgarskiia alpinist: Poema v 32 monologi* (The Search for the Bulgarian Alpinist: A Poem in 32 Monologues, 1985); and *Kazvam se Malcho: Prikazki, pritchi, anekdoti* (My Name Is Malcho: Fairy Tales, Fables, Anecdotes, 1989). Stoianov has also written much poetry and prose for children and young readers.

Translations: Two poems, in versions by Roy MacGregor-Hastie, in *Modern Bulgarian Poetry*, comp. Bozhidar Bozhilov (Sofia: Sofia Press, 1976), 176–81, a Bulgarian–English edition.

Stoica, Ion (b. 1936) Romanian poet. Stoica was born in the village of Amărăştrii de Sus, in the Dolj district. He attended secondary schools in Craiova and Caracal and then went on to Bucharest University, where he studied philology. He received his doctorate in 1973. Stoica served for a number of years as director of the Central University Library in Bucharest. Apart from his many contributions to professional journals in the areas of library science and literature, he has published several volumes of poetry: *Casa de vînt* (House of Air, 1981); *Porţile clipei* (*Gates of the Moment*, 1982); *Paşi peste ierburi* (Stepping over Grass); *A două viaţă* (A Second Life, 1995); and *Vorbind cu tine* (Talking with You, 1995). As a poet, Stoica is lyrical, generally traditional in his metrics, keenly aware of the passage of time yet tranquil, a poet for whom nature—above all, in spring—evokes intimations of the infinite. Two of Stoica's more noteworthy publications in the field of library scholarship are *Modernismul în literatura română: Contribuţii bibliografice* (Modernism in Romanian Literature: Bibliographical Contributions, 1968) and *Alma mater librorum: Rolul şi locul bibliotecii universitare* (The Alma Mater of Books: The Role and Place of a

University Library, 1979). Stoica is also the editor of an anthology of English translations of newer Romanian poetry titled *Young Poets of a New Romania: An Anthology*, translated by Brenda Walker with Michaela Celea-Leach (1991).

Translations: *As I Came to London One Summer's Day . . . : Poems by Ion Stoica*, trans. Brenda Walker (London: Forest, 1990); *Gates of the Moment: Poems of Ion Stoica*, trans. Brenda Walker and Andrea Deletant (London: Forest, 1984), a Romanian–English edition.

Stojanović, Radosav (b. 1950) Serbian poet, short-story writer, and novelist. A native of Crna Trava in Kosovo, Stojanović graduated from high school in Niš and then studied Serbo-Croatian language and Yugoslav literature at Priština University. He eventually made his home in Priština and worked in the city, at least until the Serbian assault in late March and early April 1999. Stojanović has published poems, short stories, and one novel. His poetry includes the volumes *Inoslovlje* (The Allegory, 1979); *Rukopis čemerski* (The Manuscript from Čemer, 1982); and *Djavolska škola* (Devil's School, 1988). His one novel, *Kraj sveta* (The End of the World), appeared in 1993. It is, however, primarily in the short story that Stojanović has made his mark as a writer. The first of his collections, *Aritonova smrt* (Ariton's Death), appeared in 1984. It contains fourteen fairly short stories narrated in the first-person singular or plural and depicting the lives of ordinary people in Stojanović's native town, many of whose sons have left to become migrant workers, like Ariton's three sons. Stojanović's skill lies in his ability to bring vividly to life the inhabitants of the town; their quarrels and fights, often over boundary disputes; and their frequent drinking bouts. *Mrtva straža* (The Dead Sentinal, 1988), his second collection of stories, is set in the same southeastern Serbian region that Stojanović knows so well. In it, individual portraits become even more vivid, and events from World War II as well as relations between Serbs and Albanians form the material of several of the stories. With the deterioration of these relations much on his mind, Stojanović, in 1990, published a chronicle of the anti-Albanian campaign in Kosovo in the 1980s under the title *Živeti s genocidom: Hronika kosovskog beščašća, 1981–1989* (Living with Genocide: A Chronicle of the Dishonor in Kosovo, 1981–1989). The title of Stojanović's third volume of stories, *Gospodar uspomena: Rukoveti* (The Master of Memories: Handfuls, 1996), derives from the title story about a retired railroad worker whose passion is a detailed map of his native region that demands frequent revisions because of an ever-changing landscape. The lesson of the map, as one of his sons puts it, is that the world is not as it appears to us but as the soul sees it.

Translations: "The Clock in the Roofbeam of Hvosno," trans. Radmila Gorup and Halie Stein, in *The Prince of Fire: An Anthology of Contemporary Serbian Short Stories,* ed. Radmila J. Gorup and Nadežda Obradović (Pittsburgh: University of Pittsburgh Press, 1998), 278–83.

Stojčevski, Sande (b. 1948) Macedonian poet, essayist, and critic. Born in Studena Bara, near Kumanovo, Stojčevski studied literature at Skopje University. His professional employment has been mainly with Radio Skopje, the Saint Clement of Ohrid National and University Library, the publishing house Misla, and the literary journal *Stremež.* Stojčevski made his debut as a poet with the collection *Kralot na lebedite* (The King of the Swans, 1972), which won the Kočo Racin Prize. His subsequent volumes of poetry include *Feneri niz maglata* (Lanterns Through the Mist, 1977); *Zlatna granka* (The Golden Bough, 1980); *Večerna*

(Evening Prayer, 1985); *Abor gora* (Mount Abora, 1987); *Golemata bukva* (The Big Inducement, 1994); *Kuboa* (1993); and *VRV* (1996). Several editions of Stojčevski's selected poems have also been published: *Glamja* (1989); *Napravi čudo za mene* (Make Me a Miracle, 1990); *Trepeti vo žedna pesok* (Tremors in Thirsty Sand, 1990); and *Orač medju skeleti* (A Plowman Among Skeletons, 1992), for which Stojčevski himself made the selection and wrote the introduction.

Notwithstanding his solid reputation in his own country, Stojčevski is a difficult poet for a reader who knows no Macedonian. Fascinated, if not obsessed, with language and speech, he experiments with different linguistic layers in Macedonian—the medieval church language, the Ovče-Pole-Kumanovo dialect of his native area, and the contemporary standard language—so that an inextricable bond is forged among language, idea, and image that in translation accentuates the complexity and enigmatic character of much of his verse. The layers and patterns of association from the mundane to the metaphysical may be discernible to the native reader, but are simply lost on the foreigner. Although he plumbs the resources of dialect and folk tradition, Stojčevski is not a "rural" poet in the usual sense of the term.

Apart from his poetry, Stojčevski is the author of four books of literary essays, mainly about Macedonian poetry. These writings, which help shed light on his own concept of poetic creativity, are contained in such volumes as *Golemata pobuda* (The Big Stimulus, 1988); *Vozbudata na jadroto* (The Excitement of the Heart, 1982); *Pofalba na razgovorot* (In Praise of Conversation, 1994); and *Strav od tišina* (Fear of Silence, 1995), in which he discusses his ideas about the place and role of silence in poetry. Stojčevski has also brought out an anthology of contemporary Macedonian poetry under the title *Problesoci na noumenot* (Illumination of the

Noumenon, 1981) as well as an erudite and at the same time poetic book about the identification of mushrooms in Macedonia, *Ni den bez gabi* (Not a Day Without a Mushroom, 1991). Stojčevski has also translated extensively from Polish and Serbo-Croatian.

Literature: Miodrag Drugovac, *Tragacot, cestakot i jatkata* (Skopje: Misla, 1997), the sole monograph on Stojčevski.

Translations: *A Gate in the Cloud* (Skopje: Detska Radost, 1993); six poems in *Contemporary Macedonian Poetry,* ed. and trans. Ewald Osers (London: Forest, 1991), 157–62.

Stratiev, Stanislav (real name Stanko Stratiev Miladinov; b. 1941) Bulgarian playwright, novelist, short-story writer, and poet. Born in Sofia, Stratiev completed his secondary-school education in that city in 1959 and then received a degree in Bulgarian literature from Sofia University in 1968. After a few editorial positions from 1964 to 1976, he became director of the State Theater of Satire in Sofia. As a creative writer, Stratiev is best known for his grotesque and absurd humor and social satire cultivated in a variety of literary genres, from the feuilleton to the full-length play. His first published work was a collection of stories for young people under the title *Samotnite viaturni melnitsi* (Lonely Windmills, 1969). It was followed by his first collection of humorous short stories, *Troianskiiat kon* (The Trojan Horse, 1971). Stratiev subsequently published another eight collections of humorous stories: *Peeshtiiat korab* (The Singing Ship, 1973); *Kapitanite ot Biskaiskiia zaliv* (The Captains from the Bay of Biscay, 1982); *Peizazh s kuche* (*Landscape with Dog,* 1986); *Bulgarskiiat model* (*The Bulgarian Way,* 1991); *Uprazhneniia po drugost* (Exercises in Otherness, 1992); *Litse ot Greco* (Portrait by Greco, 1997); *Podrobnosti ot peizazha* (Details of a Landscape, 1978); and *Posledno kino* (The

Last Movie House, 1991). His plays, contemporary social comedies a few of which are set in the world of the Bulgarian theater, include *Rimska bania* (*The Roman Bath,* 1977); *Sako ot velur* (The Velour Jacket, 1979); *Reis* (*The Bus,* 1982); and *Maksimalistut* (The Maximalist), all published in a single volume in 1984 as *Piesi* (Plays). A second collection of Stratiev's plays appeared in 1990 containing *Zhivotut, makar i kratuk* (Life, Even Though It's Short); *Podrobnosti ot peizazha*; and *Balkanski sindrom* (Balkan Syndrome). Stratiev also wrote longer works of prose fiction along the lines of his stories: *Diva patitsa mezhdu durvetata* (A Wild Duck Among the Trees, 1972); *Puteshestvie bez kufar* (A Trip Without Luggage, 1972); *Stoian* (Stoian, 1995); and *Motivi za klarinet* (Themes for Clarinet, 1997). Fortunately, three of his best works—*Reis, Bulgarskiiat model,* and *Rimska bania*—are available in English translation.

Translations: *The Bus,* trans. Iglika Vassilieva (Sofia: Press and Information Center of the Committee of Culture, 1982); *Landscape with Dog. The Bulgarian Way,* trans. David Jenkins (Turnovo: Faber, 1997), a Bulgarian–English edition; *Roman Bath,* trans. Marguerite Alexieva (Sofia: Centre of Propaganda and Information of the Directorate "Theatre and Music," 1979); "A Bulgarian Tourist Chats to an English Pigeon in Trafalgar Square" (from *The Bulgarian Way*), trans. Galina Holman, in *Description of a Struggle: The Vintage Book of Contemporary Eastern European Writing,* ed. Michael March (New York: Vintage, 1994), 223–31.

Strezovski, Jovan (b. 1931) Macedonian poet, novelist, short-story writer, and playwright. Known especially as the director of the Struga Poetry Evenings Festival from 1971 to 1993, Strezovski was born in the village of Podgorci, Struga. He was educated in local schools before earning his university degree at the Faculty of Philosophy in

Skopje in 1960. From 1949 to 1955, he worked as an elementary-school teacher in several village schools before joining Radio Skopje as a journalist. From 1960 to 1963, he was the principal of the Brothers Miladinov Elementary School in Struga and then, until 1971, principal of the Niko Nestor Construction Engineering Secondary School in Struga. From 1971 until his retirement in 1993, he was the director of the Struga Poetry Evenings Festival.

Strezovski made his literary debut with his first collection of poems, *Šepoti* (Whispers), in 1958. This was followed by such other volumes of poetry as *Šareni pesni* (Dappled Poems, 1959); *Šareno ogledalo* (The Dappled Mirror, 1965); *Od Severen do Južen pol* (From the North to the South Pole, 1966); *Cekori vo vremeto* (Timely Actions, 1968); *Orfej na beskrajot* (Infinite Orpheus, 1971); *Velebilje* (Atropa Belladonna, 1985); *Nokjniot voz* (Night Train, 1989); *Prva ljubov* (First Love, 1995); and *Blik* (The Source, 1999). Strezovski writes of the soul, love, death, pain, dreams, earth, shadow, and thought. He is philosophical while plainly demonstrating a certain disdain for formal philosophy and philosophers. Plants of many kinds appear in his poetry and have their own lives and their own souls. On the whole, Strezovski's poetry offers a unified transcendental vision that integrates his metaphysics, epistemology, politics, and aesthetics.

Strezovski has also distinguished himself as a writer of prose fiction. He brought out a collection of stories, *Lugje so luzni* (People with Scars), in 1961, but then concentrated mostly on the novel, publishing such well-received works as *Družinata bratsko steblo* (The Brotherly Tree Gang, 1964), his most acclaimed novel, for which he received the Skopje Radio and Television Award; *Voda* (Water, 1972), which won the 11 October Award; *Sveto prokleto* (The Holy and the Damned, 1978), a winner of the Stale Popov

Award; *Zarek* (The Oath, 1981); *Jandza* (Fever, 1986); *Tajni* (Secrets, 1989); *Zlodobro* (Good and Evil, 1990); *Eretik* (Heretic, 1994; republished, 1998, in a slightly augmented text); and *Tajni sili* (Mysterious Powers, 1998). Strezovski was also honored in 1991 with the Goce Charter of the Days of Goce Cultural Event for his lifetime achievement. In 1991 he published a book about the history of the Struga Festival and his own role in it under the title *Poetska Struga: 1962–1991* (Poetic Struga: 1962–1991, 1991).

Translations: Six poems in *Contemporary Macedonian Poetry*, ed. and trans. Ewald Osers (Forest, 1991), 71–76; three poems, trans. Herbert Kuhner and Duško Tomovski, in *Reading the Ashes: An Anthology of the Poetry of Modern Macedonia*, ed. Milne Holton and Graham W. Reid (Pittsburgh: University of Pittsburgh Press, 1977), 94–95.

Strittmatter, Erwin (1912–1994) German novelist and playwright. A native of Neuruppin, Strittmater was trained as a baker, his father's profession, but worked at a variety of odd jobs until called to military service in World War II. Strittmatter, however, deserted from the army near the end of the war. After the war, he found employment first as a baker and then as a small farmer, at which he also had previous experience. His literary career began in provincial journalism within a few years after his entry into the East German Communist Party. In 1951 he became the regional editor of the *Märkische Volksstimme* in Senftenberg. Largely self-educated and drawing heavily on his own experiences in his fiction, Strittmatter published his first novel, *Ochsenkutscher* (The Oxcart Drivers), a bleak picture of the village proletariat during the Weimar Republic, in 1950. His thematically related play, *Katzgraben: Szenen aus dem Bauernleben* (The Village of Katzgraben: Scenes from Peasant Life, 1953), dealing with the modern class struggle in the village, was produced by Bertolt Brecht at the Berliner Ensemble in the 1952/1953 season. This was followed by the novel *Tinko* in 1955. Beginning in the late 1950s, most of Strittmatter's writing turned autobiographical. This includes the autobiographical trilogy *Der Wundertäter* (The Miracle Workers, 1957, 1974, 1980); *Schulzenhofer Kramkalender* (A Village Almanac, 1966); *Die blaue Nachtigall oder der Anfang von etwas* (The Blue Nightingale, or The Beginning of Something, 1972); *Meine Freundin Tina Babe* (My Friend Tina Babe, 1977); a second autobiographical trilogy, *Der Laden* (The Shop, 1983, 1987, and 1992); and *Grüner Juni: Eine Nachtigall-Geschichte* (Green June: The Story of a Nightingale, 1985). Of a more patently autobiographical and personal character are such works from the 1980s as *Selbstermunterungen* (Self-Stimuli, 1981); *Wahre Geschichten aller Art* (True Stories of Every Kind, 1982); and *Lebenszeit: Ein Brevier* (Life Term: A Breviary, 1987). Strittmatter's last published work, *Die Lage in den Lüften: Aus Tagebüchern* (The Situation Up Above: From My Diaries, 1990), covers the period from January 1973 to 30 December 1980. Although his autobiographical fiction and personal reflections make interesting, at times engrossing, reading, Strittmatter's greatest literary success was his controversial novel *Ole Bienkopp* (Ole Beehead, 1963), which is also on a peasant theme and in which he seems to question the dominant role of the Party in the German Democratic Republic. Strittmatter won numerous awards for his writing: the Lessing Prize (1966); the Fontana Prize of the Potsdam District (1966); and the National Prize for Literature (1953, 1955, 1964, 1976). He was also given the Order of Karl Marx in 1974. In 1959 Strittmater became the first secretary of the German Writers Association of the GDR.

Literature: Erwin Strittmatter, *Nur, was ich weiss und fühle*, Zeugen des Jahrhunderts (Witnesses to the Century), ed. Ingo Hermann (Göttingen: Lamuv, 1994), a conversation with Alexander U. Martens; *Erwin Strittmater: Leben und Werk: Analysen, Erörterungern, Gespräche* (East Berlin: Volk und Wissen, 1977, 1984; West Berlin: Das europäische Buch, 1984).

Translations: "Electric Power," trans. Jan van Heurck, in *The New Sufferings of Young W. and Other Stories from the German Democratic Republic,* ed. Therese Hörnigk and Alexander Stephan (New York: Continuum, 1997), 91–103.

Strniša, Gregor (1930–1987) Slovenian poet and playwright. One of the most highly regarded contemporary Slovenian writers, Strniša was born and educated in Ljubljana. He began writing poetry at a very young age and published his first poems in the youth magazine *Naš rod* when he was twelve. Strniša's education was interrupted in 1949 when he was imprisoned, ostensibly for political reasons. He was released on parole in 1951 and the following year entered Ljubljana University, where he majored in German. He received his master's degree in 1961. He subsequently became a member of the *Beseda, Revija 57,* and *Perspektive* group, which included the poets Kajetan Kovič, Rudi Šeligo, Veno Taufer, and Dane Zajc. Strniša's first collection of poems, *Mozaiki* (Mosaics), appeared in 1959. It clearly fulfilled the promise of his early verse and demonstrated a characteristically fertile imagination nurtured by archetypical myths and symbols. *Mozaiki* was followed by eight other volumes of original verse: *Odisej* (Odyssey, 1963); *Zvezde* (Stars, 1965); *Želod* (Acorn, 1972); *Mirabilia* (Wonders, 1973); *Oko* (The Eye, 1974); *Škarje* (Scissors, 1975); *Jajce* (The Egg, 1975); and *Rebrnik* (Rib Cage, 1976), a collection of poems and plays. In addition, five collections of Strniša's selected poetry have been published: *Severnica* (North Star, 1974), which Strniša himself edited; *Pesmi* (Poems, 1976), which also contains works by Kovič and

Zajc; *Pesmi* (Poems, 1976); *Vesolje* (The Universe, 1983); and *Balade o svetovjih* (Ballads of Universes, 1989), these later volumes evidencing Strniša's strong predilection for the mystical and cosmic. Apart from his poetry, Strniša was the author of several well-regarded plays, among them *Samorog* (Unicorn, 1967); *Žabe ali prilika o ubogem in bogatem Lazarju* (The Frogs, or The Story of Poor and Rich Lazar, 1969); *Ljudožerci* (Man-eaters, 1972), and *Driada* (1976). The best of these are the symbolic and metaphysical medieval poetic dramas *Samorog* and *Driada,* about the life of a poet in a small town. Strniša also wrote radio plays and children's fiction and was well known for his popular song lyrics. In 1962 one of his texts won first prize at the First Festival of Slovenian Popular Song, held in Bled. Strniša was awarded the Prešeren Prize for lifetime achievement in 1986. In 1986, the year before his death, he received a Fulbright Fellowship to visit the United States, but had to postpone the trip and in fact never made it.

Translations: Three poems, trans. Michael Biggins, in *The Imagination of Terra Incognita: Slovenian Writing, 1945–1995,* ed. Aleš Debeljak (Fredonia, N.Y.: White Pine, 1997), 206–11; two poems, including "The Vikings" and "Brobdingnag," trans. Veno Taufer and Michael Scammell, in *New Writing in Yugoslavia,* ed. Bernard Johnson (Harmondsworth: Penguin, 1970), 284–88.

Stryjkowski, Julian (b. 1905) Polish novelist and short-story writer. A native of the town of Stryj in Galicia, Stryjkowski was educated at the university in Lwów (now Lviv, Ukraine), where he earned a graduate degree in Romance philology in 1932. His earliest writings were poems in Hebrew, which he cultivated at the time in keeping with his strong Zionist leanings. He subsequently switched to Polish, in which all his major literary works were written. Stryjkowski worked for a time for local newspapers as a literary and theatrical critic. He was also employed in nearby Płock as a schoolteacher. It was in Płock that he joined the Communist Party of the Eastern Ukraine. The organization was then illegal, and Stryjkowski's activities on behalf of it landed him in prison for over a year. In 1937 Stryjkowski moved to Warsaw, where he was employed as a librarian and translator (Celine was one of the authors he translated into Polish). During World War II, Stryjkowski sought refuge in the Soviet Union, where he worked for various Polish-language communist publishing organizations. From 1946 to 1949, he was employed by the Polish Press Agency in Katowice, Silesia, which later sent him to Rome as a correspondent.

Stryjkowski's first novel, *Bieg do Fragala* (The Race to Fragal, 1951), deals with the revolt of people living in the south of Italy against the miserable conditions of their lives. Stryjkowski was declared persona non grata because of the novel and was expelled from Italy. Upon his return to Warsaw, where he was honored for the novel, he wrote an account of his experiences as a journalist in Italy; it was published under the title *Pożegnanie z Italią* (Goodbye to Italy, 1956). In 1956 he also published *Głosy w ciemności* (Voices in the Dark), which he had written years earlier during his wartime residence in the USSR and which is widely regarded as his greatest work of fiction. Set in Hapsburg Galicia in the year 1912, the novel explores the impact of modern ideas and changing economic structures on the traditional Jewish shtetl. Three of Stryjkowski's subsequent novels—*Austeria* (*The Inn,* 1966); *Sen Azrila* (Azril's Dream, 1975); and *Echo* (1988)—deal with similar material and together with *Głosy w ciemności* form a tetralogy. After *Głosy w ciemności,* Stryjkowski dedicated himself wholly to his literary career, dividing his time between heading the prose section of the prestigious Warsaw monthly *Twórczość* and writing novels and short stories. A collection of stories, *Imię własne* (The Right Name), appeared in 1961; another collection of short stories, *Na wierzbach ... nasze skrzypce* (Our Fiddles ... on the Willows), appeared in 1974. Stryjkowski's first novel after *Głosy w ciemności, Czarna róża* (The Black Rose), came out in 1965. It was followed by *The Inn*; *Sen Azrila*; *Przybysz z Narbony* (The Arrival from Narbona, 1978); and a series of autobiographical works, including *Wielki strach* (The Great Fear, 1980), which could be published in Poland only in 1989; *To samo, ale inaczej* (The Same, but Different, 1990); and *Ocalony na Wschodzie* (Saved in the East, 1991), a long interview with the writer Piotr Szewc. Stryjkowski's autobiographical writings shed considerable light on the experiences of growing up Jewish in Poland before World War II and the hazards of life in occupied Poland under the Germans and, in the postwar period, under the communists. Stryjkowski followed his tetralogy on the transformation of traditional Jewish life in Poland in the twentieth century with a trilogy of novels set in biblical times: *Odpowiedź* (The Reply, 1982), a short novel set in the time of the ancient Hebrews in Egypt; *Król Dawid żyje!* (King David Lives, 1984); and *Juda Makabi* (Judas Maccabeus, 1986), another short novel on an Old Testament subject. A homosexual, Stryjkowski has attempted to deal with his homosexuality in two short works of fiction: *Tommaso del Cavaliere* (1982) and *Milczenie* (Silence, 1993), the more forthright of the two. Stryjkowski has also published a collection of Polish homoerotic writings titled *Dyskretne namiętnosci: Antologia polskiej prozy homoerotycznej* (Discrete Passions: An Anthology of Polish Homoerotic Prose, 1992).

Translations: *The Inn,* trans. Celina Wieniewska (New York: Harcourt Brace Jovanovich, 1971). *Przybysz z Narbony* is available in Italian as *L'uomo venuto da Narbona,* trans. Giorgio Origlia (Rome: Edizione e/o, 1985).

Sugarev, Edvin (b. 1953) Bulgarian poet and literary critic. Sugarev was born in Sofia, where he studied Bulgarian language and literature at Sofia University. After graduating in 1978, he worked for a year as a librarian at the Academy of Medicine and, from 1980 to 1981, as a teacher of Bulgarian at the Institute for Foreign Students. In 1981 he became a doctoral candidate at the Literary Institute of the Bulgarian Academy of Sciences and received his degree with a dissertation on Bulgarian literature and German expressionism before World War I (published in book form in 1989). Sugarev began teaching modern Bulgarian literature at Sofia University in 1987 and since 1989 has been active as an editor affiliated primarily with such liberal publications as *Most,* an almanac that was considered illegal by the communist regime; *Literaturna misul*; and the daily *Demokratsiia.* Sugarev has served on the executive committee of the environmentalist journal *Ecoglasnost* and has been a member of the Bulgarian Independent Literary Society. He has also served as a delegate to the Bulgarian parliament, the Narodno Subranie. Sugarev's career has been divided between literary scholarship and creative writing. As a scholar, he has worked on literary programs and currents in Bulgaria after World War I, explored Bulgarian modernism and expressionism, and written studies of such Bulgarian writers as Nikolai Rainov, Lamar (pseudonym of Laliu Marinov Ponchev, 1898–1974), Geo Milev (pseudonym of Georgi Milev Kasabov, 1895–1925), and Chavdar Mutafov (1889–1954). His particular field of interest has been poetic language. Sugarev made his own debut as a poet in 1980 in the pages of the journal *Septemvri.* He subsequently published such collections of verse as *Loshi sunishta* (Bad Dreams, 1988); *Vodni krugove*

(Water Circles, 1989, 1991); *Vulcha pamet* (A Wolf's Memory, 1989); *Kaleidoskop* (Kaleidoscope, 1990); and *Dzhaz* (Jazz, 1998). Intellectual and philosophical, often conveying a sense of existential fragility and impermanence, Sugarev's poetry has been motivated by a strong spirit of protest against any curtailment of individual freedoms and social action. His articles on the state of Bulgaria in the immediate postcommunist period, published in the 1993 issues of *Demokratsiia,* were reissued that year in book form under the title *V kakvo shte viarvat detsata ni: Otvoreno pismo do prezidenta na Bulgariia* (In What Will Our Children Believe: An Open Letter to the President of Bulgaria).

Translations: Two poems, trans. Edward Hirsch, in *Window on the Black Sea: Bulgarian Poetry in Translation,* ed. Richard Harteis, in collaboration with William Meredith (Pittsburgh: Carnegie Mellon University Press, 1992), 169–170; six poems in *Young Poets of a New Bulgaria: An Anthology,* trans. and ed. Belin Tonchev (London: Forest, 1990), 125–31.

Sugarev, Rashko (b. 1941) Bulgarian short-story writer, novelist, and essayist. A native of Plovdiv, Sugarev completed high school in his native city in 1959 and then studied medicine at the Institute of Military Medicine, also in Plovdiv. From 1968 to 1972, he headed a psychiatric clinic in the city of Smolian, thereafter serving as editor of the periodical *Trakiia* (1973–1975), an employee of the Writers Association in Ruse (1976–1977), an editor at the Narodna mladezh publishing house (1978–1980), and an editor at the Military publishing house (1980–1982). His first literary efforts appeared in the journal *Komsomolska iskra* in 1962. Sugarev thereafter published several novels and collections of stories. His novels include *Nie, pravednite* (We, the Righteous, 1971); *Dunavsko horo* (Danubian Round Dance,

1976); *Otkaz ot nasledstvo* (Rejection of Heritage, 1984); and *Preobrazheniia gospodni* (The Lord's Transfigurations, 1988). Among his collections of stories and novellas are *Starshinata i sluntseto* (The Sergeant and the Sun, 1973), a collection of six longer stories, most set in wartime; *Sineva i sniag* (Azure and Snow, 1978); *Balada za kniaze: Raskazi i povesti* (Ballad for Princes: Stories and Novellas, 1982); and *Svetlinata na onezi dni* (The Light of Those Days, 1988).

His vision of reality shaped largely by the post–World War II changes to Bulgarian society, Sugarev in his fiction addresses primarily the subjective processes by which the individual adapts to or resists social changes imposed by historical circumstances, as well as the impact of these changes on his or her attitude toward the past. His emphasis on the moral and psychic aspects of this issue owes much to his medical and psychiatric training. Sugarev's most recent publications extend his basic sphere of inquiry into the postcommunist period. They include the collection *Svoboden do nepravdopodobnost: Statii, eseta, miniaturi, nabroski* (Unimaginably Free: Articles, Essays, Miniatures, Sketches, 1996), composed of pieces, some quite short, written mostly in 1992 and 1993. They deal with Bulgarian literature and history, love (the "Miniatures"), and, in the largest section of the book, social and political themes related to contemporary Bulgaria and the new democracy. His latest novel, *Litse na ugodnik* (The Face of a Sycophant), was published in 1999.

Sükösd, Mihály (b. 1933) Hungarian essayist, short-story writer, and novelist. Although he has written fiction, Sükösd is perhaps better known as an essayist. A graduate in humanities from Eötvös Lóránd University, he in fact began his literary career with a book of studies and essays published in 1958 in the volume *Tudós Weszprémi István* (The Scholar István

Weszprémi), dealing with Archbishop Stephano Weszpremi (1723–1799). A volume of short stories, *Ólomketrec* (Leaden Cage), appeared in 1960, followed in 1962 by the short novel *Fától fáig*, a World War II story about the Russians in Hungary. These were eventually overshadowed by one of the books for which he is best known, his account of the hippie phenomenon published under the title *Hippivilág* (Hippie World, 1979), which appeared in an expanded second edition in 1985 under the new title *Beat, hippi, punk* (Beat, Hippie, Punk). Other works include *Babilon hercege* (Prince of Babylon, 1981); *A törvénytevő* (The Lawmaker, 1981); *A kivülálló; Viszgálati fogság: Két regény* (The Stranger; Detention on Remand: Two Novels, 1983); *Seregszemle* (Review, 1985), a substantial collection of literary and literary-political essays mostly devoted to contemporary Hungarian writers but also covering such Russians as Mikhail Bakunin, Maxim Gorky, and Boris Pilnyak, and the Americans Joseph Heller, Bernard Malamud, William Styron, John Updike, and Gore Vidal; *Halottak napja feltámadás* (All Souls' Day Resurrection, 1986); and *Halottak gyorsan lovagolnak* (The Dead Ride Fast, 1987).

Translations: "All Souls' Day: The Resurrection," trans. Gillian Howarth, in *Present Continuous: Contemporary Hungarian Writing*, ed. István Bart (Budapest: Corvina, 1985), 96–109.

Suško, Mario (b. 1941) Bosnian Croatian poet, novelist, and translator. Suško was born and educated in Sarajevo and did postgraduate study in the United States. He received his doctorate in English from the State University of New York at Stony Brook, and also taught at Nassau Community College on Long Island. He subsequently became professor of English at Sarajevo University, but left in 1993 to take up permanent residence in the United States, where he is currently a member of the Department of English at Nassau Community College. As a poet, Suško is the author of a number of volumes of verse, including *Prvo putovanje* (First Journey, 1965); *Drugo putovanje* (Second Journey, 1968); *Fantazije* (Fantasies, 1970); *Preživljavanje* (Survival, 1974); *Ispovijesti* (Confessions, 1976); *Skladbe i odsjevi* (Compositions and Reflections, 1977); *Zemlovidenje* (Land Vision, 1980); *Gravitacije, 41* (Gravitations, 41, 1982); *Izabrane pjesme* (Selected Poems, 1984); *Izabrane pjesme* (Selected Poems, 1986); *Physika Meta* (Meta Physics, 1989); *Priručnik za poeziju* (A Handbook of Poetry, 1994); *Majke, cipele i ine smrtne pjesme* (*Mothers, Shoes, and Other Mortal Songs*, 1997); and *Versus Exsul* (1999). The last two are of particular interest in view of their relationship to the Bosnian War of the 1990s. *Mothers, Shoes, and Other Mortal Songs* was written during the siege of Sarajevo and vividly captures the inhumanity and unreality of war. *Versus Exsul* is a sort of retrospective of Suško's poetry arranged in two sections, the first ("Versus") covering the period 1982 to 1994, and the second ("Exsul"), 1992 to the present. Apart from his poetry and a book of essays published in 1978 under the title *Duh i glina* (Spirit and Clay), Suško is widely known for his many translations from American and British literatures. He has translated works by Theodore Roethke, e. e. cummings, Donald Barthelme, William Styron, James Baldwin, E. L. Doctorow, Kurt Vonnegut, and Bernard Malamud, and has edited seven volumes of Saul Bellow's selected works. He has also published an anthology of American poetry, *Savremena americka poezija* (Contemporatry American Poetry, 1990), and, with David Harsent, an anthology of British poetry, *Savremena britanska poezija* (Contemporary British Poetry, 1988). His anthology *Contemporary Poetry of Bosnia and Herzegovina*, which includes several of his own poems, appeared in 1993. In 1997 Suško won the *Nassau*

Review Poetry Award, and in 1998 the Italian Premio Internazionale di Poesia e Letterature "Nuove Lettere."

Translations: *Mothers, Shoes, and Other Mortal Songs* (Stamford, Conn.: Yuganta, 1996); *Versus Exsul* (Stamford, Conn.: Yuganta, 1998); seven poems in *Contemporary Poetry of Bosnia and Herzegovina,* trans. and ed. Mario Suško (Sarajevo: International Peace Center, PEN Club Bosnia and Herzegovina, 1993), 87–91.

Sütő, András (b. 1927) Hungarian playwright, short-story writer, and essayist. Although he has published several volumes of essays, travel musings (as he calls them), and short stories, Sütő is best known as a dramatic writer. His major work is a trilogy of plays dealing with the rebellion of an individual against an existing order, usually one newly established and hence still fragile. In the first play, *Egy lócsiszár virágvasárnapja* (*The Palm Sunday of a Horse Dealer,* 1976), subtitled "A Drama in Three Acts After the Novella of Heinrich von Kleist" and indeed based on Kleist's famous story *Michael Kohlhaas,* the existing order is the new Lutheran movement recently allied with the nobility. In the second play, *Csillag a máglyán* (*Star at the Stake,* 1976), it is John Calvin's new theocratic state in Geneva, Switzerland, the stability of which Calvin sees threatened by his close friend Michael Servetus (ca. 1511–1553). And in the third play, *Káin és Ábel* (Cain and Abel, 1978), which is a new interpretation of Cain's murder of Abel, the new order is that of Genesis and Cain kills Abel in order to end the practice of human sacrifice, which Abel had defended as based on the authority of God.

Collections of Sütő's many essays, articles, and other prose writings include *Engedjétek hozzám jönni a szavakat: Jegyzetek hómezőn és porban* (Let the Words Come to Me: Jottings in the Snow Field and on Dust, 1977); *Rigó és apostol: Úti tűnődések* (Thrush and Apostle: Travel Reflections, 1973); *Istenek és falovacskák: Esszék, újabb úti tűnődések* (Gods and Hobby-Horse Riders: Essays and Newer Travel Musings, 1973); *Évek, hazajáró lelkek: Cikkek, naplójegyzetek (1953–1978)* (Years, Homecoming Spirits: Articles, Memoranda [1953–1978], 1980); *Gyermekkorom tükörcserepei* (The Cracked Mirror of My Childhood, 1982); and *Az idő markában: Esszék, naplójegyzetek* (In the Mark of Time: Essays, Diary Notes, 1984). Three collections of his occasional writings were also prepared for publication by László Ablonczy: *Omló egek alatt: Arcképvázlatok és tűnődések: Gyászőrségben* (Beneath the Heavens: Portrait Sketches and Jottings: On Bereavement Watch, 1990); *Sárkány alszik veled: Beszélgetések könyve* (The Dragon Sleeps with You: A Book of Conversations, 1991); and *Csipkerózsa ébresztése: Arcképvázlatok, esszék, útitűnődések* (The Dog-Rose Wake-up Call: Portrait Sketches, Essays, and Travel Musings, 1993). Available editions of Sütő's plays include: *Színművek* (Plays, 1989); *Színművek* (Plays, 1992); and *Színművek* (Plays, 1995).

Translations: *The Palm Sunday of a Horse Dealer,* trans. Eugene Brogyányi, in *Drama Contemporary: Hungary,* ed. Eugene Brogyányi (New York: PAJ Publications, 1991), 17–63; *Star at the Stake* (Binghamton, N.Y.: Max Reinhardt Archive/State University of New York at Binghamton, 1980). SOUND RECORDING: A sound recording, dated 1992, of Sütő reading from his work is available at the Recorded Sound Reference Center, Library of Congress.

Svetina, Ivo (b. 1948) Slovenian poet and playwright. Svetina was born in Ljubljana, where he was educated through university. He graduated from Ljubljana University in 1977 with a degree in comparative literature and literary theory. He subsequently worked as a freelance writer and was involved with the Pupilija Ferkeverk and Pekarna theaters.

It was at the Pekarna in 1972 that he directed a theatrical version of the ancient Sumerian epic *Gilgamesh*. Svetina later became dramaturg of the Slovenian Youth Theater and then its artistic director. From 1993 to 1998, he served as undersecretary of the Ministry of Culture, whereupon he became director of the Slovenian Theatrical Museum in Ljublana. Svetina's first book of poetry, *Plovi na jagodi pupa magnolija do zlatih vladnih palač* (The Magnolia Puppet Sails on a Strawberry to Golden Rulers' Palaces), appeared in 1971. It was followed by *Heliks in Tibija* (Helix and Tibiia, 1973); *Botticelli* (1975), for which he won the Zlata ptica award; *Vaš partijska ljubezen, očetje! Herojska smrt življenja . . .* (Your Party Love, Fathers! The Heroic Death of Life, 1976); *Joni* (To Jonah, 1976); *Dissertationes* (Dissertations, 1977); *Bulbul* (The Song Thrush, 1982); *Marija in živali* (Maria and the Animals, 1986); *Péti rokopisi* (Manuscripts Sung, 1987), which won the Prešeren Prize; *Knjiga očetove smrti* (The Book of Father's Death, 1990); *Almagest* (1991); *Disciplina bolečine* (The Discipline of Pain, 1993); and *Glasovi snega* (The Voices of Snow, 1993). Svetina's poetry is predominantly satirical, political, erotic, and exotic. The last two features, combined with a strong bent toward the poetic, philosophical, and classical, also characterize much of his playwriting. Svetina is the author of some ten plays, several of which have enjoyed wide resonance in Slovenia and beyond. Three of them—*Biljard na Capriju* (Billiards on Capri, 1987), which is clearly based on the life of the Russian revolutionary writer Maxim Gorky; *Vrtovi in golobica* (The Gardens and the Dove, 1992); and *Tako je umrl Zaratuštra: Oslovska žaloigra* (*Thus Died Zarathustra: An Assinine Tragedy*, 1996)—have won the Slavka Gruma Award. The Slovenian Youth Theater production of his play *Šeherezada: Vzhodna–zahodna opera* (Sheherezade: An East–West Opera, 1989) was one of the most successful Slovenian theatrical productions of the late 1980s and early 1990s and has been widely performed in other countries. Svetina's other plays include *Lepotica in zver* (Beauty and the Beast, 1985); *Kamen in zrno* (Stone and Grain, 1990); *Tibetanska knjiga mrtvih* (The Tibetan Book of the Dead, 1992), which is based on Svetina's own translation of the original; and *Ojdip v Korintu* (Oedipus in Corinth, 1998). In 1998 Svetina also published his translations of three Tibetan mysteries. Svetina's plays with ancient and biblical settings such as *Thus Died Zarathustra*, The Tibetan Book of the Dead, Sheherezade, and Oedipus in Corinth are colorfully exotic and bring to mind the spectacle films of Cecil B. DeMille.

Translations: *Thus Died Zarathustra: An Assinine Tragedy*, trans. Alan McConnell-Duff with Ivo Svetina and Lili Potpara, in *Contemporary Slovenian Drama* (Ljubljana: Slovene Writers Association, 1996), 205–88, which contains synopses of *Šeherezada: Vzhodna–zahodna opera* and *Vrtovi in golobica*.

Świetlicki, Marcin (b. 1961) Polish poet. Widely known and popular as the lead singer of the rock band Świetliki (Glowworms), Świetlicki was born and educated in Kraków, where he serves as a member of the editorial board of the influential Catholic weekly *Tygodnik Powszechny*. He has been associated with the Kraków-based "Barbarian" group of poets, who publish in the quarterly *bruLion*. Some of his poems also appeared in the anthology *Przyszli barbarzyńcy!* (The Barbarians Have Arrived!, 1991). His first independent volume of poems came out in 1992 under the *bruLion* imprint. It was followed in 1998 by *Pieśni profana* (Songs of a Profane Man) and, more recently, by the fifty-six-page collection *Czynny do wołania* (Subject to Recall, 2001).

Translations: Ten poems in *Young Poets of New Poland: An Anthology*, trans. Donald

Pirie (London: Forest, 1993), 164–78; five poems, trans. W. Martin, *Chicago Review* 46, nos. 3–4 (2000): 276–79.

Swir, Anna (real name Anna Świrszczyńska; 1909–1984) Polish poet. Born in Warsaw, the daughter of a painter, Swir knew poverty at first hand and had to begin work early in life in order to put herself through university. While at Warsaw University, she studied medieval and Baroque Polish literature—an interest that, together with her experience of art at an early age, is reflected in a number of poems in such collections as *Lyriki zebrane* (Collected Lyrics, 1958); *Cudowna broda szacha* (The Shah's Splendid Beard, 1959); *Z dawnej Polski* (From Ancient Poland, 1963); and *Czarne słowa* (Black Words, 1967). During World War II, Swir, who survived the German occupation and the devastating Warsaw Uprising of August and September 1944, served as an orderly and a nurse in hospitals and was a member of the Resistance. She also contributed to underground publications. It was during this period that she wrote three poems inspired by three prominent figures in the cultural life of Silesia that were broadcast to Opole (Silesia) over Radio Warsaw. Based on typewritten texts, the poems were finally published in 1982 under the title *Śląskie opowieści* (Silesian Tales). Swir's wartime memories are graphically recounted in the short poems of her collection *Budowałem barykadę* (*Building the Barricade*), which appeared thirty years after the events, as if Swir needed the distance of time to commit her recollections to print. In her subsequent volumes of poetry *Wiatr* (Wind, 1970); *Jestem baba* (I Am a Woman, 1972); *Szczęśliwa jak psi ogon* (*Happy as a Dog's Tail*, 1978); *Poezje wybrane* (Selected Poems, 1973), for which the poet herself made the selection; and *Wybór wierszy* (Selected Verse, 1980), Swir reveals another very important facet of her personality that also

had to wait a long time before finding appropriate literary expression—a powerful sense of femininity and sensuality. Her poems in these later volumes are usually short, simple in language, often addressed to physical love, obsessed with the body (e.g., "A Woman Talks to Her Thigh" and "Large Intestine" from *Jestem baba*) and the miracle of birth, and keenly aware of the passage of time, which manifests itself in those poems dealing with old age and terminal illness. Political and social concerns fall outside Swir's field of vision. Posthumously published collections of Swir's poetry include *Radość i cierpienie: Utwory wybrane* (Joy and Suffering: Selected Works, 1985, 1993) and *Poezja* (Poetry, 1997), edited by Czesław Miłosz, who is a great admirer of Swir and has co-translated a number of her poems into English. A small volume of Swir's verse plays was published in 1984 as *Teatr poetycki* (Poetic Theater).

Literature: Czesław Miłosz, *Jakiegoż to gościa mieliśmy: O Annie Świrszczyńskiej* (Kraków: Znak, 1996), an affectionate appreciation of Swir's poetry by one of the greatest Polish poets of the twentieth century, illustrated with several photos of Swir; Anna Świrszczyńska, *Anna Świrszczyńska*, Poeci polscy (Polish Poets) (Warsaw: Czytelnik, 1984), a succinct introduction to the poet's life and work. The biographical and critical material in the various English editions of her poetry collectively represent the most extensive literature on Anna Swir in English.

Translations: *Building the Barricade,* trans. Magnus J. Krynski and Robert A. Maguire (Kraków: Wydawnictwo Literackie, 1979), a Polish–English edition; *Fat Like the Sun,* trans. Margaret Marshment and Grazyna Baran (London: Women's Press, 1986); *Happy as a Dog's Tail,* trans. Czeslaw Milosz with Leonard Nathan (San Diego: Harcourt Brace Jovanovich, 1985); *Talking to My Body,* trans. Czeslaw Milosz and Leonard Nathan (Port Townsend, Wash.: Copper Canyon, 1996)

Sýs, Karel (b. 1946) Czech poet. One of post–World War II Czechoslovakia's most prolific and well-regarded poets, Sýs was born in the village of Rychnov nad Kněžnou. After graduating from high school in Písek in 1964, he studied at the Prague College of Economics. He received his degree in 1970 and for the next four years worked for the art-exporting company Art Centrum. From 1974 to 1983, he edited a column on cultural topics for the weekly *Tvorba*. He thereafter held editorial positions at several journals in Prague and elsewhere, especially *Kmen, Literární měsíčník, Práce,* and *Profil,* and at such publishing houses as Mladá fronta, Československý spisovatel, and Severočeské nakladatelství. As a result of the political changes in Czechoslovakia in November 1989 and his communist affiliations, Sýs gave up these positions. From 1990 to 1992, he edited the erotic magazine *Sextant.* In 1993 he worked for the biweekly *Domácí lekař.* Two years later, with the writers Daniel Strož and Pavel Burian, Sýs founded the journal *Obrys/Kmen* (previously a supplement to the communist newspaper *Haló noviny*) as a publication fundamentally opposed to Czech post–November 1989 political and literary development. In 1996 he stood as a candidate for parliament in national elections.

After publishing his early poems in a large number of journals, Sýs came out with his first book of verse in 1969 under the title *Newton za neúrody jablek* (Newton During the Bad Apple Harvest). It was followed by *Pootevřený anděl* (The Half-Open Angel, 1972); *Dlouhé sbohem* (Long Goodbyes, 1977); *Nadechni se a leť* (Take a Deep Breath and Fly, 1977; enl. ed., 1980), for which Sýs borrowed the title of a Raymond Chandler detective novel; *Poštovní holubi paměti: Výbor z milostné poezie* (Carrier Pigeons of Memory: Selected Love Poems, 1978); *Ame-*

rický účet: Verše rodinné a jiné (American Account: Family and Other Poems, 1980); *Básník a spol* (The Poet and Co., 1981); *Ohrada snů* (The Yard of Dreams, 1982); *Stroj času* (The Time Machine, 1984); *Kniha přísloví* (A Book of Proverbs, 1985); *Písecká domovní znamení* (Písek City House Signs, 1985); *Pero nikoli za kloboukem* (A Feather Not at All in the Cap, 1985), history and criticism; *1 + 1, aneb nesoustavný rozhovor o poezii* (1 + 1, or An Unsystematic Conversation About Poetry, 1986), with Jiří Zacek; *Atomový pléd* (The Atomic Plaid, 1986); *Rodné číslo Homéra: Výbor z poezie, 1962–1983* (Homer's Home Number: A Selection of Poems, 1962–1983, 1986); *Ze Země na Měsíc a zpátky* (From Earth to Moon and Back, 1988); *Pražský chodec II* (The Prague Pedestrian II, 1988), a chronicle of sorts of Sýs's romance with the Czech capital; *Ztráty a nálezy: Z intimní lyriky, 1985* (Lost and Found: Intimate Lyrics, 1985, 1989); *K. ještě po deseti letech* (K. Even After Ten Years, 1989), a collection of aphorisms; *Soulet a jiné básně aneb Židovská kuchařka* (Soulet and Other Poems, or The Jewish Cook, 1991), which is based in part on the Jewish Talmud; *Milování v Čechách* (Love in Bohemia, 1991), selected love lyrics; *Zasklené kalhoty dospělého muže* (The Glazed Pants of a Mature Man, 1992); *Kapsa: Kniha utkvělých představ (26.7. 1946–9.7.1986)* (The Pocket: A Book of Fixed Ideas [26 July 1946–9 July 1986], 1992); *Píšu básen zatímco za oknem padá muž* (I Write Poetry Because a Man Is Falling Past the Window, 1992); *Načas v očistci* (Short Stay in Purgatory, 1993*); Pet let v mtrvém domě* (Five Years in the Death House, 1995); and *Nediskrétní poezie: Výbor z veršů z let 1969* (Indiscreet Poems: Selected Verse from 1996, 1996).

Besides his considerable body of poetry, Sýs has edited several volumes of Czech poetry and written critical pieces on Czech literature, generally of an unconventional and irreverent nature. The best collection of his literary as well as political writings, *Nová kronika aneb Bordel v Čechách* (A New Chronicle, or The Bordello in the Czech Lands, 1994), appeared under the pseudonym Kosmas. As a poet and prose writer, Sýs is lively, playful, colorful, opinionated, outrageous, and fond of thumbing his nose at conventional attitudes and ideas. In a down-to-earth and conversational style, his works convey a real zest for life and an utter lack of prudishness that was popular with readers whatever their political persuasion. Many of his poems are about love, and more often than not the love is highly charged with eroticism. In 1986 Sýs published an edition of the poetry of one of his Czech literary idols, Vítězslav Nezval (1900–1958). He is also an indefatigable translator whose interests range from Mongolia to France. He has a particular fondness for such French poets as Guillaume Apollinaire, Paul Éluard, and Jacques Prévert.

Translations: "The Time Machine," trans. Ewald Osers, in *The New Czech Poetry: Jaroslav Čejka, Michal Černík, Karel Sýs* (Newcastle upon Tyne: Bloodeaxe, 1988), 53–62. Conceived in Paris in 1982, "The Time Machine"—one of Sýs's best poems and an excellent introduction to his work—is a brash, freewheeling survey of civilization some thirty-five years after the events of World War II.

Szabó, Magda (b. 1917) Hungarian novelist and short-story writer. A native of Budapest, Szabó was a secondary-school teacher of Hungarian and Latin for many years. She began her literary career as a poet, publishing several volumes of poetry between 1947 and 1949. In response to the worsening political and cultural climate in Hungary in the early post–World War II period, Szabó withdrew from a public literary career until 1958, when her first novel, *Freskó* (Fresco), appeared. It was a timely treatment of the problems of intellectuals—the milieu Szabó knew best—trying to come to grips with the great changes taking place in Hungary at the time. Szabó reurned to this period in subsequent novels. In *Mondják meg Zsófikának* (Let Them Tell Sophie, 1958; translated as *Tell Sally . . .*), she drew on her own experiences as a teacher to tell the story of the difficult adjustments a young girl has to make in her relations with her mother and others after her father's death. *Az őz* (*The Fawn*), which appeared a year after *Tell Sally*, is a first-person narrative by a woman addressed to her deceased husband recalling their families, their past loves, and their life together. One of her most popular works, the novel *Disznótor* (*Night of the Pig Killing*, 1960), takes place on a single day in postwar Hungary and chronicles the enmity between two families joined by a failed marriage that ends in a murder of passion. *Az ajtó* (*The Door*, 1987), another of her better-known novels, is an intriguing if overdrawn portrait of an eccentric elderly housekeeper who gradually becomes an integral part of the narrator's life. As in most of her works, Szabó's interest is strong in psychological portraiture. Szabó's other novels include *Pilátus* (Pilate, 1963); *A Danaida* (The Danaides, 1964); *Mózes egy, huszonkettő* (Moses 1:22, 1967); *Katalina utca* (Katalin Street, 1969); *Ókút* (The Ancient Well, 1970); *Abigél* (Abigail, 1970, 1973); *A szemlélők* (The Onlookers, 1973); *Régimódi történet* (An Old-fashioned Story, 1978); *Kívül a körön* (Outside the Circle, 1982); and *A pillanat* (The Moment, 1990). Szabó is also the author of a volume of short stories, *Alvók futása* (The Race of the Sleeping, 1967); several plays, *Kígyómarás* (Snake Bite, 1960); *Vörös tinta* (Red Ink, 1959); *Fanny hagyományai* (The Memoirs of Fanny, 1965); *Eleven képe a világnak* (A Vivid Picture of the World, 1966); and *Béla Király* (King Béla, 1986), a historical trilogy based on the life of Bela IV (1206–1270); and two travelogues, *Hullámok kergetése* (Chasing the Waves,

1965) and *Zeusz küszöbén: Úti jegyzetek* (On Zeus's Doorstep: Travel Notes, 1968). Her literary and critical essays have been collected in three volumes: *Kívül a körön* (Outside the Circle, 1982); *Záróvizsga* (Final Exam, 1987); and *A félistenek szomorúsága* (The Sorrow of the Demigods, 1992), which also contains essays on drama and theater.

Translations: *The Door*, trans. Stefan Draughon (Boulder, Colo.: East European Monographs, 1994); *The Fawn*, trans. Kathleen Szasz (New York: Knopf, 1963); *Night of the Pig-Killing*, trans. Kathleen Szasz (London: Cape, 1965; New York: Knopf, 1966); *Tell Sally . . .* , trans. Ursula McLean (Budapest: Athenaeum, 1963); "At Cockcrow," trans. Lily Halápy, in *44 Hungarian Short Stories*, ed. Lajos Illés (Budapest: Corvina, 1979), 470–501. *Freskó* is available in French as *Fresques*, trans. Georges Kassai (Paris: Seuil, 1963); *Katalina utca* as *Rue Katalin*, trans. Elisabeth Kovacs (Paris: Seuil, 1974); *Mozes egy, huszonkettő* as *Les Parents perdus*, trans. Tibor Tardos and Remi Dreyfus (Paris: Seuil, 1970); and *Pilatus* as *La Ballade de la vierge*, trans. Tibor Tardös and Hélène Fougerousse (Paris: Seuil, 1967).

Száraz, György (b. 1930) Hungarian essayist, playwright, and novelist. Chief editor of the literary monthly *Kortárs*, Száraz, who is known most for his nonfictional and essayistic writing, published his first book, *A vezérkari főnök* (Chief of Staff), in 1969. It deals with the career of Aurél Stromfeld, commander of the Hungarian Republic of Councils under the communist leader Béla Kun. His similar documentary novel, *A tábornok* (The General, 1981), offers a portrait of a prominent Hungarian figure, György Pálffy, who was a victim of the purges in the time of the "cult of personality" of the 1950s. Száraz's major collection of seven plays (two of them written for televi-

sion) appeared in 1979 under the title *A Rókus-templom harangjai* (The Bells of the Temple). Mostly historical (real or imaginary) in nature, the plays include *A nagyszerű halál* (The Splendid Death); *Ítéletidő* (Judgment Time), a comedy set in Transylvania in 1849; *Királycsel* (Royal Ruse), another comedy, this time about the relations between the Hungarian king Zsigmond and the rival papacies in Rome and Avignon; the made-for-television *Worafka tanácsos úr* (Worafka the Wise), set in Pest in 1859 and 1861; the also made-for-television title play *A Rókus-templom harangjai*, which is set in 1809 and 1810 in Vienna, Tübingen, and Paris, and has the Austrian diplomat Metternich as one of the leading characters; *Az élet vize* (The Water of Life), a tragicomedy with Beowulf among the cast of characters; and *A megoldás* (The Solution), a play with a Russian setting featuring Count Leo Tostoy and his wife. Száraz resumed serious documentary and essay writing in 1981 with *A tábornok*. It was followed by *Egy furcsa könyvről* (About a Strange Book, 1983), a small book, written in 1982, in which Száraz polemicizes with the Romanian writer Ion Lăncrănjan, the author of a book about Transylvania published in 1982 by a Bucharest sports and tourism publishing house. In his huge volume of essays *Történelem jelenidőben* (History in the Present Tense, 1984), the longest of which is "Egy előítélet nyomában" ("On the Trail of Prejudice," 1976), Száraz presents a broad sweep of Hungarian politics and culture through World War II and the postwar period. It also includes, among others, pieces on Tolstoy, the Vietnam War, the Hungarian writer Gyula Illyés, and Polish–Hungarian relations.

Translations: "Roast Pheasant with Groats," trans. András Boros-Kazal, in *Present Continuous: Contemporary Hungarian Writing*, ed. István Bart (Budapest: Corvina, 1985), 58–69.

Szczypiorski, Andrzej (1924–2000) Polish novelist, essayist, and short-story writer. A prolific and widely translated writer, Szczypiorski was born and educated in Warsaw. He participated in the Warsaw Uprising of 1944 and was subsequently imprisoned in the Sachsenhausen concentration camp. He began his career as a journalist in 1946 and published his first collection of stories in 1955. There are two major facets to Szczypiorski's career: his activist role in the Solidarity movement of the 1980s and subsequent participation in the political life of postcommunist Poland, and his work as a writer of fiction. Szczypiorski's views on Solidarity and postcommunist Polish political culture are contained in a collection of his essays published under the title *Grzechy, cnoty pragnienia* (Sins and Virtues of Desire, 1997). The essays cover a wide variety of political and social topics grouped into two sections: "Z notatnika stanu przemian" ("From a Notebook of a State of Affairs"), which was originally published in 1983 and deals with the plight of political prisoners during the time of Solidarity and martial law, and "Grzechy bliźnich, cnoty własne" ("The Sins of Others, My Own Virtues"), which includes later pieces.

As a writer of fiction, Szczypiorski is best known for his novels dealing with the behavior of Poles, Germans, and Jews in occupied Poland during World War II. Although vivid and often graphic in his depiction of the brutalities of the occupation, Szczypiorski, while hardly an apologist for the Germans, nevertheless tried to see the events of 1939 to 1945 from a philosophical perspective. This allowed him to find good and bad in all people and to suggest that in the right circumstances the roles of victim and oppressor might easily be reversed. Underlying this point of view (which in his novel *The Beautiful Mrs. Seidenman* leads him to portray Israeli soldiers victimizing Palestinian fedayeen during an Arab–Israeli conflict)

was Szczypiorski's patent desire to achieve a truly united Europe with the horrors of the past consigned to history.

Szczypiorski's published novels include *Za murami Sodomy* (Beyond Sodom's Walls, 1963); *Podróż do krańca doliny* (Journey to the Edge of the Valley, 1966); *Msza za miasto Arras* (*A Mass for Arras,* 1971), an allegory, based on the persecution of Jews and witches in the town of Arras, France, in October 1461 in the wake of the plague, that alludes to the anti-Semitic campaign in Poland in 1968; *I ominęli Emaus* (A Detour Around Emmaus, 1974); *Złowić cień* (Hunting Shadows, 1976; translated as *The Shadow Catcher*), a fairly slight novel about a fifteen-year-old Polish boy coming to maturity on the threshold of World War II who, among other things, thinks about Poland's large Jewish community, which he regards as an integral part of his nation; *Trzej ludzie w bardzo długiej podróży* (Three People on a Very Long Trip, written 1977; and published 1980), a rumination about the lessons to be drawn from World War II in the form of a slight novel about a few people caught up in a murky hostage drama; and *Początek* (The Beginning, 1986; translated as *The Beautiful Mrs. Seidenman*), possibly Szczypiorski's best novel, about an Aryan-looking Jewish woman who survives the German occupation of Warsaw by living as a Christian outside the walls of the Jewish ghetto and the ironies of her postwar life.

A series of interviews with Szczypiorski, conducted by Tadeusz Kraśko, that deal in part with issues raised by *The Beautiful Mrs. Seidenman,* came out in 1991 under the title *Początek raz jeszcze* (Beginning Again). The same year, Szczypiorski published the novel *Noc, dzień i noc* (Night, Day and Night), a first-person narrative in which the device of interviews in a foreign setting (here Switzerland) serves as the pretext for a series of recollections and observations on, for example, attitudes toward Jews in postwar

Poland. *Noc, dzień i noc* was followed by *Czas przeszły* (Past Tense, 1993), a thin novel divided into two parts, the first set in occupied Poland in 1944 and the second mostly in postwar Germany in 1959. Szczypiorski follows certain German and Polish survivors of a foiled wartime plot to execute a German officer in order to advance the idea that it was time for people to put World War II, with all its atrocities, behind them in order to move forward into a new era. In 1994 Szczypiorski published *Autoportret z kobietą* (*Self-Portrait with Woman*, 1994), which chronicles the love affair between a Pole invited to Switzerland for a series of interviews about the changes in Poland and Eastern Europe, brought about by the collapse of communism, and the Swiss woman who conducts the interviews. The work is essentially a long personal reflection by a Pole who went through World War II, the Holocaust, and the evils of the communist system and for whom the pain and suffering represented by those events was of no spiritual benefit. Its autobiographical character is unmistakable, and Szczypiorski's aim in writing it was to disabuse Western readers of the notion that the calamities that the Poles—as, indeed, other Eastern Europeans—lived through from 1939 to 1989 had some enduring moral and/or spiritual value.

Szczypiorski's later volumes of short stories, on subjects familiar from his novels, include *Amerykańska whisky i inne opowiadania* (American Whiskey and Other Stories, 1990); *Trzy krótkie opowiadania* (Three Short Narratives, 1990); and *Polowanie na lwy* (Hunting for Lions, 1995). Perhaps the most interesting collection of this group is *Amerykańska whisky i inne opowiadania*, in which, in his attempt to sketch the newest history of Poland, Szczypiorski sets aside a judgmental approach in favor of an analysis of the circumstances that might have shaped people's behavior. His best-known novel outside Poland, *The Beautiful*

Mrs. Seidenman, won the Austrian State Prize for European Literature as well as the Nelly Sachs Prize, also from Austria.

Translations: *The Beautiful Mrs. Seidenman,* trans. Klara Glowczewska (New York: Grove Weidenfeld, 1989); *A Mass for Arras,* trans. Richard Lourie (New York: Grove, 1993); *The Polish Ordeal: The View from Within,* trans. Celina Wieniawska (London: Croom Helm, 1982); *Self-Portrait with Woman,* trans. Bill Johnston (New York: Grove, 1995); *The Shadow Catcher,* trans. Bill Johnston (New York: Grove, 1997).

Szécsi, Margit (1928–1990) Hungarian poet. A native of Budapest, and the wife of the poet László Nagy, Szécsi was born into poverty, which explains her early enthusiasm for socialism and her strong feelings about social justice. She attended Budapest University on a scholarship for "proletarian students," but did not stay for a degree. After she left the university, she joined the editorial staff of the literary magazine *Csillag,* the successor of *Nyugat.* It was about this time, in 1949, that her first poems began appearing. Szécsi's early poetry breathes with the spirit of socialist realism. Genuinely committed to the cause of socialism, she demonstrated her sincerity in 1951 by volunteering to help build the steel-mill complex in the village of Dunapentele, which was subsequently renamed Sztálinváros (Stalin City; now Dunaújváros). As Szécsi developed as a poet, lyrical and romantic motifs came more often to the fore, reflecting a real zest for life and love and a greater openness to the folk tradition. Szécsi's first published collection of poetry appeared in 1955 under the title *Március* (March). It was followed by eleven more volumes of verse: *Angyalok strandja* (Angels' Beach, 1956); *Páva a tűzfalon* (Peacock on the Partition, 1958); *A trombitákat összesöprik* (They'll Sweep Up the Trumpets, 1965); a volume of collected poems, *Új heraldika* (New Heraldry, 1967); *A nagy virágvágógép* (The Great

Flower-Cutting Machine, 1969); *A madaras mérleg* (Scales with Bird, 1972); *A szent buborék* (Holy Bubble, 1974); *Birodalom* (Empire, 1976); *A rózsaszinű dzsip* (The Rose-Colored Jeep, 1982); *Költő á holdban* (The Poet in the Moon, 1984); and *A Betlehem-Blues* (The Bethlehem Blues, 1986), She was awarded the Attila József Prize for poetry in 1957 and 1968.

Translations: Two poems in *The Face of Creation: Contemporary Hungarian Poetry*, ed. Jascha Kessler (Minneapolis: Coffee House, 1988), 142–45; eight poems in *In Quest of the "Miracle Stag": The Poetry of Hungary*, ed. Adam Makkai (Chicago: Atlantis-Centaur, 1996), 837–42; four poems in *Modern Hungarian Poetry*, ed. Miklós Vajda (New York: Columbia University Press, 1977), 221–24.

Székely, János (1929–1992) Transylvanian Hungarian poet, novelist, playwright, and essayist. A native of Tîrgu Mureş (Hungarian, Marosvásárhely), Székely attended the military academy in his native town and, while still in his teens, was drafted into the army and thrown into combat in World War II. He was captured on the western front and was able to resume his education only after the war's end and his repatriation. His book *A nyugati hadtest* (The Western Division) is an account of his wartime experiences. In 1952 Székely graduated from the Hungarian Bolyai University in what was then the city of Kolozsvár (now Cluj-Napoca, Romania). Until his retirement in 1989, he worked in the Cluj-Napoca office of a Bucharest-based Hungarian-language newspaper. Székely's works, most of which are on historical themes, include *Profán passió* (Profane Passion, 1954); the long poem *Dózsa* (1964), about the leader of the peasant rebellion of 1514; *Caligula helytartója* (Caligula's Lieutenant, 1972); *Protestánsok* (The Protestants, 1978); *Irgalmas hazugság* (The Merciful Lie, 1979); and *Vak Béla király*

(King Béla the Blind, 1981). In 1973 he published *Ars Poetica*, in which he argued that poetry was dead and rejected even much of his own poetry as lacking purpose. Thereafter spurning poetry, Székely concentrated on literary translation, rendering into Hungarian the works of such Romanian writers as Mihai Beniuc and Mircea Eliade. Székely has also translated from German and Russian. A collection of Székely's poetry from 1948 to 1986 was published as *Semmi, soha: Versek, 1948–1986* (Nothing, Never: Poems 1948–1986, 1994, 1999). Székely's essays, most of which deal with literature, were published in three collections: the two-volume *Könyvek között: Gondolatok könyvről, olvasásról, tanulásrol, nyomdászatról* (Among Books: Thoughts on Books, Reading, Learning, and Printing, 1961); *Rögeszme genezise* (The Genesis of Obsession, 1978), a volume of essays and reviews; and the posthumous *Mítosz értelme* (The Reason of Myth, 1996).

Translations: Three poems in *In Quest of the "Miracle Stag": The Poetry of Hungary*, ed. Adam Makkai (Chicago: Atlantis-Centaur, 1996), 842–46.

Szép, Ernő (1884–1953) Hungarian poet, novelist, and playwright. Born in Huszt, in the eastern part of the Austro-Hungarian Empire, Szép began his literary career in 1902 with a volume of poems titled *Első csokor* (First Bouquet). Once settled in Budapest, he went on to become one of Hungary's most popular and prolific writers, with over thirty volumes of poetry, prose fiction, and plays to his credit. Before World War I, he was associated with the important and innovative literary journal *Nyugat*, which was dominated by the poet Endre Ady. Although almost all his literary work preceded World War II, Szép wrote a straightforward, unsentimental, but vivid memoir of what he experienced as a Jew when, after the fall of the government of Miklós Horthy, on 15 October 1944, the extremist Arrow Cross Party of Ferenc Szálasi took power and then joined forces with the Germans in a desperate three-month defense of Budapest against the approaching Soviet army. Sixty years old at the time, Szép was forced to dig earthworks around the outskirts of Budapest along with thousands of other Hungarian Jews who had not been deported to death camps in the massive German roundup on 19 March 1944. Szép's memoir, *Emberszag* (*The Smell of Humans*), was first published in 1945 and was reprinted in 1984. It is the only work by Szép available in English. Although Szép was not popular with Hungary's Marxist literary critics in the late 1940s, his reputation as a writer has gained immeasurably from the ardent championship of his work, beginning in the late 1970s, by the very important writer Dezső Tandori.

Translations: *The Smell of Humans: A Memoir of the Holocaust in Hungary,* trans. John Bátki, with an introduction by Dezső Tandori (Budapest: Central European University Press, 1984).

Szewc, Piotr (b. 1961) Polish novelist, poet, and essayist. Born in Zamość, where he received his early schooling, Szewc graduated from the Catholic University in Lublin in 1986 with a degree in Polish studies. He has published extensively in such journals and newspapers as *Twórczość, Tygodnik powszechny, Akcent,* and *Życie Warszawy,* and is currently editor of the periodical *Nowe Książki.* His first published book was a volume of poems, *Świadectwo* (Witness), which appeared in 1983. It was followed by his first novel, *Zagłada* (*Annihilation,* 1987), which attracted considerable attention and has been translated into English, French, German, and Italian. *Annihilation* is a slight novel whose goal is to capture the mood of a July day in 1934 in the Jewish district of the southeastern Polish town of Zamość. With the extermination of the once very large Jew-

ish community of Poland during World War II, little of Jewish life and culture remains in Poland. Poles and Jews alike have joined in an effort to preserve what they can of the past. In literature, this has taken the form of works such as Szewc's, which attempt to re-create the way of life of the Jews of Poland before the Holocaust. Along with preserved visual documentation, such fiction constitutes a record of the Jewish past in Poland for new generations of Poles who will not have any direct experience of the scope and nature of the Jewish presence in the country. Szewc's novel is a quiet, almost lyrical, act of nostalgia in which a single day in the life of a Jewish community in Poland is warmly re-created with barely a hint at what the future holds. Szewc's second novel, *Zmierzchy i poranki* (Sunsets and Sunrises, 1999) is, like *Annihilation,* a painstakingly detailed portrait of a single summer day in a town in southeastern Poland. Although the small Jewish community is an element in the town's landscape, Szewc does not focus on it as such in this novel. Instead, he explores modes of femininity as represented by several dominant female characters and as seen through the eyes of the young boy Piotruś. So realistic in its detail is the image of the town evoked by Sunsets and Sunrises that its very reality becomes suspect, as if something sinister and threatening lurks just around the corner, as in *Annihilation.* In 1991 Szewc also published, in Montricher, Switzerland, a fascinating and candid series of interviews with the Polish writer Julian Stryjkowski under the title *Ocalony na Wschodzie: Z Julianem Stryjkowskim rozmawia Piotr Szewc* (Saved in the East: Piotr Szewc Converses with Julian Stryjkowski). This was followed in 2001 by an eighty-seven-page personal reminiscence of Stryjkowski under the title *Syn kapłana* (The Chaplain's Son).

Translations: *Annihilation,* trans. Ewa Hryniewicz-Yarbrough (Normal, Ill.: Dalkey Archive Press, 1993).

Szilágyi, Andor (b. 1955) Hungarian play-wright, novelist, and short-story writer. Szilá-gyi was born in Szolnok and in 1983 com-pleted a course of study in history and adult education in a teachers college in Eger. He subsequently moved to Budapest, where he worked as a journalist, stock clerk, bricklayer, and lumberman. From 1986 to 1993, he was employed by Radio Hungary, after which he became a freelance writer. His first published work was *A világtalan szemtanú* (The Blind Eyewitness, 1989), subtitled *Naivregény* (A Naive Novel). It was followed in 1993 by a col-lection of short stories titled *Ezotérema.* Szilágyi's first play, *Rettenetes anya* (The Dreadful Mother, written 1988; staged 1990), which bleakly portends the postcommunist changes in Eastern Europe, set the pattern for much of his subsequent playwriting, which is grotesque, surreal, often enigmatic, with much linguistic play, inventiveness, and an abandonment of traditional norms of drama-turgy. *El nem küldött levelek* (*Unsent Letters,* staged 1993), his only work thus far available in English, is a play about the missed oppor-tunities in life. A man and a woman, both "angels" (Angelus and Angelina), meet at a railway station, fall in love and part, presum-ably forever, only to meet on other occasions and in different circumstances without rec-ognizing each other. In 1997 Szilágyi pub-lished a rather weak moralizing novel about the Bosnian War, *Shalim,* in which the titular character, a small boy, is the only member of his family across several generations to sur-vive the war. Szilágyi was awarded the Szép Ernő Prize in 1994.

Translations: *Unsent Letters,* in a version from a translation by Ildikó Pathy, in *Hun-garian Plays: New Drama from Hungary,* selected and introduced by László Upor (London: Nick Hern, 1996), 77–122.

Szilágyi, Domokos (1938–1976) Transylva-nian Hungarian poet. Szilágyi was born in Satu Mare, Romania, where he received his early education. After graduating from Satu Mare high school in 1955, he moved to Cluj, where he earned a degree from the Babes-Bolyai University a few years later. In 1958/1959, he was on the staff of the review *Igaz Szó* and in 1960 joined the Hungarian-language Bucharest daily *Előre.* He remained with the newspaper until ill health forced his retirement in 1970. Although he published his first book of poetry in 1962, it was only with the collection *Búcsú a trópusoktól* (Farewell to Tropics, 1969) that he gained recognition as one of the best poets of his generation. *Búcsú a trópusoktól* was followed by such additional collections as *Fagyöngy* (Mistletoe, 1971); *Sajtóértekezlet: Versek, 1956–1971* (News Conference: Poems, 1956–1971, 1972); and *Felezőidő* (Half Time, 1974). A disciplined, generally accessible poet, who combines elements of the tradi-tional and the modern, Szilágyi often writes of untenable illusions and the reluctant but inevitable need to recognize that trying to find a meaning to life is bound to be thwarted. In 1975 Szilágyi published a vol-ume of translations of poems by Walt Whit-man, *Walt Whitman legszebb versei* (Walt Whitman's Best Poems), and translated from modern Romanian poetry. Posthumous col-lections of his poetry and prose began ap-pearing soon after his death. They include *Szilágy Domokos legszebb versei* (Domokos Szilágyi's Best Poems, 1978); *Tengerparti lakodalom: Hátrahagyott versek/Szilágyi Domokos* (Wedding by the Sea: Unpublished Poems by Domokos Szilágyi, 1978); *Kényszer-leszállás* (Emergency Landing, 1976); *Élnem adjatok: Vers, próza, esszé, 1956–1970* (Let Me Live: Poetry, Prose, Essays, 1956–1976, 1990);-and *Magyarok* (The Hungarians, 1997). In 1979 a collection of his poems was published in Romanian translation by Constantin Olariu, with a foreword by the well-known Romanian writer Nichita Stănescu.

Translations: Three poems in *The Colon-nade of Teeth: Modern Hungarian Poetry,* ed. George Gömöri and Goerge Szirtes (Newcastle upon Tyne: Bloodaxe, 1996), 193–96.

Szymborska, Wisława (b. 1923) Polish poet. Hailed as one of the greatest Polish poets of her time, and the winner of the Nobel Prize in Literature in 1996, Szymborska was born in Bnin, in western Poland, where she lived until her family moved to Kraków in 1931. During World War II, she attended classes in an illegal underground Polish school network. After the war, she studied Polish literature and sociology at the Jagiellonian University in Kraków. From 1953 to 1981, she worked at the Kraków literary weekly *Życie Literackie* as poetry editor and a columnist.

Szymborska has published ten volumes of poetry: *Dlatego żyjemy* (That's Why We're Alive, 1952); *Pytania zadawane sobie* (Questions I Put to Myself, 1954); *Wołanie do Yeti* (Calling the Yeti, 1957); *Sól* (Salt, 1962); *Sto pociech* (A Hundred Joys, 1967); *Wszelki wypadek* (Chance, 1972); *Wielka liczba* (A Great Number, 1976); *Tarsjusz i inne wiersze* (Tarsius and Otther Poems, 1976); *Ludzie na moście* (*People on a Bridge*, 1986); and *Widok z ziarnkiem piasku* (*View with a Grain of Sand*, 1996). Several editions of selected poems by Szymborska have also appeared: *Poezje wybrane* (Selected Poems, 1967); *Poezje* (Poems, 1970); *Poezje* (Poems, 1977); *Poezje wybrane* (Selected Poems, 1983); and *Wieczór autorski* (Author's Evening, 1992), a selection made by Szymborska herself. Szymborska has also published a three-volume collection of feuilletons and book reviews on Polish and other literatures under the title *Lektury nadobowiązkowe* (Essential Readings, 1973, 1992). Most of them originally appeared over a fourteen-year period in the journal *Życie Literackie;* in the 1980s, in the short-lived *Pismo;* and finally in *Odra.* She is also the author of a short book about herself, *Wisława Szymborska* (1970).

A splendid poet of unpretentiousness and human everydayness, of the miraculousness of the ordinary, Szymborska is fond of juxtaposing the seemingly small and trivial to the monumental, the unimportant to the presumably important. She does so with wry humour and the eloquence of understatement. Her attitude toward grandiosity is nowhere better expressed than in one of her most famous poems, "Wielka liczba" ("Big Numbers"). In "Jawa" ("Reality"), she touts the greater power of reality over the dream:

The volatility of dreams
allows memory to shake them off,
Reality needn't fear being forgotten.

Her poetic credo is aptly encapsulated in "Pod jedną gwiazdką" ("Beneath One Little Star") where she writes: "Speech—don't blame me for borrowing big words / and then struggling to make them light." The poem "Ludzie na moście" ("People on a Bridge") was inspired by the famous print by the Japanese artist Hiroshige Utagawa.

Literature: Małgorzata Antoszewska-Tuora, *Niektórzy lubią Szymborską: Mały przewodnik po twórczości* (Warsaw: Stentor, 1996), a useful short guide through Szymborska's poetry; Stanisław Balbus, *Świat ze wszystkich stron świata: O Wisławie Szymborskiej* (Kraków: Wydawnictwo Literackie, 1996), a solid critical study; Stanisław Balbus and Dorota Wojda, eds., *Radość czytania Szymborskiej: Wybór tekstów krytycznych* (Kraków: Znak, 1996), a collection of critical articles; Małgorzata Baranowska, *Tak lekko było nic o tym nie wiedzieć: Szymborska i świat* (Wrocław: Wydawnictwo Dolnośląskie, 1996); Jacek Brzozowski, ed., *O wierszach Wisławy Szymborskiej: Szkice i interpretacje* (Łódź: Wydawnictwo Uniwersytetu Łódzkiego, 1996); Marta Fox, *Zdarzyć się mogło, zdarzyć się musiało: Z Wisławą Szymborską spotkanie w wierszu* (Katowice: Towarzystwo Zachęty Kultury, 1996), mostly on Szymborska's influence on other Polish poets; Ewa Krajska, *Dwie twarze Wisławy Szymborskiej* (Warsaw: Wydawnictwo Św. Tomasza z Akwinu, 1996); Jerzy Kwiatkowski, *Wisława Szymborska: Życie na poczekaniu* (Kraków: Wydawnictwo Literackie, 1996); Anna Legeżyńska, *Wisława Szymborska,* 2nd ed. (Poznań: Rebis, 1996); Anna Węgrzyniakowa, *Nie ma rozpusty większej niż myślenie: O poezji Wisławy Szymborskiej* (Katowice: Towarzystwo Zachęty Kultury, 1996); Aneta Wiatr, *Syzyf poezji w piekle współczesności: Rzecz o Wisławie Szymborskiej* (Warsaw: Kram, 1996); Dorota Wojda, *Milczenie słowa: O poezji Wisławy Szymborskiej* (Kraków: Universitas, 1996), a good short study; Leszek Żuliński, *Lekcje z Szymborską* (Bochnia: Prowincjonalna Oficyna Wydawnicza, 1996).

Translations: *Nic dwa razy: Wybór wierszy/Nothing Twice: Selected Poems,* trans. Stanisław Barańczak and Clare Cavanagh (Kraków: Wydawnictwo Literackie, 1997), a Polish–English edition; *People on a Bridge,* trans. Adam Czerniawski (London: Forest, 1990); *Poems,* trans. Magnus J. Krynski and Robert A. Maguire (Kraków: Wydawnictwo Literackie, 1989), a Polish–English edition; *Poems: New and Collected, 1957–1997,* trans. Stanisław Barańczak and Clare Cavanagh (New York: Harcourt Brace Jovanovich, 1998); *Sounds, Feelings, Thoughts: Seventy Poems by Wisława Szymborska,* trans. Magnus J. Krynski and Robert Maguire (Princeton, N.J.: Princeton University Press, 1981); *View with a Grain of Sand: Selected Poems,* trans. Stanisław Barańczak and Clare Cavanagh (New York: Harcourt Brace Jovanovich, 1995).

T

Tadić, Novica (b. 1949) Serbian poet. One of the most respected Yugoslav poets of the postwar generation, Tadić, a native of Montenegro, has lived for most of his life in Belgrade. He published his first volume of poetry, *Prisustva* (Presences), in 1974, at the age of twenty-five. The collection *Smrt u stolici* (Death in a Chair) appeared the following year. Tadić subsequently published another eleven books of poetry: *Ždrelo* (Maw, 1981); *Ognjena kokoš* (Fiery Hen, 1982); *Pogani jezik* (Foul Language, 1984); *Ruglo* (The Object of Ridicule, 1987); *O bratu, sestri i oblaku* (About Brother, Sister, and a Cloud, 1989); *Ulica* (Street, 1990); *Kraj godine: Groteske* (The End of the Year: Grotesques, 1990); *Kobac* (Sparrow Hawk, 1990); *Noćna svita* (Night Suite, 1990; translated as *Night Mail*); *Napast* (Assault, 1994); and *Ulica i potukač* (The Street and the Tramp, 1999), which also includes a number of short prose texts. Clearly a protégé of the great Serbian poet Vasko Popa, Tadić is known above all for short lyric poems full of strange, grotesque, and often menacing images, as the "Maker of Faces" cycle in *Smrt u stolici*. Some of the most disturbing images appear in poems with an urban setting. Motifs of disfigurement, horror, and an abysmal sense of emptiness and futility are also common. Typical of Tadić's combination of brevity of form and unsettling imagery are "Fiery Hen":

Jesus
Our Jesus
Our Jesus a pincushion.

and "The Object of Ridicule":

I threw
A single die
On the table
Of black marble-Saw
Not one side
Of the cube
Had a mark or number
There was
Nothing.

and "Sparrow Hawk":

> He turns the pages of books
> And examines the poems there
> Saying my god
> All this has already been written.

Translations: *Night Mail: Selected Poems,* trans. Charles Simic (Oberlin, Ohio: Oberlin College Press, 1992), which consists of excerpts from virtually all of Tadić's books of poetry.

Talev, Dimitur (pseudonyms Dimo Bolgarin and Dimitur Palislamov; 1898–1966) Bulgarian novelist. A highly popular writer in his time, Talev was born in Prilep, Macedonia. Uprooted by the Balkan wars and World War I, he was educated in Prilep, Salonica, Skopje (where he published his first literary work, a short story, in 1917), Stara Zagora, and Bitola, where in 1920 he finally completed secondary school. After studying medicine and philosophy for a semester each in Zagreb and Vienna in 1920 and 1921, he earned a degree in Slavic philology at Sofia University in 1925. Talev began his literary career as an editor at several journals and as a writer of short stories in the Bulgarian rural and patriarchal tradition. Stories in this vein were collected in the volumes *Zlatniiat kliuch* (The Golden Key, 1935); *Staraia kushta* (The Old House, 1938); and *Zavrushtane* (The Homecoming, 1944). His promising career was interrupted, however, by a series of jail and work-camp terms lasting from October 1944 to February 1948. Although no specific charges were brought against Talev, his arrest and incarceration were generally related to his deep Macedonian sympathies and what was regarded at the time as a politically incorrect "Great Bulgarian" chauvinism. After his release from detention, he and his family were forcefully relocated from Sofia to Lukovit from 1948 to 1952; it was there, in relative social isolation, that Talev completed the first novel in his major tetralogy, *Zhelezniiat svetilnik* (*The Iron Candlestick*, 1952), and wrote two other novels in the series: *Ilinden* (1953) and *Prespanskite kambani* (*The Bells of Prespa*, 1954). The fourth volume, *Glasovete vi chuvam* (Your Voices I Hear), was undertaken later and appeared in 1966. Together they constitute an impressive national epic, chronicling the struggle to liberate Macedonia from Turkish rule. Prior to the tetralogy, Talev had written a trilogy of novels under the general title *Usilni godini* (Hard Years) on the subject of the ill-fated Macedonian Ilinden (Saint Elijah's Day) and Preobrazhenie (Feast of the Transfiguration) Uprising of August 1903. The trilogy includes *V drezgavinata na utroto* (The Morning's Dawn, 1928); *Podem* (Revival, 1929); and *Ilinden* (1930). Long interested in ancient Bulgarian history, as evidenced by his 1937 collection of historical tales, *Velikiiat tsar* (The Great Czar), Talev also wrote another trilogy set in the reign of Czar Samuil (997–1014). It consists of the novels *Shtitove kamenni* (Shields of Stone, 1958); *Pepeliashka i tsarskiiat sin* (Cinderella and the Czar's Son, 1959); and *Pogibel* (Downfall, 1960). A revised 1966 edition of the trilogy was titled *Samuil: Roman-letopis za kraia na Purvata bulgarska durzhava* (Samuil: A Novel-Chronicle About the End of the First Bulgarian State). Apart from his two trilogies and tetralogy, Talev wrote a large number of fictional and nonfictional short works on Macedonia and was well known for his children's stories.

Literature: Aleksandur Spiridonov, *Dimitur Talev* (Sofia: Nar. mladezh, 1982), primarily a biography; Kosta Tsurnushanov, *Dimitur Talev v moite spomeni* (Sofia: Makedoniia, 1992), a book of memoirs by someone who knew Talev well.

Translations: *The Bells of Prespa,* trans. Mihail Todorov (Sofia: Foreign Languages Press, 1966); *The Iron Candlestick,* trans. Marguerite Alexieva (Sofia: Foreign Languages Press, 1964); "The Last Journey," in *The Peach Thief and Other Bulgarian Stories*, trans. Radost Pridham and Jean Morris (London: Cassell, 1968), 45–96.

Tandori, Dezső (pseudonyms Nat Roid, Tradoni, and D'Tirano; b. 1938) Hungarian poet, novelist, short-story writer, essayist, and translator. A cosmpolitan, prolific, innovative, challenging, and often entertaining writer, Tandori was born in Budapest and studied German and Hungarian at Eötvös Lóránd University in that city. He taught German in a Budapest high school for several years after obtaining his degree. His first book, *Töredék Hamletnek* (Fragment for Hamlet, 1968), was a bold attempt to de-poeticize the poetic text by making it as prosaic as possible by such means as a heavy use of run-on verse, digressions of every kind imaginable, a breezy style, and an abuse of lexical and grammatical conventions. His next collection, *Egy talált tárgy megtisztítása* (Cleansing of a Found Object, 1973), was praised by critics for its postmodern qualities. This pattern of freewheeling formal innovation continued into his next book of poems, *A mennyezet és a padló* (The Ceiling and the Floor, 1976), in which he experimented mostly with such lyric forms as the sonnet. Tandori's first collection of short stories, and one of his best, appeared in 1977 under the typical Tandorian title *Itt éjszaka koalák járnak* (The Koalas Roam at Night Here), although in this case koala bears do indeed figure prominently in the book.

The offbeat nature of much of Tandori's poetic writing—evident, for example, in the frequent appearance of birds inspired by the nine sparrows that share his apartment—is carried over into his writings about horse racing, a relatively later interest, soccer, tennis, and gambling. They include *Döblingi befutó* (Winner at Döbling, 1992), a collage-like work (in fact, a hodgepodge of autobiographical fragments, references overt and otherwise to world and Hungarian events, artwork, and so on) reflective of Tandori's enthusiasm for horse racing in all its manifestations, while demonstrating a greater awareness of the outside world than in his previous writing; *Nem lóverseny!* (They're Off!, 1999), more narrowly focused on racing and gambling in Great Britain and France and illustrated with photographs; *Gombfocikönyvek* (Football Books, 1980–1985), about the Sunday matches of English soccer teams; and *Játek történet* (Gambling Stories, 1998). He has written a number of perceptive, clever, and at times exasperating essays brought together in such collections as *Madárzsoké* (Bird Jockey, 1995) and *Evidencia történetek* (Story Files, 1996) and novels overweighted with the trivia and verbiage characteristic of much of his prose writing, among them *Miért élnél örökké* (Do You Want to Live Forever?, 1977); *Helyből távol* (From a Faraway Place, 1981); and *Vér és virághab* (Blood and Blossoms, 1998). Tandori has also written a few mysteries under the pen name Nat Roid, among them *Azt te csak hiszed, bébi!* (Keep the Faith, Baby!, 1982) and *Bízd a halálra* (Trust unto Death, 1985). Tandori is an able, professional translator who has translated extensively from German and English. American and British authors he has translated include Wallace Stevens, e. e. cummings, John Berryman, J. D. Salinger, Sylvia Plath, Randell Jarrell, John Keats, Lord Byron, Virginia Woolf, Samuel Beckett, and Robert Browning. His most recent book of poetry, *Koppar Köldüs*, appeared in 1991. In 1966 Tandori won second prize in an international competition for younger poets organized by PEN International. His other awards are the Graves Prize (1972); the Milán Füst Creative Award (1975); the Sándor Weöres Prize (1990); the Getz Prize (1994); and the Kossuth Prize (1998).

Translations: *Birds and Other Relations,* ed. Bruce Berlind (Princeton, N.J.: Princeton University Press, 1986), a Hungarian–English edition; *Selected Poems,* trans. Bruce Berlind (Princeton, N.J.: Princeton University Press, 1986); five poems in *The Colonnade of Teeth: Modern Hungarian Poetry,* ed. George Gömöri and George Szirtes (Newcastle upon Tyne: Bloodaxe, 1996), 202–5; four poems in *Modern Hungarian Poetry,* ed. Miklós Vajda (New York: Columbia University Press, 1977), 265–67; five poems in *Ocean at the Window,* ed. Albert Tezla (Minneapolis: University of Minnesota Press, 1980), 361–66; two poems in *Turmoil in Hungary: An Anthology of Twentieth-Century Hungarian Poetry,* ed. and trans. Nicholas Kolumban (St. Paul, Minn.: New Rivers), 54–56; "Baalbeck Hotel," in *Thy Kingdom Come: 19 Short Stories by 11 Hungarian Authors,* ed. Peter Doherty, Gyöngyi Köteles, and Zsófia Bán, trans. Eszter Molnár (Budapest: Palatinus, 1999).

Tar, Sándor (b. 1941) Hungarian poet and short-story writer. Tar was born in Hajdúsámson. After graduating from a technical secondary school for the machine industry, he was employed as a factory worker for a number of years, an experience that stood him in good stead when he began depicting in his fiction the harsh conditions suffered by laborers. Tar began his literary career as a poet, his first poems appearing in the Debrecen monthly *Alföld.* He eventually settled in Debrecen, where he became a freelance writer best known for his short stories and social documentaries. His first volume of stories, *A 6714-es személy* (Person No. 6714), appeared in 1981 and was followed by two other collections, *Ennyi volt* (There Were So Many) and *A te országod* (This Land of Yours), a collection of new and old stories, both published in 1993. Tar's world is mainly that of the Hungarian peasantry and the urban poor in the Great Plains area of northern Hungary, whose wretched life he depicts in unflinching, down-to-earth terms. Of particular concern to him is the ruinous impact on peasant life and agriculture of the forced collectivization of the communist years. However, Tar surprised his readers with his first novel, *Szürke galamb* (The Gray Pigeon, 1996), a change-of-pace murder mystery with all kinds of surprise twists and elements of the absurd and surreal. Although known for his realism, Tar puts on an unexpected and impressive display of stylistic pyrotechnics in his best work to date.

Translations: "Enclosure," trans. Judith Sollosy, in *The Kiss: Twentieth Century Hungarian Short Stories,* selected by István Bart (Budapest: Corvina, 1993), 374–96; "Sermon on the Mount," trans. Krisztina Horvath and Martin Baker, in *Give or Take a Day: Contemporary Hungarian Short Stories,* ed. Lajos Szakolczay (Budapest: Corvina, 1997), 187–96; "Thy Kingdom Come," in *Thy Kingdom Come: 19 Short Stories by 11 Hungarian Authors,* ed. Peter Doherty, Gyöngyi Köteles, and Zsófia Bán, trans. Eszter Molnár (Budapest: Palatinus, 1999); "A Winter's Tale," trans. Eszter Molnár, in *Present Continuous: Contemporary Hungarian Writing* ed. István Bart (Budapest: Corvina, 1985), 261–77.

Tartler, Grete (b. 1948) Romanian poet. A Bucharest native, and a member of Romania's ethnic-German community, Tartler studied the viola at the Conservatory of Music, from which she graduated in 1972. While a teacher of the viola at a secondary school, she enrolled in Bucharest University to study Arabic and English. By the time she got her degree in 1976, she had published two volumes of verse. Four more volumes followed: *Hore* (Dancing the Hora, 1977); *Scrisori de acreditare* (Credentials, 1982); *Substituiri* (Entailed Estates, 1983); and *Achene zburătoare* (Winged Achenes,

1986). In addition to her poetry, Tartler has published two books of essays, several books of nursery rhymes for children, an anthology of contemporary German poetry, and a number of translations of German and Arabic poetry. In 1978 and 1985, she was awarded the Poetry Prize of the Writers Union. She was also honored by the Romanian Academy in 1982 and has served as Romania's cultural attaché in Vienna. Motifs reflecting Tartler's musical and Arabic interests appear often in her poetry, which while generally weightier intellectually than that of other contemporary Romanian women poets is also marked by whimsy, playfulness, and greater accessibility.

Translations: *Orient Express,* trans. Fleur Adcock (Oxford: Oxford University Press, 1989); seven poems, trans. Liviu Bleoca, in *An Anthology of Romanian Women Poets,* ed. Adam J. Sorkin and Kurt W. Treptow (New York: East European Monographs, 1994), 87–95; seven poems in *15 Young Romanian Poets: An Anthology of Verse,* trans. and ed. Liliana Ursu (Bucharest: Eminescu, 1982), 81–87; ten poems in *Silent Voices: An Anthology of Contemporary Romanian Women Poets,* trans. Andrea Deletant and Brenda Walker (London: Forest, 1986), 131–41.

Tatarka, Dominik (1913–1989) Slovak novelist. Born in Plevník, near Považská Bystrica, Tatarka received his undergraduate degree from Charles University in Prague in 1938, following which he studied at the Sorbonne in Paris for a year. When he returned to Czechoslovakia, he settled in Bratislava where he taught French from 1939 to 1944 and worked as an editor, a position he held until 1963. In 1963/1964, he was employed as a dramatic adviser in the film industry in Bratislava, after which he became a full-time freelance writer. His first major publication was the novel *V úzkosti hľadania* (In the Anguish of the Search, 1941). His next work, which appeared only after the war and the communist takeover of Czechoslovakia, was *Farská republika* (The Parish Republic, 1948), a caustic look at the World War II "independent" Slovak republic under Josef Tiso. Tatarka then came out with a socialist realist hack work, *Prvý a druhý úder* (The First and Second Blow, 1950), a solid communist war novel in which the hero, Reptiš, becomes a partisan first in the Ukraine and then in Slovakia and later becomes a mighty builder of socialism as a builder of bridges. It was followed by *Radostník* (A Cheerful Man, 1954) and two more works in the 1950s of a nonfictional character: *Človek na cestách* (A Man on the Road, 1957), a description of travel through Europe and Mongolia, and *Rozhovory bez konca* (Conversations Without End, 1959). Tatarka's next major novel, *Panna zázračnica* (The Miraculous Maiden, 1964), about the impact of an offbeat young woman named Anabella on a sardonically portrayed circle of young artists and intellectuals, anticipated the literature of the 1960s and won Tatarka a prize. He later wrote a screenplay based on the novel for a film by Stefan Uher.

One of Tatarka's most personal and interesting works, *Démon súhlasu: Fantastický traktát z konca jednej epochy* (The Demon of Conformism: A Fantastic Treatise from the End of an Epoch), published first in journals in 1956 and then in book form in 1963, was in fact a confessional in which he ruminates in a spirit of deep disenchantment on those factors that inclined him to cooperate with totalitarianism by writing socialist realist novels in the 1940s and 1950s and the impact of the revelations at the Soviet Twentieth Party Congress of 1956. Similarly personal is *Prútené kreslá* (Wickerwork Chairs, 1963), the title referring to the chairs of Parisian outdoor cafés. The book is a rather lyrical and nostalgic evocation of the year Tatarka spent as a young man at the Sorbonne in Paris not long before the outbreak of World War II. In 1968, five years after *Prútené kreslá,* Tatarka published *Proti démonom: Výber stati o literatúre a výtvarníctve* (Against the Demons: A Collection of Essays About Literature and Painting). The essays in the collection, some dating from as early as 1940, deal with a wide variety of writers, including Dostoevsky, Knut Hamsun, François Mauriac, and Rilke, as well as with architecture and painting. The volume also includes a "Manifesto of Socialist Humanism" in which Tatarka expresses a qualified support for the doctrine of socialist realism, which in his view would permit free experimentation.

In response to his denunciation of the Soviet invasion of Czechoslovakia in 1968, Tatarka was denied permission to publish after 1969. His response to the ban appeared only later and outside Czechoslovakia in the form of his most provocative literary work, *Písačky* (Jottings, 1984), published in Cologne, Germany. Regarded as a singular event in Slovak prose, Jottings is one long celebration of and hymn to freedom in the form of an autobiographical novel of a totally uninhibited sexual nature. It is divided into three volumes: *Písačky* (Jottings); *Sám proti noci* (Alone Against the Night, 1984); and *Listy do večnosti* (Letters to Eternity, 1988). *Písačky* was followed by the less explosive *Navrávačky* (Tapings, 1986), also published in Cologne. As evidence of Tatarka's official status as a "nonperson," even as late as 1987 his name was completely excluded from the multivolume *Dejiny slovenskej literatúry 4: Slovenská literatúra po roku 1945* (History of Slovak Literature 4: Slovak Literature After 1945), published by the Slovak Pedagogical Publishing House in Bratislava.

Literature: Peter Petro, "The Audacity of Tatarka," in *Modern Slovak Prose: Fiction Since 1954*, ed. Robert B. Pynsent (London: Macmillan, 1990), 50–58. In 1980 the French journalist Bernard Noël visited Tatarka in Bratislava and wrote a brief account of his meetings with the Slovak writer under the title *La Recontre avec Tatarka* (Encounter

with Tatarka, 1986), actually an excerpt from a larger travel book on Czechoslovakia that appeared separately to coincide with the French publication of *Démon súhlasu: Fantastický traktát z konca jednej epochy* as *Le Démon du consentement; La fin d'une époque: Traité fantastique,* trans. Sabine Bollack (Le Roeulx, Belgium: Talus d'approché, 1986).

Translations: "The Demon of Conformism" (abridged), trans. Peter Petro, *Cross Currents* 6 (1987): 285–97; "Mystery," trans. Milan Pomichalek and Peter Schermer, in *Good-bye, Samizdat: Twenty Years of Czechoslovak Underground Writing,* ed. Marketa Goetz-Stankiewicz (Evanston, Ill.: Northwestern University Press, 1992), 47–49.

Taufer, Veno (b. 1933) Slovenian poet, playwright, critic, and translator. Taufer was born in Ljubljana and graduated from Ljubljana University with a degree in comparative literature in 1960. He served as editor of the review *Revija 57* until it was banned in 1959. From 1966 to 1969, Taufer worked for the BBC in London. When he returned to Slovenia, he accepted a position in the cultural section of Slovenian Radio and Television. He was also a manager of the experimental theater group Oder 57. After Slovenia became independent, Taufer was employed by the Ministry of Foreign Affairs and the Ministry of Culture. His books of poetry include *Svinčene zvezde* (Stars of Lead, 1958); *Jetnik prostosti* (Prisoner of Freedom, 1963); *Vaje in naloge* (Exercises and Assignments, 1969); *Podatki* (Data, 1972); *Pesmarica rabljenih besed* (Songbook of Second-Hand Expressions, 1975); *Ravnanje žeblev in druge pesme* (Hammering Nails and Other Poems, 1979); *Tercine za obtolčeno trobento* (Tercets for a Dented Trumpet, 1985); *Vodenjaki* (Water Sprites, 1986; translated as *Waterlings*), for which he won the Jenko Prize of the Slovene Writers Association; *Črepinje* *pesmi* (Shards of Poems, 1989); *Še ode* (More Odes, 1996); and the haiku-like *Kosmi* (Flakes, 2000). Four volumes of his selected poetry have also been published: *Prigode* (Occasions, 1973); *Sonetje* (Sonnets, 1979); *Pesmi* (Poems, 1980); and *Nihanje molka* (Swinging a Rosary, 1994). As a poet, Taufer began as an exponent of modernism but soon became known for his avant-garde experimentation. Typical of his style is the poem "Koncert v naravi" ("Open-Air Concert") from the *Jetnik prostosti* collection, whose first stanza reads:

> she with tin legs
> with an hourglass in her mouth and an
>   aquarium in her head
> he with all the town's staircases on his
>   back
> under his arm a heart that is easily
>   wound up or stopped.

Taufer's translations of such American and British poets as T. S. Eliot, Ted Hughes, and Wallace Stevens are highly regarded, as are his translations from the Croatian, Macedonian, and Serbian. Taufer is also the author two plays, both variations of classical myths: *Prometej ali tema v zenici sonca* (Prometheus, or The Darkness in the Pupil of the Sun, 1968) and *Odisej in sin ale Svet in dom* (Odysseus and Son, or The World and the Home, 1990). He has also written two books on the theater: *Ob londonskem gledališkem poldnevniku* (On the London Stage of the Meridian, 1970) and *Avantgardna in eksperimentalna gledališča: Opis tiskane dokumentacije* (Avant-garde and Experimental Theaters: A Description of Printed Documentation, 1975). In 1995 Taufer was awarded the Central European Prize in Vienna, and the following year, the Prešeren Prize for lifetime achievement.

Translations: *Waterlings,* trans. Milne Holton and Veno Taufer (Evanston, Ill.: Northwestern University Press, 2000); three poems, including the nine-part "Non-Metaphysical Sequence," trans. Milne Holton, in *The Imagination of Terra Incognita: Slovenian Writing, 1945–1995,* ed. Aleš Debeljak (Fredonia, N.Y.: White Pine, 1997), 220–28; six poems, trans. Veno Taufer and Michael Scammell, in *New Writing in Yugoslavia,* ed. Bernard Johnson (Baltimore: Penguin, 1970), 179–84.

Ťažký, Ladislav (b. 1924) Slovak novelist, short-story writer, and essayist. A solid and extraordinarily prolific writer, Ťažký was born in Čierny Balog, where he received his early education. He worked for a time as a forester (his father's profession) until caught up in World War II and ordered to the eastern front. During the Slovak National Uprising, he was taken prisoner by the Romanians, but escaped from an internment camp in Romania, only to be captured by the Hungarians. He was sent to a labor brigade in Austria and took part in the rebuilding of Vienna until the end of the war. After working at different jobs for a few years, in 1948 he entered the Advanced School of Politics and Economics in Prague, where he studied law, economics, history, and diplomacy. Following his studies, he settled in Bratislava. From 1952 to 1957, he was employed as a reporter in the cultural section of the Central Committee of the Slovak Communist Party, following which he pursued further studies for the next three years at the Institute of Social Studies in Prague. After graduating, Ťažký devoted the next several years to writing. In 1967 he became an editor at the daily *Smena,* but his condemnation of the Warsaw Pact invasion of Czechoslovakia cost him his position, his membership in the Communist Party, and the right to publish or hold a regular position. It was only in 1973 that he could accept a job with the central office of the State Folk Art Company, which he held until 1979. He subsequently resumed his career as an imaginative writer and a journalist on a full-time basis. After the political upheaval of November 1989, he became honorary chairman of the Association of Slovak Writers and a member of the governing board of the Matica slovenska state publishing house and cultural institution. He now holds the honorary chairmanship of the presidium of Matica slovenska. Ťažký was twice a candidate for the presidency of the Slovak Republic.

Ťažký's literary career began relatively late, with a book of short stories about the war published in 1962 under the title *Vojenský zbeh* (The Army Deserter). But neither this work nor *Hosť majstra čerta* (The Guest of Master Devil), which was published the same year, attracted much attention. He did better, however, with his longer story *Dunajské hroby* (Danubian Graves, 1964) largely, in the view of critics, because he drew on his own experiences during World War II instead of merely acting as a conduit for those of others, as in his two previous works. *Dunajské hroby* relates the attempt by several Slovak soldiers who have escaped German capture to reach home across the frozen Danube. Ťažký repeated the same basic approach with even greater success in his most highly regarded work, the overdrawn trilogy *Ámenmária, samí dobrí vojaci* (Amen Mary, All Good Soldiers, 1964). Set during the war, the novel addresses the fate of the Slovak army, ordered by the wartime Slovak fascist state to fight with German troops against the Soviets. The subject of Slovak–German collaboration was a literary taboo, which Ťažký was among the first to break. The novel's not fully convincing narrator-hero is the army sergeant Matúš Zraz, who is meant to typify those Slovak soldiers who refused to fight against the Soviets and indeed wanted to give up fighting altogether. Toward the end of the novel, which has a strong finish, Zraz openly defies his German officers by neglecting his military duties in order to continue writing his account of his experiences, which in fact survives his death. *Ámenmária, samí dobrí vojaci* is generically related to Vladimir Mináč's mythopoeic treatment of the Slovak National Uprising of 1944 in his unabashedly procommunist trilogy *Generácia* (Generation, 1958, 1959, 1961) and that part of Rudolf Jašík's huge *Mŕtvi nespievajú* (The Dead Do Not Sing, 1961) that deals with the fate of two Slovak divisions on the eastern front.

Ťažký's next publication, *Kŕdeľ divých Adamov* (The Tribe of Wild Adams, 1965), comprises the previously published *Dunajské hroby* in addition to two new stories, *Divý Adam* (Wild Adam) and *Hriešnica žaluje tmu* (The Sinner Laments the Dark). Ťažký's obsession with Slovakia during World War II, while as strong as ever, now assumes a more balladic treatment. The novel *Pivnica plná vlkov* (Cellar Full of Wolves, 1969) traces the destiny of a family of farmers during the war and in the period of the postwar collectivization of their village. Communist critics complained, however, that in its too narrow focus the novel ignored the broader social dimensions of the issue. As if chastened by the criticism, Ťažký returned to the war theme in such subsequent novels as *Pochoval som ho nahého* (I Buried Him Naked, 1970) and *Evanjelium čatára Matúša* (The Gospel of Sergeant Matuš, 1979). But he then abandoned it in favor of more socially oriented subjects beginning with the story collection *Márie a Magdalény* (Marys and Magdalenes, 1983), which pays homage to Slovak women as the saviors of the race and nation. The novel *Aj v nebi je lúka* (There's a Meadow Even in the Sky, 1985), about a very poor man's stoic acceptance of his fate, was Ťažký's next work and was followed by another novel, *Pred potopom* (Before the Deluge, 1988), dealing this time with the personal relations among workers at a Danubian hydroelectric plant. Two novels of a contemporary social character, both with a youth orientation—*Smrt obchádza štadióny* (Death Avoids Stadiums, 1990) and the psychological detective novel *Kto zabil Ábela* (Who Killed Abel, 1991)—marked Ťažký's literary entry into the 1990s. These works were followed, in turn, by a series of novels devoted to the subject of Slovak emigration in past and more recent times: *Fantastická Faidra (Žena, ktorá strašne seba ľubila)* (Fantastic Faidra: The Woman Who Loved Herself Terribly, 1991); *Dvanásť zlatých monarchov* (Twelve Golden Monarchs, 1992); and *Maršalova dcéra* (The Marshal's Daughter, 1993).

Ťažký's nonfiction prose consists mainly of essays gathered in such collections as *Ozvena svedomia* (Echo of Conscience, 1970) and *Literárne vrásky: Spomienkové eseje* (Literary Wrinkles: Recollective Essays, 1996), which contains three lengthy essays from 1976 and sheds light especially on Ťažký's work in film. *Testament svedomia* (Testament of Conscience), which appeared in 1996, is a book of conversations between Ťažký and Jozef Leickert, the spokeman of the Slovak president. Ťažký's most recent works are the novels *Zjavenie sabiny* (The Sabine's Revelation, 1997); *Vystúpila z obrazu* (She Stepped Out of the Picture, 1998); and *Útek z Neresnice* (Flight from Neresnica, 1999). Ťažký has been honored on several occasions for his writing: in 1968 with the Matica slovenska Prize; in 1994 with the Jozef Cíger Hronský Prize; and in 1966 with the Ľudovit Štúr Prize for his journalistic work.

Temesi, Ferenc (b. 1949) Hungarian novelist and short-story writer. A native of Szeged, Temesi was trained as a teacher of Hungarian and English. He eventually moved to Budapest, where, since 1975, he has worked wholly as a freelance writer and translator. His first book of short stories, *Látom nekem kell lemennem* (I See I Have to Go Down Myself), appeared in 1977. In 1993 he re-ceived the Novel of the Year Prize for the two-volume *Por I–II* (Dust I–II). His second novel, *Pest*, was published in 1996.

Translations: "A Story that K. Did Not Like At All," trans. Georgia Greist, in *Present Continuous: Contemporary Hungarian Writing*, ed. István Bart (Budapest: Corvina, 1985), 334–43; "What Did Bloodthirsty Bill, High School Student, Do Monday Night, 16 October 1972?," trans. Paul Olchváry, in *Give or Take a Day: Contemporary Hungarian Short Stories*, ed. Lajos Szakolczay (Budapest: Corvina, 1997), 197–204.

Teodorescu, Cristian (b. 1954) Romanian novelist and short-story writer. A native of Medgidia, near Constanţa on the Black Sea,. Teodorescu received his degree in Romanian language and literature from Bucharest University in 1980. He then spent the next five years teaching at a school in Ciocăneşti, Dâmboviţa district, after which (excluding a six-month period of unemployment) he became first a reader for the literary reviews *România literară* and *Contemporanul* and then, in 1988, an editor at *România literară*, to which he has regularly contributed. Teodorescu began his writing career in 1983 when some of his works were included in a collection of stories by young writers (*Desant '83*) compiled by the literary critic and professor Ovid S. Crohmălniceanu. His first published volume of short stories, *Maestrul de lumini* (Light Director, 1985), received the Writers Union Prize for a first work. In 1988 Teodorescu came out with his first novel, *Tainele inimei* (Mysteries of the Heart). A second volume of short stories appeared in 1996 under the title *Povestiri din lumea nouă* (Stories from the New World), for which he was awarded the prize of the Constanţa literary review, *Tomis*, and the prize of the Constanţa branch of the Writers Union. Teodorescu has also received the Liviu Rebreanu Foundation Prize; the prize of the literary review *Ateneu;*

and the Romanian Academy Prize. In the spirit and style of photographic realism, much of Teodorescu's writing exposes the contradictions between the grim social realities and injustices of the Nicolae Ceaușescu period and the images of Romanian life in official propaganda.

Translations: "Dollinger's Motorcycle," in *The Phantom Church and Other Stories from Romania,* ed. and trans. Georgiana Farnoaga and Sharon King (Pittsburgh: University of Pittsburgh Press, 1996), 62–66.

Teodorescu, Virgil (pseudonyms Virgil Rareș and Cocoi Taalat; 1909–1987) Romanian poet. An important figure in pre– and especially post–World War II Romanian literary surrealism, Teodorescu was born in Cobadin in the Constanța area. After his early education in local schools and high school in Constanța, he studied literature and philosophy at Bucharest University, from which he graduated with a master's degree in 1935. He made his first important debut, under the pseudonym Virgil Rareș, with poems published in 1928 in the poet Tudor Arghezi's (1880–1967) literary review, *Bilete de papagal.* Rareș was but one of a series of pseudonyms Teodorescu used at various times in his career. In 1932 he edited the avant-garde Constanța review *Liceu,* only two numbers of which appeared, and in which he published poems under the pseudonym Cocoi Taalat. He subsequently joined the editorial staffs of several progressive literary reviews of the time. In the 1940s he was a member of the Bucharest surrealist group, which also included Gellu Naum, Paul Păun, Gherasim Luca, and Trost (Adolf Trost). Two of his poems written in 1940, "Poema în leopardă" ("The Poem in the Leopard"), a text in Romanian and a nonsense language, and, with Păun and Trost, "Diamantul conduce mâinile ("Diamonds Guide the Hands"), remain unpublished except for short excerpts. In 1945 Teodorescu

published two books of poems, *Blănurile oceanelor* (The Cloaks of the Oceans) and *Butelia de Leyda* (The Electric Jar), in the Surrealist Collection. These were followed by another two collections of poems in French, *Au lobe du sel* (To a Pinch of Salt) and *La Provocation* (The Provocation), both published in 1947 in the avant-garde collection *Infra-Noir.* Teodorescu's later volumes of poetry include *Scriu negru pe alb* (I Write Black on White, 1955); *Drepturi și datorii* (Rights and Obligations, 1958); *Semicerc* (Semicircle, 1964); *Rocadă* (Castling, 1966); *Corp comun* (Common Body, 1968); *Vîrsta cretei* (The Age of Chalk, 1970), an anthology of poems from his previous collections, as well as a number of previously unpublished poems from the period 1931 to 1941; *Poemul întîlnirilor* (The Poem of Encounters, 1971); *Sentinela aerului* (Sentinel of the Air, 1972); *Ucenicul nicăieri zărit* (The Missing Pupil, 1972); *Heraldica mișcării* (The Heraldry of Motion, 1973); *Poezie neîntreruptă* (Uninterrupted Poetry, 1976); *Legea gravitației* (The Law of Gravitation, 1979); and *Culminația umbrei* (The Culmination of Darkness, 1980). In 1968 Teodorescu was appointed vice president of the Romanian Writers Union; in 1972, editor in chief of *Luceafărul;* and in 1974, president of the Writers Union.

Translations: Four poems, trans. Leon Levițchi, in *Like Diamonds in Coal Asleep: Selections from Twentieth Century Romanian Poetry,* ed. Andrei Bantaș (Bucharest: Minerva, 1985), 213–19.

Țepeneag, Dumitru (b. 1937) Romanian novelist and short-story writer. Țepeneag was in the forefront of the younger generation of writers at the end of the 1960s who were opposed to the rigid social and cultural controls of the Communist Party and sought to break out of the narrow confines of socialist realism in literature. He had published two novels, *Exerciții* (Exercises,

1966) and *Frig* (Cold, 1967), before his collection of stories *Aşteptare* (Waiting, 1971) was withdrawn from Romanian bookstores in official censure of his increasing radicalism in the early 1970s. He was then permitted to travel to Paris, where he subsequently learned of his loss of Romanian citizenship. Despite his new status as an exile in the French capital, Ţepeneag's literary activity continued unabated. From 1975 to 1980, he held the position of editor of *Cahiers de l'Est,* a journal for Eastern European writers in exile. He also published several works in French, among them *Exercices d'attente: Récits* (Exercises in Waiting: Stories, 1972), a French version of *Aşteptare; Arpièges* (Arpeggios, 1973); and *Les Noces nécessaires* (The Shotgun Wedding, 1977). After 1980, when he left the editorship of *Cahiers de l'Est,* Ţepeneag withdrew from further public activity, devoting his time mainly to chess, about which he also published a book, *La Défense Alékhine* (The Alekhin Defense, 1983). He resumed his career as a creative writer with the publication in 1984 of the novel *Le Mot sablier* (The Hourglass Word). *Roman de gare* (The Train-Station Novel) followed in 1985.

After the fall of the regime of Nicolae Ceauşescu in 1989, Ţepeneag, again able to publish in Romania, came out with two books in the early 1990s recounting his exile from Romania and his early experiences as an exile in Paris: *Zadarnică e arta fugii* (The Futile Art of Running, 1991) and *Român la Paris: Pagini de jurnal, 1970–1972* (A Romanian in Paris: Pages of a Journal, 1970–1972, 1993). In 1997 the Cartea Românească publishing house of Bucharest brought out a valuable collection of short articles and other materials by Ţepeneag and the poet Leonid Dimov titled *Momentul oniric* (The Oniric Moment). Dating from the period 1968 to 1971, the articles are related to the neosurrealistic oniric movement in postwar Romanian literature. Edited by Corin Braga,

the volume also includes previously unpublished pages of Ţepeneag's diary from 2 to 25 August 1974. In 1998 Ţepeneag published *Călătorie neizbutită* (An Unsuccessful Trip), a description of a return trip to Romania in late 1995 when he and the French writer Alain Robbe-Grillet (some of whose works Ţepeneag had translated into Romanian) were invited to the French Cultural Institute in Timişoara for "Francophone Days." Subsequent acrimonious interviews in the press and elsewhere during Ţepeneag's stay in Cluj and Bucharest, mostly turning on the place of the émigré/exile writer in Romanian literature, soured Ţepeneag on his return to Romania, hence the title of the work. Ţepeneag subsequently published two more novels in France, *Hotel Europa* (1996) and *Pont des arts* (The Bridge of Art, 1998).

Translations: "The Accident," in *The Phantom Church and Other Stories from Romania,* ed. and trans. Georgiana Farnoaga and Sharon King (Pittsburgh: University of Pittsburgh Press, 1996), 112–19. *Aşteptare* is available in French as *Exercices d'attente: Récits,* trans. Alain Paruit (Paris: Flammarion, 1972); also available are *Hotel Europa,* trans. Alain Paruit (Paris: P. O. L., 1996); *Les Noces nécessaires,* trans. Alain Paruit (Paris: Flammarion, 1977); and *Pont des arts,* trans. Alain Paruit (Paris: P. O. L., 1998).

Tetzner, Gerti (b. 1936) German novelist and short-story writer. Tetzner was born in the village of Wiegleben, Thuringia, and received her early education both there and in nearby Gotha. In 1955 she began legal studies at Leipzig University, receiving her degree in 1959. After practicing law for three years, she gave up the profession in favor of a literary career, studying for two years at the Johannes R. Becher Institute of Literature in Leipzig. However, uncertain as to whether she could succeed as a writer, she worked at a variety of odd jobs until the success of her first (and most highly regarded) novel, *Karen W.* (1974), enabled her to devote full time to writing. She subsequently settled in Berlin. The story of a woman who agonizes over her decision but finally breaks out of a marriage she feels has no future, *Karen W.* situates Tetzner in the ranks of such East German feminist writers as Brigitte Reimann, Irmtraud Morgner, and especially Christa Wolf, a major influence on her career. Tetzner's other works include *Maxie* (1979); *Das Verwandlungshaus* (The Makeover House, 1985); *Im Lande der Fähren* (In the Land of the Ferries, 1988), which she wrote with her husband, Reiner Tetzner; *Bilder aus Dänemark* (Pictures from Denmark, 1988); *Mit dem Fahrrad übers Meer* (Across the Sea by Bike, 1989); and *Eines schönen Sonntags* (One Fine Sunday, 1993).

Translations: "Karen W." (excerpt from *Karen W.*), trans. Dorothy Rosenberg, in *Daughters of Eve: Women's Writing from the German Democratic Republic,* ed. and trans. Nancy Lukens and Dorothy Rosenberg (Lincoln: University of Nebraska Press, 1993), 23–29.

Tišma, Aleksandar (b. 1924) Serbian novelist, short-story writer, and playwright. A native of Horgoš , Tišma studied philosophy at Belgrade University and then went into journalism. He has served as director of the Matica Srpska publishing house in Novi Sad and as an editor of the journal *Letopis matice srpske*. The great majority of Tišma's works deal with the German and Hungarian occupation of Serbia during World War II and the atrocities carried out against the Jewish population. Although Tišma began his literary career in 1951 with his story "Ibikina kuća" ("Ibika's House"; reprinted, 1973, in the collection *Mtrvi ugao* [The Dead Angle]), his reputation began to develop only with the publication in the 1960s of such novels as *Krivice* (Guilt, 1961) and *Za crnom devojkom* (In Search of the Dark Girl,

1969), and a collection of short stories under the title *Nasilje* (Violence, 1965). His most resonant novels about the war and the Holocaust include *Knjiga o Blamu* (*The Book of Blam*, 1972), about a converted Jew named Miroslav Blam who survives the brutal Hungarian occupation of his native Novi Sad, a major provincial town on the eastern Danube; *Upotreba čoveka* (*The Use of Man*, 1980), a denser novel than *The Book of Blam* in which the diary of a lonely German-language teacher in Novi Sad frames a tale of the interlocking fortunes of members of different families, Jewish and gentile, during and immediately after the war; and *Kapo* (1987), a somber novel about a Bosnian Croatian Jew raised as a Catholic who degrades himself as a kapo (or prisoner guard) in Auschwitz and becomes obsessed after the war with tracking down a Jewish woman he abused and humiliated in the concentration camp and who survived the war. Between *The Use of Man* and *Kapo*, Tišma wrote the rather melodramatic, and weaker, novel *Vere i zavere* (Trust and Betrayal, 1983), about the son of a Novi Sad dentist whose practice was built on that of a murdered Jew. During the war, the son (Sergije) falls in love with a partisan fighter who is eventually captured and shot. After the war, Sergije, now a diplomat in Warsaw, becomes involved in a romantic intrigue that culminates in the death of a colleague. He is returned to Yugoslavia, where he begins a new career as an editor in a publishing house specializing in popular romances. But his misfortune with women results in an unhappy marriage and a troublesome relationship with the German-Austrian wife of a former Nazi's son.

Tišma's novels about the Holocaust in Yugoslavia, and in Novi Sad in particular, contain some of the most graphic depictions of the atrocities to appear in postwar Yugoslav literature and offer at the same time a bleak perspective on the plight of the human spirit in a world of unspeakable barbarism and cruelty. Tišma was honored with the NIN Prize for *The Book of Blam* in 1977 and, two years later, with the Andrić Prize for *Škola bezbožništva* (The School of Atheism), a depressing tale of Tolstoyan fatalism about a small government clerk who cannot get ahead because his father was a peasant who refused to surrender his land to the collective and, when the land is taken away from him anyway, commits suicide.

Tišma has also published a book of essays, *Pre mita* (Before the Myth, 1989), dealing with nationalism in Yugoslavia, especially Serbia, and three other collections of stories set in the wartime and postwar periods: *Povratak miru* (Return to Peace, 1977); *Bez krika* (Without a Cry, 1980); and *Iskušenja ljubavi* (Temptations of Love, 1995). Tišma's stories are peopled with average citizens burdened with problems of everyday existence over which they have little or no control. Tišma has little good to find in Yugoslavia under the communists and depicts a socialist society as drab and spiritless, a society in which the individual has few incentives to try to improve his or her lot.

Translations: *The Book of Blam,* trans. Michael Henry Heim (New York: Harcourt Brace Jovanovich, 1998); *Kapo,* trans. Richard Williams (New York: Harcourt Brace Jovanovich, 1993); *The Use of Man,* trans. Bernard Johnson (San Diego: Harcourt Brace Jovanovich, 1988); "Personality," trans. Celia Williams, in *New Writing in Yugoslavia,* ed. Bernard Johnson (Harmondsworth: Penguin, 1970), 143–62. *Vere i zavere* is available in German as *Treue und Verrrat,* trans. Barbara Antkowiak (Munich: Hanser, 1999).

Titel, Sorin (1935–1985) Romanian novelist and short-story writer. One of the most highly regarded prose writers of the post–World War II period, Titel was born in the village of Margina, in the Timiş region.

He attended schools in Lugoj (1945–1948) and Caransebeş (1948–1953), receiving his high-school diploma in the latter, and then went on to study Romanian literature at Bucharest University from 1953 to 1956. He interrupted his studies to work for a year in Cluj, after which he taught school in Cârpa, in the Caraş-Severin region, as a substitute teacher. In 1962 he took a state examination that qualified him for his undergraduate degree. Titel then found employment as an editor for *Orizont* magazine in Timişoara and held the position from 1962 to 1971. He then moved to Bucharest, where he became an editor at *România literară*. His first collection of stories, *Copacul* (The Tree), appeared in 1963 and was at once compared with the writings of Alan Fournier and Antoine-Marie Saint-Exupéry, in their spare compressed style with elements of the lyrical and symbolic. *Copacul* was followed by the novella *Reîntoarcerea posibilă* (The Possible Return, 1966), which is particularly interesting for Titel's abandonment of linear narration in favor of a multiple narrative structure; another collection of short prose, *Valsuri nobile şi sentimentale* (Noble and Sentimental Waltzes, 1967); two more novellas, *Dejunul pe iarbă* (The Lunch on the Grass, 1968) and *Noaptea inocenţilor* (The Night of the Innocents, 1970); and Titel's first novel, and arguably his best, *Lunga călătorie a prizionerului* (The Prisoner's Long Journey, 1971), a work reminiscent of Kafka, and to some extent Beckett, and one in which critics have seen the influence of the French *nouveau roman*.

After *Lunga călătorie a prizionerului,* Titel produced another novella, *Mi-am amintit de zăpadă* (I Am Reminded of Snow, 1973), before returning to the novel with such texts as *Ţsara îndepărtată* (The Far-off Land, 1974); *Pasărea şi umbra* (The Bird and the Shadow, 1977), which was awarded the Writers Union Prize; *Clipa cea repede* (The Sudden Moment, 1979); *Femeie, iată fiul tău*

(Woman, Behold Your Son, 1983), which deals with the mythology of the decline of the Hapsburg monarchy; and *Melancholie* (Melancholy, 1988). Titel's talents as an essayist are much in evidence in his essay on Herman Melville, *Herman Melville, fascinația mării* (Herman Melville and the Fascination of the Sea, 1975), who appealed to Titel as a kindred writer of allegory and parable, and in his collection of critical pieces, *Pasiunea lecturii* (The Joy of Reading, 1976).

Translations: "She Wants Me to Climb the Stairs," in *The Phantom Church and Other Stories from Romania,* ed. and trans. Georgiana Farnoaga and Sharon King (Pittsburgh: University of Pittsburgh Press, 1996), 69–73. *Lunga călătorie a prizonierului* is available in French as *Le Long Voyage du prisonnier,* trans. Marie-France Ionesco (Paris: Denoël, 1975).

Todorovski, Gane (b. 1929) Macedonian poet, essayist, and critic. A prolific poet and prose writer, Todorovski was born in Skopje and educated in that city university's Faculty of Philosophy, from which he eventually received his doctorate. He began his career as a journalist in 1947 and from 1954 to 1992 taught Macedonian and Croatian literatures at the Faculty of Philosophy. A member of the Macedonian Academy of Arts and Sciences, Todorovski has also served as his country's ambassador to Russia. His first published volume of poetry, *Vo utrinite* (In the Dawns), appeared in 1951. Although it conforms for the most part to the conventions of then obligatory socialist realism in both its contents and its classical metrics, Todorovski introduced the subjective elements that became more prominent in his subsequent poetry. This is especially evident in his simple but moving "In Place of Flowers," on the death of his sister. Todorovski's second volume, *Trevožni zvuci* (Notes of Alarm, 1954), was full of the restlessness, pessimism, and sense of hopelessness then fash-

ionable in Macedonian poetry. These moods, however, became muted in such subsequent collections of poems as *Spokoen čekor* (A Quiet Step, 1956); *Božilak* (Rainbow, 1960); *Apoteoza na delnikot* (Apotheosis of the Working Day, 1964); *Čas po pcosti i nežnosto* (A Time for Curses and Tenderness, 1966); *Gorčlivi goltki nepremolk* (Bitter Gulps of Utterance, 1970); *Sneubaven den* (Unbeautified Day, 1974); *Skopjani* (Skopje People, 1981); *Zborovi od zemja i od zlato* (Words of Earth and Gold, 1985), an edition of selected poems from most of his collections through 1981; *Nevolici, neverici, nesonici* (Needfulness, Heedfulness, Sleeplessness, 1987); *Neka se rodi čovek* (Let a Man Be Born, 1993); and *Nedostižna* (An Unapproachable Woman, 1995).

As his career developed, certain trends became discernible in Todorovski's poetry. Although he occasionally abandoned conventional meters for free verse, he remained faithful to the simplicity of syle and diction for which he has long been admired. Often personal and confessional, Todorosvki also has demonstrated a capacity for humor, as is evident, for example, in "Poem to a Robot" from *Gorčlivi goltki nepremolk* and in his personal poetic credo "The Poem I Ought to Write" from the same collection:

> My poem should be attractive,
> with a bit of laughter, a bit of rage and
> sin . . .
> It should be attractive enough for
> writers to envy it,
> for publishers to republish it
> and, having once been heard, to be
> forever embraced
> by listeners.

Todorovski is also an ardent Macedonian patriot who has made his country's troubled history, its long struggle for freedom, its culture, and its monuments the subject of a number of his poems.

Besides his poetry, Todorovski has published over eleven volumes of essays, literary criticism and history, and Macedonian historiography. They include such works as *Traktati za sonceljubivite: Esei i zapisi na makedonski temi* (Tractates on the Heliotropes: Essays and Notes on Macedonian Themes, 1974); *Veda Slovena* (The Wisdom of the Slavs, 1979); *So zbor kon zborot: Prilozi kon makedonistikata* (With Words Toward Words: Contributions to Macedonian Studies, 1985); *Neodlazni ljubopitstva* (Urgent Curiosities, 1987); *Istoriografski temi* (Historiographical Themes, 1990); *Zborot i nepokorot: Panorama na makedonskata poezija vo XIX veka* (The Word and Disobedience: A Panorama of Nineteenth-Century Macedonian Poetry, 1993); and *Stranici za makedonofilstvo* (Partisans for Macedonofilism, 1994), on the Macedonian question during the period 1878 to 1912. Macedonian poets and revolutionary figures such as Dane Gruev (1871–1906), Gorce Petrov (1864–1921), Konstantin Miladinov (1830–1862), Kočo Racin (1909–1943), and Raiko Žinzifov (1839–1877) figure prominently both in his poetry and in his critical and historical writing. Todorovski was also the author of a biography of the Croatian poet Antun Matoš (1873–1944). An active translator throughout his career, Todorovski has published over thirty books of translations of poetry from Albanian, Czech, Bulgarian, Croatian, English (Edgar Allan Poe, Robert Frost), German, Russian, Serbian, and Slovenian. He has been the recipient of such Macedonian literary honors as the 11 October, 13 November, Brothers Miladinov, Clement of Ohrid, and Dimitar Mirev prizes.

Literature: Miroljub Stojanović, *Gane Todorovski, poezija i poetika* (Skopje: Makedonska revija, 1990).

Translations: *Lonely Voyager,* ed. Ljubica Todorova-Janešlieva, trans. Graham W. Reid, Ljubica Todorova-Janešlieva, and Peggy Reid (Skopje: Detska Radost, 1996); *Poems* (Bradford: Bradford University Press, 1976).

Țoiu, Constantin (b. 1923) Romanian novelist, short-story writer, and essayist. One of the most gifted and highly regarded contemporary Romanian prose writers, Țoiu was born in Urziceni. After graduating from high school in Brașov, he studied in the Faculty of Letters and Philosophy at Bucharest University, from which he graduated in 1946. He subsequently worked as an editor with such journals and reviews as *Luceafărul, România literară*, and *Secolul XX*. He broke into print with short stories published in *Gazeta literară* in 1958. His first novel, *Moartea în pădure* (Death in the Woods), appeared in 1965. Neither it nor Țoiu's collection of stories, *Duminica muților* (The Sunday of the Mute, 1968), attracted much critical attention, and he spent the next several years writing his most celebrated novel, *Galeria cu viță sălbatică* (A Gallery of Wild Vine, 1976). Widely praised as one of the most significant Romanian literary events in decades, the novel was awarded the Writers Union Prize in 1977 and a prize of the Romanian Academy in 1978. Dense and richly textured, the work in essence traces the downfall of a literary editor (Chiril Merișor) who becomes innocently involved in what the authorities regard as a political conspiracy. The editor is believed to have taken his own life by hanging at the end of the novel, but the manuscript of an important work by him has been successfully smuggled out of the country by an Italian journalist and is eventually published. *Galeria cu viță sălbatică* was followed by another four novels between 1981 and 1999: *Însoțitorul* (The Companion, 1981); *Obligado* (1984); *Căderea în lume* (The Descent into the World, 1987); and *Barbarius* (1999). A fine craftsman, admired for his elegance of style, Țoiu often uses his characters to address the matter of narration itself, as in

Însoțitorul. This is especially evident also in his most recent novel, *Barbarius,* in the figure of Rânzei, a kind of alter ego of the central character, the seventy-three-year-old Cezar Zdrăfculescu, a former overzealous public prosecutor during the Stalinist period who immigrated to Italy in the 1960s and returned to Romania only after the downfall of Nicolae Ceaușescu. Much of the novel, which Romanian critics have compared with Thomas Mann's *Death in Venice,* is taken up with Zdrăfculescu's revisiting places and people linked to his past. Comic and erotic at the same time, *Barbarius* is arguably Țoiu's finest novel after A Gallery of Wild Vine. Țoiu's essays, generally short, incisive, and concerned with questions of aesthetics and literature, predominantly Romanian, appear in the collections *Destinul cuvîntelor* (The Fate of Words, 1971); *Pretexte* (Pretexts, 1973); *Alte pretexte* (Other Pretexts, 1977); *Prepeleac* (The Peg, 1991); *Caftane și cafteli: Prepeleac doi, trei* . . . (Caftans and Capes: Peg Two, Three . . . , 1994); and *Morsus diaboli: Prepeleac patru* (Morsus diaboli: Peg Four, 1998), which won the essay prize of the Romanian Writers Union in 1998. Țoiu participated in the University of Iowa's International Writing Program in October and again in December 1978 and published short articles about his experiences in the United States in his *Prepeleac* columns.

Translations: *Galeria cu vița sălbatică* is available in French as *L'Exclu,* trans. Georges Barthouil and Llinca Barthouil-Ionesco (Paris: Nagel, 1981).

Tokarczuk, Olga (b. 1962) Polish novelist. One of the most highly regarded contemporary Polish literary figures, Tokarczuk was trained in psychology at Warsaw University. She made her literary debut in 1993 with her metaphysical novel *Podróż ludzi księgi* (The Journey of the People of the Book), which won a prize in the literary competition sponsored by the Association of Polish Book Publishers. This was followed by the novel *E. E.* (1995), which is set in Wrocław (formerly Breslau) in the first decade of the twentieth century and features a fifteen-year-old heroine named Erna Eltzner (E. E.) who suddenly acquires parapsychological abilities. *Prawiek i inne czasy* (Prawiek and Other Times, 1996), her first work so far to have attracted international attention, plays with concepts of time and place. Tokarczuk's goal is to demonstrate that everything that happens, every individual event, is an instrument of time that is ultimately unnecessary to time, which moves on regardless. Prawiek, the name of a small town where the novel is set, can also mean "distant or remote time" in Polish. It is in a sense the universal past. Further emphasizing the element of space in time is the division of the novel into a large number of small units each called *czas* (time) and bearing the name of the individual character who figures in it. The result is an intriguing picture of small-town relationships that are relativized into meaninglessness when taken in the totality of the time process.

Dom dzienny, dom nocny (*House of Day, House of Night,* 1998) was nominated for the prestigious NIKE Prize for the best novel of the year and on 25 June 2002 was awarded the Berlin Brücke Prize. Set in Nowa Ruda, an out-of-the-way town on the Czech border, where Tokarczuk herself lives, the novel addresses essentially the same issues of time and space as *Prawiek i inne czasy.* It is arranged in small units, each separately titled and each devoted to a past, present, or future event in the lives of individuals, various aspects of the town physically and topographically, and even the author herself. Of the many discrete units of which the novel is composed, the most curious is a fifteen-page "Life of Saint Kummernis (Also Known as Wilgefortis)," which Tokarczuk says she picked up in a bookstore in Wambierzyce and faithfully reproduces. The likelihood is that the saint's life is an invention of Tokarczuk herself. As in *Prawiek i inne czasy,* every individual thing, no matter how small, is part of something bigger, which, in turn, is part of something even bigger, so that no matter how small something may be it has a place in the general scheme and meaning of things. The search for that greater meaning of life occupies all the characters who in various ways straddle the border between the everyday and the fantastic. *Szafa* (The Closet), which also appeared in 1998, consists of three stories: the very short title story about the mysterious magnetic power of a particular closet; "Numery" ("Numbers"), the longest story of the three, built around the narrator's fascination with hotel rooms and what they reveal of their occupants; and "Deus ex," about the curious inventions of a computer whiz. Tokarczuk's most recent work, *Lalka i perła* (The Doll and the Pearl, 2001), is not a piece of fiction but an unconventional reading of the famous nineteenth-century Polish novel *Lalka* (*The Doll,* 1888) by Bolesław Prus (real name Aleksander Głowacki) inspired by Czesław Miłosz's free translation (1983) of "The Hymn of the Pearl."

Translations: *House of Day, House of Night,* trans. Antonia Lloyd-Jones (London: Granta, 2002). *Prawiek i inne czasy* is available in French as *Dieu, les temps, les hommes et les anges,* trans. Christophe Glogowski (Paris: Laffont, 1998).

Tomov, Aleksandur (b. 1944) Bulgarian novelist, poet, short-story writer, screenwriter, and playwright. Tomov was born in Sofia, where he completed high school in 1962 and graduated from Sofia University in 1970 with a degree in Bulgarian literature. From 1971 to 1981, he worked as an editor at Radio Sofia and, from 1981 to 1991, as a screenwriter for Bulgarian Feature Film Studios. After publishing a poem for children and a fairy tale, both in 1973, Tomov published his first major

collection of stories, *Ulitsa kum predgradieto* (Street to the Suburb), in 1977. It was followed in 1978 by the volume of poems *Kvartal Nadezhda* (District Hope); in 1983, by *Elegiia za ptitsi* (Elegy for Birds), another collection of stories; and in 1984, by *Luminestsentii baladi* (Luminescent Ballads), a book of ballads, and *Svetata Ana* (The Holy Ana), his third volume of stories. *Pamet* (Memory), a collection of stories, and *Melnitsa za vetrovete* (The Windmill), a novel, appeared in 1985 and 1986, respectively. *Koruptsiia* (Corruption), a two-volume novel, came next in 1989 and 1990; it was expanded to three volumes in 1991. *Absurdna liubov* (Absurd Love), Tomov's fourth collection of prose fiction, appeared in 1990; *Zdrach i pechal* (Dusk and Sorrow), an intriguing collection of sixteen tales with elements of the mythological, bizarre, and macabre, in 1992; *Siankata na edin sun* (The Specter of a Dream), a volume of stories, in 1994; *Razkazi* (Stories), another volume of stories, in 1995; *Novobogatashi* (Nouveaux Riches), a novel, in 1997; and *Esenta na surtseto* (The Autumn of the Heart), a volume of selected stories, in 1998. Tomov's only volume of essays, *Arhipelazi na duha* (Archipelagos of the Spirit), was published in 1995. Tomov is essentially an urban writer with a strong interest in exploring the social and psychological dimensions of conflicts and currents in the big city's poorer outlying neighborhoods, which to Tomov represent squalor and boredom. Apart from the more serious aspects of his writing, Tomov is a good storyteller who reads easily. Although his works have been translated into several languages, including German and Spanish, he has yet to appear in English.

Topalov, Kiril (b. 1943) Bulgarian novelist. A native of Sofia, Topalov was educated in local schools and graduated from Sofia University in 1968 with a degree in Bulgarian literature. From 1969 to 1971, he worked at the Institute of Bulgarian Language of the Bulgarian Academy of Sciences and, from 1971 to 1974, pursued graduate studies in Bulgarian literature at Sofia University. In 1974 he defended his dissertation on the poetry of the Bulgarian National Revival, and in 1982 he became a docent at Sofia University specializing in the literature of the National Revival. An authority also on contemporary Greek literature, Topalov spent the academic year 1978/1979 teaching at Athens University. He has also taught at the University of Provençe in France (1992–1994).

Apart from his fictional writing and his work as an editor at the Sofia publishing house Bulgarski pisatel (1977–1988), Topalov is a well-known literary scholar who has published a number of studies of Bulgarian literature, most dealing with the National Revival and liberation. They include the two-volume *Vuzrozhdentsi* (The Awakeners, 1988, 1990); monographs on such major literary figures as Hristo Botev (1848–1876) and Peto Slaveikov (1827–1895); a biography of Georgi Stoikov Rakovski (1821–1867), one of the leading figures in the drive for Bulgarian independence; two books on outstanding Bulgarian churchmen, *Svetogorskiiat buntar: Neofit Bovzeli* (The Svetogorski Rebel: Neophyte Bovzeli, 1982), about Archimandrite Neofit Bovzeli (ca. 1780–1848), and *Grigor Purlichev: Zhivot i delo* (Grigor Purlichev: Life and Work, 1982); and *Ventsenosetsut* (Wreathed in Laurel, 1993), about Saint Grigor Purlichev (1830–1893). Topalov first attracted attention as a creative writer with his short novel for children and young readers, *Biagai . . . Obicham te* (Flee . . . I Love You, 1976), which was made into a film. His serious interest in children and especially in the plight of abandoned illegitimate children is reflected in such subsequent works of fiction as *Budi blagoslovena* (Be Blessed, 1979) and *Ne se surdi, choveche* (Don't Get Angry, Man, 1982).

Topalov's critical attitude toward contemporary moral and social values, his sense of the growing aliention of the individual, his interest in crime and punishment, and his ability to create intrigue and psychologically complex characters come together nicely in his novels *Od tuk do horizonta* (From Here to the Horizon, 1980); *Staina temperatura* (Room Temperature, 1985); *Razminavane* (Exchange, 1986); and *Nervi* (Nerves, 1989; rev. ed., 1994). His most recently published novel is the satirical *Maimunska istoria* (Story of a Monkey, 1997). Topalov has also had a successful career as a dramatist on the basis of such generally "light" plays and comedies as *I esen idat shturkeli* (Storks Come Even in Autumn); *Pritcha za filosofa* (A Fable About a Philosopher); *Svobodno suchinenie za sluntseto* (Free Composition on the Sun); *Eksperimentut* (The Experiment); *Viva akademiia* (Long Live Academia); *Strashniiat sud* (The Terrible Judgment); *Nervi za liubov* (Nerves for Love); *Biznes* (Business); *Igra na muzh i zhena* (A Play of Husband and Wife); and *Znak, che sme zhivi* (Sign of Life). In June 1998, Topalov was named Bulgarian ambassador to Greece.

Topol, Jáchym (b. 1962) Czech novelist, poet, and journalist. The son of the dramatist Josef Topol, Topol was born and educated in Prague. One of the bright stars of the postcommunist Czech cultural scene, Topol did investigative reporting for the weekly *Respekt* before founding his own review, *Revolver*. He was also the lyricist for such rock groups as Národní třída; Psí vojáci, led by his younger brother Filip; and Naěva. His three collections of poetry, which were originally published in samizdat between 1985 and 1988, were reissued in 1991 under the title *Miluju tě k zbláznění* (I Love You Madly). In 1992 he published a new collection, *V úterý bude válka* (The War Will Be on Tuesday). His first novel, *Sestra* (Sister, 1994; translated as *City Sister Silver*), was a critical success. A huge explosive work of the imagination, free form in structure and at times almost hallucinogenic, it offers the best view yet of the amoral, hedonistic, hustling, and cynical postcommunist Czech youth. The novel won the prestigious Egon Hostovský Prize for best novel of the year. It was followed in 1995 by the novellas *Výlet k nádražní hale* (*A Trip to the Train Station*) and *Anděl* (Angel), in which Topol again demonstrates his knowledge of and skill at depicting the seamy underside of postcommunist Prague, with its foreign hustlers and native criminal element.

Literature: Tomáš Weiss, *Jáchym Topol: Nemůžu se zastavit* (Prague: Portal, 2000), an interesting book of interviews with Topol that sheds much light on his life, career, and outlook.

Translations: *City Sister Silver*, trans. Alex Zucker (North Haven, Conn.: Catbird, 2000); *A Trip to the Train Station*, trans. Alex Zucker (Brno: Petrov, 1995), an illustrated Czech–English edition.

Topol, Josef (b. 1935) Czech playwright. A talented, if not very well known, dramatic writer, Topol was born in the small town of Poříčí, on the Sázava River near Prague, and moved to the capital at the age of eighteen to work in the theater run by the renowned Czech director E. F. Burian. His first play, *Půlnoční vítr* (The Midnight Wind, 1956; premiere 1955), was a Shakespearean historical tragedy in verse written for this theater. In the late 1950s, the director Otomar Krejča encouraged Topol to write for the Prague National Theater, of which he had become head in 1956 (Krejča remained in this position until 1961 and was also the theater's principal director until 1964). Topol obliged him by writing two of his best plays, *Jejich den* (Their Day, 1962; premiere 1959), a Chekhovian social drama set in a provincial town on a single day about young people attempting to deal with identity crises, and *Konec masopustu* (End of Carnival, 1963; premiere 1964), arguably

Topol's best work for the stage, which was also performed in Vienna and Paris but to lackluster response. An intricate, dark, and in some ways elusive play about collectivization of farms in a small village, *Konec masopustu* is set against the annual Shrovetide carnival, whose masks and symbolism form an integral part of the dramatic action. When Krejča opened a new theater, Divadlo Za branou (Theater Beyond the Gate), in 1965, Topol wrote his well-regarded *Kočka na kolejích* (*Cat on the Rails*, 1965) for the occasion. This is a bleak play essentially about a young man and a woman who seem to lack purpose in life, love but cannot commit to marriage, and at the end appear to opt for suicide while sitting on rails in the path of an oncoming train. Its relative brevity, stark simplicity, focus on essentials, and nonpolitical character are typical of Topol's dramatic writing after 1963. This is evident in his two short plays, *Slavík k večeři* (Nightingale for Supper, 1967) and *Hodina lásky* (Hour of Love, 1968), both deeply pessimistic in outlook. The first is a Gothic tale of horror; the second, an intensely expressionistic work about the illusion of the permanence of love and the relentless, irreversible passage of time. Although Theater Beyond the Gate was closed in the 1970s in the wake of the invasion of Czechoslovakia in 1968, Topol continued working as a translator (he had translated Shakespeare and Chekhov for Krejča) until 1977, when as a signatory of Charter 77 he was not permitted to publish or perform any more works for the stage. During this period, he wrote *Dvě noci s dívkou, aneb, Jak okrást zloděje* (Two Nights with a Girl, or How to Rob Thieves, 1972), which was inspired by the opera *The Marriage of Figaro*; *Sbohem, Sokrate!* (Goodbye Socrates!); and *Hlasy ptáků* (The Voices of Birds). Despite the prohibition on Topol, *Dvě noci s dívkou, aneb, Jak okrást zloděje* was performed a few times outside Prague, whereas the other two works could reach the stage only after the collapse of communism in Czechoslovakia.

Translations: *Cat on the Rails,* trans. George Voskovec and Christine Voskovec, in *Czech Plays: Modern Czech Drama,* selected and introduced by Barbara Day (London: Nick Hern, 1994), 95–138. *Konec masopustu* is available in French as *Fin de carnaval,* adapted by Milan Kepel, Avant-scène, no. 438 (Paris, 1969); *Dvě noci s dívkou, aneb, Jak okrást zloděje* in German as *Zwei Nächte mit einem Mädchen, oder, Wie man Diebe bestiehlt* (Vienna: Universal, 1972); and *Hodina lásky* as *Stunde Liebe: Ein Traum im Spiel* (Vienna: Universal, 1969).

Tozaj, Neshat (b. 1943) Albanian novelist and short-story writer. A native of the village of Kallarat, near Vlorë, Tozaj studied law at the Faculty of Political Science in Tirana. He is known primarily for spy novels and short stories reflective of Albanian paranoia about foreign and domestic plots against the regime in the time of Enver Hoxha. These include such collections of stories as *Takimi i fundit* (The Last Meeting, 1976); *Në gjurmë të të tretit* (On the Track, 1979); *Rrëmbimi i arkivit* (The Theft of the Archives, 1977); and *Bisede për një shok* (Talks About a Friend, 1988) and the novels *Dora e ngrohtë* (The Warm Hand, 1983); *Në emër të popullit* (In the Name of the People, 1984); *Mes nesh* (In Our Midst, 1986); *Thikat* (The Knives, 1989); *Pragu i tjetërsimit* (The Other Threshold, 1994); and *Turpi* (Shame, 1998). Several of Tozaj's works have been made into films. Arguably the best of his tales of intrigue is *Thikat,* a fictionalized treatment of the case involving the explosion of a bomb on the grounds of the Yugoslav Embassy in Tirana. What would appear to be nothing more than the isolated act of a deranged person turns into a monstrous power play by the Ministry of the Interior (for which Tozaj worked), intent on uncovering a nonexistent plot against the state. The candor with which Tozaj exposes the mind-set of people in power in Albania in the time of the novel made the work a considerable success and elicited a favorable review from Ismail Kadare in the Tirana literary newspaper *Drita.* Since the downfall of communism in Albania, Tozaj has written a book of memoirs, *Pse flas: Retrospektivë* (Why Talk? Retrospectives, 1993); a collection of three novellas (a "triptych") titled *Pervërset* (Perversity, 1994); a political commentary, *Diktatura dhe demokracia në Shqipëri* (Dictatorship and Democracy in Albania, 1996); and a novel, *Turpi* (Shame, 1998).

Trefulka, Jan (b. 1929) Czech novelist, short-story writer, literary critic, and screenwriter. A native of Brno, Trefulka studied literature and aesthetics in Prague and Brno and worked as a tractor driver before serving as editor (1962–1968) and then editor in chief (1969–1970) of the journal *Host do domu.* He made his debut as a writer of fiction with the novella *Pršelo jim štěstí* (It Rained Luck for Them, 1962), which offered a sombre picture of young people in the Stalinist period. This was followed by *Třiatřicet stříbrných křepelek* (Thirty-Three Silver Doves, 1965), the title being a well-known Czech tongue twister, and the short-story collections *Výmysly* (Contrivances, 1966) and *Nálezy pana Minuse* (The Discoveries of Mr. Minus, 1966). After 1968 he was prohibited from publishing his works in Czechoslovakia, and so his first book after the ban, *Velká stavba* (The Great Construction Project), which like *Pršelo jim štěstí* is set in the Stalinist period, could appear first only in an Edice Petlice samizdat edition in 1971 and then in book form in Cologne in 1982. In similar fashion, his next book, *O bláznech jen dobré* (Speak No Ill of Fools), a portrait of a kindhearted eccentric in a provincial town in southern Moravia, which appeared first as an underground publication in 1973, came out in print in Toronto in 1978. His next book, *Zločin pozdvížení: Variace na staré téma* (The Crime of Disturbance: Variations on an Old Theme), about a social revolution, first circulated in manuscript form in 1976 until it was printed in Cologne in 1978. *Svedený a opuštěný* (Seduced and Abandoned), which first appeared underground in 1983, was published in Toronto in 1988.

Translations: "Belleview" and "The World's Glory: A Feuilleton About a Festive Day," trans. Jan Drabek, in *The Writing on the Wall: An Anthology of Contemporary Czech Literature,* ed. S. Antonin Liehm and Peter Kussi (Princeton, N.J.: Karz-Cohl, 1983), 176–211, 212–16; "A Czech Fairy Tale," trans. Milan Pomichalek and Anna Mozga, in *Good-bye, Samizdat: Twenty Years of Czechoslovak Underground Writing,* ed. Marketa Goetz-Stankiewicz (Evanston, Ill.: Northwestern University Press, 1992), 37–41.

Tribuson, Goran (b. 1948) Croatian novelist, short-story writer, playwright, essayist, and art historian. A prolific and popular representative of Croatian postmodernism, Tribuson was born in Bjelovar where he was educated through high school. He then went on to earn a degree in the Faculty of Philosophy of Zagreb University, where he also pursued postgraduate studies. After a period of employment in a marketing agency, he became a freelance writer. In 1978 he joined the Croatian Writers Association. Tribuson's first important publication was the short-story collection *Zavjera kartografa* (The Mapmaker's Conspiracy, 1972). He subsequently published five additional collections of stories: *Praška smrt: Groteske* (Death in Prague: Grotesques, 1975), which as the title suggests is situated in the city of Kafka; *Raj za pse* (A Dogs' Paradise, 1978); *Spavaća kola* (The Sleeping Car, 1983); *Klasici na ekranu* (Classics on Screen, 1987); and *Zvijezda kabareta* (Cabaret Star, 1998). He is also the author of fourteen novels: *Snijeg u Heidelbergu* (Snow in Heidelberg, 1980); *Čuješ li nas Frido Štern* (Do You Hear Us, Frido Štern, 1981); *Ruski rulet I i II* (Russian Roulette I and II, 1982); *Polagana predaja* (Slow Surrender, 1984); *Legija stranaca* (The Foreign Legion, 1985); *Zavirivanje* (Peeping, 1985); *Uzvratni susret* (Rematch, 1986); *Made in U.S.A.* (1986); *Povijest pornografije* (The Story of Pornography, 1988); *Siva zona* (Gray Area, 1989); *Potonulo groblje* (The Sunken Grave, 1990), for which he won the K. S. Gjalski Award in 1991; *Dublja strana zaljeva* (The Farther Side of the Bay, 1991); *Sanatorij* (Sanatorium, 1993); and *Noćna smjena* (Night Shift, 1996).

Tribuson is a lively, energetic writer who borrows freely from the techniques of fantastic literature, the horror genre, the mystery novel, and intertextuality. He is easily situated in the postmodernist current influenced, for example, by the Argentine writer Jorge Luis Borges, and is also grouped by Croatian critics with other Croatian admirers of the American novelist J. D. Salinger. Tribuson is very much at home in the world of pop culture, especially American pop culture. His works brim with allusions to American films, and jazz and rock music are common leitmotifs in his fiction. Musicians such as Miles Davis, Coleman Hawkins, John Coltrane, Bruce Springsteen, Bob Dylan, Eric Clapton, the Beatles, and the Rolling Stones are all part of the fabric of his writing. Tribuson is a skilled writer of mystery fiction, which usually has a definite social dimension in his work; he has said that his favorite detective is a "cynic and moralist along the lines of [Raymond Chandler's] Philip Marlowe."

In 1997 Tribuson published a book of autobiographical notes titled *Rani dani* (Early Days); in 1999, a new collection of short stories, *Trava i korov: Novi zapisi o odrastanju* (Grass and Weeds: New News on Growing Up), which includes the three longer texts

"Kuća koja je otputovala u Ameriku" ("The House that Traveled to America"), "Škola gitare" ("The School of Guitar"), and "Dnevnik rock freaka" ("The Diary of a Rock Freak"); and in 2000, a new mystery novel, *Bijesne lisice* (Savage Foxes). Tribuson is also the author of a monograph on the Croatian watercolorist Antun Mates (b. 1945), published in 1996, and, perhaps surprisingly, a play about the Croat–Serb conflict during the wars of the 1990s, "Dovidjenje u Nustru" ("Till We Meet Again in Nuštar," 1992), which brings together on the front lines two Croats who live elsewhere and who rediscover their roots in the circumstances of battle.

Tryzna, Tomek (b. 1948) Polish novelist. Tryzna's reputation as an intriguing storyteller rests wholly on his much praised first novel, *Panna nikt* (*Miss Nobody*, 1993), subtitled *Tajemnicza powieść o dojrzewaniu* (A Mysterious Novel About Reaching Maturity). It is a sensual, erotic work about lesbian love, sensitively written by a man in the naive, simpleminded style of his heroine, a fifteen-year-old Polish girl whose life gradually assumes a nightmarish aspect when her family moves to a new town (Walbrzych). After reading the novel, Czesław Miłosz wrote that the subtitle should include "Only for Adults" or "Only for Readers over 40," the age in which it was permitted pious Jews to read the books of the Cabala.

Translations: *Miss Nobody,* trans. Joanna Trzeciak (New York: Doubleday, 1999).

Tsanev, Stefan (b. 1936) Bulgarian poet, playwright, and essayist. A native of the village of Chervena voda, in the Ruse region, Tsanev completed high school in Ruse and then studied journalism at Sofia University, graduating in 1959. He subsequently graduated in dramaturgy from the Moscow Film Institute, in 1965. From 1959 to 1960, he was a correspondent for *Narodna mladezh* in the Rodope Mountains; he then worked as an editor at Bulgarian Feature Film Studios (1965–1967) and as dramatic adviser to the Bulgarian State Satirical Theater (1967–1970), the Theater of the Provinces (1970–1973), the Theater Sofia (1973–1984, 1991), and the Dramatic Theater in Plovdiv (1984–1991). Tsanev's first published book was *Chasove* (Hours. 1960), a collection of poetry. It was followed by another eleven volumes of poems: *Kompozitsii* (Compositions, 1963); *Hroniki* (Chronicles, 1965); *Perigei ili nai-goliamoto priblizhavane do zemiata* (Perigei, or The Biggest Arrival on Earth, 1967); *Parapeti* (Parapets, 1968); *Az pitam! Stihotvoreniia i poemi* (I Ask: Shorter and Longer Poems, 1975); *Rekviem* (Requiem, 1980); *Lirika* (Lyrics, 1983); *Poemi* (Poems, 1984); *Nebesni premezhdiia* (Heavenly Mishaps, 1986); *Sezonut na iliuziite: Liubovni stihotvoreniia* (The Season of Illusions: Love Poems, 1988); and *Spasete nashite dushi!* (Save Our Souls!, 1992).

Tsanev's sometimes bitterly ironic poetry is characterized by a questioning attitude toward the abstract ideals of communism and a willingness to address such issues as the social and technical revolution and its impact on the individual, the nature of authority, and people's right to spiritual freedom. In the interest of humanity, Tsanev denounces war, decries the ease with which humans kill one another, and laments the wrongs of the world. Some of his poetry is in a style reminiscent of the expressionistic militancy of the Russian revolutionary poet Vladimir Mayakovsky, whose works Tsanev has translated into Bulgarian.

Tsanev's plays, in which parody and the grotesque appear frequently and a few of which are built around historical personages, deal with much the same themes as his poetry. They include *Istinkiiat Ivailo* (The Real Ivailo, 1962); *Protsesut protiv bogomilite* (The Case Against the Bogomils, 1969); *Subota '23* (Saturday the 23rd, 1978); *Poslednata nosht na*

Sokrat (Socrates's Last Night, 1986), un-
doubtedly Tsanev's best-known play outside
Bulgaria; *Tainata vecheria na Diakona Levski*
(The Last Supper of Deacon Levski, 1987);
Strashniat sud (Judgment Day, 1988); and
Drugata smurt na Zhana d'Ark (The Other
Death of Joan of Arc, 1989–1990). A volume
of Tsanev's plays, *Piesi*, published in 1992,
contains *Protsesut protiv bogomilite*,
Poslednata nosht na Sokrat, *Dragata smurt na
Zhana d'Ark*, and *Zhivotut—tova sa dve zheni*
(That's the Life—Two Wives). In 1991 Tsanev
wrote a play titled *Paranoia* specifically for
the English stage; it was performed by the
Royal Court Theatre in London. His book of
essays, *Ubiitsite sa mezhdu nas: Eseta i pritchi*
(Murderers Among Us: Essays and Stories),
which came out in 1996, is a collection of very
short, breezy pieces, many in dialogue form,
on a wide variety of subjects, including a few
of his speeches on Bulgarian drama, on why
the Bulgarians have lacked jesters, his participation in a contemporary international poetry festival in Australia in 1982, the debit side
of the introduction of democracy in Bulgaria, the alienation of the intelligentsia from
the people, and the suicide of Mayakovsky.

Translations: Six poems in *Clay and Star:
Contemporary Bulgarian Poets*, trans. and
ed. Lisa Sapinkopf and Georgi Belev (Min-
neapolis: Milkweed, 1992), 91–97; two
poems, trans. Roland Flint, in *Poets of Bul-
garia*, ed. William Meredith (Greensboro,
N.C.: Unicorn, 1985), 80–83; three poems,
trans. Marvin Bell, in *Window on the Black
Sea: Bulgarian Poetry in Translation*, ed.
Richard Harteis, in collaboration with
William Meredith (Pittsburgh: Carnegie
Mellon University Press, 1992), 173–75.

Tudor, Corneliu Vadim (b. 1949) Romanian
poet, essayist, and political figure. An ultra-
nationalist and former "court poet" of the
Romanian communist dictator Nicolae
Ceauşescu, Tudor attracted considerable attention nationally and internationally when
he became a candidate for the Romanian
presidency in the December 2000 runoff
election as head of the Partidul România
Mare (Greater Romania Party). Known for
his unapologetic nationalism and his tirades
(mostly in the unsigned "Ideals" section of
the weekly *Săptămîna*) against Hungarians,
Jews, and Gypsies, Tudor is not an untal-
ented writer or a mere political hack. He has
a commendable grasp of Romanian history,
which serves as the basis of his claim that
Romania and Romanians have been dealt
with unfairly through the ages, and he takes
deep pride in the accomplishments of Romanian poets and artists and in the richness
of the Romanian language. In his book of
essays *Istorie şi civilizaţie* (History and Civilization, 1983), he cites pridefully the evidence of a growing interest in the United
States, for example, in Romania and its culture and presents himself throughout as a
staunch communist and supporter of the
Ceauşescu regime. A second book of essays
along similar lines, *Mîndria de a fi români:
Eseuri, recenzii, medalioane* (The Pride of
Being Romanians: Essays, Reviews, Portraits), was published in 1986. The same
year, a collection of Tudor's poetry from
1976 to 1986 appeared under the title *Mira-
cole* (Miracles), with a foreword by the similarly nationalistic writer Eugen Barbu, for
whom Tudor has high praise in an essay in
*Mîndria de a fi români: Eseuri, recenzii,
medalioane*. As a poet, Tudor is conservative
in style and metrics and writes primarily of
traditional Romanian virtues, the nobility
of the Romanian people, the beauty of the
Romanian language (e.g., "Ode to the Romanian Language"), the Romanian past, his
love of the Romanian landscape in the different seasons, fresh and faded love, his
youth and family, and so on. Tudor's personal account of the tumultuous days of
1989 and 1990 is recorded in *Jurnalul Revo-
luţiei, de la Crăciun la Paşte* (The Journal of
the Revolution, from Christmas to Easter,

1999). This is a diary of events from 22 December 1989 to 16 April 1990, replete with a large number of photographs of Tudor, especially with members of the Romanian Orthodox hierarchy and prominent political figures, both Romanian and foreign. The jacket of the book has a color photograph of Tudor, in the presence of the head of the Romanian Orthodox Church, Patriarch Teoctist, giving Pope John Paul II a copy of an anthology of his own poems published in Turin in eight languages on 8 May 1999.

Tyrmand, Leopold (1920–1985) Polish novelist, journalist, essayist, and music critic. A popular writer in his time, Tyrmand left Poland in 1966, settled in the United States, and thereafter became a stern critic of communism in Poland and Eastern Europe as a whole. A native of Warsaw, he graduated from high school in 1937 and the following year left for Paris to study architecture. When World War II broke out, he was taken into custody by the Germans and sent to Germany as a forced laborer, in which capacity he worked at a variety of jobs, including seaman. He escaped from a German merchant ship in 1944 while in a Norwegian port, but was captured and sent to a concentration camp. After the liberation of Norway, he made his way back to Poland via Denmark in 1946. Once in Warsaw again, he became active as a journalist and contributed to such well-known periodicals and newspapers as *Słowo Powszechne, Expres Wieczorny,* and *Tygodnik Powszechny.* He made his literary debut in 1947 with a story published in *Przekrój,* on whose editorial staff he served from 1947 to 1949. In 1950 he began collaborating with *Tygodnik Powszechny* on a regular basis but gave up journalism in 1953 in order to devote his time to creative writing and music criticism.

As an imaginative writer, Tyrman turned to novel writing after the publication in 1947 of a book of short stories titled *Hotel Ans-*

gar. He turned out four novels: *Gorzki smak czekolady Lucullus* (The Bitter Taste of Lucullus Chocolate, 1957); *Filip* (Phillip, 1961); *Zły* (The Evil One, 1966; translated as *The Man with the White Eyes*); and *Siedem dalekich rejsów* (Seven Distant Voyages, 1975), published in London. The best known of these and a sensation when it first appeared was *The Man with the White Eyes,* the kind of hard-hitting crime novel, about the criminal underworld in contemporary Warsaw, that had no peers in Poland at the time.

After he immigrated to the United States in 1966, Tyrmand published a series of books in English and Polish (with émigré presses in London and Paris) unmasking the realities, as he saw them, of communist tyranny in Eastern Europe and describing conditions in the United States based on his own experiences. They include *Życie towarszyskie i uczuciowe* (Social and Emotional Life, 1967), published in Paris; *Explorations in Freedom: Prose, Narrative, and Poetry from Kultura* (1970) and *Kultura Essays* (1970), both based on materials published originally by the Polish émigré periodical *Kultura* in Paris; *The Rosa Luxemburg Contraceptives Cooperative: A Primer on Communist Civilization* (1971); *Tu w Ameryce, czyli dobre rady dla Polaków* (Here in America, or Good Advice for Poles, 1975), published in London; *Notebooks of a Dilettante: Encounters and Confrontations of a "US Immigrant in America"* (1976), published posthumously in Poland as *Zapiski dyletanta* (1991); and *Cywilizacja komunizmu* (The Civilization of Communism, 1992), published posthumously in London. In 1980 Tyrmand also published, in London, a two-volumes-in-one "diary" of the year 1954 (*Dziennik, 1954*), which contains much personal information against the background of the Stalinist period. *Dziennik, 1954* appeared in Poland in 1981 during the time of martial law as an underground publication. After the lifting of martial law, the entire

Dziennik, 1954 was published by a small independent press with the new subtitle *Kondycja własna* (Personal Condition).

During his years in the United States, Tyrmand turned ever more conservative in his political outlook and became a critic of American liberalism. In order to better promote his views, he founded the Rockford Institute, which published the journals *Rockford Papers* and *Chronicles of Culture*. In 1985, the year of his death, his book of antiliberal essays, *The Ugly Beautiful People: Essays in Liberal Culture,* was published.

Literature: Lidia Burska, "Leopold Tyrmand," in *Sporne postaci polskiej literatury współczesnej,* ed. Alina Brodska and Lidia Burska (Warsaw: Instytut Badań Literackich, 1996), 179–91, a good short piece on Tyrmand.

Translations: *The Man with the White Eyes,* trans. David Welsh (New York: Knopf, 1959).

Works in English: *Explorations in Freedom: Prose, Narrative, and Poetry from Kultura* (New York: Free Press, 1970); *Kultura Essays* (New York: Free Press, 1970); *Notebooks of a Dilettante: Encounters and Confrontations of a "US Immigrant in America"* (New York: Macmillan, 1976); *The Rosa Luxemburg Contraceptives Cooperative: A Primer on Communist Civilization* (New York: Macmillan, 1971); *The Ugly Beautiful People: Essays in Liberal Culture* (Lanham, Md.: University Press of America, 1985).

Udovič, Jože (1912–1986) Slovenian poet, essayist, and translator. Born in Cerknica, Udovič graduated from high school in Šentvid, near Ljubljana, and earned a degree in Slavic studies at Ljubljana University. He was interned in Italy during the early years of World War II, but in 1943 was able to return to Yugoslavia and join the partisans. After the war, he earned his living mostly as a freelance writer. A major presence in postwar Slovenian literature, Udovič began publishing poems and short prose pieces as early as 1936. His first published volume of poetry, *Ogledalo sanj* (The Mirror of Dreams), came rather late in 1961 and spans nearly a twenty-year period of time. On the basis of it, he was awarded the Prešeren Prize in 1962. Udovič's second collection, *Darovi* (Gifts), was also slow to appear, coming out only in 1975. Apart from the poems printed with those by his fellow poets Anton Vodnik and Cene Vipotnik in the volume *Pesmi* (Poems, 1975), Udovič brought out only one more collection of verse before his death, *Oko in senca* (Eye and Temples, 1982). A posthumous collection of his poems was published in 1988 as *Pesmi* (Poems). Deeply influenced by European modernism and surrealism, the latter of which he is credited with introducing into Slovenian poetry, Udovič was inspired by his wartime experiences; the world of classical antiquity; and nature, which provided a rich palette of colors and spiritual sustenance. His poems are generally short, as are his lines of verse, and his images finely chiseled, as in these excerpts from the poem "In vendar" ("And Yet") from the collection *Darovi*:

And yet throw nothing away.
Everywhere are hidden signs.
Look behind the rotted fence, behind
　　the wooden wall,
behind the old picture, into the empty
　　jug.
. . . somewhere a shelter, still
　　unknown, is hidden,
a soft lap of feathers and poems,
of azure moss and breath,
from which may arise
a new presence.

Virtually all of Udovič's postwar prose was published posthumously in such volumes as *Spremembe* (Changes, 1991), a collection of short stories; *Zapisi v tišino* (Noted in Silence, 1992), diary notes; and *Brazda na vodi* (Furrow in the Water, 1993), a book of essays. A talented and highly regarded translator, Udovič translated works by Hermann Broch, Franz Kafka, Federico García Lorca, Pablo Neruda, and Dylan Thomas, among others.

Translations: Nine poems, trans. Michael Biggins, in *The Imagination of Terra Incognita: Slovenian Writing, 1945–1995*, ed. Aleš Debeljak (Fredonia, N.Y.: White Pine, 1992), 186–93.

Ugrešić, Dubravka (b. 1949) Croatian novelist, short-story writer, author of children's books, and translator. A prominent writer before she left Croatia, Ugrešić, a Zagreb native, went into exile after being denounced for her independent views and her refusal to yield to the spirit of nationalism of the new post-Yugoslav Croatian state. Her major works of prose, which have been widely translated, reflect her liberal outlook on the Yugoslav wars of 1991 to 1995. They include *Forsiranje romana-reke* (*Fording the Stream of Consciousness*, 1991); *Na raljama života* (*In the Jaws of Life*, 1992); *Americki fikcionar* (My American Fictionary, 1993; translated as *Have a Nice Day: From the Balkan War to the American Dream*), which also deals with her travels in the United States; *Kultura laži: Antipolitički eseji* (*The Culture of Lies: Antipolitical Essays*, 1996), a collection of witty and breezy short pieces covering a wide range of contemporary Croatian and Yugoslav cultural and political topics; and *Muzej bezuslovne predaje* (*The Museum of Unconditional Surrender*, 1998), Ugrešić's first published work of fiction since the breakup of Yugoslavia and a novel in the form of fragments of various sorts (including self-contained short stories) that splendidly conveys the emotional and intellectual

dilemmas of an exile's homelessness. A highly respected translator and scholar of modern Russian literature, Ugrešić, with Aleksandar Flaker, published a study of the Russian avant-garde in 1984 and, in 1988, came out with her own book on new Russian prose of the 1970s. Her children's book *Stefica Cvek u raljama života* (Stefica Cvek in the Plows of Life, 1990) was made into a film by Art Film (Belgrade) under the direction of Rajko Grlič. Ugrešić also wrote a book on the fairy tale titled *Život je bajka: Metaterxies* (Life Is a Fairy Tale: Metaxerxes, 1983).

Translations: *The Culture of Lies: Antipolitical Essays* (London: Phoenix House, 1998); *Fording the Stream of Consciousness*, trans. Michael Henry Heim (London: Virago, 1991); *Have a Nice Day: From the Balkan War to the American Dream*, trans. Celia Hawkesworth (London: Cape, 1994; University Park: Pennsylvania State University Press, 1998); *In the Jaws of Life*, trans. Celia Hawkesworth and Michael Henry Heim (London: Virago, 1992; Evanston, Ill.: Northwestern University Press, 1993); *The Museum of Unconditional Surrender*, trans. Celia Hawkesworth (London: Phoenix, 1998); "Balkan Blues," trans. Celia Hawkesworth, in *Storm Out of Yugoslavia*, ed. Joanna Labon (London: Carcanet, 1994), 2–35.

Uhde, Milan (b. 1936) Czech playwright, short-story writer, screenwriter, poet, and literary critic. One of post–World War II Czechoslovakia's better known dramatic writers, Uhde was born in Brno, Moravia, where he studied at Brno University's Faculty of Philosophy and where, as a dramatist, he was associated with Evening Brno, a theater that began basically as a cabaret in the Moravian capital. After serving as an editor of the literary journal *Host do domu* from 1958 to 1970, he became a freelance writer in 1971. Besides radio plays (a few of which were broadcast in other countries) and film scripts, Uhde has written short stories. His fame, however, rests mainly on his play *Král Vávra* (King Vávra, 1964), which he wrote for Evening Brno. Freely based on a satirical poem by the nineteenth-century Czech writer Karel Havlícek Borovský that, in turn, was inspired by an Irish fairy tale about a king's attempt to conceal his donkeylike ears by growing his hair long, in Uhde's hands the play became a none too subtle absurdist commentary on totalitarian power. *Děvka z města Théby* (The Wench from the Town of Thebes, 1967), Uhde's second (and artistically and critically less successful) play, is a free adaptation of Sophocles' *Antigone,* intended to serve as a parable on power and the failure of idealism. Disillusioned at the end by the pointlessness of her conspiracy against Creon, Antigone turns to sensual pleasures in a vain attempt to find happiness. Uhde's other dramatic writings include *Záhadná věž* (The Mysterious Tower, 1967); *Obloha samej cvok* (Heaven of Buffoons, 1967); *Hra na holuba* (Playing at Pigeons, 1974), originally published in samizdat; *Pán plamínků* (Lord of the Flames, 1977), a television play, originally published in samizdat, from the series *Okřídlený tramvaják; Velice tiché Ave a jiné hry* (The Winged Tram Conductor: A Very Quiet Ave and Other Plays), published first in samizdat in 1986 and then in Toronto in 1988; *Hanba Angličanům: Dvě komedie z Velké Británie a Irska* (Shame on the English: Two Comedies from Great Britain and Ireland, 1987), originally published in samizdat, which includes *Král Vávra* and *Zvěstování* (The Annunciation); and *Modrý anděl* (*The Blue Angel,* 1985, 1991), an increasingly jarring dramatic work in the form primarily of a monologue spoken by a woman who is cheated out of an uncle's property by her brother and looks for recourse against him within the bureaucracy. In January 1990 Uhde became publisher of Atlantis publishers in Brno and, in June 1990, Czech minister of culture.

Translations: *A Blue Angel,* trans. Vera Pech, in *Drama Contemporary: Czechoslovakia,* ed. Marketa Goetz-Stankiewicz (New York: PAJ Publications, 1985), 127–41; *The Blue Angel,* trans. George Theiner (Brno: Atlantis, 1991); "My Desk," trans. Milan Pomichalek and Anna Mozga, in *Good-bye, Samizdat: Twenty Years of Underground Czechoslovak Writing,* ed. Marketa Goetz-Stankiewicz (Evanston, Ill.: Northwestern University Press, 1992), 110–13.

Uhse, Bodo (1904–1963) German novelist, essayist, and journalist. Born in Rastatt, Uhse was the descendant of a noble family with a long military tradition. He joined the National-Socialist German Workers' Party (NSDAP) in 1927 and edited the Nazi Party's first daily paper in northern Germany. His Nazi affiliations ended abruptly in 1930, however, when he became a member of the German Communist Party and secretary of the German Peasant Committee. When Hitler came to power, Uhse joined the large number of German antifascists immigrating to France. Like many of them, he participated in the Spanish Civil War of 1936 to 1938. With the outbreak of World War II, Uhse left Europe for Mexico, joining Anna Seghers and other left-wing German émigrés in Mexico City. His editorship of the German émigré journal *Freies Deutschland* stood him in good stead when he returned to Germany in 1948 and became editor of the journal *Aufbau.* He was also a member of the Kulturband zur demokratischen Erneuerung Deutschlands (Cultural Association for the Democratic Renewal of Germany). After the formation of the German Democratic Republic, he became politically active and served as a delegate to the East German parliament from 1950 to 1954. He was also prominent in the East German PEN Club and the Writers Union. In 1963, he took over the editorship of the journal *Sinn und Form.*

Uhse's early Nazi sympathies and subsequent turn to the political left form the subject of his autobiographical novels *Söldner und Soldat* (Mercenary and Soldier, 1935) and *Wir, Söhne* (We, Sons, 1948). "Christian Klee, der Soldat des Friedens" ("Christian Klee, Soldier of Freedom"), which is also autobiographical, remains unpublished.

As with those of other German writers who spent the war years in Mexico, some of Uhse's works have Mexican backgrounds. They include primarily a collection of stories on Mexican themes, *Mexikanische Novellen* (Mexican Novellas, 1957). Uhse's best-known work of fiction, and the only one available in English, is *Leutnant Bertram* (*Lieutenant Bertram*, 1943). Heavy on military action and the contrast between the mentality of the Nazis and that of the Germans who opposed Hitler, the novel deals with the adventures of a German Luftwaffe pilot, mostly in Spain during the Civil War. Bertram eventually harbors some doubt about the German and Italian intervention on the side of General Francisco Franco and at the end of the novel is shot down and taken prisoner by German members of the International Brigades who presumably begin his ideological reeducation. Uhse's other major works include *Die erste Schlacht* (The First Battle, 1939) and *Die Patrioten* (Patriots, 1954).

Literature: The best overview of Uhse's life and career is Klaus Walther's short *Bodo Uhse: Leben und Werk* (Berlin: Volk und Wissen, 1984). Also useful as a short introduction to Uhse's work, in particular the novels *Lieutenant Bertram* and *Die Patrioten,* is Gunter Albrecht and Karl Heinz Berger, eds., *Bodo Uhse. Eduard Claudius: Abriss der Spanienliteratur* (Berlin: Volk und Wissen, 1961), which is, however, an orthodox East German interpretation. Interesting information can also be found in the collection of correspondence between Uhse and the Czech-German writer F. C. Weiskopf: Günter Caspar, with the assistance of Margit Stragies, eds., *Briefwechsel, 1942–1948: Bodo Uhse F. C. Weiskopf* (Berlin: Aufbau, 1990). Much of the correspondence between the two writers during the war years was conducted in English when Uhse was in Mexico City and Weiskopf, a fellow exile, lived in New York City. Weiskopf's reviews of *Lieutenant Bertram,* including those in English for the *Saturday Review of Literature* and *Books Abroad,* appear in an appendix. Renata von Hanffstengel, *Mexiko im Werk von Bodo Uhse: Das nie verlassene Exil* (New York: Peter Lang, 1995), is a good account of Uhse's Mexican exile and his writings of that period.

Translations: *Lieutenant Bertram: A Novel of the Nazi Luftwaffe,* trans. Catherine Hutter (New York: Simon and Schuster, 1944).

Ujkani, Qerim (b. 1937) Kosovo Albanian poet. Born in Peć in 1937, Ujkani studied law at Belgrade University and then went to work for Radio Priština, where he was in charge of the literary section. He made his debut as a writer in 1963 with the verse collection *Hullinat* (The Furrows). Several other books of poetry soon followed, among them *Deti ose poeme e shqetsueme* (The Sea, or The Uneasy Poem, 1967); *Prralla e votrës* (The Oaken Hearth, 1968); *Pagëzimet* (Baptisms, 1969); *Antisonete* (Anti-Sonnets, 1972); *Pasthirrmë* (Interjection, 1975); *Lartësi toke* (The Height of the Earth, 1979); *Gjaku im* (My Blood, 1980); *Hije e këputur* (Torn Shadow, 1982); and *Dielli që po e krijoj* (The Sun that I'm Discovering, 1983). Two of his books have appeared in Serbo-Croatian translation, and he has translated from Serbo-Croatian into Albanian. During the turmoil in Kosovo in the 1990s, Ujtani became involved in politics and emerged as the head of the Albanian National Democratic Party (PNDSH).

Urban, Milo (1904–1982) Slovak novelist, short-story writer, and memoirist. Urban is most highly-regarded for his interwar writings, notably the trilogy *Živý bič* (The Living Whip, 1927); *Hmly na úsvite* (Mists at Dawn, 1970); and *V osídlach* (Ensnared, 1971). The best of these by far is *Živý bič*, about the changes experienced in the traditional Slovak village in part as the result of World War I. In such post–World War II novels as *Zhasnuté svetlá* (Extinguished Lights, 1957) and *Kto seje vietor* (Who Sows the Wind, 1964), Urban sought to link these works with his prewar writing by tracing social developments in Slovakia from the end of the 1930s to the outbreak of the Slovak National Uprising of 1944. But these novels in the mode of socialist realism fell below the creative level of *Živý bič*. Urban fared better, however, with his memoiristic writing, especially *Zelená krv: Spomienky hájnikovho syna* (Green Blood: Remembrances of a Gamekeeper's Son, 1970), in which he warmly describes his youth from childhood to secondary-school years. Other books of memoirs by Urban include the four-part posthumously published *Kadetade po Halinde: Neveselé spomienky na veselé roky* (Here and There Across Halinda: Unhappy Memories for Happy Years, 1992); *Na brehu krvavej rieky: Spomienky novinara* (On the Shore of a River of Blood: A Journalist's Memoirs, 1994); and *Sloboda nie je špás: Spomienky dochodcu* (Freedom Is No Joke: A Pensioner's Memoirs, 1995), completed in 1977, five years before Urban's death. In some ways it is the most interesting of his later memoirs, covering as it does the turbulent period from 1948 to the late 1970s. Apart from what it reveals of his own creative work, and his political difficulties, the volume is striking for Urban's candor in what he has to say about the wartime Slovak fascist state and, above all, its treatment of the Jews. While acknowledging that the Slovak Jews were never integrated into mainstream Slovak society, what the Slovaks did to them "under German pressure," he writes, "exceeded the limits of humanity." Urban also published two volumes of novellas, *Výkriky bez ozveny* (Shrieks Without Echoes, 1965, 1973, 1989) and *Z tichého frontu* (From the Quiet Front).

Urbánek, Zdeněk (b. 1917) Czech essayist, short-story writer, novelist, and translator. A close friend and confidant of Czech president Václav Havel, Urbánek is a highly original prose writer at home in small sketches and feuilletons and a skilled practitioner of interior monologue. His first major work was the novel *Cestou za Quijotem* (The Road to Don Quixote, 1949), which is loosely based on Quixote's young years in an Algerian prison. In his introduction to an English edition of Urbánek's short prose pieces, published as *On the Sky's Clayey Bottom* (1992), Havel wrote that when he discovered the novel in prison "I was struck by the prophetically modern quality of the work and the imaginative sense captured by a writer of fiction of what it really feels like to be a prisoner." When for political reasons Urbánek was unable to publish anything after the 1950s, he came close to becoming a forgotten writer. However, interest in him reawakened in the aftermath of the "Velvet Revolution" of 1989, when his feuilletons began appearing in the newspaper *Lidové noviny*. The same year, he also published the first volume of his novelistic trilogy, *Stvořitelé světa* (Creators of the World). In 1992 a large collection of Urbánek's short stories was published under the title *Ztracená země: Kniha próz* (The Lost Land: A Book of Prose). This was followed by a book about the Czech writers Jiří Orten (1919–1941) and Ivan Blatný (b. 1919), *Zvláštní případy* (Special Cases, 1993), and a volume of essays on the theater, *Domy plné události: Eseje o divadle a dramatu* (Houses Full of Happenings: Essays on the Stage and Drama, 1995). The second and third parts of *Stvořitelé světa* appeared in 1996 and 1997, respectively. Apart from his considerable talent as a writer of fiction and as an essayist with great literary sensitivity as well as keen political insights, Urbánek is well known as a translator of English and American literature. He has translated works by Shakespeare, T. S. Eliot, Walt Whitman, William Saroyan, and James Joyce, among others.

Translations: *On the Sky's Clayey Bottom: Sketches and Happenings from the Years of Silence,* trans. William Harkins, with a foreword by Václav Havel (New York: Four Walls Eight Windows, 1992), an excellent introduction to Urbánek that contains thirty-six short pieces selected mainly from *Ztracená země: Kniha próz.*

Uricariu, Doina (b. 1950) Romanian poet and literary scholar. Born in Bucharest, Uricariu studied French and Romanian at Bucharest University and later worked as an editor for the Eminescu publishing house. She has published seven volumes of verse: *Vindecarile* (Healings, 1977); *Jugastru sfială* (Common Maple, Shyness, 1977); *Vietați fericite* (Happy Creatures, 1980), for which she won the National Prize for Poetry; *Natura moartă cu suflet* (Animated Still Life, 1982); *Ochiul atroce* (The Evil Eye, 1985); *Institutul inimii* (The Institute of the Heart, 1995); and *Puterea leviatanului* (The Power of Leviathan, 1995). A poet of small forms, Uricariu is especially striking in poems exploring the complex emotions of a new mother toward her child before and after birth. Uricariu has also been very active as a literary scholar. She has edited several works by the Romanian writer Emil Botta (1911–1977) and is the author of a book on modern Romanian poetry titled *Ecorseuri: Structuri și valori ale poeziei românești moderne* (Appearances: The Structures and Values of Modern Romanian Poetry, 1989) and

a study of the contemporary Romanian poet Nichita Stănescu, *Nichita Stănescu: Lirismul paradoxal* (Nichita Stănescu: Paradoxical Lyricism, 1998).

Translations: Six poems in *15 Young Romanian Poets: An Anthology of Verse,* trans. and ed. Liliana Ursu (Bucharest: Eminescu, 1982), 89–93; seven poems in *Silent Voices: An Anthology of Contemporary Romanian Women Poets,* trans. Andrea Deletant and Brenda Walker (London: Forest, 1986), 143–50.

Urošević, Vlada (b. 1934) Macedonian poet, short-story writer, novelist, essayist, critic, and translator. Of Serbian origin, Urošević was born and educated in Skopje, where he has been a member of the Faculty of Philology of Skopje University since 1982. During World War II, the Bulgarians deported Urošević and his family to Serbia. In 1947, after their return to Skopje, his father, an educator, was invited by the new Macedonian government to join the recently established Faculty of Philosophy. Urošević began publishing poetry as early as 1954, three years before graduating from Skopje University. He wrote his earliest poems in Serbo-Croatian, but then switched to Macedonian as his principal vehicle of literary expression. Between 1959 and 1986, Urošević published seven volumes of poetry: *Eden drug grad* (Another City, 1959); *Nevidelica* (The Unexpected, 1962); *Leten dožd* (Summer Rain, 1967); *Dzvezdena terezija* (The Tailor's Dummy, 1973); *Nurkačko dzvono* (Diving Bell, 1975); *Sonuvačot i prazninata* (The Dreamer and the Void, 1979); and *Hipnopolis* (Hypnopolis, 1986). Highly respected as a poet, Urošević operates with a broad range of subjects of a more universal than local character.

Urošević has also published four collections of short stories, many fantastic in nature—*Znaci* (Signs, 1969); *Nokjniot pajton* (The Night Coach, 1972); *Lov na ednorozi*

(Hunting Unicorns, 1983); and *Skopski raskazi* (Skopje Tales, 1988)—and a well-regarded novel, *Vkusot na praskite* (The Taste for Peaches, 1965). He has published six volumes of essays, three of which deal mostly with Macedonian literature: *Vrsnici* (Contemporaries, 1971); *Mreža za neulovlivoto* (Net for the Uncatchable, 1980); and *Niškata na Arijadna* (Ariadne's Thread, 1986), as well as two quite interesting collections addressed to the theoretical and literary-historical aspects of the literature of the fantastic and science fiction: *Podzemna palata* (The Underground Palace, 1987) and *Demoni i galaksii* (Demons and Galaxies, 1988). His interest in the fantastic and science fiction began in earnest in the late 1960s when he spent nearly a year and a half in France on a French government scholarship. In 1976 he published an anthology of fantastic short stories in the literatures of Yugoslavia, and in 1987 completed his doctoral dissertation for Skopje University on the subect of fantastic literature and science fiction.

While in France in 1967/1968, Urošević developed a love of French poetry that led him to translate such authors as Baudelaire, Rimbaud, and Henri Michaux. In 1972 he also published an anthology of contemporary French poetry in Macedonian translation. Apart from his translations from French, Urošević has been a major translator of Macedonian literature into Serbo-Croatian. Urošević's most recent book is *Aldebaran* (1991), a collection of essays written between 1960 and 1989 and originally published in various journals. Their topics range from discussions of Skopje and the Lake Ohrid region, to his travels in the Mediterranean, his stay in Paris, his interest in the fantastic, and a "sentimental panorama" of surrealism.

Urošević has won several awards for his writing: the Mladost Prize for young poets in 1967 for his first volume of poems, *Eden drug grad*; three Gold Laurels (1967, 1973, 1986) of the Struga Poetry Evenings festival for *Leten dožd, Dzvezdena terezija,* and *Hipnopolis*; the Grigor Purlichev Prize twice for translating, in 1974 for his translations of Baudelaire, and in 1989 for his translations of Alain Bosquet; and, in 1981, a separate award for his book *Kiril Pejčinović: Tetoets* (Kiril Pejchinović: Man of Tetovo) at the international conference of literary translators in Tetovo (Macedonia). In 1982 Urošević was invited to join the Faculty of Philosophy of Skopje University as a professor of comparative and general literature.

Translations: "The Tailor's Dummy," in *The Big Horse and Other Stories of Modern Macedonia,* ed. Milne Holton (Columbia: University of Missouri Press, 1974), 191–97; seven poems in *Contemporary Macedonian Poetry,* ed. and trans. Ewald Osers (London: Forest, 1991), 85–94; nine poems, trans. by various hands, in *Reading the Ashes: An Anthology of the Poetry of Modern Macedonia,* ed. Milne Holton and Graham W. Reid (Pittsburgh: University of Pittsburgh Press, 1977), 71–76.

Ursachi, Mihai (b. 1941) Romanian poet. Born near Iași, Ursachi graduated from Iași University in philosophy and German studies. A literary "lone wolf" who long distanced himself from the Bucharest litrerary community, and who has published little, Ursachi nonetheless has a solid reputation in Romania both as a poet and for his resistance to the regime of Nicolae Ceaușescu. He was imprisoned for four years during the 1960s. His first book of poems, *Inel cu enigmă* (A Ring with Enigma, 1970), won the prestigious Eminsecu Prize. His next volume, *Missa solemnis* (1971), was awarded the Writers Association Prize. In 1972 he published a collection of poems (*Poezii*) that includes most of his previous verse. This was followed in 1974 by one of his best collections, *Poemul de purpură și alte poeme* (The Purple Poem and Other Verse), and in

1977 by *Marea înfățișare* (Grand Appearance). In 1981 Ursachi succeeded in immigrating to the United States, where he lived for nine years, teaching comparative literature part of the time at the University of San Diego. He returned to Romania only after the overthrow of Ceaușescu. Ursachi subsequently became director of the National Theater in Iași and has been active in the opposition Civic Alliance. Ursachi's reputation for strangeness as a poet relates to a certain inclination toward the enigmatic and phantasmagoric in which a fascination with death combines with rich colors and textures.

Translations: *Some Poems of Magister Ursachi Translated by His Friends,* trans. Don Eulert and Cornelia Hîncu (Iași: Junimea, 1980); eight poems and the short prose piece "The Myth of Demiurgos," in *46 Romanian Poets in English,* trans. and ed. Ștefan Avădanei and Don Eulert (Iași: Junimea, 1973), 286–93; the ten-part "Imperium," in a version by Paula Meehan, in *When the Tunnels Meet,* ed. John Fairleigh (Newcastle upon Thyne: Bloodaxe, 1996), 105–12.

Ursu, Liliana (b. 1949) Romanian poet, short-story writer, and translator. One of the foremost Romanian poets who came to prominence in the 1970s, Ursu is a native of the Transylvanian town of Sibiu. In 1972 she graduated from Bucharest University with a degree in English. She now teaches English at the university. Her first book of poetry, *Viață deasupra orașului* (Life Above the City), appeared in 1977. It was followed by *Ordinea clipelor* (Time Sequences, 1978); *Piața aurarilor* (The Goldsmiths' Market, 1980); *Zona de protecție* (Safety Zone, 1983); *Corali* (Coral, 1987); *Port Angeles* (1992); *Visul* (The Dream, 1995); and *Înger călare pe fiară* (Angel Riding the Beast, 1996). In addition, Ursu has published two books of short stories, including *La jumătatea drumului*

(Half Way There, 1986), and six books of translation from American, English, and Flemish poets. She has also translated Romanian writers into English for her anthology *15 Young Romanian Poets: An Anthology of Verse* (1982). And in 1992, with Adam Sorkin, she published a Romanian–English anthology of seven poets from her native Sibiu: *Focuri pe apă: 7 poeti din Sibiu* (*Fires on Water: 7 Poems from Sibiu*). Since 1980 Ursu has had a popular weekly literary program on Romanian Radio that features interviews, poetry, and book reviews. She also writes for children and works for Romanian Radio as an editor of cultural programs. In 1992/1993, she was a visiting professor at Pennsylvania State University on a Fulbright grant.

A sensitive and delicate poet, most at home in short poems often no more than a dozen lines long, Ursu writes about poetry and the crafting of poetry; love present and past; her American friends, above all the poet Tess Gallagher, with whom she collaborated on translations of her own poetry; her native Sibiu at different times of the year; the long-persecuted Romanian philosopher Constantin Noica (1909–1987); and, in one of her long poems, the eminent Romanian pianist and writer Cella Delavrancea and the Romanian novelist Gabriela Melinescu. Ursu has never been overtly political, yet a number of her poems lament the lack of liberty and the privations of the Ceaușescu period. But Ursu never despairs, never gives way to resignation; hers is a belief in the ultimate triumph of the human spirit. "Art like faith starts with liberty," she writes in one poem. "Oh, how I craved it—Libertate—even before I was born."

Translations: *Angel Riding a Beast,* trans. Liliana Ursu and Bruce Weigl (Evanston, Ill.: Northwestern University Press, 1998); *The Sky Behind the Forest: Selected Poems,* trans. Liliana Ursu with Adam J. Sorkin and Tess Gallagher (Newcastle upon Tyne:

Bloodaxe, 1997); six poems in *15 Young Romanian Poets: An Anthology of Verse,* trans. and ed. Liliana Ursu (Bucharest: Eminescu, 1982), 95–100; ten poems in *Silent Voices: An Anthology of Contemporary Romanian Women Poets,* trans. Andrea Deletant and Brenda Walker (London: Forest, 1986), 151–61.

Utassy, József (b. 1941) Hungarian poet. Utassy was born in Ózd near the Czechoslovak border, where his father, a laborer who died on the Russian front in 1943, was employed at the time. The future poet was reared in nearby Bükkszenterzsébet and graduated from high school in Eger in 1959. He then worked at odd jobs until 1961, when he entered Budapest University. Poor attendance nearly cost him his degree, but he eventually graduated in 1967. For the next five years, he worked first in the library of the Hungarian Ship and Crane Factory and then as a teacher in a vocational school. In August 1972 he made up his mind to become a freelance writer. Utassy published his first book of poetry, *Tüzem, lobógóm!* (My Fire, My Flag!), in 1969. His light deft touch, feeling for the simple joys of life, sense of humor, and understanding of the impact of Hungary's calamities on its people inform this volume as well as such subsequent books of poetry as *Csillagok árvája* (Orphan of the Stars, 1977); *Áve, Éva!* (1981); *Pokolból jövet* (On the Way Here from Hell, 1981); *Judas idő: Összegyűjtott versek* (The Age of Judas: Collected Poems, 1984); *Ragadozó föld* (Predatory Earth, 1987); *Hungária kávéház?/Kávéház Hungária!* (Hungaria Coffeehouse?/Coffeehouse Hungaria!, 1988); *Íratlan ég alatt* (Under the Unwritten Sky, 1988); *Hóemberség* (Snowman, 1989); *Rezeda-álom* (Mignonette-Dream, 1991); *Keserves: Versek, 1986–1989* (Painful: Poems, 1986–1989, 1991); *Hol ifjúságom tűnt el* (Where My Youth Disappeared, 1992); *Kálvária-ének* (Song of Calvary, 1995); and

Földi szivárvány (The Earthly Rainbow, 1996). In 1978 Utassy edited a volume of poems commemorating the Hungarian uprising of 1848: *Haj, ne hátra, haj előre: 1848 emlékezete* (Hey, Not Backward, Forward! In Memory of 1848).

Translations: Four poems in *Ocean at the Window: Hungarian Prose and Poetry Since 1945,* ed. Albert Tezla (Minneapolis: University of Minnesota Press, 1980), 375–77.

V

Vaculík, Ludvík (b. 1926) Czech novelist and journalist. Vaculík was born in the village of Brumov in Moravia. Although he trained as an apprentice shoemaker at the famous Bata company in Zlín from 1941 to 1946, he left shoemaking for the study of journalism at the Institute of Political Science and Sociology in Prague from 1946 to 1950. After a stint as a reporter with *Rudé Právo,* the *Pravda* of Czechoslovakia, he served as editor of the influential Czech literary journal *Literární noviny* from 1965 to 1969. His first work of fiction, the novella *Rušný dům* (The Busy House), appeared in 1963 and attracted no great attention. Matters changed with the publication in 1966 of his novel *Sekyra* (*The Axe*). The work is narrated in the first person by a Prague journalist who angers the authorities because of his candid reporting of the suicide of a girl denied admission to a high school. The narrator's return to his native Moravian village becomes an act of self-discovery as he recalls the life of his deceased father, a sincere communist of great integrity whose faith is ultimately shattered by the sacrifices demanded of him in the name of socialism. The novel is notable for its multiple narratives (the father's letters and extended first-person narration in addition to the journalist's narration itself) and its extensive use of the regional speech patterns of Vaculík's native Moravia. By means of the interlocking narratives of the son and his father, Vaculík's indictment of the corrupt Stalin-like Czech bureaucracy of his own time acquires an added, historical dimension.

Like other Czech and Slovak literary reformers of the time, Vaculík supported the campaign for a relaxation of censorship and greater political freedom in the Writers Union. He also aired his views in *Literární noviny* and in the journal *Literární listy,* with which he was affiliated. His bold remarks in favor of democratization at the Fourth Congress of the Writers Union in June 1967 resulted in his ouster from the Communist Party. He was readmitted in 1968, but again courted the disfavor of the Party by joining a number of his fellow writers in active support of the reformist policy of Alexander Dubček. When it appeared that Dubček was about to cave in to Soviet pressure to curtail reform, Vaculík composed the *Dva tisíce slov* (Two-Thousand-Word Manifesto). The defiant manifesto was published in *Literární listy* in June 1968. Party conservatives in Czechoslovakia and the Soviets interpreted it as a deliberate and dangerous provocation engineered by Dubček himself. That the manifesto, which had broad public appeal and made Vaculík famous, was a factor in the Soviet decision to intervene in Czechoslovakia seems beyond reasonable doubt.

In the aftermath of the Soviet invasion, Vaculík was again expelled from the Party and prohibited from publishing his books in his native land. In the 1970s, he established the so-called Edice Petlice (Padlock Editions) as an outlet for writers unable or unwilling to publish with the state publishing houses. Edice Petlice books were distributed only in typewritten copies. It was also via Edice Petlice that Vaculík circulated his

Český snář (A Czech Dreambook) in 1980. The work explores the intellectual opposition in Prague in the decade after the Soviet invasion. The first printed edition of it appeared in Toronto in 1982.

Vaculík's bleak outlook during this period is nowhere more evident than in his Kafkaesque novel *Morčata* (*The Guinea Pigs*), which was written as a response to the brutal suppression of the "Prague Spring." Denied permission for publication in Czechoslovakia, *The Guinea Pigs* first circulated in typewritten copies in 1970 before appearing in a German printed translation (as *Die Meerscheinchen*) in Lucerne, Switzerland, in 1971. An English translation of the novel was published in 1973. A Czech edition of the work was finally issued in Toronto in 1977.

Narrated mostly in the first person in a simple style appropriate to the novel's central figure, a modest clerk in a state bank, *The Guinea Pigs* is a dark, unsettling work. The clerk is soon beset by two obsessions. One has to do with his belief that bills stolen from the bank by its employees and confiscated by bank guards are not returned to the bank's treasury but are part of some monstrous conspiracy by unknown forces to destroy the country through financial depletion and mass unemployment. The clerk's other obsession has to do with guinea pigs he raises after buying one for a family pet as a Christmas present on an acquaintance's suggestion. The more nightmarish the great plot involving the bank becomes, the more bizarre the clerk's treatment of his guinea pigs. From innocent curiosity about them, his interest progresses from play to torture.

Literature: Antonin J. Liehm, "Ludvík Vaculík and His Novel *The Axe*," in *Czech Literature Since 1956: A Symposium,* ed. William E. Harkins and Paul I. Trensky (New York: Bohemica, 1980), 91–102.

Translations: *The Axe,* trans. Marian Sling (London: Deutsch, 1966); *A Cup of Coffee with My Interrogators,* trans. George Theiner (London: Readers International, 1987); *The Guinea Pigs,* trans. Káča Poláčková (New York: Penguin, 1975); "In Retirement" and "A Padlock for Castle Schwarzenberg," trans. Milan Pomichalek and Anna Mozga, and "The Last Say," trans. A. G. Brain, in *Good-bye, Samizdat: Twenty Years of Czechoslovak Underground Writing,* ed. Marketa Goetz-Stankiewicz (Evanston, Ill.: Northwestern University Press, 1992), 114–29.

Vámos, Miklós (b. 1950) Hungarian novelist, short-story writer, and playwright. A native of Budapest, Vámos graduated from high school in 1968 and then worked as a printer at a Budapest publishing house until 1970. He was admitted to the law school of Eötvös Lóránd University in 1970 and received his degree in 1975. From 1975 to 1991, he was employed as a literary adviser to the Mafilm Objektiv film studios. Vámos received a Fulbright Fellowship and spent the academic years 1988/1989 and 1989/1990 at Yale University. In 1990 he was also appointed East European correspondent for *The Nation.* Since 1991, he has headed the Ab Ovo publishing house in Budapest. Vámos's first literary work, a collection of short stories and sketches titled *Előszó az ábécéhez* (Foreword to the Alphabet) appeared in 1972, before Vámos left law school. Five more collections of stories appeared between 1973 and 1997: *Jelenleg a tizenharmadík a listán* (At Present Thirteenth on the List, 1973); *Váltás Pé és Em* (Exchange [P and M], 1977); *Valaki más: Válogatott novellák* (Somebody Else: Selected Stories, 1981); *Szenvedélyes emberek* (Passionate People, 1985); and *135 lehetetlen történet* (135 Impossible Stories, 1997). Vámos's first novel, *Borgisz* (Borgis), came out in 1976. It was followed by *Én és én* (Me and Myself, 1979); *Zeng az ének* (Sing the Song, 1984), one of Vámos's best works in which he addresses the matter of his gen-

eration's awakening consciousness; *Félnóta* (Half a Song, 1986); *Jaj* (Oh!, 1985), a short novel; *Egybesült államok* (Congealed States, 1991); *Ha én Bródy volnék* (What If I Were Bródy, 1994); and *Anya csak egy van* (You Have Only One Mother) and *A New York–Budapest métro* (The New York–Budapest Metro), both released in 1995. Vámos has also published two works of nonfiction: *Ki nem küldött tudósítónk jelenti* (Our Undispatched Reporter Reports, 1985), a collection of articles and other journalistic writings, and *Teniszsezz velem* (Tennis Play With Me, 1988), a book of essays. As a playwright, Vámos has written for radio and the stage. Six of his radio plays were produced from 1970 to 1976, and two of his plays have been produced (one in 1975, and the other the following year). A collection of his dramatic writings was published in 1981 under the title *Háromszoros vivát: Drámák, hangjátékok* (Three Cheers! Dramas and Radio Plays). Many of Vámos's stories and novels are built around the problems of the young in everyday life and tend toward the satirical. As his career progressed, his outlook became more compassionate and empathetic. Generally, Vámos's works are long on dialogue and short on narration, which enables him to display his obvious enthusiasm for experimentation with language. Vámos was awarded the Attila József Prize in 1984.

Translations: "Keresztes" and "Little Boys, Big Boys," trans. Albert Tezla, in *Ocean at the Window: Hungarian Prose and Poetry Aince 1945,* ed. Albert Tezla (Minneapolis: University of Minnesota Press, 1980), 433–37; "A Very Private Affair," trans. J. E. Sollosy, in *Present Continuous: Contemporary Hungarian Writing,* ed. István Bart (Budapest: Corvina, 1985), 383–91.

Vas, István (1910–1991) Hungarian poet, essayist, critic, memoirist, and translator. Born in Budapest, Vas first studied in Vienna for a business career before returning to Budapest and employment in the civil service. He eventually gave these up to become a writer and to work in publishing. A descendant of rabbis, Vas had converted to Catholicism and managed to survive the war, in part due to the good offices of his friend Géza Ottlik, a novelist. Although his earliest literary leanings were toward the avant-garde, Vas's first book, *Őszi rombolás* (Autumnal Destruction, 1932), signaled a return to more traditional forms. He published one more volume of poems before the outbreak of World War II, *Levél a szabadságról* (Letter About Freedom, 1935). After the war, a single volume of poems, *Kettős ösvény* (Double Path, 1946), appeared before communist criticism of his alleged bourgeois attitudes kept him out of the literary mainstream and forced him to earn a living for several years as a translator, mostly from English and French. His return to active literary life came with the publication of the poetry volume *A teremtett világ* (The Created World, 1956). After that, Vas published four more volumes of poetry: *Önarckép a hetvenes évekből* (Self-Portrait from the Seventies) and *Itt voltam* (I Was Here), both published in 1976; *Ráérünk* (We Still Have Time, 1983); and *Mégis* (Nevertheless, 1985). His collected poetry from 1930 to 1962 was published in 1963 as *Összegyűjtött versei*. A two-volume collection of his poetry appeared in 1970 under the title *Mit akar az ez ember?* (What Does This One Man Want?). Other collected/selected volumes of his poems include *A földalatti nap* (The Underground Sun, 1969); *A kimondhatatlan: Válogatott versek* (The Unspeakable: Selected Poems, 1972); *Ki mást se tud: Versek, 1930–1945* (Who Even Knows Another: Poems, 1930–1945, 1977); *Rapszodia a hűségről: Versek, 1945–1959* (Rhapsody on Loyalty: Poems, 1945–1959, 1977); *A tűzlopó: Versek, 1960–1976* (The Fire Gourd: Poems, 1960–1976, 1977); *Ném számít* (It Doesn't

Count, 1979); and *Válogatott versek* (Selected Poems, 1990).

Besides poetry, Vas published several volumes of literary criticism, among them *Igen is, nem is* (Yes and No, 1987); *Vonzások és választások: Tanulmányok* (Attractions and Selections: Studies, 1978); *Tengerek nélkül: Tanulmányok* (Without the Seas: Studies, 1978); and *Körül-belül: Tanulmányok* (Just About: Studies, 1978). A collection of his essays and criticism came out in 1974 titled *Az ismeretlenisten* (The Unknown God). Arguably Vas's most impressive writing can be found in his autobiographical trilogy: *Nehéz szerelem* (Difficult Love, 1964); *A félbeszakadt nyomozás* (The Interrupted Investigation, 1967); and *Miért vijjog a saskeselyű?* (Why Does the Vulture Screech?, 1981). Apart from its self-revelatory character and urbane style, the trilogy is of considerable value for its insights into interwar and post–World War II Hungarian literary and cultural life. Vas's complete works began to be published in 1977. Eleven volumes appeared between 1977 and 1983 under the general title *Összegyűjtött munkái*. Vas enjoys the distinction of being the first critic in Hungary under the communists to write appreciatively of the exiled poets after the 1956 uprising. Vas is also admired for his excellent translations of English poetry from Shakespeare to Eliot.

Literature: István Fenyő, *Vas István* (Budapest: Akadémiai Kiadó, 1976), a critical study; Zoltan Sumonyi, *Vas Istvan* (Budapest: Szépirodalmi Könyvkiadó, 1982), a biography.

Translations: *Through the Smoke: Collected Poems*, ed. Miklós Vajda (Budapest: Corvina, 1989); six poems in *The Colonnade of Teeth: Modern Hungarian Poetry*, ed. George Gömöri and George Szirtes (Newcastle upon Tyne: Bloodaxe, 1996), 78–84; thirteen poems in *The Face of Creation: Contemporary Hungarian Poetry*, ed. Jascha Kessler (Minneapolis: Coffee House, 1988), 150–62; sixteen poems in *In Quest of the*

"Miracle Stag": The Poetry of Hungary, ed. Adam Makkai (Chicago: Atlantis-Centaur, 1996), 725–40.

Vasiliu, Lucian (b. 1954) Romanian poet and novelist. A native of Puiești-Bîrlad, in the Vaslui district, Vasiliu graduated in 1981 from Iași University, where he studied philology. From 1976 to 1980, he worked as a librarian at the Iași Polytechnic Institute and, from 1980 to 1990, was curator of the Moldova Literary Museum. Since 1990. he has been the director of the Museum of Romanian Literature in Iași and editor of the review *Dacia Literară* in Iași. Vasiliu first appeared in print in 1973 in the literary review *Convorbiri literare* with a small selection of poems. His first collection in book form was *Mona-Monada* (1981), in fact a series of love poems inspired in part by the philosopher Gottfried Leibniz's theory of monads. It was followed by *Despre felul cum înaintez* (My Way of Going Forward, 1983); *Fiul omului* (The Son of Man, 1986); *Verile după conachi* (Summers After Conachi, 1990); *Mierla de la Casa Pogor* (The Blackbird at Pogor's, 1994), a retrospective selection of poems; *Dincolo de disperare* (Beyond Despair, 1995); and *Lucianograme* (Lucianograms, 1990). His one published novel is *Să alergăm împreună* (Let's Run Together, 1985). Vasililu has won several awards for his poetry: the Nicolae Labiș Prize (1979); the Mihai Eminescu Prize (1983); and the Iași Writers Association Prize for Poetry (1990, 1994). He is a member of the Writers Union and the Romanian PEN Club.

Translations: Five poems in *Young Poets of a New Romania: An Anthology,* trans. Brenda Walker with Michaela Celea-Leach, ed. Ion Stoica (London: Forest, 1991), 41–46.

Vegri, Saša (real name Albina Dobršek; b. 1934) Slovenian poet. Born in Belgrade, Vegri received her early education in Celje and graduated from high school in Ljubljana. She then received a degree in art history from Ljubljana University, after which she pursued the career of a freelance writer in the Slovenian capital until 1968, when she became a librarian. Vegri published her first book of poetry, *Mesečni konj* (The Moonstruck Horse), in 1958. It was followed by *Naplavljeni plen* (Abandoned Booty, 1961); *Zajtrkujem v urejenem naročju* (We Breakfast in Style, 1967); *Ofelija in trojni aksel* (Ophelia and the Triple Axel, 1977); *Konstelacje* (Constellations, 1980); and *Tebi v tišino* (To You in Silence, 2001). She has also published several books of poetry for children. As a poet, Vegri addresses a broad range of women's experiences from adolescence to maturity. With the exception of the more avant-garde and experimental poetry in *Konstelacje,* she has tended to favor short poems written in short lines often consisting of only a word or two in a highly compressed style. A poem frequently encompasses just a single image, usually drawn from natural phenomena. This is a typical poem from the *Naplavljeni plen* collection:

"Women"—Are like lutes
tranquil and devoted,
that wait for
their bodies
to begin singing.
And when
Someone
plays harmoniously
on them
they sing
of the sadness
of silver nights
which perhaps
they themselves release,
of birth
which they weave
in themselves,
and of love
chords
like strings
from their mouths
to their hips.

Velea, Nicolae (1936–1987) Romanian short-story writer, screenwriter, and novelist. Velea studied forestry at Braşov University before earning a degree in philology at Bucharest University in 1958. In the 1960s he worked as an editor at such literary magazines as *Gazeta literară* and *Viaţa nouă*, later joining the Bucureşti film company as a journalist and a screenwriter. His first book, the short-story collection *Poartea* (The Gate, 1960), won the Romanian Academy Prize. Here and in such subsequent collections of short stories as *Opt povestiri* (Eight Stories, 1963); *Paznic la armonii* (Keeper of Harmonies, 1965); and *Zbor jos* (Flying Low, 1968), he dealt mainly with the privations and dislocations experienced by rural people after the communist takeover in 1945. Velea's first novel, *În război un pogon cu flori* (An Acre of Flowers at War), appeared in 1972 and was followed by *Dumitraş şi cele două zile* (Dumitras and Those Two Days, 1974), a small collection of stories for children; *Călător printre înţelepciuni* (Sojourner Among the Wise, 1975), a selection of pieces published originally in *Luceafărul; Întîlnire tîrzie* (Late Encounter, 1981), a collection of novellas; and *Olina* (1992), a short novel. His most recent collection of stories, *Povestiri* (Stories), appeared in 1997. Acknowledging his talent, some Romanian critics have lamented Velea's preference for the short story over the novel.

Translations: "Carefree" (from *Opt povestiri*), in *The Phantom Church and Other Stories from Romania*, ed. and trans. Georgiana Farnoaga and Sharon King (Pittsburgh: University of Pittsburgh Press, 1996), 24–32.

Velikić, Dragan (b. 1953) Serbian novelist, short-story writer, and essayist. Born in Belgrade, Velikić began his literary career in 1983 with the publication of his first book of stories, *Pogrešan pokret* (The Erroneous Movement). His second collection of stories, *Staklena bašta* (The Greenhouse), ap-

peared in 1985. His novels include *Via Pula* (1988), which won the Miloš Crnjanski Prize in 1988; *Astragan* (Astrakhan, 1991), a largely autobiographical work in which Velikić reconstructs his own life growing up in Belgrade, Rijeka, and Pula through the story of his central character, Marko Delić; *Hamsin 51* (1993); *Severni zid* (The Northern Wall, 1995); and *Danteov trg* (Dante's Square, 1998). Velikić's strong interest in paranormal phenomena and in creating puzzles out of his characters' lives and then putting them together is evident in much of his fiction, as in his most recent novel, *Danteov trg*. This is essentially the story of a single person, a Serbian writer who dies in exile in a Bavarian town. His life is reconstructed as a puzzle, pieces of which are fit into place by a succession of characters who knew him at various stages in his life. The novel takes a curious twist with the introduction of an American professor who tours Eastern Europe, obsessed with the idea of constructing an image of the archetypical East European. This he hopes to do through a fictional blend of the lives of three regional writers, one of whom is the Serb who dies in Bavaria. In an epilogue, Velikič ties together the various strings of his complex narrative and resolves the mysteries he is always fond of elaborating.

Translations: "A Woman from a Catalogue," trans. Dragan Milivojević, in *The Prince of Fire: An Anthology of Contemporary Serbian Short Stories*, ed. Radmila J. Gorup and Nadežda Obradović (Pittsburgh: University of Pittsburgh Press, 1998), 300–313.

Velmar-Janković, Svetlana (b. 1933) Serbian novelist and essayist. A major representative of the so-called modernist writers who appeared in Serbian literature in the 1950s in opposition to socialist realism, Velmar-Janković was born and educated in Belgrade. She studied French and Latin at Belgrade University, following which she

worked as a journalist before joining the editorial board of *Literatura*. She was also affiliated for a number of years with the
Prosveta publishing house as an editor. A
talented novelist and short-story writer,
Velmar-Janković explored in her first novel,
Oziljak (The Scar, 1956; 2nd rev. ed., 1999),
the psychological and emotional impact of
World War II on a young girl. In 1969 she
won the Isadora Sekulić Prize. Her second
major literary award, the Ivo Andrić Prize,
was awarded to her for the short-story collection *Dorćol, imena ulica* (Dorćol, Names
of Streets, 1986), which is set in a largely
Jewish Belgrade neighborhood. Her next
most successful publication was *Lagum*
(*Dungeon*, 1990), a well-crafted, absorbing
novel that begins in November 1944 and
moves back and forth in time between the
early 1940s and 1984 in a sweep of Belgrade
history from the German wartime occupation through the communist takeover of the
country and the subsequent changes in Yugoslavia under their rule and during the first
years after Tito's death. The novel is narrated in the first person by the wife of a professor of art history who is accused of and
eventually executed for collaboration with
the wartime quisling Serbian government. Patently autobiographical, *Dungeon*
is especially effective in its depiction of the
outlook and mores of the interwar Serbian
cultured middle class and its fate under the
communists after the war. Velmar-Janković
won the Meša Selimović Prize for *Dungeon*
in 1991, as well as the National Library Prize
for most read book in 1992. Velmar-
Janković's other novels include *Ukletnici*
(The Bewitched, 1993); *Vracar* (1994), which
deals with the Belgrade district of Vracar
from 1594 to 1994; *Knez Mihailo: Neistorijska
drama o istorijskom zbivanju* (Prince
Maihailo: An Unhistorical Drama About a
Historical Assassination, 1994); and *Bezdno*
(Abyss, 1995). The last two works are based
on the asassination of the Serbian prince

Mihailo III (1823–1868). Velmar-Janković
won the NIN Prize for best novel of the year
for *Bezdno* in 1996. A literary critic and historian, Velmar-Jankovič is the author of the
two-volume *Književnost izmedju dva rata*
(Literature Between the Two Wars, 1965,
1966); a short study on the poetry of Ivan
V. Lalić (1987); and a book of essays titled
Savremenici   (Contemporaries,   1968).
Velmar-Janković's most recent work of fiction is *Glasovi* (Voices), a collection of short
stories published in 1998. Additional literary
awards Velmar-Janković has won are the
Djordje Jovanović Prize (1994) and the Bora
Stanković Prize (1995).

Translations: *Dungeon,* trans. Celia
Hawkesworth (Belgrade: Dereta, 1996);
"Sima Street," trans. Bogdan Rakić, in *The
Prince of Fire: An Anthology of Contempo-
rary Serbian Short Stories,* ed. Radmila J.
Gorup and Nadežda Obradović (Pitts-
burgh: University of Pittsburgh Press, 1998),
84–90.

Verona, Dan (b. 1947) Romanian poet.
Verona received his degree in philology from
Bucharest University and started working as
an editor for the radio. He is the author of
five books of poems: *Noptile migratoare*
(Migratory Nights, 1972); *Zodia măslinului*
(Under the Skin of the Olive, 1974); *Cartea
runilor* (The Book of Runes, 1976), a collection of poems singing the praises of the Romanian nation and its political and cultural
heroes from its ancient beginnings to modern times and conceived as a tribute to "Our
Goddess, the Romanian Language"; *Daţi
ordin să înflorească magnolia* (Order the
Magnolia to Bloom, 1977); and *Viaţa la
treizeci şi trei de ani* (Life at Thirty-three,
1980). At home generally in longer poems,
Verona writes often of love and melancholy,
life and death, in historical as well as ancient
and mythological contexts. He is an admirer
of the classical antique world, much in evidence, for example, in *Zodia măslinului*. In

his more recent writing, Verona has trained his sights on modern society, for which he has nothing but contempt. Appropriately, this newer poetry parts company with the classical rhythms of his previous writing in preference for free verse and an idiom shaped by everyday contemporary life.

Translations: Four poems in *15 Young Romanian Poets: An Anthology of Verse*, trans. and ed. Liliana Ursu (Bucharest: Eminescu, 1982), 101–9.

Vészi, Endre (1916–1987) Hungarian poet, novelist, and playwright. Vészi was born in Budapest, where he apprenticed as a steel engraver. He soon opted, however, for a career in journalism, writing for such newspapers as *Népszava, Magyar Hírlap,* and *Pesti Napló.* After publishing his first poems in various reviews, Vészi came out with his first collection of poetry, *Végy oltalmadba* (Take Me Under Your Protection), in 1935. His novel *Felszabadultál* (You Were Liberated) appeared in 1937 and won the Mikszáth Prize. From 1937 to 1940, Vészi wrote mainly for *Népszava* and in 1945 became a regular member of the newspaper's staff. After World War II, his collected poems were published in 1974 under the title *A teljesség igézetében* (Utterly Enchanted), and his plays were collected in the volume *A piros oroszlán* (The Red Lion, 1971). Although he successfully combined social and psychological analyses in the many stories and novels he published in the postwar period, none ever achieved the fame of his novel *Angi Vera* (Vera Angi, 1977), named for the main female character, in which the grim realities of Hungarian life in the Stalinist 1950s are presented in an unflinching, painfully truthful way. The novel served as the basis for one of postwar Hungary's most successful and widely known films, directed in 1978 by Pál Gábor. Vészi was awarded the Attila József Prize in 1950, 1955, and 1965, and the Kossuth Prize in 1978.

Translations: "Ólmosi-Bleier's Last Work," trans. László T. András, in *Present Continuous: Contemporary Hungarian Writing,* ed. István Bart (Budapest: Corvina, 1985), 199–214; "Stonemusic," trans. Caroline Bodóczky, in *44 Hungarian Short Stories,* ed. Lajos Illés (Budapest: Corvina, 1979), 448–59.

Vezhinov, Pavel (real name Nikola Delchev Gugov; 1914–1983) Bulgarian novelist and short-story writer. Best known as a writer of detective and mystery fiction as well as science fiction, Vezhinov was born in Sofia and received his early education there. Because of his leftist political convictions, he was not permitted to enter a public high school in the city and had to be privately educated. After completing high-school requirements in 1938, he entered Sofia University the following year and graduated with a degree in philosophy in 1944. The same year, he was sent to the front as a war correspondent and editor of the military paper *Frontovak.* After the war, from 1947 to 1951, he was assistant editor in chief of the journal *Sturshel* and, from 1951 to 1954, worked for *Septemvri.* His next major employment (1954–1972) was with Bulgarian Cinematography as a screenwriter and administrative official. In 1973 he became editor in chief of the journal *Suvremenik.*

Although he began publishing in various literary reviews and journals as early as 1932, Vezhinov's first breakthrough as a writer came in 1938 with the appearance of a collection of short stories titled *Ulitsa bez pavazh* (Unpaved Streets). It established him as a journalistically oriented urban writer with a strong social conscience whose subjects were drawn mostly from the lives of the capital's poorer neighborhoods. His next collection of stories, *Dni i vecheri* (Days and Nights, 1942), demonstrated a broadening of his social outlook and a growing interest in the psychological makeup of his characters. A similar collection of stories,

Chudnoto otkritie (The Wonderful Discovery), appeared in 1946. The following year, 1947, Vezhinov published his first novel, *Siniiat zalez* (Blue Sunset), which was severly criticized for its emphasis on criminality and its sensational as well as erotic elements, tendencies that were in general out of sync with official socialist realism and the new postwar communist society. Undeterred by such criticism, Vezhinov nevertheless toned down the sensationalism of his writing and offset the fuss raised by *Siniiat zalez* with humorous and parodistic tales about everyday contemporary life as well as with a wartime novel, *Vtora rota* (The Second Brigade, 1959), and novels of an antifascist character, such as *V poleto* (In the Field, 1961) and *Daleche ot bregovite* (*Far from the Shore*, 1967). One of Vezhinov's more popular works, *Far from the Shore* is an improbable adventure story set in the 1930s about a small band of Slav communists who commandeer a boat from Bulgaria with the purpose of making their way to the Soviet Union and the "free life." Vezhinov's other works include *Chovekut v siankata* (The Man in the Shadow, 1965), a collection of detective and mystery stories; *Zvezdite nad nas* (The Stars Above Us, 1966); *Duh na bademi* (The Scent of Almond, 1966); *Nauchnofantastichni novelli* (Science-Fiction Novellas) and *Sinite peperudi* (The Blue Butterflies), a collection of science-fiction stories, both published in 1968; *Prilepiti letiat noshtem* (Vampires Fly at Night, 1969); *Malkite prikliucheniia* (Small Adventures, 1970); *Kutiia za enfie* (Snuffbox, 1973); *Samopriznanie* (Self-Confession, 1973); *Gibelta na Aiaks* (The Death of Aax) and *Nad vsichko* (Above All), two science-fiction novellas, both published in 1973; *Goliamata stupka* (The Big Step, 1974), a sports novel; *Beliiat gushter* (The White Geese) and *Siniiat kamuk* (The Blue Stone), both issued in 1977; *Ezernoto momche* (The Boy from the Lake, 1978); *Noshtem s belite kone*

(At Night with the White Horses, 1981), a novel; *Az sum atomna* (I Am Atomic, 1981), another science-fiction novel; and *Malki semeini hroniki* (Small Family Chronicles, 1988), subtitled "An Ironic Novel." A collection of Vezhinov's novellas, *Izbrani povesti* (Collected Novellas), was published in 1964, followed by a collection of stories, *Izbrani razkazi* (Collected Stories), in 1965 and another collection of stories, *Razkazi* (Stories), in 1969. A four-volume edition of Vezhinov's collected works (*Izbranie proizvedeniia*) was published in 1984.

Literature: Svetlozar Igov, *Pavel Vezhinov* (Sofia: Narodna prosveta, 1990), a useful short critical study; Atanas Svilenov, ed., *Kniga za Pavel Vezhinov* (Sofia: Bulgarski pisatel, 1986), a large collection of materials on Vezhinov; Rumiana Uzunova, *Pavel Vezhinov: Literaturno-kriticheski ocherk* (Sofia: Bulgarski pisatel, 1980), a good slightly older study.

Translations: *Far from the Shore*, trans. Gregor Pavlov (Sofia: Foreign Languages Press, 1967); "The Boy with the Violin" and "Spanish Cholera," trans. Gregor Pavlov, in *Introduction to Modern Bulgarian Literature: An Anthology of Short Stories*, ed. Nikolai Kirilov and Frank Kirk (New York: Twayne, 1969), 269–99, 299–309; "The Late Visitor," trans. Petko Drenkov, in *The Balkan Range: A Bulgarian Reader*, ed. John Robert Colombo and Nikola Roussanoff (Toronto: Hounslow, 1976), 270–82; "My Father," in *The Peach Thief and Other Bulgarian Stories*, trans. Radost Pridham and Jean Morris (London: Cassell, 1968), 145–70.

Vida, Viktor (1913–1960) Croatian poet. Born on the island of Kotor off the Dalmatian coast, Vida was educated in secondary schools in Kotor and Podgorica, after which his parents resettled in Zagreb. He studied South Slavic and other languages and literatures at Zagreb University and graduated from the Faculty of Philosophy in 1937. He then left for Rome on a scholarship from the Italian Institute in Zagreb. When he returned to Croatia two years later, he began work as a librarian at the Italian Institute. In 1941 he taught at a Zagreb high school and then quit in 1942 when he resettled in Rome and joined the Italian-Croatian News Agency. When the agency closed in 1943 after the fall of Italy in World War II, Vida remained largely unemployed until, in 1946, he found a job as a clerk at the Pontificia Commissione Assistenza. Obviously restless, Vida packed himself and his family off to Argentina, arriving in Buenos Aires at the beginning of 1948. Although he lived a threadbare existence in Argentina, Vida began publishing poems, essays, and reviews in a variety of émigré journals, becoming in time a frequent contributor to the *Hrvatska revija*, edited by Vinko Nikolić. His first books of poetry, *Svemir osobe* (The Universe of a Person, 1951) and *Sužanj vremena* (Slave of Time, 1956), were published with the help of friends. In response to the growing, largely political divisions within the Croatian émigré community in Argentina, Vida, always an able essayist, collaborated with Ivo Bogdan on *Obrana hrvatske cjelokupnosti i javnih radnika* (A Defense of Croatian Integrity and Public Workers, 1954). In 1960, for reasons never successfully clarified, Vida committed suicide by throwing himself under the wheels of a train. Despite deep feelings of emptiness and isolation as an émigré, Vida apparently never seriously considered returning to postwar Yugoslavia. He chose instead to deal from the distance of emigration with many of the questions with which contemporary Croatian writers in Croatia itself and elsewhere were absorbed. The long neglect of Vida's poetry in Croatia ended in 1962 with the publication of his collected poems (*Sabrane pjesme*) preceded by a sensitive analysis by the critic Ivo Lendić in which he demonstrated Vida's

modernity and contemporaneity. While nurtured in the mainstream of European symbolism and modernism—he was conversant with the works of such poets as Paul Valéry, Giuseppe Ungaretti, Eugenio Montale, Salvatore Quasimodo, Rainer Maria Rilke, and T. S. Eliot—Vida sought and achieved his own distinct style.

Translations: *Viktor Vida, Collected Poems*, trans. Magda Osterhuber (Zagreb: The Bridge, 1998), which also contains quite good companion pieces on Vida and his poetry by Božidar Petrač and Andjelko Novaković.

Viewegh, Michal (b. 1962) Czech novelist. Viewegh's first novel, *Názory na vraždu* (Thoughts About Murder), appeared in 1990. Narrated in the first person (as is almost all of Viewegh's fiction), the short novel is about the mysterious death of a young schoolteacher. Typical of Viewegh's style, apart from the brevity of his novels, is the feeling his works convey of contemporary postcommunist Czech and, especially, Prague life. His leading characters are mostly young people and usually include offbeat individuals, such as a few Vietnamese in *Názory na vraždu* and a homebred Mafia type in *Výchova dívek v Čechách* (*Bringing Up Girls in Bohemia*, 1994). *Báječná léta pod psa* (The Blissful Years of Lousy Living, 1992), Viewegh's second novel, became an immediate success and was translated into Dutch and German. It also won the Jiří Orten Prize. Set in the communist period, the work is a kind of abbreviated contemporary bildungsroman whose "hero" is a young writer named Quido (Czech, Kvido) who was born to an actress mother during a stage performance. Interspersed with excerpts from Quido's diary are pages of play-like dialogue between characters, adding to the texture of the narrative. Viewegh has subsequently published a collection of literary parodies under the title *Nápady laskavého čtenáře* (Ideas of the Kind Reader, 1993); his most successful novel to date, *Bringing Up Girls in Bohemia*, an entertaining book about the relationship that develops when a Prague crime big shot hires a writer to help his very independent daughter satisfy an ambition to become a writer herself; and *Účastníci zájezdu* (The Tour Group, 1996), a shrewdly observant and entertaining study of the relations among a mixed bag of tourists from different walks of life at an Italian sea resort.

Translations: *Bringing Up Girls in Bohemia*, trans. A. G. Brain (London: Readers International, 1997); excerpts from *Báječná léta pod psa*, trans. O. T. Chalkstone, in *This Side of Reality: Modern Czech Writing*, ed. Alexandra Büchler (London: Serpent's Tail, 1996), 154–64.

Vilikovský, Pavel (b. 1941) Slovak novelist. One of Slovakia's most respected contemporary writers, Vilikovský is perhaps known best for the Slovak–English dictionary that he and his wife, Júlia Vilikovská, published in 1971. The dictionary has had several editions, the most recent an expanded edition published in 1991. Vilikovský was born in Palúdzka and was educated through high school in Bratislava. He studied Slovak and English at Comenius University and after graduating in 1965 became editor of the journal *Slovenské pohľady,* a position he held until 1970. He subsequently worked for the Tatran publishing house and, from 1976 to 1996, edited the journal *Romboid*. As a writer of imaginative literature, Vilikovský made his debut in 1965 with the story collection *Citová výchova v marci* (A Sentimental Education in March), which deals mostly with contemporary youth and their problems. After devoting almost the next two decades to translating from English and American literatures, he resumed writing fiction and in 1983 came out with the novella *Prvá veta spánku* (The First Sentence of Sleep), a

combination detective and psychological novel. In 1989 Vilikovský published two of his most interesting texts: the two-part *Kon na poschodi, slepec vo Vrabloch* (A Horse on the Staircase, a Blind Man in Vrabel) and the independently published *Večne je zelený...* (Ever Green Is the ...). *Kon na poschodi, slepec vo Vrabloch* is a humorous, ironic work, with elements of the grotesque and absurd; it is built around the story of a horse that someone claimed to have seen on a staircase in which every chapter begins with a citation from an equestrian manual. *Večne je zelený...* is, according to the author, a "satire on spies, secret police, Slovaks, Romanians (especially chambermaids), Leninism, Nazism, Balkan homsexuality, and police informers among university students." Vilikovský's next major work was the lighthearted romantic-erotic *Slovenský Casanova* (A Slovak Casanova, 1991), which also includes stories from the collection *Okno po erotických snoch* (A Window on Erotic Dreams, 1991) by the Slovak-Hungarian writer Lajos Grendel (b. 1948). Vilikovský's next book, *Pesí príbeh* (Adventure of a Dog, 1992), is essentially an antitotalitarian political satire in the form of a criminal novel. It was followed by *Krajní osamelost* (Extreme Loneliness, 1996) and the well-received story collection *Krutý strojvodca* (The Cruel Engine-Driver, 1996).

Translations: *Kon na poschodi, slepec vo Vrabloch* is available in French as *Un Cheval dans l'escalier,* trans. Peter Brabenec (Paris: Nadeau, 1997).

Vinca, Agim (b. 1947) Kosovo Albanian poet and literary scholar. Vinca was born in Veleshtë, near Struga, Macedonia, where he completed his secondary-school education. He then studied Albanian language and literature at Priština University and later joined the university's Faculty of Philology. He currently heads the Department of Albanian Literature and has served as deputy minister of education for Kosovo. Vinca's career embraces the writing of poetry and literary criticism. His first collection of poems, *Feniksi* (The Phoenix), was published in 1972 and was followed by *Shtegu i mallit* (The Path of Longing, 1975); *Në vend të biografisë* (In Place of a Biography, 1977); and *Buzëdrinas* (Along the Shores of the Drin River, 1984). As a poet, Vinca draws on native Kosovo sources for his inspiration and subjects and employs a style shaped to a large extent by the popular tradition. His formidable critical and scholarly contributions include *Aspekte të kritikës* (Aspects of Criticism, 1977); *Qasje* (Approach, 1980); *Struktura e zhvillimit të poezisë së sotme shqipe, 1945–1980* (The Development of Contemporary Albanian Poetry, 1945–1980, 1985); and *Orët e poezisë* (Poetry Hours, 1990), a nearly 600-page collection of essays on Albanian-language and foreign poetry and on poetic theory. Vinca has also edited a useful anthology of contemporay Albanian poetry in Yugoslavia in Serbo-Croatian translation, *Iz savremene albanske poezije u Jugoslavii* (1985). In May 1995, Vinca was arrested by the Serbian authorities and jailed for fifteen days because of an "illegal" visit to Albania in October 1993. He is widely known for his vigorous advocacy of self-determination in Kosovo and his denunciation of Serb-instigated human-rights abuses there.

Virk, Jani (b. 1962) Slovenian poet, novelist, essayist, and translator. A native of Ljubljana, Virk graduated from Ljubljana University with a degree in German and comparative literature and subsequently taught both at the university. He was editor in chief of the review *Literatura* in 1988/1989, cultural editor and editor in chief of the daily *Slovenec,* and subsequently head of cultural broadcasting at TV Slovenia. An avid sportsman and former member of the Yugoslav junior ski team, Virk has published a book of poems, *Tečeva čez polje* (Let's Run Through the Field, 1994); a novel, *Rahela* (Rachel, 1989); two collections of short stories, *Preskok* (Jump Over, 1987) and *Vrata* (The Door, 1991); and a book of essays, *Na robu resničnosti* (On the Edge of Reality, 1992). Virk also translates from German, English, and Serbo-Croatian. In 1994 he edited a book (in Slovene) on myths in the legends of the American Indians: *Moški nad prepadom* (The Man Above the Abyss). *Smeh za lešeno pregrado* (The Smile Behind the Wooden Fence, 2000), Virk's most recent book, is an affectionate first-person narrative about the small town in Slovenia in which Virk grew up, his family background, the local public school, the accidental drowning of his friend Leon, and the townspeople and the impact on them of the last years of World War II and the beginning of collectivization under Tito. A running dialogue with his alter ego, the lively, and earthy, young boy Pavel—which is printed in italics—adds another dimension to the narrative and functions as the prism through which the past is often viewed.

Translations: "The Door," "Rošlin and Verjanko," and "Regatta," trans. Lili Potpara, in *The Day Tito Died: Contemporary Slovenian Short Stories* (London: Forest, 1993), 79–101.

Višnjić, Miroslav Josić (b. 1946) Serbian novelist, short-story writer, poet, and playwright. A talented and idiosyncratic writer, Višnjić was born in Stapar in the Vojvodina region of Serbia. He received his early education in his native town and then studied at a teachers college in Sambor. He subsequently earned a degree in world literature and literary theory at Belgrade University. Višnjić has had extensive experience as an editor and a publisher. He served as secretary of the journal *Student,* editor in chief of the periodical *Relations,* and editor of *Novi Albatros,* and became one of the first private publishers in post–World War II Yugoslavia when he founded the Književna fabrika "MJB i deca" (Book Factory "MJB and Sons"). Višnjić began his literary career in 1966 with a volume of poems, *Azbuka smeha* (The Alphabet of Laughter). It was followed by two collections of short stories: *Lepa Jelena* (Beautiful Helen, 1969) and *Dvanaest godova* (Twelve Rings, 1975). A popular work when it first appeared, *Lepa Jelena* is narrated by the eponymous heroine, a young village woman of casual morals who describes her life in the big city: nightclubs, where she spends much time; romantic encounters, especially with soldiers; and everyday trials and tribulations. The hedonism and shallowness of her life and the candor of her narrative are the stories' major source of appeal and a social commentary on the times. The work was awarded the Isadora Sekulić Prize in 1970.

Višnjić's first longer prose work was the novella *Roman o smrti Galerije* (Novel About the Death of an Art Gallery), which he completed in 1970 but which was regarded as controversial and kept out of bookstores in the Republic of Serbia despite its sales elsewhere in Yugoslavia in 1972 to 1974. In 1971 Višnjić published the novel *Češka škola* (The Czech School), which won the prize of the newspaper *Mladost* in 1972. It was followed by *Rečima po platnu svetu* (Like Words on a Canvas World, 1978), a book about the painter Milan Konjović, and the idiosyncratic *Pristup u svetljost (TBC, prvi zglob)* (Access to the Light [TBC, the First Joint], 1980), a 280-page work consisting entirely of very short sketches, some containing only a single word. Many of the sentences resemble lines of poetry with rhymes and patterns of repetition reminiscent of the oral tradition, as

The water was cold
And the sand was moist.
And the sky was blue.

And I was naked.
And she was naked.
So see: we were naked.

Višnjić says he began working on the text on 9 May 1970 and finished it at the end of January 1975. In 1982 Višnjić published, at his own expense, another curious text with the title *Pro/za 30* (Pro/For 30).

Višnjić's most highly regarded work is *Odbrana i propast Bodroga u sedam burnih godišnjih doba* (The Defense and Fall of Bodrog, During Seven Turbulent Seasons, 1990), on which he worked from 1976 to the spring of 1989. Set in the Serbian Vojvodina in the time of the Serbian and Hungarian revolutionary campaigns of 1848/1849, the novel traces the defeat of the Serbs at Bodrog by the Austrians and Hungarians, the subsequent outbreak of cholera in the region in the summer of 1849, and the ultimate crushing of the Hungarian uprising by combined Austrian and Russian armies. Bodrog (Bodrok), which no longer exists, arose in the eastern Vojvodina in the sixteenth and seventeenth centuries. A splendidly constructed novel merging the lyrical and epic, *Odbrana i propast Bodroga u sedam burnih godišnjih doba* has won several awards: the NIN Prize as novel of the year and the Boris Stanković and Stanislav Vinaver prizes for the best book of prose in the Serbian language; the newspaper *Borba* also named it best book of prose for the year. Višnjić's own drama based on the novel was performed by Radio Belgrade in 1991. Radio Belgrade had previously performed Višnjić's play *Služba oca Radoslava* (The Service of Father Radoslav, 1970) and in 1974 TV-Belgrade aired his film *Pogledaj me, nevernice* (Look at Me, Faithless Woman). Višnjić is also the author of a literary reference work titled *Azbučnik prideva u srpskoj prozi dvadesetog veka* (An Alphabetical List of Adjectives in Serbian Prose of the Twentieth Century, 1991). His most recent publication is the collection of nineteen stories *Novi godovi* (The New Rings, 1998). Although the stories reflect the war in Yugoslavia and the political situation in the Balkans in the 1990s, and in one case harks back to the political turmoil of 1948 and the Yugoslav–Soviet break, Višnjić's sense of humor and literary playfulness offset the somber reality of much of the subject matter.

Translations: "The Forest of Perpetual Darkness," trans. Henry R. Cooper Jr. and Gordana B. Todorović, in *The Prince of Fire: An Anthology of Contemporary Serbian Short Stories*, ed. Radmila J. Gorup and Nadežda Obradović (Pittsburgh: University of Pittsburgh Press, 1998), 230–37.

Voiculescu, Vasile (1884–1963) Romanian poet, short-story writer, and playwright. A native of Pîrscov, in Buzău county, about sixty-five miles north of Bucharest, Voiculescu studied in Buzău and Bucharest and in 1902 entered the Faculty of Letters and Philosophy of Bucharest University. However, he switched to medicine and received his degree in 1910. While pursuing his medical career in the provinces, Voiculescu began devoting increasingly more time to his writing. He began his literary career as a poet, publishing his first volume of poetry, *Poezii* (Poems), in 1916. A similarly titled collection appeared in 1944. Voiculescu published another five volumes of poetry before World War II: *Pîrgă* (Ripening, 1921); *Poeme cu îngeri* (Poems with Angels, 1927); *Destin* (Destiny, 1933); *Urcuș* (Ascent, 1937); and *Intrezăriri* (Glimpses, 1939). In 1941 he was awarded the Great National Prize for Poetry. A frequent writer for radio, he became manager of the Romanian Radio Broadcasting Company in 1930. He also published several plays in the 1930s, among them *Fata ursului* (The Bear's Daughter, 1930); *Duhul pămîntului* (The Earth Spirit, 1932); and *La pragul minunii* (On the Threshold of Wonder, 1932), followed by *Demiurgul* (The Demiurg, 1943) and *Gimnastică sentimentală*

(Sentimental Exercises, 1972). Like several of his prose works, Voiculescu's dramatic works deal with the striving for self-perfection of the individual or the human race.

After World War II, Voiculescu's attempt to resume his literary career was thwarted by the politics of communist Romania. Sharing the fate of other prominent literary figures of the interwar period, he was blacklisted and, beginning in 1947, unable to publish his works for the rest of his life.

Although he was regarded primarily as a writer of the interwar period, and largely overlooked, posthumous publication of Voiculescu's postwar writings attracted considerable attention and won him an entirely new audience. The first of these posthumous publications, and perhaps the most impressive, was *Ultimele sonete închipuite ale lui Shakespeare în traducere imaginară de V. Voiculescu* (*Shakespeare's Last Fancied Sonnets in V. Voiculescu's Imaginary Translation*), which came out in 1964, a year after the poet's death. The ninety sonnets in the collection, representing a collective exploration of all the manifestations of love, were composed between 1954 and 1958 and merit recognition as a remarkable literary fiction as well as poetic achievement. Shakespeare wrote 154 sonnets. What Voiculescu did was to construct an imaginary series of Shakespearean sonnets, numbered 155 to 244, in a Romanian much alive with the spirit and themes of Shakespeare's own sonnets. Equally impressive an achievement in prose was the stylistically rich two-volume collection of tales of fantasy and magic published in 1966 under the title *Povestiri* and containing "Capul de zimbru" ("The Aurochs's Head") and "Ultimul Berevoi" ("The Last of the Berevois"). Lively and entertaining, Voiculescu's tales transform the traditional village of Romanian realism into a realm of myth and legend. Some Romanian critics see in Voiculescu's "magical village" a kind of antireality juxtaposed to the grim reality of

Stalinist Romania in the decade of the 1950s. The publication of Voiculescu's tales of fantasy and magic also coincided with the renewal of Romanian prose writing in the early 1960s. The conjuring of a mythical and symbolic interpretation of village life typical of this writing and exemplified by works of such writers as D. R. Popescu, Fănuş Neagu, and Ştefan Bănulescu, owed much to Voiculescu's example. The growing interest in Voiculescu, since the publication of his posthumous works in the 1960s, is evident in the new editions of his texts in the 1970s, 1980s, and 1990s. A small volume of his plays was published in 1972 under the title *Teatru* (Theater); a collection of his tales of magic and fantasy, *Iubire magică* (Magic Love), came out in 1975 and again in 1984; a two-volume collection of his poetry (*Poezii*) appeared in 1983; another volume of his prose fiction was published in 1991 as *Toiagul minunilor* (The Wand of Miracles); and a volume of his religious poetry, *Calatorie spre locul inimii* (Journey to the Seat of the Heart), was issued in 1994. Voiculescu's last written work was the strong novel *Zahei orbul* (Zahei the Blind, 1970). Recapitulating themes found elsewhere in Voiculescu's writing, it is a kind of religious parable indebted in part to the fairy-tale tradition about a man for whom injustice and protracted suffering become the way to self-discovery.

Translations: *Shakespeare's Last Fancied Sonnets in V. Voiculescu's Imaginary Translation,* trans. Christina Tătaru (Cluj-Napoca: Dacia, 1990); *Tales of Fantasy and Magic,* trans. Ana Cartianu (Bucharest: Minerva, 1986); "The Last of the Berevois," in *The Phantom Church and Other Stories from Romania,* ed. and trans. Georgiana Farnoaga and Sharon King (Pittsburgh: University of Pittsburgh Press, 1996), 3–17; six poems, including three of the Shakespeare sonnets, trans. Andrei Bantaş, Dan Duţescu, and Leon Leviţchi, in *Like Diamonds in Coal Asleep: Selections from Twentieth Century Romanian Poetry,* ed. Andrei Bantaş (Bucharest: Minerva, 1985), 75–80. A collection of Voiculescu's poems is available as *Poesies,* trans. Paul Miclau (Bucharest: Minerva, 1981), a French–Romanian edition.

Vopěnka, Martin (b. 1963) Czech novelist. A native of Prague, Vopěnka was trained as a nuclear physicist but gave up science for a career in literature. Besides his fictional writing, he is the owner of a small publishing house in the Czech capital. He made his first appearance on the Prague literary scene in the 1980s as a participant in authors' evenings at the Rubín club. His first published work was *Kameny z hor* (Rocks from the Mountains, 1989), a small book of lyric prose resembling a diary. A continuation of *Kameny z hor, Balada o sestupu* (*Ballad of Descent,* 1992), his best-known work, traces the Kafkaesque journey of two young men from Prague on a Christmas Day to "that other country." The society they leave behind is one of repressed individuality, but in "that other country," which is very near and is obviously intended to represent Romania (its inhabitants have Romanian names and occasionally utter words and phrases in Romanian), they find far worse repression and the chaos of great civil unrest. However, a passionate love affair between the narrator of the novel (one of the two men on the journey) and a woman he meets and ultimately loses in "that other country" assumes a transcendant significance, investing a symbolic and metaphoric quest for self-discovery with meaning. In his most recent novel, *Hotel uprostřed života* (Hotel in the Midst of Life, 1999), which was written between 1990 and 1996, Vopěnka explores the traumatic effects on his parents, close friends, and himself of a young man's tormented relationship with a married woman.

Translations: *Ballad of Descent,* trans. Anna Bryson (Evanston, Ill.: Northwestern University Press, 1995).

Vostrá, Alena (b. 1938) Czech novelist and playwright. A native of Prague, Vostrá graduated from high school in 1956 and then studied surveying for two years at the Czech Technical College in Prague before switching over to the Theater Faculty of the Academy of Musical Arts with the intention of studying the lute and lute making. However, she was expelled from the institution in 1960 on the grounds of "individualism" but was later permitted to reenter it in the summer of 1962 after a protracted appeal process. Since she was not encouraged to continue in her previous field of specialization, she instead pursued the study of dramaturgy and finally graduated in 1966. During the period of her exclusion from the Academy of Musical Arts, Vostrá became actively involved in children's entertainment, an interest she resumed somewhat later in her career.

Vostrá made her literary debut in 1964 with the novella *Bůh z reklamy* (God from an Ad). It was followed by *Vlažná vlna* (The Tepid Wave, 1966), which continued her interest in depicting the banality of everyday life but with a greater emphasis on stylistic and structural experimentation. The novel is about an attractive hairdresser whose innocent relationship with her boss, who is romantically interested in her, becomes a source of malicious gossip. When the boss's wife, who is in the hospital, dies unexpectedly of a pulmonary embolism, there is even speculation about the cause of her death. Ordinary, even banal people, petty intrigues, ill-founded gossip, and sometimes suspicious deaths are as commonplace in Vostrá's fiction as her use of dialogue as the principal means of character delineation. After publishing two plays in the 1960s—*Na koho to slovo padne* (On Whom the Word Falls, 1967) and *Na ostří nože* (On the Cutting Edge, 1968)—and a series of works for children, she resumed writing novels and in 1988 came out with *Než dojde k vraždě* (Before It Comes to Murder) and *Tanec na ledě* (Dance on Ice), both of which operate with formulas of the mystery genre.

Vrhovac, Duška (b. 1947) Bosnian Serb poet. A native of Banja Luka, Vrhovac graduated from Belgrade University, where she studied world literature and literary theory. Although she began publishing poems as early as 1966, her first volume of poetry, *San po san* (Dream by Dream), appeared only in 1986. It was followed by *S dušom u telu* (With a Soul in the Body, 1987); *Godine bez leta* (Years Without Summer, 1988); and *Glas na pragu* (Voice on the Threshold, 1990). A resident of Belgrade, where she works as a freelance journalist and critic as well as an editor of television documentaries, Vrhovac has also translated from twentieth-century German and Italian literatures. A poet of well-crafted miniatures, Vrhovac writes of love, separation, loss and loneliness, and the solace of the written word.

Translations: *I Wear My Shadow Inside Me*, trans. Richard Burns with Vera Radojević (London: Forest, 1991), a selection from Vrhovac's four published volumes of poetry.

Vrkljan, Irena (b. 1930) Croatian poet, memoirist, translator, and film and radio scriptwriter. Born in Belgrade, Vrkljan studied archaeology and German at Zagreb University. She also graduated from the Film and Television Academy of Berlin in 1969. Since then, she has divided her time between Berlin and Zagreb and writes in both Croatian and German. Apart from her several volumes of poetry and her translations into German of works by Croatian authors, Vrkljan is the author of a stunning and innovative autobiography. Written originally in Serbo-Croatian, and comprising so far the two works *Svila, škare* (Silk and Shears, 1984; translated as *The Silk, the Shears and*

Marina; or About Biography) and *Marina, ili, o biografiji* (Marina, or, On Biography, 1986; translated as *Marina, or, On Memory*), the closely related small volumes are at once an autobiography and a biography of another woman writer, the distinguished Russian poet Marina Tsvetaeva (1892–1941), in which biographical writing is explored as literature and as memory. *The Silk, the Shears and Marina; or About Biography,* which was greeted with high praise on its publication and was awarded the K. Š. Gjalski Prize in 1986, consists of a three-part collection of autobiographical fragments covering Vrkljan's childhood in Belgrade before World War II, her well-off family's move to Zagreb in 1941, the war itself, her life in postwar socialist Yugoslavia, and her subsequent career as a writer in Zagreb and Berlin. In *Marina, or, On Memory,* Vrkljan turns her attention to the life and career of Tsvetaeva, to whom she was attracted by both her poetry and her suicide in 1941. Vrkljan's other writings include such books of poems as *Paralele* (Parallels, 1957); *Soba, taj strašan vrt* (The Room, This Frightful Garden, 1966); and *U koži moje sestre: Berlinske pjesme* (In My Sister's Skin: Berlin Poems, 1982) and the novels *Stvari već daleka* (Matters Now Distant, 1962); *Doba prijatelstva* (Time of Friendship, 1963); *Dora ove jeseni* (Dora, 1991); *Pred crvenim zidom, 1991–1993* (Before the Red Wall, 1991–1993, 1994); and *Posljednje putovanje u Beć* (The Last Trip to Vienna, 2000), a short mystery novel.

Translations: *Marina, or, On Memory,* trans. Celia Hawkesworth (Zagreb: The Bridge, 1991); *The Silk, the Shears and Marina; or About Biography,* trans. Sibelan Forrester and Celia Hawkesworth (Evanston, Ill.: Northwestern University Press, 1999). SOUND RECORDING: A sound recording, dated 1964, of Vrkljan reading her poetry is available in the Woodberry Poetry Room, Harvard University.

Wander, Maxie (1933–1977) German short-story and documentary writer. A native of Vienna, Wander quit school before graduating in order to join the workforce. In 1958 she and her husband, the writer Fred Wander, moved to East Germany and settled in Klein-Machnow, near Potsdam. She worked as a secretary, a journalist, a writer of scenarios, and a photographer. Her premature death from cancer in Berlin in 1977 ended a literary career that had just begun but had already established Wander as one of the most influential East German writers of her time. Her one and only short story, "Martine," appeared in the journal *Das Magazin* in 1968. Although it attracted favorable attention, it was her sensational collection of interviews with seventeen East German women from different walks of life, *Guten Morgen, du Schöne: Frauen in der DDR* (Good Morning, My Lovely: Women in the GDR, 1977), that really established Wander's literary fame. A groundbreaking, extraordinarily candid glimpse into virtually every facet of the life of the East German woman, the book—in which only the responses of the interviewees are recorded—quickly achieved the status of a canonical text of German feminism on both sides of the Berlin Wall (it was published in West Germany in 1978). This despite the fact that Wander advances no feminist agenda in *Guten Morgen, du Schöne: Frauen in der DDR* and offers no theoretical postulates. Wander's women seek self-definition beyond the confines of stereotypical gender roles and often do so in concert with, rather than in opposition to, the men in their lives. Love, which looms large in Wander's outlook, usually operates as a key motivational factor. The contribution of *Guten Morgen, du Schöne: Frauen in der DDR* to the development of a strong women's literature in the German Democratic Republic can be seen in the fact that it preceded such important texts in this area as Sarah Kirsch's *Die Pantherfrau* (*The Panther Woman*) and novels by Irmtraud Morgner, Brigitte Reimann, and Gerti Tetzner. Two years after Wander's death, her husband, Fred, selected and published a collection of her previously unpublished writings under the title *Maxie Wander: Tagebücher und Briefe* (Maxie Wander: Diaries and Letters, 1979). *Leben wär eine prima Alternative* (Life Would Be a Great Alternative), in which Wander writes about the death of her daughter Kitty and her own struggle with cancer, appeared in 1980.

Translations: "The Fear of Love" (from *Guten Morgen, du Schöne: Frauen in der DDR*), trans. Jan van Heurck, in *The New Sufferings of Young W. and Other Stories from the German Democratic Republic,* ed. Therese Hörnigk and Alexander Stephan (New York: Continuum, 1997), 184–89; "Ute G., 24, Skilled Worker, Single, One Child" (from *Guten Morgen, du Schöne: Frauen in der DDR*), trans. Nancy Lukens, in *Daughters of Eve: Women's Writing from the German Democratic Republic,* ed. and trans. Nancy Lukens and Dorothy Rosenberg (Lincoln: University of Nebraska Press, 1993), 39–48.

Wat, Aleksander (real name Aleksander Chwat; 1900–1967) Polish poet and short-story writer. A major figure in the development of the interwar Polish avant-garde, Wat was born in Warsaw where in 1918 he graduated from high school. He then went on to study philosophy, psychology, and logic at Warsaw University, but because of several interruptions he did not graduate until 1926. A cofounder of the Polish futurist movement, he was coeditor of the journal *Nowa Sztuka* in 1921/1922 and of the *Almanach Nowej Sztuki* (Almanac of *Nowa*

Sztuka) in 1924/1925. A number of his early writings first appeared in these publications. Wat's first published collection of futurist poetry, *Ja z jednej strony i Ja z drugiej strony mego mopsożelaznego piecyka* (Me from One Side and Me from the Other Side of My Pug Iron Stove), appeared in 1920. It was followed in 1927 by *Bezrobotny Lucyfer* (*Lucifer Unemployed*), a collection of experimental short stories. In 1929 Wat became the editor of *Miesięcznik Literacki,* the most important communist journal in Poland between the wars. It was closed down in 1932, and Wat was briefly imprisoned.

Between 1933 and the outbreak of World War II in September 1939, Wat worked as literary director at the distinguished Polish publishing house Gebethner & Wolff. After being separated from his wife and son as they were fleeing the invading Germans, Wat went to Lwów in eastern Poland in search of them. By then, Lwów had fallen to Soviet forces after the USSR's march into Poland on 17 September 1939. Wat succeeded in reuniting with his family and worked for a while for the newspaper *Czerwony Sztandar.* However, he was arrested by the Soviet authorities in 1940 and again separated from his family, who were deported to Kazakhstan. Wat was transferred to prison in Kiev and then Moscow. After the German invasion of the Soviet Union on 22 June 1941, he was imprisoned in Saratov, where he converted to Christianity from Judaism. He was released from prison in late 1941 and again reunited with his family in 1942. In 1943 the Wats settled in Ili, Kazakhstan, returning to Warsaw in April 1946 when Wat resumed his literary career. His first postwar publication, *Wiersze* (Poems), appeared in 1957 and won the *Nowa Kultura* Prize that year. The following year, 1958, he became editor in chief of the state publishing house, Państwowy Instytut Wydawniczy. He was also now a member of the governing body of the Polish Writers Union, the presidium of the Council of Artists Unions, and the executive committee of the Polish PEN Club.

Wat had spent the years 1955 to 1957 in France for medical reasons and resettled there permanently in 1963. His next collection of poetry, *Wiersz śródziemnomorskie* (*Mediterranean Poems*), appeared in Poland in 1962, but not long afterward a ban was placed on further publication of Wat's works in Poland in response to his alleged anticommunist activity in emigration. In 1964/1965, Wat was in Berkeley on invitation from the University of California's Center for Slavic and East European Studies. While there, he spent many hours taping his memoirs in the company of his fellow Polish poet Czesław Miłosz. With Miłosz's assistance, the memoirs were edited for publication and appeared in London in 1977 under the title *My Century*. Wat died in Paris in 1967. The following year, a collection of his poems from the period 1963 to 1967 was published in Paris under the title *Ciemno świecidło* (Dark Trinkets).

Literature: Tomas Venclova, *Aleksander Wat: Life and Art of an Iconoclast* (New Haven, Conn.: Yale University Press, 1996), a good critical biography of Wat that includes a number of his poems in translation.

Translations: *Lucifer Unemployed,* trans. Lillian Vallee (Evanston, Ill.: Northwestern University Press, 1990); *Mediterranean Poems,* ed. and trans. Czesław Miłosz (Ann Arbor, Mich.: Ardis, 1977); *My Century: The Odyssey of a Polish Intellectual,* trans. Richard Lourie (Berkeley: University of California Press, 1988); *With the Skin,* trans. and ed. Czesław Miłosz and Nathan Leonard (New York: Ecco Press, 1989).

Ważyk, Adam (1905–1981) Polish poet, playwright, novelist, and essayist. A native of Warsaw, Ważyk was a prominent member of the prewar avant-garde and one of the foremost representatives of cubism in Pol-

ish poetry of the 1920s. He began his literary career in 1924 with a volume of poetry titled *Semafory* (Semaphores), followed two years later by his second volume, *Oczy i usta* (Eyes and Lips). Despite his impact on Polish poetry at the time, Ważyk all but stopped writing verse in the 1930s, opting instead for prose fiction. He published two novels before the outbreak of World War II: *Latarnie świecą w Karpowie* (Lamps Are Lit in Karpów, 1930) and *Mity rodzinne* (Family Myths, 1938). Ważyk spent the war years in the Soviet Union, where he resumed writing poetry. When he returned to Poland, it was as an officer in a Polish communist-backed army raised in the USSR and a proponent of Soviet-style socialist realism. The poems Ważyk wrote during the war were published in a single volume in Lublin in 1944 under the title *Serce granatu* (The Heart of a Grenade). One of the poems, "Szkic pamiętnika" ("Sketch for a Memoir"), is notable for its picture of the interwar Polish literary scene and its poetic schools and debates. Years later, in 1977, Ważyk returned to the avant-garde of which he had been a prominent member in one of his more important literary works, *Dziwna historia awangardy* (The Strange History of the Avant-garde), a nearly 100-page essay about Polish avant-garde poetry accompanied by a small anthology of representative texts.

Although regarded as a militant proponent of socialist realism in Poland after the war, Ważyk published few new poems during the Stalinist period, busying himself instead with a well-regarded translation with the poet Julian Tuwim of Aleksandr Pushkin's *Eugene Onegin,* one of the masterpieces of classical Russian literature. The translation appeared in 1977. A volume of Ważyk's selected verse appeared in 1947, followed in 1950 by *Nowy wybór wierszy* (A New Selection of Poems). In 1955 Ważyk stunned the Polish literary world with his controversial *Poemat dla dorosłych* (A Poem for

Adults), an astonishing repudiation of political and cultural totalitarianism. The work is generally acknowledged as signaling the beginning of the post-Stalinist cultural "thaw" in Poland. Ważyk subsequently resumed writing poetry and published an additional four volumes before his death: *Wiersze i poematy* (Lyrics and Poems, 1957); *Wybór poezji* (Selected Poems, 1967); *Zdarzenia* (Occurrences, 1977), his last volume of original poems; and *Wiersze wybrane* (Selected Poems, 1978). His later poetry is distinguished by a symbiosis of prewar avantgarde techniques and contemporatry themes, including politics. Apart from *Dziwna historia awangardy*, Ważyk published other studies of Polish poetry and literature, among them *Esej o wierszu* (An Essay on Verse, 1964); *Kwestia gustu* (A Question of Taste, 1966); *Eseje literackie* (Literary Essays, 1982); and *Amfion: Rozważania nad wierszem polskim* (Amphion: Thoughts on Polish Poetry, 1983).

Translations: Five poems in *Polish Poetry of the Last Two Decades of Communist Rule: Spoiling Cannibals' Fun,* ed. and trans. Stanisław Barańczak and Clare Cavanagh (Evanston, Ill.: Northwestern University Press, 1991), 18–21.

Wegner, Bettina (full name Bettina Wegner-Schlessinger; b. 1947) German songwriter and poet. A native of Berlin, Wegner studied librarianship from 1964 to 1966 and then enrolled in the Actors Studio in Berlin. She was dismissed, however, because of her participation in demonstrations protesting the Soviet invasion of Czechoslovakia in 1968. She was also given a sixteen-month suspended sentence. In 1972/1973, she earned her diploma in song from the Central Studio of Entertainment Art and thereafter became a full-time songwriter and poet. She again ran afoul of the authorities in 1976 when she joined a number of other East German artists in protesting the

government's action in the Wolf Biermann matter and was banned from further public performances. Thereafter, her records and books could be published only in West Germany. Wegner's publications include her first collection of poems, *Wenn meine Lieder nicht mehre stimmen* (If My Songs Can No Longer Be Heard, 1979), which includes texts from the period 1963 to 1978 and carries an introduction by the poet Sarah Kirsch. Borrowing from the traditions of folklore, children's literature, and popular song, Wegner's lyrics make a strong appeal to the private life and are not for the most part overtly political. Despite the ban on her public performances, Wegner developed an enthusiastic "private" following and in time became immensely popular for her songs and poems. In the 1980s, she was regarded by many of her admirers as the spiritual voice of her generation. Her other published works include *Traurig bin ich sowieso* (I'm Sad Anyway, 1982); *Als ich gerade zwanzig war* (When I Was Just Twenty, 1986); *Von Deutschland nach Deutschland: Ein Katzensprung* (From Germany to Germany: A Stone's Throw, 1986); and *Es ist so wenig: Lieder, Texte, Noten* (It's So Little: Songs, Texts, Scores, 1991).

Weil, Jiří (1900–1959) Czech novelist. Born near Prague, Weil eventually studied at Charles University, where in 1928 he received his doctorate for a dissertation on the Russian writer Nikolai Gogol and the English novel. In the mid-1930s, Weil wrote *Moskva—hranice* (From Moscow to the Border, 2nd ed., 1991), which was based on his experiences in Moscow working for the Czech section of the Comintern publishing house. He was expelled from the Czech Communist Party as a result. *Dřevěná lžíce* (The Wooden Spoon), a sequel to *Moskva—hranice,* remained unpublished for some thirty years until it appeared in an Italian translation in 1970. It was published in a

Czech samizdat edition in 1980 and was reprinted by a commercial house in Prague in 1992. In 1942, during the German occupation of Czechoslovakia, Weil feigned suicide to avoid a callup for transportation to a concentration camp with the rest of Prague's Jews, and succeeded in hiding until the end of the war. In the late 1950s, Weil was appointed director of the Jewish State Museum in Prague. He was also readmitted to the Writers Union. But he remained largely reclusive until his death in 1959.

Apart from *Vzpomínky na Julia Fučíka* (Recollections of Julius Fučík, 1947), a book of reminiscences about his friend Julius Fučík (1903–1943), a Czech writer, Weil's most important post–World War II writings are the novels *Život s hvězdou* (*Life with a Star,* 1949) and *Na střeše je Mendelssohn* (*Mendelssohn Is on the Roof,* 1960), both set in Prague in the period of the German occupation. Patently autobiographical, *Life with a Star* is a first-person account of how the everyday world of a Jewish former bank clerk is grotesquely transformed by the occupation. *Mendelssohn Is on the Roof* is a grimly ironic novel about what happens when a young SS officer is ordered to pull down the statue of the Jewish composer Felix Mendelssohn from among those atop the roof of Prague's concert hall and erroneously topples the statue of the great German composer Richard Wagner based on the length of his nose.

Translations: *Life with a Star,* trans. Ruzena Kovarikova with Roslyn Schloss (New York: Farrar, Straus and Giroux, 1989); *Life with a Star,* trans. Rita Klímová with Roslyn Schloss (Evanston, Ill.: Northwestern University Press, 1998); *Mendelssohn Is on the Roof,* trans. Marie Winn (New York: Farrar, Straus and Giroux, 1991; Evanston, Ill.: Northwestern University Press, 1998).

Weöres, Sándor (1913–1989) Hungarian poet and playwright. One of the most gifted and versatile twentieth-century Hungarian poets, Weöres was born into a small-landowning family in Szombathely, near the Austrian border, but was raised in the nearby village of Csönge. He studied law and then geography and history at Pécs University and eventually earned a doctorate in philosophy and aesthetics. His dissertation, *A vers születése* (The Birth of the Poem), was published in 1939 and sheds interesting light on his attitude toward poetic creativity. His first book of poetry, *Hideg van* (It Is Cold), was published in 1934. In recognition of his growing stature as a poet, he was awarded the prestigious Baumgarten Prize in 1935 and again in 1936. *Hideg van* was followed by such highly acclaimed books of poetry as *A teremtés dícsérete* (In Praise of Creation, 1938); *A fogak tornáca* (The Colonnade of Teeth, 1947); and *A hallgatás tornya* (The Tower of Silence, 1956).

Drafted into a labor force during World War II, he never saw front-line duty. During the darker days of postwar Hungarian communism, when his refusal to go along with the doctrine of socialist realism earned him denunciation as a "nihilist," Weöres was limited to earning his living by writing children's books and translating. He published a great deal of verse for children that has long enjoyed considerable popularity. As a translator, Weöres was as indefatigable as he was global. He had traveled extensively through Europe and Asia in the 1930s and drew on a broad knowledge of different cultures, from American to Japanese. His strong interest in Asian philosophy and religion is reflected not only in his own poetic creativity but also in his versions of Chinese and Japanese poetry. Weöres's impressive learning also grew out of his long employment as a librarian first in Pécs, then in Székesfehérvár, and finally in Budapest Weöres's enthusiasm for translating was shared by his wife, the poet Amy Károlyi. In 1977 both poets visited the United States as guests of the Translation Center of Columbia University. This was the year in which Columbia University Press published *Modern Hungarian Poetry,* edited by Miklós Vajda. The Hungarian poets Ferenc Juhász and István Vas were also along on the trip and, with Weöres and Károlyi, gave readings of their poems at the Guggenheim Museum in New York and elsewhere. Two collections of Weöres's translations have been published: *A lélek idezése* (The Conjuring of the Soul, 1958) and *Egybegyűjtött műfordítások* (Collected Translations, 1976).

After his collection of poems *Tűzkút* (Fire Pump) was published in Paris in 1964 because of the ban on Weöres in Hungary, the poet was able to reenter the Hungarian literary mainstream in the late 1960s, beginning with the volume *Merülő Saturnus* (Saturn Descending, 1968). Subsequent books of poems by him include *Áthallások* (Overhearing, 1976); *Harmincöt vers* (Thirty-Five Poems, 1978); *Ének a határtalanról* (The Song of the Boundless, 1980); *Posta messziről* (Mail from Far Away, 1984); *Magyar etűdök: Száz kis énekszöveg* (Hungarian Etudes: One Hundred Small Texts, 1985); *Kútbanező* (Well Gazer, 1987); *A sebzett föld éneke* (The Song of Wounded Earth, 1989); and the posthumously published *A teljesség felé* (Toward Wholeness, 1995). Weöres's astonishing range—from children's verse to deeply philosophical poems centered largely on humans' place in the universe—and great mastery of language and form eventually earned him official recognition when in 1970 he was awarded the coveted Kossuth Prize. In 1983 Weöres's collected dramatic works were published under the title *Színjátétok* (Plays)

Two of Weöres's more interesting publications date from the 1970s. In *Psyche: Egy hajdani költőnő írásai* (Psyche: Writings by a Poet of Yore, 1972), a witty and linguistically brilliant literary hoax, Weöres claimed that the texts contained in the volume had been written originally by an early-nineteenth-century Hungarian poet by the name of Erszébet Lónyay, whom he called Psyche. The book is a miscellany of "Psyche's" poetry, translations, personal notes, and letters, and even includes a biographical account of her by a putative contemporary. In a postscript, Weöres related the circumstances surrounding the "discovery" of the long-lost collection. A genuine literary tour de force, *Psyche* not only re-creates the carefree, cosmopolitan ambience of the rococo and Biedermeier styles of the late eighteenth and early nineteenth centuries, but also constructs an astonishingly convincing portrait of a woman by entering her mind and soul. In 1977 Weöres published a different sort of tour de force, a gigantic anthology of forgotten or previously unknown gems of Hungarian poetry with critical commentary titled *Harom veréb hat szemmel* (Three Sparrows with Six Eyes).

Of the many poems by Weöres available in English translation, perhaps the finest introduction to his outlook and style is "Az elveszített napernyő" ("The Lost Parasol," 1953), one of his longer texts (ten pages in English). The poem relates the transformation of a red parasol—the symbol of their love—left behind by a young woman after a romantic tryst with her lover at the edge of a steep gorge. Abandoned to the forces of nature, the parasol disintegrates, a piece of red silk all that remains. In a parallel transformation, the lovers themselves are destined to molder into one after death.

Literature: Zoltán Kenyeres, *Tündérsíp: Weöres Sándorról* (Budapest: Szépirodalmi Könyvkiadó, 1982), a standard biography of the poet; János L. Nagy, *Ismétlések és értelmezések Weöres Sándor verseiben* (Budapest: Akadémiai Kiadó, 1996), and Attila Támas, *Weöres Sándor* (Budapest: Akadémiai Kiadó, 1978), both books of criticism; Imre Bata, *Weöres Sándor közelében* (Budapest: Magvető, 1979); Vera Zimáné

Lengyel, *Weöres Sándor: Bibliografia* (Budapest: Fővárosi Szabó Ervin Könyvtár, 1979), a bibliography of Weöres's writings; Mátyás Domokos, ed., *Magyar Orpheus: Weöres Sándor emlékezetére* (Budapest: Szépirodalmi Könyvkiadó, 1990), a collection of essays by various hands, and *Egyedül mindenkivel: Weöres Sándor beszélgétesei, nyilatkozatai, vallomásai* (Budapest: Szépirodalmi Könyvkiadó, 1993), a collection of interviews with Weöres.

Translations: *Eternal Moment: Selected Poems,* ed. Miklós Vajda (London: Anvil, 1988), which contains "The Lost Parasol," 69–78; *If All the World Were a Blackbird: Poems by Sándor Weöres,* trans. Alexander Fenton (Aberdeen: Aberdeen University Press, 1985); *Selected Poems of Sandor Weöres,* trans. Edwin Morgan [and] *Selected Poems of Ferenc Juhasz,* trans. David Wevill (Harmondsworth: Penguin, 1970); thirty poems in *The Face of Creation: Contemporary Hungarian Poetry,* trans. Jascha Kesler (Minneapolis: Coffee House, 1988), 166–86.

Wiens, Paul (1922–1982) German poet and essayist. A native of Königsberg, Wiens emigrated with his family from Germany in 1933, the year Hitler became chancellor, because of concerns about his Jewish origin. After living for a few years in Switzerland, Italy, France, and England, he returned to Germany where he was promptly arrested and put in a concentration camp. After his liberation near the end of the war, he settled in what became East Germany and later became active in literary theoretical debates in the 1950s and 1960s. An avowed Marxist, he took issue nevertheless with communist dogmatists over the matter of the creative autonomy of the artist. Early in his career, Wiens had embraced the doctrine of socialist realism and composed "agit" (agitational) poetry and propagandistic texts for mass songfests. However, his interesting collection of poems, *Nachrichten aus der dritten Welt* (Reports from the Third World, 1957)—the "third world" representing the present—reflected the East German literary thaw of 1956/1957 in its more lyrical and personal character, so atypical of socialist realist "monumentalism," with its emphasis on the collective as opposed to the individual. Wiens's next two books of poetry, *Dienstgeheimnis* (Professional Secret, 1968) and *Vier Linien aus meiner Hand: Gedichte, 1943–1971* (Four Lines from My Hand: Poems, 1943–1971, 1972), showed him capable of an impressive range artistically, of vivid and striking imagery, satirical talent, and a surprisingly optimistic worldview. Two more works by Wiens were published posthumously in the year of his death, 1982, by the East German publishing house Aufbau: *Innenweltbilderhandschrift: Gedichte und Musterzeichnungen* (A Picture Manuscript of the Inner World: Poems and Model Drawings) and *Einmischungen: Publizistik, 1949–1981* (Interferences: Journalistic Writings, 1949–1981), the latter of particular value in assessing the role that Wiens played in major East German literary debates.

Wirpsza, Witold (1918–1985) Polish poet, novelist, and short-story writer. Known for his writings in German as well as Polish, Wirpsza was born in Odessa. He studied law at Warsaw University and then music at the College of Music. He made his literary debut as a poet in the journal *Kuźnia Młodych* as early as 1935, but the German invasion of Poland in September 1939 drastically changed his life. He took part in the September campaign but was captured by the Germans and imprisoned until 1945. With the end of the war, he settled briefly in Kraków before accepting the editorship of the army weekly *Żołnierz Polski* in Warsaw. From 1947 to 1955, he lived in Szczecin where he was in charge of the cultural section of Radio Poland. He returned to Warsaw in 1956 and became a member of the editorial board of the important weekly *Po prostu*. From 1957 to 1958, he was also on the editorial board of the weekly *Nowa Kultura*. In 1969 Wirpsza left Poland and settled mainly in West Germany, where he became closely identified with the anticommunist Polish émigré press.

Although he eventually became better known for his prose, Wirpsza wrote and published a great deal of poetry and was well regarded as an original and innovative poet. His first volume of poetry appeared in 1949 under the title *Sonata* and set the pattern for his mostly socialist realist collections through 1956: *Stocznia* (The Shipyard, 1949); *Polemiki i pieśni* (Polemics and Poems, 1951); *Dziennik Kożedo* (Kożedo's Diary, 1952); *Pisane w kraju, 1950–1951* (Written in Poland, 1950–1951, 1952); *List do żony* (Letter to a Wife, 1953); *Poematy i wiersze wybrane* (Poems and Selected Lyrics, 1956); *Z mojego życia* (From My Life, 1956); and *Mały gatunek* (A Small Species, 1960), a collection of his poetry from 1943 to 1959. Beginning with his long poem *Don Juan* (1960), Wirpsza moved beyond socialist realism to a discovery of his own poetic voice, as is evident in such subsequent books as *Komentarze do fotografii: The Family of Man* (Comments on Photography: The Family of Man, 1962); *Drugi opór* (The Second Line of Resistance, 1965), a collection of poems from 1960 to 1964; *Przesądy* (Prejudices, 1966); *Traktat skłamany* (The False Treaty, 1968); and *Wagary* (Vagabonds, 1970).

Although interesting for its revelations of his personal life and experiences and for its broad humanitarian concerns, Wirpsza's poetry eventually became overshadowed by his prose text *Pomarańcze na drutach* (Oranges on Wires, 1964). This is a first-person narrative based on his experiences in a German concentration camp during World War II and notable especially for its exploration of the absurdity of the notion of a differentation between freedom of time and freedom of space as represented by different groups of inmates. The text became widely known

through its German translation in 1967. Wirpsza's first published work of prose fiction was the novel *Na granicy* (On the Border, 1954), which was followed by a collection of short stories titled *Stary tramwaj i inne opowiadania* (The Old Streetcar and Other Stories, 1955) and a volume of stories and dramatic texts, *Morderca* (Murderer, 1966).

In 1971, after he had left Poland for the West, Wirpsza published, in German, *Pole, wer bist du?* (Pole, Who Are You?, 1971), a general book divided into a large number of small sections intended to satisfy greater interest in Poland and Eastern Europe in the wake of the upheavals of 1956 (Hungary), 1968 (Czechoslovakia), and 1970 (the Polish workers' demonstrations in December of that year). The book reaches far back into the Polish past and comes up to World War II and postwar reconstruction. It also includes an analysis of the weak foundations of Polish communism. Needless to say, the book was roundly attacked in Poland. Wirpsza was also the author of a book of literary essays, *Gra znaczeń* (Interplay of Meanings, 1965), which while concerned mainly with theoretical issues, proved highly controversial in Polish literary circles in part because of Wirpsza's intrusion into politics as well.

Translations: Five poems in *Polish Poetry of the Last Two Decades of Communist Rule: Spoiling Cannibals' Fun*, ed. and trans. Stanisław Barańczak and Clare Cavanagh (Evanston, Ill.: Northwestern University Press, 1991), 37–40. *Polak, kim jesteś?* is available in German as *Pole, wer bist du?*, trans. Christa Vogel (Lucerne: Bucher, 1971); *Pomarańcze na drutach* as *Orangen im Stacheldraht*, trans. Maria Kurecka (Munich: Carl Hanser, 1967); and a collection of Wirpsza's poems as *Drei Berliner Gedichte* (Three Berlin Poems) (Berlin: Literarisches Colloquium, 1976).

Wojdowski, Bogdan (1930–1994) Polish novelist and essayist. A survivor of the Holocaust, Wojdowski is best known for his deeply disturbing novel *Chleb rzucony umarłym* (*Bread for the Departed*), a detailed account of life in the Jewish community in occupied Warsaw between 1940 and 1942. The last part of the book is devoted to the mass deportation of Jews from the ghetto to the death camps. The novel was completed during the "anti-Zionist" campaign in Poland in 1968 and 1969 and was published in 1971. Wojdowski, who was in the Warsaw Ghetto from age ten to twelve, focuses on the central role of bread in a community subjected to systematic starvation and the attempts by children, above all, to obtain the precious commodity by any and all means. Episodic in structure, virtually without plot, the novel splendidly captures the rhythms of life inside the ghetto walls and the daily confrontation with death. The work is also remarkable for its complex linguistic and stylistic mixture of standard and substandard Polish, Yiddish, and Hebrew.

Translation: *Bread for the Departed*, trans. Madeline G. Levine, with a foreword by Henryk Grynberg (Evanston, Ill.: Northwestern University Press, 1997).

Wolf, Christa (b. 1929) German novelist and essayist. Arguably the twentieth-century German woman writer best known outside Germany, Wolf was born in Landsberg on the Wartha (now part of Poland). In January 1945, her family took up residence in Mecklenburg, in northeastern Germany. She studied German language and literature at the universities of Jena and Leipzig, after the establishment of the German Democratic Republic, subsequently working as a researcher and an editor. She became involved in the Bitterfeld movement and for a time worked in a factory and participated in a Working Writers' Circle. She began her literary career as an editor of anthologies of East German writers and traveled extensively before going freelance in 1962. Her first published literary

work was the weak, socialist realist *Moskauer Novelle* (Moscow Novella, 1961), a hidebound moral tale about a love affair between an East German physician and her Russian translator, whom she had met years earlier as a soldier during the Soviet occupation. *Der geteilte Himmel* (*Divided Heaven*, 1963), Wolf's next work of fiction, marks a significant aesthetic advance. Although still conforming to socialist realist ideological norms, and an outgrowth of the Bitterfeld Conference, the story—about a young woman's recovery physically and mentally from an ostensible factory accident—employs a complex and sophisticated narrative strategy that foreshadows Wolf's later experiments with form. Five years after *Divided Heaven*, Wolf brought out *Nachdenken über Christa T.* (*The Quest for Christa T.*), the work that at once established her literary fame on both sides of the Berlin Wall and stamped her as a bold and controversial writer. An innovative and far-reaching breakout from the socialist realist formal straitjacket, *The Quest for Christa T.* has been widely (and in part erroneously) interpreted as a negative critique of the GDR. Conceived in the spirit of Marxist humanism, the highly personal novel about the narrator's relationship with Christa T. and her attitude toward her death is set primarily in the post–World War II period and the efforts to construct a socialist state in East Germany. The negative reception of *The Quest for Christa T.* in the GDR, and the politicized readings of it in the West, prompted Wolf to try to explain her intentions with it in several essays, primarily those included in her collection *Lesen und Schreiben: Aufsätsze und Betrachtungen* (Reading and Writing: Essays and Observations, 1972; translated as *The Reader and the Writer: Essays, Sketches, Memories*).

Wolf's next major work of fiction was the autobiographical *Kindheitsmuster* (*Patterns of Childhood*, 1977). Deliberately eschewing first-person narration as a psychological impossibility, Wolf attempts in the book to come to grips with her own experience as a young girl growing up in Nazi Germany and living through World War II. Notwithstanding a largely negative reception in the GDR and misinterpretations in West Germany, *Patterns of Childhood* remains a work of pivotal importance in Wolf's development as a writer and thinker. It was followed by the three-story collection *Unter den Linden: Drei unwarscheinliche Geschichten* (Under the Linden Trees: Three Improbable Tales, 1974); *Gesammelte Erzählungen* (Collected Stories, 1974), a volume of collected stories; and *Kassandra* (*Cassandra*, 1983), a novella. A prolific and thought-provoking essayist, who addresses literary, cultural, and political issues with equal ease, Wolf's volumes of essays, apart from *The Reader and the Writer*, include *Till Eulenspiegel* (1972), with Gerhard Wolf; *Kein Ort. Nirgends* (No Place. Not Anywhere, 1979; translated as *No Place on Earth*); *Fortgesetzter Versuch* (Experiment Continued, 1979); *Ins Ungebundene gehet eine Sehnsucht: Gesprächsraum Romantik* (A Longing Reaches for the Unbound: About Romanticism, 1985), also with Gerhard Wolf; *Störfall: Nachrichten eines Tages* (*Accident: A Day's News*, 1987); *Die Dimension des Autors: Essays und Aufsätze, Reden und Gespräche, 1959–1985* (*The Author's Dimension: Essays and Articles, Speeches and Talks, 1959–1985*, 1987); *Ansprachen* (Lectures, 1988); *Sommerstück* (Summer Piece, 1989); *Reden im Herbst* (Speeches in the Fall, 1990); and *Was bleibt* (*What Remains*, 1990).

Wolf's political troubles with the GDR regime began when she joined other writers and intellectuals in denouncing the expulsion of the poet and songwriter Wolf Biermann in November 1976. After first being censured by the Party, she and others were expelled from the board of directors of the Berlin branch of the Writers Union. She thereafter became an active participant in the International Writers Conferences on Peace in the 1980s and has been widely honored in Germany and Austria. She has also held several writer-in-residence awards in American colleges and universities.

Literature: Anna K. Kuhn, *Christa Wolf's Utopian Vision: From Marxism to Feminism* (Cambridge: Cambridge University Press, 1988).

Translations: *Accident: A Day's News*, trans. Heike Schwarzbauer and Rick Takvorian (New York: Farrar, Straus and Giroux, 1992); *The Author's Dimension: Selected Essays*, ed. Alexander Stephan, trans. Jan Van Heurck, with an introduction by Grace Paley (New York: Farrar, Straus and Giroux, 1993); *Cassandra: A Novel and Four Essays*, trans. Jan van Heurck (New York: Farrar, Straus and Giroux, 1984); *Divided Heaven*, trans. Joan Becker (Berlin: Seven Seas, 1965); *No Place on Earth*, trans. Jan van Heurck (New York: Farrar, Straus and Giroux, 1982); *Patterns of Childhood*, trans. Ursula Molinaro and Hedwig Rappolt (New York: Farrar, Straus and Giroux, 1985); *The Quest for Christa T.*, trans. Christopher Middleton (New York: Farrar, Straus and Giroux, 1970); *The Reader and the Writer: Essays, Sketches, Memories*, trans. Joan Becker (New York: International, 1977); *Selected Essays* (London: Virago, 1991); *What Remains and Other Stories*, trans. Rick Takvorian and Heike Schwarzbauer (New York: Farrar, Straus and Giroux, 1993); "Revised Philosophy of a Tomcat" (from *Unter den Linden: Drei unwarscheinliche Geschichten*), trans. Nancy Lukens, in *Daughters of Eve: Women's Writing from the German Democratic Republic*, trans. and ed. Nancy Lukens and Dorothy Rosenberg (Lincoln: University of Nebraska Press, 1993), 111–33.

Wolter, Christine (b. 1939) German novelist and short-story writer. A native of Königsberg, East Prussia (now Kaliningrad, Russia), Wolter grew up in East Berlin. She studied

Romance languages and then worked as an editor for several East German publishing houses and translated from Italian. She began her literary career in the early 1970s with a book based on her Italian travels, *Meine italienische Reise* (My Italian Journey, 1973). It was followed in 1976 by a collection of stories of a completely different character, *Wie ich meine Unschuld verlor* (How I Lost My Innocence), which deals with women living alone after failed marriages or the deaths of their husbands. In 1977 Wolter published a second Italian travel book, *Juni in Sicilien* (June in Sicily). Not long afterward, she succeeded in emigrating from the German Democratic Republic. In 1978 she married an Italian architect and together with their son resettled permanently in Milan, where she taught German at the university. Apart from her Italian travel books, her novels and stories have addressed primarily two themes: the situation of women and relations between the two Germanys. Her work, which became immensely popular, is heavily autobiographical. *Die Hintergrundsperson oder Versuche zu lieben* (The Person in the Background, or Attempts at Love, 1979; reprinted, 1983, in West Germany as *Stückweise leben* [Living Piecemeal]); *Die Alleinsseglerin* (The Solo Woman Sailor, 1982); *Areopolis* (1985); and *Strasse der Stunden: 44 Ansichten von Mailand* (Street of Hours: 44 Views of Milan, 1987) were all published by the East German publishing house Aufbau after Wolter's immigration to Italy. Of her last three books, *Piazza Brà* (1988), a collection of short first-person narratives from between 1974 to 1977 and 1984, was published in Switzerland, whereas *Das Stendahl-Syndrom* (The Stendahl Syndrome, 1990) and *"Italien muss schön sein": Impressionen, Depressionen in Arkadien* ("Italy Must Be Lovely": Impressions and Depressions in Arcadia, 1993), another in her series of Italian travel books, were published in unified Berlin. Without doubt, Wolter's most popular work remains the collection of ten stories contained in the volume *Wie ich meine Unschuld verlor*. In writing about ordinary women in everyday situations, as in *Wie ich meine Unschuld verlor,* Wolter is matter-of-fact, unsentimental, and inclined toward a less than favorable depiction of the male species.

Translations: "Early Summer" (from *Wie ich meine Unschuld verlor*), trans. Dorothy Rosenberg, in *Daughters of Eve: Women's Writing from the German Democratic Republic,* trans. and ed. Nancy Lukens and Dorothy Rosenberg (Lincoln: University of Nebraska Press, 1993), 97–102; "I Have Married Again," trans. Jan van Heurck, in *The New Sufferings of Young W. and Other Stories from the German Democratic Republic,* ed. Therese Hörnigk and Alexander Stephan (New York: Continuum, 1997), 208–15.

Woroszylski, Wiktor (1927–1996) Polish poet, novelist, and essayist. Woroszylski was born in Grodno, in eastern Poland, and remained in the city until March 1945 when he was repatriated to Łódź in central Poland. He completed his early schooling in Grodno and attended university in Łódź for a year, studying first medicine and then Polish literature. He made his literary debut with a war poem published in 1945 in *Trybuna Robotnicza* and the same year began working as a reporter for the daily *Głos Ludu.* In 1947 he moved to Warsaw and resumed his study of Polish literature for a year at Warsaw University. An ardent supporter of the new Polish communist regime in the 1940s and 1950s, Woroszylski held several "official" literary positions during these years: secretary of the editorial board of the journal *Po prostu;* instructor in the cultural section of the Central Committee of the Polish Workers Party (later the Polish United Workers Party), under whose auspices he published in 1951 the anthology *O Polsce Ludowej: Zbiór wierszy i pieśni z lat 1941–1951* (On People's Poland: A Collection of Poems and Songs from the Years 1941–1951); and, after transferring to Szczecin in 1949 and then returning to Warsaw, a member of the editorial staff of *Sztandar Młodych* and then of *Nowa Kultura* until 1952. In 1950 he received the State Prize, Third Class, and from 1952 to 1956 studied in Moscow at the Institute of Literature, where he wrote a dissertation on Vladimir Mayakovsky and Russian poetry of the 1920s. He returned to Warsaw in July 1956 and rejoined the journal *Nowa Kultura,* serving as editor in chief from 1957 to May 1958.

Woroszylski's volumes of poetry from the late 1940s and early 1950s were faithful to the spirit and letter of socialist realism. They include *Noc komunarda* (The Night of a Communard, 1949); *Śmierci nie ma! Poezje, 1945–1948* (There Is No Death! Poems, 1945–1948, 1949); *Weekend Mister Smitha: Satyry i fraszki* (Mr. Smith's Weekend: Satires and Trifles, 1949); *Pierwsza linia pokoju: Poezje, 1949–1950* (The First Line of Peace: Poems, 1949–1950, 1951); *Ojczyzna* (Fatherland, 1953); *Wiersze i poematy wybrane* (Selected Lyrics and Poems, 1955); and *Z rozmów, 1955* (From Conversations, 1955, 1956). He was also the author of works extolling the USSR and the GDR, notably, *Szkoła dwustu milionów: Notatki z podróżej do ZSRR* (A School of Two Hundred Million: Notes from a Journey to the USSR, 1950) and *Przyjaciele zza Odry: Notatki z podróży do NRD* (Friends from Beyond the Oder: Notes of a Journey to the GDR, 1952).

Woroszylski's experiences as a correspondent in Budapest during the Hungarian uprising of 1956, coupled with the impact on him of the civil unrest in Poland the same year, changed his political perspective and transformed him into a champion of reform. Soon after, he became a cofounder and editor of *Zapis,* the first uncensored, dissident literary periodical in Poland. After the imposition of martial law in Poland in 1981, he was held in detention for a year because of his agitation in the huge Ursus automobile plant in Warsaw. Woroszylski's new outlook, opposed to repression and extolling freedom, yet unwilling to break completely with a socialism he believed capable of reform, is conveyed in a rhythmically more conversational style, usually free of punctuation and with touches of irony. These qualities are much in evidence in such verse collections as *Okrutna gwiazda* (Cruel Star, 1958); *Zagłada gatunków* (Extermination of the Species, 1970); *Poezje wybrane* (Selected Poems, 1982), with the selections made by Woroszylski himself; and *Z podróży, ze snu, z umierania: Wiersze, 1951–1990* (From Travel, from Sleep, from Dying: Poems, 1951–1990, 1992).

An able prose writer, Woroszylski published several book of essays, among them *Dzisięć lat w kinie: Felietony filmowe* (Ten Years in Cinema: Film Feuilletons, 1973) and *Powrót do kraju: Kartki z dziennika, wspomnienia, artykuły* (The Return Home: Pages from a Diary, Reminiscences, Articles, 1979). He was also the author of a novel about literature titled *Literatura: Powieść* (Literature: A Novel, 1977). Woroszylski's strong interest in Russian poetry and popular music led him to write four major works on Russian writers: the poet Sergei Esenin (1973); the nineteenth-century novelist Mikhail Saltykov-Shchedrin (1980), which could appear only in a samizdat edition; the poet Vladimir Mayakovsky (1984); and on the death of Aleksandr Pushkin (1983). The biography of Mayakovsky, Woroszylski's only major work to be translated into English, is typical of his innovative style of biography, consisting primarily of documentary materials linked by the author's narration. Woroszylski also edited collections of the songs of such once immensely popular Soviet singers as Bulat Okudzhava (1924–1997) and Vladimir Vysotsky (1938–1980).

Translations: *Life of Mayakovsky,* trans. Boleslaw Taborski (New York: Orion, 1970);

two poems in *The Burning Forest: Modern Polish Poetry*, trans. and ed. Adam Czerniawski (Newcastle upon Tyne: Bloodaxe, 1988), 135–37; eight poems in *Polish Poetry of the Last Two Decades of Communist Rule: Spoiling Cannibals' Fun,* ed. and trans. Stanisław Barańczak and Clare Cavanagh (Evanston, Ill.: Northwestern University Press, 1991), 116–22.

Wygodzki, Stanisław (1907–1992) Polish poet, short-story writer, and novelist. A writer best known for his poetry inspired by the Holocaust, Wygodzki was born in Będzin, Silesia. His studies at a Hebrew secondary school were interrupted in 1924 when he was expelled for alleged communist activity. During the interwar period, he became part of the left-wing artistic avant-garde and joined the Communist Party. His political affiliation resulted in his arrest and brief imprisonment in the 1930s. He began his literary career with a book of poems, *Apel* (Appeal), which had to be published in Moscow in 1933. His next two volumes, *Chleb* (Bread, 1934) and *Żywioł liścia* (The Element of Leaves, 1936), were published in Kraków. During the German occupation of Poland in World War II, Wygodzki was imprisoned in Auschwitz and other concentration camps along with his family. At one point, during their confinement in Auschwitz, Wygodzki attempted suicide, along with his wife and daughter, by taking arsenic. They died, but he survived—a grim turn of events that he describes in a poem in his collection *Pożegnanie* (Farewell, 1979). After two years in convalescent homes in Germany immediately after the war, Wygodzki returned to Poland in 1947 and was employed for a time by the Ministry of Culture. From 1948 to 1953, he served as literary editor of Polish Radio, subsequently becoming a freelance writer. His first postwar literary work was a volume of poetry, *Pamiętnik miłości* (A Memoir of Love, 1948), in which in a spare style markedly different from that of his interwar poetry he attempted to convey his understanding of what had befallen the Jews. Wygodzki was awarded the prize of the Polish Writers Union for the book. After *Pamiętnik miłości,* Wygodzki wrote a series of novels and short stories devoted almost wholly to World War II and the immediate postwar years. They include *Widzenie* (Vision, 1951); *Powrót do domu* (The Return Home, 1954); *Milczenie* (Silence, 1958); *O świcie* (At Dawn, 1959); *Upalny dzień* (A Sultry Day, 1960); *Koncert życzeń* (Request Concert, 1961), which was awarded the prize of the Warsaw weekly *Nowa Kultura; Serdce mego rodzeństwa* (The Hearts of My Siblings, 1961); *Człowiek z wózkiem* (Man with a Wagon, 1961); *Opowiadania* (Stories, 1961); *Nauczyciel tańca* (The Dancing Teacher, 1963); *Basy* (The Double Bass, 1965); and *Powrót na ziemię* (Return to Earth, 1967), a collection of stories.

The Polish "anti-Zionist" campaign of 1968 was the last straw in terms of Wygodzki's disillusionment with communism. A harsh treatment of Stalinism in his novel *Zatrzymany do wyjaśnienia* (Held for Questioning) necessitated his publishing the book in 1968 with the Polish émigré publishing house Instytut Literacki in Paris. The same year, Wygodzki left Poland for Israel. A frequent contributor to the Polish-language weekly *Nowiny,* Wygodzki also wrote several literary works while in Israel, among them *Pieskin został pisarzem* (Pieskin Became a Writer, 1973), a satirical novel published in London, and three volumes of poetry: *Drzewo ciemności* (Tree of Darkness, 1971); *Podróż zimowa* (Winter Journey, 1975); and *Pożegnanie* (Farewell, 1979). All three volumes were also published in London. These later works by Wygodzki are preoccupied with death and with profoundly troubling but unanswerable questions about the meaning of life. The poet laments the loss of his family in the concentration camps, especially his daughter; he voices his nostalgia for his native Poland; and he further vents his hatred of the Stalinist system.

X

Xoxa, Jakov (1923–1979) Albanian novelist. A native of Fier, in the Myzeqe plain region, Xoxa studied French language and literature at Sofia University in Bulgaria. He began his literary career as the author of a volume of short stories published in 1949 under the title *Novela*. However, his reputation rests primarily on two Soviet-style novels about the plight of the peasantry both before and after World War II. *Lumi i vdekur* (The Dead River, 1965), a huge novel in three volumes and regarded as a landmark of Albanian socialist realism, is set in the time of the monarchy and presents a grim picture of the dispossession and degradation that a peasant endures at the hands of corrupt officials and merchants. Xoxa's next novel, *Juga e bardhë* (The Southern Spring Wind, 1971), is about Soviet-style agricultural collectivization in post–World War II Albania. It brims with melodramatic touches, including the sabotaging of a canal that causes a peasant village to be flooded. Xoxa is also the author of the novel *Lulja e kripës* (The Salt Flower, 1981). Xoxa's collected works (*Vepra letrare*) were published in six volumes in Tirana in 1983.

Translations: *Juga e bardhë* is available in French as *Le Vent blanc* (Tirana: 8 Nëntori, 1974), and *Lumi i vdekur* in Italian as *Il fiume morto* (Tirana: 8 Nëntori, ca. 1972).

Z

Zagajewski, Adam (b. 1945) Polish poet, novelist, and essayist. Regarded by many as the most important poet of his generation, Zagajewski was born in Lwów (now Lviv, Ukraine). His family resettled in Silesia, in western Poland, the year of his birth. In 1963 he moved to Kraków, where he graduated from the Jagiellonian University and where, while a student, he edited the dissident journal *Zapis*. In 1979 he was invited to Berlin by the Berliner Künstlerprogramm, returning to Poland only in September 1981. He became actively involved in the Solidarity opposition movement while living in Kraków in the 1980s. In December 1982 Zagajewski immigrated to Paris, where he became editor of the quarterly Polish-language literary magazine *Zeszyty Literackie / Cahiers Littéraires* (Literary Notebooks), which relocated to Poland in the early 1990s. He has visited the United States on several occasions and has taught in the University of Houston's Creative Writing Program. Perhaps his best-publicized visit to the United States was the lecture and poetry reading he held, on 14 February 1989, at the Guggenheim Museum in New York City, where he was introduced by the writer Susan Sontag, who also read some of his poems.

Zagajewski's first volume of poetry, *Komunikat* (Communiqué) was published in 1972. It was followed by *List* (A Letter, 1979), which was reprinted in 1982 with *Oda do wielości* (Ode to Greatness) and *Nowe wiersze* (New Poems); *Cieńka kreska* (Upstroke, 1983); *Jechać do Lwowa i inne wiersze* (Traveling to Lwów and Other Poems, 1985); *Dzikie czereśnie: Wybór wierszy* (Wild Cherries: Selected Verse, 1992); and *Ziemia ognista* (Fiery Land, 1994). Zagajewski is a poet of great clarity, intellectual refinement, and moral responsibility whose outlook was shaped by the horrors of World War II—to which he refers time and again—and by the political turmoil during the era of Solidarity and martial law. Chords of anxiety, sorrow, and loneliness are struck often as the poet reflects on the terrible cost to human life and dignity of war and dictatorial repression. Similar concerns are addressed in Zagajewski's many essays, which have been more widely translated than his poetry and encompass a broader range of expression. It is also in his essays that Zagajewski's fine sense of wit and irony are splendidly accommodated. His first highly regarded collection of essays was written with Julian Kornhauser and published in 1974 under the title *Świat nie przedstawiony* (Unrepresented World). Four subsequent volumes appeared in the period 1978 to 1998: *Drugi oddech* (Second Wind, 1978), a collection of articles and reviews; *Solidarność i samotność* (Solidarity and Solitude, 1986; translated as *Solidarity, Solitude*); *Dwa miasta* (*Two Cities: On Exile, History, and the Imagination*, 1991); and *W cudzym pięknie* (In Alien Beauty, 1998; translated as *Another Beauty*) Ranging widely over literature and the arts, in Poland and elsewhere, a keen observer of life in foreign cities, and an implacable foe of dictators and totalitarianism whose best weapons are irony and mockery (see, for example, his little essay "I Killed Hitler"), Zagajewski is an immensely readable essayist, light in manner yet intellectually engaging. His talents as an essayist are perhaps nowhere better demonstrated than in his fine piece (in *Two Cities*) on the Polish Jewish writer Bruno Schulz, who was shot to death in November 1942 on a street in his native city of Drohobycz in a random act of mindless brutality by a German SS officer.

Translations: *Another Beauty*, trans. Clare Cavanagh (New York: Farrar, Straus and Giroux, 2000); *Canvas*, trans. Renata Gorczynski, Benjamin Ivry, and C. K. Williams (New York: Farrar, Straus and Giroux, 1991); *Mysticism for Beginners*, trans. Clare Cavanagh (New York: Farrar, Straus and Giroux, 1997); *Solidarity, Solitude: Essays by Adam Zagajewski*, trans. Lillian Vallee (New York: Ecco Press, 1990); *Tremor: Selected Poems*, trans. Renata Gorczynski (New York: Farrar, Straus and Giroux, 1985); *Trzej aniołowie* (*Three Angels*), selected by Adam Zagajewski, trans. Clare Cavanagh et al.

(Kraków: Wydawnictwo Literackie, 1998), a Polish–English collection of poems; *Two Cities: On Exile, History, and the Imagination*, trans. Lillian Vallee (New York: Farrar, Straus and Giroux, 1995); *Without End: New and Selected Poems*, trans. Clare Cavanagh, Renata Gorczynski, Benjamin Ivry, and C. K. Williams (New York: Farrar, Straus and Giroux, 2002), which includes the English-language collections *Tremor, Canvas,* and *Mysticism for Beginners* as well as Zagajewski's most recent work and new translations of some early poems. SOUND RECORDING: A sound recording, dated 14 February 1989, of Zagajewski's lecture and poetry reading at the Guggenheim Museum is available from the Academy of American Poets, which also published the text of the lecture.

Zajc, Dane (b. 1929) Slovenian poet and playwright. A major figure in Slovenian literature after World War II, Zajc was born in Zgornja Javorščica and completed his secondary schooling in Ljubljana. He subsequently worked for a number of years as a librarian. He helped found and was affiliated with such leading literary reviews of the period as *Mladinska revija, Beseda, Revija 57, Perspektive,* and *Problemi*. Zajc made his literary debut in 1958 with his first published volume of poems, *Požgana trava* (Burned Grass), which in part was shaped by his dark memories of World War II and stood at considerable variance with the officially mandated socialist realism. Two more collections appeared in the 1960s: *Jezik iz zemlje* (Earth Language, 1961) and *Ubijavci kač* (Snake Killers, 1969). The emergence of a new Slovenian avant-garde in the 1960s won Zajc a number of new readers who were drawn to the subtle wordplay and highly imaginative style of such later collections of his poetry as *Pesmi* (Poems, 1974); *Rožengruntar* (Master of the Roses, 1975); *Si videl* (You Have Seen, 1979); *Zarotlive* (Conspiracies, 1985); and *Pesmi* (Poems, 1990).

Four volumes of his selected poems were also published in 1971, 1976 (a volume containing texts as well by his fellow poets Kajetan Kovič and Gregor Strniša), 1979, and 1984.

As a playwright, Zajc is known best for such poetic dramas as *Otroka reke* (The River Children, 1962); *Potohodec* (The Roadwalker, 1971); *Likvidacija* (Liquidation, 1971); *Voranc* (1978); and *Grmače* (*Rocky Peak,* 1995) as well as for his own interpretation of the Finnish national epic poem, *Kálevála* (1985), and the ancient Greek classic *Medea (Medeja,* 1988). One of his most popular theatrical works is the puppet play *Mlada Breda* (Young Breda, 1981). In 1981 Zajc received the Prešeren Prize for lifetime achievement, and in 1990 a five-volume edition of his collected works was published. Zajc at one point held a Fulbright Fellowship to Columbia University.

Translations: *Rocky Peak,* trans. Evald Flisar, in *Contemporary Slovenian Drama* (Ljubljana: Slovene Writers Association, 1997), 372–422, which also contains synopses of *Medeja* and *Kálevála*; *Scorpions: Selected Poems,* trans. Sonja Kravanja; *Scorpions: Poèmes choisis,* trans. Zdenka Štimac (Ljubljana: Slovene Writers Association, 2000); eleven poems, trans. Erica Johnson Debeljak, in *The Imagination of Terra Incognita: Slovenian Writing, 1945–1995,* ed. Aleš Debeljak (Fredonia, N.Y.: White Pine, 1997), 195–205; six poems, trans. Veno Taufer and Michael Scammell, in *New Writing in Yugoslavia,* ed. Bernard Johnson (Harmondsworth: Penguin, 1970), 243–49.

Zaniewski, Andrzej (b. 1940) Polish poet and novelist. One of the best-known contemporary Polish writers on the strength of his novel *Szczur* (*Rat,* 1993), which attracted considerable attention at the Frankfurt International Book Fair in 1994, Zaniewski was born and educated in Warsaw, where he studied art history at Warsaw University. He made his literary debut as a poet in 1958 with his first poems published in the Gdańsk *Głos Wybrzeża.* He founded the poetry group Hybrydy (Hybrids) while a student at Warsaw University and eventually headed the poetry section of the monthly *Poezija.* Zaniewski's first book of poetry, *Przed siebie* (Before Oneself), appeared in 1967 and was followed by *Podróż* (Journey, 1968); *Poemat dzisiejszy* (A Poem for Today, 1978); *Treny* (Laments, 1979); *Zwierzenia starszego inspektora* (The Senior Inspector's Animals, 1983); *Cień wysypiska: Światło i mgła* (Shadow of a Mound: Light and Mist, 1987); and *Krawędź* (The Edge, 1989), a four-part collection of poems consisting of "Krawędź," by far the largest part of the collection, "Mity" ("Myths"), "Sonety" ("Sonnets"), and "Treny" ("Laments"). A number of the poems, especially in "The Edge," reflect Zaniewski's growing ecological concerns and fondness for animals apparent in his subsequent novels. One poem, for example, is titled "Szczury" ("Rats") and anticipates— indeed, synopsizes—Zaniewski's later novel *Rat.* Another poem, "Cywilizacja ptaków" ("The Civilization of Birds"), similarly anticipates his novel *Cywilizacja ptaków* (The Civilization of Birds, 1996). Despairing over what humans have done with their world through the centuries, Zaniewski foresees the coming of a civilization of birds,

approaching from all sides
above the dumping ground of our daily
    sins . . .
You don't believe me,
that birds are the future of Earth . . .
The Civilization of birds will overtake us
    and remain
long after we have gone.

Rat, on which Zaniewski's international reputation is based (it was issued simultaneously in nine countries around the world), is a fictional history of a rat from birth to death narrated in the first person by the rat. It is anything but pleasant reading, with its graphic naturalistic detail. In his preface to the novel, Zaniewski explains that he was compelled to write the novel because of his growing obsession with the similarities and parallels between humans and rats. Widely traveled, including a stay in war-ravaged Vietnam in 1977, Zaniewski had ample opportunity to observe rats. Moreover, he was well aware of the recurring motif of the rat's fate, as parallel to that of man, in works of fiction by such writers as Franz Kafka, T. S. Eliot, James Joyce, and Albert Camus. Zaniewski argues that humans should give up the belief that civilization is "supreme and perfect" and recognize that they are another species of animal and that among animals rats are very close to humans biologically and psychologically. "Thanks to their vitality, strength, and intelligence," he writes, both species "have not only survived millions of years of evolution, but also taken control of our planet."

Apart from *Rat*, Zaniewski attracted attention in the late 1990s with the publication of the first two volumes of a projected five-part autobiographical cycle about his own family titled *Commedia dell' morte* (Comedy of Death). The novels that have appeared so far are *Król Tanga* (King Tanga, 1996) and *Śmierć Harlekina* (The Death of Harlequin, 1998). The remaining three novels have tentatively been titled "Ucieczka Colombiny" ("Columbine's Flight"), "La camparsita," and "Syn tancerki" ("Son of a Dancer"). The first two novels are devoted to the life story of Zaniewski's mother (1918–1970), a dancer, through the German occupation of World War II. *Śmierć Harlekina*, which focuses on the precariousness of his mother's situation under the Germans as a half-Jew, is the more compelling of the two works. Short on description and long on dialogue, candid, and graphic, it has a definite immediacy, strengthened by

Zaniewski's use of second-person address throughout most of the novel, as if he were writing a memoir with his mother's help.

Zaniewski won the prestigious Władysław Reymont Prize in 1995 for *Rat*. He also received the Red Rose Prize of Gdańsk in 1996. In 1981 Zaniewski founded the Stowarzyszenie Kultury Słowiańskiej (Association for Slavic Culture), which he continues to head, and he is also an active member of the Association of Polish Writers. Since 1996, he has also served as vice president of the Association Against Crime in the Name of Jolanta Brzozowska, named for a young Polish woman who was brutally murdered and whose murderers have not yet been sentenced. Zaniewski's most recent publication is the collection of poems *Wyschnięte drzewa też płaczą* (Dried Out Trees Also Cry, 1999), which contains for the most part previously unpublished poems from the last dozen years. The poems echo the concerns for justice, human dignity, and the care of the world of which Zaniewski has become a passionate champion.

Translations: *Rat,* trans. Ewa Hryniewicz-Yarbrough (New York: Arcade, 1994).

Závada, Pál (b. 1952) Hungarian novelist. A sociologist whose specialty has been village life, Závada became an overnight literary sensation on the basis of his novel *Jadviga párnája* (Jadviga's Pillow, 1997). A dense, linguistically challenging work that is anything but an easy read, the novel consists mainly of the diary of a well-off Slovak farmer, András Osztatni, in northern Hungary. Závada himself is a native of the same Slovak-minority community in which the novel is set. In his diary, Osztatni chronicles the dire effects on several people of his marriage to the strange Jadviga (his father's adopted daughter) from 1915 to 1922 and continuing to the year 1987. The crux of the problem in the relationship between András and Jadviga is her stubborn refusal to consummate their marriage. When she finally yields and eventually bears a son, Marci, she then resumes her previous rejection of marital sex, to András's profound consternation. When András ultimately discovers that throughout his marriage Jadviga had kept up relations with a former lover, a Jewish friend of the family named Franci, he leaves his family and property in 1922 and retreats to a wretched existence on a remote farm. As the novel progresses, more truths are revealed about the psychologically complex and even disturbed Jadviga, whose secret love life included more than just Franci. After András's death, Jadviga comes across his diary and "edits" it, supplying her own commentaries on the events. A further redaction of the diary takes place years later, when Marci, who has since become a Stalinist-era informer, writes his own interpretation of the family history. Despite its narrative complexity and different layers of language—from the more restrained classical style of András himself to the tough contemporary idiom of Marci—Jadviga's Pillow is compelling reading and marks one of the more significant Hungarian literary achievements of the late 1990s. A film based on the novel and directed by Krisztina Deák was released in 2000.

Translations: Excerpts from *Jadviga párnája*, trans. Judith Sollosy, *Hungarian Quarterly* 421 (2000): 22–37.

Zelinka, Milan (b. 1942) Slovak novelist. Born in Igram, Zelinka finished secondary school in Trnava and then went to work as a telephone mechanic in Humenný. After making his literary debut with the short-story collection *Druhý dych* (Second Breath) in 1972, Zelinka went on to publish several short novels, among them *Smädné serdce* (The Thirsty Heart, 1974); *Belasé ráno* (Azure Morning, 1978); *Slamienky z Makova* (Immortelles from Makov, 1980); *Kvety ako*

drobný sneh (Flowers Like Snowflakes, 1982); *Povest o strykovi Kenderešovi* (A Tale About Uncle Kendereš, 1985); *Z Havranieho dvora* (From Havraný's Courtyard, 1988); and *Krajina* (Countryside, 1992) as well as another collection of short stories under the title *Mechanici: Príbehy zo zabudnutého priečinka* (Mechanics: Stories from a Forgotten Quarter, 1983). A number of Zelinka's works are set in the fictitious town of Makov, which critics have likened to Ladislav Ballek's Palánk (although minus the mythic element of Palánk) and which he peoples with a whole gallery of Slovak provincial types whose mores he knows well and affectionately animates. The weakest work in this respect is the novel *Z Havranieho dvora*, in which hyperbole as a compositional principle and simplistic characterization are carried to excess. In *Mechanici: Príbehy zo zabudnutého priečinka*, a collection of six mostly humorous and simply written stories in which the lead characters are mechanics, Zelinka drew on his own experiences as a telephone mechanic in Humenný. Arguably the best of these tales is "Príbeh Adriána Berilu" ("The Story of Adrián Berila"), in which the now old Adrián Berila tells the narrator about his problems with and on account of his lovely and exotic-looking wife, whom people take for a Turk or Yugoslav. *Kvety ako drobný sneh* is undoubtedly Zelinka's best piece of fiction. It is about an actor, Alfred Merjavý (the name crops up in other works by Zelinka), who fails to complete his studies as an actor but works in a hospital where he entertains the dying and small children. At a certain point, he believes that he has contracted an incurable fatal illness, but later learns that his illness was induced by autosuggestion. He then decides to leave, believing that his work in the hospital was in vain.

Zhiti, Visar (b. 1952) Albanian poet. Zhiti was born in Durrës but grew up in Lushnjë, where he finished high school in 1970. He then began teaching in Kukës, in northern Albania near the Kosovo border. In 1973, just as he was preparing to publish his first book of poems, *Rapsodia e jetës së trëndafilave* (Rhapsody of the Life of Roses), he fell victim to the purge of Albanian artists and intellectuals triggered by the Fourth Plenary Session of the Albanian Communist Party. His manuscript was rejected by the Naim Frashëri publishing house, to which he had submitted it, as ideologically unacceptable. Unable to publish anything, Zhiti continued to live and teach in Kukës until his arrest there in November 1979. After several months in solitary confinement, he was sentenced in April 1980 to ten years' imprisonment. He was released in 1987 and allowed to work in a brick factory in Lushnjë. While in solitary confinement, and denied writing implements, Zhiti composed and committed to memory nearly 100 poems reflecting his harrowing experiences. He was finally able to publish these poems in book form in 1993, two years after the downfall of the Albanian communist regime, under the title *Kujtesa e ajrit* (The Memory of the Air). A second volume of prison poems, *Hedh një kafkë te këmbit tuaja: Poezitë e burgut* (I Toss a Skull at Your Feet: Prison Poems), appeared in 1994.

Zhiti's prison poems are a grim record of ideological persecution under the Enver Hoxha regime and at the same time a testimony to the poet's strength of will and character in creating a dispassionate but powerful poetic account of what he lived through. *Kujtesa e ajrit* also contains a cycle of poems written after Zhiti's release and dealing in part with his visits, for the first time, to Austria and Italy. Zhiti's subsequent works include *Mbjellja e vetëtimave* (Sowing Lightning, 1994); *Valixhja e shqyer e përrallave: Rrëfenja për ato që rriten* (The Tattered Traveling Bag of Tales: Stories for Grownups, 1996); and *Si shkohet në Kosovë: Poezi* (Getting Around in Kosovo: Poems,

2000), a guide to Kosovo in verse. Zhiti has won several literary prizes, among them the Italian Leopardi Gold Prize for Poetry (1991) and the Ada Negri Prize (1997). In 1996 he was elected a delegate to the Albanian parliament and currently holds the position of cultural adviser to the Albanian Embassy in Rome.

Translations: Seven poems, the majority from the time of Zhiti's imprisonment, in *An Elusive Eagle Soars: Anthology of Modern Albanian Poetry*, ed. and trans. Robert Elsie (London: Forest, 1993), 191–99. Two volumes of Zhiti's poetry are available in Italian translation by the Italo-Albanian (Arberesh) writer Elio Miracco: *Croce di carne* (Pomigliano d'Arco: Oxiana, 1997) and *Passeggiando all'indietro* (Pomigliano d'Arco: Oxiana, 1998).

Žiak, Miloš (b. 1959) Slovak novelist, poet, and political writer. A native of Bratislava, Žiak was educated in local schools before graduating from the Faculty of Philosophy of Comenius University in his native city. He then worked at the Institute of Art Criticism and Theatrical Documentation in Bratislava and joined the editorial staff of the journal *Fragment K*. Žiak became something of a public figure when he served as an adviser to President Václav Havel of Czechoslovakia. After the separation of the Czech and Slovak republics, in 1994 he became an adviser to the Slovak prime minister, Jozef Moravčik. After publishing poems in several journals, Žiak came out with his first book of poetry, *Oheň až požiar* (From the Frying Pan into the Fire), in 1982. His verse grotesque, *Don Quijote v pekle* (Don Quixote in Hell, 1989), addresses serious contemporary issues beneath a mask of frivolity. Žiak demonstrated his literary erudition and essayistic skill in his next publication, *Svet v názorach Goetheho* (The World in Goethe's View, 1989). A father–son conflict in his controversial novel, *Bojim sa mat' strach* (I'm Afraid to

Be Afraid, 1990), serves as the pretext for another exploration by Žiak of contemporary social issues, particularly the question of Jews and Jewishness in Slovak society. He returned to the Jewish issue several years later in his provocative and revealing *Jewropean* (1997). A small book, written in a personal style, it considers the place of the Jew in postwar Slovakia and Europe as a whole, but deals primarily with those Slovak Jews who survived World War II, remained in the country, and gave their support to the Slovak Communist Party. Apart from his poetry and prose fiction, Žiak is well known for such incisive political and social writings as *Pad komunizmu na Slovensku a najmä co se dialo potom* (The Fall of Communism in Slovakia and Especially What Happened Afterward, 1994); *Slovensko: Od komunizmu kam?* (Slovakia: From Communism to Where?, 1996); and *Slovensko medzi napredovaním a úpadkom* (Slovakia Between Progress and Decline, 1998). In his most recent work, the novel *Gold, Zlatko a Zlatoústy* (Gold, Goldie, and Golden-Mouth, 1999), he views the individual and society in Czechoslovakia against the background of such tumultuous events as the Soviet-led invasion in 1968, the upheaval in November 1989 that toppled communism, and the division in 1993 of Czechoslovakia into two separate republics.

Živančević, Nina (b. 1957) Serbian poet, journalist, literary critic, and translator. Born in Belgrade, Živančević began her literary career with the publication of a small volume of poems (*Pesme*) in 1983. A second volume, *Mostovi koji rastu* (Bridges that Rise Up), appeared in 1985. Her third volume of poems, of generally more cosmopolitan spirit, *Duh renesanse* (The Spirit of Renaissance), was published in Belgrade in 1989. The preceding year, Živančević had come out with a fifty-six-page critique of contemporary Serbian lit-

erature issued by independent publishers: *Gledajući knjige nezavisnih izdavaca* (Reviewing the Books of Independent Publishers). Živančević came to the United States in 1974 and lived for several years in the country before eventually moving to France. While in the United States, she learned English well enough to write original poetry in it. Her collection of poems in English, *More or Less Urgent,* was published in 1988. While a few of the poems in the volume relate to events in Yugoslavia going back to World War II, most were inspired by her experiences in the United States—for example, living on the Lower East Side in New York City. In 1994 Živančević also published *Inside & Out of Byzantium,* a collection of her own short stories, translated by her or with others into English. Most of the stories are of a personal nature; some are set in Paris; and the last deals with the fighting between Serbs and Croats in 1991 and 1992. Another volume of Živančević's writings in English, *Living on Air Fiction,* came out in 1998. Her most recent work, in Serbian, *Podavtsi snova* (Dream Merchants, 2000), is an account of a trip from New York to Paris before she knew French; the colorful characters, mostly in the arts, she meets in Europe; and her ill-fated, drug-filled trans-Atlantic romance with her French lover.

Translations: *Inside & Out of Byzantium,* trans. Nina Zivančević with Ken Jordan or Dawn Michelle Baude (New York: Semiotext [e], 1994).

Works in English: *Living on Air Fiction* (Brooklyn, N.Y.: Cool Grove, 1998); *More or Less Urgent* (St. Paul, Minn.: New Rivers, 1988).

Zografi, Vlad (b. 1960) Romanian playwright. A native of Bucharest, Zografi graduated from Bucharest University in 1985 with a degree in physics. In 1990 he received a scholarship to study in France and earned a doctorate from the University of Paris XI (Orsay) in physics in 1994. He has published articles on theoretical atomic physics in such journals as *Physical Review, Physics Reports,* and *Surface Science.* Encouraged by the influential literary critic Nicolae Manolescu, Zografi made his debut as a creative writer in 1990 in the literary periodical *România literară.* Between 1990 and 1995, he continued to publish in *România literară* as well as in other major periodicals. His first published book was a collection of short stories, *Genunchiul stîng sau genunchiul drept* (The Left Knee or the Right Knee), which appeared toward the end of 1993. It was followed by his first novel, *Omul nou* (The New Man). Zografi's debut as a dramatist came in 1996 with the publication of the three-play collection *Isabela, dragostea mea* (Isabela, My Love). One of the plays in the volume, *Petru* (Peter), won the Critics Award of the Romanian Section of the International Association of Theater Critics. In 1997 the same play was honored by the Romanian Writers Union. After *Isabela, dragostea mea,* Zografi published two more plays, *Oedip la Delphi* (Oedipus at Delphi, 1997) and *Regele și cadavrul* (The King and the Corpse, 1998), which had its premiere at the National Theater in Bucharest in March 1999, and the play collection *Viitorul e maculatură* (The Future Is Garbage, 1999), which includes, in addition to the title play, *Sărută-mă* (Kiss Me), a dramatic monologue, and the one-act *Creierul* (The Brain). *Petru* has had the most exposure of any of Zografi's plays. It premiered in September 1997 in the Theater of the North in Satu Mare and was highlighted at the Mittlefest theater festival in a production by the highly regarded Bulandra Theater of Bucharest (Teatrul Lucia Sturdza Bulandra), directed by Catalina Buzoianu. It recounts the long journey of Peter I from Russia to the France of Louis XV in the hope of regenerating his native country by blending the knowledge and intellectualism of western Europe and the soul of still barbaric Russia. Toward this goal, he seeks out the cynical and much misunderstood French philosopher Pierre de la Manque, from whom he hopes to learn the art of "civilizing" a "barbaric" people. Although set in the early eighteenth century, the play has obvious referents to the present day.

Zupan, Vitomil (1914–1987) Slovenian playwright, novelist, poet, screenwriter, and essayist. Zupan was born and educated in Ljubljana. During World War II, he was in Italian internment for a while but later joined Slovenian partisans in 1943. After the war, he worked for Radio Ljubljana until 1947, when he became a freelance writer. In 1948 he was taken into custody by the communist regime as a suspicious intellectual and in 1949 was sentenced to ten years in prison. He was released in 1954, whereupon he continued his education, receiving a degree in civil engineering from Ljubljana University in 1958. He soon resumed his career as a freelance writer. Although he had begun to write before the war, most of Zupan's early work was published for the first time in the 1970s, beginning with the verse collection *Polnočno vino* (Midnight Wine, 1973). It was followed by the first of a number of prose works, *Andante patetico* (1945), a psychologically interesting novella with a wartime partisan setting but critically dismissed as "decadent." After *Andante patetico,* Zupan published such novels as *Vrata iz meglenega mesta* (The Gate of a Misty Town, 1968), an exercise in socialist realism; *Potovanje na konec pomladi* (Journey to the End of Spring, 1972); *Klement* (Clement, 1974); *Menuet za kitaro* (Minuet for Guitar, 1975); *Zasledovalec samega sebe* (His Own Pursuer, 1975); *Duh po človeku* (The Smell of Man, 1976); *Mrtva mlaka* (The Dead Pool, 1976); *Igra s hudičevim* *repom* (Playing with the Devil's Tail, 1978), an autobiographical novel; *Komedija človeškega tkiva* (The Comedy of Human Tissue, 1980); *Levitan* (1982), about his own imprisonment; *Človek letnih časov* (A Man of Summer Seasons, 1987); and *Apokalipsa vsakdanjosti* (Apocalypse of the Everyday, 1988). He was also the author of two collections of stories: *Sonče lise* (Sun Spots, 1969) and *Gora brez Prometeja* (The Mountain Without Prometheus, 1983). Probably the best known of Zupan's novels is Minuet for Guitar, which weaves an interesting narrative out of the recollections of two former combatants, a Slovene partisan and a German officer, who meet by chance in a Spanish resort decades after the war.

As a playwright, Zupan is best known for his neonaturalistic drama, *Bele rakete lete na Amsterdam* (White Rockets Fly Toward Amsterdam, 1973), which won an anonymous play competition sponsored by three Yugoslav theaters in 1972. Other plays include *Aki* (1944); *Punt* (Revolt, 1944); *Tri zaostale ure* (Three Lost Hours, 1944), a partisan play; *Rojstvo v nevihti* (Birth in a Storm, 1945); *Stvar Jurija Trajbasa* (The Creation of Jurij Trajbas, 1947), which was dismissed as "decadent"; *Ladja brez imena* (Ship Without a Name, 1972), a morality play; and *Angeli, ljudje, živali* (Angels, Humans, Beasts [Barbara Nives], 1974).

Translations: Excerpt from *Menuet za kitaro*, trans. Harry Lemming, in *The Imagination of Terra Incognito: Slovenian Writing, 1945–1995*, ed. Aleš Debeljak (Fredonia, N.Y.: White Pine, 1997), 320–31; "The Measures of the Soul: Ljubljana Through Poets 1993," trans. Irena Zorko Novak, in *The Slovenian Essay of the Nineties*, selected by Matevž Kos (Ljubljana: Slovene Writers Association, 2000), 73–80.

Zweig, Arnold (1887–1968) German novelist, short-story writer, and playwright. Zweig's career developed mainly in the in-

terwar period, when his strong novel about the German army in World War I, *Der Streit um den Sergeanten Grischa* (The Case of Sergeant Grisha, 1927), became a great success and brought him international acclaim. A Jew who wrote extensively about Jewish and Zionist issues, Zweig and his family fled Berlin in 1933 and resettled in Palestine. Before World War II broke out, Zweig made several return visits to Europe. In 1939 he attended a PEN Club meeting in New York and later met President Franklin Roosevelt in the White House. Zweig began serious study of Marxism in 1940 and soon became actively pro-Soviet. When the war was over, he returned to a divided Germany and established residence in Berlin. When the German Democratic Republic was created, Zweig won election to the Volkskammer, or East German parliament. His espousal of communism and active support of the politics of the GDR brought him several honors, among them the National Prize for Literature in 1950 and the presidency of the German Academy of Arts the same year. In 1958, six years after his first visit to the USSR, Zweig received the Lenin Peace Prize. Zweig's literary works after World War II fall far below the standard of his interwar fiction. Revealingly, two of the three novels he published in the postwar period—*Die Feuerpause* (Ceasefire, 1954) and *Die Zeit ist reif* (The Time Is Ripe, 1957)—are set in the period of World War I and relate to earlier works. *Die Feuerpause* is a badly flawed attempt at a sequel to *The Case of Sergeant Grisha*. *Die Zeit ist reif*, which Zweig conceived as early as 1929, is even worse, as muddled artistically as it is unconvincing politically. Even his last novel, *Traum ist teur* (The Price of Dreaming, 1963), although set during World War II, draws heavily on Zweig's earlier fiction. Politically correct in the Stalinist sense, the novel attempts to transpose the central character of *The Case of Sergeant Grisha* to the Greek army in World War II and to portray the ideological transformation of a German Jewish psychiatrist with the telling name of Karthaus (house of cards) from a believer in capitalism into an ardent communist. A moderately gifted writer with a profound moral sense, Zweig never approached the fame of *The Case of Sergeant Grisha* with any other literary work. Although sincere in the political beliefs that made him a strong supporter of the GDR, Zweig was utterly unable to find a way to remain true to his ideological convictions without seriously compromising the integrity of his writing. He remains, however, one of the most compelling German writers on World War I.

Literature: George Salamon, *Arnold Zweig* (Boston: Twayne, 1975), the only monograph on Zweig in English. There is an extensive secondary literature on him in German.

Translations: Much of Zweig's pre–World War II fiction and nonfiction has been translated into English, but none of the post–World War II novels are available in English.

Zwerenz, Gerhard (pseudonyms Gerd Gablenz, Peter Lauenhaim, Leslie Markwart, and Peter Tarrok; b. 1925) German novelist, short-story writer, and essayist. Zwerenz was born in Gablenz and as a young man trained as a boilermaker. He volunteered for military service in 1942 but deserted two years later. However, he was taken prisoner by the Soviets and held in the USSR until 1948. After his return to East Germany, he became a member of the Volkspolizei (People's Police) and about the same time joined the Socialist Unity Party. In 1952 he enrolled in Leipzig University in order to study philosophy. Zwerenz thereafter threw his lot in with reformers within the Communist Party, making his views known in a series of journalistic and satirical

works. When the short-lived thaw in East German cultural life peaked in 1957 and Zwerenz feared that he might share the lot of GDR writers being arrested and imprisoned, he fled to West Germany, although he regarded himself as an East German writer who had been forced into involuntary exile.

Zwerenz's works fall into several distinct categories. His works of fiction of a largely satirical nature addressed to various aspects of life in the GDR include *Aufs Rad geflochten: Roman vom Aufstieg der Neuen Klasse* (Spun on a Wheel: A Novel About the Rise of the New Class, 1959), arguably his best piece of fiction, and *Casanova, oder der Kleine Herr in Krieg und Frieden* (Casanova, or The Little Fellow in War and Peace, 1966; translated as *Little Peter in War and Peace*), in which the modern Casanova figure embodies the right of humans to happiness. Zwerenz wrote books of an erotic or a pornographic character, in part intended to demonstrate the power of the sexual urge to undermine even a politically repressive regime, such as *Bürgertum und Pornographie* (The Bourgeoisie and Pornography, 1971); *Erotische Schriften* (Erotic Writings, 1976); *Die Freiheit einer Frau* (A Woman's Freedom, 1981); *Lang verlorenen Gefühle* (Long-Lost Feelings, 1981); *Auf den Tod ist kein Verlass: Erotischer Thriller* (Death Is Unreliable: An Erotic Thriller, 1982); *Abschied von den Mädchen* (Leaving the Girls, 1982); and *Berührungen: Geschichten vom Eros des 20. Jahrhunderts* (Contacts: Tales of Eros of the Twentieth Century, 1983). Political texts reflective of Zwerenz's passion for politics as great as his enthusiasm for the erotic include *Walter Ulbricht* (1966); *Lust am Sozialismus: Ein Wahlgeschenck* (The Desire for Socialism: An Election Present, 1969); *Kopf und Bauch: Die Geschichte eines Arbeiters, der unter die Intellektuellen gefallen ist* (Head and Stomach: The Story of a Worker Who Fell in Among the Intellectuals, 1971); *Für die*

Anerkennung der DDR (For the Recognition of the GDR, 1967); *Plebejische Intellektuelle: Essays* (Plebeian Intellectuals: Essays, 1972); *Politische Schriften* (Political Writings, 1975); *Westdeutschen: Erfahrungen, Beschreibungen, Analysen* (West Germans: Experiences, Descriptions, Analyses, 1977); *Rückkehr des toten Juden nach Deutschland* (The Return of the Dead Jew to Germany, 1986); *Soldaten und Mörder: Die Deutschen und der Krieg* (Soldiers and Murderers: The Germans and the War, 1988); *Vergiss die Träume deiner Jugend nicht: Eine autobiographische Deutschlandsaga* (Don't Forget the Dreams of Your Youth: An Autobiographical Saga of Germany, 1989); and *Rechts und dumm?* (Right Wing and Stupid?, 1993).

Zwerenz also wrote several books reflective of his interest in drama and the performing arts, among them *Aristotelsche und Brechtsche Dramatik* (Aristotelian and Brechtian Drama, 1956); a work about actors, publishers, and Frankfurt and its annual book fair, *Wozu das ganze Theater: Lustige geschichten von Schaupsielern, Verlegern, Von Frankfurt, seiner Buchmesse und vom lieben schönen Tod* (Why All the Theater: Merry Tales About Actors, Publishers, About Frankfurt, Its Book Fair, and About Dear Lovely Death, 1977); a biography of the well-known satirist and cabaret writer Kurt Tucholsky (1979); and a "report" on the death of the German filmmaker Rainer Werner Fassbinder (1982). He is also the author of the autobiographical *Widerspruch: Autobiographischer Bericht* (Contradiction: An Autobiographical Report, 1974) and the novels *Rasputin* (1970), under the pen name Peter Tarock; *Erde ist unbewohnbar wie der Mond* (Earth Is Uninhabitable Like the Moon, 1973); *Grosselternkind* (Grandparents' Child, 1978); and *Chinesische Hund* (The Chinese Dog, 1981).

Translations: *Little Peter in War and Peace,* trans. William Whitman (New York: Grove, 1970); *Remembrance Day: Thirteen Attempts in Prose to Adopt an Attitude of Respect,* trans. Eric Mosbacher (New York: Dutton, 1966).

Selected Bibliography

Individual author entries contain extensive bibliographic information on available literature about the writers and translations of their works into English. English-language anthologies are listed in this bibliography by literature, apart from their citations in the
"Translations" section of the individual author entries. This bibliography includes only
studies in English on Eastern Europe as a whole, including the former German Democratic
Republic (East Germany); works of a historical and/or political nature, with particular reference to World War II and the postwar period; and studies of national literatures. Because
of the political separation of Czechs and Slovaks in 1993, entries for "Czech" and "Slovak"
are grouped separately under "Czechoslovakia"; similarly, entries for the successor states of
the former Yugoslavia are grouped individually under "Yugoslavia."

Eastern Europe

Banac, Ivo, ed. *Eastern Europe in Revolution*. Ithaca, N.Y.: Cornell University Press, 1992.
Cottey, Andrew. *East-Central Europe After the Cold War: Poland, the Czech Republic,
Slovakia and Hungary in Search of Security*. New York: St. Martin's Press, 1995.
Crnković, Gordana. *Imagined Dialogues: Eastern European Literature in Conversation
with American and English Literature*. Evanston, Ill.: Northwestern University Press, 2000.
Garton Ash, Timothy. *The Magic Lantern: The Revolution of '89 Witnessed in Warsaw,
Budapest, Berlin and Prague*. New York: Vintage, 1993.
———. *The Uses of Adversity: Essays on the Fate of Central Europe*. New York: Vintage, 1990.
Hawkesworth, Celia, ed. *Literature and Politics in Eastern Europe: Selected Papers from
the Fourth World Congress for Soviet and East European Studies, Harrogate, 1990*. New York: St.
Martin's Press, 1992
Konrád, George. *The Melancholy of Rebirth: Essays from Post-Communist Central Europe, 1989–1994*.
Selected and translated by Michael Henry Heim. San Diego: Harcourt Brace Jovanovich, 1995.
March, Michael, ed. *Child of Europe: A New Anthology of East European Poetry*. New York: Viking
Penguin, 1990.
———, ed. *Description of a Struggle: The Picador Book of Contemporary East European Prose*. Lon-
don: Picador, 1994.
Mihailovich, Vasa, ed. *White Stones and Fir Trees: An Anthology of Contemporary
Slavic Literature*. Rutherford, N.J.: Fairleigh Dickinson University Press, 1977.
Pynsent, R. B., and S. I. Kanikova, eds. *The Everyman Companion to East European Literature*. Lon-
don: Dent, 1993.
Serafin, Steven, ed. *Twentieth-century Eastern European Writers*. First series. Detroit: Gale, 1999.
———, ed. *Twentieth-century Eastern European Writers*. Second series. Detroit: Gale, 2000.
———, ed. *Twentieth-century Eastern European Writers*. Third series. Detroit: Gale, 2001.

Albania

Biberaj, Elez. *Albania: A Socialist Maverick*. Boulder, Colo.: Westview, 1990.
———. *Albania in Transition: The Rocky Road to Democracy*. Boulder, Colo.: Westview, 1998.
Bihicu, Koçu. *A History of Albanian Literature*. Tirana: 8 Nëntori, 1980. [An "official" communist his-
tory of Albanian literature to the 1970s]

Elsie, Robert. "Albanian Literature in English Translation." *Slavonic and East European Review* 70, no. 2 (1992): 249–57.

———. *Dictionary of Albanian Literature*. Westport, Conn.: Greenwood, 1986.

———. *A Dictionary of Albanian Religion, Mythology, and Folk Culture*. New York: New York University Press, 2001.

———. *History of Albanian Literature*. 2 vols. Boulder, Colo.: East European Monographs, 1995.

———. *Studies in Modern Albanian Literature and Culture*. Boulder, Colo.: East European Monographs, 1996.

———, ed. and trans. *An Elusive Eagle Soars: Anthology of Modern Albanian Poetry*. London: Forest, 1993.

Hutchings, Raymond. *Historical Dictionary of Albania*. Lanham, Md.: Scarecrow, 1996.

Pipa, Arshi. *Contemporary Albanian Literature*. Boulder, Colo.: East European Monographs, 1991.

Raifi, Mensur, ed. *The Roads Lead Only One Way: A Survey of Modern Poetry from Kosova*. Translated by John Hodgson and Fiona Cullen. Priština: Kosova Association of Literary Translators, 1988.

Vickers, Miranda, and James Pettifer. *From Anarchy to a Balkan Identity: Albania*. New York: New York University Press, 1997, 2000.

Bulgaria

Bell, John D., ed. *Bulgaria in Transition: Politics, Economics, Society, and Culture After Communism*. Boulder, Colo.: Westview, 1998.

Bozhilov, Bozhidar, comp. *Modern Bulgarian Poetry*. English version by Roy MacGregor-Hastie. Sofia: Sofia Press, 1976.

Crampton, R. J. *A Concise History of Bulgaria*. Cambridge: Cambridge University Press, 1997.

Detrez, Raymond. *Historical Dictionary of Bulgaria*. Lanham, Md.: Scarecrow, 1996.

Markov, Georgi. *The Truth that Killed*. Translated by Liliana Brisby. Afterword by Annabel Markov. London: Weidenfeld and Nicolson, 1983.

Miller, Marshall Lee. *Bulgaria During the Second World War*. Stanford, Calif.: Stanford University Press, 1975.

Moser, Charles A. *A History of Bulgarian Literature, 865–1944*. The Hague: Mouton, 1972.

———. *Theory and History of the Bulgarian Transition*. Sofia: Free Initiative Foundation, 1994.

Slavov, Atanas. *The "Thaw" in Bulgarian Literature*. Boulder, Colo.: East European Monographs, 1981.

Tempest, Peter, trans. *Anthology of Bulgarian Poetry*. Sofia: Sofia Press, 1980.

Czechoslovakia

Kovtun, George J. *Czech and Slovak Literature in English*. Washington, D.C.: Library of Congress, 1988.

Nesvadba, Josef. *The Lost Face: Best Science Fiction from Czechoslovakia*. New York: Taplinger, 1971.

Czech

Büchler, Alexandra, ed. *Allskin and Other Tales by Contemporary Czech Women*. Seattle: Women in Translation, 1998.

———, ed. *This Side of Reality: Modern Czech Writing*. London: Serpent's Tail, 1996.

French, Alfred. *Czech Writers and Politics, 1945–1969*. Boulder, Colo.: East European Monographs, 1982.

Goetz-Stankiewicz, Marketa. *The Silenced Theatre: Czech Playwrights Without a Stage*. Toronto: University of Toronto Press, 1979.

Harkins, William E., and Paul I. Trensky, eds. *Czech Literature Since 1956: A Symposium*. New York: Bohemica, 1980.

Lappin, Elena, ed. *Daylight in Nightclub Inferno: Czech Fiction in the Post-Kundera Generation*. North Haven, Conn.: Catbird, 1997.

Liehm, Antonin, and Peter Kussi, eds. *The Writing on the Wall: An Anthology of Contemporary Czech Literature*. Princeton, N.J.: Karz-Cohl, 1983.

Sayer, Derek. *The Coasts of Bohemia: A Czech History*. Princeton, N.J.: Princeton University Press, 1998.

Theiner, George, ed. *New Writing in Czechoslovakia*. Baltimore: Penguin, 1969.

Trensky, Paul. *Czech Drama Since World War II*. White Plains, N.Y.: Sharpe, 1978.

Slovak

Cincura, Andrew, ed. *An Anthology of Slovak Literature*. Riverside, Calif.: University Hardcovers, 1976.

Petro, Peter. *A History of Slovak Literature*. Montreal: McGill–Queens University Press, 1995.

Pynsent, Robert B. *Modern Slovak Prose: Fiction Since 1954*. London: Macmillan, 1990.

Rzhevsky, Nicholas, ed. *Transitions: Slovak Stories*. Stony Brook, N.Y.: Slavic Cultural Center Press, 1999.

German Democratic Republic

Atkins, Robert, and Martin Kane, eds. *Retrospect and Review: Aspects of the Literature of the GDR, 1976–1990*. Amsterdam: Rodopi, 1997.

Bathrick, David. *The Powers of Speech: The Politics of Culture in the GDR*. Lincoln: University of Nebraska Press, 1995.

Firchow, Peter E., and Evelyn S. Firchow, trans. and eds. *East German Short Stories: An Introductory Anthology*. Boston: Twayne, 1979.

Flores, John. *Poetry in East Germany: Adjustments, Visions, and Provocations, 1945–1970*. New Haven, Conn.: Yale University Press, 1971.

Fox, Thomas C. *Border Crossings: An Introduction to East German Prose*. Ann Arbor: University of Michigan Press, 1993.

Hallberg, Robert von, ed. *Literary Intellectuals and the Dissolution of the State: Professionalism and Conformity in the GDR*. Translated by Kenneth J. Northcott. Chicago: University of Chicago Press, 1996.

Hamburger, Michael, ed. *East German Poetry: An Anthology*. New York: Dutton, 1973.

Hell, Julia. *Post-Fascist Fantasies: Psychoanalysis, History, and the Literature of East Germany*. Durham, N.C.: Duke University Press, 1997.

Hörnigk, Therese, and Alexander Stephan, eds. *The New Sufferings of Young W. and Other Stories from the German Democratic Republic*. New York: Continuum, 1997.

Leeder, Karen. *Breaking Boundaries: A New Generation of Poets in the GDR*. Oxford: Clarendon Press, 1996.

Lukens, Nancy, and Dorothy Rosenberg, trans. and eds. *Daughters of Eve: Women's Writing from the German Democratic Republic*. Lincoln: University of Nebraska Press, 1993.

Reid, J. H. *Writing Without Taboos: The New East German Literature*. New York: Wolff, 1990.

Tate, Dennis. *The East German Novel: Identity, Community, Continuity*. Bath: Bath University Press, 1984.

Hungary

Basa, Enikő Molnár, ed. *Hungarian Literature*. Review of National Literatures. New York: Griffon, 1993.

Brogyányi, Eugene, ed. *Drama Contemporary: Hungary*. New York: PAJ Publications, 1991.

Cox, Terry, ed. *Hungary 1956: Forty Years On*. Portland, Ore.: Cass, 1997.

Gömöri, George. *Polish and Hungarian Poetry, 1945 to 1956*. Oxford: Oxford University Press, 1966.

Gömöri, George, and George Szirtes, eds. *The Colonnade of Teeth: Modern Hungarian Poetry*. Newcastle upon Tyne: Bloodaxe, 1996.

Györgyey, Clara, trans. and ed. *A Mirror to the Cage: Three Contemporary Hungarian Plays*. Fayetteville: University of Arkansas Press, 1993.

Hoensch, Jörg K. *A History of Modern Hungary, 1867–1994*. 2nd ed. Translated by Kim Traynor. London: Longmann, 1996.

Hungarian Plays: New Drama from Hungary. Selected and introduced by László Upor. London: Nick Hern, 1996.

A Hungarian Quartet: Four Contemporary Short Novels. Budapest: Corvina, 1991. [The collection includes Géza Ottlik's *Logbook*, Ivan Mándy's *Left Behind*, Miklós Mészöly's *Forgiveness*, and Péter Esterházy's *The Transporters*]

Illés, Lajos, ed. *44 Hungarian Short Stories*. Budapest: Corvina, 1979.

———, ed. *Nothing's Lost: Twenty-five Hungarian Short Stories*. Translated by Richard Aczel. Budapest: Corvina, 1988.

Kessler, Jascha, trans. *The Face of Creation: Contemporary Hungarian Poetry*. Minneapolis: Coffee House, 1988.

The Kiss: Twentieth Century Hungarian Short Stories. Selected by István Bart. Budapest: Corvina, 1993.

Makkai, Adam, ed. *In Quest of the "Miracle Stag": The Poetry of Hungary. An Anthology of Hungarian Poetry in English Translation from the Thirteenth Century to the Present in Commemoration of the 1100th Anniversary of the Foundation of Hungary and the Fortieth Anniversary of the Hungarian Uprising of 1956*. Chicago: Atlantis-Centaur, 1996.

Ray, David, ed. *From the Hungarian Revolution: A Collection of Poems*. Ithaca, N.Y.: Cornell University Press, 1966.

Szakolczay, Lajos, ed. *Give or Take a Day: Contemporary Hungarian Short Stories*. Budapest: Corvina, 1997.

Tezla, Albert, ed. *Ocean at the Window: Hungarian Prose and Poetry Since 1945*. Minneapolis: University of Minnesota Press, 1980.

Thy Kingdom Come: 19 Short Stories by 11 Hungarian Authors. Selected and edited by Peter Doherty, Gyöngyi Köteles, and Zsófia Bán. Translated by Eszter Molnár. Budapest: Palatrinus, 1998.

Vajda, Miklós, ed. *Modern Hungarian Poetry*. New York: Columbia University Press, 1977.

Varnai, Paul, ed. *Hungarian Short Stories*. Toronto: Exile Editions, 1983.

Poland

Barańczak, Stanisław, and Clare Cavanagh, eds. and trans. *Polish Poetry of the Last Two Decades of Communist Rule: Spoiling Cannibals' Fun*. Evanston, Ill.: Northwestern University Press, 1991.

Czerniawski, Adam, trans. and ed. *The Burning Forest: Modern Polish Poetry*. Newcastle upon Tyne: Bloodaxe, 1988.

Czerwinski, Edward, ed. *Dictionary of Polish Literature*. Westport, Conn.: Greenwood, 1994.

Davies, Norman. *Heart of Europe: A Short History of Poland*. Oxford: Oxford University Press, 1986.

———. *The Polish Revolution: Solidarity*. Rev. ed. New York: Viking Penguin, 1991.

Gömöri, George. *Polish and Hungarian Poetry, 1945 to 1956*. Oxford: Oxford University Press, 1966.

Kott, Jan, ed. *Four Decades of Polish Essays*. Evanston, Ill.: Northwestern University Press, 1990.

Milosz, Czeslaw. *The History of Polish Literature*. 2nd ed. Berkeley: University of California Press, 1983.

Polonsky, Antony, and Monika Adamczyk-Garbowska, eds. *Contemporary Jewish Writing in Poland: An Anthology*. Lincoln: University of Nebraska Press, 2001.

Sanford, George, and Adriana Gozdecka-Sanford. *Historical Dictionary of Poland*. Lanham, Md.: Scarecrow, 1994.

Segel, Harold B., ed. *Stranger in Our Midst: Images of the Jew in Polish Literature*. Ithaca, N.Y.: Cornell University Press, 1996.

Tighe, Carl. *The Politics of Literature: Poland, 1945–1989*. Cardiff: University of Wales Press, 1999.

Wechsler, Lawrence. *The Passion of Poland: From Solidarity Through the State of War*. New York: Pantheon, 1984.

Romania

Avădanei, Ștefan, and Don Eulert, trans. and eds. *46 Romanian Poets in English*. Iași: Junimea, 1973.

Bodiu, Andrei, Romulus Bucur, and Georgeta Moarcăs, eds. *Romanian Poets of the '80s and '90s: A Concise Anthology*. Pitești: Paralela 45, 1999.

Cartianu, Ana, trans. *Romanian Fantastic Tales*. Bucharest: Minerva, 1981.

Catanoy, Nicholas, ed. *Modern Romanian Poetry*. Oakville, Ont.: Mosaic Press/Valley Editions, 1977.

Ciopraga, Constantin. *The Personality of Romanian Literature*. Iași: Junimea, 1981.

Cornis-Pope, Marcel. *The Unfinished Battles: Romanian Postmodernism Before and After 1989*. Iași: Policrom, 1996.

Cu bilet circular/With Circular Ticket: Romanian Short Stories. Translated by Fred Nadaban and John W. Rathbun. Edited by Mircea Zaciu. Notes by Sever Trifu. Cluj: Dacia, 1983.

Deletant, Andrea, and Brenda Walker, trans. *An Anthology of Contemporary Romanian Poetry*. London: Forest, 1984.

——, trans. *Silent Voices: An Anthology of Contemporary Romanian Women Poets*. London: Forest, 1986.

Dutescu, Dan, ed. and trans. *Romanian Poems: An Anthology of Verse*. Bucharest: Eminescu, 1982.

Fairleigh, John, ed. *When the Tunnels Meet: Contemporary Romanian Poetry*. Newcastle upon Tyne: Bloodaxe, 1996.

Farnoaga, Georgiana, and Sharon King, eds. and trans. *The Phantom Church and Other Stories from Romania*. Pittsburgh: University of Pittsburgh Press, 1996.

Galloway, George. *Downfall: The Ceausescus and the Romanian Revolution*. London: Futura, 1991.

Georgescu, Vlad. *The Romanians: A History*. Columbus: Ohio State University Press, 1991.

Giurescu, Dinu. *Illustrated History of the Romanian People*. Bucharest: Edit. Sport-Turism, 1981.

Kellogg, Frederick. *The Road to Romanian Independence*. West Lafayette, Ind.: Purdue University Press, 1995.

Lamb, Ruth Stanton. *The World of Romanian Theatre*. Claremont, Calif.: Ocelot, 1976.

Lefter, Bogdan. *A Guide to Romanian Literature: Novels, Experiment and the Postcommunist Book Industry*. Pitești: Paralela 45, 1999.

Like Diamonds in Coal Asleep: Selections from Twentieth Century Romanian Poetry. Compiled and introduced by Andrei Bantaș. Translated by Andrei Bantaș, Dan Dutescu, and Leon Levitchi. Bucharest: Minerva, 1985.

MacGregor-Hastie, Roy, trans. and ed. *Anthology of Contemporary Romanian Poetry*. London: Peter Owen, 1969.

Părvu, Sorin. *The Romanian Novel*. New York: East European Monographs, 1992.

Rady, Martyn. *Romania in Turmoil: A Contemporary History*. London: Taurus, 1992.

Romanian Fiction of the '80s and '90s: A Concise Anthology. Pitești: Paralela 45, 1999.

Sorescu, Marin. *Hands Behind My Back: Selected Poems*. Translated by Gabriela Dragnea, Stuart Friebert, and Adriana Varga. Oberlin, Ohio: Oberlin College Press, 1991.

Sorkin, Adam J., and Kurt W. Tretow, eds. *An Anthology of Romanian Women Poets*. New York: East European Monographs, 1994.

Steinberg, Jacob, ed. *Introduction to Rumanian Literature*. New York: Twayne, 1966.

Teodorescu, Anda, and Andrei Bantaș, trans. *Romanian Essayists of Today*. Bucharest: Univers, 1979.

Treptow, Kurt, and Marcel Popa. *Historical Dictionary of Romania*. Lanham, Md.: Scarecrow, 1996.

Trifu, Sever, and Dumitriu Ciocoi-Pop, eds. *Romanian Poems: A Bilingual Anthology of Romanian Poetry*. Cluj: Dacia, 1972.

Young Poets of a New Romania: An Anthology. Translated by Brenda Walker with Michaela Celea-Leach. Edited by Ion Stoica. London: Forest, 1991.

Yugoslavia

Banac, Ivo. *The National Question in Yugoslavia: Origins, History, Politics*. Ithaca, N.Y.: Cornell University Press, 1984.

Johnson, Bernard, ed. *New Writing in Yugoslavia*. Baltimore: Penguin, 1970.

Lenski, Branko, ed. *Death of a Simple Giant and Other Modern Yugoslav Stories*. New York: Vanguard, 1965.

Lukić, Sveta. *Contemporary Yugoslav Literature: A Sociopolitical Approach*. Edited by Gertrude Joch Robinson. Translated by Pola Triandis. Urbana: University of Illinois Press, 1972.

Magaš, Branko. *The Destruction of Yugoslavia: Tracking the Breakup, 1980–1992*. London: Verso, 1993.

Mihailovich, Vasa D. *A Comprehensive Bibliography of Yugoslav Literature in English, 1592–1980*. Columbus, Ohio: Slavica, 1984. [Supplements published separately in 1988 and 1992]

———, ed. *South Slavic Writers Before World War II*. Detroit: Gale, 1995.

———, ed. *South Slavic Writers Since World War II*. Detroit: Gale, 1997.

Mihailovich, Vasa D., and Steven Serafin, eds. *South Slavic and East European Writers*. Detroit: Gale, 2000.

Mikasinovich, Branko, ed. *Five Modern Yugoslav Plays*. New York: Cyrco, 1977.

Mikasinovich, Branko, Dragan Milivojević, and Vasa D. Mihailovich, eds. *Introduction to Yugoslav Literature: An Anthology of Fiction and Poetry*. New York: Twayne, 1973.

Milivojević, Dragan. "Recent Yugoslav History in the Works of Contemporary Yugoslav Writers: Vuk Drašković, Slavenka Drakulić, and Slobodan Blagojević." *Serbian Studies* 9, nos. 1–2 (1995): 122–39.

Ramet, Sabrina P. *Nationalism and Federation in Yugoslavia, 1962–1991*. 2nd ed. Bloomington: Indiana University Press, 1992.

Silber, Laura, and Allan Little. *Yugoslavia: Death of a Nation*. Rev. ed. New York: Penguin, 1997.

Wachtel, Andrew Baruch. *Making a Nation, Breaking a Nation: Literature and Cultural Politics in Yugoslavia*. Stanford, Calif.: Stanford University Press, 1998.

Woodward, Susan. *Balkan Tragedy: Chaos and Dissolution After the Cold War*. Washington, D.C.: Brookings Institution Press, 1995.

Bosnia-Herzegovina

Agee, Chris, ed. *Scar on the Stone: Contemporary Poetry from Bosnia*. Newcastle upon Tyne: Bloodaxe, 1998.

Hawkesworth, Celia. *Voices in the Shadows: Women and Verbal Art in Serbia and Bosnia*. Budapest: Central European University Press, 2000.

Topčić, Zlatko, ed. *Forgotten Country 1: A Selection of Bosnian-Herzegovinian Stories*. Sarajevo: Association of Writers of Bosnia-Herzegovina, 1997.

———, ed. *Forgotten Country 2: War Prose in Bosnia-Herzegovina (1992–1995)*. Sarajevo: Association of Writers of Bosnia-Herzegovina, 1997.

Croatia

McMaster, Graham, trans. *Croatian Tales of Fantasy*. Zagreb: The Bridge, 1996.

Stallaerts, Robert, and Jeannine Laurens. *Historical Dictionary of Croatia*. Lanham, Md.: Scarecrow, 1995.

Macedonia

Andonovski, Venko, ed. *The Song Beyond Songs: Anthology of Contemporary Macedonian Poetry*. Prilep: Stremež, 1997.

Drugovac, Miodrag. *Contemporary Macedonian Writers*. Translated by Militsa Moyich Rekalich. Skopje: Macedonian Review, 1976.

Holton, Milne, ed. *The Big Horse and Other Stories of Modern Macedonia*. Columbia: University of Missouri Press, 1974.

Holton, Milne, and Graham W. Reid, eds. *Reading the Ashes: An Anthology of the Poetry of Modern Macedonia*. Pittsburgh: University of Pittsburgh Press, 1977.

Lunt, Horace G. "A Survey of Macedonian Literature." *Harvard Slavic Studies* 1 (1953): 363–96.

Serbia

Gorup, Radmila J., and Nadežda Obradović, eds. *The Prince of Fire: An Anthology of Contemporary Short Stories*. Pittsburgh: University of Pittsburgh Press, 1998.

Hawkesworth, Celia. *Voices in the Shadows: Women and Verbal Art in Serbia and Bosnia*. Budapest: Central European University Press, 2000.

Holton, Milne and Vasa D. Mihailovich. *Serbian Poetry from the Beginnings to the Present*. New Haven, Conn.: Yale University, Center for International and Area Studies, 1988.

Judah, Tim. *Kosovo: War and Revenge*. New Haven, Conn.: Yale University Press, 2000.

Simic, Charles, ed. and trans. *The Horse Has Six Legs: An Anthology of Serbian Poetry*. St. Paul, Minn.: Graywolf, 1992.

Šutić, Miloslav, ed. *An Anthology of Modern Serbian Lyrical Poetry (1920–1995)*. Belgrade: Serbian Literary Magazine, 1999.

Vickers, Miranda. *Between Serb and Albanian: A History of Kosovo*. New York: Columbia University Press, 1998.

Slovenia

The Day Tito Died: Contemporary Slovenian Short Stories. London: Forest, 1993.

Debeljak, Aleš, ed. *The Imagination of Terra Incognita: Slovenian Writing, 1945–1995*. Fredonia, N.Y.: White Pine, 1997.

Jackson, Richard, and Rachel Morgan, eds. *The Fire Under the Moon: Contemporary Slovene Poetry*. 2nd rev. ed. Chattanooga, Tenn., and Elgin, Ill.: Poetry Miscellany/Black Dirt, 1999.

Plut-Pregelj, Leopoldina, and Carole Rogel. *Historical Dictionary of Slovenia*. Lanham, Md.: Scarecrow, 1996.

Predan, Alja, ed. *Contemporary Slovenian Drama*. Ljubljana: Slovene Writers Association, 1997.

The Slovenian Essay of the Nineties. Selected by Matevž Kos. Ljubljana: Slovene Writers Association, 2000.

Zawacki, Andrew, ed. *Afterwards: Slovenian Writing, 1945–1999*. Buffalo, N.Y.: White Pine, 2000.

Author Index

Hungary

Macedonia

Poland

Romania

Serbia (and Montenegro)

Slovenia